1,000,000 Books
are available to read at

www.ForgottenBooks.com

Read online
Download PDF
Purchase in print

ISBN 978-1-5278-6971-4
PIBN 10921946

This book is a reproduction of an important historical work. Forgotten Books uses state-of-the-art technology to digitally reconstruct the work, preserving the original format whilst repairing imperfections present in the aged copy. In rare cases, an imperfection in the original, such as a blemish or missing page, may be replicated in our edition. We do, however, repair the vast majority of imperfections successfully; any imperfections that remain are intentionally left to preserve the state of such historical works.

Forgotten Books is a registered trademark of FB &c Ltd.
Copyright © 2018 FB &c Ltd.
FB &c Ltd, Dalton House, 60 Windsor Avenue, London, SW19 2RR.
Company number 08720141. Registered in England and Wales.

For support please visit www.forgottenbooks.com

1 MONTH OF FREE READING

at

www.ForgottenBooks.com

By purchasing this book you are eligible for one month membership to ForgottenBooks.com, giving you unlimited access to our entire collection of over 1,000,000 titles via our web site and mobile apps.

To claim your free month visit:

www.forgottenbooks.com/free921946

* Offer is valid for 45 days from date of purchase. Terms and conditions apply.

English
Français
Deutsche
Italiano
Español
Português

www.forgottenbooks.com

Mythology Photography **Fiction**
Fishing Christianity **Art** Cooking
Essays Buddhism Freemasonry
Medicine **Biology** Music **Ancient Egypt** Evolution Carpentry Physics
Dance Geology **Mathematics** Fitness
Shakespeare **Folklore** Yoga Marketing
Confidence Immortality Biographies
Poetry **Psychology** Witchcraft
Electronics Chemistry History **Law**
Accounting **Philosophy** Anthropology
Alchemy Drama Quantum Mechanics
Atheism Sexual Health **Ancient History**
Entrepreneurship Languages Sport
Paleontology Needlework Islam
Metaphysics Investment Archaeology
Parenting Statistics Criminology
Motivational

Vol. 4 No. 1   Attend the January Furniture Exhibitions   JANUARY, 1914

Canadian FURNITURE WORLD AND THE UNDERTAKER

Published by the Commercial Press, Limited, 32 Colborne Street, Toronto

Furniture of Dignity and Grace

Constructed on a basic principle of lasting elegance, McLagan Furniture links the dealer with the user through the common bond of good service.

McLagan reliability is a sales force of value to any good dealer.

Quartered oak and mahogany China and Parlor Cabinets in pleasing variety, fully described in our large catalog of complete lines. Ask us to send you a copy if you have not got one on your desk.

Western buyers can save on freight charges by ordering through the Stratford Shipping Combination. Write to any of the Stratford Furniture Manufacturers for particulars.

THE
GEORGE McLAGAN FURNITURE CO.
LIMITED

STRATFORD   ONTARIO   CANADA

John C. Mundell & Co., Elora, Ont.

Will Have Something to Interest You in the Furniture Line During January

IT has been decided to hold a Furniture Exhibition in the Toronto Exhibition Grounds during January, which will be in itself an Exposition of the Furniture Trade and its developments up to the year 1914, and showing the latest ideas and triumphs in the designing of furniture.

This Exhibition will be decidedly a representative one. It will be participated in by a majority of the leading manufacturers of Ontario, who are taking space in the Exhibit, and contributing in various ways to make it a Success.

We want all of our customers to attend on this occasion. To the Furniture Man, what can there be more interesting than Furniture? New designs, new ideas, new points in Finish and Upholstering, new coverings, new grades of Leather, new Artificial Leathers of all kinds and in the new shades.

We ask you to come and see the Mundell Exhibit on this occasion—the results will amply repay you—your welcome will be cordial—in short, you will be glad you came.

Time—January 12th to 24th
Place—Exhibition Grounds, Toronto

John C. Mundell & Co., Elora, Ont.

It will pay any dealer many times over to inspect the new lines early in the season

STRATFORD FURNITURE EXHIBITION JAN. 12-24, '14

The entire Exhibition will be shown under one roof —in the new four storey brick building just completed for the Farquharson-Gifford Company, containing 40,000 feet of floor space.

All the Stratford Furniture Manufacturers will show their entire lines for 1914, resulting in the most comprehensive Exposition of Furniture ever held in Canada, and one that will do full justice to the Furniture Industry in this country.

The Berlin-Waterloo Furniture Exhibition will be in progress concurrently, offering an opportunity of visiting both exhibits on the one trip.

The Exhibition Building will be specially lighted, and a noon-day luncheon will be served to visitors right on the spot.

Dealers will be our guests while in the city. Let us know the day you will arrive, and we shall have a warm room and a warm reception awaiting.

By all means come to Stratford, the home of good furniture, you'll learn much of value and interest.

George McLagan Furniture Co. Limited
Imperial Rattan Co., Limited
Stratford Chair Co., Limited
Globe-Wernicke Co.
Stratford Desk Co.
Farquharson-Gifford Co.
Stratford Bed Co.
Frame & Hay Fence Co.
Classic Furniture Co., Limited
Stratford Manufacturing Co., Limited

CANADIAN FURNITURE WORLD AND THE UNDERTAKER.   January, 1914

Yes! It's—
"Enthusiasm" Bedding

¶ The enthusiasm of our dealers sells more Antiseptic Bedding because back of that eagerness to sell is the inspiring influence created by the higher workmanship embodied in our goods—plus substantial profits and unexcelled service.

¶ We guarantee Antiseptic Mattresses and Pillows to be moth-proof, germ proof, antiseptic, sterilized and comfort promoting—as well as anything else asked for in good bedding.   Enquire about Antiseptic now.

THE
Antiseptic Bedding Co.
187-189 Parliament Street
Toronto, Ont.

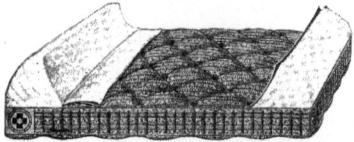

A Special For This Month

THIS BEAUTIFUL COUCH.   QUARTERED OAK FRAME.   SPRING EDGE.
Deep Tufted or Plain Top

In
Genuine
Leather
$55.00
List

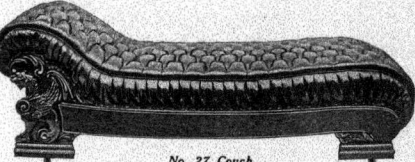

No. 27 Couch

In
Genuine
Spanish
$60.00
List

This is only one of our many designs that we manufacture. Look up our goods and prices before you place your Spring order. It will pay you.

Our New Catalogue will be ready to mail on the 20th of this month

The Montreal Upholstery Company
1611 Clarke Street,   -   -   Montreal, Canada.

January, 1914   CANADIAN FURNITURE WORLD AND THE UNDERTAKER.   5

Attend the Furniture Show, Jan. 12-24
All Factories Showing Under One Roof

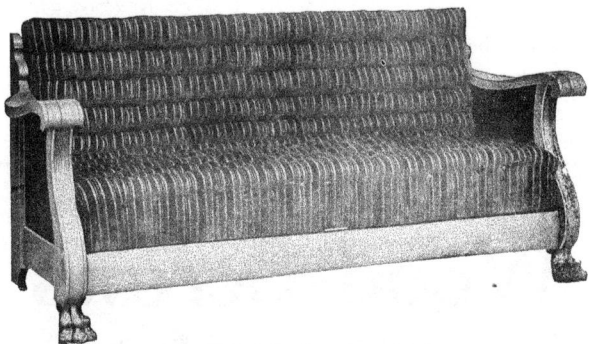

We manufacture all the frames for all our various lines, and carry the most comprehensive stock of Imported Tapestries in Canada. This combination of economy and Variety enables us to produce, at lower prices, a range of Upholstered Furniture second to none in the Dominion. The famous Stratford Davenport Bed is made up in Tapestries, Silk Velours and Leathers.

Come to the Stratford Furniture Exhibition, January 12 to 24

We will show many new designs in Upholstered Reed Chairs and Rockers; English Overstuffed Chairs and Chesterfields; Stratford Davenport Beds; leather and imitation leather Chairs and Rockers.

White Enamel

For All Purposes.

Made in Flat, Egg Shell and High Gloss Finish.

Can be rubbed in forty-eight hours.

Works free and easy, and does not brush mark.

Write for Prices and Samples.

The Ault & Wiborg Co., of Canada
Limited
Varnish Works
Montreal   TORONTO   Winnipeg

ROBERTSON SOCKET HEAD
Wood Screws

See That Square Hole

Pat. Feb. 12, 1909

THIS IS A REAL WOOD SCREW

It is driven by a simple square bit, and is the only one of its type on the market.

Driver fits snugly into the square hole and positively cannot slip and cut the fingers, or disfigure costly furniture or woodwork. It is driven with less exertion. No ragged slots after driving. Saves time, labor, money and material. We make the drivers in all suitable styles.

Drivers sent free with first order. Write for catalogue and prices.

P. L. Robertson Mfg. Co., Limited
MILTON :: ONTARIO

January, 1914   CANADIAN FURNITURE WORLD AND THE UNDERTAKER.

We Will Show Many New Designs
at the
Stratford Furniture Exhibition

In addition to the attractive Box Seat Diners in quartered oak shown here, we will display at the Stratford Furniture Exhibition, in 5,000 feet of floor space, our entire representation consisting of many new designs in Diners, Den, Library and Office Chairs, complete Dining-room Suites, Dressers and Stands in plain and quartered oak and quartered gum.

The Stratford Chair Company's range sells while others are only seen. Stock this line and turn lookers into buyers.

Buyers at Western points can save on freight charges by buying through the Stratford Shipping Combination. Ask us for particulars

SPECIALISTS IN FURNISHING FABRICS

Telephone:
CITY 2514 (4 Lines)

Cable Address:
"BOTCHERY, CENT., LONDON"
A.B.C. Code 5th Edition

TAPESTRIES

The demand for Chesterfields, Lounge Chairs and other pieces of comfortable upholstered furniture for the living room calls for the use of Tapestry.

Our stock of Silk, Wool and Cotton Tapestries, carefully selected to harmonize with the prevailing designs and color schemes of carpets and wall decorations is the largest in the trade.

We shall be pleased to submit samples and are able to promptly ship large or small orders.

Mr. Dodd will visit the leading Trade Centres in the Spring and will show an entirely revised and up-to-date collection at the lowest London Prices.

**MOQUETTES, CAR PLUSH, CORDUROYS, CRETONNES
PRINTED LINENS, SHADOW TISSUES**

Our "Fadenomore" fabrics, consisting of Tenasserims, Velours, Casements, Bolton Sheetings, Repps, etc., etc., are the last word in the modern dyers' art. They are absolutely impervious to Sunshine and Washing. Patterns on application.

Canadian Buyers visiting London are especially welcome

STONARDS LIMITED

7, 8, 9, 10, Paternoster Buildings, London, E.C., Eng.

OTHER OVERSEAS REPRESENTATIVES
South Africa: Mr. H. S. Potter, Freemans Chambers, Cape Town: Pinn's Buildings, Johannesburg. Australasia: Mr. G. H. Lander, 31 Queen St., Melbourne. India and Far East: Mr. T. Adair, 38 Kiangse Road, Shanghai.

January, 1914   CANADIAN FURNITURE WORLD AND THE UNDERTAKER.   9

Mr. Furniture Dealer :—

We cordially invite you to attend the Stratford Furniture Exhibition to be held in our new factory building, January 12th to 24th.

Samples of our lines will be ready for your inspection and, we believe, will meet with your approval.

Arrangements have been completed for your entertainment, and we want you to come and be our guests during your stay in Stratford.

Write for Special Dealers' Proposition at once!

You Can Sell Them at a Moderate Price to Net a Handsome Profit

Nagrella Kitchen Cabinets

Every furniture dealer should get in touch with us right away to learn about our new Nagrella Kitchen Cabinets. We are filling orders just as fast as possible and the quicker you get in touch with us and place your order, the sooner we will be able to make you a shipment. Every dealer who sees the new kitchen cabinets is anxious to get them in his store, because the Nagrella is the very last word in kitchen cabinet construction. It embodies all the good points of all the other cabinets on the market and none of their weak points.

The table top is covered with solid aluminum; it is 44 inches wide and has two end-hinged flaps, making a total table width of 66 ins.

It is furnished in Elm, Black Ash, and solid Oak with golden, antique, or early English finish.

Write at once for special dealers proposition

Nagrella Mfg. Co., Limited
HAMILTON, ONT.

January, 1914   CANADIAN FURNITURE WORLD AND THE UNDERTAKER.   11

A Beautiful Art Mission Style

The Art Mission Style of Sectional Bookcase is a creation of beauty and service. It lends itself to the furnishings of most any living room or library, adding to their tone of refinement as well as utility.

Globe-Wernicke "firstness" is exemplified to a high degree in Art Mission, embodying many new innovations that enhance their selling power.

Dealers are asked to write us for catalogs giving full details of many combinations of these quick-selling Sectional Bookcases.

Complete Showing at the Stratford Exhibition, January 12-24th

We will have on display a most complete range of Globe-Wernicke Sectional Bookcases and Filing Cabinets. We devote our entire time and efforts to the perfecting of these two lines as sales producers, and have some interesting features to demonstrate. Come to Stratford.

THE ELLIS FURNITURE COMPANY

MANUFACTURERS
INGERSOLL, ONT.

Dec. 30th, 1913

To our Friends and Patrons:

    We take this opportunity, thru "The Furniture World", of thanking our numerous customers for the liberal patronage they have given us during the past year. We desire, also, to wish our friends and clients everywhere, a bright New Year, more prosperous and successful than any that has gone before.

    As in the past, our motto for 1914 will be "Quality always First". Hoping to merit your continued confidence,

              Yours sincerely,

                  THE ELLIS FURNITURE COMPANY.

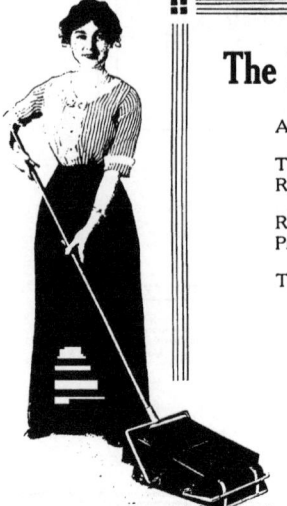

The Livingston Vacuum Sweeper

A Real Vacuum Sweeper, ball bearings, runs as easily as a carpet sweeper.

Three bellows that suck in all the dirt and dust.

Removable sweeper brush picks up all hairs, threads, etc.

Rubber furniture protectors.

Pressed steel top, nickel trimmings, beautiful mahogany finish.

The best finished and the best made.

Big Profit   Big Seller

Write for prices and sample

J. H. Connor & Son, Limited
OTTAWA, ONTARIO

Manufacturers of Washing Machines and Clothes Wringers

January, 1914   CANADIAN FURNITURE WORLD AND THE UNDERTAKER.   13

Opportunities in Portable Assembly Seating

FURNITURE DEALERS now recognize our Portable Assembly Seating as an exceedingly profitable addition to their lines. It is used extensively in Halls, Theatres, Lecture Rooms, Gymnasiums and Y.M.C.A.'s; it is strong and light in weight, is easily removed, and occupies a minimum amount of storage space.

Portable Assembly Seating will form an important part of the showing of our complete lines at the Stratford Exhibition. Come and see us.

These Beds Have Selling Arguments

A *Stratford* Bed will sell every time a *good* bed is wanted. Have a variety of "Stratfords" for those who appreciate the finer qualities.

When you visit our space at the Stratford Furniture Exhibition you'll be favorably impressed with our lines for 1914. We'll expect you.

No. 855X. List Price $11.20

No. 853. List Price $9.80

No. 852X. List Price $8.20

Money Invested in Ontario Iron Beds, Springs and Mattresses

will yield the investor good returns. Ontario Beds and Bedding have a reputation with the purchasing public not alone for quality, but service as well—a combination hard to beat.

Win the Good Will

of your customers and you win success in business. Ontario Bedding will help you do this. It is of the kind that sells readily at a good profit and stays sold.

Write for 1914 Catalogue

FOR All of Our Friends and Patrons We Wish a Happy and Prosperous New Year.

The Ontario Spring Bed & Mattress Co.
Limited

The Largest Bedding House in Canada

LONDON **ONTARIO**

"Classic" Woven Wire Bed Springs
"Best for Every Use"

Attention is called to our car combination for Western shipments. We ship with any of the Stratford factories, effecting material savings in freight charges.

WE manufacture a line of Wire Bed Springs and Cots that reach a high standard of excellence.

Our exhibit at the Stratford Furniture Exhibition will demonstrate why they should be placed on your floors this year.

We have issued a catalog covering our various lines which we shall be pleased to mail you.

Exclusive Brass Furniture Trimmings

in designs to harmonize with any style of furniture. The exquisite finish of our trimmings sells them on sight. Special designs to order.

We will Show New Designs for 1914 during the Stratford Furniture Exhibition.

Has it occurred to you to look back to September 1911, when the first issue of the

CANADIAN FURNITURE WORLD
WAS MAILED TO THE TRADE

Time passes quickly but the FURNITURE WORLD keeps pace with the time and already has nearly 1800 paid subscribers on its subscription list.

Any Furniture Manufacturer or Dealer, knowing a Dealer who is not already a subscriber, will do us a favor by sending us the Dealers' name and address. The FURNITURE WORLD aims at 100 per cent. efficiency.

Mattresses

"SWEET DREAMS"

See The Laced Opening

Comfort Sanitation Economy

YOUR customers do not always know the particular make of good Mattress they will purchase when they enter your store. When they do, it's pretty sure to be a Kellaric, and when they don't specify, you can sell them Kellarics with very little effort when you show the goods. Kellaric Mattresses are big trade-pullers in any Furniture Store.

Start in at once to sell the Kellaric and our three popular priced lines, the **Model Box** spring, the **Hair-in-Cotton** and the **Common Sense** for a good year's profits in Mattresses.

See our Display at the Toronto Furniture Exhibition February, 12th to 24th, 1914.

The McKellar Bedding Co., Limited,
Fort William, Ontario
Eastern Branch: BERLIN BEDDING CO., LIMITED, 31 Front St. E., Toronto

TORONTO FURNITURE EXHIBITION

The Gold Medal Line

No. 684. Hard Edge, Deep Spring Seat, Pillow Spring Back.

No. 685. Deep Spring Edge Seat, Silk Floss Cushion; Pillow Spring Back.

WHEN once seen by your customer, the manifest goodness of the GOLD MEDAL LINE of EASY CHAIRS creates in his or her mind a desire to possess, even while giving a perfunctory inspection to other lines. The choice eventually will be GOLD MEDAL.

Write us to-day and have our goods ready for those "new" GOLD MEDAL customers.

Parlor Furniture, Couches and Easy Chairs, Felt and Mixed Matresses, Upholstered Box Springs.

See Our Display at the Toronto Furniture Exhibition

Gold Medal Furniture Mfg. Co., Limited

Head Office and Factory: TORONTO, ONT.
Factories also at: UXBRIDGE, MONTREAL, and WINNIPEG

JANUARY 12th to 24th, 1914

"Crown" Dining Room Furniture is "Different"

Buffet No. 630

THE choicest oak and mahogany—the exquisite matching—the rich, soft finish—the many sought for styles, all combine in making "Crown" Furniture very easy to sell to people who seek quality in the furniture for their homes.

If you will not be able to see our display at the Toronto Furniture Exhibition, January 12 to 24, drop us a postcard and we will send you one of the nifty catalogues we have just received from the printer.

OUR PERMANENT FACTORY SHOWROOMS

are open to you at any time, and you are cordially invited to visit us when in Preston.

Crown Furniture Company :: Preston, Ont.

Quality First!—
Material, Workmanship and Finish Guaranteed

The Elmira Line

New Lines for 1914
Neat and Newest Designs

This is the line you cannot afford to miss seeing at The Toronto Furniture Exhibition.

We invite you all to call at our exhibit in the Horticultural Building.

We have in store for you an entire new line for 1914, which will interest every buyer.

We are not illustrating any line herewith, but want you to see the genuine article finished complete.

It will be a pleasure to us to meet you and show you the goods that will increase your sales, and make your most critical customers your best customers.

Remember The Elmira Line on Exhibit in the Horticultural Building, Toronto Furniture Exhibition, Jan. 12-24, 1914

The Elmira Furniture Co., Ltd.

Elmira  Ontario

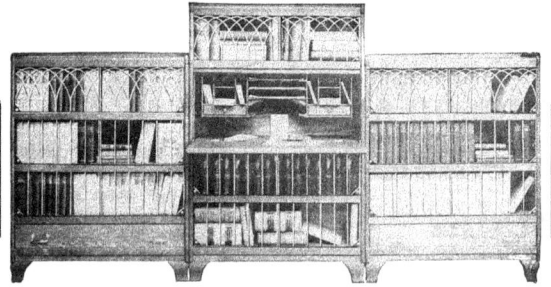

Weis Slide Door Sectional Bookcases Have The Selling Points You Want

They are the most simple in construction; most practical, elegant and profit-producing Sectional Bookcases made. When you stock the "Weis" you have the blue ribbon in Bookcases. Many people who visit your store will buy some make of bookcases during 1914. They will buy the "Weis" if you show them the many exclusive features of this great line. It's to your advantage, too, there's more profit selling "Weis" Sectional Bookcases.

Fitted with the sliding glass doors that cannot bind and are nearest to being dust-proof, are shipped knock down, saving in freight charges and floor space in your store.

They are easily set up by anyone in one minute; absolutely rigid when assembled, besides presenting an attractive, dignified substantial appearance recognised by all.

OUR DISPLAY AT THE TORONTO FURNITURE EXHIBITION WILL CONTAIN MANY SAMPLES WHICH YOU OUGHT TO SEE

The Knechtel Furniture Co., Limited
Hanover, Ont.

TORONTO FURNITURE EXHIBITION

We'll Have a Worthy Display

Furniture Dealers visiting the Toronto Furniture Exhibition will expect to see much that is new and praiseworthy. We are confident that in the Kindel line of DAVENPORTS, DIVANETTES, CHAIR BEDS, COUCHES, etc., they will find many effects worthy of their approval and admiration. We invite you, Furniture Men, to come and visit us.

"The bed that makes itself"

Kindel Convertible Parlor Furniture is not surpassed on the continent. It comes to you with a purpose of most satisfactorily filling a specific want, and providing a good profit on every sale.

The Kindel Bed Co., Limited, Toronto

See our new lines and prices at the

TORONTO FURNITURE EXHIBITION

January 12th to 24th, 1914

The

North American Bent Chair Co., Limited

Owen Sound, Canada

No. 942   No. 940

TORONTO FURNITURE EXHIBITION

The Ashburnham

The Ashburnham visualizes the aristocracy of the old British families—their tastes for luxuriousness and sociability. An Ashburnham is built for cosiness and comfort—years and years of it. Let us have your name and we'll be pleased to tell you more about this splendid line of Upholstered Furniture.

See Us at the Exhibition

New designs just coming out will form an attractive feature of our show space at the Toronto Furniture Exhibition. It will include a very high grade of upholstered Living Room, Den and Library Chairs, Settees, Davenports and Couches—probably the most appealing display you've ever seen. We cordially invite your inspection.

We Sell To The Trade Only

Quality Furniture Makers, Limited
ED. JEFFRIES, Managing Director
WELLAND :: CANADA

JANUARY 12th to 24th, 1914

Comfort

is one big factor in closing a sale of furniture. The moment you get your customer to **try** "Canada" Upholstered Goods the sale is just about 90% finished.

Then the price,—

This is the other 10%. The price at which you can offer "Canada" Goods always surprises your customer with its reasonableness, and it always leaves you a nice profit.

Catalogue ready for you if you want a copy.

Canada Mattress Mfg. Co.
Victoriaville
Que.

The Big Five Mixed Carload Center

| January 12th to 17th 1914 | **BERLIN WATERLOO FURNITURE EXHIBITION** | Our Third Annual Show |

Do Your 1914 Buying at the Berlin-Waterloo Furniture Exhibition

Berlin and Waterloo, with their two dozen furniture factories, are the furniture manufacturing centres of Canada, and their Furniture Exhibition Building, with 22 fine displays, together with the displays in factory showrooms, and the opportunities of seeing factory processes of furniture in the making, offer advantages second to no place in Canada to Furniture Buyers.

Attend the "German Smoker" on Thursday Evening, January 15th

A better investment cannot be made by any Furniture Dealer than to attend the January Furniture Exhibitions, the greatest of which is the Berlin and Waterloo Show. Less than an hour from Stratford and two hours from Toronto.

Come with the crowd to Berlin and Waterloo and we'll do our best to entertain you in real old German Style. Two dozen Furniture Manufacturers invite you

BERLIN FURNITURE EXHIBITION

AN INVITATION

TO our many friends and customers, and to those with whom we hope to enter into more close business relations during this new year, we extend our hospitality on your visit to the Berlin-Waterloo Furniture Exhibition, Jan. 12th to 17th.

Our complete range of attractive pieces in good grade furniture will be shown, and we believe it will be to our mutual interests that you inspect our display.

The Lippert Furniture Co., Limited
Berlin   -:-   Ontario

JANUARY 12TH TO 17TH, 1914

BAETZ BROTHERS AND COMPANY
BERLIN :: ONTARIO.

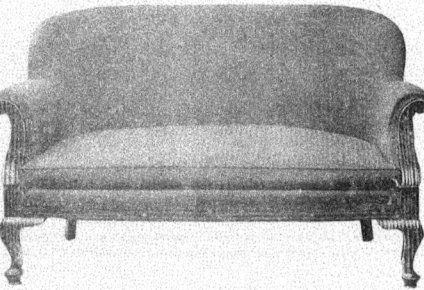

CHAIRS
DINING
BEDROOM
PARLOR
MISSION
BUNGALOW

SUITES
PARLOR
MISSION
BUNGALOW

Visit Our Exhibit at Our Factory, Berlin, During the Berlin-Waterloo Exhibition, January 12 to 17, 1914.

"SPECIALIZING IN CHAIRS."

Sure, You're Welcome
to our "At Home" of

In our permanent factory showrooms during the Third Annual

Berlin-Waterloo Furniture Exhibition
January 12th to 17th, 1914

Our "Latest Beauties" Will be There

and few there are in the furniture trade but have good things to say of the "Waterloo Monimaker" beauties of former years.

Our Den, Living and Drawing Room Furniture

offers opportunities for profit making unequalled by any other line on the Canadian market.

Come and Have a Double Look

The Waterloo Furniture Co., Limited
Waterloo   *Write for a copy of our "Monimaker" Booklet*   Ontario

Brighten Your Stock

For the Holidays
WITH A SELECTION FROM THE

KRUG LINE

Library Tables, Writing Tables, Parlor Tables, Hall Chairs, Footstools, Dining Chairs, Davenport Sofas, Morris Chairs, Couches, Rockers and Chairs, Reception Chairs, Parlor Furniture. Office, Side, Arm, Rotary Chairs and Settees.

Designed and built with a care that seems to be just a little more than necessary, but at prices that are well within the moderate limit.

Our new Supplement will be mailed in a few days

The H. Krug Furniture Co., Limited
BERLIN, ONTARIO

CANADIAN FURNITURE WORLD AND THE UNDERTAKER.   January, 1914

"The Compliments of the Season to You"

See this new mattress at the Toronto Furniture Exhibition

Illustration shows mattress with top ticking removed

The Trade Acclaims It

⇒ Arrows indicate Ventilators

"NEVERSPRED"
(Patent Applied for)

Like all great inventions, the principle of the "Neverspred" mattress is exceedingly simple. It consists of a series of bands that run cross-wise and length-wise over the felt and under the ticking. These bands are so arranged as to form a reinforcement which positively prevents stretching or sagging or the falling away of the edge. In this wise: the band is cut to the absolute length of the mattress, so that the mattress itself cannot vary in width or in length in the slightest degree.

Nevertheless, the only indication that these bands are there comes from the fact that they form a handle on the top, bottom and sides of the mattress, and in this way serve a double purpose.

Another big feature of the mattress is its series of rubber ventilators.

Finally, every "Neverspred" mattress is finished with the famous "Ideal" Imperial Edge, and every mattress is covered with a very fine grade of art ticking.

THE IDEAL BEDDING CO. LIMITED
2-24 JEFFERSON AVENUE — TORONTO

Canadian Furniture World and the Undertaker

PUBLISHED THE FIRST OF EACH MONTH BY

THE COMMERCIAL PRESS, LIMITED
52 COLBORNE STREET, TORONTO
Phone Main 4978

D. O. McKinnon, *President.*	Weston Wrigley, *Manager.*
W. L. Edmonds, *Managing Ed.*	Geo. H. Honsberger, *Advertising Mgr.*
James O'Hagan	George G. Colvin
Wm. J. Bryans	John A. Gibson
Associate Editors	*Advertising Representatives*

F. C. D. Wilkes (Phone Main 6559), Room 704, Unity Bldg., Montreal.
E. J. MacIntyre, Room 659, 122 South Michigan Avenue, Chicago.
Gotham Advertising Company, 95 Liberty Street, New York.

Subscriptions
Canada, $1.00 a year. Other Countries, $2.00 a year

Publishers' Statement—2000 copies of this issue of the Canadian Furniture World are printed, over 1900 of these being mailed to furniture dealers, salesmen, etc., and the balance to advertisers and exchanges. An average of 2000 copies has been printed every month during 1913. Itemized statement, showing distribution according to provinces, will be furnished on request.

Vol. 4   JANUARY, 1914   No. 1

The Forthcoming Furniture Exhibitions. That the forthcoming exhibitions at Stratford, Berlin, Waterloo and Toronto will be a success there can scarcely be any doubt.

As far as the manufacturers themselves are concerned, they certainly are sparing no effort. They are not only working even harder than they did last year, but they are working more together. This of course applies to the manufacturers in Berlin, Waterloo and Stratford.

Toronto is making its first venture in furniture exhibiting, but there are indications that it will be a successful one. At any rate the space demanded has overtaxed the supply, with the result that some manufacturers will be unable to exhibit.

At Stratford an innovation will be introduced. Heretofore each manufacturer has exhibited in his own factory. At the forthcoming exhibition all exhibits will be under one roof, and luncheon will be served there as well.

The promoters of the exhibition at Berlin have secured a central building for the exhibits of outside manufacturers. Local manufacturers will, as before, exhibit in their own factories. It is quite probable that this building will become a permanent furniture exchange.

Take a note of the dates and make up your mind to attend. Stratford, January 12 to 24; Berlin, January 12 to 17; Toronto, January 12 to 24.

He will be a wise retailer who makes up his mind to visit all three. It will pay him.

He who believes he knows all about his business that it is possible to learn is exhibiting signs of commercial paresis.

Talks at Exhibitions on Selling Methods. The suggestion made in the last issue of The Furniture World to the effect that provision should be made at the forthcoming exhibitions for a conference of those in the trade is meeting with endorsation. The opinion is that it would be a good thing.

A manufacturer who is not directly interested in any of the exhibitions which are to be held makes the further suggestion that the manufacturers who are directly interested should make arrangements whereby one or more addresses on retail selling methods might be given during the exhibition.

The suggestion is a timely one. It would make the exhibitions doubly attractive to retail dealers and would consequently tend to increase the attendance.

It should not be a difficult thing to arrange both for the conference and the addresses or talks on retail selling methods. It is to be hoped the suggestion will be acted upon.

One cannot lag in business, any more than one can lag in a race, and expect to win the highest honors.

The Furniture Trade and Better Housing. Those engaged in the furniture business, either as manufacturers or retail dealers, can scarcely be uninterested spectators of the world-wide movement for better housing conditions for workmen.

It necessarily follows that better housing conditions will demand better home furnishings. There can be no doubt about that. Experience proves it. As it is natural for tumble-down houses and tumble-down furniture to accompany each other, so it is natural for bright, clean and sanitary homes to possess furniture that is in keeping with them.

But the movement for better housing conditions is not concerned alone with the welfare of the lower class of workmen: it embraces that of the skilled worker and the clerk. Its ramifications are therefore wider than many people may suppose.

In no one country has the movement for better housing conditions generated the impetus that it is likely to do before a great while. And in Canada we are at any rate far behind the Mother Country in this respect. But in some of the centres of population we are making a promising start.

In their own interests as well as that of the people who are to be directly benefited, those in the furniture trade can well afford to lend the movement all the co-operation they can. The greater the number of those who co-operate the better, for the movement will only advance as public opinion forces it.

An automatic machine may manufacture goods, but it calls for a man with brains to make sales.

Unique Exhibition of Loyalty. In a business where there is an all-round loyalty between employer and employees there is a potent factor for success. This is the heartiest kind of co-operation, for co-operation is one of the fruits of loyalty. Everybody is doing his level best to build up big business.

In going over an advertising magazine the other day I came across a reprint of a unique circular letter signed by the salesmen of a certain large and long established store. It was unique in two particulars. In the first place it revealed the spirit of "hearty service" on the part of the eight salesmen who signed it. And in the second place it showed the use that could be made of the selling staff where loyalty really existed in advancing the interests of the firm.

It appears that the firm had been in business about 57 years, and that some of the salesmen had been in its employ about 25 years. One of the salesmen conceived the idea that this evidence of loyalty on the part of employer and employee could be utilized to the advantage of the firm. The others fell into line and as the fall season was approaching it was decided to take advantage of it for advertising purposes.

First of all it was decided to appoint a committee to examine the goods that had been taken into stock for the season's trade. When this had been done the result was embodied in a circular together with a statement regarding the number of years the firm had been in business and the length of time several of the salesmen had been in its employ. The circular closed with an invitation to their customers to call and inspect the stock.

That it sold goods as well as attracted attention may be taken for granted.

There are scores of stores throughout Canada in which all-round loyalty obtains. Why cannot the clerks in many of them emulate their brethren of the store to which reference is made above?

If done well it would take well. Its uniqueness alone would give it advertising value.

The business that has in it the leaven of ability and enterprise will swell to successful proportions

Necessity for Stock-taking
Stock-taking is to many a merchant a nightmare and only to be gone through from a sense of necessity. Occasionally one comes across so-called business men who are so obsessed with the magnitude of the undertaking that they ignore it altogether and go on year after year in ignorance as to their actual financial standing. If they have a small balance in the bank they are satisfied. They think they are doing well.

The president of a large commercial corporation tells how many years ago when he first became a director of the concern of which he is now the head that the then president announced to the board that it was proposed to pay the shareholders a dividend of seven per cent., which was something they had not done for several years.

"Where is your financial statement?" asked the new director.

"We haven't one, but we've got the money in the bank," was the answer that came back.

After a determined fight the new director obtained the promise from the president that a financial statement should be prepared before any further action was taken in regard to the payment of dividends.

When the promised statement appeared it showed that instead of being in a position to pay a dividend the company was in a hole to the extent of nearly fifty thousand dollars. That nipped in the bud the dividend-paying proposition.

The company is in business to-day and regularly pays dividends, but not until stock has been taken and a financial statement prepared.

This may be an extreme case, but it establishes the fact that no business man can know for a certainty where he stands until he has taken stock.

A good many of the large retail firms, like the banks, now take stock every six months. All retailers should at least do so once a year.

He who would be a good salesmen must learn the rudiments that make one.

Loyalty of Employers and of Employees.
Loyalty is a factor in the success of all business enterprises. Loyalty of the right brand is not a jug-handled affair. It approximates more to the loving-cup with its two or more handles rather than to the jug with its one handle.

In other words there should be a loyalty of the employer as well as a loyalty of the employee.

An employer cannot expect loyalty from his clerks if he is disloyal to them. Neither can clerks expect loyalty from their employer when they are disloyal to him.

"Hearty service in friendship or love" is one of the definitions the dictionary gives of loyalty.

In every business, no matter what its nature may be, "hearty service" is necessary in order to secure success.

"Hearty service" every clerk should give. That is what he is paid to do. No clerk was ever employed under terms and conditions which stipulated that he should only render a half-hearted service.

Even if his remuneration is not commensurate with the quality of his service that is no reason why he should not do the very best he can for the business in which he is employed.

On the other hand the employer must be loyal to his clerks. He must treat them as human beings, not as machines. He must treat them not as slaves, but as free men. And he must pay them what they are worth. That is loyalty.

Clerks who are not loyal are dear at any price, and should be given their "walking ticket" at the first convenient moment.

The best thing a clerk can do with a disloyal employer is not to be lax in the performance of his duties, for that will probably do himself as much harm as it will his chief, but to obtain another place of employment at his earliest convenience.

Let your windows reflect in the concrete the articles you have in the store that are suitable for the holiday trade.

Co-operative Advertising
A great deal could be accomplished in combating the competition of the mail order houses if the merchants in the small towns and villages were to combine for the purpose of advertising the advantages that accrue from buying in the home town.

Advertising rates in local newspapers are low and the cost of a quarter, half or whole page would amount to little if divided among the home merchants.

The space should be used not for the purpose of advertising merchandise, nor for "knocking" mail order houses, but for the purpose of educating the local residents to the importance of patronizing the merchants in the home town.

At one time it occurred to but few people that purchases made at the mail order stores in the large cities that could have been made at home were derogatory to the interests of the town generally as well as to the merchants specifically. This wider phase of the matter is now being more generally recognized. But there are still a great many to whom this aspect of the case has yet to be brought home.

An advertisement run once a week in the local papers setting forth this and other reasons why the home stores should be patronized would undoubtedly exercise in time a great deal of influence for good.

Such advertisements should not interfere with the regular advertisements of the individual merchants. This should be still kept up, its purpose being to advertise the merchandise of each individual merchant.

Whatever may be done in a general way to educate the public in regard to the reasons for buying at home no merchant can afford to neglect that which advertises his own goods and stamps his own personality on his business.

The Business Situation in Canada

BY W. L. EDMONDS

The Business Adjusting Process. Business in Canada is gradually adjusting itself to the new conditions obtaining in the financial world. This is the outstanding feature of the business situation as it stands to-day.

This process of adjustment is not going on without causing some disturbance. Now conditions cannot be brought about without it. It is natural.

There is, however, no need for alarm. The basic conditions are sound. One does not require a microscope to discover this. This must be apparent to everyone who will for a moment stop and think.

It is true that in most of the manufacturing industries the decline in business has necessitated either the shortening of the hours of labor or the reduction of staffs. But it is not because there is as a rule throughout the country an excess of goods in the hands of the retail distributors.

The condition of business as it is to-day in Canada is due to the weakening of credit, chiefly owing to the stringency of the money market. The goods are wanted, but the money necessary for the payment of the same is not forthcoming with the same freedom as formerly. That is the situation in a nutshell.

* * * *

Foundations are Sound. That the foundations of business are sound there can be no doubt.

A grain crop of over half a billion bushels and of a quality higher than ever experienced in the history of the country is no mean foundation. At any rate it gives strength to the faith of the commercial and financial interests of the country.

The bank clearings, the official banking returns issued by the Government and the railway earnings, are on the whole of a character which tends to optimism rather than to pessimism.

In spite of the undoubted recession in business, the bank clearings for the first ten months of the year are still ahead of those for the same period of 1912; and last year was an abnormal year. The explanation of this is the large deliveries of this year's grain crops and the improvement which has taken place during the last couple of months in collections. But whatever the cause may be, the clearing house barometer indicates that large sums of money are being turned over, even if the uniform increases which were recorded week by week last year are not now so much in evidence.

Neither are the bank returns of a depressing character. Following the lead of the Bank of England the banks in this country are in a stronger position than they were even a year ago. Their liabilities are $34,097,000 smaller than a year ago while their assets are $14,826,000 greater.

That, in spite of the conservatism that is being made, the banks are still taking care of the commercial interests of the country is evidenced by the increase of $8,714,000 in note circulation, and of nearly $7,000,000 in loans to mercantile concerns.

Up to a couple of months ago the gross earnings of the C.P.R. showed some rather uncomfortable decreases, but since then, on account of the movement of the new crop, there has been a steady increase, until up to the end of the first week in November the gain for the year to date was $1,388,000.

The increase for the three transcontinental railways for the year up to the end of the first week in November was $3,164,302. This indicates anything but a paralized condition of business.

* * * *

Not an Unmixed Evil. As far as the money stringency is concerned, it is not altogether an unmixed evil. During the extraordinary prosperity which this country has enjoyed the last few years, evils have been allowed to creep in which could only be eradicated or cured by the inability to obtain a further supply of the money upon which they fed.

Money is now barely in sufficient supply for the regular needs of legitimate and established business enterprises. Wildcat enterprises are therefore dying of starvation, and to take up a subscription to rescue them from their fate is the farthest from anybody's mind.

But in spite of the stringency Canada has fared extraordinarily well. In fact much better than, under the circumstances, might have been expected. Up to the end of October we had borrowed about $210,000,000 in London, which is larger than the amount obtained last year up to the same time. Last year Canada borrowed about $31,000,000 in the United States, but this amount, it is estimated, will be exceeded by the borrowings of this year. France also promises to become a larger purchaser of Canadian securities.

From a monetary standpoint it cannot by any means be said that the outlook for Canada is bad.

It may be some months before the world's money market returns to a normal condition, but when it does we may confidently expect an active resumption of trade in Canada.

* * * *

A Growing Foreign Trade. Although there is a recession in trade on the home market, there is no sign of a falling off in our foreign trade.

The latest official returns issued for the present fiscal year only cover the four months ending July. These show the aggregate foreign trade to be $358,486,286, an increase of over $30,000,000 compared with the same period in 1912.

The imports were $227,675,273, an increase of $16,808,816; the exports $130,811,013, an increase of nearly $13,000,000.

The exports of manufactured goods during the four months were larger than in any corresponding period. They were $16,054,895, which is $3,392,000 in excess of those for the first four months of the previous fiscal year.

With the home market demanding less attention we may expect the manufacturers of Canada to devote a little more time to the cultivation of the foreign market. Last year the value of the exports of Canadian-made goods was $43,692,708. Twelve years ago it was only about equal to that which we are now doing in one-third of a year. If the ratio of increase the first four months is maintained, it will be $64,000,000 for the twelve months. So mote it be—and more.

The Coming Stratford Furniture Exhibition

The new Farquharson-Gifford building, where the exhibition will be held.

The furniture manufacturers of Stratford have decided that the 1914 exhibition of their products, which they will make during the fortnight from January 12 to 24, will be the greatest and best exposition of furniture lines they have even brought together, and that for comprehensiveness, beauty, utility and arrangement of display the exhibition will rank high in comparison with similar expositions in any other furniture centre.

All the lines displayed will be shown under one roof —in the Farquharson-Gifford furniture manufacturing building—a brand new structure, conveniently located in the midst of the Stratford furniture factory district, handy to the railway station, and not far from the retail section and big hotels.

This Farquharson-Gifford building is a four-storey

CHARLES FARQUHARSON
President, The Farquharson-Gifford Co., Stratford.

white brick structure, 164 x 60 feet, and giving a clear floor space of 40,000 square feet. It will be specially lighted for the exhibition, so that the finer points and features of the lines displayed may be suitably set off and strikingly shown,

A feature that will be appreciated by those attending the Stratford exhibition is the noon-hour lunch, which it is proposed to give daily in the exhibition building. This will enable visitors to spend the whole day at the exhibition in comfort and also save time in allowing them to devote their attention to the various lines displayed.

Furniture dealers visiting Stratford during the period of the exhibition will be the guests of the manufacturers of the Classic city, and not only will they be made welcome at the exhibition hall, but carriages will be at their disposal to take them to and from the station to their hotels, the exhibition and the factories. As well, members of the entertainment committee will be at their service in the evenings to act as guides in directing the visitors to any of the club or lodge meetings they may wish to attend.

Of course the exhibition hall will be the centre of things. A visit there, if only to look over the new lines, will prove an invaluable help, as the information to be obtained by visitors, and especially by furniture

> There is no place like an exhibition to get a grasp of the vogue of furniture.

trade visitors, will be such as can not readily be gathered through any other means. All the new goods for 1914 will be shown, and the dealer will have an opportunity of meeting the makers and designers of the lines displayed, thus making new friends for mutual profit. Besides, should the visitor desire, he may visit the factories where the goods are turned out, and there learn a lesson in salesmanship that will be specially useful on the floor of his store by seeing the raw material turned into furniture items in the rough, and finally their transformation when they make their appearance after leaving the finishing room.

During the first week of the Stratford exhibition the Berlin-Waterloo furniture show will also be on, and as Stratford and Berlin are but an hour apart visitors can with convenience visit the two centres and, if they wish, have an opportunity of visiting 35 furniture factories turning out goods for every room in the house and store.

The list of exhibitors who will show at Stratford is made up of:
George McLagan Furniture Co., Ltd.
Stratford Chair Co., Ltd.
The Imperial Rattan Co., Ltd.
The Globe-Wernicke Co., Ltd.
Stratford Desks Co., Ltd.
The Stratford Mfg. Co., Ltd.
Stratford Bed Co.
The Farquharson-Gifford Co., Ltd.
The Classic Furniture Co., Ltd.
Stratford Brass Co.
Frame & Hay Co.

And all these factories will show their full lines, making the exhibition one of the most comprehensive furniture displays ever made in Canada, and a display that will be a credit to the Canadian furniture industry.

The Stratford furniture factories have set the exhibition pace, and they propose to lead the procession. "By all means visit Stratford, the home of good furniture," say the manufacturers. Let them know the day you are to arrive, and they will have a warm room and a warm reception awaiting you.

There will be four new furniture exhibitors in the Stratford display this year—Stratford Desk Co., Stratford Bed Co., Farquharson-Gifford Co., and Classic Furniture Co.

Each of the factories is sending individual invitations to the trade, and in other ways they are doing all in their power to make the exhibition a success. Visiting dealers remaining over night in Stratford will be taken care of by entertainments provided for them.

The arrangements for those contemplating visiting Stratford make sure that the dealer will be put to small expense. Besides, he will see the new offerings for spring and summer—and in some cases goods a year in advance. There are some who believe that in the near future dealers from the United States will make Stratford a visiting point during the January exhibition season to see what are the new things being put out by Canadian furniture factories.

The interior of the exhibition hall has been painted white for the occasion, and it will be splendidly lighted by 100-watt electric lamps.

The Stratford Chair Co. will make a display covering 5,000 square feet of space. They will show their entire chair line of diners, rockers, den and library, bedroom and office chairs. Many new designs will be shown for the first time. They will as well make a display of an entirely new line of inexpensive oak case goods, both plain and quartered, and also a line of quartered gum case goods.

The retailer who loses most by furniture exhibitions is he who stays away.

F. M. GIFFORD
Sec.-Treasurer, The Farquharson-Gifford Co., Stratford.

STRATFORD EXHIBITION'S STRONG POINTS

Good hotel accommodation; all goods shown under one roof; all factories showing their complete lines; noonday lunch under same roof.

Interior of Farquharson-Gifford building, showing possibilities of display. There are four floors like this.

Method of Keeping a Perpetual Inventory

Simple System Which Will Show Approximate Standing of Business at any time.

IT is of greatest assistance to a merchant to be able at all times to keep in close touch with the progress of his business. The closer he can keep in touch with all the details which will show him what advance is being made, the greater will be the advantage to him. The progressive business man will agree that it is a valuable asset to be able to tell at intervals the standing of his business. It is for this reason that an annual inventory is taken. A large number of dealers would like to know this oftener, but the labor involved is so great that most dealers have to be satisfied with one inventory a year.

Simple Plan Gives Approximate Standing.

Herewith is given a method whereby the retailer may tell approximately at all times throughout the year the standing of his business. In this way, if there are any leaks they will be discovered and rectified before they have run very long. It enables a dealer at any time, and with little work, to find out how his business compares with the last time he took stock, and if progress is favorable.

The plan is not by any means a complicated one, and while not giving this information just as exact as the annual inventory, it gauges it closely enough to show how the business is proceeding. Then, again, at the end of the year the annual inventory can be taken the same as usual.

Three Accounts Necessary.

The accompanying cuts will explain the plan. First, we have Stock Account. On January 1, when stock was taken, we found we had $1,500 worth of stock on hand. During January we purchased $800 worth as shown by the invoice book. During the same time we sold $1,200 worth, which, with the estimated profit on the same deducted, shows amount of goods taken from stock during that month.

How do we find the amount of profit? During the previous year we sold, say, $14,400 worth of goods, on which, according to our annual inventory, we made a gross profit of $2,160, which means 15 per cent. This will vary with different stores, but for to illustrate our plan, we take the average profit in this case as 15 per cent.

The amount on the books at the end of January is simply found. When inventory was taken on January 1 the amount was $1,000. There was sold for credit in January $500, while $600 was received on account, so that the amount remaining on the books at the end of the month is $900.

The third account is that of the Amount Owing. On January 1 the amount was $800. There was bought on credit during January $800, while there was paid on account owing $1,000. This leaves debts of $600 at the end of January.

How the Plan Works Out.

Thus, at the end of January we have the amount of stock, the amount on books and the amount owing, so that with the other resources and liabilities such as cash in bank and on hand, notes payable and receivable, etc., we are ready to make a complete inventory. At the end of February the same thing may be done, and in this manner at any time throughout the year the merchant may tell with a fair degree of accuracy the standing of his business. In other words, he has a perpetual inventory.

Of course, every dealer will recognize that this perpetual inventory may not be exactly accurate, as the percentage of profit may vary, but by taking his annual inventory at the end of the year, the same as usual, he will be able to ascertain how correct it is. One of the important features is to get the average profit as accurate as possible.

It is quite evident that this perpetual system has to be commenced immediately after the annual stock-taking and inventory, when all the necessary facts to commence with are available.

The three accounts necessary in keeping perpetual inventory as explained on this page.

Make up your mind that even if you don't sell more goods this year, that you will sell as many goods, but of better quality and at a higher price. You can make from ten to twenty-five per cent. more than last year by adopting this plan.

Collins' Course in Show Card Writing

Second of a series of articles specially prepared for this journal.

Plate 9 is the same style of letters as Plate 8, but is "condensed." That is, each letter is high and narrow. There are many occasions where this style of letter will work in to better advantage than those of Plate 8. Practise this style of letter, noting carefully that the bodies of all the letters are the same height.

Plates 10 and 11 are among the most useful styles of letters there are. They are known as italics, and are used where a card may have considerable matter on it. Plate 10 is not blocked as Plate 11 is. These can be made with one of your small brushes. You may hold it as instructed in last lesson by restig one hand on the other. Or you may hold it in the same manner you would hold a pen or pencil, resting your hand on the card.

Plate 12 is a full block alphabet of what some call the "thick and thin" style of letters. By that is meant that some of the lines are thicker than others. Blocked letters are not advisable for general use in card writing as they cannot be made rapidly. However, for one or two words or a line that needs bringing out prominently, this type of letter will work in most admirably.

In practising with your brush always make your strokes continuous and as long as possible. Do not make a short stroke, then go back and "lap" or "join" onto it. Practise speed as well as accuracy in forming each letter. In all the plates thus far you should make each part of the letter with one stroke. You may find the curved lines hardest to do, but make as much of each curve as you can with one stroke of your brush. Work as rapidly as you can, even though at first your lines may be crooked and uneven. Practise making a vertical stroke about three or four inches long, doing it as rapidly as possible; then practise a horizontal stroke. Make these by the hundred for speed and accuracy. Remember patience and practice are just as necessary in learning to write showcards as in learning to play some musical instrument.

We offer three cards as a suggestion for the Christmas trade. The style of cards to be used for this particular season must be determined largely by the line of goods one has for sale. The special Christmas stocks such as toys, candies and other lines that are considered strictly Christmas presents, are not difficult to advertise. Other lines must be treated differently. Many of these must be advertised under the heading of useful presents. Two of the cards offered belong to

Sample of seasonable window card which may be finished in a variety of colors.

The price in red and the wording in black makes a strong combination on display card.

The History of Furniture

Recent displays of period furniture made by the T. Eaton Co., Toronto. Upper picture depicts Sheraton period 1750-1800, beautiful, simple, dainty and classic lines. Tapering brass carpet legs, brass rods, galleries on sideboards, curved, barred doors and "fanbone" work. Lower picture (Gothic 1100-1500) architectural period of furniture. Purity of outline and solidity of build. Massive chairs and sideboards, tracery carving, oak. Suitable for dining room, library and hall.

Although we pass our lives in houses of our own or those of others, very few, indeed, have any idea of the origin of the homely articles with which we are surrounded. But, from attic to kitchen, in nearly all of them, there is to be traced quite a romantic beginning. Take the pictures hanging on the wall, for instance. They date back to about 500 years, when monks painted their living rooms round with Scriptural subjects. One day someone suggested nailing a piece of wood in between the paintings to separate the subjects. Then came gilding, and the modern picture frame followed as a matter of course.

The drawing-room is very fertile in romance. As most people know, its real and true title is the "withdrawing room," i.e., the room to which you withdraw after dinner. The origin of antimacassars is also common history. One hundred and fifty years ago it was the fashion to dress the head liberally with macassar oil. Housewives, objecting to the damage caused to their chairs by this grease, placed strips of lace over the backs, and the word and article antimasacar came into being.

The chairs themselves are very interesting. They date back to the time when knights and ladies, wishing to keep their feet off the draughty floors, brought in the use of the stretcher. Originally the stretcher was only raised a few inches above the rush-strewn ground, but gradually the form was altered, and by the time that carpets were common the stretcher had evolved into a high-legged and high-backed chair. The cosy armchair came last of all. At first only a cushion was placed over the wooden seat. Then they carved the legs of the seat possessing the cushion, and finally they padded back and arms. Chairs were always very important articles of furniture. To-day "taking the chair" denotes taking the head of affairs, and is reminiscent of the time when only the most imporant personage present sat on a four-legged seat, the lesser fry having to put up with three-legged stools.

Window curtains, or, rather, the European idea, came from China in the Middle Ages, when some adventurous traveller returning from that country mentioned the Chinese habit of fastening a piece of cloth across the window.

Table drawers owe their being to the gamblers of former days. A place was wanted to keep the cards when not in use, and an aperture beneath the table top was utilized.

Kitchen is derived from an Anglo-Saxon word, being to cook. Scullery has nothing to do with scullion, but comes from a word meaning a bowl; while "hall"—meaning a covered-in place—has just the same root as—the infernal regions.—Pacific Furniture Trade.

"I talk with my department heads, not at them," expresses the knack by which one general manager gets big men to work with him.

Before he starts a conference which involves the personality of either man in the conference, he trys to eliminate the personal factor. He supposes that the difference of opinion over policy or method is the idea of a third party. Then both he and his department head discuss that third party's point of view and work as impersonally as possible.

Selling Methods in the Furniture Store

Some Experiences and Suggestions

SELLING OFFICE FURNITURE

Practically every dealer in office furniture to-day realizes that the best aid in selling his goods on the floor is to display them in some way that will attract the attention and please the eye of the prospective buyer. An effort should be made to group pieces into sets that belong together. Even if the grouping is nothing more than a roll-top desk with a swivel chair in front of it, an effort is made to effect something of this nature. Many wide-awake dealers are showing their office furniture grouped in model offices: a desk, swivel chair, typewriter desk and chair, waste-basket, filing devices, etc. Some displays show how the furniture is adapted to some particular line of business. It is well to have a filing device in every display. If the display is to represent a real estate office, files that should be used in that line of business should be in that display. Legal blank sections, document-file sections, card sections with the proper labels in each label-holder, so the prospect can see without being told just what each file is to be used for and how much of a time and labor-saving device it really is.

LET TICKETS TELL THE PRICE

There is a feeling in the breast of nearly every human being that rebels against going into a store to ask the price of an article displayed in a show window.

If, on the other hand, the article displayed looks good and the price looks reasonable, it sells itself to a great many people.

Few merchants nowadays advertise special bargains or specials of any kind, without giving the price after the description. Price is the final clincher for the sale. In the merchants' advertising, something definite must be told.

Show window advertising is much the same as newspaper advertising. The description of the goods is given by their display. Even where goods are displayed, sometimes a word or two of printed description is necessary. But to our minds, the display of anything, no matter how good it may be, is very incomplete without the price ticket.

We believe in the generous use of price tickets inside the store also. People like to see them, and the tickets very often lead to the sale of an article that would not sell otherwise on account of the timidity existing on the part of the would-be-but-afraid-to-ask-the-price customer.—Trade Outlook.

KNOW YOUR COST OF DOING BUSINESS

Every merchant should keep an expense sheet which will show every actual fixed or running expense, such as rent, light, insurance, interest on the investment, clerk hire, his own salary, etc., for month and year.

Your own salary should be equivalent to what you would get if you worked for someone else. Your real profit, the thing you should be in business for, must be figured over your salary. If you own the building your store is in don't forget to charge yourself rent for it equivalent to what you could obtain by renting it to someone else. Donations and contributions are also a consistent part of the cost of doing business and must not be forgotten.

Compare your monthly expense reports frequently with the report for the corresponding month of the preceding year. In this way many excessive climbing expenses without a corresponding increase in profit can be detected and cut down.—Selling Power.

DUTCH MILL SELLS DUTCH CHINA

The Burroughes Furniture Co., Toronto, just previous to the Christmas season made a push on their chinaware department, suggesting china dinner and tea sets as holiday gifts. They advertised a 100-piece delft blue Dutch dinner set worth $25 for $12—and at an instalment rate of $1 down and $1 a week. Proper newspaper publicity was given, and good window displays

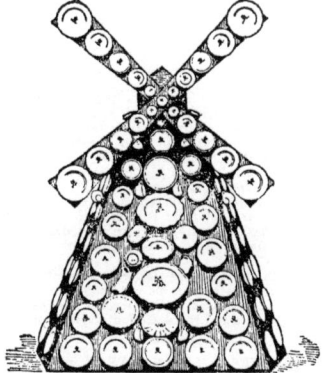

Burroughes Dutch China Windmill.

were made. Especially attractive was the moving wind-mill of chinaware, which occupied a prominent position in the various window displays. It was made of old packing cases covered with yellow cloth, the chinaware in blue and white setting off well, and being attached to the mill with brass hooks. The arms of the mill were free, of course, and moved about with the aid of a small motor. The Dutch mill advertised the Dutch china set, and effectively drew attention to the display.

The Burroughes Company also made an offer of 50 pieces of china free with every $100 purchase in the store.

AS WANAMAKER DOES IT

John Wanamaker has written "Nine Rules for Honest Merchandising," which are as follows:
1. Trustworthy merchandise sold at actual value.
2. True advertisements and salesmanship.
3. No sale settled to stay a sale until the buyer cared to have it so.
4. Goods returnable for cash refunding.
5. One price rigidly, and that the lowest, marked in plain figures.
6. The customer should take the goods at the price named or leave them.
7. Genuine labels on goods and, whenever possible, indicating the character of component parts.
8. A new sense of relations between customer and storekeeper, giving personal freedom to the visitor without obligation to purchase
9. A recognition of a duty to an employee beyond the mere payment of wages.

No one would claim that Mr. Wanamaker has a monopoly on these worthy ideals, but whoever formulates such standards and backs them up by his example, renders a service not only to his own business, but to the business world generally.

SCRUTINIZE YOUR FREIGHT BILLS?

How many retailers scrutinize freight bills carefully? The question is asked by an American trade journal, which points out the large losses to retailers arising from this negligence.

"It is well known that the tariffs of the railroads and other transportation companies are complicated affairs," says this paper, "and that the average railroad billing clerk is far from knowing all the details which affect the method of classification alone is probably no overstatement. Yet in the classification a large difference in the rate may be involved. Usually, moreover, when the clerk is in doubt he decides the question in favor of his employers—by charging the higher rate. We have heard it stated that in order to encourage such action transportation companies compel their clerks to pay out of their own salaries any losses which the company may suffer from undercharges.

"The difficulty with the average merchant is that his own employers are not fully posted in the details of routing, classification, rates, etc. And the dealer may well ask, 'What are we going to do when we have not such facilities?'

"For one thing, when the dealer is a member of a local merchants' association, he can induce his fellow members to join in providing facilities for the examination of freight bills and the detection of overcharges."

GIVES 5c TABLETS FREE.

Giving a 5c tablet free with each 50c purchase was the means adopted by a southern merchant to interest children in his store.

A number of people bought more than they really intended to in order to get the tablet without cost.

It is extremely interesting to see to what trouble some people will go to get something for nothing.

This is a principle of advertising which no merchant should overlook.

SPECIAL "HOUR SALE" SUCCESS

"Glasgow House" (R. H. Williams & Sons, Ltd.), Regina, Sask., recently conducted a novel "hour sale," which proved to be a valuable advertising stunt. Ten pieces of furniture were put on sale at special prices for one hour on a Saturday evening. There was no profit on the items placed on special sale, but as 600 people visited the furniture department, drawn thereto by the newspaper advertising, and as they spent $700 on other furniture items, the department made a very satisfactory showing.

THE FIXED RETAIL PRICE

More and more comment is being heard in favor of selling furniture at fixed retail prices, and the question of its advisability is having close attention of the most successful members of the trade. An argument in support of the branded goods and fixed retail price is given by a furniture manufacturer, who, in an interview in Furniture Worker, says:
1. General distribution of branded articles of merit, placing such articles within ready reach of the public at a fixed, fair price is a condition distinctly advantageous to the public.
2. Fixed prices for branded articles do not kill competition. On the contrary, they create a competition of brains and skill, which is infinitely more valuable to the public than a sporadic and unhealthy competition of dollars and cents.
3. Any manufacturer who attempts to maintain unduly high retail prices will inevitably invite—and as certainly will secure—the competition of substitute articles at more popular prices.
4. A majority of the best retail dealers favor price-maintenance because it enables them to buy staple goods with confidence, knowing that their profits are assured, if not large.
5. Practically all opposition to price-maintenance comes from dealers who make a practice of price-cutting for their own selfish reasons, regardless of the moral rights of manufacturers and the legitimate profits of other dealers, and with no purpose whatever to serve the public legitimately, but, on the contrary, with the idea of misleading the people as to their ability to sell goods below the market.
6. Fair, fixed prices are really a guarantee against high prices. When people know the standard price of any article they are safeguarded against overcharge.

CHECKING UP ON LOST SALES

A large firm of merchandisers in a well known American city make it a point to find out the real reason for every order they lose. The purpose is not to ply the lash on the unfortunate salesman, but to keep in constant, active touch with the weak spots in their own stock and service. To this end the salesmen themselves are instructed to seek, tactfully, the real objections to the goods which have prevented any given deal or purchase. When the plan was first tried, a few salesmen even had to be "jacked up" for blaming themselves rather than the lines they had failed to sell. "Dig down; get at the root of it" was the department manager's order. The result to-day in that store is a system by which every turn and drift in popular preference is constantly known by the purchasing department—and the stock itself is "turned over" with surprising regularity. By assuming its fallibility and trying to improve on it, the establishment has perfected a service which is well nigh perfect. And the complaint department is reduced to a clerk and a boy assistant. Oddly enough, it has also tended to improve the courtesy of the salesmen themselves.—Office Appliances.

The Art of Display

Suggestions for Window and Interior Arrangements.

SEASONABLE WINDOW TRIMS

That well trimmed windows, or displays are of prime importance in modern merchandising, no one will deny. In the larger cities we find highly paid experts who have developed window trimming to a marvelous degree of artistic beauty, as well as compelling sales in no uncertain measure.

The furniture man, or home furnisher in the small town can take a lesson from the larger towns and, by paying careful attention to the windows, create even greater attention than would be the case in the more metropolitan city. It will pay, and pay well, to give your windows every attention. If you still have an old-fashioned front, poorly lit windows and lack of proper display space get busy and have the windows enlarged.

The proper idea, according to a writer in an exchange, is to have as large an expanse of glass as possible, without interfering frames or posts. Have the windows made to take in at least one complete room scene, if store space will possibly permit. Remember the advantage of an unobstructed view from across the street, do not have the awnings hang too low.

The character of trade catered to determines to a considerable extent the character of the window trim. If an exclusive shop, of the higher grade, rich backings of velours, brocades and fewer pieces, can be utilized. For more general stocks and the more popular priced trade the windows may be arranged in a number of ways, all effective and compelling.

In constructing the window bear in mind that ever troublesome question of frost. Have the window effectively cut off from the store. Use for this purpose either plain or paneled partitions to the ceiling. These panels or partitions should have glass filled spaces at the top to afford as much light as possible, into the store itself. Artificial lighting is becoming more important every day. Some artificial lighting systems are so good in fact, they supersede daylight, but for the ordinary store these systems are rather expensive and elaborate, so daylight must be figured on.

And above all things, whether daylight or artificial light is used, keep the store well lit at all times. The size of your windows will depend largely upon the size and shape of your store, but a show window should not be less than six feet high to give the best results. Windows nearly flush with the sidewalk or main floor level are coming more into use. This affords the passerby a much better opportunity for intimate inspection of the wares.

KEEPING WINDOW FREE FROM FROST.

The time of year is now near at hand when the question of keeping the store window free from ice incrustations will face a good many retailers. Among the methods suggested by one authority is that known as absorption. This can be done with two inexpensive chemicals:—

Calcium Chloride, 10 lbs. (not Chloride of Lime).
Zinc Chloride, 1 lb.

Place in a granite kettle on a hot stove and stir frequently for about an hour or until it begins to stiffen, but is still thin enough to pour. In another room which must be thoroughly dry, place eight or ten sheet-iron baking pans. Pour the mixture into the pans to a depth of about ¼-inch, and allow to cool. When it has set sufficiently but not quite hard, loosen the compound with a knife and break it into small pieces, then pass through a coarse sieve, breaking the large pieces with a hammer. Fill 16-ounce tins half full. Place covers on and seal apertures with paraffine wax until needed. When needed remove cover and place can in window. In from twelve to sixty hours, depending on the amount of moisture, etc., the compound will have absorbed all the moisture from the air that it can. Then place the can on a hot stove, and evaporate the water until the compound is com-

The furnished room in the window makes for increased sales. Tasty seasonable arrangement of living room furniture for Winter selling goods.

January and February Furniture Sales

Some Examples of Advertising done by retailers to attract business, and some comments in regard thereto

BY A. B. LEVER

As soon as the Christmas holiday trade is over furniture dealers throughout the country will naturally be preparing to push their January and February sales.

A January or February special furniture sale without advertisement is, of course, inconceivable. May as well endeavor to get up steam without fuel as for a furniture dealer to run a special sale, be it in January or in December, without advertising.

In business advertising is the impelling force. It is wanted at all times, but at no time so much so as when a special sale is being conducted.

If well done there is scarcely anything a dealer can do to get business which costs him relatively less than advertising. But one can no more expect to do bad advertising and reap good results than good results can be obtained from cultivating poor soil or using bad seed in good soil.

Advertising, in order to be well done, must be carefully thought out. It is not a difficult matter if one takes time to do it properly.

On the next page will be found grouped a number of advertisements which have been used by different furniture dealers. Although each ad. is very much reduced from the original, it is sufficiently clear to serve as a basis for other dealers in preparing their advertising copy.

The advertisement of D. A. Smith, Limited, stands out well, and is, generally speaking, a good one, even though it does not contain a single illustration. In fact, this advertisement looks more attractive without an overloading of any kind than one which has a surfeit of illustrations. There is, however, just one suggestion I would offer, and that is that should any other dealer be disposed to make it the basis of an ad. for his own firm that he leave out the rules which are underneath the seven lines in the table, naming articles and prices. Without these rules the lines will stand out much more clearly. The original was 6½ by 8 inches.

The advertisement of Sheridan's (Brockville) was a simple, newsy little ad., of 4⅜ by 5¼ inches. To prepare an ad. of this kind does not require great skill. It requires common sense. Had the first line been made to read "Annual Furniture Sale," "Money Saving Opportunities," or some other more striking phrase than "Sale of Furniture" I think it would have improved the ad.

The little ad. "A Snap in Wood Beds," is submitted to show how effective even small space like that can be made. The original, which was only 1½ by 4½ inches, was taken from a department store ad. Put in 2½ inch space it would make an attractive little ad. indeed.

The Tobey ad. is of course the best in the group. The Tobey Furniture Company is located in Chicago, and their ad. is reproduced here as a specimen of what is being done by a firm outside Canada. In writing advertisements it does not interfere with one's originality to know what furniture dealers abroad are doing. The original, which was 4 by 13¼ inches, was an all round good ad. It looks well and is well written. Note its neat and artistic appearance, and particularly the engraving and the table giving the former and the present prices of the articles on sale. The engraving, which is of zinc, costs less than a half-tone and on news print shows the details of the piece of furniture much better than if it was of the latter description.

The advertisement of Murray-Kay, Limited, is not only an artistic and attractive one, but it contains a regular budget of news. As the ad. was 6½ by 14¼ inches, the space at their disposal allowed them to do this. The news of the store is what every advertisement should tell in simple and plain language. Prices should also as a rule be included. An ad. with prices named is much more effective than one which is without them. Never mind your competitors; think only of your customers.

ADVERTISING A RETAIL BUSINESS

Where local advertising is concerned, the retailer has little or no trouble in making a selection. Newspaper-advertising rates are based in nearly every case upon so much per thousand circulation, and if there is more than one medium in your town, you will find enough good circulation in the other propositions to merit using them. It is a mistake to take it for granted that you are going to reach the entire buying public by confining your advertising to one particular paper, unless that paper is entirely without opposition, a condition seldom met with.

Small copy, sixty or seventy lines, single space, or fifty or sixty lines, double space, should suffice to tell your story. Whenever possible, illustrations and prices should be used. Large copy, of course, is in order, especially at holiday periods, when down-to-date retailers can exploit various articles of every-day use for men and women.

Good advertising will help establish your credit. Good advertising will not stoop to sharp practice or misrepresentations, because sooner or later the deception will be found out. No business that can not be exploited honestly can ever hope to be permanently successful. Good advertising thus will help build up your own character as well as your business.

After all, advertising is only reputation, and can not show results in a day any more than an individual can show his true character in the same period. It is purely accumulative, and can only prove fruitful as we become acquainted with the proposition.

Do not look upon the money spent on advertising as a gamble. In the majority of advertisements, it is true that immediate results can not be observed; but when you plant seed of any kind, you certainly do not expect to see the fruits immediately spring up; it is necessary to wait a season, and, in the meantime, water and constantly guard the planting. When we see the amount spent by advertisers of known successes, both national and local, in the exploitation of their wares, it seems hardly necessary to add that consistent and persistent advertising will pay in the long run if the merchandise has merit.

THE ROAD TO PROFITS

It costs a retail merchant (except in rural districts) between 18 and 30 per cent. to do business. Generally speaking, the larger the city the higher the cost, because customers expect more in the way of service and display, because store rents are higher, and advertising and delivery more expensive. This cost of doing business must be taken care of before the merchant can make a profit for himself. The publishers of the Saturday Evening Post assert that there are two ways in which this cost can be taken care of:

(1) By charging high prices to the customer.

(2) By charging moderate prices, but selling goods fast, so that although less money is made on each article, so many are sold that the aggregate returns at the end of the year are sufficient to cover both costs and profits.

The latter method is known as "getting more turnovers." Advertised merchandise usually yields more turnovers. Customers, having read about the goods in their favorite publications, take them by preference, to others less known.

PURPOSE IN ADVERTISING

Random advertising like random shooting in the woods, fails to bring down the game. Advertising—the real kind—is a continuous campaign closely related to salesmanship, and no business house would hire salesmen just for a day or a week.

Advertising is a steady drive for business. How to do it most intelligently is an important subject of consideration in every successful business.

Suggestions of great value often come from most unexpected sources. The man who prepares copy must ever be on the lookout for new ideas or his efforts will be commonplace or obsolete. The clever salesman is constantly looking for good points about his goods or new and attractive ways of presenting them, while the advertiser, who prepares the "salesmanship on paper," must do likewise.

Have a purpose in your advertising for the holiday trade.

CLEAN UP SALE WAS OMITTED.

F. I. Fletcher, at a Sphinx club dinner in New York, told an advertising story.

"A man," he said, "entered a shop one bitter cold day and bought a woolen muffler. When he opened the muffler he found inside it the photograph of a beautiful girl, together with a note saying:

"'If you are single, please write to me.'

"A name and address followed, and the man smiled. He was single, and he put the photograph on his sitting room mantel. There, every evening, looking up from his book, he beheld it. It was very beautiful, and in a week he has fallen head over heels in love.

"So he wrote to the girl. Another week passed, a week of anxious nerve racking suspense. Then the love sick man received the crushing letter:

"'The Mary Smith to whom you wrote was my grandmother. She died nine years ago, aged 86. Yours truly.'

"Our heart-broken bachelor, on looking into this strange matter, found that he had foolishly bought the muffler from a dealer who didn't advertise."

Samples of actual advertisements used to promote January and February furniture sales by Canadian dealers

Beds and Bedding

PURE BEDDING PLUS QUALITY

The good work started in enacting laws regulating the manufacture of bedding has had many followers. Alonzo E. Yout, secretary of the Home Furnishers' Association of Massachusetts, writing on this subject says:

Pure bedding laws will have action and re-action. Action in favor of the merchant who puts quality as one of the fundamental principles of his establishment, and re-action against the unscrupulous dealer who is intent upon obtaining the price regardless of quality.

Imagine the Jones family in suburban Boston; they are in moderate circumstances. Mr. Jones has a good living income and is typical of the ordinary American citizen, the keenest judges of good values and quality in the world, they decide that it is time to replenish their household effects; Mrs. Jones wants a new parlor suite and some new bedding, mattresses, etc., they make the usual rounds of the furniture houses and department stores, comparing prices. Mr. Up-to-date Salesman in the house where quality is a cardinal principle says: "Mr. Jones, we can sell you mattresses at any price you wish to pay, and we particularly pride ourselves on the quality of the goods we have for your selection. You will please note the label on each mattress which tells you exactly what the contents are, and we want to assure you that this house stands back of those labels, when it says white cotton it means positively white cotton, and South American hair is not pigs' bristles.

"It is the same with the parlor set and any other merchandise on our floors. We insist upon dealing with reputable manufacturers, and we guarantee that the interior and upholstering is clean and sanitary, the workmanship right, and the quality is there." This appeals to Mr. Jones, who has been following the pure food agitation, the pure bedding legislation, and the sale is consumated.

This also appeals to the progressive merchant. With his goods standardized and labelled the sale is half made, because there is that feeling of confidence and trust inspired at the very start.

The buyer who follows this plan of quality and the right prices need have no fear of a dead stock, the merchandise man will not have to camp on his trail, he will find that the sales record has vindicated his good judgment.

The complaint man will also find his duties less strenuous, and the reason is obvious. The customer who has been sold quality has no legitimate reason for complaint for the quality goods stand the only real test—time.

With the merchant co-operating with the manufacturer along these lines we have a selling proposition that must impress itself forcibly upon the buying public, and the result is a satisfied customer. They are the backbone of our business reputation and the foundation of continued prosperity.

NEW MATTRESS ON THE MARKET

Introduced on the market just at the commencement of the Christmas shopping season, The Ideal Bedding Co., Ltd., Toronto, are now manufacturing a new mattress, called the "Neverspred," which already has obtained a hold on the trade. It is a felt-filled mattress built on exceedingly simple lines.

For a long time manufacturers have experimented with felt and mixed mattresses trying to produce one that would not sag, spread or stretch. The principle of this new mattress is that a series of bands run crosswise and lengthwise over the felt and under the ticking. These bands are so arranged as to form a reinforcement which prevents stretching or sagging or falling away at the edge. The bands are cut to exact length

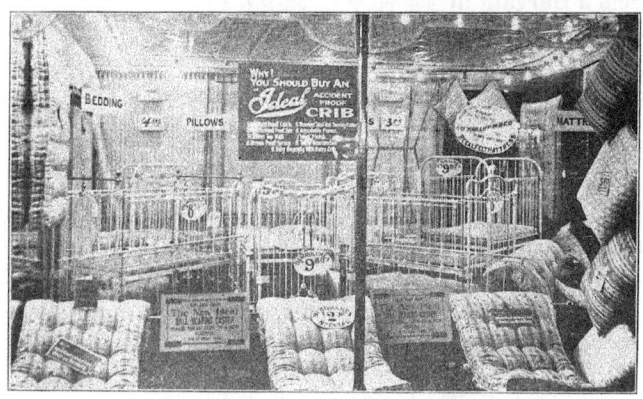

Bedding display made by the Burroughes Furniture Co., Toronto, as a supplement to the window display shown last month—"from raw material to finished product."

and width of the mattress so that the mattress cannot vary in length or width in the slightest degree.

The only indication that these bands are on the mattress comes from the fact that they form a handle on the top, bottom and sides of the mattresses, and thus serve a double purpose. A series of rubber ventilators is set in the edges of the mattresses all round, and the mattress is finished off with the Ideal imperial edge and covered with high grade art ticking.

The company's travellers carried samples for the first time on November 15, and since that time, the management says the factory has been running almost exclusively on the making of "Neverspred" mattresses.

SELLING BEDS THROUGH DISPLAY

Eighty-nine beds sold in ten days is the result of a display put on by B. W. Woon, of the Ideal Bedding Co., Toronto, in Logan's furniture store at St. Catharines, recently. Mr. Woon and Mr. Logan got together on the proposition in advance; Mr. Woon looked after the display and Mr. Logan handled the customers. One or two advertisements in the local newspaper gave the publicity and started the crowd.

Mr. Logan, commenting on the display, stated the result was beyond his expectations. Not only were 89 beds sold as a direct result of the demonstration, but sales of beds have been very fair ever since.

HOW ONE DEALER DISPLAYS BEDS

J. C. Locke, of Ridgetown, has fitted up a room to set up the better class of iron beds, springs and felt mattresses. By having this separate room for the beds, he not only shows the goods actually set up, but places them in much better light than shown in a room crowded with other furniture.

NEW BEDDING COMPANY IN WEST

The Swift Current Bedding and Mfg. Co., Ltd., Swift Current, has been incorporated with a capital of $50,000.

NEW FOLDING DAVENPORT AND DIVANETTE

The "Thorobed" is one of the newest and latest designs of folding davenport and divanette to be offered to the furniture trade by a Canadian manufacturer. Snyder Bros.' Upholstering Co., Ltd., of Waterloo, have secured the manufacturing rights for Canada of this famous bed, and are now making up a full line of samples to be displayed at the Berlin and Waterloo exhibition in January. The "Thorobed" contains many new and desirable features, chief of which is its mechanical construction. The operating devices have been so skilfully concealed as to give it the appearance of a stationary davenport. A wardrobe sufficiently large enough to store pillows and bedding is constructed in the back, this being an entirely new departure. "Thorobeds" are sanitary in every respect, easily operated, and altogether make a handsome piece of living-room or library furniture.

There is a whole lot of solid satisfaction about it when a customer comes back long after having bought something from you and says: "You made me pay a price for that stuff, but it was worth it." Also, it is some compliment to your salesmanship.

Floor Coverings

HANDLING FLOOR COVERINGS

Floor coverings are, to-day, in far greater demand than ever. On every hand we see, in place of the old time "one line" store, which handled nothing but furniture, dry goods, or hardware, the big department stores, house furnishing concerns, and general stores.

Each of these establishments carries, or should carry, a line of floor coverings, and that many of them do so, is proof conclusive of the success of the line as a profit producer.

One of the prime factors for the success of the largest mail order concerns, is the fact that they cater to practically every human need, and to offset mail order competition, the wise dealer should make every effort to carry as large a variety of merchandise as is consistent with his class of trade.

Newly-weds, in furnishing their home, prefer to buy everything under one roof, as far as possible. It is more convenient in regard to the credit contract, deliveries, and selection of goods.

In the larger cities the department stores now sell larger quantities of Oriental rugs and higher priced floor coverings than formerly, as evinced by the large amount of newspaper advertising carried, which is devoted to this class of goods. This is a significant fact and should be borne in mind by dealers; the catalogue stuff of the mail order concerns is usually of the cheapest character, and the dealer can, by practical demonstrations and skilled salesmanship, cater to a better class of trade than the catalogue firms secure.

The dealer in the small town need not fear to put in a line of floor coverings on account of the expense. Persons purchasing carpets, rugs and linoleums in the smaller centres are usually willing to wait, at least a short time, for deliveries. They certainly would have to wait if they sent to the mail order concerns or to the large city store, and here is where the small town dealer wins out. By carrying a well assorted line of samples and catalogues, he can offer a wide variety to the prospective purchaser, taking measurements himself and laying the floor covering himself. This is all appreciated by the customer, and instead of seeing the order go to out of town customers, the local man can pocket the profit on the transaction.

In stocking floor coverings, a careful study of the class of trade to be supplied is the part of wisdom. In some communities none of the really high priced coverings can be disposed of at all. In other communities the very cheap goods would prove simply dead stock. In ordering, the dealer should make a careful scrutiny of the homes in his neighborhood, and size up the situation, and then place his orders for the actual staples as the stock on hand, with the novelties and special grades carried only by sample, or sold from catalogue as suggested. H. K. H.

THE ORIENT AND ITS RUGS

To those who have visited the Orient, its rugs hold us in captivating charm. For it is only by a visit that we can judge the reverence the true Oriental has for his rug. He knows the love, the patience, the skill, the art that each rug has taken to make, and so great is his reverence for the floor covering that he will never tread upon it with his shoes. It is due to this that rugs have come down to us, hundreds of year old, as beautiful as when they were new. The famous mosque at Adrianople, Sultan Selim's Mosque, now captured by the Balkan states, treasures a number of rugs said to be 800 years old. Many beautiful, almost priceless, rugs are in the famous art collections of the world, and for the last thousand years the history of the Orient has been closely interwoven with the history of its rugs. Rugs are to the Orientals what paintings are to us. While our great painters immortalized their creations on canvas, the Oriental made rugs, sometimes spending a lifetime on one masterpiece. These fine rugs were works of love, finished but never perfect. Often deliberately the rug was made to show a defect, in proof that Allah alone is perfect. Such is the explanation of the irregular rugs, the one warp of lighter dye or the slight imperfections of the finest rugs that often puzzle the amateur rug collector.

In order to appreciate the beauty and value of Oriental rugs it is interesting to know how they are made and with what infinite patience and skill the bits of wool are knotted into the warp, knot after knot, and tie after tie, until the prefect rug is finished. The method of weaving is simple. The warp is stretched on a wooden frame. The knotting is begun at the bottom and worked from right to left. A bit of wollen yarn about two inches long is twisted between the strands of the warp, then tied in a secure knot and the ends left free. This knot is then secured in place by one or more twists of the end of the warp; another knot is then begun, and so on ad infinitum until the bottom row is finished and the second row begun. Not until the rug is completed are the ends of the knots cut according to the length of the nap desired. When one square inch of the rug has been finished there have been laboriously tied from one hundred to sometimes a thousand knots, according to the fineness of the rug and the yarn. All this time the weaver works with his brain as well as his hands, for he carries the design and color in his head. To-day often whole families, from the smallest child to the grandparents, make these rugs in their homes, to be sold either to the rich Orientals or exported to Europe and America. It is a fact that America imports more Oriental rugs and of finer quality than all the other continents combined.

In order of importance and general excellence Persian rugs come first. They include the Kirman, Sehna, Kurdistan, Khorassan, Serabend, Youraghan, Feraghan, Shiraz, Gulistan, Mousal, etc. The term "Iran" is the old name for Persian, and is used as a term for general classification.

Among the Turkish rugs, which are mainly from Asia Minor, come the Gheordez, Koulahs, Kenjahs, Latiks and the Bergamas; also others which are sometimes generalized as Anatolians.

From Turkestan come the Bokharas and the more uncommon Samarkands. Afghanistan supplies the Afghans, Kivas and Yamond-Bokharas.

Beluchistan sends out but one type which is generally unmistakable, though Afghans, Bokharas and Beluchistans (sometimes called the Blue Bokharas) all have a family resemblance.

To Caucasia, in Southern Russia, are credited the Kabistans, Shirvans, Chichis, Darbends, Karabaghs, Kizaks, the Gengias and the Cashmeres. The first four are quite similar and are sometimes classed together as the Daghestans.

India supplies modern rugs and fine, large carpets, the designs being often imitations of Persian or Occidental patterns.

The dye, the tone, the richness and color value of a rug is an essential characteristic of the weaving of each class and region, and formerly was not only characteristic but exclusive,. the dyes being often family or tribe secrets. Of course all know that the dyes of the good Oriental rugs are from vegetable or animal origin, and to that is due their beauty and durability. The yarn is dyed and not the wool. In obtaining, for example, the rich, unapproachable blue of the Persians, called imperial blue, the wool is dyed many times, and after each time has to be thoroughly air dried. When one considers that all this is done by hand, with the help of only the most primitive tools, and the patience, the skill and the time it takes, to say nothing of the secrets of the art, is it no wonderful how cheap Oriental rugs really are?

For the Oriental rug is not for the collector alone. Modern transportation facilities have brought the finest of these rugs within the reach of almost every home, and their price, although a trifle higher than that of the machine-made local floor coverings, in view of their beauty and marvellous lasting qualities, is really very economical.

While paintings have signatures and marks by which experts may determine their age and value, rugs must speak for themselves and go on their own intrinsic values. For that reason study of Oriental rugs can never be an exact science, and in their purchase one must rely entirely on his own judgment and the dealer's advice.

RUGS IN ROLLS

The fact that probably a few isolated stores here and there practice the plan suggested by the Dry Goods Economist (New York), makes it none the less worth while to call attention to a way of keeping rugs that is not as common as it ought to be:

In a prominent Cincinnati store the Economist man found the entire rug stock rolled on poles and placed in a leaning position against the walls. Upon asking the reason for this mode of stock-keeping, the buyer replied that he thought it best. The air in this city was so full of soft coal smoke, he added, that no other means of keeping the stock seemed quite as satisfactory.

"I tried having my stock in piles, as many other stores do, and I don't like it," he continued, "for the rugs in one pile could be shown to only one customer at a time, and, at that, the services of two men were desirable, if not imperative. Now, by keeping my stock in this way, I find one man can wait on a customer unaided, inasmuch as a single rug is easily handled, even in the largest stock sizes. Furthermore, a customer likes to see the rug unrolled before her.

"It is much the same way, to my mind," continued the department head, "in selling a good domestic rug as in selling a fine Oriental. If the customer sees the rug unfolded or unrolled, as the case may be, she is more impressed with it than if it were merely the next one in the pile turned up for her inspection.

"I also find that while one salesman is showing a half dozen to a dozen rugs, say of floral design, another salesman can be showing rugs of the same quality of medallions perhaps, or plain centers, or whatever; and neither customer has to wait until the other gets through before she can see what we have to offer.

"I know some of the stores accuse us of being old-fashioned in showing our goods this way, but our customers like it; and, after all, that's the main thing."

SALESPEOPLE

DIPLOMACY AND TACT
By J. A. Conrey

Diplomacy and tact. How many of you use them? I walked into a furniture store a few weeks ago, in the city. A lady came in and asked for a commode. The salesman said, "We don't keep them—haven't got them." She turned and walked out. I thought, "What a fine salesman." I followed her—I wanted to see the difference. She walked into another store. She was met by a salesman. She asked for a commode. He said, "We just sold the last one this morning. We have some on the way. I will show you just what they are." He went back, got a little cut and showed it to her. She asked the price. It was a little bit more than she wanted to pay. He said, "I know the kind you want. We had them. We concluded our customers wanted something a little bit better and got this better one. It is well made, well polished, perfectly odorless, and it's only $1.50 more, and I am sure you would like it better than the cheaper one. I would like to send one out to you." "Well," she said, "you may send it up." The facts were he did not have any coming. He went and ordered one for her. I happened to know who the lady is. The last time I was in the store that salesman said to me: "Do you remember about that lady who came for the commode? She's one of our customers now."

That's what came of a little tact. It always makes me tired when a salesman says, "We haven't got it. We don't keep it." That man has something to learn. There are so many things that enter into this game. What an interesting study the furniture game is; so many possibilities, and I am always glad to see a body of men organized, that come together and talk over those things. There's an organization worth while, if they never do another thing but regulate anything but themselves. I sometimes think the worst competitor the retail dealer has is just himself, if he is not progressive, if he is not studying his game.

QUALITIES OF SALESMANSHIP

The following was recently issued by a manufacturing firm to their salesmen:

"Salesmanship consists of brain work; it is mind, not muscle, which does the business. A salesman does not make permanent friends by yielding to demands for cut prices. It is a sign of weakness, and weakness excites pity rather than admiration.

"Make your selling talk practical. Use facts and figures; they are convincing. If you get a chance, travel along the road in company with your competitor, the better you know him the more you will think of yourself.

"Don't rely upon the introduction of another salesman to influence business for you. You stand on firmer ground if you introduce yourself.

"Jumping ahead of your competitor doesn't pay; he gets all you leave behind, and you leave behind more than you get.

"When selling one man in a town forget all others until you have done your work thoroughly with the one.

"Remember the principal qualifications that equip a salesman to establish confidence, and don't forget that 'cheerfulness' is not only good medicine, but is food for mind and body; it is a character that thrills every atom with new life, and is to the facilities and talents of the mind what sunshine is to the flowers and trees.

"When you are plumb discouraged in the effort to land a customer, bear in mind that he is as near giving up as you are. Don't be the first to 'cave.' Forget the words that signalize surrender; recall the story of the two Irishmen who got mixed up in a little difficulty and decided to fight it out. The referee was chosen and said: 'Let the man who is licked say "sufficient,"' and I will stop the fight.' The two went at each other with hammer and tongs. Soon both were exhausted and landing jabs in the air. Mike was about to keel over, but managed to place one more punch on poor Pat's nose when Pat yelled, 'Sufficient!' 'Begory,' said Mike, 'it's meself that's been trying to think of that darn word for the last tin minutes.' Moral— Don't be a quitter.'

"Let the red blood of determination run riot in your veins and its very energy will force aside the blues."

A NATIONAL DEMAND

A number of traveling salesmen were sitting in a hotel lobby when one began to boast that his firm had the largest number of people pushing its line of goods.

This statement, of course, created much argument until one drummer, who had not much to say before, rose and said: "I'll bet anyone in the lobby that my firm has the largest number of people pushing its line of goods!"

The bet was accepted by the boastful one and the money put up. Then the boastful drummer asked: "Now, what is your firm's line of goods?"

"Baby carriages," said the quiet man as he took the money and departed.

SAYS THE YOUNG SALESMAN—
By Ross Ellis

Off on the start of a seven weeks' trip again,
Hotels and sleepers to be my abode.
How my arm thrills to the tug of my grip again!
Gee! But it's good to be back on the road.
No one to tell me to do this or not do that,
No one to care where I sleep or I dine;
Office hours—open wherever I hang my hat;
Orders are wanted and that's where I shine!

Back where the sidewalks are plank, or just gravel trails,
Where one big plant is the life of each town;
Where folks seem pleased when I tell 'em my travel tales.
Ask me to draw up a chair and sit down.
None of this wasting my time on some sassy clerk!
Head of the firm is the man I will see
Smoke my cigars, while I get in my classy work.
That's the way business is done believe me!

How the hotel clerk will beam when I register,
While the proprietor, jolly and fat,
Stretches his face 'till its whiskery edges stir
Makes me feel good to be welcomed like that!
Back where my notions are thought of immense account,
Where my new clothes will establish the mode;
Back where the house lets me have an expense account
Say! It is great to be back on the road!

Suing to Recover Insurance Money

Insurance companies, as a general thing, don't like law suits. They would much rather create the impression that they are easy to deal with, because that has a directly helpful effect on business, while a reputation for contentiousness has the opposite.

Nevertheless, if the amount at stake is substantial, the average insurance company will fight rather than pay, if it considers that it has a good defence, and when an insurance company sets itself against the payment of a claim nobody on earth takes fuller advantage of every known technicality. It deliberately lays the foundation for that in its complicated policy, which imposes all sorts of duties on the holder, the ignoring of any of which—without the company's consent—is ground for refusing to pay.

The Company's Policy in Disputed Cases.

Nevertheless, the company's policy in most disputed cases is to settle, if it can do so on terms that it considers reasonable. It can be laid down as a rule that in most cases it also pays the holder of the policy to settle, rather than fight the company in court, even though he has to take less than he thinks himself entitled to. I am looking at the matter now not as one of principle, but as one of cold business—dollars and cents in other words.

Every one of the large insurance companies maintains a legal bureau of high-salaried lawyers retained by the year. The company has every advantage in litigation—unlimited means, the best counsel, unlimited time and the possession of the plaintiff's insurance money. In the average case it can tire out the ordinary man so far that he will be weary unto death, and even if he finally gets his money he will have spent a large part of it, or possibly all, in the court.

With other men I should like to be able to look at these matters from the standpoint of pure principle. "No matter if the sum at stake is only 5 cents, and it will take $500 to recover it, I will still go ahead, for my cause is right." If a man has the $500 to spare, and can afford to assume the burden of a worrisome and time-consuming lawsuit, very well, then let principle be vindicated. The average man, however, has to view the matter as one of financial expediency—which course will yield the most money in the end?

As a Rule It Pays the Insured to Settle.

I cannot refrain from referring to a case in which I was recently retained to bring action against an insurance company. My client claimed that his loss was $2,800, but the company disputed this and contended that it was only $2,100. They offered, however, $2,400 to settle the case.

I advised my client to accept it, for two reasons: First, because though the case seemed strong, litigation is always uncertain, and he might lose entirely; second, even if he won all he claimed the company would undoubtedly appeal, and by the time the case was concluded in the highest court he would have spent far more than the $400 difference between his claim and the company's offer.

I could not convince the client of the wisdom of the advice, and he instructed me to refuse the offer and bring suit. A verdict was rendered in the lower court for $2,600 and interest, from which the company appealed. To make a long story short, three years elapsed between the time suit was brought and the day when the Supreme Court finally upheld the verdict of the lower court, and my client had spent $800 in ways which he could not tax against the company as costs. His account with the case therefore stood like this:—

Amount of verdict $2,600
Interest three years 488

                                   $3,088
Expenses   800

Net return $2,288

In other words he had fussed and fought for three years, and was $122 worse off than when he started. To be sure he had the satisfaction of having made the company pay out considerably more than it had offered to, but I question whether it was worth what it cost.

Every Insurance Policy Prescribes Certain Things

which must be done by the holder before suit can be brought. If even one of these conditions is ignored the courts will hold the suit prematurely brought and throw it out.

For instance, there is always a condition that suit shall not be brought until notice and proof of loss are furnished. As stated in a preceding article, however,

---

Those who are not orthodox in regard to fire insurance matters may have a hot time when they least expect it.

---

both notice and proofs can be waived by the company. But if not waived they must be forthcoming before suit can be brought.

Some policies also contain a condition that suit shall not be brought until the approximate amount of loss shall have been ascertained by some form of appraisal or arbitration. This, too, will be binding on the policyholder in the majority of cases.

Practically all policies provide that no suit shall be brought until after a certain time, usually 60 or 90 days. Unless there is something in the case to take it out of the fire, any policyholder beginning suit in advance of the time named will be thrown out of court. This condition, like others, can be waived by the company—not only by words but by actions. For instance, under the law, if the company denies all liability for the loss, it is a waiver of the time limit and suit can be brought at once.

There is also another condition that suit cannot be brought after a certain time. This has always been upheld by the courts unless the time limit prescribed is unreasonably small.

Some insurance companies have endeavored to go even further than this, by compelling a policyholder, through a condition in the policy, to bring suit only in such courts as the company chose. This condition has always been overthrown, because it would unduly fetters a citizen in his right to use whatever court would have jurisdiction over his case.

A Trick Sometimes Tried.

In my own experience I have known insurance companies—not the largest and best, however—to endeavor to trick a policyholder into going past the time limit without bringing suit. For instance, they would open negotiations with a policyholder who had had a loss, thus leading him to believe they were going to pay. Of course we would not bring suit, and when the time limit had expired they would abruptly cease the negotiations and figuratively put their thumb to their nose.

Whenever the policyholder carries a case like this into the courts he will win, for all courts refuse to uphold the company in any such course.

When sued on an insurance claim, the company can defend on the ground that the policyholder failed to comply with some condition in the policy. The policyholder must then prove one of two things: First, he did not violate the condition; or second, if he did violate it, the company consented. If he is helpless on both these points he will lose his case.

Editor's Comment.—While this article contains much truth, it misses the great point, the trouble in these losses usually arises through the assured being ignorant of the proper procedure to take in case of loss or in his having a badly drawn contract. Prevent all this by having your policies put in proper shape to fully protect you, and when you have a loss recognize that you are dealing with a subject of which you know nothing, not the hardware business, but fire loss adjustment.—Editor Canadian Furniture World and the Undertaker.

WHAT THE LIVE MERCHANT ASKS HIMSELF.

By G. S. Buck

Have I found a way to cut expenses?
Have I cleaned up any of the old stickers?
Have I used enough for leaders?
Have I seen that the store is kept clean and in order?
Have I marked all the new—and old—goods in plain figures?
Have I done anything to get new people into the store?
Have I given my advertising and show windows proper attention?
Have I overstocked on any article?
Have I really placed my orders where price and quality are best?
Have I explained the talking points of the goods to the salespeople?
Have I dealt squarely with them?
Have I been pleasant to everyone to-day?
Have I made plans for a better day to-morrow?
Am I a better merchant—and a better man—than I was yesterday?

THE WHITE BEDROOM

Some woman with a predilection for daintiness in the bedroom furnishings has expressed her taste as follows:

After all is said and done, the all-in-white bedroom is a joy forever. It is not entirely practical if the room is of that convertible type used as sitting room and sleeping apartment alternately; but when the bedroom is used to sleep in only, or, perchance, as a dressing room, too, there is no more perfect scheme than white furnishings.

Cottage furniture has returned, and a while enameled bed will look well with a bureau and a washstand that have been retouched with wood enamel in white. Even the washstand china may be an all-white porcelain of a more than usually shapely design. The woodwork may be whitened, even if it first requires the application of a paint remover and the work that entails.

Curtaining and wallpaper will present no difficulty since the wallpaperer can now supply both plain and glossy white papers, and the qualities of swiss for sash curtains are practically numberless. That paper having a satiny surface or an invisible pattern will prove less monotonous, and the drapery of the dressing bureau should match the curtains.

Now, the introduction into this "colorless" scheme of the occasional picture or the bit of delicate pottery or metal ware will break what may prove monotony, but an excess of ornamentation is to be decried, since the main object and purpose of this purity in coloring is the accomplishment of an entirely sanitary room.

THE RENOVATING DEPARTMENT

A lady with an abundance of means and a mania for collecting antiques, according to the "Furniture Record," found an old battered maple bureau which the owner had discarded as worthless trash, purchased it for a small sum, sent it to a neighboring city, and for twenty-five dollars had it re-dressed into a thing of beauty. The grain of the curly maple was all restored, and those who had wondered what she could want of the old truck were amazed at the results, while she was well rewarded in the knowledge that for the same money she could not get anything new which would be as well worth the price.

The result set others to thinking. They resurrected old cast-offs from the attic and polished them up at home to the best of their ability, but few had the money to pay the expenses of the professional in a distant city. Had there been some one at home who could do this work, they would have been only too glad to employ him, but the crating and shipping, the chances of damage in transit, the correspondence or personal interview with the city man, all these look like larger tasks to those unfamiliar with this work than they really are. And so the old bureau stays old, and is tolerated only because it is as good as that on which the rich Mrs. B. lavished so much care.

What could a man skilled in this sort of work accomplish? He would soon be astonished at the amount of material gathered into his establishment as the result of a single piece refinished in a worthy manner. Good work is always a good advertisement. And if he doubted, an excellent test would be to place the oldest and most unpromising piece obtainable in his front window, half re-polished and the remainder left with all the dullness acquired in a century. This would invite curiosity, interest, and there is no question but that other work would speedily come. More, it would be the means of enthusing many in the beauty of good furniture. The old piece thus brought into prominence would lead its owner to want more good furniture. It would create more demand for the well furnished home.

ADVERTISING

There was a man in our town,
And he was wondrous wise;
He swore (it was his policy)
He would not advertise.
But one day he did advertise,
And thereby hangs a tale:
The ad was set in quite small type,
And headed "Sheriff's Sale."

—Havana Post.

It is certain that the dealer who doesn't have the goods can't sell them. And yet there are dealers who keep the goods, and they keep them because they don't let the public know that they keep them. That's doing business with a sort of keeps.

Getting at the Basis of Profits
By F. M. Taussig

Few business men know precisely what profits are. They are willing to take what they regard as profits, but most of them have a false idea concerning the actual amount that should be credited on the right side of the ledger each year.

Some economists even go so far as to sharply distinguish business profits from wages. Part of what a business man gets is thought to be simply wages; but part is neither wages, nor interest, nor rent; it is different from these. This peculiar element is regarded as profits. The method of separating business wages from profits is artificial.

Looking over the whole varied range of earnings among those engaged in business careers, it is simplest to regard them all as returns for labor—returns marked by many peculiarities, among which the most striking are the risks and uncertainties, the wide range, the high gains from able pioneering.

In some cases business profits are separated from wages by considering as wages that amount which the individual would have been paid if hired by some one else. An independent business man's actual earnings are likely to exceed that sum; the excess is business profits. Here emphasis is put on the element of risk. Profits differ from wages in that they are the result of the assumption of risk and are the reward for that assumption.

To know what dividends you are really entitled to draw, it is necessary to look the facts in the face, avoid all fallacies, count in every expense, and get the price that will pay the profit. This is no small order, but if you have the courage to study your business just as critically as though it were a competitor's, it is possible to discover the real facts—and make real profits. Search for the expenses that get away and you will know what your business really pays.

The average business does not really pay what it is supposed to pay, because the owner lacks sufficient business training to discover the hidden leaks. His premises are wrong, his principles wrong, and his calculations often wrong.

The first and most general fallacy is that which, in spite of figures, repeats to itself: "I am making 10 or some other per cent. When this form of self-hypnosis is so common that it has almost the force of a trade custom.

"If I ever want to sell out," the owner reasons, "I can't sell a business that does not pay. Then, too, if I claim my business is not paying, it is a reflection on my ability." So he makes the claim of a mythical 10, or 20 or 25 per cent. until he actually believes he is earning that much.

A tradesman celebrated this winter his forty-fifth anniversary in his town and shop. It is his proud boast that he has made, year in and year out, his 20 per cent. So firmly is this fixed in his mind that he resents, as a disloyal act, the attempt of his son—a skilled accountant—to show him that last year's business paid him but 14½ per cent. and that he has had years when he actually lost money. The son, used to calculating the profits of city concerns, sees in a glance what his father has not seen in forty-five years of business in one place.

A second fallacy is the assumption that all, or a great part, taken in over the cost price is profit.

The master barber of a five chair shop found one of his men calculating. "I'm going to start a shop," he announced. "Last Saturday I did $4.80 worth of work for which you gave me $1.20, consequently you made $3.60 profit out of me. I am going to start a shop and get all the profit."

This journeyman barber, having omitted to note that he had drawn $1.20 for Tuesday's work—which day he took in but 50 cents—he was a surprised man when the new shop was sold five months later to pay wages and rent.

Third on the list of profit eating fallacies is the belief that every expense incurred because of the business should not be charged in the expense to run. Thus a caterer neglected to charge in the wages of his wife and children in running the business. His oversight is duplicated every day. Where a business owns a building, the rental is frequently neglected in calculations; window displays, particularly where the display is depreciable, often fail to connect with a charge; and interest on investment is never reckoned by fully 60 per cent. of business men to-day.

A fourth fallacy is to take the price paid the supplier as the actual price of goods, neglecting various other items, such as railway charges. The cost price goods of is their cost when on the shelves ready to sell.

Fifth—and one of the greatest fallacies of business—is the theory that profit percentages are reckoned on the price paid for merchandise. That overactivity in one department is successful in overcoming loss, neglect, or lack of method in another, is a sixth fallacy that misleads many in an honest attempt to determine the real profit. "Extra business necessitates extra expenses," rectifies the seventh fallacy. Almost every business man has his eye on a point ahead where he will round out profit by a little more business. But increase of business is not necessarily followed by increase of profits. There are other factors to reckon with.

Interviewed lately on the subject of profits, a printer who had previously expressed this faith, observed:—

"Extra business costs extra money to handle. No printer or manager in any other line of business can force more profits merely by adding to volume. It may work out on paper, but it won't work out in the shop. I calculate it this way: The manager of any well regulated business, as mine, is kept fairly busy. Each year he is growing busier. Additional business calls for more oversight and more oversight calls for more time—which is not to be had without more expense. When you start out to add to profit by any other method than by cutting expense you have a ticklish road to travel—unless you can get a greater amount of work done for the same money, in which case you are cutting expense by short cuts disguised."

It is not enough to be able to avoid the sophistries which tend to disguise expenses as profits or inflate a 1 per cent. dividend until it looks like 10. Knowing what to avoid is only half the game; knowing what route to take and how to take it is the other half. Profit, as distinguished from theory, is what is left of the selling price after all costs and expenses have been paid.

WELL DIRECTED ADVERTISING.

A well directed advertising campaign will increase the sales of any product, but beyond increased sales, the right kind of advertising has a far-reaching effect. It standardizes the product; it establishes a sale of the articles on a firm foundation; it puts the article advertised on a basis where the dealer that handles it will not have to contend with unfair competition; it enables the dealer to maintain a price that is at all times profitable; and it also helps the dealer to decrease his selling cost.—Doorways.

Knobs of News

W. H. Blair, furniture dealer and woodworker, Davidson, Sask., has moved into new premises.

The King Furniture Co. have commenced business at Fort William, Ont.

Turner & Farrell have taken over the furniture and undertaking business formerly carried on by Geo. H. Lawrence, Dauphin, Man.

The stock of the estate of Frank Betts & Co., furniture dealers, Warman and Yorkton, Sask., has been sold to the Standard Furniture & Undertaking Co., of the same places.

Beach Furniture, Ltd., Cornwall, has been incorporated, with a capital of $99,900. The provisional directors are Robt. Henderson Perry, Jas. Freeman, Margaret Perry, Julius Miller, and Dora Martha Beach.

Bernier & Brisley, furniture dealers, Montreal, have dissolved partnership.

M. B. Judson has purchased the retail business of The Gibbard Furniture Co., at Napanee.

The Lander Hardware Co., Oshawa, have purchased the furniture store and stock of Disney Bros., who in future will devote their energies to their undertaking business.

The Durham Furniture Co. have installed a $4,500 joining and glueing machine in their factory. As the company spent $2,400 last year on glue alone they hope to save half of this amount in next year's bill.

The furniture business of Dunford & May, Clinton, Ont., has been taken over by Ball & Atkinson. Both men are well known to the buying public, having been connected with this same store during previous years.

W. H. Blair, Davidson, Ont., has taken up new premises on Washington street, where he has erected a new building 24 by 50 feet. Mr. Blair will continue his business on a larger scale as a woodworker and furniture manufacturer.

"The Saskatchewan Purchasing Co., Ltd., will be closed out. This company started at Broadview, and has been operating 14 co-operative stores.

G. Loveridge, of The Great West Furniture Co., Saskatoon, Sask., was a recent visitor to Toronto.

W. F. Lawrence, furniture dealer, Maple Creek, Sask., who was burned out several months ago, has his new premises completed.

J. A. Hicks, furniture dealer, of Essex, Ont., is making extensive improvements and additions to his store, necessitated by his rapidly increasing business. The width of the store is being increased, a new front put in, and another storey added, and when completed he will have one of the most commodious and up-to-date furniture stores in Western Ontario.

S. T. Holmes, who has been manager of the Broadfoot & Box Co., furniture dealers, Seaforth, Ont., for the past twenty years, is going into business for himself and is opening up premises in the Cady Block in that place. James Dunford, who has been in the furniture business at Clinton, Ont., for the past 12 years, has taken over the management of Broadfoot & Box's furniture store at Seaforth.

A. Barrie, furniture dealer, of Midland, Ont., has moved into his new store. The new building is a brick structure with a glass front and presents a very attractive appearance. Mr. Barrie hopes to carry a more complete and larger stock, and is preparing to give the best possible service to customers.

The Hudson Bay Co. will increase their capital by $5,000,000 to increase their trade and extend their retail stores in the West.

Some 34 branches of the Retail Merchants' Association have been established in Alberta since September 1.

W. A. Wright, furniture dealer, Port Arthur, Ont., was elected first vice-president of the newly organized branch of the Retail Merchants' Association formed in that city.

L. A. Ball's furniture store at Aylmer, Ont., had a close call from fire on the evening of Dec. 11, when some boxes which were piled in the basement near the furnace ignited from the heat. The fire brigade, attracted by the big smoke, soon had the blaze extinguished, though not before some of the stock on the floor above had been badly smoked. The loss is covered by insurance.

Mr. Henry of the Blowey, Henry Co., furniture dealers, Edmonton, Alta., was a visitor to Toronto during the week before Christmas.

The Ontario Furniture Co., London, have secured property adjoining their present premises, and early in the new year will enlarge their quarters, making a modern and up-to-date drapery department.

WANTS FURNITURE CATALOGUES

J. W. Richardson, North Bay, who recently added furniture to his hardware stock, wishes to receive catalogues.

NEW FURNITURE COMPANY

The Sudbury Furniture Co., Ltd., is the name of a new company which recently received an Ontario charter to sell furniture of every description at Sudbury, Ont. The capital is set at $40,000, and the provisional directors are Geo. Levesque, L. P. Levesque, Nap. L. Adams, E. G. Levesque and Wm. Brazeau.

FURNITURE STORE BURNED

One of the worst disasters in the history of Smithville, Ont., occurred on Dec. 13, when fire, which is said to have originated in Gracey's furniture store and undertaking establishment, destroyed $40,000 worth of property in a number of nearby stores. H. Gracey's own loss was $8,000.

SELLING SEATS FOR PICTURE SHOWS

That some furniture dealers are alive to the interests of their business outside their stores is shown by the fact that not a few are looking after the selling of seats for public halls and moving picture theatres. Some recent sales of this line of goods have been made by W. R. Orr, Portage la Prairie, Man.; Berlin Furniture Co., Berlin, Ont.; The Zoelner Sons Co., Prince Albert, Sask.; The Chas. Austin Co., Chatham, Ont., and D. Courville, Alexandria, Ont.

A HAPPY NEW YEAR

To every furniture dealer in Canada The Furniture World extends a Happy and Prosperous New Year. May 1914 usher in an era of good health, good business and much happiness to every member of the trade.

SELLING OFFICE FURNITURE

Are you securing your share of this end of the business?

Many a concern is making a good thing out of office furniture alone; no reason why you should not add this line to your others, if you have not already done so.

There are many things to consider in this regard. In buying the desks for instance, study well local conditions. See what local trade demands. In the larger centres a larger variety may be safely carried than in the smaller towns. If you find on investigation the lower priced numbers are about all that you feel you can sell, stick to them. The catalogues will help land the orders of the chap who wants something better, or special.

Filing devices are ready sellers; modern business demands system, and there are so many good things in these lines that only need display in the store and windows to make some fine sales.

If you install furniture for the office, or have such

Parlor cabinet made by The George McLagan Furniture Co.

a department, see that the lines have their share of the window trims.

A plain blotter with the statement that you have office furniture, liberally distributed among the offices will help. Or address a direct letter to business men and call attention to the lines you have on hand. Let the men know you are alive to their interests; that you have the articles desired.

There's just as much satisfaction and profit in furnishing up an office as a room in a home. All you have to do is to "be on the job" and you will land your share of the business. If you wish to know anything about office furniture and how to push this end, ask us; we will be pleased to assist you in a practical manner in this regard.

FIRE IN WINGHAM FURNITURE FACTORY

Fire of unknown origin recently destroyed the offices and warerooms of Walker & Clegg, upholstered furniture manufacturers, near the Grand Trunk station, at Wingham, Ont. The building burned was a two-storey frame structure, about 90 by 90, and the loss is $10,000; insured. The main building, adjoining, was saved principally by two steel doors. It was a four-storey building until Good Friday's storm, when the gale lifted a whole storey and dropped it on the frame structure, which has now been burned.

The firm has been rushed with work, and the men have been putting in overtime four nights a week, preparatory to the Christmas holidays. Most of the hands are employed in the main building, but about 20 will be temporarily out of work. The best class of goods turned out at the factory were stored in the warerooms and sample-rooms, which makes the loss particularly severe.

LARGER QUARTERS FOR JOHNS-MANVILLE CO.

The Toronto branch of The Canadian H. W. Johns-Manville Co., Ltd., has removed to more spacious quarters at 19 Front Street East. This new store and warehouse has a floor area of approximately 35,000 sq. ft., and is situated in the heart of the wholesale district. In their new quarters this firm will be able to carry a larger stock and have ample space for the display of their complete line of J-M asbestos roofings, packings, pipe coverings, building materials, electrical and railroad supplies, automobile plumbing specialties, and other lines. The entire building will be lighted by their Frink and J-M linolite system, and one room will be used for exhibiting these systems of lighting.

BEDROOM SUITES, BUFFETS, CHINA CABINETS

The Gibbard Furniture Co., Napanee, Ont., have just issued a new catalogue (No. 14) descriptive of their bedroom suites, buffets and china cabinets in mahogany and oak. The line is fully illustrated in this new booklet, and some idea can be gleaned of the various articles produced. They are a popular priced line, too, which adds to their popularity.

CROWN FURNITURE CATALOGUE

"To manufacture goods of the highest quality has always been our ambition," says the introduction to the new catalogue just published by The Crown Furniture Co., Preston, Ont., and, judging by the illustrations, they have attained a high standard. The company pride themselves on the fact that their business has been built on the foundation of "quality," and they mean to retain and uphold their reputation. The catalogue contains 32 pages of illustrations of their furniture items, and as these are printed on superfine paper the finer points are strikingly emphasized. Buffets, china cabinets, dressers, somnoes, chiffoniers, dressing tables, washstands, all have their place, many of them—most of them, in fact—having decidedly new and novel features. To mention only one: In a new-style colonial buffet there is a special drop front for holding the tray while putting away the table articles, with a drawing and sliding silver and cutlery lined tray above. Enamelled white and French grey bedroom furniture is also pictured and described, as also are some new designed desks in white oak, fumed oak, and Early English finish.

DEATH OF PROMINENT FURNITURE MAKER

One of the leaders of the furniture trade in Canada in the person of A. B. Hay died recently at Owen Sound in his 57th year. He was formerly in business at Woodstock, his factory being taken over by the Canada Furniture Manufacturers. Moving to Owen Sound with his brother John, he established and built up the North American Bent Chair Co.

The Furniture Manufacturer

A Department of News and Ideas

Gossip for the Furniture Manufacturer

THE Canadian commercial agent at Rotterdam is hoping that with the opening of the Panama canal there will come a demand in Holland for Canadian lumber. He says that since the advance in Canadian spruce, buyers have not found it remunerative to import from Canada. "Lumber from British Columbia," he says, "with the high freight rates now ruling, cannot be imported with the possibility of competing with the countries of Northern Europe and of the Southern States."

Referring to furniture woods he says: "The following woods are used extensively in the manufacture of furniture:—Mahogany, walnut, oak, American poplar, ebony, rosewood, teak, beech, elm, hickory, ash, maple and basswood. The price of these woods has advanced considerably during the past few years, mahogany, for instance, is now 40 per cent. higher than it was six years ago. Importers will be glad to receive samples of Canadian beech, birch, maple and ash, with quotations of prices delivered here."

Unfortunately the supply of Canadian lumber for furniture manufacturing purposes is not equal to the demand. Our manufacturers have in consequence to draw upon foreign markets for a great deal of their supply.

In Nova Scotia, according to an investigation made by Dr. B. E. Fernow, 70 per cent. of the area of that province is actual or potential forest land, but nevertheless the merchantable timber will be exhausted in twenty-five years at the present rate of cutting.

SPEAKING of the condition of the furniture trade in the United States, the Furniture Manufacturer says: "Most of the salesmen have made their last trip for the current year, and where factories are not already sold up to the limit of their producing capacity for the ensuing thirty days, mail orders are keeping many a factory more than busy. This is particularly the case with the factories the products of which make a holiday appeal. It is well to keep in mind that manufacturers have operated their factories on a conservative basis throughout the year. They have permitted very little accumulation of stock, but although there have been intervals when the outlook was not promising, when drouth threatened to cut off trade from one part of the country, and financial uncertainty from another, and flood and disaster from some other, the aggregate result is by no means bad, and the volume for the year promises not to be below the average of recent years. Here and there will be found manufacturers who show a gain, but these are exceptional. More are given to comparing records to establish that they are 'up to our sales last year.' In the factories where samples for the January exhibitions are in preparation, designers, cabinet-makers and photographers are as busy as the finishers and packers and shipping on the going lines. There is abundant reason for the announcement that the new lines will be very strong. The far-seeing manufacturers are adopting this policy to forestall any demand which may be presented for lower prices based on recent reductions in the tariff."

C. F. REILLY, a furniture manufacturer in the United States, is out with an article in the Furniture Manufacturer against the holding of two exhibitions a year.

He is of the opinion that the practice of holding two markets a year results in a strenuous and wasteful competition between manufacturers, and has developed a fictitious demand for a new line every six months which is not only the source of great expense to the manufacturer, but subjects the retailer to trouble and loss as well. As a result of this custom, many successful designs are rejected to make room for new patterns of problematical value, at a heavy expense to the manufacturer, while the retailer suffers loss through depreciation of his stock and the inability to match up broken sets which should really be staple for years.

"The spring season in the furniture trade," he says, "is steadily growing shorter, and the bulk of goods sold are now disposed of in the fall. On account of this fact, the larger buyers are finding it impossible to wait until the mid-summer market for placing their orders, owing to the crowding at the factories during the fall months, making satisfactory deliveries impossible. With this condition a fact, would it not be the part of wisdom for our manufacturers to settle on one line and one exhibit a year, the market season to be in the early summer, say, commencing May 1st or May 15th, with a positive closing date which would be acceptable both to the buyer and exhibitor? This would enable the manufacturer to book his heavy volume of business at an advanced date, which would give him the advantage of fully two additional months in which to take care of his fall season's trade."

In Canada there is probably no one who favors holding furniture exhibitions more frequently than once a year. At any rate that is the opinion that one would gather from the discussion which took place in the columns of The Furniture World early in 1913.

A FURNITURE manufacturer tells in Printers' Ink how his firm helps the retailer. Briefly his method is as follows: In the first place they do what most manufacturer at any rate try to do, and that is give the dealer a fair profit, while should an order come to them direct from a consumer they turn the order in to the nearest dealer. In small towns they give dealers exclusive rights.

As the average dealer cannot afford to carry a heavy stock of furniture, this particular manufacturer makes illustrations in detail, showing all features of the furniture. This serves the double purpose of permitting patrons to see exactly what they might be getting and of allowing dealers to order at need and secure in short order. It is not an advantage to carry a large stock at the factory, but it is practically unavoidable, and the dealer appreciates any improvement in catalogue service and deliveries. They have, in consequence, paid more than ordinary attention to the development of their correspondence department, which handles this phase of the business.

This firm, when occasion demands it, send their furniture experts to assist local dealers in closing important orders. They go out with books and photo-

Separating Shavings and Dust
By J. C. Taylor

In the older times, when practically everything in the form of shavings, dust and waste went into the fire box of the boiler to help make steam, there was a disposition to concentrate. The sawdust and shavings were all sent through the same blower system and delivered through the same spout to the shavings bin or the fire box. We are creatures of habit, so this older habit stays with us yet even at times when it is evident it would be worth while to separate the shavings from the dust for the sake of better handling and better returns. An idea in this connection was furnished recently by a man operating a small plant who put in electric drives, buying outside current. In figuring out the matter of disposal of his shavings and dust, he found that he could get more out of them by separating the waste. So he now handles his shavings with one blower system and his sawdust with another.

New buffet with rest tray feature made by the Crown Furniture Co., Preston.

Some of his shaving he sells loose, some in bales. His sawdust finds ready sale at so much per barrel in his home town. He takes his scrap wood and sells it for kindling. From all this he gets enough to more than pay for his entire power bill. The point here is the idea of separating the shavings and the sawdust. There are uses for each kind of waste which are developing and enlarging every day. Generally, these uses are for each material separately. Consequently, this waste product is in a better marketable shape if the sawdust is kept clean and apart from the shavings, and this is the case with the shavings if kept clean and apart from the dust or kindling wood. Sometimes this may call for two blower equipments instead of one, but even that should not call for any more power and only a little more for the installation.

Where the machines are up above the floor and the dust can be spouted down through them, the dust can be handled by belts and various machinery conveyors with less power than is required to handle it through the blower system. Consequently, it will be a good idea where the blower system is getting to be pretty heavily loaded, to cut all the saws off from the blower system and handle the dust with machine conveyors and spouts, and leave nothing for the blower to handle but the shavings. This gives you both products separated and in beter condition for marketing.

VARIOUS WOODS AND SUITABLE STAINS
By H. Mader

Such a large number of stains are on the market that it is often difficult to decide which of them to use for certain work, and the following article will give a brief review of suitable stains for certain woods.

For low grade oak veneer work, stains composed of mild chemicals, i.e., composed mostly of pure coal tar dyes, will give best results. If other stains, containing acidic chemicals, are used, the glue used for veneering is discolored and the wood will show poor results. It will become too rough and will then need sandpapering to obtain the original finish.

Effect of Fumed Furniture

It is often required to imitate the effect of fumed furniture by means of the ordinary water stains. Where the so-called fumed stains cannot be used, the ordinary coal tar dye stain can be used, provided the wood is treated before staining by a solution of 10 to 15 g. soda to one liter of water, and is sandpapered after drying.

In all the wood stains, the nature of the wood itself is of course of prime importance. Maple wood for example can be stained gray without any trouble at all, while oak will not give the right gray color in most cases, since its color tends too much toward yellow, and the gray stain after waxing and shading and matting shows greenish.

When light stains are used on oak it is often noticed that they turn yellow, especially if the stain is not light-proof, and if it consists in the main of coal tar dyes.

All woods stained gray with iron salts take on a brown color with time. Most stains are made with some such additions as potassium chromate, copper sulphate, etc., as also many metallic salts.

Most coal tar dyes are either mixed at the shop or, which is better, bought ready mixed. With the great number of shades and stains now on the market, it is almost useless for any shop to mix stains at the same, unless for some special purpose and unless the mixer is an expert at it.

If the stains are mixed at the shop, care must be taken in the first place to get light-proof colors, and that these colors are as nearly alike as possible in their resistance to the influence of light. For example, if a brown stain is mixed from black, yellow red, then the stained wood will gradually take on a much lighter shade than desirable if the red was less light-proof than the other colors.

The same thing can be observed with the products of many paint supply houses, for their paints and stains are also mixed from the fundamental colors. Brown colors consist as a rule of red, yellow and black dyes; gray colors of blue-black, yellow a little red, and sometimes a little green. It depends on the preponderance of some color in the dye whether the final stain will have one shade or another.

If in a brown color red is in excess then the final shade will be reddish brown. The modern greenish brown shades similar to the fumed finish are usually mixed with green. Green deadens all colors. If too much of it is used, the shade will have too great a greenish hue, and red may be used to offset the green.

Coal tar dyes may be deepened in shade by adding a little potassium chromate or a little sodium hydroxide. Most colors may be made by using the fundamentals red, yellow and blue. Since the blue colors are, however, less light-proof than the others, they are avoided wherever possible, and other colors are substituted.

It is impossible to get exactly the same color on a wood with the same stain. A piece of furniture will show considerable differences in shades in the various parts, a state which is not very obvious in the completed product. If the different parts were laid side by side, however, the enormous differences in stain would be at once apparent.

The reason lies, of course, in the natural difference of wood itself. Oak, for example, shows such a difference even when taken from the same trunk that it is impossible to get a uniform shade over the entire surface. A good stain is not supposed to cover the natural grain of wood but is presumed to show it up more clearly. The stain should stain the wood uniformly over the entire surface, but it cannot be expected to produce an absolutely uniform effect.

Stain Maker and Woodworker

Often woodworker and stain manufacturer have long arguments and differences about the nature and quality of the stain, merely because the woodworker demands something of the stain which he has no right to demand. This is especially true if he is required to stain two pieces of furniture alike. He may not allow for the difference in grain and structure, and then lays the blame at the door of the stain manufacturer.

Every experienced finisher knows that in staining, veneers always remain lighter than solid wood, and that such differences must be eliminated by different manipulations. This can be done by adding a second coat of stain, using either the same stain or some oil or spirit stain. An experienced stainer can prevent the darkening of cross-grained wood or carvings by moistening the wood with water just before staining to prevent the stain from penetrating too deeply. It is true in general that moistening the wood prevents irregularity in final effect of stains to some extent.

All vivid stains containing many alkaline ingredients or even potassium chromate should be avoided, as they fade rapidly under the influence of light and show many drawbacks which appear only after a long time. For example, the chromate and the soda in the hydroxide destroy the shellac layer, and with very strong solutions of these chemicals yellow and gray spots appear after a time, which are hard to eliminate.

Stains from coal tar dyes have the disadvantages of leaving the pores in the wood lighter than the rest of the wood, but this can be remedied by waxing the surface after staining. Too much wax should not be used either, as then the pores become too dark and the surface of the wood takes on a dirty brown appearance.

VARNISH MAGNIFIES DUST SPECKS

Go into a spotlessly clean room that has not been used for weeks. Notice the innumerable atoms of dust, which may be seen floating in the streak of light made by a stray sunbeam, and which were invisible otherwise. So, just because you cannot see any dust on the surface of the work, don't conclude that there is none. And these specks of dust, which are invisible when there is no varnish on the surface, will be visible after varnish is applied. When the varnish is put on over the dust specks, it is slightly raised by them, and forms a concave-convex lens, which magnifies the small grain of dust many times, sufficiently at least, until it becomes large enough to be visible to the naked eye, and many such specks make the finished work look seedy.

The thorough removal of dust is impossible simply by sweeping with a duster. The accepted way is to pour a little oil in the hollow of the hand, with which slightly moisten the ends of the bristles of the duster. Then, with a gliding movement rather than a sweeping motion, go over the work several times. The dust will then adhere to the oiled bristles. If one will violently rub the ends of the bristles back and forth on the hand for several moments before moistening with oil, the dust will adhere better. The friction electrifies the bristles, imparting to them a magnetic property which draws the fine particles of dust to them.—Pratt & Lambert's Varnish Talks.

SMALL STEAM RETORTS

The steaming or vulcanizing of wood is a subject of interest to the progressive veneer user to-day, and because of this there is an idea comes to mind in connection with a certain steaming retort used in making bent wood. The old-time wasteful boiling vat and wood steam box is giving way in these days of higher efficiency to a metal retort which can be closed up tightly and some steam pressure used in preparing of stock. It sometimes happens that the veneer user in the furniture trade may need one of these retorts anyway for the preparing of material for certain articles of bent wood, and that these same retorts may be used for steaming or vulcanizing veneer and other products which enter into the face work to uniform and deepen the color tone.

One of the best examples of the new idea in oak, with this grayish tint to it, shown lately, was produced by this vulcanizing process, by steaming the oak in an inclosed steam tank under pressure with certain acids. The man presenting the work said that he found it difficult to get oak which would run uniform enough in color for some of the high-grade work, and he was resorting to this process to bring a mixed stock of oak into a harmony of color tone and getting excellent results.

Among the manufacturers of hardwood lumber for the furniture trade there is now being used quite extensively a steaming treatment preparatory to drying, the general effect of which is to uniform the color tone as well as facilitate seasoning. This same idea ought to be good in connection with veneer, and it has been demonstrated by experiment that one can use ammonia and other acids along with the steam and thus produce various stain effects which are deep and well fixed into the wood. If the right stains can be secured there is no question but what this should be the best way to do it, because it saves the risk of endangering glue joints on made-up work by the use of surface stains afterward, and it is more thorough and satisfactory, anyway. Whether or not it is practical to use some of these smaller retorts made for preparing bent wood work is not known to the writer, but they suggest possibilities along a new line of work. So those that have them might try some experiments along this line, and those that have not might on investigation find the prospects for good work justify installing one and trying it out. Veneers.

Who Owns Three Lindermans?

KNECHTEL FURNITURE CO., Hanover, again shows its appreciation of a good thing by installing a Linderman Dovetailer in its SOUTHAMPTON FACTORY.

Hanover Machine	shipped	Oct. 28th, 1911
Walkerton Machine	"	May 9th, 1912
Southampton Machine	"	Dec. 15th, 1913

"The Proof of the Pudding is the Eating"
AND A $13,000 PUDDING IS SOME PUDDING

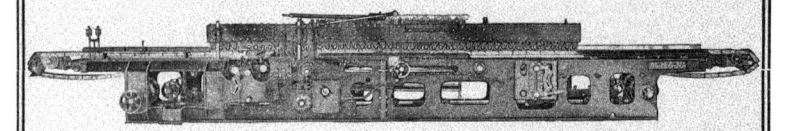

THE LINDERMAN

is the greatest furniture factory money-saver on the market to-day

It joints, glues, clamps and sizes in one operation, saving not only from 60% to 70% of your annual glue bills, and from 5% to 10% of your lumber waste, but also 40% to 60% of labor.

*Eventually you will get one.
Why not now?*

Canadian Linderman Co., Limited

Woodstock :: Ontario

IT'S OUT!

OUR New Catalog No. 105 C.F. is out. It is new in every sense of the word. It offers a new and simplified way of ordering—tabulated so that you can find in a moment the kinds of casters desired, the various styles of casters, etc., are faithfully illustrated in half-tone engravings. But best of all it puts before you the recent additions, and improvements made in the "Universal" Line, *the greatest variety of casters ever offered to the trade.*

The following list will give an idea as to the styles and varieties of casters:

BALL BEARING GRIP NECK
NON-BALL BEARING GRIP NECK
BALL BEARING PHILADELPHIA
NON-BALL BEARING PHILADELPHIA
BALL BEARING OBLONG PLATE
DISC BEARING PLATE

BALL BEARING METALLIC BEDSTEAD
DEEP SOCKET AND SHALLOW SOCKET
BRASS AND IRON PLATE
BRACKET AND IRON BED
PIANO AND TRUCK
ENGLISH PATTERN

MISCELLANEOUS ITEMS

FURNITURE SLIDES
CASTER RINGS AND SOCKETS
SANITARY DESK SLIDES AND SHOES

TABLE BRACKETS
BALL BEARING STOVE TRUCK
SHELF BLOCKS

Catalog No. 105 C.F. will be found at once the most convenient as well as the safest guide to caster selection ever offered. Write for a copy.

Universal Caster & Foundry Co.

29 West 42nd Street (Aeolian Building)

New York

BIG DEMAND FOR LOW PRICED FURNITURE

We are the largest manufacturers of low priced oak DRESSERS, Chiffoniers and Ladies Desks in the NORTH.

This enables us to sell our line on a very small margin.

LOOK AT THE PRICES ON PIECES SHOWN
ALL OUR PRICES ARE IN PROPORTION

202
Price $5.00. Weight 95 lbs.
Top 18x33. Height 64 in.
French bevel plate mirror 12x20.
Same, with imitation quart. oak front and top. Price $5.25.

102
Price $5.45. Weight 110 lbs.
Top 18x30. Height 69 in.
French bevel plate 12x16.

215
Price $6.50. Weight 110 lbs.
Top 18x38. Height 67 in.
French bevel plate 20x22.

WE ALSO MANUFACTURE A LINE OF THE ABOVE GOODS IN THE COLONIAL STYLE

Terms: F.O.B. CHICAGO. 60 days net—2% for cash in 20 days

Our location is the most convenient in the U.S. to supply the Canadian Trade
Send for our illustrated catalog. It means PROFIT FOR YOU.

J. D. FREESE & SONS CO.
2501-2523 HOMER ST.   **CHICAGO, U.S.A.**

BUYER'S DIRECTORY

When writing to advertisers kindly mention the Canadian Furniture World and the Undertaker

ARTS AND CRAFTS FURNITURE
Geo. McLagan Furniture Co., Stratford.

ASBESTOS TABLE COVERS.
Canadian H. W. Johns-Manville Co., Toronto.

BABY CARRIAGES.
Gendron Mfg. Co., Toronto.

AWNINGS
Stamco, Limited, Saskatoon, Sask.

BENT WOOD FURNITURE.
John C. Mundell & Co., Elora.
J. & J. Kohn, Toronto (W. Craig).

BOOKCASES.
Knechtel Furniture Co., Hanover.
Geo. McLagan Furniture Co., Stratford.
Meaford Mfg. Co., Meaford, Ont.

BUFFETS.
Bell Furniture Co., Southampton, Ontario.
Kensington Furniture Co., Goderich.
Knechtel Furniture Co., Hanover.
Geo. McLagan Furniture Co., Stratford.
Meaford Mfg. Co., Meaford, Ont.
Peppler Bros., Hanover.
Stratford Chair Co., Stratford.
Victoriaville Furniture Co., Victoriaville, Que.

BEDS (Brass and Iron).
Canada Beds, Ltd., Chesley.
Ideal Bedding Co., Toronto.
Farquharson-Gifford Co., Stratford, Ont.
Quality Beds, Limited, Welland, Ontario.
Ives Modern Bedstead Co., Cornwall Ont.
Stamco, Limited, Saskatoon, Sask.
Stratford Bed Co., Stratford, Ont.
S. Weisglass, Ltd., Montreal, Que.

BEDS (Modern Wood).
Elora Furniture Co., Elora.
Knechtel Furniture Co., Hanover.

BED SPRINGS.
Knechtel Furniture Co., Hanover.
Frame and Hay Fence Co., Stratford.
Gold Medal Furniture Co., Toronto
Leggett & Platt Spring Bed Co., Windsor.
Ideal Bedding Co., Toronto.
Stamco, Limited, Saskatoon, Sask.
Steel Furnishing Co., New Glasgow, N. S.
S. Weisglass, Ltd., Montreal, Que.

BED ROOM CHAIRS.
Baetz Bros., Berlin.
Bell Furniture Co., Southampton, Ontario.
Elmira Furniture Co, Elmira, Ont.
Lippert Furniture Co., Berlin.

BED ROOM SUITES.
Bell Furniture Co., Southampton, Ontario.
Kensington Furniture Co., Goderich.
Knechtel Furniture Co., Hanover.
Victoriaville Furniture Co., Victoriaville, Que.

CARD AND DEN TABLES.
Geo. McLagan Furniture Co., Stratford.
John C. Mundell & Co., Elora, Ont.

CARPET RACKS
Steel Furnishing Co., New Glasgow, N. S.

CAMP FURNITURE.
Stratford Mfg. Co., Stratford.
Ideal Bedding Co., Toronto.

CEDAR BOXES
D. L. Shafer, St. Thomas, Ont.

CELLARETTES
John C. Mundell & Co., Elora, Ont.

CHAIRS AND ROCKERS
Bell Furniture Co., Southampton, Ontario.
Baetz Bros., Berlin.
Knechtel Furniture Co., Hanover.
John C. Mundell & Co., Elora.
Stratford Chair Co., Stratford.
Waterloo Furniture Co., Waterloo.
Canadian Rattan Chair Co., Victoriaville.

Gold Medal Furniture Co., Toronto.
Elmira Furniture Co, Elmira, Ont.
Imperial Furniture Co., Toronto.
Lippert Furniture Co., Berlin.
Victoriaville Chair Mfg. Co., Victoriaville.

CHESTERFIELDS.
Imperial Furniture Co., Toronto.

CHIFFONIERS.
Bell Furniture Co., Southampton, Ontario.
Knechtel Furniture Co., Hanover.
Meaford Mfg. Co., Meaford, Ont.
Stratford Chair Co., Stratford.
Victoriaville Furniture Co., Victoriaville, Que.

CHINA CABINETS.
Bell Furniture Co., Southampton, Ontario.
Peppler Bros., Hanover.
Geo. McLagan Furniture Co., Stratford.
Meaford Mfg. Co., Meaford, Ont.

COMFORTERS.
Toronto Feather & Down Co., Toronto.
Stamco, Limited, Saskatoon, Sask.

COTS
Frame and Hay Fence Co., Stratford.

COUCHES.
J. P. Albrough & Co., Ingersoll.
Ellis Furniture Co., Ingersoll.
Gold Medal Furniture Co., Toronto.
Imperial Furniture Co., Toronto.
John C. Mundell & Co., Elora, Ont.
Steel Furnishing Co., New Glasgow, N. S.
S. Weisglass, Ltd., Montreal, Que.

COUCHES (Sliding).
Ideal Bedding Co., Toronto.
Farquharson-Gifford Co., Stratford, Ont.
Gold Medal Furniture Co., Toronto.
Stamco, Limited, Saskatoon, Sask.

CRADLES.
Knechtel Furniture Co., Hanover.

CRIBS (Brass and Iron)
Ideal Bedding Co., Toronto.
John C. Mundell & Co., Elora, Ont.
Stamco, Limited, Saskatoon, Sask.
S. Weisglass, Ltd., Montreal, Que.

CUSHIONS.
Stamco, Limited, Saskatoon, Sask.

DAVENPORT BEDS.
Farquharson-Gifford Co., Stratford, Ont.
Montreal Upholstering Co., Montreal, Que.
Imperial Rattan Co., Stratford.
John C. Mundell & Co., Elora.

DEN FURNITURE
Elmira Furniture Co. Elmira, Ont.
Farquharson-Gifford Co., Stratford, Ont.
John C. Mundell & Co., Elora, Ont.

DIVANETTES.
Lippert Furniture Co., Berlin.

DESKS.
Bell Furniture Co., Southampton, Ontario.
Elmira Interior Woodwork Co., Elmira.
Knechtel Furniture Co., Hanover.
Geo. McLagan Furniture Co., Stratford.
John C. Mundell & Co., Elora.
Stratford Desk Co., Stratford, Ont.

DINING-ROOM FURNITURE
Farquharson-Gifford Co., Stratford, Ont.

DINING SUITES.
Bell Furniture Co., Southampton, Ontario.
Knechtel Furniture Co., Hanover.
Geo. McLagan Furniture Co., Stratford.
John C. Mundell & Co., Elora.
Peppler Bros., Hanover.
Stratford Chair Co., Stratford.

DINNER WAGONS.
Geo. McLagan Furniture Co., Stratford.
Peppler Bros., Hanover.

DRESSERS.
Bell Furniture Co., Southampton, Ontario.
Knechtel Furniture Co., Hanover.
Stratford Chair Co., Stratford.
Victoriaville Furniture Co., Victoriaville, Que.
Meaford Mfg. Co., Meaford, Ont.

EXTENSION TABLES.
Bell Furniture Co., Southampton, Ontario.
Peppler Bros., Hanover.
Berlin Table Mfg. Co., Berlin.
Meaford Mfg. Co., Meaford, Ont.

FILING DEVICES.
Elmira Interior Woodwork Co., Elmira.
Geo. McLagan Furniture Co., Stratford.

FYLING CABINETS
Globe Wernicke Co., Stratford, Ont.

FYLING CABINETS, Supplies
Globe Wernicke Co., Stratford, Ont.

FOLDING CHAIRS.
Stratford Mfg. Co., Stratford.
Ideal Bedding Co., Toronto.

FOLDING TABLES.
Stratford Mfg. Co., Stratford.

FOOTSTOOLS
Elmira Furniture Co, Elmira, Ont.

FURNITURE HARDWARE
Stratford Brass Co., Stratford.

HALL SEATS AND MIRRORS.
Geo. McLagan Furniture Co., Stratford.
Meaford Mfg. Co., Meaford, Ont.

HALL TREES.
Geo. McLagan Furniture Co., Stratford.

HAMMO-COUCHES.
Ideal Bedding Co., Toronto.

INVALID CHAIRS.
Gendron Mfg. Co., Toledo, Ohio.
Victoriaville Chair Mfg. Co., Victoriaville, Que.

IRONING BOARDS AND DRYERS.
Stratford Mfg. Co., Stratford.

JARDINIERE STANDS.
Elmira Furniture Co, Elmira, Ont.
Elora Furniture Co., Elora.
Geo. McLagan Furniture Co., Stratford.
Meaford Mfg. Co., Meaford, Ont.

KITCHEN CABINETS.
Hamilton Ideal Mfg. Co., Hamilton.
Knechtel Kitchen Cabinet Co., Ltd., Hanover, Ont.

KITCHEN TABLES.
Knechtel Furniture Co., Hanover.
Victoriaville Furniture Co., Victoriaville.

LADIES' DESKS
Meaford Mfg. Co., Meaford, Ont.

LAWN SEATS AND SWINGS.
Stratford Mfg. Co., Stratford.

LIBRARY TABLES.
Bell Furniture Co., Southampton, Ontario.
Peppler Bros., Hanover.
Elmira Furniture Co, Elmira, Ont.
Geo. McLagan Furniture Co., Stratford.
Meaford Mfg. Co., Meaford, Ont.
John C. Mundell & Co., Elora, Ont.

LUXURY CHAIRS.
Lippert Furniture Co., Berlin.

MATTRESSES.
Berlin Bedding Co., Toronto.
Gold Medal Furniture Co., Toronto.
McKellar Bedding Co., Fort William, Ont.
Stamco, Limited, Saskatoon, Sask.
Standard Bedding Co., Toronto.
Antiseptic Bedding Co., Toronto.
Ideal Bedding Co., Toronto.

MAGAZINE RACKS AND STANDS.
Geo. McLagan Furniture Co., Stratford.

MEDICINE CABINETS.
Meaford Mfg. Co., Meaford, Ont.

MISSION FURNITURE.
Ellis Furniture Co., Ingersoll.
Baetz Bros., Berlin.
John C. Mundell & Co., Elora.
Waterloo Furniture Co., Waterloo.

MORRIS CHAIRS.
Ellis Furniture Co., Ingersoll.
Imperial Rattan Co., Stratford.
Knechtel Furniture Co., Hanover.
John C. Mundell & Co., Elora.
Waterloo Furniture Co., Waterloo.

MUSIC CABINETS.
Geo. McLagan Furniture Co., Stratford.
Knechtel Kitchen Cabinet Co., Ltd., Hanover, Ont.

OFFICE CHAIRS.
Bell Furniture Co., Southampton, Ontario.
Elmira Furniture Co, Elmira, Ont.
Knechtel Furniture Co., Hanover.
Stratford Chair Co., Stratford.
J. & J. Kohn, Toronto (W. Craig).
John C. Mundell & Co., Elora, Ont.

OFFICE TABLES
Stratford Desk Co., Stratford, Ont.

PARK SEATS.
Stratford Mfg. Co., Stratford.

PARLOR CHAIRS and ROCKERS
Ellis Furniture Co., Ingersoll.
Elmira Interior Woodwork Co., Elmira.
John C. Mundell & Co., Elora, Ont.
Waterloo Furniture Co., Waterloo.

PARLOR SUITES.
Elmira Interior Woodwork Co., Elmira.
Ellis Furniture Co., Ingersoll.
Knechtel Furniture Co., Hanover.
Waterloo Furniture Co., Waterloo.
Gold Medal Furniture Co., Toronto.
Lippert Furniture Co., Berlin.

PARLOR TABLES.
Geo. McLagan Furniture Co., Stratford.
Meaford Mfg. Co., Meaford, Ont.
Elora Furniture Co., Elora.
Elmira Furniture Co, Elmira, Ont.
Knechtel Furniture Co., Hanover.
Peppler Bros., Hanover.

PEDESTALS
Peppler Bros., Hanover.
Geo. McLagan Furniture Co., Stratford.

PILLOWS.
Toronto Feather & Down Co., Toronto.
Ideal Bedding Co., Toronto.

PILLOW SHAM HOLDERS.
Tarbox Mfg. Co., Toronto.

RATTAN FURNITURE.
Imperial Rattan Co., Stratford.
Canadian Rattan Chair Co., Victoriaville, Que.
Gendron Mfg. Co., Toronto.

RECLINING CHAIRS.
Ellis Furniture Co., Ingersoll.
Knechtel Furniture Co., Hanover.
John C. Mundell & Co., Elora, Ont.

RUG RACKS
Steel Furnishing Co., New Glasgow, N. S.

SECTIONAL BOOKCASES
Globe Wernicke Co., Stratford.

SCHOOL FURNITURE.
Bell Furniture Co., Southampton, Ontario.

SIDEBOARDS.
Knechtel Furniture Co., Hanover.
Meaford Mfg. Co., Meaford, Ont.
Stratford Chair Co., Stratford.

TABLES.
Bell Furniture Co., Southampton, Ontario.
Elora Furniture Co., Elora.
Knechtel Furniture Co., Hanover.
John C. Mundell & Co., Elora.
Orillia Furniture Co., Orillia.
Stratford Chair Co., Stratford.
Victoriaville Furniture Co., Victoriaville, Que.

TABLE SLIDES
B. Walter & Co., Wabash, Ind.

TABOURETTES
Elora Furniture Co., Elora.
Kensington Furniture Co., Goderich.

TELEPHONE STANDS.
John C. Mundell & Co., Elora, Ont.

TENTS
Stamco, Limited, Saskatoon, Sask.

TYPEWRITER DESKS.
Elmira Interior Woodwork Co., Elmira.
Stratford Desk Co., Stratford, Ont.

UPHOLSTERERS' SUPPLIES
Ellis Furniture Co., Ingersoll.
Gold Medal Furniture Co., Toronto.

UPHOLSTERED FURNITURE
Baetz Bros., Berlin.
Ellis Furniture Co., Ingersoll.
Farquharson-Gifford Co., Stratford, Ont.
Imperial Furniture Co., Toronto.
John C. Mundell & Co., Elora.
Knechtel Furniture Co., Hanover.
Waterloo Furniture Co., Waterloo.
Gold Medal Furniture Co., Toronto.

VACUUM CLEANERS.
Onward Mfg. Co., Berlin.

VERANDAH FURNITURE.
Imperial Rattan Co., Stratford.
Stratford Mfg. Co., Stratford.

Continued on page 92

Dominion Casket Co., Limited

Telephones: Day No. 1020. Nights and Sundays and Holidays No. 1069

Guelph, Ont.

RUSH ORDERS SOLICITED

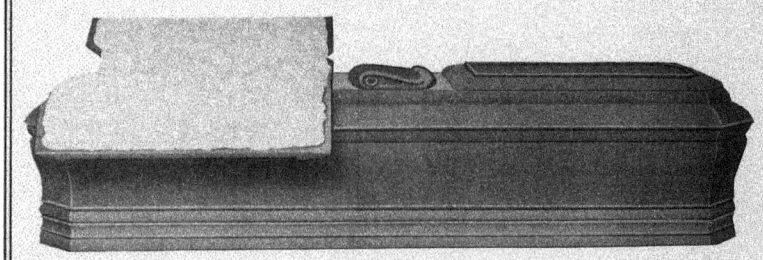

No 174

The two styles shown upon this page are of a quality and design used almost daily throughout the Dominion. Why not carry in your showroom such styles, instead of those which are entirely devoid of all mechanical good looks. This casket can be made in any of the popular panels and covered with any of the numerous materials that may be desired in quality or color.

A trial order of any of our lines will convince the funeral director that we have the goods

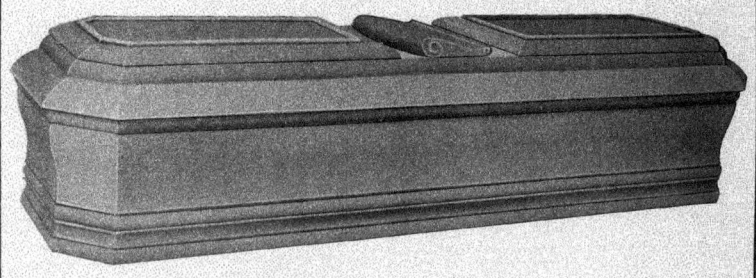

No. 172

OUR FACTORY IS ALWAYS OPEN

Undertakers' Department

Problems affecting the Undertaking Profession are here discussed and readers are invited to send letters expressing their views on any of the subjects dealt with—News of the profession throughout Canada.

CURRENT UNDERTAKING TOPICS

Embalming Case in Court. A case has recently been decided in the Colorado Court of Appeals which is of more or less interest to undertakers and embalmers everywhere.

A body had been embalmed in Colorado and shipped to Pennsylvania, but on arrival at destination it was found to be so badly decomposed that the coffin containing the remains had to be left outside the house in which the funeral services were conducted.

The widow of the deceased, claiming that the embalming had been improperly done, brought suit for $10,000 for injury to her feelings. The question of breach of contract did not figure in the claim at all. She was awarded $1,000. On appeal, however, this verdict was set aside, the court holding that as wilful negligence had not been shown, the plaintiff was not entitled to more than nominal damages for injury to feelings.

An Undertaker's Suggestions. While the case for injury to feelings in the Colorado court absolves the embalmer from wilful negligence, it conveys this lesson: Undertakers cannot be too thorough in their work. Most of them realize this, but as there are possibly some who do not, it is perhaps not out of place to here quote an extract from an address recently delivered by F. W. Walker on the "Shortcomings of the Undertaker."

"First of all," he said, "I may say it seems to me that too many funeral directors fail to make good from the fact that they enter upon the work from the seeming monetary consideration and not that they have any special fitness for the same. Misfits in business very often occur and it is as true of ours as any other. It occurs to me that one entering upon the duties of this profession should think rather of the opportunity for service to his fellow man in the various and intricate duties which are sure to devolve upon him at this time most trying of all times, when diplomacy and tact count for so much, and without which no man can in the largest sense expect to make good.

"While we should have every detail well in hand and be master of the situation at all times, performing our duties with precision, punctuality and dispatch, yet we should remember that we are serving the people and that their wishes should be complied with, unless they are wholly out of harmony with the fitness of things, when by suggestion and not over-persuasion we may convince them our way is better. Thus seeking rather to serve than to antagonize, thereby losing the good will and confidence of those with whom we come in contact.

"Another thing which might be termed a cause of prejudice and fail to impress people that we are making good is the tendency of some of us to neglect the details incident to a funeral of the poorer class of work. You may sometimes think that this is a small matter, but let me suggest that we cannot tell how far-reaching this may be. Unsuspecting ones may notice this and we may be justly criticised for this seeming oversight. I think that we should give our best efforts to all alike.

"Thus will we make good, not only with those whom we are serving, but with all who may demand our services and entire community in which we live, for as our success is locally so shall we become known to the profession at large, and I am sure that it is our wish to make good and eliminate all possibility of prejudice that may be held against our profession, remembering that it is our shortcomings which might be the cause of public prejudice."

Educating the Profession. It is one of the significant things in connection with the embalming profession that at convention after convention efforts are made to impress upon those engaged in it the importance of vocational education. At the recent convention of the Funeral Directors' Association of Michigan it was the subject of much consideration, and the resolution that was adopted spoke in no uncertain tones in regard to the matter. It read: "Recognizing the advantage, to both our profession and the public, that a certain definite educational standard be made a requirement preliminary to the granting of an embalmer's license, and believing that such standard should be of the same grade as that which is required for entrance to other professional courses, we heartily approve the effort of the Michigan Funeral Directors' and Embalmers' Association in arranging for the establishing of a course in embalming in their State University, and we pledge our support by every legitimate means to the maintenance of the educational standard therein adopted, and we compliment the Michigan Association and the University on the step taken."

At the annual Conference of North American Embalmers' Examining Boards, a pronouncement equally strong was made. "Embalmers," said the president, "must be qualified. If we ask the various states to adopt more rigid rules, regulating the transportation of dead human bodies, we must exact a high standard in the qualifications of the embalmer. This means a more thorough and extended course of study and schooling for the applicant, and we should recognize and encourage our embalming schools by giving applicants credit for completing and passing a certain specified course. If we ever expect to have a chair of embalming established in our state university we must offer such inducement as will eventually demand it.

WAS A LUCKY HEARSE

Lord Charles Beresford told of one of his tenants who conducted a small undertaker's establishment in Waterford. One day he asked how business was. "Grand, me lord!" he exclaimed. "I have now the luckiest little hearse you ever saw. Glory be to goodness, it was never a day idle since I got it."

G. S. Thompson   A. W. Robinson   G. H. Lawrence

The Western Casket Co.
Limited

Cor. Emily St. and Bannatyne Ave.
Winnipeg - Manitoba

WE desire to announce to the profession of Western Canada that our new warehouse is now completed with a full line of Funeral Supplies on hand and ready to receive your valued orders.

Our travellers will shortly call upon you; in the meantime send us your orders: until we have our catalogues ready to be placed in your hands, use the catalogues and numbers that are at present in use and we will know requirements.

Our designs in a great many instances are superior to the old styles.

In placing these new designs before the profession in Western Canada, we ask for a fair share of your patronage and kind consideration in the way of a trial sample order, we are quite sure on our part that the goods will please you.

We will give special attention to telegraph and phone orders, one of the principals of the firm being in charge of office day and night, assuring you of prompt and careful attention to your orders at all times, we will never miss a train for express orders.

Yours truly,

The Western Casket Co., Limited

Phone Day and Night
Garry 4657

Winnnipeg, Manitoba

A Matter of Interest to Undertakers

By J. C. Van Camp

Is it wise for the undertakers to encourage the manufacturers to make so many kinds of cheap caskets? The caskets known as "No. 409" and "No. 411" are cheap cloth-covered cases; many of the undertakers consider them almost too cheap and do not use them for fear of injuring their reputation. These cases are covered in a cheap broadcloth, and when properly trimmed, make a very good looking case; yet, they are cheap goods, and I have often said to the makers, that I would rather pay two or three dollars more and have them made with a little more care, and a little better trimming inside, so that a satin lining can be used to match the goods put in by the maker or manufacturer.

So far, in Canada, the manufacturers have agreed that no cheaper goods in the casket line should be made than those I have mentioned; and we believe this to have been wise. If cheaper goods are needed for certain kinds of trade, the cloth-covered coffin is what has been used, and I think should still continue to be used for this cheaper trade.

I have noticed once in a while, a cheap casket coming in from the United States, covered in crepe cloth. They always have a cheap appearance, and I have always been at a loss to know why any maker of caskets should spoil a good or well-designed casket, with good woodwork, by covering it with such a cheap, common-looking material.

I understand, from pretty good authority, that the manufacturers in the United States have come to realize that they have made a mistake in trying to put these goods on the market. I also understand that the undertakers have come to see their mistake, in trying to sell these goods. It has cheapened the business, and it has been a loss to them financially. The crepe goods cost the undertaker within a dollar or so of what the cloth-covered goods cost him, and in selling them he will make the price from five to ten dollars less than for cloth-covered. So he is out just that much cash and at the same time cheapens the trade.

We understand now, that many of the manufacturers in the United States are loaded up with these cheap goods, and would like to be able to dispose of them at a loss, to get them out of the way.

I think that we—the undertakers in Canada—should take a stand in this matter, and not encourage the manufacturers who are making these goods in Canada just now. I understand that this class of goods are now being made and offered for sale, and it is quite likely that some of the undertakers have been induced to buy.

After thinking this matter over, I have come to the conclusion that a great majority of undertakers will see this as I do, and the time to put a check on this practice is now. It will be better for those who are making these goods, to realize that the undertakers do not require this class of goods, and they would much prefer that they should not be put on the market.

CREMATION CONGRESS IN GERMANY

The seventeenth congress of the Association of the Cremation Societies of the German-speaking countries was held recently at Strassburg, capital of Alsace-Lorraine. Delegates from the various societies of Germany, Austria and Switzerland were present. Encouraging reports were made in regard to the progress of the societies. Attention was called to the significant vote of the city of Zurich, where the referendum vote in favor of the cremation law was 23,000 in favor and only 3,000 opposed.

This German Association of Cremation Societies was formed 27 years ago, and now embraces 140 societies. Thirteen societies have been added since the last meeting. The present total membership is 70,674, a gain of 7,496 in the last year. The largest societies are those of Berlin, 6,281 members; Nuremburg, 5,090 members; Munich, 4,292 members; Chemnitz, 1,668 members. The Strassburg society numbers 520, Mulhausen 340, Metz 170, and Colmar 73 members.

The number of crematories embraced in the district of this association has increased during the last year from 29 to 36, and 25 other crematories, mostly municipal, are projected or actually under construction. There were 7,555 incinerations in 1912.

No precise general statistics of cremations are said to have yet been compiled, but Mr. March, city construction advisor, has compiled statistics of the incinerations that have been made in the German-Speaking countries up to July 30, 1913. As far as exact information has been obtained the total number of cremations in this association district is 59,731. The cities showing the largest figures are as follows: Basle, 1,136; Bremen, 2,840; Chemnitz, 3,911; Coburg, 1,600; Dresden, 1,229; Eisenach, 1,157; Gotha, 8,088; Hamburg, 6,133; Heidelberg, 2,483; Jena, 3,044; Karlsruhe, 1,148; Leipzig, 3,061; Mainz, 3,153; Mannheim, 1,629; Offenbach, 2,406; St. Gaul, 1,284; Stuttgart, 1,269; Ulm, 1,967; Zurich, 4,853.

BANQUET FOR "GEORGE"

A number of friends and business acquaintances of George H. Lawrence, the well known funeral director and furniture dealer of Dauphin, Man., and formerly of Lucknow, Ont., gathered at Allan's Cafe, in Dauphin, to wish him success on his departure from town. The long table was well filled, and after partaking of an excellent supper the toastmaster, Robert Crues, M.P. for Dauphin district, called on each person at the board to express his feeling at Mr. Lawrence's departure.

After all had wished Mr. Lawrence a continued life of happiness and success in his new venture, J. W. Johnstone presented him with a smoking set on behalf of those assembled. Mr. Lawrence made a suitable reply, and the rest of the evening was taken up in singing old-time songs by impromptu quartettes, trios, etc. Mr. Lawrence shortly after left for Winnipeg, to assume his new duties in connection with The Western Casket Co., Ltd.

TESTING REALITY OF DEATH

A remarkable new method of testing absolutely whether an apparently dead person is really dead and thus avoiding the possibility of premature burial, just announced by Dr. Icard of Marseilles, France, has been received with great interest by his colleagues in Paris.

Dr. Icard's system depends on the question whether the blood is still in circulation or not, and consists of a subcutaneous injection of a small quantity of fluorescein, which is quite harmless, but one of the most violent coloring matters known.

If there be the slightest motion of the blood the fluorescein, carried around the body, stains it a vivid golden yellow, while the eyes become a deep emerald green. If, on the other hand, there is no movement of the blood the coloring matter is not dispersed, and produces no effect. Half an hour is stated to be enough to make this test.

Dominion Manufacturers
Limited

MANUFACTURERS OF

Fine Funeral Requisites

Extend to the profession

The Season's Greetings

and Best Wishes for

A Happy New Year

BRANCHES

The Globe Casket Co., and Branches	London, Ontario
The Semmons & Evel Casket Co. & Branches,	Hamilton, Ontario
The National Casket Co.	Toronto, Ontario
Jas. S. Elliot & Son	Prescott, Ontario
Girard & Godin and Branches	Three Rivers, Quebec
Christie Bros. & Co.	Amhest, N. S.

FRED W. COLES
General Manager

D. M. ANDREWS
Secretary Treasurer

HEAD OFFICE

468 King Street W., Toronto

Indiscriminate Use of the Trocar
By H. S. Eckels, Ph.G.
Dean of Eckel's College of Embalming, Philadelphia, Pa.

No habit is more wide-spread, more destructive of good embalming or more inimical to the best interests of the profession than the indiscriminate use of the trocar. I say "habit" advisedly, because I am convinced from long experience and contact with embalmers in all sections of the country, that nine-tenths of the time the use of the trocar is totally unnecessary, even where a raw formaldehyde fluid is used. Where a penetrating and tissue-saturating fluid, with peroxide of hydrogen as its base, is used, practically every time the trocar is employed its use is gratuitous and unnecessary.

Unquestionably the promiscuous puncturing of the bodies in the embalmer's care with the barbarous trocar is a survival of the day when cavity embalming was practically universal. A few years ago no embalmer felt absolutely safe—or, indeed, was absolutely safe—unless he had taken some precaution and had assured himself that his fluid had penetrated into every cavity of the body.

Now, happily, due to the improvement in embalming fluids—and this applies to no one brand, but in a measure, at least, to all of the standard fluids—arterial embalming, particularly through the axillary artery, insures such a distribution of the embalming medium, that all of the gases will be taken care of naturally in ninety-nine cases out of a hundred. It is only in the exceptional case that the trocar need be employed to-day.

Consider the Family

Quite aside from any humane aspect of the question, the effect upon the family should be considered by every undertaker. Where the use of the trocar is absolutely essential, not even the family can make it a legitimate objection. Where its use is unnecessary, no one can view its employment without disgust and dissatisfaction. It should be regarded by the funeral director as a last resort and should be employed under no other circumstances.

If the embalmer wishes to avoid increasing the pressure upon the weakened capillaries and wishes to reduce to the minimum the staining effect of the blood, he should by all means drain blood freely from the superior vena cava itself by way of the axillary vein. The use of the trocar is neither sane nor scientific. It never should be resorted to except in extreme cases, and then preferably not until the day after the injection of the fluid.

Many undertakers are prone to believe that where much abdominal gas exists that the use of the trocar is inevitable. Experience has shown that this is not true. A few days ago, I had the opportunity of embalming a case in which the abdomen was greatly distended by gas. About two hundred and fifty undertakers were present; most of them men of wide experience. I raised the axillary artery and vein and used the Genung-Eckels Axillary instruments. I did not use the trocar. Many of the audience expressed extreme skepticism of my ability to secure satisfactory results in this case. This fear was not confined to those who never had used the method. Even those who had practised it for years seemed to doubt its efficiency in such drastic circumstances as this. The result, however, justified my assertion that the gas-destroying chemicals in Dioxin were amply sufficient to take care of the case.

Personally, I never had the slightest fear, but as the body was immediately removed to the establishment of the undertaker who furnished it for the demonstration, I was unable to personally make a second examination. This was on Thursday. On the following Sunday, the embalmer who had charge of the body wrote to me as follows: "Complying with your request, I take pleasure in stating that the body of Mr. ——, which you embalmed Thursday by your non-trocar method, was to-day absolutely perfect in every detail, and the family was well pleased. Naturally, I was also. I kept a close watch upon it and not once was there any indication that I should use a trocar. I further take pleasure in stating that as you said at the time, the intestines would relieve themselves of gas as soon as the fluid had had a chance to act. I found this to be true, and the abdomen to-day has dried and hardened up greatly to my satisfaction."

Indiscriminate Use of Trocar Harmful

I feel as I have long felt that the indiscriminate use of the trocar is much more apt to do harm than it is to do good. Let us for a moment analyze the conditions found in the case just cited. The abdomen was greatly distended by gas. Fluid was injected plenteously, with the result that for a moment the distention was increased. Certain signs showed me that the circulation had been thorough—more thorough indeed than would have been possible had the fluid had a base of raw formaldehyde. I did not use the trocar. The fluid took care of the gas, and all trouble was obviated.

Had the trocar, however, been inserted, what would have been the result? Not only would the gas have been relieved by what I may call unnatural means, but unquestionably some of the fluids also would have escaped. Even if none were immediately observable, there certainly would have been leakage. This need not necessarily have been external. The fluid easily might have drained from the tissue into the cavities. It was not needed in the cavities; it was needed in the tissue, and by remaining there did its work. Had I used the trocar, I do not believe that it would have been possible to have secured nearly so satisfactory results, because I would have relieved the pressure throughout the body with the result that reflushing possibly would have occurred, even as far away as in the face and hands, and a putty color have resulted.

About one letter in three which the average teacher of embalming receives deals with some peculiar discoloration for which the undertaker cannot account, and for which he is prone to blame his fluid. Where a raw formaldehyde fluid is used, his contention frequently is justified, but this is true only in one class of cases—those in which the surface of the skin shows considerable blotches with a brown and burned appearance. In many of such cases even the trouble could have been avoided in a great measure, had the undertaker made the first part of his injection with fluid greatly weakened, following this up immediately, if need be, with a normal quantity of fluid in the strength called for by the directions on the bottle.

Effect of Fluids Uneven

It is an unfortunate fault of raw formaldehyde fluids that their astringency is so great that circulation is extremely uneven. The embalmer discovers that sufficient fluid has not reached some particular part of the surface and, therefore, continues his injection with the result that he gets too much fluid in other places. To this circumstance is attributable a large portion of the discolored spots. Of course, there is a remedy for this.

Burglar Proof and Water Tight

"The St. Thomas"

Original, Quick Closing End Vault

MANUFACTURED BY

The St. Thomas Metallic Vault Company, Limited
ST. THOMAS, ONTARIO

Springfield's New Toncan Metal Caskets

The Biggest and Best Value Ever Offered

This new design is a winner. For a moderate priced casket it has no equal.

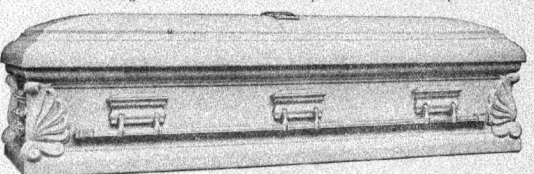

The "JACKSON"

Broadcloth Covered. Made without inner top. Trimmed complete with Antique Silver extension handles and name plate, lined with figured Artsilk Pillow Set. Face Cap hinged and lined to match pillow set.

The "JORDAN." Made with an inner top which contains half length glass and can be sealed air tight. Lined and trimmed same as the "Jackson." ¶ Toncan Metal possesses greater strength than copper, is a worthy substitute for copper, and in every instance is superior to rolled steel. It is noncorrosive because of its purity, is made to withstand the climatic and atmospheric effects of today. ¶ Toncan Metal Caskets are good for all time. Send for full description and large illustration. ¶ Springfield All Steel Welded Grave Vaults, seven styles in all, are the best selling grave vaults on the market, try them.

Springfield Products for Sale by all Leading Jobbers

The Springfield Metallic Casket Co'y   SPRINGFIELD OHIO, U.S.A.

In fact, practically every one of these bodies could have been preserved absolutely without this surface discoloration had a more penetrating fluid like Dioxin been used, because the distribution of the fluid would then have been much more uniform, due to the superior distributing qualities of the peroxide of hydrogen, which forms its basic disinfectant substance.

Where this type of fluid is employed, there is little liability of one part of the body getting too much fluid and still less liability of even an over-supply burning the surface tissue. There are, however, discolorations which appear and for which the fluid is not to blame. Happily they are not common, and an undertaker with a good business even may go years before encountering one.

It is an axiom in the prefession that if accidents are to occur, they almost invariably happen upon the bodies where we can the least afford them. A letter I received some time ago calls to my mind one form of discoloration, however, which it would be difficult to foresee. The writer says: "We write you to get a little information in regard to a case we had last week. It was that of a young lady, nineteen years old. Pneumonia following measles caused death. She was in good flesh, weighing about one hundred and thirty-five pounds, and had been ailing only a few days. We were called immediately after death to embalm her. We used the axillaries, withdrawing half a gallon of blood, and injecting seven pints in the axillary artery. After the embalming was finished, she had a fine color with a good capillary circulation in the face. On the following day we went back to dress the body and place it in the casket, when we noticed two spots on her face, different from any discoloration we had ever seen. One was on her cheek about the size of a half dollar and extending into her eyelid; the other, not so large, under the other eye. These spots seemed to be dry and crispy as if burned with something. They had a deep red color. The flesh was firm and well preserved and we knew of nothing to do but to bleach it. We used Kresoling, which produced extremely satisfactory results. We then used our paint outfit and blended the tints so that the spots were practically undiscoverable. We have had such great success with Dioxin that we feel sure that it was not the fault of the fluid, but would appreciate it if you would let us know just what the trouble was, so that we can avoid it if we should encounter a similar case in the future."

The answer to this was exceedingly simple. The deep red color gave a clue that it could not possibly have been burned by the fluid, no matter in what strength it had been used. Therefore, the explanation had to be sought in the conditions which obtained previous to death. Unquestionably the effect produced was due to the vasation of blood and fluid into the superficial tissue—in other words, a form of purpura. Blood had been forced through the walls of the capillaries into the tissue itself, there it had rested and had produced the deep red color.

Cause of Extra Color

Had exactly this same condition existed and had any other than a peroxide of hydrogen fluid been used, this blood would have turned a dark purple, due to the action of the raw formaldehyde. The oxygen in the peroxide of hydrogen, however, acting much as the oxygen which the lungs extract from the air, purifying the dark venous blood in the superficial tissues to its natural red tint. Extra vasation means forced-out blood, and as applied here means that the blood was forced out of the capillaries and lies between them and the surface. The only remedy for this is exactly the one which the embalmer who writes used.

Purpura is a condition most frequently seen in women. Almost never is it found in the body of a man. It was produced in this instance, I am sure, by the abnormal conditions of measles and pneumonia, the combination of which would produce in the blood a severe toxic state. This would be especially apparent during menstruation, and when combined with the toxic condition of the blood, due to measles and pneumonia, would furnish a poison which would render the capillaries extremely permeable. Through this weakened tissue, therefore, even the slight pressure used to inject fluid would force the blood.

Another form of facial discoloration which should not be mistaken for fluid burns is found in chloasma. Here the discolorations of the skin are found in irregular blotches, and vary in color from a light yellow to a pronounced brownish yellow hue. They are due to the decomposition of the stagnant blood in the finer capillaries which has produced a condition somewhat similar to the ordinary "black and blue" mark which results from a blow. Where chloasma is found and where the body is not embalmed, this blotch would make its appearance and remain soft. When the body is embalmed, however, and the fluid has acted, the spot becomes hard and doesn't change its color. In its color, formation, extent and general appearance it is quite like the callous in the palm of the hand of a laboring man.

In old persons, and especially those who have cardiac valvular trouble of a chronic nature, we often observe conditions which betray hemorrhagic purpura. This is not dissimilar to the first case cited. In plain English, hemorrhagic purpura means blood leaks in the capillaries. This condition is more frequently found than in the combination described in the early part of this article, and betrays itself in small, dark spots of a bluish tinge over the face and forehead. They seldom are larger than a pin-head. This condition is not one found alone after death. Its presence is merely disclosed by the changes in the color of the blood, which result after life has passed out of the body. They existed to quite as great an extent before death as after, but the discolorations do not appear so prominently, due to the fact that the blood is in its normal color. The spots are then light red. If a strong formaldehyde fluid be used, these, of course, deepen to an extremely dark hue. Even where a peroxide of hydrogen fluid is used they are not totally obliterated, although the property of peroxide of hydrogen does much to soften the disquieting tint.

PROFESSIONAL NOTES

John Simpson, the well known funeral director of Neepawa, Man., paid a visit to Winnipeg recently.

At a meeting of the Western Casket Co., Ltd., held at Winnipeg, Man., G. L. Thompson was elected president, A. W. Robinson vice-president, and G. H. Lawrence secretary-treasurer.

The Globe Casket Co., Ltd., London, has received an Ontario Charter, with a capital of $40,000. The provisional directors are Frederick W. Coles, R. L. Watson, F. H. Coles, C. H. Ivey and R. H. G. Ivey.

B. H. Greenwood, of Saskatoon, Sask., has started in the undertaking business in Transcona, Man. Mr. Greenwood is a brother of the well known funeral director of the same name in Stratford, Ont. The Western Casket Co., Winnipeg, secured the opening order.

FRIGID Automatic Control Safety Lowering and Raising Device

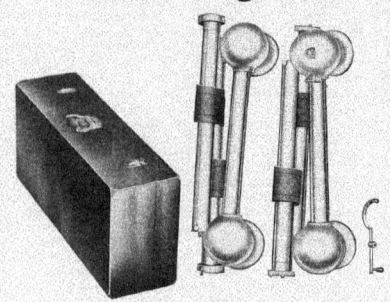

For the first time in the history of lowering devices, we offer an automatic or self-controlled lowering device that can by its peculiar construction also be used as a raising device. The particular advantage of the FRIGID Automatic, however, lies in its perfect safety.

"Safety First"   "Safety First"

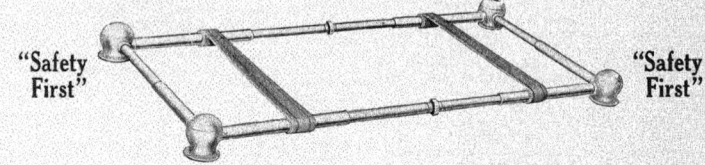

"Safety First" is necessary. When, with safety you have dignity in the slow descent of the casket into the grave, you have beauty in the design and richness of the finished device, you have simplicity of operation, ease of control, and you have a device whose operation lends itself to any ritual—then you surely have a device that helps to reach the ideal in funeral work.

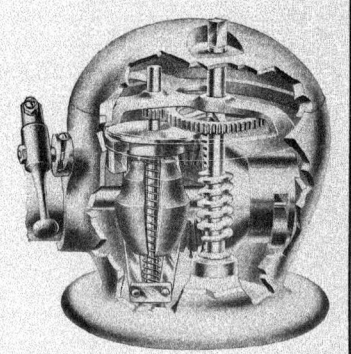

FRIGID FLUID CO.,   Chicago, Illinois

The Old-Time Undertaker

Address delivered by H. S. Stone, Secretary-Treasurer Alberta Funeral Directors, before recent annual convention of that body

As time goes on, one wonders if the day of the old-time undertaker has gone, never to return. To a great extent I believe it has, and as years roll by I believe he will disappear altogether and a different class of men, with broader view, will take his place.

The undertaker of the moving-picture shows is a joke, but, at the same time, they depict almost to life the men who, years ago, carried on the profession or business of undertaking; and the type with some exceptions (but I am glad to say that not all by any means) were of the kind that has in the past made a joke of the undertaker.

I believe that the time is now here when the professional funeral director will no longer be held up for ridicule in either fiction or moving-picture shows. Why should those in the profession dress or act so as to draw attention to themselves, singling themselves out from others wherever they go? Why not the funeral director dress and act as any other professional man? I see no reason why he should not dress in neat business attire, not only when in the office, but also in making his calls and up to the time he is required to conduct the funeral.

Does it lend any more dignity to the profession or the man to go on his professional call, where he is expected often to take hold and see after everything from the very start, dressed in his Prince Albert, etc.? Will he not feel more at ease and less conspicuous dressed in a neat business suit? Will not the family think just as much of him in the one dress as the other? Certainly. For it is not the dress a man has on that is respected at these times, but it is the man in the dress. If the man himself is not able or competent of gaining the respect of those who in time of sorrow require his services, then surely the clothes will not gain this respect for him. Therefore, why should we as professional funeral directors and embalmers, when not actually conducting a funeral, dress differently than other professional or business men?

Certainly the funeral director should, as a gentleman and a man of business, dress neatly and in quiet colors —colors that would not in any way be out of place even in a house of mourning. A man of good taste will always know how to dress becomingly, and in these days when we can get such a large assortment of patterns and styles to choose from, surely it is not a hard matter to choose a neat and becoming suit, suitable for the business you are conducting.

To-day we see our ministers and doctors doing away with their black suits as every-day wearing apparel. The minister of to-day mingles amongst the people the same as other business men, and you are seldom able to distinguish him amongst other men you meet, the clergy of the Anglican and Roman Catholic Churches excepted. Are not these men just as much respected when in their business or every-day clothes as those who wear the black clerical dress? Certainly they are. Again it is not the dress that makes the man, but the man that is in the dress.

In all classes or professions you will find men that are no credit to their calling, but here is one thing I could never understand. Consider the man we call into our home when our hearts are full of sorrow and grief for some loved one (perhaps a wife, a mother or a daughter); the man whom we expect to handle and look after our loved one, who will see and hear that which is strictly confidential and which you would not care to have made public. Often this man has to be the friend of the family for the time being and will share some family secrets and confidences, to say nothing of his being intrusted to lay out and care for the body of wife, daughter or mother. Now why should this man who is placed in this position owing to the fact that he is a professional undertaker or funeral director so often be made the butt of a joke by some brainless fool who thinks he is getting off something smart?

For instance. A few days ago I was spending a few hours at one of our summer resorts and someone spoke of going boating on the lake. Some smart Alec replied, "Well, it's alright, we have got the undertaker with us." Can you tell me where the joke or the laugh comes in? I certainly fail to see any. For let the case be reversed and the time come when these same people who are always ready to make ridicule of things that are full of sorrow and grief, have to come themselves to the man they have all had a joke over, they are the very ones who, when death enters their homes, feel keenly their loss and see little then to joke over, very often feeling ashamed of themselves for making light of the one who, in their time of trouble, showed them so much kindness and tried to make their sorrow as light as possible by taking away from death so much that is unpleasant.

Let those who contemplate entering into the profession of embalming and funeral directing think well before they take the step, for not every man who can embalm a body will make a successful funeral director. Often they are two different men.

You do not have to put on that sanctimonious look as if you were just bubbling over with sympathy for the family and wanted everyone present to know it, nor do you have to go about your work with a face as long as a fiddle making people feel like giving you a lift with the toe of their boot. Nor do you have to put on a sort of smirk expression in your face and rub your hands together to show your patrons how much pleasure it gives you to be able to sell them an expensive coffin or casket. It is this kind of men who act like simpering fools who are never a success. Nor do other people care much to have a man of this description amongst them.

Again, it's the man himself along with business ability and neatness of dress and appearance who is not always thinking of the "Almighty Dollar" and what he is going to get with it—who has gained the good will and respect of those he comes in contact with in the course of his business life by his manner of doing his work and conducting his funerals—I say he is the man who makes the successful funeral director.

And here again it is not the silk hat and Prince Albert alone, but "The Man Under the Hat."

George Hendren, of Creston, B.C., has started in the undertaking business in that town.

John Thomson, of the J. Thomson Co., Winnipeg, has left to spend the winter on the Pacific Coast.

G. J. Wainwright has retired from the undertaking business at Kamloops, B.C. His hearse, casket wagon, and ambulance were purchased by Campbell Bros., of Vernon, B.C.

R. A. Logan, of Dorchester, Ont., writes to correct the information published in the last issue of The Furniture World and The Undertaker in regard to the purchase of the furniture and undertaking business there. Mr. Logan is the purchaser and sole proprietor of the business at one time conducted by Mr. McNiven, the latter gentleman having retired from the business some time ago.

DIOXIN
IS PLEASANT TO USE!

IF DIOXIN had no other superiority over the ordinary formaldehyde fluids, the fact that it is safe and pleasant to use should insure it a place in the affections of every embalmer.

If there is any one feature in the care of the dead human body that is more annoying than any other, it is the fact that, except DIOXIN, practically every fluid in the market will literally pickle the hands of most operators, no matter how careful they may be, and, particularly in cold weather, will open up painful sores which it is practically impossible to heal.

DIOXIN users are free from this great annoyance and danger—for every open cut or sore affords a hiding and breeding place for the germs of disease.

CONSIDER YOUR ASSISTANT

Perhaps your assistant does the most of your embalming. Consider his comfort and his health for selfish if for no other reasons. A good assistant, familiar with your wants, your methods and your customers, is a jewel. Make his work as safe and pleasant as you can.

Preserve his delicacy of touch. It may save you the embarrassment of an unsatisfactory result, or even of a spoiled body. There are enough risks in embalming, enough chances for mistakes, enough opportunities for error, without adding others unnecessarily.

Formaldehyde does not dangerously affect the hands of every embalmer, but it must deaden, must dull, the sensitive and delicate nerves of the fingers and render the worker less sure of touch, less certain of results, particularly in difficult cases. You can wash your hands in DIOXIN without injury.

NO TORTURED EYES WITH DIOXIN

The fumes of most fluids, too, in addition to attacking the hands, have a particularly irritating effect upon not only the mucous membranes of the eyelids, but upon the eyes themselves. This is particularly offensive and harmful when the work is done in a warm or brilliantly-lighted room.

DIOXIN DOES NOT EMBALM Your LUNGS

DIOXIN has no injurious effect upon the eyes or eyelids of the operator. The embalmer does not embalm his own eyesight when he uses it. If you or your assistant have suffered from the pungent effects of ordinary raw formaldehyde fluids, try DIOXIN. What little fumes arise from it are pleasant and positively non-irritant. Indeed, we feel that we cannot too strongly recommend DIOXIN to all embalmers who are troubled with failing eyesight—and most users of raw formaldehyde fluids are literally pickling their eyes.

Most of us are almost overcome when entering a room filled with the fumes of formaldehyde. We may not realize it, but we really are literally embalming our own lungs. In DIOXIN, what formaldehyde the fluid does contain, is purified and modified into formochloral, while peroxide of hydrogen, the great bleacher and disinfectant, replaces a very great proportion of this irritating agent.

As a result, DIOXIN has absolutely no deleterious effect upon either the lungs of the operator or the mucous membranes of nostrils and throat.

Dioxin comes in Bulk and Concentrated and RE-Concentrated.

Did we mention the fact that DIOXIN does not fill the house with offensive odors? That is another of its many virtues. And did we say that it makes the body firm, but pliable, rendering posing in the casket easy. Rigidity is not essential to preservation; in fact, it retards the circulation of the fluid.

But we've told you enough—although only a small part of the virtues of DIOXIN. Try it yourself—that is the great convincer. Order to-day!

H. S. ECKELS & CO.
1922 Arch St., Philadelphia, Pa.   241 Fern Ave., Toronto, Ont., Can

Undertakers Shipping Directory

ONTARIO

Aurora—
Dunham, Charles.
Barrie—
Smith, G. G. & Co.
Bowmanville—
Disney, R. S.
Brockville—
Quirmbach, Geo. R., 162 King St.
Campbellford—
Irwin, James.
Campden—
Hansel, Albion.
Clinton—
Walker, Wesley.
Coboconk—
Greenley, A.
Copper Cliff—
Boyd, W. C.
Dungannon—
Sproul, William
Dutton—
Schultz, B. L.
Elmira—
Dreisinger, Chris.
Fenelon Falls—
Deyman, L. & Son.
Fenwick—
H. A. Metler.
Fergus—
Armstrong, M. F.
Thomson, John & Son.
Fort William—
Cameron & Co., 711 Victoria.
Morris, A.
Haileybury—
Thorpe Bros.
Galt—
Anderson, J. & Son.
Hamilton—
Green Bros., 124 King St. E.
Robinson, J. H. & Co., 19-21 John St. N.
Hanover—
Wunnenberg, Norman.
Hastings—
Howard, P. N.
Hepworth—
Downs, E. J.
Inwood—
Lorriman, E. S.
Kemptville—
McCaughey, Geo. A.
Kenora—
Horn & Taylor.
Kingston—
Corbett, S. S.
Lakefield—
Hendren, Geo. G.
Little Current—
Sims, J. G.
Markdale—
Oliver, M.
Newmarket—
Millard, J. H.
North Augusta—
Wilson, J. R.
North Bay—
St. Pierre, E.
Oakwood—(Mariposa Station G.T.R.) Wilmot F. Webster.
Ohsweken—
Johnson, F. L.
Oshawa—
Disney Bros.
Luke Bros.
Ottawa—
Rogers, Geo. H., 128 Bank
Petrolia—
Steadman Bros.
Port Arthur—
Collin Wood, 36 Arthur St.
Morris, A.
Prescott—
Rankin, H. & Son.
Renfrew—
O'Connor, Wm.
St. Mary's—
N. L. Brandon.
St. Thomas—
Williams, P. R. & Sons, 519 Talbot St.
Seaforth, Ont.
W. T. Box & Co.
Scotland—
Vaughan, Jos. H. M.
Sudbury—
Henry, J. G.
Toronto—
Cobbledick, N. B., 2068 Queen St. East and 1508 Danford Ave. Private Ambulance.
Humphrey, E. J. Burial Co. Head Office, 359 Yonge St.; Branch, 407 Queen St. W. Private ambulance.
Stone, Daniel (formerly H. Stone & Son), 82 Bloor St. West.
Vancamp, J. C., 30 Bloor St. West.
Waterloo—
Klipper Undertaking Co.
Welland—
Sutherland, G. W.
Woodstock—
Meadows, T. & Sons.
Mack, Paul.

QUEBEC

Buckingham—
Paquet, Jos.
Cowansville—
Judson, M. B.
Montreal—
Tees & Co., 912 St. Catherine St. West.
St. Hyacinthe—
Cadorette, Mongeau & Leary.
St. Laurent—
Gougeon, Jos.

CANADIAN FURNITURE WORLD AND THE UNDERTAKER

NEW BRUNSWICK
Petitcodiac—
 Jonah, D. Allison.
Welland—
 Sutherland, G. W.
Woodstock—
 Van Wart, Jacob.

NOVA SCOTIA
Ferrona—
 Fraser, D. & Co.
Halifax—
 Snow & Co., 90 Argyle St.
Sydney, C.B.—
 Beaton, A. J. & Son, 374-384 George St.

MANITOBA
Brandon—
 Campbell & Campbell.
 Vincent & McPherson.
Swan River—
 Paull, Geo.
Winnipeg—
 Bardal, A. S., 834 Sherbrooke
 Thompson, J. C., 501 Main
 Clark-Leatherdale Co., Ltd., 232 Kennedy St.

SASKATCHEWAN
Gull Lake—
 Morrow, Fred. A.
Saskatoon—
 Young, A. E.

Kamsack—
 Russell, G. E. I.
Lanigan—
 Robertson, Wm.
Moose Jaw—
 Broadfoot Bros.
Rush Lake—
 Friesen, John M.
Prince Albert—
 Howard, A. C.
 Hadley, C. L.
Regina—
 Speers, George.
Semans—
 Haygarth, Jas.
Welwyn—
 Leavens, Merritt.
Wolseley —
 Barber, B.

ALBERTA
Calgary—
 Graham & Buscomb, 611 Centre St.
Castor—
 Winter, W. G.

BRITISH COLUMBIA
Hosmer—
 Cornett, T. A.
Victoria—
 Hann & Thompson, 827 Pandora Ave.

IF YOU WANT TO BUY OR SELL

A Furniture or Undertaking Business, try our Classified Pages. The Canadian Furniture World and The Undertaker is read by practically every furniture merchant and undertaker in Canada every month.

The Original Patented Concentrated Fluid

Patented Formula
Strongest and Best

Essential Oil Base, combined with Alcohol, Glycerine, Oxidized Formaldehyde and Boron-Dioxide.

Ask others for their Formula

Special Canadian Agents

National Casket Co.
Toronto, Ont.

GLOBE CASKET CO.
London, Ont.

SEMMENS & EVEL CASKET CO.
Hamilton, Ont.

GIRARD & GODIN
Three Rivers, Que.

JAS. S. ELLIOTT & SON
Prescott, Ont.

CHRISTIE BROS.
Amherst, N.S.

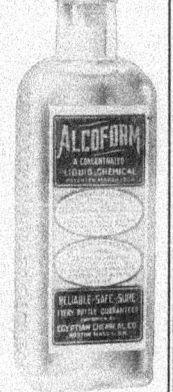

Larger Bottles filled up with water

Egyptian Chemical Co. Boston, U.S.A

Interesting and Profitable *To You Mr. Undertaker*

KELLER CHEMICAL CO.,
Philadelphia, Pa.

Gentlemen:—
It might interest you to know that eight months ago, I embalmed the body of a man with NITROZONE and still have him on view in my morgue. He is in splendid condition, and as soon as we get a pleasant day for out-of-door work, I think I will call a photographer in, and have a picture taken. I only made one injection, and did not expect to keep him, but after reading an article in reference to the failure in the case of King Edward, I thought I would watch this fellow for a while. Those who have seen him, have expressed surprise at his lifelike appearance. Yours very truly,
Perth Amboy, N.J. Ferd Garretson

Clipping from Perth Amboy Chronicle

A double funeral was held from the Morgue of Coroner Ferd Garretson yesterday afternoon when the unidentified man who died at the police headquarters last Sunday was buried, and Christopher Edge, who died one year ago, yesterday, was also buried.
Edge had been at the Morgue during the entire time, and yesterday, when he was buried he looked the same as the day he died, due to an Embalming Fluid which the Coroner was trying, having worked to perfection. Edge was a Seaman and died aboard a barge which was anchored off the Raritan Yacht Club. He was an Englishman, and had no relatives in this country. Since the body has been at the Morgue, it has been viewed by a large number of people who were astonished at its preserved state. Officials from the state board of health also viewed the remains of the man out of curiosity and thought that the experiment of Coroner Garretson was a very good one.

Note Price and Convince Yourself by Ordering a Trial Case

KELLER CHEMICAL CO. Date ....
1914 ARCH STREET, PHILA.

Gentlemen:

Please ship the following Via, Freight/Express to

Name ....

Address ....

F.O.B. Philadelphia. Terms 2%, 15 days.
Subject to draft after 30 days.

Mark the quantity wanted by making (X) in front of the line

1 case cont'g 1 doz bottles Concentrated Nitrozone, @ $4.00				
1 " 2 " " " " " " 4.00 per doz
2 " 4 " " " " " " 4.00 "
3 " 6 " " " " " " 3.90 "
6 " 12 " " " " " " 3.75 "
12 " 24 " " " " " " 3.50 "

The Freight on 4 dozen is the same as on any smaller quantity

NITROZONE may be returned at anytime if not satisfactory

Signed

Index to Advertisements

A
Adams & Raymond..........i.b.c.
Albrough & Co., J. P..........30
Antiseptic Bedding Co..........4
Ault & Wiborg..........6

B
Baetz Bros. & Co..........39
Batavia Clamp Co..........i.b.c.
Berlin Exhibition..........38
Berlin Table Mfg. Co..........42

C
Canada Mattress Mfg. Co..........35
Canadian Linderman Co..........76
Canadian Furniture Mfrs..........21
Can. H.W. Johns-Manville Co..........43
Can. Rattan Chair Co..........36
Connor & Son, J. H..........12
Crown Furniture Co..........22

D
Dominion Casket Co..........80
Dominion Mfrs., Limited..........84

E
Eckels & Co., H. S..........90
Egyptian Chemical Co..........91
Elmira Interior Woodwork Co..........32
Elmira Furniture Co..........22
Elora Furniture Co..........27
Ellis Furniture Co..........12

F
Farquharson-Gifford..........9
Esame & Roy..........15
Freere & Sons Co., D. S..........78
Frigid Fluid Co..........88

G
Gibbard Furniture Co..........31
Globe Wernicke..........11
Gold Medal Furniture Mfg. Co..........19
Gendron Wheel Co..........i.b.c.
Gendron Mfg. Co..........24

H
Hourd & Co..........43

I
Ideal Bedding Co..........44
Imperial Furniture Co..........30 i.b.c.

J
Jamieson & Co., R. C..........24

K
Kawnee Mfg. Co..........33
Kindel Bed Co. Limited, The..........28
Knechtel Furniture Co..........23
Kohn, J. & J..........23

Krug Furniture Co., H..........41
Kellar Chemical..........91

L
Lackawana Leather Co..........i.b.c.
Lippert Furniture Co..........39

M
Menford Mfg. Co..........26
Mundell & Co., John C..........i.f.c.
McLagan Furniture Co..........o.f.c.
McKellar Bedding Co..........18
Montreal Upholstering Co..........4

N
Nagrella Mfg Co..........10
North American Bent Chair Co..........28

O
Onward Mfg. Co..........43
Ontario Spring Bed..........14

Q
Quality Furniture Makers Ltd..........29

R
Robertson, P. & L., Mfg. Co..........6

S
Scafe & Co., A. J..........42
Shafer, D. L..........32
Springfield Metallic Casket Co..........80
Standard Bedstead Co..........34
Stratford Exhibition..........3
Stratford Brass Co..........15
Stratford Bed Co..........13
Stratford Mfg. Co..........13
Stratford Chair Co..........7
St. Thomas Metallic Vault Co..........86
Stonards, Ltd..........8
Steel, Limited, James..........i.b.c.
Steel Furniture Co..........30

T
Toronto Feather & Down Co..........i.b.c.
Toronto Furniture Exhibition..........16-17
Toronto Furniture Co..........o.b.c.

U
Universal Caster Co..........77

V
Victoriaville Chair Co..........36
Victoriaville Furniture Co..........37

W
Walter & Co., B..........43
Waterloo Furniture Co..........40
Western Casket Co..........82
Weisglass, S., Limited..........26

BUYERS' DIRECTORY
(Continued from page 79)

WARDROBES
Knechtel Furniture Co., Hanover.
Measford Mfg. Co., Measford, Ont.
Stratford Chair Co., Stratford.

FACTORY SUPPLIES

CLAMPS
Batavia Clamp Co., Batavia, N.Y.

FURNITURE SHOES
Onward Mfg. Co., Berlin.

DRY KILNS
Morton Dry Kiln Co., Chicago

GLUE JOINTING MACHINES
Canadian Linderman Co., Woodstock.

NAILS
P. L. Robertson Mfg. Co., Milton, Ontario.

PLATING
P. L. Robertson Mfg. Co., Milton, Ontario.

RIVETS AND SCREWS
P. L. Robertson Mfg. Co., Milton, Ontario.

SPRINGS
James Steele, Guelph.
Ideal Bedding Co., Toronto.

SPANISH LEATHER
Lackawana Leather Co., Hackettstown, N. J.

STERILIZED HAIR
Griffin Curled Hair Co., Toronto.

TRUCKS
W. I. Kemp Co., Ltd., Stratford.

VARNISHES
R. C. Jamieson & Co., Montreal.
Ault & Wiborg, Toronto.

VENEERS
Adams & Raymond Veneer Co., Indianapolis, Ind.

VENEER PRESSES
Wm. R. Perrin & Co., Toronto.

UNDERTAKERS' SUPPLIES

AMBULANCES
Mitchell & Co., Ingersoll.

BURIAL ROBES
James S. Elliott & Son, Prescott.
Evel Casket Co., Hamilton.
Globe Casket Co., London.
Semmens & Evel Casket Co., Hamilton.

CLOTH CASKETS
Michigan Casket Co, Detroit, Mich.

CEMENT CASKETS
Canadian Cement Casket Co., Prescott.

CASKETS AND COFFINS
Dominion Casket Co., Guelph.
Evel Casket Co., Hamilton.
Globe Casket Co., London.
Semmens & Evel Casket Co., Hamilton.

EMBALMING FLUIDS
Egyptian Chemical Co., Boston.
Michigan Casket Co., Detroit, Mich.
H. S. Eckels Co., Philadelphia.

HEARSES
Mitchell & Co., Ingersoll.

SCHOOLS OF EMBALMING
Canadian School of Embalming, Toronto.

STEEL GRAVE VAULTS
St. Thomas Metallic Vault Co., St. Thomas, Ont.
Michigan Casket Co, Detroit, Mich.

UNDERTAKER'S CHAIRS
Stratford Mfg. Co., Stratford.

WASHERS
P. L. Robertson Mfg. Co., Milton, Ontario.

WHEN YOU WANT TO SELL YOUR BUSINESS

You want to get the best possible offer. The more possible buyers you get in touch with the better chance you have of making a good sale. The "For Sale" and "Want" ads. in the CANADIAN FURNITURE WORLD are read every month by over two thousand manufacturers, travellers, retail dealers and store salesmen.

Four Cents a Word — One Insertion
Ten Cents a Word — Three Insertions

For Sale
Wanted

TERMS FOR INSERTION
4 Cents per word one insertion
10 Cents per word three insertions
MINIMUM 50 CENTS

TRAVELLER, covering Western Ontario, is open for lines in case goods, extension tables and chairs. Address—728 Cannon St. E., Hamilton, Ont.

Is Yours a Growing Store?

Here are ideas which will help it grow faster. Here are suggestions for the young man starting in business in Northwest Canada, as well as for the dealer with an established trade.

BUILDING A FURNITURE BUSINESS

is a cloth bound book of 205 pages, every one of which contains helpful hints for the furniture dealer. Though written in easy narrative style as the story of "Bobby Burton, Successful Furniture Dealer," the book is neither fiction, theory or dry preachment. The incidents, plans and experiences are woven together from actual practice in widely separated localities.

If your trade is in a rut you will find here a suggestion for a new sales plan, a new advertisement or something to start people talking about your store.

Every man who is looking for new ideas in furniture merchandise and methods will find something worth while in this book.

Postpaid, $1.00.

The Commercial Press, Ltd.
Publishers of The Canadian Furniture World and The Undertaker

Invalid Chairs and Tricycles of every description.

This has been our study for thirty-five years. We build chairs that suit the requirements of any case. Write us for catalogue No. 20 and prices, if interested.

Gendron Wheel Co., Toledo, O. U.S.A.

The Toronto Feather & Down Co.
LIMITED

Manufacturers of PILLOWS, DOWN AND COTTON FILLED COMFORTERS, CUSHIONS

Write for price list and catalogue

35 Britain St., Toronto

CONSULT THE BUYERS DIRECTORY

The Buyers Directory of CANADIAN FURNITURE WORLD AND THE UNDERTAKER contains much valuable information.

Sometimes an advertiser makes several lines—and only ONE line will be represented in his advertisement—but if you will refer to the Directory in most cases you will find just what you are looking for.

IMPERIAL FURNITURE CO.

Manufacturers of

Turkish Rockers, Leather Upholstered Couches High Grade English Chairs and Chesterfields.

585 QUEEN ST. W. TORONTO

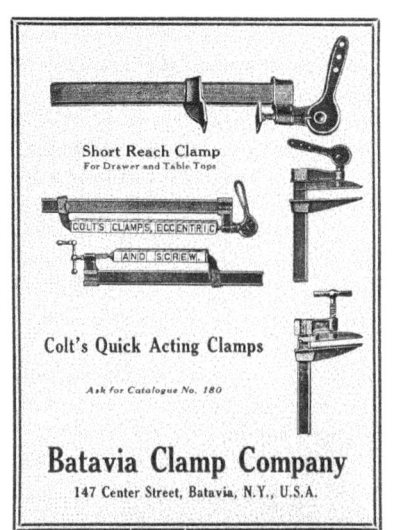

Short Reach Clamp
For Drawer and Table Tops

COLT'S CLAMPS, ECCENTRIC AND SCREW.

Colt's Quick Acting Clamps

Ask for Catalogue No. 180

Batavia Clamp Company
147 Center Street, Batavia, N.Y., U.S.A.

We are now producing elegant results in **Goat Grain** *effects from large Spready Steer Leather. Finish sun and water proof.*

The
Lackawanna Leather Co.
Hackettstown, N.J.

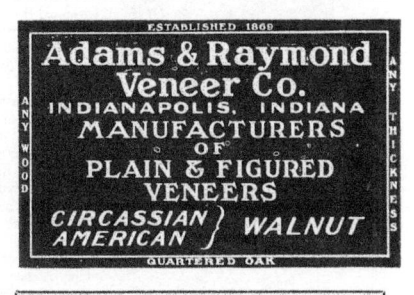

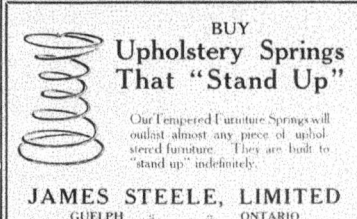

ESTABLISHED 1869

Adams & Raymond Veneer Co.
INDIANAPOLIS, INDIANA

MANUFACTURERS OF
PLAIN & FIGURED VENEERS

CIRCASSIAN } WALNUT
AMERICAN

QUARTERED OAK

ANY WOOD — ANY THICKNESS

BUY
Upholstery Springs That "Stand Up"

Our Tempered Furniture Springs will outlast almost any piece of upholstered furniture. They are built to "stand up" indefinitely.

JAMES STEELE, LIMITED
GUELPH :: :: ONTARIO

AN INVITATION TO
ATTEND THE TORONTO FURNITURE EXHIBITION

January 12th to 24th, 1914

YOU are cordially invited to visit our permanent exhibit of Fine Period Furniture in our showrooms on Dufferin Street during the big January exposition or any time you are in the city. This is the only display we will have as we gave up our reservation in the Transportation Building in order that as many as possible of the out of town manufacturers could be accommodated.

To make inspection both pleasant and easy, we have grouped the different pieces into periods. Thus you will find Sheraton represented by a bedroom suite, Adam by a diningroom suite and so on, each attractively set out and each separate from the other.

This year we are showing three new designs in Colonial, Queen Anne and Adam which are splendid examples of the combined skill and intelligence of the Canadian craftsman. An exceptional opportunity is afforded of studying, under one roof, the various styles of cabinet making in vogue during the seventeenth and eighteenth centuries from picked specimens of the most characteristic types of each period.

It is interesting to see here examples of the work of Chippendale, Sheraton, Hepplewhite and of the Brothers Adam—styles which have done more than anything else to give period furniture the great vogue that it enjoys to-day.

THE OPEN DOOR
to our Factory Showrooms where we will be making an extensive display of PERIOD FURNITURE
Right opposite where the street cars stop in front of Exhibition Grounds

TORONTO FURNITURE COMPANY
LIMITED
OFFICES AND FACTORY: DUFFERIN ST., TORONTO

Vol. 4 No. 2   FEBRUARY, 1914

Canadian Furniture World
AND THE UNDERTAKER

Published by the Commercial Press, Limited, 32 Colborne Street, Toronto

---

Stratford Chairs Open Up in Perfect Shape

We take no chances on rough usage en route. Our chairs and furniture are wrapped and packed to create a buying impression as soon as the coverings are removed.

We are showing some pleasing designs in our entirely new line of inexpensive Buffets, Extension Tables, China Cabinets, Dressers and Stands in plain and quartered oak and in quartered gum.

Reap the Benefit of Our Better Service. It's a Valuable Asset to You.

Stratford Chair Company, Ltd.
Stratford   Ontario

Western Buyers can save on Freight Charges by ordering through the Stratford Shipping Combination. Write us for details.

JOHN C. MUNDELL & CO. LIMITED, ELORA, ONT.

WHAT ABOUT Settees, Davenports, Couches, **ETC., FOR SPRING?**

We manufacture most kinds, in many different designs,—some plain, in polished Oak, others all upholstered, others partly upholstered only. The prices vary, keeping pace with the amount of the upholstering.

Thus we can give you a fine Settee of polished quartered Oak for $10.00, and so on up the scale. In upholstered Settees we make a handsome all-upholstered Settee in reliable Pantasote of fine quality for $12.50.

All furniture dealers are interested in these lines. Drop us a card for Blue Prints.

Our new Price List will reach you in a few days.

John C. Mundell & Co., Limited, Elora, Ont.

Every Principle Behind the "Red Cross" is Reflected in—

Made to render the kind of service to the user that will result in more Antiseptic Bedding business to the dealer and us.

Antiseptic Bedding

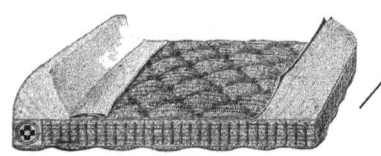

A Profitable Line for Any Dealer to Sell

THE
Antiseptic Bedding Co.
187-189 Parliament Street
Toronto, Ont.

STRATFORD

Western Buyers can save Freight Charges by ordering through the Stratford Shipping Combination. Write us for particulars.

McLagan Furniture has Stood the Crucial Test of Long Service

ENTHUSIASM will sell anything, and if the article sold will render in good service the equivalent of the price paid for it, the result is good business to Maker and Dealer, and pleasure to the User.

We are enthusiastic about our splendid showing of Hall, Parlor, Dining Room, Living Room and Library Furniture, because we know before it leaves the factory, that there's big value in store for every party concerned in the process of marketing.

Feature McLagan Furniture--you'll be enthusiastic, too.

The Geo. McLagan Furniture Company, Limited
Stratford, Ontario

We Mean You, Mr. Dealer

Before placing your Spring order anywhere else, it will pay you to examine our line of Couch Pullman Davenports, Beds and Duofold Divanettes first. We have our complete line on our Sample Floor and a visit from you, Mr. Dealer, will be greatly appreciated.

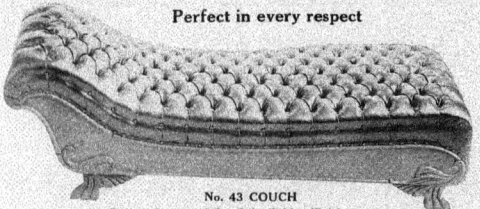

Perfect in every respect

No. 43 COUCH
Frame; Quartered Cut Oak, Golden Finish.
Fabricoid - - - $24.00 List
Genuine Leather - - $46.00 List

If you have not received our new Catalogue yet, write for it and we will mail it to you at once.

The Montreal Upholstering Company
1611-1613 Clarke St., MONTREAL, Que
Opposite Weinglass, Ltd.

PRESTIGE AND PROFIT

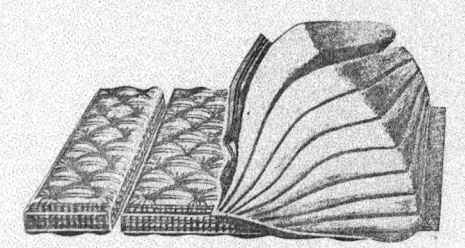

THAT is what you get, Mr. Furniture Dealer, when you stock the Ontario line of Mattresses.

Each and every grade satisfies your customers in every respect, and embodies those profit producing features which make it

THE ONE DESIRED LINE

WRITE FOR FURTHER INFORMATION

The Ontario Spring Bed & Mattress Co., Limited
London   THE LARGEST BEDDING HOUSE IN CANADA   Ontario

STRATFORD

Western Buyers can save on freight charges by ordering through the Stratford Shipping Combination.

The Stamp of Leadership that Proclaims Big Sales

Our Upholstered Furniture Ranks With the Most Select Shown on the Continent

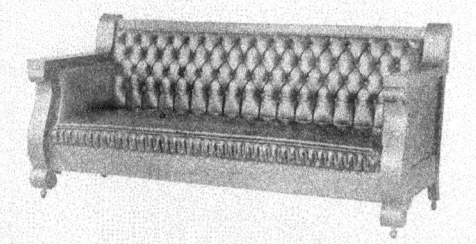

The best is certainly none too good for your business, providing you can buy it right and sell it right. When you direct your attention to the Imperial Rattan Company line, you'll find an abundance of reasons why it offers more opportunities for fair profits than anything else you can handle.

We know you would be interested in our many new designs in upholstered Reed Chairs and Rockers; English Overstuffed Chairs and Chesterfie'ds; Stratford Davenport Beds; Upholstered Chairs and Rockers, and we want you to hold over the placing of orders until you see our line.

Imperial Rattan Company, Ltd.
Stratford   Ontario

An unequalled line of fine beds for 1914

which gives an exceptionally wide range of choice for discriminating furniture dealers. We are confident that ours is the most comprehensive line of metal beds and of bedding made in Canada.

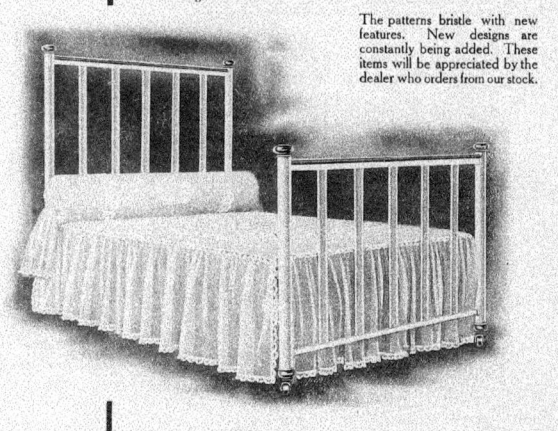

The patterns bristle with new features. New designs are constantly being added. These items will be appreciated by the dealer who orders from our stock.

906
One of hundreds of patterns, it shows Gale distinction even in its most simple lines. Gale's Beds are the evolution of Canada's Pioneer Bed Makers.

Geo. Gale & Sons
Waterville, Que.

Warerooms at Montreal, Toronto, Winnipeg

February, 1914   CANADIAN FURNITURE WORLD AND THE UNDERTAKER.

STRATFORD

Western Buyers can save Freight Charges by ordering through the Stratford Shipping Combination. Write us for particulars.

The Home of the New Line of

Davenport Beds and Living Room Furniture

Travelers handling our line are now calling on the trade throughout Canada.

We trust that you give the F-G man a hearty hand-shake and promote a feeling of good fellowship that will be appreciated by us, and more than returned in good service to you in any business we may do together.

Our Davenport Beds merit your consideration.

The Farquharson-Gifford Co., Ltd.
Stratford, Ontario

A Word of Thanks

To the large number who viewed our exhibit in the Horticultural Building at the Toronto Furniture Exhibition, we desire to extend our appreciation of the interest and expressions on the excellence and selling qualities of our goods.

We will illustrate in the next issue of The Furniture World, some of the new lines displayed at the Exhibition.

The Elmira Furniture Co., Ltd.

Elmira　　　　　　　　　Ontario

There's concentrated goodness in every can of

Jamieson's Varnishes

These are the Varnishes to sell to your customers when they want something that will wear well.

These are the varnishes you should use yourself—if you want "real genuine" value. They are the result of years of experiment, years of study in correct processes. They are varnishes we are proud of.

We want you to try them. Will you?

R. C. Jamieson & Co., Limited

Montreal　　　　ESTABLISHED 1858　　　　Vancouver

Owning and operating P. D. DODS & CO., Limited

STRATFORD

Western buyers can save on Freight Charges by ordering through the Stratford Shipping Combination. Write us for particulars.

Worthy a Place in any Home
Globe-Wernicke Sectional Bookcases

An Attractive Standard Style Combination

In the Standard Style the book units are finished in a shapely oval, the top section having a slightly projecting curve. The number of finishes in oak and mahogany gives wide latitude to those seeking to carry out color schemes in decoration.

We shall be pleased to send you our catalogs and price lists, wherein the innumerable exclusive selling features of Globe-Wernicke Elastic Bookcases are fully described. Write us, we can interest you in this well-known, profitable line.

Stratford   Ontario

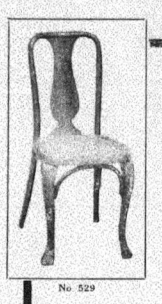

KOHN'S
Imported Bentwood Furniture
SELLS BECAUSE SATISFACTORY

Made of selected Austrian Beechwood, famed for its toughness.

Seasoned by a special process that retains the strength and prevents the warping and splitting usually occasioned by climatic changes.

Leg joints reinforced with steel screws sunk into the wood.

Seats hand caned or hardwood veneered in cross layers.

Durable in the extreme yet artistic, ornamental and light in weight.

No. 529

Exclusive in Style Because Imported to Order

To be had in special finishes and colors to fit unusual requirements.

Will lend tone to your store and prove a satisfactory source of profit.

CATALOGUE MAILED ON REQUEST

JACOB & JOSEF KOHN
215-219 Victoria Street, TORONTO

| VIENNA | 110-112 West 27th St. | 1410-1418 So. Wabash Ave. | Keeler Building | 418 Maritime Building |
| AUSTRIA | NEW YORK | CHICAGO | GRAND RAPIDS | SEATTLE |

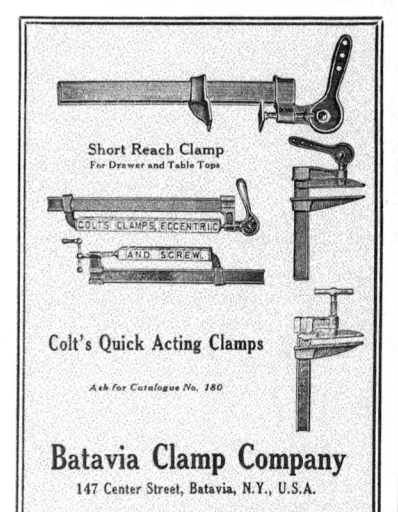

Short Reach Clamp
For Drawer and Table Tops

COLT'S CLAMPS, ECCENTRIC AND SCREW

Colt's Quick Acting Clamps

Ask for Catalogue No. 180

Batavia Clamp Company
147 Center Street, Batavia, N.Y., U.S.A.

We are now producing elegant results in

Goat Grain

effects from large Spready Steer Leather. Finish sun and water proof.

The
Lackawanna Leather Co.
Hackettstown, N.J.

STRATFORD

Western Buyers can save on Freight Charges by ordering through the Stratford Shipping Combination. Write us for particulars.

New Money For You

Our Portable Assembly Seating is making gigantic strides in volume of sales. You can obtain a part of this good business and create much more. It sells wherever portable seating is required. Write for our Catalog and Prices.

We manufacture profitable lines of Lawn Swings, Gliding Settees, Garden and Park Seats, Folding Chairs, Camp Stools and Chairs, Verandah Furniture, Folding Tables, etc.

Stratford Manufacturing Co., Limited
Stratford   Ontario

When Your Customers Want Bed Springs That Won't Sag or Creak, Sell Them

Classic
Woven Wire Bed Springs

A High Standard of Quality in every Spring.

We Guarantee Every Spring We Send Out.

Send for Our Catalogue and Price List

The Frame & Hay Fence Co., Limited
Stratford   Ontario

Onward Sliding Furniture Shoes

Will not injure any floor covering, nor wrinkle the rug on a polished floor.

Made to Fit Perfectly Any Size of Post.

Mott metal and glass bases in styles and sizes for use with any furniture.

Used by leading hotels and hospitals everywhere. Why not meet the profitable demand for these shoes that so economically and efficiently replace the old style wheel castors?

Send for a sample order.
Literature on request.

Onward Mfg. Co. : BERLIN, ONT.

"Acme" Folding Table

This neatly made, compact Folding Table weighs only 10-lbs., and is the strongest of its weight on the market. Notice the folding device eliminating the leg braces. Tops covered with green felt or leatherette. A dozen Acme Folding Tables represents a small outlay, but the turnover will surprise you.

Drop us a card for prices

HOURD & COMPANY, Limited
WHOLESALE FURNITURE MANUFACTURERS
LONDON, CANADA
Sole Canadian Licensees and Manufacturers

Quality is Economy—
Push Scafe Lines

YOU can't put a minute's time and a postal card to better business use than to ask us how you can make substantial profits on our English upholstered Lounge Chairs and Chesterfields.

¶ Complete line in many attractive designs and coverings.

A. J. SCAFE & COMPANY
Berlin   Ontario

STRATFORD

Western Buyers can save on Freight Charges by ordering through the Stratford Shipping Combination. Write us for particulars.

Quality First

Yet with that quality, you'll also find in Stratford Beds, all the other essentials necessary in a really worth while, profit making line.

The Stratford Bed Company

Distinctiveness in Brass Furniture Trimmings

The exquisite finish of our Brass Trimmings is obtained by secret processes known only to ourselves.

Anything you require on a "guaranteed-to-please" agreement.

The Stratford Brass Co., Limited

The only trade paper in its field in Canada quoting its circulation in plain figures on its editorial page each month is the

Canadian Furniture World
and The Undertaker
The circulation of this issue is TWO THOUSAND COPIES

An Old Store with a New Front

54 years the Appeldoorns did business behind this old Front—always did a good business and made money—but when they installed their KAWNEER STORE FRONT their business was increased 40%. The new Front actually paid for itself in eight months. Now and for years to come the profits on the increased sales will go straight to the profit column. Think of the sales this one Store lost because of the old Store Front—and if yours is an old Front you are losing sales just as the Appeldoorns did. Let their experience (together with the experience of thousands of other Merchants behind KAWNEER FRONTS) help you to increase your business.

Within three doors of the Appeldoorn Store, a KAWNEER FRONT is making money for Max Livingston. In a letter he said, "We are very much pleased with our new Front that you have installed for us, are only sorry that we did not have it done years ago as we can now see it is the best asset a Merchant can have—it is better advertising than a newspaper."

Never before could a KAWNEER STORE FRONT do you so much good as now—never before could one pay you such big returns on the investment. The success of every commodity is dependent upon its usefulness—in the case of Store Fronts it's *sales*. If you intend to install a new Store Front, let the experience of 30,000 KAWNEER users help you. Don't let sentiment move you—guide yourself by the paid-for experience of other Merchants.

kawneer STORE FRONTS

Store Front Book

For eight years we've specialized in the designing, manufacturing and installing of modern KAWNEER STORE FRONTS—our experience has been the experience of Merchants and by this we believe we are competent to help you with your new Front. Don't risk the amount of money you will necessarily spend for any kind of Store Front when you can secure "Boosting Business No. 2" for a mere post-card. "Boosting Business No. 2" is compiled expressly for you Merchants —it contains photographs and drawings of many of the best paying Store Fronts in the country—both big and little. See what other Merchants have done in erecting dividend paying Store Fronts. Just a post-card for "Boosting Business No. 2" will bring it to you by return mail. No obligation.

kawneer Manufacturing Company
Francis J. Plym, President
Dept. S
1197 Bathurst Street
TORONTO, CAN.

Possible in Any Home

—Electric Grate Mantels

No Chimney Required.
No Tiling Necessary.

Can be installed in any room: wired for electric lighting. Just set it against the wall and it presents the appearance of a coal grate mantel—but with **no dust, dirt** or **smoke.**

All ready to connect, three and four burners. Many Furniture Dealers have been quick to see the big selling possibilities in Elmira Electric Grate Mantels, and are earning splendid returns for their enterprise. Why not you?

Let Us Have Your Name for Our Catalogue and Price List

The Elmira Interior Woodwork Co.
G.T.R.   ELMIRA   ::   ONTARIO   C.P.R.

In Your Search for the Most Saleable Parlor, Den and Living Room Furniture You'll Find That the

Waterloo Monimakers

Are the Line That Will "Put Across" the Most Ready Sales

They're finished in dull and polished Mahogany, and if you didn't look them over or place an order during the BERLIN-WATERLOO EXHIBITION ask *now* for prices and a copy of our "Monimaker" Booklet.

The "Monimakers" are built to a standard above the ordinary, but they're readily saleable at a price that will net the dealer a handsome margin of profit.

Get acquainted with the line that pleases. They're your one best bet during 1914

Waterloo Furniture Company, Limited

Waterloo   Our Salesmen Get Credit on Mail Orders   *Ontario*

Weisglass Beds

The Important and Outstanding Feature of the Spring Season

Points of eminence characteristic to the line:—

1. Structural Beauty
2. Perfect Workmanship and Construction
3. Superior Finish with Guaranteed Acid-proof Lacquer

OUR Representative will be with you soon,— wait for him and see our line.

OUR new catalogue will be out in February. Be sure you get yours.

No. 709

Our line of High Grade Springs, Couches, Davenports, Divans, Cot Beds and Cabinet Beds shows remarkable values, backed by our **Blue Ribbon Label**, your guarantee of Quality.

Our Latest Quotations will be of Interest to you.

S. Weisglass Limited

1620 Clarke Street
Montreal, Que.

Our mark of quality and our Guarantee on Brass Beds

Our Guarantee of Quality on Springs, Couches, etc.

The Gold Medal Line

Now Ready to Ship

A VERY FINE LINE OF

Living Room Chairs and Rockers

Our New Importations of French and English Tapestries have arrived, and we offer you an unrivalled collection of newest patterns to choose from.

No. 686—Rocker and Chair to match. Deep Spring Edge Seat, Pillow Spring Back.

SAMPLES MAILED ON REQUEST.

OUR SPECIALTIES ARE THE MANUFACTURE OF

Upholstered Furniture
Steel Couches
Gold Medal Felt Mattresses
and
Hercules Bed Springs

The Gold Medal Furniture
Mfg. Co., Limited

TORONTO   MONTREAL   WINNIPEG   UXBRIDGE

Head Office—Van Horne St., Toronto

No. 687—Quarter Cut Oak. Chair and Rocker to match.

BAETZ BROTHERS AND COMPANY
BERLIN :: ONTARIO.

CHAIRS

DINING
BEDROOM
PARLOR
MISSION
LIVING
   ROOM
BUNGALOW

SUITES

PARLOR
LIVING
   ROOM
MISSION
BUNGALOW

No. 263
This shows the Sofa of one of our New Suites, in Solid Mahogany

ASK OUR REPRESENTATIVE ABOUT OUR NEW LINES

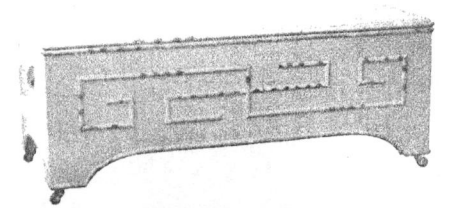

Red Cedar Bedroom Boxes and Chests

Light in weight but strongly made and will not warp. Tops panelled and nicely padded. These matting covered boxes possess big selling value.

Write for prices

D. L. SHAFER
St. Thomas - - Ontario

BUY
Upholstery Springs That "Stand Up"

Our Tempered Furniture Springs will outlast almost any piece of upholstered furniture. They are built to "stand up" indefinitely.

JAMES STEELE, LIMITED
GUELPH :: :: ONTARIO

WHEN YOU WANT TO SELL YOUR BUSINESS

You want to get the best possible offer. The more possible buyers you get in touch with the better chance you have of making a good sale. The "For Sale" and "Want" ads. in the CANADIAN FURNITURE WORLD are read every month by over two thousand manufacturers, travellers, retail dealers and store salesmen.

Four Cents a Word   *Ten Cents a Word*
One Insertion   *Three Insertions*

COLLERAN PATENT SPRING MATTRESS CO.

LONG DISTANCE PHONE
MAIN 4750

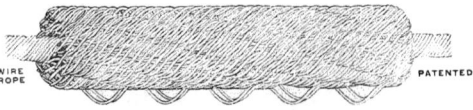

WIRE ROPE — PATENTED

WOVEN WIRE BEDS AND COTS

HAYTER AND TERAULAY STREETS
TORONTO................................ 191....

To the Furniture Trade

Dear Sirs :--

The Gold Medal Furniture Co., through their Solicitors, Messrs. Heyd, Heyd & McLarty, have issued a letter to the trade under date of Nov. 25th, warning the trade of infringing patents for Spring Beds held by the Gold Medal Furniture Co., Ltd., and particularly the Patent of Rimmington No. 147,226 (Re-issue)

We have to state that we are not manufacturing according to the said Patent of Rimmington on which infringement is claimed against us, and the following is the opinion of the eminent Patent Counsel, Mr. Fred B. Fetherstonhaugh, of Fetherstonaugh & Co.

"I have carefully considered the Bed which you have submitted to me, and which I understand you are manufacturing, and after a careful examination of the same I find that it is made in accordance with the Isreal Kinney Patent No.36,831 of June 16th, 1891. This Patent expired through lapse of time on June 16th, 1912, as may be found out from enquiry at the Patent Office. The invention covered thereby is, therefore, public property, and the trade generally can manufacture the said invention as covered by the above recited Patent without fear of let or hinderance.

I am also of the opinion that the suit brought by the Gold Medal Furniture Co. is with the object of harassing and annoying you in your business, and interfering with your trade."

You will, therefore, see the object of this letter, and we may further state that we are prepared to protect you against any action for damages or otherwise in connection with the Spring Beds which we are now supplying to the trade.

Yours truly,

The Colleran Patent Spring Mattress Co.

Victoria-ville

Standard Beds for the "Great Majority"

BIG FIVE

It doesn't take much figuring to determine what class of people buy **most often** and the most of standard lines. Our whole policy is to concentrate on straight forward, reliable furniture at a price to meet this big demand from the working classes,—the "great majority."

The cut shows a simple, substantial design which has much to recommend it besides the price,—and we are continually bringing out **new** designs. All our salesmen carry photos of these, so be sure and see them before ordering.

437

If you don't want to wait for the regular call of the salesman in your territory, drop us a line and we'll have him make a special trip to help you out.

Mixed Carload Center

The
**Standard
Bedstead Co.**
Limited

Victoriaville
Que.

Upholstered Comfort

This is the outstanding feature of "Canada" Upholstered Goods. The rest-producing comfort that steals over any customer who **trys** our goods is 90% of the selling argument. The other 10% is divided between price and the fine construction, with price a "bad second." In fact, the price (always reasonable) hardly ever is a factor except as a "sales clincher."

Have a stock of "Canada" goods on your floors—they won't stay there long!!

Canada Mattress
Manufacturing Co.
Victoriaville   Quebec

The Big Five Mixed Carload Center

Isn't it a Beauty?

Just one of our comprehensive range of elegant upholstered chairs and furniture.

You can keep your store filled with buying people when you display these goods in your windows.

Let us quote you prices. You'll find them very attractive.

Imperial Furniture Co.
585-591 Queen St. West, Toronto

When your business is big—when you have placed thousands of pieces of furniture in homes throughout your district, there's a world of satisfaction and peace of mind in knowing that **every** customer has received good service from the goods purchased from you.

Albrough Upholstered Chairs and Rockers will help you to big business and give satisfaction too.

Send for blue-prints and prices

J. P. ALBROUGH & CO.
MAKERS OF
Quality Couches and Easy Chairs
INGERSOLL   CANADA

No. 310

The "20th Century" Rug Rack

The best Rug Rack on earth. Opens like a book and folds up neatly against the wall. No better investment could be made.

A Rug Rack will repay its initial cost in a very short time and after that pay perpetual dividends to the owner.

It does not matter whether you are located in the east or the west we guarantee satisfaction and make up any capacity Rack required. Ask for catalogue and prices.

The Steel Furnishing Company
New Glasgow, N.S.

A large rack holding 12 Rugs of all sizes. We make racks holding 12 Rugs and over.

Their "Built-in" Superiority Will Assert Itself

Quality Furniture

Not only "Stands Out" in illustration, it commands "buying attention" wherever it is displayed.

The Hampton Court

Part of a two-piece suite made in many desirable coverings. The loose cushion is filled with goose down, and the seat, which is of extra depth, is even more comfortable than it appears.

The Chedwick

An excellent example of a high quality English Easy Chair. Splendid selections in leather and tapestry coverings. Write us for further information concerning these lines.

We Sell Through Dealers Only—We Do Not Sell Direct to the Consumer.

Quality Furniture Makers, Limited

ED. JEFFRIES, Managing Director

WELLAND .. CANADA

Weis Slide Door Sectional Bookcases Sell Well Throughout the Winter Months

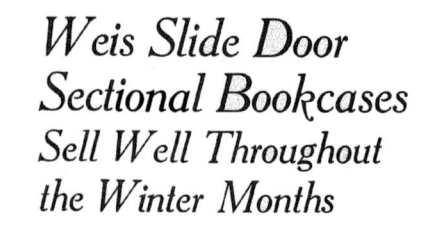

DURING the cold weather when the family spend much more time together in the home, the householder is naturally more inclined to see that he is well provided with those pieces of furniture which best promote pleasant hours.

In the Weis Slide Door Sectional Bookcases he is offered a splendid example of beauty and service carefully combined.

There is nothing to get out of order in the "Weis." The book shelves cannot sag and the doors operate quietly and do not stick.

Saving in material and economy in construction do not sacrifice quality in Weis Slide Door Sectional Bookcases, but make the low prices possible.

Why not write us about the opportunities for steady profits in the sale of this line in your locality?

The Knechtel Furniture Co., Limited
Hanover, Ont.

Making TABLE-SLIDES is a Specialty Business

For more than TWENTY-FIVE YEARS we have made TABLE SLIDES exclusively. Our Factory is equipped with Special Machinery which enables us to make SLIDES,—BETTER and CHEAPER than the furniture manufacturer.

Canadian Table makers are rapidly adopting WABASH SLIDES

Because { They ELIMINATE SLIDE TROUBLES
Are CHEAPER and BETTER

Reduced Costs | BY USING
Increased Out-put | **WABASH SLIDES**

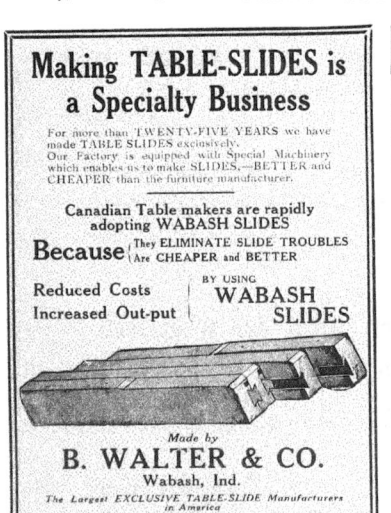

Made by
B. WALTER & CO.
Wabash, Ind.

The Largest EXCLUSIVE TABLE-SLIDE Manufacturers in America
ESTABLISHED 1887

Quick Sales—Big Profits

Here's a line that practically sells on sight.

The careful housewife knows the necessity of protecting her dining table against hot dishes—and in most cases she simply can't resist buying if you attract her attention by a display of

J M ASBESTOS
Table Covers and Mats

You eliminate competition when you handle this line. And you satisfy your customers because you give them the very BEST at a lower price than they would pay for ordinary goods.

Yet you realize bigger profits than you could make with a cheaper line. Being the largest manufacturers of asbestos goods, we quote you lowest prices.

Write Our Nearest Branch for Special Proposition to Dealers.

THE CANADIAN
H. W. JOHNS-MANVILLE CO., Limited

Manufacturers of Show-Case, Show-Window and General Illuminating Systems, Asbestos Table Covers and Mats; Pipe Coverings, Dry Batteries, Fire Extinguishers, Etc.

TORONTO   MONTREAL   WINNIPEG   VANCOUVER

The Automatic Top

was again the feature of the Furniture Exhibition.

Their substantial construction, beauty of design and perfect finish, together with the easy slide, were highly commended by every dealer present.

Both sides of the top are opened by drawing lightly on one side.

The top is always automatically centered on the pedestal, it cannot get off centre. The increasing sales show the growing popularity of these tables.

Complete your Stock by having an assortment of our Tables on your floor for the Spring trade.

The Berlin Table Manufacturing Co., Limited
BERLIN :: ONTARIO

—HERE—

is an illustration of our bed number 500. Remember the number. What strikes you particularly as you look at this Bed?

Are not these your thoughts—

It is strongly put together and it will wear well

It is handsome without being ostentatious

It has an *"air of Solidity"* **about it**

All of these are fine selling points. Moreover your customer can only judge your business by the goods you sell. With such goods as this on your floor that **"air of solidity"** is imparted to your whole store.

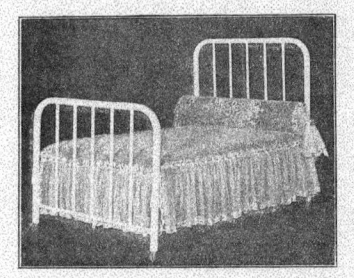

It is by considering points like these that we have built up our extensive business. They have made Stamco a power to be reckoned with in the bedding trade, and they will do the same for you.

Stamco Limited,   Stamco of Regina Limited
Saskatoon, Edmonton   Regina

Kellaric Mattresses

"SWEET DREAMS"

There's Nothing to Equal Their Comfort, Sanitation and Economy

THE Mattress that is open to the inspection of the world through the laced opening at the end. It discloses to everybody their big selling features—the firm, soft, sanitary, resilient cotton felt and the heavy, serviceable covering.

There will be a lacking element in your big profit-making lines during the new year if you do not stock these popular mattresses.

Our consumer advertising and other dealers' helps make additional reasons why you should attend to it at once.

Order Your Kellarics Now

The McKellar Bedding Co., Limited,
Fort William, Ontario

Eastern Branch: BERLIN BEDDING CO., LIMITED, 31 Front St. E., Toronto

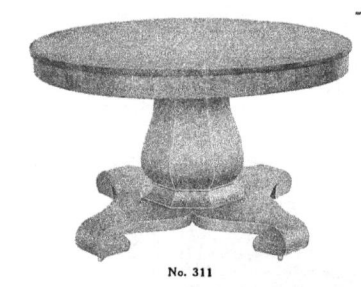

No. 311

No. 310

No. 640

One of the "Hits" at the Toronto Furniture Exhibition

Many were the expressions of congratulation tendered us by visitors to the Toronto Furniture Exhibition at showing such excellence in a new line.

PEPPLER DINING ROOM FURNITURE

Includes Extension Tables, Diners, Buffets, China Cabinets, Dinner Wagons, Library and Parlor Tables.

The Designs of Peppler-made Furniture are most attractive, hence the line is a Quick Seller.

The Quality is in the goods and the Finish is Right—yet the Price is Reasonable

You cannot do better during 1914 than to give the new and Popular Pepplar Line a place on your floor. It will make profit for you.

Peppler Bros., Limited
HANOVER, ONTARIO

Our Display at the Furniture Exhibition

was beneficial from both our customers' and our own standpoint, we being able to demonstrate to hundreds of dealers the **wide variety** of hall, dining, bed and living room furniture comprised in **The Meaford Line.**

WE THANK the Furniture Dealers of Canada for the privilege of so convincingly demonstrating the superior features of our Imitation Mahogany, Golden, Early English, and Fumed Oak Furniture, as well as our White Enamel and French Grey bedroom suites at the Toronto Furniture Exhibition.

The Meaford Line of popular priced goods owes its splendid success to the thoroughly substantial workmanship and the special process of painting, staining, and finishing we employ in its manufacture. The surface of Meaford Imitation Furniture will not chip. It is as permanent as that of real oak and mahogany, and in graining, color and tone is a perfect imitation.

In high grade Imitation Oak and Mahogany Furniture at a very reasonable price, you will find your choice in **The Meaford Line.**

The Meaford Manufacturing Co., Limited
MEAFORD :: ONTARIO

WHERE "IDEAL" LINES ARE SOLD IN CANADA

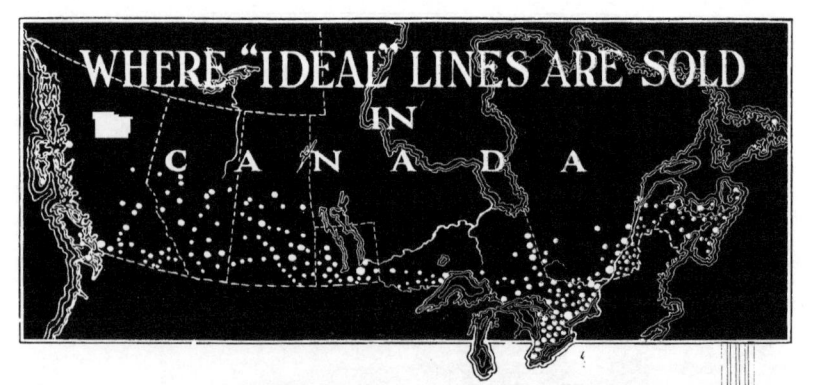

IN every city, in every town, and in almost every village in Canada, one or more progressive dealers sell and recommend the "Ideal" lines of Beds and Bedding.

The reason is simple. No other line is, we believe, so well-made, so extensively advertised, so satisfying to one's customers, and so profitable to handle from a quality standpoint as the "Ideal" line.

We closed the year 1913 with the largest volume of business in our history, and we take this opportunity of thanking the trade for its cordial support.

We shall endeavor in this year to co-operate with you to a greater extent than ever before, and we look forward with pleasure to receiving your continued patronage.

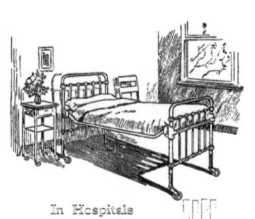

IDEAL BEDDING CO. LIMITED
SOHO AVENUE — TORONTO

In Hotels   In Private Homes   In Hospitals

Where "IDEAL" Lines are used

Canadian Furniture World and the Undertaker

PUBLISHED THE FIRST OF EACH MONTH BY

THE COMMERCIAL PRESS, LIMITED
32 COLBORNE STREET, TORONTO
Phone Main 4973

D. O. McKinnon, *President.* Weston Wrigley, *Manager.*
W. L. Edmonds, *Managing Ed.* Geo. H. Honsberger, *Advertising Mgr.*

James O'Hagan   George G. Colvin
Wm. J. Bryans   John A. Gibson
Associate Editors   *Advertising Representatives*

F. C. D. Wilkes (Phone Main 638), Room 704, Unity Bldg., Montreal.
E. J. MacIntyre, Room 659, 122 South Michigan Avenue, Chicago.
Gotham Advertising Company, 95 Liberty Street, New York.

Subscriptions
Canada, $1.00 a year. Other Countries, $2.00 a year

Publishers' Statement—2900 copies of this issue of the Canadian Furniture World are printed, over 1900 of these being mailed to furniture dealers, salesmen, etc., and the balance to advertisers and exchanges. An average of 2900 copies has been printed every month during 1913. Itemized statement, showing distribution according to provinces, will be furnished on request.

Vol. 4   FEBRUARY, 1914   No. 2

Taking Back Unsatisfactory Furniture.

As a dealer is likely in the long run to lose more by refusing to take back a piece of furniture that has not proved satisfactory than if he takes it back, there should not be much question in his mind as to what he should do under the circumstances.

Customers are no doubt often unreasonable, but even the most unreasonable of customers should be dealt with in a tactful way. In fact the greater the unreasonableness the greater should be the tactfulness exercised. It is mental skill against mental dullness and stupidity. It is worth something for the former to obtain the victory, and especially when it means holding instead of losing a customer.

A dissatisfied customer, whether a reasonable or unreasonable person, is dangerous to be abroad. That he may go to a competitor is perhaps not the worst of it. The worst of it is in the harm that may be done by the gossiping tongue of the dissatisfied customer.

It pays to take back unsatisfactory goods even though an immediate loss may be entailed in doing so.

Success in business comes only to those who employ methods that are conducive to success.

Meddlesome Employers.

The failure of heads of departments in large stores to make good is not always due to their incapacity. Sometimes it is due to the action of the management.

When a man is given charge of a department he should be given a free hand. If the employer is, to use a slang phrase, always "butting in" and interfering with and upsetting the plans of the department manager, there is bound to be friction and ultimate failure. And yet one occasionally meets with employers who do this. They are as a rule hard workers themselves and get the idea into their heads that no one can do anything right but themselves. The centre and circumference of their confidence is reposed in themselves. Consequently they cannot keep from meddling.

The first essential of good management is the ability to relegate to others the duty of looking after details, reserving to themselves the planning of campaigns and the general oversight of the business.

This is the policy of the large department stores, and it is the only policy that will succeed in any store which is departmentalized.

The head of a department that cannot be given responsibility should not be appointed to such a position. If he has been appointed and does not make good he should be superseded. But when appointed he should be given a chance to make good, which he is not given when the employer is meddlesome.

The dealers who lost the most money were those who stayed away from the furniture exhibitions.

The Dealer Who Thinks.

Those who succeed in the retail furniture trade are those who think about furniture.

They may not think about it all the time. But they think about it and plan for it when they should be doing so. They may have a time for recreation and for the pursuit of intellectual subjects. But they do not permit these to interfere with the legitimate demands of business. They are not like the enthusiastic golfer who declared that business should never be permitted to interfere with golf.

It was never intended that a dealer should be the slave of his business. It was intended, however, he should be its master. This can only be done by giving it proper attention and studying ways and means of successfully doing so.

The beginning of a New Year is a particularly appropriate time for mapping out a plan of campaign for the ensuing twelve months.

A little thought given now may save a great deal of regretful retrospect later on.

That evolution is busy at work in the furniture manufacturing industry of Canada must have been quite apparent to those who made the rounds of the recent exhibitions.

Right Use of Small Windows.

One would think that because their windows are small some furniture dealers were of the opinion that they cannot be utilized for selling purposes.

At any rate that is the conclusion that one must reach when a store window is used more for storage than for selling purposes.

The dealer whose window is small may not be able to make the elaborate displays that he can who possesses large store frontage. But there is no reason why he should not make displays that are attractive and good selling factors.

It isn't the size of a window after all that determines its possibilities for display. It is the skill and judgment that are exercised in arranging the displays.

Even into large windows it is a mistake to crowd a conglomeration of furniture. One piece of furniture is better than a score, particularly if it is well arranged and is accompanied by a good window card or two.

In window displays it is that which arrests the attention and grips it that is as a rule the most effective. For example one mattress with the wax figure of a woman reclining upon it or an easy chair with the figure of a man at rest upon it is a thousand times more attractive than a window that is crowded with mattresses or easy chairs.

If you have hitherto been in the habit of crowding your window with a conglomeration of furniture, try what can be done with a little ingenuity and care in the way suggested.

Window space costs money. It should therefore be a money getter.

The measure of success that attends this year's business will be largely determined by the quality and the amount of energy that the dealers of the country put into their business.

An Expert's View of Our Financial Position. The address of Sir George Paish, before the Canadian Club, Toronto, the other day, was marked by three outstanding features.

The one was his clear and comprehensive grasp of the financial situation in Canada. The second was his optimism in regard to the future of the Dominion, and the third was his sound and sane advice.

While quite recognizing that Canada had reached a period when her borrowings for railway construction would naturally decline for the time being, he felt that before long large sums of money would again be required to provide the ways and means of building railways in order to supply the transportation needs of the country.

The amount of money Canada has borrowed during the last ten years for the construction of railways he placed at $900,000,000, while our total indebtedness to all countries for money obtained for railway and industrial development and for municipal undertakings was $3,000,000,000. The annual interest charges which we have to meet is $135,000,000, or at the rate of about 4½ per cent., a much lower rate than would have been probable had it not been for the favor in which Canada is held by the capitalists of England.

As to Canada's natural and potential wealth, he had no doubt as to its future. Partly due to the condition of the money markets of the world a halt had to be called for the present, but he believed that before a great while an increased period of activity would set in.

As to his advice to the business men of Canada, there can be no doubt of its soundness. He urged that for the present at any rate caution should be exercised in order that the capital of the country might be conserved and an outflow of gold prevented. Because of the timidity of capital, gold in large amounts had recently been driven out of Brazil. Canada could avoid this by not crowding on sail. At present, in the opinion of Sir George, Canada is well able to meet her interest charges of $135,000,000 a year.

Canada is fortunate in having the counsel and advice of such a high and eminent financial authority as Sir George Paish.

Anything that interests the public in your store will help to draw trade. It is this that makes schemes profitable.

Railway Building and Business. Railway construction in Canada is still going on apace. In spite of the tightness of the money market and the recession in trade, 1913 will be numbered among the record years in railway development.

A statement given out at Ottawa the other day tells us that no less than six thousand miles of railway have been under construction during the year. At present, we are informed the Canadian Pacific and Grand Trunk Pacific have each at least 1,000 miles in hand, the Canadian Northern 2,000 miles and the Hudson's Bay Railway 500 miles. Besides this there is the National Transcontinental the Government are constructing from Moncton to Winnipeg, and which is now nearing completion.

Just how much money has been expended this year on railway construction cannot at present be ascertained. Last year the amount was $23,712,000, and in 1911 it was $24,760,000. This year's outlay, one is pretty safe in assuming, will approximate to that of the last few preceding years.

Whatever the amount may be it is certain that many millions of it will ultimately be exchanged for merchandise, to the benefit of the retail merchant and the business of the country generally.

One's pessimism begins to dissipate in the face of facts like these.

The best thing dealers can do who did not attend any of the recent furniture exhibitions is to make a solemn league and covenant with themselves to the effect that nothing short of sickness shall prevent them from attending next year.

Basis of Agreement re Cartage Charges. That there will be general satisfaction over the arrangement whereby the railway companies will continue the cartage service practically goes without saying.

The arrangement was brought about, we are told, by the agreement of shippers to pay the exact cost of cartage. The shippers had hitherto, it will be remembered, objected to paying the increase.

Had an agreement not been reached a most serious state of affairs would have existed after the beginning of the New Year, as the railways had positively refused to again postpone the discontinuance of the cartage service.

For a time at any rate the discontinuance of the cartage service would have been tantamount to a strike. In the large cities it would have badly dislocated business until such time as an adequate service could have been developed. And that could not have been accomplished in a day. Fortunately the danger is now averted.

The opposition of the shippers was based on the assumption that the increase in the cartage would have to come out of their own pockets as the added charges could not be made an additional charge on the goods shipped.

As the new rates have not yet been fixed, there will, of course, have to be further negotiations. But as the railways have come down a step or two in agreeing not to charge more than cost of cartage service, and the merchants have agreed to go up a step or two, a point has been reached where there is reasonable assurance of a final and satisfactory arrangement being concluded.

WITH THREE FURNITURE exhibitions going at the same time, the dealers of Canada never had such an opportunity of acquiring knowledge regarding the latest effects and styles. Neither did those who stayed away ever before miss such an opportunity of gathering a fund of useful information.

Impressions of the Furniture Exhibitions

BY W. L. EDMONDS

The Attendance of Retailers. While making a tour of the furniture exhibitions that were held in Stratford, Berlin and Toronto during the second and third weeks in January, I heard a good many complaints in regard to the comparative paucity of retailers who attended.

Undoubtedly there was some ground for these complaints. There were not as many retailers in attendance as there should have been. That was quite obvious. But it is quite doubtful if on the whole the attendance was smaller than it was a year ago. On the contrary, I do not think it was.

One thing is certain, there were both more larger buyers and more buyers generally from as far west as Winnipeg and as far east as Halifax.

The fact that there was this year an exhibition at Toronto as well as at Berlin, Waterloo and Stratford may mean that the falling off is more apparent than real.

It is probable, therefore, that while at some points the attendance of retailers was not as numerous as last year, yet taken on the whole the number of Canadian furniture dealers who visited exhibitions this year was larger than before.

But whether this was so or not it does not alter the fact that there were all too many dealers who stayed away. Many faces, for example, that were seen last year were this year noted for their absence.

* * *

Encouragement From Retailers. It is to be regretted in many ways that there are still so many retail dealers who take little or no interest in furniture exhibitions.

The exhibitions this year were undoubtedly superior to those of former years. This is beyond question. The manufacturers, therefore, who go to the trouble and expense of exhibiting are entitled to all the encouragement they can get.

They neither ask nor expect that every dealer who visits their exhibits shall place an order for furniture. It would be unreasonable if they did expect it.

The chief end of every manufacturer is to give to the retail dealers of the country an ocular demonstration of the particular kind of furniture which he is making. His aim, of course, is ultimate business. Having faith in the goods he manufactures, he believes that sometime, if not now, the dealer will order at least some of the lines which have attracted his attention on the floor of the showroom or exhibition.

And for the faith that is in him he has reason. Dealer after dealer who visited last year's exhibitions acknowledged during those recently held that he had within the last twelve months placed orders for lines which he had merely taken numbers of at last year's exhibition.

The educational value of a furniture exhibition is enormous; but the work of educating is discouraging when, relatively speaking, so many retailers do not even grace the exhibitions with their presence.

* * *

What Retailers Lose. Of course the manufacturer is not the only one who loses through certain retail dealers staying away. It is decidedly doubtful if he is even the chief loser.

At any rate those dealers who regularly attend furniture exhibitions are of the opinion that they would lose enormously if they did not attend. In fact they are of the opinion they could not "keep in the swim" if they did not. And it is significant that among those dealers who value furniture exhibitions are those from the far East and far West; in other words, those whom it costs the most to reach the points where the exhibitions are held.

Catalogues and advertisements in the trade papers are excellent. No progressive manufacturer can do without them. Neither can he do without travellers. They are indispensable.

But there is no place like the floor of an exhibition to get a real conception of a line of furniture. The dealer can there see it and handle it. And even if he does not buy a single stick of furniture he will go home with a fund of knowledge regarding the latest ideas in furniture that cannot be but of great value to him.

It is the knowledge of this fact that regularly brings so many retail dealers from far and near to attend furniture exhibitions.

* * *

A Place for Inspiration. It is not only direct knowledge of styles and so-forth that a furniture dealer obtains by visiting furniture exhibitions.

He gets inspiration.

Inspiration to handle better and more profitable lines; inspiration to employ better business methods; and inspiration to push Canadian-made furniture.

This is the experience of many dealers. One ran across dealers at the recent exhibitions who confessed what others had confessed at previous exhibitions, namely, that their efforts to sell better quality furniture, as the result of inspiration received at previous exhibitions, had been successful. In other words, they had sold furniture which, as far as quality is concerned, they had not hitherto deemed possible.

They came, they saw and were conquered. And they were glad of the fact.

* * *

The Furniture Exhibition Idea Growing. Although the retail dealers of Canada have not yet got the habit of attending furniture exhibitions as well cultivated as it ought to be, yet it by no means follows that the exhibitions held last month were features. As a matter of fact they were on the whole fairly successful.

Scarcely anything worth while can be brought to a high degree of success by initial effort. It is true that efforts to run furniture exhibitions made a dozen years ago in Toronto proved abortive. But the present movement only began three years ago with the exhibition opened by the manufacturers at Stratford. Berlin and Waterloo and Elora fell into line, and this year Toronto caught the fever. Viewing it, therefore, from every aspect, the results are encouraging rather than otherwise.

* * *

Pleased Stratford Manufacturers. At Stratford there were no signs of discouragement. In fact the manufacturers there were fairly well pleased with both the attendance and the business done.

But the conditions under which they held their exhibition were rather more favorable than were those at any other of the three points at which exhibitions were held.

Their exhibition was held under one roof. That in itself was a distinct advantage. But that was not the only advantage. The local manufacturers also pulled together like a crew in a boat. When A, for example, got through with a dealer he saw that he was passed on to B. The latter saw that he was passed on to C, and so on down the line.

"We are all as one happy family here," remarked one manufacturer to me. But he need not have told me this. It was so obvious that even the most cursory visitor could not fail to recognize it. And then the fact that a full course dinner was provided on the spot for all visitors and their hotel bills paid if they remained in the town over-night put the finishing touch on the hospitality of the furniture manufacturers of Stratford.

* * *

Improved Conditions in Berlin. At Berlin the factory building which Williams, Greene & Rome have vacated was utilized for the exhibits of the outside manufacturers. This was a great improvement over the market building utilized for the same purpose a year ago. But to use it for the score of furniture factories which are located in Berlin and Waterloo was, of course, out of the question.

The need of a central building for their exhibits is, however, fully recognized by the manufacturers of Berlin and Waterloo. And that they will eventually have it there can scarcely be any doubt.

The men who have found the ways and means of building up a furniture industry such as that which flourishes in the twin cities will certainly not fail to find the ways and means of providing adequate facilities for an up-to-date furniture exhibition building.

Some of the manufacturers are of the opinion that it should lie with the retailers as to whether or not a central building should be provided. As one manufacturer remarked: "If the retailers demand it we'll get the building."

Let me put it another way: If the building for a central exhibition is provided the retailers will visit it. There isn't any doubt about that.

The furniture manufacturers of Berlin and Waterloo have the goods, and where the goods are the retailers will come. They would be sacrificing their own interests if they didn't.

As a matter of fact, Berlin is remarkably well situated for holding a central exhibition. In Berlin, Waterloo. Elmira and other places in Waterloo county are located between thirty and forty furniture manufacturers. Their natural centre for exhibition purposes is either Berlin or Waterloo. And at the "Smoker" Mr. Edwards, of Elmira, no doubt voiced the sentiments of other manufacturers in the county when he declared that they would exhibit in no other place than Berlin.

* * *

Conditions at the Toronto Exhibition. The furniture manufacturers who exhibited at Toronto had ample space at their disposal, but they were to some extent handicapped by the buildings in which the exhibition was held being located so far from the centre of the system. In the summer this would probably not have mattered so much.

But what was probably the greatest drawback of all as far as the exhibitors themselves were concerned was the difficulty of properly heating the large transportation and agricultural buildings in which the exhibits were located. On account of this some damage was done to certain lines of furniture by the cold snap of the 13th, when the thermometer suddenly dropped to 22 degrees below zero. But this was the result of an unexpected freak of Nature.

But in spite of all handicaps quite a number of retailers travelled out to the exhibition during the two weeks which it was open and a good deal of business was booked. This was particularly true of the second week of the exhibition. As a business venture the exhibition at Toronto was on the whole a success.

* * *

Three Central Exhibitions. At the "Smoker" held in Berlin some of the retailers openly expressed themselves in favor of a central exhibition in one of the large centres, notably Toronto, in which the manufacturers from all parts of Canada could exhibit the products of their factories.

From a retailer's standpoint this is quite natural. But from a manufacturer's standpoint it is a horse of another color—at any rate from the standpoint of manufacturers who are grouped in such manufacturing centres as Berlin, Waterloo and Stratford.

They simply will not forego their own exhibitions for the purpose of participating in an exhibition at Toronto or any other large centre. The manufacturers of Berlin, Waterloo and Stratford have emphatically stated this, and never more emphatically than during the recent exhibitions.

One thing that must now be patent to all who have given any study to the matter is this: No one centre, large or small, will have a monopoly of furniture exhibitions. Toronto, now that a start has again been made will continue to hold an annual furniture exhibition. So will Stratford, Berlin and Waterloo.

The outlook for the present, at any rate, is three central exhibitions, not one. And if held concurrently there is no reason why retailers should not attend all three.

* * *

Educating the Public Regarding Canadian Furniture. One thing that struck me while making the rounds of the recent exhibitions was the importance of educating the consuming public in regard to Canadian-made furniture.

That they need educating along this line there cannot be any doubt. Canadian-made furniture, particularly that of medium and lower grade, is on the whole, the equal of that produced anywhere.. In many respects it is better. But comparatively few of the people who use furniture are aware of this. Even dealers when they visit furniture exhibitions frequently express surprise at what they see. If those in the trade are sometimes surprised, what must be the measure of knowledge which the average man and woman outside the trade possess?

It seems to me that very few of the furniture manufacturers of the country are doing what they might or should do to educate the public. If manufacturers were to exhibit one or more of their distinctive lines at such annual fall exhibitions as London, Ottawa and Toronto much could in time be done in the desired direction.

* * *

Display Cards on Exhibits. I noticed when making my rounds that a manufacturer here and there had a tasty, well-printed and epigrammatically phrased display cards placed on his furniture. It added so much to the attractiveness and life of the displays that I was surprised that more manufacturers did not do likewise.

It is to be hoped that next year they will all keep it in mind.

* * *

An Appreciative Dealer. Coming down in the train one night I overheard a retailer who sat behind me remark to a traveller: "I'll tell you it pays to go to these furniture exhibitions. I've seen things on this visit in connection with the furniture trade I never saw before. There was not only many new things in furniture which I saw, but in the factories there were the processes of manufacture to be seen. One thing, for example, that interested me very much was a machine which, with a round augur, bored a square hole. Now I never would have believed that possible had I not seen it with my own eyes."

He was only one of many who saw things that surprised him. All who visit furniture exhibitions learn something.

* * *

Business Done. As far as I was able to gather, a fair amount of business was done at all three of the exhibition points, although some manufacturers seem to have been more favored than others. One of the outside manufacturers who exhibited at Berlin had all his exhibit sold by the second day. While the buyer of a large department store is said to have purchased heavily, I have reason to believe that more or less caution characterized most of the buying.

The dealers I spoke to from all parts of the country were looking for a good year's business, but that, until the next crops were assured, they felt it wise to "make haste slowly." This was particularly true of the dealers from the West. Some of the dealers from the Maritime Provinces assured me that their business in 1913 was the largest on record. But it must be remembered that the Maritime Provinces did not feel the recession in trade to the extent that the Western part of Canada did during the past year. And dealers down there are expecting that business during 1914 will be equally as good as that of 1913.

MINNESOTA FURNITURE DEALERS MEET

The Minnesota Retail Furniture Dealers' Association held their ninth annual convention at Minneapolis on Jan. 28 and 29, and in commemoration of the event issued a very neat program of the convention embossed in gold.

THE MODERN STORE BEAUTIFUL

The modern store of to-day is far ahead of the old-fashioned shop of ye olden times. It is as few things represents, a change from crudeness and shiftlessness to the store beautiful. It is a striking picture of the public's protest against ugliness.

Shoppers of to-day show preference for the neat, and artistically furnished store, and with that inviting air that denotes due appreciation of the patronage of the public.

You may not think that such things count quite as much as giving good values, yet you must acknowledge in the face of present facts, that as an artistic store lures the customer to come see the goods, it is the most important factor in selling. Other things are likewise important, and possibly should not be subordinated to the artistic idea, yet for permanent success an eye to the beautiful is an eye on the main chance of making your store the leading store of your town.

LARGE RANGE OF FURNITURE ITEMS

A beautiful catalogue of furniture items is that recently put out by The Andrew Malcolm Furniture Co., Ltd., Kincardine and Listowel, Ont. The firm has been making furniture for fifty years now, and their continued growth demonstrates the worth of the goods put out by the company's factories. Chamber, dining-room and library sets, as well as desks, are specialties of the two plants, and in detail and finish, workmanship and material, these Malcolm goods hold a position all their own. The catalogue covers some 64 pages of illustrations and descriptions, which will give a faint idea of the big range of articles embraced in this company's lines.

Value of Trade Exhibitions

By Weston Wrigley

I attended three exhibitions of Canadian-made furniture last week and was disappointed in only one thing—the failure of furniture retailers to take advantage of the educational opportunities offered by spending a few days away from business during a dull season and attending the Exhibitions.

I met many of the most wide-awake manufacturers and travelers in the Dominion and found them ready and willing to give freely of their time and knowledge to any visiting retailers, to explain the methods of manufacture, the various finishes, the new goods and designs, and the trend of trade in their particular line. I also found the manufacturers and salesmen ready to lend a willing ear to suggestions and criticisms as to how goods could be improved, methods of shipping or invoicing improved, etc. While willing to book orders, selling was treated by the manufacturers as a secondary consideration.

I also met some of the livest furniture dealers in Canada at the Exhibitions. Buyers were there from Canada's largest mail order house, as well as from the largest stores in Halifax, St. John, Fredericton, Moncton, Sherbrooke, Montreal, Portage La Prairie, Brandon, Moose Jaw and other large centres; but the retailers from the smaller places in Ontario weren't there in sufficient numbers, although hundreds could have attended at the expense—or rather the investment—of $20 to $50.

While Eaton's buyers were on the job, keeping up-to-date, hundreds of furniture dealers who suffer more or less from mail order competition stayed at home to save the $20 or so the trip might have cost them. But it wasn't a saving—it was a lost opportunity to learn and get abreast of the times, and chances are that the small saving made now will be lost many times over during the coming year.

The more a merchant knows about the goods he sells, the more sales he will make and the fewer lost opportunities he will have to regret. And how can a retailer know as much as he should by doing all his buying in his own store, without taking any trips to conventions, trade exhibitions or manufacturing plants, where the goods he sells are made?

If it pays the Big Stores to have their buyers attend trade exhibitions to study the new lines and be abreast of the times, it should more than pay the smaller dealers, who do not have the same opportunity of buying to advantage in their stores as the Big Store buyers have behind their desks.

The merchant who tries to make money by staying home from trade exhibitions adopts a very shortsighted policy and leaves the door wide open for catalogue house competition.

Furniture Men Smoke and Discuss Trade Matters

Nothing scarcely could have been more successful than the "smoker" which was held on the night of January 15, under the auspices of the manufacturers of Berlin and Waterloo.

Strictly speaking, the word "smoker" does not convey a correct idea of the entertainment. It was more than a "smoker" in its ordinary accepted sense. In reality it was a "smoker" and trade conference combined.

The entertainment part of the program was good. Bennett, the professional entertainer, was brought up from Toronto, and he certainly entertained. At "half time" refreshments were served, and there again "mine host," the local furniture manufacturers, were again prodigal in their liberality.

But from the standpoint of the practical the really important part of the program was the free and open discussion of subjects appertaining to the furniture trade, which took place between character stunts of Entertainer Bennett.

Mr. D. Hibner, of D. Hibner & Co., Berlin, was in the chair, and a happy chairman he made. He had the happy knack of saying the right thing in the right place. He was never lengthy in his remarks, and he frequently employed the epigram to express his thoughts.

"Honesty and fair dealing is the corner stone of the furniture trade" was one of the epigrams he got off, and it was vigorously applauded.

Mr. A. Edwards, of the Elmira Interior Woodwork Co., Elmira, Ont., opened the business end of the program with an interesting paper, in which he traced the development of the furniture industry in Canada. This paper will be found in full in another part of this issue.

Criticism of Manufacturers Invited

Mr. E. O. Weber followed with an address to the retail furniture dealers, and, like the chairman, he urged the dealers to freely criticise the manufacturers if they felt disposed to do so.

"Our purpose as manufacturers," he said, "is to raise the standard of furniture manufacturing in Canada."

He pointed out that if retailers would advise manufacturers what lines they liked best it would assist them (the manufacturers) materially, for by being thus advised they would be able to specialize on the desirable lines, and thus be able to ship more promptly.

The Question of a Permanent Exhibition

Referring to the subject of a permanent furniture exhibition, he said: "Retailers should freely express their opinion as to where furniture exhibitions should be held. As far as the furniture manufacturers of Berlin and Waterloo are concerned, we have decided that we will exhibit in Berlin and nowhere else. What would you retailers think of us if we were to exhibit in Toronto and then at the close of the exhibition dispose of our exhibit at a big discount to the large buyers, and the goods we thus sold were to compete with you?

"A permanent exhibition building will be erected here when a demand for it comes from the retail trade. When that demand comes we'll form a joint stock company and erect the building."

Some of the Best Furniture in Canada

"I have just come from Toronto, where I visited the furniture exhibition, and I want to say to you that right here in Berlin I have seen some of the best furniture manufactured in Canada." (Applause)

He said he had not many criticisms to make. There was one, however, he had to make, and that was in regard to the crating of furniture. Sufficient care, he declared, was not always taken. He suggested that if about half an inch of space was allowed between the goods and the crate there would be less damage done to tops and other parts of furniture.

A Word for Furniture Exhibitions

Mr. N. J. Boyd, of Mitchell, said he was strongly in favor of furniture exhibitions. "More benefit is to be derived from a personal inspection of the goods on the floor than is possible in any other way," he declared.

Coming to the subject of a permanent exhibition, he said that this not only necessitated a building of sufficient size, but in his opinion it meant that such building should be located in a large centre, where the exhibitors could readily dispose of their goods.

Referring to retailing methods, he said: "One of the best things I have in my store is Eaton's catalogue. If a customer says she can buy a certain piece of furniture at Eaton's at a lower figure than I quote, I produce the catalogue, and should the price I quote be higher I draw her attention to the advnatages which she derives of being able to see and examine the goods on the floor of the store instead of in the catalogue and also of direct delivery from our store to her home. The customer is usually convinced. Of course," he added, "I do not bring the catalogue out and show it to the customer. I only bring it out when it is policy to do so." (Laughter)

During a brief hiatus in the proceedings Mr. Hibner referred to the habit of the railways of putting heavy goods in cars which were partly filled with furniture. With the sudden stopping and starting of the cars

D. Hibner the genial chairman of the evening.

these heavy goods were sometimes jammed against the furniture, frequently causing damage.

A Voice from Winnipeg

Mr. W. H. Rennie, of Winnipeg, who boasted that his native province was Nova Scotia, did not favor confining furniture exhibitions to any one centre. "I think," he remarked, "that there will be exhibitions at three cities—Stratford, Berlin and Toronto."

Mr. H. G. Walker, Peterboro, one of the Waterloo Furniture Co.'s travelers, was introduced as "a man who can sell a retailer goods whether he wants to buy them or not." Mr. Walker prefaced his remarks by urging that the commercial traveler should always wear a smile whether he got orders or not. Manufacturers, on the other hand, should always greet travelers with a glad hand even when they occasionally returned to the house with few orders.

Three Essentials for Travelers

There are, he said, three things every traveler should possess. In the first place he must have good health. In the second place he should know that he has the loyal support of his house behind him, and thirdly, he must have good morals.

"There is no place in Canada to-day," he added, "for the commercial traveler who is a debauchee. Neither is there any place for the grouch." (Loud applause).

Mr. Walker concluded by urging care in the packing of goods. "I have known," he said, "thousands of dollars to be lost to manufacturers because of their losing dealers as a result of improperly packed goods."

Retail Organizations

The subject of retail organizations was introduced by Mr. F. Pond, of the Furniture Journal, who urged that retailers should throw in their lot with the Retail Merchants' Association. Mr. Weston Wrigley, of The Furniture World, who followed, favored the formation of a district furniture dealers' association, and pointed out the benefits that had accrued to the retail hardware and stove dealers of Ontario as the result of forming a distinct association about eight years ago.

The "smoker," which was held in the central exhibition building, was brought to a conclusion about midnight amid the manifestation of much enthusiasm.

THOSE REGISTERED AT BERLIN EXHIBITION

A. Lutes, Hamilton.
W. A. Coltart, Chatham.
C. T. Trout, Woodstock.
W. A. Stewart, Toronto.
J. B. Hincy, Elmira.
J. L. Matthews, Pt. Arthur
F. Henderson, Drayton.
Jas. Lambo, Montreal.
J. W. Turner, Hillsburg.
E. A. Wilson, Halifax.
E. A. Nath, New Dundee.
W. A. Wright, Pt. Arthur.
W. H. Rennie, Winnipeg.
E. Bussell, Toronto.
C. S. Crawford, Chalham.
W. J. Beys, Mitchell.
Mr. Lappin, Montreal.
R. W. McDonald, St. Thomas.
A. Broadfoot, Moose Jaw.
A. F. Stager, Hespeler.
A. E. McSweeney, Moncton.
J. W. Everett, Halifax.
Mr. Jennings, Fredericton.
Thos. Little, Galt.
D. S. Wilhelm, New Hamburg.
E. C. McMurtry, London.
Mrs. W. Patten, London.
Mae G. Griffiths, London.
W. C. Letter, Waterloo.
Wilterson & McKay, Stratford.
S. E. Grine, Preston.
A. Edwards, Elmira.
G. E. Shaw, Hamilton.
W. C. Honderich, Milverton.
J. P. Bender, Milverton.
R. MacPherson, Brandon.
W. J. Draper, Brandon.
M. Hilborn, Elmira.
D. P. McColl, Regina.
D. M. McPhail, Renfrew.
Geo. Hohmeier, Goderich.
J. M. Adams, Goderich.
L. Yolles, Toronto.
J. Cohan, Toronto.
O. C. Lumsden, Vancouver
P. W. Arnold, Brantford.
J. P. McNally, Brantford.
Jas Jackson, Arkona.
F. L. Kelly, Hamilton.
Jas. O'Hagan, Toronto.
W. H. Anderson, Galt.
E. Wilder, Montreal.
W. W. Wilder, Montreal.
H. P. Graham, Montreal.
E. Trudeau, Montreal.
Geo. W. Bannerman, Winnipeg.
R. D. McLean, Buffalo.
T. J. Savage, Guelph.
Geo. N. Jocken, Leamington.
W. F. Jackson, Leamington.
Mr. Harris, Shelburne.
R. Boney, Galt.
B. Wolf, London.
H. I. Krug, Berlin.
J. K. Edwards, Sherbrooke, P.Q.
S. N. Edwards, Sherbrooke. P.Q.
N. C. Disney, Berlin.
C. M. Church, Berlin.
A. A. Perrin, Berlin.
P. Zinn, Hanover.
M. Wunder, Berlin.
A. S. Nixon, Beamsville.
Theo Linder, Stratford.
P. F. Turner, Toronto.
Harry Thorp, Montreal.
J. H. Whitlam, Toronto.
Jno. P. McCammon, Paris.
Jas. Baird, Plattsville.
H. C. Baird, Plattsville.
C. F. Coryell, Toronto.
L. Epstein, Ottawa.
O. Y. Keene, London.
W. E. Cassidy, Toronto.
W. F. Wheaton, London.
J. Werlick, Preston.
W. K. Patton, London.
J. Stemmeler, Detroit, Mich.
S. Hansen, Toronto.
H. Hansen, Toronto.
H. Peppler, Hanover.
A. L. Stager, Hespeler.
Geo. Gildner, Berlin.
H. J. Schreider, Berlin.
E. B. Foster, Berlin.
Jos. Winterhalt, Berlin.
D. Becker, New Hamburg.
Jas. Acton, Toronto.
L. Solomon, Montreal.

This list is not complete, it representing only one and a half days' registrations.—Editor.

A COUPLE OF PERSONAL NOTES

On his way to Berlin Albert Evans lost his grip containing a clean collar and a toothbrush. He was compelled to go to bed wrapped in a postage stamp—the only covering he had with him.

"Kellarie" Ingles must have lost his purse as well as his grip. He was noticed walking forlornly along King street opposite the Walper House about 3 a.m. with no definite place in view.

STOP KICKING YOUR TOWN AROUND

There is profound wisdom in the following verse. This is good gospel to preach in your own town.

In every town some folks keep a houn' around,
And every time strangers come to town—
Some folks go to kicking the town around.
It's even worse'n kickin' a houn' aroun',
Stop your kickin', be hopeful and profoun';
It's a mighty poor way to build up a town-
To keep kickin' public interest aroun',
But, like others, we have a few old houn's
Who get at the stranger that comes to town -
Says the town's a houn', and kicks it aroun,.
If a houn's a houn', then a town's a town,
And can't build up if kicked aroun' and aroun',
You have a right to kick your own houn',
But it hurts us all if you kick your town.
Now let's pull together for the good home town,
And stop kickin' our town aroun',
Tho' the town, if a myth'll make no soun',
If you don't stop kickin' we'll get no strangers in town.

Evolution of Canada's Furniture Industry

By A. EDWARDS, Elmira, Ont.

Paper read at the "Smoker" in connection with the furniture exhibition on January 15.

I would like to give you this evening a few thoughts along the line of the evolution of the furniture industry, and of the Furniture Dealer.

My connection with this business extends back to the 60's.

In those days the Furniture Dealer was the cabinet maker of the town, and if anyone wanted an article of any pretension it was made to his order, mainly by main strength, though not always by ignorance.

My own father, who is still living, commenced business by making in the attic of his house, the goods required for his customers, mostly after the orders were placed. In those days a furniture man was not only required to be a mechanic or cabinet maker, but an upholsterer, a finisher, an undertaker and general jack of all trades.

Among my earliest recollections were that I had the recaning of chairs as the task for my holidays, and in those days cane work was laced through, and woven by hand on the individual piece.

My next recollection was the connection with the undertaking end of the business; it also was an unheard of thing for an undertaker to be prepared with ready made caskets or coffins in those days. It was only after the American civil war and when the American factories had a surplus stock in this line that they solicited orders for undertaking supplies in Canada. I well remember the first coffins and caskets we imported from Allegheny, Pa., and the excitement locally, when a coffin of the old-fashioned rosewood finish was first used.

At this time only one furniture factory, Jacques & Hays, was in operation in the city of Toronto. Their work was good, and many an old wood chair with a whole seat is yet to be found throughout Ontario, in active use, which was made by this firm. These were days when most farmers and many townspeople has as their best, a wood chair or possibly a cane chair.

The designs at this time were not so bad, and often followed what we are now following—Old Country ideas.

A period immediately following produced some horrible goods, particularly when the making of furniture became an established fact in this Province.

After Jacques & Hays time the Upper Canada Furniture Co., at Bowmanville, and the Oshawa Cabinet Factory, at Oshawa, held the honors of makers of high class goods, and a tremendous business for those days was done by these factories.

I remember as a boy, just coming into the business, the trouble I had to decipher a letter from the manager of the Upper Canada Factory, than a Mr. McArthur. This was before the days of the typewriter, and the managers usually wrote their own letters. It looked for all the world as if a spider had dropped into the ink and crawled over the pages afterwards.

It is said this manager never could tell what he had written, when once the subject passed from his mind. It was sometimes a boom to his customers I believe that he couldn't.

After the passing of these two factories, in fact before, we commenced to hear, as the boom of distant thunder, of the establishment of furniture factories at points such as Berlin, Waterloo, Seaforth, Lucknow, Harriston; in fact we down easterners thought that west of Toronto furniture factories grew as thick as gooseberries on the bush, and we daily lived in expectations of hearing of a new establishment, or two.

There are no doubt men here, in plenty, who remember well this transition period in the furniture industry and the part the pioneers played in the ultimate development of the industry.

The Hays, Simpsons, Andersons, Gibbards, Kreiners, Hesses, Krugs and Knechtels were all names to conjure with in those days, and we know how they have builded.

Not to weary you too much with these reminiscences let us look for a moment at the present, and at the future. I believe that with the great development of this, our glorious country, the furniture business has kept pace, and that we stand on the threshold of even greater things.

It is often said that in unity there is strength, and in the development of this industry in the County of Waterloo we are looking to the lead of you men in the Grand Rapids of Canada for inspiration. We factory men in outside towns appreciate the lead you have given us, and our interests in always keeping the County of Waterloo, and this district, to the forefront in furniture matters.

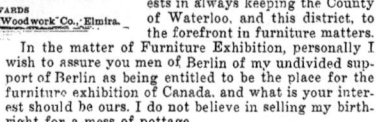

In the matter of Furniture Exhibition, personally I wish to assure you men of Berlin as being entitled to be the place for the furniture exhibition of Canada, and what is your interest should be ours. I do not believe in selling my birthright for a mess of pottage.

What Grand Rapids is to the United States Berlin should be to Canada, and if you Berliners fail in your duty in this respect we will have to annex you to Elmira and we will have the exhibition there, as the next best place.

Even now our Mayor has his eye on Berlin, and he may yet get after our local member to have Berlin annexed to our thriving burg. But as the mills of the gods grind slowly, we may have yet to wait for a generation or two. But at any rate we of the northern burg will continue to stick together with you for the making this more than ever the centre of the furniture industry of Canada—and we can do it, too.

A. EDWARDS
Manager Elmira Interior Woodwork Co., Elmira.

The time will, in my opinion, not be far distant when with permanent quarters for the exhibition and better hotel accommodations, which I believe is at hand, Berlin need fear no rival in this respect, and dealers will not in their own interest pass Berlin by.

Personally I wish to thank my Berlin co-manufacturers for their kindly feelings on all occasions, and wish them one and all a prosperous year, and with them I extend the same wish to our good friends—the retailers. I have been a retailer myself and know something of their trials and difficulties. I thank them most heartily for their support in 1913, and wish them every success.

Now, as a Canadian of English descent, coming among my fellow-Canadians of German extraction, I wish to emphasize the fact that I have observed, that no matter whether we prefer "The Watch on the Rhine" or "Britania Rules the Waves," we all agree on the "Maple Leaf Forever." As it is for our native country, so should it be for our own country, our own community, or city, or town, and I trust that all the manufacturers of this great country will so see eye to eye, that we will not again see one deserting his own country for the flesh pots of Egypt, but all pull together and make Waterloo County the furniture centre of Canada.

THAT BOWLING MATCH

On Wednesday night of Exhibition week at Berlin the travellers representing the Berlin and Waterloo furniture factories invited the visiting dealers to play a bowling match at Rowling's bowling alleys, fixing up a plan beforehand how they were to defeat the retailers, but they reckoned without taking into consideration the prowess of their opponents. The bowling began on four alleys at 8.30 and continued until three minutes past eleven, when the dealers were declared the victors by three pins. The high score of 163 was made by Harry Graham, Montreal.

Berlin citizens who retire early complained to the police of the noise in the vicinity of the alleys, and the police force when he opened the door was almost blinded with smoke, so much so that he rang in a fire alarm. When the air was cleared it was noted that Bill Beney had been handing out some bungalow perfecturas. He was notified to quit or take the next car down to Galt.

Mr. Coltart of Chatham was there with the goods. He made a sewer shot followed by a three shot, which almost put him out of the game.

Percy Brown, the bowling expert, showed his skill on three alleys. He was kept off the fourth only through his fear of Charlie Coryell.

But the real bowling was done by Louie Yolles. He was in the game from the drop of the hat until the close. He took off everything but his undershirt, despite the efforts of Jake Cohen, who tried to persuade him to desist.

Among the dealers who took part at one time or another through the night were: W. A. Coltart, Chatham; W. W. Wilder, Montreal; Harry Graham, Montreal; Chas. Coryell, Toronto; L. Yolles, Toronto; J. Cohen, Toronto; J. Kelly, Falconer Furniture Co., Hamilton; Oliver Keene, London; C. S. Crawford, Chatham; A. Schreiter, Berlin; and Messrs. Turner and Vanderbilt of the Reliable Furniture Co., Toronto.

The travellers in part were represented by H. G. Walker, W. J. Whyte, Peter Zinn, Doc. Clemens, Dick S'ont, Bill Beney, Herb. Snyder, C. F. Ott, Jimmy Dore, Martin Anthes, Percy Brown, and some few others.

Songs Sung at the Smoker.

THE GOOD OLD SUMMER TIME

There's a time in each year that we always hold dear,
   Exhibition time,
When we see the new goods and buy our spring stocks,
   Exhibition time,
When stocktaking is over and we are in clover,
   And life is one beautiful rhyme,
No troubles annoying each one is enjoying,
   Our exhibition time.

In exhibition time,
In exhibition time,
Meeting together once each year,
   With a crowd so fine,
You shake our hand and we'll shake yours
   And that's a very good sign,
We're bound to be bigger and greater than ever
   Next exhibition time.

YIP-I-ADDY

Yip-I-Addy-I-Ay-I-Ay,
Yip the Exhibition,
It's the market that beats them all,
Standing together we have the call.
Yip-I-Addy-I-Ay-I-Ay,
We feel just like shouting "Hurray! Hurray!"
Numbers growing each year,
We have nothing to fear,
Yip the Exhibition.—Repeat.

DOWN IN JUNGLE TOWN

Stand, with stein in hand,
And drink the toast
We love the most,
It's a health to furniture men,
To furniture dealers all.
Cheer, come on au cheer,
A three times three, with laughter free,
We'll be true, and loyal through and through
To the good furniture trade.

STEIN SONG

For it's always fair weather when good fellows meet together,
With a stein on the table, and a good song ringing clear.
For it's always fair weather when good fellows meet together,
With its crowd of good fellows, and its good songs ringing clear.

OUR CHAIRMAN

What's the matter with Weber, he's alright,
What's the matter if Percy's hair isn't white,
He's very strong for the other sex,
But Weber's the fellow that signs his checks,
What the matter with Weber, he's all right.

DOWN WHERE THE WURZBERGER FLOWS

Take Scully down, down, down where the Wurzberger flows, flows, flows;
Let him drown, drown, drown all his troubles and cares and woes;
Just order two seidels of beer for him,
If he don't want to drink it's merely a whim;
The Rhine may be fine but it's Seagram's for mine,
Down where the Wurzberger flows.

FURNITURE AULD LANG SYNE

Of "Auld acquaintance" we are proud,
   But here today we sing,
Of new acquaintance with a crowd,
   That happiness should bring.
A proof of furniture faith may we,
   In earnest give and swear
That as we are, we'll always be
   Because we're on the square.

Three Big Canadian Furniture Exhibitions

*Features of the displays at Stratford, Berlin and Toronto—
New goods shown for the first time in the Dominion—
Tendency of the times and movement of the lines.*

Fortnight's Display Under One Roof at Stratford.

STRATFORD'S 1914 Furniture Exhibition was unquestionably the best of the series of annual furniture displays, which the manufacturers of the Classic City have undertaken.

In point of attendance, in point of business transacted; and in point of convenience of display, this year's Stratford show sets a new record which must in future be lived up to.

It was the fourth of the series, and the manufacturers were exceptionally well fixed in that they had a splendid new building in which to display their goods to the best advantage, and all under one roof.

The new Farquharson-Gifford furniture factory proved an ideal location for the show, situated as it was in the midst of the furniture factory district, and its four floors lent themselves admirably to the classification of the exhibits.

A new feature introduced this year—and a splendid one it was, too, was the appetizing and tasty daily luncheon served in a specially equipped dining-room on the ground floor. Through this feature buyers and visiting dealers were enabled to spend the whole day at the exhibition hall and leisurely inspect the various items shown without the least hint of hurry. The evenings were filled up with amusements of various sorts accommodated to the tastes of the visitors. From the time the visitor stepped off the train at Stratford and was whisked off to the exhibition in one of the special sleighs he felt he was in the hands of friends who looked after his welfare until he departed again from the Classic City. One outstanding feature at Stratford was the loyalty and harmony existing among the manufacturers there.

Desks, Beds and Park Seats.

The first floor of the hall was given over to exhibits of the Stratford Desk, Stratford Bed, Frame & Hay, Stratford Manufacturing, Classic Furniture and Globe-Wernicke Companies. On entering, the first display was the combined one of the Stratford Desk and Globe-Wernicke Companies, occupying one-third of the whole lower floor space.

The Desk Co. made an extensive showing of their desk lines, which this year are notable for their high grade, the company cutting out the cheaper grades and devoting their attention to better and higher lines. Among the new goods were some mahogany office desks with roll tops, and mahogany typewriters' desks with a new horizontal bed feature, enabling the typewriter to remain upright without the use of screws even when placed away out of use, the bed sinking down horizontally instead of turning with a roll. They also showed a complete line of mahogany and oak desks, both roll and flat tops, as also office tables, desk chairs and bookkeepers' stands. For a concern which has been in existence for only a year, the Stratford Desk Co. has made splendid progress, and they contemplate adding to their line the whole range of office equipment. Among the recent additions to their line, samples of which were shown at the exhibition, were a new oak office wardrobe, new costumiers, new oak desks with letter and card files, and a splendid flat top double desk.

Book Cases and Filing Devices.

The Globe-Wernicke Co. showed a splendid assortment of sectional book cases in all woods, finishes and combinations. One of the features of these cases is the equalizer, which allows of the glass front being opened by taking hold anywhere, and the roller doors prove a convenience. Some decidedly pretty specimens were shown in oak—golden and fumed—early English and mahogany. A sample art mission style book-case came in for a deal of favorable comment. The adjustable shelves in many of the combinations also proved a striking feature.

In office filing cabinets an extensive range was shown adaptable for all kinds of business and uses, and a number of new combinations in leg and base sets were displayed. A base desk with book-case stack was an outstanding feature. The filing cabinets were in horizontal, unifyle, vertical and upright—in fact all styles and combinations; and in all woods and finishes. The combined exhibit of the Stratford Desk and the Globe-Wernicke Co. were in charge of Mr. Mason, Sr., F. Mason and E. C. Rohfritsch.

New Bedroom Furniture.

The latest addition to Stratford's industries—the Classic Furniture Co.—made a showing of samples only, as their plant has just started. These samples were seen for the first time. The various items—all bedroom pieces—are strictly high-grade, and the materials and workmanship are first class. Bedsteads, chairs, chevals dressers and stands of unique designs in mahogany, Circassian walnut, quartered oak and quartered gum were among the goods shown, and they proved a source of great attraction. J. G. Davies was in charge of the display. The company will be ready to ship about the middle of February.

Brass Bed Display.

The Stratford Bed Co.'s display was in charge of Mr. Heincke, and it consisted of about 36 brass beds. Being a new concern it goes without saying that the lines shown were new. The styles seemingly run to simple lines, though the tubing is quite substantial. The beds—most of them—have the satin finish, and this finish seemed to have the preference of most of the dealers, though some splendid polished samples were also displayed. Quality is the keynote of the company's output.

Stratford Manufacturing Co.

The Stratford Mfg. Co. made a comprehensive display of their various lines, including lawn swings, with and without cover; park seats, garden settees, portable chairs, lawn benches, assembly chairs, etc. These latter are now being made very extensively by the company for church and theatre seating, and a good line it is too, particularly a new portable assembly chair in birch and oak. This chair line comes in natural golden and mahogany finishes. The company are making also a line for moving picture shows.

Verandah swing seats with heavy chain attachments are comparatively new with them. They are both attractive and substantial looking. Lawn canvas seats with and without backs also have a big hold.

Then the ladder line is a big thing with the company. They are made for all purposes—stationary, extension, folding, fruit-picking etc., as well as the strongly-built and braced stepladders of various sizes. The folding chair-ladders, while not exactly new, are as popular as ever. A full range of ironing and bake boards, clothes bars and racks, and other kitchen woodenware was shown. Chas. Moore and Roy Harris were in charge of the exhibit. Some interesting information was given in regard to the order for 700 park seats filled for the Toronto Exhibition last fall. The seats were delivered exactly on the day specified and proved entirely satisfactory. In their construction some 43,000 belts were used in the 700 seats.

Woven Wire Bed Springs

The Frame & Hay Fence Co. made a showing of their various bed spring lines, James M. Miller looking after the display. A couple of samples of their new "Clas the display. A couple of samples of their new "Clas prominent. Another prominent line was the all-kiln-dried maple frame bed spring, with a two-inch side rail and springs in all weaves. Folding cots, too, in two sizes, were shown, and a couple of dozen of high quality samples of various weave springs.

Upholstered Furniture Goods

On the second floor of the building the Farquharson-Gifford Co. made their display. The company is already turning out goods, and a very extensive range of samples were set out. These included davenports in leathers and velours, couches in many designs and coverings, parlor suites, rockers, arm chairs, fancy chairs—all upholstered articles—in mission, art silk, shadow cloth and tapestry coverings. A beautiful three-piece Circassian walnut parlor suite was one of the best groupings on the floor. Other handsome things were the ladies' rockers covered in striped velours.

Besides the couch and davenport line there was shown a davenport bed line in padded leathers and tapestries, in oak, fumed and mahogany. All these goods are new —most of them, in fact, being samples turned out during the days previous to the exhibition, and they are certainly a good upholstered line.

McLagan's Wonderful Exhibit

The entire third floor was given over to a splendid display of furniture items by The George McLagan Furniture Co. The exhibit numbered thousands of articles, and was one of the best displays ever put out by a Canadian furniture factory anywhere in this country.

A very extensive range of Gunn sectional bookcases in all woods and a variety of designs was shown. They made, too, just as extensive a display of their own patented filing cabinet goods on sanitary and full bases. In this section, too, were set out office and library tables and accessories.

The table line was a most comprehensive one. It covered the home library, some with desk drawers all ready for use; parlor and hall tables; card tables with swing top, giving double space and size; hollow-top tables for storing cards; reversible swing top tables for cards or chess; folding tables; smokers' tables and sets; and tables round, square and oval for all uses and places. Cellarette cabinets were also displayed in this section.

Ladies' secretaries, desks, and writing tables had a section devoted to themselves, and some splendid specimens of workmanship were shown in these goods. A big range of fancy parlor tables of varied shapes and sizes, made of all kinds of wood and finishes, were also displayed.

Hall racks and stands had a large corner of the floor given over to them. One side wall was entirely devoted to trees and racks, seats and tables. In this section, too, were set out umbrella stands, hall chairs and hall mirrors. Colonial style is very much the vogue in this line as well as other lines, and the satin finish was noted on many of the items in various departments.

The music cabinet section was made up of cabinets for disc and phonograph records in three different styles for each, and each of these made in three different ways. Cabinets, too, for player-piano rolls and sheet music cabinets found a place in this section.

Adjoining were a number of fancy parlor items, embracing silver cabinets, one of these for the centre of the room being practically all of glass. In these goods, too, were noticed the colonial touch.

Dining-room furniture, of course, because of bulk and great variety of design, occupied the biggest portion of the space in this exhibit. Some of the newest samples were of period designs, with Jacobean predominating. These were in fumed oak. Mission designs and the newer Colonial found a large place also. A number of oak tables and a variety of china cabinets, some for corner places, were also shown here. The newer Colonial buffets have an extra doily drawer, and some of them have extra shelves for small fancy pieces. Many of the tables, particularly those falling into period groups have massive and elaborately carved pedestals.

Where the hall rack display left off in wall space the remainder of the space was taken up with china cabinets and combinations. These were of big range and varied designs.

Reed and Rattan Goods

On the fourth floor the Imperial Rattan Co. and the Stratford Chair Co. made a big display of their products, and especially of their new goods—those lines and items which have been added of late for 1914 selling.

The Imperial Rattan Co., which occupied one-half of this floor had a number of furnished rooms down one side of their display, in which were housed different grades and styles of reed furniture for bed living, parlor and dining-room, as well as verandah items. The partitions between the booths were hung in art silks, tapestries and velours—coverings of the furniture goods displayed.

One of the very new things shown was a suite of reed furniture in mahogany color. The line embraced flower stands, book racks, ladies' desks, library and other tables, rockers, and chairs of various designs. These articles were also shown in a variety of colored and plain reeds. In addition there were also shown cribs, couches and work tables, wholly or in part composed of reed goods, upholstered and cushioned.

Another novelty was a suite of wicker furniture in white enamel; a third showed rattan fumed effect; and there were various items in plain, padded and upholstered effects—window boxes, foot stools, dinner trays, and general furniture articles. The reed chair and rocker line was shown in hundreds of different styles and designs.

The upholstered goods covered the whole range of living-room items, covered in tapestries and leathers, with removable cushions if desired. All kinds of finishes and designs were seen, from the mission to the most ultra conventional; and a splendid assortment of bed-davenports were demonstrated by Mr. Strudley and his assistants.

Invalids' couches and easy chairs in reed, with tapestry upholstering, and a wooden frame bed couch with spring and mattress for sanitarium or hospital use are a new line now being made; as also is a big easy chair in red upholstered leather with padded seat, back and arm rest.

Stratford Chair Display

The Stratford Chair Co., occupying the other half of the fourth floor, made a showing of almost 300 different styles of chairs. Like the Rattan Co., the Chair Co. had a series of five furnished rooms ranged alongside their exhibit, in which they made a showing of their dining-room and bedroom furniture. Case goods are practically a new line with them, and for this year the chair company are making a more extensive range and of a higher quality.

The chair display mostly diners, come in an immense range in plain and padded seats and backs, slat, rung and ornamental backs, in all woods and finishes.

The case goods comprise a full line in oak—washstands, desks, bureaus, dressers, kitchen cupboards, buffets, dining tables, suites, clothes cabinets and wardrobe. The dining tables come in round and square extension shapes, and other tables in fancy designs were shown for bedroom, writing and card playing, some of these latter of folding varieties.

Some nice samples of the better grade of chiffoniers, dressing tables, and clothes cabinets were seen in maple with walnut finish, and mahogany; also dining-room furniture in fumed and quartered oak.

Besides the extensive diner line of chairs there were displayed fancy and parlor chairs in arm, rocker and lightweight ladies' designs; mission, padded, all-wood, hollow seats, library reading with paper pockets, high and low-backed, in fumed and polished oak.

An immense range of ladies' chairs were exhibited in hollow and cobbler seats, as well as upholstered, wood, and cane. These also were shown in children's designs, and parlor chairs of mahogany. Two old-fashioned kitchen chairs with broad fronts, narrow depth and high rung backs in fumed oak were novelties. They are said to have sold rapidly.

Office chairs and stools of all kinds—stationary, revolving and screw seats, high or no backs, are an extensive line with this company, and they were shown in a great many designs.

SOME OF THOSE WHO WERE AT STRATFORD

O. H. Becker, D. Becker, New Hamburg.
W. E. Long, W. E. Long Furnishing Co., Brantford.
Mrs. W. Patten, London.
Miss Griffith, London.
A. Broadfoot, Broadfoot Bros., Moose Jaw, Sask.
S. Shupe, C. Austin & Co., Chatham.
Geo. W. Jackson, Leamington.
W. Foster Jackson, Leamington.
W. R. Orr, Portage la Prairie, Man.
H. G. Grahame, Wilders, Ltd., Montreal.
J. E. Wilder, Wilders, Ltd., Montreal.
W. N. Wilder, Wilders, Ltd., Montreal.
E. Trudeau, Ontario Furnishing Co., Montreal.
E. Bussell, T. Eaton Co., Toronto.
W. J. Southworth, T. Eaton Co., Toronto.
W. S. Partridge, Trafford Furniture Co., London.
C. H. Christie, Trafford Furniture Co., London.
Jas. Jackson, Arkona.
T. Kelly, Faulkner Furniture Co., Hamilton.
R. E. Venables, Reliable Furniture Co., Toronto.
W. F. Turner, Reliable Furniture Co., Toronto.
E. J. Coles, Woodstock.
C. F. Traut, Jr., Woodstock.
W. E. Artindale, Toronto.
G. W. Simpson, Toronto.
Geo. W. Honsberger, Can. Furniture World, Toronto.
Herb. Schreiter, Schreiter Ftr. Co., Berlin.
J. K. Edwards, Edwards Furniture Co., Sherbrooke.
G. N. Edwards, Edwards Furniture Co., Sherbrooke.
Jas. O'Hagan, Furniture World, Toronto.
Jno. H. Laughton, Canadian Bag Co., Toronto.
Bert. Stadelbaurer, Worchester, Mass.
B. Wolf, H. Wolf & Sons, London.
A. E. Everett, St. John, N.B.
W. L. Jennings, Lemont & Sons, Ltd., Fredericton.
Gordon Thomas, Peoples' Outfitting Co., London.
Roy Thomas, Peoples' Outfitting Co., London.
R. Macpherson, Vincent & Macpherson, Brandon, Man.
W. J. Draper, Vincent & Macpherson, Brandon, Man.
E. Weinheim, Textileather Co., New York City.
Weston Wrigley, Can. Furniture World, Toronto.
F. Schmidt, Textileather Co., Berlin.
A. L. Hixon, Onward Mfg. Co., Berlin.
Mrs. Orr, Ingersoll.
A. Hermiston, A. Hermiston & Co., Listowel.
A. E. McSweeny, Peter McSweeny Co., Moncton, N.B.
W. H. A. Patton, London.
A. E. Uren, Furniture World, Toronto.
A. Lutes, Hamilton.
F. C. Abbott, London.
A. M. Tanmer, J. A. Banguild, Winnipeg.
W. J. Warren, Western Furnishing & Supply Co., Ltd., Kurobot.
H. G. Coomber, Tillsonburg.
L. Solomon, H. Solomon & Co., Montreal.
E. Solomon, H. Solomon & Co., Montreal.
J. N. Archambeault, Montreal.
W. I. Luket, The McLaren Co., St. Catharines.
H. Hoffman, Simcoe.
Mrs. H. Hoffman, Simcoe.
W. Dunlop Stewart, Hamilton Cotton Co., Toronto.
W. M. White, R. White & Co., Stratford.
W. A. Wright, Port Arthur.
W. H. Rennie, Winnipeg.
C. F. Coryell, Adams Furniture Co., Toronto.
W. E. Cassidy, Adams Furniture Co., Toronto.
O. S. Crawford, Chatham.
G. A. Browne, The Interlake Tissue Mills, Toronto.
R. C. Williams, London.
Justin Duggan, J. A. Duggan, Stratford.
D. A. Souter, A. M. Souter & Co., Hamilton.
A. E. Reeves, Hamilton.
W. McDonald, Baldwin-Robinson Co., St. Thomas.
O. S. Keene, Ontario Furnishing Co., London.
P. Zohm, Hanover.
W. L. Edmonds, Commercial Press, Ltd., Toronto.
C. N. Greenwood, Greenwood & Vivian, Stratford.
Thos. Stephenson, Ailsa Craig.
E. A. Wilson, N. S. Furnishing Co., Halifax, N.S.
E. S. Wegensast, Reinhorn Bros., Regina, Sask.
S. A. Hewitt, Mitchell.

Berlin's Exhibition of Fine Furniture Productions

BERLIN and Waterloo furniture manufacturers held their third annual exhibition during the week commencing January 12th. The out-of-town manufacturers were accommodated in the special show rooms on Queen Street, which had been placed at the disposal of the committee by the Williams, Greene & Rome Co., who lately put up a new building and hastened on its construction to completion so as to move their plant and give the Queen Street showrooms to the furniture men. It was a gracious act, and the members of the exhibition committee felt highly gratified at the co-operation of the W., G. & R. people; as well it was favorably commented upon by the visitors to exhibition hall.

Secretary P. Scully was a busy man all the week, and the success of the exhibition may safely be laid at his door. The details of arrangements were left with him and he acquitted his work well.

Seventeen firms exhibited in the showroom, and they occupied all the available space. These, with the 23 Berlin and Waterloo factories, which showed in their own buildings, made a comprehensive and extensive display of all lines of furniture.

Vacuum Cleaners and Furniture Shoes

One of the first booths on entering the Queen Street exhibition hall was that of the Onward Mfg. Co., Berlin, makers of furniture shoes and slides and vacuum cleaners. In the latter line of goods the Onward Co. are putting on the market this year their new "Eureka" power cleaner, and their new "Onward" hand-power combined vacuum cleaner and carpet sweeper—a cleaner which resembles in some respects a carpet sweeper and works like one, but which has an adjustable feature which makes it different. This adjuster is attached to the brush, giving it action like a vacuum cleaner. The "Eureka" electric vacuum cleaner was demonstrated by T. A. Witzel and A. L. Hixon, who were in charge of the booth, and they were kept pretty busy answering the questions put to them regarding the merits of the machine.

The Onward Mfg. Co. also made an extensive showing of furniture shoes in mott metal base and glass base, with short stem for wood furniture and wishbone bushing for metal beds. Mott metal is a non-rustable, hard metal, with a high polish. It works on any kind of floor. For very light weight furniture the new "Onward" slides are now made. They are small, light metal shoes without long shanks and are adaptable for use where casters cannot be used.

Furniture and Wood Polish

In an adjoining booth the Canadian Wood Polishing Co. made a display of "Re-Nu-All." G. E. Shaw was in charge, and the exhibit was made in conjunction with the Onward Mfg. Co.

Kitchen Cabinets

The H. E. Furniture Co., Milverton, Ont., made a display of some nine samples of their fifteen designs of kitchen cabinets. These come in oak and gum-wood.

All the cabinet fronts are different, and in most of them so are the interiors—some having added features not existing in the cheaper grades. One special rolling front cabinet was strongly featured. The interior of all cabinets are finished in white enamel paint, and the tops are finished in plain wood, aluminum, nickeloid and white. Some of the cabinets have mirror fronts, others plain or fancy frosted glass. W. C. Honderich was in charge.

Mantels and Grates

The Elmira Interior Woodwork Co.'s display of mantels and grates was a novel and striking exhibit and demonstration. The whole display was sold in the first couple of days of the show. The company also make office tables, desks, filing cabinets and sections, dining and parlor frames, chairs, and costumiers in birch, mahogany, Circassian and oak. A. Edwards, the manager, was present all the week and took personal charge of the booth.

The mantels and grates with electric attachments were the most prominent goods shown, and they were made of various woods. In desks a combination filing and typewriter desk was a useful novelty. Practically all the desks and office tables shown were of the sanitary variety.

Bedsteads, Springs and Mattresses

Shurly-Dietrich Co., Ltd., Galt, manufacturers of "Maple Leaf" iron and brass beds, made an extensive showing of their various bed products, including mattresses and springs, two new lines they have recently begun to manufacture. They also made a demonstration of two sample hammo-couches, which they are making in the highest grade only.

In iron enamelled beds with brass trimmings Shurly-Dietrich are making some 50 different styles and designs. Besides they are also making a dozen styles of children's cribs with stationary, swing and drop sides. The latter have a patented grip attachment for supporting the sides by which they can be adjusted to any height desired. This attachment is simple, though it cannot be dislodged by a child. The cribs now are made with heavier filling and the old woven wire springs are displaced by "National" rustless and non-corrosive springs, which are more sanitary. The patented side adjuster is being wanted by a U. S. bed maker.

Institution beds of ten or more designs are made, and in connection with this the company are making a new line—sanitary hospital screens of any dimension and in any number of sections. When not in use these screens can be folded into small space. When placed about a bed they can be opened either back-ward or forward and used to completely surround a bed.

In connection with this line Shurly-Dietrich are also making sanitary hospital tables with porcelain tops, cast iron frames and rubber or other style of foot tips.

The "Maple Leaf" sanitary springs are made in six styles; "Maple Leaf" comfort mattresses in nine styles—with any number of ticking colored coverings; and four styles of baby comfort crib mattresses.

Roy Torrance, Peter Zinn, and Jas. Dore were in charge of the display.

Lippert Tables and Furniture.

The largest and most extensive display in Exhibition Hall was that of the combined exhibit of the George Lippert Table Co. and the Lippert Furniture Co., one whole floor of the annex being occupied. The table company made a special demonstration of their patented dining table, equalizer and folding top, called "Lippert Handy Leaf and Equalizer," so called from the convenient contrivances they embody in caring for the extra leaves when not in use, and the simple equalizing contrivance for keeping the top of the table always exactly centred over the pedestal. The storing of the extra leaves under tables is not an entirely new feature, as some square and rectangular tables have had such equipment in the past, but the Lippert "handy leaf" is said to be the only round dining table yet designed that has this equipment. Under the top of the table is a well for holding the leaves, the latter being hinged for folding. When not in use the extra leaves are entirely out of sight, though right at hand for instant use when required. The equalizer attached to the key leaf regulates the extra leaves, centreing the table exactly over the pedestal, no matter how many or how few leaves are used. There is no danger of the slides becoming stiff to interfere with the equalizer, as the latter has nothing to do with the slides. The centre pedestals of these diners are of both round and square patterns. and the tables are made in two sizes—45x45 inches, extending to 6½ feet, and 48x48 inches, extending to 8 feet. Equalizers can be put on dividing pedestal tables extending up to 12 or 14 feet.

The table company also showed a full range of library and centre tables in a variety of woods, pedestals, jardiniere stands, and a new piano lamp stand for electric light. the stand consisting of a female figure, with concealed wires, the boring being done by a special machine. George J. Lippert and Matt. Brown looked after the exhibit.

The Lippert Furniture Co. had a display of hall racks, trees. seats. and mirrors surrounding three walls of their booth. These were of various woods and many designs. A very large showing was also made of parlor furniture items, suites and chairs of elaborate and rich upholstery. some with pearl inlaid, others plain wood, but all with rich and beautiful effects. Gold and presentation furniture had a goodly space, and settees, sofas and couches in profusion were well set out.

Leather-covered furniture for living-rooms in mission effects. and in highly polished woods were shown in large range. Easy chairs and rockers in Chesterfields. and the new Hemco chairs were given much attention. the latter chairs especially, with their newly-patented device for lending comfort to the user, being much sought after. The removable cushion line of chairs and couches. too, were most comfortable and enticing.

In period furniture there were displayed some Sheraton designs in chairs—simple and neat lines of rockers and ornamental stationary chairs. Other fancy chairs in Circassian for bedroom, dining-room and parlor were as well displayed. These come in upholstered and cane seats and backs. Messrs. Lippert, senior and junior, were in charge.

Club and Living-Room Furniture

A. J. Scafe personally superintended the display of English living-room and club furniture made by A. J. Scafe & Co. An exclusive club chair with a broad, long seat was the centre of attraction. This chair has been in demonstration use all over Canada for the past 18 months, and the use and abuse it has had in its day should have sent it to the hospital long ago.' Mr. Scafe walked all over it—arms, back, top and seat—but it survived and looked just as good as ever. This chair, as well as the other furniture items embracing this line—sofas, lounges, davenports, comfort chairs—are made principally of steel frames, the upholstering being of French tapestries specially imported. Extra cushions are supplied for all the den and living-room furniture.

New Mattress Line

The Schreiter Bedding Co., a new concern in Berlin, made a display of their various makes of mattresses— "Royal," "Success," "National," "Faultless," "Elite," "Imperial," "Soft-nap" and "Excel" brands. Mr. Schreiter, Jr., was in charge of the booth, which was set up in the shape of a large tent made of art ticking. These different mattresses had open ends to show the filling and how they are constructed. Some were filled with hair and felt, others with white felt, all wool, curled grass and wool, and grass and felt.

Desks and Office Furniture

The Berlin Interior Hardwood Co., while specialists in interior bank and office fittings, made a display of desks and general office furniture, including book cases, costumiers, flat and roll top, and typewriter desks, office seats, clothes cabinets, umbrella stands, directors' tables, waste paper baskets, and bookkeepers' standing desks (double and single). The book cases are made with sliding roller doors.

This company also make opera and assembly folding chairs in singles and in groups. While most of the items displayed were in oak, with satin finish, and mahogany, the various lines are made in all woods to correspond with the interior fittings. A. C. Clemens was in charge of the booth.

Durham Furniture Co.

In charge of Clarke Washburn, the Durham Furniture Co. made a very nice showing of dining-room and bedroom furniture. There were shown buffets, china cabinets and combinations in many designs, some of the latter with glass doors and fronts. Oak was the predominating wood. Tables, both round and square, with upholstered chair sets and all-wood rockers also had a place in the display.

All the bedroom furniture shown was in either oak or mahogany, though a nice white enamelled bedroom suite made a striking display. There were shown, too, some attractive golden oak and mahogany case goods articles and several ladies' desks and baby cradles.

Upholstered Parlor Furniture

In conjunction with the Durham line, Mr. Washburn also assisted Mr. Hachborn to look after G. H. Hachborn & Co.'s display of upholstered goods. These were parlor suites in mahogany with slat and padded backs, velour, tapestry and art silk seats; also leather and fancy arm chairs with removable cushions; settees and fancy corner chairs. The suites were in three and five pieces. A number of easy and reclining chairs for the living-room were a feature of the display, as particularly was the "Duofold" divanette with two chairs, a new product of their factory.

Cane panels come in for a lot of embellishment on many of the newer styles of parlor furniture, and soft, downy upholstering in the new living-room suites. The woodwork runs to fumed and Early English effects, and colored leathers are more generally used.

Bedroom boxes and stools have a place in the Hachborn line, and about 33 different styles of couches are put out. They also make a large line of fumed oak mission furniture, with upholstering to match.

Berlin Table Display

Looking at the large array of tables in the Berlin Table Co.'s booth, it does not take long to note that the "Colonial" style holds a high place. This company is specializing in non-divisable pedestal tables, mostly in quartered oak, for dining-rooms. These are extension, of course, and all of them are fitted with the new automatic self-centreing slide, the feature of which is that when a new leaf or leaves are wanted in the table these can be inserted and the table centred automatically. The mechanism controlling this is on the ratchet principle, and is completely out of sight. While shown a year ago for the first time, the mechanism has now been improved and perfected. The simplicity of its operation was shown by connecting one of the tables up with a small water motor and running it throughout the whole exhibition. The tables can be extended to 7½ feet. Manager Ed. Scully was in charge of the exhibit, and he was assisted by J. W. Bailey, superintendent; Henry May, secretary, and Wm. May. Their representatives from various sections of Canada were as well helping with the exhibit—F. M. Anthes, Montreal; W. H. Beney, Toronto; W. H. Gross; W. Cline, Vancouver, and T. H. Prosser.

Kellaric Mattresses

The Berlin Bedding Co., Toronto, and McKellar Bedding Co., Ft. William, with A. E. Ritchie in charge, showed how their mattresses looked when set up on a bed. They also displayed their "Kellaric," with laced opening, making it possible to see the inside. The Kellaric mattress is built upon scientific principles by a new web process. Machinery especially constructed cards the cotton into clean, buoyant, elastic sheets, which are built layer upon layer until the required weight (45 lbs.) is reached. These layers, when ready, stand two-and-a-half feet high. They are then compressed to a thickness of five inches, making the mattress soft, yet firm, so that while it sustains the body comfortably at every point of contact, it is soft without yielding. Some splendid samples of art ticking covers for these mattresses were also shown.

Oil Tempered Upholstering Springs

The Waterloo Spring Co., whose booth was in charge of J. J. Cress, made a display of their oil-tempered upholstering springs. Samples of all sizes from 3 to 16 inches were shown in gauges running from 9 to 14.

Artificial Leather

One of the most interesting exhibits in the Queen Street showrooms was that of the Textileather Co., New York, the vice-president of which company, Emil Weinheim, was on hand to tell of its merits and value. He was assisted by the Canadian representative, F. Schmidt. To show the hold Textileather has obtained in the United States Mr. Weinheim stated that though only organized five years ago the company has been compelled to enlarge its plant four times. Textileather is an artificial leather, not an imitation article, and takes the place of leather at half the cost. It is sanitary and waterproof and is not affected by weather or climate in any way, the product being manufactured on natural lines. It is made in a variety of weights for all classes of work in which leather is used and can be had in all colors and grains, which will not fade nor lose their shape.

Motor Washing Machines

S. Brubacher gave a demonstration of the Excello Motor Washer Co.'s washing machines. For this purpose a couple of these washers were connected to the one tap and, being filled with old rag carpets and heavy pieces of clothing, were set in motion. Mr. Burbacher said he had been told by one visitor that he had an "Excello" in his home for seven years without a repair. The tub is made of red cypress and the motor of brass.

Quality Mattresses

The Quality Mattress Co., who have just moved into their new factory at Waterloo, put on display a large number of their high and medium grades of mattresses, together with some demonstration mattresses to show construction. A big range of art ticking samples was shown and the representatives present looked after visitors, explaining the merits and describing the variety of the company's lines. They were A. L. Dantzer, M. H. Monthe, W. H. Grosz and J. E. Reinhardt.

A Visit to the Waterloo Furniture Factories

THE Waterloo factories held exhibitions of their products in their own factory showrooms.

Snyder Bros. are among the biggest makers of mission furniture items, and their display of these goods was very extensive. A large portion of their showroom floor, occupying one whole flat of their building, being devoted to a showing of these goods. Mission tables in fancy, library, hall, card, den and smoking room designs were there in profusion; and magazine stands, newspaper racks, book shelves, umbrella stands, waste paper baskets, jardiniere and flower stands, costumiers, cigar stands and stools were novelties out of the ordinary. Strong on mission goods, Snyder Bros. added several new tables and desks within the past few months, and they are continually bringing out new goods.

Another addition to this line is a three-piece mission suite—couch, rocker and armchair, and these were shown to advantage, as was an immense range of couches and individual chairs, nearly all covered in goat skin. The skins used in covering and padding were ranged about the walls of the room to help out the decorative effect.

In rockers, armchairs and reclining chairs in mission and living-room furniture there was a splendid showing, as there was of general upholstered goods. Fancy parlor pieces and suites in three and five pieces, with couches covered in tapestry and art silks were shown in gorgeous profusion. A decidedly novel morocco-covered English club chair was a feature. Two samples were shown in green and in maroon colors. They were exceedingly soft, being stuffed with floss, and had removable cushions.

The firm are specializing on down cushions, and their davenports and Chesterfields are equipped with them. Pretty three-piece living-room suites are also padded with these cushions, giving a good effect and comfort as well. In living-room coverings, Snyder Bros. as using 200 different tapestry designs.

This firm is continuing to make Snyder wire-back chairs in all the popular designs, which proved attractive in the past, and these occupied quite a space in the hall.

The big new line on which they are pushing at present, however, is the "Thorobed" revolving seat davenport and divanette—the latest addition to the Snyder line, and for which a new two-story factory was built and rushed to completion in five weeks. The factory, which is 80 x 100, gives 16,000 square feet of floor space. "Thorobeds" are made in two sizes; are fitted with "Simmons" steel fabric, and are supported by oil-tempered, helical springs. It carries a 35-pound mattress, and has a large dust-proof wardrobe in the back for storing pillows and bedding. It is simple in operation, compact and sanitary. The fixtures are of steel, are finished in aluminum, and the mechanical device is concealed.

School Outfits and Office Desks.

J. B. Snider made a double display in his showroom. A school outfit was displayed in regular form, with teachers' chair, desk and pupils' desks. He also made a showing of his main line of office furniture, flat and roll top desks both single and double; bookkeepers' standing desk in six, seven and eight feet lengths, single and double; board room and directors' tables; also stools and chairs—in fumed, golden and early English finishes. The desks had both full and sanitary bases. One of the desks with Hungarian ash writing top was a feature, as were the rotary filing features of the higher class of office desks, these latter were splendid articles.

Office chairs with and without arms and back, in swing and pivotal styles were shown; and a good feature in the standing desks was the set of book files and drawers down the side.

Living-room and Parlor Furniture.

At the Woeller, Bolduc & Co. plant Mr. Woeller showed the company's line of high-grade living-room, dining-room and parlor furniture. In upholstered goods some old Dutch designs of chairs in plain and strapped leather effects were new. They had broad seats and wide rolling arms, and to sit in were springy and comfortable. They were of reclining patterns. A few old English easy chairs were also new. These, too, were very comfortable with their round padded backs and removable cushions.

Mission couches and other living-room furniture in all-over tapestry coverings looked what they were intended for, and a new three-piece set with spring seats and padded backs were decidedly comfortable.

Other upholstered items were parlor suites and fancy individual pieces in mahogany, Chesterfields and single chairs. Parlor and fancy tables also had their place; so had dining chairs in leather, cane and upholstered seats.

One whole room was devoted to mission furniture items for den, hall, library and living-room in chairs, couches, tables, jardiniere stands, costumiers, folding card tables, etc. Office swivel and typewriters' chairs were also shown, as were bedroom tables and piano benches in mahogany, and cane seated ladies' rockers and dressing chairs.

"Monimaker" Parlor Suites.

The Waterloo Furniture Co.'s display of their goods was an elaborate one. The walls alone were decorated with silks and skins valued at $7,000. Fumed oak goods in living-room furniture were displayed at one end. Many of these were in three-piece suites covered in leather and tapestry. The rockers and arm chairs in this section were particularly striking.

New steel construction Morris chairs with soft, pillowy backs and seats looked comfortable, and a fine large davenport for the den with smokers' chairs to match were favorably commented on.

Judging by the high price and scarcity of leather, tapestry is to be the covering this year in all the factories, and the Waterloo Furniture Co. is no exception. They showed some splendid tapestry effects. There was a fine line of Colonial design chairs in the exhibit—massive—for the living-room, also some quartered oak in leather for club and hotel. Some of the suites had tables to match.

The company is strong on club and rotunda chairs, living-room furniture and three-piece solid mahogany parlor suites. In coverings there are about 200 different designs.

Something decidedly new this year is the bungalow furniture line in oak with grey finish and cane panel backs and seats. This line may be had upholstered, too, or with loose cushions; and it may be had in fumed. Other new items are period styles in fancy and odd pieces of Sheraton and Hepplewhite designs.

In dining-room goods, solid mahogany, Circassian and fumed oak lead in finishes. One beautiful parlor suite had a covering with a gold thread running through that made it specially attractive.

Ladies' desks and writing tables, in all woods and finishes, fancy and bedroom chairs in rockers and hair dressers were another big line. They came in shell, wood, and cane backs with cane seats.

The exhibit was looked after by E. O. Weber, C. F. Ott, Percy Brown and H. G. Walker. The Waterloo Furniture Co. also had a display of upholstered goods in the Berlin exhibition hall.

Tour of Berlin's Many Furniture Making Plants

THE Berlin furniture factories not exhibiting in Exhibition Hall made displays of their productions in their factory, sales and warerooms. Baetz Bros., making a specialty of upholstered chairs and parlor suites, showed some excellent samples in this line, as also did they of a number of new diners. These new dining chairs were mostly in solid oak, with black leather padding, though a number of high-class mahogany veneer diners, also upholstered in black leather, were as well shown. These new dining chairs tended much to simplicity and straight lines.

Chesterfields in two and three piece sets—with arm-chair and rocker to match davenport—were worthily represented by some samples in the living-room furniture display. Their soft filling and removable cushions proving a great attraction.

The most recent Baetz line is a bungalow suite, samples of which only have as yet been made, and these were shown in a number of articles. The silver grey color of this line with their cretonne and tapestry covering caught the eye immediately. The cane panelling on the sofa and chair backs showed the prevailing tendency of the new furniture styles. This bungalow line comes in all furniture items—davenport sofas, tables, chairs, rockers, magazine, flower and book stands, and parlor, living and dining-room pieces.

Another attractive display was the white enamel parlor suites and individual pieces for ladies, with cane seats or cretonne upholstered coverings. Other parlor suites included Chippendale, which, while not new this year, are put out in some new coverings. A three-piece Adams suite in blue silk covering, however, is decidedly new this year, and shows the hold period furniture is taking in Canada. Several new modern styles were as well shown in the parlor furniture section, as also were five-piece mahogany sets of heavy frame and a variety of colored coverings.

Baetz Bros. also made an extensive showing of their

Circassian and black walnut—the only woods they use. Bed and dining-room furniture are specialties, and in the former they make some 20 different suites, all in period style. In fact almost every article in the exhibit was in Adam, Colonial or Louis XIV. design. Some beautiful beds, dressing tables, chiffoniers, bureaus, chairs and ladies' writing desks were displayed, and two bedroom suites of black walnut were very rich.

The drawers in all the furniture pieces made by Anthes & Co. have dustproof partitions, and it is impossible to reach a drawer from any other drawer. There are, too, guides along the bottom of drawers which prevent them falling down when pulled out even to the length of the drawer.

In dining-room suites there are 20 different styles made, principally in mahogany, though one or two are

Waterloo Furniture Co's. display of their "Moninaker" line in factory showrooms.

mission line for living-room, den, library, dining-room and hall. J. H. Baetz and W. H. Bency looked after the display.

Big Hall Furniture Display.

The Wunder Furniture Co. are this year featuring hall furniture, and in their showrooms made an extensive display of this line. Hall mirrors with racks and hall seat to match seems to have a vogue, judging from the many varied samples shown. Something new in the line is a four-piece set—hall rack, umbrella stand, sofa and chair—and a beauty was a mahogany rack with fine hardware, built on straight, massive lines.

Parlor suites in all finishes and coverings is also a big line, and some splendid specimens were shown, as also were a number of gold furniture, single items and parlor suites.

Diners in all finishes were displayed, a new one in fumed, golden and mahogany with tan or other colored leather upholstery to match looked well. There were also shown a great many rockers in bent wood and upholstered seats and backs. The color effects run to plain designs, though the material itself is richer than usual.

Period Furniture.

Anthes & Co. showed in their big factory a large range of high-class furniture items in oak, mahogany,

in oak. Here the period styles find full play in Adams, Sheraton, Chippendale, Jacobean and Colonial. Hand carving predominates on the various items, no two of which, except the suits, were exactly alike. Fancy tables and ladies' desks and secretaries were also shown built on period lines.

Jacobean Period Furniture.

The H. Krug Furniture Co. this year are giving great prominence to Jacobean and William and Mary styles, this period furniture being new with them this year. The Jacobean with its dignified outlines and the William and Mary in simple though beautiful designs are decidedly classy. Both these periods run the whole range of hall seats and chairs, combination book shelf and clock, armchairs and rockers, desks, tables and stools for dining-room, bedroom, parlor and living-room, the cane panelling carrying out the lines of the furniture construction.

The Jacobean dining-room suites were splendid; so were the fancy pieces for every hall and room in the house all were high class. Even the upholstered living-room furniture is being built on period lines. Rockers and diners come in leather, cane or plain wood seats, and ladies' bedroom chairs, though built on lighter lines, carry along the same designs.

Modern furniture lines, particularly in new parlor goods, run to straight lines with carved finials. The upholstery, too, is simple, but rich in colored tapestries and denims. Couches and davenports are constructed on the same beautiful lines with exquisite patterns and designs in leather and denim coverings and mahogany and oak woods.

In the den, club and general living-room furniture mission styles still hold strongly; and in office chairs the Krug lines show variety from the simplest to the most elaborate.

Library Tables and Ladies' Desks.

Kreiner & Co. made an exhibit, and a good one, of their library tables, ladies' desks, bookcases and parlor tables—in all woods and finishes. A circular card table with circular-backed chairs that fit right snug under was the novelty. It has sold well in the west for homes and clubs, and also for restaurants, where space oft times is at a premium. Pedestal and leg tables are also made in large variety, and a great many sundries of mission design in cellarettes, magazine stands, newspaper racks, and things that fit in well with the other items of this class were both novel and seemed good sellers.

In the desk line some very odd designs were shown with slat effect and cane panel effect; and in book cases a great variety of designs in fronts were shown in mission and other finishes. The doors were both sliding and hinge opening. A very fine line was the combined desk and book cases.

Kreiner & Co. will show in Exhibition Hall next year.

The Hibner Line.

The D. Hibner Furniture exhibit was one of the largest in the Berlin district. It embraced in the first showroom parlor tables, library tables, fancy tables, ladies' desks, hall racks, upholstered parlor furniture and pedestals, in mahogany and oak. Some of the parlor frames were massive and heavy with elaborate carvings, though most of this line was along straight lines. All the sofas and chairs were large and roomy, and had a big range of coverings in plush and leathers.

The fancy tables for library, hall, parlor and den were of many designs, in square, round and oval shapes, with novel folding card and compartment tables for convenient corners.

In the bedroom and ladies' chair section there were shown many dainty items in writing and dressing tables and chairs, jardiniere stands, pedestals, etc.

The second showroom was devoted to the main Hibner line—dining-room and library furniture. Next year the showroom will be enlarged so as to bring all the display in the one big room.

The company is strong on extension tables and the display surely showed it, as they were there in all finishes and in all woods. An endless range of buffets also was shown, many of them new this year.

A beautiful satin walnut Sheraton dining-room suite was on display. All the articles of the suite were inlaid, and the effect was beautiful. Another suite in mahogany on the same lines was richer and more elaborate. Where these two suites were set out was a section devoted to all mahogany dining-room suites.

A third room was given over to sectional book cases, combinations, and ladies' desks. The book cases were of Humphrey-Widman patent, and they came in Colonial, art craft and standard styles; all woods and finishes.

Clocks and Bedroom Furniture.

The Berlin Furniture Co. in their well-appointed showroom, made a striking and fine display of their bedroom furniture lines and other items. Mission, cathedral and colonial design clock cases set off the exhibit well, and the striking of the chimes gave life to the whole floor.

The company is going into the wood bed line, and these will be put out in five different styles, a couple of splendid samples were shown in the exhibit. Some fine new specimens of dressing tables, chiffoniers, chevals and writing tables were displayed in black walnut and solid mahogany. They were strictly high grade; and some medium grade high and low dressers, desks, bedroom tables in oak and mahogany were both new and attractive.

As with other makers, a great many of the articles shown run to Colonial design. Even the new costumiers have this feature. Some nice bedroom items in medium and cheaper grade were set out, and but for the fact that they are in oak one could not find such a great distinction between them and the better grades.

Sheraton and Colonial bedroom suites in black walnut were among the chief items of interest in the exhibit. Mr. Jacques, the manager, and A. E. Evans, representative, looked after the display and brought forward the features of the exhibit.

New Goods at Toronto Furniture Exhibition

FOR the first time in many years Toronto made a furniture display in the Transportation and Horticultural Buildings in the Industrial Exhibition grounds--and a most varied, unique and highly satisfactory exhibition it was. A long corridor, walled with green burlap, ran down the centre of both buildings. Off these were the exhibition booths of the various manufacturers, also separated one from the other by green burlap partitions.

A series of numbers was used to distinguish the booths, and these were correspondingly described in the combined guide and order book which visitors received on registering at the entrance to the exhibition. These order books were unique in their way, the forms being uniform in size and encased in an Arabian leather covering made by The Cotton Mfg. Co.

Booths 1 to 16 were located in the Transportation Building, and 17 to 37 in the Horticultural Building; but as in some of the booths two and in others three exhibits were made there were all told some 50 exhibitors represented at the show.

Carpets and Rugs.

Exhibit No. 1.—Toronto Carpet Mfg. Co. made an extensive and varied display of their goods—not the showy lines, but the carpets and rugs which they are making every day for sale throughout Canada. The designs are beautiful enough for any exhibition, however, and as they come in all colors and designs and grades the line is almost inexhaustible. There are four grades of Brussels, four of Wiltons, tufted rugs, wool rugs and rag rugs—all were seen to good advantage. The rich designs of the Persian and Oriental patterns were strikingly set forth, and after seeing them no one wonders at their growing popularity.

Tans and browns are the most popular colorings in

regular carpet lines, but the reproductions of Eastern patterns lend themselves so effectively to harmony in any room that here again is their popularity shown.

Wool rugs and rag rugs in any color or design may now be had, and leading decorators have of late been using these very extensively. To see how the old-fashioned rag carpets are now treated in this modern process would make our grandmothers rub their eyes with surprise. They certainly look classy.

The representatives present stated that the company were very busy, their output at present being 8,000 yards a day. A. J. Balfour, J. M. Greenwood and L. W. Veale were in charge of the booth.

Bedroom Furniture and Tables.

Exhibit No. 2.—Malcolm & Souter Furniture Co., Hamilton. The full manufactured line of this company consists of bedroom furniture in Circassian walnut, mahogany, quartered oak and gum; parlor and library tables, cabinets, writing desks and wardrobes. A Circassian bedroom suite of ten pieces at the entrance to the booth was a beauty; as also were the enamelled line in ivory, white and French grey.

A new line in suites was a curly birch in natural finish. This comes in three pieces—dressing table, chiffonier and dresser. Mahogany suites, of course, hold their own, some of the new ones are treated with cane panel effects, especially the bedsteads.

A quartered gumwood suite, which started a few months ago with three pieces, has now grown to eleven, so popular has the line become.

Walnut music cabinets, pedestals, five o'clock tea tray, topped tables, parlor and library tables in dull and polished finishes of many shapes and designs, invalid trays, bedroom chairs and umbrella stands are among others of many samples of goods shown. Inlaid holly and satinwood on quartered gum bedroom furniture are new, two samples of the latter being the only articles of the line so far made.

Besides Messrs. Malcolm and Souter, both of whom spent some days at the show, the exhibit was in charge of R. W. Higginbottom and Ed. Bagshaw.

Kitchen Cabinets

Exhibit No. 3—Universal Cabinet Co., Chatham, Ont., showed their No. 6 and No. 7 sanitary cabinets, the latter of which are equipped with metal flour bin with detachable sifter; large cupboards; glass automatic sugar bin; glass spice, coffee and tea jars; two large drawers, one containing compartments; sliding shelf; cutting board; aluminum-covered sliding table top that will not rust or tarnish. No. 6 has in addition two sliding shelves, door rack and two large cupboards. No. 61 has extra equipment over the No. 6, and No. 71 extra articles over No. 7. Ed. Bagshaw was in charge of this exhibit and the other displays in the booth.

Popular Case Goods Line

The Markdale Furniture Co., makers of case goods in surface oak, imitation mahogany and white enamel, had their display also in Booth No. 3, where they showed a well assorted range of their productions. They displayed a fine line of buffets and combination china cabinets and buffets, some of the former with fancy glass doors, and all of the latter, of course, so furnished.

They also showed some combination desk and book cases of varying designs. For the bedroom very neat dressers and chiffoniers were set out, also clothes cabinets with mirror doors.

Medicine chests for bathrooms, jardiniere stands for living-room, and hall seats and racks were other furniture items shown, some of them in mission designs and finish.

Chairs of all Kinds

Also in Booth No. 3 was the display of the McGill Chair Co., Cornwall, Ont. Among other things were shown oak and mahogany all-wood rockers, high chairs for children, kitchen and diners in all-wood, and some bedroom chairs.

In upholstered diners were shown quite a number of fumed and surface oak patterns in leather (this is a big line with them); and for den and living-room, fumed in padded and all-wood were displayed. Couches to match for sets were as well numbered in this division. Office and desk chairs and stools held a prominent place in the grouping. They ran the whole range from the plain oak to the upholstered revolving and tilting chairs.

Patent Spring Mattresses

A fourth exhibit in this booth was that of the Colleran Patent Spring Mattress Co., Toronto, makers of wire mattresses and cots. A showing of some 15 sample wire mattresses was made on a demonstration stand. This does not complete the line, however, but gave some idea of the range. Some of these were cross reinforced, and all are guaranteed not to sag. The wire rope edge on the mattresses was a feature. The "Excelsior" lock weave divan proved popular, and when Tom Colleran gave his afternoon talks his demonstrations were attentively followed.

Popular Period Suites.

Exhibit No. 4.—Andrew Malcolm Furniture Co., Kincardine, are makers of popular priced period suites in mahogany and oak for dining and bedrooms. They are also makers of desks. All of these were shown in sample and a great many in complete suites. A lovely thing was a birdseye maple bedroom suite; there were also some splendid specimens of mahogany, Circassian and ivory enamel. Cane panelling was quite prominent in many of the items.

The dining-room furniture ran to period suites in Adams, Jacobean, Elizabethan, Sheraton and Colonial styles, though two Adams bedroom suites in Circassian were new also. A Sheraton suite in 11 pieces with cane panels, and the items inlaid was very pretty.

A beautiful bedroom suite of 11 pieces in polished mahogany and a dining-room set in fumed mahogany were much noticed. Oak dining pieces in buffets, china cabinets and combinations, book cases, clothes closets, etc., were also favorably commented on .

An inlaid library mission suite in fumed finish—desk, chairs, table and couch—was about the best seen in the exhibition; and individual library tables and ladies' desks in fumed and mahogany were very fine, as were two cellarettes in fumed and mission. Office desks also had their place.

Andrew Malcolm, James and A. E. Malcolm and Thos. Ingles looked after the display.

Living-room, Den and Office Furniture.

Exhibit No. 5.—F. E. Coombe Furniture Co., Kincardine, displayed some very fine samples of their productions. A Jacobean inlaid suite in fumed with cane-seated chairs and backs was one of the best things shown.

Mission furniture, too, is a heavy line, and many splendid items were shown in this department. In upholstered living-room stuff, sofas with rounded corners were the last word in comfort. The coverings are running a lot to tapestries this year, and the company are using only No. 1 genuine Spanish leather and tapestry. Much of the mission line in leather is furnished with square cushions, removable.

The comfort chairs are fine, the soft padding making them unusually attractive. Stools, leather-topped, in mission designs, go well with the living-room articles.

In tables all shapes, patterns and designs of the mission line were shown, and a number of very comfortable bedroom and den couch-boxes and couch seats for any space were shown. In couches, too, there was a full range displayed for den and living-room; and large all-over upholstered tapestry club chairs were shown in this section. The couches and sets come in automobile or loose cushion seats.

The office chair line consists of all kinds of chairs and stools for business purposes, some perforated leather over cane seats being new. Rockers and mission chairs also had a place in this department. F. E. Coombe and H. R. Magwood looked after the visitors.

Dining Extension Tables.

The Lucknow Table Co. occupied space in the same booth with the Coombe Furniture Co. They made a showing of ten of their dining tables in round and square extension designs. The round extension tables have two new features—some are equipped with an equalizer device for inserting extra leaves and keeping the table exactly centred over the top; and others have extra leg sets, which fold under the centre of the table when not in use, for carrying steady the table when extended to its utmost length. All the tables may be had in surface, plain, quartered or golden oak. Messrs. Shantz and Honderick looked after the booth.

North American Chair Line.

Exhibit No. 6.—North American Bent Chair Co., Owen Sound, makers of chairs of all kinds, showed specimens of their productions from the cheapest kitchen chair to a medium-priced diner. Surface oak rockers and oak diners in padded seats and backs, fumed finish, are among some of the newer staple lines being made. Circular seated chairs in bent wood, too, were displayed in light weight diners. Fumed birch in diners and rockers are the newest productions of this company's plant, and equally new are the imitation mahogany diners.

The company are also putting out a cheap line of white enamel and mahogany bed and bathroom chairs, and a new inlaid cork-seated bath stool. Stools and small tables in oak and cobbler-seated rockers are also products of the North American factory. D. A. and W. G. Hay were in charge of the exhibit.

Enamel Beds.

Canada Beds. Ltd., Chesley, also made an exhibit in Booth No. 6. of their white enamel beds. G. N. Griffin. the manager of the plant, looked after the visitors, and he stated he was more than pleased with the reception his line had received, and appreciated the business he had done. It was beyond his expectations. His company is specializing on medium-priced beds, which is also their staple line.

They made a display of 16 different designs, though these do not cover all the patterns made. Some are brass tipped; others have brass rods, but the line does not at all compete with the brass line. They are, however, made of the best material and workmanship possible to get into a bed made to sell at a low price.

Dining-room, Bedroom and Library Suites.

Exhibit No. 7.—The North American Furniture Co., Owen Sound, made a showing of their dining-room suites along one side wall of their booth, and of their bedroom suites along the side wall. opposite; these suites were set out in compartments separated by costume screens. Buffets in golden oak of many patterns and designs had a portion of the booth all to themselves, along with some combinations and individual dining-room pieces.

Half a dozen different styles of ten-piece sets in fumed oak were set out to advantage in compartments, as also were several Sheraton inlaid dining suites in gumwood.

The bedroom suites, too, came in some period designs. A suite in ivory enamel with prima-vera mahogany tops, cane panels in bed, and tapestry covered chairs was very beautiful. A Circassian walnut, inlaid, suite was another fine thing; the chairs were cane seated. A plain patterned Circassian suite looked classy, as did also an oak and a dull mahogany suite. A dull finished Circassian suite was a novelty.

Individual pieces ran to ladies' desks, writing cabinets, odd-fashioned cellarettes, umbrella stands, etc. These were in mahogany and oak, and a great many pieces were fumed, these latter running to plain or straight line. W. Pearson, J. M. Weber and J. Black looked after the display.

Chairs for all Purposes

The Owen Sound Chair Co. occupied space in the same section with the North American Furniture Co., and the display was looked after by the same representatives. This company is particularly strong on medium-priced dining chairs, and also on some chairs in the living-room class. Cane-seated chairs in all styles, especially dining, bedroom and dressing chairs, and baby high chairs were shown in many designs.

In the living-room chairs there were shown a big line of fumed upholstered easy chairs, and both fumed and polished oak frames formed a large proportion of the leather-covered dining line.

Stools and office chairs of all kinds—wood, cane, and upholstered—in revolving, screw and stationary are another large line put out by this company.

Extension and Library Tables

The National Table Co., Owen Sound, also made a display in booth No. 7. There was made a showing of a great many of their extension dining and library tables. A great many of the dining tables were in fumed and golden oak. Library and card tables, in the same wood and finishes, were also shown extensively; a leather-topped den table was novel and odd.

Parlor tables, round, square and of fancy designs on pedestal and fancy legs were shown in great number. Many of these were in mahogany, dull and finished, and fumed.

Hall and bedroom pedestals and book racks in oak—fumed and golden—were well represented in the display, which was a very fine one.

Upholstered Couches and Chairs

Exhibit No. 8—Maple Leaf Couch Co., Toronto, had their booth in charge of W. McFarquhar, in which was displayed some knock-down and stuff-over chairs of every description. Club, living-room and easy chairs in leathers, velours and tapestry were well displayed, as were also some representative couches and rockers with removable cushions. A davenport bed with pull-out back was used for demonstration purposes; also some smoking and den chairs, the rockers having paper and magazine racks in the arms. An English pillow back settee was one of the best in the Chesterfield class shown.

High Grade Bed and Dining-room Suites

Exhibit No. 9—The Hespeler Furniture Co. are strong on period suites in Colonial, Jacobean, Elizabethan, Sheraton and Adams styles, and both dining-room and bedroom suites representative of these periods were shown. One bedroom suite inlaid with oak was an especially strong thing on display. Other bedroom suites in fumed, built on modern lines, showed plain straight lines. These were very neat. One of the suites had the popular cane panels.

In buffets two high class samples were shown, both with top glass cabinets, which gave a rich effect. Other buffets with extra doily drawers were very attractive. China cabinets, too, were shown in beautiful designs, some for corner places being especially so.

All woods were seen in the goods displayed—oak, mahogany and Circassian—in fumed, dull and polished. An Elizabethan dining suite of ten pieces looked a beauty, as also did a Colonial in mahogany. Mr. Grentzner himself looked after the booth and he had helping him his first lieutenant, Percy Brown.

Bent Wood Furniture

In the same booth, Jacob and Joseph Kohn, of Vienna, Austria, made a display under the charge of Joseph Sauer, of their varied products of cane-seated and bent wood chairs for parlor, office and bedroom. A church sanctuary set in cane backs and seats was a special. All the chairs shown were hand-polished, and they come in all wood finishes.

As in other furniture lines, period styles are coming to the front. A great many of the items are made of beech, which lends itself so readily to bending, but the finishes come in all colors. A black-gray was a new color; a green was another. There were, too, many gold chairs in bent and cane shown. These latter are in the parlor class. In this section, too, were displayed suites in leathers, plushes, and other upholstered coverings.

Costumiers are a new line, the samples displayed having never before been shown. The nest of stools—three of them fitting one upon another under a fourth was a novel necessity where space is to be considered. Restaurant tables with wood or marble tops, umbrella stands, parlor stands, enamelled chairs, and children's and baby high chairs were as well displayed. Slip-seated chairs—a removable upholstered seat over a cane seat—were a source of attraction.

Folding Bed Davenports and Chairs

Exhibit No. 9—The Owen Daveno Bed Co., Hespeler, beside their usual bed-davenport, made a display and demonstration of a new davenport bed, shorter than the regular line, and which when opened has an extra fold which fits under the back of the davenport. For use as a bed the sleeper lies with head to back of davenport; in the regular he lies lengthwise with it. This new short bed-davenport is 4 feet 3 inches long, convenient for bungalows or rooms where space is contracted. A chair to match accompanies the bed to make a living-room set. As with the regular line, this new davenport is made of mahogany and fumed oak, with a variety of coverings in tapestry and leather.

Slumber chairs in leather with smoker's box and paper rack in arm, make these fine for dens. Wm. Wingfield and Percy Brown explained the features of the exhibit.

The Gold Medal Line

Exhibit No. 10—The Gold Medal Furniture Mfg. Co., makers of parlor furniture, couches, bed springs and mattresses, had their booth placed in charge of Geo. Hughes, J. Byron, R. Wright and Wm. Dalby. Theirs was a most comprehensive display of their varied productions.

In living-room sets and pieces there were a great many fine tapestry upholstered items shown, some of the new things being beautiful two-piece suites—davenports and chairs to match. For small rooms the davenport gave place to a sofa. Individual chairs and rockers in leather and tapestry were inviting and comfortable.

Couches are another big line with the Gold Medal Co. They make them for den, smoking and living-room, upholstered in leather, tapestry, and velours, one for den with newspaper rack at head was a fine one. They come principally in fumed this year.

The living-room davenport-bed, with easy chair and rocker to match, has a number of features to attract. The bed is dressed ready for use at all times, the opening process only being necessary, and this operation can be done in a few seconds. The mattress is detachable. The bed folds up just as it opens, and with all the clothes folded with it there is yet eight inches of air space inside. It is made in oak and mahogany in a great many designs. In cities, where space is all important and rooms are small, a divanette takes the place of the davenport. This, too, is ready at all times for occupancy, and the mattress may be detached. It gives a bed 6 feet 2 inches long by 4 feet 6 inches wide.

In parlor and drawing-room furniture some splendid mahogany frames were shown, and an upholstered suite of Louis XV. design was a beauty. Many fine examples of leather, tapestry and art silk upholstered stuff were shown. In this section, too, was displayed the Smith adjustable rocker—one with long, high runners and adjustable head and back cushions, enabling a person to rock back to a position horizontal with the floor without any danger of tipping.

In the bed and mattress section was shown the original Hercules woven spring mattress, which the company has been making for the past 16 years. This comes in a number of weaves. The "Neversstretch" mattress, too, is another prominent line. This mattress, composed of separate compartments joined at each tuft, is, as its name implies, one that will not stretch or its contents get out of place. The "Gold Medal" and other filled mattresses were well set off.

Morris chairs, in leather and velours; easy and rocking chairs in fumed and oak; wire construction leather-covered chairs; and a big range of tapestry coverings completed the exhibit.

Baby Carriages and Reed Goods

Exhibit No. 11—The Gendron Mfg. Co., makers of baby carriages, children's wagons and reed goods, made a comprehensive showing of these goods. A reversible coach gear is new in the carriage line. These may be had with or without artillery wheels. The reed hoods, too, are new and are meeting with favor. Most of the carriages have the coach gear, though they come with or without the reversible body. The artillery wheels,

too, are colored to match the body of the carriage to which they are attached.

Some of the carriages have an automobile hood made of French cloth which is indestructible, being unaffected by rain or frost. The line of wood body carriages are done up in combination colors—tan and buff, green and green, blue and carmine—and are full size with stationary or sleeper backs.

In go-carts a new one is shown in the reversible folder. There was also shown a full line of metal folding carts. New sulkies, too, with stationary or collapsible bodies, with or without hoods, were shown. A new artillery wagon, 14½ x 34 inches, makes a good delivery wagon for a boy. Dolls' carriages in wood, reed and metal were shown.

Reed furniture in fancy, parlor and verandah chairs and pieces had a section to themselves, as also did velocipedes, tea trays and reed tables.

Thos. Chadwick, J. Smith, W. H. Bateman and E. Roy were in charge of the exhibit.

The Kindel Bed

Exhibit No. 12—Kindel Bed Co., makers of Kindel beds, davenports, divanettes and chair beds, besides showing a full line of their somersault beds with their three features—bed, davenport, and clothes box—a demonstration of the new action "Kindel de luxe" parlor bed, which is to be placed on the Canadian market later on in the year, was given. A spring at the bottom, when touched, throws up the bed ready for opening. The rest of the action is like the regular Kindel bed, though the mattress is a removable one. It has interchangeable ends, too.

The divanette and chair bed as well were shown to advantage. All kinds of coverings were shown—plain and art leathers, tapestries and denims.

Furniture Polish

Ronuks, Ltd., also had a small booth in this section. Here was made a display of furniture polish, floor wax, metal and other polishes, also steel wool and steel shavings. A. R. Hughes and Ed. Keeble explained the merits of the products.

Bed and Dining-room Goods

Exhibit No. 13—The Crown Furniture Co., Preston, manufacturers of bedroom and dining-room furniture,

The Alaska brass and enamel bed display.

in oak and mahogany, made an elaborate display of many of their goods. Buffets in colonial and mission effects were striking, and the new buffet with drop tray for holding cutlery drawer or extra tray is a taking feature. China cabinets in fumed; and bedroom suites, also fumed, as well as in mahogany and oak, were attractive.

An ivory enamelled five-piece bedroom suite drew a deal of attention, as did a new dressing case, in mahogany, with three folding mirrors. This was new

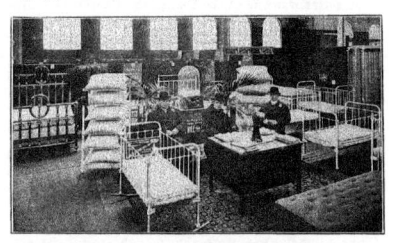

Exhibit of Alaska cribs, pillows and bedding goods.

and it made a striking feature. R. A. McGillivray, A. Moss, H. Linall, R. Stout, S. S. Nash and J. James looked after the exhibit.

Metal Beds and Bedding

Exhibit No 14.—The exhibit of the Alaska Feather and Down Co., Montreal, attracted much favorable comment because of the clever arrangement for display of the various lines shown. Their booth was effectively divided by screens or partitions forming numerous aisles, and against these backgrounds on either side the various designs of beds were shown off to splendid advantage. In one of the aisles could be seen a selection of the newest designs in high grade brass beds, and in another the most popular designs in brass beds; while in other aisles were arranged the enamelled iron designs, shown off to the best advantage against the plain, green background. Naturally the newest ideas attracted the most attention, and the exhibit was distinguished for its novelties and up-to-date improvements.

Almost the first thing to catch the eye was the new "Alaska Cradle Crib"—an enamel crib set on non-tipping steel rockers, which are interchangeable with casters, so that the outfit can be either a crib or a cradle as desired. Another novelty was the "Swinging Crib" or "Cradle," which can be instantly adjusted by the turning of a simple catch, to serve the purposes of a stationery crib. A still further idea in the bed line was an enamelled chilless "Bungalow Bed," which seemed to meet with great favor. The "Hospital Cot," with high bed was also quite new. It is set on three-inch rubber-tired wheels, and the bed can be raised or lowered to any desired height, being adjustable in this manner from the head, foot or side.

"Bnaner" and other Alaska springs were effectively displayed on a unique, space-saving display rack, while the popular lines of "Alaska" mattresses were suspended from a wall-rack in a similarly effective manner. Another interesting feature of the exhibit was the "Ostermoor" mattress, shown in various styles and tickings, several samples being open to show the filling. The Alaska Company does its own carding and cleaning. the white cotton used in filling the "Ostermoor" being baked in an oven at 120 degrees to make it non-absorbent. Samples of the upholstered "Chateau,"

"Waldorf" and "Banner" box spring beds were also displayed and demonstrated.

Double-deck bunks of angle iron showed the great advance which has been made of late in promoting sanitary conditions in construction camps. Much interest was also shown in a new box lounge, as well as a splendid line of Alaska iron couches, davenports, etc. A special display of made-up beds attracted a great many buyers. Here were featured new twin brass, and new twin enamel beds, as well as a sample brass and enamel, and an all-enamel bed.

The Alaska line of pillows was prominently displayed in the special racks, which were specially designed for the store exhibit of this line. The manager, W. P. Bennett, came up twice from Montreal to meet customers and friends, and was assisted by W. W. Arrowsmith and C. R. Woodburn. Every visitor to the "Alaska" exhibit was presented with a carnation, while a commodious rest and desk room was fitted up at the entrance for the convenience of visiting dealers.

Upholstered Parlor Furniture

Exhibit No. 15—Morlock Bros., Ltd., Hanover, showed in parlor suites and individual items some fine specimens of mahogany upholstered stuff in art silk and tapestry coverings; and in living-room suites in fumed frames. For this room, too, were shown a full line of wire-backed chairs in leather coverings. This line is a specialty with Morlocks. A number of steel-construction couches of varied designs were attractively displayed.

L. E. Morlock and L. Miller, eastern representative, looked after the display.

Bedroom and Dining-room Furniture

In the same booth as above was the splendid display of Peppler Bros., Ltd., Hanover. Making a big line of fumed buffets and extension dining tables, the display of these naturally was large and varied and the samples shown were decidedly attractive. Hall racks and dinner wagons in fumed and golden oak also were displayed in big number. A great many of the items, particularly those for the dining-room, were designed in colonial style.

Fumed book cases and china cabinets had a large section devoted to these attractive goods, and some very pretty china cabinet and buffet combinations were set off to advantage. Umbrella stands to match hall furniture suites in new and novel designs were well represented.

The round extension dining tables with extra new drop legs were, of course, the principal feature of the exhibit. During the past few months great improvement has been made with this feature until now it is almost automatic in action. When extended these extra legs take care of the extra weight and steady the table without dividing the pedestal. When not in use the legs fold under the table entirely out of sight.

L. E. Morlock and H. Rapp looked after the booth and display.

Surface Oak and Imitation Mahogany Goods

Exhibit No. 16—The Hepworth Mfg. Co., makers of bedroom and dining-room furniture, in surface oak and imitation mahogany, made a comprehensive display of their goods—buffets, square extension dining tables; kitchen cabinets, with and without tops; kitchen cupboards and dining-room sideboards; folding leaf kitchen tables, etc.

In bedroom furniture were shown some imitation mahogany suites. Also individual bureaus, dressers, chiffoniers, cradles, wash stands, and ladies' desks. For goods made to sell at a price the line made a nice display. J. Clark was in charge.

Displays in the Horticultural Building

Exhibit No. 17—The Ideal Bedding Co.'s booth was in charge of Otto Thies, F. J. Mackie and B. W. Woon. These representatives expressed themselves as well pleased with the business done at the booth, although the display was purely an exhibition.

In new goods there were shown two new fold-away cots, one with and the other without head and foot hold. These cots can be made ready for use in a second or two, and when not wanted can be folded away and placed in storage in a clothes closet—the space occupied by it being practically nil. Another new item is a folding camp cot, which when folded occupies a space only six inches square. It is shipped in a paper carton, and can be made ready for use in half a minute.

The Ideal duplex spring bed is another new product. It is simply like a twin mattress for a double bed. It comes in two patterns—woven wire and in link fabrics. Several new designs in panel beds were shown. That is brass beds with wood panels, head and foot. These designs follow the popular period styles. Two of the notable patterns were a French and a Chippendale. These period beds were made up with the lines bedding productions, chief among which were the new "never-spread" mattress.

The Hammo-couch has several new features for this year. First there is the scalloped edge; then it has folding legs filled with casters, whereby it can be made to serve also the purpose of a bed as well as a swing couch; and it is now equipped with chain hangers which swing direct from the springs.

The children's crib line showed several new brass and enamel designs, and the new safety device on all cribs is now colored in red. As well the Auto Couch, a foot-power folding double bed, was demonstrated.

The brass and enamelled bed line were shown in a series of separate rooms, where a person could judge the merits of the items in the different sections without confusion. Several new designs were shown in iron with brass trimmings, and new enamelled iron costumieres were also displayed.

Furniture for Living and Dining-room

Exhibit No. 18—J. C. Mundell & Co., Elora, made an elaborate and comprehensive display of all their lines—living-room, den, library and dining-room furniture—and it was attractively set off, too. The Robt. Simpson Co., Toronto, bought the whole exhibit.

In bedroom and ladies' rockers a great many different designs were shown in all woods. Most of them had cane or bent wood seats. Some fine leather-sealed rockers for the den were also displayed.

For the living-room and the den there were a number of splendid black padded seats and backs shown, and some fancy arm and easy chairs in velour coverings. Morris chairs appear to be as popular as ever, and samples shown came in velours and leathers.

Club and smoking-room suites were represented in some nice pieces with tables for cards of the folding variety. Library lines, too, were shown in abundance. A couple of these suites were set out in homelike surroundings with table to match in nine pieces—one in all-over leather upholstery, and the other in upholstered seats only. A fumed suite, in Colonial style, with Spanish leather coverings was particularly fine. Fine, too, were the individual library pieces—tables, desks, chairs, etc., nearly all in fumed oak.

Library lamps is another line. In mission and art crafts designs many splendid specimens were shown.

sweeper and is operated by one person. It is easy-running, light and powerful. The combination machine also is operated by one person and is easily adjusted. The electric machine, equipped with extra attachments, can be used on walls, furniture, draperies, bedding and everything in the home.

One minute Washing Machines

Exhibit No. 21—The One Minute Mfg. Co., in charge of F. Ehrhardt, displayed and demonstrated their "One Minute" washing machines and wringers. The hand power washing machine is an easy running washer, and

Waste paper baskets, foot stools and book cases were among the other items in the exhibit.

The dining suites were just as fine as were the library lines. Here also fumed was the popular finish, the chairs being covered in leather and upholstery. A restaurant set or card table set was a novelty with its round table and five circular-backed, three-cornered chairs, which, when not in use, fit close under the table.

A mahogany parlor period suite upholstered in green was a beauty, and with a Jacobian library suite, which was set out near the entrance to the booth, was one of the best things in the display.

Art Modern Wood Beds

In the same booth was the display of the Elora Furniture Co., both of the exhibits being in charge of John Stockford. The Elora Furniture Co. are makers of art modern wood beds, tables, pedestals and taborettes, and these goods were represented by splendid samples and specimens of the wood turners' art. In bedsteads were shown oak, mahogany and white enamelled in modern art and period styles, some splendid samples in these now being offered. In tables, too, some of the finest parlor tables in the whole exhibition were set out in this booth. They come in nearly all woods, especially mahogany, and in all shapes with centre pedestals and with legs for parlor and library.

The pedestal and taborette line is a big one, and in this group, too, were the umbrella stands and footstools —all of them in artistic designs of many shapes. Bedroom rockers and dressing chairs in mahogany and white enamel in a few choice patterns were set out. Those with the cane seats being very pretty, neat and seemingly useful. The beauties of this exhibit were commented upon favorably.

Vacuum Cleaners

Exhibit No. 19—Clement Mfg. Co., Toronto, showed and demonstrated their Cadillac machines, the exhibit being in charge of K. J. Pettit. These were the Cadillac vacuum sweeper, the combination vacuum cleaner and carpet sweeper, and the electric vacuum cleaner. The first is a hand cleaner which runs like a carpet

is able to take care of the ordinary family washing with the minimum of labor. The water-power machines will, of course, look after themselves and do the work while the housewife is busy with her other household duties.

The "One Minute" wringer is so built that it can be attached easily to the washer. This wringer has warranted rubber rolls vulcanized to the shafts. The cog wheels are covered so that they cannot become clogged, and it has the best steel spring. The wringer is easy-working and is a valuable adjunct to the washing machine.

Vacuum Washing Machines

The Easy Washer Co., Toronto, had also a display of two of their machines, a hand-power washer and a power motor washer. The principle of the machine is a vacuum one—two vacuum washer basins attached to a metal yoke on a metal staff mounted on a ratchet wheel. A ratchet dog attached to the lever engages the ratchet wheel and gives the basins a turn at the top of every washing stroke, causing them to take a new position on the clothes at every downward movement. Hand or foot power runs one machine and electricity or small gasoline engine runs the power machine. The former is made of galvanized iron and the latter of copper with wringer and all attachments. A removable gas attachment may be had for either washer. This keeps the water hot all through the washing operation. L. P. Gates explained the working of the washers.

Bowser Storage and Filling Systems

In the same booth S. F. Bowser & Co. gave a demonstration of five of their oil storage and measuring machines. One of these was for paints, oils and varnishes; another for an auto-filling station; a hand filtering system was another; a battery of fillers was a fourth; and a Bowser non-overflow filler for hand oilers. All of these storage and filling systems caused much comment, especially those showing economies in the factory.

Fischman Patent Mattress

Exhibit No. 22—The Fischman Mattress Co., Toronto, had a display of their new patent mattress, the features of which are the little coil contained in cotton pockets and arranged in rows, each row being wrapped in cotton felt, which makes it impossible for the springs to touch one another or tear the pockets by friction. Thus the springs are noiseless and the mattress a springy one. There are some 460 springs in each mattress—22 rows of them with cotton felt layers top and bottom— each spring acting independently, and allowing the mattress to automatically adapt itself to the contour of the body. The mattress has been subjected to severe tests, one of them being to bear a ton weight for two weeks, which left it unaffected. The mattresses may be rolled into small compass. J. McLaughlin, of McLaughlin & Scott, was in charge of the booth.

Red Cedar Bedroom Boxes

Exhibit No. 23—D. L Shafer & Co., St. Thomas. In this booth was displayed the new line of bedroom boxes and cedar chests, made by this company. These boxes and chests are made in 32 different sizes and styles, some on casters and some on pediments. Some have trays, and some have only the deep box. The boxes are made of British Columbia red cedar, the outside being covered with Japanese matting bound with white rattan in fancy designs. The three classes of box— utility, nursery and bedroom—made a splendid exhibit. To this line will be added a new moth-proof red cedar box in the spring. D. L. Shafer was in charge of the display

Pictures and Mouldings

Exhibit No. 24—Matthews Bros., Ltd., Toronto, made a showing, under the supervision of C. F. Matthews, of their pictures and mouldings. Of the pictures many of new, are still very popular. Mirrors are a big line with this firm, but there were few on display.

Brass Beds

Exhibit No. 25—S. Weisglass, Ltd., Montreal, consisted of a big representation of their various brass bed designs, not a full one by any means, as they have about 200 different designs, but a fine one nevertheless. One of the most striking of the beds was placed at the entrance to the booth. It was a horseshoe design, and was a beauty, high class throughout.

The new velvet finish was a popular feature, the surface of the beds in this finish shining like a mirror. As well, there were some fine specimens of satin finish beds. Brass cribs and costumiers were also much commented on favorably. In all the exhibits the characteristic features noticeable were their structural beauty, their high class workmanship and construction, and their splendid appearance, finished as they are with their guaranteed acid-proof lacquer.

One section of the booth was given over to their high grade springs, auto couches, davenports, divans, cat beds and cabinet beds. The dispay was in charge of C. G. Sinclair, C. H. Miller, Max Levinson and R. W. Menzie.

Upholstered Furniture

Exhibit No. 26—Quality Furniture Makers, Welland, made an interesting and excellent display of their upholstered products, especially in their English living-room chairs and settees, in Chadworth, Rivington, Lyndale and Hampton Court designs. Sofas and lounges

The H. K. Furniture Company's display of kitchen cabinets.

the colored ones were of English publication, the rest being Matthews' own reproductions.

The new picture frames show imitation Circassian walnut; embossed machine-carved moulding in oak and gumwood; veneered mouldings in all woods, some of the most popular being rosewood, Circassian, mahogany and burl. Antique Roman golds, too, are new and popular. The gilt and enamel frames, while not for club, smoking-room and den also were shown in splendid specimens, in tapestry and leather, as were a nice range of leather-covered couches.

Settees in leather with removable cushions and easy chairs in new designs of tapestry were set out attractively. Many of the items shown, especially in the living-room class, would look well in the parlor or drawing-room, as the lines of the furniture were not only

One of the best arranged displays was that of the Meaford Manufacturing Co.

comfortable, but tasty as well. Ed. Jefferies, J. A. McLaughlin and W. Gowdy looked after the display.

Kitchen Cabinets

Exhibit No. 27—The H. E. Furniture Co., Milverton, made a showing of ten of their cabinets, all different one from the other. They are making fifteen different designs, the newest one being a double roller front. The cabinets come in gum and oak. Not only are the fronts different, but the interiors are different also, so far as equipment and arrangements are concerned, though all are finished in white enamel paint, the tops coming in plain wood, aluminum nickeloid and white enamel. The ornamentations are mirror-fronts, plain and frosted glass in various designs. M. H. Honderick explained the features of the H. E. cabinet to visitors calling at the booth.

Bedding Goods.

Exhibit No. 28—Canadian Feather & Mattress Co., Toronto, in their booth showed their Royal line of mattresses, pillows, box springs and down comforters. W. H. and H. L. Smith looked after the display. In the combination felt mattress their "Special," "Princess" and "Fidelity" brands were shown; their high-grade goods consisting of the "Empress," "Queen," "Royal" and "Canfealine." High-grade specials with imperial edge are the "Queen Imperial," "Canfealine Imperial," "Royal Imperial" and "Lambs' Wool Imperial." They also make a sanitary mixed mattress filled with seagrass and a combination of jute and felt in five sizes, single and double.

Camp cots, cot and crib mattresses, and divans are also products of the company, as are the "Royal" feather bed pillows in about a dozen different varieties. These pillows are boxed in pairs, one pair in a carton, so that they need not be handled unnecessarily. Cambric cushions are another line.

The "Royal" box spring is made of oil-tempered springs, each spring being tied and double cross tied and edged with cane. It is upholstered with felt and covered with high-grade art ticking. The "Royal" springs are made of woven wire and twin link fabric.

Standard Mattresses.

Exhibit No. 29—Standard Bedding Co., Toronto, displayed their "Hygienic" line of mattresses and their "Maydwell" line of bed springs, and gave demonstrations of their worth. In the mattress line the various grades were shown uncovered so that the felt and other filling, of which they are composed, could be seen and inspected. These "Hygienic" mattresses come in about 15 different styles.

The bed springs come in nine styles and sizes. Box springs, too, are a production of the Standard Bedding Co., also cots with and without head rest. James Burrell looked after the booth.

Arabian Leather

Exhibit No. 30—Cotton Mfg. Co., under the supervision of W. Pertle, showed a big range of their Arabian leather furniture coverings in all colors and thicknesses. The order and guide book handed to every dealer visiting the exhibition was covered with some of this company's product—black Arabian leather.

Upholstered Furniture.

Exhibit No. 31—Imperial Furniture Co., Toronto. In this booth was shown a full range of this company's production, which covers the whole line of upholstered furniture. Among others we display a number of knock-down framed leather upholstered rocking and easy chairs in all colors. Couches, in leather and tapestry, too, were shown, and some splendid specimens of Chesterfields in sets for living-rooms. Individual items in this latter class, covered in denim, looked very pretty, as also did a three-piece set in purple.

On nearly all the pieces, whether leather or tapestry, the cushions were made removable. Oak and mahogany predominated in the frames, and judging by the fine display English easy chairs for comfort in the living-room is a very big line with this company. J. L. O'Malley and W. G. Mulheron were in charge.

Dining and Bedroom Chairs.

Exhibit No. 32—Elmira Furniture Co., makers of dining and bedroom chairs, library suites and tables, office tilters, jardiniere stands, etc., showed a representative grouping of the productions. S. B. Frey, H. M. Rapp, J. E. Newton and E. M. Arnold were on hand to answer inquiries. A big line is their oak, fumed and mahogany diners, about a dozen new suites in these being shown, and three new all wood diner sets now coming through the factory.

Two cobber-seated rockers are also new; and there is, too, a lot of new fumed dining chairs in open and upholstered backs this season. Fumed rockers are as well new.

Upholstered slip seats were noticed on a great many of the suites shown, and not a few shaped seats n the all-wood. Mission goods for den were shown, and three new rockers on modern lines, two of them shaped and one upholstered.

Bedroom rockers in mahogany were pretty, and in library sets and tables and desks and some parlor and office chairs and seats, mahogany, also held favor. Hall chairs in oak and mahogany constructed on modern lines were new.

Dining Chairs and Parlor Furniture.

Exhibit No. 33—Schierholtz Furniture Co., New Hamburg, represented by E. and L. Schierholtz and J. S. Shantz, are featuring diners, and they showed a large assortment in fumed and golden oak. They also displayed den rockers and chairs, drawing-room chairs, parlor suites in all the latest coverings, individual chairs, sofas and rockers. The coverings matched the various items—art silks, tapestries and leathers being used.

The company also make a select line of davenports upholstered in leather and tapestry for living-rooms, and a line of velour and leather covered couches.

Extension Dining Tables.

The Orillia Furniture Co. also made a display in this booth of their dining extension tables in quartered and fumed oak; buffets in the same woods, also mahogany; and parlor tables in quartered and mahogany.

Chiffoniers and dressers in quartered and Empire mahogany with dressing tables to match were as well shown. The imitation mahogany products looked fine in the samples shown.

Office Furniture.

Exhibit No. 34—Collier, Cockerill, Co., Aurora, a new concern of 18 months' standing, made a display of their new office equipment goods—desks, tables, filing devices, costumieres, book cases, typewriter desks, correspondence trays, telephone stands and wardrobes. They intend to extend the line in the near future and make a complete line of office furniture needs. The samples shown in the exhibition, while few in number, showed good workmanship and material. The woods used were oak and mahogany. J. H. Noble was in charge of the exhibit.

Surface Oak and Imitation Mahogany Goods.

Exhibit No. 35—Meaford Mfg. Co. in their booth made one of the finest displays in the whole exhibition. A set of rooms down one side of their compartment set off to advantage a number of bed and dining-room suites in white and ivory enamel, mahogany, fumed and golden oak.

Clothes closets and cabinets with single and double doors, book cases, tables for dining-room in extension round and square, hall seats and racks, desks and combinations of a great many designs were shown.

This company has been making for years a golden oak line of furniture that has obtained a good trade hold, and they are building up a good line of surface and mahogany also, and this year will make a strong bid for favor with their fumed goods. A strong point with their goods is the durability of their finish, due to the special process of manufacture. The way in which this was demonstrated with the use of a hammer was certainly convincing. The company use extensively maple wood, finishing the products by printing direct from the veneer.

One strong line with this company is their bureaus, cupboards, buffets, wash-stands and medicine chests, in all finishes. Another big line is their parlor table and pedestal stands. These were shown to great advantage, and were the cause of a great deal of decidedly favorable comment. Geo. Graham, eastern representative, and J. Montgomery, Toronto representative, looked after the booth.

Big Furniture Manufacturers.

Exhibit No. 36—The Knechtel Furniture Co., Hanover, had one of the largest displays in the Horticultural Building. They make all kinds of case goods, chairs, upholstered furniture, desks, kitchen cabinets. Weis filing cabinets and sectional book-cases—many samples of which were shown in their exhibit, which was in charge of W. R. Deeton, E. J. Rose, Chas. Knechner and Dan. Schroeder.

In their sectional book-cases they lay particular stress on the sliding door feature, the receding door having a special equalizer which makes it automatic in working. To this line should also be added the Weis-Knechtel filing case line, which has all the features of the Weis

EXHIBITORS AND REPRESENTATIVES WHO LOOKED AFTER DISPLAYS IN HORTICULTURAL BUILDING.

In the back row will be seen John Stockford and J. Smith of J. C. Alundell & Co.; Ted and James Jeffery of Quality Furniture Makers; C. H. Miller of S. Weisglass, Ltd.; Geo. Graham and J. Montgomery of Meaford Mfg. Co.; Adam Godfrey of Imperial Furniture Co.; and R. and G. Thomas of People's Outfitting Co., London. In the front row, among others, will be noticed W. C. Wilson, Meaford Mfg. Co.; G. Mulheron, Imperial Furniture Co.; J. A. McLaughlin; D. L. Slinfer, St. Thomas; J. Minaker, Picton; Max Levinson, S. Weisglass, Ltd.; and F. Ehrhardt.

patents, which are controlled in Canada by the Knechtel Co. These and the book-cases come in sanitary and full base, and as well in combinations.

The Knechtel line of office desks covers the whole range of roll and flat tops in single and double. Typewriter desks, book-keepers' stands, board-room tables and other office furniture lines were shown in extenso.

In bedroom furniture there was displayed a large line of quartered oak in beautiful finishes. All their bedroom items come in five different finishes: surface, empire mahogany, natural maple, white enamel and walnut, and even in the cheap and medium grades these finishes are added. A new cheap line is now made in Colonial style. A new line is one in golden elm, natural finish. These goods were in a class by themselves, as also were the mahogany veneer. In gumwood finishes may be had in natural, satin, walnut and Kyonyx. Wooden bedsteads are included in the suites, and a big white enamel line in these goods was shown.

In the dining-room line the chairs come upholstered and in all wood. Buffets, china cabinets, tables and suites were shown in fumed and golden on Colonial and modern lines, a big range being shown. Clothes cabinets had a display by themselves, and a couple of kitchen cabinets—the Knechtel special—were also displayed.

Toronto Furniture Co.

The Toronto Furniture Co., makers of dining-room, library and chamber suites and odd pieces in mahogany, Circassian walnut and oak, made their exhibit in their own factory showrooms on Dufferin street. They specialize on period styles, and so have divided their floor space into rooms or small compartments, in which are set out complete suites of bed and dining-room furniture in various woods and in different styles.

Two sides of the showroom, which covers one of the factory floors, are devoted to bedroom suites, and a double tier of rooms down the centre are used to show to advantage the beauties of the dining suites. The odd pieces are given one end of the floor to themselves.

In bedroom goods were shown suites in Louis XVI. of grey enamel; white enamel with blue trimmings, and plain white enamel. An Adams enamel set was also shown, an odd effect being given to one suite because of the mahogany polished top on enamel Sheraton, inlaid, was another, and some splendid Circassian, mahogany and prima vera in Sheraton style were set out. Queen Anne, turned Colonial with rush-seated chairs, and William and Mary designs were among other bed suites.

In odd pieces a great many mahogany tables, desks, music cabinets were shown in Chppendale, Hepplewhite and Adams designs, and in dining-room suites in Circassian, fumed and mahogany, a number of William and Mary, Adams, Jacobean, Old English, Chippendale and Sheraton were shown. It was a fine display.

Canada Furniture Manufacturers.

This company made a display of their varied furniture goods in their Toronto warehouse on King Street East. Four floors of the building being given over to the exhibit. Among other things shown were a number of enamel-finished bedroom suites in white, ivory and French grey, in period styles—Adams and Sheraton predominating. A lady's boudoir set in French grey enamel was a feature.

In dining-room suites, period styles also held sway. Adams sets in gumwood with satin walnut finish, antique mahogany, and Circassian in Louis XVI. were splendid samples. A bedroom suite in the latter style, and one in tuna mahogany Sheraton style, natural finish were fine. Other suites for bed and dining-room, in Adams and Colonials—all woods—were well set off. A mahogany Chinese Chippendale dining suite looked nice with its odd carving.

In den and living-room furniture the styles seem to run to fumed. Much of the drawing and living-room stuff is covered in denim as sample to set off from, and are finished in any covering to suit the buyer. New parlor goods in Adams, Colonial, Hepplewhite, Louis XV. and XVI. were shown in graceful designs and beautiful frames. Cane-seated furniture in period style was new and novel.

Miscellaneous lines for hall, den, bed and living-room were shown, and a big line of couches, too, were displayed, as well as cheap and medium bed and dining-room suites.

The reed and rattan furniture line is a big one, and in baby carriages and go-carts about 125 different designs and samples were displayed, a new carriage being made of Hong-Kong grass. These carriages come in reed, wood and this new grass.

Exhibition Notes.

The Chair Craft Co., of Traverse City, Mich., showed a couple of new reclining chairs in the Transportation Building, which they were trying to interest manufacturers in. These were called the "Rest-Fest" and "Rex" recliners. The former was an easy chair which ran on a circular frame, enabling the user to recline at any desired angle, even with the feet higher than the head. The "Rex" had a back which could be lowered flat and even with the seat, making of it a bed-chair. Both chairs are equipped with folding foot-rests.

In the same building The Thompson Co., of Belleville, set up two of their kitchen cabinets, fully equipped with jars and utensils for keeping foods, spices and sundries.

THOSE REGISTERED AT TORONTO EXHIBITION.

W. I. Luke, McLaren & Co., St. Catharines.
R. M. McPherson, Vincent McPherson, Brandon, Man.
W. J. Draper, Vincent McPherson, Brandon, Man.
John Leslie, John Leslie, Winnipeg.
W. H. Rennie, J. Robinson & Co., Winnipeg.
G. M. Smith, G. G. Smith Co., Barrie.
A. N. Tanney, J. A. Banfield, Winnipeg.
Tourigny & Tourigny, Victoriaville.
J. K. Edwards, Edwards Furn. Co., Sherbrooke, Que.
G. M. Edward, Edward Furn. Co., Sherbrooke, Que.
D. N. McPhail, D. M. McPhail & Co., Renfrew, Ont.
E. J. Johnston, Noden Hallett & J., Toronto.
O. G. Keene, Ontario Furn. Co., London.
J. Warrin, Western Furn. S. Co.
J. H. Williman, M. E. Long, Brantford.
H. R. Sills, M. E. Long, Brantford.
A. Lutes, Thos. C. Watkins, Hamilton.
F. C. Abbott, Thos. C. Watkins, Hamilton.
E. Solomen, H. Solomen & Co., Montreal.
L. Solomen, H. Solomen & Co., Montreal.
J. W. Buck, Beamsville.
Peter McSweeney, Moncton, N. B.
J. N. Archambault, Montreal.
J. F. Wildman, Office Specialty, Toronto.
H. G. Coomber, Coomber & Co., Tillsonburg.
F. G. Wilcox & Co., Waterford.
R. W. MacDonald, Baldwin, Robinson, St. Thomas.
W. A. Jennings, Jennings Furn. Co., St. Thomas.
W. J. Lindsay, Woodstock.
G. J. Little, G. Little & Son, Galt.
G. W. Jackson, G. W. Jackson, Leamington.

W. T. Jackson, Leamington.
J. E. Wilder, Wilder & Co., Montreal.
E. Trudeau, Montreal.
W. J. Davidson, A. F. Davidson, Lucknow.
G. T. Aitchison, Lucknow Table Co., Lucknow.
A. L. Pouliet, Harrison Furn. Co., Montreal.
S. Sharp, C. Austin Co., Chatham.
A. Bradfoot, Moose Jaw.
J. Britton, Lucknow.
Fred Skinner, Schomberg.
C. B. Tadman, Home Furn. Co., Toronto.
R. L. Adoph, Home Furn. Co., Toronto.
Chas. Cooke, Lord Furn. Co., Ottawa.
I. Friedman, Garden City Furn., St. Catharines.
E. Luke, F. C. Burroughs, Toronto.
B. Wolf, H. Wolf & Son, London.
Geo. Holmere, Goderich.
J. Boles, Ingersoll.
D. Becker, New Hamburg.
S. A. Hewitt, Mitchell.
Mr. Hislop, Hagersville.
W. H. Manning, Coldwater.
W. J. Lewis, Smallman & Ingram, London.
A. J. Freeman, Ottawa.
J. Robb, R. Simpson Co., Toronto.
H. Turk, Kingston.
E. Cohen, Hamilton.
B. C. Burroughs, Burroughs Furn. Co., Toronto.
A. Watts, Burroughs Furn. Co., Toronto.
J. S. May, Burroughs Furn. Co., Toronto.
A. E. Everett. St. John, N.B.
W. L. Jennings, Lamont & Co., Fredericton, N.B.
R. P. Taylor, F. C. Burroughs Co., Toronto.
M. D. Gilbert, Gilbert & Co., Picton.
S. C. Blacklock, Murray-Kay Co., Toronto.
D. T. Henderson, Adams Furn. Co., Toronto.
J. J. McKinnon, R. Simpson Co., Toronto.
A. K. Thomas, Rockwood.
G. C. Wilkinson, T. Eaton Co., Toronto.
J. H. Butler, T. Eaton Co., Toronto.
Mr. Witeman, Fort William.
A. A. Schreiter, Berlin.
W. Rath, M. E. Long Co., Brantford.
M. E. Long, M. E. Long Co., Brantford.
W. H. Hash, Hamilton.
N. H. Keen, Keen Bros., London.
A. H. Keen, Keen Bros., London.
J. A. Genest, P. T. Lagare, Quebec.
N. Bilsky, Can. House Furn., Ottawa.
Mr. Jackson, Georgetown.
N. L. Brandon, St. Mary's.
A. G. Laing, Laing & McKid, North Bay.
J. Jackson, Woodhouse & Co., Montreal.
Mr. Wilkinson, Tillsonburg.
J. Hammer, Newsted.
N. J. Roadhouse, Newmarket.
C. Bussell, T. Eaton Co., Toronto.
Mr. Scott. T. Eaton Co., Toronto.
Mr. McKillop, McKillop & McIntyre, Brampton.
Mr. McIntyre, McKillop & McIntyre, Brampton.
C. F. Trout, E. J. Cole & Co., Woodstock.
Mac McPherson, Delhi.
C. R. Sheddon, Sheddon Furn. Co., Woodstock.
W. J. Gillott, Millbrook.
E. A. Waterman, Weiler Bald. Ltd., Victoria.
W. A. S. Tagart, Wensley & Cowan, Milden, Sask.
A. G. Tagart, Wensley & Cowan, Milden, Sask.
R. Healey, Kingsville.
H. Carnaham, Elmvale.
C. W. Marsh, W. Marsh & Son, Morrisburg.
J. C. Marlatt, Grimsby.

E. Miles, E. Miles & Co., Walkerton.
W. A. Hunt, Belmont.
F. Bedell, F. Bedell & Co., Toronto.
J. T. Romp, Font Hill.
T. Pursell, Pursell & Co., Brantford.
Mr. Pollard, Pursell & Co., Brantford.
A. H. Miller, Berlin.
R. E. Smith, W. Smith & Son, Leamington.
W. J. McConvey, F. C. Burroughs, Toronto.
R. C. Tarrance, S. & D., Galt.
A. Johnston, Washington & J., Toronto.
E. J. Patrick, Guelph.
L. Yolles, Toronto.
H. W. Curtis, Curtis & Wilson, Toronto.
E. Buckley, Buckley & Co., Niagara Falls.
L. Roenick, C. McCullough, Trenton.
W. C. Wood, R. H. Williams, Regina, Sask.
E. B. Williams, R. H. Williams, Regina, Sask.
E. F. Kelly, G. W. Robinson, Hamilton.
J. A. Forbes, J. A. Duggan, Stratford.
E. Renaud, Renaud, King & Patterson, Montreal.
Mr. Loeselle, Henry Morgan, Montreal.
R. Thomas, Peoples Furn. Co., London.
G. Thomas, Peoples Furn. Co., London.
K. Reid, Kingston.
M. B. Judson, Napanee.
M. Steinburg. Dom. House Furn. Co., Montreal.
A. E. Stager, Hespeler.
Mr. Thompson, Belleville.
R. M. Patterson, R. Simpson Co., Toronto.
E. J. Johnson, Kenmore.
L. Hahan. New Hamburg.
Chas. Durham, Aurora.
H. Kemer, Windsor.
L. Bileddeau. Dupuis Bros., Montreal.
W. H. Anderson, Galt.
Mr. Lindsay, Woodstock.
J. Paquin, Hull, Que.
W. Hilder, Hilder & Co., Welland.
R. Breckenridge, Owen Sound.
W. R. Wilson. Curtis Wilson, Toronto.
J. A. Sutherland. Curtis Wilson. Toronto.
H. Hoffman. Simcoe.
Mr. Noden, Noden, Hallitt & J., Toronto.
Mr. Thompson, Belleville.
Mr. Dale. Dale Furn. Co.. Toronto.
Mr. Disney. Bowmanville.
Arthur Smith. Bowmanville.
Smith Furn. Co., London.
G. S. Wilson. Norwich.
F. Kilkenney. Bradford.
Mrs. Herminson. Listowel.
G. M. Baldwin. St. Thomas.
Mr. Baxter. Collingwood.
F. C. Dance, Shelburne.
Gertzshein Bros., Toronto.
H. C. Bissontz. St. Catharines.
N. G. Love. Ogilvy & Son. Montreal.
E. W. Williamson, Burlington.
W. L. McCaul. St. Williams.
Mr. A. Walker. Guelph.
G. H. Brett. Dunnville.
B. Swinton. Orillia.
Mr. Hendry. Sudbury.
F. Crawford. McDonald Fur. Co., Chatham.
W. F. Tinard, Reliable Fur Co., Toronto
F. A. Walsin, Nova Scotia Furn., Halifax.
W. A. Wright, Wright & Hepburn, Port. Arthur.
I. Mathews, Port Arthur.
F. C. Cressman. The Cressman Co., Ltd., Peterboro.
C. F. Coryell. Adams Furn. Co., Toronto.

C. R. Montgomery, Toronto.
N. J. Boyd, N. J. Boyd, Mitchell.
F. Jackson, Sudbury.
J. Lappin, Goodwin, Limited, Montreal.
T. T. Allison, C. Duprie Co., Toronto.
W. Doherty, Sarnia.
F. E. Walker, P. E. Walker Co., Ltd., Hamilton.
W. L. Stern, F. E. Walker Co., Ltd., Hamilton.
I. L. Matthews, Port Arthur.
R. W. McDonald, Baldwin Robinson, St. Thomas.
F. Goodwin, St. Thomas.
J. B. Hoodless, The Hoodless Furn. Co., Hamilton.
W. M. Tomlins, The Tomlins Furn., Toronto.
R. Nusboin, Brantford.
S. Sharp, O. Austin Co., Chatham.
N. M. Steinman, Baden.
A. Humsleys, Baden.
A. Black, Orillia.
Jno. Dalton, Deseronto.
C. J. Broderick, Deseronto.
J. D. Craig, Peterboro.
G. W. Bernett, Peterboro.
G. Davis, F. C. Burroughs, Toronto.
W. G. Beach, F. C. Burroughs, Toronto.
S. Foremoin, Toronto.
W. R. Orr, Portage la Prairie.
S. A. Hewitt, S. A. Hewitt, Mitchell.
J. D. Hill, Rouleau, Sask.
P. E. Brown, Toronto.
T. J. Webster, Reliable Furn. Co., Toronto.
Mr. Faconyell, Bedell Furn. Co., Toronto.
J. C. Shortell, Winnipeg.
Howard Rogers, Howard Rogers, Fredericton.
H. H. Wrightman, W. H. Whalen Co., Fort William.
W. Knechtel, F. C. Burroughs, Toronto.
F. L. Willson, Geo. McLay Co.
Chas. L. Bustin, St. John, N.B.
J. Hardy, Danville, Que.
J. Jackson, Woodhouse & Co., Montreal.
Chas. W. Marsh, W. Marsh Co., Morrisburg.
W. R. Valiguette, N. G. Valiguette Co., Montreal.
A. Desnoyen, N. G. Valiguette Co., Montreal.
J. H. Jackson, Georgetown.
D. A. L. Parsons, W. J. I. Parsons, Sarnia.
Jno. Hammer, Neustadt.
R. W. Waldon, Neustadt.
J. C. Richardson, Weston.
D. H. Bernhard, Walkerville.
R. Healey, Healey & Crawford, Kingsville.
E. J. Patrick, Guelph.
J. C. Marlett, Grimsby.
F. H. Winmaker, Buchanan & Winmaker, Picton.
C. H. Bryon, F. C. Burroughs, Toronto.
O. N. Bomberg, Hamilton.
W. J. Palmer, Northway Co., Tillsonburg.
F. Schmot, Berlin.
E. Miles, Walkerton.
F. Pollard, Brantford.
L. Yolles, Toronto.
Henry Gordon, F. C. Burroughs, Toronto.
W. E. Tuer, F. C. Burroughs, Toronto.
W. B. Jennings, St. Thomas.
Fred Reid, Kingston.
P. Dowsley, Kingston.
N. McCabe, Kingston.
Wm. Lalonde, J. S. Price Co., Montreal.
W. E. Cassidy, The Adams Furn. Co., Toronto.
W. S. Partridge, Wm. Trafford Co., London.
Jos. Baird, Baird Bros., Plattsville.
Mr. Gillespie, Gillespie Bros., Orangeville.
T. E. Simpson, F. E. Simpson Co., Sault Ste. Marie.

J. G. Henry, Sudbury.
J. B. Dangall, Barrie.
R. Baxter, Collingwood.
S. A. Webster, Waterloo.
Sam Avery, Caledonia.
H. T. Falls, Simcoe.
W. Comstock, A. Comstock, Peterboro.
R. A. Breckenridge, Owen Sound.
J. A. Donadson, Caledon East.
W. R. Wilson, Toronto.
G. S. Wilson, G. S. Wilson, Norwich.
F. Kickenny, Bradford.
W. A. Corpin, The Curtis Wilson, Toronto.
G. F. Sutherland, Sutherland & Son, Welland.
G. W. Baldwin, Baldwin Robinson, St. Thomas.
A. J. Smith, Smith Furn. Co., London.
J. A. Wendover, Wendover & Sons, Frankford.
H. C. Bissontz, St. Catharines.
J. Smith, Marshal Field & Co., Chicago.
Jas. Cholmondeley, Warings, Ltd., London, Eng.

SECOND WEEK'S REGISTRATION AT STRATFORD FURNITURE EXHIBITION

I. L. Matthews, Jr., I. L. Matthews & Co., Pt. Arthur.
J. H. McCammon, Paris.
N. J. Boyd, N. J. Boyd, Mitchell.
H. H. Mightmann, W. H. Whalen Co., Ltd., Ft. William.
T. E. Simpson, T. E. Simpson, Ltd., Sault Ste. Marie.
J. S. Henry, Sudbury.
J. G. F. Dale, Dale Furniture Co., Toronto.
S. C. Blacklock, Murray-Kay, Ltd., Toronto.
John Leslie, Leslie & Co., Winnipeg.
W. J. Nash, J. Hoodless Furn. Co., Hamilton.
G. H. Hetherington, Langton.
F. Goodwin, St. Thomas.
Geo. T. Sheppard, St. Thomas.
W. T. Jennings, St. Thomas.
Jas. Baird, Baird Bros., Plattsville.
H. C. Baird, Baird Bros., Plattsville.
B. C. Burroughes, F. C. Burroughes & Co., Toronto.
F. C. Burroughes, F. C. Burroughes & Co., Toronto.
J. M. Struthers, Guelph.
J. G. Cress, Waterloo Spring Co., Waterloo.
E. F. McIntyre, McKillop & McIntyre, Brampton.
P. McKillop, McKillip & McIntyre, Brampton.
J. U. Dore, Hamilton.
Warren Andrews, Anderson Co., Ltd., St. Thomas.
D. H. Bernhardt, Walkerville.
N. J. Johnston, Kenmore.
J. A. Genest, P. T. Ligare, Ltd., Quebec.
C. R. Montgomery, Adams Furn. Co., Ltd., Toronto.
W. J. Walker, Seaforth.
J. O. Mitchell, St Mary's.
Jos. Dunford, Seaforth.
E. L. Box, Seaforth.
C. Hewitt, Hewitt & Son, Mitchell.
J. A. Duggan, J. A. Duggan, Stratford.
Thos. Simpson, J. A. Duggan, Stratford.
J. A. Forbes, J. A. Duggan, Stratford.
L. Phippen, Phippen & Simpson, Sarnia.
J. Edwards, Alberts, Ltd., Montreal.
A. Renaud, Renaud, King & Patterson, Montreal.
P. Loiselle, H. Morgan & Co.. Ltd., Montreal.
W. Comstock, A. Comstock, Peterborough.
J. B. Hoodless, J. Hoodless Furn. Co., Hamilton.
M. Steinberg, Dom. House Furnishing Co., Montreal.
Joseph Gibson, Stratford.
A. Wood, Remer, Sask.
J. Neault, Jno. Watt, Millbank.
E. B. Williams, Regina, Sask.

Buy Honest Made-in-Canada Furniture

Canada imported over $3,000,000 worth of furniture last year; 92 per cent. of it from the United States. Five years ago Canada bought slightly over $500,000 from abroad.

Some of it was brought in as samples by manufacturers; some by those who worship at the shrine of the antiquarian. The great bulk of the imports, however, were on behalf of the retail trade.

According to the census of 1911 Canada had 172 furniture factories, with a capital of $13,746,262 and an output of $12,369,366. To its 9,000 employees $4,044,236 was paid in wages.

These conditions bring up the question why Canadian retailers are buying so much furniture from the United States?

In the exceptionally costly and period furniture the United States maker has an advantage over the Canadian because of the extent of his market. Canada will be an importer of this class of goods for many years.

In the medium and lower grades of furniture Canada need not take second place to any country in the world. The workmanship in Canadian furniture factories is so superior that their product boasts a finish and stability which enables the Canadian product to stand up against any ompetition.

The Canadian furniture manufacturer is, however, facing competition that is hard to meet. In the Southern States a line of exceptionally cheap furniture, which looks much like the medium priced lines made here, but which is poorly made by cheap and unskilled colored workers.

The Canadian retailer should hestitate before buying these lines. To sell an inferior article, even at a slightly lower price does not help to build up a reputation or extend one's business.

"Quality is remembered long after the price is forgotten."

The retailers of Canada have it to say whether Canadian money will remain at home to keep Canadian workmen busy producing honest furniture or whether inferior goods, made by the inefficient and cheap colored labor, will take its place.

In considering the comparative cost of furniture f.o.b. Canadian points and f.o.b. United States points it is necessary, also, to remember that a duty of 30 per cent. has to be paid on the latter.

The Canadian Furniture World recommends the honest furniture "Made-in-Canada."

Collins' Course in Show Card Writing

Third of a series of articles specially prepared for this journal.

For those who feel they would like to try some real card writing we will offer some general rules that will apply at all times. The white card you use should be 8 ply for large sizes, but for smaller ones and price tickets 6 ply will answer. The standard size of cardboard is 22 in. x 28 in. Half sheets are 14in. x 22 in. or 28 in. x 11 in. For panels a size that cuts without waste is 11 in. x 17 in. You can get three cards this size out of a full sheet. First cut one off the top, 11 in. x 22 in. This leaves a piece 22 in. x 17 in., which will cut into two 11 in. x 17 in. Trim your first cut to 17 in. and you will have three panels 11 in. x 17 in. each. The cutting will make price tickets.

In making window cards there is usually two important features to be brought out prominently—the name of the article and the price. All other reading on the card is subordinate to these. If it be a chair you are advertising and you word the card as follows: "An Unusual Bargain, This Chair $6.50," the two main features are This Chair, and $6.50. The other wording, "An Unusual Bargain," should be written in small lettering while the words and the price should be brought out prominently. Any of the styles of alphabets given in this and previous lessons will suit admirably for a card of this description.

We have intimated that the plain card is more in demand than the fussily ornamented one. As a rule the beginner is inclined to make too fancy letters or put on too much ornamentation. If you find this is your fault, strive to make your cards too plain, and you will then hit a happy medium. All ornamentation should be made in a subdued color. But of coloring we will say more in the next lesson.

The laying out, or arranging of the lettering on a card is almost as important as the formation of the letters. Frequently the beginner is inclined to spread the matter out equally all over the card. This will tend to destroy the effect of emphasizing the article and price advertised. While a card writer has unlimited license in the matter of laying out a card, there is one rule that should always be borne in mind, that is, that each subject matter should be kept by itself. This is particularly true if there is much to go on the card. If you have three or four lines of lettering in small type, keep these compact and do not have too much space between each line. With upper case do not have the space between each line greater than the height of the letters. If lower case is used the space may be a little deeper than the depth of the body of the letters to allow for the letters that extend above and below the lines.

Do not be afraid to leave a good wide margin on your cards. A special display line may run to the edge of the card, but even then the card as a whole should have a margin and this line should be worked over or into it. In cases where you have a great quantity of reading matter to go on to a card, it may

Suggestive card for early February sales.

Striking bargain sale window card.

Plate 12.—Combination of capitals and numerals.

A B C D E F G H I J K L M N O P Q R S T U V W X Y Z ?

Plate 13.—Alphabet of capital letters.

not be necessary to emphasize any particular word or line. In such cases you should keep the reading matter well in the centre of the card and have a liberal margin outside. The general appearance of the card will be better than if the matter were spread all over it in larger type.

It frequently occurs that you will have a long space to fill with a short word or the reverse, a long word to fit into a short space. This may be accomplished by "condensing" or "extending" the letters. The alphabet given this month shows a moderately condensed letter and a sample line of "extended" in the same style, which will show you the possibilities of extending and condensing letters. See plates 13 and 14.

Window card which speaks for itself.

Plates 13 and 14 are among the styles of most general use for display lines and words, but are not easily enough made to be sufficiently rapid for general use. They are very clean cut and will always look well.

In the general conduction of any business it is always well to take advantage of any situation that may be turned to advertising advantage. Conventions, gatherings, political meetings, picnics, all holidays, etc. The month of February is one of those sort of between-season-months in which business drops down to a pretty low ebb. However there is one day—St. Valentine's—that may be used as a handle to wield a little advertising with. No matter what the nature of business may be, your store will stand a little decorating with hearts and cupids and ribbons, etc. Use some cupid or heart design on your cards. You may also, with profit, arrange a special sale for the month of February that will clear out your odd lines and slow

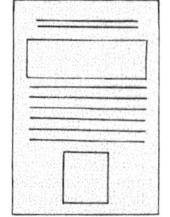

Example of poor layout. 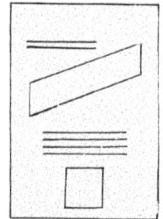 Good layout with same matter.

sellers, and make room for your new spring goods.

The sample cards are suggestive for any line of business you may be engaged in. The 50c. card may be adapted to any article or price during the valentine season. The design is made with an air brush which we will take up later. The other two cards are also air

A poorly laid out card.  The same attractively set out.

brush work. The February Sale card is suggestive for a sale of any line of goods. You may use it for any special article and quote the price of it. These should be helpful in stimulating business during the quiet business month of February.

a b c d e f g h i j l m n o p q r s t u v w x y z

Plate 14. Alphabet of lower case letters.

The Art of Display

Suggestions for Window and Interior Arrangements.

Christmas Window Competition

On this page is published the prize-winning window in our Christmas competition, the winner of which is G. P. Chamberlain, of Chilliwack, B.C. The window represents a bedroom on Christmas Eve. Mr. Chamberlain's boys enter in their night gowns, hang up their stocking, then after going over to the fireplace to get warm, go to bed. In a short time Santa Claus enters (by the fireplace), seeing the boys asleep he proceeds to fill the stockings. After looking around, brushing out his whiskers, etc., he departs the same way he entered. The boy awakening shortly after, and, thinking it is morning, get their stockings from the fireplace and climbing back into the bed commence to unpack them. It was at that moment that the camera snapped, and the picture is the result.

The points considered in the competition were attractiveness, originality and selling power—and on these three points the judges considered that Mr. Chamberlain's window was the best submitted. Some few photographs sent in for the competition did not get high points because they were folded and creased, thus spoiling them for publication purposes; others had not been given sufficient exposure, and thus their striking features were not clearly brought out.

It speaks well for The Furniture World that the competition brought photographs from all parts of Canada.

The prize winners in the order of merit were:

G. P. Chamberlain, Chilliwack, B.C., $10.

J. Lettee & Son, Waterloo, Ont., two years' subscription to The Furniture World.

C. J. Learight, Norwood, Ont., two years' subscription to The Furniture World.

A GOOD WINDOW TICKET AND SOME

In a Muswell Hill furnisher's window, says the Review, of London, there is a window ticket, plain and bold, and worded as follows:

{ f
{ t's not
{ n the window
{ t's
{ nside.

Simple, but very effective!

Memo, to new men who keep on spelling it "Adams." It is "Adam," not "Adams."

Why not a sign, "We pay good money for advertising. Come in and look around. Your personal inspection is worth far more to us than even good newspaper advertising."

Another tocsin: "Shop early. It may take some inspection to decide on that holiday gift."

The gift department is a fixture. Why not a children's department, with high chairs, little carts, "Little Mother" baby tenders, and juvenile furniture. A section for the children will make it easy to shop and sell a lot more children's furniture.

The furniture store is coming into its own for the holiday trade. What a wonder it is that it has been so long delayed.

The right use of a small or moderate sized space in the local papers now by a house that really has something to say is worth twice the space indifferently used,

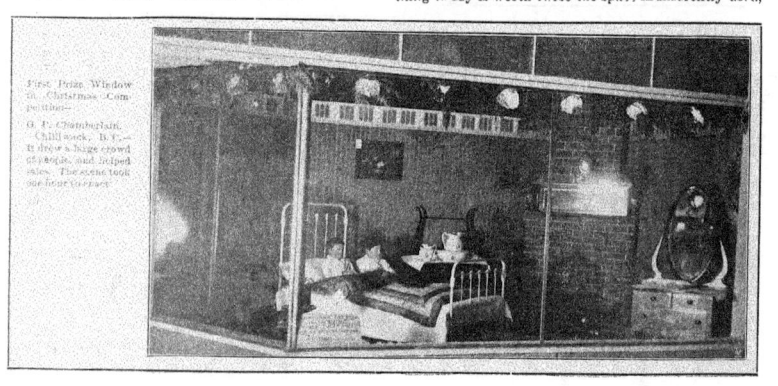

First Prize Window in Christmas Competition—
G. P. Chamberlain, Chilliwack, B.C.—It drew a large crowd of people, and helped sales. The scene took one hour to enact.

or with simply a lot of illustrations and prices. Illustrations and prices are all right, but a little talk on your goods and policies, with holiday suggestions, day after day, in a small or moderate space, will bring the business at the psychological moment.

KEEP FIRST IMPRESSIONS IN MIND

"In dressing a window, remember that one is preparing for the prospective customer, his first impression of the stock," remarks the Furniture World of New York. An attractive display will catch his eye and lead him to study the window and incidentally the goods that are offered; but a freakish display will not. The impression carried away by the passer-by is not one of the things you have in stock. The reason is obvious. The freak is a separate attraction in itself, something that might be seen in a circus side show, but entirely unrelated to your goods. Guard against this delusion in regard to what constitutes a successful window. Let the whole effect be harmonious, instead of over-emphasizing the setting. The merchant who neglects his windows, or fails to make the best use of them, is losing an important means of advertising, which is but another way of saying that he is losing sales and the money they would bring him. The unwisdom of such a policy is obvious.

PREVENT SHOW WINDOWS FROM FROSTING

A great many merchants find difficulty in preventing their windows from frosting or sweating in cold weather, which practically renders them useless for publicity purposes at a time when they are of the most value.

The physical cause of the deposits of moisture upon windows is the great difference in the temperature between the surface of the glass and the air. This is especially true when the air that comes in contact with the glass bears a relatively high portion of moisture.

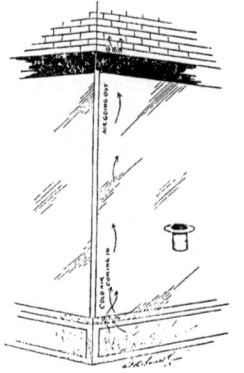

As long as the glass is as warm as the circulating air, or near that temperature, there will be no deposits.

Warm air is able to carry a much larger portion of water than cold air, and the problem therefore resolves itself into the question of keeping the glass as near the temperature as the air on the outside of the window, or, reverse the reasoning, to keep the air on the inside of the window near the temperature of the coolness of the glass.

At all times try to keep as even a temperature as possible on both sides of the glass, as the cold air on the outside of the glass condenses the moisture in the warm air inside, which causes moisture or sweat to deposit on the inner surface of the pane. This sweat when freezing causes frost.

A very practical and safe solution of this problem is to have the windows so ventilated that the air on both sides of the glass is kept at about the same temperature. In order to accomplish this result, the windows must be shut off or boxed in from the inside of the store and ventilated from the outside. All of the new modern metal window construction is equipped with these ventilating tubes. In fact, one of the strongest points in favor of metal strip show window construction is the ventilating feature.

In a series of windows, where they are all connected, a 24 x 6 inch opening at either end of the series will in most cases answer nicely and obviate any further trouble.

The accompanying illustration shows a fixture designed to prevent this difficulty. This can be purchased from fixture houses or it can be made by practically any metal concern that deals in pipes or lighting fixtures. This shows a row of small tubes with screen protections at either end run through the show window sash at top and bottom. In case the window sash is not deep enough the tubes can be set in below the flooring of the window. This will require an elbow made especially for this purpose. If the window is large, these tubes should be placed at equal distances along the upper and lower portions of the sash.

The diagram shows how the cold air circulates through the tubes across the inside window fronts and out of the tube. The screen shields are placed at each end of the fixture in order to prevent insects from getting into the windows and to prevent mischievous boys from pushing sticks and other articles into the tube.

As windows rarely sweat in the summer, a cap can be placed over the inside opening to prevent dust from accumulating on the merchandise shown in the window.

Other Methods

Other remedies that have been tried where the show window has not been properly constructed are as follows:

Rub the glass with a solution of equal parts of alcohol and glycerine, allowing the solution to remain on the glass.

Set an electric fan on the inside of the window, so that it will blow directly on the glass.

The best solution is to see that your show windows are properly ventilated, and in order to be properly ventilated they must be cased in.—Hardware Age.

SHELVES INCREASE WINDOW DISPLAY SPACE.

As a means of increasing the display space in their windows, the Alexander Hardware Co., Hamilton, Ont., have had shelves placed at the rear of their windows. When small articles are being shown this allows the display of a much larger number of articles. The shelves are made of glass and can be raised or lowered to any position in the window. Thus if the display proper rises up quite a distance, the shelves may merely be used at the top for a supplementary display.

Advertising Furniture Clearance Sales
BY A. B. LEVER

For another month or six weeks a good many furniture dealers throughout the country will be conducting clearance sales. In order that these sales may be successful a certain amount of advertising must be done. The advertisements which I am reproducing this month are among the best which have appeared in newspapers published in different parts of the country. They are in styles and descriptions various and are likely, therefore, to be of interest to nearly all readers of the Furniture World.

The advertisement of Luke Bros. was 6¾ by 15 inches, and is a good example of what can be done with fairly large space in bringing before the public, in a simple, straight-forward manner, the bargains which the dealer is offering. The advertisement has two commendable features. It first of all stands out well and in the second place it is "newsy." There are some advertisements which stand out well, but they are not "newsy," and therefore neither impress the public nor sell goods. I came across an advertisement the other day which occupied a half-page in a daily newspaper. But it was a jumble of words and type which distracted instead of attracted. I do not think I ever saw an advertisement of Luke Bros. which was of this kind. While I believe in using illustrations in furniture advertisements, yet this advertisement is a good example of what can be done without an engraving of any kind. I might further say that this is a good style of advertisement for dealers in small towns, where only weekly papers are published.

Much the same can be said of the second advertisement in the group. It is clipped from a department store announcement, and was 6¼ by 3½ inches. There is one thing I particularly like about this ad., and that is the terse and pointed way in which reference is made to the service the sales staff of the firm are prepared to render. It is a good thing to impress service, provided the service is rendered.

The advertisement of the Hastings Furniture Co., Limited, Vancouver, is, taking it all round, the best in the ground. Artistically it is practically all that can be desired. At any rate it ranks high in this respect. Here its chief purpose is to emphasize one thing, and that is that the firm are offering a suite of furniture that cost them the price at which they are prepared to sell it. This sounds better than saying they are offering it below cost, and is probably more assuring to the public. Although a great many dealers are no doubt uttering a truism when they say they are advertising below cost, yet there has occasionally been a reckless use of the term, until among the public there are a good many "Doubting Thomases." The original ad. was 6¾ by 6.

Gordon & Keith, Halifax, have made good use of their 4¾ by 6 inch space. They have not attempted to get too much matter into it, and the whole is arranged with good judgment. The engraving is just large enough to be in keeping with the size of the ad. I think, however, the last line, "Furniture, carpets, stoves, ranges," might have been dropped and the address put in a little larger type. It would have given a little better balance to the ad. This is not, however, a serious defect, as the ad. is on the whole a good one.

The advertisement of the Lord Furniture Co., Ottawa, is a good example of how small space can be utilized with good effect. The original was only 2¼ by 3⅝ inches, but it arrested the attention. It is an encouraging ad. for those who do not advertise because they think they cannot afford large space in daily newspapers.

The advertisement of Freiman, Ottawa, is an example of how, with the exercise of a little skill in arrangement, a great deal of matter can be crowded into an ad. without giving it a bewildering appearance. The ad. is also well written and no doubt drew business. The original was 6½ by 7 inches.

The advertisement of D. A. Smith, Limited, Vancouver, could not fail to arrest attention, and particularly that of people who were furnishing their home. "Furnish your Home at Half-Price" is a catching phrase, and is original as far as I am aware. If I may, however, be allowed to make a suggestion I would say that the ad. would have been a little more in keeping with its purpose if the lines devoted to desks and go-carts had been left out and the space used by lines strictly appertaining to home furnishings. The original size of the ad. was 6⅝ by 9½ inches.

The dining-room furniture ad., which is next in order is from a department store announcement, and is another example of an effective one-line advertisement. It is also to be commended for the briefness and terseness of its phraseology. There is no waste of words.

The advertisement of J. M. McDonald is another of those little "newsy" ads. The display type used in the first three lines might have been improved upon, three different series being employed, but that is the fault of the printer.

Brager's ad. is another good instance of the wisdom of devoting moderate-sized space in a daily newspaper to advertising one line of goods, and it is made all the more effective by the illustration at the top. The ad. is neat, artistic and should have brought business to the store. The original was 4¼ by 6 inches.

ADVERTISING FURNITURE IN A SMALL TOWN

The average country merchant advertises in his home weekly newspaper because he feels that he ought to give the editor some encouragement.

Therefore, because he takes little or no interest in what the advertisement says, he seldom changes it, and still more seldom does he have anything in the advertisement that grips the reader, and thereby brings him trade.

The ordinary advertisement in a weekly newspaper reads like a label. Few of them deal in anything but generalities. Such advertisements are probably not worth anywhere near what they cost. About all they do is keep the name of the dealer before the reader. But in a small community nearly everyone knows a merchant who has been in business any length of time, so simply keeping his name before the public is of little use.

Many furniture dealers leave the writing of their advertisements to the editor. They order their space, sometimes amounting to a page, and tell him to write a "good strong ad." They do not furnish him with a single price, description, or selling argument of any kind. All he gets is orders to fill the space.

When the country merchant learns to write snappy advertising, filled with plain talk and prices, then he will have less cause to sit by the stove in the rear of the store and assail the mail-order houses.

TALKS TO TRADE PAPER ADVERTISERS
By Frank Farrington

You cannot put into your advertising space any talk that will do more to make the dealer appreciate the advertisement than a good selling argument for him to use.

The dealer who has your goods in his store will welcome at any time any tips on how to make more sales.

The dealer who has none of your goods will be the more apt to take them on if you show him how he can easily persuade the consumer to buy.

Even the dealer who has carried your line and thrown it out because it did not sell may be shown selling arguments which will cause him to think that the reason the line did not move may have been because he did not understand how to sell it.

Make your trade advertising talk a help to the dealers, and the dealers will make them a help for you.

It is more than likely that by asking the dealers to bring you samples of the selling talks they have used, you will get hold of a lot of new arguments that you and your office force have never uncovered.

The more selling ability the dealers possess, the more of your goods they will be able to sell.

It is very likely that the dealers do not know all the uses of your product. See that it is no fault of yours they don't. The more uses they know, the more uses the consumer will know and follow.

ADVERTISING AND REPUTATION

A man who advertises dishonestly is looking for present profits regardless of his future. The honest merchant who intends to remain in business cannot afford to make his sales in that way. He has too much to lose and nothing to gain in the long run.

It is to be said to the credit of the advertising agencies that scarcely an agency can be found which is willing to handle extravagant, dishonest advertising. They are opposed to dishonesty on general priciples, and they also do not care to risk their own reputations by helping along a business of this kind.

A close scrutiny of statements made through the public press will do much to increase the prestige of the reputable merchant.

Examples of special and clearance sale advertisements made by Canadian Furniture Dealers.

Beds and Bedding

NEW ALASKA REPRESENTATIVE IN EAST

The Alaska Feather & Down Co., Ltd., Montreal, have appointed G. L. Towner to represent them in eastern Quebec, in place of H. V. Bernier, who has resigned from the service of the company. Mr. Towner has been with Alaska Feather & Down Co. since boyhood—joining the staff in 1904—in which time he has occupied various positions, mostly in connection with sales department work. He was for some years on the Montreal city order desk; later he had charge of the country orders, and afterwards was warehouse salesman, besides having some knowledge of manufacturing details. In all of these positions Mr. Towner has had ample opportunity of learning all about Alaska bedding, and so is qualified to introduce and sell Alaska products.

NEW QUEBEC BEDDING COMPANY

The "Victoriaville Bedding Co., Ltd.," Victoriaville, Que. is the title of a new concern recently incorporated at Ottawa to make furniture, beds, mattresses and accessories. The capital stock is $150,000, and the incorporators are Paul Tourigny, D. H. Pennington and J. Z. Auger.

ADDING NEW GROUND.

H. W. Hare, who works Northern Ontario for the Ideal Bedding Co., will in future cover the counties of Grey and Dufferin, with the exception of Hanover, in Grey County, which will continue to be worked by Mr. Thies. This change became effective on January 1st.

NEW GEORGIA MATTRESS

The Ideal Bedding Co., Ltd., Toronto, recently announced that "effective January 1st our 'Dixie' mattress will be withdrawn from the market and we will substitute the "Georgia" mattress at the same price." This new mattress is said to be superior in many ways to the one which it replaces, being finished with a roll edge, for which no extra charge is made. All orders calling for "Dixie" mattresses, after the first of the year, will be filled with these "Georgia."

NEW WEISGLASS TRADE MARK

S. Weisglass, Ltd., Montreal, are directing the attention of the trade to their new trade mark, which they have adopted for the bed springs they manufacture. This company has been turning out high grade springs for some time, but it was just recently that they decided to direct more energy to this department in an effort to produce the best springs in the country. They have spent a large sum of money in equipping that department with modern and up-to-date machinery and with a staff of skilled workmen. They expect the springs to meet with favor.

SLIDING SHOES ON IDEAL BRASS BEDS.

To meet the wishes of some of their customers who have requested them, the Ideal Bedding Co., Toronto, are furnishing when required, glass sliding shoes with all their two-inch post brass beds. This will add 35 cents to the price of the bed. However, they will also furnish a set of casters with each bed, in case the user desires to make a change at any time. These sliding shoes are made wholly of glass. They are locked into the tubing with a notch, so that they cannot become loose, although they can be easily taken out. They are specially recommended where a bedroom has a hardwood floor, because they do not scratch, neither will they damage a rug or carpet.

TWO NEW BED FACTORIES

There is talk in the trade to the effect that the bed factory erected at Preston for the Anchor Bed Company will be taken over by a new company including representatives of the T. Eaton Co. and the Page Hersey Iron and Tube Company. The Ingram bed spring may be one of the lines manufactured, but brass beds will probably be the main product.

The Mesereau Metal Bed Co., of Jersey City, N.J., propose, it is said, to erect a factory in Toronto for the making of metal beds. They will confine themselves to the brass line at first. For the past two years the company have had a warehouse in Toronto.

"SAFETY FIRST."

Following the lead of the big railway companies, which are now emphasizing the great principle of "safety first," the Ideal Bedding Co., Toronto, have decided that in future all their "Ideal" cribs equipped with the patented safety catch will have that catch painted red instead of having it brass-plated. The touch of color makes the crib look effective, but the great point is that the dangerous part of the crib is the latch. If it is not secure the side may drop and the baby fall out. The red spot will draw attention to safety.

A man without ambition is like a bird without wings. He can never soar in the heights above, but must walk like a weakling, unnoticed with the crowd below.—Walter H. Cottingham.

Knobs of News

The Battleford Furniture & Plumbing Co., Battleford, Sask., has dissolved.

Schwartz & Co., furniture dealers of Waldeck, Sask., have sold their business to Peters & Janzen.

Shillington Bros., of Laura, Sask., furniture and hardware dealers, are selling their hardware stock to J. C. Gordon.

The stock of the estate of Frank Betts & Co., furniture dealers, of Yorkton, Sask., has been sold to Rindeknecht & Wilson.

James Ramsay, Ltd., Edmonton, have purchased part of the stock of the Cope-Fletcher Co., of Saskatoon, Sask., valued at $40,000.

W. H. Heath & Son, furniture dealers of Wilkesport, Ont., will continue his Sombra, Ont., business under the same management.

H. Gracey contemplates erecting a furniture store and undertaking parlors at Smithville, Ont., to replace the building destroyed by fire recently.

Jonas Howe, a prominent citizen of St. John, N.B., and for many years a member of the furniture manufacturing firm of J. & J. D. Howe, died December 15th, at the age of 74.

H. T. Rapp, formerly with the Hepworth Furniture Co. for many years, is now covering Western Ontario for Peppler Bros., Hanover. He is making Stratford his headquarters.

Joseph Meyers, an employee of the Knechtel Furniture Co., Walkerville, was instantly killed recently while unloading logs from a car at the company's siding at the G. T. R. depot.

The Vegreville Furniture Co., Vegreville, Alta., has sold out to the National Co-Operative Co., Limited, Vegreville. The taking over of furniture is a new venture for the last named concern.

J. Critelli, Thorold, Ont., is building a solid brick store in that town, 47 x 60 feet for retailing purposes. It is understood that the upper floor will be used for furniture and the lower floor as a general store.

R. G. Grieve & Co., Tofield, Alta., announce that they have disposed of an interest in their furniture, hardware and implement business to Geo. Meizanghlin, and the firm will in future be known as Grieve-McLaughlin, Ltd.

J. M. Weber, formerly with the Hobbs Mfg. Co., is now representing the North American Furniture Co., the Owen Sound Chair Co., and the National Table Co., all of Owen Sound, covering Western Ontario for them, and making his headquarters at London.

At the completion of the half-mile in the indoor races held at the Windsor rink, Windsor, N.S., recently, H. B. Tremain, M.P., on behalf of the Windsor Furniture Co.'s employees, presented Frank Ettinger with a handsome silver dish for his excellent showing in the Halifax to Windsor race.

E. F. Best, of Best & Son, Thamesville, Ont., has bought H. Huffman's furniture business at Simcoe, Ont. Mr. Best is a believer in advertising and contemplates having an up-to-date service to push his new business. As he expresses it, "the kind that will bring grist to the mill."

W. D. Thomas, proprietor of the People's Outfitting Co., London, has had such an increase in business that he has found it necessary to build 100 feet on to his store, making the total length of the basement and main floor 165 feet. In connection with these alterations, Mr. Thomas has carried out a very enterprising scheme for the attractive display of the various line he carries. On the west side of the building, he has had erected a gallery 100 feet long. The space underneath this gallery has been divided into rooms, which Mr. Thomas has furnished in most tasteful manner with beds, and various other articles of household furniture that he has for sale.

SOUTHAMPTON FURNITURE BY-LAW CARRIED

The by-law submitted to the ratepayers of Southampton, Ont., guaranteeing the bonds of the Steel Furniture Co., was carried by a vote of 206 to 13.

PRESENTATION TO MR. MOORE

The employees of the Stratford Manufacturing Co., Stratford, Ont., recently presented Chas. A. Moore, manager and secretary-treasurer of the company, with a handsome club bag as a slight token of the esteem in which he is held by the employees of the firm.

FURNITURE FACTORIES WANTED

Ft. William, Ont., Darmody, Forgray, Linstrom, Melville, Rowletta, and Stoney Beach, Sask.; Edmonton and Tofield, Alta., and Port Edward, B.C., are said to want furniture factories. Ft. William and Melville want as well school furniture plants.

WANT FURNITURE STORES IN WEST

Openings for furniture stores are said to exist in Allan, Cudworth, Grandora, Leney, Meacham, Talmage and Young, Sask. Also in Beiseker, Holden, Huxley, Mirror and Wabamun, Alta. Those interested should write the secretaries of the boards of trade at these places.

FURNITURE FACTORY BURNED

A general alarm brought out the whole Quebec fire brigade for a fire that had broken out in the Valliere Furniture Company's factory at St. Roch and St. Valliere streets, on the night of Jan. 12. The sawmill was completely gutted. The furniture factory was also destroyed, and the showrooms on St. Valliere street, with the valuable contents. All the buildings destroyed were four-storey brick structures. Nothing is left standing but the walls. A conservative estimate places the loss at $100,000. Insurance was carried.

FURNITURE MEN IN MUNICIPAL LIFE

The municipal elections held recently throughout the country brought to the front a number of furniture men who will act as legislative leaders in their communities during this present year. Among those elected as mayor are the following: D. Lippert, Neustadt; J. J. Marsh, Smith's Falls; and F. W. Lippert, Walkerton.

D. M. Wright, of the McLagan Co., Stratford, was elected alderman; so was G. A. Grentzner, of the Hespeler Furniture Co., at Hespeler, H. H. Scott was elected to the council at Smith's Falls; James Malcolm to the Kincardine council, and C. Woeller to Waterloo council.

S. M. Smyth, of the Strathroy Furniture Co., was made a water commissioner in his home town.

BIG BED BUSINESS BOOKED

A token of the Brightening Business Outlook was the splendid volume of orders for Beds given us at our display at the

TORONTO FURNITURE EXHIBITION

We were delighted to demonstrate our moderate priced line of Iron Beds to several hundred furniture dealers, and were gratified at the many and large orders given us.

1914 WILL BE A GOOD YEAR

for us, and it will be an equally good year for you if you put in a stock of Canada Beds.

M. A. Halliday, President   *We'll soon publish a new Catalogue. Send us your name.*   G. N. Griffin, Manager

CANADA BEDS, LIMITED   CHESLEY, ONT.

The Furniture Exhibition a Gratifying Success

To the Furniture Dealers of Canada who made the Toronto Furniture Exhibition a splendid business success we voice our sincere appreciation. Many customers showed their faith in Kindel Convertible Parlor Furniture by ordering several samples from the pieces shown.

Literature gladly furnished

The "KINDEL" Kind

Where Quality Counts

Made up to a standard —not down to a price.

The Kindel Bed Co., Limited
Toronto   Ontario

A Display of H.E. Kitchen Cabinets Produces Sales

WHEREVER they are shown—at the Furniture Exhibitions, on your floors, in the home of the user—the outstanding merits of H.E. Kitchen Cabinets draw attention and develop more profitable business.

Displaying H.E. Kitchen Cabinets at the Toronto Furniture Exhibition. Note the many attractive combinations and their exclusive conveniences.

H.E. Kitchen Cabinets incorporate the removable flour bin; clean, smooth, washable, sanitary interiors and the roller curtain doors. Write us for complete descriptions of these sure profit-makers.

H. E. Furniture Co., Limited
Milverton   Ontario

Cost Figures—
Do You Know Them?

One Linderman User writes:

"Here is the result of our experience with the 'Linderman' at this plant in the manufacture of case goods as promised when you were here last.

On an average output of 15,000 lineal feet of joint per day, we find by actual test that our GLUE COST figures 19 cents per thousand lineal feet of joint.

On a consumption of 6,000 feet of $23 per M lumber per day, we find a daily saving of $15.00, including the blocks which we utililize in core stock, by means of the variable cut device on the 'Linderman,' which does away with the edging waste on the rip-saw.

The trimmings from the cut off saw, as short as 2 inches, which we formerly had to dispose of for fuel purposes, are now being used in cores. Including labor and glue and handling, these cores stand us $3.85 per M feet of lumber. This is a saving that is patent to any good furniture manufacturer.

The 'Linderman' permits us to manufacture lumber to 24-inch widths from random sizes, and any length desired for the work. This original method gives us an ample supply of stock at all times to be ripped to any bill sizes."

Twenty-nine Furniture Plants in Canada will testify to the benefits they receive. Let us show you what you can do

Canadian Linderman Co., Limited

FACTORIES AT

Muskegon, Mich.   Woodstock, Ont.

Anglo Rubbing and Polishing Varnish

None Better Made

A RECENT addition to the many world-known lines of Ault & Wiborg manufacture. Produced after years of experimenting and testing, it will afford you the most pleasing results.

Made to rub in twenty-four hours, two days and three days. Works free and easy. Polishes with a beautiful finish.

There's economy with a high standard of excellence in the use of our Varnishes, Enamels, Graining Colors, etc.

Write for Prices and Samples

Ault & Wiborg Company of Canada, Limited
Varnish Works,
MONTREAL   TORONTO   WINNIPEG

ROBERTSON SOCKET HEAD Wood Screws

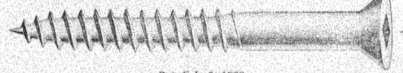

See That Square Hole

Pat. Feb. 2, 1909

THIS IS A REAL WOOD SCREW

It is driven by a simple square bit, and is the only one of its type on the market.

Driver fits snugly into the square hole and positively cannot slip and cut the fingers, or disfigure costly furniture or woodwork. It is driven with less exertion. No ragged slots after driving. Saves time, labor, money and material. We make the drivers in all suitable styles.

Drivers sent free with first order. Write for catalogue and prices.

P. L. Robertson Mfg. Co., Limited
MILTON :: ONTARIO

Dominion Casket Co., Limited

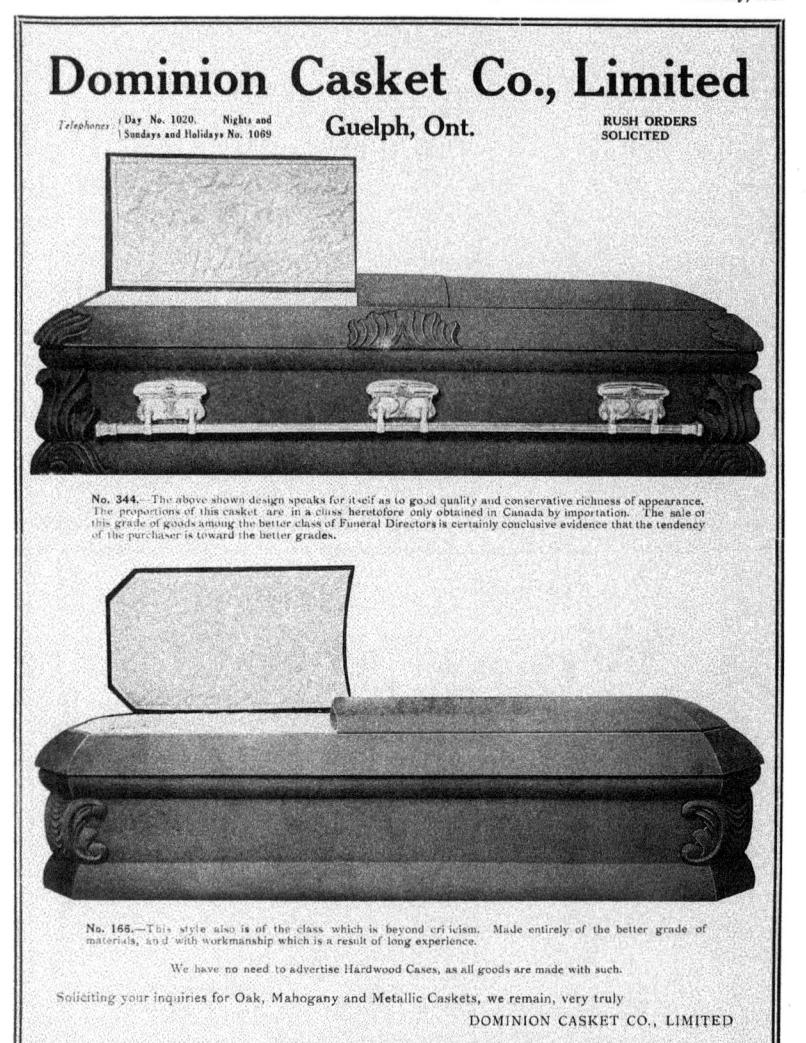

Telephones { Day No. 1020. Nights and Sundays and Holidays No. 1069 }

Guelph, Ont.

RUSH ORDERS SOLICITED

No. 344.—The above shown design speaks for itself as to good quality and conservative richness of appearance. The proportions of this casket are in a class heretofore only obtained in Canada by importation. The sale of this grade of goods among the better class of Funeral Directors is certainly conclusive evidence that the tendency of the purchaser is toward the better grades.

No. 166.—This style also is of the class which is beyond criticism. Made entirely of the better grade of materials, and with workmanship which is a result of long experience.

We have no need to advertise Hardwood Cases, as all goods are made with such.

Soliciting your inquiries for Oak, Mahogany and Metallic Caskets, we remain, very truly

DOMINION CASKET CO., LIMITED

Undertakers' Department

Problems affecting the Undertaking Profession are here discussed and readers are invited to send letters expressing their views on any of the subjects dealt with—News of the profession throughout Canada.

CURRENT UNDERTAKING TOPICS

He Set a Good Example. Mr. A. J. H. Eckardt, of the National Casket Company, Limited, was a candidate for the Board of Control at the last municipal elections in Toronto.

Although he was not elected, he received nearly eight thousand votes, a creditable number indeed, in view of the fact that Mr. Eckardt entered the arena at the eleventh hour.

Mr. Eckardt is to be commended for his courage.

He is also to be commended for something else. He is to be commended for setting an example to manufacturers in particular and business men in general.

Business men with the civic spirit are all too rare, and when a new case of it develops we should not be backward in tendering congratulations.

* * * *

Undertakers and Their Associations. In The Casket of recent date a writer says: "It is a sad fact, but true that among a given number of embalmers and undertakers, three-fourths of them are at loggerheads. Why such a condition of affairs should exist is beyond the knowledge of the writer. There is no objection to a healthy competition, in fact such a competition has the tendency to keep the embalming profession and the undertaking business at its best, which if it did not exist would soon show signs of nonprogression and retrogression. Destructive competition is a benefit to no one, in fact it is a great detriment, not only to the men personally and professionally, but also to their clientage."

While this applies directly to undertakers and embalmers in the United States the statement should not be without some interest to members of the profession in Canada.

That three-fourths of the embalmers and undertakers in Canada are at loggerheads we do not for one moment believe, but that there are some who are not on the best of terms is equally certain.

But even were the number large or small the importance of organization cannot be denied. There are now good organizations in every part of Canada, so that no undertaker has any excuse for not belonging to one.

Membership in a funeral directors' organization does not destroy competition, but it tends to strip it of its most objectionable features and to develop among the members a laudable esprit de corps instead of a spirit of bitter antagonism.

* * * *

Lady Assistants. A good deal is heard these days in all civilized countries about lady assistants in the undertaking profession. As Canada is no exception to the rule, we take the liberty of giving the opinion of a woman (Mrs. E. L. Hahn) who is engaged in the undertaking profession, in regard to the subject.

"An undertaker," she says, "should be careful in selecting a lady assistant, else it might not prove to be a good business proposition, in fact being detrimental. First, she should be a lady; second, she should have reasonably good health, dress plain and neat; third, to be able to successfully cope with any and all conditions. I find that she must be endowed with a disposition to readily adjust herself to conditions as she finds them, in other words she should be able to move with as much grace and ease in the house of the rich as in that of the poor. She should be a lady of a strong personality, and one who is able to say and do the right thing at the right time, and above all things to say only what is necessary. It is very necessary that she be conservative and patient, always ready to carry out the wishes of the family and to be kind and tender to all. To be a successful proposition, let your lady understand when she leaves the house of mourning that what she has seen and heard at that home shall be left as much a secret as is possible; for at that particular time those experiences to that family are sacred and not intended as material for gossip. To be a successful proposition it is necessary that you select the lady to do all your work. Don't pick up Miss Smith this time, Miss Jones next time and Mrs. Brown next time, and so on. That is an injustice to both Miss Jones and yourself. No two ladies will do work alike, and you do not get a chance to become accustomed to each other's work, and the work is in a great many instances unsatisfactory. Use great care in selecting some good lady in your neighborhood (if you have not work for her all of the time), tell her what you expect of her and call her on every case, thereby allowing her to become accustomed to the work, and in that way give you better service."

* * * *

Services at Cremations. The Bishop of Rochester, England, is quite friendly to cremations. In fact he thinks its future is assured. But he is of opinion that the burial services, where cremation is employed, should be held after cremation, the urn containing the ashes being treated just as the coffin was treated in the Prayer Book service, buried out of sight in the churchyard, the burial registered in the parish register, and the place of interment kept a sacred spot for the pious care of relatives. They should be prepared to secure that the practice be not associated with any carelessness on the religious side. "It might help them ultimately," he said, "to a closer connection with our sanctuaries of Christian prayer and hope than in these days of vast and crowded cemeteries. Our cathedrals and our churches might, like our closed churchyards, once more become the resting-place of our sacred dead, under the very shadow of the church."

A. M. Shaver, lately of Shaver, Armstrong & Macpherson, undertakers and embalmers, Calgary, stopped off for a day or two on his way to New York recently, whither he went on business.

Western Service

Always at Your Service

UNDERTAKERS handling *Western* Caskets and Funeral supplies know that with every order they get *Quality* — the assurance that they are right and that their customers will be pleased.

Our stock is fast being completed and by end of month we expect to be in full swing.

We have to thank the trade at large for their many enquiries and also for the large volume of business which has already reached us.

The Western Casket Co., Limited

Cor. Emily St. and Bannatyne Ave.   Winnipeg, Manitoba

Open Day and Night

G. S. Thompson   A. W. Robinson   G. H. Lawrence

Blood Draining
By H. S. Eckels, Ph.B

I suppose that at this late day I should preface any talk about blood drainage, the axillary method with an apology to those who for years have found in it by far the most satisfactory method of embalming yet devised. Really it does seem at this advanced day that any argument on the subject is superfluous. Under normal circumstances, I should make none. To me and to the thousands of others who have used the axillary artery for injection and the axillary vein for drainage, it would seem that this method had so many advantages that they would be apparent to everyone. More than one-half of all the embalmers of America to-day rely almost exclusively on this system.

Naturally a good many of those who learned the art before the invention of the axillary tubes still cling to the old way of injecting fluid through the brachial artery and draining what blood they do drain through a trocar barbarously thrust into the heart—when they hit the heart, which I beg to assure you is very far from invariable.

I certainly have no fault to find with those who cling to the old customs. There is a saying as old as history that "You can't teach an old dog new tricks." This really should read "You can't teach some old dogs new tricks," for in my experience I have found that the most apt pupils were some who, while old in years, were decidedly young and progressive in spirit. Age is no criterion. The progressive man is as progressive at ninety as he is at nineteen.

But I started to talk about the axillary method. I am impelled to do this because my attention has recently been called to addresses delivered before two state associations by two supposedly eminent lecturers, in which the axillary method was scoffed at to the limited limit of the ability of the speakers. To say that I was surprised is putting it rather mildly. It was rather to be expected, as I have said, that a few undertakers would still cling to old methods, but that a lecturer and would-be teacher should try to tell an intelligent audience that the axillary tubes were of no utility and were exploited only because the inventor was the manufacturer of them would be laughable if it were not pathetic.

Injection in Normal Cases

Now, let us for a moment analyze the situation dispassionately and see where that analysis brings us. To insure preservation the embalmer must inject in normal cases about one quart of fluid to each fifty pounds of body weight. Personally, I think that he would better inject a little more of a little milder fluid because I believe that better effects can be produced; but in general practice, the average embalmer uses about the quantity I have mentioned.

The first question to arise is: Into what artery shall this fluid be injected? We have our choice of many, and on some bodies it is necessary for us to take up several. On ninety-five cases out of a hundred, however, one artery will suffice, if the injection be carried on carefully and continued until signs of embalming are everywhere apparent. What artery then shall we select?

In the earlier days of embalming, when preservation only was aimed at, the femorals and the iliacs were most largely used. It soon became evident, however, that by the use of these arteries preservation was no more thorough than with some others, and also that cosmetic effect was pretty nearly an absolute impossibility. There was a further objection that on the bodies of women and children, an unnecessary and offensive exposure was inevitable. The choice of arteries then shifted and the radial was, for a short time, quite commonly use. Common sense soon demonstrated, however, that to inject fluid into the radial artery, one of the smallest of the main trunk arteries in the body, was to inject your embalming medium through the small end of the funnel. It was only natural, therefore, that the embalmer soon began to follow the course of this trunk artery upward and raise it higher in the arm and nearer the heart.

The Axillary Now Used

The brachial artery held its sway longer perhaps than did any other, until the axillary was used. Indeed, the brachial is still used to a limited extent, although why, it is difficult to understand, for by its use the embalmer merely went a little higher up the funnel.

After the carotids had been tested and the objections to their universal use carefully considered, the axillary was selected by a very great proportion of the really progressive directors of the country. The reasons for this were many, but among them may be cited the following facts:

1.—That the incision need be only a small one, since both vein and artery lie very near the surface in the axillary space (the armpit).

2.—That at no point of the body does a large trunk artery come so near the surface as here.

3.—That the incision is more easily concealed from the inspection of the curious than at any other point in the body.

4.—That by the use of the flexible arterial tube, it is easy for the embalmer to inject fluid directly into the arch of the aorta.

5.—That injecting fluid directly into the arch of the aorta starts the fluid in its course through the arterial system at the same point at which Nature begins the circulation of the blood and that, therefore, it reaches all of the trunk arteries, their branches and sub-branches, with the same relative pressure which Nature gives to the blood in life.

6.—That by using the axilarry artery, we are, therefore, approaching as closely as possible to Nature's own method.

7.—That through this same incision the axillary vein may be picked up and by means of the G.E. axillary drainage tube blood may be drained directly from the superior vena cava, the main blood reservoir in the upper portion of the body and the one into which drain all of the veins from those portions of the body which it is desirable to beautify for funeral purposes.

8.—That by the use of those tubes, the drainage of the blood is absolutely controllable at the will of the operator, who can start or stop the drainage at any instant he wishes without the withdrawal of the tubes.

9.—That by having the drainage of the blood absolutely at his control, reflushing can be absolutely prevented.

10.—That by withdrawing blood from the superior vena cava, it is possible to drain more blood from the points where it is most objectionable to cosmetic effect than is possible by any other method.

There are a hundred other reasons why the axillary method should commend itself to every lecturer and teacher of embalming, but I shall not go into it at this time. Rather I would like to discuss the general subject of blood drainage and its advisability, a proposition which was denied by one of the lecturers to whom I referred earlier.

It must be apparent that two bodies cannot occupy the same space at the same time. If, therefore, we are

Dominion Manufacturers
Limited

MANUFACTURERS OF

Fine Funeral Requisites

We guarantee

The Highest Quality

and the

Quickest Possible Service

*Night or Day Orders
given Prompt Attention*

BRANCHES

The Globe Casket Co., and Branches	London, Ontario
The Semmons & Evel Casket Co., and Branches,	Hamilton, Ontario
The National Casket Co.	Toronto, Ontario
Jas. S. Elliot & Son	Prescott, Ontario
Girard & Godin and Branches	Three Rivers, Quebec
Christie Bros. & Co,	Amherst, N. S.

FRED W. COLES
General Manager

D. M. ANDREWS
Secretary Treasurer

HEAD OFFICE

468 King Street W., Toronto

to inject from three-quarters of a gallon to a gallon of embalming fluid into the average body, it should be very apparent that it is desirable for us to withdraw at least as nearly the same quantity of blood as possible, if only to make room for the fluid. This, however, is not the only reason for blood drainage. It is true that to inject a gallon of fluid into many bodies without withdrawing blood would be to give a puffed and swollen appearance, which would be alike displeasing to the family and to the conscientious undertaker.

Embalming Fluids Astringent

There is, however, a still greater reason and one far more vital to good embalming. This is that all embalming fluids are more or less astringent in their action, and that raw formaldehyde fluids in particular have the peculiar faculty of pasting, as it were, the red corpuscles of the blood against the walls of the smaller arterial branches and of sealing up the blood corpuscles in the capiliaries. The chemical action of these fluids upon the corpuscles also assists the natural tendency of the corpuscles to become darker in color. The result is, as this pigment is visible through the skin, it gradually turns from a reddish color to a very dark tint where it is present in large quantities and shows a putty color through the skin everywhere else. This objectionable putty color can be obviated in only two ways, or rather by a combination of two ways. One is the drainage of every possible bit of blood from the upper part of the body—the face and the hands. The second is the injection of a fluid which is blood solvent in its nature (preferably a peroxide of hydrogen fluid) which will force these corpuscles of blood ahead of it and wash them out from the tiny corpuscles into the superior vena cava whence they will be drained through the axillary artery and into your blood bottle. If they stay in the capiliaries they inevitably will stain the skin and inevitably will show a putty color or worse.

To me and those fifteen or twenty thousand undertakers who have had success with them, the use of the axillary vein tubes are so logical and the results obtained so satisfactory that it seems positively laughable to have a so-called doctor and a so-called professor denounce them. It was but natural that when these tubes were first introduced, nearly ten years ago, that they should have been met with skepticism on the part of some and hostility on the part of others. This was to have been expected and is the fate of every innovation. It is too late now, however, for any man, no matter what his motive, to assail them. They have demonstrated their efficiency so thoroughly and are used by progressive undertakers so universally, that for a "teacher" to attack either their value or their manufacturer is to say the least absurd.

ECKELS' DEMONSTRATION AT BUFFALO

A very successful series of lectures and embalming demonstrations were given by Prof. H. S. Eckels, of Philadelphia, in the parlors of the Central Casket Co., at Buffalo, during the week January 5 to 10. There were in attendance 200 undertakers and embalmers from territory in Ontario and nearby states adjacent to Buffalo, and every person present felt greatly benefited by the lectures and work performed.

Of those present there were at least a dozen ladies, and the Ontario profession was represented by sixteen undertakers and embalmers.

Some of the up-to-the-minute subjects Prof. Eckels discussed and demonstrated were: "How to handle that most difficult of all difficult cases—jaundice—so as to restore a life-like complexion and to prevent the yellow and green color usually found in such cases"; "how to embalm a dropsy case in the quickest, cleanest and most satisfactory manner"; "how to lift twenty years from the appearance of a consumptive or other greatly emaciated cases"; "how to restore to a life-like appearance bodies which show disfigurements from accidents and from cancer and similar diseases"; "how to inject fluid directly into arch of aorta, at the same time draining blood directly from the superior vena cava through the same incision—and that incision in the most obscure part of the body—the arm pit'"; "how to secure the perfect and permanent preservation of the body without the sacrifice of the cosmetic effect"; "how to care for sunken eyeballs and how to restore them to their proper shape and fullness without the use of eyecaps or other devices which the family might discover."

Assisting Prof. Eckels was G. W. Bates; and other speakers were Dr. Wm. Jacobs, Buffalo, an authority

Prof. H. S. Eckels, Philadelphia, who conducted the lectures.

on post mortem, who gave a splendid address on "Autopsy," as also did W. C. Harrington, who spoke on "Skin-slip."

Among the Ontario men registering were: C. M. G. Smith, Barrie; Norman Craig, Toronto; David Clark, Orillia; J. M. Taylor, Tillsonburg; C. E. St. Aucour, Montreal; J. H. Cameron, Fort William; Ross Craig and wife, Toronto; H. Ellis, Toronto; Mr. Guernsey and wife, Hamilton; H. Gracey, Smithville; G. W. C. Graham, Toronto; Robt. Flint, Toronto; Robt. Stone, Toronto; C. R. Woodburn, Ottawa; Geo. H. Hensberger, Toronto, and J. H. Atwood, Bridgeburg.

EMPTY COFFIN BURIED

A strange burial incident is reported from Burton-on-Trent. The child of a domestic servant died in the workhouse infirmary. A coffin was prepared, and eventually there was a funeral.

Some days afterwards it was discovered that the body supposed to have been buried was still in the house, and that the service had been held over an empty coffin. The second interment took place in the same grave, on the top of the empty coffin.

Burglar Proof and Water Tight

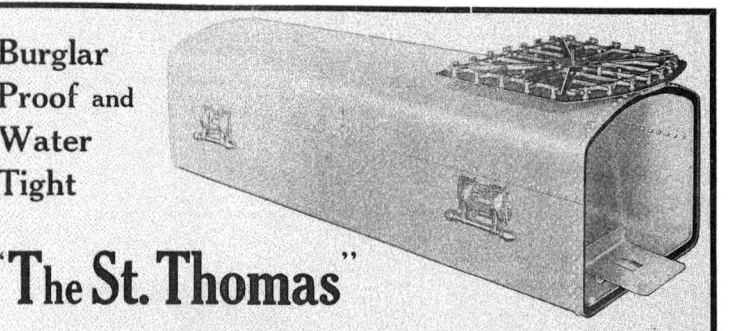

"The St. Thomas"

Original, Quick Closing End Vault

MANUFACTURED BY

The St. Thomas Metallic Vault Company, Limited
ST. THOMAS, ONTARIO

Springfield's New Toncan Metal Caskets

The Biggest and Best Value Ever Offered

This new design is a winner. For a moderate priced casket it has no equal.

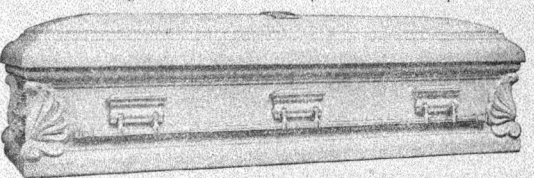

The "JACKSON"

Broadcloth Covered. Made without inner top. Trimmed complete with Antique Silver extension handles and name plate, lined with figured Artsilk Pillow Set. Face Cap hinged and lined to match pillow set.

The "JORDAN." Made with an inner top which contains half length glass and can be sealed air tight. Lined and trimmed same as the "Jackson." ¶ Toncan Metal possesses greater strength than copper, is a worthy substitute for copper, and in every instance is superior to rolled steel. It is noncorrosive because of its purity, is made to withstand the climatic and atmospheric effects of today. ¶ Toncan Metal Caskets are good for all time. Send for full description and large illustration. ¶ Springfield All Steel Welded Grave Vaults, seven styles in all, are the best selling grave vaults on the market, try them.

Springfield Products for Sale by all Leading Jobbers

The Springfield Metallic Casket Co'y SPRINGFIELD OHIO, U.S.A.

Undertakers' Association Doings

The Alberta Funeral Directors and Embalmers' Association is evidently a progressive organization, judging by the activity of its officers. The following is a form letter, which the secretary recently sent out, and a couple of replies thereto. They are published with the object of helping other associations in their organization work:—

Alberta Funeral Directors' & Embalmers Association.
Red Deer, Oct. 1913.
Mr. ....
....

Dear Sir:—At our Convention held in the city of Calgary during the month of September, the question came before the meeting of what to do with the members whose dues were in arrears.

This has become a serious matter in connection with the finances of the Association, as the amount outstanding on our books at that time amounted to over $700.

Now you, as a business man, know that it requires money to conduct our yearly Conventions and carry on the work of the Association, pay bills, etc., from year to year. The sum of $5.00, you must admit, is not large when you consider what the Association has done—perhaps not personally for YOU, as you may be one of the few in the Province who, at the time the Association started its work, knew how to embalm a body, and to conduct a funeral—but outside of a few to whom this may apply, the large number of practically new men with little or no knowledge of embalming, etc., have the Association and its work to thank for their success and standing to-day as practical funeral directors and embalmers in the Province of Alberta. —Will you not then continue to help the good work that is being done by the association by keeping your dues paid up that we may have the use of this money which belongs to the association? It is not much to ask for what we are giving, and we wish to keep the name of every funeral director in Alberta and those members in our sister provinces in good standing. This can only be done by their remitting the dues now in arrears.

I have been instructed to collect these dues, and although you may not be aware of the fact, the Alberta Funeral Directors' and Embalmers' Association is an incorporated company, and each member is a stockholder. His stock consists of one share, which, to begin with, costs him $10, and then $5 each following year, as long as he remains a member. This money can legally be collected through the courts, but we would much prefer to have each member send his dues direct to the secretary-treasurer, thereby saving any publicity as well as expense. Then, if they feel that they do not care to remain a member of the association any longer, after paying their indebtedness to the association, they are at liberty to request that their name be struck from the membership roll.

You must also understand that only those members in good standing will have their names sent to the Provincial Board of Examiners, appointed by the Provincial Government, who will grant licenses to all those funeral directors and embalmers who are duly qualified and in business at the time the Embalmers' Act comes in force. This may mean much or nothing to you, therefore you are the best judge as to whether it is worth your while to keep your name on the roll of this association or not. Trusting you will see there is nothing of a personal nature intended by this letter, and only the good of the association. I sincerely hope you will not fail to remit your dues as per statement enclosed before November 1st, 1913.

I remain, your respectfully,
H. G. Stone, Sec.-Treas.

The Replies

"Your letter and statement of Oct. 11th to hand, and was very pleased to receive the same, although it did remind me of my neglect. However, I wish to say that I believe it to be one of the best investments I ever made, and I certainly do not wish to ask for my name to be struck off the roll.

I regret very much that I was unable to attend either of the last two conventions, but, strange to say, on both occasions I have been called out just when I should be thinking of getting ready for the train.

Enclosed please find check for the amount of my dues as per statement received, and I hope I'll need to send you quite a few more yet. Trusting yourself and family are in the best of health, I beg to remain,
".................."

"I am just in receipt of your circular letter in reference to the dues of the above association. Please allow me to say I agree heartily with all you have to say and

Mr. and Mrs. H. G. Stone, of Red Deer, Alta.

my only regret is that it was not possible for me to have been with you at the last convention. I myself at previous conventions always gained considerable more good than could be estimated in the moneys paid for dues, etc. And I sincerely hope that the members will come forward promptly with the money necessary to carry on the very good work of the association. The reason I have not sent my own before is an oversight on my part. I also wish to personally thank you and express my appreciation for all you have done in behalf of the association, and sincerely hope that I shall be able to be with you all at the next convention."

SCATTERED HIS ASHES

The ashes of Charles W. Presley, a rich contractor, were thrown by an undertaker's assistant from the middle of Brooklyn bridge. It was Presley's last request.

DIOXIN
IS PLEASANT TO USE!

IF DIOXIN had no other superiority over the ordinary formaldehyde fluids, the fact that it is safe and pleasant to use should insure it a place in the affections of every embalmer.

If there is any one feature in the care of the dead human body that is more annoying than any other, it is the fact that, except DIOXIN, practically every fluid in the market will literally pickle the hands of most operators, no matter how careful they may be, and, particularly in cold weather, will open up painful sores which it is practically impossible to heal.

DIOXIN users are free from this great annoyance and danger—for every open cut or sore affords a hiding and breeding place for the germs of disease.

CONSIDER YOUR ASSISTANT

Perhaps your assistant does the most of your embalming. Consider his comfort and his health for selfish if for no other reasons. A good assistant, familiar with your wants, your methods and your customers, is a jewel. Make his work as safe and pleasant as you can.

Preserve his delicacy of touch. It may save you the embarrassment of an unsatisfactory result, or even of a spoiled body. There are enough risks in embalming, enough chances for mistakes, enough opportunities for error, without adding others unnecessarily.

Formaldehyde does not dangerously affect the hands of every embalmer, but if must deaden, must dull, the sensitive and delicate nerves of the fingers and render the worker less sure of touch, less certain of results, particularly in difficult cases. You can wash your hands in DIOXIN without injury.

NO TORTURED EYES WITH DIOXIN

The fumes of most fluids, too, in addition to attacking the hands, have a particularly irritating effect upon not only the mucous membranes of the eyelids, but upon the eyes themselves. This is particularly offensive and harmful when the work is done in a warm or brilliantly-lighted room.

DIOXIN DOES NOT EMBALM Your LUNGS

DIOXIN has no injurious effect upon the eyes or eyelids of the operator. The embalmer does not embalm his own eyesight when he uses it. If you or your assistant have suffered from the pungent effects of ordinary raw formaldehyde fluids, try DIOXIN. What little fumes arise from it are pleasant and positively non-irritant. Indeed, we feel that we cannot too strongly recommend DIOXIN to all embalmers who are troubled with failing eyesight—and most users of raw formaldehyde fluids are literally pickling their eyes.

Most of us are almost overcome when entering a room filled with the fumes of formaldehyde. We may not realise it, but we really are literally embalming our own lungs. In DIOXIN, what formaldehyde the fluid does contain, is purified and modified into formochloral, while peroxide of hydrogen, the great bleacher and disinfectant, replaces a very great proportion of this irritating agent.

As a result, DIOXIN has absolutely no deleterious effect upon either the lungs of the operator or the mucous membranes of nostrils and throat.

Dioxin comes in Bulk and Concentrated and RE-Concentrated.

Did we mention the fact that DIOXIN does not fill the house with offensive odors? That is another of its many virtues. And did we say that it makes the body firm, but pliable, rendering posing in the casket easy. Rigidity is not essential to preservation; in fact, it retards the circulation of the fluid.

But we've told you enough—although only a small part of the virtues of DIOXIN. Try it yourself—that is the great convincer. Order to-day!

H. S. ECKELS & CO.
1922 Arch St., Philadelphia, Pa.   241 Fern Ave., Toronto, Ont., Can.

To Canadian Funeral Directors

We were favored with an attendance of nearly a score of the leading Embalmers of Ontario at our Annual School in January, when we had Professor Eckles, of Philadelphia, with us. We will expect an even larger number next year, as the number of our customers in Ontario, Quebec and the other Provinces is steadily increasing.

A FULL LINE READY FOR PROMPT SHIPMENT

The "CENTRAL" Line of mahogany, oak, plush and cloth covered caskets covers a wide variety of designs in the newest of styles. We can also supply anything desired in Casket Linings, Burial Robes and a general line of Undertakers' Supplies.

Special attention given to telegraph or phone orders. We never miss a train on express orders

CENTRAL CASKET COMPANY
Bridgeburg, Ont.   R. S. Flint   Canadian Representative: 241 Fern Ave., Toronto

NEW PALATIAL UNDERTAKING PARLORS

Center & Hanna, undertakers, Vancouver, recently completed the appointments in their new parlors at 1049 George street, and held a formal opening. The newspaper men of the city were conducted through the new building the first day, and on the second day the doctors, nurses and clergy of the city were welcomed The three following days the building was thrown open to the general public, who thus had an opportunity to inspect what is beyond a shadow of a doubt one of the most thoroughly modern and at the same time completely artistic undertaking establishments in the West, if not in the whole of the Dominion of Canada.

The building is located in a quiet district which at the same time is within close touch of the central districts of the city. It represents an expenditure of $100,000, and as the result of this expense the firm has produced an epoch-making structure in their particular line of business.

In the building of this structure the one thought throughout has been to utterly eliminate any objectionable feature. For the bereaved relatives who would attend the funeral of their late beloved one there is every facility offered, with the view to eliminate each objectionable detail and every contact with the affairs of others. The building is so arranged that three funerals may be conducted at the same time without the least overlapping and with absolute privacy, one from the other. The feature of privacy for families has been considered throughout. Those who have lost their loved ones may enter the building, transact their affairs regarding the funeral and leave without coming into contact with any jarring force.

Entering the front of the building the visitor finds him or herself in a large reception room with lofty ceilings. Comfortable furniture and shaded lights lend the room a soothing charm. Beyond is seen a much larger room with massive furniture and a high fireplace in which burns a cheerful fire. In this room is telephone communication for the public, roomy chairs and convenient writing tables.

The entrance to the chapel can be effected either through this room or through another entrance from the street. This second entrance opens into a spacious corridor which runs the entire length of the building and which offers a splendid space for lodges attending funerals in which to form their ranks in case of wet weather, instead of outside in the rain. The chapel can be entered from this corridor or from the room where caskets are placed while lying in state. In this latter room the casket is placed in an alcove while a softly-colored light sheds a gentle radiance from above. When the visitor enters this room an atmosphere of sanctity impresses him. Immediately in front of this chamber is the chapel, a beautifully designed place capable of seating 250 persons. The walls and ceiling are of softly-toned woods, while the lights, unseen, shed a gentle twilight.

In the basement the storerooms, the automobile garage, the mausoleum and the columbarium are located. The mausoleum and the columbarium are places for the storing of bodies and the cremated bodies, respectively. In the columbarium small glass-faced cement receptacles are prepared for the urns which will hold the ashes of cremated persons. Each of these two rooms are absolutely fireproof.

The building is a four-storey structure, each floor being complete in its equipment. The ventilating system of the building cost $3,500 alone, and it pours a constant flood of freash air into every part of the structure. A complete change of air is provided for every room in the space of fifteen minutes, which is the record for any building on the Coast by three minutes.

EMBALMERS: ATTENTION.

It has again been rumored that under "The Embalmers' Act," the Board of Examiners will shortly be appointed, and forthwith proceed to prepare the first examination.

The Canadian School of Embalming, under the Principalship of Mr. R. U. Stone, anticipating this event, would bring to the notice of the Embalmers who will have to appear before the Board in order to obtain a License, the necessity of being well versed in Theory as in the practical work, in order to be successful.

The object to be attained should have the serious thought of each and every young Embalmer in the Province who expects to still follow this vocation, and also of every Undertaker who has started in business since March 14th, 1911.

The School gives a thorough course, covering the entire ground, yet plain and short, and the fees are comparatively moderate.

It would be well if those who contemplate preparing themselves for the examinations by taking a course of instruction with Mr. Stone, would arrange to take it at once, thereby having the advantage of individual tuition, which is more satisfactory than when given before a large class.

OPENINGS FOR UNDERTAKERS

The following Western towns are asking for undertaking establishments: Grandora and Melville, Sask., and Edson, Holden, Huxley, Mirror and Wabamun.

Gossip of the Profession

A. B. Purdy, of Provost, Alta., has purchased the undertaking business of C. L. Hadley, of Prince Albert, Sask.

Scheiner & Wilson, of Prince Albert, Sask., have opened a new undertaking business.

W. C. Edwards & Co., Funeral directors, Saskatoon, Sask., have opened a branch of their business at Hanley, Sask.

Waddell & Co., Humboldt, Sask., have purchased the furniture and undertaking business of Messrs. Smith & Cox, in that town.

A third undertaking establishment has been opened in Saskatoon by G. H. McKague and Sons, who for some years have conducted a similar business at Outlook, Sask. The new establishment is in the Travelers' Block, on 3rd Avenue, where Mr. McKague has secured ground space and large rooms in the upper story.

Nunn & Thompson, undertakers, Vancouver, are succeeded by Nunn, Thompson & Clegg.

M. N. Powers, St. John, N.B., has added a new funeral car to his equipment. Mr. Powers is of the fourth generation of his family in the undertaking profession in St. John.

R. U. Stone, Toronto, performed a demi-surgical case for Fred Myers, North Toronto's undertaker, on two men recently killed in an accident in the brickyards at Eglinton. The face of one of the men was greatly battered, but a natural shape was brought back again.

Undertakers Shipping Directory

ONTARIO

Aurora—
 Dunham, Charles.
Barrie—
 Smith, G. G. & Co.
Bowmanville—
 Disney, R. S.
Brockville—
 Quintabush, Geo. R., 162 King St.
Campbellford—
 Irwin, James.
Campden—
 Hansel, Albion.
Clinton—
 Walker, Wesley.
Coboconk—
 Greenley, A.
Copper Cliff—
 Boyd, W. C.
Dungannon—
 Sproul, William
Dutton—
 Schultz, B. L.
Elmira—
 Dreisinger, Chris.
Fenelon Falls—
 Deyman, L. & Son.
Fenwick—
 H. A. Metler.
Fergus—
 Armstrong, M. F.
 Thomson, John & Son.
Fort William—
 Cameron & Co., 711 Victoria.
 Morris, A.
Haileybury—
 Thorpe Bros.
Galt—
 Anderson, J. & Son.
Hamilton—
 Green Bros., 124 King St. E.
 Robinson, J. H. & Co., 19-21 John St. N.
Hanover—
 Wunnenberg, Norman.
Hastings—
 Howard, P. N.
Hepworth—
 Downs, E. J.
Inwood—
 Lorriman, E. S.
Kemptville—
 McCaughey, Geo. A.
Kenora—
 Horn & Taylor.
Kingston—
 Corbett, S. S.
Lakefield—
 Hendren, Geo. G.
Little Current—
 Sims, J. G.
Markdale—
 Oliver, M.
Newmarket—
 Millard, J. H.
North Augusta—
 Wilson, J. R.
North Bay—
 St. Pierre, E.
Oakwood—(Mariposa Station G.T.R.) Wilmot F. Webster.
Ohsweken—
 Johnson, F. L.
Oshawa—
 Disney Bros.
 Luke Bros.
Ottawa—
 Rogers, Geo. H., 128 Bank
Petrolia—
 Steadman Bros.
Port Arthur —
 Collin Wood, 36 Arthur St.
 Morris, A.
Prescott—
 Rankin, H. & Son.
Renfrew—
 O'Connor, Wm.
St. Mary's—
 N. L. Brandon.
St. Thomas—
 Williams, P. R. & Sons, 519 Talbot St.
Seaforth, Ont.
 W. T. Box & Co.
Scotland—
 Vaughan, Jos. H. M.
Sudbury—
 Henry, J. G.
Toronto—
 Cobbledick, N. B., 2068 Queen St. East and 1508 Danford Ave. Private Ambulance.
 Humphrey, E. J. Burial Co. Head Office, 359 Yonge St.; Branch, 407 Queen St. W. Private ambulance.
 Stone, Daniel (formerly H. Stone & Son), 82 Bloor St. West.
 Vancamp, J. C., 30 Bloor St. West.
Waterloo—
 Klipper Undertaking Co.
Welland—
 Sutherland, G. W.
Woodstock—
 Meadows, T. & Sons.
 Mack, Paul.

QUEBEC
Buckingham—
 Paquet, Jos.
Cowansville—
 Judson, M. B.
Montreal—
 Tees & Co., 912 St. Catherine St. West.
St. Hyacinthe—
 Cadorette, Mongeau & Leary.
St. Laurent—
 Gougeon, Jos.

NEW BRUNSWICK
Petitcodiac—
 Jonah, D. Allison.
Welland—
 Sutherland, G. W.
Woodstock—
 Van Wart, Jacob.

NOVA SCOTIA
Ferrona—
 Fraser, D. & Co.
Halifax—
 Snow & Co., 90 Argyle St.
Sydney, C.B.—
 Beaton, A. J. & Son, 374-384 George St.

MANITOBA
Brandon—
 Campbell & Campbell.
 Vincent & McPherson.
Swan River—
 Paull, Geo.
Winnipeg—
 Bardal, A. S., 834 Sherbrooke
 Thompson, J. C., 501 Main
 Clark-Leatherdale Co., Ltd., 232 Kennedy St.

SASKATCHEWAN
Gull Lake—
 Morrow, Fred. A.
Saskatoon—
 Young, A. E.
Kamsack—
 Russell, G. E. I.
Lanigan—
 Robertson, Wm.
Moose Jaw—
 The Bellamy Co.
 Broadfoot Bros.
Rush Lake—
 Friesen, John M.
Prince Albert—
 Howard, A. C.
 Hadley, C. L.
Regina—
 Speers, George.
Semans—
 Haygarth, Jas.
Welwyn—
 Leavens, Merritt.
Wolseley —
 Barber, B.

ALBERTA
Calgary—
 Graham & Buscomb, 611 Centre St.
Castor—
 Winter, W. G.

BRITISH COLUMBIA
Hosmer—
 Cornett, T. A.
Victoria—
 Hana & Thompson, 827 Pandora Ave.

The Original Patented Concentrated Fluid

Patented Formula
Strongest and Best

Essential Oil Base, combined with Alcohol, Glycerine, Oxidized Formaldehyde and Boron-Dioxide.

Ask others for their Formula

Special Canadian Agents
National Casket Co.
 Toronto, Ont.
GLOBE CASKET CO.
 London, Ont.
SEMMENS & EVEL CASKET CO.
 Hamilton, Ont.
GIRARD & GODIN
 Three Rivers, Que.
JAS. S. ELLIOTT & SON
 Prescott, Ont.
CHRISTIE BROS.
 Amherst, N.S.

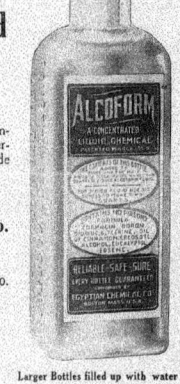

Larger Bottles filled up with water

Egyptian Chemical Co. Boston, U.S.A.

IF YOU WANT TO BUY OR SELL

A Furniture or Undertaking Business, try our Classified Pages. The Canadian Furniture World and The Undertaker is read by practically every furniture merchant and undertaker in Canada every month.

February, 1914 CANADIAN FURNITURE WORLD AND THE UNDERTAKER 85

BUYER'S DIRECTORY

When writing to advertisers kindly mention the
Canadian Furniture World and the Undertaker

ARTS AND CRAFTS FURNITURE
Geo. McLagan Furniture Co., Stratford.
John C. Mundell & Co., Elora.

ASBESTOS TABLE COVERS.
Canadian H. W. Johns-Manville Co., Toronto.

BABY CARRIAGES.
Gendron Mfg. Co., Toronto.

AWNINGS
Stamco, Limited, Saskatoon, Sask.

BENT WOOD FURNITURE.
John C. Mundell & Co., Elora.
J. & J. Kohn, Toronto (W. Craig).

BOOKCASES.
J. D. Freese & Son Co., Chicago, Ill.
Knechtel Furniture Co., Hanover.
Geo. McLagan Furniture Co., Stratford.
Meaford Mfg. Co., Meaford, Ont.

BUFFETS.
Bell Furniture Co., Southampton, Ontario.
Kensington Furniture Co., Goderich.
Knechtel Furniture Co., Hanover.
Geo. McLagan Furniture Co., Stratford.
Meaford Mfg. Co., Meaford, Ont.
Peppler Bros., Hanover.
Stratford Chair Co., Stratford.
Victoriaville Furniture Co., Victoriaville, Que.

BEDS (Brass and Iron).
Canada Beds, Ltd., Oheslsy.
Ideal Bedding Co., Toronto.
Farquharson-Gifford Co., Stratford, Ont.
Quality Beds, Limited, Welland, Ontario.
Ives Modern Bedstead Co., Cornwall Ont.
Ontario Spring Bed & Mattress Co., London, Ont.
Stamco, Limited, Saskatoon, Sask.
Stratford Bed Co., Stratford, Ont.
S. Weisglass, Ltd., Montreal, Que.

BEDS (Modern Wood).
Elora Furniture Co., Elora.
Knechtel Furniture Co., Hanover.

BED SPRINGS.
Knechtel Furniture Co., Hanover.
Frame and Hay Fence Co., Stratford.
Gold Medal Furniture Co., Toronto
Leggett & Platt Spring Bed Co., Windsor.
Ideal Bedding Co., Toronto.
Ontario Spring Bed & Mattress Co., London, Ont.
Stamco, Limited, Saskatoon, Sask
Steel Furnishing Co., New Glasgow, N. S.
S. Weisglass, Ltd, Montreal, Que.

BED ROOM CHAIRS.
Baetz Bros., Berlin.
Bell Furniture Co., Southampton, Ontario.
Elmira Furniture Co, Elmira, Ont.
Lippert Furniture Co., Berlin.

BED ROOM SUITES.
Bell Furniture Co., Southampton, Ontario.
Kensington Furniture Co., Goderich.
Knechtel Furniture Co., Hanover
Victoriaville Furniture Co., Victoriaville, Que.

BUNGALOW CHAIRS & SUITES
Baetz Bros. & Co., Berlin, Ont.

CARD AND DEN TABLES.
Geo. McLagan Furniture Co., Stratford.
John C. Mundell & Co., Elora, Ont.

CARPET RACKS
Steel Furnishing Co., New Glasgow, N. S.

CAMP FURNITURE.
Stratford Mfg. Co., Stratford.

CEDAR BOXES
D. L. Shafer, St. Thomas, Ont.

CELLARETTES.
John C. Mundell & Co., Elora, Ont.

CHAIRS AND ROCKERS.
Bell Furniture Co., Southampton, Ontario.
Baetz Bros., Berlin.
John C. Mundell & Co., Elora.
Stratford Chair Co., Stratford.
Waterloo Furniture Co., Waterloo.
Canadian Rattan Chair Co., Victoriaville.
Gold Medal Furniture Co., Toronto.
Elmira Furniture Co, Elmira, Ont.
Imperial Furniture Co., Toronto.
Lippert Furniture Co., Berlin.
Victoriaville Chair Mfg. Co., Victoriaville.

CHESTERFIELDS.
Imperial Furniture Co., Toronto.

CHIFFONIERS.
Bell Furniture Co., Southampton, Ontario.
J. D. Freese & Son Co., Chicago, Ill.
Knechtel Furniture Co., Hanover
Stratford Chair Co., Stratford.
Victoriaville Furniture Co., Victoriaville, Que.

CHINA CABINETS.
Bell Furniture Co., Southampton, Ontario.
Peppler Bros., Hanover.
Knechtel Furniture Co., Hanover.
Geo. McLagan Furniture Co., Stratford.
Meaford Mfg. Co., Meaford, Ont.

CLOCK CASES
Elmira Interior Woodwork Co., Elmira, Ont.

COMFORTERS.
Toronto Feather & Down Co., Toronto.
Stamco, Limited, Saskatoon, Sask.

COTS
Frame and Hay Fence Co., Stratford.

COSTUMERS
Elmira Interior Woodwork Co., Elmira, Ont.

COUCHES.
J. P. Albrough & Co., Ingersoll.
Ellis Furniture Co., Ingersoll.
Gold Medal Furniture Co., Toronto.
Imperial Furniture Co., Toronto.
John C. Mundell & Co., Elora, Ont.
Steel Furnishing Co., New Glasgow, N. S.
S. Weisglass, Ltd., Montreal, Que.

COUCHES (Sliding).
Ideal Bedding Co., Toronto.
Farquharson-Gifford Co., Stratford, Ont.
Gold Medal Furniture Co., Toronto.
Ontario Spring Bed & Mattress Co., London, Ont.
Stamco, Limited, Saskatoon, Sask.

CRADLES.
Knechtel Furniture Co., Hanover.

CRIBS (Brass and Iron)
Ideal Bedding Co., Toronto.
John C. Mundell & Co., Elora, Ont.
Ontario Spring Bed & Mattress Co., London, Ont.
Stamco, Limited, Saskatoon, Sask.
S. Weisglass, Ltd., Montreal, Que.

CUSHIONS.
Stamco, Limited, Saskatoon, Sask.

DAVENPORT BEDS.
Farquharson-Gifford Co., Stratford, Ont.
Montreal Upholstering Co., Montreal, Que.
Imperial Rattan Co., Stratford.
John C. Mundell & Co., Elora.

DAVENPORT FRAMES
Elmira Interior Woodwork Co., Elmira, Ont.

DEN FURNITURE
Elmira Furniture Co., Elmira, Ont.
Farquharson-Gifford Co., Stratford, Ont.
John C. Mundell & Co., Elora, Ont.

DIVANETTES.
Lippert Furniture Co., Berlin.

DESKS.
Bell Furniture Co., Southampton, Ontario.

Elmira Interior Woodwork Co., Elmira.
Knechtel Furniture Co., Hanover.
Geo. McLagan Furniture Co., Stratford.
John C. Mundell & Co., Elora.
Stratford Desk Co., Stratford, Ont.

DINING-ROOM FURNITURE
Farquharson-Gifford Co., Stratford, Ont.

DINING SUITES.
Bell Furniture Co., Southampton, Ontario.
Knechtel Furniture Co., Hanover.
Geo. McLagan Furniture Co., Stratford.
John C. Mundell & Co., Elora.
Peppler Bros., Hanover.
Stratford Chair Co., Stratford.

DINNER WAGONS.
Geo. McLagan Furniture Co., Stratford.
Peppler Bros., Hanover.

DRESSERS.
Bell Furniture Co., Southampton, Ontario.
J. D. Freese & Son Co., Chicago, Ill.
Knechtel Furniture Co., Hanover.
Stratford Chair Co., Stratford.
Victoriaville Furniture Co., Victoriaville, Que.
Meaford Mfg. Co., Meaford, Ont.

EXTENSION TABLES.
Bell Furniture Co., Southampton, Ontario.
Peppler Bros., Hanover.
Berlin Table Mfg. Co., Berlin.
Meaford Mfg. Co., Meaford, Ont.

FILING DEVICES.
Elmira Interior Woodwork Co., Elmira.
Geo. McLagan Furniture Co., Stratford.

FYLING CABINETS
Globe Wernicke Co., Stratford, Ont.

FYLING CABINETS, Supplies
Globe Wernicke Co., Stratford, Ont.

FOLDING CHAIRS.
Stratford Mfg. Co., Stratford.
Ideal Bedding Co., Toronto.

FOLDING TABLES.
Stratford Mfg. Co., Stratford.

FOOTSTOOLS
Elmira Furniture Co. Elmira, Ont.

FURNITURE HARDWARE
Stratford Brass Co., Stratford, Ont.

HALL SEATS AND MIRRORS.
Geo. McLagan Furniture Co., Stratford.
Meaford Mfg. Co., Meaford, Ont.

HALL TREES.
Geo. McLagan Furniture Co., Stratford.

HAMMO-COUCHES.
Ideal Bedding Co., Toronto.

INVALID CHAIRS.
Gendron Mfg. Co., Toledo, Ohio.
Victoriaville Chair Mfg. Co., Victoriaville, Que.

IRONING BOARDS AND DRYERS.
Stratford Mfg. Co., Stratford.

JARDINIERE STANDS.
Elmira Furniture Co., Elmira, Ont.
Elora Furniture Co., Elora.
J. D. Freese & Son Co., Chicago, Ill.
Geo. McLagan Furniture Co., Stratford.
Meaford Mfg. Co., Meaford, Ont.

KITCHEN CABINETS.
Hamilton Ideal Mfg. Co., Hamilton.
Knechtel Kitchen Cabinet Co., Ltd., Hanover, Ont.

KITCHEN TABLES.
Knechtel Furniture Co., Hanover.
Victoriaville Furniture Co., Victoriaville.

LADIES' DESKS
J. D. Freese & Son Co., Chicago, Ill.
Meaford Mfg. Co., Meaford, Ont.

LAWN SEATS AND SWINGS.
Stratford Mfg. Co., Stratford.

LIBRARY TABLES.
Bell Furniture Co., Southampton, Ontario.
Peppler Bros., Hanover.
Elmira Furniture Co. Elmira, Ont.
Elmira Interior Woodwork Co., Elmira, Ont.
Geo. McLagan Furniture Co., Stratford.
Meaford Mfg. Co., Meaford, Ont.
John C. Mundell & Co., Elora, Ont.

LUXURY CHAIRS.
Lippert Furniture Co., Berlin.

MAGAZINE RACKS AND STANDS
Geo. McLagan Furniture Co., Stratford.

MATTRESSES.
Berlin Bedding Co., Toronto.
Gold Medal Furniture Co., Toronto.
McKellar Bedding Co., Fort William, Ont.
Ontario Spring Bed & Mattress Co., London, Ont.
Stamco, Limited, Saskatoon, Sask.
Standard Bedding Co., Toronto.
Antiseptic Bedding Co., Toronto.
Ideal Bedding Co., Toronto.

MANTELS—Wood, Tile
Elmira Interior Woodwork Co., Elmira, Ont.

MANTELS—Electric
Elmira Interior Woodwork Co., Elmira, Ont.

MEDICINE CABINETS.
Meaford Mfg. Co., Meaford, Ont.

MISSION FURNITURE.
Ellis Furniture Co., Ingersoll.
Baetz Bros., Berlin.
John C. Mundell & Co., Elora.
Waterloo Furniture Co., Waterloo.

MORRIS CHAIRS.
Ellis Furniture Co., Ingersoll.
Imperial Rattan Co., Stratford.
Knechtel Furniture Co., Hanover.
John C. Mundell & Co., Elora.
Waterloo Furniture Co., Waterloo.

MUSIC CABINETS.
Geo. McLagan Furniture Co., Stratford.
Knechtel Kitchen Cabinet Co., Ltd., Hanover, Ont.

OFFICE CHAIRS.
Bell Furniture Co., Southampton, Ontario.
Elmira Furniture Co., Elmira, Ont.
Knechtel Furniture Co., Hanover.
Stratford Chair Co., Stratford.
J. & J. Kohn, Toronto (W. Craig).
John C. Mundell & Co., Elora, Ont.

OFFICE TABLES
Stratford Desk Co., Stratford, Ont.

PARK SEATS.
Stratford Mfg. Co., Stratford.

PARLOR CHAIRS and ROCKERS
Ellis Furniture Co., Ingersoll.
Elmira Interior Woodwork Co., Elmira.
John C. Mundell & Co., Elora, Ont.
Waterloo Furniture Co., Waterloo.

PARLOR FRAMES
Elmira Interior Woodwork Co., Elmira, Ont.

PARLOR SUITES.
Elmira Interior Woodwork Co., Elmira.
Ellis Furniture Co., Ingersoll.
Knechtel Furniture Co., Hanover.
Waterloo Furniture Co., Waterloo.
Gold Medal Furniture Co., Toronto.
Lippert Furniture Co., Berlin.

PARLOR TABLES.
Geo. McLagan Furniture Co., Stratford.
Meaford Mfg. Co., Meaford, Ont.
Elora Furniture Co., Elora.
Elmira Furniture Co., Elmira, Ont.
Knechtel Furniture Co., Hanover.
Peppler Bros., Hanover.

PEDESTALS.
Peppler Bros., Hanover.
Geo. McLagan Furniture Co., Stratford.

PILLOWS.
Ontario Spring Bed & Mattress Co., London, Ont.
Stamco, Limited, Saskatoon, Sask.
Toronto Feather & Down Co., Toronto.
Ideal Bedding Co., Toronto.

PILLOW SHAM HOLDERS.
Tarbox Mfg. Co., Toronto.

RATTAN FURNITURE.
Imperial Rattan Co., Stratford.
Canadian Rattan Chair Co., Victoriaville, Que.
Gendron Mfg. Co., Toronto.

RECLINING CHAIRS.
Ellis Furniture Co., Ingersoll.
Knechtel Furniture Co., Hanover.
John C. Mundell & Co., Elora, Ont.

RUG RACKS
Steel Furnishing Co., New Glasgow, N. S.

SECTIONAL BOOKCASES
Globe Wernicke Co., Stratford, Ont.

SCHOOL FURNITURE.
Bell Furniture Co., Southampton, Ontario.

SIDEBOARDS.
Knechtel Furniture Co., Hanover.
Meaford Mfg. Co., Meaford, Ont.
Stratford Chair Co., Stratford.

BUYERS' DIRECTORY

Index to Advertisements

TABLES
Bell Furniture Co., Southampton, Ontario.
Elora Furniture Co., Elora.
Knechtel Furniture Co., Hanover.
John C. Mundell & Co., Elora.
Orillia Furniture Co., Orillia.
Stratford Chair Co., Stratford.
Victoriaville Furniture Co., Victoriaville, Que.

TABLE SLIDES
B. Walter & Co., Wabash, Ind.

TABOURETTES
Elora Furniture Co., Elora.
J. D. Freese & Son Co., Chicago, Ill.
Kensington Furniture Co., Goderich.

TELEPHONE STANDS
John C. Mundell & Co., Elora, Ont.

TENTS
Stamco, Limited, Saskatoon, Sask.

TYPEWRITER DESKS
Elmira Interior Woodwork Co., Elmira.
Stratford Desk Co., Stratford, Ont.

UPHOLSTERERS' SUPPLIES
Ellis Furniture Co., Ingersoll.
Gold Medal Furniture Co., Toronto.

UPHOLSTERED FURNITURE
Baetz Bros., Berlin.
Ilhe Furniture Co., Ingersoll.
Farquharson-Gifford Co., Stratford.
Imperial Rattan Co., Stratford.
Imperial Furniture Co., Toronto.
John C. Mundell & Co., Elora.
Knechtel Furniture Co., Hanover.
Waterloo Furniture Co., Waterloo.
Gold Medal Furniture Co., Toronto.

VACUUM CLEANERS
Onward Mfg. Co., Berlin.

VERANDAH FURNITURE
Imperial Rattan Co., Stratford.
Stratford Mfg. Co., Stratford.

WARDROBES
Knechtel Furniture Co., Hanover.
Meaford Mfg. Co., Meaford, Ont.
Stratford Chair Co., Stratford.

FACTORY SUPPLIES

CLAMPS
Batavia Clamp Co., Batavia, N.Y.

FURNITURE SHOES
Onward Mfg. Co., Berlin.

DRY KILNS
Morton Dry Kiln Co., Chicago

GLUE JOINTING MACHINES
Canadian Linderman Co., Wood stock.

NAILS
P. L. Robertson Mfg. Co., Milton, Ontario.

PLATING
P. L. Robertson Mfg. Co., Milton, Ontario.

RIVETS AND SCREWS
P. L. Robertson Mfg. Co., Milton, Ontario.

SPRINGS
James Steele, Guelph.
Ideal Bedding Co., Toronto.

SPANISH LEATHER
Lackawanna Leather Co., Hackettstown, N. J.

STERILIZED HAIR
Griffin Curled Hair Co., Toronto.

TRUCKS
W. L. Kemp Co., Ltd., Stratford.

VARNISHES
R. C. Jamieson & Co., Montreal.
Ault & Wiborg, Toronto.

VENEERS
Adams & Raymond Veneer Co., Indianapolis, Ind.

VENEER PRESSES
Wm. R. Perrin & Co., Toronto.

WASHERS
P. L. Robertson Mfg. Co., Milton, Ontario.

UNDERTAKERS' SUPPLIES

AMBULANCES
Mitchell & Co., Ingersoll.

BURIAL ROBES
James S. Elliott & Son, Prescott.
Evel Casket Co., Hamilton.
Globe Casket Co., London.
Semmens & Evel Casket Co., Hamilton.

CLOTH CASKETS
Michigan Casket Co., Detroit, Mich.

CEMENT CASKETS
Canadian Cement Casket Co., Prescott.

CEMETERY SUPPLIES
Frigid Fluid Co., Chicago, Ill.

CASKETS AND COFFINS
Dominion Casket Co., Guelph.
Evel Casket Co., Hamilton.
Globe Casket Co., London.
Semmens & Evel Casket Co., Hamilton.

EMBALMING FLUIDS
Egyptian Chemical Co., Boston.
Frigid Fluid Co., Chicago, Ill.
Michigan Casket Co., Detroit, Mich.
H. S. Eckels Co., Philadelphia

EMBALMERS' SUPPLIES
Frigid Fluid Co., Chicago, Ill.

HEARSES
Mitchell & Co., Ingersoll.

LOWERING DEVICES
Frigid Fluid Co., Chicago, Ill.

SCHOOLS OF EMBALMING
Canadian School of Embalming, Toronto.

STEEL GRAVE VAULTS
St. Thomas Metallic Vault Co., St. Thomas, Ont.
Michigan Casket Co., Detroit, Mich.

UNDERTAKER'S CHAIRS
Stratford Mfg. Co., Stratford

UNDERTAKERS' SUNDRIES
Frigid Fluid Co., Chicago, Ill.

A
Albrough & Co., J. P. 22
Antiseptic Bedding Co. .... i.f.c.
Ault & Wiborg 73

B
Baetz Bros, & Co. 18
Batavia Clamp Co. 10
Berlin Table Mfg. Co. 25

C
Canada Beds Limited 70
Canada Mattress Mfg. Co. 21
Canadian Linderman Co. 72
Can. H. W. Johns-Manville Co. .. 25
Central Casket Co. 82
Colleran Patent Spring Mat. Co. 19

D
Dominion Casket Co. 74
Dominion Mfrs., Limited 78

E
Eckels & Co., H. S. 82
Egyptian Chemical Co. 84
Elmira Interior Woodwork Co. 14
Elmira Furniture Co. 8

F
Farquharson-Gifford 7
Frame & Hay 11
Freese & Sons Co., J. D. 79

G
Gale & Son, Geo. 6
Globe Wernicke 9
Gold Medal Furniture Mfg. Co. 17
Gendron Wheel Co. 86

H
H. E. Furniture Co. 71
Hourd & Co. 12

I
Ideal Bedding Co. 30
Imperial Furniture Co. 22
Imperial Rattan Co. 5

J
Jamieson & Co., R. C. 8

K
Kawneer Mfg. Co. 14
Kindel Beds Co., Limited 70
Knechtel Furniture Co. 24
Kohn, J. & J. 10

L
Lackawanna Leather Co. 10

M
Meaford Mfg. Co. 29
Mundell & Co., John C. .... i.f.c.
McLagan Furniture Co. 3
McKellar Bedding Co. 27
Montreal Upholstering Co. 4

O
Onward Mfg. Co. 12
Ontario Spring Bed 4

P
Peppler Bros., Limited 28

Q
Quality Furniture Makers Ltd .. 23

R
Robertson, P. & L., Mfg. Co. .. 3

S
Scafe & Co., A. J. 12
School o Embalming 86
Shafer, D. L. 18
Springfield Metallic Casket Co. 80
Stamco, Limited 26
Standard Bedstead Co. 30
Steel Furniture Co. 22
Steele, James Limited 18
Stratford Brass Co. 13
Stratford Bed Co. 15
Stratford Chair Co. .... o.f.c.
Stratford Mfg. Co. 11
St. Thomas Metallic Vault Co. 80

W
Walter & Co., B. 25
Waterloo Furniture Co. 15
Western Casket Co. 76
Weisglass, S., Limited 16

Canadian School of Embalming
Instruction in Practical Embalming and Funeral Directing
PREPARATION FOR EXAMINATIONS
ENTER AT ANY TIME
R. U. STONE   32 Carlton Street
Principal   Toronto

Invalid Chairs and Tricycles of every description.
This has been our study for thirty-five years. We build chairs that suit the requirements of any case. Write us for catalogue No. 20 and prices, if interested.
Gendron Wheel Co., Toledo, O. U.S.A.

For Sale / Wanted

TERMS FOR INSERTION
4 Cents per word one Insertion
10 Cents per word three Insertions
MINIMUM 50 CENTS

WANTED—Well established Funeral Directing Business; wouldn't object to good furniture Business in connection with the Undertaking. Apply, giving all particulars as regards amount of business done in both lines. R. Summerfeldt, Unionville, Ont. 14/1/1.

FOR SALE—Undertaking business, excellent place to live, 12,000 population, one competitor, best location, and equipment, doing good business, taking over large city business. Cash price, $3,000. Box 124, Canadian Furniture World and The Undertaker, 32 Colborne St., Toronto, Ont. 14/1/1.

FOR SALE—Furniture and Undertaking in town of Stayner; established twenty years, forced to give up business on account of getting disabled—act quick—low rent. Address—D. Mathers, Stayner. 14/1/1.

FURNITURE FACTORY SUPERINTENDENT open for engagement March 1st. Best reasons for changing. Best references as to ability for handling men, designing, etc. Address, Box 125 Canadian Furniture World and The Undertaker, 32 Colborne Street, Toronto, Ont. 14/1/1

CONSULT THE BUYERS DIRECTORY
The Buyers Directory of CANADIAN FURNITURE WORLD AND THE UNDERTAKER contains much valuable information.
Sometimes an advertiser makes several lines—and only ONE line will be represented in his advertisement—but if you will refer to the Directory in most cases you will find just what you are looking for.

February, 1914   CANADIAN FURNITURE WORLD AND THE UNDERTAKER

Low Priced Furniture

A growing country has a great market for low priced but well built furniture.

Our line is built strong and well. The oak pieces are all built of **SOLID OAK** and the imitation Mahogany of **SOLID BIRCH**.

We are the largest manufacturers of low priced Dressers, Chiffoniers and Ladies' Desks in the North.

This enables us to sell on a very small margin.

LOOK AT THE PRICES ON PIECES SHOWN
All Our Prices are in Proportion.

202
Price $5.00. Weight 95 lbs.
Top 18x33. Height 64 in.
French beVel plate mirror 12x20.
Same, with imitation quart. oak front and top. Price $5.25.

102
Price $5.45. Weight 110 lbs.
Top 18x30. Height 69 in.
French beVel plate 12x16.

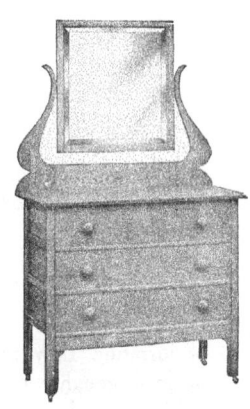

215
Price $6.50. Weight 110 lbs.
Top 18x38. Height 67 in.
French beVel plate 20x22.

We also manufacture a line of the above goods in the Colonial Style.
Terms: F.O.B. Chicago. 60 days net—2% for cash in 20 days.
Our location is the most convenient in the U.S. to supply the Canadian Trade. Order one of the above pieces to-day as a sample, then look over our illustrated catalog. It means **PROFIT FOR YOU**.

J. D. FREESE & SONS CO.
2501-2523 HOMER STREET
CHICAGO, U.S.A.

A FURNITURE BUYERS' DIRECTORY

To Furniture Dealers

Have you ever searched high and low, and everywhere, for the names of manufacturers making a line of goods for which you have a customer, or which you need for your own requirements? Most furniture dealers have had that experience.

A Special Announcement

The Canadian Furniture World will shortly publish a Special Buyers' Directory Number, containing a colored paper supplement in which will be indexed for the convenience of the twenty-five hundred Buyers of Furniture in Canada, the names of the various manufacturers making the many lines indexed.

To Furniture Manufacturers

Canadian Furniture Manufacturers are requested to send us a full list of all the various classes and articles of furniture they manufacture, so that this index can be made thoroughly representative of the Canadian furniture industry, and enable dealers to purchase as much of their stocks in Canada as is possible for them to do.

Check over the condensed Buyers' Directory on pages 75 and 76, and send your additions to this list to the Canadian Furniture World.

CANADIAN FURNITURE WORLD

32 COLBORNE STREET
TORONTO

Vol. 4 No. 3 MARCH, 1914

Canadian FURNITURE WORLD AND THE UNDERTAKER

Published by the Commercial Press, Limited, 32 Colborne Street, Toronto

---

What Will Sell Faster Than "Good Looks"?
"Good Looks" with "McLagan Quality"

Our Goods retain longer and with less attention their original attractiveness

Do You Sell Gunn Sectional Bookcases?

We manufacture Gunn Sectional Bookcases in a good variety of designs and combinations for home and office use. There is a rapidly growing demand for good grade Bookcases at reasonable prices, and our offerings should be of interest to you. Let us suggest that you write us.

Geo. McLagan Furniture Company
Stratford, Ontario

JOHN C. MUNDELL & CO., LIMITED, ELORA, ONT.

Upholstered Easy Chairs, Rockers, Settees

We manufacture these in sets, in pairs and in single pieces, — in new designs that are attractive and in demand. The covers range in variety from Drill, Pantasote and Imitation Spanish Leather, up through the intermediate grades to No. 1 Spanish Cowhide, and come in almost every desirable shade.

For the Living Room, Library or Den, Upholstered pieces like these are indispensable. A set of three, made up of Rocker, Arm Chair and Settee, not only completely furnish such a room, but give it an air of elegance and comfort. ¶ The prices are so inviting in view of the appearance of the Chairs, that the goods seem to sell themselves. $7.75, $9.00, $10.50 and on up, according to the quality of cover used. For speedy sales and satisfactory returns for your investment these upholstered pieces are indeed Leaders.

Blue Prints ready for mailing

John C. Mundell & Co., Limited, Elora, Ont.

THE FISCHMAN PATENT MATTRESS

Can. Pat. March 16, '09. U.S. Pat. Feb. 16, '09

Our Guarantee

We give a Five Year Guarantee with each Mattress that it will not sag or spread and that it is absolutely noiseless.

Mechanically Constructed

FISCHMAN PATENT SPRING MATTRESSES are composed of little coil springs which are contained in strong cotton pockets, scientifically arranged in rows, each row being wrapped in finest cotton felt, making it impossible for the springs to touch one another and tear the pockets by friction, and thereby making it the only noiseless spring mattress built.

Each spring acts independently, thus allowing the mattress to automatically adopt itself to the contour of the body, ensuring the utmost in comfort and repose.

You can easily double your mattress business by selling the Fischman—the mattress of five years' guaranteed service at a popular price.

McLaughlin & Scott, Canadian selling agents. Samples can be seen at their show-rooms on 67-71 Adelaide Street West.

The Fischman Mattress Company
569 Queen St. W.   Toronto, Ontario

March, 1914.   CANADIAN FURNITURE WORLD AND THE UNDERTAKER.

STRATFORD

Upholstered Reed Furniture
Made Complete in the Imperial Factories

THIS Imperial Upholstered Reed Suite, and **all** Imperial Furniture, is made up complete, frames and all, in in our own workshops. That is **one** reason why the "Imperial" make comes to you such pronounced elegance at prices which will allow you a most liberal profit on the turnover.

Stratford, Ontario

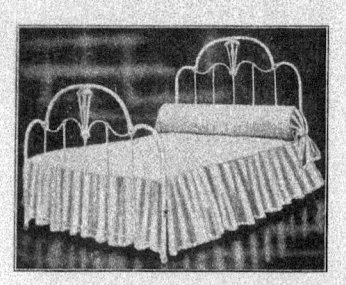

A Better Profit

When you are buying a line of goods to sell you are making an investment that should yield profit.

However, you can make no profit until you make sales at a fair advance upon cost. Therefore the line you can sell easiest—turn over the oftenest—under this condition is

The Profit Producer

You will like Ontario Iron Beds because of their profit producing quality, and your customers will like them because of their style and utility.

Iron Bed No. 852 x
Height of Head 61 in.   Height of Foot 45 in.
Brass Spindles ½ in.   Widths 4 ft. and 4 ft. 6 in.
List Price $8.30

The Ontario Spring Bed & Mattress Co., Limited
London   THE LARGEST BEDDING HOUSE IN CANADA   Ontario

A Handsome Parlor Davenport and a Full Sized Comfortable Bed

This handsome piece of furniture serves every purpose of a bed and a sofa. Occupies only half the space and costs only half as much as both. The bed is full size, 72 by 17 in. It is simply mechanically perfect, easily changed from sofa to bed or from bed to sofa. It is luxuriously comfortable as a bed, no ridges or hard spots. Plenty of room for bedding within sofa, when bed is closed. Sanitary construction. You do not sleep on the upholstering, but on a soft mattress, which is easily removed for airing. Advise your customers to buy a Duofold and they will be able to move into a smaller apartment or get along with one less room. We have a style and price to suit your needs exactly.

Frames: Quartered Cut Oak or Birch Mahogany.
Finish: Fumed Oak, Golden Oak, and Mahogany.

Fabricoid or Velour
$49.00

Imitation Spanish
$50.00

Genuine Leather
$60.00

Genuine Spanish
$63.00

(List Prices)
Try a Sample Order.

No. 81—Duofold (Divanette)

If you have not received our new Catalogue, write us and we will mail you a copy.

The Montreal Upholstering Company
1611-1613 Clarke St., MONTREAL, Can.

STRATFORD

Designs that Pull Trade

The designing in Stratford Chairs, with their many other excellent sale-creating advantages, has always proven a popular subject for admiration both with the dealer and the ultimate user.

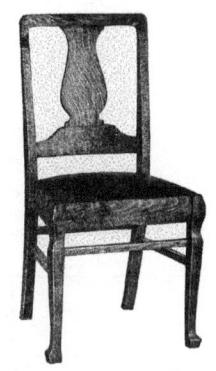

Obey that impulse—

to write us about the new lines of inexpensive dining-room and bedroom furniture we are now manufacturing. It is an impulse that will repay you well. Write us a card NOW.

Stratford   Ontario

Are your customers millionaires, or working-men or both?

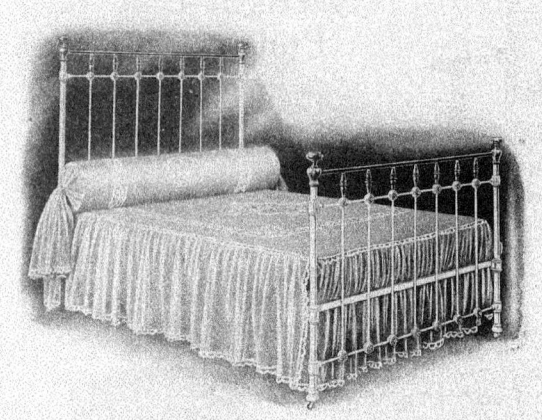

There's a Gale Bed for every purse

No. 880

IRON BEDSTEAD
No. 880

Pillars - - - 1 1-16 inch
Filling - - - 5-16 inch
Top and Bottom Rods - ⅝ inch
Head - - - - 60 inches
Foot - - - - 39 inches
Sizes 3 ft., 3 ft. 6 in., 4 ft., 4 ft. 6 in.
Shipping Weight - 110 lbs.

BRASS TRIMMINGS
Door Knob Vases 3 inches
Top Rod ⅝ inch
Mounts and Spindles

This is the claim we make for the Gale Line—the most comprehensive line of beds ever offered any furniture trade. A line backed up by a catalog from which it is easy and a pleasure to sell beds. No need for more than a representative stock,—the catalog and our prompt shipments from large stocks put practically every bed in our line on your floors.

Geo. Gale & Sons
Waterville, Que.

Warerooms: TORONTO, MONTREAL, WINNIPEG

STRATFORD

An Important Link in the Chain of Stratford's Busy Furniture Industries

¶ The Farquharson-Gifford Company is especially well equipped to manufacture a line of furniture that will afford genuine pleasure to the purchaser, and to maintain a service to dealers that will cover every phase of fair dea'ing and sub.tantial profit-making.

Our Specialty is

Davenport Beds, Couches and Living Room Furniture

¶ It is our aim to produce a par'icularly good grade of these lines at prices which will appeal to most people.

Our travelers are now calling on the trade. Give them an opportunity to prove the above claims.

Stratford,   Ontario

Jamieson's Turpentine Stains

The Best
of the good stains

R. C. Jamieson & Co., Limited
Established 1858
Montreal   Vancouver

Cabinet No. 30

"Usefulness" in Every inch of Space

NO other one piece of furniture in the home is of more practical utility to the housewife than the Kitchen Cabinet—and no other Kitchen Cabinet, we believe, exemplifies this so strikingly as the "H.E."

It has the removable flour bin, which eliminates the overhead lifting of heavy flour sacks.

Glass receptacles for sugar, spices, tea and coffee, perfectly sanitary, and all showing the quantity each contains.

Roller front, which does away with doors opening out on the working surface of the cabinet.

See that you have the H. E. make on display for the early spring demand.

The H. E. Furniture Co., Ltd.
Milverton   Ontario

STRATFORD

Globe-Wernicke Art-mission Bookcase with Desk Unit

The good reader is frequently a good writer. He studies and reviews books, making frequent notations from the authorities he consults. All studious persons have use for a Desk as well as a Bookcase.

This Art-mission 12¦ Desk Unit occupies no additional floor space, yet affords all the conveniences of a compact desk. Write for our catalogs and price lists of complete Globe-Wernicke combinations—the ideal line to sell.

Stratford   Ontario

Kohn's Imported Bentwood Furniture

THE QUALITY LINE

High grade in design, construction and finish. Inexpensive enough to sell well. Certain to give satisfactory service.

Steel Screw Leg Joints

that will not loosen—solid one-piece backs—hand caned seats.

Made of specially seasoned Austrian beechwood, bent by a strength-retaining process.

Finished in any color desired. Hand polished.

Light weight, convenient, comfortable, sanitary. All periods and modern art characteristics represented.

Complete variety of grades and styles.

Write for Catalog   SPECIAL DESIGNS IMPORTED TO ORDER   *Visit Our Showrooms*

JACOB & JOSEF KOHN
OF VIENNA, AUSTRIA
215-219 VICTORIA STREET, TORONTO, CANADA

| 110-112 West 27th St. NEW YORK CITY | 1410-1418 So. Wabash Ave. CHICAGO, ILL. | Second Floor, Keeler Building GRAND RAPIDS, MICH. | 418 Maritime Building SEATTLE, WASH. |

ELLIS QUALITY
ALWAYS TO THE FORE ..

The new lines we just have out are quite the most up-to-the-minute and improved possible. That you may see the latest photos, ask for our representative to call.

Nothing But Fine Upholstered Furniture

THE ELLIS FURNITURE COMPANY
INGERSOLL   ONTARIO

STRATFORD

Quality First

Yet with that quality, you'll also find in Stratford Beds, all the other essentials necessary in a really worth while, profit making line.

"CLASSIC"
Woven Wire Bed Springs

The best all round Bed Springs for every specific use that brains and up to the hour equipment can produce.

+ **Plus** +

Write Us for Catalogue.

A feeling that the dealer is the most important factor in the distribution, and our consequent policy of making our lines really profitable to him.

Stratford   Ontario

"View it with the Eye of the Passer-by"

Size it up from the outside—from the view-point of the person who buys for the pleasure of using it. Then you will see the wisdom of placing this and others of our line of Upholstered Chairs and Chesterfields in your stock to sell.

They **produce profits** because they **please people.**

A. J. Scafe & Co. - Berlin, Ontario

The Top is Always Centered
A gentle pull on one side opens both sides

The substantial construction, beauty of design and perfect finish of Berlin Tables, together with the easy slide, is a sales force of great value to every furniture dealer.

Stock an Assortment of Berlin Tables for the Spring Trade.

The Berlin Table Manufacturing Co., Limited
BERLIN :: ONTARIO

STRATFORD

Order Stratford Folding Chairs

YOU can quickly turn these Folding Chairs into cash whenever crowds assemble for an impromptu affair—providing you have the chairs in stock to deliver on short notice. *Order Now.*

What about your lines of Lawn Swings, Garden and Verandah Furniture for this season?

Write for our Catalog and Price List

Stratford Manufacturing Co., Limited
Stratford   Ontario

Brass Furniture Trimmings For Every Use

In any design and finish required, and the best results in every instance. | Let us quote you prices on your next Brass Furniture Trimming order.

The only trade paper in its field in Canada quoting its circulation in plain figures on its editorial page each month is the

The circulation of this issue is TWO THOUSAND COPIES

Spring Beds, Cots and Divans
OUR SPECIALTY

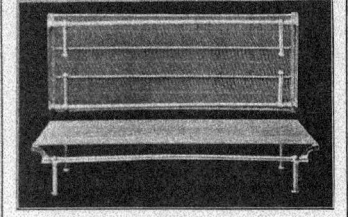

No. 10 DIVAN
Rope Edge Patented in Canada and United States

Our representatives are now calling on the trade with complete lines of our specialties for 1914.

REPRESENTATIVES
Ed. Bagshaw, Western Ontario   A. McNab, Eastern Ontario
J Clarke, Northern Ontario   J. A. McLaughlin, Quebec

Colleran Patent Spring Mattress Co.
TORONTO, ONT.

Every Up-to-date Housewife is a Live Prospect For These Covers

Every woman in your town knows that the ordinary silence cloth will NOT protect the polished top of her dining table against hot dishes.

J-M Asbestos Table Covers and Mats

afford better protection against heat than any other. They are also the most durable. They invariably give satisfactory service. The line of J-M Asbestos Table Covers and Mats is so complete that you can cater to all pocket books. And you won't have to tie up a lot of money in stock, as our branch right near you will fill rush orders in any quantity, without delay. Our prices are so low that you can undersell competitors besides giving your customers better value than they can get in any other make of cover.

Write Nearest Branch for Booklet and Special Dealer Proposition

THE CANADIAN H. W. JOHNS-MANVILLE CO., Limited
TORONTO   MONTREAL   WINNIPEG   VANCOUVER

? Isn't it Human-like to Patronize the Store with a Good Front?

You're paying a big rental and it is for no other reason than to be located where you can show your merchandise to the greatest number of people. Attraction results in a greater number of sales today than any other store element. If your Store Front is merely keeping out the snow and rain and not selling your merchandise you could just as well be located on a back street. Every inch of your street frontage is valuable—more valuable than any other space in your Store—be sure you are using it.

Here are two photographs of the Economy Store—one before and the other after the installation of a KAWNEER STORE FRONT. Is it paying dividends—is it making sales? This Front increased the business of this Store 35%—and not one cent additional clerk expense was added—the profit on the increased business is net.

If you intend to put in a new Store Front go at it in a business-like way—don't let some sentiment (your desire to be noted) run away with your good judgment—make your new Store Front fit your business. Let the experience of the owners of 30,000 KAWNEER STORE FRONTS help you. We understand Store Fronts thoroughly—we've helped thousands of Merchants solve their problems and thoroughly believe we are deserving of your confidence—deserving of the opportunity to co-operate with you. Every KAWNEER FRONT that makes good does us nearly as much good as it does the Merchant behind it. We want to give you Merchants the benefit of our specialized experience.

Kawneer STORE FRONTS

Authentic Store Front Book

The first logical step for you to take is to read "Boosting Business No. 2"—it's the most instructive and interesting Store Front book ever published. It contains photographs and drawings of many of the best-paying Store Fronts in the country—both big and little. Learn more about the metal KAWNEER STORE FRONTS—only solid copper, brass, bronze or aluminum is used—they're permanent (no repair or paint expenses), leak-proof and they *sell* merchandise.

Just drop a card for "Boosting Business No. 2"—don't risk the money it takes to install a modern Store Front of any kind until you have seen this Store Front book. You won't be obligated by requesting us to send "Boosting Business No. 2."

Kawneer Manufacturing Company
Francis J. Plym, President
Dept. S
1197 Bathurst Street
TORONTO, CAN.

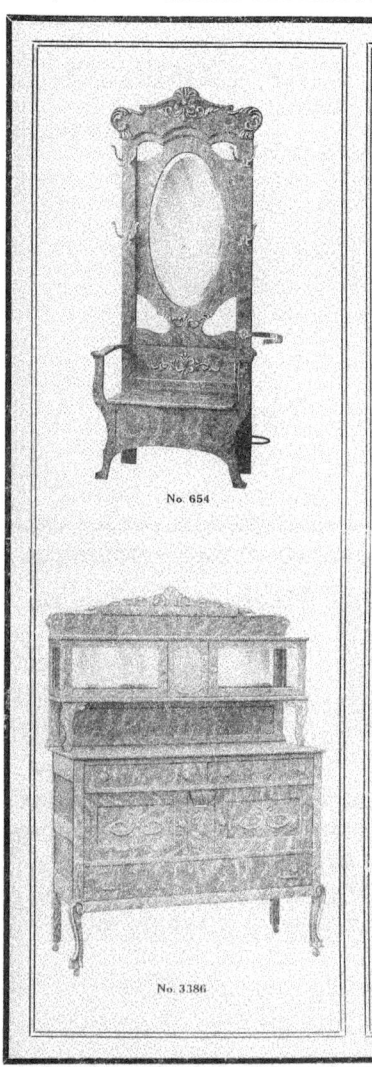

March, 1914. CANADIAN FURNITURE WORLD AND THE UNDERTAKER. 15

Yes it's Imitation But—

¶ It is an imitation that fulfils every element of attractiveness, usefulness and serviceability of the real oak and mahogany.

¶ Select white maple is used in our furniture, and by our process of staining and finishing we obtain a finish that is absolutely permanent, non-chippable and perfectly true in shade and grain.

¶ When the Meaford Line Man calls—better write for us to send him—listen to his sales plan. He can show you the way to bigger business—no matter what your class of trade—by utilizing this popular priced line.

The
Meaford Mfg., Co.
Limited
Meaford, Ontario

No. 654

No. 3386

BAETZ BROTHERS AND COMPANY
BERLIN :: ONTARIO

No. 707

English Bungalow Furniture

HAVE YOU SEEN IT? BRIGHT, NEW, TASTY DESIGNS.   MADE IN COMPLETE SUITES

Representatives:—J. A. RUMBALL   W. H. BENEY   J. H. CLARKE   M. F. ANTHES   J. H. HALEY

Bedroom Boxes

The cedar box trade should be a Valuable adjunct to your business. Is it?

Send for our cata'og, prices and discounts on these attractive B.C. Red Cedar Matting covered Boxes.

Made for beauty, utility and long service at a low price.

D. L. SHAFER
St. Thomas - - Ontario

READ THIS ISSUE FROM COVER TO COVER

Then you will agree that this Paper is worth ten times the price.

$1.00 January next year
Send your Subscription in to-day

THE COMMERCIAL PRESS, LIMITED
32 Colborne Street, Toronto

WHEN YOU WANT TO SELL YOUR BUSINESS

You want to get the best possible offer. The more possible buyers you get in touch with the better chance you have of making a good sale. The "For Sale" and "Want" ads. in the CANADIAN FURNITURE WORLD are read every month by over two thousand manufacturers, travellers, retail dealers and store salesmen.

Four Cents a Word   *Ten Cents a Word*
One Insertion   Three Insertions

The Gold Medal Line

HERCULES BED SPRINGS

and

STEEL COUCHES

GOLD MEDAL FELT MATTRESSES

and

A FULL LINE OF MIXED MATTRESSES

No. 697

One of our Six

New Den Sets

(Quarter-Cut Oak)

Loose Automobile Spring Cushions

Blue prints of these sets will be sent to any dealer interested upon request.

We now have the most varied and up-to-date line of Upholstered Furniture in the Dominion, and we can make prompt shipments.

Gold Medal Furniture Co., Limited

Toronto, Montreal, Winnipeg and Uxbridge   *Head Office:* TORONTO

The Highest Plane of Beauty and Service

The Kindel Bed

"The bed that makes itself" comes in most pleasing design — just as pronounced as the real bed comfort which has made it famous.

Our four types are the Somersaultic, Divanette, Parlor Bed and Chair Bed.

Write for details of the new 1914 sales advantages of the "Kindel."

An aristocrat of the 24 hour day service in convertible parlor furniture

The Kindel Bed Company, Limited
Toronto - Ontario

No Sagging—No Rolling to Centre

The Right Principle--The Single Cone

Each Spring Cone bears the weight directly over it—sagging is impossible because there is no "end and side" pull. L. & P. Bed Springs are essentially "comfort and service" springs.

Protect yourself from the troubles resulting from "wrong principle" Bed Springs. Order L. & P. goods made from the best Premier Spring Steel Wire on a "Better Satisfaction" Guarantee.

LET US SEND YOU OUR CATALOG

Leggett & Platt Spring Bed Company, Limited
WINDSOR :: ONTARIO

Isn't It a Fact

that the bulk of your customers are included in the phrase "the working classes"? We have found it so all along the line and have built up our business by producing beds to suit the purses of this large majority.

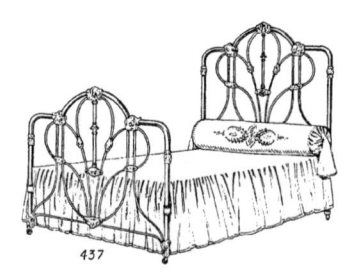

437

In doing so, however, we have not overlooked the large part that new and pleasing designs play in making sales. The result is a line of bedsteads that is practically unbeatable at the price they command. And this price, while within reach of all, leaves a good margin of profit for those dealers that stock our Beds.

*We are in a position to serve you well.
Will you give us a chance to prove this?*

The Victoriaville Bedding Company, Limited

Victoriaville
Que.

The Big Five Mixed Carload Center

Every Line of Our Upholstery Suggests Comfort

We cannot emphasize too strongly this feature of comfort. Every furniture dealer knows how much it enters into the sale of a piece of furniture such as a couch or a chair.

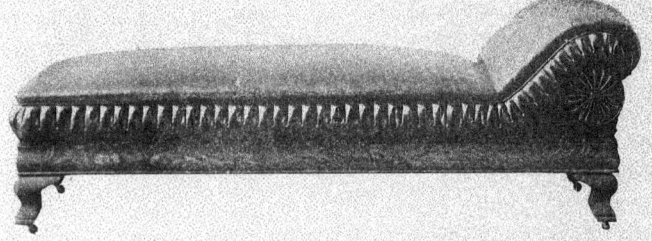

Every piece of our upholstery gives solid comfort both to the body and to the purse. The design, and care in making, take care of the former, while the price suits the latter in every case.

Watch for our travellers or, if in a hurry, drop us a line. We will be glad to make a special trip to your store.

The Victoriaville Bedding Co., Limited
Victoriaville
Que.

The Big Five Mixed Carload Center

The Big Five Mixed Carload Center

Something for 1914

Group No. 103, comprising 1 Buffet, BB Mirror, leaded glass; 1 China Cabinet; 1 Pedestal Table; 5 Diners, upholstered seats; 1 Arm Chair.

Price $32.50

Get a good showing Victoriaville Furniture on your floors and you'll quickly find that in design, quality and price, those pieces are just what your customers have been looking for.

See the many new designs we have for Spring selling.

The Victoriaville Furniture Co.
Victoriaville, Que.

Chairs that wear like iron !

The **service** you render your customers is a prime factor in their repeat orders. You cannot render them better service than by selling them Victoriaville Chairs. These are made from sound, flawless lumber in a plant devoted exclusively to chairs that "wear like iron" and give complete satisfaction.

Victoriaville Chair Mfg. Co.
Victoriaville
Que.

The Big Five Mixed Carload Center

Get your orders in early for this Verandah Chair

Indications show that even bigger sales of this popular chair will be made this year than in 1913. For this reason we urge your placing your orders before the big Spring Rush. Our salesmen are on the road, showing as fine a line of Reed Furniture as is possible to produce. Wait for them or

Get our new catalogue, just off the press—full of new things in Reed Furniture

The Canadian Rattan Chair Co., Limited
Victoriaville
Que.

The Big Five Mixed Carload Center

Weisglass Beds

Represent the Maximum Result in

Construction, Durability and Design

DEALERS everywhere advise us of the success attending the sale of the Weisglass line.

Our "Acid Proof" Lacquer is something more than a talking point, its splendid wearing qualities have been demonstrated successfully everywhere. Have you given your Spring order yet? Our salesmen are now on the road.

Facsimile of Gold Medal Recently Awarded to Weisglass Beds

Weisglass also make Springs and Couches

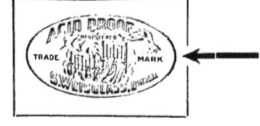

Look for these Trade Marks Your Guarantee of Quality

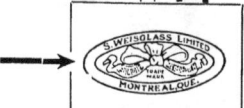

Upholstered Chairs and Furniture that is admired everywhere.

Carefully made of the highest grade materials, finished in all coverings.

Look at Our Travelers' Photographs

The Imperial Furniture Company, Toronto

No Need to *Say* It's "Fine Quality"

It tells the truth itself in every line—in every fibre. Moreover, the Albrough line of Upholstered Chairs and Rockers possess that subtle force of attractiveness that invariably results in "Closing the Sale."

Blue Prints and Prices await your request

J. P. ALBROUGH & CO.
MAKERS OF
Quality Couches and Easy Chairs
INGERSOLL   CANADA

The "20th Century" Rug Rack

Is the Greatest Silent-Salesman on Earth

You have the advantage of our 5 years' experience in manufacturing "20th Century" Rug Racks. These racks are now in use in almost every town and city in Canada, and for this reason you can be assured of receiving the highest satisfaction.

The racks are manufactured wholly of steel, and can not warp or twist, or in any way wear out, or give the least trouble. The money invested will go on paying you perpetual dividends. Ask for catalog and price delivered your station.

The Steel Furnishing Company
New Glasgow, N.S.

Three large Rug Racks holding 120 rugs each

The Grand Old Elms!

THE Good Friday wind storm brought low many of the remaining grand old Elms of Western Ontario. There will not be many Soft Elm trees left after this season's cut, and the big, large grained variety will be practically extinct.

It is one of our **Best Furniture Woods**, has a beautiful grain, soft texture, and partakes of a rich golden color and high polish. When well seasoned (as ours is) it is less liable to warp and check than most any other wood.

Our Elm Goods

Made a Great Hit at The Toronto Exhibition

WOULD advise you to stock up with goods made of this beautiful, and now, rare wood, as in less than eighteen months the supply will be practically exhausted.

Let our travellers show you the pictures, and put in a stock while they last.

Beautiful Figure   Rich Golden Finish

The Knechtel Furniture Co.
LIMITED

Hanover :: Ontario

One of our New 1914 Designs in Fine Diners

A SELECTION from our much admired display at the Toronto Furniture Exhibition.

No. 180. In quartered oak, fumed finish, leather slip seat. We have other new designs just as enticing.

Our representative will visit you soon, to show you the complete line of 1914 winners. It will pay you to wait and see.

The Elmira Furniture Co., Ltd.
Elmira   Ontario

Our New No. 180 Diner

Display Electric Mantels
They Sell to Tenants as well as Landlords

WHAT great sales possibilities! Prospects for good profitable sales in the majority of householders in your town.

Electric Mantels can be set up by **anyone** in **any** room where there is electric wiring. No chimney—no tiling necessary. Initial expense very reasonable—cost of operation very small.

A living room display in your window featuring Elmira Electric Mantels will create a new and important revenue for you.

Send for Our Catalog of Mantels, Desks Cabinets and Parlor Frames

Elmira Interior Woodwork Co., Limited
ELMIRA   ONTARIO

K-E-L-L-A-R-I-C

Mattress Luxury at a Reasonable Price

"SWEET DREAMS"

A MODERN Mattress made in a modern factory. It is entirely hand-built of the highest grade of material and is composed of **non-absorbent, long, staple, white, downy cotton**, built in thin, filmy layers, **carefully hand-stitched** and tabbed with quiet patterns of strong **sateen ticking**. Made with strap handle at each side and **turned-in seams** which leave no edge for holding dirt, making them perfectly sanitary.

We take the responsibility of Kellarics measuring up to their name. If they fail we will gladly refund the purchase price at any time.

We also manufacture a full line of **Woven Wire Springs, Model Upholstered Box Springs** and **McKellar Steel Spiral Springs.**

The McKellar Bedding Co., Limited
Fort William, Ontario

Eastern Branch: Berlin Bedding Co., Limited, 31 Front St. E., Toronto

REGISTERED
We have given it a "Backbone"
Ideal Duplex Spring
No. 2
(Patent Applied For)
An idea simple enough and clever enough to stamp it as something really great.
Now, it can't Sag
We have so much confidence in this Spring that we GUARANTEE it for 20 YEARS.
Put one on the floor. See how little effort it needs to sell it.
The high-grade "Simmons Link" fabric itself is absolutely non-stretchable.
For greater ease, and to divide the strain on the outer helical springs we run a band of steel down the middle, practically dividing the springs into two, at the same time linking each half to this steel band with helical springs. Thus, each half-spring is entirely surrounded with comfortable, yet tremendously strong helical springs, making the whole a marvel of comfort, resiliency and durability.
Same idea in Woven Wire Fabric is listed as "Ideal Duplex No. 1." Also a winner. Ask about it.
THE IDEAL BEDDING Co LIMITED
2-24 JEFFERSON AVENUE - - TORONTO

Canadian Furniture World and the Undertaker

PUBLISHED THE FIRST OF EACH MONTH BY

THE COMMERCIAL PRESS, LIMITED
32 COLBORNE STREET, TORONTO
Phone Main 4978

D. O. McKINNON, *President.*　　　WESTON WRIGLEY, *Manager.*
W. L. EDMONDS, *Managing Ed.*　GEO. H. HONSBERGER, *Advertising Mgr.*

JAMES O'HAGAN　　　　　　　GEORGE G. COLVIN
WM. J. BRYANS　　　　　　　JOHN A. GIBSON
Associate Editors　　　　　　*Advertising Representatives*

F. C. D. WILKES (Phone Main 658), Room 704, Unity Bldg., Montreal.
E. J. MACINTYRE. Room 659, 122 South Michigan Avenue, Chicago.
GOTHAM ADVERTISING COMPANY, 85 Liberty Street, New York.

Subscriptions
Canada, $1.00 a year. Other Countries, $2.00 a year

PUBLISHERS' STATEMENT — 2700 copies of this issue of the Canadian Furniture World are printed, over 1906 of these being mailed to furniture dealers, salesmen, etc., and the balance to advertisers and exchanges. An average of 2000 copies has been printed every month during 1913. Itemized statement, showing distribution according to provinces, will be furnished on request.

Vol. 4　　　　　　　　MARCH, 1914　　　　　　　　No. 3

Scientific Retailing. Scientific management in the retail trade is merely performing the different motions and acts in the most expeditious and economic way commensurate with the general welfare of the business.

To do this requires care and much intelligent thought. An outsider may assist in bringing about the desired state of affairs. But the onus is after all practically upon the merchant himself with his clerks co-operating. If he expects that a brand new system that will work with the precision of a high-priced watch can be made and installed by a so-called expert, he will be doomed to disappointment.

There is not a retail store in existence whose management is so scientific and perfect that there is no room for improvement. To the thoughtful and enterprising merchant better methods are always possible. It is only the business man who deems his methods perfect that is incapable of being taught new and better methods.

Those who think, and plan and analyze with a view to doing business on a more scientific basis, make a close study of the trade newspapers and magazines and rub shoulders with their fellows whenever opportunity affords. That is the way many new ideas are conceived and many old ones improved.

Every satisfied customer is a foundation stone to the business.

Plans to Hold Good Clerks. One of the difficulties with which nearly every business man has to contend is the holding of good clerks. In this growing country of ours, with its many new openings for young men, this is a natural condition. The lure of the West is particularly strong.

To offset this many merchants are employing various schemes and holding out various inducements whereby they hope to retain the services of trusted employes.

Among the schemes thus employed there is one by a Western Ontario merchant that might be cited. In charge of one of his departments is a man of good ability whom he is anxious to retain. Accordingly he has agreed to pay him a good salary, and, at the end of the year, provided he remains in his service, to share equally with him the net profits of the department.

Still another plan might be cited. It is that which is employed by an insurance company. This company, in brief, presents each of its clerks with a five hundred dollar life insurance policy at the expiration of a three-year term of service. At the expiration of each subsequent year another hundred dollars is added until the policy possesses a value of $2,500, which is the maximum.

These incidents are not cited in the expectation that either of them can be appropriated by retailers. It is merely for the purpose of drawing attention to what some firms are doing in order to retain the services of worthy men. To the resourceful dealer one or the other may suggest something which he may employ in his own business.

The retailer who is making the most headway is he who has time to stop and study trade papers.

Store Service. The best of advertising campaigns will be greatly minimized in effectiveness unless accompanied by effective service in the store.

The absence of this service is the explanation of many an unsatisfactory advertising campaign.

There are business men of all kinds who seem to think that all they need do is to insert an advertisement in the newspapers and then sit down and wait for customers to flock into their store in droves.

No dreamer ever had a worse delusion.

Service is the right hand of advertising. And business without either is crippled.

Time and again merchants have been known to advertise special prices for certain articles and leave their clerks entirely in ignorance of the fact. This is certainly not conducive to service. There is one thing to which it certainly does tend, and that is disorganization. This is the very antithesis of co-operation.

To make the window displays co-operate with the advertisement is to greatly enhance the value of the latter. The practice of the leading department stores and that of many retailers is a proof of this.

The one tells the story in print. The other gives an ocular demonstration.

Service implies a bright, clean and attractive store, one that will prove attractive to women as well as to men.

Good service creates confidence. That quality cannot, however, be created in a day. It comes through a process of evolution. Here a little and there a little. A little courtesy to-day. A little attention to-morrow. Goods never being other than they are represented to be, and goods delivered when it was promised they should be.

Service does not come from the right performance of one or two things. It is in the performance of many things, with the whole tenor of the store and its organization being bent in the direction of satisfying and pleasing customers.

Veneer is all right for furniture ; but it doesn't wear well on the dealer.

How He Made His Business Grow. He is a rash man who to-day thinks that the limit has been reached in anything. This is true of business enterprises as well as in the field of science. As a matter of fact, most thoughtful men are inclined to the belief that in business at any rate possibilities are only limited by the will power and resourcefulness of those who are in command.

The business of a retailer in a back country store in Ontario had reached a stage beyond which the proprietor was beginning to wonder whether or not further growth was possible. He had not reached the point at which he had abandoned hope. He wasn't made of that kind of stuff. But during his meditations he felt that even if there was further growth it could scarcely be material, particularly as the town in which he did business appeared to have reached the stand-still stage.

One day, however, in the midst of his meditations, a newspaper friend dropped in to see him. And the thing that was on his mind became the subject of discussion, during which the newspaper man suggested that he get out a small illustrated catalogue, placing one in the home of every family in the town and surrounding country.

The dealer, who was never known to turn down a suggestion, gave this one much consideration. After some deliberation he decided to make the venture. He sought and secured the co-operation of a number of manufacturers and jobbers whose goods he handled, and from them he obtained the use of a number of engravings.

When mailed the catalogue was accompanied by a short and nicely worded circular letter.

It is about a year since the venture was made, and not only has the dealer secured business from homes which had not hitherto dealt with him, but the general turnover of goods in his store has materially increased.

He does not now depend wholly upon his catalogue as an advertising medium. He has been encouraged to use the columns of the local newspapers to tell the news of his store.

That he is no longer perturbed about the future of his business may be taken for granted. He feels that his business has taken a new lease of life, and he intends to take all the advantage of it that he can.

The day a furniture dealer gets behind the times his customers begin to trek towards the store of his more progressive competitors.

Highways and Business. The Dominion Government is for the third time to introduce a bill to provide ways and means of aiding the provinces in the construction and maintenance of good roads. On the two former occasions on which the bill was introduced it passed the House of Commons, but being amended in a way that was unacceptable to the Lower House, was allowed to drop.

It is to be hoped the two parties in Parliament will be able to arrive at a basis of agreement this time. It is only hair-splitting on the part of each that has heretofore prevented the bill becoming law.

The matter is an important one. Bad roads are a detriment to the general welfare of the country. An authority in the United States a few years ago estimated that bad roads impaired the transport efficiency on public highways to the extent of 25 per cent.

Not long since, a committee investigated the effect of bad roads in a district of 750 square miles tributary to Minneapolis, and their conclusion was that the combined loss to the farmers, merchants and manufacturers therein was $1,518,000 a year.

Primarily of course the movement for good roads is designed for the betterment of the farmers. Good roads, we are told, go hand in hand with the advance in agriculture. In Massachusetts it has been found that as a result of betterment of roads, hundreds of people have come to the abandoned farms. In all parts of the world it has been found that the tendency of the inauguration of good roads has been to keep people on the farms.

It is obvious, therefore, that the movement for better roads is a matter of concern for business men as well as for farmers.

The Good Roads Association have asked the Dominion Government to set $50,000,000 aside for the improvement of highways in different parts of Canada. The sum set aside under the abortive bills of the last and preceding session of Parliament was $10,000,000. For highway improvement in Ontario the Government of that province a couple of years ago set aside the sum of $5,000,000.

The stronger public opinion becomes, the more rapidly will Parliament respond to its wishes. Being in its final analysis a business matter it is directly in the interest of the business men of the country to lend their aid to the furtherance of the good road movement.

The transportation problem may begin at the farmyard gate, but it ends at the doorway of the business man's customer.

Retailers who cause offence are in the eyes of many customers guilty of an unpardonable sin, whether the offence be intentional or not.

A Professor's Wild Statement. Prof. Dean, of the Ontario Agricultural College, is credited with saying: "It is doubtful if an honest man can successfully compete under present conditions of trade."

This is a statement that will hardly stand analysis.

There may possibly be men in business who will agree with Prof. Dean. But their number is comparatively few.

Aside altogether from ethical motives, the average business man knows that it does not pay to be dishonest in business. No matter how sharp he may be, he knows dishonesty, like murder, "will out."

But if it be "doubtful if an honest man can successfully compete under present conditions of trade," as Prof. Dean asserts, what about the great army of successful business men in all parts of Canada whose integrity is beyond dispute?

The retailers of Canada are approximately 128,200, and the recent census places the manufacturers at nearly 20,000. Besides these there are the wholesalers to be taken into consideration. All told, there must be 150,000 to 160,000 business men in Canada.

While all may not have reached the goal of success, it would, upon the face of it, be absurd to assert that those who have had travelled by the dishonest route.

But is it not true that one occasionally meets with professors whose theories have no foundation in fact?

Taken straight through, quality considered, the country merchant has the mail order house beaten on prices. It is ridiculous to say that retail mail order houses quote the lowest prices on all types of merchandise. If that is so, why do they advertise so strenuously? If their catalogues contained nothing but lowest prices, their hard work to secure trade would be superfluous; trade would flow to them as naturally as water flows down hill.

Large Oaks From Small Acorns Grow

AN outstanding feature of most successful Canadian stores is the fact that they have evolved from modest beginnings. Scores of instances can be seen from one end of Canada to the other where men have launched into business in a small way, and with little financial backing, but who have, despite these handicaps, made remarkable onward strides. Such men have all the more reason to be congratulated on their success, for there is nothing that the broad-minded person of to-day admires more than to see men, handicapped on the start by lack of funds, struggle on to success in spite of this drawback.

Canada is a country of self-made men—men who though sparsely endowed with this world's goods, have not allowed it to interfere with their ambitions, and in the hardware and kindred trades there are many outstanding instances of big stores evolved from very modest beginnings. In nearly every district, instances are to be found. This fact should prove an incentive to other dealers now running comparatively small establishments, for when other men have made big successes from small starts, there is always chances for the same thing to be repeated. True, the remarkable progress by the country itself, and in a few instances specially favorable conditions have helped in some degree the success of many men, but the country gives every promise of great progressiveness and many opportunities for years to come.

While we may never equal the success of some of the most notable cases that can be cited, we can at least put forth our best effort, and who knows—some of the successful men of to-day did not really on the start expect to reach the heights which they have attained, but they had dreams and aspirations which proved a wonderful force in carrying them upward.

Dreams and aspirations, however, will not of themselves win success. The man who would reach the summit of the mountain Success—who would scale the pinnacle of his ambitions—must tackle the undertaking with a willingness for work. He must call into action the best that is in him, and undaunted by any adversities that may cross his path, struggle onward in the race. Persistent and determined effort are essentials in the man who has his own way to make in this world.

No man in Canada to-day need allow his ambitions to be curbed by the fact that he must start at the bottom of the ladder—make a modest beginning. The instances of those who have accomplished great things from small beginnings should give him confidence and encouragement. He should ever bear in mind that "large oaks from small acorns grow."

Collins' Course in Show Card Writing

Fourth of a series of articles specially prepared for this journal.

We presume that the students will have a proper table or place on which to do their work. Some may prefer to work standing up. If so, the height should be equivalent to that of sitting, that is, the top of the table should be a little above the elbows. A very little

Fig. 4—Showing first method of ruling.

slant like a desk top, is desirable. An ordinary kitchen table makes a very suitable work bench. The stool can be made the proper height.

Making Your Own Colors

We intimated in last issue that we would say more about colors in this part. The colors used for card writing are water or distemper colors. These are more suitable than oil, as they are more easily worked, brushes are easier cleaned after use and the colors will not spoil through standing. They will dry out, but can be re-mixed by adding water. It must be remembered that water colors will not do for use outside. You may buy the various mixed colors known as distemper colors at any paint store in small jars of about a half-pint each. They are ground very fine in water. When you buy them they are hard, but can be softened with water. You must add sufficient mucilage to them to make them hold to the card, so they will not rub off after they are dry. A little experience will soon determine the amount. A jar of color will do many hundred cards.

The average student will not need so great a quantity of color at one time. It is possible for you to mix your own colors. Buy 10c. worth of good Canadian Vermilion, 5c. worth each of blue, green and chrome yellow, all in dry colors. Get wood alcohol and mix each color into a thick paste with it, then add a little water, stir and let stand for a time. If necessary it can be used immediately, but it improves by standing. Add to this enough mucilage to make it adhere to the card without rubbing when dry. The object of using wood alcohol is to cut the color, as dry colors are all more or less oily in nature. If you cannot obtain the spirits, use borax water or washing soda water. For white, buy the best flake white. Do not accept whiting, white lead, nor white zinc. Insist on flake white and see that it is not lumpy. Mix exactly as directed with other colors. You will need more white and black than any other colors—red possibly next.

Fig. 5—Showing second method of ruling.

The blue, as you buy it, will be very dark. You can lighten it with white. For shading, ruling and ornamentations, scrolls, etc., make it very light. Green

ABCDEFGHI
JKLMNOPQR
STUVWXYZ?
123456789

Plate 15—Tuscan block, upper case.

March, 1914.   CANADIAN FURNITURE WORLD AND THE UNDERTAKER   33

makes the best all-round color to shade with, also for borders, decorations, scrolls, etc. It must be made very pale by mixing with white. These are what are known as "subdued" colors.

For special color or shade effects, it may be well to know that red and yellow make orange; yellow and blue make green; red and black make brown; red and blue make violet; red and white make pink. The knowledge of these colors will be of great assistance to you.

Ruling

There are various methods for ruling with a brush. Each one has its advantages. Figure 4 is the one most generally in use. By this method you possibly may make a longer line than by any other. Lay your rule on the card about a half-inch from the line you wish to draw. Hold it firmly with your left hand. Take the brush between your thumb and forefinger. Place the tips of your other fingers against the edge of the rule for a guide and draw your line carefully. See Figure 4.

Figure 5 is another method. Notice the rule is raised on the front side and held in position by resting on the fingers of the left hand. Rest the back of the fingers of the right hand on the top of the rule and the brush against the edge. Draw the brush along where the line is desired. A little practice will enable you to become proficient in this.

Sample Cards

The sample cards shown herewith are in keeping with the season. They are suggestions that can be utilized in almost any kind of a retail business. Every merchant who has house-cleaning requisites to sell should begin in March to advertise them. Don't wait until the house-cleaning season is over before you start. There are at least four merchants who should make extra advertising efforts for the house-cleaning trade. Furniture, hardware, groceries, and drugs. The furniture dealer will likely have, in addition to furniture, which house-cleaning usually boosts the sale of, polishes, window shades, dustless mops, vacuum

Seasonable opening card for March.

Drawing attention to the spring house-cleaning season.

ABCDEFGHI
JKLMNOPQR
STUVWXYZ?
123456789

Plate 17. Half block, upper case.

abcdefghijklmn opqrstuvwxyz

Plate 16—Tuscan block, lower case, to match plate 15 on previous page.

cleaners, carpet sweepers, etc. Hardware—pails, mops, brushes, brooms, soaps, paints, kalsomines, varnishes, polishes, stoves, linoleums, oilcloths and many other articles. The grocer has many of the lines the hardware dealer has, and the druggist has cleaning powders, soaps, disinfectants, brushes, sponges, etc.

Make a window with the various needs in it and price ticket every article. The house-cleaning card will make an attractive centre. Make it not less than 14 in. x 22 in. The figure may be in colors, yellow skirt with red waist and white spots. Blue head cloth. The main background of card may be brown and the circle white with red or black letters.

We suggest that every merchant should do a little decorating in the month of March. St. Patrick's Day comes, which makes possible the use of shamrocks, hats, pipes, harps, etc., for decorating purposes. The harp card is somewhat unique. The pattern for the design is cut out of heavy paper, and the scroll pattern is cut separate from the harp. These are laid on the card and air-brushed around. The patterns being separate permits the harp being lifted off and the edge of the scroll being air-brushed where it touches the harp, giving the effect of the harp being behind the scroll. The strings are gold cord passing under and over the scroll, giving the effect of the scroll passing through or between them. The harp can be in gold with a green air-brushed background. The scroll should be in white, or the color of the card. With appropriate wording this design will do for any class of merchandise.

The $7 card is another distinctive St. Patrick's Day card. This may also be used for any line of goods. The shamrocks are in green, the coat of the man should be dark green, the vest red, tie a shade of green, and the breeches corduroy color or light green. Hat green. This will make a very attractive figure. If you find it difficult to draw the figure, cut one from some paper or magazine and paste it on. The letters may be in red with outlining in green. The figure 7 may be in black and the small letters should be in black.

The suggestions these cards offer should assist you in producing others equally as good.

The alphabets shown with this part of the course are the Tuscan Block and the Half Block. The Tuscan is suitable for feature words or lines, but is too hard to make to be of general use. The same may be said of the Half Block. The latter is an excellent style for "Cutting In," which we will take up next month.

Do your employees treat your customers with the same courtesy when they do not purchase as when they do? Are they just as pleasant when making a small sale as they are when making a large one? Do your clerks give short answer to your poorly dressed customers? If you are not able to answer these questions, it's up to you to find out, whether these conditions exist or not.

abcdefghijklmn opqrstuvwxyz

Plate 18—Half block, lower case, to accompany alphabet plate 17, on previous page.

How to Figure Costs in the Furniture Store

BY H. YOUNG

Almost without exception, the object in establishing and organizing any business is for one purpose only, namely, to make a profit on the capital invested. There may be other reasons sometimes, but very seldom.

When a person, firm or corporation engages in any business, the first question to be considered is, "What will it pay on the amount of capital invested?" Of course, the more uncertain the investment the larger percentage of profit is demanded.

things to be considered, among others, four very prominent ones:

To properly answer this question, there are many

1. What are the gross profits to be made from the investment?
2. What will be the cost of operating such a business?
3. What will be the loss from bad accounts?
4. What will be the depreciation and losses on the assets after the capital has been invested?

These are questions that must be successfully answered to arrive at, even approximately, the net profits to those who invest their capital.

I feel sure that very few businesses are organized until these figures are so adjusted, at least on paper, as to show a liberal return on the amount invested. Inasmuch, however, as about 90 per cent. of mercantile businesses are a failure, and a large portion of the other 10 per cent. make very little money, it is readily seen that most of these figures are incorrect.

In my opinion there are more errors made and more failures due to the lack of correct knowledge of what the actual cost of doing business is than from any other source.

The cost of doing business is the obstruction between the capital invested and the net returns on same. It is the enemy of the real purpose for which all businesses are organized. It prevents the proper return on the amount of capital invested. The proper treatment of it does not lie in an effort to minimize it in discussions or on paper, but the good to be accomplished is in the proper application of the items of expense to the different departments of your business to arrive at a correct cost upon which to base your actual profit.

As you all know, the percentage of expense to the volume of business has materially increased during the past few years. This is due to several reasons, and is partly explained by reason of the decrease in values during the past decade. It is now necessary to sell a much larger quantity of merchandise to equal the sales of 20 to 25 years ago.

Among other causes of increased expense is the number of distributors, increased sometimes to a greater extent than seems necessary to supply the demands of the trade. As a result, the average value or amount of the individual order decreases with the consequent increase of the cost of handling, making necessary a more expensive organization to conduct the business.

The publication of expensive catalogues, which a great many of the jobbers in our line of business are now doing, has added considerably to the expense account, as have also modern advertising methods, which are now more necessary than formerly.

Again, the much-talked-of higher cost of living, through the general advance of prices in foodstuffs and other commodities of life, has resulted in a necessary advance in the scale of salaries, and wages to be paid all classes of help. It has also largely increased expense accounts of traveling salesmen, due to advanced hotel rates.

And another item is the increased rent, caused by the increased value of realty in the central and business district of our cities. This, of course, means additional selling expense, hence the increased proportion of expense to gross sales.

Therefore, with these conditions before us, it is the more necessary that we adopt a system of cost that will take care of these items, which seem absolutely impossible to avoid. If we are confronted with a condition unavoidable, we must devise a proper method to take care of the condition. The only method is to properly apply the cost of doing business to the invoice cost of goods, plus freight, and upon the total of these figures, base your profit. If freight rates increase, we take care of it by adding to the invoice cost of goods. Why not do the same when other items of cost advance?

To do so, in my judgment, it is necessary to provide a proper accounting system to determine exactly what is the actual cost of doing business based upon the goods, according to class and other conditions.

I think the first item of expense to be considered is the necessity for charging interest on the capital invested. Certainly if the real object is to earn interest on the capital invested, this item should be provided for first.

Then, properly provide for the salaries of those who manage and operate the business, whether they be partners, officers or employes. Certainly if a person devotes his time to an enterprise in which his capital is invested, he is also entitled to a proper remuneration for his services.

Some firms or corporations, where there are three or four principals only, have been in the habit of charging little or nothing to the expense account for the salaries of these principals. I do not think this correct. The business should afford proper remuneration for those who conduct it. You should then charge rent for the building, whether it is owned by the company or not. Certainly a building in any Southern city could be rented for its rent value, and if it is occupied by the owner, a proper amount should be charged to expense to take care of the rent.

A proper amount should be charged to the expense account for interest on borrowed money and exchange.

A charge of the average percentage of losses should be made to the expense account to take care of bad debts, as it is necessary to include this in the cost to make the result satisfactory at the end of the year.

Also add a reasonable amount for depreciation on stocks of goods after they have been placed in your building.

The cost of doing business can be largely decreased by the proper care and handling of goods from the time they are delivered to you by the transportation companies until you have sold and made shipment of them to your customers.

There are numerous other expense items which we might discuss, but I consider time is too limited to undertake to enumerate the numerous items of different expense which are all well known to each of us. I consider that methods and the application of same far more important than the mere enumeration of the various and sundry expense items. I shall, therefore, devote my arguments to what I consider a practical remedy.

I consider it more important to devise a practical method to be applied than the suggestion of the numerous details in connection with the same. The details must be handled by each individual after all. Then after you have figured out your actual expense at the end of the year, you can easily tell the actual percentage of doing business based upon the gross volume of sales.

I do not think it a proper method, however, to apply the same percentage of the cost of the expense account to the gross sales to every item of your business. It should be borne in mind that the expense sustained by a business house during the year gives the average percentage of expense of selling of goods, but does not give the percentage of expense of selling any particular one of the many lines of goods handled.

It is unquestionable that certain staples in continual demand are less expensive to handle than are small goods on which the demand is lighter and the cost of handling greater. The cost of handling bulky goods, seasonable goods and items where the volume of sales is small is much more than the cost of handling other classes of goods which are easily handled without any packing or without waste.

Then, too, should be taken into consideration the number of times a line of goods can be turned over in a given period. For instance, the cost of selling goods that can be turned over at least 12 times per annum is much less than selling a line of goods which cannot be turned over more than one and a half times per annum.

It therefore, is best to departmentize your business as much as possible and charge specifically to each department or line of goods the true proportion of expense to the volume of business, with due consideration for the actual cost of handling each department as a whole.

Interest on the amount invested, insurance and taxes, rent for floor space, according to the amount of space occupied; proper amount for the bad debts; salaries and other expenses incurred exclusively, including any travelers engaged especially for the department; advertising, according to the amount spent for advertising such department; proper proportion of all the general traveling expenses calculated on the basis of the cost of sales made; proper proportion of all other general salaries and expenses of the house based on the cost of total sales of the house and calculated on the cost of sales in each department.

The sum total of these general expenses must be divided among the various departments in proportion to the cost of the goods sold, for the reason that it is considered a more equitable basis than the amount of sales, because it would be unfair to charge a department which bears a good rate of profit and fair rate of expense in consequence as compared with a department showing a lower rate of profit.

In dividing traveling salesmen's salaries and expenses a less proportion is segregated against a department comprising heavy staples, for the reason that less time is necessary for selling these articles than the general line of goods.

By means of this close calculation the actual cost of handling merchandise in each department can be arrived at, and a percentage representing the total of this expense must be added to the flat cost of the goods in each department in order to obtain the actual cost of the goods to you.

It will not require a high priced statistician to figure the cost down to the one-hundredth part of one per cent., but the cost of handling the different classes of goods may be readily ascertained by a careful calculation and consideration of the conditions under which they are handled and sold.

If this plan is carried out, which can be done unquestionably by the co-operation of all dealers, in my opinion, we will arrive at the actual cost of doing business and a proper solution of this most important subject.

Undoubtedly merchants do sell goods down to almost cost, but it is seldom that a merchant will sell goods at actual cost. Therefore, if your catalogue cost or working cost covered all items of expense, including a reasonable return upon the investment, then it would be an easy matter to obtain a reasonable profit upon the volume of business done and for the amount of risk taken.

This may seem impractical at first glance, but it is only a mathematical proposition to be handled by the heads of departments, who are certainly in a better position to know and figure the actual cost than are your salesmen and others to whom you are leaving the responsibility of fixing the future destiny of your business.

It is my opinion that all manufacturers adopt this plan, and if it works well for them, why should not it work well for us? Can any of you give a good reason why each individual item should not take care of the actual cost of doing business and show for itself?

You all know that every one of us is selling many articles below the actual cost of doing business. Why should we not add the actual cost, the same as we add the actual freight? Certainly you would not leave it to your salesmen to add the freight without a knowledge of what the freight is. Why, then leave it to them to add a much more important item, the actual cost of doing business? They have no idea of what it is, and they are therefore not in a position to handle this important subject.

You will not stop demoralization, it is my belief, until you fix the cost as above outlined. Then your salesmen will not go very far below that cost. This is the first great, strong, powerful step for us to take—put on a cost that includes all fixed charges of doing business. When you do this, you will have solved the problem.

HOW A GROUCHY BOSS INJURES BUSINESS

J. T. Templeton

One of the greatest drawbacks of any business is a grouchy boss. It not only drives away trade, but it disorganizes the entire force, and the only one who seems to be benefited in any way is the grouch who imagines that by those tactics he is considered a great man by everyone with whom he comes in contact. It does not cost much to smile, therefore, if I were managing a business and felt that I just had to be grouchy at some time during the day, I would get me a good cigar, a big red apple, and take a walk during my grouchy spell; at least I would not be seen around my place of business in that frame of mind. I think the retail salesman is the worst neglected member of the human family. No one takes very much interest in a boy who is struggling to become a salesman; that is to say, no one devotes very much time to instructing him as to how he should sell goods. Did you ever stop to think what salesmen come from—I venture to say that a large majority of you came from the same place that I did; namely, the corn field.

Selling Methods in the Furniture Store

Some Experiences and Suggestions

HOW A DEALER MISSED SALES

In a furniture store four sales were lost in one day recently, according to an exchange, because the dealer did not have the goods the customers wanted, and was unable to locate the catalogues showing them while the parties were in the store. After the first "misfire" a salesman started to look up the catalogues, and finally found the exact goods required, illustrated and described in two of them, published by two different manufacturers. This was small satisfaction, however, as the people had left the store. Had these catalogues been kept in a handy place and a card index made showing who manufactured specific lines, the pictures could have been presented and the goods ordered. Some other dealer in that city, better prepared for emergencies of this kind, doubtless got one or more of those orders.

A dealer cannot keep all kinds of furniture. But the least he can do is have the information about their origin at his fingers' ends. Some people have a vague, half-formed idea of what they want, and go from store to store groping for something new—something stylish and inexpensive. Of course, the intelligent salesman will do everything possible to help them select from his present stock, but if he sees they are determined to go elsewhere, he ought to impress on his parties the fact that he can get them exactly what they want in a reasonable time. Then, if he has his catalogue file in proper shape he can quickly show them just what they want and secure the order.

This sequence of events does not always follow that way, but it is admitted by experienced dealers that the inability to locate catalogues for the purpose of rescuing a sale has lost much profitable business to dealers who could ill afford to lose it.

No matter how you do it, get a filing system for your catalogues, and in addition compile a list of sorts and kinds of furniture and who makes them.

A FURNITURE TIP

A salesman for a furniture store handling a high grade of merchandise spends much of his spare time in outside solicitation, says a writer in System, and one of his sources of business is through co-operation with architects specializing in residence building.

His acquaintance with these architects enables him to keep in touch with people who are building houses of the kind likely to be fitted with a good class of furnishings, for it is a well known fact in the furniture trade that a new home is certain to result in at least some buying of furniture, if nothing but curtains and a rug or two. Quite often, there is much replacement at the time of going into the new home or soon afterward.

Very often, too, architects making a specialty of home building are asked to make suggestions as to furniture which would be most suitable in combination with the house and its decorations. In this connection, the furniture house is sometimes directly recommended as the place to go, for the salesman sees to it that the architects are well informed as to the newest and best things he has to offer. Some similar information is obtained from building permits issued by the city building department for houses whose cost and location show that the owners are able to buy good furniture.

A NOVEL FURNITURE SALE

A correspondent sends the following interesting account of "a very novel sale." He says: "One morning (some weeks ago) about 9.30, a very tall, broad, and heavy man, with a very little, mild and gentle-mannered woman, came into the shop, asking in a broad Scotch accent to see some bedroom suites. Being a cainy Scot, he was careful not to in any way give me any idea of the type of suite he was likely to want, and all my leading questions were quite barren of result. I therefore set myself to expound on the virtues of each suite as we came to it, but after a good half-hour's enthusing I was as far off as ever, as all he would do was to grunt, and the little woman merely followed along without any sign of interest whatever.

"At the end of that time, I was getting desperate and asked him point blank if there was any particular style or make of suite he would like to see. His reply was: 'Have you no more?' I said 'Yes,' and took him into a little room at the back of the shop, where one or two suites are usually stored. He then, for the first time, showed some sign of life, and going directly up to one, and putting his great hand on the dressing-chest, turned to his wife, saying, 'How do you like it?' She, poor soul, seemed fearful of speech, in case she made an error, and only looked without replying. Thinking I had got a likely sale at last, I talked hard for twenty minutes or so about the virtues of this particular line, but was surprised at the end of that time by him saying he had already carefully examined it. My surprise was natural in the circumstances.

"I asked him when; said he, 'To-day.' Seeing that it was then only 10.30, and I had been in the shop since opening, I quite failed to follow his remark, and it was only after a considerable time I got the story of his previous visit. He said he was a sergeant of police, and, passing the shop at 2.30 in the morning, he had found the front door unlocked, came in, and had a good look round, thinking, no doubt, someone was in who had no business there. In his tour of the premises, he had seen this bedroom suite, liked it, and as stated, came back for a further examination, and eventually bought it, after haggling about the price, etc. His wife told me later that they had been looking out for a suite for over three years, but she could never get him up to buying point, and it was only when he himself saw the suite under the peculiar circumstances related that he decided to buy. And I think I am right in saying it was 'A very novel sale.'" I agree.—Aitchee, in Furniture Record, London.

AN OPENING OFFER

F. A. Gummer, of Stockton, Cal., had a formal opening recently, and extended a general invitation in the shape of a formal engraved invitation. With this in, vitation was enclosed a card, containing the following offer, which seems to have been an excellent method of obtaining a mailing list:

"We request that you register your name and address on a card which will be handed to you as you enter the store on the opening night. We will give away on this night to some one person, to be decided upon by a committee of representative citizens, the complete furnishings of a four-room bungalow, displayed on our opening night on the third floor of our new building."

MISTAKEN IDEAS.

Some men have a "mistaken idea" that they are running their business. The facts are that the business is running them—soul, mind and body, says an exchange.

Some have a "mistaken idea" that fifteen to twenty hours a day brings the most business success. The fact is that the man who only works twelve will win out in the long run, with a healthy body to boot. A tired mind is a poor affair from which to evolve new ideas, and a tired body does not make very fast time.

Some have an idea that selling cheap is the great magic stone to bring success; forgetting that profits after all are the great end in view.

There is a "mistaken idea" that trade gotten this way is O. K. because it comes quickly. It leaves also just as quickly in most cases, for new and more enticing fields.

There is a "mistaken idea" that the former times were better than these; but there are just as many poor getting poorer and rich getting richer to-day as there were fifty years ago.

There is a "mistaken idea" abroad that the furniture business is a "cinch," yet how many who have tried it for themselves can advise differently.

"Mistaken ideas" are disastrous affairs if not soon taken in hand. They generally come from inexperience and are very costly affairs. We can profit by them if we will. Fools only repeat a "mistaken idea" when once discovered.

Business is like a battle; the general who can keep his head and miss no opportunities is the successful one. One mistake often loses a battle or dissolves a business.

So if you have any "mistaken ideas" get rid of them at once and get hold of the sensible and practicable kind.

DUPLICATE PURCHASE ORDER FORMS

Some system of keeping track of orders given for goods is valuable, if not a necessity, in every well conducted store; it will save trouble and money. It is especially valuable in giving orders for future delivery, as it eliminates the possibility of ordering the same goods twice, a bad mistake which loads not a few dealers up with more of a line than they require. It also eliminates "leading up" of orders by wholesale houses. While most jobbers try to fill orders exactly as they are given, some of them in their zeal send more goods than the dealer orders. Unless he has a purchase order, he can hardly say anything as he has no proof.

A CLEAN SWEEP SALE

One of the secrets of success in the furniture store is something new all the time. One merchant boosted sales one dull month by a seven day Clean Sweep Sale. He says that it increased his sales during the seven days just 33 1/3 per cent.

Some little advertising was done to catch the eye of the regular as well as the prospective customer. In addition, he made the Clean Sweep idea felt throughout his store by the free use of yellow price tickets with a picture of a broom on them. These price tickets were placed on all merchandise in both the store and windows.

A quantity of new goods was bought for the sale to give increased interest to the event, and with it was sold a number of items that were entering the dead stock stage.

GAVE RANGE AS ADVERTISEMENT

A Missouri furnitureman, ever ready to grasp an opportunity that will in any manner increase his business, recently advertised a sale.

At a recent fair held in his town he had a booth, and as a drawing feature gave away every day a small wagon to some youngster on the grounds. The last day of the fair he gave a range to one of the housewives present. His booth was the most popular, and the amount of interest created was very great. He had a range in operation, and hot biscuits were served to all who wished them; at the same time he had a force of salesmen talking about the range. During the three days he sold 12 ranges, and the results of the advertisement brought him more than double that amount of range and stove business in the first few weeks following the fair.

CONVENIENCES STORE PROVIDES

A general merchant gives customers the following advantages of dealing at his store:

Why it is that people like to trade at our store better than any other store in the county? We'll tell you:

Because it is so convenient. Because they get so many things here they do not have to pay for. Because they know they will not be importuned to buy, and we're always glad to see them even if they come here only to visit. Really, though, have you stopped to think of the many ways we make you welcome and the numerous little services we perform without asking or expecting a cent of remuneration? For instance, these:

We cash your checks. We sell you postage stamps. You can leave your packages here when in town. You can meet your friends here. Write your letters here—we furnish stationery. Tired? Rest in our easy chairs.

In short, this is your store. We are running it for you. Somebody has to be at the head of anything, and so why not us? The modest profit—and there is one, for we do not claim to do business for nothing—goes to us to pay us for our work. In this way, we all are happy and prosperous, and each transaction makes us regard each other all the more highly.

The store is yours. Use it.

S. L. Marcus & Co., house furnishers, St. John, N.B., have sold their business to Maurice Rubin.

A LITTLE MORE EFFORT on each of the three hundred business days of the New Year will give greater bulk to the dealer's revenue at the close of the year.

The Art of Display

Suggestions for Window and Interior Arrangements.

USE AND VALUE OF WINDOW SIGNS

A retail dealer buys a stock of merchandise and places the goods on his shelves. Then getting them off those shelves immediately becomes the one big object—the thing worth while. This, in brief, is merchandising.

The most successful manufacturers have come to realize that lending a hand in this second phase of merchandising pays big dividends. For when they aid in moving the goods which they have sold they help materially in speeding up the turnover—and the good will of the retail trade is an important by-product. This is the sole object of all advertising done by manufacturers—helping not only to make their own sales grow, but unavoidably helping the retail dealer's sales in the process.

But what I started out to talk about was the uplift in store display—the advertising which is done right where the goods are on sale. Until comparatively few years ago any old sort of printed sign or marking pot art was considered good enough to tack up on the wall of the average store. Whether or not the sign got any real attention—or whether or not that attention, if secured, was favorable—was not seriously considered.

However, that the retail merchants of those days recognized even in this crude form an attempt to help them move the goods which they had bought and paid for is evidenced by the fact that so many of them allowed their walls to be patched over with matter of this sort. This sort of sign advertising has gone, however, with the days when all crackers came packed in wooden boxes—and the cracker-box politician ruled the Dominion from his perch by the store's stove.

To-day the merchant demands that store advertising done in his establishment by manufacturers must not only far outstrip the store advertising of a few years ago in actually selling the goods thus advertised, but the hangers, transparents, window trims and counter stands must be so attractive as to be a credit to his store as well. When they live up to this standard the wise merchant welcomes such selling helps with open arms, for the modern retailer realizes that, if he is to meet competition and run his store on an up-to-date basis he must take advantage of all the real selling helps he can get.

The circulation of window advertising is something enormous. I have a business associate who has placed men with hand-counting machines in front of the stores in all classes of communities, excepting the central business districts of cities. These men have counted the people who pass those stores during the hours when the average citizen is up and about; and the actual count shows that thirty-five people per walking hour—or five hundred or more per day—actually pass the windows. What an opportunity some merchants and some manufacturers are missing!

For those manufacturers and merchants who know how to handle it the show window has proved itself the most forceful and direct of all advertising media—as with all other media, results depend on the plan, the copy and seeing to it that proper use is made of the material. In this connection it is surprising the amount of expensive matter of this sort which is allowed to go to waste simply for lack of knowledge as to how to get it into the hands of the dealers who are waiting to put it to work—if it comes up to the standard.

If the goods for which store advertising is to be provided by the manufacturer are sold only at certain restricted seasons, the sign or display must be of a

A natural and homelike display of dining-room furniture made by a large American furniture house. Note effect of appropriate surroundings, all the details helping out the attractiveness of the window picture and the worth of the goods from the buyer's standpoint.

temporary nature and must deliver a forceful, timely message—or possibly several messages in quick succession—changing the copy just as is considered essential in street car, billboard, newspaper or any other sort of advertising. But suppose the article is one which is in demand just as much at one time of the year as at another; it is then that a permanent sign is the logical thing—with possibly a temporary hanger or display every now and then to stimulate the demand and renew the interest.

Merchants these days are asking for store advertising which not only ties up their establishments with such other advertising as the manufacturer may be doing, but which have real sales-making elements for other lines which the merchant carries. As a result an innovation in the line of permanent signs is a display for the top of the show window featuring the manufacturer's advertising on one panel of a transparent, and devoting panels on each side to the dealer's other lines. Such displays show a healthy spirit of co-operation on the part of the manufacturer, and earn the good will of the merchant.

Besides temporary and permanent displays for use right on the front window—where the circulation is, of course, largest—progressive advertisers are now using extensively cardboard stands for sitting on the counter or showcase and holding actual packages of their goods, thus bringing them politely, but more effectively, to the attention of the retailer's customers.

Store advertising is just beginning to receive the attention which is due it as a medium which does its work at the very place where goods are traded for dollars. It does away with the problem of the relation between the advertising and the distribution of merchandise. It does away with waste circulation, for it marks the actual spot where the goods are on sale. And it speeds up the turnover.—J. F. Myers, Canadian Manager The International Sign Co.

Diagram Showing Method of Scientific Lighting

LIGHTING THE SHOW WINDOW

The good display which is not properly lighted is less effective in drawing prospective customers to the store than is the poor display which is lighted after plans suggested by a really efficient store illuminating specialist. The old days of the gas light, or the arc lamp hung in the window, to greet the eye of the passer directly with its glare, have long since passed. The old style of lighting which lined the frame of the window with gas or electric lights about a foot apart has also taken to cover. It is a universally acknowledged fact to-day that the source of the light in a show window must be hidden from the sight of the person outside the window. This is, of course, not for the purpose of causing the person to wonder where the light comes from, thereby arousing his curiosity. A window which is well and evenly lighted, with the light well diffused over the display at all points, and with the light shining into the eyes of the "looker" nowhere, either directly or by reflection, is a merchandizing beacon for the weary eye at night. It reaches out quietly and grasps the attention of the passer. It sells goods with the same unexplainable facility that is the birthright for the natural born salesman. And, best of all, this window is lighted economically. The modern lighting system is both best and cheapest.

The best informed among the trade, whether they be buyers or sellers of merchandise, are quick to discover, even by the show windows which line a business thoroughfare, which of the establishments back of those show windows are progressive and which are not, writes Harold Cantwell, a lighting expert. Even the shopping public is able to discriminate in this respect; in fact, the average shopper does thus discriminate, even though he or she may not be conscious of the fact.

The average merchant is not alive to the possibilities of high-class scientific window lighting and to the improvements in show window lighting which have been made within the last two or three years.

Most retailers, however, are more or less cognizant of the immense advertising value of the show-window, which is evidenced in numerous instances by the elaborate fittings which characterize modern display windows, and also by the constantly increasing demand for thoroughly competent window-dressers.

Eloquent testimony to the merchant's appreciation of the advertising value of his window frontage is shown in the frequent alterations of old-time storefronts, involving in many instances the sacrifice of beautiful monolithic marble columns and other artistic and massive structural features, in order to gain a few more feet of window space.

That a show window attractive by day can be made doubly attractive by night is realized by some concerns, but few merchants are fully aware of the possibilities of staging this effect to the best advantage and with the minimum cost of maintenance. It is now coming to be more generally recognized that the window display can best be brought out in sharp relief by focusing the light upon the merchandise, and, at the same time, without the light source being visible to the eye.

It is a well-known fact that visual acuity is lessened by the eye being directly exposed to a brilliant source of light; and that details clearly discernible with the light source shaded are frequently lost and always dimmed when a bright light is directly exposed to the retina.

The explanation of the phenomenon is simple; the pupil of the eye requires time in which to accommodate itself to a strong light and is, under that light, unable to at once clearly distinguish details. A person looking in the direction of the sun is unable to distinguish details until the eye has accommodated itself to the glare which confronts the retina. Persons accustomed to motoring at night will recall that, by means of the illumination of the usual acetylene lamps, objects in the road ahead are clearly visible, but when approaching an arc lamp these same objects become less prominent and at times almost invisible.

This result is not brought about because there is a lessening of the illumination, but the objects appear less distinct because the brilliant illumination from the arc light is in the direct line of vision and there is a partal blinding of the vision.

An important factor in the effectiveness of an evening display is found in the distribution of the light in such a way as to materially affect the tone of the illumination. Many a show-window is well lighted in the front half, while the display in the back of the enclosure is in comparative shadow.

Frequently these conditions are reversed, with an excess of illumination in the rear of the window and a low degree of intensity at the front, near the plate glass. The window that is ideally illuminated is the one in which there are no light streaks or shadows.

Because the average merchant has given little attention to the matter it is difficult for him to realize what a slight variation in a reflector design will bring about in the way of improved illumination for his window display. A small difference, however, in the design of a reflector will frequently effect a considerable difference in the window illumination.

A common old style method of lighting up the windows has been to use "border" lights; that is bulbs placed along the top, bottom or sides of the glass. This is not satisfactory, however. The light is placed between the eye and the goods on display with the result that the display is not illuminated to advantage, says another writer.

Outside lighting has also been attempted, but the results are not good. Gas arcs placed outside the store will undoubtedly light up the windows, but the goods displayed within will not be seen with any degree of distinctness.

It has been effectually demonstrated that the lights and reflectors should be placed as close to the plate glass as possible and so arranged that the rays will slant towards the goods. In other words, the rays should strike the goods from the same direction in which the people will look. By this means it is possible to get a "spot light" effect, practically eliminating all shadows.

Figure 1 shows the cross-section of a window eight feet high and 16 feet deep, and the other diagrams show the suggested system of lighting this window as outlined in the American Architect. The light is placed at the top and near the front with a scoop reflector. The curve of the scoop reflector is traced on the sketch, and it will be noted that the distribution of light covers the entire line of the trim, that is the space which would be occupied by the display of goods. This distribution curve shows that the downward candle power directly underneath the reflector would be about 275. At an angle of 45 degrees the candle power is about 235, and where the light would strike the upper part of the line of trim, the candle power delivered would be about 225, that is with a 60-watt clear bulb Mazda lamp.

The intensity of illumination desired would determine the number of reflectors used. Where the street would be brilliantly lighted, neighboring windows well lighted and the background and fixtures would be of a medium color, that is not too dark, the window would be well lighted by using the reflectors every 15 inches apart.

In Fig. 2 is shown a window of considerable height. In a case of this kind it is generally found that the upper part of the background is made of glass in order to admit light into the store. This is an important factor in arranging for the illumination of the window. The light should not be thrown on the glass part. Otherwise it would flood into the store and be wasted.

In Fig. 3 is shown the method of properly illuminating the window shown in Fig. 2. The light and reflectors are placed from 12 to 14 feet above the floor. A reflector of the shape shown would, when used in

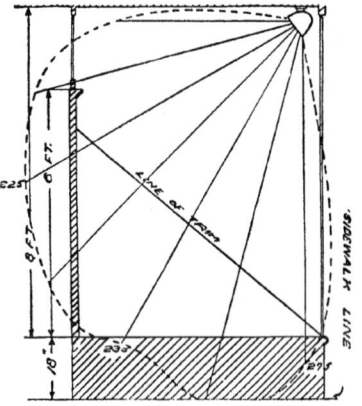

This Light would not Bother the Customer

conjunction with an 80-candle power lamp, throw over 800 candle power downward. This is one of the most powerful reflectors ever designed for window illumination.

VACUUM THEOLOGY

A colored Baptist was exhorting. "Now, breddren and sistern, come up to de altar and hab yo' sins washed away."

All came but one man.

"Why, Brudder Jones, don' yo' want yo' sins washed away?"

"I done had my sins washed away."

"Yo' has. Where yo' had yo' sins washed away?"

"Ober at de Methodist church."

"Ah, Brudder Jones, yo' ain't been washed; yo' jes' been dry cleaned."

———

A woman entered a department store, sought out the men's furnishing counters, and said:—

"I wish to buy a bathing suit for my husband."

"Yes, madam," said the salesman, "and what chest measure?"

The woman frowned and bit her lip.

"Well, now," she said, "how provoking that is! I've forgotten the chest measure."

"Twenty-eight inch, madam?" suggested the salesman.

"Why, yes, of course!" she cried, beaming. "How on earth did you know?"

"Gentlemen who let their wives shop for them," he answered, "always have twenty-eight-inch chests."

Advertising House Cleaning Lines
BY A. B. LEVER

In the course of a few weeks spring house-cleaning will be in vogue and retailers will be drawing attention to articles of various kinds which will be required either for carrying on the house-cleaning process or for furnishing the homes afterwards.

Advertising is, of course, a necessary adjunct to every house-cleaning sale campaign. I have selected for reproducing in this issue ads. which have been used by furniture dealers in different parts of the country when pushing goods for the house-cleaning season. These ads. come from firms in four of the provinces.

I tried to get a vacuum cleaner ad., but was unsuccessful in my search. I regret this, as vacuum cleaners are coming more and more into use. I would be glad if dealers would send me copies of any vacuum cleaner ads. which they have run.

The advertisement of L. Bertrand, Amherstburg, Ont., is an all-round good one. Its appearance is good, but I think its probable strongest point is the suggestion that after renovating the home new furniture is needed. The original was 4⅜ by 5¼ inches.

The advertisement of Greenwood & Vivian, Limited, Stratford, makes an appeal to the women in the home, upon whom the burden of house-cleaning falls. This is its strong point, and is further strengthened by the list of prices furnished. There is one suggestion, however, which I would like to make, and that is in regard to the top line. If the line "O-Cedar Mop Polish" had been given first place and the name of the firm confined to the bottom line the ad. would have been stronger and at the same time been even better in appearance. I would suggest that in future ads. Greenwood & Vivian confine their name to the bottom of the ad. The original was 4⅜ by 5 inches.

The advertisement of Gordon & Keith, Halifax, catches the eye. That is one good thing in its favor. Another good point is the reminder that "now is the time" to buy carpets and rugs. But the advertisement would have been even stronger than it is if the outstanding line on the top had been "Carpets and Rugs for Your Home," instead of the name of the firm. I would make the same suggestion to Gordon & Keith as I have to Greenwood & Vivian.

The outstanding feature of the advertisement of the Home Outfitting Co., Limited, Hamilton, is of course the engraving on the top. The housewife's attention would be immediately arrested by it, and this done, her eye would naturally follow the rest of the advertisement to its bottom. The advertisement is a good one, but it would have been all the more complete has a section or two of the space been devoted to such articles as vacuum cleaners and mops. The original was 8¾ by 17¼.

The advertisement of J. L. Gordon, Kamloops, B.C., is an example of how a good ad. can be secured, even when illustrations are not used. The advertisement is an exceeding good one. Both ad. writer and printer did their work well. While it does not name prices, it should have accomplished what it was evidently designed to do, namely, remind housewives that house-cleaning might necessitate new floor coverings and furniture. The original was 4¼ by 7¾ inches.

The ironing board advertisement is a section from a department store announcement and may furnish a suggestion to retailers when preparing their copy.

"Fine Rugs Make Attractive Homes" is a good one, and is well calculated to excite the aesthetic taste of housewives. It is the strong feature of the ad. The preparing of advertising copy, like letters, require some thought, but it does not always get it. F. P. Scratch & Co. have evidently exercised this thought, and the result is a good, all-round ad. The original was 4¼ by 7¼ inches.

Ads that Make the Right Start
By S. Roland Hill

In advertising, as well as in running, considerable depends on getting a good start.

If we had any way of knowing the facts we should probably know that a great many advertisements are missed altogether just because they don't start strongly.

Some time, just for fun, count the number of advertisements in your favorite newspaper or magazine, average up the amount of time that a copy of the publication gets from you, and then figure out the chance that any one of the advertisements has to attention. The figuring will surprise you—will probably impress on you the importance of the good start for a piece of copy.

The eye doesn't pore down into the body matter of an advertisement unless it is drawn there by some conspicuous feature or by a generally attractive appearance. On the contrary, the eye skims around on the pages of a publication with remarkable speed, and if you are to catch attention, and command the reader's interest you must have "the point of contract" in the beginning of your story.

Of course the good illustration often serves admirably as an attention-getter, but even when illustrations are used, a great deal depends on the displayed starting-point of the word-message.

There is nothing surer than that as time goes on increased attention will be paid to the headlines or "catch lines" of advertisements.

It is a mighty fine thing when you are building an advertisement to ask yourself: "What question or suggestion about the need, benefit or use of this article is most likely to command the favorable attention of readers?"

DEAD QUIET.

The little chap was playin "store"
   Along with other boys;
And as they romped around the floor
   They made a lot of noise.
"Keep that store quiet," mother said.
   The little chap was wise.
"All right," quoth he, "we'll just pretend
   That we don't advertise."

ONE-TIME ADVERTISING

One-time advertising pays only in exceptional cases, says Furniture World, New York. It takes vigorous and persistent follow-up. The newspaper representative should point this out to the new advertiser.

It is usually best to start advertising on small persistent space. A dealer did not believe in advertising. He started newspaper advertising, as he said, because he liked the solicitor and wanted to see if it would pay. His five-inch space in a daily newspaper was changed daily. At the end of the first month he could see no effect except the monthly statement of $48.00. He was persuaded to keep on. At the end of the second month he was sure of two regular customers who came entirely because of a special price in an ad. This merchant had not missed an issue for five years. His ads. are timely and forceful.

WHY PEOPLE ADVERTISE

Advertising is done, among other reasons: To establish trademarks, good will, etc. To create acquaintance and confidence. To identify products and makes. To prevent substitution. To dominate the field. To insure against domination by others. To create an automatic demand. To increase sales, either by direct influence, or assist dealers, or both. To keep up sales that may be declining, due to depression, indifference or inroads of competition. To control and direct the demand to dealers, as against leaving them free to push favored goods. To own your own business and good will and control distribution. To tell your own story as you want it told. To discount or annihilate time in establishing a new or wider market.—Printer's Ink.

HOW THE FARMER VIEWED ADVERTISING.

The Hardware Trade in a recent issue told this incident:

A merchant met a farmer carrying an express package from a Chicago mail order house. "Why, didn't you buy that bill of goods from me?" he asked, "I could have saved you the express charges, and, besides, you would have been patronizing a home store."

The farmer looked at the merchant for a full minute and then said: "Why don't you patronize your home paper and advertise? I read them and did not know you had this particular line."

In lieu of moral, this comment is made: The retailer thinks that the business of his territory belongs to him, and so it does, but the same kind of support you expect the farmer to give you, you should be willing to extend to your local publisher.

Examples of House Cleaning Sales Ads. in daily newspapers used by Canadian Furniture Dealers.

STOVES AND HOUSE FURNISHINGS

HOW TO SELL A STOVE OR RANGE
By F. L. Edman in Iron Age Hardware

Salesmanship is a part of the service buyers demand, pay for and have a right to expect. It is always important in supplying the requirements of the consuming public; not alone because goods are being disposed of and dollars added to the till, but also because of the prestige it establishes. People learn that your store is a desirable place to trade, which means increased business and more profits.

The stove salesman will find it greatly to his advantage to prepare a selling talk on stoves, as well as other items which require more than ordinary skill in salesmanship. This does not mean that he should hand out a cut and dried speech to all prospects, but rather that he should have a definite, logical plan of procedure. He should study the merits of the line he is selling; anticipate objections and be prepared successfully to meet and overcome them.

Everyone makes mistakes, but the wise man profits by his errors, using them as stepping stones to success. If a sale is lost through lack of an adequate argument to cover an objection, that means there is a vulnerable point in your selling talk and not a stone should be left unturned until the weak spot is properly reinforced.

The Buyer's Viewpoint

Many arguments are ineffective because the viewpoint of the buyer is not considered. The man who is in the market for a stove understands very little, and cares less, about the various processes which certain parts undergo in the course of construction. It is therefore a waste of time to direct your talk along this line. What he does want to know is how well the stove will meet his requirements.

If he is in need of a heating stove, the element of comfort should be the basis for the construction of your selling talk. He is interested in learning of any special features it may possess that make for greater efficiency in the production and radiation of heat.

If the prospect wants a range the cooking and baking facilities are most important. A large, roomy oven is a point of merit that will bear special emphasis, also the manner in which the heat is distributed to all parts.

Bringing Imagination Into Play

Just ordinary statements of cold facts are not sufficient. It is essential that you bring your imagination into play. For instance, you state that the stove is a good baker. This assertion may be true, but it is advisable to enlarge on this a little. Picture the delicions pies, cakes, pudding, etc., it is possible to make in an oven so perfectly constructed as the one with which this particular stove is equipped. In this way your talk will be more interesting and forceful.

Inasmuch as everyone is susceptible to an argument that suggests economy, it is always well to make prominent the fuel-saving properties of a stove.

The average housewife likes a plain stove, as the work of keeping it clean is greatly facilitated. Therefore something along this line should be incorporated in your selling talk, providing, of course, the stove will bear you out in your assertions.

Handling the Question of Price

The price objection is one with which the stove salesman is constantly coming in contact. The prospect may be apparently well pleased with the stove; is satisfied that it is just what he or she wants, but thinks the price is prohibitive; had figured on getting one for less money.

Salesmen have various way of meeting this objection. Some try to make the prospect believe that there is no other stove worth carrying home; others refrain from mentioning any competitive line whatever, but talk their stove from an investment standpoint, preferring to make the sale rather on the merits of their line than on the defects, real or assumed, of competitive goods. The latter is, of course, the logical method. To knock another man's product is to advertise it, and no merchant has time to assist his competitor in this way.

Clinching the Sale

Not infrequently sales are lost through the salesman's inability to close the deal. It must be remembered that the buyer is usually on the defense. When he makes his final decision it means the battle is at an end; one of the two contending forces has succumbed to defeat, the other pronounced victor. Right at this climax everything depends on the salesman's ability to properly put on the clinchers. He should never consider his selling talk complete until this point is mastered, for here is where the fight is won or lost. By a carefully planned, well-executed maneuver the salesman may here turn the tide in his favor, even though he may have been apparently beaten up to this time. A single blunder, however, is likely to lose all that has heretofore been gained.

The dropping of a remark which will convey the idea that you consider the deal closed will often be instrumental in leading the customer to a favorable decision. Care must be exercised, however, to see that this is not done in an offensive manner. It is well to get the buyer to do some talking before an attempt is made to clinch the sale, as the effort is then more apt to be successful.

New Salesman Scores Over a Tough Customer

A retail hardware merchant located in a small town in northern Indiana relates the following story, which affords an excellent illustration of one way to close a sale, as well as presenting some other very strong points:

"If there was one man we all hated to see come into the store it was old John Walker. He was always on the lookout for trouble; seldom made purchases amounting to anything and was forever kicking about what he did buy. It was his special delight to have us show him various articles and then tell how much cheaper he could buy the same thing, or something just as good, of catalogue houses.

"A short time ago I added a new man to my selling force—a young fellow by the name of Bright, who claimed to have had experience in a city hardware store. He had not been with me very long until an opportunity to demonstrate his selling ability was afforded.

"Walker entered the store one morning, and as none of us was overly anxious to wait on him we hung back to give the new clerk a chance. Bright went forward promptly, greeting him courteously, and succeeded in selling him a pound of nails.

"'If you can spare a few minutes,' said Bright, as Walker was in the act of leaving the store, 'I would like you to see our line of base burners.'

"Walker replied that he had no objection to looking at the stoves, but that he could tell him before hand that he wouldn't have one in his house, because he had never seen one yet that was any good.

"This did not seem to worry Bright in the least, however. He conducted Walker to a seat, and, pulling one of the stoves out in front of him, began pointing out some of the special features of this particular burner.

"Walker said he had very little faith in them. He had bought one ten years ago and the only thing it was good for was to consume fuel. It burned six tons of coal in one winter; the house was seldom comfortable, and the floor was always like a cake of ice.

"Bright here took the trouble to explain the special flue construction of this stove, which made it an especially efficient floor heater, and insured the very best results from the fuel consumed.

"'This is a powerful heater,' he continued. 'With the check draft in you can heat three large rooms in zero weather: then, during the warmer days of spring and fall, the heat may be easily regulated to suit. This stove requires very little attention and you can keep your home in a comfortable, healthy condition at all times. You are not too hot one minute and freezing the next. The length of time it will hold fire is really remarkable. It is handsome, durable, an efficient heater; a stove we know you can use with pleasure and satisfaction.'

"'What's the price of such a stove?' inquired Walker, with a faint spark of interest.

"'Forty-five dollars,' replied Bright.

"Walker threw up both hands, emphatically declaring that he could get one in Chicago just as good for $30.

"Bright did not lose his temper nor get the least bit excited, but took the matter as calmly as though he had anticipated just such an outburst. It was evident he had handled tough customers before. He did not dispute Walker's statement; did not tell him that the stove he could buy in Chicago for $30 was inferior in quality to this one; in fact he said nothing at all about it. What he did do, however, was to produce a pencil and paper and demonstrate by actual figures that this stove at $45 was a mighty profitable investment, showing the real economy of purchasing a stove that was long-lived and would save him fully 25 per cent. on his fuel bill. This sort of an argument appealed uncommonly strong to Walker, whose heart was most easily reached through his purse.

"At just the right time, when Walker appeared somewhat puzzled to know what to do, Bright explained that the stove was made in three sizes, and politely asked which he would prefer. After considerable hesitation Walker stated his choice and the sale was made."

Manager (five-and-ten-cent store) What did that lady who just went out want?

Shopgirl—She inquired if we had a stove department.

TRADE MEDDLING BY QUEBEC LEGISLATURE

Piano men generally in Quebec have grown heartsick of the continual dabbling and meddling of the legislature of the province in all laws affecting liens on goods sold by instalment. So much so that they have been willing for the last two or three years to give it all up, resting all their faith in the landlord law, so-called, or notification law, which when legally acted upon, saves the piano from third parties claiming it for debts due by the purchaser.

Some time ago a bill was introduced into parliament, requiring that no repossessions be made unless the merchant repossessing the piano was willing to refund four-fifths of the amount paid by the instalment. This bill was fought strenuously by the piano men, under the leadership of A. P. Willis, president of Willis Co., Ltd., and was thrown out. Last year, another bill was brought up, which was then defeated, but it has been brought forward this session with double force and determination that it shall pass the legislature. This is the bill that many piano men have allowed to give the go-by. However, in the opinion of Mr. Willis, it is a very bad and injurious bill—the thin edge of the wedge that would eventually break up the whole instalment system. Asked to define the practical result of this bill if it ever became law, Mr. Willis said: "Well, it is just like this: You sell goods, but you cannot collect for them outside the district in which you reside, that is the real meaning of the 'Domicile Bill,' for that is the name of the bill before the legislature. This bill is in the interest of country lawyers and country courthouses, who have no business, who are briefless, and who wish to encourage litigation in their own districts, without any regard to the interests of trade in general. Under the present system, a merchant in Montreal or Quebec, doing business 500 miles away, within the province, can elect Domicile at Montreal or Quebec. Under the proposed law, the country people snap their fingers at the manufacturer or merchant, because they know it would never pay a man in Montreal to go far away from home to the lawyer or the court-house to attend a law suit. In this way, numberless customers may refuse to pay balances on pianos, $50, $25, $10. People would say, 'Well, we have paid enough on that piano, I guess they will not want to come and sue me here, 300 miles away,' and so the very profits, the only profit in the transaction would be jeopardized. The whole discussion in Quebec Parliament has brought up all the objectionable arguments that are ever raised against the instalment system."—Canadian Music Trades Journal.

Furniture men as well as piano men are interested in legislation of this kind, and they should take just as much interest in protecting their business.—Editor Furniture World.

I believe in knowing just what I am doing and where I hope to land. I always strive for something a little farther ahead, but I always know the exact point which I hope to attain, and I have figured out the steps I must take to reach that point.—Walter H. Cottingham.

Selfish interests, if they are our pilots, will betray us. Vainglory will destroy us. Pride will wreck us. Expedients are for an hour, but principles are for the ages. Nothing can be permanent and nothing safe in this exigency that does not sink deeper than politics and money. We must touch the rock or we shall never have firm foundations. Beecher.

Floor Coverings

A GOOD CARPET SALESMAN
By W. L. Harris

The best salesman I ever knew was a man in my own line of business. In showing a carpet, for instance, he took a roll from the shelf—that was in the days when we did not show by samples, but by strength—rolled it out deftly and gracefully, matched it up with the utmost dexterity, but never for a moment did he watch his carpet, his eye was on his customer, and he knew his merchandise so well, and had practised by himself so thoroughly the way to properly exhibit it, that he could, and did, focus his entire attention on his customer.

Seldom did the salesman referred to show more than one carpet, and never more than two or three. What does the crude, green salesman do? Pulls down the whole stock, roll after roll, or sample after sample; gets the customer all mixed up; is himself in a stew, so that when he should be at the point of clinching the sale, he is in no sort of condition, and all he really had time to notice about his customer was that he was a two-legged creature, and that he's been giving a rehearsal instead of a finished performance—and a pretty poor rehearsal at that.

Another point. It isn't the price of merchandise to-day which counts so much, as quality, coupled with faith in the salesman, and it is, in my judgment, a poor salesman who emphasizes over-strongly the question of price. In fact, to-day people don't shop around for price: they assume that the price will be all right, and don't waste time in dealing with harlequins, quacks, fakirs or hypnotists.

MAKE GRASS FURNITURE AND RUGS

The Winnipeg Grass Rug Co., Ltd., Winnipeg, has received a Manitoba charter to manufacture and deal in grass-twine, matting and other products of grass, and also to make furniture composed wholly or partly of grass. Emil H. Steiger, of Oshkosh, Wis., is interested, as also are a couple of St. Paul, Minn., men. A local capital will be raised to carry on the industry, which is capitalized at $100,000.

CHINESE RUGS

The demand for Chinese rugs, which several years ago reached the proportions of a well-developed fad, is still an important factor to be reckoned with by dealers in Oriental rugs, says the American Carpet and Upholstery Journal.

The colorings of Chinese rugs harmonize particularly well with Chippendale furnishings, and it is perhaps largely owing to the fact that there is a continued call for this type of furnishing that Chinese rugs, both in antiques and reproductions, continue in favor.

Chinese antique rugs, on account of their soft, rare colorings and long-wearing qualities, command a high price in the market; so high, in fact, that in sizes larger than 6 x 9 feet there is a very limited selling field. Chinese reproductions are priced to reach a larger trade, and these are moving well at the present time.

Before Chinese rugs came into high favor, there was the same craze for India rugs. These, too, were good sellers for a time, but now very few are moving. One Oriental rug dealer claims that those who have a stock of India rugs at the present time are satisfied if they get fifty cents on the dollar for them.

During the last few months there has been a noticeable call for Oriental rugs shading on a mulberry color. Formerly, brown colorings were the popular ones, but it is now believed in the trade that this mulberry, or crushed strawberry color, as it is sometimes called, will supersede the browns for next season at least. Owing to the recent demand for these new shadings, it is impossible to obtain them from stock, but many orders have already been placed.

SOME ORIENTAL RUG SYMBOLS

The medallion in an Oriental rug is said to symbolize space generally, a lozenge or square in the medallion, the earth, and the branches protruding from it mountains and rivers or land and sky.

The tree of life seen so often in Persian rugs is always a religious symbol. The tree is generally a cypress because this tree typifies immortality, its wood being so little affected by the progress of time. Cypress trees are very common in Oriental countries. Willow trees are also employed to suggest ending life.

A pitcher or jug of water is often represented near the tree of life, the idea being that after death the spirit may use the water to wash his eyes and thus shut out the evil he has seen in his life, wash his ears to remove the evil he has listened to, and his mouth to cleanse it from the evil he has uttered.

The pomegranate is frequently used in Oriental rugs. This fruit was dedicated to Juno, perhaps because of the wealth of seeds it contains, as Juno was the patroness of marriage, riches and fertility.

Animal figures are most common in Chinese rugs. The star and crescent together form a Turkish symbol, the star representing the earth and the crescent the continued growth of Turkish power. The unicorn and antelope are symbols of the moon, and the phenix represents life.—Ex.

"Then you don't like a folding affair?"
"I do not. It's trouble enough at night to undress yourself without having to undress the bed."—Washington Herald.

"I am afraid, madam, we have shown you all our stock, but we could procure more from our factory."
"Well perhaps you'd better. You see I want something of a neater pattern one quite small—just a little square for my bird-cage."—Punch.

Beds and Bedding

BIG BEDDING PLANT AT VANCOUVER

The new plant of the Alaska, B.C., Bedding Company, Limited, was formally opened by his Worship Mayor Baxter, at Vancouver recently, and the machinery throughout the large plant was put in motion for the first time that day. Mayor Baxter poured the metal for the first metal bedstead to be manufactured in British Columbia, and, considering his inexperience, his Worship performed the task very satisfactorily, although Ald. Crowe and Ald. Hepburn both remarked that they could do it without spilling so much of the molten liquid on the ground instead of into the moulds.

The opening ceremony was performed in the presence of the leading officials of the plant and of a large number of citizens.

In conversation, W. I. Crombie, the managing director, stated that the total cost of the plant and equipment was about $225,000. One hundred employees would be engaged from the outset and he believed this number would be materially icnreased before very long.

The plant comprises seven buildings. The main building is 155 feet long by 75 feet wide. The foundry is 80 feet by 55 feet, the warehouse, 150 by 40 feet; the excelsior mill, 36 by 36 feet; the picker house, 24 by 24 feet; the boiler room, 30 by 30 feet; and the stable, 75 by 40 feet. All but the last-named are completed. They are of red brick on reinforced concrete.

MOVED TO LARGE NEW PLANT

The Quality Mattress Co., Berlin, on February 1, began operations in their newly-erected plant at Waterloo, where now is located their head office and factory. The new plant is capable of turning out from 100 to 150 mattresses a day.

IRON BED PLANT BURNED

The Shurly & Dietrich Works, at Galt. Ont., was destroyed by fire early in the morning of February 6. the loss totalling $250,000. The insurance carried amounts to $85,000. The company makes iron beds and saws. The only part of the plant saved was a detached warehouse filled with stock. J. C. Dietrich, senior member of the company, who also controls the R. H. Smith Co., St. Catharines, announces that orders in hand will be filled at the latter plant and that most of the Galt employees will be moved to St. Catharines temporarily.

IDEAL BEDDING NOTES.

The February issue of The Ideal Bulletin is an "Institutional Bed" number, containing as it does much information on this particular bedding line. The front page of the Bulletin is devoted to a number of illustrations of Canadian hospitals.

The company was well pleased with the result of their showing at the Furniture Exhibition. They got business where it was not sought after, and opened several new accounts.

By an actual test recently made with a "Neverspred"

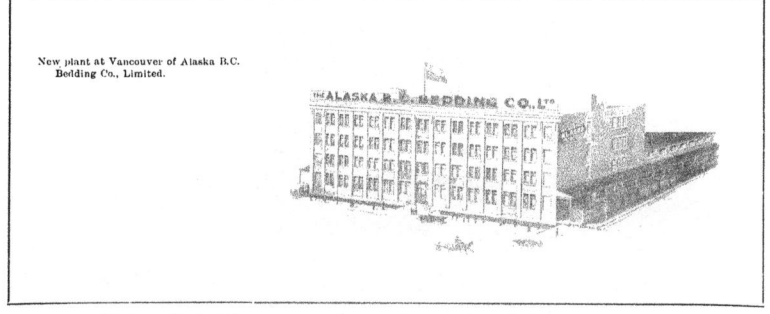

New plant at Vancouver of Alaska B.C. Bedding Co., Limited.

All the machinery is electrically driven, and the most up-to-date automatic machines have been installed in all departments. Some of these machines have been brought from England. The plant is steam-heated throughout.

The company intends to manufacture everything in metal bedsteads, children's safety cribs, woven wire and link fabric springs, coil springs, upholstered box springs, wood and metal frame cots, sliding couches, davenports, "Health" brand mattresses, felt mattresses, etc.

The company has factories in Montreal and Winnipeg, and branches at Regina and Calgary. The president is J. H. Parkhill, Winnipeg; and the vice-president, J. H. Sherrard, Montreal.

mattress, in which one of these makes was sent out from the factory and put into use for three months and then returned, it was found that the mattress was exactly as it had been sent out, the edges holding up, not being displaced even a quarter of an inch. New designs of art ticking are being put on as covers for this season. The double Imperial square edge gives a finish to this product.

The "Fold-Away" cot is one of the latest productions of The Ideal Bedding Co. As its name implies, it is a cot which can be folded away and placed in a corner or closet when not in use, thus taking up little or no noticeable space. It can be made ready for use in an instant. It is built of steel tubes, bronzed or enamelled at choice, and with either canvas or wire link fabric spring mattress. Mounted on rollers and being easily folded, it can be moved about and operated by a child. Head and foot also fold automatically with the opening and closing of the "Fold-Away." Last year's sales in New York State totalled 11,00.

This wire link fabric is an important and big line with The Ideal Company, as they use it in a great many of their various bed springs, as well as woven wire. It carries a guarantee, and is used extensively in the United States. It is a special feature of the new "Duplex" spring—another new Ideal line, by the way—which is working its way into favor rapidly throughout the country.

The "Duplex" is made in woven wire as well as link fabric. The essential feature is, as its name implies, a double or duplicated spring of the twin variety— two individual bed springs being attached with a steel device which makes it possible for a heavy person to use one side of the bed without bringing down the whole mattress on a slant or disturb a lighter weight on the other half of the mattress. This spring made of link fabric carries a twenty-year guarantee.

A new feature is being added to the Ideal "Harinfelt" mattress this season. The "Harinfelt" has always been reckoned the highest production of the company. This year the special features of the "Neverspred'—the strapped filling and the side ventilators—are being added without any extra charge. Some new designs in art ticking are as well being used.

A unique new line of children's cribs with an added accident proof feature is being put out this year. This is a mesh side crib, the sides being composed of mesh instead of rod fillers. With the bringing of the fillers closer together and the adding of the new lock device (now colored in red, as an extra precaution) the children's crib was brought pretty close to perfection. The Mesh side makes this essentially so, particularly as regards safe-guarding against accidents.

The very latest in popular sellers is the new "Perth" woven wire mattress, first manufactured in February. This mattress has reinforced copper wires running through it and a copper rope edge.

UNIQUE CHILDREN'S VOTING CONTEST

The Bedells Furnishing Co., Toronto, are conducting a unique voting contest at present in their Yonge Street store, in which every boy and girl in the city under 16 years of age is eligible for entry. For every cent spent in the store between January 26 and April 6 the purchaser is given a coupon entitling him or her to one vote for any candidate—which means practically any child in Toronto, excepting only employees and relatives of employees of the store—as all are eligible for entry. At the close of the contest the ballot box will be unlocked and three responsible newspaper men will count the votes and award the prize to the child who has gained the largest number of votes. The prize, which is well worth striving for, is a Shetland pony, a stylish carriage, and a set of harness.

Any child wishing to enter the contest may enroll name personally or have a friend do so. A number of pony picture postcards are given the contestant for distribution among relatives and friends asking them to buy from Bedells and cast votes for the sender.

The contest has been given publicity through the press, through circular distribution, and through window announcements, and already quite an interest has been stirred up among the children of the city, which, no doubt, will bring quite a bit of business to the store, this being, of course, the real purpose of the contest.

In connection with the contest a special inducement is being offered to instalment buyers to increase their payments, double votes being given for all "excess" payments. That is if one dollar is due and two dollars are paid the customer is entitled to 300 voting coupons —100 for the due payment and 200 for the excess payment.

The contest is run in conjunction with the Dunlap Pony Co. of Greenfield, Ohio, they obtaining some advertising publicity for their pony farm through the avenue of this competition.

Good all-round bedding and mattress display made by Henry Hoffman, Simcoe, Ont.

C. F. Emde has sold his furniture and hardware business at Imperial, Sask.

Hints for the Office Man

CASH DISCOUNTS AND INVOICE PRICE
By an Old Retailer

Cash discounts should not be deducted from invoice price before applying the cost of doing business; to do this would cause the dealer to lose the cash discount—provided he add the same net profit. If the dealer's expense account includes all the real expense of his business, then interest is charged in this account for all money invested and all money borrowed, and it is this money that enables the dealer to secure the cash discounts. The fact that the dealer creates an expense to secure money to take his discounts is proof that the cash discount should protect this expense, and the dealer who deducts the cash discount before applying the cost of doing business loses the discount. The cost of doing business cannot be measured entirely by the total amount of the expense account. Many times dealers do certain things in business that does not cause them to add anything to their expense account in dollars and cents, but it is not prepared to give good service to the trade; the dealer who does not study the line of goods he sells; the dealer who does not place quality above price; the dealer who is continually changing, selling one make of goods this year and another next; the dealer who sacrifices his profit to secure a greater volume of business; the dealer who sells goods all year without checking his sales and stock against goods on hand and from inventory and goods received during the year, then he may discover goods delivered without settlement; the dealer who neglects to take his cash discounts, even if he has to borrow the money; the dealer who neglects to make a demand for settlement of note and account when due; the dealer who is not able to meet his customers with a smile, no matter what his own troubles may be, all add to their cost of doing business.

HANDLING MONTHLY ACCOUNTS SPEEDILY

Every day of delay in the preparation of statements means that they will get into the hands of customers late, and that remittances will not come in promptly.

The time consumed in making out statements consists of transcribing the items on the statement blank, entering the date and afterwards going over them and adding the amounts.

Here is a method of making up statements which has proved a most efficient one in practice:

When the dates and the amounts have been transcribed on the statement, it is torn off and dropped into the ledger opposite the account from which the amounts have been taken. The edge is left projecting slightly above the page so that it will serve as a marker. In this manner all the statements are dropped into the ledger opposite the respective accounts. When the adding and listing of the amounts has been completed, the bookkeeper turns to the first account and enters the name on the statement, which completes it.

But there is another important point just here that should not be overlooked. Since all the items taken from a customer's account have been added and listed on the statement, the total should agree with the ledger total.

By making the comparison between the statement and the ledger totals when the names are filled in, the bookkeeper is enabled to check both his statement total for items transcribed and to check up his ledger footing at the same time.

This very important feature of this method of making out statements is incidental to the method itself and does not require any extra time for the check. Besides, it enables the bookkeeper to get out his statements much more quickly and with far less effort.

A SHORT CUT IN ADDITION

Memorizing combinations of figures greatly simplifies the work of addition. At first, says a writer in System, it is best to attempt only one column combinations rather than those of two columns, although, after practice, the latter can be used. But when one learns combinations of numbers as he has already learned combinations of letters in words, he can add as quickly as he reads print. Thus, two 2's coming together in a column are thought of only as 4; 3 and 4 as 7; 4 and 5 as 9; 2, 4, and 5 as 11; and so on.

Another method is to add by tens. Although this is slower than adding by combinations it is quicker and more accurate than the ordinary method.

The rule is to add up the first ten, commencing at the bottom, placing a dot opposite the last figure, to drop the ten, to add until another ten is reached, and to place a second dot, each time carrying the unit into the next ten. To illustrate:

One Column	Two Columns	Three Columns
3	2 3	1 2 3
7	4 7	2 4 7
4	3 4	5 3 4
2	7 2	1 7 2
6	2 6	2 2 6
9	1 9	3 1 9
31	2 2 1	1 6 2 1

A SIMPLE METHOD OF ACCOUNTING

In keeping his customer's ledger accounts in check one bookkeeper used a series of consecutive numbers to designate each settlement, marking the number in a small check column opposite each of the debit and credit items covered by the payment.

These numbers did nothing more than identify the items. By making the numbers express dates, however, such as 7/12 for July 12th, he could tell at a glance the date each charge was paid without having to look for the corresponding number on the credit side.

SHORT HINTS ON STOCK-TAKING

Try to get the work over as soon as possible, but be sure and do it accurately.

If you take stock during business hours, be sure not to neglect customers.

Prepare ahead as far as possible. Put like articles together—have cost marked on goods—have bins and boxes weighed.

If you have occasion to leave some line until later before listing, make a note of it, so it will not be forgotten.

Loose leaf stock sheets are the best, as they allow several people to do listing. Afterwards they can be bound together.

Don't guess at quantities or cost price. Guesswork has no place in stock taking.

Take other particulars of your business needed in making out a financial statement, at the same time as you take stock.

SALESPEOPLE

RANDOM TALKS FOR AND ABOUT CLERKS
By Frank D. Smith

MY early training in selling goods was secured in a country town. In the store next door there were a couple of young fellows who thought that the world owed them a good time, and who decided to take it as they went along. Whenever they got a chance during business hours they slipped down to the barber shop to talk and play checkers. Some days they would spend practically a quarter of their time there, but when Saturday night came they would take their money without a thought that they hadn't earned it—in fact they were constantly expecting a raise.

I don't know why the boss didn't kick up a fuss, but he was one of those easy going fellows, and while I know he frequently called them down, they managed to hold their jobs.

A Lost Opportunity

It was too bad that they didn't apply themselves, for if either of them had taken any interest in the business he would have been given the chance to take charge of the store. The boss took ill, and couldn't stay at the store much, and so had to get someone to manage it. He would have certainly given one of them the chance if they had proved themselves at all capable, but they believed in taking things easy as they went along—and so lost one of the best opportunities of their lives.

How One Clerk Succeeded

In the same town was another fellow who took an interest in his work and in the business, and did his best to get along. Probably it was because his father was dead. and realizing that he had no one to fall back on, he felt that he just had to get along. His employer was very strict, but he stood more than most young fellows would have done, but in the end it proved all to his own good, for the competent knowledge of the business which the boss required of him proved very valuable once he got started climbing. He took a position in a larger store in a larger town as assistant in a department. In two years he had advanced to manager of the department, just because back in the little town he had completely mastered all the fundamental points of the business.

The Dissatisfied Fellow

Clerks do become dissatisfied with their positions at times, it is true. Sometimes they can see no chance for any advancement in the store they are in, and feel like seeking another position. There was one such clerk in a store in a small city last year. He was next to the manager in the department, but could see no chance for further advancement there. He decided to go West, and wanted the fellow who was next to him to go too. but the latter decided to stick for a while longer. The other went.

Two months afterwards, the manager of the department left to accept a better position, and the under-clerk who had decided "to stick" was given his position. He is now getting more money than his senior who felt there were no possibilities in the store.

Don't Mix Ambition and Discontent

There is also the fellow who is always seeing greater possibilities in other lines of endeavor than the one he is following. He has heard or read of someone who has made a lot of money in a short time in some way, and he too is anxious to tackle the same thing. He forgets that he hears only of the ones who have made a success—not of the many who have tried it and made a miserable failure.

It is all very well for the young man to have ambition, and plenty of it, but not a few mistake discontent for ambition.

Decide on a line of endeavor that you feel you can succeed at and stick with it persistently, ever attempting to improve your knowledge of that particular business.

SALESMAN AIDED BY GOOD AIM
By George F. Barton

Here is an instance told by the buyer and gun department manager of one of the large retail stores of how he made a sale by unusual salesmanship:

"One day a man loked at the air guns which were in a rack on the counter.

"'Could I sell you one, sir?' I inquired.

"'I guess you could if they shot straight, but of course they're a hopeless case when it comes to accuracy.'

"'I am a fair shot myself, so I said: 'Do you see that calendar down at the end of the aisle?' pointing at one which hung on the wall some seventy-five feet away with an illustration of two Indians in a canoe. 'I'll bet you the price or the gun that I can shoot the left eye out of the Indian with the red feather in his hair.'

"'You're on,' he said, incredulously.

"I loaded, aimed the gun, and pulled the trigger.

"The calendar flapped as it was hit. We went over to it. The tiny bit of lead had hit exactly in the designated spot. The left eye of the Indian with the red feather was nothing more than a ragged little hole!

"He looked at the picture and then at me with bulging eyes.

"'Wonderful!' he said, 'I'll take two of them.'

"I couldn't duplicate the shot again in a thousand chances without some streak of luck, but I felt that I could hit near enough so that he would not claim the wager and buy a rifle besides. The result was even better than I had hoped for."

HOW TRAVELLER HELPED RETAILER

Scores of men enter business in Western Canada without much or any knowledge of fundamental business principles.

The representative of a Winnipeg wholesale house a few months ago ran across a hardware dealer whose only books were his bank and cheque book. The merchant's wife had been a school teacher, and the traveller explained to them a simple system of keeping books.

Under advice they took stock, entered the value of all goods received, kept track of sales and figured a certain margin of profit.

A few months later a fire occurred and the possession of the rough set of books enabled them to collect the full amount of their insurance and keep their credit good with the wholesale house.

ENGLISH STYLES IN DEMAND IN AMERICA

The demand for English furniture and furnishings in the styles made classic by the early cabinetmakers still continues strong in America. The Georgian period, including the work of Chippendale, Heppelwhite and Sheraton, seems most in favor, says our Grand Rapids namesake, probably because it lends itself more easily to the uses of the day, probably because it gives the decorator a wider scope in which to exercise his inventive and adaptive genius. The earlier English styles, the Tudor, the Elizabethan, the Jacobean, and in some instances William and Mary, are reserved for special treatment where the size and character of the room permit them to be used as they should.—The Furniture Record, London.

EVOLUTION OF THE BABY CARRIAGE.

The early nineteenth century car looks primitive enough to us in the year 1912, but compared with prototypes of baby cars at the present day in use among the Hudson Bay Indians and the natives of Siberia it is indeed luxurious, remarks a writer in an English publication. It would be interesting to get the Siberian mother's opinion of one of the latest all-steel, nickel-plated collapsible cars. She, good woman, would probably be very scared at it and far prefer to strap her infant on to the boat-shaped board. The cradles used by the Hudson Bay Indians are carried on the backs of the women, and in the rude churches in that part of the world the visitors may see stout nails in the walls; on these the babies are hung in their respective carriers from the beginning of the service until the clergyman has pronounced the benediction. Although, at the present day, the individual carriage is only used for infants and invalids, in the eighteenth century the Sedan chair was very generally employed, and many of them were very beautifully decorated. The Sedan chair is eastern in origin, and its introduction into this country from Naples is ascribed to a certain Sir Sanders Duncombe, who was granted a monopoly for fourteen years for letting such chairs on hire in London. When the owner was not taking the air these Sedan chairs occupied a permanent place in the hall, and were decorated elaborately and upholstered in rich stuffs. In England the Sedan never reached the high artistic level which it did in France.

That the makers of baby carriages have borrowed many ideas from coach and carriage builders is patent from the very names employed, such as landau, landaulette, and barouche, coach finish, etc., and if one looks at very early carriages, such as the Continental example, made about 1700, one sees how that came about. These, the center part hung on the elaborate under framing to which the wheels are attached, take the exact shape of a double-seated perambulator with a well between.

"Here we take the opportunity," concludes the writer, "of entering a protest against the constant cry for something cheaper in perambulators. We have no hesitation in saying that there is absolutely no need for this, for when a baby carriage is bought the very best that money can procure is constantly demanded.

IS GOLD FURNITURE COMING BACK?

A salesman for an American upholstered furniture house, who covers the Western States, recently returned from his trip, and noted what he thought looked like the beginning of a revival of the demand for gold furniture, which is as unexpected as it is hard to account for. His house closed out its gilding department some time ago because of a lack of demand for that part of the product. He referred to one incident that is interesting. Some three years ago he sold a high-priced gold suite to a leading buyer, and it had remained on the floor in its glory of increasing age for about three years. The salesman had been approached by the house a number of times to do something to get the aforesaid suite off his hands, but it seemed glued to the floor tighter than ever. What was the surprise of the salesman on his last trip to this place to secure an order for two more suites of the same pattern, the original suite having been sold in the meantime. His house filled the order, but had to send out the goods to be gilded. and now they are trying to find out if there really is a new demand springing up.

In Canada, at least in the east, there does not appear to be any renewal of this business. In fact, furniture dealers spoken to state they do not expect to see a revival of this or any other garish line. There may be, it is true, an occasional sale for a gift gilt chair, but none of the dealers interviewed would like to stock this line unless there was more evidence of a demand for it. Furniture dealers say they are "from Missouri" on this question.

ART IN FURNITURE.

Do we realize, even in a moderate degree, what a factor the furnishing of the home is in the scheme of modern civilization? Frankly it seems we have as plain and manifest a duty in educating the homemaker in the selection of furniture as in preaching civic beauty. When we assist in creating the home of taste, we are ministering to culture and intelligence. It is impossible that one should continue without the other. No homemaker can associate with household goods in which the kindred quality of each is well established and interrelated, without being improved by the contact. Mental efficiency, moral breadth and the sheer pagan joy of life are all promoted by our intimate environments. So important, indeed, is the effect of environment upon mental and bodily health that in the not far distant future our most successful physicians may sometimes prescribe proper furniture and home decoration as aids to digestion and disposition.—A. T.

Plenty of business men every year fail, not because they could not see far enough ahead to avoid disaster, but because they would not look ahead.

ADVANTAGES OF RETAIL ORGANIZATION

A Saskatoon merchant makes the point that if the retailers in Western Canada were better organized they would be able to make their influence felt upon the bankers and others largely responsible for the business conditions of the country.

"We retailers," he said, "have to carry the load of this over speculation in land. The wholesalers are organized into the Credit Men's Association and can act unitedly on matters of common interest. If we had a strong retail association we could present our views to the government, the bankers and the credit men more intelligently."

SHORT SHOP TALKS.

By Frank Farrington

It is better to refuse to deliver goods at all than to deliver them in an unsatisfactory way. What is worth doing at all is worth doing well.

It is a good plan to offer bargains but it is well to remember that unless there are some bargains for the seller as well as for the buyer, the business cannot prosper.

The man who thinks that he can learn all he needs to know about business without any outside help forgets that two heads are better than one.

If you find that you cannot get time in the store to read your trade papers carefully, why not take them home with you. You certainly need to read them.

Every dollar you spend each year for trade papers ought to pay you a return of ten or even a hundred dollars. If it fails to do so, the fault probably lies with you.

The clerk who spends his half day off sitting around the smoky hotel or club room will go back to work worse off than as if he had not had the time off.

How do you know you don't want any of the drummer's goods unless you look them over? He may have the very thing you are looking for.

Be careful how you under-estimate your new competitor. Just because he has little money and a small stock that is no sign that he may not have lots of business getting ability.

Do you want to know what will be of great value in helping you to build up your business and yet will not cost you a single cent to use? It is cordiality.

The more lines of goods you can handle well, the more customers you will have. But remember that I said handle well.

If you are cold-blooded in your way of handling customers, don't be surprised if the customers fail to get warmed up about buying.

The grouchy employer must expect grouchy clerks and grouchy clerks will make a grouchy employer.

Clerks can help the management by finding out what has brought customers in to buy, whether certain advertisements have pulled well or not.

Do people get waited on right away when they come into your store or do they have to stand around until half of their buying inclination is gone before they have a chance to buy?

There are two sides to every offer and often times the Something-for-nothing offer carries its most important features on the under side.

This Year
Let Us Improve in Every Way:

1 Physically	2 Mentally	3 Morally	4 Financially	5 Socially
By	By	By	By	By
1. Eliminating bad food and not eating too much.	1. Learning from the experiences of others.	1. Being honest with ourselves and others.	1. Working more systematically and intelligently.	1. Choosing the right kind of friends.
2. Breathing plenty of fresh air.	2. Reading good books, magazines and newspapers.	2. Remembering that right is right and wrong is wrong.	2. Decreasing unnecessary expenses.	2. Avoiding associates that discourage us.
3. Using plenty of water inside and outside.	3. Observing events that make for the world's progress.	3. Helping others. (The more we know and the more we have, the more strictly will we be judged.)	3. Following more closely Company methods.	3. Taking more interest in the neighborhood.
4. By letting more sunlight into our houses.	4. Discussing our problems with others who can help us.	4. Being charitable. (Charity begins at home but must not end there.)	4. Taking advantage of all our many opportunities.	4. Taking more interest in the city, the state, the nation and the world.
5. By exercising for health, not for strength.	5. Thinking only of things that will help us.	5. Keeping away from temptation.	5. Make our business so absorbing that all other interests are incidental.	5. Treating others as we would have them treat us.

From the N. C. R. Weekly, published by the National Cash Register Company, Dayton, Ohio.

HOW TO REDUCE FAILURES
By Walter Weiss

The chart of intelligible statistics is the only guide to reduction of expenses. Knowledge of such statistics will enable either the reduction of expenses or the development of more or better paying business.

It is necessary for everyone in business to know the exact cost in detail of doing business, in all departments of his business. We have found it so in our business.

Business men hire bookkeepers to keep their accounts straight. What reason have they for not hiring a cost system man to keep their production straight? They hire clerks to check in all shipments made them, so as to be sure they get all they pay for. What reason have they for not hiring a cost system man so as to be sure their labor is giving them all they pay for? They hire accountants to see that all purchases check in O.K. and that billing has been made on all out-going shipments, but let their stock on hand "go hang" because they have a lock on the front and back door. Then at the close of the year they throw their force into an inventory to see where they stand. What reason have they for not having a cost system man who carries a continuous inventory, being able at any time, within a few minutes, to give them an accurate check on any item?

Any one of these items is as important as the other. They all represent their cash value.

It is easy to overestimate or underestimate a man if one does not study and know his ability and capacity. Do not expect your workmen to take the lead and put all the ginger into your business, and make money for you while you show indifference. Show them ways and means, causes and effects, profits and expenses and losses, and watch them come through. Spirit them on as you take them into your confidence and they will then stay with your house.

Much ruinous competition comes from the clerk, salesman or foreman of a department launching into business for himself after having saved up some money working for you. He has seen only a part and believes the game is easy money without the proper insight to figure what really constitutes costs. Take him into your confidence, show him the difficulties of your line of business, he will appreciate it and will not likely launch out if he realizes what is before him. If he does; he is going to be legitimate competition wherever he lands.

Thorough knowledge of all your operations is the only safe guide to the maximum production and minimum of overhead expenses, whether it be departmental or general.

It is possible to get each workman's production, the actual condition of each piece of machinery in a plant, the exact amount of make-ready time, the running time, the amount produced and the idle time with the cost of operating same. This enables one to detect all leaks and produce the highest possible efficiency, thereby enabling one to bill work on a square deal basis.

The departments a customer's work goes through is the basis on which he pays, and he gets all he pays for, or his money's worth. Occasionally he may think a charge is a little high; but as a whole he will find his work very satisfactory, even from a price standpoint, for he receives the benefit of the efficiency. Especially if one assembles the time spent in running around for prices. And right here enters one fine thought, "The Efficiency of One's Own Time." This, however, is a subject in itself.

The thing that should interest all business men, is not to know just how to do every detail of the work in their establishment, but what is each of my help doing and what are the results in each of my departments? The statement of costs gives it in a nutshell.

That business man who, after he asks his bookkeeper how much cash is on hand and is told and is handed the list of collections and disbursements to be made, then asks the cost system man for his results, and is handed his continuous inventory, showing all stock on hand, the result in detail of each department, whether machinery or hand work, with his statement of cost, can very quickly see where he stands.

I am sure the reason for so great a number of business men in any line making a failure is due to their not knowing their costs. I cannot conceive the idea that any sane man is going to sell his goods at a loss if he knows it. I firmly believe the reason for so many business men not knowing their costs is due to their throwing up their hands at the suggestion of getting a detailed knowledge of their costs, saying it is too much work, too much expense, nothing gained, Smith forces me to sell at certain prices anyway, what is the use, and so on. These are only a few excuses some business men are making every day. Such men are a menace to their line of business.

The man without a speed indicator either has to do a lot of figuring to find the speeds of the different machines, or a lot of guessing at it, and too often it is the guessing that is done.

"YOU CAN'T BEAT CIVILITY."

THESE are words which ought to be lettered in gold or illumined with fire, and hung in every office, shop, factory, corporation and institution in the world. They ought to be a motto for 1913, 1914, 1915 and so on to the end of time.

They were uttered in a flash of inspiration by a man in London whose business is the selling of licensed properties. He was explaining why foreigners—Frenchmen and Italians in particular—are ousting Englishmen in the management and ownership of British hotels and restaurants. "The Englishman can't bow and scrape like the foreigner," said—I've forgotten his name. And then with an intensity which I recall to this day, he exclaimed: "You can't beat civility!"

Think out for yourself the significance and truth of this bit of wisdom. Then apply it in your own case. When you are tempted to be "smart," sneering, ungracious, rude, short, surly, rough, truculent, remember that "you can't beat civility" in your choice of a weapon of offence and defence. It is as oil on troubled waters. It is the sun which thaws out the frost in others. It is the check on hasty tempers. It is the solvent of resistance. If you are the one canvassed, be civil. When you grow hot under injustice, rough treatment, discourtesy or malice, remember that the exercise of civility will win you more triumphs than explosions of wrath, or acts of retaliation. Think it out. Test the aphorism. Practise its implied behest. And if you find the words and the message good, pass them on.

—*John C. Kirkwood.*

Are You Insured Against Fire?

Savings of a lifetime are frequently lost by lack of sufficient insurance.

HOW frequently do we hear of a merchant having the savings of a life time collected together by years of long hours and strenuous labor wiped out by fire, in the twinkling of an eye, as it were. Instead of the enjoyment of pleasures from the little nest egg which he had gradually been laying aside, by neglect to carry sufficient insurance, he is perhaps left in a state of bankruptcy, or at least much disheartened and discouraged, and with little heart or ambition to take up the struggle of strenuous business activities again.

Why Merchant Should be Well Insured

In justice to himself and the business he is fostering, the family which depends on him, and the wholesalers who have extended credit to him, the dealer should see that he is fully and well insured against loss by fire. Surely the very thought of the pitiable tales of other dealers overcome by fire—the dearly bought experiences of other merchants—should awaken in every business man the necessity of carrying sufficient insurance.

The Question of Rates

The time to consider the question is now—and not after a fire has occurred. It is true that insurance costs money, but it is a necessary expense for the safeguard of the business, and should be charged up to the expense account just the same as rent, light and other expenditures. The excuse that premiums are high is absolutely no reason for carrying insufficient insurance. If rents are high, the merchant simply has to get a larger percentage of profit, and if insurance is high, in the same way the fact will have to be taken into consideration in figuring profits.

The dealer by consulting his insurance agent can frequently ascertain certain precautions that, if complied with, will assist somewhat in the reduction of the rate. Especially when a new building is being constructed, it should be found out what character of construction will give the lowest insurance rate.

Appropriate Time to Deal With Problem

This is a particularly appropriate time to take up the question of carrying sufficient insurance. Around the first of the year most dealers take stock, and are thus in a position to gauge whether the amount of insurance is sufficient for the stock carried. This is one value of taking stock, and in addition the stock sheets are a means of proving loss in case of fire, thus allowing a rapid settlement of claims.

If stock is increased for any one season of the year, insurance should be increased. Short term policies are available for this purpose. There are several fire insurance companies that allow a percentage off the premium when 80 per cent. of stock is kept insured during entire year. Insurance up to 80 per cent. of stock is considered fairly good protection.

Be Not Only Fully, but Well, Insured

In addition to being fully insured, the merchant should make certain that he is well insured—that his insurance really insures and gives him protection. A reliable company should be selected. Policies should be carefully examined, so that in case of fire he will really receive the amount he expects.

If the dealer is insured in more than one company, he should see that each has notice of the insurance carried by the other. This should be looked after, because in the past some companies have used it as a reason for default of payment.

Then again, see that policies read concurrently—that the description of your stock and premises are worded in the same way in each policy if insured with more than one company.

Fire is something in which the dealer wants to use the ounce of prevention. No matter how well he is insured, the honest dealer does not want to have a fire, because it interferes with business to a considerable extent. Every precaution should be taken.

Premises should be kept clean and free from rubbish and waste paper. Clerks should be instructed to be careful in the use of matches. Electric wiring needs attention. Flimsy decorations should be eliminated.

This may all seem like a good deal of "preaching," but it is all worthy of the attention of the dealer. Every dealer should protect his savings from years of hard work from being wiped out.

WORTH OF CATALOGUES TO THE MERCHANT

The general merchant, if he wants to keep trade at home, must attempt to supply all the requirements of his customers. If he does not carry a line in stock, he should offer to secure it for a customer, for if they cannot get it from the local merchant they will probably order it from the city by mail and thus is mail order buying started. The customer will probably not only order the one article, but others besides. She will say to herself, "I don't want to pay the express on that one article, I will order enough to get the charges paid."

Catalogues of manufacturers and wholesalers can be made use of in supplying customers with goods not carried in stock. If an enquiry is made for something you have not got, turn up to the catalogue and attempt to sell it to the customer, informing her how soon you can get it for her.

For this reason it would be well for the merchant to put all the catalogues he receives on file. Perhaps at the time he may feel that he will find no use for it, but he can never tell when he will receive an enquiry for some of the articles listed in it.

VALUE OF ENTHUSIASM

Enthusiasm is the greatest business asset in the world. It beats money and power and influence. Single-handed the enthusiast convinces and dominates where the wealth accumulated by a small army of workers would scarcely raise a tremor of interest, says the Melting Pot.

Enthusiasm tramples over prejudice and opposition, spurns inaction, storms the citadel of its object, and like an avalanche overwhelms and engulfs all obstacles.

Enthusiasm is nothing more nor less than faith in action. Faith and initiative rightly combined remove mountainous barriers and achieves the unheard of and miraculous.

Set the germ of enthusiasm afloat in your institution; carry it in your attitude and manner; it spreads like contagion and influences every fibre of your business before you realize it; it begets and inspires effects you did not dream of; it means increase in production and decrease in costs; it means joy and pleasure and satisfaction to your workers; it means life, real and virile; it means spontaneous bed rock results—the vital things that pay dividends.

Knobs of News

D. Woodrow has opened a furniture store at Kincaid, Sask.

Gould & McClinton have added a furniture agency to their implement business.

Edward Reith, of Rainy River, Ont., has moved his furniture stock to Fort Frances.

Mrs. Elie Badeau has registered the furniture business of Elie Badeau & Cie, Maisonneuve, Montreal.

The retail merchants of British Columbia held a big convention in the Empress Hotel, Victoria, on February 9 and 10.

H. M. Christie, having purchased all the stock of the World Furnishing Co., Orillia, Ont., is now sole proprietor. T. H. World has retired from the business.

J. Rung, whose store was recently damaged by fire, has sold out the balance of his stock to Jacob Fritz, of the same town, who will continue the business.

Damage to the extent of $3,500 was done to the building and contents of the Elora Textile Co.'s factory at Elora, on Feb. 8. The loss is covered by insurance.

Hollenberg Bros., house furnishers, Fort William, are erecting an addition to their store, 50 x 70 feet, in which they will carry a full line of hardware and kitchen goods.

Fire damaged the stock of C. L. Bustin, furniture dealer and storage agent, recently at St. John, N.B., as also it did the stock of W. O. Dunham, upholsterer, of the same place. Both were fully insured.

At the annual meeting of the Winnipeg R.M.A. election of officers resulted as follows: President, J. A. Banfield; vice-presidents, John H. Treleaven and C. H. Mulvey; treasurer, J. McNeil; secretary, J. F. Kennedy.

J. A. McLaughlin, of McLaughlin & Scott, furniture jobbers, Toronto, while calling on the trade in Hamilton, recently fell on the icy sidewalk and wrenched his knee. He had to stay in his bed for a couple of weeks, but is now about again.

The Restmore Manufacturing Company, Vancouver, have taken out a permit to amend the plans for their mattress and furniture factory calling for a further expenditure of $7,000. Their original permit was for a factory costing $150,000.

CALGARY'S NEW FURNITURE STORE

The opening of the Calgary Furniture Company's new store introduces to the public one of the largest and one of the finest furniture stores in Canada. It is somewhat of a distinction for the city, which only comes sixth in Canada in the matter of population, to have what is, perhaps, the largest retail furniture store within the Dominion.

This building which will be occupied entirely by the Calgary Furniture Company is 100 by 130 feet, with six storeys and basement. It is of reinforced concrete construction, the exterior of terra cotta and tapestry brick, which makes one of the finest looking buildings in this city. Ornamental iron entrances and show windows add much to the exterior appearance and give it a most substantial and attractive look.

The interior finish is of quartered-oak with maple floors. The building is provided with a modern sprinkling system throughout which makes it absolutely fireproof. There are five elevators which should facilitate the transaction of business with the least possible delay.

The Calgary Furniture Company deserve great credit for the successful manner in which they have conducted their business. This business was only established in 1895 and has several times had to enlarge its quarters to cope with its growing trade.

The new building will involve a cost of something like $350,000.00, and will be one of the most attractive business houses in the West. The contractors were Fyshe, McNeill, Martin & Trainer.

DISSATISFIED WITH CARTAGE CHARGES.

The new Canadian railway cartage schedule, which went into effect on January 1 last, is the cause of much dissatisfaction to furniture, bed and bedding manufacturers in the larger centres, particularly Montreal. Toronto and Winnipeg, where outspoken complaint has been made. The increased cartage rates have caused dealers to pay higher freight charges, and these charges are now listed as "cartage" and "freight," whereas in the past the charges in the bill came under the one head "freight." The dealer wants to know why he should pay cartage at the shipping point and is apt to threaten discrimination because of this.

A case in point—on a bill of goods shipped from Toronto to Cobourg recently the shipping charges were 65 cents—40 cents cartage at Toronto and 25 cents freight from Toronto to Cobourg. It cost more to transport the goods from the factory to the railway car, less than a mile. than from shipping point to destination, about 40 miles away.

To offset these unfair charges, the manufacturers of beds and furniture at Toronto have arranged to do their own carting practically, chopping the railway companies' cartage charges in half, with a minimum placed at 20 cents. They are doing this because they feel that the railway companies are making an exorbitant charge, and as a matter of protection to their customers. The railway companies' new cartage charge in Montreal is four cents per hundred pounds—an increase of one cent over the old rates.

The rates in other centres are: Toronto, 3¼ cents; Hamilton, 3 cents; and the following points also 3 cents: Bothwell, Brantford, Glencoe, Guelph, Hamilton, Kingston, London, Ottawa, Sarnia, St. Catharines, St. Hyacinthe, St. Thomas, Thamesville, Valleyfield, Walkerville, and Windsor.

The minimum in all cases is set at 20 cents. Additions to the list of exceptions to the flat tariff include baskets, empty packages and furniture (except brass and iron bedsteads.

The request of shippers has been met by the customs authorities to hand the delivery of customs parcels over to one carrying agent under orders from the customs examining warehouse, and thus cheapen the cartage importers have agreed to pay.

THE GALE COMPANY INCORPORATED

Geo. Gale & Sons, Ltd., Waterville, Que., makers of beds and cots of all kinds, as well as mattresses, pillows, cushions and furniture, have received Dominion incorporation at Ottawa. The capital is set at $500,000, divided into 5,000 shares of $100 each.

REDUCE EXPRESS CHARGES

The Railway Commission has issued an order reducing express charges for the handling of freight bills of lading and collection of moneys thereunder. At present the express companies forward bills of lading for freight shipments, they, however, charging for the collection and return of money under the bill of lading 1 per cent.

By the order now signed a change in the express classification has been made. A new rule provides for the charge of one-eighth of 1 per cent., with a minimum of 1 per cent. on $100 on one company's line, and 1½ per cent. when carried by more than one company. In practice the present and the proposed rules will work out as follows: On $100—present, $3; proposed one line, $1; two lines, $1.50. On $300—present, $3; proposed one line, $1; two lines, $1.50. On $500—present, $5; proposed one line, $1; two lines, $1.50. On $1,000 present, $10; proposed one line, $1.25; two lines, $1.50. On $2,000—present, $20; proposed one line, $2.50; two lines, $2.50.

A STEEL DISPLAY RUG RACK

A convenient machine for furniture stores which handle stocks of rugs and carpets is the "20th Century" rug rack made by The Steel Furnishing Co., of

Large rack holding 120 rugs of all sizes.

New Glasgow, N.S. It is built on lines similar, though simpler, to those described at various times in our columns. A number of steel arms, holding on each side a rug, swing open like a book, making it possible to view any and every one of the rugs hung in the rack in a very short time. When not in use the arms fold up with the rugs against the wall, thus occupying a minimum amount of space. These racks are made in various sizes to hold any number of rugs required or carried in stock. With slight effort the rack can be so arranged with the addition of a few furniture items to give the appearance of a furnished room.

WILY WIDOW

In the window of a pretty villa residence in a Lancashire town is a notice: "This house to let; only young couples need apply." But, strange to say, the occupancy of the house never changes.

"I think you ask too much rent for your villa, Mrs. W.," the next-door neighbor ventured to suggest to

the owner, a shabbily-dressed widow. "You could easily let it if you reduced the price a little."

"But I don't want to let it," the widow said, calmly. "I'm quite comfortable here, thank you."

The neighbor's face expressed amazed incredulity.

Library table made by the George McLagan Furniture Co.

"Don't want to let it!" she replied. "Then why insert that notice in the window?"

"Well, you see, I'm a lonely widow, with only myself to depend on, and I'm obliged to make a living somehow," the widow answered, confidentially. "So I write down the names and addresses of all the young couples who call, and sell them, at a fair price to a firm of house furnishers."

NEW CATALOGUE OF UPHOLSTERED GOODS

A new catalogue has just been published by The Montreal Upholstering Co., 1611 Clarke Street, Montreal, makers of upholstered furniture goods, which reflects credit on that company, describing and illustrating as it does a splendid line of up-to-date upholstered furniture items. The catalogue is sent to the trade on request.

DOING IT NOW

Every time you decide to do something and fail to do it you weaken the force called will. Do this often enough and irresolution will become a habit. On the other hand, every time you decide or resolve to do and then do it, your will power strengthens. Every resolution kept, every wish formed into action, makes it easier for you. If you decide to drop a bad habit or form a good one, to add another customer to the list,

Another library table made by the Geo. McLagan Co.

to increase the sales of your particular line, do it now. Once you have held to your purpose of doing things, your task of accomplishment becomes easier every day that follows.

The Furniture Manufacturer

A Department of News and Ideas

Gossip for the Furniture Manufacturer

THE manufacturers who do not advertise when business is brisk are usually the ones who do not advertise when business is quiet.

The time to advertise is all the time. This applies to the furniture trade as much as it does to many others. That this is recognized is evidenced by the continuous advertising which so many of the furniture manufacturers do.

Advertising splurges for a special purpose are all right in their place. But the use of moderate space continuously is better. It is the regular and continuous hammering away that builds up the reputation of manufacturers and the furniture they turn out.

All that an advertisement does for a manufacturer can, with mathematical accuracy, never be known. But advertising well done is always at work influencing buyers.

"I have never in my entire career seen a single direct result from my advertisement," once remarked a manufacturer who was a regular advertiser, "but I do know that my business is increasing every year, and the boys on the road tell me that the advertised line is easier to sell than anything they carry."

That's it. The manufacturer who advertises to the trade is blazing the way for his travellers.

IT appears that some of the furniture manufacturers in the United States consider that their best interests are not served by the use of the word "veneer" in explaining the construction of their goods. They claim that the use of the word "veneer" gives to the public mind the impression that there is something shoddy in the construction of the article in question, and that it will not stand up to the test of time, and that it is really but a poor imitation of something that ought to be better.

They would substitute for 'veneer" the words "reinforced wood," contending that veneer is really reinforced wood in that the piano, table top or other article in which veneer is used is really made of several layers of veneer, one reinforcing the other.

While recognizing this contention to be true, the Hardwood Record is of the opinion that "it is extremely doubtful if the establishment and maintenance of such a policy will be of any benefit to the furniture manufacturers, and it is practically certain that it would be anything but a benefit to manufacturers of veneer.....'Veneer is coming to command more and more popularity, but such popularity should be founded on a proper understanding of its value, purpose and application and not upon any false pretenses such as are being suggested as above noted."

THE question of costs is always an interesting one to manufacturers, for a perfect system no man has ever devised. We therefore print the following interview with a furniture manufacturer which appeared in an exchange.

"The general profit on cheap and medium classes of furniture," said this particular manufacturer, "will not average over 5 per cent. on the sales, yet these people are offering goods 10 to 20 per cent. less than we can afford to—and we have been refusing a lot of orders after our product has been sold up. They will doubtless wake up only after they have been in business six months to a year and take account of stock, when sad experience will tell them exactly where they stand. There is no necessity for prices of this kind with any kind of a sales management, in these days when we have found the demand for furniture greater than the supply. Come over here," he continued, "and I will give you an object lesson. Here is a dresser case, 42 inches, full swell, quartered oak top and front, 22x28 pattern or oval plate, sold in the South, in gloss finish, at $11.25. A corresponding case, as large in every detail, in bird's-eye maple and mahogany veneers, is being made by two or three very short-sighted houses and sold at from $9.25 to $9.75. Think of the difference! Our price, $11.25—theirs $9.25 to $9.75. Our factory is a notably successful one, although we only pay 6 per cent. dividends on our capitalization. We buy for spot cash, take all discounts, have the best machinery, systems and administration. Where can a concern get off which names such prices? Here is another dresser on which our net cost is $9.80, without any allowance for overhead charges or profit. That same dresser is being also sold at from $9.25 to $9.75. What a pity it is that any concern will do business on this basis, and not only make no profit, but head direct for the bankruptcy court! Happily, there are only two or three of these and there is a limit to their production. They have an interest greater than any one else can possibly have in getting a cost expert into their factory."

FURNITURE manufacturers, like manufacturers of all kinds, try to employ methods that will produce the greatest expedition in the delivery of materials between the various departments of their factory. A writer in The Furniture Manufacturer briefly describes the system employed by a Detroit manufacturer. He built a small electric storage battery car to handle loads of 1,000 to 2,000 pounds. Inside of a week it had replaced five hand trucks and eight men and was paying dividends on the investment. I am thinking about this one instance of cutting the costs of handling material, because it touches a phase of plant operation that is too often underestimated—a problem which every furniture factory has and few have satisfactorily solved.

Perhaps the possibility of a similar saving may open in your own plant the whole question of handling materials economically.

SANDING OAK

Oak, whether plain or quartered, is a comparatively easy wood to work smooth. It is not a soft wood, but what is meant is that oak can be worked on the planer and get a smooth finish with knives that are a little dull. The same thing is true in working it with saws. When it comes to gum and some of the other woods, the knives and saws must be perfectly keen to give good results. Now, when it comes to sanding, it is the other way. You may sand gum, or some other even-grained wood, with comparatively smooth or even slick sand paper and get fair results, but when it comes to sanding oak, to get a good finish the sand paper should be fresh and sharp. This is because of the unevenness in the texture of the wood. If it is plain oak, there are the hard streaks and the soft streaks of the annual rings of growth, and if they are sanded over with dull paper, it will cut down into the soft streaks and the hard ridges be all right for a certain kind of finish, but where a perfectly smooth face is wanted, one should sand oak with a sharp, clean paper. If it is quartered oak, it is the same thing in a different way. There is a hard film which makes the splash line which nothing but sharp paper will touch. If the wood is sanded over with dull or slick paper, it will simply dig down between the splash lines and leave them standing up in waves. To get good results, you should not only have sharp paper, but you should get the sanding across the grain or splash line to reduce the tendency to cut down the soft places between.

A WELL PROTECTED BAND SAW

A band saw, recently built by Cowan & Co., Galt, for the C.P.R., carries out the "Safety First" idea since the workman is protected from the revolving parts. A reference to the illustration will show how these parts have been covered.

The machine has a stiff, square column back with wheel 36 in. in diameter and a 2 in. face. The top one is fitted with weighted knife edge tension. The lower wheel is solid, and, being heavier than the upper one, controls the movement of same. The table is of iron 34 in. x 30 in., and can be tilted and clamped without the use of wrench.

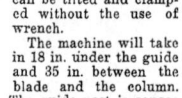

The machine will take in 18 in. under the guide and 35 in. between the blade and the column. Length of saw, 20 ft. 4 in. The guide post is square and fitted for counterweight. Adjustable back and lateral guides are provided both above and below the table.

Well-protected band saw supplied the C.P.R. by Cowan & Co., Galt.

CUTTING DOWN THE GLUE COST
J. W. Belger in "Veneers"

Few realize what can be accomplished by scientific methods of testing and using glue. The practical application of these methods and the surprising results obtained will be of unusual interest to large consumers of glue.

The concern alluded to had for the past ten or twelve years been buying its glue from one company, and it had given very good results. I say, good results, but not economical. It was found after sending this glue to an expert to be analyzed that they were paying 9½c for an article that could be duplicated for 8½c. That loss, without any doubt, had been going on for a good many years. Therefore, it was advisable to install a laboratory for testing and introduce new methods to cut the glue cost. After the installation of the laboratory, samples of glue were received from many of the glue manufacturers, and radical differences in value to the consumers, at the price quoted on the glues, were discovered. I will here give a few values showing the wide variation in values of some of the glues on the market:—

Glue.	Price quoted in cents.	Worth to the consumer.
No. 1	8.5	8.5
No. 2	9.5	8.5
No. 3	9.5	9
No. 4	9.5	8.5
No. 5	9.6	10.2
No. 6	10	10.6
No. 7	10	9
No. 8	10	8.2
No. 9	10	10.88
No. 10	10.5	8.2
No. 11	10.5	10.4
No. 12	11	10.1

This table will speak for itself to those who will take the time to study it.

All of the above glues are used in some plants, and, as was the experience at this plant, so it will be at many others, that the glue they are using can be placed by another one at less money, and give the same results.

One word in regard to the method used in determining values. A glue, to work well, has to be made up so as to have a certain body—we call it our standard body—and for that body it must have the proper strength. By the use of the laboratory, within twenty-four hours, a glue can be analyzed, and just the per cent. of dry glue required of any sample, to give the proper mixture, may be determined. In this way it is easy to figure which glue is the most economical to use, and the above prices are all based on comparison with one standard glue. That standard has been selected as an average of values, therefore some of the glues are quoted above and some below.

The glue selected to be used made a saving of 20 per cent. in the buying, and as the glue bill was about $10,000 a year, it is easy to see that the laboratory paid for itself in a very short time.

This was, of course, only the beginning, for thus far nothing has been said as to the saving accomplished out in the plant.

Taking samples of liquid glue as they were being used out in the plant and analyzing them for value, showed that the method of handling glue allowed it to deteriorate in value to such an extent that the joint made with the glue had a very small factor of safety. On the first day that this analysis was made there was about $56 worth of glue in solution, and the real value of that glue to the company by tests was only $44. Upon changing the method of mixing glue, as best we could before our final system was installed, and doing away with the greatest part of the heat damage, the cost of glue work was cut about 20 per cent., which, of course, is the cost of work with the old glue that they had been using.

The next step taken was to install a central mixing station, where all the glue for the plant is made. This makes it possible for all the bench men to get fresh glue in the morning at 7 and start at once to work. Previously the different bench men made their own glue and a great deal of time was wasted, and the glue was made up by guesswork, each man thinking that his own way of making and keeping glue was the best. At times, when a man had been working on a certain job and was either put to other work or did not come to work, the liquid glue remained in solution for several days before it was all used up. Often the glue would spoil and have to be thrown away.

Under the present system, all glue from the bench men, as well as from the supply tanks to the glue-spreaders, is brought back to the central mixing station. The glue is put in cooling trays and the buckets are all washed out good and clean. This glue in the cooling trays is the first glue used next morning, and the object is to have just as small an amount on hand as possible. Fresh glue is made three or four times a day, and no glue is at any one time in solution over a very few hours. In this way the heat damage is cut to a small amount and all the glue through the plant is of a good quality. The total saving made at this plant was about 45 per cent. and the quality of the work was greatly improved.

CUT PRICE VS. SALESMAN'S POLICY
By M. Wulpi

It is notorious that the salesman's "Tale of Woe," on high prices and competitor's low prices only too often influence "the Office." Have you considered what that means, and have you shown your salesman what it means for him? Read this over twice and see what you think of it:

Assume that your salesman sells $100,000 annually, at prices on a basis of 10 per cent. manufacturer's profit, from which the salesman is paid on a 3 per cent. basis.

Result—manufacturer's profit, $7,000; salesman's salary, $3,000. To maintain the manufacturer's profit and the same salary—

If he cuts 1 per cent. he must sell $111,111, or 11 per cent. more goods.

If he cuts 2 per cent. he must sell $125,000, or 25 per cent. more goods.

If he cuts 3 per cent. he must sell $142,857, or 43 per cent. more goods.

If he cuts 5 per cent. he must sell $200,000, or 100 per cent. more goods.

If he doesn't sell more than before, and to retain for the manufacturer the same profit (which should be), it will be necessary to cut his salary—

On a 1 per cent. cut of price from $3,000 to $2,000.
On a 2 per cent. cut of price from $3,000 to $1,000.
On a 3 per cent. cut of price from $3,000 to 0
and
On a 5 per cent. cut of price he should owe the manufacturer $2,000 at the end of the year.

Great, isn't it? Is it not a fact, though? Talk this over with "Billy" the next time he complains about your "prices being too high" and he attempts to break down your determination to "stick to prices and terms." Suggest to him that the above works the other way, too, if he can sell above your prices. Good "Nervine."

SELLING THE SAWDUST

Not many years ago saw-mills were glad to get their sawdust carted away even if they had to pay for it. Now, however, a wide-awake concern will create a market for the waste and dispose of it at a good profit.

One day the owner of a string of saw-mills in Tennessee noticed a woman sweeping up the dusty floor of a public room with wet leaves to keep down the dust. He asked if wet sawdust would not do just as well, and was answered affirmatively.

The next week this man shipped a carload of sawdust to Knoxville. This was peddled around to the various retail stores, to saloons, and to meat shops, with a request to moisten and try a sample of it for keeping down the dust when sweeping.

Most of those who tried it, liked it, and placed a standing order for sawdust at a nominal price.—Business.

RED CEDAR FUR CHEST
By W. Berry

The accompanying illustration shows a B. C. red cedar fur chest. It is 38 in. long, 20 in. wide, 24 in. deep, inside measurement. The top section is 6 in. deep. The drawers are each 7¼ in. deep.

The top section has a matched bottom and glue joined, while the drawer bottoms are glue joined. The chest is built entirely of red cedar and is strictly moth proof. This style is much handier than the old type with two or three trays to lift out to get to articles at bottom.

The hardware should be of a polished brass. The drawer handles should be of a light neat pattern and

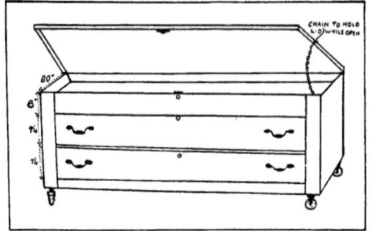

British Columbia red cedar fur chest.

locks of the cylinder type without key plate. Some prefer handles at ends of chest, but such spoils the beauty of the finish, as this class of wood is very pretty if finished in its natural color and polished. I usually put a glass ball caster on these chests, thus adding greatly to the appearance.

ATTENTION TO DETAILS PRODUCES RESULTS

It's attending to the little things in the factory that creates efficiency and increases profits. An owner of a woodworking plant sees that the floors in his plant are kept clean and in good condition in order that there may be no time lost in pushing trucks around piles of rubbish or in getting the wheels out of ruts in the floor. It often happens in some plants that in moving trucks around, a machine has to be stopped because of some material lying in the way. Every time a machine is forced to cease running, owing to a cause such as this, money is lost.

This same man also sees that his trucks are fitted with pin or roller bearings, so designed as to make them run smoothly. By this observance of the minutest details the standard of shop work is raised and a greater perfection in work is obtained.

A Few Points About

STAMCO LIMITED

First we have, beyond all dispute, the most up-to-date factory in Canada—we repeat, in big letters—

The Most Up-to-date Factory in Canada

For the Manufacture of

BEDS and BEDDING

We have the most centrally situated factory in the West. We are on all three Transcontinental lines and we have our own siding. We want to point out to the Western Merchant that modern plant and shipping facilities, plus central situation, mean

Quality, Service and Quick Delivery

Our 1914 illustrated catalogue is just out. A post card will bring you a copy of it per return.

Stamco Limited, **Stamco of Regina Limited**
Saskatoon and Edmonton   Regina

Manufacturers of

Beds, Springs, Mattresses, Pillows, Tents, Awnings, and all kinds of Canvas Goods

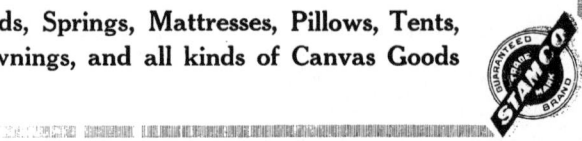

Making TABLE-SLIDES is a Specialty Business

For more than TWENTY-FIVE YEARS we have made TABLE SLIDES exclusively. Our Factory is equipped with Special Machinery which enables us to make SLIDES,—BETTER and CHEAPER than the furniture manufacturer.

Canadian Table makers are rapidly adopting WABASH SLIDES

Because { They ELIMINATE SLIDE TROUBLES
Are CHEAPER and BETTER

Reduced Costs
Increased Out-put } BY USING **WABASH SLIDES**

Made by
B. WALTER & CO.
Wabash, Ind.

The Largest EXCLUSIVE TABLE-SLIDE Manufacturers in America

ESTABLISHED 1887

LACKA-TAN SPANISH LEATHER now in its 8th year of Unquestionable Success. Many Imitations of Course.

To get the genuine, see that your furniture carries a leather label, size and design as above.

The Lackawanna Leather Co.
Hackettstown, N.J.

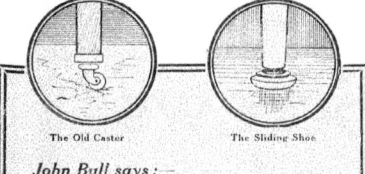

The Old Caster   The Sliding Shoe

John Bull says:—

$250,000 worth of carpets and matting are destroyed yearly by fire, but $500,000 worth are destroyed by casters.

Onward Sliding Furniture Shoes

have proven their superiority over the old wheel casters and are used by leading Hotels, Hospitals, etc., in large quantities.

Hotel Astor, New York - 2,500 sets
I.O.F. Temple Building, Toronto - 350 "
Sick Children's Hospital, Toronto - 250 "

and many others in all parts. Made in all styles and sizes.

Write for our literature and prices

Onward Mfg. Co., Berlin, Ont.

Is Yours a Growing Store?

Here are ideas which will help it grow faster. Here are suggestions for the young man starting in business in Northwest Canada, as well as for the dealer with an established trade.

BUILDING A FURNITURE BUSINESS

is a cloth bound book of 205 pages, every one of which contains helpful hints for the furniture dealer. Though written in easy narrative style as the story of "Bobby Burton, Successful Furniture Dealer," the book is neither fiction, theory or dry preachment. The incidents, plans and experiences are woven together from actual practice in widely separated localities.

If your trade is in a rut you will find here a suggestion for a new sales plan, a new advertisement or something to start people talking about your store.

Every man who is looking for new ideas in furniture merchandising and methods will find something worth while in this book.

Postpaid, $1.00.

The Commercial Press, Ltd.
Publishers of The Canadian Furniture World and The Undertaker

Anglo Rubbing and Polishing Varnish

None Better Made

A RECENT addition to the many world-known lines of Ault & Wiborg manufacture. Produced after years of experimenting and testing, it will afford you the most pleasing results.
Made to rub in twenty-four hours, two days and three days. Works free and easy. Polishes with a beautiful finish.
There's economy with a high standard of excellence in the use of our Varnishes, Enamels, Graining Colors, etc.

Write for Prices and Samples

Ault & Wiborg Company of Canada, Limited
Varnish Works,
MONTREAL · TORONTO · WINNIPEG

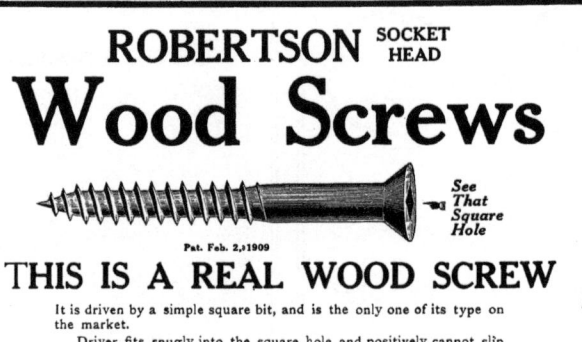

ROBERTSON SOCKET HEAD
Wood Screws

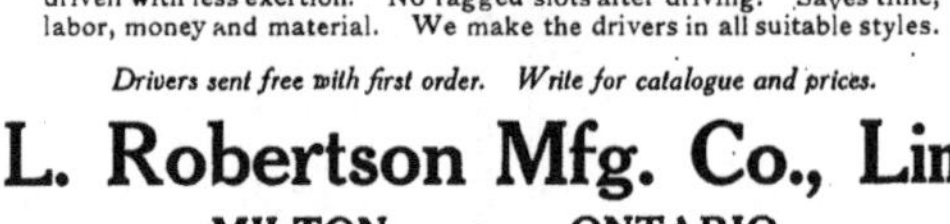

Pat. Feb. 2, 1909

See That Square Hole

THIS IS A REAL WOOD SCREW

It is driven by a simple square bit, and is the only one of its type on the market.
Driver fits snugly into the square hole and positively cannot slip and cut the fingers, or disfigure costly furniture or woodwork. It is driven with less exertion. No ragged slots after driving. Saves time, labor, money and material. We make the drivers in all suitable styles.

Drivers sent free with first order. Write for catalogue and prices.

P. L. Robertson Mfg. Co., Limited
MILTON :: ONTARIO

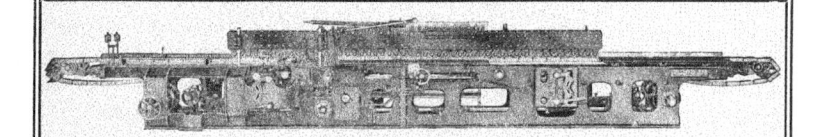

The Universal Linderman

The only machine that joints, glues and clamps in one operation. We have, from time to time, been telling you what the LINDERMAN is doing for others.

Give us an Opportunity to tell you what it will do for *you*

Without the slightest obligation on your part, one of our staff will, with your permission, make a survey of your plant. This will present data on which you can base the real value of the LINDERMAN process in connection with your plant.

Write us to-day

Canadian Linderman Company, Limited

Works at

Muskegon, Michigan   Woodstock, Ontario

Dominion Casket Co., Limited

Telephones { Day No. 1020. Nights, Sundays and Holidays Nos. 1069-1101

Guelph, Ont.

RUSH ORDERS SOLICITED

No. 514½

The polished oak casket to-day is without doubt a class of goods for which there is no substitute. The design shown above is one of a grade from which seventy-five per cent. of the sales of oak cases are made.

This is plain sawed solid white oak finished in a dark golden, rubbed and polished, with half couch trimmed with a fine grade of crepe "Louisine" or satin. A trial order of any one of our styles will convince the most critical that we lead in this class of work.

No. 516

This is also of the same grade but different corner can be furnished with "K" panel or half couch.

Soliciting your business, we are, very truly,

DOMINION CASKET CO., LIMITED

Undertakers' Department

Problems affecting the Undertaking Profession are here discussed and readers are invited to send letters expressing their views on any of the subjects dealt with—News of the profession throughout Canada.

CURRENT UNDERTAKING TOPICS

The Mournful Funeral Sermon. If there is anything that is to be deprecated in connection with funeral services it is the long and mournful nature which some of them partake. That tactful undertakers can do much to prevent this goes without question. They may not be always able to succeed, but they can most of the time if they try.

Apropos of this subject is the experience of an undertaker, who, writing in the Embalmers' Monthly, says: "Several weeks ago a lady came to me for my services in the burial of her husband. She requested me to secure a clergyman and to inform him that a long and sorrowful sermon was not desired, and that the family wished that no bells be tolled the day of the funeral. She said their affliction was sad enough without adding a solemn sermon and mournful bells. I consider her request one of the best I ever received and believe undertakers could use her suggestion in many cases. One of the most eloquent funeral sermons I ever heard was in a little country church. The minister held the funeral party by his eloquence, his words had an influence upon the relatives of the deceased and there were very few wet eyes. At the conclusion of his remarks the choir sang one of the most mournful songs I ever heard. It occurred to me: Why such a song? Everyone knows our feeling in time of death, and why add to them in mournful song? Would it not be a good plan for every undertaker to have a selection of songs to submit to the choir and do away with those heart-breaking hymns we so often hear in our country villages at funerals?"

* * * *

Relative Cost of Dying and Living. One occasionally comes across squibs in the daily papers regarding what they term the high cost of dying. A few days ago, however, we came across an article in a Wisconsin daily paper in which it was shown that it was cheaper to die than to live.

"Do you know," begins the article, "it costs more to live than die—that the expenses of death have decreased, while those of life are constantly increasing? It's a fact.

"High grade undertaking supplies have shown but slight advance in cost during the past few years, while beef and bread have soared. Again, the quality of caskets, coffins, shrouds, chin rests and name plates has grown better while the grade of beef has and is deteriorating—that is, those cuts within reach of the average purse.

"You may walk into any undertaker and have a 'nice right-up-to-now' funeral for $125, and this includes the cost of embalming, two or three carriages and a dandy coffin of latest design. Of course you may be buried for less money and they'll 'plant' you decently, but you'll not get the same material as is used in the $125 'outfit.' You can get more for your money in 'grave equipment' than in what you need to live.

"If you are married and have, say, a couple of kiddies, it costs you $75 every month to keep the home going, and if wife needs a new bonnet and the youngsters have to have shoes your bill will be nearer $100. You can die for less money—very much less. In fact they can lay you away for $70, and persons who do not know the ins and outs of the undertaking business would think you were paying $200."

If the privilege of getting off jokes about the high cost of dying are permissible, surely one like the above, maintaining that it is cheaper to die than to live, is equally allowable. At any rate both are jokes, neither one of which is founded on fact.

* * * *

A Word to Assistants. Two things are necessary in an ideal undertaker's assistant. The one is loyalty to his employer and the other is desire for perfection in the practice of his profession. At a recent convention a speaker dwelt on the relationship that should exist between employee and employer, during which he made this apt remark: "You owe it to yourself, your profession and your employer to endeavor to be up-to-date—by study of new methods and texts; to be original, able to do things right without having to be told how; to be prompt, at all times to keep engagements; to be neat in your personal appearance; to be patient under all circumstances; to be polite, because it is your nature to be so; to be cheerful, but not boisterous; to be busy, because the busy man is usually the happy man, and people have a sort of habit of patronizing the hustler."

* * * *

Sunday Funerals. Referring to the agitation in Great Britain for putting an end to Sunday funerals, the Undertakers' Journal, London, expresses the opinion that there are other lines of business in which Sunday labor is employed which should be first given attention.

There is some logic in this. There is undoubtedly other lines of business in which labor is more regularly employed on Sunday. But that being true it by no means follows that no movement should be made to put a stop to Sunday funerals until greater transgressors in other lines of business have been persuaded to mend their ways.

In Canada no such arguments have been used. Undertakers, realizing that labor is entitled to a rest on Sunday, discourage as much as possible funerals on that day. As a consequence funerals in many parts of Canada on the first day of the week are uncommon. In Toronto, for example, notwithstanding its population of nearly half a million, a funeral on Sunday is scarcely ever seen.

Western Service

Always at Your Service

UNDERTAKERS handling *Western* Caskets and Funeral supplies know that with every order they get *Quality* — the assurance that they are right and that their customers will be pleased.

Our stock is fast being completed and by end of month we expect to be in full swing.

We have to thank the trade at large for their many enquiries and also for the large volume of business which has already reached us.

The Western Casket Co., Limited

Cor. Emily St. and Bannatyne Ave.   Winnipeg, Manitoba

Open Day and Night

G. S. Thompson   A. W. Robinson   G. H. Lawrence

Practical Derma-Surgery

Professor Eckels gives complete details of the handling of an interesting and typical case

I have just attended the funeral of a particularly interesting case, in which I was called upon to practice derma-surgery. It may be instructive, and certainly should be interesting, for me to detail the circumstances of this case in extenso. The body was that of a man about fifty years of age. He was rather above the average weight and had a full, round face. Three days before he had been struck and run over by a train. The body was almost cut in two, and both legs and both arms were hanging in shreds. The lower lip was split in about the center, the cut extending down over the chin and neck to the point of the breast bone. The frontal bone over the right eye was crushed in and the flesh of the eyebrow was torn in a dozen places. A piece of flesh had been dug out from the forehead on the left side about two inches long and a half-inch wide, the mark running diagonally over the left eye toward the ear. The man was almost bald, and to complicate matters, there were two scalp wounds about an inch apart and extending from ear to ear. These abrasions looked very much like the incisions made for autopsical purposes, except that they were so far forward that they could not be hidden by the pillow.

Our work was complicated in several ways. In the first place, embalming would have been exceedingly difficult because of the mangled condition of the body. Second, to do good derma-surgical work, it is highly desirable, and indeed almost essential, that the flesh be rendered firm by the use of embalming fluid. Third, a church funeral with the corpse to be shown in daylight was an essential, yet, at the same time, we were forced to so guard and guide our work that those of his friends who were not able to attend the daylight funeral could view the body at the home during the previous evening.

Here then were practically all possible complications present. We decided not to embalm the trunk of the body, the weather being such that it was comparatively easy to hold it for three days if the room were kept at the temperature of the outside air. To get the proper derma-surgical effect, however, we were compelled to take up the carotid arteries and inject fluid upward, thus preserving and plumping out the facial tissues and putting them in a condition to receive and hold the derma-surgical preparations. Another complication, however, arose at this point. When we began our work, we, of course, removed the body from the room in which it had been kept beside an open window and brought it into a warmer apartment. The change of temperature produced "body sweat," rendering the operation much more tardy and difficult than it otherwise would have been.

Body Same Temperature as Room

Naturally it is very much easier to do tinting on a body which is of the same temperature as the room in which it is lying. I spent part of the first hour in trying to fill out the tissue over the eye, where the bone had been crushed in, by means of injections of melted wax. This was not the success I had anticipated, although I am confident that the method would have worked out finely but for the many cuts and holes, through which the liquid would leak out while hot. Had the superficial facia not been broken, this method I am sure would have been the easiest of all by which to obtain the proper conformation of the head, and would have provided an easy means of restoring the natural contour of the face. It also would have provided an additional advantage in that it would not have been necessary to have painted it over, which always is necessary when any substance like wound filler is employed. This would have saved much time in painting and blending out the tinting to match the natural complexion of the face.

In this instance, however, the wax would not hold in the cuts and abrasions long enough to chill and produce the desired effect. It was necessary, therefore, to employ the wound filler. This was used in abundance and despite the fact that it could not be worked so rapidly, eventually produced a highly satisfactory effect.

In the old days, we were wont to use Plaster Paris. This also was a very tedious operation, and in this particular location extremely difficult to handle satisfactorily. Moreover, it gives far too metallic a finish for use around the eyes, forehead and temples, because the finish usually must be done by a spatula, leaving a moulded or cast effect. Employing the wound filler, we entirely overcame this, because the filler was shaped with the fingers and the "wooden" effect obviated.

It was during the handling of this case that I made a discovery which was invaluable. It was that the wound filler should be of the consistency which could be most easily moulded, even after it had been reduced to the temperature of the body, thus permitting the re-moulding after the eyebrow had been painted on. Had we followed our old-time methods in this case, we would have rigidly moulded the eyebrow of Plaster Paris, then after we had painted in the eyebrow, we doubtless would have discovered for the first time that it and the natural brow on the other side did not match. Our work thus would have gone for nothing, and we should have had to file and sandpaper it down and re-tint it.

Difficult to Work When Flesh Cold

Another discovery which this case brought about was that to make a smooth, even, flat finish to the edges of the wound filler, which is applied to fill out the tissues, was an exceedingly difficult matter where the flesh was cold. Naturally for this reason, the wound filler did not adhere as readily as it did to the warm finger with which I was trying to spread it. It was necessary, therefore, to use something on my finger which would prevent the wound filler from adhering, and which at the same time would tend to increase the adhesive qualities of the wound filler to the cold flesh. I did this by employing an oily substance which would dry out quickly. This preparation, which I have called blending, I have added to my derma-surgery set, together with full directions for its use.

Shaping this wound filler over the eye and pressing some of it into the abrasions on the skin to hold it fast and firm, I then worked out the edges as described above with the aid of blending. Fifteen minutes were allowed to elapse for it to set firmly and for the surface oil to completely evaporate. As I expected, this resulted in a splendid foundation for the tinting, which must of necessity follow. For this tinting, I find artist's flesh paints of the highest and finest grade the best adapted. They should be applied liberally in order to get a good foundation or priming coat and to furnish sufficient material to blend out evenly and carefully to the color of the tissue of the face surrounding the wounds.

In this particular case, it was very valuable to have the different preparations all of one harmonious character, so that all blended into each other in color with

Dominion Manufacturers
Limited

MANUFACTURERS OF

Fine Funeral Requisites

We guarantee

The Highest Quality
and the
Quickest Possible Service

*Night or Day Orders
given Prompt Attention*

BRANCHES

The Globe Casket Co., and Branches	London, Ontario
The Semmons & Evel Casket Co., and Branches	Hamilton, Ontario
The National Casket Co.	Toronto, Ontario
Jas. S. Elliot & Son	Prescott, Ontario
Girard & Godin and Branches	Three Rivers, Quebec
Christie Bros. & Co,	Amherst, N. S.

FRED W. COLES   D. M. ANDREWS
General Manager   *Secretary Treasurer*

HEAD OFFICE
468 King Street W., Toronto

such a texture as to permit the use of the accompanying harmonious surface tints. In this first operation, the wound filler was in some parts of the eyebrow as much as three-quarters of an inch in thickness. It was far superior to Plaster Paris, yet was hardly fitted to fill in the abrasions over the left part of the forehead, which I already have mentioned. This was a skin wound, not a flesh wound, and, therefore, did not need to be sewed together. Indeed, there were places where the wound was not more than one-sixteenth of an inch in depth.

Remember that the head was properly embalmed and that the tissues were more or less firm; therefore, these abrasions had to be filled up and made level and smooth, so that there would be no shades or reflections to show up the tinting after we had carefully applied them. Here again I had to dip into my derma-surgical kit to find a satisfactory preparation. A moment's reflection convinced me that enameline was the proper thing to use, since it was of the desired color; hence, comparatively little tinting would be necessary after the wound had been entirely covered with this preparation. Some little tinting, however, was of course desirable, in order to blend the surrounding tissue and the enameline in a satisfactory manner. The paint, which was used to cover the wound filler over the right eyebrow again was employed here, and since enameline and wound filler worked in harmony with each other they also worked harmoniously with the tinting. Therefore, the same shade was gotten to perfection.

Filling the Crevices

There were three other places which needed careful attention. These were the chin and the top of the head. The wounds here had been carefully sewed up by the embalmer, previous to the injection of the fluid. It had been necessary to sew these parts together with strong thread and naturally the stitches showed on either side of the incision for perhaps a quarter of an inch. There also was a natural crevice to fill from one end of the stitched incision to the other. Here we found the wound filler especially adapted for our purpose. A strip about as thick as a lead pencil was rolled between the palms of the hands until it had become warm and correspondingly soft and flexible. To press this into every crack and crevice was the work of but a moment, but here again the preparation was spread out so thinly that it had a tendency to adhere to the warm finger, rather than to the cold tissue of the body. Therefore, we did this work very rapidly with just sufficient pressure to set the wound filler in place. We allowed it to remain some little time until it had cooled off to more nearly the body temperature. A little of the blending was put on the tip of the finger and then the wound filler rubbed into place and smoothed off. It was not at all difficult then to press it firmly and properly around the threads and into the incision. As it continued to cool off, it became still firmer. A few deft touches with a blending-anointed finger, and, except for the tint, it was difficult to tell just where it had been spread. All three of these long incisions were covered in this way.

It would have been a long and tedious job to finish them off with the oily paints, as was done with the smaller incisions, because of their length and prominence. It was much easier and more satisfactory to spread a very thin coating of enameline over the wound filler. In fact, it was but the work of a moment to properly cover it, which I again want to point out was done with materials which will adhere to either flesh or to the wound filler and work harmoniously in conjunction with the oil, as well as with the paint which it afterwards was necessary to apply in small quantities in certain places, in order to blend out the proper shade of the skin. This work was done in daylight and it was finished with the paints thinned down with oil, so that they could be blended out to the skin color without showing where the line of paint ended and the uncolored skin began. A few moments' wait allowed all of these to dry, when all of the work was covered with a powder of a harmonious chemical composition. The result was that the powder was not absorbed, nor was a sheen or shiny surface left.

Having the distribution of this surface powder just right, we found that when we turned on the artificial light, that the body looked just as well as it did in the daylight. If a body is to be shown in daylight, it is absolutely necessary that ultra-embalming work be done in daylight. The body then can be shown by either natural or artificial light. If the work is done at night, the body can be shown only by artificial light.

Gossip of the Profession

Sam. Harris has sold his undertaking and furniture business at Streetsville, Ont.

Frank Batts & Co. have sold out their furniture business at Yorkton, Sask.

H. Hoffman has sold his furniture and undertaking business at Simcoe, Ont., to E. F. Best.

J. E. Disney, Oshawa, has purchased the undertaking and furniture business of Tordiff Bros., Brooklin, Ont.

F. L. Cocks who has been promoted to the management of the Toronto plant of Canadian Manufacturers Limited.

Mr. Disney's son, Stanley, of Bowmanville, will assist in handling the business. The Tordiff brothers intend going to British Columbia.

J. Van Camp, Toronto, was recently elected president of the Retail Merchants Assn. of that city.

W. J. Bollon, of Rainy River, Ont., has opened in the undertaking business in that town. The Western Casket Co., Ltd. Winnipeg, Man., secured the opening order. They also supplied the opening order of goods to Wm. Yele, who, formerly in the undertaking business at Owen Sound, Ont., has opened in the same business at Swift Current, Sask.

Burglar Proof and Water Tight

"The St. Thomas"

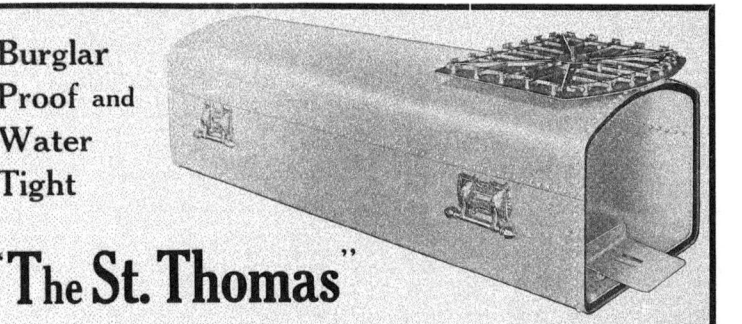

Original, Quick Closing End Vault

MANUFACTURED BY

The St. Thomas Metallic Vault Company, Limited
ST. THOMAS, ONTARIO

The Original Patented Concentrated Fluid

Patented Formula
Strongest and Best

Essential Oil Base, combined with Alcohol, Glycerine, Oxidized Formaldehyde and Boron-Dioxide.

Ask others for their Formula

Special Canadian Agents
National Casket Co.
Toronto, Ont.
GLOBE CASKET CO.
London, Ont.
SEMMENS & EVEL CASKET CO.
Hamilton, Ont.
GIRARD & GODIN
Three Rivers, Que.
JAS. S. ELLIOTT & SON
Prescott, Ont.
CHRISTIE BROS.
Amherst, N.S.

Larger Bottles filled up with water

Egyptian Chemical Co. Boston, U.S.A

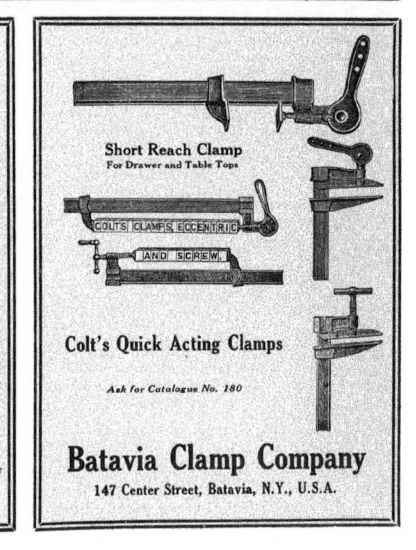

Short Reach Clamp
For Drawer and Table Tops

Colt's Quick Acting Clamps

Ask for Catalogue No. 180

Batavia Clamp Company
147 Center Street, Batavia, N.Y., U.S.A.

REMEMBERED OLD FRIENDS

Before giving up on February 1 the active management of the National Casket Co., Toronto, which recently became part of Dominion Manufacturers, Ltd., A. J. H. Eckardt marked the occasion by distributing among his friends, relatives, employees and agricultural societies and churches of York County between $55,000 and $60,000.

While severing his connection with the management of the above company to devote his time to his many other interests, Mr. Eckardt is still heavily financially interested as a stockholder in Dominion Manufacturers, and is a director of that organization. He has been connected with the National Casket Co. for the past thirty-five years, joining the staff of that company when it was known as Richard Philp, in 1879, he being then about 18 years of age. After a year's experience in the office and warerooms Mr. Eckardt went on the road for the firm, being one of the youngest commercial travelers in the country at that time, as it was not regarded then that a man had experience enough until he was 40 years of age.

Mr. Philp formed his business into a company in April, 1882, giving interests in the business to L. C. Hockey, Robt. Watson, F. W. Coles and Mr. Eckardt. The concern then became known as R. Philp & Co. Messrs. Coles and Eckardt did all the traveling up to that time and continued in that capacity for some time afterward.

In 1883 the partners bought out Mr. Hockey's interests, and in 1890 Messrs. Watson and Coles' interests were purchased and the name changed to Philp & Eckardt. In 1896 Mr. Eckardt bought out Mr. Philp's interests, and the company's name was changed to the Eckardt Casket Co.

When Mr. Eckardt first went with the company their factories were located at Richmond and Sheppard Streets, with offices and warerooms at 12 Jordan Street. Still later, in 1882, the office and warehouse was moved to 100 Front Street West, next the Queen's Hotel, the factory remaining on Sheppard Street.

In the year 1896 Mr. Eckardt became sole proprietor of the Eckardt Casket Co. He moved the whole plant, office and warerooms to the Jacques & Hay furniture factory at the foot of Bay Street, which he had purchased for that purpose. This building was completely destroyed in the big fire of 1904, which consumed the entire wholesale business section of Toronto.

Mr. Eckardt was out of business for three years, due to the fire and resultant law suits, but in the fall of 1906 he purchased the present structure and plant on Niagara Street, which he completely remodelled and fitted up in elaborate style with all manner of conveniences for out-of-town visitors. The firm then became known as The National Casket Co., and The National Silver Plate Co. Mr. Eckardt sold out his interest to Dominion Manufacturers, Limited, at the close of 1913.

Mr. Eckardt is a Canadian by birth of the sixth generation and in distributing the presents he naturally remembered his old birthplace at Unionville. He first paid off the mortgage on the Lutheran Church there, and is also installing therein a handsome mahogany pipe organ, and has erected a big new bell, in memory of his forefathers, who came from the Genesee Valley, N.Y., in 1792, to settle in York County. Other churches and associations of Unionville, Markham and vicinity also benefit through Mr. Eckardt's liberality, as well do his employees.

Mr. Eckardt has opened temporary offices to look after his other interests at room 700, Empire Building, 64 West Wellington Street, Toronto, and intends taking larger quarters in the new Dominion Bank Building, at King and Yonge Streets, when that structure is completed. He will also look after some of his business at his home, 500 Huron Street. Mr. Eckardt hopes, in the near future, to take his family on a holiday trip round the world to get a rest from his labors of the past few years.

In his new office he is taking up Toronto and Northern Ontario real estate and securities, and will act in the capacity of adviser to those intending to enter upon commercial pursuits, as well as other matters connected with business law and dealings. Some of this work will take him from town occasionally.

Always a friend and supporter of the various undertakers' and embalmers' associations throughout Canada, Mr. Eckardt hopes to continue the pleasant relationship now that he is not in direct touch with them.

WHAT WOULD YOU HAVE DONE?

At the recent convention of Ohio Funeral Directors' Association a member said: Talking of advertising. I can take you to a little place in Ohio where a little coffin is in the window and a sign reads "Coffins for sale."

Not long ago I had a little experience I want to tell you about: One evening about 5 o'clock three brothers came in to the office and one of them said, "I want you to go out to my mother's at Bodkins; my mother is dead; well, she is not dead yet, but she was dying when I left, and she will be dead by the time you get there." Well they got in their buggy and drove away, going to one or the other's homes. Next morning, about 9 o'clock, David, one of the boys, came in and asked the time of the funeral, and I said, "What funeral," and they wanted to know if I had gone out to their mother's home and I said "No."

Well, do you know that old lady lived for six months after, but when she did die I did not get the funeral. You see I had lost their friendship by not going.

What would you have done, would you have gone? And would that have been advertising?

PRACTICAL "JOKER" CAUGHT

John Brewster, of 111 South Sixth Street, Newark, N.J., recently got six months in jail when sentenced for sending fake telephone calls to undertakers and doctors.

"I thought it great fun to see an undertaker crawl out of his bed at 1 o'clock in the morning and drive off to some distant part of the city," said Brewster. "After awakening an undertaker I would watch the fuss that followed."

"Perhaps you will enjoy your stay as well as you did your 'phone work," observed Judge Herr in sentencing the man.

Brewster was arrested three months ago for the same offense, but was put on probation.

AN AUTOMOBILE FUNERAL CAR

A patent recently granted to Ida Schmidt Marvin, of Detroit, Mich., presents a funeral car in which a compartment to receive a casket is located in rear of the space for the chauffeur and a large compartment is provided in the rear of the casket space for passengers.

W. P. Eckardt, son of A. J. H. Eckardt, has resigned from the National Casket Co.'s force. He joined his father's business in 1906, after completing his college course.

To Canadian Funeral Directors

We were favored with an attendance of nearly a score of the leading Embalmers of Ontario at our Annual School in January, when we had Professor Eckles, of Philadelphia, with us. We will expect an even larger number next year, as the number of our customers in Ontario, Quebec and the other Provinces is steadily increasing.

A FULL LINE READY FOR PROMPT SHIPMENT

The "CENTRAL" Line of mahogany, oak, plush and cloth covered caskets covers a wide variety of designs in the newest of styles. We can also supply anything desired in Casket Linings, Burial Robes and a general line of Undertakers' Supplies.

Special attention given to telegraph or phone orders. We never miss a train on express orders

CENTRAL CASKET COMPANY
Bridgeburg, Ont.   R. S. Flint   Canadian Representative: 241 Fern Ave., Toronto

---

DIOXIN
IS PLEASANT TO USE!

IF DIOXIN had no other superiority over the ordinary formaldehyde fluids, the fact that it is safe and pleasant to use should insure it a place in the affections of every embalmer.

If there is any one feature in the care of the dead human body that is more annoying than any other, it is the fact that, except DIOXIN, practically every fluid in the market will literally pickle the hands of most operators, no matter how careful they may be, and, particularly in cold weather, will open up painful sores which it is practically impossible to heal.

DIOXIN users are free from this great annoyance and danger—for every open cut or sore affords a hiding and breeding place for the germs of disease.

CONSIDER YOUR ASSISTANT

Perhaps your assistant does the most of your embalming. Consider his comfort and his health for selfish if for no other reasons. A good assistant, familiar with your wants, your methods and your customers, is a jewel. Make his work as safe and pleasant as you can.

Preserve his delicacy of touch. It may save you the embarrassment of an unsatisfactory result, or even of a spoiled body. There are enough risks in embalming, enough chances for mistakes, enough opportunities for error, without adding others unnecessarily.

Formaldehyde does not dangerously affect the hands of every embalmer, but it must deaden, must dull, the sensitive and delicate nerves of the fingers and render the worker less sure of touch, less certain of results, particularly in difficult cases. You can wash your hands in DIOXIN without injury.

NO TORTURED EYES WITH DIOXIN

The fumes of most fluids, too, in addition to attacking the hands, have a particularly irritating effect upon not only the mucous membranes of the eyelids, but upon the eyes themselves. This is particularly offensive and harmful when the work is done in a warm or brilliantly-lighted room.

DIOXIN DOES NOT EMBALM Your LUNGS

DIOXIN has no injurious effect upon the eyes or eyelids of the operator. The embalmer does not embalm his own eyesight when he uses it. If you or your assistant have suffered from the pungent effects of ordinary raw formaldehyde fluids, try DIOXIN. What little fumes arise from it are pleasant and positively non-irritant. Indeed, we feel that we cannot too strongly recommend DIOXIN to all embalmers who are troubled with failing eyesight—and most users of raw formaldehyde fluids are literally pickling their eyes.

Most of us are almost overcome when entering a room filled with the fumes of formaldehyde. We may not realize it, but we really are literally embalming our own lungs. In DIOXIN, what formaldhyde the fluid does contain, is purified and modified into formochloral, while peroxide of hydrogen, the great bleacher and disinfectant, replaces a very great proportion of this irritating agent.

As a result, DIOXIN has absolutely no deleterious effect upon either the lungs of the operator or the mucous membranes of nostrils and throat.

Dioxin comes in Bulk and Concentrated and RE-Concentrated.

Did we mention the fact that DIOXIN does not fill the house with offensive odors? That is another of its many virtues. And did we say that it makes the body firm, but pliable, rendering posing in the casket easy. Rigidity is not essential to preservation; in fact, it retards the circulation of the fluid.

But we've told you enough—although only a small part of the virtues of DIOXIN. Try it yourself—that is the great convincer. Order to-day!

H. S. ECKELS' & CO.
1922 Arch St., Philadelphia, Pa.   241 Fern Ave., Toronto, Ont., Can.

THE CHURCH FUNERAL
By George W. Wyatt

A funeral service has primarily two objects—to offer comfort and consolation to the living and to show our respect and honor for the dead. To accomplish these most successfully we must have the proper environments.

In the church are the necessary arrangements—the pew, the pulpit, the organ, the choir, in fact, the things to do with as the thing ought to be done. Contrast such a church with the close, stuffy rooms of some of our homes—25 or 30 people in a 12 x 15 foot room, little or no ventilation, often as many men outside as there are women inside, and the church must have the preference for such service. It is therefore most desirable, because of these accommodations, for those who really desire to hear what may be said on such occasions.

It is eminently proper when the deceased is a member of a fraternity and that society is present to assist in the service, and especially appropriate when the church mourns the loss of a Christian member and his family are Christian folks.

In our large cities where conditions demand or favor private funerals, such an arrangement is preferable; but in the smaller cities, towns and rural districts they are unusual, hence the necessity of a place for a large gathering, and the church is the logical place for such a meeting. If we can educate the people to the custom of closing the casket at the home and thus relieve them from the nervous strain of the exhibition of the form of their loved one to the public at the church, a strong objection to the church funeral will be removed. I believe we should use our best efforts to abolish the custom of opening the casket in front of the chancel, and asking the people to parade before it.

To take our loved dead into God's house, sit quietly down with our friends and from song and gospel message receive that consolation so much desired and needed at this hour, and then as quietly go to the city of the dead and lay the form away with soothed and comforted hearts, is to reap the rich results of any funeral service.

Accepting the church funeral as proper and desirable, I will speak of the next topic—its direction and management. To make it effective it must be orderly, dignified and sacred.

We will suppose that there are the usual floral offerings and that such as you do not desire to place upon the casket have been removed to the church and placed in a decorative manner at the altar.

We are in a city or town large enough to have hacks to accommodate the family and guests. The funeral car is halted just past the entrance to the church. As the casket bearers and minister come from their conveyance to their place near the car, the director will place the truck in the vestibule and return to the car door; at a signal to the drivers they will open the cab doors, the family and friends alight as the casket is removed from the car.

The minister leads, unless he did not accompany the cortege from the house, in which event he meets us at the church door, and after the casket is placed on the truck, passes down the aisle, followed by the casket bearers, the family following directly behind the casket; an usher will seat the bearers and another the family and friends. When all are seated, at a signal from the director, the minister takes charge of the services. At the conclusion the minister, closely followed by the bearers and they by the casket and family, pass out, and having been placed in their respective conveyances, proceed to the cemetery for the interment, the extra flowers being taken care of by an assistant.

If, for good reasons, the face of the dead must be exposed at the church, it is best to have the family pass the ordeal of the final good-bye in the privacy of the home. In that event the casket may be removed to the vestibule of the church and the audience allowed to pass by it and out of the house, and whenever practical, have the family leave the church by another exit, take their carriages, and by the time this has been done, the audience is out, the casket is in the car, and everything is in readiness to proceed to the cemetery; but if the family insist upon being the last to look upon the face of their dead, they can come to the vestibule in reverse order from their entrance, thus bringing the immediate family last, then the casket can be quickly closed and removed to the funeral car. If, however, the casket must remain at the church altar, there being no vestibule or space other than this, at the close of the services, the director will arrange it, and stepping to the most advantageous point will have the audience pass by it, allowing them to return to their seats; if an order is present, it will pass next and out of doors; the bearers will follow and take their positions at the door, and if the family must go through this part of the service personally, the more distant relatives come first, leaving the immediate family to the last, the casket is closed and minister precedes it, and we retire in the order of our entrance.

For the church funeral in the smaller towns and rural churches, the only difference is in the outside care of the conveyances for the family, they, in most instances, being of private ownership.

My ideal church funeral is conducted in the Roman Catholic church of our little city. The family take the final leave at home, and understand that promptness is desired so we are at the church on time; the casket is placed in the vestibule on the truck, all flowers are removed therefrom and placed on tables provided for the purpose. The casket of every member goes before the altar unadorned, no difference what his station in life may have been. The reverend, with the altar boys, meet us at the door, and after a simple service, precede us to the altar; the casket bearers follow them and are seated to the left; the casket is placed in its proper position, and the family are seated to the right. At the close of the regular service I pass to the casket, signal the bearers, who arise and pass out; as I follow with the casket, I speak softly to the family, who follow me to the vestibule, where the flowers are re-arranged and we proceed to the conveyances and to the cemetery.

The casket is never opened in the church. If, however, the deceased was a resident of some other city and it should be so desired, it may be opened in the vestibule and the audience passes out; it is then closed, and the family, having remained seated, are notified, when we pass to the conveyances in the regular order.

DARKLY HINTED

The host was talking to a newly-married couple who were spending their honeymoon at Scarborough. "You mustn't leave until you have seen the cemetery," he said; "it's well worth a visit." They said they would go. I forgot about it until too late; then the young wife reached her husband, saying, "Dear, you have not taken me to the cemetery yet." "Well, dearest," was the reply, "that is a pleasure I must have in the future."

CANADIAN FURNITURE IN WEST INDIES

The Canadian Trade Commissioner in the British West Indies writes as follows from Barbados:

Furniture to the value of £20,000 a year is imported into these colonies. The greater part is credited to the United Kingdom, some of which however is foreign bentwood furniture. As this comes knocked down and closely packed, it reaches its destination with low transportation charges. Canadian furniture in the cheaper lines would have a much greater sale if it were realized by the manufacturers that the question of freight is all important. A small consignment from Ontario which recently came via Halifax to Barbados was found to cost about sixty per cent. of its value in freight charges. This was due to the fact that bulky pieces of cheap furniture were packed without being knocked down. Had the shipment been manufactured for export and packed in small bulk, the freight would have been reduced so that repeat orders might have been possible.

Mattress Packing

The same complaint is also made in regard to spring mattresses purchased from Canadian manufacturers. The supply is now coming from England for the reason that English mattresses are shipped knocked down and closely packed and the ocean freight correspondingly low. Canadian mattresses are shipped on the frames strained, ready to sell, and on account of the size of the package the through freight amounts to about fifty per cent. of their value. Your Commissioner's attention was called by a firm here to a recent shipment of Canadian mattresses received, on which the size of the packages occasioned an excessive ocean freight and made a profit on the sale of the goods impossible.

In the cheaper lines manufactured from elm and birch there will be a continued demand, and will warrant some firm taking the matter up and preparing a line for these markets to be shipped knocked down and closely packed. The more expensive furniture, however, will only find sale in these colonies if made from mahogany or cedar, as these are the only woods that will withstand the wood ant. No buyer would think of purchasing expensive furniture in any other woods, as under favorable conditions, the wood ant will invariably destroy in a few years anything made except from these two named woods.

Rattan Furniture

Madeira supplies most of the rattan ware, which is cheaply made there and comes here packed with the onion. The furniture is open and cool and suited to a tropical country. It is seen in every furniture store and offered at a low price. Some of this kind of furniture comes from the United States but is much higher in price. Chair manufacturers have learnt the need of close and inexpensive packing, and it is hoped that the time will come when Canadian manufacturers of other lines of furniture will learn the same lesson.

"Was your wife angry at you for getting home last night?"
"Angry! Why she actually threw flowers at me."
"Well, how do you account for that black eye?"
"Oh! she forgot to take them out of the pots."

SITUATION WANTED.

YOUNG Man wants position as Embalmer and Assistant with firm requiring first class services, preferably in Ontario, but will go anywhere. Address Embalmer, c/o Furniture World and The Undertaker, 32 Colborne St., Toronto.

THE FURNITURE WORLD BRINGS RESULTS

"We have had some very good Enquiries through our ad in the Canadian Furniture World."

HOURD & COMPANY

London, Ont., Jan. 20, 1914

Undertakers Shipping Directory

ONTARIO
Aurora—
 Dunham, Charles.
Barrie—
 Smith, G. G. & Co.
Brockville—
 Quirmbach, Geo. B., 162 King St.
Brooklin—
 Disney, R. S.
Campbellford—
 Irwin, James.
Campden—
 Hausel, Albion.
Clinton—
 Walker, Wesley.
Coboconk—
 Greenley, A.
Copper Cliff—
 Boyd, W. C.
Dungannon—
 Sproul, William
Dutton—
 Schultz, B. L.
Elmira—
 Dreisinger, Chris.
Fenelon Falls—
 Deyman, L. & Son.
Fenwick—
 H. A. Metler.
Fergus—
 Armstrong, M. F.
 Thomson, John & Son.
Fort William—
 Cameron & Co., 711 Victoria.
 Morris, A.
Haileybury—
 Thorpe Bros.
Galt—
 Anderson, J. & Son.
Hamilton—
 Green Bros., 124 King St. E.
 Robinson, J. H. & Co., 19-21 John St. N.
Hanover—
 Wunnenberg, Norman.
Hastings—
 Howard, P. N.
Hepworth—
 Downs, E. J.
Inwood—
 Lorriman, E. S.
Kemptville—
 McCaughey, Geo. A.
Kenora—
 Horn & Taylor.
Kingston—
 Corbett, S. S.
Lakefield—
 Hendren, Geo. G.
Little Current—
 Sims, J. G.
Markdale—
 Oliver, M.
Newmarket—
 Millard, J. H.
North Augusta—
 Wilson, J. R.
North Bay—
 St. Pierre, E.
Oakwood—(Mariposa Station G.T.R.) Wilmot F. Webster.
Ohsweken—
 Johnson, F. L.
Oshawa—
 Disney Bros.
 Luke Bros.
Ottawa—
 Rogers, Geo. H., 128 Bank
Petrolia—
 Steadman Bros.
Port Arthur—
 Collin Wood, 36 Arthur St.
 Morris, A.
Prescott—
 Rankin, H. &. Son.
Renfrew—
 O'Connor, Wm.
St. Mary's—
 N. L. Brandon.
St. Thomas—
 Williams, P. R. & Sons, 519 Talbot St.
Seaforth, Ont.
 W. T. Box & Co.
Scotland—
 Vaughan, Jos. H. M.
Sudbury—
 Henry, J. G.
Toronto—
 Cobbledick, N. B., 2068 Queen St. East and 1508 Danforth Ave. Private Ambulance.
 Humphrey, E. J. Burial Co. Head Office, 359 Yonge St.; Branch, 497 Queen St. W. Private ambulance.
 Stone, Daniel (formerly H. Stone & Son), 82 Bloor St. West.
 Vancamp, J. C., 30 Bloor St. West.
Waterloo—
 Klipper Undertaking Co.
Welland—
 Sutherland, G. W.
Woodstock—
 Meadows, T. & Sons.
 Mack, Paul

QUEBEC
Buckingham—
 Paquet, Jos.
Cowansville—
 Judson, M. B.
Montreal—
 Tees & Co., 912 St. Catherine St. West.
St. Hyacinthe—
 Cadorette, Mongeau & Leary.
St. Laurent—
 Gougeon, Jos.

NEW BRUNSWICK
Petitcodiac—
 Jonah, D. Allison.
Welland—
 Sutherland, G. W.
Woodstock—
 Van Wart, Jacob.

NOVA SCOTIA
Ferrona—
 Fraser, D. & Co.
Halifax—
 Snow & Co., 90 Argyle St.
Sydney, C.B.—
 Beaton, A. J. & Son, 374-384 George St.

MANITOBA
Brandon—
 Campbell & Campbell.
 Vincent & McPherson.
Swan River—
 Paull, Geo.
Winnipeg—
 Bardal, A. S., 834 Sherbrooke
 Thompson, J. C., 501 Main
 Clark-Leatherdale Co., Ltd., 232 Kennedy St.

SASKATCHEWAN
Gull Lake—
 Morrow, Fred. A.
Saskatoon—
 Young, A. E.
Kamsack—
 Russell, G. E. I.
Lanigan—
 Robertson, Wm.
Moose Jaw—
 The Bellamy Co.
 Broadfoot Bros.
Rush Lake—
 Friesen, John M.
Prince Albert—
 Howard, A. C.
 Hadley, G. L.
Regina—
 Spoors, George.
Semans—
 Haygarth, Jas.
Welwyn—
 Leavens, Merritt.
Wolseley—
 Barber, B.

ALBERTA
Calgary—
 Graham & Buscomb, 611 Centre St.
Castor—
 Winter, W. G.

BRITISH COLUMBIA
Hosmer—
 Cornett, T. A.
Victoria—
 Hanna & Thompson, 827 Pandora Ave.

For Every Furniture Man

HOW TO KNOW PERIOD STYLES IN FURNITURE

A Helpful, Thoroughly Practical Book, Written by an Authority—

150 Pages 317 Illustrations

Price, $1.50

Designers will find illustrations of the work of celebrated designers of history. Examples are taken from the recognized collections and museums of the world.
Buyers—The book is arranged for easy reference with the distinguishing features of each period clearly shown.
Salesmen—The information in "How to Know Period Styles" will enable you to talk authoritatively on the subject.
Students—The confusing element has been eliminated, but all necessary information is included.

Send us $1.50. Keep the book 10 days and if it isn't worth the price, return it and get your money back.

The Commercial Press
Publishers The Canadian Furniture World and The Undertaker
32 Colborne Street, Toronto

IF YOU WANT TO BUY OR SELL

A Furniture or Undertaking Business, try our Classified Pages. The Canadian Furniture World and The Undertaker is read by practically every furniture merchant and undertaker in Canada every month.

BUYER'S DIRECTORY

When writing to advertisers kindly mention the Canadian Furniture World and the Undertaker

ARTS AND CRAFTS FURNITURE
Geo. McLagan Furniture Co., Stratford.
John C. Mundell & Co., Elora.

ASBESTOS TABLE COVERS.
Canadian H. W. Johns-Manville Co., Toronto.

BABY CARRIAGES.
Gendron Mfg. Co., Toronto.

AWNINGS
Stamco, Limited, Saskatoon, Sask.

BENT WOOD FURNITURE.
John C. Mundell & Co., Elora.
J. & J. Kohn, Toronto (W. Craig).

BOOKCASES.
Knechtel Furniture Co., Hanover.
Globe Wernicke Co., Stratford.
Geo. McLagan Furniture Co., Stratford.
Meaford Mfg. Co., Meaford, Ont.

BUFFETS.
Bell Furniture Co., Southampton, Ontario.
Knechtel Furniture Co., Hanover.
Geo. McLagan Furniture Co., Stratford.
Meaford Mfg. Co., Meaford, Ont.
Peppler Bros., Hanover.
Stratford Chair Co., Stratford.
Victoriaville Furniture Co., Victoriaville, Que.

BEDS (Brass and Iron).
Canada Beds, Ltd., Chesley.
Ideal Bedding Co., Toronto.
Geo. Gale & Son, Waterville, Que.
Ives Modern Bedstead Co., Cornwall Ont.
Ontario Spring Bed & Mattress Co., London, Ont.
Standard Bedstead Co., Victoriaville, Que.
Stamco, Limited, Saskatoon, Sask.
Stratford Bed Co., Stratford, Ont.
S. Weisglass, Ltd., Montreal, Que.

BEDS (Modern Wood).
Elora Furniture Co., Elora.
Knechtel Furniture Co., Hanover.

BED SPRINGS.
Colleran Spring Mattress Co., Toronto.
Knechtel Furniture Co., Hanover.
Frame and Hay Fence Co., Stratford.
Gold Medal Furniture Co., Toronto.
Leggett & Platt Spring Bed Co., Windsor.
Ideal Bedding Co., Toronto.
Ontario Spring Bed & Mattress Co., London, Ont.
Stamco, Limited, Saskatoon, Sask.
S. Weisglass, Ltd., Montreal, Que.

BED ROOM CHAIRS.
Baetz Bros., Berlin.
Bell Furniture Co., Southampton, Ontario.
Elmira Furniture Co, Elmira, Ont.
Lippert Furniture Co., Berlin.

BED ROOM SUITES.
Bell Furniture Co., Southampton, Ontario.
Knechtel Furniture Co., Hanover
Meaford Mfg. Co., Meaford.
Victoriaville Furniture Co., Victoriaville, Que.

BUNGALOW CHAIRS & SUITES
Baetz Bros. & Co., Berlin, Ont.

CARD AND DEN TABLES.
Geo. McLagan Furniture Co., Stratford.
John C. Mundell & Co., Elora, Ont.

CARPET RACKS
Steel Furnishing Co., New Glasgow, N. S.

CAMP FURNITURE.
Stratford Mfg. Co., Stratford.
Ideal Bedding Co., Toronto.

CEDAR BOXES
D. L. Shafer, St. Thomas, Ont.

CELLARETTES.
John C. Mundell & Co., Elora, Ont.

CHAIRS AND ROCKERS.
Bell Furniture Co., Southampton.
Baetz Bros., Berlin.

CHAIRS
Knechtel Furniture Co., Hanover.
John C. Mundell & Co., Elora.
Stratford Chair Co., Stratford.
Waterloo Furniture Co., Waterloo.
Canadian Rattan Chair Co., Victoriaville.
Gold Medal Furniture Co., Toronto.
Elmira Furniture Co, Elmira, Ont.
Imperial Furniture Co., Toronto.
Lippert Furniture Co., Berlin.
Victoriaville Chair Mfg. Co., Victoriaville, Que.

CHESTERFIELDS.
Imperial Furniture Co., Toronto.

CHIFFONIERS.
Bell Furniture Co., Southampton.
Knechtel Furniture Co., Hanover.
Meaford Mfg. Co., Meaford, Ont.
Stratford Chair Co., Stratford.
Victoriaville Furniture Co., Victoriaville, Que.

CHINA CABINETS.
Bell Furniture Co., Southampton, Ontario
Peppler Bros., Hanover.
Knechtel Furniture Co., Hanover.
Geo. McLagan Furniture Co., Stratford.
Meaford Mfg. Co., Meaford, Ont.

CLOCK CASES
Elmira Interior Woodwork Co., Elmira, Ont.

COMFORTERS.
Toronto Feather & Down Co., Toronto.
Stamco, Limited, Saskatoon, Sask.

COTS
Ideal Bedding Co., Toronto.
Ontario Spring Bed and Mattress Co., London.

COSTUMIERS
Elmira Interior Woodwork Co., Elmira, Ont.

COUCHES.
J. P. Albrough & Co., Ingersoll.
Ellis Furniture Co., Ingersoll.
Gold Medal Furniture Co., Toronto.
Kindel Bed Co., Toronto.
Imperial Furniture Co., Toronto.
John C. Mundell & Co., Elora, Ont.
Montreal Upholstering Co., Montreal.
Steel Furnishing Co., New Glasgow, N. S.
S. Weisglass, Ltd., Montreal, Que.

COUCHES (Sliding).
Ideal Bedding Co., Toronto.
Farquharson-Gifford Co., Stratford. Co., London, Ont.
Stamco, Limited, Saskatoon, Sask.
Gold Medal Furniture Co., Toronto.

CRADLES.
Knechtel Furniture Co., Hanover.

CRIBS (Brass and Iron)
Ideal Bedding Co., Toronto.
Ontario Spring Bed & Mattress Co., London, Ont.
Stamco, Limited, Saskatoon, Sask.
S. Weisglass, Ltd., Montreal, Que.

CUSHIONS.
Stamco, Limited, Saskatoon, Sask.

DAVENPORT BEDS.
Farquharson-Gifford Co., Stratford.
Kindel Bed Co., Toronto.
Montreal Upholstering Co., Montreal, Que.
Imperial Rattan Co., Stratford.
John C. Mundell & Co., Elora.

DAVENPORT FRAMES
Elmira Interior Woodwork Co., Elmira, Ont.

DEN FURNITURE
Elmira Furniture Co, Elmira, Ont.
Farquharson-Gifford Co., Stratford.
John C. Mundell & Co., Elora, Ont.

DIVANETTES.
Lippert Furniture Co., Berlin.

DESKS.
Bell Furniture Co., Southampton.
Elmira Interior Woodwork Co., Elmira.
Knechtel Furniture Co., Hanover.
Geo. McLagan Furniture Co., Stratford.
John C. Mundell & Co., Elora.
Stratford Desk Co., Stratford, Ont.

DINING-ROOM FURNITURE
Crown Furniture Co., Preston.
Farquharson-Gifford Co., Stratford.

DINING SUITES.
Bell Furniture Co., Southampton.
Knechtel Furniture Co., Hanover.
Geo. McLagan Furniture Co., Stratford.
John C. Mundell & Co., Elora.
Peppler Bros., Hanover.
Stratford Chair Co., Stratford.

DINNER WAGONS.
Geo. McLagan Furniture Co., Stratford.
Peppler Bros., Hanover.

DRESSERS.
Bell Furniture Co., Southampton.
Knechtel Furniture Co., Hanover.
Stratford Chair Co., Stratford.
Victoriaville Furniture Co., Victoriaville, Que.
Meaford Mfg. Co., Meaford, Ont.

EXTENSION TABLES.
Bell Furniture Co., Southampton.
Peppler Bros., Hanover.
Berlin Table Mfg. Co., Berlin.
Meaford Mfg. Co., Meaford, Ont.

FILING DEVICES.
Elmira Interior Woodwork Co., Elmira.
Globe Wernicke Co., Stratford.
Knechtel Furniture Co., Hanover.
Geo. McLagan Furniture Co., Stratford.

FILING CABINETS
Globe Wernicke Co., Stratford, Ont.

FOLDING CHAIRS.
Stratford Mfg. Co., Stratford.
Ideal Bedding Co., Toronto.

FOLDING TABLES.
Hourd & Co., London.
Stratford Mfg. Co., Stratford.

FOOTSTOOLS
Elmira Furniture Co, Elmira, Ont.

HALL SEATS AND MIRRORS.
Geo. McLagan Furniture Co., Stratford.
Meaford Mfg. Co., Meaford, Ont.

HALL TREES.
Geo. McLagan Furniture Co., Stratford.

HAMMO-COUCHES.
Ideal Bedding Co., Toronto.

INVALID CHAIRS.
Gendron Mfg. Co., Toledo, Ohio.
Victoriaville Chair Mfg. Co., Victoriaville, Que.

IRONING BOARDS AND DRYERS.
Stratford Mfg. Co., Stratford.

JARDINIERE STANDS.
Elmira Furniture Co., Elmira, Ont.
Elora Furniture Co., Elora.
Geo. McLagan Furniture Co., Stratford.
Meaford Mfg. Co., Meaford, Ont.

KITCHEN CABINETS.
H. E. Furniture Co., Milverton.
Nagrelia Mfg. Co., Hamilton.
Knechtel Kitchen Cabinet Co., Ltd., Hanover, Ont.

KITCHEN TABLES.
Knechtel Furniture Co., Hanover.
Victoriaville Furniture Co., Victoriaville.

LADIES' DESKS
Meaford Mfg. Co., Meaford, Ont.

LAWN SEATS AND SWINGS.
Stratford Mfg. Co., Stratford.

LIBRARY TABLES.
Bell Furniture Co., Southampton.
Peppler Bros., Hanover.
Elmira Furniture Co, Elmira, Ont.
Elmira Interior Woodwork Co., Elmira, Ont.
Geo. McLagan Furniture Co., Stratford.
Meaford Mfg. Co., Meaford, Ont.
John C. Mundell & Co., Elora, Ont.

LUXURY CHAIRS.
Lippert Furniture Co., Berlin.

MAGAZINE RACKS AND STANDS.
Geo. McLagan Furniture Co., Stratford.

MATTRESSES.
Berlin Bedding Co., Toronto.
Canada Mattress Co., Victoriaville, Que.
Gold Medal Furniture Co., Toronto.
McKellar Bedding Co., Fort William, Ont.
Ontario Spring Bed & Mattress
Stamco, Limited, Saskatoon, Sask.
Standard Bedding Co., Toronto.
Antiseptic Bedding Co., Toronto.
Ideal Bedding Co., Toronto.
Fischman Mattress Co., Toronto.

MANTELS—Wood, Tile
Elmira Interior Woodwork Co., Elmira, Ont.

MANTELS—Electric
Elmira Interior Woodwork Co., Elmira, Ont.

MEDICINE CABINETS.
Meaford Mfg. Co., Meaford, Ont.

MORRIS CHAIRS.
Ellis Furniture Co., Ingersoll.
Imperial Rattan Co., Stratford.
Knechtel Furniture Co., Hanover.
John C. Mundell & Co., Elora.
Waterloo Furniture Co., Waterloo.

MUSIC CABINETS.
Geo. McLagan Furniture Co., Stratford.
Knechtel Kitchen Cabinet Co., Ltd., Hanover, Ont.

OFFICE CHAIRS.
Bell Furniture Co., Southampton.
Elmira Furniture Co., Elmira, Ont.
Knechtel Furniture Co., Hanover.
Stratford Chair Co., Stratford.
J. & J. Kohn, Toronto (W. Craig).
John C. Mundell & Co., Elora, Ont.

OFFICE TABLES
Stratford Desk Co., Stratford, Ont.

PARK SEATS.
Stratford Mfg. Co., Stratford.

PARLOR CHAIRS and ROCKERS
Ellis Furniture Co., Ingersoll.
Elmira Interior Woodwork Co., Elmira.
John C. Mundell & Co., Elora, Ont.
Waterloo Furniture Co., Waterloo.

PARLOR FRAMES
Elmira Interior Woodwork Co., Elmira, Ont.

PARLOR SUITES.
Elmira Interior Woodwork Co., Elmira.
Ellis Furniture Co., Ingersoll.
Knechtel Furniture Co., Hanover.
Waterloo Furniture Co., Waterloo.
Gold Medal Furniture Co., Toronto.
Lippert Furniture Co., Berlin.

PARLOR TABLES.
Geo. McLagan Furniture Co., Stratford.
Meaford Mfg. Co., Meaford, Ont.
Elmira Furniture Co., Elora.
Elmira Furniture Co., Elmira, Ont.
Knechtel Furniture Co., Hanover.
Peppler Bros., Hanover.

PEDESTALS.
Geo. McLagan Furniture Co., Stratford.

PILLOWS.
Ontario Spring Bed & Mattress Co., London, Ont.
Stamco, Limited, Saskatoon, Sask.
Toronto Feather & Down Co., Toronto.
Ideal Bedding Co., Toronto.

PILLOW SHAM HOLDERS.
Tarbox Mfg. Co., Toronto.

RATTAN FURNITURE.
Imperial Rattan Co., Stratford.
Canadian Rattan Chair Co., Victoriaville, Que.
Gendron Mfg. Co., Toronto.

RECLINING CHAIRS.
Ellis Furniture Co., Ingersoll.
Knechtel Furniture Co., Hanover.
John C. Mundell & Co., Elora, Ont.

RUG RACKS
Steel Furnishing Co., New Glasgow, N. S.

SECTIONAL BOOKCASES
Knechtel Furniture Co., Hanover.
Globe Wernicke Co., Stratford.

March, 1914. CANADIAN FURNITURE WORLD AND THE UNDERTAKER.

Index to Advertisements

A
Albrough & Co., J. P. 21
Ault & Wiborg 62

B
Baetz Bros. & Co. 16
Batavia Clamp Co. 70
Berlin Table Mfg. Co. 12

C
Canadian Linderman Co. 62
Canadian Rattan Chair Co. 23
Can. H.W. Johns-Manville Co. ... 14
Central Casket Co. 72
Colleran Patent Spring Mat. Co. 11

D
Dominion Casket Co. 64
Dominion Mfrs., Limited 68

E
Eckels & Co., H. S. 72
Egyptian Chemical Co. 70
Ellis Furniture Co. 10
Elmira Interior Woodwork Co. ... 26
Elmira Furniture Co. 26

F
Farquharson-Gifford 7
Fischmann Mattress Co. ...... i.f.c.
Frame & Hay 11

G
Gale & Son, Geo. 6
Globe Wernicke 9
Gold Medal Furniture Mfg. Co. .. 17
Gendron Wheel Co. .... i.b.c.

H
H. E. Furniture Co. 8

I
Ideal Bedding Co. 28
Imperial Furniture Co. 24
Imperial Rattan Co. 3
Ives Modern Bedstead Co. .. o.b.c.

J
Jamieson & Co., R. C. 8

K
Kawneer Mfg. Co. 11
Kindel Beds Co., Limited 18
Knechtel Furniture Co. 25
Kohn, J. & J. 10

L
Lackawana Leather Co. 61
Leggatt & Platt Spring Bed Co... 18

M
Meaford Mfg. Co. 15
Mundell & Co., John C. ..... i.f.c.
McLagan Furniture Co. ...... o.f.c.
McKellar Bedding Co. 27
Montreal Upholstering Co. 4

O
Onward Mfg. Co. 61
Ontario Spring Bed 4

R
Robertson, P. & L., Mfg. Co. ... 62

S
Scafe & Co., A. J. 12
Shafer, D. L. 16
Stamco, Limited 60
Steel Furniture Co. 24
Steele, James Limited ...... i.b.c.
Stratford Brass Co. 13
Stratford Bed Co. 11
Stratford Chair Co. 5
Stratford Mfg. Co. 13
St. Thomas Metallic Vault Co. .. 70

V
Victoriaville Bedding Co. .. 19-20
Victoriaville Chair Co. 22
Victoriaville Furniture Co. 21

W
Walter & Co., B. 61
Western Casket Co. 66
Weisglass, S., Limited. 23

SCHOOL FURNITURE.
Bell Furniture Co., Southampton.
SIDEBOARDS.
Knechtel Furniture Co., Hanover.
Meaford Mfg. Co., Meaford, Ont.
Stratford Chair Co., Stratford.
STORE FRONTS
Kawneer Mfg. Co., Toronto.
TABLES.
Berlin Table Mfg. Co., Berlin, Ont.
Bell Furniture Co., Southampton, Ontario.
Elora Furniture Co., Elora.
Knechtel Furniture Co., Hanover.
John C. Mundell & Co., Elora.
Orillia Furniture Co., Orillia.
Peppler Bros., Hanover.
Stratford Chair Co., Stratford.
Victoriaville Furniture Co., Victoriaville, Que.
TABOURETTES.
Elora Furniture Co., Elora.
Kensington Furniture Co., Goderich.
TELEPHONE STANDS.
John C. Mundell & Co., Elora, Ont.
TYPEWRITER DESKS.
Elmira Interior Woodwork Co., Elmira.
Stratford Desk Co., Stratford, Ont.
UPHOLSTERERS' SUPPLIES
Ellis Furniture Co., Ingersoll.
Gold Medal Furniture Co., Toronto.
UPHOLSTERED FURNITURE
Baetz Bros., Berlin.
Ellis Furniture Co., Ingersoll.
Farquharson-Gifford Co., Stratford, Ont.
Imperial Rattan Co., Stratford.
Imperial Furniture Co., Toronto.
John C. Mundell & Co., Elora.
Knechtel Furniture Co., Hanover.
Waterloo Furniture Co., Waterloo.
Gold Medal Furniture Co., Toronto.
Quality Furniture Makers, Welland.
A. J. Scafe & Co., Berlin.
VACUUM CLEANERS.
Onward Mfg. Co., Berlin.
VERANDAH FURNITURE.
Imperial Rattan Co., Stratford.
Stratford Mfg. Co., Stratford.
WARDROBES.
Knechtel Furniture Co., Hanover.
Meaford Mfg. Co., Meaford, Ont.
Stratford Chair Co., Stratford.

FACTORY SUPPLIES

BRASS TRIMMINGS
Stratford Brass Co., Stratford.
CLAMPS.
Batavia Clamp Co., Batavia, N.Y.
FURNITURE SHOES.
Onward Mfg. Co., Berlin.
DRY KILNS.
Morton Dry Kiln Co., Chicago
FURNITURE HARDWARE
Stratford Brass Co., Stratford, Ont.
GLUE JOINTING MACHINES.
Canadian Linderman Co., Woodstock.
NAILS
P. L. Robertson Mfg. Co., Milton, Ontario.
PLATING
P. L. Robertson Mfg. Co., Milton, Ontario.

RIVETS AND SCREWS
P. L. Robertson Mfg. Co., Milton.
SPRINGS.
James Steele, Guelph.
Ideal Bedding Co., Toronto.
SPANISH LEATHER.
Lackawanna Leather Co., Hackettstown, N. J.
STERILIZED HAIR.
Griffin Curled Hair Co., Toronto.
TABLE SLIDES
B. Walter & Co., Wabash., Ind.
TRUCKS.
W. I. Kemp Co., Ltd., Stratford.
VARNISHES.
R. C. Jamieson & Co., Montreal.
Ault & Wiborg, Toronto.
VENEERS.
Adams & Raymond Veneer Co., Indianapolis, Ind.
VENEER PRESSES.
Wm. R. Perrin & Co., Toronto.
WASHERS
P. L. Robertson Mfg. Co., Milton.

UNDERTAKERS' SUPPLIES

AMBULANCES.
Mitchell & Co., Ingersoll.
BURIAL ROBES.
James S. Elliott & Son, Prescott
Evel Casket Co., Hamilton.
Globe Casket Co., London.
Semmens & Evel Casket Co., Hamilton.
CLOTH CASKETS
Michigan Casket Co, Detroit, Mich.
CEMENT CASKETS.
Canadian Cement Casket Co., Prescott.
CEMETERY SUPPLIES
Frigid Fluid Co., Chicago, Ill.
CASKETS AND COFFINS.
Dominion Casket Co., Guelph.
Evel Casket Co., Hamilton.
Globe Casket Co., London.
Semmens & Evel Casket Co., Hamilton.
EMBALMING FLUIDS.
Egyptian Chemical Co., Boston.
Frigid Fluid Co., Chicago, Ill.
Michigan Casket Co, Detroit, Mich.
H. S. Eckels Co., Philadelphia
EMBALMERS' SUPPLIES
Frigid Fluid Co., Chicago, Ill.
HEARSES.
Mitchell & Co., Ingersoll.
LOWERING DEVICES
Frigid Fluid Co., Chicago, Ill.
SCHOOLS OF EMBALMING.
Canadian School of Embalming, Toronto.
STEEL GRAVE VAULTS
St. Thomas Metallic Vault Co., St. Thomas, Ont.
Michigan Casket Co, Detroit, Mich.
UNDERTAKER'S CHAIRS.
Stratford Mfg. Co., Stratford
UNDERTAKERS' SUNDRIES
Frigid Fluid Co., Chicago, Ill.

For Sale
Wanted

TERMS FOR INSERTION
4 Cents per word one insertion
10 Cents per word three insertions

MINIMUM 50 CENTS

FOR SALE—Hearse, Harness, Cooling Board, as good as new. Photo on application. A. J. Thomson, 74 Annette St., Toronto.

BUY
Upholstery Springs
That "Stand Up"

Our Tempered Furniture Springs will outlast almost any piece of upholstered furniture. They are built to "stand up" indefinitely.

JAMES STEELE, LIMITED
GUELPH :: :: ONTARIO

Invalid Chairs and Tricycles of every description.

This has been our study for thirty-five years. We build chairs that suit the requirements of any case. Write us for catalogue No. 20 and prices, if interested.

Gendron Wheel Co., Toledo, O. U.S.A.

"STORE MANAGEMENT COMPLETE"

272 Pages **ONLY ONE DOLLAR** 13 Chapters

Tells all about the management of a Store, so that not only the greatest sales but the largest profit may be realized.—By FRANK FARRINGTON.

COMMERCIAL PRESS, Ltd., 32 Colborne St., Toronto

IVES "Regal" Beds
For Your Spring Business

Ask our salesmen to show you our newest designs in Steel and Brass Bedsteads

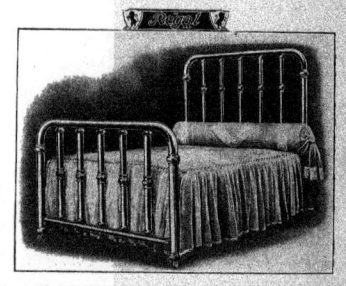

No. 857   No. 844

SEE THESE IN OUR

MONTREAL AND WINNIPEG SHOWROOMS

and remember that

IVES SERVICE

Stands out pre-eminently the *Best in Canada*

PROMPT SHIPMENTS—COURTESY
—ATTENTION TO DETAIL

Ives Modern Bedstead Co., Limited

Montreal   Cornwall   Winnipeg

Vol. 4 No. 4   APRIL, 1914

Canadian Furniture World
AND THE UNDERTAKER

Published by the Commercial Press, Limited, 32 Colborne Street, Toronto

Western Buyers! Buy through the Stratford Shipping Combination and save on freight charges.

Do Your Customers Admire Beauty?

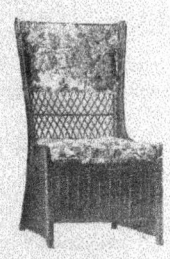

THESE are "substantial" beauties—not blanketed skeletons. You can figure on lasting admiration every time a piece of Imperial Rattan Upholstered Furniture is sold.

We make the famous Stratford Davenport Bed in a great variety of coverings.

Attractive values in English Overstuffed Chairs and Chesterfields.

Imperial Rattan Company, Ltd.
Stratford, Ontario

NEW LINES AT JOHN C. MUNDELL & CO.'S

Some Striking Jacobean Designs

DISTINCTIVENESS is the word most frequently used in describing some of the new lines we are bringing out this season. Rockers, Arm Chairs, Settees, Couches, Tables, in the graceful style in vogue during the Jacobean Period, convey an effect of Old World culture and elegance impossible to describe or to resist.

Tall, slender, and quaint are the Chairs and Rockers of this period, while the Tables and Settees harmonize with them at every point. Finished in special Old Oak finish, made with Twisted Turnings and Woven Cane Sides and Ends, and upholstered in Spanish Roan, these pieces make their appeal at once to the taste and comfort of the shopper, and at the same time give an effect of distinction and character to the dealer's Stock.

Blue Prints and Prices for the asking, and sent by return mail

John C. Mundell & Co., Limited, Elora, Ont.

Five Points in the Sale of Bedding

1.—Sanitation. 2.—A high degree of Comfort. 3.—Great Serviceability. 4.—Price Consistency. 5.—Appearance that reflects the other four points.

If the Bedding you carry does not embody these all-important factors in profit making, you are not selling the best to be had. It is time you knew the service in

Antiseptic Bedding

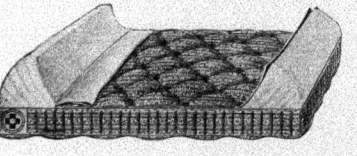

THE
Antiseptic Bedding Co.
187-189 Parliament Street
Toronto, Ont.

April, 1914　　CANADIAN FURNITURE WORLD AND THE UNDERTAKER

STRATFORD

The Stratford Shipping Combination offers big savings on freight charges to Western Buyers. Write us for details.

You'll need some of the freshness and exclusive dignity of the McLagan type to complete your Spring showing.

The many new lines in Dining Room, Hall, Parlor, Living Room and Library Furniture we now have ready in conservative and quietly unusual designs should present this opportunity to you.

GUNN SECTIONAL BOOKCASES AND FILING CABINETS

Reproductions of these lines upon request

The
Geo. McLagan
Stratford, Ontario

Make a Note Now

to investigate the new ONTARIO Brass Bed Line before placing your Spring Orders

We have equipped an up-to-the-minute plant to manufacture this line — and have secured expert workman having long experience in producing a sup rior article. We can guarantee the finish.

Successful business for the year depends on the class of goods you stock your store with.

You can't go wrong if you give **Ontario Brass Beds** a trial.

Get in Touch Now

No. 308
Pillars, 2 inches continuous
Filling, 5-8 inchs and 1/2 inch
Head, 59 inches
Foot, 37 inches
Finish Satin, Bright or Combination
Sizes 3-0, 3-6, 4-0, 4-6

The Ontario Spring Bed & Mattress Company, Limited
The Largest Bedding House in Canada
London - Ontario

Another Money Maker For You, Mr. Dealer

This is one of our May Designs that we are manufacturing. It will pay you to examine our full line, as every article we manufacture, is a money maker for the dealer. We are manufacturing the following lines: Couches, Pullman Davenports, Duofolds Divanettes, Etc.

No. 91 Couch
Frame: Quartered Cut Oak.   Finish: Early English and Fumed Oak

The Montreal Upholstering Company
1611-1613 Clarke St., MONTREAL, Can.

April, 1914   CANADIAN FURNITURE WORLD AND THE UNDERTAKER   5

STRATFORD

The Stratford Shipping Combination offers savings in freight charges to Western buyers. Write us for details.

A limitless assortment that makes choosing a matter of available space on your floors.

No. 1566.1

The wise dealer is now demanding reliable goods—and for reliability there is nothing to excel the fine line of chairs we offer to the trade. You are assured of more chair trade if you sell the Stratford Make.

No. 1566.5

We know how to make **good** chairs better than any other kind, and we are always striving to make them still better. In our box seat diners you'll find a touch of better chair making that **must** appeal to you.

Stratford   Ontario

No. 3386

Give the Meaford Line
a Chance to Sell Itself
on its Face

Display it side by side with real mahogany and real quartered oak, and see how fast it will sell itself to the majority of your customers. It sells on its face—its true graining and finish, and unusual lowness in price.

Sideboards	Jardiniere Stands
Buffets	Centre Tables
China Cabinets	Dressers
Extension Tables	Chiffoniers
Hall Racks	Dressing Tables
Hall Seats and Mirrors	Wardrobes
Library Tables	Bedroom Tables
Desks and Book Cases	Medicine Cabinets

The Meaford Mfg. Co., Ltd.
Meaford   Ontario

STRATFORD

The Stratford Shipping Combination offers big savings on freight charges to Western buyers. Write us for details.

¶ Our aim this year, our first in the manufacture of the "F.-G." lines, is to work up a satisfactory volume of sales. We have a large factory, everything needed in equipment and material, and the men to put quality into the goods.

OUR SPECIALTY IS

Davenport Beds, Couches and Living Room Furniture

and we are showing some decidedly attractive pieces.

¶ Look over the photos our traveler will show. We are sure that the lines will please you, and we are making our proposition a "good buy" in every way. *Wait* for our traveler.

Stratford   Ontario

Jamieson's Turpentine Stains

The Best of the good stains

R. C. Jamieson & Co., Limited
Established 1858
Montreal   Vancouver

The Removable Flour Bin Idea

A feature that, in itself, will sell the H. E. Kitchen Cabinet when you explain its labor-saving advantages to your customer. But

H. E. Kitchen Cabinets

possess many other valuable conveniences. Your spring stock should include a showing of this line. To-day is the day to write for our literature and trade offer.

Cabinet No. 30

The H. E. Furniture Co., Ltd.
Milverton   Ontario

April, 1914   CANADIAN FURNITURE WORLD AND THE UNDERTAKER   9

STRATFORD

The Stratford Shipping Combination offers big savings on freight charges to Western Buyers. Write us for details.

In the Globe-Wernicke make you will find the greatest variety in design, finish and combination.

Sheraton Beauty

Among the early period styles the Sheraton is perhaps the most favored. Its delicacy of outline is in itself a graceful decoration, while the patterns, though daintily proportioned, are geometrically true.

There is a decided advantage in being able to show on your floors, or by our catalogs, any style or combination desired by your customer. You can **best** do this by featuring the comprehensive Globe-Wernicke line.

Ask for Our Catalogs and Price Lists

Stratford   Ontario

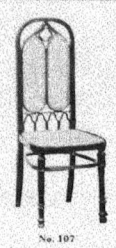

Kohn's Imported Vienna Furniture Sells

And makes permanent patrons for the store because of its beauty, comfort and durability.

Made of specially seasoned Austrian Beechwood, constructed so as to withstand the strain of constant service.

Will attract the trade of fashion leaders in your city.

No. 107

Kohn's Imported Bentwood Furniture

Is shown by leading furniture stores everywhere. Artistic in outline, high-class in finish. With steel screw leg joints. Light weight but remarkably lasting

Send for Catalogue and Price List To-day

JACOB & JOSEF KOHN
OF VIENNA
215-219 VICTORIA ST., TORONTO, CAN.

| 110-112 West 27th St. NEW YORK CITY | 1410-1418 S. Wabash Ave. CHICAGO, ILL. | Second Floor, Keeler Bldg. GRAND RAPIDS, MICH. | 418 Maritime Bldg. SEATTLE, WASH. |

No. 107E

The Mattress Built With the Little Coil Springs in the Padded Cotton Pockets

The Fischman Patent Mattress is the *comfort* mattress. With 22 rows of springs encased in cotton pockets with layers of cotton felt on top and bottom, its primary feature is *softness*.

Each spring acts independently—there is no friction caused—nothing to wear but the ticking, which can easily be renewed.

Your Mattress Business will double up *over night* if the Fischman is featured.

THE FISCHMAN PATENT MATTRESS
Can. Pat., Mar. 16, 1909   U.S. Pat., Feb. 16, 1909

A Real Guarantee

Warranted for five years against sagging or spreading. Absolutely noiseless.

Sales to-day are what count. That's the aim of the Fischman Mattress.

McLaughlin & Scott, Canadian Sellings Agents, 67-71 Adelaide St. W.

The Fischman Mattress Company
569 Queen St. W.   Toronto, Ontario

STRATFORD

The Stratford Shipping Combination offers big savings on freight charges to Western Buyers. Write us for details.

Will YOU supply the Spring Demand?

There is a big market for Lawn Swings, Verandah and Garden Furniture, such as those pieces illustrated. A little push on these lines, Mr. Dealer, will show where the real profits lie in Spring Goods. The Stratford make are the strongest sold, and good service is guaranteed. Better get in touch with us at once.

As an evidence of the superiority of our lines, we are at the present time filling an order for **15 car loads of seats** for the new grand stand at the Woodbine Race Track in Toronto. You can profit on some good business like this, too. See that the Park Board in your town know the worth of Stratford made Park Seats.

We manufacture good Ladders for all purposes. Write for our catalog and price list for Spring ordering.

Stratford Manufacturing Company, Limited

Makers of Ladders, Lawn Swings, Boyer's Gliding Settees, Folding Chairs and Tables, Chairs for Assembly Seating, Lawn, Camp and Verandah Furniture, Woodenware, Park Seats, etc.

STRATFORD · · · CANADA

HAVE YOU RECEIVED OUR CATALOG OF PICTURE FRAME MOULDINGS?

PICTURE FRAMES   PICTURES, MIRRORS
ROOM MOULDINGS   PLATE RAILS
and DECORATORS' MOULDINGS OF ALL KINDS

Wide Range of Designs, finest Workmanship employed

If you are interested in any of these lines and have not received our Catalog, kindly advise us and we will forward you one at once.

MATTHEWS BROS., LIMITED
788 Dundas Street   Toronto, Ontario

"Utility" in Office Furniture

The Elmira make of Office Desks, Filing Cabinets and Sections, and Chairs, covers a wide range of labor-saving conveniences.

An investment in these down-to-the-minute lines will make your Office Furniture Department a real live end of your business.

No. 195. Sanitary Desk. Fitted with sections for Card Index, Legal Blank and Document File to meet any requirement.

Write for Catalog of these Paying Lines

No. 203. Sanitary Desk. ¼-Quartered Oak. Single Pedestal. Size 30 x 42.

Elmira Interior Woodwork Co., Limited
ELMIRA   ONTARIO

STRATFORD

Western Buyers! Buy through the Stratford Shipping Combination and save on freight charges.

Eliminate the "Risk" in Bed Springs

THE Bed Spring will show up any "weakness" faster than any other one thing used in the bedroom. You, therefore, cannot afford to sell "risky" Bed Springs.

"Classic" Bed Springs

are guaranteed to give perfect satisfaction in every case, which insures YOU against "bad sales."

Write for Descriptions and Prices of our Various Lines of Woven Wire Springs

The Frame & Hay Fence Co., Limited
Stratford   Ontario

A Word about Brass Furniture Trimmings

Makers of furniture, who are particular about the distinctive quality and exclusive designing in the furniture, should also be particular about the brass trimmings we use. That is where we come in.

Stock designs of best quality and the famous Stratford finish for all uses.

Special lines to meet all requirements on short notice. Best service always.

The Stratford Brass Company, Limited

What about Brass Bedsteads for your Spring Trade?

Have you got a good stock of bedsteads on your floors,---bedsteads which you can sell at a price that will interest the majority of your customers,---"the working class" and still leave you a good margin of profit?

"Victoriaville" bedsteads will suit the purses of your patrons and leave you a good profit. The simple and pleasing designs which we manufacture make them sell like hot cakes.

The cut shows one of the many different designs which we manufacture.

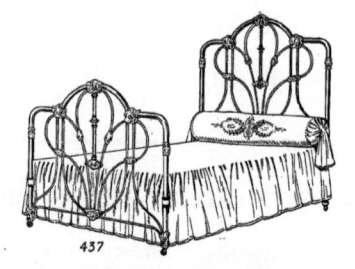

437

The Victoriaville Bedding Co., Ltd.
(Formerly The Standard Bedstead Co., Limited)

Victoriaville
Que.

The Big Five Mixed Carload Center

P.S.—Our beds are finished so that they may be cleaned with gasoline.

"Victoriaville" Upholstered Furniture

Means the height of solid comfort and first class workmanship. The style, workmanship and finish cannot be beaten at the price.

Look at the above cut, Mr. Dealer. Doesn't it look cosy? Don't you think it would pay you to have a stock of these and our other lines on your floors?

Our prices allow you to make a good profit. Watch for our travellers or, if you are in a hurry, drop us a line for our catalog.

The Big Five Mixed Carload Center

The Victoriaville Beddng Co.
(Formerly Canada Mattress Co., Ltd.) Limited

Victoriaville :: Quebec

BAETZ BROTHERS AND COMPANY
BERLIN :: ONTARIO.

No. 149
DINER

Made of Solid Quartered
White Oak
and in
Solid Cuban Mahogany

This Chair has a large comfortable Spring Seat, with Padded Back.

The Price is Right

Ask our Representative

Freedom from Complication of Mechanism

No fussing and pulling to get the *Kindel* "made up." It works easily and quickly because it is made for that purpose.
We have just added a number of additions to our lines with new mechanical features with which you should be fully acquainted.

The
**KINDEL
BED**
"Makes Itself"

The
**KINDEL
BED**
"Makes Itself Liked"

Drop us a line for information to-day

The Kindel Bed Co., Limited, Toronto, Ont.

The Gold Medal Line

With many years of popularity and undoubted good reputation for stability and comfort the "Hercules" Bed Spring is the one spring that will add to the reputation of the dealer and increase his bedding sales.

This advertisement will appear in other papers later.

Reliable goods well advertised are trade and profit producers for the wide-awake dealer.

This advertisement now running in the Daily Mail and Globe will surely bring trade to the dealer who handles "Hercules" Bed Springs and Gold Medal Felt Mattresses.

Gold Medal Furniture Mfg. Co.
LIMITED
Toronto   Montreal   Winnipeg   Uxbridge

Which Way Do You Sleep?

O "HERCULES" SPRING BED

The "HERCULES" Way
Is The Proper Way to Sleep

The weave of the "Hercules" Bed Spring is known as the "5 Times" weave. It is "5 Times" stronger than ordinary woven wire fabric, but it is also "5 Times" more resilient and restful.

A scientifically correct principle of weaving is responsible for the superiority of the "Hercules" Bed Spring—it means an equal distribution of weight. No bagging or sagging.

Ask your Dealer for the "Hercules"

HERCULES
REGISTERED
BED SPRINGS
VERMIN PROOF

Write us if you find difficulty in obtaining a "Hercules"

Buy a "Hercules" Bed Spring for your body's sake and for your brain's sake too, because proper rest means mental and physical fitness. Energise your days by taking your rest *right* at night.

The "Hercules" can be obtained from all responsible dealers, in wood or iron frame. Many purchasers prefer the "Hercules" with the basket edge which keeps the mattress from spreading and the clothes from slipping. The price is reasonable.

The Wrong Way — Don't tire yourself during the night by sleeping this way

ORDINARY   SPRING

"Hercules" Bed Springs are Manufactured by

The Gold Medal Furniture Mfg. Co. Limited
Toronto (Phone Junct. 840)—also at Montreal and Winnipeg.

Makers of The
Famous Gold Medal Felt Mattress
Which can also be obtained of any responsible Dealer.   No. 1

Will Not Sag   **Guaranteed**

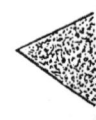

The "Natural" Spring---<u>Up and Down</u>, Not from "Ends and Sides"

That's the Difference Between

Leggett & Platt
Single Cone Bed Springs
and Woven Wire Springs

Leggett & Platt construction begins in the drafting room. Here stress and strain, design and effect are accurately estimated.

In the L. & P. Bed Springs the weight is absorbed **where** the weight **rests** by the individual coils.

It requires no special effort to sell this line when they are shown, and every sale creates the impression of good service you wish to have connected with your store.

Order Leggett & Platt Single cone Bed Springs with the "L" metal tag.

Write for our Literature

The Leggett & Platt Spring Bed Co.
Limited
WINDSOR   ONTARIO

Concentration in the Buying

Will Produce More Profit in the Selling

THE KNECHTEL LINE embraces everything in furniture for use in the kitchen, dining room, living room, library, parlor and chamber---all in great variety of design and finish, and in grades required by most people.

By Utilizing the Knechtel Line

you can derive a benefit in selection, savings in price and on freight charges, and a better service that is well worth your consideration.

Write us about the line made direct

From the Tree to the Finished Product

The Knechtel Furniture Co., Limited
HANOVER :: ONTARIO

It's Profits that Count

Wouldn't you jump at the chance to stock an exclusive line of genuine

Chinese Grass Furniture

if you **knew** you could make a quick turn over and double your money? Just try a sample order.

We stock a complete line of

**Chairs, Rockers, Tables
Work Baskets, Stools
Curates, Etc.**

in Sea Grass and Rattan. Natural or Fumed Brown finish.

Write for New Catalog and Price List

The Jennings Co.
ST. THOMAS, ONT.

WE SELL THE FURNITURE TRADE ONLY

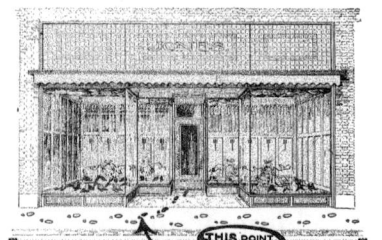

THIS POINT MEANS PROFIT OR LOSS TO YOU

Every time a person *passes by* your Store without entering, you *lose*—every time he *enters* you have the opportunity of making a sale—of making a profit.

There's a psychological point in the path of every passer-by that means a profit or loss to you—that's the point where he either *enters* or continues on his way.

It's your ideal to cause every passer-by to pause and enter—and can there be a more logical power to do that than a good Store Front.

One Merchant debated for three years whether or not a KAWNEER STORE FRONT would increase his business. Finally he put one in and now he says, "Our Front is worth $5,000 a year." And that in a small city of 12,000 people. Another Merchant says, "There is no question but what our new KAWNEER STORE FRONT sells at least $10,000 worth of merchandise a year over what we could have possibly sold with the old Front. We are more than willing to recommend your Fronts because of the great satisfaction ours has given." Another says, "Our business increased 40%—the KAWNEER FRONT **Kawneer STORE FRONTS** paid for itself in eight months." If you could only see the actual letters of recommendation that we have on file from Merchants you would not hesitate another day. There are standing today 30,000 KAWNEER FRONTS as proofs of all we claim of them. Our one claim that should interest you most is the ability of KAWNEER FRONTS to increase sales—ask any of the 30,000 Merchants if his KAWNEER FRONT has increased his business—take his word for it, not our claims.

There is such a multitude of different kinds of Store Fronts, both big and little, that you must take care lest you choose one that will not fit your business. To be of greater help to you in making this important decision, we've compiled "Boosting Business No. 2" which is without question the most complete, instructive and interesting Store Front book ever published. This book contains actual photographs of many of the best-paying large and small Store Fronts in the country—Fronts in all kinds of businesses—together with drawings and suggestions that will interest you.

Don't risk the amount of money it requires to install any kind of Front when a mere 2 cent stamp will bring to you this book of practical Store Front ideas. Your copy is in an envelope stamped with a 5 cent stamp and ready for your address. Don't delay—every day you conduct your business without a KAWNEER FRONT the people are *passing* instead of *entering*.

Kawneer
Manufacturing Company
Limited
Francis J. Plym, President
Dept. S. 1197 Bathurst Street
TORONTO, ONT.

It stays and pays

A Few Points About
STAMCO LIMITED

First we have, beyond all dispute, the most up-to-date factory in Canada—we repeat, in big letters—

The Most Up-to-date Factory in Canada

For the Manufacture of
BEDS and BEDDING

We have the most centrally situated factory in the West. We are on all three Transcontinental lines and we have our own siding. We want to point out to the Western Merchant that modern plant and shipping facilities, plus central situation, mean

Quality, Service and Quick Delivery

Our 1914 illustrated catalogue is just out. A post card will bring you a copy of it per return.

Stamco Limited
Saskatoon and Edmonton

Stamco of Regina Limited
Regina

Manufacturers of
Beds, Springs, Mattresses, Pillows, Tents, Awnings, and all kinds of Canvas Goods

Weisglass Beds

Represent the Maximum Result in

Construction, Durability and Design

DEALERS everywhere advise us of the success attending the sale of the Weisglass line.

Our "Acid Proof" Lacquer is something more than a talking point, its splendid wearing qualities have been demonstrated successfully everywhere. Have you given your Spring order yet? Our salesmen are now on the road.

Facsimile of Gold Medal Recently Awarded to Weisglass Beds

Weisglass also make Springs and Couches

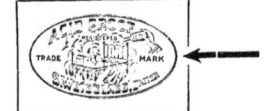

Look for these Trade Marks
Your Guarantee of Quality

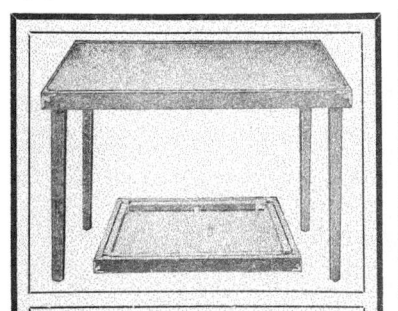

A Splendid Seller
"Acme" Folding Table

Weighs only 10 lbs., strongest folding table made. Special folding device; green felt or leatherette covered tops, nothing more practical for card playing, etc. Write for us to "show you" why you should stock these tables.

HOURD & COMPANY, LIMITED
Wholesale Furniture Manufacturers
LONDON — CANADA
Sole Canadian Licensees and Manufacturers

Every Up-to-date Housewife is a Live Prospect For These Covers

Every woman in your town knows that the ordinary silence cloth will NOT protect the polished top of her dining table against hot dishes.

J M Asbestos
TABLE COVERS AND MATS

afford better protection against heat than any other. They are also the most durable. They invariably give satisfactory service. The line of J M Asbestos Table Covers and Mats is so complete that you can cater to all pocketbooks. And you won't have to tie up a lot of money in stock, as our branch right near you will fill rush orders in any quantity, without delay. Our prices to the trade are so low that you can undersell competitors besides giving your customers better table than they can get in any other make of cover. Write nearest branch to-day for booklet and our special dealer proposition.

THE CANADIAN
H. W. JOHNS-MANVILLE CO., Limited
TORONTO   MONTREAL   WINNIPEG   VANCOUVER

Synopsis of Contents
PART I

Chapter I.—Using the Windows—The General Principles of Display. Some specific instances. Some combination window display offers.
Chapter II.—One Idea Window Displays—Advising against trying to show all the goods at once.
Chapter III.—Window Display Profits—How to make windows actually produce direct sales.
Chapter IV.—Showing the Goods—No matter what the class of merchandise, sales are increased if it is attractively displayed.
Chapter V.—Window Displays that Cost Nothing—Some special windows described and illustrated.
Chapter VI.—The Use of Window Fixtures—Displays can be made much more attractive with modern fixtures.
Chapter VII.—Let the Money in Through Your Windows—Making a success of a paint department through attractive displays.
Chapter VIII.—Keeping Frost from Windows—Suggestions on this important subject from several sources.
Chapter IX.—A Few Suggestions for Easy Displays—These can be arranged with very little expense.
Chapter X.—Window Card Pointers—Some good suggestions on the making of show cards and the correct colors to use.
Chapter XI.—Show Window Photographs—How to take good pictures, avoid reflection and get proper contrast.

PART II

Practical Displays—One hundred windows, each illustrated and described so that any clerk can arrange them with little or no expense. (145 pages.)

224 pages. 4 1-4 x 7 inches. 104 full page plates. Price $1.00 postpaid.

One Hundred Easy Window Trims

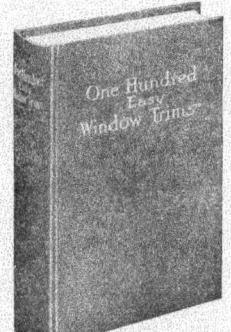

THIS handy little volume of 224 pages was written especially for the merchant who has small windows or wishes to divide large ones into sections. The displays cover all classes of goods, but there are enough suggestions to give you a change each week for almost a year.

They are all simple, inexpensive and easily arranged displays, and all the material required may be taken from stock or purchased for a few cents.

Commercial Press, Ltd.
32 Colborne St., Toronto, Ont.

Dining Room Furniture
Extraordinary

BUILT to use, cheer and endure. We manufacture our product so reliably that the dealer may absolutely depend upon its worthiness. It is correct in style, made from selected wood and material, and skilfully constructed, yet not expensive. It is Dining Room Furniture of character at a price that you may sell your customers with a certainty of perpetuating their good will.

Be sure that your Spring Display includes the Peppler Line.

Peppler Brothers, Limited
Hanover   Ontario

Soon to be the Best Seller in Canada

It must be plain to any dealer that a mattress with the unique and exclusive features of the

DIXIE NoTUFT Compartment Mattress

must appeal to the better class of trade who want a mattress that will always remain like new.

The Dixie has many successful selling points that cannot apply to any other mattress made.

Features which make it unmistakeably superior, and therefore preferable from every point of view.

Exclusive Local Selling Rights

will be granted dealers who are in a position to do justice to the splendid sales opportunities of the Dixie in their locality.

You know the value of having a mattress which can be made the biggest seller---and of being the only dealer in your neighborhood who sells it. Then write now for the particulars of our selling plan.

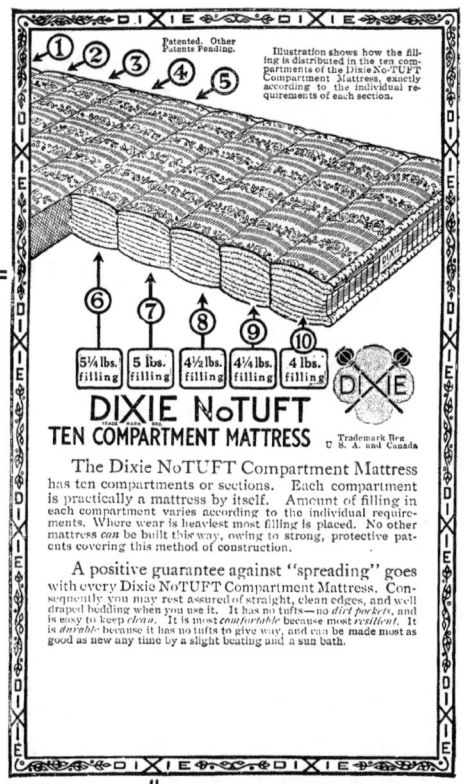

Patented. Other Patents Pending.

Illustration shows how the filling is distributed in the ten compartments of the Dixie NoTUFT Compartment Mattress, exactly according to the individual requirements of each section.

5¼ lbs. filling | 5 lbs. filling | 4½ lbs. filling | 4¼ lbs. filling | 4 lbs. filling

DIXIE NoTUFT TEN COMPARTMENT MATTRESS
Trademark Reg. U.S.A. and Canada

The Dixie NoTUFT Compartment Mattress has ten compartments or sections. Each compartment is practically a mattress by itself. Amount of filling in each compartment varies according to the individual requirements. Where wear is heaviest most filling is placed. No other mattress *can* be built this way, owing to strong, protective patents covering this method of construction.

A positive guarantee against "spreading" goes with every Dixie NoTUFT Compartment Mattress. Consequently you may rest assured of straight, clean edges, and well draped bedding when you use it. It has no tufts—no *dirt pockets*, and is easy to keep *clean*. It is most *comfortable* because most *resilient*. It is *durable* because it has no tufts to give way, and can be made most as good as new any time by a slight beating and a sun bath.

A "Dixie" News Paper Ad.

Geo. Gale & Sons, Limited

Waterville, - Que.

Montreal   Toronto,   Winnipeg

The Imperial Make Will Please Your Exacting Customers

GET on more intimate terms with the unusual quality in our Upholstered Furniture. We believe you'll find that it will fill an important phase of your business to the best advantage. Our traveler will tell you why. In the meantime write us for photos of our new lines.

Imperial Furniture Company
585-591 Queen St. West, Toronto

One of Our Attractive New Styles

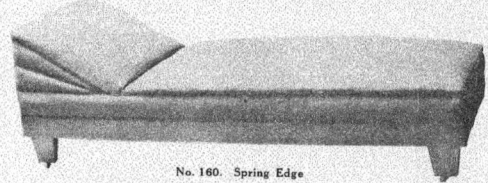

QUARTERED oak frame, fumed or in any other finish. Full spring seat and head containing 37 springs. Double stuffed. Full range of covers in tapestry, leather or imitation leather.

Blue prints of other new designs on request.

No. 160. Spring Edge

J. P. Albrough & Co. - Ingersoll, Canada
Makers of Quality Couches and Chairs

A New Line of Red Cedar Chests

Genuine Tennessee Red Cedar Chests, absolutely moth proo . Made in three sizes. Mahogany finish; best copper trimmings; serviceable brass lock.

Ask for cuts and prices

D. L. SHAFER & CO.
St. Thomas - - Ontario

Do you know of any Furniture Dealer or Funeral Director, any where in Canada, who is not a subscriber to the Canadian Furniture World and The Undertaker? If so, you will be doing him a favor by sending us his name and address so that we can send him a sample copy and subscription order blank.

KELLARIC MATTRESSES

"Makes Sleeptime Sleepfull"

Reasons

Why You should *show* the KELLARIC and
Why your customers will *buy* the KELLARIC

Because: It is unconditionally guaranteed by us through you.

Because: Our secret process of cross binding positively eliminates all possibility of spreading—a fault so common in mattresses.

Because: The laced opening at the end of each KELLARIC mattress enables them to inspect the material of which it is built.

Because: The KELLARIC mattress is altogether the product of Canadian skill.

The McKellar Bedding Co., Ltd.
Fort William   Ontario

The Berlin Bedding Company, Limited, 31-33 Front St. E. Toronto, Ont.

"Safety First"—Last and All the Time

Ideal Mesh Side Crib — No. 56

A Pronounced Success

Specifications

7/8 in. Posts. Head 46 in. high. Foot 46 in. high. Sides 21 in. high. Shipping weight, 80 lbs. Sides 1 in. square interwoven wire mesh. Sliding sides. Safety catch. Ball-bearing casters. All white enamel.

A woman is careful when purchasing a crib, because unless the baby is absolutely safe and comfortable in it, it means trouble for both parents.
This new Ideal Mesh Side Crib satisfies every conceivable requirement as to safety and convenience.
It marks a big advance in crib designing, and we anticipate many old cribs being replaced by it.
Put one on exhibition in your window. Its very novelty will attract passers-by.

THE IDEAL BEDDING CO. LIMITED
2-24 JEFFERSON AVENUE - - TORONTO

Canadian Furniture World and the Undertaker

PUBLISHED THE 1ST OF EACH MONTH BY

THE COMMERCIAL PRESS, LIMITED
32 COLBORNE STREET, TORONTO
Phone Main 4978

D. O. McKinnon		President
W. L. Edmonds		Vice-President
Weston Wrigley		Vice-President and Manager of Trade Papers
J. C. Armer		Vice-President and Manager of Technical Papers
James O'Hagan		Editor
John A. Fullerton		Associate Editor
Wm. J. Bryans	"	"

Staff Representatives
Geo. H. Honsberger, Advertising Manager — Toronto
F. C. D. Wilkes, Eastern Manager, 704 Unity Bldg. — Montreal
R. C. Howson, Western Representative — Winnipeg
E. J. MacIntyre, Room 659, 122 South Michigan Avenue — Chicago

C. G. Brandt, *Circulation Manager*, Toronto

Subscriptions
Canada, $1.00 a year. Other Countries, $2.00 a year

PUBLISHERS' STATEMENT—2000 copies of this issue of the Canadian Furniture World are printed for circulation. Itemized statement, showing distribution according to provinces, will be furnished on request.

Vol. 4   APRIL, 1914   No. 4

News of the Retail Store.

No retailer, no matter how small his business, can afford to ignore advertising.

To be located even where no newspaper is published is no excuse for not using printers' ink. Advertising is fortunately neither confined to method nor place.

"All advertising is good, but some is better" is an old saying. All that is demanded of any retailer is that he uses the best medium that is at his command. That best available medium may be a circular, a letter, or a dodger.

Whatever you do, use the local newspaper. If it is worthy of the name of a newspaper it is the best medium you can use. Should you be without a local newspaper you can scarcely be inaccessible to a printing office of some kind.

The news of your store told in plain, terse terms will always interest consumers, whether it be told through the columns of a newspaper or within the folds of a circular or letter. Good advertising is good store news.

See that at least in some way the consumers in your locality are supplied with the news of your store.

The small merchant will exist as long as he keeps going.

Service as a Factor in Business.

Chasing a price-cutter, like chasing a will-o'-the-wisp, is a dangerous as well as a foolish practice. It will in all probability eventually lead one into the quagmire.

The only safe competitor to follow is he who makes service the foundation of his business.

Other than service there is no firm foundation on which to build a successful business superstructure.

Price-cutting may momentarily bring a store into the limelight, but it will not keep it there.

Anybody can cut prices. No ability is demanded. It is merely an exhibition of the lowest type of business mentality and can only lead to ultimate failure.

To build up a business on the basis of service rendered is, on the other hand, an exhibition of brains.

Service is not the studying of ways and means of getting a big margin of profit on everything sold. It is the studying of ways and means of giving customers value for the merchandise they purchase. To do this successfully demands brains—brains that are able to appreciate the fitness of things.

Profit a merchant must of course have; but it is not by the demanding of big profits that he builds up a large and prosperous business. It is by moderate profits and a large turnover that he accomplishes this.

A dealer died in Toronto a short time ago who all his life had made the getting of big profits his ideal. Practically everything he sold was a little above in price that asked by any other dealer in his neighborhood. But he never built up a large business. His customers were chiefly those who patronized his store in emergencies and a few old friends who stood by him. And when he died his store had about the same half-dead and half-alive appearance it had the day it was opened twenty-five years ago.

The high road to success in business is neither by cutting prices nor by demanding big profits. It is by service, which inspires confidence and holds trade.

To attempt to build up a business by price-cutting methods is like attempting to strengthen a building by removing the foundation stones.

The Retailer's Surplus Capital.

Many retailers whose business has developed to the point where a surplus of capital has accumulated, have been perplexed as to what they should do with this surplus.

To allow it to lie in the bank earning merely 3 per cent. interest is neither businesslike nor profitable. He is a poor business man indeed who could not put it to better use than that.

As to what a retailer who finds himself with a substantial cash surplus should do is a matter which each must decide for himself, as no hard and fast rule can be made which shall apply to all alike. There are, however, certain underlying principles which do apply to practically all cases.

In the first place everyone will probably concede that it is unwise to cripple one's business by taking from it and employing elsewhere capital that really belongs to it. A good many retailers who have been dipping deeper into real estate speculations than the condition of their capital warranted have been learning this to their sorrow of late.

On the other hand, it is also unwise to keep capital inadequately employed. Not only is it not earning as much as it should earn, but when there is a plentiful supply of cash on hand there is not always the same disposition to look closely after the collection of accounts.

A large wholesale dealer in Toronto who, when he died a few years ago, had amassed a large fortune, made it a rule, as he termed it, to "starve his business." That is, he kept as much of his capital as possible safely invested in good marketable securities. The result was that his capital inside his business was kept working hard.

Another successful dealer made it a practice of investing his money in central revenue-producing real estate upon which at any time should there have been a necessity for his doing so, he could raise money on a mortgage. He, too, died a wealthy and honored citizen.

In the employment of surplus capital outside the business it often makes all the difference in the world as to whether it is used as an investment or for speculating purposes. It is unwise to speculate when you cannot afford to take a chance. And when investing it is well to consider the possibilities of turning the investment into cash in case of emergency.

There are some who hold that the retailer should not invest in anything outside his own business. In many instances this would, no doubt, be sound advice. But to make it a hard and fast rule would not be wise. If the business is one which possesses great potentialities by all means develop it. But if its potentialities are not good: if it has about reached the limit of its possibilities, the wisest thing might be to keep the surplus capital working on another job.

There is one outstanding fact about capital these days--the demand exceeds the supply. And the chief concern for those who possess a surplus is how and where it is best to employ it.

It is a profitable thing for merchants to study to please their customers and for clerks to study those things that advance the interest of their employers.

An Opportunity in Card Writing. Every dealer should turn to good account the lessons in card writing which are appearing in each issue of this paper. These lessons are prepared by a practical man. They are simple and easily mastered. Some undoubtedly possess greater aptitude than others for card writing. But even those with the least aptitude need not despair.

In these series of simple articles we have provided the way. Any one who possesses the necessary will power can profit by them.

No clerk should allow the opportunity for acquiring efficiency in card writing to slip by. Every lesson should be carefully studied, for with practice comes perfection.

And a good card writer is worth money.

Problems beset merchants in large towns as well as those in small towns, and the only panacea is courage and perseverance.

Why He is Losing Business. Location is no doubt a contributing factor in the success of a retail business. But some men do not seem to be able to succeed however good the location may be. In such instances it is obviously the fault of the merchant and not that of the locality in which the store is situated.

We have in mind a retailer who some months ago bought out a business in one of the suburbs of a certain large city. But in spite of the fact that his predecessor had done well, he is obviously losing ground. The reason is not far to seek: He is not giving adequate service.

His particular weakness seems to be a lack of system in keeping informed in regard to his stock. He is frequently out of this or that staple article. As a large share of his business is family trade a good deal of inconvenience is being caused customers.

When on telephoning orders they are repeatedly told that he is out of this and that line it does not take a customer long to switch his patronage to a dealer who can give better service.

Of course, it is every merchant's fate to be caught short in some lines now and then. Unfortunately, however, perfect his own system may be, he cannot control the other contributing agents, such as the manufacturer, the wholesaler and the transportation company. But even then it is better to secure from a fellow-dealer the article wanted rather than to allow an order to go incomplete or unfilled.

The retailer to whom we have reference is surrounded by fellow-retailers, but he never appears to make any attempt to get from them that which he has not in stock, no matter how much a customer may need it. He is gradually, in consequence, surrendering his business to his surrounding competitors.

Price cutting practices were never known to create prestige in business.

The Knack of Getting Together. The freight rate war among the Atlantic steamship companies is said to have petered out. War of this kind usually does peter out before hostilities have been going on for long.

Steamship men seem to possess the happy knack of being able to call off a war before much damage has been done.

It is a pity business men, and particularly retailers, do not possess the same happy knack. They, year after year, go on waging bitter warfare cutting prices and striving by might and main to drive each other out of business.

True, a better day seems to be dawning. Business men are realizing that even if they can only get acquainted and rub shoulders asperities disappear, and the inclination to cut prices modifies.

Though the millenium in business may still be a long distance away, it is some satisfaction to know that the tendency is more in that direction than away from it.

Show windows were designed for the purpose of exhibiting the retailers' enterprise, not the lack of it.

Getting After Dishonest Advertisers. At a meeting of retailers in Philadelphia the other day a resolution was adopted endorsing the movement against fake advertising.

The attitude of mind toward advertising has undergone a marked change within the last decade or two.

There was a time within the memory of many people when the average advertisement was looked upon as a gross exaggeration, if not a deliberate lie. And there was some reason for this view. To at least exaggerate was deemed by not a few advertisers as an exhibition of skill. It would make people take notice.

To-day all this is changed. Aside altogether from its moral aspect the average business man knows that even to exaggerate is the height of foolishness. He knows that unless he tells the truth, the whole truth and nothing but the truth, his advertising will in time become abortive. Consequently he is quite aware that to even once attempt to fool the people would be risky.

Business men who to-day know experimentally the value of advertising, are naturally jealous for the maintenance of its good name. To see them banding together in order to clip the wings of the few advertisers who are still disposed to transgress the laws of good advertising is therefore what might be expected.

Selling Ideas of Retail Furniture Dealers

MERCHANDISING is ever rising upward to a higher plane—in the furniture as well as other lines of business. The foremost methods of yesteryear are being replaced by new and improved ones in the strenuous bid for business. The dealer who wants to hold his own in the race must keep pace with the advancing methods. Not only must he be able to adapt himself to changing conditions as they arise, but it is well that he be able to himself originate and devise new methods of merchandising.

The man who forges to the front in business to-day is the one with an active brain, who is constantly hitting on new plans of bringing his store and goods more prominently before customers to the benefit of sales and profits. Anything new and original appeals strongly to people, and for this reason is especially valuable to the dealer. One idea in itself is not going to bring success, any more than the insertion of one advertisement in a paper is going to work wonders. One swallow does not make a summer, and no more will one good plan or idea, although it may be a dandy, bring more than temporary benefit to the store. As the runner in the long distance race must keep plugging away, so must the man in the race for business.

Selling ideas include the small as well as the big ones. How often we see some simple little practical idea that is costing little, bringing in big results. A sales creating scheme does not always have to be extensively staged at big expense. It would seem that some dealers believe this to be true, and that original and business-getting selling schemes are for the big stores only, that have a good deal of money to expend in this direction. Even the big interest-compelling features have to be backed up by smaller ones. The balloon ascension may be the central feature of the village fall fair, but it is far from being the whole fair. The numerous smaller events are a necessity to its success.

And so it is in business. There are certain underlying principles for the successful conduct of all stores. For instance, goods should be kept bright, attention should be given to interior and window display, a certain amount of advertising should be done, and good service should be given. While those are the main features, there must be called into use in addition, many other selling ideas, simple though they may be, and frequently it is upon these little plans and methods that the degree of success depends.

The big stores have by no means a monopoly on new and practical innovations that help to sell goods. Many small stores in all parts of the country are constantly devising excellent plans for getting more business.

Trend of Furniture for the Spring Season

AT the present time when high-class furniture is moving slowly, and the call is largely for the cheap lines, it is difficult to obtain a decided impression of the trend of furniture styles for the coming season. The views of buyers, who care more about price than workmanship, design and materials, are of little value in this respect. Purchasers of this class are undoubtedly entitled to consideration, and they are getting more and better value for their money than ever before. At the same time, the future of the furniture industry as a whole must rest with the discriminating consumer, an increasing class every year. It is becoming more and more apparent that the medium-class buyers are no longer willing to buy anything that is highly finished and striking in appearance without regard to its harmony with other furnishings, but are beginning to know exactly what they want and to hunt around until they get it.

Arts and Crafts Big Sellers.

Among the biggest sellers to-day in medium-class goods is the general line comprehended under the term "arts and craft." There are numerous varieties of this style, ranging from the original mission style, which was found too severe and massive for the average city home, down to the very cheapest furniture, barely recognizable as such. There is, however a gratifying increase in the number of purchasers who have come to understand that high-class furniture of this type is worth a good price, the original impression having apparently been that it should be very cheap because of its straight lines and lack of carving or other ornamentation. For the dining-room, library and living-room, art-craft furniture is a leader up to a price where fine mahogany comes into active competition.

There is less seen of the very dark oak finishes which were popular a year or two since and more of the warm, red browns and fumed oak finishes. The waxed finish, too, is popular with the housekeeper, because it is so easily kept in good condition. Golden oak is still the leading staple in the cheap lines. In some quarters there is a small, but increasing demand for oak finished in the light gray stains, which are the rage in Europe. Exhibition pieces have been seen under various fancy names such as "Hungarian ash," and some dealers think favorably of these light stains for the future.

Summer rattan easy chair—Imperial Rattan Co., Stratford

They are certainly more cheerful and dainty than the very dark finishes, but their use will probably be confined to those who can afford to decorate their rooms in harmony.

White Furniture.

This tendency toward the lighter coloring is perhaps attributable to the continued demand for light-colored enamel furniture, the gray enamels apparently being popular in the better grades. In high-class goods, the manufacturers of enamel furniture have gone to extreme lengths in the matter of ornamentation and elaborate design. Nearly all the better-class shops now show white or gray enamel dining-room sets, mostly in the popular Adam style. Furniture of this period lends itself readily to profuse ornamentation, which can be very easily overdone. The carved portion of the ornament is usually along classical lines, and now in low relief, accentuating the delicate design of the piece as a whole. Floral or other designs painted upon the enamel are the rock upon which many designers are wrecked, some manufacturers apparently believing that any ornament which is "hand painted" is indubitably artistic and appropriate, be it executed ever so indifferently, whereas the original Adam furniture was decorated by some of the most eminent artists of the day.

Period Furniture.

In the better class "period furniture" for the dining-room, the Adam style is the leader at present when mahogany is desired and the late Jacobean or William and Mary in oak. The two latter styles are often more

Summer verandah rocker—Imperial Rattan Co., Stratford

or less combined; in fact, the transition is so gradual that it is difficult to make a distinction in many cases. The William and Mary style merely shows a little more of the Dutch influence which came to be felt in England upon the accession of William of Orange to the English throne. The early Jacobean style, characterized by considerable carved ornament, is not popular, but the quaint panelings, curved underframing and "pear drop" drawer pulls have caught the fancy of the public. Tables are furnished with legs rather than pedestal bases, and often have underframing, although the latter is usually confined to serving tables and dressers. Some of the chairs have this feature also. Some of the more recently exhibited sets in this class are elaborately inlaid in black and white stringings, which place them in the William and Mary period. A dull oak finish is the usual thing in furniture of this class, often being given an antique appearance by rubbing off the stain at the points of natural wear. This popular style for dining-room furniture does not seem to have taken hold in any other line.

On the other hand, the Adam style is equally popular for bedroom furnishing—in fact, some consider the mahogany Adam dining-room furniture as decidedly funereal in effect, especially when the typical Adam tableware urns are included. For dainty and rich bedroom furniture, however, it is unsurpassed, even by the Marie Antoinette style, which impresses many people as ornate and artificial. In bedroom furniture the present Adam showings are mostly in enamel with a few in mahogany. The use of caned panels is a leading feature. An exhibition set has twin beds, in severely classical outline, with little or no carved ornamentation, but artistically outlined with painted festoons and swags of floral patterns. In the centre of each large panel there is an inset medallion of Wedgewood china, showing a classical Cupid on the typical dull background. This feature is repeated on all the principal pieces of the set. The enamel is a soft old ivory shade.

Awnings for Spring Selling.

The extent to which porch furnishings and decorations have developed is astonishing. Awnings have become distinctly decorative as furniture of a spring and summer character. We heard of a firm that adopted the scheme of making up standard awning sizes during the slack months, by making a number of frames all ready equipped for the spring rush. The awning season is generally a crowded and busy season, even under the most favorable conditions, and any plan which will make use of the slack time of the winter to help out the busy rush of spring is not only a safe, but a profitable investment.

Park Seats and Lawn Swings.

Spring is the time for getting after the possible business that is to be had in park and lawn furniture. This is a line of furniture that is too often left by the dealer to take care of itself, but which if gone after persistently and in the right way, could be made profitable. It will not be many weeks before the municipal officials of the various towns and cities will have made plans as to what will be done during the coming summer in the way of park improvements. There is a demand of some kind for these goods for public purposes every

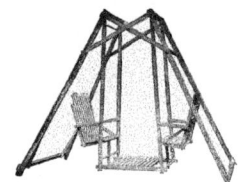

Summer lawn swing—Stratford Mfg. Co.

year. Why not get after those officials who have the necessary purchases in hand at once? Show them what you can do in this line. If you have no goods of this character in stock, secure the catalogues of the manufacturers of these lines, show them a line that you can give them. Then, when the time comes for the goods to be brought you will stand a good chance of securing the order. The present time is not one day too early to get after this trade. Let them know that you can supply them, that they need not send out of town, that you can give them just as good a price as they can secure anywhere. They will naturally look to you at least before they buy. Closely associated with these goods is the various lines of wooden swings, porch furniture, etc., which will be in demand soon. The de-

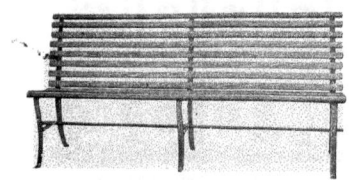

Park or garden seat—Stratford Mfg. Co.

New summer dressing chair - Baetz Bros., Berlin

mand in these goods is steady during the summer season, and the line is one that most furniture dealers could handle very profitably. Be ready with a representative selection when the buying commences.

In the country towns the man that would serve all his trade must carry cheap as well as good furniture, but in the larger towns and cities it is often better to specialize than to spread eagle and try to cover the whole range. The buyers of good furniture in such places like to feel that there is some exclusiveness about the place they trade.

Collins' Course in Show Card Writing

Fifth of a series of articles specially prepared for this journal.

AS mentioned at the close of last month's article, the letters of plate 17, the half-block style, are particularly adapted for "cutting in." "Cutting in" is a trade term known to card writers and sign writers, in which the work of lettering is exactly reversed from the ordinary way of painting letters. The background is painted, leaving the letters the color of the card. For certain classes of work, such as large letters, it is much easier to letter by this process. Fig 6 will give a good idea of how the work is executed and how it will look when completed. First, rule straight lines at the top and bottom of the letters. This finishes the letters on the top and bottom sides. Then the outside vertical lines of the letters may be ruled in. Next the inside lines and the horizontal and other strokes of such letters as F, E, K, etc. The beveled corners may be done next. This completes the ruling in or "cutting in" of the letters. It will at once be seen why this particular style of letter is so well adapted to "cutting in." There are no curved lines, which permits of all the lines being ruled. It will be necessary in doing work this way to take great care that the letters are made wide enough in the stems. The letters, when the outlining is done, will appear larger than when the entire background is filled in. The word "designs" in one of the sample cards is made by this "cutting in" method, but is a fancy type.

Gold and Aluminum Paints

Every card writer will find use for gold and aluminum paints or colors. These can be mixed as easily as other colors and are to be preferred to any you can buy. Buy a package of good bronze powder, also a package of aluminum. Do not use silver, as it will tarnish easily. Mix these separately with a little spirits. When well "cut," add mucilage of sufficient quantity to make it stick. Then after mixing, add enough water to make it work fluently. This is practically the same way as you mix the other colors. In mixing your own colors, use your own judgment in adding water. The colors should be sufficiently thin to flow easily, but should not show streaky. The beginner may experience some difficulty in getting the color to the right consistency to work well. He may also experience some difficulty in getting his brushes to work satisfactorily. Both of these obstacles will be overcome by practice and experience.

Some Suggestions on Their Use

It may be well, however, to offer a few suggestions. If the color is too thick it will work sticky and not make a straight or clean edge. If it is too thin it will be thin and streaky. So experiment until you have it the right consistency to flow easily and cover evenly. After dipping the brush into the color, spread it out well, as shown in Fig. 2 in first lesson. This will get the brush to the proper "spread." Then work it back and forth on a piece of cardboard until it will stay out flat. Apply now to your lettering. Use sufficient pressure to keep the brush to the width of the stem of the letter you are working on. Do not work too slowly. A slow stroke is more liable to be uneven and unsteady. You will get better results with a stroke drawn quickly. Keep plenty of color in your brush, but not enough to make it hold together and not spread properly. Do not be afraid of spreading your brush too much. Beginners are liable to use their brushes too much like a pen or pencil. They will make fine or narrow strokes. Get away from this method as soon as possible. There are occasions when it is well to make one side of a stem at a time, but even then it is well to make it with the brush well spread. See Fig. 3 in previous issue.

Give Artistic Effect

To return to the gold and aluminum paints—these

Fig 6.—Showing method of "cutting in".

**ABCDEFGHIJ
KLMNOPQRS
TUVWXYZ 12!**

Plate 19—Upper case, Spurred Egyptian.

are excellent for shading, and for borders and ornamentations, as they give a card a very attractive and artistic effect. It will be seen that these colors and all bronzes will show to best advantage on dark cards.

We suggest for those who are interested in this course of card writing, that each one should procure a scrap book and cut out the printed pages on which the lessons appear, and preserve them in the scrap book for future reference. The sample cards and alphabets will be found particularly helpful to refer to from time to time.

The Alphabets

Plates 19 and 20 are the upper and lower case of the Egyptian style of letters, similar to those shown in plate 7 in the first lesson. The difference is that the letters in plates 19 and 20 are "spurred." That means that the ends of the various stems are flared or made a little wider than the stem proper. This gives a letter a more finished look and greatly improves its appearance. The "spurring" is not hard to do, as one side can be done with the brush at the top when beginning the stroke and the bottom when finishing the stroke. The other two must be done separately. Plates 21 and 22 are suitable styles for small brush or pen work. They should be used on cards where much reading matter appears and the small letters should not be over half an inch high on a full size 22 in. x 28 in. card.

Some Sample Cards

The month of April brings us nearer to real spring, that period when all people and all nature seem jubilant. The revivifying atmosphere and other conditions seem to put new life into one. And this new-life feeling seems an inspiration to buying. Therefore every merchant should make some extra display or decoration that will attract trade.

It is just possible that the grocer, the hardware merchant, the furniture dealer and some other trades people do not lay enough importance on this feature of decorations. They excuse themselves with lack of time, or their lines are not suitable for special displays and decoration. To all this we say, take the time, and all these merchants mentioned have lines that can be given up to special display. The grocer could devote a certain space to display attractively certain lines of canned, bottled and other packed goods. These could have suitable and appropriate decorations around them. The same can be said of the hardware merchant. A number of fine mechanical tools will make an attractive display. And these will even stand a few strings of artificial flowers tastily woven through the display. The hardware merchant, the grocer, the furniture dealer, the druggist should not allow the milliner and dry goods merchant to monopolize all the good things in the way of decorative beauty. Break the conventionality and be different. The furniture dealer can arrange a dining suite, a bedroom suite, or the furniture for some other room and display it with an artistic arrangement of flowers that would be perfectly in keeping with the season, and at the same time get away from the old conservative methods.

Some Holiday Designs

April, in addition to ushering in spring weather, has

CANADIAN FURNITURE WORLD AND THE UNDERTAKER. April, 1914

ABCDEFGHI
JKLMNOPQRS
TUVWXYZ &?

Plate 21.—Upper case, pen or small brush style.

a special holiday—Easter—that affords a good advertising opportunity. It also opens a field for cards by way of its emblematic chicks, eggs, lilies, rabbits, etc. Purple, lilac, violet and white are its colors, which should be adhered to in window displays and other decorative features. Crepe tissue decorating paper may be purchased at trifling cost that has appropriate Easter designs in pretty colors.

The sample rabbit card is made by cutting out the design in paper and "spattering" the background on it. The pattern is then lifted and the detail put in by hand. The lettering is also done afterward. The background may be done in dark purple and the letters in a harmonizing shade to match. The rabbit should be white.

The little chick card is done the same way as the bunny card. The color of the chick should be in yellow with the background color in grey. The egg, of course, should be white. The lettering in blue or purple and shaded with a subdued blue.

The other card may be in black or brown all through, but if used for Easter designs or displays, purple or blue should be used. The "cut in" effect on the word "design" is somewhat striking. Leaving a portion of the letters open to be filled in with the imagination is also unique.

Next month we will give sample cards with less ornamentation, simpler in design and showing use of some of the alphabets already shown.

Catchy card—construction described in article.

CREDIT PHASE OF FURNITURE TRADE.

A well known furniture man of the South, speaking on the credit phase of the furniture trade, has this to say: "Lately there has been considerable discussion, pro and con, concerning the installment furniture business; and, after studying the subject carefully, I find that about three-fourths of the people have their entire holdings in furniture, and that nine-tenths buy on the installment plan. This indicates that the installment plan is not an evil, but a boon to the masses of the people. Almost anyone can pay cash for a $10 bill of groceries; but when it comes to a home and its furnishings the installment plan has to be resorted to; and it is a fact that many people would never accumulate anything or get a start if it were not for this method of investing."

How does your clerk know you appreciate the work he is doing for you? He is no mind reader.

abcdefghijklmn
opqrstuvwwxyz

Plate 22.—Lower case, pen or small brush style.

Selling Methods in the Furniture Store

Some Experiences and Suggestions

A CLEVER PUBLICITY IDEA.

The New Orleans dealer who recently started into business, has an enterprising plan for attracting the attention of housewives to the store.

This includes what has been termed "a boosters' plan," which consists in offering handsome souvenirs and premiums to women who send their friends to make purchases of furniture at this store.

The management will, upon request, present to every woman who visits the store, "a booster book." None are to be sent by mail, nor by hand. Each little book contains ten "booster certificates," about the size of a bank check.

The certificate, which has a blank for the name of the friend, as well as for the signature of the woman who holds the book, is to be filled out and given to any person the holder knows wishes to make purchases of furniture. Upon presentation at the store it serves as an introduction of the holder to the management, and counts as cash in the purchase of goods.

Each time a booster certificate is presented, the distributor will receive a present. In addition to this, handsome souvenirs, it was announced, are to be given women who, within a specified time, used one book of ten certificates.

The privileges of the plan will expire March 31, 1914. No certificates are to be rewarded or accepted after that date. All certificates, in order to be rewarded or honored, must be presented at the time the purchase is made.

Here is the suggestion the management will make to women desiring to enroll as "boosters": "Mrs. Jones, your neighbor mentions to you that she will need a gas stove soon. Tell her that we carry the largest assortment of gas stoves in the city, and that we give a signed guarantee with every stove. Giving her a 'boosters' certificate' will get her $1 in discount and you will receive free, delivered at your home, a useful present."

YELLOW STREAK SALE

When you speak of the yellow in a person you mean some one of the qualities in his makeup that keeps him from being what he ought to be.

A Minnesota merchant, though, made a very novel use of the term "Yellow Streak" by hanging a sale on it. He printed his Store Paper on yellow paper and used the term Yellow Streak Sale many times.

In an explanatory article he says:

There will be no yellow streak in the quality of the goods offered at this sale.

The yellow streak will be found in the price only. Prices will be decidedly yellow.

In other words, they will be weak.

So weak, in fact, that they cannot hurt the slimmest wallet.

Then at intervals through the paper he had expressions like this:

Nothing yellow but the prices. Only the prices are yellow.

This is a yellow streak sale and the goods will go like a yellow streak.

The idea pulled, and there was a great deal doing in that store while the sale was in progress.

He sent out his Store Paper in white envelopes which had yellow streaks printed upon them.

The people of that vicinity certainly knew there was something yellow going on at that store and that nothing but the prices were yellow.

A CANDLE BURNING CONTEST

A western dealer is attracting a good deal of attention to his store by candle burning contests. Each week a candle of varying size is put in the show window. With every 50 cent purchase, a guess is given as to how long the candle will burn. Each coupon has a perforated stub on which is printed instruction with a space for hours, minutes and seconds which the holder thinks the candle will burn. Coupons given out one week are good for guesses on the candle that is to burn the following week. This brings the customer back a second time. A cash prize or merchandise is given each week to the person guessing nearest the exact burning time of the candle.

The contest is closed promptly each Saturday afternoon, when the official time is posted in the show window. That the weekly event is popular is evidenced by the crowd which blocks the sidewalk before the announcing of the correct time.

PAY ENVELOPE WITH A FACE VALUE.

A dealer in a manufacturing town supplies all the mills with their pay envelopes free of charge for the privilege of printing on them this announcement: "If this envelope is presented at our store within twenty-four hours of the date stamped thereon, it will be good for a five-per-cent. discount on any purchase.

As a result of this publicity, the store is crowded the evening of pay day.

AN ADVERTISING SCRAP BOOK

A Montreal dealer has received good results from what he calls an "advertising scrap book." It is just an ordinary book on the front of which is inscribed, "We handle all the high grade goods."

PRICE TICKETS ON DISPLAYED GOODS.

Modern methods of business call for prices, good, plain, readable prices, prices that are so evident that to the passing public there can arise no possible question on this subject, says The Keystone.

There are still merchants who are unable to comprehend this, and to all questions regarding the subject, they have the ever-ready reply, "It tells our competitors what we sell at." Of course it does, but it also tells customers the same thing. What do you care about your competitor; ten to one he is too busy to bother about your prices, and if he isn't you can't afford to be afraid of him. If you are not able to do as well as he can, there must be something wrong about your purchasing department. Anyhow, if you competitor was really interested in your prices, it would be the easiest matter in the world to obtain them.

But these arguments have been talked and argued until every twist and turn of speech has been taken advantage of, yet there still remains merchants who will visit their wholesale house and purchase a bill of goods, because they happened to see a low price on it, and yet won't see that the same method would attract customers to their own stores. What more can be said?

HOW TO PREVENT A KICK.

A salesman called on a furniture dealer, and found the proprietor engaged in getting a dining set ready for delivery. The pieces were just being assembled from the different parts of the store, and the dealer was going over every article, carefully inspecting it and moving it from side to side. He took out all the drawers from the buffet, and refitted them, to avoid the least binding. He found one castor a little higher than the rest, and fixed it. He also carefully rubbed over each piece.

The salesman noticed particularly that all the pieces when first assembled appeared to be in a first-class condition. However, the dealer seemed to think that while it might not be necessary, it was advisable to make another overhauling before putting the goods on the wagon.

"Do you make a practice of doing this every time you deliver furniture?" asked the salesman.

"You bet I do," was the answer. "I never allow a piece of furniture to leave my store without a thorough inspection. I want to avoid even the suspicion of a kick from the customer before he gets the furniture. This is a splendid suit, made by a factory in which I have the utmost confidence, but a trifling defect, such as a tight drawer, a bent castor, or a little abrasion on the finish, while only a trifle in our eyes, would perhaps start something when the piece was put in my customer's house. So I avoid having to make any excuses; and see that the stuff is right before it leaves here."

The salesman who gave us this incident says: "What better advertisement can a dealer buy than the confidence of his customers?"

ARE SPECIAL SALES WORTH WHILE?

"Yes, our special sales pay because they are legitimate," said a department store manager, and we believe that is exactly the position every dealer must occupy before offering his goods below the ordinary price, which gives him a living profit, if these sales are to have a really beneficent effect upon his business.

It does not follow, that because the special sale is a successful feature in the conduct of a business in every-day necessities, such as food and apparel, the method can be applied with equal results in those trades supplying articles of a small per capita consumption, and having a limited demand in consequence. In the former they constitute an essential part of the regular business and conform to the policy of small profits and a quick turnover, made expedient by the larger volume of trade possible, while in the latter the margin of profit must of necessity average so much higher that the offering of a bargain, with a large reduction in price, educates the public to a belief that the profits are excessive, and it will pay to wait for such special offerings, all of which cut into the normal demand.

The members of this trade engaged in the upbuilding of a permanent service to the people of their communities will have but one or two valid reasons for concluding that a special sale will be legitimate merchandising: a lot of "stickers," a surplus of certain articles, or financial obligations making it imperative to turn goods into money. The man who uses this means to move his goods has missed his calling and should have been an auctioneer—closing out and not building up his business. The apparent need of stimulating the demand, upon investigation, will be found usually to result from faulty methods in the ordinary rendering of his service and that any sacrifice of profits he may make under the special sale will bring far better returns if distributed during the year through a lower price or better value.

If you are Progressive and must have your "Specials," feature Quality, then Value, but price least of all; no one expects to get a twenty for $14.75, nor do they expect to buy your goods for less than their real worth, at which you should sell them every day in the year.

TEN GOOD FURNITURE STORE RECIPES.

1. Advertise your store in the newspapers.
2. Make your store front so attractive that the people who saw your ad. in the newspapers will not mistake the place.
3. Show your furniture in the store as it might appear in the homes of the people who call to see it.
4. Let your employees receive visitors the minute they enter, and treat them as guests—with kindness and courtesy—until they go out.
5. Don't permit any employee to show disappointment if he fails to make a sale. Patience all the time, under every condition, is the only safe way.
6. Escort customers to the door as politely as when you received them. Be cordial, and look pleasant, sale or no sale.
7. Walls have ears. Never let a customer hear you or your employees comment on a visitor just gone out. Let the manners of your sales-force be the same in the store as you would have in your home circle. Business is business, but it can be made big business by good breeding and courtesy.
8. When a lady visits your home, you offer her your cosiest chair. Don't forget to do so when she visits your store. She is your guest in both places.
9. Think of the heat and dust of shopping along the busy street. Keep a bountiful supply of cool water and bright glasses near the entrance. How inviting to the tired woman who comes into buy of you!
10. There is scarcely an item you sell that doesn't suggest something to go with it. You sell a bed—can you not add a dressing table or somnoe? A customer buys a dining-room table—can you not get the job of refinishing her chairs to match it? And if she agrees, and you make a good job, how about selling the buffet to complete the suit? Or the china closet?

Think it over.—Northern Furniture.

WHY FURNITURE MEN DRINK

"How much is this dresser?" asked the deaf old lady.

"Ten dollars, madam."

"Eighteen dollars? Oh, that's far too dear; I'll give you fourteen."

"I said fourteen dollars!" yelled the honest dealer.

"Oh, fourteen—well, I'll give you eleven-fifty."

The Art of Display

Suggestions for Window and Interior Arrangements.

Furniture and Window Displays
By G. W. Whitcomb

One gentleman of much self-esteem once read a paper before a body of publicity agents, the title of which was, "What is Advertising?" He thought the answer was contained in his elaborate and carefully prepared symposium, but he started a discussion that has not ended and will, probably, never end. Perhaps a short definition that will answer immediate purposes is, the doing of anything that will attract intelligent attention to the thing advertised. Therefore, it does not follow that a litter of pigs or puppies in a window would be an intelligent advertisement for a fashion show, although they would draw a crowd, undoubtedly, and more or less expert comment.

Advertising has taken certain definite forms in recent years, and one of the most definite of these is window dressing. For instance, one Chicago department store, alone, spends in excess of $150,000 a year on its window dressing activities.

Window dressing has often been likened to the front page of a newspaper, where the best, most original and latest is to be displayed. The window has come to be an expression of the character of both store and business, and to such an extent that an illy-dressed window drives away trade instead of attracting it. Good window dressing manifests itself in all businesses, and is nothing more than a combination of artistic conception, technical knowledge and common sense.

Furniture dealers are beginning to learn the lesson that a brass bedstead, a dining-room table and a few chairs do not constitute the kind of window display that attracts customers. There is less originality displayed in furniture window displays than in any other commodity, and yet there is none where good taste and artistic judgment can be so happily blended. Dealers constantly crowd their windows with a conglomeration of inharmonious furniture that would be a nightmare to them if their wives arranged the home furniture in the same way.

Window dressing, as an art, has reached its highest attainment in the department stores and has done so because the managers have learned that goods well displayed are half sold. This is the reason that the window dressing staff of these big institutions is among its most important divisions, and why it is considered profitable to allow to this staff all the space it wants or needs for working out its ideas.

Go up to the top story of one of these stores and see what is going on. Step off the elevator right under the skylight and take a look around. You will see a huge studio, seventy or more feet long, lighted entirely from above. Close to the door a couple of French hair-dressers are busy arranging the coiffures of two ladies—of wax. Along the wall two mural painters are covering a canvas with a hunting scene. In a corner workmen are completing the model of an old English fireplace. A packing case contains real ferns from Maine, that have been shipped to Germany to be dyed a permanent green and then reshipped to this country. Behind a screen a sculptor is modeling a figure from the living model. In another room seamstresses are busy with fingers and needles. Beyond are cupboards filled with hundreds of glasses, metal and plaster vases, tables, baskets and ornaments of all kinds, flanked by tapestries and fabrics of every hue.

Here are worked out on paper the ideas that will soon assume concrete form in the show windows, to the delight of every passerby, who will stop and idle a moment. It is the office of the chief window demonstrator

Easter display of furniture made by J. L. Westaway, the home furnisher, Port Hope. The background is a white frame work with purple lining and purple and white festoons. Mr. Westaway is a native of Durham County, Ont., and has been a resident of Port Hope for the past 21 years. He has been in business for himself there for 14 years, each year increasing the volume of his sales. He is a firm believer in the proper use of his windows for display and sales purposes.

—one of a group of artistic men who have advanced window dressing into an art and made of it a profession in which the most gifted ones draw salaries that will magnetize the collector of income taxes.

Window dressing of the present is an evolution. It has not been long ago—and the idea has not been entirely abandoned in some stores, more's the pity!—when merchants thought they had not done their duty by themselves, and their customers until a sample of everything carried in stock was put in one window, which, if it did not give the viewer a headache, drove him away in disgust before his eyes had seen a fraction of the articles displayed. Then came the period of pigs, puppies, rabbits, chickens and window buzzers to attract attention. This result was achieved, all right, but the windows were a waste of time and effort because they sold no goods.

Then followed what might be termed the "motion era." It did not appear to make any difference what the article was that was used to attract attention, as long as it was always in motion. Toy railways, loop-the-loops, flashing electric lights and all such things were used, but they were discarded because the mer-

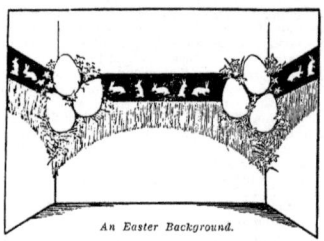

An Easter Background.

Suggestion for an Easter background described herewith.

chants at last learned that the only successful window dressing was the kind that displayed artistically the goods that were for sale, inside the store.

Under the new system, every effort is made for harmony in effects and background. It is now considered absurd to display a lot of gorgeous evening gowns in a background that depicts the snow and discomforts of winter, just as it is incongruous to expect the best from a display that shows fur coats against a background of azure skies, lazy waves, graceful palms and sleeping alligators. There must be no inharmony in window dressing or the effect will be lost.

Why furniture men have not studied this question to greater advantage is one the writer cannot answer. That they have not can be demonstrated any day by a visit to any of the large retail furniture districts, where furniture is grouped in the windows in such manner that the prospective purchaser can have no idea of what the appearance of the same furniture will be when it is installed in his home or office. Furniture dealers, like other merchants, want more trade all the time. They can get it if they will study even the elementals of window dressing and then apply the fruit of that study to the dressing of their own windows.

Some day, some genius will apply the "movies" to a new use and crowds will stand before the windows that display moving panoramas of beautifully furnished homes, where every attention has been paid to details, in which the kitchen sink is not where the ice box should be, or where the kitchen cabinet takes up space that should have been given to the parlor table and where the purchaser can have a visualized picture of his apartment or flat as he would want it to be.

BACKGROUND FOR YOUR EASTER WINDOW.

Easter gives opportunities for the sale of extra goods that should not be neglected. It is also an occasion when the dealer can well afford to devote a little extra effort to decorations. The time expended in window trimming and interior store display will pay you well in increased sales of Easter merchandise.

Herewith is reproduced, a suggestive background for an Easter window. In making this display, the background is of pure white crepe paper. A wide board runs around the top as shown in the drawing. Cover the board with purple crepe paper, thus getting the proper combination for Easter—purple and white. The next step is to cut out the Easter eggs of white cardboard and mount them in each corner, garnishing them with a display of purple and white Easter lilies. These paper lilies can be purchased at a small price. The next step is to cut the small rabbits out of carboard and mount them on the board. If you think this is too much work, use some of the rabbits sold for decorations around Easter, pinning them in place. The fringe you see hanging from the border is purple crepe paper cut in shreds.

Any variety of goods may be shown in such a window. There are, however, some specially appropriate lines which the dealer will find it most profitable to feature at this time.

VALUE OF WINDOW SPACE.

The larger the city the greater the use of show windows in retail stores, and in smaller places little or no thought seems to be given to their use; and this suggests a sore lack of the knowledge of their value. Why is this, and why do not the retailers in villages take advantage of the opportunity that is theirs?

Most dealers in small towns complain that the inhabitants go to the cities unnecessarily to make purchases, which purchases should be made in their own town. It would seem that if the merchant did all he could and copied the successful stores of the larger places, in so far as their management goes, much of this complaint would be done away with.

The rental value of a square foot of space in a show window in a village of 2,500 is less by many times than the space in the same store similarly situated in a large city, and this may in a measure account for the difference in their use; but compared with the total floor rental the one costs as much as the other.

It has been stated that some show windows are held to be worth half the total rental of an entire floor. Whether or not this is true, there can be no means of knowing, but certain it is, that the space per foot in the show window is worth many times that of any other in the store.

The window trimmer who is alive and who will take the time to study and plan, can figure windows that will pay certain profits. The windows merit as much, if not more, attention than any other phase of merchandising, and he who improves his window service is making an improvement that will show an increase in sales and in the bank account.

Getting the Best Results From Retail Furniture Advertising

BY E. J. CREEPER, Owen Sound

We live in an age of progressiveness. Modern business demands many things both unthought and unheard of in years which have passed. The subject which has been alloted to me for a few minutes is, "How to get the most out of advertising, or, as I think it might be termed, "Looking through the nickels at the dollars beyond."

Advertising is necessary to a furniture dealer as fertilizer is to the farmer; or, in other words, it is a necessity. To begin with, advertising is merely getting better acquainted with the public. There are hundreds of ways of advertising, but as a general rule it is the little things that count. By that I mean that it is not the most expensive means of advertising that always brings the best results.

If you will try and put yourself in the place of your prospective customer and discover why they purchase from your store in preference to others you will probably find it is because of one of the following reasons:—

That your store is convenient to them.
That you and your clerks are courteous.
That your smile is a little more pleasing, and your ways a little more obliging than your competitor.
That your store is neater, cleaner and more inviting than your competitor's.

The Window as an Advertisement.

Let us start with your windows. I am afraid there are too many of us that do not pay enough attention to our window advertising. It is one of the best publicity agents of any merchant. It is necessary, however, to make it so by displaying in a tempting and attractive manner the merchandise, so that people will stop and examine it. There must be some definite impression you wish to make, and this idea must be concentrated in your windows to succeed. Change your displays not less than once every week, oftener, if possible, to get the best results.

Neatness and order in your store is another latent advertising feature.

Then, again, are your clerks well informed and obliging? There is nothing impresses a casual customer more than to enter a store where the clerks are obliging, courteous and well informed. Do not keep a grouchy clerk at any cost. Courtesy pays big dividends and always gives particular attention to women customers.

Other Methods of Advertising.

There are many other ways of advertising that are inexpensive to the dealer, and of which few really avail themselves. They are ways that bring big results if properly worked.

The aim of every ambitious merchant is to obtain the greatest results from the least expenditure. Competition demands it, but anything that is worth doing is worth doing well. It is not always wise to limit your expenditures in advertising so that the impression of cheapness in your management or your actions is given to your customers. If you think of giving a customer a cigar it is far better to keep your money in your pocket than offer him a cheap one. The personal touch which you can have with your customers is a great aid to business. You can solicit trade by means of circular letters or post cards, but the actual going out and circulating among farmers, home-builders and mechanics will make a much better and more lasting impression.

Systematic Newspaper Advertising

Then again, the newspaper without question is one of the greatest factors for the upbuilding of any progressive establishment. It must be used, however, with care and system or it will be found to be an expensive luxury. Determine upon the amount you can well afford to spend and find out how much space you can get for that amount. The ordinary country and town storekeeper is apt to condemn newspaper advertising, as he has possibly not succeeded in obtaining results from his advertising, because he has allowed the same advertisement to appear time after time, and then wonders why they do not pay. The reason lies in the fact that they are stale news and nobody cares to read them the second time. Many people read the advertising columns as regular as any other part of the paper, and if you offer them in each ad. something that they need they will soon be coming around to see you. Catchy headings, good electros descriptive of goods—all help to make impression on prospective customers.

There are many other ways of advertising, such as road signs, souvenirs, in programs, and at church fairs. The last two, I believe, should be avoided, as they are simply donations and should come under that head.

The kind of advertising that brings results to-day is that which impresses the public, and the way to do it is through your store service, your window displays, your newspaper advertisements, and your personal solicitation for business.

People are pretty sure to associate flashy advertising with trashy goods. Make your advertising such that you will be willing for your goods to be judged by it.

E. J. CREEPER, Owen Sound, who contributed this article, is one of the live merchants of that town, and is a member of the firm of Canada Beds, Limited, Chesley, Ontario.

Advertising Furniture for the Spring Trade

BY A. B. LEVER

With the approach of Spring the thoughts of the furniture dealer naturally turn to ways and means of securing his share of the business which is seasonable for that time of the year.

Among his plans, advertising, of course, finds a place. In fact, without advertising of some sort he can scarcely be said to have plans. He may buy well, and even make good window displays, but unless he heralds the fact abroad, by the aid of printer's ink, his share of the Spring trade will be very much smaller than it otherwise would be.

The advertisements which I am reproducing in this issue are of such a character that every dealer will be able to find in them something that will assist him in the preparation of his own copy. It does not follow that he should strictly imitate any one of them. The purpose I have in reproducing them is that from an ad. here and there a helpful suggestion may be obtained.

The advertisement of Lemont & Sons, Fredericton, N.B., not only looks well, but is couched in language which appeals to the heart of parents who are the proud possessors of a baby. "Fresh Air Helps the Babies!" is good, and the words which follow are based upon this thought. Lemont & Sons are to be congratulated. The original was 4⅜ by 6¼ inches.

The advertisement of the Hastings Furniture Co., Vancouver, is not, like the above, of the heart-to-heart talk description. It is a good advertisement just the same. Typographically, it is excellent, and is made particularly so by the white space which surrounds it. The reading matter is simple, to the point, and is "newsy." The original was 4⅜ by 6 inches.

The strong point in the advertisement of the Blowey-Henry Co., Edmonton, is the appeal it makes to both the asthetic taste and the comfort of the housewife. This point is made with exceedingly good judgment. Typographically the ad. is also good.

I have often pointed out in this department the mistake that advertisers sometimes make of putting the firm name at both top and bottom of their ads. In none of the ads. I have reproduced in this issue has this been done. Imagine, if you will, that it had been done with any one of the ads. shown in the group and you will at once, I think, appreciate how it would have detracted from its merits.

The "Lord Nelson" rocker, advertisement of the Home Outfitting Co., Hamilton, was 11 by 18¾ inches. Some may think this a good deal of space to devote in a daily newspaper to advertising one particular article. It is seldom, however, that it is a mistake to do so. One thing is certain, when such is done, the concentrating powers of the advertisement are all the greater. In this particular instance, at any rate, it proved a success. I have the word of the company itself for this. "It gave us good results," is what they say. The ad. is not only a good one from a typographical appearance, but the selling talk which composes the reading matter is put with skill and ability of a more than usually high order. Too many people, when writing ads. seem to forget that the purpose of an advertisement is to sell goods. A salesman would no more think of putting a chair before a customer and merely remarking "Here is a chair." On the contrary, he would dilate, as the writer of this ad. does, upon its inherent merits.

The advertisement of J. Mickleborough, Limited, St. Thomas, is another of those advertisements which is both strong in its typographical appearance and in its news features. The paragraph under the first display line dwells, in brief and well-chosen language, upon the quality and variety of the carpets and rugs the firm has in stock, and then follows the details regarding each of the lines advertised. The original was 6⅝ by 10 inches.

The line, "What You Can Do," in the advertisement of J. A. Banfield, Winnipeg, at once arrests the attention by its uniqueness. The attractiveness of the ad. is further enhanced by the illustrations and the prices, the latter of which are well brought out. The original was 6⅝ by 7¾ inches.

Note—Am glad at any time to receive samples of ads. with, when possible, statements as to results which have been obtained from them.

CO-OPERATION WITH ADVERTISERS

Each year almost inconceivably large sums of money are spent by manufacturers and wholesalers in conducting national campaigns of advertising, in order to establish the sale of their products and make their brands known to every consumer in the country. These great firms are not spending this money in moments of unguided enthusiasm, but after careful consideration, the study of conditions, the weighing of mediums and the knowledge of the same work in the past. It is a sober, business proposition with them. They spend money that they may make more money.

You will notice in the trade papers much information along this line; you will find it in the advertisements of these firms. They seek the retailer with announcements of their intentions, and they ask co-operation. The attitude of a good many retailers is something like this:

"Why should I trouble myself about a proposition of that kind? If they want to advertise on the billboards of my town, and in the newspapers, and in the street cars, well and good; I'll get some of the benefits, no doubt."

We are not arguing against this "sit-tight" policy because it is selfish, although it may be, but because it is foolish and short-sighted. The retailer who takes that attitude is not materially interfering with the business of the national advertiser, but he is damming up the stream of his own profits.

It is impossible to estimate the vast sums of money the retailers lose each year because they refuse to respond to the suggestions and requests for co-operation. And they are the chief losers, too.

Advertising properly prepared and placed is effective, there can be no question of that. It has been proved over and over again; and the very fact that the big firms continue to advertise is enough evidence that it pays them to do it. It brings trade to them. But there is an opportunity here which some retailers overlook—an opportunity for themselves.

The great firms catering to the retail trade are creating business for themselves by this extensive publicity. The public sees, reads, is attracted and convinced, and wants the article, compound, preparation or whatever it may be. The public is convinced and ready to buy.

"And how am I to co-operate?" one may ask. Suppose you receive notification that during a certain week a firm whose goods you handle proposes to inaugurate a strong selling campaign. It is ready to send you matter for free distribution, hangers for your store, etc. If you admit that this campaign is apt to put the consumer in a receptive state for buying, why not get his trade, take his money and make your profit? Why not put in a window display of these goods? Why not make an extra effort to use the effort already used?

There is a psychological moment in selling, as every good salesman knows. There is the time of public indifference, of interest awakened, of half persuasion. A little effort right then turns a doubtful and hesitating customer into a buyer. The national advertiser has done the preliminary work; he asks you to do the rest, for mutual advantage. It pays to do it—to co-operate with him. It pays him and it pays you.

The real test of advertising is when business is slow—any kind of advertising will sell goods when business is good, but it takes real publicity to move stock in dull times.

WHAT JUDICIOUS ADVERTISING DOES.

Reduced to tabular form, some of the chief economic operations of judicious advertising, in the opinion of The New York Furniture Journal are:

Expansion of markets.—It increases production and reduces the cost of the product and consequently lowers the price at which it can be sold at a profit.

Saving in service.—When the customer goes to the store knowing exactly what he is after, fewer clerks are needed. This lowers the labor charge which the retailer figures into his expense before fixing his prices. Quicker turnovers of the stock are also accomplished, reducing the overhead expenses.

Competition is stimulated, resulting in improved quality.

Standardization of goods.—Responsibility is fixed. The consumer knows just who is at fault if the goods are not up to the mark. Instead of blaming the dealer, he blames the manufacturer, an incentive for the latter to keep goods up to standard.

Publicity.—The people know more about their necessities than they ever did before. Result: Better goods.

Economy in time.—The advertising page is the customer's market place. It informs him where he can get what he wants at a price he can pay. It simplifies shopping.

QUALITY CIRCULATION IS WHAT COUNTS.

Perhaps mine is not a typical case, for I do not consider circulation volume in the same light that I think other advertisers do. It matters little to me whether a paper has 5,000 or 50,000 circulation. Where it circulates and what it circulates is much more important. C. C. Winningham in "Printers' Ink."

The man who thinks writing his advertisements is a thing he can do at any odd time will be lucky if he gets them read even at odd times.

The Demoralization of Canadian Brass Bed Prices

Brass Bed Demoralization.

There does not appear to be any let up to the price cutting in brass beds which has now been going on for some time. On the contrary, it is, if anything, more general, and consequently worse.

The situation is regrettable. It not only breeds discord among those who are engaged in it, but it has a demoralizing effect upon business generally, and particularly in regard to the line whose price is being cut.

Upon buyers in general the effect is a distinct undermining of confidence in prices. When they see the price of certain lines of bedsteads being cut down to the low figures which they have of late they naturally conclude that the figures which previously ruled were excessive. They consequently deem that the prices now ruling should be the normal ones.

Should there ever be an attempt—as there undoubtedly will be at some time—to get prices back to their normal status it will be found that buyers will resent it. They will declare that a combination is at work and the public are being swindled.

The trouble with price cutting is that no one manufacturer or retailer can monopolize it. He cannot, "cuss" words because they have not at their command a sufficient number of reputable words. Whether this fact is based on scientific data does not matter.

But there can scarcely be any doubt about the reasonableness of the assertion that those who engage in price cutting in order to build up business are attempting to erect a superstructure on an unsound foundation.

That price-cutting is unsound economically we have never heard anyone deny. It is too obvious to deny it. And the more we analyze it the more difficult does the task of denying it become.

Sound business economics demand that the business man, be he manufacturer, wholesaler or retailer, should pare his costs down to the lowest possible point commensurate with efficiency. There isn't any doubt about that. He owes it to the consuming public as well as to himself. No man has a right to be prodigal in regard to his cost of doing business.

Neither has be any right to do business without a fair margin of profit over and above his costs.

He who cuts prices as ordinarily understood, is not obtaining a fair margin of profit. He may be getting business, but it is at the expense of profits. And it

Beds in the window—A demonstration of Ideal Cribs made by The Whitten Co., Bracebridge, Ont.

therefore, maintain any advantage it may give him, for ten chances to one when he starts others will follow in his train, until they are all again on an equal footing, and each, instead of making money on the lines affected, are losing it.

It is altogether a horse of another color when, because of improved and better facilities, his cost of manufacturing is reduced a manufacturer is able to put his goods on the market at a lower figure than his competitors. That is sound economically, and he is entitled to all the advantages which may thereby accrue. Under such conditions as these he may, as is often the case, be making a larger profit on the output of his factory than those of his competitors who are struggling along ever at the old and higher figures.

* * * *

True Business Foundations.

It has been said that profanity is an evidence that those who practice it are deficient in their vocabulary. In other words, they are compelled to resort to

is not only at the expense of profits, but at the expense of himself.

No man can live unto himself in business. If he resorts to unsound methods in business, he is not the only one to suffer: His fellow business men suffer as well.

Price cutting is not only unsound economically, but it is based on selfishness, that and nothing else. It presumes, if it does not so profess, that no one else has any right to have a share of the business in the particular line affected.

It is the duty of every business man, whether he be manufacturer or dealer, to get every dollar's worth of business that he can get. He cannot develop unless he does.

He who has reached a stage where he decides that he wants no more business has reached a stage where there will be devolution instead of evolution. One cannot stand still in business. If the movement is not forward it is backward.

Cutting prices is attempting by a backward movement to go forward, whether the article be brass beds or anything else.

There is only one way to go forward, and that is to employ going forward methods.

Make or sell an article that is good, that will give satisfaction and will ensure a moderate profit. Through advertising mediums that reach them, tell in plain, simple language those to whom you wish to sell the merits of your goods, and in your selling methods employ the most modern and progressive possible. That will be building on a good foundation.

C. N. Greenwood, elected president of Stratford Bed Co.

STRATFORD BED CO. INCORPORATED

The Stratford Bed Co., Ltd., Stratford, has received an Ontario charter to manufacture and sell furniture and bedding of all kinds. The capital is set at $40,000, and the provisional directors are C. N. Greenwood, Fred C. Hennicke, Geo. McLagan, H. W. Strudley and D. M. Wright.

C. N. Greenwood is president, secretary-treasurer and general manager; F. C. Hennicke is vice-president and superintendent, and the other three will be members of the board of directors. The Stratford Bed Co. will continue to occupy the present premises, and on the road throughout Canada will be represented by the following Geo. McLagan Furniture Co.'s traveling salesmen: Messrs. Dobson, Burns, Chown, Friendship, Stewart, Truscott, Higginbottom and Griffin.

NEW BEDS AND SWINGING COUCH

The Ideal Bedding Co.'s March bulletin is featuring cribs of various designs and styles for many purposes.

The company is adding a dozen or fifteen new designs to their brass and iron beds, some of the new brass trimmings showing open spaces with copper effect underneath.

For summer trade their new hammo-couch this year has several improvements; among others the hanging chains have been extended and are now attached to the seat; folding legs under the couch may be let down to make a bed at night, and a valance across the front edge adds a finish that was thought lacking by some people on last year's hammo-couch.

NEW ALASKA REPRESENTATIVE IN ONTARIO

The furniture trade in Eastern Ontario is being visited by R. W. Johnston, the new representative of the Alaska Feather and Down Company, Ltd. Mr. Johnston has for several years past been connected with the Alaska organization in various capacities—in office, warehouse and factory. He has thus had a good opportunity to become thoroughly well posted on what Alaska manufacturing facilities and service mean to the retail trade.

His knowledge of the line, his personality and unbounded enthusiasm, have won for him many friends among the company's customers, and should win many more friends and customers. Mr. Johnston is just now making the first trip through his territory, and is showing some of Alaska's latest designs and novelties for the first time.

BEDDING NOTES

A winding-up order having been granted the Anchor Mfg. Co., bed manufacturers, Preston, it is said the concern has been taken over by a new company representing the T. Eaton Co., Toronto, and the Page-Hersey Iron and Tube Co., Welland.

The McGeough Mfg. Co., Ltd., Toronto, has received an Ontario charter to make and sell all kinds of bedding, spring mattresses, park seats, cushions, and all materials used in their manufacture. The capital is set at $150,000.

A spark from a carding machine in the James Purvis Company, Limited, mattress factory, 2 Esplanade

R. W. Johnston, New representative in Eastern Ontario for Alaska Feather & Down Co.

Street, Toronto, started a fire that gave the eastern section of the fire brigade a stiff two hour fight recently, resulting in $10,000 damage. The building, a wood skeleton, one storey, iron covered place, suffered to the extent of $2,000, and the machinery, stock, and contents, $8,000.

Story of the Metal Bed Industry
By A. H. Plante

Iron beds have been made in England for one hundred years or more. They were first adopted by prisons and poor houses about the year 1812. These beds were made in the crudest possible manner, composed of ¾ and ⅞ inch bar iron for posts and ⅜ by 1½ inch flat bars for sides, sheet iron head and foot boards, the whole being forged and riveted together. On the frame was laced canvas sacking, making, on the whole, a very comfortable bed.

About the year 1820 an enterprising Wolverhampton man put on the market a (sand) cast iron sofa that could be converted into a bed. This may be said to be the root from which sprang one of England's greatest industries; namely, the iron bedstead trade of Birmingham. In a short time iron men in a small way of business introduced iron beds as a side line. They were generally made of ⅜ and ½ inch rail work, and, as I have said, were forged and riveted together. A cast iron vase surmounted the posts, no casters being used. To one of these small manufacturers in the city of Birmingham, in 1830, belongs the credit of introducing the first cast iron corner and dove-tail. To

One of the Ives Modern Bedsted Co.'s new productions.

the same man also belongs the credit of introducing the hollow cast iron flowers that made so marked a change. The flowers were drilled out to fit the crossrods, and uprights were threaded thereon and pressed or pinned together to make the rail firm. Thus, with but slight changes in designs, the industry made slow progress until about the year 1840, when John Davis revolutionized the whole system of manufacturing these goods.

Mr. Davis conceived the idea of casting the whole end together by means of iron stocks, or chills, the same system in general use to-day. Up to this time, it will be understood, the iron bedstead was a luxury enjoyed only by the well-to-do. The Davis method brought it within the reach of the masses, and from that time on old wooden beds were a thing of the past, and capitalists were not slow to recognize that fact. In a very few years bedstead factories began to start up like mushrooms. This, of course, created an increased demand for pig iron, round iron and angles, and by the year 1850 the Black country (a district within thirty miles of Birmingham, and so called for its products of coal, iron, etc.,) was ablaze with puddling furnaces, rolling mills and tube mills.

With the advent of the Davis method came also the idea of trimming beds in brass and shortly afterwards the making of all-brass bedsteads. This, in its turn, created a new departure in the already enormous brass business in Birmingham. As the years rolled on the industry grew apace, and to-day it may truly be said to be the greatest of the many great enterprises in the largest manufacturing city in the world.—Southern Furniture Journal.

HOW TO DISTINGUISH COLONIAL DESIGNS

Colonial furniture, as far as it is to be distinguished from the English furniture of the same period, is characterized by greater simplicity, by the preference for curved rather than straight outlines, and by its large expanses of polished surface, says Eleanor Allison Cummins, in "Keith's Magazine." Sofas with spreading arms and claw feet and backs elaborately curved are Colonial. So are pillared and claw-footed tables, and little sewing tables with lids, which raise to discover trays of many small compartments, and hanging bags of fluted silk. Bureaus, desks and sideboards often have pillars continued down the corners ending in claw feet, and have curving fronts, reminiscent of the French styles of the seventeenth century. Pomegranates and pineapples are common decorative motives, being used for the ends of bed posts and as parts of table legs. Some decorative motives are distinctly patriotic, like the eagle's feathers and stars found on the frames of mirrors. The banjo clock is native, so are several varieties of spindle back chairs, notably the effective Windsor chairs, with wooden seats and curving banistered backs. Secretaries, combining the functions of a desk and a bookcase, are made in large numbers by cabinet makers, and though usually very simple, depending for their beauty upon the fine grain of the wood and the brilliant polish of their brasses, are still very desirable possessions.

NEW MORRIS AND INVALID CHAIRS

M. B. Dodd, a well known young man, of Arnprior, Ont., has completed models for a Morris and an invalid's chair. Those who have been privileged to see them are loud in their praise of the work. The seats and backs of both chairs are so simply contrived that the mere pressure of a little lever will adjust them to any angle, and no matter in what position they may be, the back, shoulders and head receive support and rest. The Morris is equipped with a new arrangement for resting the legs and feet, and when not in use this part is very simply slipped conveniently under the chair.

OLD LACQUER FURNITURE IN DEMAND

One of the latest of London's fashion freaks is a demand for old lacquer furniture. A drug on the market until a few weeks ago, lacquer cabinets are now bringing from $5,000 to $15,000, and the demand is so great that the big furnishing firms are turning out large quantities of modern lacquer in the hope of meeting the new fashion.

There is a right place for everything that comes into your store and it is your business to decide where that place is.

Picture Framing

PROGRESS IN PICTURES.

It is such a big subject, such an important subject, that of the gathering of pictures, the proper placing of pictures, and the choice of the fitting frames.

It is not only that all this is important to the proper appearance of the home. It is important in its influence on the home-dwellers. For pictures in their influence make unmistakably for mental strengthening and advancement, or else for the reverse.

And, in addition to all that, they are capable of giving a high degree of pleasure, which alone would be reason sufficient for care in their choice.

With most people the greatest obstacle to the proper enjoyment of pictures, to gaining the best advantages from pictures, is the curious and absurd disinclination to get rid of poor ones already in their possession. For, with them, it is once a picture, always a picture. They will change their furniture and their wall-paper, their window-curtains, their table-china, their gowns, their hats. But the picture that hangs on the wall is sacred! As soon as their walls are full it is a case of thus far and no farther. Henceforth they stagnate along what ought to be a line of steady advance. Their pictures jumble time and space—give them space and they remain for all time.

And yet, to continue the acquisition of pictures, to raise the standard, and to do this with the least possible expense—for there are few to whom expense is not a consideration—is not such a difficult matter, after all. If a picture or a frame is too bad to keep, why should you keep it? Get rid of it. Give it away—throw it away—sell it—do anything with it. Even if it was a present it is not incumbent on you to keep it; at least not to keep it in sight. No one, whether relative or friend, has the right to give any article of house or personal adornment except with the distinct risk that, if the taste does not meet approval, the gift shall not be kept in sight. To permit otherwise were tyranny indeed. Who was it that drolly and happily suggested that impossible presents of any sort be taken out at night, one by one, and buried? And so, be firm! Get rid of an impossible picture or frame as swiftly as you would of an impossible gown or hat. Don't let it make a strata-like journey: first floor, second floor, third floor, attic.

There are no definite rules or standards. What is one man's meat may be another man's aesthetic poison. What is one man's Carlyle may be another man's Erasmus. Individual taste, individual standards, must determine in each case what to put to the fore and what to banish.

A fixed rule in the business world is that you don't get anything for nothing. A pleased customer is a valuable asset, but you don't get him for nothing. He costs effort.

Choose a worthy object and work towards it persistently, with the assurance that success must reward your efforts. The man who never gives up always wins.—R. J. Blaine.

PICTURE FRAMES.

There are people in the panel business to-day who can perhaps look back to a time when they enjoyed an excellent trade in built-up picture frames. This was quite a strong feature and a good line to manufacture one time, and included some beautiful and artistic work as well as some plain and comparatively cheap work. Some have drifted out of it of late years because they claim too many people have gotten into it, and, with a cheap product, have spoiled the trade.

There is still a lot of built-up veneered work used in picture frames, and perhaps there are more opportunities to develop good business here than the panel man of past experience is inclined to believe. There is something doing in this line all the time, and when the winter season comes on there is a little more than usual, because people begin to furnish and refurnish and give more attention to the inside of their homes, and there is more trade in pictures and picture frames. It is true that there are many cheap products in this line, but there is always something of this kind in every line, and even if there are, there always remains a chance to sell a product which has merit, regardless of the cheaper thing.

Why not take a new grip on this picture frame proposition and go after it this fall with new lines of samples bringing out new ideas, different finishes and artistic effects of various kinds? The built-up picture frame is an excellent product that will live a long time, and the quantity used is likely to depend more or less directly on the efforts and the exploitation of the manufacturers. Why not get into the game this fall and try pushing this branch of the business along a little?

CARTAGE CHARGE DISCRIMINATION

The new railway cartage schedule, which went into effect on January 22 last, and which was mentioned in the last issue of The Furniture World as being not satisfactory to furniture manufacturers, is proving itself no more satisfactory to retail furniture men. Furniture retailers who last year paid three cents per hundred pounds on less than thousand-pound consignments are this year compelled to pay double that rate. They want to know why they should be asked to pay six cents per hundred when the general merchandise was raised only from three to three and a quarter cents. They do not charge that the rate is entirely an exhorbitant one, but they want to know the reason of the discrimination.

Railway officials and officers of the Toronto Board of Trade, when interviewed, stated that this whole cartage matter is not yet settled. The railways wished to cut out the cartage arrangements entirely, and it was only at the solicitation of the various trade organizations that the arrangements were continued at the increased rate. Exception was made of furniture and some other lines in the general classification because of the bulk of these goods, it being averred that on account of the space occupied by furniture it was more costly to transport and cart this line than those coming under the general classification.

The Retail Merchants' Association has promised its help in trying to bring about a reduction in the rate on furniture, that body contending that in addition to this specific complaint, retailers have an added ground for complaint on the double cartage charge which is made at both shipping and receiving point.

BIG ORDER FOR SEATS

The Stratford Mfg. Co., Ltd., are at present working on an order for fifteen carloads of seats for the new grandstand which is being erected by the Ontario Jockey Club at the Woodbine race track at Toronto. This is one of the biggest orders placed in Canada for some time.

STOVES

AFTER STOVES SELL ACCESSORIES

Setting up housekeeping, I bought a home at the very start. It cost me $1,400 cash down. When the dicker was finished and the money paid, the widow lady who sold the house called attention to a neat little walnut cupboard.

"This would be very handy, don't you think?" she urged:—and quoted her price.

I took the cupboard. I took a lot of kitchen utensils, a croquet set, a lawn mower. I took approximately seventy-two dollars worth of stuff, a good part of it junk that I didn't need.

That woman had the right selling idea. Had she been a bit younger, she would have made a fortune behind the counter.

Initiative

For it is the clerk with the initiative and the energy and the enthusiasm to suggest extras that builds business for the store. It is comparatively easy to sell the article the consumer first asks for. It is another matter to suggest things additional. Yet it is the sale of these additional things that marks the difference between the half-salesman and the thorough-salesman.

It takes a good salesman to sell a stove—no doubt of it. Yet too often the salesman, once the stove is sold, is so elated that he forgets lesser opportunities to which the first sale opens the door.

The Alert Salesman

Every coal range or coal heater should be accompanied by a coal scuttle. The alert salesman suggests a coal scuttle before the customer leaves the store. The salesman not quite so alert waits until the customer comes back complaining of oversight—and then sets a bad example by throwing in the scuttle for good measure.

Wood stoves in these latter days are comparatively scarce; yet with the wood stove the dealer might just as well sell an axe. There is also a possibility of selling a hatchet for chopping kindling. If the purchaser already has an axe, it may need a handle. Sell him one, and get the job of fitting it. A timely suggestion will mean a little extra, perhaps two or three extras, on the original stove sale.

There is, too, the job of putting up the stove. Your men can do this work in less time, and can do it far better than the average purchaser. Most men now-a-days will appreciate being relieved of the job. Not merely is there the putting up of the stove you sell—there may be, also, other stoves to put up.

Many purchasers of new stoves use old pipe. Such pipe is pretty sure to be worn thin; in many cases it is as full of holes as a sieve. With any stove this means risk of fire; with coal or gas there is the added risk of suffocation. A timely word, after you have sold that stove, will usually induce the customer to let you look over his stock of pipe and replace what needs replacing.

Every stove needs a stove brush, and a supply of stove polish. The woman who spends sixty dollars for a new range will start well, whatever she may do later. The bright steel ornamental work on the heater needs attention—a little polish now and then will keep it clean; far easier than cleaning after dirt and rust has once affected it. See that you sell the polish.

Then, too, the new range is a sort of stepping stone to a host of kitchen utensils. The woman who has replaced an old cook stove with a new range is probably using the limited supply of utensils available twenty years ago. Talk to her of replacing the graniteware that is worn out, the pots, kettles and wash-boilers on which time and usage have laid relentless fingers. Interest her, too, in modern kitchen devices that go to make housework easier. You may not land her order at the immediate moment, but you have paved the way —and a circular letter now and then will keep her in line for goods of this sort.

Suggestions have endless possibilities, to the clerk who is wide awake. From the articles sold in the first place, the mind jumps quickly to other articles customarily associated with the first. Not every suggestion means a sale, but every suggestion paves the way for a future sale.

This is better than selling merely a range or heater. Though it's mighty good policy to cinch your sale of the range or the heater first and settle all the terms—for if you don't, you'll have the customer asking that the extras be thrown in for good measure.

A FRIEND IN "NEAD."

Herewith is reproduced, minus the original hieroglyphics, a letter that reached a well-known retail hardware man, coming from a customer who was in sore "nead." It is worthy of perusal, both as showing what the hardware man is often up against, and because of the unique terms the writer has coined to give expression to his troubles:

Sir

reseved the litel stove i bought of you last thursday and find it no good the door at the Bottom will not close the snib is to Short

i thought i did not put it up right so i went and got a stove tinker or plumber to look at it as soon as he seed it he told me thar hed been a mistake eather in the Foundry or at the Setting it up as it would take 4 or 5 aights to raise it at the heal that is at the Hangrs and the wire is to small for the Hols in the Caston and that the Snib at the Front of the door is 5 aights to Short

it will have to come back to you, . What will you do about it tell me when to ship it and if you will give me one in its place do tend to it as we are in nead of it and i will come and See it

yours Resp

EFFICIENCY A PROCESS OF DEVELOPMENT

The making of a real stove salesman is not the work of a day. Even though a man may be born with special talent along this line, a great deal of education and training are necessary before he can hope to develop any great degree of efficiency. He must have experience with the crafty buyer; learn his likes and dislikes, and be able to fit his talk to each particular individual. To a great extent he must be his own guide and teacher, never neglecting an opportunity to add to his fund of knowledge anything that will tend to increase his efficiency.

INVENTED NEW HOTEL RANGE

Z. Franks, a Vancouver second-hand stove dealer, has invented a new hotel range which he is calling the "Dreadnought." He is trying it out in three local hotels, and so far reports speak of it favorably.

The Making of Chinese Grass Furniture
By W. A. Jennings

From the far off Flowery Kingdom come the new and attractive designs in sea grass furniture illustrated in these columns. This cool and neat-looking product of the weaver's skill fills a long-felt want for a really artistic, yet inexpensive, verandah and living-room furnishing.

The foundation of sea grass furniture is a peculiar flexible framework of Malacca cane. This cane is exceedingly strong, and is further reinforced wherever it is subject to excessive strain. Over this strong, springy frame is woven in and out the fibre cords made of braided sea grass. This grass is a peculiar growth that flourishes in the innumerable bays and baylets of the Chinese Sea. It is long, very tough, and tenacious, consequently it possesses excellent wearing qualities. The grass is cut at the proper season, goes through an extended curing and bleaching process, and is shipped inland to the factories. Here the coolies, or natives, sit in long rows and build up the chair or other article line for line from models before them. They are expert at copying designs, and can now turn out patterns similar to the most expensive rattan products. There are practically no nails used in construction, the finishing being done by cleverly concealed binding of rattan.

This line has proven a success wherever it has been stocked, and from all appearances promises to become a staple all-the-year-round seller. It is especially good, however, when the balmy days of spring extend the irresistible invitation into the open. On verandah, in living porch and summer cottage this furniture adds the finishing touch; combining as it does simplicity, durability and comfort. As there is no varnish or stain used on the natural finished product it is impervious to all weather.

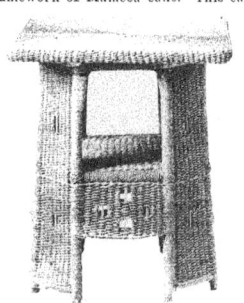

Table made of Chinese grass.

NEW FACTORIES AT STRATFORD.

By an almost unanimous vote, the ratepayers of Stratford recently carried three industrial by-laws, two of which will add an upholstering factory and a furniture frames plant, and the third means the enlarging of the Stratford Manufacturing Company's plant to more than double its present size.

The proposals were to fix the assessment of the Stratford Manufacturing Company for ten years at $7,500, and allow part of College Street to be closed, in return for the company adding a new factory 160 by 60, three stories high, and employing 75 hands in the manufacture of lawn-swings, ladders and porch furniture. This by-law was carried by 1,584 votes to 87.

Charles Diebel of Hanover is to erect a factory 150 by 50, three stories in height, employing 50 hands in the manufacture of furniture frames. The city grants $3,500 towards a site, and fixes the assessment at $7,500 for ten years for general taxes. The vote was. for 1,557, against 114.

John Morlock, also of Hanover, is to build, for the purposes of high-class upholstering, two factory buildings, one 100 by 45 and the other 50 by 45, and to employ 50 hands. The city grants $2,500 for site, and fixes the assessment at $7,500, except for schools and local improvements. This by-law received 1,550 favorable votes and 121 contrary.

ENGLISH FURNITURE HOUSE AT COAST

Announcement has been made by J. Wentworth, of Montreal, representing Waring & Gillow, Ltd., of London, England, said to be the largest upholstery manufacturers in the world, that his firm had practically decided to establish a manufacturing and distributing branch at either Vancouver or Victoria. This firm supplies the Royal households in England, and in addition has a large colonial and general trade. It employs thousands of men.

"The growth of our business in Western Canada," said Mr. Wentworth, "has led to the decision to establish a branch on the Coast. Another reason is that a

Light, summery, rocker made of Chinese grass.

branch factory here will put us in a good strategic position to go after orders in the Orient. This is a business which is capable of great expansion in the future."

The Furniture Record tells of a furniture display in New York that included a card bearing the line "The Acme of Refinement in Furniture—Sheraton Period." A young couple looked for a long time at the exhibit and then the man said, "Gee, but ain't that Acme wood beautiful."

STOVES

AFTER STOVES SELL ACCESSORIES

Setting up housekeeping, I bought a home at the very start. It cost me $1,400 cash down. When the dicker was finished and the money paid, the widow lady who sold the house called attention to a neat little walnut cupboard.

"This would be very handy, don't you think?" she urged;—and quoted her price.

I took the cupboard. I took a lot of kitchen utensils, a croquet set, a lawn mower. I took approximately seventy-two dollars worth of stuff, a good part of it junk that I didn't need.

That woman had the right selling idea. Had she been a bit younger, she would have made a fortune behind the counter.

Initiative

For it is the clerk with the initiative and the energy and the enthusiasm to suggest extras that builds business for the store. It is comparatively easy to sell the article the consumer first asks for. It is another matter to suggest things additional. Yet it is the sale of these additional things that marks the difference between the half-salesman and the thorough-salesman.

It takes a good salesman to sell a stove—no doubt of it. Yet too often the salesman, once the stove is sold, is so elated that he forgets lesser opportunities to which the first sale opens the door.

The Alert Salesman

Every coal range or coal heater should be accompanied by a coal scuttle. The alert salesman suggests a coal scuttle before the customer leaves the store. The salesman not quite so alert waits until the customer comes back complaining of oversight—and then sets a bad example by throwing in the scuttle for good measure.

Wood stoves in these latter days are comparatively scarce; yet with the wood stove the dealer might just as well sell an axe. There is also a possibility of selling a hatchet for chopping kindling. If the purchaser already has an axe, it may need a handle. Sell him one, and get the job of fitting it. A timely suggestion will mean a little extra, perhaps two or three extras, on the original stove sale.

There is, too, the job of putting up the stove. Your men can do this work in less time, and can do it far better than the average purchaser. Most men now-a-days will appreciate being relieved of the job. Not merely is there the putting up of the stove you sell—there may be, also, other stoves to put up.

Many purchasers of new stoves use old pipe. Such pipe is pretty sure to be worn thin; in many cases it is as full of holes as a sieve. With any stove this means risk of fire; with coal or gas there is the added risk of suffocation. A timely word, after you have sold that stove, will usually induce the customer to let you look over his stock of pipe and replace what needs replacing.

Every stove needs a stove brush, and a supply of stove polish. The woman who spends sixty dollars for a new range will start well, whatever she may do later. The bright steel ornamental work on the heater needs attention—a little polish now and then will keep it clean; far easier than cleaning after dirt and rust has once affected it. See that you sell the polish.

Then, too, the new range is a sort of stepping stone to a host of kitchen utensils. The woman who has replaced an old cook stove with a new range is probably using the limited supply of utensils available twenty years ago. Talk to her of replacing the graniteware that is worn out, the pots, kettles and wash-boilers on which time and usage have laid relentless fingers. Interest her, too, in modern kitchen devices that go to make housework easier. You may not land her order at the immediate moment, but you have paved the way —and a circular letter now and then will keep her in line for goods of this sort.

Suggestions have endless possibilities, to the clerk who is wide awake. From the articles sold in the first place, the mind jumps quickly to other articles customarily associated with the first. Not every suggestion means a sale, but every suggestion paves the way for a future sale.

This is better than selling merely a range or heater. Though it's mighty good policy to cinch your sale of the range or the heater first and settle all the terms— for if you don't, you'll have the customer asking that the extras be thrown in for good measure.

A FRIEND IN "NEAD."

Herewith is reproduced, minus the original hieroglyphics, a letter that reached a well-known retail hardware man, coming from a customer who was in sore "nead." It is worthy of perusal, both as showing what the hardware man is often up against, and because of the unique terms the writer has coined to give expression to his troubles:

Sir

reseved the litel stove i bought of you last thursday and fend it no good the door at the Bottom will not close the snib is to Short

i thought i did not put it up right so i went and got a stove tinker or plumber to look at it as soon as he seed it he told me thar hed been a mistake eather in the Foundry or at the Setting it up as it would take 4 or 5 aights to raise it at the heal that is at the Hangrs and the wire is to small for the Hols in the Caston and that the Snib at the Front of the door is 5 aights to Short

it will have to come back to you, . What will you do about it, tell me when to ship it and if you will give me one in its place do tend to it as we are in nead of it and i will come and See it

yours Resp

EFFICIENCY A PROCESS OF DEVELOPMENT

The making of a real stove salesman is not the work of a day. Even though a man may be born with special talent along this line, a great deal of education and training are necessary before he can hope to develop any great degree of efficiency. He must have experience with the crafty buyer; learn his likes and dislikes, and be able to fit his talk to each particular individual. To a great extent he must be his own guide and teacher, never neglecting an opportunity to add to his fund of knowledge anything that will tend to increase his efficiency.

INVENTED NEW HOTEL RANGE

Z. Franks, a Vancouver second-hand stove dealer, has invented a new hotel range which he is calling the "Dreadnought." He is trying it out in three local hotels, and so far reports speak of it favorably.

The Making of Chinese Grass Furniture
By W. A. Jennings

From the far off Flowery Kingdom come the new and attractive designs in sea grass furniture illustrated in these columns. This cool and neat-looking product of the weaver's skill fills a long-felt want for a really artistic, yet inexpensive, verandah and living-room furnishing.

The foundation of sea grass furniture is a peculiar flexible framework of Malacca cane. This cane is exceedingly strong, and is further reinforced wherever it is subject to excessive strain. Over this strong, springy frame is woven in and out the fibre cords made of braided sea grass. This grass is a peculiar growth that flourishes in the innumerable bays and baylets of the Chinese Sea. It is long, very tough, and tenacious, consequently it possesses excellent wearing qualities. The grass is cut at the proper season, goes through an extended curing and bleaching process, and is shipped inland to the factories. Here the coolies, or natives, sit in long rows and build up the chair or other article line for line from models before them. They are expert at copying designs, and can now turn out patterns similar to the most expensive rattan products. There are practically no nails used in construction, the finishing being done by cleverly concealed binding of rattan.

This line has proven a success wherever it has been stocked, and from all appearances promises to become a staple all-the-year-round seller. It is especially good, however, when the balmy days of spring extend the irresistible invitation into the open. On verandah, in living porch and summer cottage this furniture adds the finishing touch; combining as it does simplicity, durability and comfort. As there is no varnish or stain used on the natural finished product it is impervious to all weather.

Table made of Chinese grass.

NEW FACTORIES AT STRATFORD.

By an almost unanimous vote, the ratepayers of Stratford recently carried three industrial by-laws, two of which will add an upholstering factory and a furniture frames plant, and the third means the enlarging of the Stratford Manufacturing Company's plant to more than double its present size.

The proposals were to fix the assessment of the Stratford Manufacturing Company for ten years at $7,500, and allow part of College Street to be closed, in return for the company adding a new factory 160 by 60, three stories high, and employing 75 hands in the manufacture of lawn-swings, ladders and porch furniture. This by-law was carried by 1,584 votes to 87.

Charles Diebel of Hanover is to erect a factory 150 by 50, three stories in height, employing 50 hands in the manufacture of furniture frames. The city grants $3,500 towards a site, and fixes the assessment at $7,500 for ten years for general taxes. The vote was, for 1,557, against 114.

John Morlock, also of Hanover, is to build, for the purposes of high-class upholstering, two factory buildings, one 100 by 45 and the other 50 by 45, and to employ 50 hands. The city grants $2,500 for site, and fixes the assessment at $7,500, except for schools and local improvements. This by-law received 1,550 favorable votes and 121 contrary.

ENGLISH FURNITURE HOUSE AT COAST

Announcement has been made by J. Wentworth, of Montreal, representing Waring & Gillow, Ltd., of London, England, said to be the largest upholstery manufacturers in the world, that his firm had practically decided to establish a manufacturing and distributing branch at either Vancouver or Victoria. This firm supplies the Royal households in England, and in addition has a large colonial and general trade. It employs thousands of men.

"The growth of our business in Western Canada," said Mr. Wentworth, "has led to the decision to establish a branch on the Coast. Another reason is that a branch factory here will put us in a good strategic position to go after orders in the Orient. This is a business which is capable of great expansion in the future."

Light, summery rocker made of Chinese glass.

The Furniture Record tells of a furniture display in New York that included a card bearing the line "The Acme of Refinement in Furniture Sheraton Period." A young couple looked for a long time at the exhibit and then the man said, "Gee, but ain't that acme wood beautiful."

SALESPEOPLE

Why Wiggins Secured The Order

"Business is rotten," the heavy set chap with the big black case, scowled and gazed out of the window at the passing scenery.

He was covering some new territory for the house and orders had been scarce, for a fact. His lines were right up to the minute, he had good prices and worked hard, but there seemed a snag somewhere, some "nigger in the wood pile" was responsible for the lack of business.

Reaching the next town he swung down from the train—lugged the big sample case over to Gordon, sought the buyer, who happened to be J. J. Gordon, a wide-awake, alert man with hair streaked with gray. He met Wiggins cordially, asked him back to the office and went over the salesman's proposition attentively.

"Well, Mr. Wiggins, I haven't heard much of your house, but your goods look right and the prices seem O.K. What are you doing in advertising and sales helps?"

Wiggins drew a long breath, he was literally up against it. Advertising and sales-helps were not a part of his stock in trade; his concern hired the best men possible and handled quality lines at fair prices. It was up to the men in the field to get the business. It was up to the dealer to sell the goods when purchased.

"Mr. Gordon," said Wiggins, making a desperate attempt to face down the matter. "I don't believe you appreciate one fact. The goods I offer you are sold at such a close margin my firm cannot afford to put money into advertising. If we add a large advertising expense to the goods, you have to pay it. We find our trade can sell goods without the added expense and you can make more money. I am certain you will agree with me."

Wiggins knew the argument was weak, and furthermore he knew that GORDON knew it was weak.

"Let's see," answered Gordon, turning to his catalogue files. "I am handling several standard advertised lines in the store, and I have the price lists here of various makers of similar goods. Let's compare some of them." Running his finger down list after list Gordon showed Wiggins conclusively that prices for the advertised lines were as low—in some instances lower than "stock lines."

Turning finally to the discomfited salesman, Gordon said. "Mr. Wiggins, modern business methods differ from those of even a few years ago. Once we felt somewhat about advertised lines as you say your house does. To-day we know differently.

"We welcome the efforts of the manufacturer who not only produces good goods, but who comes out in the open and co-operates with us and gives us sales and advertising aids.

"I have stocked nearly all the standard, advertised lines in various departments and our records show sales away ahead on the advertised lines as against the unknown brands we try to push ourselves. It is a business policy to work along the lines of least resistance, and, therefore, I will have to pass you up."

Wiggins sighed. He had found the cause of his failure to land business. He had a strong standing with his house, and determined to go in and have a heart-to-heart talk with the general manager. If other concerns were gathering in the shekels by co-operating with the dealers, his house must fall in line, or Wiggins would connect with a concern that DID do so.

"Mr. Gordon," Wiggins spoke very earnestly. "I believe after all you are right. I have seen the tendency of manufacturers and wholesalers along advertising lines, and candidly I have had to buck mighty hard to overcome the thing. I will ask you candidly, as man to man, if my concern uses a sales plan among your trade to introduce and popularize their lines will you give it favorable consideration?"

"Gladly, gladly. Your goods are all right and your prices, and I am certain there will be no necessity for a raise if your house goes after the business right, increased output will take care of the expense end. Come and see me if your house wakes up and I'll be sure to look you over."

Wiggins shook hands heartily and went out. He made no more stops at any station, but hiked straight into the house. He had a long talk with the manager, a conference was held. An advertising man was called in and details were raked over with a fine tooth comb.

Several months later Wiggins was seen coming from Gordon & Gordon's, a smile on his face. His order book contained a fat order, not only from Gordon's, but from dealers all along the line. His concern had seen the light and had acted vigorously with the result that the "nigger in the wood pile" had been chased across lots and was seen no more on any of the routes of the boys of Wiggins' house.—Furniture Retailer and House Furnisher.

DO YOU LIKE YOUR JOB?

There are to-day any number of men who do not like their jobs. Yet it's no fault of the job. It's no fault of the man who provided the job. It's the fault of the job owner—you. You're disgruntled and sour and indifferent because you don't go to work. You'd like your job all right if you let yourself out. You're in the hum-drum stage. Day after day you do the same things and think the same thoughts. You arrive on the minute maybe, but you surely quit on the minute. These are your troubles, sir. Just as soon as you start something, just as soon as you pull yourself together, make some noise and clear out of your old rut—you'll like your job. You see, you want the firm to take some notice of you, but you don't do anything to command notice. If you want to get talked about and consulted with and advanced, throw your whole heart and energy into your work and you'll begin to love it in spite of yourself.—The Courier.

WILL WHYTE'S NEW LINE.

The Hepworth Manufacturing Co., Hepworth, Ont., is now represented in Western Ontario by Will J. Whyte, of Strathroy, the author of the catchy and suggestive phrase: "Let's chit and chat and tarry a while." He still continues to represent the Strathroy Furniture Co.

Some of the boys at the recent furniture exhibition wanted Whytie to explain what "chit" meant, and it cost him about a dollar and thirty cents to do so.

But it costs most dealers more than that to "tarry a while" with W. J. W., as if they tarry he usually gets an order.

How to Proportion Profit on Selling Price to Cost

Subscriber asks for method of finding out what percentage must be added to cost to equal certain percentage on selling price

MERCHANTS are beginning to realize the great importance of figuring profits correctly in their business. Failure to realize that advance on cost does not mean the same percentage on sales has meant disaster to not a few business men. This is something that should constantly be kept in mind—25 per cent. on cost only means 20 per cent. on sales. For the reason that expenses are figured on the selling price, merchants are beginning to realize that the safe method is to always figure profits on the selling price.

Reader Asks for Method of Figuring

Here is a letter from a dealer to this paper asking for a quick method of finding out what percentage must be added to cost to equal a certain percentage on the selling price:

Editor:

I realize that profits should be figured on the selling price, because it is the safest, as I figure expenses on selling price. However, I would like to know the method of how you change a percentage on sales to a percentage on cost basis. For instance, I know that to make 20 per cent. on selling price I must add 25 per cent. to cost of goods, but what is the formula for arriving at this? I can find it by frequent "tries" until I get it right, but would like a "short cut" method.

Yours truly,
Yours for Profit.

Method of Reasoning it out

This is a question that has puzzled not a few dealers. They know that 20 per cent. on sales means 25 per cent. on cost, but have no method of arriving at it only by frequent "tries," as in the case of this dealer. If they wanted to find what 27 per cent. on selling price meant on cost price, they would have a great deal of figuring. We will take 20 per cent. on selling price and follow the method of reasoning by which it is reduced to percentage on cost.

You want to make 20 per cent. on selling price or 20 cents on $1.00.

Cost of article must, therefore, be 80c.
Therefore figuring on cost:
On 80c. you make 20c.

On $1.00 you make $\dfrac{100 \times 20}{80}$ equals 25c.

This equals 25 per cent.

Therefore 20 per cent. on selling price equals 25 per cent. on cost.

Must Add 25 per cent. to Cost to Make 20 per cent. on Selling Price

If an article costs $2.00 and you want to make 20 per cent. on the selling price, you must add 25 per cent. to the cost price. The selling price is $2.50—you make 50 cents or 20 per cent. on selling price.

Let us figure out another problem. You buy goods at $2.25. You have figured your average expenses at 19 per cent. and want to make 6 per cent. net profit. The total per cent. you must make on the sales price is 25 per cent. What will you have to add to the cost to make this?

If you made 25 per cent. on a dollar, goods would have to cost 75 cents. Figuring on cost:

On 75 cents you make 25c.

On $1.00 you make $\dfrac{100 \times 25}{75}$ equals 33 1-3 cents.

Therefore you will have to add 33 1-3 per cent. to cost ($2.25), which equals 75 cents. The selling price would have to be $3.00.

Table Showing Equivalent

It is rather a bother for a dealer to have to figure out percentage on selling price to a percentage on cost basis each time he wants to mark any goods or ascertain if a certain line allows a sufficient amount of profit. Here is a table showing the equivalents, that the dealer would do well to keep in a handy place. It shows the per cents. to add to gross cost to get per cents. on the selling total of from 5 up to 50 per cent.:

To make 5 p.c. on selling price add 5.263 to cost
To make 6 p.c. on selling price add 6.383 to cost
To make 7 p.c. on selling price add 7.527 to cost
To make 8 p.c. on selling price add 8.696 to cost
To make 9 p.c. on selling price add 9.89 to cost
To make 10 p.c. on selling price add 11.11 to cost
To make 11 p.c. on selling price add 12.36 to cost
To make 12 p.c. on selling price add 13.63 to cost
To make 13 p.c. on selling price add 14.94 to cost
To make 14 p.c. on selling price add 16.27 to cost
To make 15 p.c. on selling price add 17.64 to cost
To make 16 p.c. on selling price add 19.04 to cost
To make 17 p.c. on selling price add 20.48 to cost
To make 18 p.c. on selling price add 21.95 to cost
To make 19 p.c. on selling price add 23.45 to cost
To make 20 p.c. on selling price add 25   to cost
To make 22 p.c. on selling price add 28.2   to cost
To make 24 p.c. on selling price add 31.58 to cost
To make 25 p.c. on selling price add 33.33 to cost
To make 28 p.c. on selling price add 38.9   to cost
To make 30 p.c. on selling price add 42.85 to cost
To make 33 1-3 p.c. on selling price add 48.42 to cost
To make 35 p.c. on selling price add 53.846 to cost
To make 40 p.c. on selling price add 66.67 to cost
To make 50 p.c. on selling price add 100   to cost

Cost Means More Than Invoice Price

This table if kept at hand will allow the merchant in a moment's time to find out what he must add to the cost of his goods to make a certain per cent. of profit. It should always be borne in mind that cost means the gross cost and not merely the invoice price. You must know the exact cost of your goods laid down in the store ready for sale, with freight and other charges added. There is often a material difference between the invoice price and the actual cost of the goods which must be taken into consideration in figuring profits. It should also be remembered that percentage on cost does not mean the same percentage on sales.

THE DEALER who courts success must concern himself with profits. Failure to understand the correct figuring of profits has been the shoal on which many a merchant has gone aground. Make certain that you understand the question thoroughly.

Ontario Retail Merchants Hold Annual Convention

In Toronto on Feb. 25 and 26—Many questions of interest to the retail trade brought up and dealt with—J. C. Van Camp, of Toronto, elected president for ensuing year.

BY A STAFF REPRESENTATIVE

THE fifteenth annual convention of the Ontario Provincial Board of the Retail Merchants' Association of Canada was held in the Temple Building, Toronto, on Wednesday and Thursday, February 25 and 26, when a big variety of questions of general interest and concern to retail merchants were discussed and dealt with. A feature of the convention was a banquet on Wednesday evening, when a much-appreciated address was delivered by A. F. Sheldon, the well-known business educator of Chicago, Ill., on "The Science of Building a Retail Business."

Need of Organization.

Wednesday morning was taken up with the registration and reception of delegates. When the session opened in the afternoon, the address of welcome of J. C. Van Camp, President of the Toronto branch, was read by F. C. Higgins. It referred to the progress made during the past year, and pointed out that never before has there been more need of a strong organization than to-day, especially with the big cry regarding the high cost of living, for which the retailer is being blamed.

B. W. Ziemann, President of the Dominion Board, in replying, referred to the wonderful strides made during the past few years, and hoped that the association would soon take the place in the commercial world that it is destined to. He touched upon the question of the high cost of living, placing much of the blame on the changing conditions that have added to cost.

Advocates Fire Insurance Inspector.

E. C. Matthews, retiring President, in his address, pointed out that the retailers were the largest commercial class in the Province, and were so necessary that they could not be dispensed with. He referred to the value of association work, and trusted that retailers would not only become members, but take a real interest in the work. He advocated the engaging of a first-class fire insurance inspector to go from town to town and inspect the policies and premises of retailers.

The considering of resolutions began on Wednesday afternoon. The first question was the proposed appointment of a fire marshal for the Province of Ontario by the Government. It was felt that such a fire marshal should be appointed under the direction and authority of a Minister of the Crown, so that in the event of any severe restrictive measures being imposed by the fire marshal, or his deputies, that retail merchants may have access to the Minister, and be able to lay their complaints before him, and a resolution was passed to this effect.

Workmen's Compensation and Parcel Post.

The association will ask that the proposed Workmen's Compensation Act be amended, so that retail merchants cannot be included by the Board, as is possible according to the act at present proposed, but only through an amendment to the act itself, passed by the Government. G. B. Ryan of Guelph said he had gone through the proposed bill, and believed that it would be a heavy expense to maintain.

Many of the daily newspapers have been clamoring for an increase in the first zone in the parcel post system, and also for an increase in the maximum weight of parcels carried. The convention passed a resolution that no change should be made in the present parcel post system, as recently adopted by the Government, until it has been fully worked out and tested, and that it would be insisted, that as far as possible, it be self-sustaining.

Much Discussion on Pedlar Question

The question of pedlars was one that came in for a good deal of discussion, and views on the matter were many and varied. Some thought that the farmers should not be privileged to peddle if competition with the retail grocer who pays a business tax, even if they do produce their own goods, but it was considered an unwise time to ask that any license be put on them, as there is such a cry at the present time about bringing producers and consumers together in an effort to reduce the high cost of living. Some thought that nothing should be done to prevent farmers from coming into town. Some suggested that the merchant, wherever possible, should buy the farmers' produce himself. One thing was agreed upon—that the Pedlars' Act should be put in English that can be interpreted.

Retailer Paying Cartage at Both Ends

When the convention opened on Thursday morning, the question of cartage being paid for at both ends by the retailer came up, and many views on the matter were expressed. Eric Jamieson, of Hamilton, pointed out that many dealers look at invoice and set selling price accordingly without taking cartage, etc., into consideration. If cartage was paid by wholesaler and included in invoice, it would eliminate this mistake. T. B. Cramp, of Orillia, would like to have goods delivered free at home station, thus eliminating possibility of making any mistake in setting prices. The question will be passed on to the Dominion Board after views of retailers have been secured.

Payment of Freight and Express Claims

Following this, the securing of payment of claims from express and freight companies, was taken up. T. B. Cramp, of Orillia, thought that much of the diffi-

---

OFFICERS ELECTED.

The officers of the Ontario Provincial Board of the Retail Merchants' Association elected for the ensuing year were as follows:—

President: B. W. Ziemann, Preston.
First Vice-President, A. M. Patterson, Brockville.
Second Vice-President, R. D. Cameron, Lucknow.
Treasurer, F. C. Higgins, Toronto.
Secretary, E. M. Trowern, Toronto.

culty could be overcome by seeing that claims were put in, in proper form. It was pointed out by a Midland man that where there is only one railroad, that you do not get as prompt consideration as if two, and he finds it an excellent plan to put claim in through the wholesale house, letting them send you a credit note for amount.

New Proposal in Place of Bulk Sales Act

It was reported that the proposed Bulk Sales Act in Ontario had been abandoned by the Canadian Credit Men's Association, and that in its place the joint committees from the Retail Merchants' Association and the Canadian Credit Men's Association had agreed on a new proposal, thought to give the desired protection to wholesalers, but without any great burden on the retailer. The new proposal is simply that all retail merchants who propose selling out their businesses, should be compelled by law, to give all their creditors fifteen days' notice of their purpose. Several members thought that it would be a serious matter to have to give notice to "all" their creditors, for as one man expressed it, "Even if a man was willing to do this, and happened to forget one creditor of a small amount, he would be liable to prosecution." The proposal was referred back to the committee to have the proposed bill framed up and submitted to the association before being submitted to parliament. Mr. Trowern pointed out that it was proposed to include farmers and boarding house keepers in the act, so that it would also give protection to the retailer, as well as the wholesaler.

A resolution was passed recommending that the retail trade assist themselves and also the wholesalers and manufacturers by reporting to the head office of the association all cases of severe price-cutting, and all cases wherein the merchants know there is likelihood of any retailer offering his goods in such a manner as to demoralize the trade and eventually deceive his creditors.

Many Resolutions Passed

Other resolutions passed by the convention were as follows:

That the question of reducing the business tax rate to 10 per cent. throughout the province be again taken up with the government.

That information be secured as to whether retail merchants are favorable to a special tax on large mail order catalogue houses, and that the money so secured would be paid into the various municipalities from which it is taken.

That more consideration be given to retail interests in literature sent out by municipalities.

That the head office be consulted before subscribing to any collecting associations or agencies.

That proposed legislation of the city of Toronto, to place a special tax on all vehicles used by retailers be strenuously opposed.

That the Ontario Government be again urged to appoint a Minister of Inland Trade.

Commend Dominion Board in asking for legislation that will make false advertising of merchandise a crime.

That further steps be taken to press the amendments to the Division Court Act, regarding garnishees and simplifying the collection of small debts.

That customers should be made equally responsible as merchants for violating law regarding Sunday selling.

Finance Committee Appointed

Mr. Dargavel, member of the Provincial House for Leeds, was one of the speakers of the afternoon. The secretary's and treasurer's reports were also presented outlining and giving particulars of what had been done during the year. Messrs. J. C. Van Camp and Thos. Bartrem, of Toronto, and R. J. McCrea, of Guelph, were appointed a finance committee to examine the treasurer's report and report on same to each branch association. Instructions were also passed that a copy of the secretary's and treasurer's reports be sent to each member of this committee before the next annual meeting, so that they may examine same and bring in a report to the convention while in session.

The representatives on the Dominion Board appointed were: A. Weseloh, of Berlin; R. D. Cameron, of Lucknow; F. C. Higgins, Toronto; A. M. Patterson, Brockville, and Secretary Trowern. Henry Watters, of Ottawa, was appointed as representative on the Toronto Exhibition Board.

ABOUT HONESTY

It is a fine thing for a store to have the reputation of being entirely honest in all of its dealings, but we doubt if such a reputation can be acquired through advertising, says Show Window. We are inclined to believe that the "holier than thou" advertising that is used by some merchants fails to accomplish any very great results. If a store is honest, the people will find it out soon enough—and an inclination to dishonesty will be discovered quite as quickly. The occasion for these remarks lies in an argument that has been running in the advertisements of two stores in an eastern city as to which is the more honest—at least that is what their arguments amount to. Both claim to have preceded the other in the matter of establishing the one-price system. As their arguments take them back nearly half a century, it seems hardly probable that the present day shopper will become wildly excited as to which store has the prior claim to the contested distinction. This sort of advertising, if such it can be called, seems all the more useless since both stores are widely known for their honesty.

WANT LEGISLATION TO ENABLE THEM TO SECURE WEEKLY HALF-HOLIDAY.

Eric C. Jamieson, of Hamilton, Ont., introduced a resolution at the Retail Merchants' Convention to secure legislation that will enable merchants to close their stores on any one afternoon of the week. At the present time, if 75 per cent. of the merchants in any municipality apply to the council, they must pass a resolution compelling the early closing of stores in the evening. It is desired that the same legislation be extended to include one afternoon of the week as well as nights, and a resolution along this line was passed.

Mr. Jamieson has been heading a movement in Hamilton to secure the Wednesday half-holiday, all-the-year-round, and several meetings of grocers and butchers have been held. Mr. Jamieson and his supporters in the movement are trying to get all stores to close by mutual agreement, but failing in this, they think they should have recourse to a by-law to compel them.

Dominion Board R.M.A. Meeting

The Ninth Annual Convention of the Dominion Board of the Retail Merchants' Association of Canada was held in the Chateau Laurier, Ottawa, on Feb. 16th and 17th, during the time of the Hardware Convention and Manufacturers' Exhibition.

In order to return the courtesy of the Hardware dealers, the Dominion Board gave a banquet, to which they invited the leading hardware men, both dealers and manufacturers, at which the most friendly feelings prevailed. The necessarily short addresses all emphasized the importance of a better understanding of the relations of the manufacturer, wholesaler and retailer, and more union in their efforts to secure better methods, in order to render the best service to the people.

Some very important subjects were taken up by the Board at their several meetings. Among other matters they decided to press for legislation during the present session making false advertising a criminal offence.

They also desire the Criminal Code amended to prevent the giving of voting contest tickets, which is considered deceptive to the customers.

They approved of the proposed cold storage bill, with the exception of several clauses which affect the retailer.

They have very little fault to find with the parcel post as recently put in operation.

They will again present their requests to the Government, asking them to abolish the fees charged the retailer for the inspection of scales and measures.

They will also ask the Government to institute a department under a Minister of Trade and Commerce similar to the departments that are now in operation for the protection of the laboring and agricultural classes.

They also feel the necessity of an educational movement to show the consuming public the need of retail stores, and that the service depends largely on their support.

They also recommended that further steps be taken to press on amendments to the Division Court Act regarding garnishees, and simplifying the collection of small debts.

The following officers were elected for the ensuing year :—
President, B. W. Ziemann, Preston.
First Vice-President, W. U. Boivin, Montreal.
Second Vice-President, A. Weseloh, Berlin.
Treasurer, J. A. Beaudry, Montreal.
Secretary, E. W. Trowern, Toronto.
Auditor, J. G. Watson, Montreal.

CONVENTION OF B. C. RETAIL MERCHANTS
Discuss Bad Debt Problem

The British Columbia Retail Merchants' Association held their annual convention in Victoria, B.C., on Feb. 9 and 10, when a number of important resolutions dealing with trade problems were passed and put before the B. C. Government by a strong delegation. One of the things asked for is an amendment to the Capias Act, which at present does not effectively protect claims under $100. It is desired that the minimum amount should be changed to $10. They also want an amendment to the Garnishee Law re Exemption, in order that it may be more in favor of retail merchants. They want protection where wages are paid weekly or fortnightly, or where part of wages are advanced before regular pay day. It was also considered that the wife should be jointly liable for goods sold for the maintenance of the home.

Other Questions Considered

In addition to these questions regarding the collection of bad debts, other forms of protection for the retail trade were considered. It was asked that greater powers be given to municipal councils governing transient traders and peddlers, and that there be a special specific law governing advertising, so that same may be kept more within the bounds of truth.

That something should be done to prevent the spread of the habit, which was said to be becoming more general, of signing cheques without having the funds to cover them, was another conclusion. While there is recourse at present under the Criminal Code through the police court, it was reported as difficult to obtain convictions.

For the protection of the trade, it was thought that collection agencies should be bonded for an adequate sum by the Provincial Government.

The question of uniform closing of stores was another one that received considerable discussion.

FINE UPHOLSTERED FURNITURE CATALOGUE

The Montreal Upholstering Co., Montreal, are sending out to the trade their newest and latest catalogue of upholstered furniture, which has been considerably enlarged since its last issue. All manner of upholstered goods are illustrated and described. One of the new things is the Duofold divanette sofa bed, which is always ready for the unexpected guest, and is also a nice piece of furniture for the home, particularly in large cities, where space is at a premium. The Duofold comes in individuals and in suites. But this is but one line; others are the revolving seat bed davenports, library and den suites, couches, bed lounges, sofa beds, etc.

NORTH AMERICAN BENT CHAIR ENLARGE

A new wing, 200x100 feet, giving another 30,000 square feet, has been added to the North American Bent Chair Co., Ltd., Owen Sound. The entire plant has also been remodelled and newly-equipped, and new office furnished. J. G. Hay is now president; Jas. Garvie, secretary-treasurer, and the directors are W. G., D. A. and J. M. Hay and J. H. Bovell.

CONVENTION OF SASKATCHEWAN RETAIL MERCHANTS AT MOOSE JAW ON MARCH 23, 24 AND 25.

The second annual convention of the Saskatchewan Retail Merchants' Association was held in Moose Jaw on March 23, 24 and 25. There was a big attendance. Since the organization at Regina last year, one of the benefits that has been received in Saskatchewan through the efforts of this organization was the passage of an act at the last session of the Legislature creating a small debts court for the collection of sums of money under fifty dollars. This court is conducted by a magistrate or justice of the peace, and has already been placed in operation.

Furniture Manufacturing in B.C.

By James Hart

THE question has been raised many times as to the future of furniture-making in Vancouver and other coast towns in the Province of British Columbia, and has been answered many times and generally in the negative. It is claimed that furniture to be made profitably must be made at or near the point of supply for raw material. The bulk of the furniture business of the Province in certain lines at the present time is maintained by Grand Rapids, Toronto, the East and by England. The woods principally used in furniture manufacture are mahogany, oak and birch.

Now mahogany is not grown in Eastern Canada or Grand Rapids, and must be imported. None of the woods mentioned in this article are grown in commercial quantities in England and have all to be imported. Still Eastern Canada, Grand Rapids and England can and do ship furniture into this Province and at a price which the jobber, wholesale and retail merchants claim cannot be approached by the manufacturer in British Columbia. This does not sound reasonable, nor is it reasonable. Every business man knows that present freight rates debar the British Columbia manufacturer from the prairie markets, but with the seaboard this Province has, ocean freights should be in its favor. Take mahogany for instance. This timber is grown in South America, Central America and the Philippines, and oak is got from the East and from Japan and Manchuria. Shiploads could be brought in here cheaper or at least as cheap as to England, Eastern Canada or Grand Rapids; and although labor is higher, this item is offset by the cheaper ocean freight and the fact that the raw material after it is brought here has not to be reshipped after manufacture, but has the market at the door. Again this Province is enormously wealthy in timber, some of which is certainly suitable for the rougher and poorer grades of furniture.

It will appear, therefore, that the freight rate is not the stumbling block so far as British Columbia is concerned. Higher wage rate does not figure as shown above. It is not the lack of labor, as there is and always has been a sufficient supply of skilled labor to meet the demand. Then what is it? Does the trouble lie in the want of enterprise or the method of the British Columbia manufacturer? Or is it the fault of the merchant and the public not creating the demand? I do not think it is the want of enterprise, as Vancouver has a number of shrewd men in the business. The fault lies with the merchant and the public. It is claimed that at present that furniture made in British Columbia is dearer than imported furniture of the same grade. This may be admitted, and can also be explained. Furniture makers in England, America and Eastern Canada have been long established, have obtained such a market for their products that they can divide the business amongst the various factories and still maintain prices. This is done by standardizing and specializing. The demand has become so great for certain standard lines that a factory makes one line alone and specializes in that line and has all it can do to keep the demand supplied. Those lines are turned out by the thousand and naturally much cheaper than from the factory where a mixed class of furniture is made and where a large stock cannot be carried.

The merchants and furniture dealers here state they are willing to patronize home industry if they can get the price, the quality and the workmanship. That is a poor stand to take, and is not logical. Let any of the large merchants place an order with a local firm for a year's supply, deliveries to be at stated periods. They are all business men and when ordering will naturally insist on a certain standard and specification. If the first delivery is not to standard, it will be his option to cancel the order, and the manufacturer will have himself to blame. But until such an order is given it is not fair play to condemn. The practice at present is to give the local man orders for furniture which is not standard and therefore not in stock. This is special work, and because the price is higher than Eastern standard stock material, the British Columbia goods are condemned. Let a merchant send East, however, for the special article and see how the price compares after the freight is taken into account, without even mentioning the loss of time in obtaining the article, and in these days time is money. High rent and excessive charges for factory sites are deterrents in the way of this as well as other industries, but if those can be obtained anyway reasonable, I think this is the time to start the business on an extensive scale. New transcontinental railways coming here will undoubtedly reduce freight and open the prairie Provinces (Alberta and Saskatchewan should be British Columbia furniture territory). Money stringency is opening the eyes of the public to the necessity of patronizing home industries. The opening of the Panama Canal will, we hope and expect, give us better rates for shipping the raw material to the Province, and the recent establishing of an up-to-date tannery overcomes the upholstering difficulty.

At present there are approximately three hundred men employed in furniture manufacturing in British Columbia. The market in British Columbia alone warrants the employment of at least three thousand men, and it does not need much thought to arrive at the benefit to the province at large of the addition to the population of three thousand skilled artisans with constant employment. With the opening of prairie markets and other advantages mentioned, there should be in the next ten years at least six thousand men in the furniture business, and it is up to the purchasing public to see that this becomes an accomplished fact. This can only be through the encouragement of existing factories by purchasing their product.—*Industrial Progress and Commercial Record.*

CATALOGUES HANDY FOR SPECIAL ORDERS

The furniture merchant who doesn't sell anything but what he has right in the store, is almost unknown.

Every dealer is willing to take orders for other goods than those in stock, and most merchants are looking for such orders.

This special order business can be developed just as far as the dealer likes.

Most dealers take special orders only when a customer comes in and asks for something not in stock. Under these conditions the dealer says: "We haven't got a dresser exactly like that, but we can easily get it for you." This is good, but not good enough.

Your catalogue file should be so handy, so well indexed and cross-indexed by name, subject and kind, that you can show your party a picture of the thing he wants, and get the order.

There should be no delay in finding the book and the illustration. You have it in front of your customer before he has time to say, "Well I'll see."

A catalogue in a customer's hands acts as a display of goods might act in developing and making sales.

Knobs of News

The Great Western Furniture Co. are erecting a five-storey warehouse at Saskatoon.

Toronto Upholsterers and Furniture Dealers is a concern recently incorporated at Toronto.

Mrs. J. W. Herbert, Montreal, has disposed of her furniture stock.

Betts, Frank & Co., Yorkton, Sask., have sold their furniture business.

Studer & Co., Didsbury, Alta., suffered a loss through fire in their furniture store recently.

A big fire at Didsbury, Alta., destroyed J. X. Berscht's furniture store. The store and stock were partially insured.

Wilders & Son, Toronto, are building a new furniture warehouse.

The Department of Trade and Commerce, Ottawa (Enquiries Branch), report that a Havana, Cuba, brokerage firm want the names of Canadian furniture manufacturers.

J. S. Prince Co.'s furniture store, Montreal, was damaged by fire recently.

The North Vancouver Furniture Co, have removed from their old stand to 830 Granville Street, Vancouver.

Chas. Shapiro has become sole proprietor of the Hamilton House Furnishing Co., Hamilton, S. Cohen having retired.

The Dupont Fabrikoid Co., Inc., Wilmington, Del., have taken over the Cotton Mfg. Co.'s business and plant at Toronto, and will conduct same as a Canadian branch of their concern. W. A. Cotton will continue as manager and W. Purtle as traveling salesman.

The Cooper Furniture Co., Saskatoon, has bought out the business of the Nelan Furniture Co., of the same place.

Robert McJannett, formerly with the Cope Fletcher Furniture Co., Ltd., Saskatoon, has been appointed manager and buyer for the furniture department of the F. R. Macmillan department store, Saskatoon

Bruno Graffunder, for some time buyer and manager of the furniture department of the Hudson Bay Co., at Kamloops, B.C., has resigned his position to take full charge of the Howson Furniture Co., Ltd., Revelstoke, B.C. The change took place on March 1.

C. H. Vrooman, Boisevain, Man., recently held a dispersion sale of his furniture stock at that place, and has purchased the furniture and undertaking business of Robertson & Son, Manitou, Man.

Dewitt Bros., Napinka, Man., are succeeded by Dewitt & Dunbar.

Higgins & Webster, Morris, Man., are succeeded by the F. H. Higgins Co., Ltd., and are enlarging their furniture department.

J. M. Baum & Co., furniture dealers, 1022 Granville St., Vancouver, have just installed an entirely new front of two windows. The entire interior is surrounded by a balcony, adding greatly to the floor space. The exterior and interior is in white, which lends greatly to the furniture display.

Canadian Baby Car Co., Ltd., Montreal, is the name of a new company recently incorporated at Ottawa to make baby carriages, bicycles, etc. The capital is set at $300,000, and the incorporators are: Napoleon Nantel, engineer; Joseph Arthur Myette, jeweler; Henri de Lanauze, machinist; Georges Serouille de Ber, agent, and Gaspard Thouin, all of Montreal.

George Cooper has purchased the furniture business of J. H. McCalpin, at Killarney, Man.

R. McLellan has commenced a furniture and undertaking establishment at Neville, Sask.

Lande Bros.' furniture stock at Montreal was damaged by fire recently. It was fully insured.

Letters patent have been issued incorporating George McLagan, David Mackenzie Wright, Julian Griffith Davies and Hugh Shaw Robertson, manufacturers, and Frederick George Scrimegour, superintendent, all of Stratford, as the "Classic Furniture, Limited," with a capital stock of $200,000.

The big gale on March 1 did considerable damage in and around Woodstock. About 20 feet of brick wall on the north side of the Canada Furniture factory gave way, a lot of debris falling into the packing-room, destroying considerable stock. The loss is estimated at $1,000.

On either side are two new living-room chairs made by J. P. Albrough & Co., Ingersoll.

In the centre is one of the latest diner productions of Baetz Bros., Berlin.

On either side two china cabinets; in centre library table—three new items in The Geo. McLagan Furniture Co.'s lines.

Fox Bros., Melville, Sask., have sold out their furniture business.

Baum & Brody, furniture dealers, Windsor, Ont., have added 4,000 square feet of floor space to their Sandwich Street store, taking in the second and third storeys over what was formerly the Oddfellows' temple.

The Home Furnishing Co., at Redcliff, Alta., have sold out their business.

Sill, Paterson & Millar, Ltd., have opened a furniture and undertaking parlors at Vancouver. D. A. Smith Co. secured the opening furniture order. Mr. Sill, senior member of the new firm, is well known throughout the trade of Eastern Canada and the United States.

The Kemp Furniture, Amherstburg, Ont., have added an automobile agency to their business.

Ben Hollenburg, of Hollenburg Brothers, furniture dealers, Fort William, has returned from a business trip to New York, Buffalo, Montreal, Hamilton and Toronto.

Geo. Gale & Sons have removed their Toronto stock from the old warehouse at 189 Queen Street East, to their own new building, at 370-374 Pape Avenue.

Owing to other business, Robert Doan is offering his stock of stoves and furniture, at Welland, for sale, in order to clear out. Also he is offering his shop for rent, as well as three automobiles.

The furniture business which has been conducted during the past couple of months by J. Fritz, at Clifford, Ont., has again changed hands, the former proprietor, Mr. Runge, having re-purchased the business. Mr. Runge, after visiting a number of places, decided that there was no better location for his line of business than right in Clifford, and decided to again embark in the trade. He will, as soon as spring opens, erect a new store for his trade, which was an extensive one previous to the fire last fall.

Ald. Matt. Watt has disposed of his furniture business at Galt to J. H. Rutherford, who has taken possession and in future will conduct the establishment. Mr. Rutherford was formerly with F. H. Chapple and A. E. Willard, and is thoroughly experienced in the business he has entered. He will deal in both new and second-hand furniture.

The Board of Managers of the Kincardine General Hospital acknowledged with thanks a donation of $50 in aid of the general fund from Andrew Malcolm.

The Elmira Furniture Company have started working overtime in order to get out the orders on hand.

LETTER BOX

Old Hickory and Sea Grass Furniture.

H. Hilder & Co., home furnishers, Welland, Ont., write The Furniture World asking the names of some makers of old hickory and sea grass furniture.

Old Hickory Furniture Co., Martinsville, Ind., make the former, and The Jennings Co., St. Thomas, Ont., import the latter.—Editor.

One-piece Chiffonier Wardrobe Wanted

The Edwards Furniture Co., Sherbrooke, Que., write The Furniture World asking the name and address of a manufacturer who makes "a chiffonier-wardrobe that is, a single piece of furniture having a mirror with drawers underneath on one side, and a wardrobe with door on the other."

Can any of our readers supply the information?—Editor.

PREPARING FOR BIG SEASON

The Durham Furniture Company, according to a recent despatch, is getting an immense amount of timber this winter. At their four mills, Dornoch, Rock Mills, Ceylon and Durham, the yards are all filling up rapidly, and the total turning will be much larger than in any former season. From their own timber lands they have taken out over a million feet, and they expect before the close of the winter to have over four and a half million feet of logs in their four yards.

FAVORITE FURNITURE FASHIONS.

The Orillia Furniture Co., Ltd., Orillia, Ont., have in their newest catalogue a pictorial description of their furniture products. A big line with them is their extensive line of dining extension tables, all of which are supplied with solid pedestal up to six feet, and fitted with duostyle patent lock in eight or ten feet. The line is almost wholly made up of oak, either plain or quartered. Buffets are another big line, as also are fancy all-wood parlor and library tables. The bedroom line embrace washstands, dressing tables, dressers, chiffoniers, etc., all of them illustrated by sample in the catalogue.

The Furniture Manufacturer

A Department of News and Ideas

Gossip for the Furniture Manufacturer

IT is unfortunate that manufacturers in Ontario find it necessary to oppose the Workmen's Compensation bill, as it has been prepared by Sir W. Meredith for submission to the Legislature at its present session. But that there is a necessity, there can be no doubt.

Manufacturers are not, as a whole at any rate, opposed to legislative action on the subject of compensation. On the contrary, they realize that the present system is not only out of date, but is cumbersome and costly to all concerned.

The average manufacturer desires to deal fairly with his workmen, but he doesn't want a burden imposed upon him which promises to be serious in its consequences. This the draft bill threatens to do if adopted by the Legislature as it stands at present.

To carefully study the draft bill is not perhaps a pleasant task, particularly to the lay mind. But it is a necessary task, which no manufacturer should hesitate to undertake. The legal department of the Canadian Manufacturers' Association has made his way comparatively easy by the copies of the draft bill with annotations which it has issued. And when the provisions of the bill have been digested the next step should be a letter to his representative in the Legislature setting forth his conclusions. To talk the matter over with him would be still better.

FURNITURE manufacturers have learned that one of the great sources of expense, and conversely, of profit, lies in unnecessary handling of lumber. A writer in The Furniture Manufacturer, dealing with this subject, says that one of the best devices he has seen for handling lumber into a box or flat car consists of an upright of hardwood about three by six inches in size, at the top end of which are attached two hooks, set at an angle, which are thrown over the edge of the roof of a box car or over the top of a car stake. About twelve inches apart on the flat side of the piece are set eye-rings. Into alternate eye-rings the two supports of a steel arm about two and one-half feet long, terminating in a roughened point, fit. The horizontal portion of the arm terminates in a hook which fits into one eye-ring, while the brace of the arm fits into a second eye-ring below. This arm can instantly be slipped out or raised to higher eye-rings, as the load of lumber is increased in height. The arm is not constructed exactly horizontal, but at a slight angle, so that its weight throws it out at right angles with the car. In use, a board about one-third of its length from the man handling it, is lifted on the end of the arm, and the other end pushed forward onto a flat car or across the regulation roller into a box car door. This pushes it around nearly parallel to the car. When the board is released the arm drops back into position at right angles with the car. It is believed that with one of these rigs one man can handle more lumber off a wagon, lorry or truck than two men can handle without its use.

The subject is one which may interest furniture manufacturers in Canada.

DR. J. W. ROBERTSON, chairman of the Royal Commission, is now going up and down the country preaching the evangel of technical education. He realizes that the report, excellent and all as it may be, will not in itself bring about that industrial efficiency which the necessities of the country demand.

Public opinion must be stirred, for the Federal and Provincial Governments will only keep pace with what they deem the demands of the people.

To get ahead of public opinion may sometimes be the quality of individuals, but of Governments, never. They only move as the spirit of public opinion impels them.

A movement is now on foot to organize technical education associations throughout Canada whose object will be to not only stir up public opinion, but to back up the recommendations of the Royal Commission in regard to Federal, Provincial and local aid in regard to establishing technical and vocational schools.

We may naturally expect that the leaders in this movement will be the manufacturers. As a class they have the most to gain, and from the interest many of them have already exhibited, there can be no doubt where they will stand in this great industrial movement, which promises soon to be under substantial heading.

PROFIT-SHARING seems to be gradually getting more fashionable. Among the most recent to fall into line is a furniture company in Pennsylvania. It has notified its employees that it has decided to recognize its employees in proportion to their faithfulness and efficiency by giving them a share in the profits. The company offers to present to each employee in its employ at the close of the year 1914 3 to 5 per cent. on the total amount of the wages received by such employees from the company during the year 1914. The company does not obligate itself to extend this recognition to its employees. It is subject to the faithfulness and efficiency of the employees and depends upon the successful outcome of the year's business.

A FINISHING ROOM COST SYSTEM
By Edmund Chase in the Furniture Manufacturer

The right stain and the right finish are the desire of every furniture manufacturer and paint shop foreman. These two items are more important than construction or style, for without them, no matter how well designed or made the product may be, it will not have a commanding sale. Many manufacturers and their foremen feel that they have attained this stain and finish. Since their goods sell in increasing amounts this supposition is fairly correct. Granting that their finish and color are correct, what does it cost them?

You ask the foreman in many shops as to what it costs him to finish his golden oak or any other color, and he replies that it takes about so much of this and so much of that to finish a dozen or a hundred pieces. Up to a certain degree, and a varying one, he is correct. For if you ask him how he knows, his reply is apt to be that when that pattern first came through the shop he measured the amounts of the various materials used on a certain number of pieces. This is the end so far as costs go. He has made no allowance for differences in the quality of the materials used, the great variation in wood textures even in the same kind of wood, the effect of temperature and humidity on the varnishes. His were right, but only for that one time.

Where the conditions under which the materials are being used are such an important factor in the amount used a more accurate system of costs should be established. Such a system I believe is embodied in the following outline and will be of service to manufacturers and foremen.

Some changes may be necessary if varnish dip tanks are not used or if varnish drying kilns have not been installed. These changes will not affect the utility of the system, however.

The Beginning of the Cost System

The first step is to take a complete inventory of all the material used in finishing the stock after having left the finish sanding department. This inventory includes all the material in the shop or in the stock room. Second: Keep a record of all material in the line of finishing supplies that are received each day at the plant. This can be obtained from the foreman or stock clerk.

Third: At the end of any fixed period of time of some duration, two weeks or a month, take an inventory of all material on hand. Take this in the same manner as the one at the beginning.

The inventory taken at the end of the period can be carried forward so as to be used as the inventory to start the next period with.

Fourth: Open up accounts with the following:
No. 1. Sanding in the white.
No. 2. Each of the different stain tanks.
No. 3. Filling department.
No. 4. Each of the different varnish tanks, (if dip tanks are used.)
No. 5. Varnish drying department, (if varnish kilns are used.)
No. 6. Sanding between coats of varnish.
No. 7. Each of the brush coat finishes.
No. 8. Rubbing and polishing.
No. 9. Wrapping and bundling.
No. 10 Barn and cartage (if any.)
No. 11. Shipping.
No. 12. Foremen.
No. 13. General shop expense.
No. 14. Costing.

The following expansion of the above accounting titles explains more fully the method of keeping them.

No. 1. Sanding in the white. Keep an account of all sandpaper used on this work, so as to show the average cost per dozen or hundred. Take stop watch tests on various kinds of material and patterns going through to get the average time required to do each kind of stock and style.

No. 2. Each of the different stain tanks. Open accounts with each of the different tanks and keep them in the same form as the attached form No. 1. This will show the amount used during the month and will also show just what the mixture averages to cost for the month. It will also show just what the mixture is costing every day and also the cost for staining the different kinds of stock.

No. 3. Filling department. Keep an account so that at the end of the month it will show the amount used: the average amount used on the various patterns and the average time required to do the work in dozen or hundred lots.

No. 4. Each of the different varnish tanks. Keep accounts with these tanks the same as with the stain tanks.

No. 5. Varnish drying department. Keep an account of the total number of pieces dried to get the average cost per dozen or hundred.

No. 6. Sanding between coats of varnish or shellac. Keep this account the same as sanding in the white.

No. 7. Each of the brush coat finishes. Open up accounts with each of the different finishes such as: brush coat gloss; brush coat polish; brush coat shellac; also any other finishes that are used.

Always make a distinction between golden oak, mahogany, weathered oak and varnishing on the wood.

On each of the accounts for hand finishing, be sure and show the number of pieces finished and the amount of material used (see Form No. 2.)

This hand finishing requires close attention, and it would be a good plan for the cost man to measure the varnish each morning and to watch the hand finishing very closely during the day.

No. 8. Rubbing and polishing. This account must show the total amount of material used during the month so as to show the average cost per dozen or hundred on each style.

No. 9. Wrapping and bundling. Keep a record of all pieces wrapped and all bundled K. D. Also show the total amount of material used on this work during the month. Be sure and make a distinction between wrapped and bundled.

No. 10. Barn and cartage. Have this account show the total labor and material in this department. (This will, of course, include hay, straw, grain, shoeing, repairs on wagons and harnesses, etc.) At the end of the month show the average cost per dozen or hundred for cartage. The total number carted can be obtained from the shipper.

No. 11. Shipping. At the end of the month show the cost for shipping per dozen or hundred. Besides the shipper's time, all other time spent on the shipping must, of course, be included.

No. 12. Foremen. This will, of course, include the foreman's time, but if the foremen do any finishing be sure and charge it to the account to which it belongs.

No. 13. General shop expense. Charge to this account all labor spent in moving stock and miscellaneous shop items not chargeable to any particular account.

No. 14. Costing. This account will show the cost of labor for costing which, of course, includes the cost man's time and other labor spent in helping him.

The Operation of the System

By opening the different accounts at the time of and charging to each account the amount of material in each department, and keeping account of the material received in each department, at the end of the month it is easy to determine just the amount used in each department.

By doing this way, at the end of the month each process can be compared with the amount used and the amount allowed for the same.

On all day labor the costs must show the amount of work done. Care must be taken to charge to each account all the day labor chargeable to same together with the amount of work done.

All the piece work earnings can be charged each day to one account under the head of Piece Work Payroll.

At the end of the month, when making out the balance sheet, get from the bookkeeper the amount of the office payroll and the piecework payroll. These deducted from the total payroll will represent the day work payroll, which should balance with the amount of the day work charged to the different departments. Make up an exhibit at the end of each month showing just how each account figures out, showing the amount used with the amount allowed.

If the allowances are deficient in any of the processes they will have to be increased so as to agree with

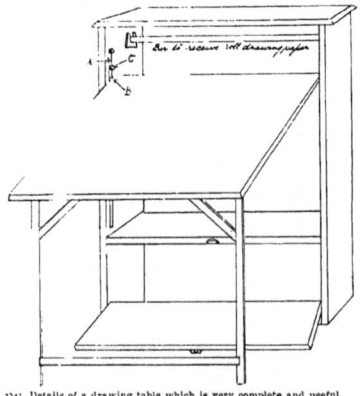

Details of a drawing table which is very complete and useful. A—¼" Groove; B—⅛" Dowel; C—Notch to receive dowel and hold back of drawing board.

the amount used. The new allowances will be used in comparing the next month's report. If the allowances are excessive they will of course be decreased and used in the same manner.

The cost man will, of course, keep costs on large lots going through the different processes so that in case he should increase or decrease his allowances he would have something to base his new allowances on. At the end of the month the expense accounts will be added together so as to show the total expense of the shop.

After the total expense is obtained then show the total general expense per dozen or hundred. The expense for each department, also the total shop expense and the expense per dozen must show on monthly report. The expense accounts are as follows: barn and cartage, shipping, foremen, moving stock and general shop expense, costing.

At the end of several weeks or months, depending on how long it is desired to run the costs, the cost man, will be able to draw off a very complete set of allowance tables from which it will be possible to make up very accurate process sheets for every finish and style.

These tables can be very easily verified and brought up to date at any time to meet with purchasing prices or new conditions.

HANDY DRAWING BOARD AND CABINET

The accompanying drawings show a handy drawing board and cabinet which I constructed for my own use. It takes up very little space and keeps unfinished drawings clean since they are turned inward when the cabinet is closed.—Chas. H. Bailey.

INSPECTION PREVENTS ILL-KEPT MACHINERY

Systematic investigation of conditions in manufacturing plants usually shows a great difference between departments in regard to the care of machinery. While many foremen are very particular that the equipment under their control is maintained in the best condition, others are much less careful. The difference in degree of depreciation is therefore marked, and the efficiency of one department must fall below that of another, because the ill-kept machine will not produce up to its standard of results. Occasionally the case arises of a foreman who crowds machines without giving proper attention to the tools which they use, thus placing upon them a burden which is abnormal, though the speeds and feeds employed would be wholly proper were the work carried on scientifically.

In one works which uses large numbers of machine tools a system of getting at information such as this revealed pronounced inequalities as between the foremen, and it was determined to check up all departments with periodic inspections under the direction of a practical mechanical expert. This is another example of the value of centralized authority. If a department is continually expecting a call from the inspector of machinery, the workmen as well as the foreman are apt to see that they are not caught with dull tools or unoiled moving parts or found lacking in cleanly care. Naturally the inspection develops cases where a machine is used too carefully, so that its product is below

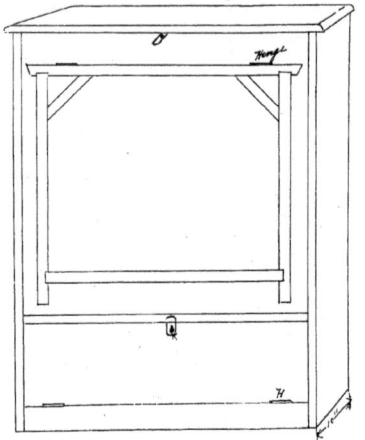

Sketch of drawing cabinet closed up.

the standard of practice, which constitutes another evil in the directing of machinery operations. In any case the system should pay a large return as compared with the cost of its maintenance.—Iron Age.

A belt that either wobbles or flops has but little business in the modern factory, for there are comparatively easy ways to prevent these things, and it is worth while to make use of them.

The "Onward" Way is the Modern Way

Sliding Furniture Shoes

For Metal Beds

Replace Wheel Castors

Wheel castors are fast becoming a thing of the past. Their days of "dis-usefulness" in damage to floor covering and floors are about over.

Take advantage of this trend of the times to supply your customers with the Onward Sliding Furniture Shoe. Made in all sizes for any size or style of post.

Write us for folder and prices.

Onward Mfg. Co., Berlin, Ont.

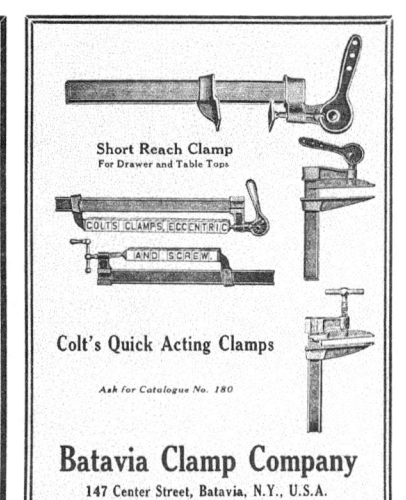

Short Reach Clamp
For Drawer and Table Tops

Colt's Quick Acting Clamps

Ask for Catalogue No. 180

Batavia Clamp Company
147 Center Street, Batavia, N.Y., U.S.A.

Is Yours a Growing Store?

Here are ideas which will help it grow faster. Here are suggestions for the young man starting in business in Northwest Canada, as well as for the dealer with an established trade.

BUILDING A FURNITURE BUSINESS

is a cloth bound book of 205 pages, every one of which contains helpful hints for the furniture dealer. Though written in easy narrative style as the story of "Bobby Burton, Successful Furniture Dealer," the book is neither fiction, theory or dry preachment. The incidents, plans and experiences are woven together from actual practice in widely separated localities.

If your trade is in a rut you will find here a suggestion for a new idea, a plan, a new advertisement or something to start people talking about your store.

Every man who is looking for new ideas in furniture merchandising and methods will find something worth while in this book.

Postpaid, $1.00.

The Commercial Press, Ltd.
Publishers of The Canadian Furniture World and The Undertaker

---

Making TABLE-SLIDES is a Specialty Business

For more than TWENTY-FIVE YEARS we have made TABLE SLIDES exclusively. Our Factory is equipped with Special Machinery which enables us to make SLIDES,—BETTER and CHEAPER than the furniture manufacturer.

Canadian Table makers are rapidly adopting WABASH SLIDES

Because They ELIMINATE SLIDE TROUBLES Are CHEAPER and BETTER

Reduced Costs
Increased Out-put

BY USING
WABASH SLIDES

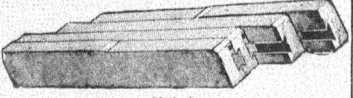

Made by
B. WALTER & CO.
Wabash, Ind.
The Largest EXCLUSIVE TABLE-SLIDE Manufacturers in America
ESTABLISHED 1887

SHELLACS

If you are in the market for first-class Shellac we believe it would be to your advantage to get in touch with us.

HIGH GRADE VARNISHES
FILLERS and GRAINING INKS

THE AULT & WIBORG CO. OF CANADA, LIMITED

MONTREAL   TORONTO   WINNIPEG

ROBERTSON SOCKET HEAD
Wood Screws

Pat. Feb. 2, 1909

See That Square Hole

THIS IS A REAL WOOD SCREW

It is driven by a simple square bit, and is the only one of its type on the market.

Driver fits snugly into the square hole and positively cannot slip and cut the fingers, or disfigure costly furniture or woodwork. It is driven with less exertion. No ragged slots after driving. Saves time, labor, money and material. We make the drivers in all suitable styles.

Drivers sent free with first order. Write for catalogue and prices.

P. L. Robertson Mfg. Co., Limited
MILTON :: ONTARIO

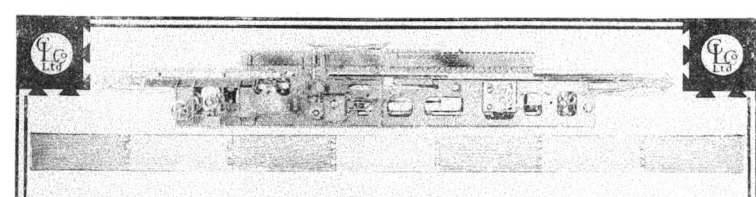

The Linderman Dovetailer and its Users

Twenty-nine of the Leading Progressive and Successful Canadian Factories, manufacturing furniture and kindred lines by the most efficient and economic method, who will frankly and willingly upon receipt of request from you, tell you of the many advantages and economies they are receiving by its use, are:—

The Knechtel Furniture Co.,	Hanover, Ont.
The Knechtel Furniture Co.,	Walkerton, Ont.
The Knechtel Furniture Co.,	Southampton, Ont.
The Canada Furniture Co.,	Woodstock, Ont.
The Canada Furniture Co.,	Wiarton, Ont.
The D. Hibner Furniture Co.,	Berlin, Ont.
Peppler Bros. & Co.,	Hanover, Ont.
Krug Bros. & Co.,	Chesley, Ont.
Chesley Furniture Co.,	Chesley, Ont.
Durham Furniture Co.,	Durham, Ont.
Goderich Organ Co.,	Goderich, Ont.
Meaford Mfg. Co.,	Meaford, Ont.
North American Bent Chair Co.,	Owen Sound, Ont.
Globe Furniture Co.,	Waterloo, Ont.
Canada Office & School Furn. Co.,	Preston, Ont.
H. E. Furniture Co.,	Milverton, Ont.
National Casket Co.,	Toronto, Ont.
Beach Furniture Co.,	Cornwall, Ont.
Victoriaville Furniture Co.,	Victoriaville, Que.
Eastern Townships Furn. Co.,	Arthabaska, Que.
J. W. Kilgour & Bro.,	Beauharnois, Que.
Dominion Furniture Mfg. Co.,	Ste. Therese, Que.
St. Lawrence Furniture Co.,	Riviere-du-Loup, Que.
W. F. Vilas	Cowansville, Que.
Singer Mfg. Co.,	St. John, N.B.
Windsor Furniture Co.,	Windsor, N.S.
C. F. Czerwinski Co.,	Winnipeg, Man.
Western Mfg. Co.,	Regina, Sask.
C. P. Ry. Co., Angus Shops,	Montreal, Que.

If desired, we can also give you addresses of fifteen other concerns who are using the Linderman machine for work not so particular as the furniture line.

Can you afford, in the face of this evidence, to continue in the old unsatisfactory and uneconomic way?

Twelve to Eighteen months' saving will pay for the machine in your factory. Ask us to prove it to you.

Canadian Linderman Co. - Woodstock, Ont.

BUYER'S DIRECTORY

When writing to advertisers kindly mention the Canadian Furniture World and the Undertaker

ARTS AND CRAFTS FURNITURE
Geo. McLagan Furniture Co., Stratford.
John C. Mundell & Co., Elora.

ASBESTOS TABLE COVERS.
Canadian H. W. Johns-Manville Co., Toronto.

BABY CARRIAGES.
Gendron Mfg. Co., Toronto.

AWNINGS
Stamco, Limited, Saskatoon, Sask.

BENT WOOD FURNITURE.
John C. Mundell & Co., Elora.
J. & J. Kohn, Toronto (W. Craig).

BOOKCASES.
Knechtel Furniture Co., Hanover.
Globe Wernicke Co., Stratford.
Geo. McLagan Furniture Co., Stratford.
Meaford Mfg. Co., Meaford, Ont.

BUFFETS.
Bell Furniture Co., Southampton, Ontario.
Knechtel Furniture Co., Hanover.
Geo. McLagan Furniture Co., Stratford.
Meaford Mfg. Co., Meaford, Ont.
Peppler Bros., Hanover.
Stratford Chair Co., Stratford.
Victoriaville Furniture Co., Victoriaville, Que.

BEDS (Brass and Iron).
Canada Beds, Ltd., Chesley.
Ideal Bedding Co., Toronto.
Geo. Gale & Son. Waterville Que.
Ives Modern Bedstead Co., Cornwall Ont.
Ontario Spring Bed & Mattress Co., London. Ont.
Standard Bedstead Co., Victoriaville, Que.
Stamco, Limited, Saskatoon, Sask.
Stratford Bed Co., Stratford, Ont.
S. Welsglass, Ltd., Montreal, Que.

BEDS (Modern Wood).
Elora Furniture Co., Elora.
Knechtel Furniture Co., Hanover.

BED SPRINGS.
Colleras Spring Mattress Co., Toronto.
Knechtel Furniture Co., Hanover.
Frame and Hay Fence Co., Stratford.
Gold Medal Furniture Co., Toronto.
Leggett & Platt Spring Bed Co., Windsor.
Ideal Bedding Co., Toronto.
Ontario Spring Bed & Mattress Co., London. Ont.
Stamco, Limited, Saskatoon, Sask.
S. Welsglass, Ltd., Montreal, Que.

BED ROOM CHAIRS.
Baetz Bros., Berlin.
Bell Furniture Co., Southampton, Ontario.
Elmira Furniture Co, Elmira, Ont.
Lippert Furniture Co., Berlin.

BEDROOM ROCKERS
Lippert Furniture Co., Berlin, Ont.

BED ROOM SUITES.
Bell Furniture Co., Southampton, Ontario.
Knechtel Furniture Co., Hanover.
Meaford Mfg. Co., Meaford.
Victoriaville Furniture Co., Victoriaville, Que.

BUNGALOW CHAIRS & SUITES
Baetz Bros. & Co., Berlin, Ont.

CARD AND DEN TABLES.
Geo. McLagan Furniture Co., Stratford.
John C. Mundell & Co., Elora, Ont.

CARPET RACKS
Steel Furnishing Co., New Glasgow. N. S.

CAMP FURNITURE.
Stratford Mfg. Co., Stratford.
Ideal Bedding Co., Toronto.

CEDAR BOXES
D. L. Shafer, St. Thomas, Ont.

CELLARETTES
John C. Mundell & Co., Elora, Ont.

CHAIRS AND ROCKERS
Bell Furniture Co., Southampton.
Baetz Bros., Berlin.
Knechtel Furniture Co., Hanover.
John C. Mundell & Co., Elora.

Stratford Chair Co., Stratford.
Waterloo Furniture Co., Waterloo.
Canadian Rattan Chair Co., Victoriaville.
Gold Medal Furniture Co., Toronto.
Elmira Furniture Co, Elmira, Ont.
Imperial Furniture Co., Toronto.
Lippert Furniture Co., Berlin.
Victoriaville Chair Mfg. Co., Victoriaville.

CHESTERFIELDS.
Imperial Furniture Co., Toronto.

CHIFFONIERS.
Bell Furniture Co., Southampton.
Knechtel Furniture Co., Hanover.
Meaford Mfg. Co., Meaford, Ont.
Stratford Chair Co., Stratford.
Victoriaville Furniture Co., Victoriaville. Que.

CHILDRENS' SULKIES
Jennings Co., St. Thomas

CHINA CABINETS.
Bell Furniture Co., Southampton, Ontario
Peppler Bros., Hanover.
Knechtel Furniture Co., Hanover.
Geo. McLagan Furniture Co., Stratford.
Meaford Mfg. Co., Meaford, Ont.

CLOCK CASES
Elmira Interior Woodwork Co., Elmira, Ont.

COMFORTERS.
Toronto Feather & Down Co., Toronto.
Stamco, Limited, Saskatoon. Sask.

COTS
Ideal Bedding Co., Toronto.
Ontario Spring Bed and Mattress Co., London.

COSTUMIERS
Elmira Interior Woodwork Co., Elmira, Ont.

COUCHES.
J. P. Albrough & Co., Ingersoll.
Ellis Furniture Co., Ingersoll.
Gold Medal Furniture Co., Toronto.
Kindel Bed Co., Toronto.
Imperial Furniture Co., Toronto.
John C. Mundell & Co., Elora, Ont.
Montreal Upholstering Co., Montreal.
Steel Furnishing Co., New Glasgow, N. S.
S. Weisglass, Ltd., Montreal, Que.

COUCHES (Sliding)
Ideal Bedding Co., Toronto.
Farquharson-Gifford Co., Stratford.
Ontario Spring Bed & Mattress Co., London, Ont.
Stamco, Limited, Saskatoon, Sask.
Gold Medal Furniture Co., Toronto.

CRADLES.
Knechtel Furniture Co., Hanover.

CRIBS (Brass and Iron)
Ideal Bedding Co., Toronto.
Ontario Spring Bed & Mattress Co., London.
Stamco, Limited, Saskatoon, Sask.
S. Weisglass, Ltd., Montreal, Que.

CUSHIONS.
Stamco, Limited, Saskatoon, Sask.

DAVENPORT BEDS.
Farquharson-Gifford Co., Stratford.
Kindel Bed Co., Toronto.
Lippert Furniture Co., Berlin, Ont.
Montreal Upholstering Co., Montreal, Que.
Imperial Rattan Co., Stratford.
John C. Mundell & Co., Elora.

DAVENPORT FRAMES
Elmira Interior Woodwork Co., Elmira, Ont.

DEN FURNITURE
Elmira Furniture Co., Elmira, Ont.
Farquharson-Gifford Co., Stratford.
John C. Mundell & Co., Elora, Ont.

DIVANETTES.
Lippert Furniture Co., Berlin.

DESKS.
Bell Furniture Co., Southampton.
Elmira Interior Woodwork Co., Elmira.

Knechtel Furniture Co., Hanover.
Geo. McLagan Furniture Co., Stratford.
John C. Mundell & Co., Elora.
Stratford Desk Co., Stratford, Ont.

DINING-ROOM FURNITURE
Crown Furniture Co., Preston.
Farquharson-Gifford Co., Stratford.
Lippert Furniture Co., Berlin, Ont.

DINING SUITES.
Bell Furniture Co., Southampton.
Knechtel Furniture Co., Hanover.
Geo. McLagan Furniture Co., Stratford.
John C. Mundell & Co., Elora.
Peppler Bros., Hanover.
Stratford Chair Co., Stratford.

DINERS
Lippert Furniture Co., Berlin, Ont.

DINNER WAGONS.
Geo. McLagan Furniture Co., Stratford.
Peppler Bros., Hanover.

DRESSERS.
Bell Furniture Co., Southampton.
Knechtel Furniture Co., Hanover.
Stratford Chair Co., Stratford.
Victoriaville Furniture Co., Victoriaville, Que.
Meaford Mfg. Co., Meaford, Ont.

EXTENSION TABLES.
Bell Furniture Co., Southampton.
Peppler Bros., Hanover.
Berlin Table Mfg. Co., Berlin.
Meaford Mfg. Co., Meaford, Ont.

FILING DEVICES.
Elmira Interior Woodwork Co., Elmira.
Globe Wernicke Co., Stratford.
Knechtel Furniture Co., Hanover.
Geo. McLagan Furniture Co., Stratford.

FILING CABINETS
Globe Wernicke Co., Stratford, Ont.

FOLDING CHAIRS.
Stratford Mfg. Co., Stratford.
Ideal Bedding Co., Toronto.

FOLDING TABLES.
Hourd & Co., London.
Stratford Mfg. Co., Stratford.

FOOTSTOOLS
Elmira Furniture Co., Elmira, Ont.

GRASS FURNITURE (Chinese)
Jennings Co., St. Thomas

HALL RACKS
Lippert Furniture Co., Berlin, Ont.

HALL SEATS AND MIRRORS.
Geo. McLagan Furniture Co., Stratford.
Lippert Furniture Co., Berlin, Ont.
Meaford Mfg. Co., Meaford, Ont.

HALL TREES.
Geo. McLagan Furniture Co., Stratford.

HAMMO-COUCHES.
Ideal Bedding Co., Toronto.

INVALID CHAIRS.
Gendron Mfg. Co., Toledo, Ohio.
Victoriaville Chair Mfg. Co., Victoriaville, Que.

IRONING BOARDS AND DRYERS.
Stratford Mfg. Co., Stratford.

JARDINIERE STANDS.
Elmira Furniture Co., Elmira, Ont.
Elora Furniture Co., Elora.
Geo. McLagan Furniture Co., Stratford.
Meaford Mfg. Co., Meaford, Ont.

KITCHEN CABINETS.
H. E. Furniture Co., Milverton.
Nagrella Mfg. Co., Hamilton.
Knechtel Kitchen Cabinet Co., Ltd., Hanover, Ont.

KITCHEN TABLES.
Knechtel Furniture Co., Hanover.
Victoriaville Furniture Co., Victoriaville.

LADIES' DESKS
Meaford Mfg. Co., Meaford, Ont.

LAWN SEATS AND SWINGS.
Stratford Mfg. Co., Stratford.

LIBRARY TABLES.
Bell Furniture Co., Southampton.
Peppler Bros., Hanover.
Elmira Furniture Co., Elmira, Ont.
Elmira Interior Woodwork Co., Elmira, Ont.
Geo. McLagan Furniture Co., Stratford.
Meaford Mfg. Co., Meaford, Ont.
John C. Mundell & Co., Elora, Ont.

LIVING-ROOM FURNITURE
Lippert Furniture Co., Berlin, Ont.

LUXURY CHAIRS.
Lippert Furniture Co., Berlin.

MAGAZINE RACKS AND STANDS.
Geo. McLagan Furniture Co., Stratford.

MATTRESSES
Berlin Bedding Co., Toronto.
Canada Mattress Co., Victoriaville, Que.
Gold Medal Furniture Co., Toronto.
McKellar Bedding Co., Fort William, Ont.
Ontario Spring Bed & Mattress Co., London, Ont.
Stamco, Limited, Saskatoon, Sask.
Standard Bedding Co., Toronto.
Antiseptic Bedding Co., Toronto.
Ideal Bedding Co., Toronto.
Fischman Mattress Co., Toronto.

MANTELS—Wood, Tile
Elmira Interior Woodwork Co., Elmira, Ont.

MANTELS—Electric
Elmira Interior Woodwork Co., Elmira, Ont.

MEDICINE CABINETS.
Meaford Mfg. Co., Meaford, Ont.

MORRIS CHAIRS.
Ellis Furniture Co., Ingersoll.
Imperial Rattan Co., Stratford.
Knechtel Furniture Co., Hanover.
Lippert Furniture Co., Berlin, Ont.
John C. Mundell & Co., Elora.
Waterloo Furniture Co., Waterloo.

MUSIC CABINETS.
Geo. McLagan Furniture Co., Stratford.
Knechtel Kitchen Cabinet Co., Ltd., Hanover, Ont.

ODD CHAIRS
Lippert Furniture Co., Berlin, Ont.

OFFICE CHAIRS.
Bell Furniture Co., Southampton.
Elmira Furniture Co., Elmira, Ont.
Knechtel Furniture Co., Hanover.
H. Krug Furniture Co., Berlin.
Stratford Chair Co., Stratford.
J. & J. Kohn, Toronto (W. Craig).
John C. Mundell & Co., Elora, Ont.

OFFICE TABLES
Stratford Desk Co., Stratford, Ont.

PARK SEATS.
Stratford Mfg. Co., Stratford.

PARLOR CHAIRS and ROCKERS
Ellis Furniture Co., Ingersoll.
Elmira Interior Woodwork Co., Elmira.
John C. Mundell & Co., Elora, Ont.
Waterloo Furniture Co., Waterloo.

PARLOR FRAMES
Elmira Interior Woodwork Co., Elmira, Ont.

PARLOR SUITES.
Elmira Interior Woodwork Co., Elmira.
Ellis Furniture Co., Ingersoll.
Knechtel Furniture Co., Hanover.
Waterloo Furniture Co., Waterloo.
Gold Medal Furniture Co., Toronto.
Lippert Furniture Co., Berlin.

PARLOR TABLES.
Geo. McLagan Furniture Co., Stratford.
Meaford Mfg. Co., Meaford, Ont.
Elmira Furniture Co., Elmira, Ont.
Knechtel Furniture Co., Hanover.
Peppler Bros., Hanover.

PEDESTALS.
Lippert Furniture Co., Berlin, Ont.
Geo. McLagan Furniture Co., Stratford.
Peppler Bros., Hanover.

PILLOWS.
Ontario Spring Bed & Mattress Co., London, Ont.
Toronto Feather & Down Co., Toronto.
Ideal Bedding Co., Toronto.

PILLOW SHAM HOLDERS.
Tarbox Mfg. Co., Toronto.

RATTAN FURNITURE.
Imperial Rattan Co., Stratford.
Canadian Rattan Chair Co., Victoriaville, Que.
Gendron Mfg. Co., Toronto.

RECLINING CHAIRS.
Ellis Furniture Co., Ingersoll.
Knechtel Furniture Co., Hanover.
Lippert Furniture Co., Berlin, Ont.
John C. Mundell & Co., Elora, Ont.

RUG RACKS
Steel Furnishing Co., New Glasgow, N. S.

SECTIONAL BOOKCASES
Knechtel Furniture Co., Hanover.
Globe Wernicke Co.-Stratford.

THE EDGE THAT NEVER SAGS

Is the edge that sells the Springs. Examine your representative before placing your next order. We Springs and see if they have **Colleran's Rope Edge**, carry a complete line of woven wire springs with which is the only real rope edge. If not, see our wood or steel frames. Cots and Divans.

COLLERAN PATENT SPRING MATTRESS CO., TORONTO, ONT.

SCHOOL FURNITURE
Bell Furniture Co., Southampton, Ontario.

SIDEBOARDS
Knechtel Furniture Co., Hanover.
Meaford Mfg. Co., Meaford, Ont.
Stratford Chair Co., Stratford.

STORE FRONTS
Kawneer Mfg. Co., Toronto.

TABLES
Berlin Table Mfg. Co., Berlin, Ont.
Bell Furniture Co., Southampton, Ontario.
Elora Furniture Co., Elora.
Knechtel Furniture Co., Hanover.
John C. Mundell & Co., Elora.
Orillia Furniture Co., Orillia.
Peppler Bros., Hanover.
Stratford Chair Co., Stratford.
Victoriaville Furniture Co., Victoriaville, Que.

TABOURETTES
Elora Furniture Co., Elora.
Kensington Furniture Co., Goderich.

TELEPHONE STANDS
John C. Mundell & Co., Elora, Ont.

TYPEWRITER DESKS
Elmira Interior Woodwork Co., Elmira.
Stratford Desk Co., Stratford, Ont.

UPHOLSTERERS' SUPPLIES
Ellis Furniture Co., Ingersoll.
Gold Medal Furniture Co., Toronto.

UPHOLSTERED FURNITURE
Baetz Bros., Berlin.
Ellis Furniture Co., Ingersoll.
Farquharson-Gifford Co., Stratford, Ont.
Imperial Rattan Co., Stratford.
Imperial Furniture Co., Toronto.
John C. Mundell & Co., Elora.
Knechtel Furniture Co., Hanover.
Waterloo Furniture Co., Waterloo.
Gold Medal Furniture Co., Toronto.
Quality Furniture Makers, Welland.
A. J. Scafe & Co., Berlin.

VACUUM CLEANERS
Onward Mfg. Co., Berlin.

VERANDAH FURNITURE
Imperial Rattan Co., Stratford.
Stratford Mfg. Co., Stratford.

WARDROBES
Knechtel Furniture Co., Hanover.
Meaford Mfg. Co., Meaford, Ont.
Stratford Chair Co., Stratford.

FACTORY SUPPLIES

BRASS TRIMMINGS
Stratford Brass Co., Stratford.

CLAMPS
Batavia Clamp Co., Batavia, N.Y.

FURNITURE SHOES
Onward Mfg. Co., Berlin.

DRY KILNS
Morton Dry Kiln Co., Chicago.
FURNITURE HARDWARE
Stratford Brass Co., Stratford.
GLUE JOINTING MACHINES
Canadian Linderman Co., Woodstock.

NAILS
P. L. Robertson Mfg. Co., Milton.

PLATING
P. L. Robertson Mfg. Co., Milton, Ontario.

RIVETS AND SCREWS
P. L. Robertson Mfg. Co., Milton.

SPRINGS
James Steele, Guelph.
Ideal Bedding Co., Toronto.

SPANISH LEATHER
Lackawanna Leather Co., Hackettstown, N. J.

STERILIZED HAIR
Griffin Curled Hair Co., Toronto.

TABLE SLIDES
B. Walter & Co., Wabash, Ind.

TRUCKS
W. I. Kemp Co., Ltd., Stratford.

VARNISHES
R. C. Jamieson & Co., Montreal.
Ault & Wiborg, Toronto.

VENEERS
Adams & Raymond Veneer Co., Indianapolis, Ind.

VENEER PRESSES
Wm. R. Perrin & Co., Toronto.

WASHERS
P. L. Robertson Mfg. Co., Milton.

UNDERTAKERS' SUPPLIES

AMBULANCES
Mitchell & Co., Ingersoll.

BURIAL ROBES
James S. Elliott & Son, Prescott.
Evel Casket Co., Hamilton.
Globe Casket Co., London.
Semmens & Evel Casket Co., Hamilton.

CLOTH CASKETS
Michigan Casket Co., Detroit, Mich.

CEMENT CASKETS
Canadian Cement Casket Co., Prescott.

CEMETERY SUPPLIES
Frigid Fluid Co., Chicago, Ill.

CASKETS AND COFFINS
Dominion Casket Co., Guelph.
Evel Casket Co., Hamilton.
Globe Casket Co., London.
Semmens & Evel Casket Co., Hamilton.

EMBALMING FLUIDS
Egyptian Chemical Co., Boston.
Frigid Fluid Co., Chicago, Ill.
Michigan Casket Co., Detroit, Mich.
H. S. Eckels Co., Philadelphia.

EMBALMERS' SUPPLIES
Frigid Fluid Co., Chicago, Ill.

HEARSES
Mitchell & Co., Ingersoll.

LOWERING DEVICES
Frigid Fluid Co., Chicago, Ill.

SCHOOLS OF EMBALMING
Canadian School of Embalming, Toronto.

STEEL GRAVE VAULTS
St. Thomas Metallic Vault Co., St. Thomas, Ont.
Michigan Casket Co., Detroit, Mich.

UNDERTAKER'S CHAIRS
Stratford Mfg. Co., Stratford.

UNDERTAKERS' SUNDRIES
Frigid Fluid Co., Chicago, Ill.

For Sale — Wanted

TERMS FOR INSERTION
4 Cents per word one insertion
10 Cents per word three insertions
MINIMUM 50 CENTS

FURNITURE: China and undertaking business for sale. For particulars write, Mrs. A. Metcalf, Treherne, Man. 14/4/1

FOR SALE: Furniture and undertaking, good business. House and store. Only twelve hundred dollars. Terms cash. Snap, J. H. Beal, Claremont. 14/4/1

TRAVELLERS—Wanted for the Maritime Provinces, Western Ontario and Eastern Ontario, to handle a side line of upholstered goods, in couches, davenports, duofolds, divanettes, etc., on a commission. Apply to Montreal Upholstering Co., 1611 Clarke Street, Montreal, Can. 14/4/1

BUY Upholstery Springs That "Stand Up"

Our Tempered Furniture Springs will outlast almost any piece of upholstered furniture. They are built to "stand up" indefinitely.

JAMES STEELE, LIMITED
GUELPH :: :: ONTARIO

Invalid Chairs and Tricycles of every description.

This has been our study for thirty-five years. We build chairs that suit the requirements of any case. Write us for catalogue No. 20 and prices, if interested.

Gendron Wheel Co., Toledo, O. U.S.A.

Every Furniture Manufacturer

Installs new equipment in his plant from time to time—the old breaks down. There is no way to dispose of it so economically and effectively. Let's tell you.

Canadian Furniture World, 32 COLBORNE ST. TORONTO

Dominion Casket Co., Limited

Telephones: Day No. 1020. Nights, Sundays and Holidays Nos. 1069-1101

Guelph, Ont.

RUSH ORDERS SOLICITED

No. 342

We are the only manufacturers in the Dominion of Canada making in our own factory a metallic casket of any description. The Combination Metallic Casket shown in accompanying illustration is a result of much study as to requirements of such goods and economical construction. These goods are made in the best manner possible from very heavy sheet metal, with sealed inner top and handles bolted to metal sides and all punctures sealed. These goods have developed much popularity, and we realize, with the ever increasing demand for cases of this class, that the public sentiment is in favor of caskets that are air, water and vermin tight. The cost is but a trifle more than for the ordinary wood caskets now on the market and can be had in any of the numerous designs shown in such. The metallic case forms a constant protection to the public at funerals and during shipment of bodies to any part of the universe. "You," Mr. Funeral Director, being the medium of distribution to the public, must not overlook the advantages to be derived from having these goods to show the public. The combination metallic casket is especially designed to meet all financial conditions. Do not delay in placing in your showroom one or more of these cases, and through the sale of such goods not only increase the circle of your friends but start an ever increasing income for your business.

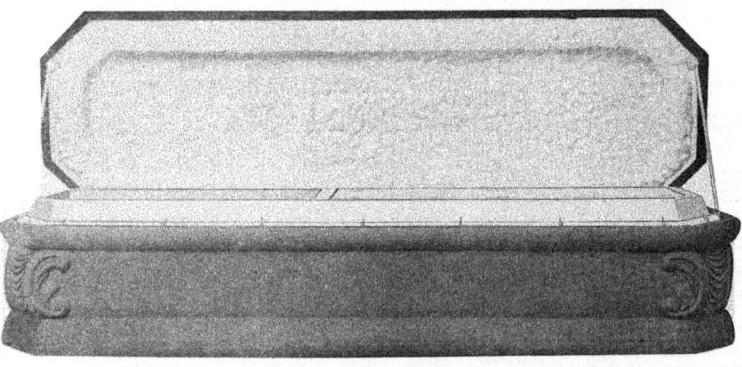

No. 165

Undertakers' Department

Problems affecting the Undertaking Profession are here discussed and readers are invited to send letters expressing their views on any of the subjects dealt with—News of the profession throughout Canada.

CURRENT UNDERTAKING TOPICS

AT a funeral in England recently, there was quite a rumpus between the rector of the church and some Non-conformist ministers which were present. It appears the trouble arose over the question of the relative status of the conflicting parties. Evidently another outburst of the jealous spirit which two thousand years ago led the question to be asked the founder of Christianity: "Who is the greatest in the Kingdom of Heaven?"

It is fortunate that it was not funeral directors that made fools of themselves.

* * * *

THAT petty jealousies exist among some of those engaged in the undertaking profession is well known. It is equally well known that these jealousies often disappear as acquaintanceships improve. One of the best mediums for bringing about these acquaintanceships is conventions. Referring to this phase of conventions a speaker recently said:

"Enough cannot be said about this common brotherhood, and what is of benefit to one in our profession, is a help to all. Let us get together and discuss our experiences—the failures as well as the successes. Possibly it would be to our best advantage to talk about cases that have given us some difficulty since we are seeking mutual improvement. By telling of one's shortcomings others may be able to advise and help us."

* * * *

University Course for Embalmers. To have suggested even a few years ago an embalming course in connection with an university would have probably been accounted ridiculous. At any rate, whether it would or not, a course in embalming has been opened by the University of Minnesota. The time of the course is about six weeks, and takes the place of the short course schools usually held under the direction of the Minnesota Funeral Directors' Association. The profession "do move."

* * * *

Caskets by Parcel Post. Shipping caskets by Parcel Post is something that has probably not entered the minds of many undertakers. It has, however, been made possible by the amended regulations in the United States to ship caskets of child's size, the weight limit now being fifty pounds. With the weight limit only eleven pounds it is, of course, impossible to use the mails for any such purposes in Canada.

* * * *

Treating Dropsical Cases. A lecturer, in giving his experiences recently in the treatment of cases where dropsy had been the cause of death, said: "When I want to remove water from the subcutaneous tissues I first cover the carpet, if there is one on the floor, with a rubber blanket, which should be at least six feet square. I then place a similar one over the embalming board. On this I put the body, and then roll up the sides of the blanket. I then bring the blanket to a point at the foot of the board, and place a bucket to receive the water as it escapes from the body. These simple preparations cost but little, and may save your reputation, for if you spill blood or water on the carpet and stain it, your reputation as a tidy workman is seriously impaired. Now, to remove water from the tissues, insert a pen pointed trocar at the inner side of the leg, near the ankle joint and push the instrument forward and upward, thereby lifting the skin from the tissues beneath it. This done, make several other incisions at the inner and outer side of the knee and raise the skin in the same manner. Now, if the arms and hands are dropsical, raise them as high as possible, and press the water downward by rubbing in this way. It may sound strange to some of you, but I have removed many gallons of water from the tissues of dead bodies, simply by gravitation. The water from the head and face and all other upper portions of the body will in a very short time gravitate to the dependent parts and pass out of the openings made in the skin. Some people say that they never remove water from dead bodies, but embalm them while the water still remains in the tissues, aspirating from the cavities only. Perhaps they can do this, and keep their bodies indefinitely, but I think it risky. A man told me the other day that he kept a bad dropsical case three days and did not remove any water. I do not dispute it, but I do say it is a dangerous experiment."

We can all learn something from the experiences of others.

* * * *

Embalmers and Surgery. An embalmer, writing to the Undertakers' Journal, London, England, thinks that the average undertaker is unfitted for so scientific an operation as embalming, and suggests that before becoming an embalmer he should undergo a course in surgery.

A course of surgery would in all probability be helpful. The more an embalmer knows about the human body the better. But surgery is not embalming, and a poor fist at embalming indeed would a surgeon make of it unless he had been properly trained in the art. As a matter of fact, in Canada at any rate, the prescribed courses of training, if intelligently followed and put to good use in practice, will create men well qualified for the embalming profession without recourse to courses in surgery.

———

M. McFadden, furniture dealer and undertaker, Hunter Street, Peterborough, has received a singular article for use in his undertaking department, in the form of a steel grave vault. This is one of the first to be introduced into that city, and it has many points of interest. It is burglar proof, water proof and also air proof.

Western Service

Always at Your Service

UNDERTAKERS handling *Western* Caskets and Funeral supplies know that with every order they get *Quality* — the assurance that they are right and that their customers will be pleased.

Our stock is fast being completed and by end of month we expect to be in full swing.

We have to thank the trade at large for their many enquiries and also for the large volume of business which has already reached us.

The Western Casket Co., Limited

Cor. Emily St. and Bannatyne Ave.   Winnipeg, Manitoba

Open Day and Night

G. S. Thompson   A. W. Robinson   G. H. Lawrence

Undertaking in the Next Decade

Professor Eckels takes a dispassionate view into the future

So much has been accomplished and such progressiveness shown by the undertakers of America during the past ten years that it may not be amiss to take a view into the future and to try at least to discern what the next decade will bring forth. Ten years ago the embalmer was struggling along with faulty methods, inadequate instruments, and, to say the least, fluids which necessarily lacked uniformity. Considering these things—and they should be considered—the results which he attained were really marvelous. Even to-day there are a few undertakers sufficiently lacking in progressiveness to cling to the methods, instruments and fluids of that bygone era; but they are the exception rather than the rule, and in almost every case it will be found that their business is either going backward or is not progressing in proportion to the business and population of their communities.

There is an old saying that "Youth must be served." Unquestionably this is true in a broad general sense. Youth is much more apt to mean progressiveness than the reverse, but how often do we find it in our profession that progressiveness is linked with experience, and that the man of fifty is much more ready to grasp the importance of newer methods and newer materials than many of the newer generation. To this latter class, "All Hail," for in them lie the great hope of the profession. Their standing as undertakers gives their every action an influence for good which is not possible, even from the most progressive young man.

Ten years ago, the embalmer had not settled upon any specific artery as the best. We would find one man invariably using the radial, another would use the brachial on every case, no matter what the circumstances; others held to the carotids, while the iliacs and the femorals likewise had their devotees. To-day this is changed. Practically no progressive embalmer inflexibly uses any one artery, although the greater proportion have come to use the axillary on a very large percentage of their cases. There is, however, thanks to our ever-widening circles of education, a general tendency to judge each case upon its merits and to choose the artery best suited for that particular body. Almost every embalmer is able to use any of the main trunk arteries with equal facility; and while, in the course of this evolution, the radial, femoral and iliac have been almost entirely discarded as between the axillary and the carotids, he is guided only by the exigencies of the case.

Embalming to-day, especially with the axillary draining tubes, is a much more cleanly and satisfactory operation than it used to be. Moreover, even to-day the tendency to drain the blood is very much more universal than it was then. During the next decade I believe that every undertaker who pretends to do embalming will as invariably drain blood as he injects fluid. In a measure, this will be forced upon the unprogressive part of the profession by the successes and the results along cosmetic lines which will be attained by those who will demand the best regardless of the amount of trouble involved or the time required.

The advantages of draining blood and of ridding the arterial system of this incumbrance to good work are too obvious not to secure even wider and more nearly universal use in years to come. In methods, therefore, we have progressed, and there certainly is no reason to doubt that the next decade will see even greater progress. The instruments of to-day, too, are vastly superior and secure much more nearly uniform results than those of the past. What the instrument manufacturer of the future will do it is impossible to foresee, but it requires no stretch of the imagination to realize that whatever he may do will be along lines which will increase the usefulness of his product, which will facilitate the work of the embalmer, and secure results which are unattainable to-day, no matter how careful the embalmer may be.

The fluid situation is likewise hopeful, despite the fact that there lately has been a tendency on the part of some undertakers to "wander after strange gods" and to fail to support the experienced and reputable chemists in their efforts to secure a better product and more nearly uniform results. Those of us who have been manufacturing fluids for years have seen a constant procession of alleged wonder-working chemicals foisted upon the undertaking profession; have seen strange fluids flourish for a day and then vanish, never again to be heard of. We have seen cellars of even progressive undertakers filled with "cats and dogs" of fluid which some glib salesman, with a mouthful of promises, had persuaded them to buy. I know of nothing easier to manufacture than claims. Compounding an embalming fluid is an extremely difficult proposition compared with making claims. All that seems necessary to convince some undertakers that a new fluid is a wonder-worker is to sound him carefully as to wherein he has had his most recent failures and then stoutly assert that the fluid you have to sell is compounded especially to meet such an emergency.

A glib salesman, going out with a new fluid, will meet one undertaker who just has had a jaundice case transformed into a beautiful green and will open up a convincing line of argument to show that this never

Mack Paul and his undertaking parlors at Woodstock, Ont. Mr. Paul holds embalmer's licenses in Ontario, New York and Michigan. He headed the poll as alderman of his city this year, and is also chairman of the Charity Commission of Woodstock. Originally with W. H. Tanton, Strathroy, where he learned his business, Mr. Paul finished his course in Detroit. He has been located at Woodstock for the past 4 years.

Dominion Manufacturers
Limited

MANUFACTURERS OF

Fine Funeral Requisites

We guarantee

The Highest Quality

and the

Quickest Possible Service

*Night or Day Orders
given Prompt Attention*

BRANCHES

The Globe Casket Co., and Branches	London, Ontario
The Semmons & Evel Casket Co., and Branches,	Hamilton, Ontario
The National Casket Co.	Toronto, Ontario
Jas. S. Elliot & Son	Prescott, Ontario
Girard & Godin and Branches	Three Rivers, Quebec
Christie Bros. & Co,	Amherst, N. S.

FRED W. COLES
General Manager

D. M. ANDREWS
Secretary Treasurer

HEAD OFFICE

468 King Street W., Toronto

could have happened with his own peculiar product. A moment later he will be expounding a dropsy argument concerning the same fluid to some funeral director whose most recent bitter experience has been with skin-slip. I have seen some of these amateur fluids which started off fairly satisfactorily and which, for a time, gave reasonable satisfaction. I expect to see fewer of them during the next ten years than I have seen in the past ten.

(To be continued)

MOTOR FUNERALS

At the annual meeting of the British Undertakers' Association the President made the following reference to motor funerals:

"The advent of motor vehicles into the funeral business is a matter of the utmost importance to those engaged in the business," he said. "To those who have much capital invested in horses and horse-drawn funeral equipages, the uncertainty as to the development of funeral motor traffic naturally causes anxiety as to possible losses by depreciation.

"Whether we like it or not it is absolutely necessary for the undertaker and carriage master to look the question of motor funerals fully in the face. It is undeniable that in many cases a motor hearse or motor van is a convenience both to the undertaker and to the public, leading as they do at times to quicker transit, and the avoidance of the removal from and to road and rail. There are, however, two aspects of the matter to which I would briefly draw your attention. First, it is certain that if any considerable section of the public desires motor vehicles for funerals—those wishes will in the long run have to be met. Therefore it will be far better for carriage masters and undertakers themselves to be adapted to the times and meet the public demands. If this is not done there will inevitably follow an influx of those not at present in the business with resulting ruinous competition.

"The second aspect which we should most carefully consider is what action should undertakers take regarding the advocacy of motor funerals. In order to do this we must realize the unique position of the funeral business. While at times a motor conveyance is an unquestioned advantage, it is also the fact that in the great majority of funerals it is not only not essential, but not desirable. To most people the present system of horse-drawn funeral conveyances gives a dignity not possessed by mechanical vehicles which far more than compensates for the difference of time taken for ordinary distances. It would be wise for undertakers to let "caution mark the guarded way" regarding motor funerals. While being progressive and entering for what are real public interests, it is unnecessary to go to the other extreme simply for the sake of novelty, encouraging changes ahead of public sentiment, thereby entailing loss and hardship to many undertakers. Much could be said on this subject, but as we are fortunate in having a trade association, I trust that the matter in all its bearings will be discussed by the various centres with the view of some uniform policy and action being adopted."

HOME-BUILT COFFIN TOO SMALL

For Sale—A second-hand coffin that is too small for its owner, who built it for himself. Apply to Sunbury County Man.

The above is just the kind of an advertisement the Gleaner is likely to be asked to publish any day since a well known resident of the parish of Sheffield, Sunbury county, has found that a coffin which he constructed for his own personal use in now too small for him.

The gentleman in question thought that he might as well employ himself profitably in his spare time, and therefore set about to build his own coffin. The work took a little longer than he anticipated, and he did not allow in his measurements for the fact that as he grows older he is becoming more portly.

Recently investigation showed him that the coffin was too small for him, or rather that he has become too big for the coffin. Just what means he used for ascertaining that interesting piece of information is not disclosed, but possibly it was by "trying it on," so to speak. At any rate on a recent visit to Fredericton he told his friends that the coffin he had built was too small and that he would sell it at a bargain rate because he was going to start upon the construction of a larger one for himself.—Gleaner, Fredericton, N.S.

STOLE A CORPSE

While G. N. Dubreuil, undertaker, of 2763 St. Hubert Street, Montreal, stepped into his house to warm up, preparatory to making a trip to the cemetery with the body of an infant that he had been commissioned to bury recently, two men made off with his horse and cutter unaware of the gruesome contents. The cutter was found by Lieut. Tetrault, of the Ahuntsic police station in the possession of Frank Paquette, 17 years of age, and a companion. The two were said to be making their way as fast as possible towards the bridge over the Back River at Ahuntsic. Lieut. Tetrault fired his revolver in the air to bring the alleged thieves to a stop.

When arraigned in court charged with the theft of a horse and cutter, and the little corpse, Paquette pleaded not guilty and was remanded. When Lieut. Tetrault made the arrest the coffin containing the corpse was found lying intact beneath the seat of the vehicle. The body was that of a new-born babe that died shortly after birth. Doubtless, if the men had been aware of their gruesome load they would have abandoned their booty in horror.

GERMANY'S MOTOR CREMATORIES

After thousands of years of being buried with honors on the field of battle, soldiers in the future will be incinerated in portable crematories mounted on motor trucks. At least this is the plan of the German general staff, following the report submitted to it by an army surgeon who accompanied the Bulgarian army and who witnessed the various assaults on Adrianople. He reported that had it not been for the cold weather, which prevented the bodies from decaying on the battlefield, the vapors arising from them would have caused disease, with untold results among the survivors. In the future this contingency will be met by the use of motor crematories, capable of incinerating at one operation from 10 to 25 bodies, and able in the entire 24 hours of each day to dispose of from 300 to 500.

CHASE PROFESSIONAL "FUNERAL GOERS"

It is estimated that there are five hundred women in Grand Rapids, Mich., who are professional funeral goers. These women haunt cemeteries and watch funeral processions and crowd up to grave sides, gazing morbidly at casket and mourners. The park commissioners decided to start a movement to keep these women out of the cemeteries on the ground that they have made themselves "public pests."

Burglar Proof and Water Tight

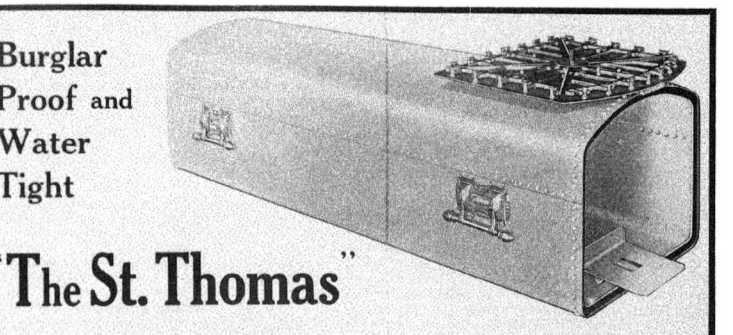

"The St. Thomas"

Original, Quick Closing End Vault

MANUFACTURED BY

The St. Thomas Metallic Vault Company, Limited
ST. THOMAS, ONTARIO

The Original Patented Concentrated Fluid

Patented Formula
Strongest and Best

Essential Oil Base, combined with Alcohol, Glycerine, Oxidized Formaldehyde and Boron-Dioxide.
Ask others for their Formula

Special Canadian Agents

National Casket Co.
Toronto, Ont.
GLOBE CASKET CO.
London, Ont.
SEMMENS & EVEL CASKET CO.
Hamilton, Ont.
GIRARD & GODIN
Three Rivers, Que.
JAS. S. ELLIOTT & SON
Prescott, Ont.
CHRISTIE BROS.
Amherst, N.S.

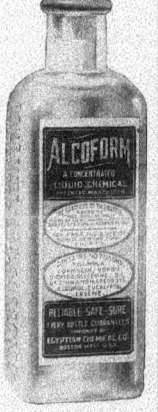

Larger Bottles filled up with water

Egyptian Chemical Co. Boston, U.S.A.

For Every Furniture Man

A Helpful, Thoroughly Practical Book, Written by an Authority—

HOW TO KNOW PERIOD STYLES IN FURNITURE

150 Pages   317 Illustrations

Price, $1.50

Designers will find illustrations of the work of celebrated designers of history. Examples are taken from the recognized collections and museums of the world. Buyers—The book is arranged for easy reference with the distinguishing features of each period clearly shown. Salesmen—The information in "How to Know Period Styles" will enable you to talk authoritatively on the subject.
Students—The confusing element has been eliminated, but all necessary information is included.

Send us $1.50. Keep the book 10 days, and if it isn't worth the price, return it and get your money back.

The Commercial Press
Publishers The Canadian Furniture World and The Undertaker
32 Colborne Street, Toronto

CHRISTIAN BURIAL.

(By Rev. J. J. McDermott, Sussex, N.B.)

Our duties towards the faithful do not cease when the soul has left its earthly mansion. In the rubrics, the Church expresses her desire concerning the dead. She directs us to care for the bodies of our departed brothers, she bids us to honor and treat their mortal remains that have been the temple of the Holy Spirit as the relics of saints. Regarding the corpse of a Christian as a sacred thing, the Church goes into minute details as to how it should be laid out and reverently guarded with vigils and sacred rites before the earth receives it. On the day of burial the body is carried to the church; the holy sacrifice of the Mass is offered for the repose the soul, and the body sprinkled with holy water, and incensed. There is nothing more pathetic and consoling for mourners than the solemn rites over the remains of their loved ones.

The dead Christian visits for the last time the church where he was born to God in baptism, where sin-stained he was cleansed, where he so often nourished his soul with the Bread of angels and knelt in humble devotion to adore the Immaculate Victim upon the altar. The Church now parts with him in peace and hope: eternal rest grant him, O Lord; let perpetual light shine upon him.

From the church the funeral train moves slowly and solemnly to the cemetery, where the ashes of Christians are sacredly guarded until the day of resurrection. The procession to the cemetery should be thoroughly Christian. How can a Christian engage in frivolous conversation as he is winding his way to the burial grounds, his own future home?

Into its furrows shall we all be cast,
At the great harvest, where the arch-angels blast
Shall winnow, like a fan, the chaff and grain.
—Longfellow.

The funeral director is called upon to bury the bodies of saints. Those bodies will rise again, united to their souls, glorious and immortal, as we trust, for all eternity. Is not your calling a sacred one? See to it then that you keep yourselves always worthy of your calling.—The Funeral Director.

NEW UNDERTAKING PARLORS AT SASKATOON.

Furnished and stocked on an elaborate scale, and prepared to carry on business and guarantee general satisfaction, G. H. McKague & Sons have opened up undertaking and embalming offices and a chapel in the Travellers' Block, 240 Third Avenue, Saskatoon, which cannot be surpassed in that city. The new firm were located first at Outlook, Sask., where they carried on business for four years. In their new showrooms they display every line of casket, ranging from an elegant state bronze casket, costing over $2,000, down to the ordinary coffin. The stock also includes solid mahogany caskets, mission oak and golden oak, besides the same class covered with royal purple, black and steel gray material.

On entering the office one is immediately struck by the rich and costly appearance of everything. The furniture is of mission oak style and is entirely new. To the left is a private room, large and well lighted, fitted with luxurious lounging chairs and which is used for a private office, the waiting room being similarly furnished. The chapel arrangements are particularly impressive. It is carpeted and supplied with new chairs, a new chapel organ and a pulpit rest for the minister when conducting service. Chairs for the pall-bearers and the mourners are on either side of the rest for the casket. Paintings depicting scriptural scenes most appropriate for the room are also nicely arranged. Directly at the rear of the chapel, which is curtained off from the front waiting room, is the embalming room, equipped with everything necessary; it is well lighted and ventilated.

G. H. McKague holds diplomas from the Canadian School of Embalming, Toronto, where he took a special course, and also from The Western Canada Funeral Directors and Embalmers' Association.

TORONTO'S HEALTH BETTER.

Toronto's bill of health is much better than it was a year ago, according to the figures of the Department of Medical Health. There was an increase of six cases in diphtheria and nine in scarlet fever, these being the only diseases showing an increase. There was a big drop in the number of cases of measles, and also in smallpox and chickenpox. Though there were 100 cases of mumps reported this February, there were none in February, 1913, and there were nine cases of erysipelas, with none reported in February of 1913.

	Feb. 1914	Feb. 1913
Diphtheria	87	81
Scarlet fever	154	145
Measles	208	431
Smallpox	2	11
Tuberculosis	51	54
Chickenpox	38	79
Whooping cough	22	23
Mumps	100	..
Erysipelas	9	..

Not so Many Burials.

The Toronto General Burying Grounds trustees give the following number of burials in three cemeteries as compared with February, 1913. It will be noticed that the number of burials are less than last year in each case:

	Feb. 1914	Feb. 1913
Mount Pleasant	113	130
Necropolis	7	24
Prospect	108	137

FROM UNDERTAKER TO COMEDIAN.

From an employee in an undertaker's establishment to principal comedian of a big musical comedy is rather a unique advancement. This distinction, however, has befallen Frank Tinney, chief funmaker of the "Ziegfeld Follies," which recently played at one of the Toronto theatres. Tinney, who was born in Philadelphia, made his debut on the stage at Keith's Theatre in 1903. His style of comedy failed to evoke the necessary quantity of laughter, and the newcomer was stamped a failure. The would-be actor declared that he was disgusted with the theatrical game, and immediately busied himself in the direction of seeking employment that would at least net him a livelihood. He was hired by an undertaker at a weekly salary of fifteen dollars. Tinney was assigned to the embalming department of the establishment, and as he knew little or nothing about the business, was discharged after a month's trial. This forced him to make another attempt at "acting." Fortunately he procured an engagement in one of the popular-priced vaudeville houses, where he presented the same act he formerly tried at Keith's. Strange to say, this time he scored a success, and he continued in vaudeville for several years.

To Canadian Funeral Directors

THE CENTRAL LINE

Mahogany, Oak, Plush and Cloth Covered Caskets

WE SHIP PROMPTLY

We can also supply anything desired in Casket Linings, Burial Robes, and a general line of Undertakers' Supplies

Orders given our Canadian representative, or sent to our factory at Bridgeburg by mail, telegraph or telephone will be shipped promptly. "We never miss a train."

CENTRAL CASKET COMPANY
Bridgeburg, Ont.   R. S. Flint   Canadian Representative: 241 Fern Ave., Toronto

---

DIOXIN
IS PLEASANT TO USE!

IF DIOXIN had no other superiority over the ordinary formaldehyde fluids, the fact that it is safe and pleasant to use should insure it a place in the affections of every embalmer.

If there is any one feature in the care of the dead human body that is more annoying than any other, it is the fact that, except DIOXIN, practically every fluid in the market will literally pickle the hands of most operators, no matter how careful they may be, and, particularly in cold weather, will open up painful sores which it is practically impossible to heal.

DIOXIN users are free from this great annoyance and danger—for every open cut or sore affords a hiding and breeding place for the germs of disease.

CONSIDER YOUR ASSISTANT

Perhaps your assistant does the most of your embalming. Consider his comfort and his health for selfish if for no other reasons. A good assistant, familiar with your wants, your methods and your customers, is a jewel. Make his work as safe and pleasant as you can.

Preserve his delicacy of touch. It may save you the embarrassment of an unsatisfactory result, or even of a spoiled body. There are enough risks in embalming, enough chances for mistakes, enough opportunities for error, without adding others unnecessarily.

Formaldehyde does not dangerously affect the hands of every embalmer, but it must, deaden, must dull, the sensitive and delicate nerves of the fingers and render the worker less sure of touch, less certain of results, particularly in difficult cases. You can wash your hands in DIOXIN without injury.

NO TORTURED EYES WITH DIOXIN

The fumes of most fluids, too, in addition to attacking the hands, have a particularly irritating effect upon not only the mucous membranes of the eyelids, but upon the eyes themselves. This is particularly offensive and harmful when the work is done in a warm or brilliantly-lighted room.

DIOXIN DOES NOT EMBALM Your LUNGS

DIOXIN has no injurious effect upon the eyes or eyelids of the operator. The embalmer does not embalm his own eyesight when he uses it. If you or your assistant have suffered from the pungent effects of ordinary raw formaldehyde fluids, try DIOXIN. What little fumes arise from it are pleasant and positively non-irritant. Indeed, we feel that we cannot too strongly recommend DIOXIN to all embalmers who are troubled with falling eyesight—and most users of raw formaldehyde fluids are literally pickling their eyes.

Most of us are almost overcome when entering a room filled with the fumes of formaldehyde. We may not realize it, but we really are literally embalming our own lungs. In DIOXIN, what formaldehyde the fluid does contain, is purified and modified into formochloral, while peroxide of hydrogen, the great bleacher and disinfectant, replaces a very great proportion of this irritating agent.

As a result, DIOXIN has absolutely no deleterious effect upon either the lungs of the operator or the mucous membranes of nostrils and throat.

Dioxin comes in Bulk and Concentrated and RE-Concentrated.

Did we mention the fact that DIOXIN does not fill the house with offensive odors? That is another of its many virtues. And did we say that it makes the body firm, but pliable, rendering posing in the casket easy. Rigidity is not essential to preservation; in fact, it retards the circulation of the fluid.

But we've told you enough—although only a small part of the virtues of DIOXIN. Try it yourself—that is the great convincer. Order to-day!

H. S. ECKELS & CO.
1922 Arch St., Philadelphia, Pa.   241 Fern Ave., Toronto, Ont., Can.

Gossip of the Profession

John Wilson's undertaking parlors at Okotoks, Alta., were damaged by fire recently.

H. L. Merritt has purchased the undertaking business at Carnduff, Sask., from J. H. Taylor.

Campbell & Campbell, funeral directors of Brandon, Man., have now a lady assistant in their embalming business.

A. Boucher & Co. have been registered at Montreal to do business as undertakers at Arthabaska and Victoriaville.

J. C. Van Camp, a leading Toronto undertaker, has been elected president of the Lambton County Old Boys' Association.

Sill, Paterson & Millar, Ltd, have opened an undertaking establishment at 652-654 Broadway, West Vancouver. The Central Mfg. & Supply Co., Vancouver, secured part of the opening order.

For the first time in Canada, a motor hearse was exhibited at the Toronto Motor Show this year. It was the car which has been used in Toronto for the past four months, and owned by A. W. Myles.

A new hearse has just been added to the equipment of George Speers, the Regina undertaker. It is a costly vehicle of the very latest type, up-to-date in every particular, and is a beautiful piece of workmanship.

Maritime Mausoleum Co., Ltd., is the name of a new concern, established at Halifax, N.S., recently incorporated at Ottawa, to make, build, equip and operate burial vaults and community mausoleums. The capital is set at $500,000.

The Dominion Mausoleum Co., Ltd., Brantford, capitalized at $40,000, has received an Ontario charter to erect, construct and sell mausoleums. The provisional directors are H. H. Powell, M. M. Cleveland, Thos. Hendry, J. W. Champion and E. C. Andrich.

E. G. Cross, who has been in charge of the undertaking business of R. White & Co., Stratford, for some time, has decided to take up business for himself in Wiarton, his home town. A. E. Hunter, a Stratfordite, is taking Mr. Cross' position with White & Co.

While proceeding to a funeral at Kingston Mills, Ont., on March 1, the day of the "big wind," Rev. Father Halligan and undertaker Thomas Ronan were thrown out in a snowdrift when the hack in which they were being driven upset. The funeral party had to turn back, and the burial was postponed until the next day, owing to the snowbound roads.

J. Watkinson, of Brandon, has joined the staff at A. E. Young's undertaking establishment, at Saskatoon. Mr. Watkinson succeeds B. H. Greenwood, who has gone to Transcona to open a business for himself. Mr. Watkinson was for ten years in the service of Campbell and Campbell, Brandon, and for the past year has been Western representative for the Winnipeg Casket Company.

NEW CASKET MANUFACTURING COMPANY

The Canada Casket Co., Ltd., Wiarton, Ont., has received letters patent from the Ontario Government and a charter authorizing them to manufacture and deal in caskets, coffins, shell and undertakers' sundries and supplies, hardware, ornamental fittings and furnishings; and also to carry on the business of wood workers and cabinet makers in all its branches. The capital is set at $300,000. The promoters have applied to the town of Wiarton for a loan of $30,000.

AN APPRECIATION.

Editor Furniture World and the Undertaker:

As an old acquaintance, and friend of A. J. H. Eckardt, late proprietor of the National Casket and National Silver Plating Companies, of Toronto, permit me to say that I knew Mr. Eckardt, when he made his maiden trip as a commercial traveller. He represented R. Philp, at that time, the first man in Canada to manufacture coffins and caskets. This was some 34 years ago. At that time Mr. Eckardt was a fine-looking young man of good habits, and I am pleased to say he has not changed much in either respect. Considering the men he has been doing business with all these years, I mean the undertakers,—he certainly is entitled to great credit for retaining his early piety.

Some years after Mr. Eckardt became a partner in the business, and it became known as Philp & Eckardt. And later still Mr. Eckardt became sole proprietor. He has given close attention to the needs of the undertaking business—up-to-date office methods; a leader in new designs, and ever watchful that the prices were not in advance of the quality of goods produced, and services rendered. He is a far-seeing business man. After the big fire in 1904, which destroyed his large factory and warerooms, he was out of active business for about three years, but the manufacturing of funeral goods and undertaking supplies seemed to be his desire and ambition, and the purchase of the property on Niagara Street was an evidence of his far-seeing business ability. Mr. Eckardt did not confine his efforts to the manufacturing of funeral and undertakers' supplies alone, but has large interests in other lines of business which have proven successful, and while yet a young man has succeeded in gathering together a financial competency.

Now that he has retired, he again exhibits his thoughtfulness and big heartedness by remembering financially his employees, friends and societies. It came to my notice while acting as secretary of the Can. adian Embalmers' Association for three years that Mr. Eckardt has been a friend to organizations such as ours. The Maritime Provinces have been doing good work along association lines of an educational nature, and if the officers were to speak they would tell of assistance and encouragement extended to them by Mr. Eckardt. The Western Associations would also join in and give the same kind of testimony. A friend in years gone by, he continues to be a friend.

The latest and most important act of his toward the associations is, to instruct me to correspond with the president or secretary of each of the six associations, and ask them to accept from him for educational purposes one thousand shares of preferred and five hundred common shares in the recently formed Dominion Manufacturers, to assist the associations and help to forward the good work undertaken by them. I have promised Mr. Eckardt, to take this matter in hand, and see that each of the associations in the Dominion receive the fifteen hundred shares thus promised. And now, on behalf of the associations thus remembered beg to acknowledge his gifts.

J. C. VANCAMP,
Toronto

Undertakers Shipping Directory

ONTARIO

Aurora—
 Dunham, Charles.
Barrie—
 Smith, G. G. & Co.
Brockville—
 Quirmbach, Geo. R., 162 King St.
Brooklin—
 Disney, R. S.
Campbellford
 Irwin, James.
Campden —
 Hausel, Albion.
Clinton—
 Walker, Wesley.
Cobocouk—
 Greenley, A.
Copper Cliff—
 Boyd, W. C.
Dungannon—
 Sproul, William
Dutton—
 Schultz, B. L.
Elmira—
 Dreisinger, Chris.
Fenelon Falls—
 Deyman, L. & Son.
Fenwick—
 H. A. Metler.
Fergus—
 Armstrong, M. F.
 Thomson, John & Son.
Fort William—
 Cameron & Co., 711 Victoria.
 Morris, A.
Haileybury—
 Thorpe Bros.
Galt—
 Anderson, J. & Son.
Hamilton—
 Green Bros., 124 King St. E.
 Robinson, J. H. & Co., 19-21 John St. N.
Hanover—
 Wunneberg, Norman.
Hastings—
 Howard, P. N.
Hepworth—
 Downs, E. J.
Inwood—
 Lorriman, E. S.
Kemptville—
 McCaughey, Geo. A.
Kenora—
 Horn & Taylor.
Kingston—
 Corbett, S. S.
Lakefield—
 Hendren, Geo. G.
Little Current—
 Sims, J. G.
Markdale—
 Oliver, M.
Newmarket—
 Millard, J. H.

North Augusta—
 Wilson, J. R.
North Bay—
 St. Pierre, E.
Oakwood—(Mariposa Station G.T.R.) Wilmot F. Webster.
Ohsweken—
 Johnson, F. L.
Oshawa—
 Disney Bros.
 Luke Bros.
Ottawa—
 Rogers, Geo. H., 128 Bank
Petrolia—
 Steadman Bros.
Port Arthur —
 Collin Wood, 36 Arthur St.
 Morris, A.
Prescott—
 Rankin, H. & Son.
Renfrew—
 O'Connor, Wm.
St. Mary's—
 N. L. Brandon.
St. Thomas—
 Williams, P. R. & Sons, 519 Talbot St.
Seaforth, Ont.
 W. T. Box & Co.
Scotland—
 Vaughan, Jos. H. M.
Sudbury—
 Henry, J. G.
Toronto—
 Cobbledick, N. B., 2068 Queen St. East and 1508 Danford Ave. Private Ambulance.
 Humphrey, E. J. Burial Co. Head Office, 359 Yonge St.; Branch, 407 Queen St. W. Private ambulance.
 Stone, Daniel (formerly H. Stone & Son), 82 Bloor St.. West.
 Vancamp, J. C., 30 Bloor St. West.
Waterloo—
 Klipper Undertaking Co.
Welland—
 Sutherland, G. W.
Woodstock—
 Meadows, T. & Sons.
 Mack, Paul.

QUEBEC

Buckingham—
 Paquet, Jos.
Cowansville—
 Judson, M. B.
Montreal—
 Tees & Co., 912 St. Catherine St. West.
St. Hyacinthe—
 Cadorette, Mongeau & Leary.
St. Laurent—
 Gougeon, Jos.

NEW BRUNSWICK

Petitcodiac—
 Jonah, D. Allison.
Welland—
 Sutherland, G. W.
Woodstock—
 Van Wart, Jacob.

NOVA SCOTIA

Ferrona—
 Fraser, D. & Co.
Halifax—
 Snow & Co., 90 Argyle St.
Sydney, C.B.—
 Beaton, A. J. & Son, 374-384 George St.

MANITOBA

Brandon—
 Campbell & Campbell.
 Vincent & McPherson.
Swan River—
 Paull, Geo.
Winnipeg—
 Bardal, A. S., 834 Sherbrooke
 Thompson, J. C., 501 Main
 Clark-Leatherdale Co., Ltd., 232 Kennedy St.

SASKATCHEWAN

Gull Lake—
 Morrow, Fred. A.
Saskatoon—
 Young, A. E.

Kamsack—
 Russell, G. E. I.
Lanigan—
 Robertson, Wm.
Moose Jaw—
 The Bellamy Co.
 Broadfoot Bros.
Rush Lake—
 Friesen, John M.
Prince Albert—
 Howard, A. C.
 Hadley, C. L.
Regina—
 Speers, George.
Semans—
 Haygarth, Jas.
Welwyn—
 Leavens, Merritt.
Wolseley —
 Barber, B.

ALBERTA

Calgary—
 Graham & Buscomb, 611 Centre St.
Castor—
 Winter, W. G.

BRITISH COLUMBIA

Hosmer—
 Cornett, T. A.
Victoria—
 Hana & Thompson, 827 Pandora Ave.

Index to Advertisements

A
Albrough & Co., J. P............26
Antiseptic Bedding Co..........i.f.c.
Ault & Wiborg...................62

B
Baetz Bros. & Co................16
Batavia Clamp Co................61

C
Canadian Linderman Co..........63
Can. H. W. Johns-Manville Co...23
Central Casket Co...............74
Colleran Patent Spring Mat. Co. 65

D
Dominion Casket Co..............66
Dominion Mfrs., Limited.........70

E
Eckels & Co., H. S..............74
Egyptian Chemical Co............72
Elmira Interior Woodwork Co....12

F
Farquharson-Gifford..............7
Fischmann Mattress Co..........10
Frame & Hay....................13
Freese & Son, J. D............i.b.c.

G
Gale & Son, Geo................23
Globe Wernicke..................9
Gold Medal Furniture Mfg. Co...17
Gendron Wheel Co...............65

H
H. E. Furniture Co..............8
Hourd & Co.....................23

I
Ideal Bedding Co...............28
Imperial Furniture Co..........26
Imperial Rattan Co............o.f.c.
Ives Modern Bedstead Co......i.b.c.

J
Jamieson & Co., R. C............8
Jennings Company...............20

K
Kawneer Mfg. Co................20
Kindel Beds Co., Limited.......10
Knechtel Furniture Co..........19
Kohn, J. & J...................10

L
Leggatt & Platt Spring Bed Co..18

M
Matthews Bros..................12
Meaford Mfg. Co.................6
Mundell & Co., John C........i.f.c.
McLagan Furniture Co............3
McKellar Bedding Co............27
Montreal Upholstering Co........4

O
Onward Mfg. Co.................61
Ontario Spring Bed..............4

P
Peppler Bros., Limited.........24

R
Robertson, P. & L., Mfg. Co....62

S
Shafer, D. L...................26
Stamco, Limited................21
Steele, James Limited..........65
Standard Bedding Co............23
Stratford Brass Co.............13
Stratford Chair Co..............5
Stratford Mfg. Co..............11
St. Thomas Metallic Vault Co...72

V
Victoriaville Bedding Co....14-15

W
Walter & Co., B................61
Western Casket Co..............68
Weisglass, S., Limited.........22

IF YOU WANT TO BUY OR SELL

A Furniture or Undertaking Business, try our Classified Pages. The Canadian Furniture World and The Undertaker is read by practically every furniture merchant and undertaker in Canada every month.

April, 1914   CANADIAN FURNITURE WORLD AND THE UNDERTAKER

Low Priced Furniture

A growing country has a great market for low priced but well built furniture.

Our line is built strong and well. The oak pieces are all built of SOLID OAK and the imitation Mahogany of SOLID BIRCH.

We are the largest manufacturers of low priced Dressers, Chiffoniers and Ladies' Desks in the North.

This enables us to sell on a very small margin.

LOOK AT THE PRICES ON PIECES SHOWN
All our Prices are in Proportion

202
Price $5.00. Weight 95 lbs.
Top 18x33. Height 64 in.
French bevel plate mirror 12x20.
Same, with imitation quart. oak front and top. Price $5.25.

102
Price $5.45. Weight 110 lbs.
Top 18x30. Height 69 in.
French bevel plate 12x16.

215
Price $6.50. Weight 110 lbs.
Top 18x38. Height 67 in.
French bevel plate 20x22.

We also manufacture a line of the above goods in the Colonial Style.
Terms: F.O.B. Chicago. 60 days net—2% for cash in 20 days.
Our location is the most convenient in the U.S. to supply the Canadian Trade. Order one of the above pieces to-day as a sample—then look over our illustrated catalog. It means PROFIT FOR YOU.

J. D. FREESE & SONS CO.
2501-2523 HOMER STREET
CHICAGO, U.S.A.

CANADIAN FURNITURE WORLD AND THE UNDERTAKER   April, 1914

"Regal" BEDS

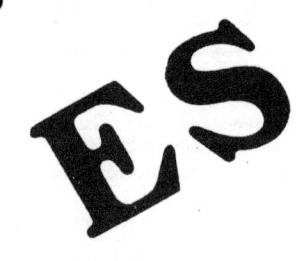

IES

Modern Bedstead Company, Limited

TRADE MARK *Regal* REGISTERED

Service

Our large stocks in Cornwall, Montreal, and Winnipeg are in first class shape for rush spring business, and

Name

Is synonymous with all that is best in Metal Beds and Bed service.

CHILLESS STEEL BED No. 540

Modern Bedstead Co., Limited

MONTREAL   CORNWALL   WINNIPEG

Vol. 4 No. 5　　　　　　　　　　　　　　　　　　　　　　　　　　　　　　MAY, 1914

Canadian Furniture World
AND THE UNDERTAKER

Published by the Commercial Press, Limited, 32 Colborne Street, Toronto

THE McLAGAN LINE offers practically unlimited possibilities for diversified selection in Dining Room Suites, Buffets, Sideboards, Library Sets; Parlor, China, Music and other Cabinets; Folding, Card, Centre, Library and Dining Tables and other Novelty pieces.

Make your floors, your windows, more attractive by displaying a few pieces from our comprehensive range

The Geo. McLagan Furniture Co.
LIMITED

Stratford　::　Ontario

MISSION FURNITURE

THE MUNDELL MAKE

WHAT strikes you about our Mission Furniture is the variety. We make Davenports and Footstools and everything between that you can think of in Mission Goods,—all grades, all descriptions.

For Spring business these Mission Lines are indispensable. Furniture for halls, dens, living rooms, libraries, dining rooms, smoking rooms—frequently more than one half of many dwellings is furnished in Mission Style, and the demand goes on increasing.

You will be pleased with our new designs in this furniture—Heavy Oak Frames, Rich Spanish Leather Upholstering, all in dark tints as if centuries old,—simple lines, heavy, substantial, rich looking, there is no doubt that this class of furniture is one of the dealer's most attractive and profitable lines.

You will find all the varieties, all grades, all prices, in the Mundell line. Let us mail you blue prints.

JOHN C. MUNDELL & CO., LIMITED
ELORA :: ONTARIO

Notice of Removal!

The Fischman Mattress Co. Have Removed from 569 Queen St. W., to 333 Adelaide St. W.

Our former plant not being adequate to meet the increasing demand for the Fischman Patent Mattress, we were obliged to obtain much larger premises and to increase our facilities.

THE FISCHMAN PATENT MATTRESS
Can. Pat., Mar. 16, 1909 U.S. Pat., Feb. 16, 1909

In our new building we have installed machinery of the most modern type, and while our output will be much greater, the well known quality of our mattresses will still be given the same attention.

McLaughlin & Scott, Canadian selling Agents
67-71 Adelaide Street West

STRATFORD

which are within the means of the great middle class—for those who are buying for to-morrow and who will pay a little more than the price for cheap goods.

That's the trade for you, Mr. Furniture Man, and Stratford Chairs will draw and hold it for you.

You'll be delighted with the beauty of design, richness in figure of selected woods and the exquisite finish of the new lines we are showing in Diners, Den and Library Chairs.

Get an order in early; the June Bride will be among those who will need Stratford Chairs.

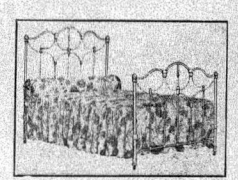

No. 855—List Price $11.20   No. 852—List Price $8.20   No. 853—List Price $9.80

Get a New Line On Profits

All of the "Ontario Line" whether Brass Beds, Iron Beds, Springs or Mattresses, can be sold at a good satisfying margin, simply because they are such obviously

Big Values

Take the three patterns of Brass Trimmed Iron Beds shown above. You will agree that they are all good, saleable designs. We have found that they seldom fail to sell on sight.

Will you not let us demonstrate the value of our line by allowing us to send on a trial order?

The Ontario Spring Bed & Mattress Company, Limited

The Largest Bedding House in Canada

London   -   Ontario

"On the Job" 24 Hours in Every Day

There is always a place and a use in every home, large or small, rich or poor, for either a Revolving Bed or a Duofold, and every wise dealer, who wants to buy better value for less money and make a large profit for himself, ought to send his orders to The Montreal Upholstering Co., where style and prices are made to suit everybody.

Try a Sample Order.   **OUR FAMOUS DUOFOLD**   Special Discount on Car Lots.

FRAME:
Quartered Cut Oak,
Finish Fumed Oak and Golden Oak.

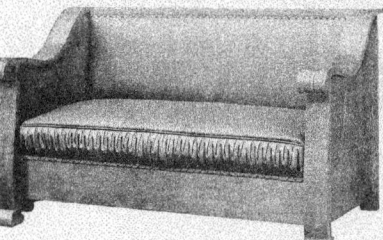

PRICES:
Genuine Leather
$71.00 List.
Genuine Spanish
$74.00 List.

WRITE FOR CATALOGUE.   No. 84—Duofold

The Montreal Upholstering Company

1611-1613 Clarke St., MONTREAL, Can.

STRATFORD

People are house-cleaning and moving these days. Most of them will require new furniture of some sort. Pieces such as these two lines illustrated are particularly strong this spring.

Upholstered Reed Chairs and Rockers are a profitable Imperial Rattan line for you. They embody thorough workmanship and are shown in all coverings.

The Stratford Davenport Bed is now looked upon as a staple, year 'round seller. Davenport Beds are desirable in any home--a necessity in small houses and flats.

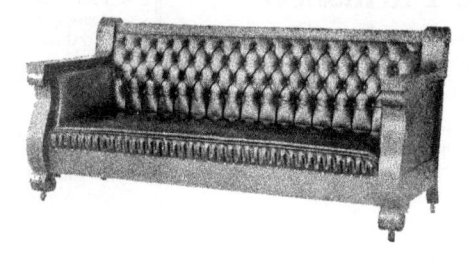

Stratford   Ontario

That We Have Weathered Two Depression Periods in the last Ten Years with
increased trade each time

PROVES beyond doubt that The Meaford Line sells in spite of the times.

¶ Surface Mahogany isn't an imitation as it may seem, any more than the so called Mahogany Furniture made of Birch Lumber, but by a special process we blend the Mahogany Stains, giving the effect of the choicest Mahogany.

¶ These stains each penetrate the wood and simply can't chip off. The after coats are the same as those used on solid mahogany and will last just as long.

Hotels Furnished

with our Mahogany Bedroom Furniture (sold through legitimate dealers only) are the best proof we have of the wear and tear our finishes will stand.

¶ From an economic standpoint nothing can replace the Meaford Line of up-to-the-minute designs and popular finishes.

No. 598

Colonial Design in Surface Mahogany

HERE'S a piece from a suite that has all the dignity, beauty and long-wearing qualities of high-priced mahogany and yet, as we produce it, is as staple a line as anything made.

Other bedroom pieces in this design: — Dresser, Dressing Table, Somnoe and Washstand.

The Meaford Manufacturing Company, Limited
Meaford - Ontario

STRATFORD

One of the Most Important Sale-Making Factors

¶ Comfort is one of the first considerations with all of us. There is nothing that can replace it because it is necessary to our health and happiness. Naturally it is one of the easiest things to sell. *Comfort* is a well developed feature of our attractive lines of

¶ That *cosiness* is built into our goods just as thoroughly as the quality and finish. You'll find the F.G. make among the easiest selling, and better profit-making lines on the market.

While waiting for our traveler to call, just send us a line for photos of the admirable pieces we are featuring.

Stratford   Ontario

The Single Cone Prevents Sagging

¶ Leggett & Platt Single Cone Spring Beds conform to the weight of every part of the body it supports, insuring the most refreshing sleep.

¶ In construction, material and workmanship, the "L" Metal Tag Trade Mark guarantees fidelity in every detail.

¶ The influence of the ultimate purchaser is always to be reckoned with. One "L" Metal Tag sale invariably leads to another.

¶ An order for "L" Trade Marked Spring Beds puts you in the "no competitors" class. They are the best paying line to which you can devote your attention.

Our complete catalogue is ready for you

The Leggett & Platt Spring Bed Company, Ltd.
Windsor, Ont.

This Metal Tag — on Every Spring

Brass Trimmings in All Finishes

Do you fully appreciate the value of solid worth and finer appearance in the Brass Furniture Trimmings you use? We do—that's why we excel in trimmings that wear longer and always look new

Our secret process of finishing is admitted to be the most artistic and lasting in the country.

Anything you want in the quickest time. Correspondence invited.

Stratford Brass Co.
Limited

Stratford   Ontario

THE MOST CONVENIENT FOLDING TABLE MADE

The Popular "Acme"

The table that presents a neater appearance when set up; is more rigid; folds most compactly; gives more service and costs less.

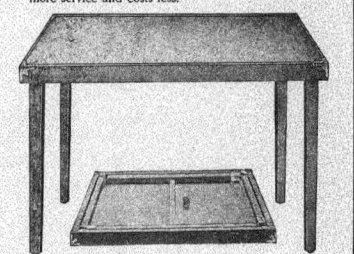

Weighs only 10 lbs. no braces, green felt or leatherette top.
Order half a dozen or more assorted finishes. Will ship them at once.

HOURD & COMPANY, LIMITED
Wholesale Furniture Manufacturers
LONDON - - CANADA
Sole Canadian Licensees and Manufacturers

STRATFORD

The Season of Big Sales in

WITH the Spring re-arrangement of living room and library comes the natural demand for Globe-Wernicke Bookcase Combinations and units for those already in use.

An attractive window showing the many harmonious arrangements obtainable in Globe-Wernicke Bookcase Units will tend to make this a record season for you.

Let us suggest that you plan out an order at once and get your share of the good business inseparable with this world-known line.

WELL ILLUSTRATED CATALOGS WITH PRICE LISTS FOR THE ASKING

Stratford   Ontario

Kohn's Imported Bentwood Furniture Builds Permanent Patronage

Sells easiest because so different and so impressing. Satisfies in service because of superior construction. Lends character to your entire showing. Not so expensive as to be confined to high-class trade.

Write for our Catalogue to-day

Our catalogue should be on your desk for comparison if nothing more. The most progressive merchants find it pays to keep posted on all lines. Writing for a copy will not obligate you in anyway.

Kohn's Imported Bentwood Furniture is artistic, light weight and sanitary. It's extreme durability is due to specially seasoned Beechwood bent by our strength retaining process. All leg joints fastened with steel screws.

JACOB & JOSEF KOHN of Vienna
215-219 Victoria St., Toronto, Canada

110-112 West 27th St., New York City.   1410-1418 So. Wabash Ave., Chicago, Ill.
Second Floor, Keeler Bldg., Grand Rapids, Mich.   418 Maritime Bldg., Seattle, Wash.

No. 3508F

The Kindel — Two Separate
Extremely Useful Articles at the Price of One.

Kindel Convertible Parlor Beds offer your customers added convenience, a saving in space and a money saving in the original purchase and in the reduction of rent.

Three types—The Somersaultic, Divanette and Parlor bed, all intended for separate and definite purposes. You'll find the prices *right* and the advertising that backs them up an added incentive to buy.

Write for our selling plan of "The Bed That Makes Itself."

The Kindel Bed Co. Ltd.
Toronto - Ontario

STRATFORD

Selling Appearance— The appearance of these

lines in your store will create a quick profitable turnover. The Stratford range will meet your customers' requirements in anything in Verandah and Lawn Furniture, Swings, etc.

Send for Our Catalog

IT WILL PAY YOU TO GET AN ORDER UP NOW

Stratford Manufacturing Co., Limited   STRATFORD

¶ Classic No. 5 Extra Fine Lock Weave, Strong 2-inch Maple frame, with two coats of varnish.

Put a few Classic Bed Springs on your floors for the Spring housecleaning trade. They are made from the toughest kiln-dried stock and best grade wire for the purpose. Every spring guaranteed to give the most efficient service.

Write at once for Catalogs and Prices of the Classic Line

One Merchant Stayed— The Other Left

Ever see a "Cut Price Sale", "Bankrupt" or "Receiver's Sale" sign nailed to a KAWNEER FRONT? No, your mind picture of KAWNEER FRONTS is one of action—one which shows prosperity and big business.

And there is a logical reason for that.

KAWNEER FRONTS create interest on the part of the passers-by—they make the people stop, then enter. After all, that's the true work of a good Store Front—to make the people *enter*.

Almost every day we see just such a condition as is shown in this illustration—one Merchant leaving—the other remaining. The departing Merchant is leaving for lack of interest in his Store. If he had been able to compel more people to enter his Store he, too, would remain.

kawneer STORE FRONTS

30,000 Merchants have staked their belief in KAWNEER by installing it in their Stores—and those same 30,000 Stores are today pointed out as the most successful. Many of the country's keenest and most conservative business men have adopted KAWNEER—they have signified their faith in KAWNEER to make business.

The type of Front your business requires can only be determined by an intelligent analysis and to help you in your first step we've compiled "Boosting Business No. 2" which is without question the most instructive and interesting Store Front book ever published. Send for it and see the actual photographs of many of the best-paying big and little Store Fronts in the country—see what other Merchants have adopted to increase their businesses—see photographs of some of the Fronts that paid for themselves in eight, ten and twelve months. The book also contains drawings of suggestions that will help you. A mere request will bring it to you—no matter what your business is or where you are located the countrywide KAWNEER organization enables us to help you wherever you are

Kawneer
Manufacturing Company
Limited
Francis J. Plym, President
Dept. S. 1197 Bathurst Street
TORONTO, CAN.

It stays and pays

Look into this Spring Mattress that Always Makes Good

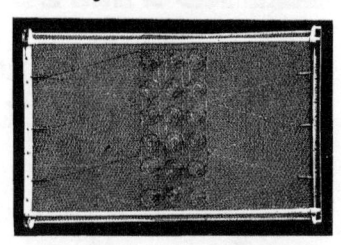

Colleran Patent Spring Mattress
No. 000

Made with a specially tempered steel frame that will resist unusual strains; Colleran patented Rope Edge; mesh of 22-gauge wire double woven; highly tempered steel cone supports six inches deep, and heavy weight-absorbing wires from cones to the tempered steel helicals. Nothing better made in Canada at any price. Unrestrictedly guaranted in any way you like.

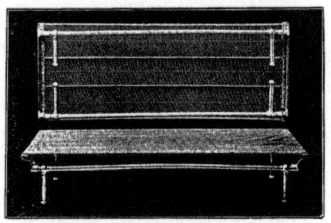

Colleran Patent Divan No. 10

All metal; Colleran patented Rope Edge. The strongest divan made. The legs fold under by a simple twist of the hand when not in use. Get our photos and selling proposition. It's a money-maker for you, Mr. Dealer.

REPRESENTATIVES
Ed. Bagshaw, Western Ontario   A. McNab, Eastern Ontario
J. Clarke, Northern Ontario   J. A. McLaughlin, Quebec

Colleran Patent Spring Mattress Co.
TORONTO, ONT.

Knechtel
No. 275—Elm Golden

Knechtel
No. 277—Elm Golden

Knechtel
No. 275—Elm Golden

Just think of our immense facilities for

Building furniture of all kinds at lower than ordinary cost, and you'll then appreciate the logical benefits resulting to *you*.

A comparison will show that *Knechtel* Furniture offers broader profits than is possible in ostensibly similar lines.

Ask our travellers to show photos of our new lines in Kitchen, Dining Room, Bed Room, Library, Parlor and Office Furniture.

You'll profit more by handling the goods direct "From the Tree to the Finished Product."

Knechtel Furniture Company
Limited
Hanover - Ontario

BAETZ BROTHERS AND COMPANY
BERLIN :: ONTARIO.

No. 608
Bedroom Chairs

This design is made in Chair, Rocker, and Dressing Table Chair. In any of these finishes:

Standard Mahogany
Old English Mahogany
Tuna Mahogany
Golden Oak
Fumed Oak
Silver Grey Oak
Kyonyx
Circassian Walnut
Black Walnut
White Enamel
Ivory Enamel

"Specializing in Chairs"

Pleasing design, beautiful finish, and solid construction, with the big practical feature of Berlin Tables

The Automatic Top

gives the dealer the advantage of being able to show his customer *more* value from every angle. Our Positive Extension Controller operates by a gentle pull on one side which opens both sides. The top is always centered.

An assortment of Berlin Tables on your floors will boost your spring business. They are becoming more popular every season

The Berlin Table Manufacturing Co., Limited
BERLIN :: ONTARIO

Lippert Davenport Beds

Two Home Comforts in One

No. 1. Length 60 inches x 32 inches deep

A NEW ADDITION TO OUR LINE

One of our very attractive designs in our line of Davenports and Davenettes. Ask our traveller to show you this line on his next trip. Get prices and prints---it will pay you.

The Lippert Furniture Co., Limited
BERLIN :: ONTARIO

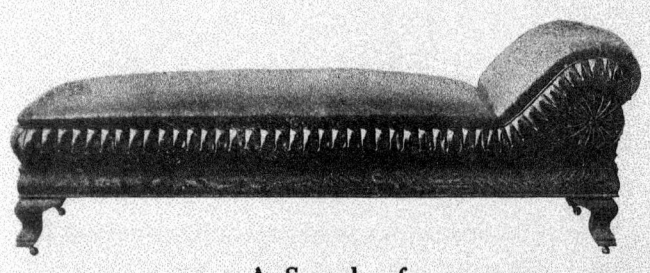

——— A Sample of ———

"Victoriaville" Upholstered Furniture

If you have not already done so, you should get a stock of this furniture on your floors.

The design, comfort and quality of Victoriaville Upholstered Furniture will appeal to your customers at sight, and when you add to this the very reasonable price at which you are able to sell them they simply cannot resist the temptation to buy.

Just send us a small order and see what a short while it will stay on your floors

The Victoriaville Bedding Co., Limited

Formerly
The Canadian Mattress Co., Limited

Victoriaville
Que.

The Big Five Mixed Carload Center

New Designs in Brass Bedsteads

We are continually bringing out new designs in Brass Bedsteads, designs that go a long way towards closing sales for you, Mr. Dealer.

Our long experience and up-to-date machinery enable us to turn out bedsteads of first class quality, at a cost which enables you to sell them at a reasonable figure and still make a good margin of profit.

Victoriaville Beds

are finished so that they may be cleaned with gasoline

Just get a small stock of these beds on your floors and see how fast they will move.

The Big Five Mixed Carload Center

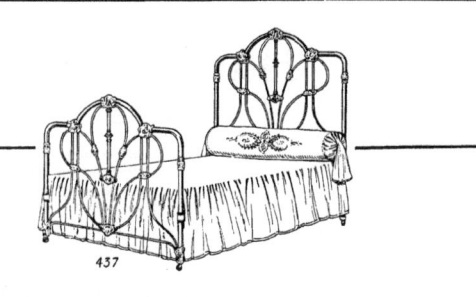

The Victoriaville Bedding Co., Ltd.
(Formerly The Standard Bedstead Co., Limited)
Victoriaville, Que.

Hardwood Chairs
Made to Wear

Our chairs are made to stand hard knocks and, owing to the fact that our plant is devoted exclusively to the manufacture of chairs, enables us to produce them at a very low price to you, Mr. Dealer.

Our catalog will give you an idea of the different designs. A post card will bring it.

The Victoriaville Chair
Manufacturing Company

Victoriaville
Que.

The Big Five Mixed Carload Center

The Good Old Summer Time will soon be here

Are you ready for the big demand for

Verandah Chairs

which this season brings with it? If not, why not send in your order before it is too late?

Nothing but first quality reeds enter into our goods, and we would be pleased to send you a copy of our new catalog of Rattan furniture, showing some splendid new lines.

The Canadian Rattan Chair Co., Limited

V.ctoriaville Que.

The Big Five Mixed Carload Center

Are you ready

With a **good** line of furniture to supply the extra demand which this season brings with it. May and June are the ideal months for weddings, and weddings mean new homes and new furniture.

The Big Five Mixed Carload Center

Victoriaville Furniture

Will fill the requirements of the majority of Newlyweds, because it is manufactured for utility rather than show, although the designs are all new and up-to-date. Our prices are the lowest (quality considered) you can find anywhere, thus allowing you to make a good profit and retail at a reasonable price.

Drop us a card for our catalog, or ask us to send a representative to tell you more about Victoriaville Furniture.

The Victoriaville Furniture Company

Victoriaville, Que.

The Story These Photos Tell

is carried out in thousands of Canadian homes to-day. It is a story of elegance and beauty with quality for a foundation, and a good profit for the dealer who sells them. Write about these new lines shown.

J. P. Albrough & Co.
INGERSOLL, CANADA

Makers of Quality Couches and Easy Chairs

A Popular Spring Design

Of generous proportions, fine appearance and substantially constructed. All materials used are selected for their special fitness in affording the maximum of comfort and service.

Order it now with davenport to match. They will help put more profit on your books *this month.*

Prices and photograph on application

The Imperial Furniture Co., Toronto

Give Your Salesmen Increased Efficiency

Install the "TWENTIETH CENTURY" RUG RACK and make selling rugs a pleasant, easy task.
The old, laborious "rug pile" method is a time waster and a severe tax upon the patience of both salesmen and customers.
By displaying your rugs on the "TWENTIETH CENTURY" RUG RACK, several customers can be waited upon at once and a demonstration is easily effected.
Send us the height of your ceiling and specify the number of rugs you wish to put on rack and we will give you full particulars as to space taken up, etc.
No matter how large or small ; our business, we have a rug rack to just suit your purpose at a price that is speedily repaid by the additional business obtained. *Write for Catalog.*

The Steel Furnishing Co., Ltd.
New Glasgow, N. S.

Manufacturers of Rug Racks, Linoleum Racks, Hearth Rug Racks and Clothing Racks.

Three large Rug Racks holding 120 rugs each

May, 1914　　CANADIAN FURNITURE WORLD AND THE UNDERTAKER　　21

Look at these High Grade Mattresses
Just What You Want For Your Better Class Trade

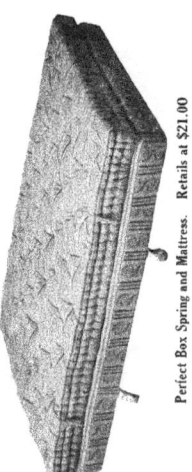

Perfect Box Spring and Mattress.　Retails at $21.00

Hair-in-Cotton Felt.　Retails at $15.00

Kapok or Silk Floss.　Retails at $15.00

Let us send you our price list and other details of our full line of Quality Mattresses.

Put these in your window and they will sell themselves.

Quality Mattresses

will increase your sales and double your profits.

Quality Mattress Co.
Waterloo and Berlin, Ont.
Head Office: Waterloo

QUALITY MATTRESSES
"Gee! this is Comfy"
DURABLE COMFORTABLE SANITARY
TRADE MARK

Every mattress is labeled, showing retail price and what it contains. We stand behind these labels. That is your customers' and your own protection.

The "Elmira" is the *Specialized* Line

You can use **Elmira** goods in your business because they are the kind that build prestige and profits while ordinary lines are becoming shop-worn.

We Manufacture Electric Mantels, Parlor Frames, Library Tables, Office Desks, Filing Cabinets and Sections.

Have You Our Catalog?

Library Table.
Made in Mahogany and Quartered Oak, beautifully finished.

No. 203
Single Pedestal Sanitary Desk

The Elmira Interior Woodwork Co., Limited
C.P.R.   Elmira, Ontario   G.T.R.

The Mattresses That "Prove Up"

You always *expect* the best in every lot of goods you buy. You lose if they don't fulfill your expectations. Our line of Mattresses combine the quality, price and service that inevitably make a *Standard* buy a most profitable one.

Lee-Burrell Rex
A Mattress to suit every taste and purse.

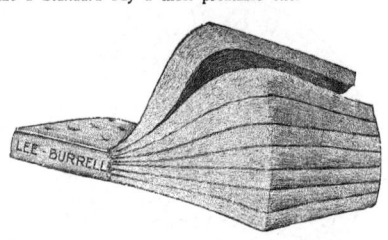

Regent Invictus
The best value possible in every grade.

The Standard Bedding Company
27-29 Davies Ave.   -   Toronto, Ont.

The Weisglass Catalogue

An Important Event for You--and Us

OUR completely illustrated catalogue, No. 1 Canadian Issue, is now ready for mailing and we shall have the greatest pleasure in forwarding a copy to all sellers of our products in the Dominion, on receipt of a postal.

Most careful attention has been given in preparing the illustrations and descriptive matter, and we are confident that a copy will prove of material assistance to your salesmen.

Please Write Us To-day

We Excel in Design, Construction, Finish

"Acid Proof" Lacquer has established a reputation for us that we are proud of. It assists you to sell beds and keep them sold.

S. Weisglass, Limited

Makers of Brass Beds, Woven Wire Springs, Steel Couches and Cabinet Beds

MONTREAL

The Gold Medal Line

SPRING TIME IS BED SPRING TIME

Keep a good supply in stock of

HERCULES
REGISTERED
BED SPRINGS

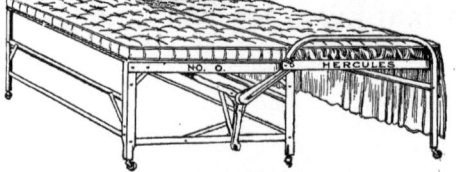

Imperial Steel Sliding Couches and Steel Folding Cots complete with cushions.

A handsome couch by day, a double bed by night. A pressure of the foot converts from the one to the other. The two articles at one cost.

"Purity" Mixed Mattresses and White Cotton Mattress.

"Gold Medal" Felt Mattresses

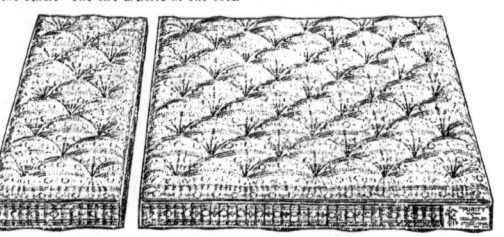

Manufacturers of Parlor and Living Room Furniture

The Gold Medal Furniture Mfg. Co.
Limited

Head office: Van Horne St., Toronto   *Factories also at* Montreal, Winnipeg and Uxbridge

NAGRELLA
Kitchen Cabinet

The Dealer's Opportunity

The Nagrella Kitchen Cabinet is a business "getter" and a business "holder." The unexcelled convenience and superior workmanship and construction make for satisfied customers—and satisfied customers mean more sales on every line you carry.

Priced to allow you a handsome margin of profit. Supplied with or without flour sifter or drop leaf.

Write at once for our Dealer Proposition

The Nagrella Mfg. Co., Ltd.
Cor. Shaw and Emerald Sts.
Hamilton, - Ontario

You Can Capture the Table Cover Trade of Your Town with J-M ASBESTOS TABLE COVERS

For years the wide-awake women of this country have known J-M Asbestos Table Covers and Mats to be absolutely the very best value obtainable in such goods. They know that we mine our own asbestos and manufacture our own asbestos articles, and that we are the largest and oldest concern in this line of business.

Why not take advantage of these facts and handle J-M Asbestos Table Covers in preference to any other line. We are prepared to make you an interesting special proposition if you will write to our nearest Branch house in your territory.

Write us TO-DAY for particulars

**THE CANADIAN
H. W. JOHNS-MANVILLE CO., Limited**
Manufacturers of Show-Case, Show-Window and General Illuminating Systems; Asbestos Table Covers and Mats; Pipe Coverings; Dry Batteries, Fire Extinguishers, Etc.

TORONTO   WINNIPEG
MONTREAL   VANCOUVER

WE are manufacturing an extensive line of Roman Stripes, Art Serge, Armure, Egyptian and Monk's Cloth, together with all grades of Tapestry curtains, and are selling direct to the trade.

Give us a chance to send our representative to you. It will be worth your while to consider the above lines. They are the best obtainable—the kind of goods that bring buyers back for more.

The Dominion Hammock
Manufacturing Company
Limited
Dunnville   Ontario

STAMCO, LIMITED

Manufacturers of

BEDS and BEDDING

with our

Modern Plant and Up-to-date Methods

we are able to guarantee

QUALITY and SERVICE

We are on all three transcontinental lines and we have our own siding. We carry large stocks and whether you want small quantities or carloads we can give you

QUICK DELIVERY

A post card will bring you our 1914
Catalogue per return

Stamco, Limited
Saskatoon and Edmonton

Stamco of Regina, Limited
Regina

Beds, Springs, Mattresses, Comforters, Pillows, Blankets, Tents, Awnings, and all kinds of Canvas Goods

Our Secret Process of Cross Binding Eliminates All Possibility of Spreading

You have probably experienced the dissatisfaction resulting from mattresses **spreading**. Mighty discouraging to have what you think is a good sale turn up **wrong** like that, isn't it?

Kellaric Mattresses are unconditionally guaranteed to keep their shape, and they last even longer than your customer expects. It pays **you,** Mr. Dealer, to sell your customers

KELLARIC MATTRESSES

The next time you are near a Kellaric, take a peek through the laced opening. It will show you why the Kellaric is a **leader** in **good** Mattresses.

Altogether the product of Canadian skill, our lines embody the best there is in comfort, sanitation and economy.

Our popular priced lines are: The **Model Spring, Hair-in-Cotton** and the **Common Sense.** *Write for further information*

The McKellar Bedding Co., Ltd.
Fort William   Ontario
The Berlin Bedding Company, Limited, 31-33 Front St. E., Toronto, Ont.

"Makes Sleeptime Sleepfull"

CANADIAN FURNITURE WORLD AND THE UNDERTAKER.   May, 1914

FRAME: Height, 5 feet 6 inches.   Length, 7 feet 6 inches.   Width, 3 feet.   WEIGHT: 50 lbs.
COUCH: Height of Windshield, 2 feet 1 inch.   Length, 6 feet.   Width, 2 feet 2 inches.
WEIGHT WITH MATTRESS, 75 lbs.
Finished in best quality tan duck.   Metal parts painted green.   Couch may be used separately as a Divan.
Spring—the famous Simmons Fabric, attached to heavy angle frame by strong helical springs.

THE ORIGINAL
1914 MODEL HAMMO-COUCH

"First in the Field and Still Leading"
The "Ideal"
HAMMO-COUCH

BEING the original and most widely advertised Hammo-Couch in Canada, it is only natural that it should be in greater demand than ever. Not only so, but this year's model has many exclusive and up-to-date features.

1. Has a real spring—strong and comfortable.
2. Mattress filled with cotton—neatly finished with Box Edge.
3. Weight so carried that couch cannot tip or give way.
4. Attractive canopy—adjustable to all positions.
5. Our own type stand—neat, compact and very strong.
6. Couch can be used indoors as a divan—having folding legs equipped with Ideal Ball Bearing Casters.
7. Has convenient magazine pockets.

Place your orders now to ensure early deliveries. We anticipate an exceedingly heavy demand as the result of our advertising.

Spring is here, and Springtime is Hammo-Couch time.

THE IDEAL BEDDING CO. LIMITED
2-24 JEFFERSON AVENUE   -   TORONTO

Canadian FURNITURE WORLD AND THE UNDERTAKER

PUBLISHED THE 1ST OF EACH MONTH BY

THE COMMERCIAL PRESS, LIMITED
32 COLBORNE STREET, TORONTO
Phone Main 4978

D. O. McKinnon	- - -	President
W. L. Edmonds	- - -	Vice-President
Weston Wrigley	-	Vice-President and Manager of Trade Papers
J. C. Armer	-	Vice-President and Manager of Technical Papers
James O'Hagan		Editor
John A. Fullerton		Associate Editor
Wm. J. Bryans	"	"

Staff Representatives

Geo. H. Honsberger, Advertising Manager	Toronto
F. C. D. Wilkes, Eastern Manager, 704 Unity Bldg.	Montreal
R. C. Howson, Western Representative	Winnipeg
E. J. MacIntyre, Room 659, 122 South Michigan Avenue	Chicago
C. G. Brandt, *Circulation Manager*, Toronto	

Subscriptions
Canada, $1.00 a year. Other Countries, $2.00 a year

PUBLISHERS' STATEMENT—2000 copies of this issue of the Canadian Furniture World are printed for circulation. Itemized statement, showing distribution according to provinces, will be furnished on request.

Vol. 4   MAY, 1914   No. 5

They no Longer Cut Prices. The want of confidence by merchants in each other is the root of many of the evils that affect the retail trade. This is probably more true of retailers in small towns than of those in the cities.

A case in point came under my observation the other day. There are a couple of merchants in a certain small Ontario town. They were keen competitors and cut prices freely. Each considered the other capable of performing any mean and unbusinesslike act. Consequently their relationship was most strained, and when passing scarcely noticed each other.

A traveling salesman, who was intimate with both, became obsessed with the ridiculousness of the situation and made up his mind to draw each of them into conversation about it. Carrying out his intention he found that each recognized the suicidal character of their present price-cutting practices, but that each hesitated to approach the other owing to his lack of confidence in him.

The next time the traveler was in the town he invited the two merchants to take dinner with him. After dinner, as they smoked their cigars, he broached the subject of price-cutting and other trade evils and pointed out how, by recognizing the right of every man to carry on business and by each exercising a little confidence in the other, there was no reason why they should not be remedied.

Each of the merchants saw the point and each was soon confessing his sins of omission and commission with the traveler presiding as father confessor.

No hard and fast agreement was drawn up as a result of the conference, but the two merchants decided to adopt the same method of arriving at costs and to add a moderate profit when fixing the selling price.

Several months have since gone by, and the desire is now to maintain prices rather than to slaughter them, for each merchant has discovered that the other fellow can, after all, be trusted.

Our Timber Prodigality. Nations, like individuals who possess great wealth, are often prodigal in their use of it. Canada has a great timber area. All told there are between 500,000,000 and 600,000,000 acres, of which 300,000,000 to 400,000,000 acres are officially estimated to be of commercial size. And yet in spite of this our waste has been so great that our supply for manufacturing purposes threatens to become inadequate.

To the furniture manufacturers this is a matter of no small importance.

The furniture and car manufacturers use between them somewhere in the neighborhood of 180,000,000 board feet of timber, approximately valued at $3,000,000. Of this quantity one-third is estimated to be imported timber.

The chief source of forest waste is, of course, fire. Some authorities are of the opinion that the waste in this respect is more than equal to the value of the timber cut. Even for firewood we cut about $50,000,000 annually, which in value is only exceeded by that of lumber, lath and shingles combined. The aggregate output of these three in 1912 was $84,000,000. The total value of all forest products in 1912 was $182,000,000.

Efficiency in the concrete is knowing how to do the trick in the best and shortest way.

Conservation Methods. The Federal and Provincial Governments are at last awakening to the importance of conserving our forest resources. Not only are they yearly making more systematic efforts to protect the forests from fires, but great areas are being reserved for the benefit of posterity. This area reserve now totals about 140,000,000 acres as compared with less than 7,500,000 thirteen years ago.

For forest protection Ontario last year spent $325,000, Quebec something like $270,000, British Columbia $375,000, New Brunswick $35,000, and Nova Scotia $8,000. These figures include amounts expended by lumber companies as well as by the various Provincial Governments.

When one considers that it requires generations to produce a tree of commercial size, one begins to realize the importance of conservation. A spruce tree twelve inches through cannot be produced in less than 120 years, while the modest looking cedar requires 175 to 200 years to come to the size necessary for the average pole.

As quality is of more importance to young home builders than price, it is quite obvious the course the furniture dealer should pursue in his selling talks when seeking the business of prospective June brides.

Nearly All Increased Profits. Reference has been made more than once in these columns to the exceptionally profitable year experienced by the banks of Canada during 1913.

A return recently issued shows that the loan and trust companies had a similar experience. In fact, speaking generally, 1913 was the most successful year on record.

All but two of the loan companies, out of thirty-six, came through the year with increased profits, and twelve out of fifteen trust companies were able to report a like result.

As with the banks, so, naturally, with the loan companies, the demand for money and its pronounced stringency enabled them to demand and obtain high rates of interest on funds loaned.

But, probably, the most satisfactory feature of the situation is the strong position which the loan and trust companies of the country occupy. Like the banks, they appear to be in a stronger position than ever. And that after a severe period of stress and storm.

It is experiences like these that help to maintain and strengthen Canada's position in the financial world.

It is not considered impolite for the furniture dealer to "get the ear" of the prospective June bride. At any rate it is considered politic that he should do so.

Great Grain-Shipping Ports. The good people of Port Arthur and Fort William have been doing a little chest expansion lately.

They have been doing some calculating for the purpose of ascertaining how the ports of the "Twin Cities" compare with those elsewhere as shippers of grain. It is the result of this figuring which has occasioned the chest expansion.

The total quantity of grain shipped last year from what might be termed the "two-in-one" ports, was 203,328,129 bushels. During the same year Buffalo received 172,138,000 bushels, Duluth-Superior shipped 115,880,000 bushels. New York received 84,994,000 bushels. Montreal shipped 54,342,000 bushels, and Chicago shipped 54,292,000 bushels.

The "Twin Cities" therefore handled 31,189,000 more bushels of grain than any other port on the continent: in fact, in the world.

Thus, while the West can boast of being the grain-growing centre of Canada, the Port Arthur—Fort William people can boast that their joint port is the world's chief grain-shipping centre.

And yet the Great West, whence the elevators at Port Arthur and Fort William get their supply of grain, still has a quarter of a billion or more acres of agricultural lands that are not yet under cultivation!

That there are still greater things in store for the ports of Port Arthur and Fort William must be patent to all who give thought to the subject.

Because Spring is lingering, it by no means follows that the business man should be late with his method for getting Spring trade.

A Business Stimulant. There is no better business stimulant than advertising. Possibly every business man could manage to get along without it, but he cannot get along as well without it as he can with it. There is no question about it.

What is to-day one of the largest firms of its kind in Canada began business a score of years ago with a very limited capital.

They managed to muddle along for a while, the growth being slow and painful. Finally the head of the firm decided that their only salvation was to advertise. Hitherto they had not spent a cent in advertising.

They decided to be systematic about the matter, and so appropriated a certain sum for the purpose. The appropriation, like their capital, was small.

The wisdom of the expenditure was soon apparent. Business began to move in a way that was foreign to all previous experience. Encouraged by this, the appropriation for advertising was at once increased two-fold; and that paid.

The firm is still growing and is still advertising.

A good window display speaks louder than words.

Death Roll of Consumers. Twelve hundred and twenty industrial workers were killed in Canada last year while engaged in their regular vocations.

This is of more than passing interest to business men. Every life lost destroyed at least a consumer if not a customer direct.

As a consumer of various forms of merchandise each victim may be estimated to be worth $500 a year to the country. If this estimate is approximately correct it means that by the death of these 1,220 persons, $610,000 was lost to the business men during the year. On the same basis $6,100,000 would be lost in ten years.

But this is not all, for by the serious accidents which befell 5,780 other persons, there was a further decrease in purchasing power.

It is quite evident that business men should have more than a passing interest in the "safety first" movement which is now becoming so general in Canada as well as in other civilized countries.

There is an economic as well as a humanitarian aspect to the subject.

A little more effort will usually bring to the store of the furniture dealer a little more of the business which arises out of June weddings.

Neglect of Potent Factors. There are hundreds of merchants throughout the length and breadth of the land who scarcely ever pay any attention to window dressing, while advertising they shun as they would the Evil One. And yet of the potency of these two factors in the development of business there can be no doubt.

If every dealer in the land who is now practically neglecting these two factors were on the morrow to come to himself and follow in the train of those who already intelligently and persistantly dress their windows well and judiciously advertise their wares and the service they are in a position to render, a revolution would be worked in a short time, and country customers, who now think it is the proper thing to buy from mail order houses, would wake up to the fact that for more reasons than one it would be to their advantage to buy at home.

Lazy-brains are responsible for more failures than lack-of-brains.

A Sign of Disintegration. The merchant who thinks he knows everything about his business that it is possible to learn is usually he whose business is no larger to-day than it was yesterday or the day he started. And so it will be until he discovers that the more he really knows the more there is for him to learn.

This principle is as true in business as in science.

The ignorant man is he who "knows it all."

Business building is one of the most interesting and fascinating games in the world to those who are daily conceiving new ideas and seeking newer and better methods.

Canadian Trade in Process of Recuperation

A Review of the Financial and Industrial Past and a Careful and Detailed Study of the Future as Far as the Different Canadian Industries are Concerned

BY W. L. EDMONDS

TRADE conditions in Canada to-day are very much different from what they were a year ago. Last Spring authorities in Canada, as well as those in other parts of the world, were scanning the financial horizon with some concern. They saw gathering premonitions of a coming storm. The money market had for some time, owing to the heavy demands which were being made upon it the world over, been exhibiting a decided tendency toward stringency and consequent higher rates of interest. To make matters worse, there was the war in the Balkans.

War doesn't turn capital over; it eats it up and destroys it. And the two wars absolutely wiped out of existence capital to the amount of half a billion dollars, or about equal to twice the sum of money Canada has been borrowing annually for government, municipal and industrial purposes.

A Clearing Sky.
Since last Spring the clouds which were peering above the horizon have enveloped the financial sky and the storm which was threatened became an actuality. And it was a rather severe storm. But it has now apparently spent its force. At any rate, the clouds are lifting, and while they have yet by no means been entirely dissipated the outlook is gradually improving. Confidence is being restored, although it may be but slowly. The stringency of the money market is practically a thing of the past.

The way Canada has weathered the storm is in many respects a matter for congratulation. We felt the effects of the storm probably less than did the United States. But we felt it keenly enough just the same. And we are still feeling it to some extent. But its centre was in the Western Provinces. And there was an obvious reason for that. Being in an earlier stage of development, they had naturally been living on credit more than any other part of the Dominion, and consequently were less able to stand the financial stringency when it appeared. But what really aggravated the situation in the Western Provinces was the inordinate spirit of speculation in real estate which prevailed there. Inordinate speculation in real estate, or in anything else for that matter, cannot be carried on all the time. A day of reckoning inevitably comes, and when it does come men who have starved their business must suffer from its effect when the money they have tied up in investments is no longer realizable.

Quick-rich methods are not conducive to permanent prosperity. What they do breed is extravagance, and where extravagance abounds capital is wasted rather than created. Thrift is the only thing which creates capital, and this is a wholesome lesson which we in Canada have yet to learn. But we are learning. Experience is teaching us.

Maritime Provinces.
One of the most gratifying things in connection with the small effect it has had upon the older provinces of the Dominion and particularly the Maritime Provinces. While of course the Maritime Provinces have been affected to some extent, yet it has been, comparatively speaking, to a small extent. As a matter of fact, instead of "marking time" the provinces down by the sea have been, and still are, advancing industrially. They have taken on a new lease of life. They have more confidence in their industrial future than they have ever exhibited before. They believe they are at last coming to their own. Not having gone to the extremes during the past few years that other parts of the Dominion have, they naturally have been in a better position during the past twelve months to weather the financial storm.

To the manufacturers in Ontario the Maritime Provinces have, during the past months of stress and strain, been, as it were, a "saving remnant." In other words, by their increased sales in Eastern, they have been, in many instances, largely recouped for their decreased sales in Western Canada.

The Furniture Industry.
The position of the furniture industry during 1913 was rather unique. During 1912 business was abnormal, and when 1913 began many of the factories found themselves with a good many of the previous year's orders unfilled. Some had at least 25 per cent. unfilled. Although some of them began to feel the money stringency as early as April, as far as their North-west trade was concerned, the furniture factories as a rule were kept busy until November or December.

There was a good deal of slaughtering in prices, particularly during the latter part of the year, but taking it on the whole the furniture manufacturers of Canada did a large business during 1913. Some at least did 20 per cent. more than in 1912. One large manufacturer, whose business in the West fell off 75 per cent., was enabled, through increased trade in the East, to show a net gain of 2 per cent. As a matter of fact, the comparatively satisfactory condition of trade in Ontario, Quebec and the Eastern provinces saved the situation for a great many manufacturers. In most instances it will probably be found that greater effort was found necessary to get business than was the case in 1912. The fact that a great many desks and a great deal of office furniture generally were thrown upon the market, through the closing of real estate offices, militated against the manufacturers of this line of goods.

In spite of the stringency in the money market and its effect on business generally, furniture manufacturers had in many instances to pay higher prices for material. This was particularly true of oak.

Unperturbed About the Future.
Furniture manufacturers are not at all perturbed in regard to the outlook for 1914. They all realize that a good deal of caution will need to be exercised, at any rate until the new crop is assured. And although orders on the books are all the way from 25 to 40 per cent. smaller than at this time last year, business has been gradually improving since the middle of January. It has, however, practically been confined to Ontario, Quebec and the Maritime provinces. An improvement in trade with the Western provinces and British Columbia is not expected at any rate until the Autumn.

Owing to the expansion which took place during 1912 and early in 1913 in factory capacity the manufacturers are now in a much better position to take care of a larger volume of business than they were, but should trade develop next Autumn, as many think it will, it is quite possible that they may again find themselves taxed to fill orders promptly, particularly in view of the light stocks which are now generally in dealers' hands throughout the country and the influx of immigration.

Up to the time the decline in business took place furniture manufacturers were receiving business at about 10 to 20 per cent. in excess of their factory capacity.

One thing that has been disturbing the manufacturers of late is the low grade furniture that is being imported from the southern States particularly, where cheap colored labor is employed. This furniture has been coming into all parts of Canada, and as it has been sold at incredibly low prices it is suspected that it is being dumped upon the market at figures lower than those obtaining in the home American market.

The Bed and Bedding Industry.
The demand for beds and bedding during 1912 and the first part of 1913 kept the Canadian manufacturers of these lines so busy that steps were taken by several of the leading concerns to increase their capacity, several new factories with modern equipment being erected to cope with the rapidly increasing call for beds and bedding. In the meantime, as the year progressed, the retail dealer, particularly in the West, began curtailing his purchases, with the result that as 1913 progressed, the manufacturer realized that while the demand lessened, the production increased, resulting in ridiculous price cutting on the part of the manufacturer in his effort to keep up his production.

The dealer, however, has only purchased to take care of his immediate needs, and we face 1914 with the following conditions:—The dealer is carrying meagre stock and, therefore, is in a position where he will require goods promptly as soon as business livens up. The manufacturer with improved facilities and increased capacity is ready to take care of the demand. Every day indicates an improved condition in all sections of the country, although the better tone is developing slowly, but while slow it is sure.

The industry employs in Canada some 2,500 skilled mechanics and practically all the beds and bedding used in Canada are Canadian-made.

* * * *

The Carpet Industry. Carpet manufacturers were busy in the early part of 1913 making up orders placed in 1912, but when they went to the market in May for orders for the Autumn they found a marked falling off in the demand. This applied to both the East and the West. Ontario orders were fairly good. It is expected that orders taken this Spring for Autumn delivery will be smaller than those taken a year ago, but it is the opinion that toward the end of the year business will improve and that orders for Spring, 1915, will reveal a much better condition of affairs than when bookings were being made for the Spring of 1914. When trade assumes anything like its accustomed activity it is the opinion that stocks will not be found to be equal to immediate requirements.

* * * *

The Outlook After the Storm. It is, of course, always easier to chronicle that which has passed than to forecast that which is to come. But just as it was possible last Spring to read the clouds which were at that time gathering in the financial and commercial horizon before the storm broke, so it is not venturing too far to attempt a study of the financial and commercial horizon after the storm has abated.

That the storm has abated there can be no doubt. Its after-effects are no doubt being felt. But it is gratifying to know that they are after-effects. Like a ship that has been battered by storms but not disabled, business in Canada is gradually getting under headway. Its sails may still be reefed, and while that means slower headway in the meantime, it naturally follows that it is only a question of time before full sail will again be hoisted. In fact, for a couple of months past the trade winds have been gradually blowing more favorably, but all authorities agree that until the next crop is assured it will be wiser to make headway under reefed rather than under full sail.

* * * *

Storm Came from Without. There is no reason why one should not have confidence in the industrial future of Canada. The depression of the past year did not have its origin in Canada. It originated outside Canada. It is true that it hit the West a hard blow. But that part of the Dominion was most affected because of the speculative excesses in which the business men of that part of the country had indulged. They had been travelling at too fast a gait. And communities, like individuals, are naturally most affected when an abnormal strain, after a period of excesses, is made upon their resources. The one, like the other, has to take a rest in order to recuperate. That, in a nutshell, is the situation as far as the West in particular is concerned.

Constitutionally Canada has not been affected by the experience of the past year. On the contrary she is stronger. She has been tested and tried, and has come through the ordeal in a way to excite the surprise as well as the admiration of the world's greatest financial authorities.

* * * *

Potentiality of Our Resources. But while the opinions of financial authorities are all right in their place, it is the potentiality of our natural, commercial and financial resources which is the best gauge for determining our prospects.

When Sir George Paish was in this country a few months ago he said that in his opinion Canada would have no difficulty in meeting her interest charges on money borrowed abroad. The amount of this money he placed at about $3,000,000,000, and the annual interest charges at about $130,000,000.

The amount we owe the British and foreign capitalists is undoubtedly large. But it might be large and yet not burdensome. Fortunately, unlike many of the nations of Europe, it was not borrowed for great armaments or for waging war on our neighbors. It was mainly borrowed for the purpose of developing the great natural and industrial resources of the country.

* * * *

How We Have Invested. Up to the end of 1912 over $2,250,000,000 had been invested in steam and electric railways in Canada, private and Government owned. On the construction of canals a further amount of $102,000,000 has been invested. Here is a total investment on these two branches of our transportation system of $2,352,000,000. For this investment we have about 30,000 miles of railway and 1,600 miles of canals. Per head of population no country in the world can compare with us in this respect; and the growing necessities of the country demand further expansion, both in railways and canals.

In manufacturing industries we had up to the end of 1910, when the last census was taken, invested $1,247,583,609, while the factories in which this money was invested are now estimated to be turning out finished products annually to the value of $1,600,000,000. According to the last census they are paying out in wages and salaries $241,000,000.

Here in transportation facilities and in the promotion of the manufacturing interests of the country is a total capital investment of close to $3,600,000,000. If we take into consideration the paid-up capital of the banks ($112,730,943) and that of the loan companies ($59,700,000) we have a total of nearly three and three-quarter billion dollars.

* * * *

Producing Three Billions a Year. The above shows how we have invested money in the transportation, manufacturing and financial institutions of the country. It is now worth while ascertaining as near as we can the value of what we are producing annually. For after all, it is that which we earn and not that which we borrow that determines whether we are prosperous or not. I have already shown that our factories are producing $1,600,000,000 worth of merchandise.

The official figures regarding the crops and the value of the live stock, dairy, fruit and other products sold, show that the farmers of Canada last year earned approximately $853,000,000. The latest figures we have in regard to forest products is for 1912. These show a value of $182,300,000. Then there are the fisheries. They yielded $33,389,000 in 1913. The mineral production in the same year was officially valued at over $144,000,000. All these added together produce the following results:

Manufactured products $1,600,000,000
Farm products (grain and live stock and dairy and other products sold) 853,000,000
Products of forest 182,300,000
Fisheries 33,389,000
Mineral production 144,000,000

Total $2,812,689,000

* * * *

Prospects for Increased wealth. With a country of eight million people, producing practically three billions a year, there is certainly every reason for confidence in its future. But there is also every reason to believe that the wealth that will be produced in 1914 will be greater than that of 1913. Take, for example, the agricultural possibilities of the country. In 1913 less than 35,500,000 acres were under cultivation. Yet we have available for cultivation in the three Western Provinces of Manitoba, Saskatchewan and Alberta 158,500,000 acres of surveyed farming lands, and 91,000,000 unsurveyed, while even in Ontario, according to a recent statement of the Minister of Mines and Lands, only one-fourth to one-third of the farm land of that Province is under cultivation.

Nineteen-fourteen will undoubtedly see a large increase in the land under cultivation in Canada. The favorable climatic conditions of last Autumn are in themselves a guarantee of this, to say nothing of the increase in the number of settlers. In Alberta alone, we are informed, there will be an increase of 750,000 acres under cultivation. While the figures for Saskatchewan are not yet available, we are told that the increase in that Province will be large. But without even taking into consideration the increase in acreage it must be remembered that the farms of Canada, through the introduction of improved methods in all branches of agriculture, are gradually becoming more productive. As it is, the farms of Canada produce five bushels more wheat per acre than is the average in the United States.

* * * *

The Value of the Immigrant. In considering Canada's wealth-producing qualities there is one factor at least that we have not taken into consideration, and that is the value of the immigrant. Last year over four hundred and seventeen thousand immigrants reached our shores. A great many of them, and particularly those who came from the United States, bring in a good deal of capital in the form of cash. Each American is estimated to bring in on an average a thousand dollars. A hundred thousand of these would, therefore, have a total of $100,000,000. But the number who came in from the United States was 115,000. And that does not take into account the other three hundred thousand people that came in during 1913, all of whom, even if they did not possess much money, had their economic value, and the net economic value of a workman, we are told, is $400.

* * * *

Construction Work for 1914.
In a study of the economic outlook for 1914, one cannot help being impressed with the amount of constructive work that is both under way and contemplated. All the Provinces, for example, are this year spending sums of money which will, in the aggregate, run into many million dollars for improving agricultural methods and conditions. The Department of Agriculture at Ottawa alone contemplates an expenditure of over $2,500,000 for this purpose. Then there are the great public undertakings which are going on in many parts of the Dominion, such for example, as the dry dock and harbor improvements in St. John; the docks at Halifax; the dry dock at Quebec; the harbor improvements at Toronto and Montreal; the new Welland Canal; the new dry dock at Victoria. This is merely a brief outline of the chief undertakings, most of which are already under way. In a letter from the Department of Public Works, Ottawa, I am informed that their contemplated expenditure on public works this year is $35,000,000.

The railways will hardly open up 4,000 miles of new lines as they did last year, but a great deal of constructive work will go on just the same and the outlay will run into a great many million dollars before the year is out. In British Columbia alone it is expected that 650 miles of new road will be built, not taking into account the double-tracking operations which are going on. The outlay on the construction of electric roads will be heavy in a great many parts of Canada. Over a thousand miles of electric roads were in operation at the end of 1912.

* * * *

Increasing Export Trade.
One of the gratifying features of the situation is our increasing export trade. For a dozen years in succession the balance of imports over exports has been heavily against us, to meet which it was necessary to borrow. While in the total trade for the twelve months, the balance has again been against us, there have been instances where during certain months the exports exceeded the imports. The aggregate trade for the twelve months ending December last was $1,147,648,243, of which the imports were $673,234,579, and the exports $474,413,664, compared with $645,547,152 and $378,093,990 respectively for the corresponding twelve months of 1912. The largest increase in exports was in agricultural products, $208,642,660 being exported, compared with $142,305,275 in 1912. The exports in manufactured goods also showed a substantial increase, the figures being $54,010,873, compared with $41,708,920 in 1912, a gain of 29 per cent.

* * * *

Financial Conditions and the Outlook.
The financial situation, generally speaking, is stronger than it was a year ago. A year ago the banks were putting on the brakes. Things were beginning to look ominous abroad on account of the war clouds in Europe and the consequent stringency in the money market. The wisdom of the course taken by the banks of Canada is now realized beyond all doubt. Possibly they were o'er cautious, but it was perhaps better that a reef too many should be taken in than that too much sail should be flowing in case of a squall. While the uncertainty lasted a great deal of perturbation was manifested. Now that the storm is over the banks find themselves in a decidedly strong position. In fact, in a much stronger position than six or eight months ago might have been thought possible. They not only all earned good dividends during the year, but they are all better fortified than they were at the beginning of 1913. And the business interests of the country are profiting by the lower rates of interest at which they are able to obtain accommodation. The fact that the gold holdings of the European central banks are $300,000,000 larger than a year ago, and that the bank of England rate has been thrice reduced since the beginning of the year all strengthens the belief in a period of easier money.

The outlook for the immediate future may not indicate what is termed "big business," but it certainly indicates a gradually improving business. A fairly good crop should restore to complete health the business of the country. But in the meantime, like a convalescing patient, we must employ all means to get well, and patiently and optimistically await results.

CANADA'S TRADE FOR 1913

According to figures issued by the Trade and Commerce Department, the total trade of Canada for 1913, exclusive of coin and bullion, was $1,119,578,117, an increase over 1912 of $121,022,956. Of this increase $23,469,290 was in imports, and $94,237,185 in exports of Canadian produce. The largest increase in exports was in agricultural products, which showed a gain of nearly $66,000,0000. It may be noted also that there was an increase of some $13,000,000 in the export of manufactured goods, many of which are now on the free list in the United States. In the month of December alone there was an increase of over $17,000,000 in agricultural products, and of nearly $2,000,000 in manufactured products exported.

POSITION OF BANKS AT CLOSE OF YEAR.

The statement of the Canadian chartered banks for the closing month of 1913 is a very different exhibit from the last report of 1912. In place of large increases in deposits, in business loans, and in note circulation the return for December, 1913, shows a falling off in all these items. Owing to the disappearance of the Sovereign Bank the paid up capital of the banks appears at $2,868,826 less than the previous month. The other changes are, however, representative of actual business conditions and illustrate to a great extent the unsettlement of the closing month of 1913. A decrease of over $10,000,000 in note circulation illustrates the contraction in business following the close of navigation, and the shrinkage in discounts of $8,327,000 was due partly to the slackening of grain exports. At the close of 1913 the bank loans to the Canadian commercial community had decreased by $58,944,000 from the last 1912 showing. This item should be considered in connection with an increase of $2,098,290 for the year in demand deposits, and a falling off of $7,949,000 in savings deposits. The depressed conditions of the security markets at the close of the year are partially explained by a decline of $2,739,870 in call loans in Canada during December. Call loans abroad increased $10,000,000 for the year.

The following tabulation gives the principal items of the December statement, the changes which occurred during December, the changes for the year ending December, 1913, and the changes which occurred during December, 1912.

	Dec. 31, 1913	Change dur. Dec., 1913	Change dur. year 1913	Change dur. Dec., 1912
Paid up capital	$x114,809,297	—$ 2,868,826	—$ 72,617	+$ 337,439
Circulation	108,646,425	—$10,050,896	—$ 1,041,93	—$ 8,424,743
Demand deposits	381,875,809	— 2,610,337	+ 2,098,290	+ 2,847,847
Savings deposits	624,692,326	— 1,110,824	— 7,949,014	— 3,169,393
Total deposits in Canada	1,006,567,835	— 3,721,361	— 5,850,721	— 321,546
Deposits elsewhere	103,403,085	— 3,919,924	+ 16,332,933	+ 3,711,484
Dep'ts Cent'l. Gold Res.	7,367,046			
Call loans in Canada	72,862,971	+ 2,739,870	+ 2,297,311	— 12,860
Call loans elsewhere	115,984,680	— 6,406,183	+ 10,032,579	— 5,840,751
Current loans in Canada	612,387,975	— 8,327,010	— 58,944,006	+ 6,610,388
Current loans elsewhere	58,305,308	+ 1,486,108	+ 17,318,262	+ 64,382

x Decrease in paid up capital due to omission of Sovereign Bank.

A PATRIOTIC CREED.

We Believe in our country—The Dominion of Canada.

We Believe in her Constitution, her laws, her institutions, and the principles for which she stands. We believe in her future—the past is secure. We believe in her vast resources, her great possibilities—yes, more, her wonderful certainties.

We Believe in the Canadian people, their genius, their brain, and their brawn. We believe in their honesty, their integrity and dependability. We believe that nothing can stand in the way of their commercial advancement and prosperity.

We Believe that what are termed "times of business depression" are but periods of preparation for greater and more pronounced commercial success.

We Believe in our country are being worked out great problems, the solution of which will be for the benefit of all mankind.

Satisfying the Disgruntled Customer

BY W. L. EDMONDS

THE value of a customer does not wholly lie in the quantity of goods he buys. That is, of course, his chief measure of value. But there is also to be taken into account the value of his influence.

Every customer exercises more or less influence upon his fellow men in their purchases.

Let him send the statement abroad that the service at So-and-So's store is not satisfactory and most of those in whose hearing he makes the statement will not only come to a like conclusion, but will give it further wing. In all probability they will avoid the store. On the other hand, let him express a favorable opinion, and the influence will be of a favorable nature. They will send that upon its way as well.

This emphasizes beyond all question the importance of satisfying every customer. In some instances it may be a difficult, and in a few instances, an impossible task. But its importance demands that no pains should be spared to accomplish it.

Failure to accomplish it may mean the loss of not one customer alone, but many. This is a contingency that retail dealers should keep in mind when their patience is sorely tried, even by irascible customers.

So important a matter is this that every retailer should make it a hard and fast rule to satisfy at almost any cost the customer that has become dissatisfied.

One of the largest manufacturers in Canada of his kind made this a hard and fast rule. And much of his success is attributed to this fact.

He holds that even where no real grievance exists the customer may conscientiously believe there is one. Consequently he made it a rule to satisfy every disgruntled customer if it was possible to do so, even if it entailed an actual loss of money.

This particular manufacturer is not now actively engaged in business. He looks on while others younger in years carry the "big end of the stick." But nothing pleases him better than to philosophise upon the wisdom of satisfying dissatisfied customers.

And what was good policy for a manufacturer who at one time practically possesses a monopoly in his particular line is certainly good for the average retailer who is surrounded by the keenest kind of competition.

If to satisfy a disgruntled customer concessions have sometimes to be made it by no means follows that it is a surrender for the merchant making it. It is rather the success of business diplomacy.

THE WEDDING GIFT WINDOW—DISPLAY OF FURNITURE ITEMS SUITABLE FOR PRESENTATION PURPOSES

Business From Prospective June Brides and Bridegrooms

Some ways and means suggested for enterprising furniture dealers — Importance of booklets, window displays and newspaper advertising — Compiling information about forthcoming marriages

BY W. L. EDMONDS

WHEN the little nation of Japan waged war upon the big nation of Russia no one thought they would succeed. At least no one but themselves thought they would. But they knew they would. They had simply planned to do it, and how they did it is known to everybody. Had Russia also planned, history would probably have had a different story to tell.

In business, as in warfare, it is those who plan their campaigns well who succeed.

Soon the June wedding season will be upon us, and those who marry and are given in marriage will need furnishings for their prospective homes. In fact they cannot have a home unless they have furnishings. It is possible to marry without love, but it isn't possible to have a home without furnishings.

More marriages take place in June than in any other month of the year. It is not that June is a better month in which to marry, but it is the "month of roses," and this creates a sentiment in its favor in the mind of men and maidens as the most appropriate time for tying the nuptial knot.

As in the furnishing of the home the furniture dealer plays the most important part, it naturally follows that those dealers who the most carefully and intelligently prepare their plans and carry them out with the most skill will reap the best results from the business that June weddings create.

And the time to plan is not when June weddings are being performed. In fact the earlier they are made the better.

About one of the first things to be done is the compilation of a list of prospective brides and bridegrooms.

It does not follow that such a list should be confined to June weddings. On the contrary the compiling of it should be carried on day in and day out the year round. Clerks can help in this by gathering the names of prospective brides from the circle of their acquaintances. Engagement announcements are another source of supply. In fact, there is no end of sources for those who are on the lookout for them.

Most retailers will probably find that such a list can best be kept on a card index system. The card index has many advantages. First of all it is more convenient. Secondly, memos can be more conveniently made upon a card than in a book or upon slips of paper; and thirdly, the card can be placed in another section when the marriage has taken place and it is desirable to maintain a list of home builders for further use.

For instance, newly-weds always need to make additional purchases after they have settled down to home life, and it is a wise thing for the dealer to keep an eye upon them. As it might be well to drop them a letter or send them a circular after they have settled down, the card should contain the address of the newly-married couple.

It is of course premised that every dealer who compiles a list of prospective brides and bridegrooms intends to make use of it. The question is, how can he best use it. Some may use it in one way and some in another. Circumstances will, to some extent, determine this. But there are certain general ways in which it is possible for all dealers to use it, the difference being only one of degree.

Before dealing further with this point, there is one thing I would like to suggest for the consideration of every dealer, and that is the advisability of keeping a stock of booklets on hand specially prepared for the purpose of conveying information to prospective brides and bridegrooms, stress of course being laid upon his ability to supply the furnishings in his particular line necessary to beginners in housekeeping. This booklet could be elaborated or condensed in keeping with the size or capacity of the store.

It would scarcely be wise for the dealer with stock and means limited to undertake a booklet of the size and proportions that might be expected of one whose stock was large and varied. But one can scarcely conceive a dealer whose possibilities were so limited that he could not do something along this line.

The next thing is to get these booklets distributed. And here is where the list of prospective home builders comes in.

When the names of the soon-to-be-married couples

have been obtained and entered on the regular list, a copy of the booklet should be sent them. A tactfully worded letter might also be enclosed, but the chief thing is to get the booklet in their hands. If the booklet is prepared with anything like ordinary skill it will be appreciated.

People who are about to embark upon the sea of matrimony are easily interested in anything and everything that serves to guide them in making their plans for home building.

And then there are not only the prospective brides and grooms to consider in connection with a booklet of this kind. There are their relatives and friends to be considered. They are often puzzled as to what they shall buy as a gift to the bride and groom. A booklet placed in their hands would also bring business to the dealer.

The next important thing, if not the most important, in connection with the campaign for getting business during the June wedding period, is window displays.

Here is where ingenuity comes in and fortunately there is ample opportunity for displaying it.

Everybody is interested in the subject of marriage. Those who "jumped the broomstick" a generation or more ago are almost as much interested as those who are about to make the venture or who live in hope of some day doing so.

Window displays, like everything else, should not be left to the eleventh hour. Plan them well ahead. Decide how frequently they should be changed. No window ought to go unchanged for more than one week. By beginning about the middle of May and continuing to the end of June there would be ample opportunity for six changes.

It will, probably, be found that the best results will be obtained from making each display distinctive and complete in itself. For example, one display might be devoted to bedroom furniture, another to drawing-room furniture, another to diningroom furniture, another to kitchen furniture, and so on, each being arranged as naturally as possible to represent the room in the home to which it applies.

One display might be given to showing a marriage ceremony. Dealers who have no wax figures in their possession could probably borrow them from fellow merchants. A drygoods store could probably be induced to lend a wax figure dressed as a bride and a clothing store one dressed as a bridegroom. On each figure a card might be placed stating by whom it was supplied. An advertisement of this kind would well recompense those who supplied the figures. These figures might also be used for other displays appertaining to the June wedding season.

In some instances dealers have been able to persuade a young couple to allow the marriage ceremony to be performed in the store window. That, of course, has always attracted a crowd, but its value as a selling proposition is questionable.

That the newspaper advertising should be made to co-operate with other schemes to attract business from prospective brides and bridegrooms might be taken for granted. Rightly done, this is a potent force which no dealer can afford to ignore. Advertising is the medium through which all other schemes are given publicity. It is the herald which announces what the dealer is doing and is prepared to do.

And, as in the case of the booklets above referred to, remember, it is not the prospective brides and bridegrooms alone who are concerned, but their relatives and friends as well.

These are a few suggestions which are offered with the hope that dealers may be able to extend and elaborate them in a way that will, between this and the end of June, bring them any orders from prospective brides and bridegrooms, and also from their relatives and friends who desire to help them embark upon the matrimonial sea under as favorable conditions as possible.

Largest Exclusive Furniture Store in the Dominion

Description of magnificent new housefurnishing premises of Calgary Furniture Store—Growth of store tells story of Calgary's rise from cow-town to metropolis

At 2 p.m. on Monday, March 23 last, the doors of the new Calgary Furniture store at Calgary, were thrown open to the public, and for the first time the people of that city had the opportunity of viewing one of the finest and most up-to-date exclusive furniture and housefurnishing stores in the Dominion. It is no exaggeration to say that the Calgary Furniture Store, Limited, has in its new building a home which, for hygiene, luxurious fittings, tasteful decorations and general appearance, has no equal anywhere in the West.

The story of the great store, risen with the growth of Calgary from a cowtown of a few thousand people to the populous and prosperous metropolitan centre of the present day, until it has attained such dimensions that it has overgrown its old premises, spacious though they were, and has sought requisite room for its great expansion in quarters which are the wonder of the day in Calgary, reads like a romance.

In point of architecture and appointment the establishment is the last word,—the equal of any larger eastern store.

The company has spared no pains or expense to make the store as handsome and attractive as possible. As a building it is a valuable addition to the architecture of Western Canada.

The general impression is one of luxuriousness and sumptuousness. Shades and colors have been carefully studied, and the blend on the ground floor particularly, is magnificent. Hung around the pillars are gilded cones bearing Wistaria, carnations and roses in their beautiful colors. These are intended as a permanent decoration. Grouped artistically around in-

NEW HOME OF THE CALGARY FURNITURE STORE

numerable palms is antique furniture, thousands and thousands of dollars' worth. There is nothing jarring it is laid out so as to be a positive pleasure to shop.

Model rooms have been designed at one side of the ground floor where the customer may see an ideally laid out house with just enough furniture in it to make an artistic arrangement. These rooms are an innovation in Western Canada, and it is only at the larger emporiums where space will permit of them being installed. They certainly give the prospective customer an excellent idea of what he needs in the furnishing of a home.

These rooms are furnished in different ways, being changed twice a week, one time the requirements of the millionaire being met, another time, the workingman's —which indicates the variety of stock carried by the institution. All told there are three storeys of furniture display for the prospective purchaser besides the basement, which is devoted to household furnishings. On the ground floor the antique furniture is arranged in impressive and imposing groups, with a useful display of library furniture. The mezzanine floor is devoted to rattan and willow furniture, while at the north end is a ladies' rest room enclosed in a grouping of ferns.

The second floor is devoted to bedroom and dining-room furniture and here are also the administration offices. The third floor is given over to carpets and draperies, such a vast and diverting variety as was never seen in Calgary before.

The company intend specializing upon what is known as the "overstuffed" furniture. It is a trifle more expensive than the ordinary run, but it is worth the few dollars more that are involved.

The windows are striking and beautiful, and emphasize almost every feature of furnishing. Approximately $10,000 worth of goods were used in the opening displays, including a dining-room in handsome dark mahogany. Chinese Chippendale with a fine Wilton carpet, a pattern which dates back to the beginning of the eighteenth century, decorated with pale blue velvet hangings; a library in Hepplewhite satin wood, introduced to the world about the same period; a bedroom, a window displaying rare yet useful carpets; a handsome outfit of draperies; a show of office furniture, and an exhibition of leather goods. The artistic designs which emphasize the main features in pleasing manner are done by T. Sidney Young, an accomplished designer of windows, who was assistant of H. H. Hollinsworth, head window trimmer of the Robert Simpson Company, Toronto.

Every department of the furniture line is represented. The stock carried in this up-to-the-minute establishment is the biggest and best in the West. Nothing is lacking.

The Calgary Furniture Store has been lucky in getting together as clever a combination of men in its offices and sales departments as would ensure the continued success of any firm. The advertising department is one of the most important and potent factors in the play for prosperity, for it is within the power of the advertising man to make or mar the successful sale of specific goods. That department is in charge of P. B. Malette, who joined the staff of the store with years of experience behind him in such positions as sales and advertising manager for some of the biggest concerns in the States. Mr. Malette will also handle the mail order department.

Picking up invaluable experience at Robert Simpson Company, Toronto, and with Wanamaker's, New York, George Balfour, head of the furniture department, has a complete knowledge of his department. It is conceded there are few better men in that line in the whole West.

Max H. Lockie, head of the carpet and rugs department, is also a man of extremely wide experience, having been with various well-known firms in Montreal and Buffalo.

Charles H. Coles, manager of the draperies and shades department, learned his profession in a good school—the Robert Simpson Company, Toronto, under J. W. Stevenson, head decoration expert for that firm. Mr. Stevenson is now the most noted decorator in Canada, and is part publisher of The Upholsterer. A. Abel is in charge of the art department. Mr. Abel gained invaluable experience with the Gibson-Catalach Company, of Portland, Oregon.

The Calgary, Furniture Store has made the provision

The old premises which housed the Calgary Furniture Store for 10 years.

The company's Seventh Avenue Store, which backs up directly on the Eighth Avenue store.

of securing the most expert in every department to ensure the best of service to the thousands of patrons they expect to have the privilege of entertaining in their new store.

The new building is six storeys high, though for the present the Calgary Furniture Store will occupy the three lower floors and the basement, the rest of the building being sublet.

Owing to a heavy mail order business, heavier stocks are necessary, as are also the addition of several new lines, such as stoves and ranges, trunks and baggage, cutlery, crockery, etc. Some of these lines will be handled on the consignment basis, making the carrying of a complete stock unnecessary.

The building is 100 x 130 feet; is of reinforced concrete construction; the exterior being of terra cotta and tapestry brick. Ornamental iron entrances and show windows add much to the exterior appearance and give it a substantial and attractive look. The interior finish is of quartered-oak with maple floors. The building is provided with a modern sprinkler system throughout, which makes it absolutely fire-proof. There are three elevators to facilitate the transaction of business with the least possible delay.

In connection with the opening of the Calgary Furniture Store issued an invitation to the townspeople to come and visit their store during "Calgary Furniture Week," using 14 pages of space in the local daily newspapers in which to tell of the goods exhibited. It was the greatest stunt of the kind ever pulled off in Canada by a furniture dealer. The manufacturers of the goods carried in stock co-operated in the scheme by helping with their advertising in the newspaper space.

THE GERMAN SOFA

The stranger in Germany is always impressed by the importance of the sofa in marking social distinctions. Indeed, among Germans of the more comfortable class, those who live from generation to generation in the same house, every piece of furniture has its own history and makes its own associations; but it is always the sofa that is given the prominent place in a room. Before it usually stands a round or oval table.

Should there be callers at the average German house, there ensues a certain dignified commotion. Should a caller, a woman of lower social standing than the mistress of the house, arrive, she must take a chair, while the hostess sits alone on the sofa. Should the visitor be of higher degree, however, the matter will be otherwise decided.

This method of distinction reaches its highest point when there is a tea party or Kaffeeklatsch (coffee gossip); for then the oldest woman with the biggest title must sit on the sofa, and the next in rank occupies the place nearest her.

As the proudest usually arrives latest, a general stir is likely to take place. For if the Frau Doktorin, the wife of a physician or scholar, is sitting on the sofa, she must vacate her position should a Frau Professorin appear. The Frau Majorin, or wife of a major, may be thoroughly enjoying the seat of honor; but she must yield it without hesitation when the Frau Generalin comes in. The whole company rises in such an event to do honor to the distinguished guest, and there must necessarily follow a general readjustment of places.

Neither unmarried men nor very young women can expect to enjoy the privilege of sitting on a German sofa.

The piece of furniture that stands next in honor to the sofa is the easy chair, which is sometimes called Sorgenstuhl or chair of cares. Should a German sit down to worry, he must have a comfortable seat, that so important a mood may be endured with dignity. A common chair would not serve his purpose in the least. But the Sorgenstuhl is, so to speak, for domestic and personal use only; the sofa is the part of the entire social framework, never to be carelessly regarded.

If buyers of expensive goods like to sit down and talk their purchases over with the salesman, see they have the chance.

Collins' Course in Show Card Writing

One of a series of articles specially prepared for this journal.

THE object in shading letters is to make them stand out in relief, or to give them a "raised" appearance. It adds very materially to the attractiveness of a card or sign. Without shading the letters appear thin or flat. It is very easy to accomplish when the principle is understood.

Shade Letters to Give Raised Appearance.

There is a mistaken idea that letter-shading is affected by an imaginary light, the same as mechanical and other classes of drawing. In those cases it is assumed that the light falls upon the object from the upper left hand corner of the material being worked on. Therefore, all portions of the drawing on which the imaginary light strikes must be made in lighter shade, tint or color. In mechanical drawings, all lines on which the light falls are made lighter (thinner) than those on the opposite side. But in shading letters, the object, as stated above, is to give them the appearance of being raised, and the light has nothing to do with it. One good way to get the correct idea in shade effect is to imagine you are looking at letters cut from an inch board.

Method of Shading Letters.

The style of shading used in lettering is known as isometric, which means that all the bevelled lines or projections are parallel. The angle is generally about 45 degrees. In Figure 7 it will be seen these lines touch the letters at the various extreme points. For convenience in general use the great majority of card and sign writers shade the letters on the left and bottom sides.

No matter where a stroke may appear in a letter the left side and bottom must be shaded unless the angle of the stroke is 45 degrees or near it, as in the letters Y, K, V, A, W, Z and M. The width of the shading will not be the same on the side of all the strokes, but the bottom shade will be the same in all cases. The width of the side shading can be determined by drawing two horizontal lines, AA, BB, Fig. 7, below the top and bottom of the letters the width you want the shading.

Next draw lines at 45 degrees from the various points of the letters as shown in Fig. 7. The point where these lines touch the lines AA and BB will determine the width of the shading on the side of the various strokes of the letters. You will note that the left top stroke of the Y has a wider shade than the vertical part and the right stroke. The latter is scarcely visible. Had it been at the angle of 45 degrees, it would not have been seen at all. Observe the same conditions in the letters A, W, M, R and O.

Examples of Shading.

Fig. 8 is a splendid example of various finishes or embellishment of letters, and the corresponding shading. Letters from 1 to 7 need very little explanation as the same rule applies to them as to the letters in

May, 1914   CANADIAN FURNITURE WORLD AND THE UNDERTAKER   41

abcdefghijklmn
opqrstuvwxyz

Plate 24.—Spurred half block—lower case.

Figure 7. Letters 8 and 9 in Figure 8 are examples of shadow shading. In this case it is assumed that the light falls from the upper left hand corner. But note carefully that this is a SHADOW and not a shade, in the sense of being relief work.

Letter 9 is a drop shadow. No. 10 is a double shade which must be worked in two colors. No. 11 is an old style of shading that has dropped into disuse. Too many lines are not good as they have a dazzling effect.

To Acquire Speed in Shading.

All that has been said above is to acquaint the student with the principles of shading that he may know how and why the work is to be accomplished. In practical card writing you should never measure the shading as you will not have time to do it. Remember speed is essential to financial success in card writing, and measuring shade lines is too slow a process to be successful. In Figure 9 are examples of rapid shading. If you flatten your brush and hold it at an angle of 45 degrees all time you are shading the letters you will find it will take care of the width of the shading automatically, no matter what the angle of the stroke may be. Row 1 are unshaded letters, which have the flat appearance. Row 2 is shaded close to the letters which is not a desirable way. Row 3 leaves a narrow space between the shading and the letters. Row 4 leaves a wider space. Either of the latter is the best style. Shading of this type gives a dashiness to the whole card that is pleasingly effective. It lacks the stiffness of measured work. With some there may be a tendency with O's and periods to carry the shade lines too far to the side. The O's in Row 2 and Row 3 show this, but Row 4 is much better.

Cards Showing Samples of Plain Lettering.

The cards shown this month are chosen specially as samples of plain lettering, and illustrate splendidly, the effects of shading. If shade lines should overlap the letters in places, it will be all right to do it. Then the various lapped places may be touched up with the original color after. Or the shading may stop before reaching the letter at the point where it is about to overlap. The letter of these cards is all done in black

All New Lines
for
SPRING

Samples of plain lettering, in which shading has been used.

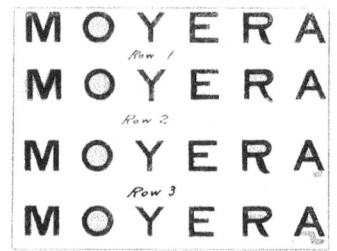

MOYERA   Row 1
MOYERA   Row 2
MOYERA
MOYERA   Row 3

Fig. 9.—Examples of rapid shading.

ABCDEFGHIJK
LMNOPQRSTU
VWXYZ & CRP

Plate 25.—Fancy full block upper case.

abcdefghijklmno
pqrstuvwxyz&

Plate 26.—Fancy full block—lower case.

and the shading is in grey which is mixed with black and white.

Alphabets Excellent for Practice Work.

The alphabets are excellent for practice work. They are not difficult to do. Plates 23 and 24 are the same as plates 17 and 18, shown before, with the exception that these are spurred, which gives them a more finish-

SPECIAL PRICE All This Week

Sample of plain lettering illustrating the effects of shading.

ed appearance. These are an excellent style for "cutting in" as explained last month.

Plates 25 and 26 are the Fancy Full Block style. Letters of this character are not good for general use, but are splendid letters for a special word or line to be brought out prominently. There is no rule to be tied to in making these letters. Notice the ending of the H, M and N, plate 26, is not the same. These various endings may be used on any of these three letters. You may use your own judgment in the various finishes of the different letters. For example, you may finish the "h" in any of the styles used in M and N. P and q may be finished like b and d; and so on, according to your own taste.

MISTAKEN IDEAS.

Some men have a "mistaken idea" that they are running their business. The facts are that the business is running them—soul, mind and body, says an exchange.

Some have a "mistaken idea" that fifteen to twenty hours a day brings the most business success. The fact is that the man who only works twelve will win out in the long run, with a healthy body to boot. A tired mind is a poor affair from which to evolve new ideas, and a tired body does not make very fast time.

Some have an idea that selling cheap is the great magic stone to bring success; forgetting that profits after all are the great end in view.

There is a "mistaken idea" that trade gotten this way is O. K. because it comes quickly. It leaves also just as quickly in most cases, for new and more enticing fields.

There is a "mistaken idea" that the former times were better than these; but there are just as many poor getting poorer and rich getting richer to-day as there were fifty years ago.

There is a "mistaken idea" abroad that the furniture business is a "cinch," yet how many who have tried it for themselves can advise differently.

"Mistaken ideas" are disastrous affairs if not soon taken in hand. They generally come from inexperience and are very costly affairs. We can profit by them if we will. Fools only repeat a "mistaken idea" when once discovered.

Business is like a battle; the general who can keep his head and miss no opportunities is the successful one. One mistake often loses a battle or dissolves a business.

So if you have any "mistaken ideas" get rid of them at once and get hold of the sensible and practicable kind.

WINDOW AND PRICE CARDS.

Window cards are of much importance to most displays. With them attention is called to new pieces of merchandise, special sales, special offers, new lines, part descriptions and, in fact, they can make a window virtually talk.

Price cards, generally speaking, are just as impor-

Big REDUCTION Sale

Special announcement card, also illustrating good use made of shading.

tant, although care should be exercised in using them on high-priced merchandise. It is quite impossible to display all the selling arguments, together with each article in the window. An article high-priced may frighten your prospective customer away; while otherwise you may have landed him with a few convincing arguments had he not seen the price previously.

Selling Methods in the Furniture Store

Some Experiences and Suggestions

SELL AUTOS AND FARM IMPLEMENTS.

The Kemp Furniture Co., Amherstburg, Ont., have added the selling of automobiles to their business. The firm have been carrying farm implements for some time, so the addition of automobiles is not entirely a venture.

Their farm implement and auto business is under a separate manager, and in an entirely separate building from that of the furniture department. W. W. Trimble,

How the Kemp Co. advertise their autos.

who is a member of the firm, spent some 15 years in the farm implement business prior to joining the Kemp Company. He has been very successful in his department.

Kemps employ two road canvassers the year round, and these salesmen push carriages and farm implements with vigor, as well as selling automobiles. The implement warehouse is 125 by 50 feet, and is acknowledged by all who have visited it to be the best kept and most up-to-date in Western Ontario.

"Since we have taken on the automobiles," writes J. H. Sutton, the manager, "our annual turnover will be $50,000 in this department, and we find it a very profitable branch of our business indeed."

PRICE IS NOT ALL.

The policy of a great many retail furniture dealers seems to be to buy discounts and terms, rather than furniture. Instead of buying an article which will bring them in several more dollars profit, because of its selling points, even if it does cost them fifty cents or a dollar more to begin with, they demand low price regardless of everything else. Then they wonder why other more discriminating dealers make more money, and why they are not building up trade as fast.

The wise dealer, nowadays, has come to realize that it is not good business to sell an inferior article, even if he can dispose of it quickly. Why? Because the customer who buys it soon finds out it is inferior, and not only never goes back to that store to buy, but tells his friends not to, and why. It may take a few more minutes to explain to a customer the difference be-

tween an inferior article and one that will be more satisfactory and last longer. The extra profit and a satisfied customer are certainly worth the little extra effort.

Take a dining table, for example. A row of dining tables, of many styles and prices, are on your floor. What can the clerk say about them? "Large, massive base, elegant design and finish"—then the price, and that's all! Then the customer says: "Yes, it looks very nice; I will call again." He goes over to your competitor's store and sees another table, which looks about the same as the one you showed him. This dealer also talks about size, design and price—only his price happens to be a dollar or so lower, so he makes the sale.

What is the remedy? Show them something different, then your competitor will have to talk something more than just size, finish and price. If he does not, then they come back to you.

BONUSING THE CLERKS.

One of the big stores in the east has adopted a scheme of paying salesmen in their floor covering department a bonus on their sales, if they equal or exceed a certain amount for a three months' period. In order that the salesman will not force a sale just for the sake of endeavoring to earn the commission a record of sales is kept, and when goods are returned the reason is investigated closely, the manager of the department having power to deduct the amount of a sale where there is any indication that unfair methods were employed.

On the other hand, an additional percentage will be awarded for the sale of "left overs," or goods carried

Canadian piano company's method of building up a mail list.

over from one season to another. The possibilities of the plan appear to be almost unlimited, and a clever scheme on the part of the management to have their salesmen do some outside soliciting among their friends' friends, thus securing a class of patronage that otherwise might be lost entirely.

Home Furnishings on Exhibition

One of the most significant happenings in the revival of interest in period furnishing and art in homes in Canada, is the campaign started last fall by the T. Eaton Company in their Toronto store. So successful was that exhibition that the manager of the store recently went to New York to see Prof. F. A. Parsons, president of the New York School of Fine and Applied Arts, and contract with him to go to Toronto to give a course of ten lectures, two a day, to the employees and heads of departments of the Toronto store, to a number who will be brought on from the Winnipeg store, and to the Eaton clientele in Toronto, the educational element of that city, and to others interested in the modern movement for the development of a better standard in home furnishing.

This "House Furnishing Exposition" began Monday, April 13, in their "Exposition Hall," on the sixth floor of the furniture building. The feature of the Exposition is a series of lectures on period and characteristic decoration. Prof. Parsons, who conducted the lectures, is considered one of the ablest authorities on this work in America, and his talks were unusually interesting. There were special displays and arrangements of period furniture, tapestries, rugs, and wall papers.

WE'LL DELIVER IT TO-DAY.

"We'll deliver it to-day" is the slogan adopted by an enterprising western merchant, who recently replaced his horses and wagons with a motor truck. The slogan appears in his newspaper advertising, in the trolley cars, on his show windows, on his trucks—in fact a complete advertising campaign is being carried on around the new and quicker delivery service.

This merchant declares that results from his enterprise in putting in a motor wagon and advertising it has proved immensely profitable. He writes that it has solved one of the weakest points in his business, namely the inability to promise delivery on the day of purchase. "Formerly we were obliged to make a rule that no promise of delivery the same day should be made to customers making purchases in the afternoon," he writes. "Many sales were actually lost because of this necessity. Now we can positively insure delivery before night of articles bought up to four o'clock, and in some cases later. Even those who really could get along without immediate delivery, will incline toward the store where they can get it. Our truck carries the appearance of enterprise and prosperity, and that draws the crowds regardless of anything else."

CLEAN UP STORE OCCASIONALLY.

Every dealer owes it to himself and his customers to give his stock a thorough renovation and cleaning up every season, or twice a season. During the rush months goods get mishandled, mixed, and in the wrong department, and the store begins to look like a junk shop.

A clean-up will show you the goods you are in need of. You will get your stock back into perfect condition. You can pick out the odds and ends, and clean them up by a special sale. You remove all dust and dirt, and use polish to freshen the stock. You make the goods look like new—as customers never take much interest in finger-marked, dusty furniture. The women like a clean, orderly store, and like to trade there. Finally, after the job is done, the boss feels better, takes on new life, is proud of his store, and is a better salesman. The same thing happens to the rest of the employees.

THE T. Eaton Company's method of drawing attention to their furniture and house furnishings—A Louis XIV room—one of the booths depicting the use and suggesting ideas for furnishing with period-styled furniture and trimmings.

THE KEY TO SUCCESS

"Your Furniture World has been a great help to me and I call it 'The Key to Success.'"
Bruno Graffunder,
Howson Furn. Co., Ltd., Revelstoke, B.C.

The Art of Display

Suggestions for Window and Interior Arrangements.

WINDOW TRIMMER TELLS HOW HE WORKS.
By W. J. Bryans

THE FURNITURE WORLD had a talk recently with a very prominent furniture window trimmer, in which he gave some very valuable hints on window trimming that will probably be of interest and value to members of the trade. He is deeply interested in window trimming, because he realizes the extreme value of it in attracting people to the store and selling goods.

The store he is now engaged in is on quite a prominent business street, and the number of people who stop to inspect his windows convinces him that they are of value. He finds that people who pass the store from day to day are on the watch for the times when he changes his displays. Then again, he frequently has customers come in the store and compliment him upon the novelty and attractiveness of his displays.

That the window does sell goods is demonstrated in a convincing manner by the direct sales that frequently come from displays.

Value of Novel Windows

He finds that novel windows with some central feature of interest are extremely valuable in directing attention to goods displayed. For instance, he put in a housecleaning goods window showing a miniature house; leading down from the front door of the house was a miniature gravel path, on each side of which was a lawn, the latter being represented by green shavings.

Plants and ferns are also made use of to give an artistic setting to certain displays. When these are not in use in the window, of course, they can be used for decorating the interior.

Study the Color Scheme of Displays

He puts a good deal of emphasis on the need of careful planning out the color schemes in displays. He says that this is something that the majority of furniture window trimmers do not give sufficient attention to, with the result that the displays they turn out do not appeal to the eye in the way they should. The trimmer should make a study of the colors that work together in the most effective way.

DISPLAYING DINING ROOM FURNITURE.

The practice of featuring an early opening display of summer furniture has now become widespread. The care with which the windows are now adorned far surpasses former efforts and the decorations are not confined to the windows alone, but likewise have transformed the floor exhibits of furniture into veritable scenes of beauty. This has become a general practice in many widely separated establishments, from one end of the country to the other.

While in the larger centres elaborate plans are laid out for displaying summer furniture items that are not possible for dealers in small towns, yet there are in these larger schemes some suggestive ideas which if adopted would prove helpful to furniture men in the less populous centres.

As to the character of the goods which are to be shown in a window, dependence must be placed on whatever goods are in stock.

Just now a dining room window would be particularly appropriate. A woman takes more pride in her dining table than in any other piece of furniture. She shows it to all her friends and tells them where she bought it. Let the women see what dining tables you have in stock by dressing up a nice window.

How do you expect to sell a table to the family who now have one? They do not want two—and the one they have answers the purpose all right and will last for years. How? Trim up your window with something different and better than she has. Show a table with all the latest devices and attachments. Her table does not lock the leaves in; she cannot get it off the

Diningroom furniture in the window, showing what a splendid display this class of goods makes when properly set out.

rug or get a rug under it; a mechanic and a kit of tools are necessary to move it; it does not have the removable top or steel bearing slides; it is shaky and unsteady, because it is not bolted together. Let the passer-by see what you have in up-to-date dining tables by making a good display, and rest assured that it will repay you for your effort to please.

CLEAN WINDOWS INCREASE SALES.

Wash the windows!

This always should be a standing order in the store, but during the summer it is especially urgent.

Dust outside the window obstructs the view. Inside the window it damages the merchandise.

Frequent washings of the outside of the glass and occasional washings of the inside will pay big dividends. Forget about soap. Put a little soda in warm water and go to it.

To keep dust out of the window, nothing is so good as an enclosed background. Better get one ready now, while you have time. Then you will be ready to keep the frost out next winter.

Background for early summer or June wedding furniture window.

PRESERVE THE SHOW WINDOW FIXTURES.

Every merchant should have a room for the window and store fixtures, and for the proper arrangement and conduct of these the trimmer should be held responsible. This is absolutely necessary, be the room in the basement or on the roof.

The size of the store and number of fixtures will determine the size of the room. In all cases it should be arranged with shelving, lockers, miscellaneous hooks to hang parts on, a tool bench and such tools and machinery as the particular store will warrant. Everything should be kept off the floor.

As the fixtures are brought from the windows or store they should be taken apart and the parts hung in separate places until again needed. When wanted for use again the fixtures should be taken down, assembled and properly cleaned before being placed. This room should be the window-trimmer's headquarters at all times when not at work in windows (unless he has other duties around the store) so the firm will have some definite place to find him when wanted, as it is sometimes difficult to find a window trimmer when needed.

If the window trimmer is a card writer also, he will, of course, have a desk in his room. The room should be under lock and key at all times, and only the window trimmer and his boy should be given access to this, outside of the night watchman. Every trimmer will, of course, arrange his room to suit himself, and can do this at practically no expense to the house.

Brass fixtures should be rubbed off with a damp cloth, and about once a month polished. In this way fixtures will always look nice and clean. All fixtures should be kept in the trimmer's room. No fixtures should be allowed to accumulate in odd parts of the store. In this way the trimmer will always have the fixtures in the proper place and ready for use. When he has a broken fixture or part missing he should at once see that the part missing be replaced or the fixture repaired.

MAKE YOUR FURNITURE SPEAK.
By J. B. Walker

All furniture attracts attention quicker when it is displayed as if in use, than if placed on the floor or window without any accessories. A dresser looks more natural with a scarf and a few simple toilet articles upon it than when it is stripped. It gives a homelike touch that goes far with the woman buyer.

In the same way, the attractiveness of a buffet is improved by placing some silverware and cut glass upon it. Sometimes an enterprising jeweler or chinaware dealer will gladly co-operate with you by loaning the articles you need, in consideration for which you should see that he gets his share of the advertising. This is secured by placing small but legible card signs near the goods, stating who loaned them. "The chinaware in this china closet is loaned through the courtesy of Blank & Company, this city," or "Sterling silverware from Jones the Jeweler," is all that is needed.

Do not make the attempt to dress all your stock on the floor in this way. It is not necessary. But select one piece of each, say, a dresser, a buffet, a china closet and sometimes a bed, which will fairly represent the kind of stock you keep.

If you cannot make the thing look right, get your wife to show you.

Don't overload the pieces with gimcracks. A bowl of bright yellow blossoms is all the decoration you want on an oak buffet, and five pieces of silverware is ample; less would be better. A tall vase of bronze or cut glass holding two or three roses is enough for the dressing table, besides the toilet bottles, brushes, combs and hand mirror.

When closing time comes, do not fail to put the "properties" carefully away, so that after the morning clean-up and dusting, they may be arranged again, bright and fresh. A good way is to put them in the drawers of the piece of furniture they are to help to sell, but don't forget to look inside before you sell the piece.

There are times in the day when this work can be done quietly, and without haste, and after you have been doing it awhile, you will be surprised to find how easy it comes, and how pleasant is the work.

However, if your store is not spotlessly clean, and your employees cannot enter into the spirit of the thing, better not attempt it, because a store with a dirty floor, and grimy windows filled with cheap wire springs or bed slats, is not the place to look for refinements in household furniture, or suggestions for making beautiful.

The Pulling Power of Good Window Display

FURNITUREMEN and their clerks are more and more coming to realize that the display window, when given the proper amount of attention, is a mighty power in attracting customers and business to the store. There are scores of progressive furniture stores from one end of Canada to the other that are daily finding their show windows attracting customers into their store, and making the cash register play a much livelier tune than it otherwise would.

The show window that begets business for the dealer must, however, be live and aggressive—must be given the necessary attention. It seems a mighty funny thing that many a merchant who would descend with a shower of wrath upon the clerk who would dare to remain idle for a minute, will allow his show windows—in some cases just as valuable as a clerk—to loaf on the job, and think nothing of it. It surely does seem gross extravagance for a dealer to allow money to slip through his fingers, as many of them do by lack of attention to the show window.

The reason for inattention does not, in many cases, lie in the fact that they do not feel that results warrant all the attention given to their window displays. On the contrary, those dealers who have given any appreciable attention to this phase of the business are loud advocates of its value. But even a good many of these merchants, who claim window display a big business factor, do not give the attention to it that they should.

Even some merchants who declare their show window their greatest asset, are not reaping the greatest possible results. It is true that they are receiving a good deal of business through them, but that is absolutely no reason why they should not reap still greater advantages, which would be easily possible by giving them more time, changing them oftener and continually aiming to make them turn every cent possible into the cash drawer.

Even the small display window can be made an effective sales medium. There are many small windows bringing in more business than the larger ones equally as well located. The explanation lies in the attention given to them. The window, like the advertisement, must be changed frequently and time given to assure proper arrangement. The many details that require attention in the store sometimes makes it difficult to give the desired attention to window display, but it should not be neglected, even if it is necessary to secure extra help to care for the various details. The extra business will more than pay for any extra cost for help.

Practical hints and suggestions, with a number of fine illustrations on how to make the window the most effective sales medium, are given in every issue of Canadian Furniture World. This special window trimming department is well worth the consideration of every furniture dealer and clerk.

Advertising Dining Room Furniture
BY A. B. LEVER

Dining room furniture sells to a more or less extent throughout the year; but probably it sells a little more freely in May and June than during any other time of the year. There are two outstanding reasons for this. One is that there is a good deal of moving by householders during those months. Consequently they often find the need of buying new furniture. The other, and probably the chief reason, is the large number of weddings that take place at that time. At any rate, whatever the cause may be, dealers throughout the country push dining room furniture a little more vigorously with the advent of spring. With this fact in mind I have this month selected for reproduction advertisements of dining room furniture.

The advertisement of Murray-Kay, Limited, is a "classy" one. It is designed, of course, to catch the trade of the wealthier class of people. But with certain modification it could be adapted to the requirements of the average dealer. The first paragraph of five lines gives in concrete form a lot of interesting information regarding period furniture and might serve as a model to dealers generally. In fact, this might be said of the ad as a whole. The original was 6½ by 11¾ inches.

The main feature of the advertisement of D. A. Smith, Limited, Vancouver, is its attractiveness. It is also well written and artistically arranged. It is at the same time simple. Its purpose is evidently not to secure direct business, but to excite the interest of the consumer in the firm's stock of dining room furniture. This is a good line of advertising for insertion in a daily newspaper, but where country weeklies are used I would urge the use of copy that is likely to bring direct business. Original was 6½ by 7¾ inches.

A good example of an advertisement that should sell dining sets is that of A. J. Freiman, Ottawa. It occupied space 6½ by 9½ inches, and was not only attractive, but brought out prices in a way that could not be overlooked by readers of the paper. Whoever prepares A. J. Freiman's copy does it well.

The advertisement of the World Furnishing Co., Orillia, is simple in construction, merely making a plain statement of fact. It is a fairly good ad just the same. That which particularly makes it so is the list of prices given. The original was 4¼ by 5¼.

The ad of the Halifax Furnishing Co. is to the point. And the point is sideboards, which customers are urged to buy before the May rush comes on and have stored free of charge until they are wanted. The original was 4¼ by 3 inches, and the firm was wise in confining the space to advertising one line of furniture. Where space is small it is usually the best thing to do.

"Dining room furniture that is appetizing" is a catching and original phrase, and the reading matter that follows is an elaboration of this thought. The original, which was 2¼ by 5, is from a department store ad.

The advertisement of the Lord Furniture Co., Ottawa, was only 2¼ by 3¾ inches in size, but it is an example of how very small space may be well utilized. Any attempt that might have been made to crowd in more reading matter would have spoilt the ad.

The advertisement of the Hastings Furniture Co., Vancouver, is an all-round good one. Typographically it is well balanced, and the reading matter, on account of the prices named, is as effective as if an effort at elaboration had been made. Original was 4⅜ by 5¾.

The ad. beginning with the line, "For the dining room and the parlor" is from a department store announcement, and only needs a firm name at the bottom to complete it.

The advertisement of the Standard Furniture Co., Vancouver, is another example of good use of 4½ by 6-inch space. The ad would, however, have probably been strengthened rather than otherwise had the two line, "Are you in need?" "Can we help a little," been omitted. More space would then have been permitted for those parts of the ad which are more important.

T. W. Currier & Co.'s ad is the only complete one in the group that is without an illustration. But it is a good advertisement nevertheless. It is well displayed and the reading matter is to the point. In a word, it is one of those simple ads which comes straight to the point without beating around the bush with useless verbiage. The original was 4⅜ by 5¼ inches.

The last ad in the group is another of those sections from a department store announcement that only needs a firm name at the bottom to make it a complete and creditable advertisement.

SIMPLICITY IN ADVERTISING.
By H. M. Howard

Advertising must be simple. When it is tricked out with the jewellery and silks of literary expression, it looks as much out of place as a ball dress at the breakfast table. The buying public is only interested in facts. People read advertisements to find out what you have to sell. The advertiser who can fire the most facts in the shortest time gets the most returns Blank cartridges make noise, but they do not hit—blank talk, however clever, is only wasted space. You force your salesmen to keep to solid facts—you don't allow them to sell muslin with quotations from Omar, or trousers with excerpts from Marie Corelli. You must not tolerate in your printed selling talk anything that you are not willing to countenance in personal salesmanship. The construction engineer plans his roadbed where there is a minimum of grade—he works along the lines of least resistance. The advertisement which runs into mountainous style is badly surveyed—all minds are not built for high-grade thinking.

Cut out clever phrases if they are inserted to the sacrifice of clear explanations—write copy as you talk. Only, be more brief. Publicity is costlier than conversation—ranging in price downward from $10 a line; talk is not cheap, but the most expensive commodity in the world. Sketch in your ad. to the stenographer. Then you will be so busy "saying it" that you will not have time to bother about the gew-gaws of writing. Afterwards take the typewritten manuscript and cut out every word and every line that can be erased without omitting an important detail. What remains in the end is all that really counted in the beginning. Cultivate brevity and simplicity. "Savon Francais" may look smarter, but more people will understand "French soap." Sir Isaac Newton's explanation of gravitation covers six pages, but the schoolboy's terse and homely "What goes up must come down," clinches the whole thing in six words.

WHAT ADVERTISING IS "NOT."

There's been a whole lot written as to what advertising IS.

There should be a few words, for the home-furnishers, and others, as to what advertising is "NOT."

To stick your name in the paper and let it go at that is certainly not advertising—for advertising is expected to bring results, and there is a real dividing line 'twixt doubtful publicity and real advertising.

Advertising is not a gamble—it is not an expense. Advertising of the right character (and only right advertising can be so termed), is an investment.

You may perform in many ways to bring attention to your store, you may campaign to your heart's content to sell your merchandise to advantage, but do not make the mistake of thinking "any old thing" in publicity is advertising.

Advertising is not to have the cheapest paid salestise him—but what good will it do you? Where is your profit in building up the other fellow's business?

Advertising is not repelling customers by obsolete methods, by lack of intelligent demonstrations. Advertising is not achieved by ignoring the trade journals or other folks' opinions and experience.

In fact, advertising is not any of a thousand and one things under which it masquerades—and by eliminating what advertising is "not" we are, if we read carefully between the lines, very thoroughly impressed with what advertising really IS.

GOOD AD. COPY
By Arthur Brisbane

Writing a successful advertisement is the most difficult thing in the business of writing. You can write an interesting story about noses and every man will

Advertising diningroom furniture by Canadian dealers. See preceding page for criticism.

force in town, the poorest display of goods and windows that lack all semblance to decent trims.

Advertising is not a mere jumble of adjectives and high-sounding phrases. It is not advertising to continually announce freak sales, and shout from the press that you are the great and only.

Advertising is not knocking your competitor save that it is advertising for him. If you want to make your competitor a success you are privileged to advertise a heater only when it is cold. He should pick the hottest day of summer and say: "It is hot as the devil to-day. Next winter will be just as cold." Then when winter comes the consumer is familiar with that particular heater.

feel his nose and look in a glass. It concerns something which is his. But in writing an advertisement you must first overcome his reluctance to read it.

The trouble with the average man is that he will advertise a heater only when it is cold. He should pick the hottest day of summer and say: "It is hot as the devil to-day. Next winter will be just as cold." Then when winter comes the consumer is familiar with that particular heater.

Beds and Bedding

IDEAS THAT HELP SALES

The following practical and business-building suggestive article appears in the first number of "The Alaskan," the new publication put out by the Alaska Bedding Co., Montreal. It speaks about service rather than price—a service that should prove profitable to the furniture dealer.

Ideas! Ideas! Ideas! What would the business of retail selling amount to without ideas. They are needed in every business, and strangely enough the more staple the merchandise, the greater the need for live, vital selling plans that connect up closely with the personal and human interest of the possible or prospective customers.

Beds are bought primarily because they are a necessity—but they also have an artistic value, which gives them a personal quality. It is just as important that the bed used in a room fit in with the furniture and general decorative scheme, as it is that a woman's hat and gown suit her personality.

You who have tried to sell beds intelligently will not doubt this. A purchaser with a sense of the fitness of things will select a bed of a design which will look well with the rest of the furniture in the room in which it is to go. Intelligent salesmanship looks not only to the utility of the goods, but also their appropriateness to their surroundings. A well informed salesman aids, suggests, and advises—intelligently and tactfully.

The up-to-date furniture dealer will strive to give his customers a complete home furnishing service of a definite nature. If this were done by more dealers it would remove the necessity for worrying about bargain sales.

Here is a practical suggestion along this line: Start in your store a 'home-beautiful library.' Any store, however small or unpretentious, can have one. In fact, the smaller the store and the town it serves, the more it needs such a library.

What is a "home-beautiful" library? It is a library containing magazines and other periodicals, and books dealing with subjects of home decoration. Most of them are beautifully illustrated. They show not only ideal room treatment, but reproductions of photographs of real rooms, real houses, real homes.

Magazines catering particularly to women have pages devoted to home furnishing and decoration. These should be carefully selected and preserved either in portfolios or in bound volumes. When the customer begins to consider this or that method of furnishing or decorating her entire house, a single room or even the hall, turn to the library and show her examples which will help her make up her mind.

Many large stores show one or more rooms decorated and furnished. To the store that cannot do this, the library offers a mighty good substitute. It is cheaper, easier to establish, and is effective in helping customers to decide. It will make definite sales before it has been in your store many months. It is really a library of ready-to-use ideas.

It could be made a feature of your store which could stand a lot of advertising. You could invite townspeople who have problems of home furnishing, or home decoration to be solved, to come and consult your library—freely, without any obligation to purchase.

The library might very well be maintained as a cosy corner arrangement near the front door, where everyone who came into the store would see it, and be invited to consult it at their leisure any time.

The mere fact that you, yourself, keep in touch with all the good books and publications devoted to home furnishing and decorating, could not fail to make a favorable impression on your customers. By reading such magazines and books yourself, you would be in a position to discuss intelligently many new and practical ideas.

It will work wonders with your regular customers, and is one of the finest and most effective result getting sources for advertising talk that you could possibly imagine.

No matter how smart you are, or how much business you are getting, there are other people getting more. They are getting it because they are smarter—they are smarter because they take suggestions from other people and other sources than their own.

So much for this suggestion—to which you are entirely welcome.

U. S. BEDDING CONCERN ENTERS CANADA

Ontario letters patent have been issued to Franklin Lincoln Groff, John Abel and Charles Bolte, all of Jersey City, N.J.; John Edmund Newton, Superintendent, and Albert Edward Knox, both of the city of Toronto, to purchase, acquire, deal in and manufacture brass, metal, spring and all kinds of beds and bedsteads, springs, mattresses, bedding, household furniture and effects and all accessories thereof; the corporate name of the company to be Canadian-Mersereau Company, Limited; the capital of the company to be $25,000; the head office of the company to be at Toronto.

FIRE AMONG BED STOCK.

One of the hardest fires that Hamilton, Ont., firemen have had to fight in many a day was that which took place in the basement of the A. M. Souter & Co.'s furniture store. There was little blaze, but plenty of smoke. Hundreds of beds were stored in the basement and, as they were wrapped in excelsior, this proved great food for the fire. The origin of the fire is unknown as it started at night after the premises were closed for the day. Several thousands of dollars damage was done.

FOR BIGGER BED AND BEDDING BUSINESS

"The Alaskan" is the name of a new publication which will be issued every once-in-a-while by the Alaska Feather & Down Co., Ltd., Montreal, together with its associated companies in Winnipeg, Regina, Calgary and Vancouver. Number 1, published under date of March 25, is an attractively-gotten-up booklet of magazine size, printed in yellow and black.

The new and standard lines of Alaska goods are illustrated and described therein, for the "Alaskan" is published in the interests of Alaskan factories and dealers, and in addition there are a number of brief articles well calculated to stir up the interest of men in the trade looking for larger and better business. Among these latter is the "Alaska service" article, showing how tab is kept on every item of stock in the factory, how the orders are handled, and the day's work completed at the day's end. Another of these is a helpful article on "Why not maintain a 'home-beautiful' library?" This article is so good that it is reproduced in this department.

If the "Alaskan" keeps up in its subsequent issues

the standard set in its first number, the magazine will surely deserve a place in the hands of all interested in "bigger business in beds and bedding."

BEDDING NOTES

Jos. E. Reinhardt is the new representative appointed to cover Western Ontario for The Quality Mattress Co., of Waterloo, Ont.

The Ideal Bedding Co. have added, during the past month, a number of new designs to their brass and iron beds; and in their spring goods have added new features to this year's "Hammo-Couch," making it stronger and more comfortable.

J. E. Brown & Co., New Westminster, B.C., received the contract for this year's mattress and bedding supplies needed by the New Westminster and Essondale hospitals.

The Fischmann Mattress Co. have removed their plant from 569 Queen Street West, Toronto, to 333 Adelaide Street West, that city, where they have installed new and improved machinery.

The Quality Mattress Co. will have their new catalogue ready about May 1, showing cuts and giving details of their full and complete lines of "Quality" mattresses. This is said to be the first catalogue of its kind in this country.

H. C. Hare, representative of the Ideal Bedding Co. in Northern Ontario, has recovered from the illness which kept him off his territory for the past month.

The Quality Mattress Company's new plant at Waterloo, Ont., is capable of turning out from 100 to 125 mattresses a day.

LETTER BOX

Chiffonier-Wardrobes

Last month we published a request from The Edwards Furniture Co., Sherbrooke, Que., asking the name and address of a manufacturer of a "chiffonier-wardrobe," and we solicited information from our readers. The following are some of the replies:

W. A. Luke, of Luke Bros., Oshawa, Ont.—Andrew Malcolm Furniture Co., Kincardine, Ont., are makers of such an article. The Cron Kills Co., Piqua, Ohio, are also makers.

The Markdale Furniture Co., Ltd., Markdale, Ont., state that this article is one of their line.

The Andrew Malcolm Furniture Co., Ltd., Kincardine, Ont., say they still make a couple of chiffonier-wardrobes.

Miss N. M. Evans (Thomas G. Watkins Co., Ltd., Hamilton) The Sprague-Smith Co., Piqua, Ohio, make some good ones, and also issue a catalogue.

Sea Grass Furniture

W. S. Beam, Selkirk, Ont., asks the names of makers of braided sea grass furniture.

The Jennings Co., St. Thomas, Ont., import this line for the Canadian trade.—Editor.

Church Furniture

Patterson & Dart, Welland, Ont., ask for names and addresses of makers of pews and other church furniture.

Berlin Interior Hardwood Co., Berlin, Ont.; John B. Snider, Waterloo, Ont.; Globe Furniture Co., Waterloo, Ont.; Canadian Office & School Furniture Co., Preston; Blonde Lumber Co., Chatham; and Bell Furniture Co., Southampton, make this class of furniture.—Editor.

Steel Filing Cabinets

Crown Furniture Co., Ltd., Quebec, want to be put into communication with a steel cabinet factory.

The Steel Equipment Co., of Ottawa, make this line of goods in their factory, at Pembroke, Ont.—Editor.

Corner Wardrobes

The Edwards Furniture Co., Sherbrooke, Que., ask the address of a firm making corner wardrobes in either oak or hardwood.

The Knechtel Furniture Co., Hanover, Ont., and Krug Bros., Chesley, Ont., make this line. Any of the furniture factories making wardrobes would be glad to make these goods to order.—Editor.

STRONG FURNITURE MAKING CONCERN

The shareholders of the Canada Furniture Manufacturers, Ltd., at their recent annual meeting held at the head office of the company in Toronto, approved of a plan for the reorganization of the company's finances, which had been prepared by a special committee of the shareholders, whereby the preferred shares of the company are to be upon a dividend paying basis, and the proceeds of $1,000,000 of securities turned into the coffers of the company. This transaction will have the effect of making the company one of the strongest financial industrial institutions in the Dominion.

ALBERTA MERCHANTS ORGANIZE.

A number of Alberta merchants have launched a movement to organize a province-wide merchants' association carrying a merchants' police force. W. E. Collier, formerly of the collection department of the John Deere Plow Co., has severed his connection with the latter firm to give his whole attention to the organization of the new league. Mr. Collier states that he will introduce new ideas into the collection end of the business which will prove a boon to the members.

It is the intention of those interested to have the new association work in conjunction with similar institutions across the line, and in this way would be able to give the merchants instant information on new arrivals. They would also be able to trace anyone who "jumped the town."

The league expects to do much to discourage the habit of writing "N. S. F." checks. The name of the association will be the Retail Merchants' Credit Association.

BUNGALOW FURNITURE.

Baetz Brothers & Co., Berlin, Ont., announce that their special catalogue of bungalow furniture is ready for mailing, and will be sent on request to any dealer.

WESTERN FIRM DOES AUTOMOBILE WORK.

The Regina Upholstery and Carpet Cleaning Works have taken on the fixing of curtains, hoods, cushions and upholstered body work for automobiles.

USEFUL IN IDEAS.

McLaren & Company, Ltd., St. Catharines, write: "We find the Canadian Furniture World very useful in getting ideas of the furniture business in general, and we are pleased to renew our subscription."

Dollar Day Brings Big Results to Wingham Merchants
BY J. O. ARNOTT

Throughout a number of Western Ontario towns there has, during the past few months, been conducted a novel local sales-provoking scheme, which has in all cases so far brought to notice been entirely successful. The latest town that has tried it out is Wingham, and there, as in other towns where it has been tried, it was a decided success in every particular.

March 17, St. Patrick's Day, was the date set, and every train brought its quota of people. From early morning until two or three in the afternoon, people journeyed from north, south, east and west to the Metropolis, where bargains were given, and where they would meet friends whom they had not seen for some time and spend a social hour. At two o'clock the day was enlivened by the Wingham Citizens' Band, which furnished music for the afternoon. There was an excellent showing of horses, many fine animals being exhibited for each special prize.

Prizes were also given among other competitions for the oldest gentleman and oldest lady coming to town; for the purchaser driving the longest distance to Wingham; to the person bringing the largest load of people to town; to the largest family coming to town; and to the most recently married couple. The prizes were all valued at five dollars each, and every merchant in the town contributed one prize.

Arrangements were made for the accommodation of horses, and in addition to the hotel barns, private barns were open for the day. The Council Chamber was heated and open all day for the accommodation of ladies and there were several horse buyers present to dicker for the purchase of the prize-winning animals.

The gentleman getting the prize for coming the longest distance was David Giddins, who travelled a distance of fifteen miles. Albert Foxton brought in the largest load of people, having thirty-one in his sleigh, and consequently receiving the prize. J. D. Anderson of Belgrave received the gold watch from W. G. Patterson for having made the largest purchase in Wingham on that day. The amount of the purchase was $97 of which $96 was for harness.

The local paper conducted a voting contest to add interest to the celebration, and the merchants of the town reaped a bountiful trade harvest. It was a grand success in every respect, and every one went away feeling satisfied, and the merchants state it is one of the best days which they ever had. The citizens of Wingham are so well satisfied that there will be another similar day here. A. H. Wilford, President, and Abner Cosens, Secretary, are the men responsible for the Dollar Day Movement, and they received the congratulations of the citizens at large on the movement, which they inaugurated, and carried to such a successful conclusion.

The Dollar Day has two objects. It means to combine business with pleasure. Wingham was on its special day the centre of attraction, and for miles around the people came for the purpose of renewing old friendships and also to enjoy the fun of shopping and getting the "Biggest Dollar's Worth" of goods ever sold. The business men entered into the suggestion with great heartiness, and before the event advertised that they were prepared to stand behind Dollar Day and give unprecedented bargains and service. Dollar Day had been successfully held in other places, so why not in Wingham, said the merchants of that town, so they made it worth the while of all to come to town that day.

All the merchants promised to sell more goods for $1.00 on that day than they ever did before. They gathered the bargains from all parts of their store and laid them before their visitors.

The people came to Wingham in great numbers and secured for themselves such bargains as will make them remember St. Patrick's Day, 1914, as one of the most enjoyable days they ever spent.

The merchants of Kincardine recently held a "Dollar Day," which they had previously extensively advertised. The Reporter, of that town, in speaking of it, says in part: "Into the scheme all the merchants heartily entered, and judging from the words of praise given by the purchasing public, the merchants gave bargains with a great big B. It was a day of genuine bargains everywhere you went. One merchant went so far as to give a $1 bill with a ten cent piece pasted on the corner for $1. He had one customer who did business for that bargain only. Not a merchant in town was heard to complain, and they got acquainted with many faces in the way of business. The turnover was big and the people were satisfied, pronouncing the advance advertising as genuine, and some stated that the merchants even went further than they promised to do. Some enthusiastic ones were heard advocating such a day once a week. The idea was to attract the people to town and show them what our merchants had and could do for them. This, with the merchants' effort to hold some of the trade, should have its effect."

STICKING TO IT
By Walt Mason, in The Butler Way

I used to run a beeswax store at Punktown-in-the-Hole, and people asked me o'er and o'er, "Why don't you deal in coal? The beeswax trade will never pay—you know that it's a sell; if you take in ten bones a day, you think you're doing well."

Thus spake these thoughtful friends of mine; I heard their rigmarole, and straightway quit the beeswax line, and started selling coal. I built up quite a trade in slate, delivered by the pound, and just when I could pay the freight, my friends again came round. "Great Scott!" they cried, "you ought to quit this dark and dirty trade! To clean your face of grime and grit we'd need a hoe and spade! Quit dealing in such dusty wares, and make yourself look slick; lay in a stock of Belgian hares, and you'll make money quick."

I bought a thousand Belgian brutes, and watched them belge around, and said: "I'll fatten these galoots and sell them by the pound, and then I'll have all kinds of kale, to pleasure to devote; around this blamed old world I'll sail in my own motor boat." But when the hares were getting fat, my friends began to hiss: "Great Caesar! Would you look at that! What foolishness is this? Why wear out leg and back and arm pursuing idle fads? You ought to have a ginseng farm, and then you'd nail the scads."

The scheme to me seemed good and grand; I sold the Belgian brutes, and then I bought a strip of land and planted ginseng roots. I hoped to see them come up strong, and tilled them years and years, until the sheriff came along and took me by the ears. And as he pushed me off to jail, I passed that beeswax store; the owner, loaded down with kale, was standing in the door. "If you had stayed right here," he said, "you'd now be doing well; you would not by the ears be led toward a loathsome cell. But always to disaster wends the man who has no spine, who always listens to his friends, and thinks their counsel fine."

GLOBE FURNITURE COMPANY TREBLE PLANT.

One of the biggest industrial propositions in he history of Waterloo was placed before the town council for consideration recently, when the Globe Furniture Co., Ltd., with improvements in view, promised to spend at least $125,000 in additional buildings and machinery and the employment of 250 hands at the end of the second year. The present number of hands is 85. With these improvements the plant would be trebled in capacity. It is understood that the line of goods to be manufactured are not being made in Waterloo.

On account of the large expenditure of money required for the purpose, the company has found it advisable to make a request of the town for a loan of $50,000.

According to the plans of the proposed additions, it is proposed to erect a wing at the north-east end of the present building 48 by 128 feet, four storeys in height. There would also be a one storey separate building, 48 by 150 feet, at the rear of the present plant. The buildings would be of mill construction, equipped with the most modern sprinkler system.

At the end of the first year 150 hands are to be employed, which would be increased to from 200 to 250 by the end of the second year. With these improvements, the company would become one of the largest industries of its kind in the Dominion.

The Waterloo town council unanimously decided to submit the big industrial proposition of the Globe Company to the ratepayers, the proposition being considered of such a magnitude that any other step would have been detrimental to the industrial progress of Waterloo.

The board of trade of the town unanimously endorsed the proposition, and no criticism has as yet been voiced against it.

ONWARD GOODS IN WEST.

The Onward Manufacturing Co., Berlin, Ont., are now carrying a stock of their Onward sliding furniture shoes and Eureka electric vacuum cleaners in Winnipeg for the convenience of customers who prefer to have shipments made from there in order to save freight. Orders are filled by their Winnipeg salesmen, Moncrieff & Endress, Ltd., Scott Building, and invoiced from Berlin.

THE OUTING COLLAPSIBLE SULKY

The W. B. Jennings Co., St. Thomas, Ont., are showing a new line of collapsible carts for children, known as the "Outing" one-motion collapsible sulkies. These folding sulkies have spring seats and reclining backs. When folded the sulky occupies the space ordinarily taken by a suitcase, and can be carried as conveniently. The frames are of finest quality steel, finished with double-baked, black bicycle enamel. Ten-inch wheels are on all sulkies, and these are fitted with half-inch rubber tires. Seat and back are of padded leatherette. Arm rests are broad and comfortable and the whole is covered with a hood adjustable to any position. Mud guards and foot rest are of latest type, and a couple of rear guide wheels guarantee against tipping the car. The "Outing" sulky makes a comfortable and convenient baby carriage.

NEW LINE OF DAVENETTES AND DAVENPORTS.

The Lippert Furniture Co., Ltd., Berlin, have added to their lines some new davenettes and davenports. They come in a large range of designs and every one of them is made up to the standard set by the company for Lippert furniture.

Globe Furniture Co.'s new plant after completion of $125,000 addition.

Knobs of News

Arthur Rouleau, furniture dealer at Plantagenet, Ont., is dead.

The assets of Z. Gendron, furniture dealer, Montreal, have been sold.

Henry Eble is reported to be considering opening a furniture store at Conestogo, Ont.

Zinger & Honsinger, furniture and harness dealers at Durban, Man., have dissolved partnership.

Zacks Brothers have opened a furniture and house furnishings store on George Street, Peterborough.

The Puffer Bros., of Norwood, have opened up a furniture shop and undertaking business at Havelock, Ont.

J. Anderson, Galt, has sold his furniture store and business to W. Allen, late of T. Lytle & Son, also of Galt.

Severine Marchand and Alma Trudel have registered at Three Rivers, Que., as La Maison Carignan & Cie., furniture dealers.

Almost $5,000 damage was done by a fire which originated in the furniture factor of Castle & Sons, at Montreal, recently.

Morrison & McPhail, furniture dealers, Kincardine, Ont., have dissolved partnership. Mr. Morrison is continuing the business.

Lewis Parker, of St. Thomas, has taken an interest with J. W. Hutchinson, Port Rowan, in his sash, door and furniture factory.

The Lucknow Table Co.'s sawmill has started cutting lumber for the season. There is quite a large stock of logs to be cut this year.

An accident to the boiler in the chair factory at Scotstown, Que., recently, made it necessary to close the factory for two days.

Nelson & Foster, Ltd., have been incorporated at Winnipeg to make and deal in office and store fixtures and furniture. Capital, $60,000.

R. Drucker, of Brunn, Austria, a large furniture manufacturer of that place, is on a tour of the world, and at present is visiting Canada.

George Cooper has purchased the furniture business of J. H. McAlpin, of Killarney, Man. Mr. McAlpin will still retain his undertaking business.

Walter Greer has recently made an extension to his business interests in Lashburn, Sask., by the addition to his furniture store of a stock of harness.

James McKay, of Egmondville, has entered into partnership with W. J. Walker, of Seaforth, in the furniture and undertaking business at the latter place.

Ben Hollenburg, of Hollenburg Bros., furniture dealers, Fort William, has returned from a business trip to New York city, Buffalo, Montreal, Hamilton and Toronto.

The National Manufacturing Co., of Ottawa and Brockville, manufacturers of stoves, sewing machines, kitchen cabinets, etc., have opened a show room in North Bay.

Mayor Anson Spotton, of Harriston, Ont., president of the Harriston Furniture Co. and a director of the Canada Stove Co., has been appointed junior judge of Wellington county.

Walker & McKay, Seaforth, Ont., have installed a rug rack in their up-to-date furniture store, for the better display of their many fine rugs which they have in stock this spring.

James McGuirl is closing out the balance of his furniture stock, after which he will close up shop at Moosomin, Sask. He intends to devote all his time and energy to the insurance business.

Veale Bros., Toronto, are opening at St. Catharines, occupying the ground floor and basement of the Masonic Building, a high-class furniture, carpets, draperies, household furnishings and stove store.

G. B. Binkley is opening a furniture store and undertaking parlors at Shaunavon, Sask. Mr. Binkley has for some time past been assistant to O. B. Dreyer, funeral director and embalmer at Swift Current.

Baldwin-Robinson have been in business in St. Thomas for nearly fifteen years, but realizing the possibilities of Sarnia, have decided to locate there also. The company handles everything required for the complete furnishing of a home.

The business section of Liverpool, N.S., had a narrow escape from destruction recently, when fire destroyed a number of stores, among others George E. Snaddon, furniture dealer. The total loss was $40,000, with insurance of $25,000.

George Kennedy has entered into partnership with W. J. Wilkins in the furniture business at Tillsonburg, Ont. Mr. Kennedy has been with Mr. Wilkins in the business over a year and understands it well. The name of the new firm is Wilkins & Kennedy.

The employees of the Knechtel Furniture Co., at Walkerton, are arranging to hold their annual celebration on May 25th, which is a public holiday. This celebration was usually held on June 3rd, but the executive this year decided to change the date.

Steadman Bros., Petrolea, Ont., last month moved their furniture store and undertaking parlors into their new quarters in the Tecumseh Block recently occupied by the Metropolitan Bank. They now have one of the finest establishments in Western Ontario.

N. D. Gilbert, of the Gilbert Furniture Co., Picton, offers a good suggestion regarding the Prince Edward Old Boys' Fair, and it is that the P. E. Agricultural Society give special prizes to the Old Boy and Old Girl that travels the longest distance to visit the fair.

Mr. Marshall, Qu'Appelle's undertaker, has removed from the Progress Building, where he has been located for some time, to the house one door east. His family have recently arrived from New York State, and they have taken up their residence on Main Street North.

The Andrew Malcolm Furniture Company, of Kincardine, purchased, last fall, the timber on a large area of land in the vicinity of Milverton. The logs are being handled at the Milverton sawmill, and it is estimated nearly 500,000 feet of timber will be teamed to Kincardine during the summer.

Jacob Werlich is having plans prepared for his new furniture store on King Street, Galt. The plans show a building 36 x 75 feet, three storeys in height and built of Milton pressed brick. Work will be commenced in the near future and when the building is completed Mr. Werlich will have one of the finest furniture stores in Western Ontario.

Building operations in a general scheme of development of the Canada Furniture Manufacturers' Woodstock plant, will proceed this season on a big scale. Material is being delivered on the ground now for a four storey factory, 10 by 60 feet, to be built as an addition to the present buildings and to be used for manufacturing purposes. The addition will entail an expenditure of $15,000.

An early morning blaze originated in the cellar under the furniture store of P. O. Fortin, St. Joseph St., Quebec, recently, and worked its way up to the store above, where there was about $2,500 worth of goods on which there was $1,800 worth of insurance. Considerable damage was done by smoke and water and the operations necessary to combat the fire.

Fred Fritzshal, sales manager; Frank Turcot, manager; Alcide Gourdea, manager; Rene Turcot, clerk, and Laura Turcot, all of Winnipeg, have been incorporated as Northwestern Housefurnishers, Limited, to carry on a general business as dealers in furniture, furnishings, and household necessaries and utensils of all kinds. The capital is set at $2,500.

The convention of the Alberta branch of the Retail Merchants' Association will be held in Regina on May 5, 6 and 7. It is expected that 200 or so delegates from all points in Alberta will be in attendance, and addresses will be delivered by a number of merchants. Secretary Bucknall has made arrangements for an exhibit of manufactured goods and merchandise in the basement of Paget hall.

George Baldwin, of Baldwin-Robinson, St. Thomas, house furnishers, visited Sarnia recently, in search of a building suitable for the opening of a large house furnishing establishment. It is the intention to construct a building large enough to accommodate the proposed company. Until more definite plans have been arranged, however, it is likely that Baldwin-Robinson will open temporary premises to meet the ever-increasing demand for this line of goods.

Lane and Eano, furniture dealers and undertakers, are now settled in their new premises at 186 Hunter Street, Peterborough. Their present quarters are extremely attractive and commodious, the work of the decorators making a transformation that must be seen to be realized. The walls have been beautifully treated, and by the removal of a partition the showroom has been greatly enlarged, making it a spacious apartment for the display of furniture. In this connection it might be mentioned that the additional floor space has made it possible for this firm to carry a larger and more varied stock than in the former store.

RATTAN AND SEA-GRASS FURNITURE.

By George E. Anderson, Hong Kong, China

The trend of Canadian and American taste toward the bungalow style of living is having a marked effect upon the furniture industry of Hong Kong and upon the rattan and grass-twine trade of South China. The increased exports from Hong Kong of rattan and sea-grass furniture, which commenced about two years ago, have been continued in increasing proportion during the past year, and the indications are that the current season will witness a larger demand than ever for such goods. Shipments of such furniture and unmanufactured rattan to America during 1913 amounted to a declared value of $180,489, of which $77.653 was of rattan and rattan furniture and $102,836 of "sea-grass" furniture, in which rattan and other materials also entered. The figures of the Hong Kong Chamber of Commerce show that shipments to continental Europe increased almost 100 per cent. during 1913 over those of 1912, while those to Great Britain were in still larger proportion. The demand for such furniture in South Africa has increased to such a point that the leading Hong Kong factory and exporting concern has opened a branch house in Durban, and is making arrangements for a similar enterprise in Cape Town. Similar enterprises are also being undertaken in various South American countries. The trade in such goods with Canada has grown especially rapidly and is now large in volume.

Trade with America in the near future promises to be on a much larger scale than ever as a result of the reduction of the tariff on furniture from 35 per cent. to 15 per cent. ad valorem. The chief interference with the further development of the trade at present is high freight. The ordinary freight charge on the average rattan or sea-grass chair made in Hong Kong at present and shipped to either America or Europe is substantially 100 per cent. of its value.

Three new McLagan productions—buffet, hall tree and china buffet.

The Furniture Manufacturer

A Department of News and Ideas

Care of Saws in Furniture Factory
By O. C. Oberberk

Scroll saws 1/4-in. in width, teeth spaced 1/4-in. apart and 21-gage in thickness, will give good results in average work. while for heavy work, such as sawing swell or sweep drawer fronts, a saw 3/4-in. wide, 19-gage thickness and 1/2-in. spacing, will give good results. As the 1/4-in. saws wear narrower, they may be used for sawing carvings. etc., while saws broken beyond repair may be cut into short lengths and used for jig saws.

In setting these saws I use an automatic set, after which the 1/4-in. saws are filed on an automatic filing machine, while the 3/4-in. saws are filed by hand. Give just as little set as is required to make the bends and set oftener, as I think the saw chattering in cut, caused by too much set, tends to crystallize the saw, which, in turn, may cause the cracking of blade.

When filing a scroll band in an automatic filer which uses the regular 6-in. slim taper file, see that the edges of file are straight, that the machine is kept clean and well oiled, and that there is no play in slide rods or bearings. I firmly believe that if the filing machine is kept in good order it will give as good results as hand filing, and more of it. Set the feed-finger to bear on second tooth to be filed, as this tends to keep teeth of a more even length. A few drops of lard oil put on the file once in a while will make it last longer and cut smoother.

In brazing the saws 1/4-in. wide I use the blow-torch method, filing the laps 1/4-in. long and using silver solder, as I think it gives a much stronger braze than spelter or brass wire. Clean the solder with a little pure muriatic acid, place it between laps, after which sprinkle with powdered borax and dampen with water. Start the torch, applying a slow flame at first, after which bring it up to a good heat or until the solder flows freely; then clamp quickly with a pair of flat-nose tongs. This tends to force all surplus solder out of the braze, making a strong joint. Care must be used in applying the tongs, as the braze will kink easily while hot. This method of brazing with torch and tongs may leave the joint in a hardened condition, so take an oilstone or piece of emery cloth, brighten the saw, and with the torch draw the steel to a blue color, when it will be about the same temper as the rest of the saw. If care was used in filing the laps and if saw is placed straight in clamps, you will have a straight saw and a braze which will last as long as the rest of the saw. In dressing down the braze, use a saw gage to determine thickness. In brazing scroll saw 1/2-in. or wider, I use the regular brazing clamps which I use for the resaws, using silver solder and "Brazine" for a flux.

The proper size of resaw to use, as to spacing of teeth, gage, etc., may be hard to determine when mixed woods are to be sawed. I would recommend the following spacings: For a 20-gage saw, teeth spaced 1 3/8-in. apart, 5/16-in. deep; for a 19-gage saw, teeth spaced 1 1/2-in. apart, 3/8-in. deep; for an 18-gage saw, teeth spaced 1 3/4-in. apart, 3/8-in. deep, with hook line of 2 1/2-in. in 6-in.

In leveling saw do not let swaged points rest on the leveling block, as it will tend to show plate slightly dished. Level the teeth as well as the rest of the plate and keep tension as even as you can, using care to see there are not tight places near the edges. Run the tension from edge to edge, using no tire in saw. Put in just enough tension that saw will lie flat on leveling block, and put a little crown in back of saw, say from 1/64-in. to 1/32-in. in 5-ft.

I swage out the points six gages wider than the saw, then with the swage-shaper bring it back to five gages of swage; in other words, a 20-gage saw will have a finished width over top of tooth of 15-gage; a 19-gage will be 14-gage, etc. Before swaging I put a small quantity of lard oil on each tooth. Generally the swage-shaper will bring all teeth back in line, although it is good practice to go over the teeth with a set-gage.

In brazing a resaw, make a lap of 3/8-in. for a 20-gage saw, 7/16-in. lap for 19 and 18-gage saws, taking care in filing to keep them free from oil, and never touching lap with the fingers, although "Brazine" will clean the laps of oil; still it is a good plan to keep the fingers off some things.

Several years ago I tried to braze a broken piece of cast iron, but it wouldn't stick, and as I had trouble with my brazing irons sticking to the saw, I decided to have a pair of cast iron ones made. Now, after using them for several years, I would use no other. Cast iron never scales in heating, does not stick to the braze, and as the irons are planed to size, there is no poor braze resulting from irons of uneven thickness. These irons are 1 1/4-in. wide, 9/16-in. thick, 18-in. long, surfaced two sides. Cast iron is brittle when hot, and if you drop it on the floor it will break, but I have given them all the pressure the brazing clamps were capable of and they would not crumble.

When the saw is placed in the clamps ready for brazing, heat irons to an orange color, slip quickly into clamp, and apply pressure. When irons turn from dark-red to black, remove them, pour machine oil over braze, and you will have plenty of temper left in braze. Dress up the braze the same thickness as the rest of the plate; put crown in back, and tension the same as the rest of the saw.

In summing up this subject, I wish to say, if a saw has a poor place in it, such as a bad crack or a braze which is open in places, don't humor it; rather have it come apart in the filing room than on the mill.—Berlin Quality.

OAK WORKING HINTS.

Here is a suggestion from a writer in the Southern Furniture Journal, which may interest some of the readers of The Furniture World : Oak, whether plain or quartered, is a comparatively easy wood to work smooth. It is not a soft wood, but what is meant is that oak can be worked on the planer and get a smooth finish with knives that are a little dull. The same thing is true in working it with saws. When it comes to gum and some of the other woods, the knives and saws must be perfectly keen to give good results. Now, when it comes to sanding, it is the other way. You may sand gum, or some other ever-grained wood, with comparatively smooth or even slick sandpaper and get fair results, but when it comes to sanding oak, to get a good finish, the sandpaper should be fresh and sharp. This is because of the unevenness in the texture of the wood. If it is plain oak, there are the hard streaks

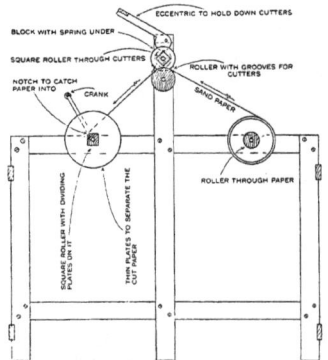

A handy sandpaper cutter, showing section through side elevation of cutter.—"At a time when belt sanders were not used so extensively we bought our sandpaper in rolls, cut the right width for the machine, say 8, 9 and 10-in., for it was a tedious job to cut the long rolls into narrow strips with the use of a long straightedge, and to buy it ready cut cost us 50c per roll. We made a machine to cut it ourselves, which I have endeavored to illustrate. It is used similar to the way paperhangers trim wallpaper. We have found it to be a very useful tool. After cutting we fasten the loose ends with common carpet tacks, and mark the number on each small roll."—E. A. Soules in The Wood-Worker.

and the soft streaks of the annual rings of growth, and if they are sanded over with dull paper, it will cut down into the soft streaks and the hard ridges be all right for a certain kind of finish, but where a perfectly smooth face is wanted, one should sand oak with a sharp, clean paper. If it is quartered oak, it is the same thing in a different way. There is a hard film which makes the splash line which nothing but sharp paper will touch. If the wood is sanded over with dull or slick paper, it will simply dig down between the splash lines and leave them standing up in waves. To get good results, you should not only have sharp paper, but you should get the sanding across the grain or splash line to reduce the tendency to cut down the soft places between.

HANDLING TIMBER WITH TRUCKS

In a woodworking establishment, for example, it has been found that it costs fifty cents a thousand feet to pick up lumber and put it down again. Hence every time an operation of picking up and putting down lumber is eliminated by introducing an extra truck, fifty cents (less the depreciation and interest charge on the truck) is saved on every thousand feet of lumber processed. And if it is easier to use a truck than not to, as it usually is in the average shop, the manager will find that apparently an unlimited number of trucks are absorbed before a surplus of empties is visible.

Other industries show corresponding savings.

The labor saving is only a portion of the total economy effected by increasing the trucking equipment to the point where material needs never to be rehandled except when processed. A large element of delay also is eliminated, greatly smoothing out the routing system and shortening the total time of processing—in cases as much as fifty per cent. The efficiency of the truckers or "move" men, too, in some instances has been more than doubled; or what is the same thing, the number of them required approximately halved.

When these several savings are integrated it is evident that a large investment in trucking equipment is justified in order to bring out the happy condition of having all material constantly on the move or ready to move on the instant.—Factory.

ADDITIONAL STORAGE OF A LUMBER MAKER

Spring and fall were the busy times for a furniture manufacturer. In summer and winter his business fell off to a very appreciable extent, and his men had little to do.

It took him from thirty to sixty days to get raw material from his sources of supply. Consequently, manufacturing at full capacity only in rush times, as was his custom, he found it almost impossible to care for his customers promptly. The superintendent, when questioned, urged him to install new machinery and increase his manufacturing facilities. Instead of doing this, however, the manufacturer built an addition to his factory and used it not for manufacturing, but exclusively for storage purposes.

Between the active shipping seasons, the manufacturer now runs full time, filling his warehouse with staple lines. The factory's capacity is no longer strained to the limit twice a year and idle the remainder of the time. Customers' orders are filled from stock. The result is really an increase in the capacity of the factory, without a corresponding increase in investment for new machinery.—Factory.

HONESTY AND FAIR DEALING WIN OUT.

That it pays to play fair at all times is proven by the experience of the sales manager of a Canadian saw manufacturer's plant who recently attended a card party at which some valuable prizes were offered. In the course of the play the saw manufacturer noticed that a salesman who had been selling supplies to his firm was doing some unfair scoring. Becoming convinced of this the saw manufacturer's representative figured it out that if the traveling salesman would not be straight in a card game he could not be depended upon in a business deal. On his return to the factory, therefore, he investigated the purchases which his company had made and his suspicions were proven to be well founded, the result being that the concern represented by the sharp card player was stricken off the list of firms from whom the saw manufacturer bought supplies.

Honesty and fair dealing will win out whether in private or business life and the traveling salesman or retail store clerk who wishes to succeed in life can draw a moral from the instance related.

Are you marching or marking time? it takes about the same amount of motion, so don't judge by that.

You should have "Twins"

Just Out!

THIS comprehensive, well-illustrated catalog is just off the press. It describes the principle of the Twin Pedestal Extension Table and shows many new designs.

¶ Our lines of Extensions, Parlor, Library Tables and Specialties are all included.

¶ Just ask us to mail you a copy. It contains a fund of practical, sale-creating information, and is well worth a place on your fyles.

Chesley Furniture Co., Limited
Chesley - Ontario

The "Twins"

Something Better in Extension Tables

Twin Pedestals

Put "Twins" on Your Floors This Spring

HERE is a principle in Extension Table Construction that places the *Twin* 'way above the ordinary kind, and gives you a selling argument that makes your customer want *nothing else* but a *Twin* Table. Consider these units of Extension Table perfectness as embodied in our lines.

A pair of pedestals, each complete in itself.
Always perfect, extended or closed.
Three-point support for each pedestal
No gaping pedestals
No unfinished surfaces when extended

¶ Get a copy of our new catalog, it is brimful of ideas for the Spring house-cleaning trade. Write a postal for it to-day.

The Chesley Furniture Co., Limited
Chesley - Ontario

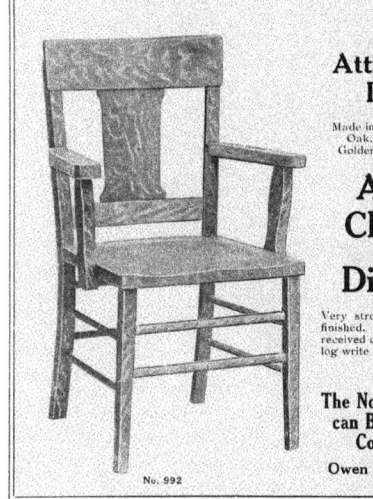

An Attractive Line

Made in Hardwood or Oak. Fumed or Golden Gloss Finish

Arm Chairs and Diners

Very strongly built, well finished. If you have not received our No. 23 Catalog write us for a copy.

The North American Bent Chair Co., Ltd.
Owen Sound, Ont.

No. 992   No. 990

This Ad Brought Results

We have had a large number of enquiries for catalogues from the one insertion of our advertisement in the April number of the *Canadian Furniture World* and we are well satisfied with the results.

Yours very truly **The Jennings Company** St. Thomas, Ontario.

Maintaining Quality *with* Big Cost Reduction

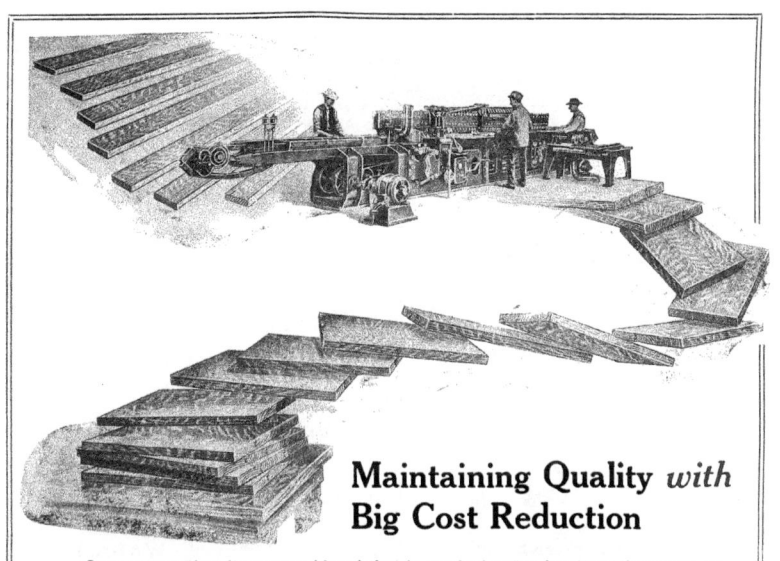

Once upon a time it was considered that in producing fine furniture there was no other way to get fine results than to do every part of the work by hand. A great many furniture manufacturers are still using hand labor where the work could be done equally as well by improved machinery. Many improvements have been made in producing furniture by automatic machinery, but the most important method, and one that completely revolutionizes former ways, is the jointing of lumber automatically on the

Linderman Automatic Dovetail Jointer, Gluer, Clamper and Sizer

Over eighty factories are producing on the latest model "Linderman" machine making the Double Cut Taper Wedge Dovetail Joint perfect and permanent furniture joints in solid quartered and plain oak; also mahogany, gum, maple and many other kinds of wood. Many of these same factories are making $10 to $25 per day by the use of the automatic method.

Taper Wedge Joint

It resolves itself to a matter of reduction in labor, lumber and glue costs that will be of great value to every furniture factory.

One automatic operation makes the completed panel, sized to the finished width with a tapered wedge dovetail glue joint that gets the glue into the pores of the wood and on every part of the jointed edge.

A new thirty-two page catalogue has just been issued in three colors, giving every detail and advantage of jointing lumber automatically, with cuts and illustrations. This will be sent upon request.

Canadian Linderman Co., Limited
Works at
Muskegon, Mich.　　　Woodstock, Ont.

A splendid new line of Genuine Tennessee Red Cedar Chests. Absolutely moth proof. Made in three sizes. Mahogany finish. Best copper trimmings.

We can put these Cedar Chests in your store on a selling basis that offers exceptional profits. Write us for photos and further information.

D. L. SHAFER & CO.　-　-　St. Thomas, Ontario

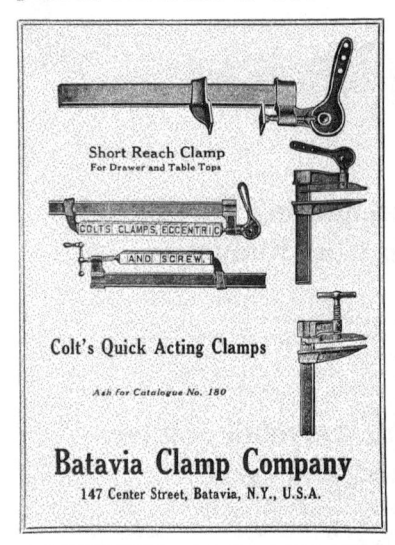

Short Reach Clamp
For Drawer and Table Tops

COLT'S CLAMPS, ECCENTRIC AND SCREW.

Colt's Quick Acting Clamps

Ask for Catalogue No. 180

Batavia Clamp Company
147 Center Street, Batavia, N.Y., U.S.A.

Making TABLE-SLIDES is a Specialty Business

For more than TWENTY-FIVE YEARS we have made TABLE SLIDES exclusively. Our Factory is equipped with Special Machinery which enables us to make SLIDES,—BETTER and CHEAPER than the furniture manufacturer.

Canadian Table makers are rapidly adopting WABASH SLIDES

Because { They ELIMINATE SLIDE TROUBLES
Are CHEAPER and BETTER

Reduced Costs
Increased Out-put

BY USING
WABASH SLIDES

Made by
B. WALTER & CO.
Wabash, Ind.

The Largest EXCLUSIVE TABLE-SLIDE Manufacturers in America
ESTABLISHED 1887

"Onward" Sliding Furniture Shoes
For all kinds of Furniture and Metal Beds.

"Onward" Slides
for chairs in place of old-fashioned carpet-tearing and floor-destroying casters.

Write for particulars, our prices will interest you.

Onward Manufacturing Company　-　Berlin, Ont.

SHELLACS

If you are in the market for first-class Shellac we believe it would be to your advantage to get in touch with us.

HIGH GRADE VARNISHES
FILLERS and GRAINING INKS

THE AULT & WIBORG CO. OF CANADA
LIMITED

MONTREAL   TORONTO   WINNIPEG

ROBERTSON SOCKET HEAD
Wood Screws

See That Square Hole

Pat. Feb. 2, 1909

THIS IS A REAL WOOD SCREW

It is driven by a simple square bit, and is the only one of its type on the market.

Driver fits snugly into the square hole and positively cannot slip and cut the fingers, or disfigure costly furniture or woodwork. It is driven with less exertion. No ragged slots after driving. Saves time, labor, money and material. We make the drivers in all suitable styles.

Drivers sent free with first order. Write for catalogue and prices.

P. L. Robertson Mfg. Co., Limited

We also manufacture Wire Nails, Rivets, Wire and Washers

MILTON :: ONTARIO

BUYER'S DIRECTORY

When writing to advertisers kindly mention the Canadian Furniture World and the Undertaker

ARTS AND CRAFTS FURNITURE
Geo. McLagan Furniture Co., Stratford.
John C. Mundell & Co., Elora.

ASBESTOS TABLE COVERS.
Canadian H. W. Johns-Manville Co., Toronto.

BABY CARRIAGES
Gendron Mfg. Co., Toronto.

AWNINGS
Stamco, Limited, Saskatoon, Sask.

BENT WOOD FURNITURE.
John C. Mundell & Co., Elora.
J. & J. Kohn, Toronto (W. Craig).

BOOKCASES
Knechtel Furniture Co., Hanover.
Globe Wernicke Co., Stratford.
Geo. McLagan Furniture Co., Stratford.
Meaford Mfg. Co., Meaford, Ont.

BUFFETS.
Bell Furniture Co., Southampton, Ontario.
Knechtel Furniture Co., Hanover.
Geo. McLagan Furniture Co., Stratford.
Meaford Mfg. Co., Meaford, Ont.
Peppler Bros., Hanover.
Stratford Chair Co., Stratford.
Victoriaville Furniture Co., Victoriaville, Que.

BEDS (Brass and Iron).
Canada Beds, Ltd., Chesley.
Ideal Bedding Co., Toronto.
Geo. Gale & Son, Waterville Que.
Ives Modern Bedstead Co., Cornwall Ont.
Ontario Spring Bed & Mattress Co., London, Ont.
Standard Bedstead Co., Victoriaville, Que.
Stamco, Limited, Saskatoon, Sask.
Stratford Bed Co., Stratford, Ont.
S. Weisglass, Ltd., Montreal, Que.

BEDS (Modern Wood).
Elora Furniture Co., Elora.
Knechtel Furniture Co., Hanover.

BED SPRINGS.
Colleraw Spring Mattress Co., Toronto.
Knechtel Furniture Co., Hanover.
Frame and Hay Fence Co., Stratford.
Gold Medal Furniture Co., Toronto
Leggett & Platt Spring Bed Co., Windsor.
Ideal Bedding Co., Toronto.
Ontario Spring Bed & Mattress Co., London, Ont.
Stamco, Limited, Saskatoon, Sask.
S. Weisglass, Ltd., Montreal, Que.

BED ROOM CHAIRS.
Baetz Bros., Berlin.
Bell Furniture Co., Southampton, Ontario.
Elmira Furniture Co., Elmira, Ont.
Lippert Furniture Co., Berlin.

BEDROOM ROCKERS
Lippert Furniture Co., Berlin, Ont.

BED ROOM SUITES.
Bell Furniture Co., Southampton, Ontario.
Knechtel Furniture Co., Hanover
Meaford Mfg. Co., Meaford.
Victoriaville Furniture Co., Victoriaville, Que.

BUNGALOW CHAIRS & SUITES
Baetz Bros. & Co., Berlin, Ont.

CARD AND DEN TABLES.
Geo. McLagan Furniture Co., Stratford.
John C. Mundell & Co., Elora, Ont.

CARPET RACKS
Steel Furnishing Co., New Glasgow, N. S.

CAMP FURNITURE.
Stratford Mfg. Co., Stratford.
Ideal Bedding Co., Toronto.

CEDAR BOXES
D. L. Shafer, St. Thomas, Ont.

CELLARETTES.
John C. Mundell & Co., Elora, Ont.

CHAIRS AND ROCKERS
Bell Furniture Co., Southampton.
J. P. Albrough & Co., Ingersoll.
Baetz Bros., Berlin.
Knechtel Furniture Co., Hanover.
John C. Mundell & Co., Elora.

Stratford Chair Co., Stratford.
Waterloo Furniture Co., Waterloo.
Canadian Rattan Chair Co., Victoriaville.
Gold Medal Furniture Co., Toronto.
Elmira Furniture Co., Elmira, Ont.
Imperial Furniture Co., Toronto.
Lippert Furniture Co., Berlin.
Victoriaville Chair Mfg. Co., Victoriaville.

CHESTERFIELDS.
Imperial Furniture Co., Toronto.

CHIFFONIERS.
Bell Furniture Co., Southampton.
Knechtel Furniture Co., Hanover.
Meaford Mfg. Co., Meaford, Ont.
Stratford Chair Co., Stratford.
Victoriaville Furniture Co., Victoriaville, Que.

CHILDRENS' SULKIES
Jennings Co., St. Thomas

CHINA CABINETS.
Bell Furniture Co., Southampton, Ontario
Peppler Bros., Hanover.
Knechtel Furniture Co., Hanover.
Geo. McLagan Furniture Co., Stratford.
Meaford Mfg. Co., Meaford, Ont.

CLOCK CASES
Elmira Interior Woodwork Co., Elmira, Ont.

COMFORTERS.
Toronto Feather & Down Co., Toronto.
Stamco, Limited, Saskatoon, Sask.

COTS
Ideal Bedding Co., Toronto
Ontario Spring Bed and Mattress Co., London.

COSTUMIERS
Elmira Interior Woodwork Co., Elmira, Ont.

COUCHES.
J. P. Albrough & Co., Ingersoll.
Ellis Furniture Co., Ingersoll.
Gold Medal Furniture Co., Toronto.
Kindel Bed Co., Toronto.
Imperial Furniture Co., Toronto.
John C. Mundell & Co., Elora, Ont.
Montreal Upholstering Co., Montreal.
Steel Furnishing Co., New Glasgow, N. S.
S. Weisglass, Ltd., Montreal, Que.

COUCHES (Sliding).
Ideal Bedding Co., Toronto.
Farquharson-Gifford Co., Stratford.
Ontario Spring Bed & Mattress Co., London, Ont.
Stamco, Limited, Saskatoon, Sask.
Gold Medal Furniture Co., Toronto.

CRADLES.
Knechtel Furniture Co., Hanover.

CRIBS (Brass and Iron)
Ideal Bedding Co., Toronto.
Ontario Spring Bed & Mattress Co., London, Ont.
Stamco, Limited, Saskatoon, Sask.
S. Weisglass, Ltd., Montreal, Que.

CUSHIONS.
Stamco, Limited, Saskatoon, Sask.

DAVENPORT BEDS.
Farquharson-Gifford Co., Stratford.
Kindel Bed Co., Toronto.
Lippert Furniture Co., Berlin, Ont.
Montreal Upholstering Co., Montreal, Que.
Imperial Rattan Co., Stratford.
John C. Mundell & Co., Elora.

DAVENPORT FRAMES
Elmira Interior Woodwork Co., Elmira, Ont.

DEN FURNITURE
Elmira Furniture Co., Elmira, Ont.
Farquharson-Gifford Co., Stratford.
John C. Mundell & Co., Elora, Ont.

DIVANETTES.
Lippert Furniture Co., Berlin.

DESKS.
Bell Furniture Co., Southampton.
Elmira Interior Woodwork Co., Elmira.

Knechtel Furniture Co., Hanover.
Geo. McLagan Furniture Co., Stratford.
John C. Mundell & Co., Elora.
Stratford Desk Co., Stratford, Ont.

DINING-ROOM FURNITURE
Crown Furniture Co., Preston.
Farquharson-Gifford Co., Stratford.
Lippert Furniture Co., Berlin, Ont.

DINING SUITES.
Bell Furniture Co., Southampton.
Knechtel Furniture Co., Hanover.
Geo. McLagan Furniture Co., Stratford.
John C. Mundell & Co., Elora.
Peppler Bros., Hanover.
Stratford Chair Co., Stratford.

DINERS
Lippert Furniture Co., Berlin, Ont.

DINNER WAGONS.
Geo. McLagan Furniture Co., Stratford.

DRESSERS.
Bell Furniture Co., Southampton.
Knechtel Furniture Co., Hanover.
Stratford Chair Co., Stratford.
Victoriaville Furniture Co., Victoriaville, Que.
Meaford Mfg. Co., Meaford, Ont.

EXTENSION TABLES.
Bell Furniture Co., Southampton.
Peppler Bros., Hanover.
Berlin Table Mfg. Co., Berlin.
Meaford Mfg. Co., Meaford, Ont.

FILING DEVICES.
Elmira Interior Woodwork Co., Elmira.
Globe Wernicke Co., Stratford.
Knechtel Furniture Co., Hanover.
Geo. McLagan Furniture Co., Stratford

FILING CABINETS
Globe Wernicke Co., Stratford, Ont.

FOLDING CHAIRS.
Stratford Mfg. Co., Stratford.
Ideal Bedding Co., Toronto.

FOLDING TABLES.
Hourd & Co., London.
Stratford Mfg. Co., Stratford.

FOOTSTOOLS
Elmira Furniture Co., Elmira, Ont.

GRASS FURNITURE (Chinese)
Jennings Co., St. Thomas

HALL RACKS
Lippert Furniture Co., Berlin, Ont.

HALL SEATS AND MIRRORS.
Geo. McLagan Furniture Co., Stratford.
Lippert Furniture Co., Berlin, Ont.
Meaford Mfg. Co., Meaford, Ont.

HALL TREES.
Geo. McLagan Furniture Co., Stratford.

HAMMOCKS
Dominion Hammock Mfg. Co., Dunnville, Ont.

HAMMO-COUCHES.
Ideal Bedding Co., Toronto.

INVALID CHAIRS.
Gendron Mfg. Co., Toledo, Ohio.
Victoriaville Chair Mfg. Co., Victoriaville, Que.

IRONING BOARDS AND DRYERS.
Stratford Mfg. Co., Stratford.

JARDINIERE STANDS.
Elmira Furniture Co., Elmira, Ont.
Elora Furniture Co., Elora.
Geo. McLagan Furniture Co., Stratford.
Meaford Mfg. Co., Meaford, Ont.

KITCHEN CABINETS.
H. E. Furniture Co., Milverton.
Nagrella Mfg. Co., Hanover.
Knechtel Kitchen Cabinet Co., Ltd., Hanover, Ont.

KITCHEN TABLES.
Knechtel Furniture Co., Hanover.
Victoriaville Furniture Co., Victoriaville

LADIES' DESKS
Meaford Mfg. Co., Meaford, Ont.

LAWN SEATS AND SWINGS.
Stratford Mfg. Co., Stratford.

LIBRARY TABLES.
Bell Furniture Co., Southampton.
Peppler Bros., Hanover.
Elmira Furniture Co., Elmira, Ont.
Elmira Interior Woodwork Co., Elmira, Ont.
Geo. McLagan Furniture Co., Stratford
Meaford Mfg. Co., Meaford, Ont.
John C. Mundell & Co., Elora, Ont.

LIVING-ROOM FURNITURE
Lippert Furniture Co., Berlin, Ont.

LOUNGES
J. P. Albrough & Co., Ingersoll.

LUXURY CHAIRS.
Lippert Furniture Co., Berlin.

MAGAZINE RACKS AND STANDS.
Geo. McLagan Furniture Co., Stratford.

MATTRESSES.
Berlin Bedding Co., Toronto.
Canada Mattress Co., Victoriaville, Que.
Gold Medal Furniture Co., Toronto.
McKellar Bedding Co., Fort William, Ont.
Ontario Spring Bed & Mattress Co., London, Ont.
Stamco, Limited, Saskatoon, Sask.
Standard Bedding Co., Toronto.
Antiseptic Bedding Co., Toronto.
Ideal Bedding Co., Toronto.
Fischman Mattress Co., Toronto.

MANTELS—Wood, Tile
Elmira Interior Woodwork Co., Elmira, Ont.

MANTELS—Electric
Elmira Interior Woodwork Co., Elmira, Ont.

MEDICINE CABINETS.
Meaford Mfg. Co., Meaford, Ont.

MORRIS CHAIRS.
Ellis Furniture Co., Ingersoll.
Imperial Rattan Co., Stratford.
Knechtel Furniture Co., Hanover.
Lippert Furniture Co., Berlin, Ont.
John C. Mundell & Co., Elora.
Waterloo Furniture Co., Waterloo.

MUSIC CABINETS.
Geo. McLagan Furniture Co., Stratford.
Knechtel Kitchen Cabinet Co., Ltd., Hanover, Ont.

ODD CHAIRS
Bell Furniture Co., Southampton.
Elmira Furniture Co., Elmira, Ont.

OFFICE CHAIRS.
Knechtel Furniture Co., Hanover.
H. Krug Furniture Co., Berlin.
Stratford Chair Co., Stratford.
J. & J. Kohn, Toronto (W. Craig).
John C. Mundell & Co., Elora, Ont.

OFFICE TABLES
Stratford Desk Co., Stratford, Ont.

PARK SEATS
Stratford Mfg. Co., Stratford.

PARLOR CHAIRS and ROCKERS
Ellis Furniture Co., Ingersoll.
Elmira Interior Woodwork Co., Elmira.
John C. Mundell & Co., Elora, Ont.
Waterloo Furniture Co., Waterloo.

PARLOR FRAMES
Elmira Interior Woodwork Co., Elmira, Ont.

PARLOR SUITES.
Elmira Interior Woodwork Co., Elmira.
Ellis Furniture Co., Ingersoll.
Knechtel Furniture Co., Hanover.
Waterloo Furniture Co., Waterloo.
Gold Medal Furniture Co., Toronto.
Lippert Furniture Co., Berlin.

PARLOR TABLES.
Geo. McLagan Furniture Co., Stratford.
Meaford Mfg. Co., Meaford, Ont.
Elora Furniture Co., Elora.
Elmira Furniture Co., Elmira, Ont.
Knechtel Furniture Co., Hanover.
Peppler Bros., Hanover.

PEDESTALS
Lippert Furniture Co., Berlin, Ont.
Geo. McLagan Furniture Co., Stratford.
Peppler Bros., Hanover.

PILLOWS.
Ontario Spring Bed & Mattress Co., London, Ont.
Stamco, Limited, Saskatoon, Sask.
Toronto Feather & Down Co., Toronto.
Ideal Bedding Co., Toronto.

PILLOW SHAM HOLDERS.
Tarbox Mfg. Co., Toronto.

RATTAN FURNITURE.
Imperial Rattan Co., Stratford.
Canadian Rattan Chair Co., Victoriaville, Que.
Gendron Mfg. Co., Toronto.

RECLINING CHAIRS.
Ellis Furniture Co., Ingersoll.
Knechtel Furniture Co., Hanover.
Lippert Furniture Co., Berlin, Ont.
John C. Mundell & Co., Elora, Ont.

RUG RACKS
Steel Furnishing Co., New Glasgow, N. S.

SECTIONAL BOOKCASES
Knechtel Furniture Co., Hanover.
Globe Wernicke Co., Stratford.

May, 1914   CANADIAN FURNITURE WORLD AND THE UNDERTAKER   65

| MOULDINGS
PICTURE FRAMES
MIRRORS
GLASS
MATBOARD
PICTURE BACKING | **MATTHEWS' QUALITY SERVING TRAYS**
Ask for our new catalogue
just out | for wedding presents. The June weddings are near at hand and all the ladies want Trays. All our Trays have glass set in with waterproof cement and are non leakable and have felt bottoms. All our latest Trays are fixed with simple screw fasteners allowing the back to be readily removed for replacing with owner's own fancy work, chintz or tapestry. Mail us an order for immediate shipment and we will send you a sample dozen assorted kinds and sizes that will not average more than $12.00 per doz. net and will retail at a good profit.
Matthews Bros. Ltd., 788 Dundas St. Toronto |

Canadian School of Embalming
Instruction in Practical Embalming and Funeral Directing
PREPARATION FOR EXAMINATIONS
ENTER AT ANY TIME
R. U. STONE   32 Carlton Street
Principal   Toronto

For Sale
Wanted

TERMS FOR INSERTION
25 Cents per line, one insertion
Four lines once for $1.00, three times for $2.00.
Cash must accompany the order
No accounts booked.
MINIMUM 50 CENTS

SCHOOL FURNITURE.
Bell Furniture Co., Southampton.
SIDEBOARDS.
Knechtel Furniture Co., Hanover.
Meaford Mfg. Co., Meaford, Ont.
Stratford Chair Co., Stratford.
STORE FRONTS
Kawneer Mfg. Co., Toronto.
TABLES.
Berlin Table Mfg. Co., Berlin, Ont.
Bell Furniture Co., Southampton, Ontario.
Elora Furniture Co., Elora.
Knechtel Furniture Co., Hanover.
John C. Mundell & Co., Elora.
Orillia Furniture Co., Orillia.
Peppler Bros., Hanover.
Stratford Chair Co., Stratford.
Victoriaville Furniture Co., Victoriaville, Que.
TABOURETTES.
Elora Furniture Co., Elora.
Kensington Furniture Co., Goderich.
TAPESTRY CURTAINS
Dominion Hammock Mfg Co., Dunnville, Ont.
TELEPHONE STANDS.
John C. Mundell & Co., Elora, Ont.
TYPEWRITER DESKS.
Elmira Interior Woodwork Co., Elmira.
Stratford Desk Co., Stratford, Ont.
UPHOLSTERERS' SUPPLIES
Ellis Furniture Co., Ingersoll.
Gold Medal Furniture Co., Toronto.
UPHOLSTERED FURNITURE
Baetz Bros., Berlin.
Ellis Furniture Co., Ingersoll.
Farquharson-Gifford Co., Stratford, Ont.
Imperial Rattan Co., Stratford.
Imperial Furniture Co., Toronto.
John C. Mundell & Co., Elora.
Knechtel Furniture Co., Hanover.
Waterloo Furniture Co., Waterloo.
Gold Medal Furniture Co., Toronto.
Quality Furniture Makers, Welland.
A. J. Beafe & Co., Berlin.
VACUUM CLEANERS.
Onward Mfg. Co., Berlin.
VERANDAH FURNITURE.
Imperial Rattan Co., Stratford.
Stratford Mfg. Co., Stratford.
WARDROBES.
Knechtel Furniture Co., Hanover.
Meaford Mfg. Co., Meaford, Ont.
Stratford Chair Co., Stratford.

FACTORY SUPPLIES
BRASS TRIMMINGS
Stratford Brass Co., Stratford.
CLAMPS.
Batavia Clamp Co., Batavia, N.Y.
FURNITURE SHOES.
Onward Mfg. Co., Berlin, Ont.
DRY KILNS.
Morton Dry Kiln Co., Chicago
FURNITURE HARDWARE
Stratford Brass Co., Stratford, Ont.
GLUE JOINTING MACHINES.
Canadian Linderman Co., Wood stock.
NAILS
P. L. Robertson Mfg. Co., Milton.

PLATING
P. L. Robertson Mfg. Co., Milton, Ontario.
RIVETS AND SCREWS
P. L. Robertson Mfg. Co., Milton, Ontario.
SPRINGS.
James Steele, Guelph.
Ideal Bedding Co., Toronto.
SPANISH LEATHER.
Lackawanna Leather Co., Hackettstown, N. J.
STERILIZED HAIR.
Griffin Curled Hair Co., Toronto.
TABLE SLIDES
B. Walter & Co., Wabash, Ind.
TRUCKS.
W. I. Kemp Co., Ltd., Stratford.
VARNISHES.
R. C. Jamieson & Co., Montreal.
Ault & Wiborg, Toronto.
VENEERS.
Adams & Raymond Veneer Co., Indianapolis, Ind.
VENEER PRESSES.
Wm. R. Perrin & Co., Toronto.
WASHERS
P. L. Robertson Mfg. Co., Milton.

UNDERTAKERS' SUPPLIES
AMBULANCES.
Mitchell & Co., Ingersoll.
BURIAL ROBES.
James S. Elliott & Son, Prescott.
Evel Casket Co., Hamilton.
Globe Casket Co., London.
Semmens & Evel Casket Co., Hamilton.
CLOTH CASKETS
Michigan Casket Co., Detroit, Mich.
CEMENT CASKETS.
Canadian Cement Casket Co., Prescott.
CEMETERY SUPPLIES
Frigid Fluid Co., Chicago, Ill.
CASKETS AND COFFINS.
Dominion Casket Co., Guelph.
Evel Casket Co., Hamilton.
Globe Casket Co., London.
Semmens & Evel Casket Co., Hamilton.
EMBALMING FLUIDS.
Egyptian Chemical Co., Boston.
Frigid Fluid Co., Chicago, Ill.
Michigan Casket Co., Detroit, Mich.
H. S. Eckels Co., Philadelphia.
EMBALMERS' SUPPLIES
Frigid Fluid Co., Chicago, Ill
HEARSES.
Mitchell & Co., Ingersoll.
LOWERING DEVICES
Frigid Fluid Co., Chicago, Ill.
SCHOOLS OF EMBALMING.
Canadian School of Embalming Toronto.
STEEL GRAVE VAULTS
St. Thomas Metallic Vault Co., St. Thomas, Ont.
Michigan Casket Co., Detroit, Mich.
UNDERTAKER'S CHAIRS.
Stratford Mfg. Co., Stratford
UNDERTAKERS' SUNDRIES
Frigid Fluid Co., Chicago, Ill.

TRAVELLERS—Wanted for Eastern Ontario and the Maritime Provinces, to handle a line on commission, of Upholstered goods. Apply to, The Montreal Upholstering Co., 1011 Clarke Street, Montreal, Canada.   14/5/1

WANTED—to hear from owner of good furniture store for sale. D. F. Bush, Minneapolis, Minn.   14/5/2

FOR SALE—Established House Furnishing Business that will stand investigating for sale in live Alberta town of 1000 with large district of prosperous farmers to draw from and no opposition. Stock will run about $5,000 and is clean and up-to-date. Last year's turnover, although a quiet year, was $12,000. For further particulars apply to Box 126, Canadian Furniture World and The Undertaker, 32 Colborne Street, Toronto, Ont.   14/5/3

UNDERTAKER WANTED—A man who has had some experience in the undertaking business, must be strictly temperate, neat in appearance and willing to make himself useful. The position is a permanent one to the right man. State age, married or single, experience and where. McIntyre & Son, St. Catharines, ontario. 14-5-1

FURNITURE BUSINESS—for sale at Sandwich where large steel plant and other industries are being established. Splendid opening, as population will grow rapidly. Good reasons for selling. E. Lassaline, Sandwich, Ont.   14-5-1

BUY
Upholstery Springs That "Stand Up"

Our Tempered Furniture Springs will outlast almost any piece of upholstered furniture. They are built to "stand up" indefinitely.

JAMES STEELE, LIMITED
GUELPH   ::   ONTARIO

Invalid Chairs and Tricycles of every description.

This has been our study for thirty-five years. We build chairs that suit the requirements of any case. Write us for catalogue No. 20 and prices, if interested.

Gendron Wheel Co., Toledo, O. U.S.A.

Dominion Casket Co., Limited

Telephones: { Day No. 1020. Nights, Sundays and Holidays Nos. 1069-1101 }   **Guelph, Ont.**   RUSH ORDERS SOLICITED

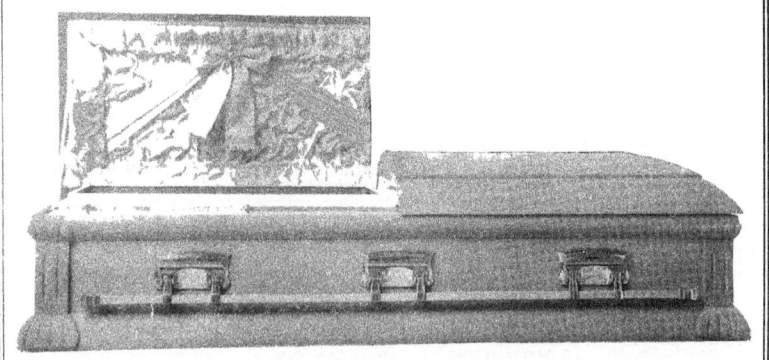

No. 365. "TONCON' STEEL CASKET

REMEMBER the hot sultry days will be here in a short time. The Combination Metallic Casket furnishes a heavy metal receptacle for burial or shipment, that is hermetically sealed. Insuring absolute safety under all circumstances, eliminating all chance of embarrassing situations.

The metal used in the casket is especially adapted to the use, as its rust resisting qualities are much greater than other metals of this class. These goods are made in Canada and are the only metallic caskets manufactured in the Dominion.

We guarantee perfect workmanship and high quality materials in all goods we place on the market. The

Combination Metallic Casket

can be furnished in any style or design with the different panel effects in appearance, the same as our wood caskets. Covered with black or colored broadcloth and embossed or silk plush of any shade. Children's cases in sizes from 3-0 to 5-0 inclusive.

Try one of these cases and be convinced that your trade will demand more

Undertakers' Department

Problems affecting the Undertaking Profession are here discussed and readers are invited to send letters expressing their views on any of the subjects dealt with—News of the profession throughout Canada.

Undertaking in the Next Decade

PART II.

By Prof. H. S. Eckels.

There is a wide variety of chemicals from which to choose in compounding an embalming fluid. A formula for "mixing" a fluid is one of the easiest things to obtain and no process could be simpler than merely mixing a fluid according to some of these formulas. Many of the chemicals employed are inexpensive in the extreme, and even a low retail price seems to offer wide opportunities to the amateur manufacturer. There is, however, a vast difference between a mixed fluid and a compounded fluid. I know of no fluid in the country, outside of four or five made by the old established, experienced, and standard manufacturers, which is not a mere mixture of three or four chemicals bottled and foisted upon the embalmer.

In the first place, comparatively few of these manufacturers of alleged embalming fluids have at their command capital sufficient to properly equip a laboratory for properly making fluid. The furnace, the vats, the caldrons, the filters, the bottling apparatus are beyond the means of most of them. But what matters this to the energetic amateur when an old whisky barrel, a convenient hydrant, and a few crude chemicals stirred together with a stick can produce a product which a glib tongue will enable him to sell to some undertakers—once.

A standard embalming fluid is a carefully-calculated chemical combination. There are not more than half a dozen manufacturers in the country making real embalming fluid in a really scientific manner. A mixed fluid cannot possibly be thoroughly and uniformly satisfactory. No two lots can be the same. The amateur may produce at one time a product which will give reasonably satisfactory results. Weather conditions, temperature, a variation in the qualities and properties of his raw materials are sure, however, to produce an entirely different result at the next mixing.

No standard manufacturer compounds his fluid by weight or by quantity. If he did his product would be as lacking in uniformity, as uncertain in result, and as inevitable in ultimate failure as are the amateur fluids with which the market is flooded. Every chemical which comes into his establishment must be carefully analyzed and tested as to percentages of efficiency, and the fluid compounded according to these percentages and not by either weight or measure.

Formaldehyde, as it comes from the manufacturers, shows a wide variation in strength, yet the embalmer (if his fluid is to be uniform, so that he may be able to secure certain definite results) must adhere to the products of the manufacturer, who has the knowledge and experience necessary to analyze this formaldehyde, who can curb its bad qualities, strengthen its weak points, and in general manipulate it so as to give absolutely uniform results. Just as the formaldehyde varies, so does every other chemical which enters into the composition of a modern and standard fluid. It is easy to realize, therefore, that the merely amateur fluid mixer cannot possibly hope to maintain his product on the market. The fluid which will be satisfactory to-day will fail utterly in the next shipment. This is the real explanation of why the coasts of the profession are strewn with the wrecks and failures of so many fluid makers. They could not keep their fluid uniform, they had neither the wide experience nor the capital necessary to instal the proper apparatus.

Just now we are having a rather unusual deluge of such fluids in the market. Each will find its few victims, each will secure its percentage of repeat orders, and each will be overwhelmed by complaints, failures, and returned goods, just as their predecessors have done in the past. The progressive funeral director of the future will realize this even more thoroughly than he does to-day. I look for the next decade to bring a great centralization of business into the hands of five or six big, able, and long-established manufacturers, just as I see the tendency in funeral directing is the elimination of the unprogressive element.

In fluid manufacturing and in funeral directing alike, the careless and incompetent cannot hope to compete with his well-equipped, largely-capitalized, and well-established neighbor. This does not necessarily mean that he will go out of business. He may drag along and will drag along until the "big fellow" fails to read the signs of the times aright and permits all of the progressiveness to be shown by his despised competitor. In every city and in many smaller towns we see young men establishing themselves and building up satisfactory clientele, but in almost every such case the real reason lies as much in the unprogressiveness of the established man as in the progressiveness of the newcomer. Where the old-established house has been alert and vigilant, we rarely see the newcomer making marked progress.

I have one large middle Western city in mind, in which a clean-cut and intelligent salesman visited practically every undertaker and showed him the first of the laying-out couches, the use of which has since become so universal. He pointed out to those directors the advisability of "doing something different." He showed them how to look at the matter from the stand-point of the family, indicated wherein it would please them—and why—and strongly insisted that the man who installed them and consistently used them would build up a reputation and make inroads into the business of the one really great and magnificently equipped establishment in the city. The funeral directors smiled, told the salesman what a good fellow he was, bought a few minor instruments from him and sent him forth without orders for the laying-out couches.

As a rule, it is the less firmly established man who most needs progressive methods and the newer and better things, and it is but natural that a salesman should make his first appeal to him. Somewhat discouraged and certainly with his optimism dampened at the reception he had had from the other directors, in desperation he went to the really big house in the

The Western Casket Co.
Limited
Winnipeg   Manitoba

Rush Express and Letter Orders Our Specialty

Our Catalogue

will be ready for the Western Funeral Director about the end of present month.

The Western Casket Co., Limited
Cor. Emily St. and Bannatyne Ave.   Winnipeg, Manitoba

Phone Night or Day Garry 4657

G. S. Thompson   A. W. Robinson   G. H. Lawrence

town. He did not tell his story well. His explanation and sales arguments were nowhere nearly so thorough and complete as they had been. He himself was beginning to lack faith in the device. But it so happened that an active executive head of the big establishment was one of the men who really deserved a high position in the profession and in the eyes of the community, and deserved it because of his own far-sightedness, judgment and ready appreciation. His first order was for ten of these laying-out couches. He since has ordered eight more and to-day practically every body which comes into his hands lies in state until the arrival of the casket. This house to-day is greater than ever and greater because it realized an opportunity which its competitors had rejected.

I believe that there will be more of this in the future than there has been in the past. I believe that this readiness of the big fellow to adopt newer methods and newer appliances, and to exercise greater care in his embalming will widen the gap between him and his competitors, just as the exercise of this same care is widening the gap between the standard fluid manufacturers and the amateur who rises to-day, droops tomorrow, and fades away before the week is out.

Saskatchewan Undertakers Organizing

James Wilson, Prince Albert, is advocating the inauguration of an undertakers' association in Saskatchewan, and a call was sent out for a convention at Regina on April 22 and 23. The objects of the association will be largely to take protective measures against the carrying of disease.

Dr. Seymour, Provincial M.H.O., has been largely instrumental in bringing the matter of organization before the undertakers of the Province. The result has been that a movement is now on foot for the formation of a provincial association. Dr. Seymour states that the department had called the attention of the undertakers to the question, and they had taken the matter up and were going ahead with organization. He stated that the association would probably be formed for the mutual benefit of the undertakers, with a view to the better carrying out of the law and the improving of the status of the profession.

George Speers, the well-known Regina undertaker, says that he has been communicating with a number of the undertakers of the Province with a view to a meeting in Regina some time this spring.

The meeting was more particularly for embalmers, and was being held with the object of discussing matters pertaining to the profession. Quite often cases were discovered where the embalming was not done properly. The meeting would discuss this and see if some way could not be arrived at whereby a higher standard of examinations would have to be passed before a person could practice embalming.

Personally, Mr. Speers stated that he was not in favor of the formation of an association. His opinion was that the Government should take the matter up and that they should see to it that no one not absolutely competent was allowed to practice. There was an association in Manitoba and if one were to be formed in Saskatchewan he thought many improvements might be suggested over that of Manitoba.

He explained that the subject had been first taken up by Dr. Seymour, of the Provincial Medical Health Department, and since then the undertakers were taking an active interest in the matter. Among those interested in the movement were Messrs. Broadfoot and Bellamy, of Moose Jaw. The meeting would probably be held in one of the local hotels. Mr. Speers stated, and a large number of the embalmers from outside points were expected.

WESTERNERS PREPARING FOR CONVENTION.

The annual convention of the Western Canada Embalmers' Association will be held in Winnipeg on July 14, 15, 16, when Prof. W. P. Hohenschuh, of Iowa City, Iowa, will demonstrate.

A meeting of the executive committee was recently held in the office of A. B. Gardiner, secretary of the association, in Winnipeg, and arrangements were made for the best convention in the history of the association. Nothing will be left undone to make this convention interesting to every funeral director. A very large attendance is looked for.

PIONEER MARITIME FUNERAL DIRECTOR.

Snow & Co., of 90 Argyle Street, Halifax, N.S., was founded as John Snow & Sons in 1883. John Snow is manager, and he is ably assisted by his three sons, E. D., assistant manager, W. H., and John R. They occupy well-appointed premises with mortuary, chapel, etc., and are the pioneer embalmers of their province, making a specialty of shipping cases. They have conducted the funerals of many notables, such as Sir John Thompson, late premier; Bishop H. Binney, Archbishop

John Snow, greatly respected leader of funeral directors in the provinces down by the sea.

C. O'Brien, and Hon. A. G. Jones, Lieutenant-Governor of Nova Scotia, and helped greatly in the embalming and shipping of many of the victims of the "Titanic" disaster.

John Snow, Sr., is ex-president of the Nova Scotia Embalmers' Association, and is business manager of the Maritime Association. W. H. Snow is a graduate of the Oriental School of Embalming, Boston.

THE REAL THING

The funeral procession was moving along the village street when Uncle Abe stepped out of a store. He hadn't heard the news.

"Sho," said Uncle Abe, "who they buryin' to-day?"

"Pore old Tite Harrison," said the storekeeper.

"Sho," said Uncle Abe, "Tite Harrison, hey? Is Tite dead?"

"You don't think we're rehearsin' with him, do you?" snapped the storekeeper.— Exchange.

Dominion Manufacturers
Limited

MANUFACTURERS OF

Fine Funeral Requisites

We guaranted

The Highest Quality

and the

Quickest Possible Service

*Night or Day Orders
given Prompt Attention*

BRANCHES

The Globe Casket Co., and Branches	London, Ontario
The Semmons & Evel Casket Co., and Branches,	Hamilton, Ontario
The National Casket Co.	Toronto, Ontario
Jas. S. Elliot & Son	Prescott, Ontario
Girard & Godin and Branches	Three Rivers, Quebec
Christie Bros. & Co,	Amherst, N. S.

FRED W. COLES
General Manager

D. M. ANDREWS
Secretary Treasurer

HEAD OFFICE

468 King Street W., Toronto

THE UNDERTAKER AND THE AUTOMOBILE

The motor-driven vehicle has made such headway in the replacing of the horse in many lines of business that so far from its use in the undertaking field exciting surprise, the wonder should rather be that the superiority of the machine over the animal was not realized there sooner. Whenever there is a distance to be traversed longer than from one part of a city to another, or longer than the usual drive over well-paved streets, the horse must give way to the motor.

Every undertaker often has occasion to make long trips into the country or to nearby towns and suburbs, the distances to which, anywhere from six or eight to twenty odd miles, take an undue amount of time and tax the strength of his horses severely. And those of the profession who serve public or semi-public institutions located at some distance from the city in which the greater part of the business is done have more than their share of these long hauls to make, and a consequently heavy burden to bear in the maintenance and replacement of horses and wagons. The solution of their difficulties is a motor-driven vehicle, to make such trips as are necessary over the longer distances, carrying the undertaker to the place of the death, and returning with the body, bringing it within a distance such as the heavy hearse and its horses can readily traverse, as from the city church or the undertaker's chapel to the cemetery. It is a rather interesting fact that some of the large city cemeteries, with their beauties of trees and flowers and their attractive and well-kept drives, do not permit automobiles of any sort within their gates, but with the rapidity with which the motor driven hearse is gaining favor this rule must soon be modified.

An undertaker in one of the larger cities of the Ohio Valley was confronted with this long-haul problem, and the solution suggested above was that adopted by him. Caring for the dead of several large institutions located at distances from the city, varying from ten to eighteen miles, he kept three wagons constantly busy answering calls from these places, in addition to taking care of his regular run of country calls; and he soon found that the three were not equal to the task, and it became the question whether to add more wagons or to take the radical step, as it was regarded in that city, of putting in a motor.

He decided on the latter alternative only after thinking the matter over, and getting a mass of data from other business men who used motor-driven vehicles on long and heavy hauls with eminently satisfactory results. He found that the department stores were using automobiles for suburban deliveries, that furniture stores were doing the same, as well as many other concerns; and he came to the conclusion that with approximately the same demands—that is, long hauls over roads that were not always in the best of condition, in all kinds of weather - his business would benefit quite as much by the use of a power wagon as any other in the city. And while the role of pioneer did not appeal to him with any great force, he thought that the benefits his business would derive from the venture would be more than sufficient to off-set any unkind criticisms that might arise from other members of the profession in the city.

The choice of a car was a matter of some difficulty, but he was assisted in this not only by the technical and helpful aid of the dealers who swarmed around him as soon as it was learned that he was in the market, but by his own experience in the handling of a touring car. The large size of body necessary to accommodate coffin boxes put the use of the smaller light delivery wagons out of the question; and at the same time heavy trucks were both too expensive and unnecessarily powerful for this purpose. He never had to carry excessive weight, while at the same time a fair rate of speed was desirable. With these requirements in view, the car finally selected was a four-cylinder, 30 h.p. affair, capable of 35 miles an hour or even more, with a special body, built to his order, along the lines of the regular undertakers' wagon body.

The machine was used, as intended, only for the longer runs, in the country, to surrounding towns, and in handling the institutions referred to above; and its advantages for these occasions became the more apparent after it had been in service a short while. Instead of taking all of a day going and coming, and having an exhausted horse on his hands to boot, the undertaker, who did most of the driving of the car, was able to make one of these runs in the course of an hour or so, depending upon the distance, leaving his time free for other matter; and that without any appreciable wear and tear on the car. This may be gathered from the fact that while the machine had been engaged in this particular service for just a year, the same set of tires, with one extra casing which has always been carried to do relief and emergency work, is still doing duty.

The undertaker referred to figures that he has accomplished a substantial economy by the use of the machine, although he has not kept exact figures on the

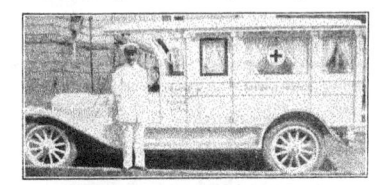

Up-to-date ambulance of P. H. Grote, Vancouver. It is equipped with stretcher and couch suspended from springs, hot and cold water, electric light and heat, warm blankets and linen which is changed every trip. Two experienced men are always in attendance.

matter; but he has before him the evidence of the actual work accomplished by the car, in handling the long runs with ease and speed, and the further fact that he has been able to dispense with two of the three wagons formerly used. It is quite possible that if he cared to do so, he says, he could get along without the remaining wagon; but he prefers to confine the use of the machine to the country and institution calls, and consequently keeps the machine idle a good deal of the time. His average of at least one long call a day, however, with several more on some days, out of his total yearly business of well over six hundred cases has made the investment well worth his while.

While, as stated, the undertaker does most of the driving himself, two of his helpers are also instructed in the use of the machine, and there is therefore no extra cost in the wages of a professional chauffeur; and, in fact, few users of motor trucks have found it necessary to pay the high prices demanded by the regular, as the ordinary driver is perfectly capable of handling a machine, given a little instruction by one who knows how.

A peculiar thing about the use of the motor car in the work of an undertaking business in this particular

Burglar Proof and Water Tight

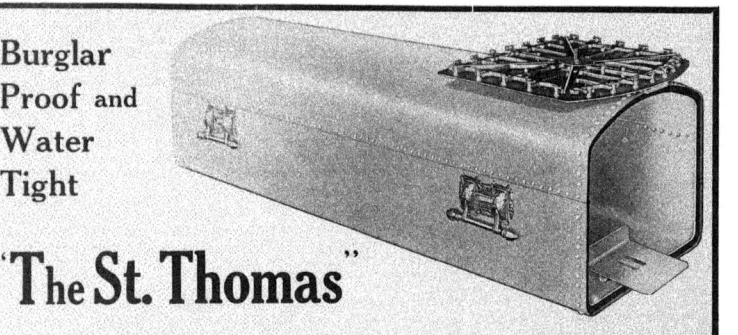

"The St. Thomas"

Original, Quick Closing End Vault

MANUFACTURED BY

The St. Thomas Metallic Vault Company, Limited
ST. THOMAS, ONTARIO

The Original Patented Concentrated Fluid

Patented Formula
Strongest and Best

Essential Oil Base, combined with Alcohol, Glycerine, Oxidized Formaldehyde and Boron-Dioxide.

Ask others for their Formula

Special Canadian Agents

National Casket Co.
Toronto, Ont.
GLOBE CASKET CO.
London, Ont.
SEMMENS & EVEL CASKET CO.
Hamilton, Ont.
GIRARD & GODIN
Three Rivers, Que.
JAS. S. ELLIOTT & SON
Prescott, Ont.
CHRISTIE BROS.
Amherst, N.S.

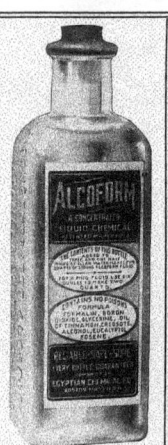

Larger Bottles filled up with water

Egyptian Chemical Co. Boston, U.S.A

For Every Furniture Man

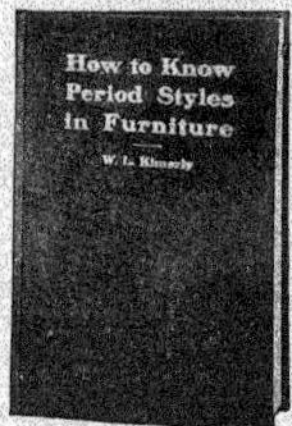

A Helpful, Thoroughly Practical Book, Written by an Authority—

HOW TO KNOW PERIOD STYLES IN FURNITURE

150 Pages   317 Illustrations

Price, $1.50

Designers will find illustrations of the work of celebrated designers of history. Examples are taken from the recognized collections and museums of the world.
Buyers—The book is arranged for easy reference with the distinguishing features of each period clearly shown.
Salesmen—The information in "How to Know Period Styles" will enable you to talk authoritatively on the subject.
Students—The confusing element has been eliminated, but all necessary information is included.

Send us $1.50. Keep the book 10 days, and if it isn't worth the price, return it and get your money back.

The Commercial Press
Publishers The Canadian Furniture World and The Undertaker
32 Colborne Street, Toronto

town is that while this is the only motor-driven vehicle in the city, in use in the undertaking business, on account of a seemingly deep-seated prejudice against such an innovation among the local members of the profession, many of them have so far overcome their opinions on the subject as to borrow the machine for use on their own country and suburban runs—thereby, of course, admitting the force of the principal arguments in its favor, and standing convicted of some inconsistency in refusing to procure similar equipment for their own use.

No objection has been heard on the part of any of the public to the use of a motor wagon by this undertaker, although it might possibly have been expected that some of the more conservative would see something at which to cavil in the employment of a vehicle capable of a forty-mile gait by a business so essentially and necessarily dignified, and therefore unhurried, as that of caring for the bodies of the dead. The limited extent to which the machine has been used, however, has appreciably reduced the chance of any such objection. The sight of a motor rushing around the city at a rate of speed which might be considered unseemly has not occurred, and only the country roads have been allowed to see what it can do when pushed. And few people would be so unfair as to object to a fairly respectable speed in making a point twelve miles or more distant.

The pioneer in the use of power vehicles in any particular business usually reaps some little reward in the way of advertising by reason thereof; that is, he makes himself honorably conspicuous as an enterprising business man—he attracts that favorable attention which is the first step toward the forming of connections that bring business. There is no reason to suppose that the undertaker in question is any exception to this rule. He disclaims, however, having had any idea of this sort of mind in adding this useful feature to his business.

"I decided to use a motor on my long runs," he declared, "simply because I had to do it, and it looked like the solution of what was becoming a ha' lem. In displacing two horses, wagons and d' performing service which they were unable ' have no doubt whatever that it has sav' erable money and enabled me to hand' more business than I could have take' the addition of other new equipmen' expected of it, and more."—Em'

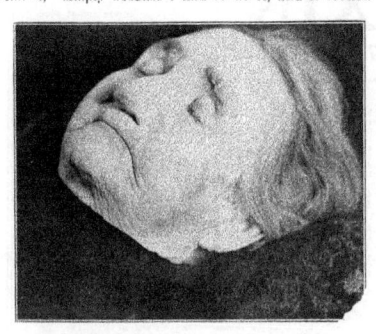

DEMI-SURGERY AFTER RADIUM TREATMENT

The two illustrations on this page are from photos depicting an interesting case of demi-surgery which Robt. U. Stone, Toronto, handled last month. It was a case of a fungous cancerous growth. The case had been treated with radium, but without avail.

Mr. Stone says the work took about three hours to complete, and was witnessed by five persons. He also took on a case for Daniel Stone, Toronto, recently on the face of a child who had been severely burned. This case, too, was successfully treated. The pictures show the advances which have taken place of late in this class of work.

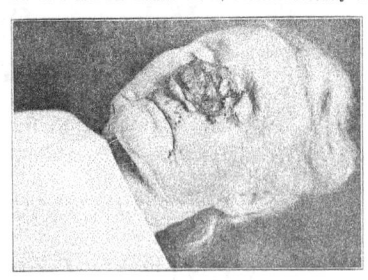

ONTARIO CEMETERY ACT AMENDED

The following is the text of a bill brought befc passed by the Ontario Legislature at its present :

"His Majesty, by and with the advice and of the Legislative Assembly of the Province tario, enacts as follows:

"1. The Cemetery Act is amended by addir 2 thereof the following section:

"38 (a) The council of any city o there is a board of park '' The Public Parks Act n' trol and manageme' poration of the n' after the cemete managers and management for the ma' to the sar' and mai this Ac

To Canadian Funeral Directors

THE CENTRAL LINE

Mahogany, Oak, Plush and Cloth Covered Caskets

WE SHIP PROMPTLY

We can also supply anything desired in Casket Linings, Burial Robes, and a general line of Undertakers' Supplies

Orders given our Canadian representative, or sent to our factory at Bridgeburg by mail, telegraph or telephone will be shipped promptly.

CENTRAL CASKET COMPANY

Bridgeburg, Ont.
Telephone 126

R. S. Flint — Canadian Representative: 241 Fern Ave., Toronto
Telephone Parkdale 3257

DIOXIN
IS PLEASANT TO USE!

F DIOXIN had no other superiority over the ordinary formaldehyde fluids, ct that it is safe and to use should insure ce in the affections of

his delicacy of touch. 's you the embarrassunsatisfactory reof a spoiled body. gh risks in emh chances for opportunities adding others

not dan hands of it must sensi the ker

hands, have a particularly irritating effect upon not only the mucous membranes of the eyelids, but upon the eyes themselves. This is particularly offensive and harmful when the work is done in a warm or brilliantly-lighted room.

DIOXIN DOES NOT EMBALM Your LUNGS

DIOXIN has no injurious effect upon the eyes or eyelids of the operator. The embalmer does not embalm his own eyesight when he uses it. If you or your assistant have suffered from the pungent effects of ordinary raw formaldehyde fluids, try DIOXIN. What 'ittle fumes arise from it are leasant and positively nonant. Indeed, we feel that nnot too strongly recomIOXIN to all embalmers troubled with failing

eyesight—and most users of raw formaldehyde fluids are literally pickling their eyes.

Most of us are almost overcome when entering a room filled with the fumes of formaldehyde. We may not realise it, but we really are literally embalming our own lungs. In DIOXIN, what formaldehyde the fluid does contain, is purified and modified into formochloral, while peroxide of hydrogen, the great bleacher and disinfectant, replaces a very great proportion of this irritating agent.

As a result, DIOXIN has absolutely no deleterious effect upon either the lungs of the operator or the mucous membranes of nostrils and throat.

Dioxin comes in Bulk and Concentrated and RE-Concentrated.

Did we mention the fact that DIOXIN does not fill the house with offensive odors? That is another of its many virtues. And did we say that it makes the body firm, but pliable, rendering posing in the casket easy. Rigidity is not essential to preservation; in fact, it retards the circulation of the fluid.

But we've told you enough—although only a small part of the virtues of DIOXIN. Try it yourself—that is the great convincer. Order to-day!

CO.
'rn Ave., Toronto, Ont., Can.

Gossip of the Profession

W. P. Currie, of Lauder, Man., has purchased the undertaking business of J. A. Morton, of that place.

Robert Gorrell has purchased the undertaking business of the W. H. Davis Estate of Crystal City, Man.

Heasman & Rowbotham have purchased the undertaking business of Mr. Charles Smith at Wawota, Sask.

Scotsburn Creamery Company, Scotsburn, Pictou Co., N.S., has added undertaking as a side line to its business.

Grey & Wilson, of Oak Lake, Man., have purchased the undertaking business of White Bros., of Maryfield, Sask.

The Maritime Funeral Directors' and Embalmers' Association will hold their 12th annual convention next August at Moncton, N.B.

The Appin Cemetery Company, Limited, has been formed at Appin, Ont., with a capital of $3,000. An Ontario charter was granted.

Murchie & Son, New Westminster, B.C., will take charge of all the embalming and all the funerals from New Westminster and Essondale hospitals this year.

E. H. Childs, of Islay, Alta., has opened an undertaking business at Vermilion, Alta. The opening order of goods was supplied by the Western Casket Co., Ltd., Winnipeg.

E. G. Cross, who has been in the undertaking business in Stratford for a number of years past, has returned to Wiarton, Ont, and will take charge of the business for his mother.

The voting at Wiarton, Ont., on the by-law for the granting of a loan of $25,000 to the Canada Casket Co., resulted in a sweeping majority for the company—325 votes for, and 40 against.

W. S. Yule has opened an undertaking office at 124 Central Ave., Swift Current, Sask., with a complete stock, including a new and modern hearse and first-class wagon. Mr. Yule has had sixteen years' experience in Gananoque and Owen Sound, Ontario, where he conducted a business.

Isaac Olive Beatteay, undertaker, died at his home at St. John, N.B., recently. Mr. Beatteay was seventy years of age and had been in the undertaking business for many years. He is survived by his wife, one son, Frederick C. Beatteay, of St. John, and one daughter, Mrs. W. B. Brown, of Montreal.

A meeting of the Dominion Mausoleum Company was held recently at Brantford when the following were elected officers of the company: H. H. Powell, president; I. Chapin, vice-president; M. M. Cleaveland, secretary and managing director; M. W. McEwen, treasurer; Thomas Hendry, director; Wilkes and Henderson, solicitors; K. V. Bunnell and Co., auditors.

Richard Langlois, 46 years of age, died from tubercular trouble recently at his late residence in Toronto. He had been incapacitated since Christmas. The deceased was born in Hamilton, moving to Toronto in 1898. Since then he had been connected with the Thompson Casket Co. and the National Casket Co. He was a member of the Queen's Own Regiment and was widely known as a yachtsman.

Work in connection with the renovating of the undertaking parlors of Hartley Field at Woodstock has been completed, and Mr. Field has now one of the most up-to-date and finest parlors in Ontario. For some weeks carpenters and painters have been at work transforming the old building and adding new and modern features which are demanded by a large and growing business, and the result of their efforts has been most pleasing.

The store recently vacated by W. Samuels, at 763 Talbot St., St. Thomas, Ont., has been leased by E. C. Killingsworth, of London, and will be opened as an undertaking parlor at an early date. Mr. Killingsworth will conduct the business as a branch of the London business. The furniture repairing and upholstering business at present carried on in the Ross street store, will be moved to the new quarters, and carried on in conjunction with the undertaking business. F. C. Killingsworth will be in charge of the local business.

W. A. Edwards, undertaker, Saskatoon, Sask., has found it necessary to enlarge his premises on Second Avenue. Mr. Edwards has secured the upper floor of the building which he now occupies, and has moved his entire stock of caskets to this portion of the premises. The interior of the ground floor has been altered and the office space somewhat cut down, so that a spacious chapel for services has been arranged. The morgue, which is maintained in connection with the establishment, has been placed in an addition to the chapel at the rear.

NEW UNDERTAKING BUSINESS IN OTTAWA.

Charles R. Woodburn, one of the best known travellers on the road, has opened an up-to-date undertaking parlor at 586 Bank St., Ottawa. Mr. Woodburn has for many years been in this line of business, and has a most practical knowledge of the profession in all its branches. He is a member of the Canadian Embalmers' Association, and holds a diploma issued by them. He recently attended Professor Eckles' special course of embalming in Buffalo. Mr. Woodburn's many friends in the trade will wish him all success in his new venture.

FUNERAL PLUMES TO GO.

It has been practically decided to abolish the use of funeral plumes on horses' heads in London. The R.S.P.C.A. caused inquiries to be made which established the fact that horses do at times suffer by reason of this plume, especially in wet weather. The Undertakers' Association (London Centre) confirmed the result of that inquiry by passing a resolution at their annual meeting condemning the use of the plume as often cruel and quite unnecessary. The personal opinion of over 300 members of the trade in London were taken, and 98 per cent. were found to hold a similar opinion.

"GIN A BODY KEN HIS BODY."

Scottish caution is illustrated in a story told in the Glasgow Herald. Two men who were going home in the dark tripped over a body lying in the road. By the light of a match they recognized the features of an acquaintance, by name Jock Henderson.

First assuring themselves that life had departed, they borrowed a wheelbarrow from the nearest cottage, and the funeral procession started for the home of the deceased. A knock at the door was answered by a familiar voice at an upper window.

Said one of the bearers, "Loch me, is thaat you, Jock Henderson? Man, we thought we had your boady here in the barra."

To this Jock replied, "Haud on a meenit till A come doon an' see."

Undertakers Shipping Directory

ONTARIO
Aurora—
  Dunham, Charles.
Barrie—
  Smith, G. G. & Co.
Brockville—
  Quirmbach, Geo. R., 162 King St.
Brooklin—
  Disney, R. S.
Campbellford—
  Irwin, James.
Campden —
  Hansel, Albion.
Clinton—
  Walker, Wesley.
Coboconk—
  Greenley, A.
Copper Cliff—
  Boyd, W. C.
Dungannon—
  Sproul, William
Dutton—
  Schultz, B. L.
Elmira—
  Dreisinger, Chris.
Fenelon Falls—
  Deyman, L. & Son.
Fenwick—
  H. A. Metler.
Fergus—
  Armstrong, M. F.
  Thomson, John & Son.
Fort William—
  Cameron & Co., 711 Victoria.
  Morris, A.
Haileybury—
  Thorpe Bros.
Galt—
  Anderson, J. & Son.
Hamilton—
  Green Bros., 124 King St. E.
  Robinson, J. H. & Co., 19-21 John St. N.
Hanover—
  Wunnenberg, Norman.
Hastings—
  Howard, P. N.
Hepworth—
  Downs, E. J.
Inwood—
  Lorriman, E. S.
Kemptville—
  McCaughey, Geo. A.
Kenora—
  Horn & Taylor.
Kingston—
  Corbett, S. S.
Lakefield—
  Hendren, Geo. G.
Little Current—
  Sims, J. G.
Markdale—
  Oliver, M.
Newmarket—
  Millard, J. H.

North Augusta—
  Wilson, J. R.
North Bay—
  St. Pierre, E.
Oakwood—(Mariposa Station G.T.R.) Wilmot F. Webster.
Ohsweken—
  Johnson, F. L.
Oshawa—
  Disney Bros.
  Luke Bros.
Ottawa—
  Rogers, Geo. H., 128 Bank
Petrolia—
  Steadman Bros.
Port Arthur —
  Collin Wood, 36 Arthur St.
  Morris, A.
Prescott—
  Rankin, H. & Son.
Renfrew—
  O'Connor, Wm.
St. Mary's—
  N. L. Brandon.
St. Thomas—
  Williams, P. R. & Sons, 519 Talbot St.
Seaforth, Ont.
  W. T. Box & Co.
Scotland—
  Vaughan, Jos. H. M.
Sudbury—
  Henry, J. G.
Toronto—
  Cobbledick, N. B., 2068 Queen St. East and 1508 Danford Ave. Private Ambulance.
  Humphrey, E. J. Burial Co. Head Office, 359 Yonge St.; Branch, 407 Queen St. W. Private ambulance.
  Stone, Daniel (formerly H. Stone & Son), 82 Bloor St. West.
  Vancamp, J. C., 30 Bloor St. West.
Waterloo—
  Klipper Undertaking Co.
Welland—
  Sutherland, G. W.
Woodstock—
  Meadows, T. & Sons.
  Mack, Paul.

QUEBEC
Buckingham—
  Paquet, Jos.
Cowansville—
  Judson, M. B.
Montreal—
  Tees & Co., 912 St. Catherine St. West.
St. Hyacinthe—
  Cadorette, Mongeau & Leary.
St. Laurent—
  Gougeon, Jos.

NEW BRUNSWICK
Petitcodiac—
  Jonah, D. Allison.
Welland—
  Sutherland, G. W.
Woodstock—
  Van Wart, Jacob.

NOVA SCOTIA
Ferrona—
  Fraser, D. & Co.
Halifax—
  Snow & Co., 90 Argyle St.
Sydney, C.B.—
  Beaton, A. J. & Son, 374-384 George St.

MANITOBA
Brandon—
  Campbell & Campbell.
  Vincent & McPherson.
Swan River—
  Paull, Geo.
Winnipeg—
  Bardal, A. S., 834 Sherbrooke
  Thompson, J. C., 501 Main
  Clark-Leatherdale Co., Ltd., 232 Kennedy St.

SASKATCHEWAN
Gull Lake—
  Morrow, Fred. A.
Saskatoon—
  Young, A. E.

Kamsack—
  Russell, G. E. I.
Lanigan—
  Robertson, Wm.
Moose Jaw—
  The Bellamy Co.
  Broadfoot Bros.
Rush Lake—
  Friesen, John M.
Prince Albert—
  Howard, A. C.
  Hadley, C. L.
Regina—
  Speers, George.
Semans—
  Haygarth, Jas.
Welwyn—
  Leavens, Merritt.
Wolseley —
  Barber, B.

ALBERTA
Calgary—
  Graham & Buscomb, 611 Centre St.
Castor—
  Winter, W. G.

BRITISH COLUMBIA
Hosmer—
  Cornett, T. A.
Victoria—
  Hana & Thompson, 827 Pandora Ave.

Index to Advertisements

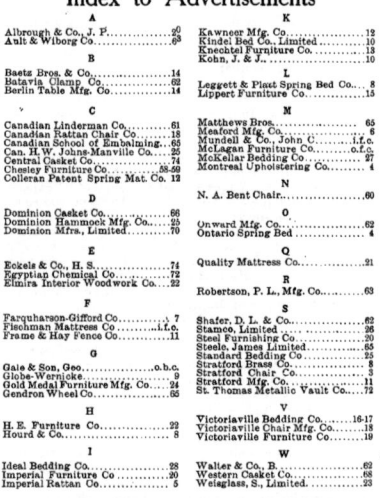

A
Albrough & Co., J. P. 20
Ault & Wiborg Co. 69

B
Baets Bros. & Co. 14
Batavia Clamp Co. 62
Berlin Table Mfg. Co. 14

C
Canadian Linderman Co. 61
Canadian Rattan Chair Co. 18
Canadian School of Embalming. 65
Can. H.W. Johns-Manville Co. 25
Central Casket Co. 74
Chesley Furniture Co. 58-59
Colleran Patent Spring Mat. Co. 12

D
Dominion Casket Co. 66
Dominion Hammock Mfg. Co. 25
Dominion Mfrs., Limited 70

E
Eckels & Co., H. S. 74
Egyptian Chemical Co. 72
Elmira Interior Woodwork Co. 22

F
Farquharson-Gifford Co. 7
Fleishman Mattress Co. ....i.f.c.
Frame & Hay Fence Co. 11

G
Gale & Son, Geo. ....o.b.c.
Globe-Wernicke 9
Gold Medal Furniture Mfg. Co. 24
Gendron Wheel Co. 65

H
H. E. Furniture Co. 22
Hourd & Co. 8

I
Ideal Bedding Co. 28
Imperial Furniture Co 20
Imperial Rattan Co. 5

K
Kawneer Mfg. Co. 12
Kindel Bed Co., Limited 10
Knechtel Furniture Co. 13
Kohn, J. & J. 10

L
Leggett & Platt Spring Bed Co. 8
Lippert Furniture Co. 15

M
Matthews Bros. 65
Meaford Mfg. Co. 6
Mundell & Co., John C. ....i.f.c.
McLagan Furniture Co. ....o.f.c.
McKellar Bedding Co. 27
Montreal Upholstering Co. 4

N
N. A. Bent Chair 60

O
Onward Mfg. Co. 62
Ontario Spring Bed 4

Q
Quality Mattress Co. 21

R
Robertson, P. L., Mfg. Co. 63

S
Shafer, D. L. & Co. 62
Stamco, Limited 26
Steel Furnishing Co. 20
Steele, James Limited 65
Standard Bedding Co. 25
Stratford Brass Co. 8
Stratford Chair Co. 3
Stratford Mfg. Co. 11
St. Thomas Metallic Vault Co. 72

V
Victoriaville Bedding Co. 16-17
Victoriaville Chair Mfg. Co. 18
Victoriaville Furniture Co. 19

W
Walter & Co., B. 62
Western Casket Co. 68
Weisglass, S., Limited 23

Every Furniture Manufacturer
installs new equipment in his plant from time to time—the old must go! There is a way to dispose of it—economically and effectively. Let's tell you!

Canadian Furniture World, 32 COLBORNE ST. TORONTO

Store Management Complete

16 Full-Page Illustrations

ANOTHER NEW BOOK

By FRANK FARRINGTON

A Companion Book to
Retail Advertising Complete
$1.00 POSTPAID

"Store Management—Complete" tells all about the management of a store so that not only the greatest sales but the largest profit may be realized.

THIRTEEN CHAPTERS

272 Pages
Bound in Cloth

Here is a sample:
CHAPTER V.—THE STORE POLICY. What it should be to hold trade. The money-back plan. Taking back goods. Meeting cut rates. Selling remnants. Delivering goods. Substitution. Handling telephone calls. Courtesy. Rebating railroad fare. Courtesy to customers.

Absolutely New   Just Published

Commercial Press, Limited
32 Colborne Street
Toronto, Ontario

'Twill Do Your Advertising

This new book on advertising will tell you all you want to know about advertising in the store.

Here's the Book that will be Your Ad. Man

Retail Advertising Complete

By FRANK FARRINGTON
$1.00 Postpaid

With this book on your desk you are never at a loss what kind of advertising to do, or how to do it. Every kind of advertising is treated fully.

272 pages
Bound in Cloth

- Chapters on Newspaper Advertising
- Making an Advertisement
- Good Specimen Ready-made Ads.
- Mail Advertising
- Window Trimming
- Advertising Novelties
- Outdoor Advertising
- Inside the Store Advertising
- Advertising Schemes
- Special Sales
- Mail Orders, etc., etc.

There is no better book of the kind at any price. You can't afford to get along without it.

Absolutely New   Just Published

Commercial Press, Limited
32 Colborne Street
Toronto, Ontario

Synopsis of Contents
PART I.

Chapter I.—Using the Windows—The General Principles of Display. Some specific instances. Some combination window display offers.
Chapter II.—One Idea Window Displays—Advising against trying to show all the goods at once.
Chapter III.—Window Display Profits—How to make windows actually produce direct sales.
Chapter IV.—Showing the Goods—No matter what the class of merchandise, sales are increased if it is attractively displayed.
Chapter V.—Window Displays that Cost Nothing—Some special windows described and illustrated.
Chapter VI.—The Use of Window Fixtures—Displays can be made much more attractive with modern fixtures.
Chapter VII.—Let the Money in Through Your Windows—Making a success of a paint department through attractive displays.
Chapter VIII.—Keeping Frost from Windows—Suggestions on this feature that cannot fail to prove useful.
Chapter IX.—A Few Suggestions for Easy Displays—Things easily arranged with but little expense.
Chapter X.—Window Card Pointers—Some good suggestions as to the making of show cards and the correct colors to use.
Chapter XI.—Show Window Photographs—How to take good pictures, avoid reflections and get proper contrasts.

PART II.

Practical Displays—One hundred windows each illustrated and described, that any store can arrange from the help of an expense. (185 pages).

One Hundred Easy Window Trims

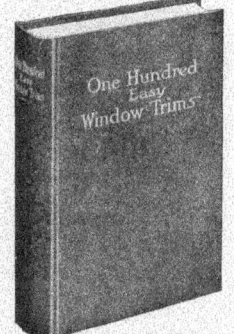

THIS handy little volume of 224 pages was written especially for the merchant who has small windows or wishes to divide large ones into sections. The displays cover all classes of goods, but there are enough suggestions to give you a change each week for almost a year.

They are all simple, inexpensive and easily arranged displays, and all the material required may be taken from stock or purchased for a few cents.

224 pages, 4 1-4 x 7 inches, 104 full page plates. Price $1.00 postpaid.

Commercial Press, Ltd.
32 Colborne St., Toronto, Ont.

The Latest Development of the Felt Mattress

The DIXIE
NO TUFT
Compartment Mattress

MADE UNDER PATENTS ISSUED, OTHERS PENDING

DIXIE NoTUFT MATTRESS

Have you followed the evolution of the mattress for the past 25 years? First the feather bed—soft and comfortable, but usually dusty and soon becoming unsanitary.

Then came hair mattresses, and while horse hair was cheap they were considered quite the proper thing. But when haircloth was invented, which put horse hair out of reach, the hair mattress was made from cattle tails, which were neither durable nor springy, even before they were cheapened by mixing with hog hair.

Then came the great revolution in mattress-making—when clean, sanitary cotton felt restored the "comfiness" of the feather bed, at half the price.

But the ordinary kind of cotton mattress has shown a discouraging tendency to spread, form holes and lumps, and make an uneven and unsightly bed.

So we have come to the latest development, the final perfection of felt mattress, in the "DIXIE No TUFT."

Tufts are always weakening, breaking and shortening the life of ordinary mattresses, so the ideal cotton felt mattresses must have no TUFTS.

The DIXIE is more than a "Tuftless" mattress. It is made up in patented independent compartments, each compartment separate and separately filled. This prevents displacement of the felt and insures a permanent, smooth, even surface.

The DIXIE has no excess width, consequently cannot spread or widen out, and always makes a handsome and comfortable bed.

The absence of tufts gives a smooth surface, easy to clean and no tuft-pockets to collect dust.

Unquestionably the "DIXIE No TUFT" is the last word, the final perfection, in high grade mattress-making. Its method of construction makes permanent the neat appearance and perfect comfort of a new cotton felt mattress.

We are the exclusive manufacturers in Canada of "DIXIE No TUFT" mattresses, and because of our unequaled manufacturing facilities, you are enabled to sell them profitably at the same price at which they are sold in the United States.

We are now arranging exclusive selling agencies for the "DIXIE" with the best dealers in each locality.

The Dixie No Tuft
is made in three grades

Retails at
"DIXIE BEST" (Gold Label) full size................$20.00
"DIXIE STANDARD" (Blue Label) full size......... 15.00
"DIXIE GOOD" (Pink Label) full size................. 12.00

Write to-day for sample outfit with display cards, and arrange to increase the sales and profits of your mattress business.

GEO. GALE & SONS, Limited
WATERVILLE, QUEBEC
MONTREAL   TORONTO   WINNIPEG

Vol. 4 No. 6   JUNE, 1914

Canadian FURNITURE WORLD AND THE UNDERTAKER

Published by the Commercial Press, Limited, 32 Colborne Street, Toronto

When You Order *Stratford* Chairs

You Take No " Slow-Selling " Risks

Stratford Chairs stand out in elegance in any company. The line shown is made of the finest quartered oak selected for beauty of graining and color. Either golden or fumed finish. Box seats braced at the corners inside, and slip seats of genuine leather.

The clinching argument, applicable to all Stratford Chairs, is that the prices are no more than ordinary particular people are willing to pay for a set that they can always admire and use for many years. You'll notice the " difference" in that first shipment.

Stratford Chair Company, Limited, Stratford, Ontario

MISSION FURNITURE

THE MUNDELL MAKE

WHAT strikes you about our Mission Furniture is the variety. We make Davenports and Footstools and everything between that you can think of in Mission Goods,—all grades, all descriptions.

For Spring business these Mission Lines are indispensable. Furniture for halls, dens, living rooms, libraries, dining rooms, smoking rooms—frequently more than one half of many dwellings is furnished in Mission Style, and the demand goes on increasing.

You will be pleased with our new designs in this furniture—Heavy Oak Frames, Rich Spanish Leather Upholstering, all in dark tints as if centuries old,—simple lines, heavy, substantial, rich looking, there is no doubt that this class of furniture is one of the dealer's most attractive and profitable lines.

You will find all the varieties, all grades, all prices, in the Mundell line. Let us mail you blue prints.

JOHN C. MUNDELL & CO., LIMITED
ELORA :: ONTARIO

Antiseptic Bedding

The hygienic principle is the most pronounced factor in bedding sales. Antiseptic Bedding attains the highest degree of excellence in all that is healthful and resting.

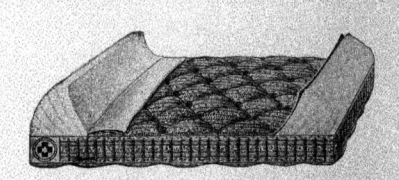

The close attention we pay to the wearing qualities of Antiseptic Bedding guarantees perfect satisfaction in every sale, yet the prices are low enough to be popular with the great middle class of people.

THE
Antiseptic Bedding Co.
187-189 Parliament Street
Toronto, Ont.

Write for prices and complete information covering our lines.

STRATFORD

STRATFORD LEADS IN REPUTABLE FURNITURE AND GOOD SERVICE

THE average dealer frequently loses sales because he does not stock the really high-class lines asked for. More frequently, perhaps, he does not obtain the better class trade because it never went to him.

It has paid many dealers with medium-class patronage to go after the exclusive trade of their particular communities. You can get it by showing the goods. The McLagan line comprises the equal of the best furniture shown in Canada, as well as the finer qualities for medium-class trade.

Write us for details of our new lines. They are bound to interest you from the standpoint of increased sales.

McLagan Furniture appeals to the Refined Taste

Stratford   Ontario

THE STRATFORD SHIPPING COMBINATION WILL INTEREST WESTERN DEALERS

CANADIAN FURNITURE WORLD AND THE UNDERTAKER   June, 1914

No. 855—Bed List Price $11.20   No. 112—Bed List Price $10.00 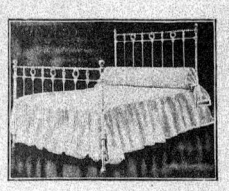   No. 222—Bed List Price $11.00

Before Placing Your Next Order for

Brass Beds, Iron Beds, Springs, Mattresses or Pillows

Send for our new Catalog. This catalog illustrates a line of Bedding you can sell **Every Day in the Week** because "Ontario" Beds and Bedding are so uniformly and carefully made of the best materials obtainable that they **Please the People.** Ontario Beds, Springs, Mattresses or Pillows are business getters and profit makers—the kind you can bank on for quick sales and satisfied customers.

Shall we send Catalog?

The Ontario Spring Bed & Mattress Company, Limited
The Largest Bedding House in Canada

London   -   Ontario

We are Specializing in Davenports and Divanettes Only

To make Davenports of such "Real Value" for the prices asked, that your trial order will prove "A Repeater," is our constant aim. The lines shown below are built to give Good Honest Service, and at prices that cannot be beat.

OUR REVOLVING DAVENPORT BED

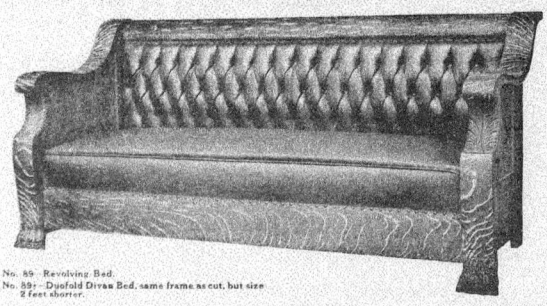

WRITE FOR PRICES

-:-

CATALOGUE IS YOURS FOR THE ASKING

No. 89—Revolving Bed.
No. 89½—Dyofold Divan Bed, same frame as cut, but size 2 feet shorter.

The Montreal Upholstering Company
1611-1613 Clarke St., MONTREAL, Can.

STRATFORD

STRATFORD LEADS IN REPUTABLE FURNITURE AND GOOD SERVICE

Imperial in Name and Character

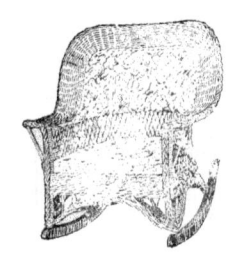

THESE lines are particularly seasonable in selling power, though their sphere of usefulness covers the entire year. Imperial Reed Furniture moves quickly **now** because its value to the user is almost doubled during the summer months.

We manufacture a wide range of Upholstered Reed Suites, Chairs and Rockers. Get your order in now and be prepared for the first of the summer business.

Stratford   Ontario

THE STRATFORD SHIPPING COMBINATION WILL INTEREST WESTERN DEALERS

AN EXCLUSIVE ADAM DESIGN AT A POPULAR PRICE

This Bedroom Suite is made in Surface Mahogany and White Enamel. Furniture critics agree that for correctness in design, richness in appearance, and durability of finish, this moderate-priced **Meaford** production equals the artistic period furniture sold at many times its price.

The Meaford Line is a Distinctive Attraction

We are now making a great variety of new designs in Period, Colonial and Modern Furniture, and at a price within the reach of those with small incomes.

The **Meaford Line** is a combination of Quality, Utility and Price Attraction that is bound to sell. If your business needs a good sales stimulant, there's nothing that will accomplish it more satisfactorily than the **Meaford Line.**

The Meaford Manufacturing Co., Limited
Meaford, Ontario

June, 1914   CANADIAN FURNITURE WORLD AND THE UNDERTAKER.

STRATFORD

STRATFORD LEADS IN REPUTABLE FURNITURE AND GOOD SERVICE

¶ We manufacture Davenport Beds, Couches, and Living Room Furniture. Although we have only had our lines on the market a few months, they have already won a place of confidence with many dealers throughout the Dominion.

¶ The reason is that we determined in the first place to give a little better than usual good value for every dollar spent with us, so that our goods would merit the good-will of the dealer and the user.

¶ If one of our travelers has not already outlined the F. G. policy in detail to you, write us for information. We are sure that our furniture will sell to a well-paying percentage of your customers.

Stratford   Ontario

THE STRATFORD SHIPPING COMBINATION WILL INTEREST WESTERN DEALERS

BAETZ BROTHERS AND COMPANY
BERLIN :: ONTARIO.

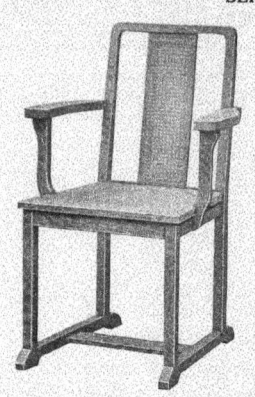

No. 711
"Bungalow" Breakfast Room Chairs

Made of solid Quartered White Oak in Silver Grey or Fumed finishes.

Seat and back in SUPERFINE open cane webbing.

Our Special "English Bungalow" Catalog is now ready. Have you one?

SATISFACTION

Satisfaction to the Dealer because of the margin of profit, and the customer-making quality of the mattress.

THE FISCHMAN PATENT MATTRESS
Can. Pat. Mar. 16, 1909   U.S. Pat., Feb. 16, 1909

Satisfaction to your customer because of its great degree of comfort and its lasting qualities.

Write to-day for our Descriptive Booklet.   We are Equipped for Speedy Delivery

The Mattress is Guaranteed for Five Years—Absolutely

The Fischman Mattress Co., Limited
333 Adelaide St. W.   Toronto

STRATFORD

STRATFORD LEADS IN REPUTABLE FURNITURE AND GOOD SERVICE

Find the Greatest Sale Among the Class of People Who Make the Most Profitable Customers

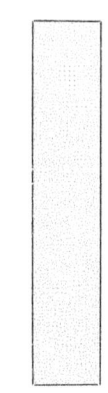

The store that carries Globe-Wernicke Sectional Bookcases is possessed of an asset that no other make of Canadian Furniture can equal. It constitutes greater prestige and more opportunities for increased profits.

Globe-Wernicke Bookcase units are made in many Period and Modern Styles for home and office use. We shall be pleased to send you our catalogs and dealer proposition. You should have a showing of this line on your floors.

Link up with Globe-Wernicke World-Wide Publicity

Stratford   Ontario

THE STRATFORD SHIPPING COMBINATION WILL INTEREST WESTERN DEALERS

The Charm of Good Bentwood Furniture

Finds expression wherever beauty of design combined with strength of construction plus extreme durability are appreciated.

KOHN'S IMPORTED BENTWOOD

is conceded to be of supreme excellence in every detail, and the demand for it is growing with rapidity. Be PREPARED for it. ¶ Built by perfected methods of the finest and toughest Austrian beechwood, by manufacturers of long experience, Kohn's Bentwood unites graceful and correct design with great rigidity and strength.

No. 4322, Cane Seat ¶ Write for our catalog, with scores of attractive designs, inexpensively priced. Don't fail, if possible to drop in at our showrooms and see the latest additions. There's a handsome profit for YOU in Kohn's Bentwood.

JACOB & JOSEF KOHN of Vienna
215-219 Victoria St., Toronto, Canada

110-112 West 27th St., New York City. 1410-1418 So. Wabash Ave., Chicago, Ill.
Second Floor, Keeler Bldg., Grand Rapids, Mich. 418 Maritime Bldg., Seattle, Wash.

No. 4345, Cane

THE
"Peerless" Folding Table
Folds in Small Space

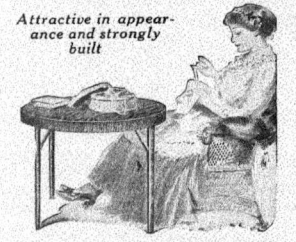

Attractive in appearance and strongly built

The "Peerless" is a splendid profit maker during the summer season. It is very light in weight, and is just the thing for the summer verandah, lawn and camp.

Get your order in at once. Our prices are right.

HOURD & COMPANY, LIMITED
Wholesale Furniture Manufacturers
LONDON,   -   -   CANADA
Sole Canadian Licensees and Manufacturers

Appropriate Designs In Brass Trimmings

OUR facilities for producing Brass Furniture Trimmings of all kinds in any quantity, design and finish you require are unequalled in Canada.

Let us quote our attractive prices on your next order, whether it is stock or special work.

Stratford Brass Co.
Limited
Stratford   Ontario

June, 1914   CANADIAN FURNITURE WORLD AND THE UNDERTAKER   11

STRATFORD

STRATFORD LEADS IN REPUTABLE FURNITURE AND GOOD SERVICE

Summer

Not a minute is to be lost if you intend to get the greatest returns from your summer stock. Order a shipment of our lines to-day—they are recognised all over Canada as the very best value in their class.

Lawn Swings, Gliding Settees, Garden Seats, Park Seats, Folding Chairs, Lawn Chairs, Camp Stools and Chairs and Verandah Furniture.

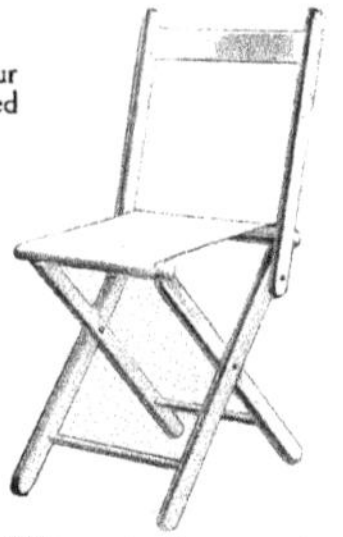

Write to-day for our catalogue of summer lines.

Stratford Manufacturing Company, Limited   ONTARIO

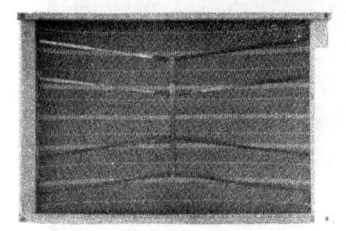

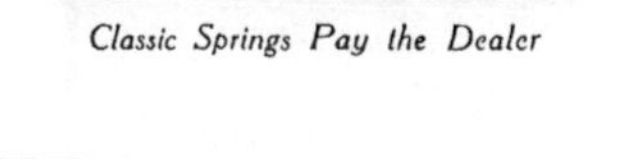

Classic Springs Pay the Dealer

SINGLE weave with extra heavy ribs every eight inches. Exceptionally strong iron support. Tin over key-way. Absolutely vermin proof.

All Classic Woven Wire Bed Springs are made of the very best materials for the popular priced trade. Every spring we turn out is fully guaranteed, and each sale affords you a generous profit.

THE STRATFORD SHIPPING COMBINATION WILL INTEREST WESTERN DEALERS

The Kindel

The Bed that Makes Itself — **Day and Night Service**

NO other Davenport can compare with the Kindel Kind where a good bed is required. The only reason in the world why a person would not buy the Kindel Parlor Bed is because he has not made a thorough investigation.

The Kindel Beds have the simplest mechanism, the easiest movement, the most comfortable seat as a davenport, and the most luxurious bed, besides the great convenience of the wardrobe feature.

Consider the Kindel itself, its range of profit, the selling plan and the fact that before you buy it, it is partly sold. Then let's get together.

The Kindel Bed Co., Ltd.
Toronto - Ontario

Authentic Store Front Book

Our eight years' experience in helping to design and build more than 30,000 KAWNEER STORE FRONTS has enabled us to compile and publish an authentic book on Store Fronts. This book contains photographs as well as drawings of many of the best paying Store Fronts in **Kawneer Store Fronts** the country and if you are interested in Store Fronts don't take another step until you have seen "Boosting Business No. 2." Let us help you build a new Store Front that will pay for itself by increasing your business.

Just a Card for "Boosting Business No. 2" will bring it without obligation

Kawneer Manufacturing Co., Ltd.
Francis J. Plym, President
Dept. S.   1197 Bathurst Street
Toronto, Ontario

The Colleran Patent All-Steel Mattress

SPECIALLY tempered steel frame; Colleran patented rope edge; double woven mesh; six-inch tempered steel cone supports.
The Colleran line will stimulate your Bed Spring Business.

Write Us for Complete Information.

REPRESENTATIVES
Ed. Bagshaw, Western Ontario   A. McNab, Eastern Ontario
J. Clarke, Northern Ontario   J. A. McLaughlin, Quebec

Colleran Patent Spring Mattress Co.
TORONTO, ONT.

WEISGLASS

Synonymous with the best in Brass Bedsteads

There is much in a name, when that name happens to be **"Weisglass."** It stands for the highest grade of Brass Beds manufactured in the Dominion of Canada: Magnificent designs, most carefully constructed, and finished with permanent indestructible **acid-proof** lacquer.

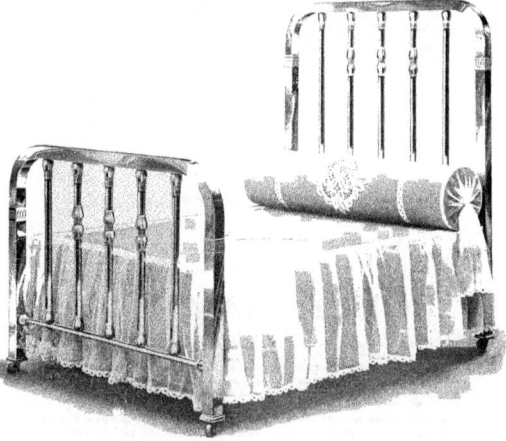

1388

We shall be pleased to quote prices on beds, as illustrated, to any responsible furniture dealer.

Our COMPLETELY illustrated catalogue is ready for mailing. Have you applied for your copy?

S. WEISGLASS, LIMITED

TORONTO   MONTREAL

Beds
Springs
Couches

Davenports
Costumers
Wall Racks

CANADIAN FURNITURE WORLD AND THE UNDERTAKER. June, 1914

No Better Value in Canada

The "Restwell No. 1"

COUCH HAMMOCK

Put a Gale Couch Hammock alongside any other couch hammock sold in Canada—compare the construction and quality of materials used—and see if it does not offer better value than any other Couch Hammock you can secure.

Material in "Restwell No. 1" is 8 oz. duck with iron-frame wire fabric spring, cotton filled mattress. Stand 1 1/16 in. tubing, height 7 ft., length 7 ft. 7 in.

List price, complete with stand, canopy, chains, windshield and pad, **$24.00**.
List price, Hammock Couch with chains, windshield and pad, **$14.00**.
List price, Stand only, **$6.00**.   List price, Canopy only **$4.00**.

GEO. GALE & SONS, Limited, Waterville, Que.
MONTREAL   TORONTO   WINNIPEG

Always a Great Seller

Few Springs can equal "The Cuban" record of 15 years' success and satisfaction

"THE CUBAN"

The Gale business began with the manufacture of spring mattresses, and no spring they manufacture has given greater satisfaction or greater service than "The Cuban."

No one ever heard of "The Cuban" going wrong, and thousands of them have been in use for over 15 years.

There are hundreds of people in your locality who would buy "The Cuban" spring if they knew how good it is.

Why not try it and see how well it sells?

Wholesale price, **$8.00** –f.o.b. factory.

Sold only to merchants who will agree to retail selling price.

GEO. GALE & SONS, Limited, Waterville, Que.
MONTREAL   TORONTO   WINNIPEG

How is Your Stock of Brass Bedsteads?

Are you keeping it up-to-date? Are you doing a profitable business in Brass beds? If not, there is something wrong and you should get to the bottom of it at once.

Just drop us a line and we will put you on the right track.

Victoriaville Beds

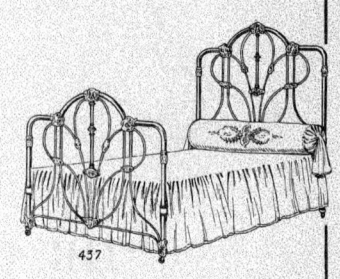

are made of the very best material. Our up-to-date facilities for manufacturing this class of furniture enable us to produce them at a cost which comes within the means of the majority of your customers, after allowing yourself a good substantial profit.

It will pay you to get acquainted with us.

The Victoriaville Bedding
(Formerly The Standard Bedstead Co., Limited)
Company, Limited
Victoriaville, Que.

The Big Five Mixed Carload Center

The Big Five Mixed Carload Center

A PROFITABLE LINE
OF
COMFORTABLE UPHOLSTERED FURNITURE

The best material, the best workmanship, and real comfort at a low price, are what we offer furniture dealers in Victoriaville Upholstered Furniture.

These are the points that count when talking to a prospective customer, and a trial order of our upholstered furniture will prove our claims. Send for our catalogue.

The Victoriaville Bedding Company
Limited

(Formerly The Canada Mattress Co., Ltd.)

Victoriaville, Que.

The Gold Medal Line

SPRING TIME IS BED SPRING TIME

Keep a good supply in stock of

HERCULES
REGISTERED
BED SPRINGS

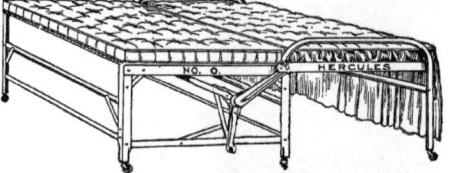

Imperial Steel Sliding Couches and Steel Folding Cots complete with cushions.

A handsome couch by day, a double bed by night. A pressure of the foot converts from the one to the other. The two articles at one cost.

"Purity" Mixed Mattresses and White Cotton Mattress.

"Gold Medal" Felt Mattresses

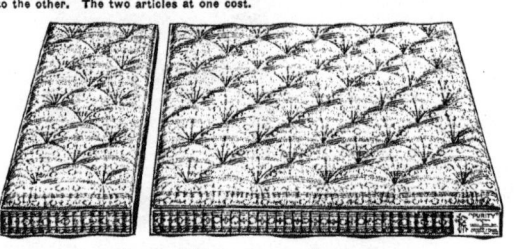

Manufacturers of Parlor and Living Room Furniture

The Gold Medal Furniture Mfg. Co.
Limited

Head office: Van Horne St., Toronto *Factories also at* Montreal, Winnipeg and Uxbridge

A Pair of Pedestals
each Complete in Itself

That's the patented feature of our TWIN PEDESTAL EXTENSION TABLE—the line that has made such wonderful advances during the past year. The Twin Pedestals present a perfect appearance and give the greatest support, extended or closed. There are no troublesome locks, no gaping pedestals and no unfinished surfaces when extended. In the

Twin Pedestal Extension Table

you can close a sale fast by showing your customers all they can desire in design, fine quality and finish; and more than they expect in utility and serviceability—all at a reasonable price, too.

You should have a copy of our large new catalog, just out. You'll like the Twin Pedestal proposition

Chesley Furniture Company, Limited
Chesley :: Ontario

"Twin" Tables make "Twin" profits

No. 555

Knechtel

Elm

Beautiful | Grain
Color
Finish

No. 280—$35.25

No. 278—$18.00

No. 278—$13.50

One of the finest cabinet woods. Orders repeated again and again. Oversold most of the time.

Knechtel Furniture Co.
Limited

Hanover :: Ontario

Knechtel

Elm

Golden Elm

No. 278 $30.00

No. 278 $26.25

No. 279 $29.25

Order right now and have your turn come earlier. Stock up and get business. Write us to-day.

Knechtel Furniture Co.
Limited
Hanover :: Ontario

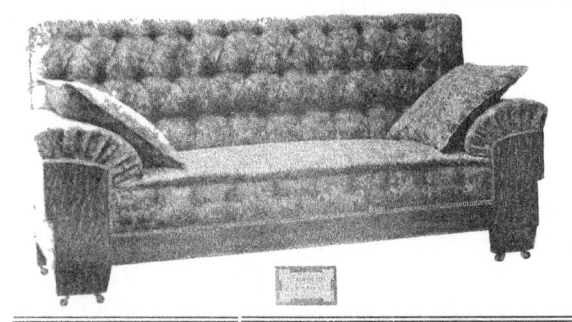

CANADIAN FURNITURE WORLD AND THE UNDERTAKER — June, 1914

Solid Comfort and Big Value

This is one of a number of new designs we have just produced. It is very attractive in appearance, substantially made, and affords the maximum of comfort.

Write for our prices.

J. P. Albrough & Co.
INGERSOLL, CANADA

Makers of Quality Couches and Easy Chairs.

Fine Upholstered Furniture

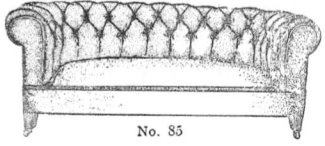

No. 85 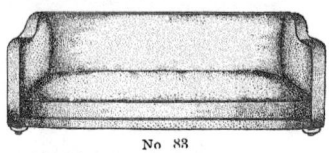   No. 88

In the Imperial make of Upholstered Furniture you'll find that touch of better finish, appearance or quality that develops the customer who is 'just looking them over to-day" into an immediate purchaser.

WRITE FOR OUR PRICES AND PHOTOS

IMPERIAL FURNITURE CO.   585-591 Queen St. W., Toronto

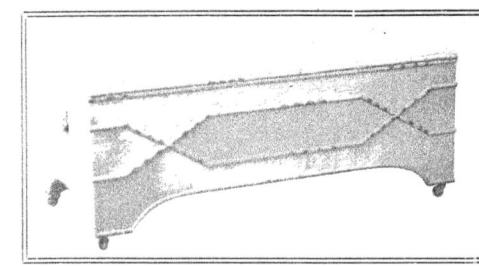

B.C. Red CEDAR Bedroom Boxes

¶ Made of ¾ in. B.C. Red Cedar covered with Japanese matting and trimmed with rattan. Bent brass hinges and casters. Top panelled and nicely padded. Made in three sizes.

Particulars of other lines on request

D. L. Shafer & Co.
ST. THOMAS   -   ONTARIO

Do you know of any Furniture Dealer or Funeral Director, anywhere in Canada, who is not a subscriber to the Canadian Furniture World and The Undertaker? If so, you will be doing him a favor by sending us his name and address so that we can send him a sample copy and subscription order blank.

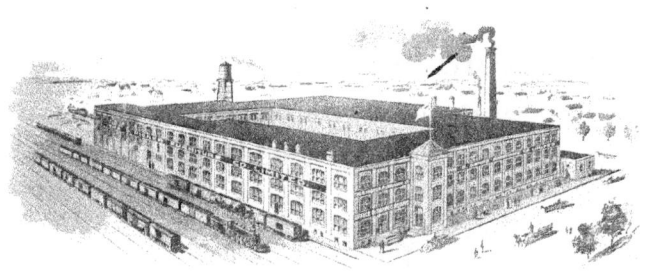

FACTORIES AT BERLIN & LISTOWEL   ESTABLISHED 1877.

The D. HIBNER FURNITURE CO., LIMITED.
MANUFACTURERS OF
HIGH GRADE FURNITURE, COMPLETE DININGROOM SUITES IN OAK & SOLID MAHOGANY, PARLOR & LIBRARY TABLES, SECTIONAL BOOK CASES & PARLOR SUITES.

BERLIN, ONTARIO,
CANADA.

April 29th, 1914

The Canadian Linderman Co.
    Woodstock, Ont.

Gentlemen:-

    Our Linderman six-foot Dovetailer has been running at our factory for over six months. During that time we have used it on all grades and classes of work, from Solid Mahogany Table Tops to core work, drawer sides, etc., and we can truthfully say that the machine has fulfilled every promise that you made us about it. Our joints are as fine as we could ask, and we have had no trouble with the machine since we installed it.

    We wish to thank you for the interest you have taken in our machine, and we surely appreciate the attention.

                Yours very truly,

                      THE D. HIBNER FURNITURE CO., LTD.

This Table is a *Splendid* Value

A handsome Library Table that reaches the top notch of excellence in its class. It is plain, yet aristocratic in design, and will never become "out of style." The drawers and book shelves are spacious and well arranged. Write for our prices and you'll be sure to order a couple at once.

Made in mahogany and quartered oak, beautifully finished. Substantially constructed and serviceable in every way.

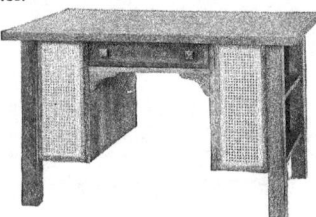

Our lines of Office Desks, Chairs, Filing Cabinets, etc., should interest you. Our catalog will be sent on application.

The Elmira Interior Woodwork Co., Limited
C.P.R.   Elmira, Ontario   G.T.R.

Sure Selling Diners

Our latest design in attractive Diners at a popular price.

Nos. 971 and 973, made in hardwood and oak with cane seats. Also made with impervious veneer seats when specified.

Get this line in stock at once. Prices on request.

No. 971   No. 973

THE NORTH AMERICAN BENT CHAIR CO., Limited
OWEN SOUND   -   -   ONTARIO

WE are manufacturing an extensive line of Roman Stripes, Art Serge, Armure, Egyptian and Monk's Cloth, together with all grades of Tapestry curtains, and are selling direct to the trade.

Give us a chance to send our representative to you. It will be worth your while to consider the above lines. They are the best obtainable—the kind of goods that bring buyers back for more.

The Dominion Hammock Manufacturing Company
Limited
Dunnville - Ontario

Are you getting YOUR share of this profitable business?

During the past year our sales of J-M Asbestos Table Covers took a tremendous jump. Some dealers **somewhere** are getting the benefit of this increased demand. Are you one of them?

J-M ASBESTOS
TABLE COVERS AND MATS

are made in our factory, from the finest grade of Asbestos in the world, taken directly from our own mines. Yet in spite of their superior quality, J-M Asbestos Table Covers cost no more and often less—than the ordinary, soon-wear-out kind.

A modest investment and a little effort on your part will quickly develop a thriving business in this line. We'll help you by supplying free attractive booklets imprinted with your own name on the cover. It isn't necessary to carry a large stock either, as our nearest branch is prepared to get quickly on hurry-up orders.

Write to-day for Booklet and Special Proposition to Dealers. Address nearest Branch.

THE CANADIAN
H. W. JOHNS-MANVILLE CO., Limited

Manufacturers of Show-Case, Show-Window and General Illuminating Systems; Asbestos Pipe Coverings; Dry Batteries   Fire Extinguishers, Etc.

TORONTO   **WINNIPEG**
MONTREAL   **VANCOUVER**

Onward Sliding Furniture Shoes

For Metal Beds

For Wood Furniture

Are **always** in good working order, and they never damage floor surfaces or coverings.

See that the furniture and metal beds you stock are equipped with Onward Sliding Shoes. Manufacturers can supply them at no extra cost.

Order a trial case to-day. Onward Sliding Shoes are well advertised and they sell quickly and profitably.

The Onward Mfg. Co.
Berlin, Ontario

Making TABLE-SLIDES is a Specialty Business

For more than TWENTY-FIVE YEARS we have made TABLE SLIDES exclusively. Our Factory is equipped with Special Machinery which enables us to make SLIDES, BETTER and CHEAPER than the furniture manufacturer.

Canadian Table makers are rapidly adopting WABASH SLIDES

Because They ELIMINATE SLIDE TROUBLES Are CHEAPER and BETTER

Reduced Costs   BY USING
Increased Out-put   **WABASH SLIDES**

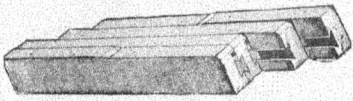

Made by
B. WALTER & CO.
Wabash, Ind.

The Largest EXCLUSIVE TABLE-SLIDE Manufacturers in America
ESTABLISHED 1887

Lippert Davenport Beds

Two Home Comforts in One

No. 1. Length 60 inches x 32 inches deep

A NEW ADDITION TO OUR LINE

One of our very attractive designs in our line of Davenports and Davenettes. Ask our traveller to show you this line on his next trip. Get prices and prints---it will pay you.

The Lippert Furniture Co., Limited
BERLIN :: ONTARIO

"Makes Sleeptime Sleepfull"

That Laced Opening Shows the Build

KELLARIC Mattresses are made of firm, soft, sanitary, resilient cotton felt, and heavy, well-wearing coverings of attractive design.

Our secret process of cross binding eliminates all possibility of spreading. Kellaric Mattresses hold their shape indefinitely.

Kellaric Mattresses are made with straps at the sides for convenience in handling.

Stock the KELLARIC now, Mr. Dealer, and get the benefit of our consumer advertising. You can handle these mattresses at a good profit. There is nothing to equal their comfort, sanitation, and economy, and they are half sold when you get them.

Our Model Spring, Hair-in-Cotton and Common Sense Mattresses will meet the demand for lower Priced goods.

Eastern Branch: BERLIN BEDDING CO., LIMITED, 31 Front St. E., Toronto

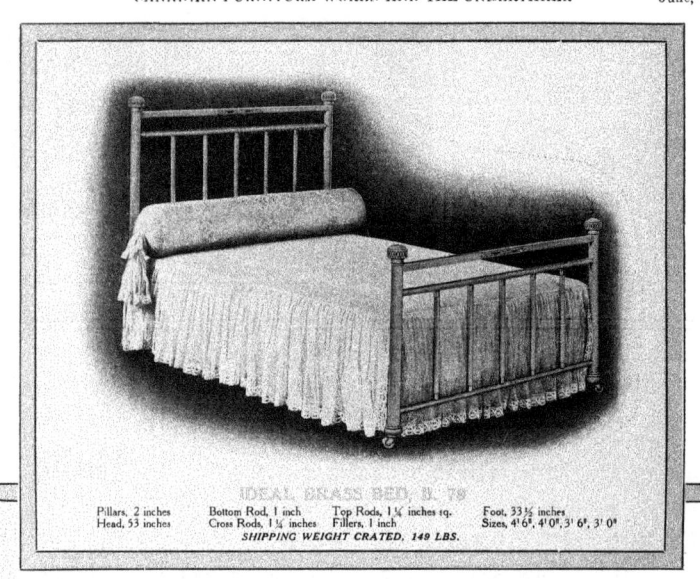

CANADIAN FURNITURE WORLD AND THE UNDERTAKER   June, 1914

IDEAL BRASS BED, B. 78

Pillars, 2 inches   Bottom Rod, 1 inch   Top Rods, 1¼ inches sq.   Foot, 33½ inches
Head, 53 inches   Cross Rods, 1¼ inches   Fillers, 1 inch   Sizes, 4' 6", 4' 0", 3' 6", 3' 0"
SHIPPING WEIGHT CRATED, 149 LBS.

> Bed is a bundle of paradoxes; we go to it with reluctance, yet we quit it with regret; and we make up our minds every night to leave it early, but we make up our bodies every morning to keep it late.—*Colton.*

OF all the beds that ever charmed the eye and appealed to one's sense of value, it would be hard to equal the IDEAL BRASS BED, B. 78, which is pictured above.

For pure simplicity of design, elegance in appearance and perfection of workmanship, we consider B. 78 a masterpiece, and you may have full confidence in recommending it to your customers. It is equipped with the very fine appearing Pierce Trimmings.

IDEAL
REGISTERED

Canadian Furniture World and the Undertaker

PUBLISHED THE 1ST OF EACH MONTH BY

THE COMMERCIAL PRESS, Limited
32 COLBORNE STREET, TORONTO
Phone Main 4978

D. O. McKinnon	President
W. L. Edmonds	Vice-President
Weston Wrigley	Vice-President and Manager of Trade Papers
J. C. Armer	Vice-President and Manager of Technical Papers
James O'Hagan	Editor
John A. Fullerton	Associate Editor
Wm. J. Bryans	" "

Staff Representatives

Geo. H. Honsberger, Advertising Manager	Toronto
F. C. D. Wilkes, Eastern Manager, 704 Unity Bldg.	Montreal
R. C. Howson, Western Representative	Winnipeg
E. J. MacIntyre, Room 1155, 122 South Michigan Avenue	Chicago
C. G. Brandt, Circulation Manager, Toronto	

Subscriptions
Canada, $1.00 a year. Other Countries, $2.00 a year

PUBLISHERS' STATEMENT—2000 copies of this issue of the Canadian Furniture World are printed for circulation. Itemized statement, showing distribution according to provinces, will be furnished on request.

Vol. 4   JUNE, 1914   No. 6

Punctuality and Success.

We print in another part of this issue a short article by J. Wilhelm, a salesman with the T. Eaton Co., on the subject of "Punctuality Essential to Success in Life." The article should be read by everyone, and particularly clerks.

Nearly every clerk is ambitious to succeed. But it is not every clerk that is willing to religiously do these things which bring success. A disregard of punctuality is one of those things.

It is just as easy to be punctual as not punctual. Either is a matter of habit. And habit, on the other hand, is a reflection of the will power.

Make up your mind to be punctual. And then develop it into a habit.

We shall be glad to hear from clerks on this or any other subject. The experience of one stimulates others.

When trade is quiet the time is opportune for getting busy on collections.

Knowing the Customer.

He who knows the goods he is selling possesses that which is an important factor in salesmanship.

But there is still another thing he should know if he is to be adequately equipped.

He should be able to "size up" his customers when they enter the store.

To do this with customers with whom he has a personal acquaintance is not a difficult matter. He has from experience learned their tastes and peculiarities. And any intelligent business men can learn by experience.

Where the test of skill comes in is when the salesman can read the customer who is a perfect stranger to him.

This may not be an easy task, but it is not an impossible one. Like everything else that is worth while, it comes by study, or the study of human nature.

And the essentials to the study of human nature are patience, perseverance, and tact, for it is not the study of a day; it is the study of a lifetime.

Probably the greatest of these essentials is tact, for without this patience and perseverance will prevail but little.

Before you can know an unknown customer that comes into your store, you have got to do a little "angling." In other words, you have got to feel him—to draw him out—in order that you may ascertain how you can secure his confidence and good-will, and ultimately obtain his order. This is tact. Patience and perseverance come to the assistance of tact when it is sorely tried by the enigmatic customer.

"Playing" to land a customer is great sport. Fishing for either bass or trout isn't to be compared with it. He who hasn't the ambition to equip himself for it had better seek another vocation, for he'll never be a salesman.

While it is unwise to allow pleasure to interfere with business, yet it is also unwise to allow business to interfere with the health of the merchant.

The Dealer Who Hides Behind Himself.

The dealer who says that he has been so long in business that he does not need to advertise is hiding behind himself. He may not realize the fact, but it is true, nevertheless. And the more persistently he hides behind himself the greater will be the number of people who will forget him.

If all dealers were to agree to refrain from publicity all would, of course, be on an equal footing. But the trouble is no really progressive dealer would agree to conform to any such reactionary policy.

Once upon a time a group of manufacturers in Canada agreed to discontinue all advertising. There were only three or four in the group, but they were the only manufacturers of the kind in the country. Even they, however, soon found that their policy was an unwise one.

Like a good many other business men, they thought that money paid out in advertising was an expenditure. Their experience, however, taught them that it was an investment. They are now all consistent advertisers.

The question naturally arises: If a group of manufacturers who monopolize the manufacture of an article find that it is an unsound business practice not to advertise, what must be the case when a retailer, who has to meet the keenest kind of competition, decides that he will not use the columns of his local newspaper? The answer is easy- he is handicapped.

Some business men have been heard to remark that if they knew how to prepare copy they would advertise.

Writing an advertisement is merely putting on paper the substance of what they would say to a customer who entered their store to buy a certain article.

True, some can do this better than others; but just as there is no one in business who is such a poor salesman that he becomes dumb when a customer enters his store, so there is no one so inefficient that he can,

not put on paper the selling points of an article that he wishes to advertise.
Where there's a will there's a way. But the trouble is that some do not appear to have the will as far as advertising is concerned.

It is only those who make adequate preparations that can expect to reap a good harvest from the summer furniture trade.

How He Made His Business Grow. He is a rash man who to-day thinks that the limit has been reached in anything. This is true of business enterprises as well as in the field of science.

As a matter of fact, most thoughtful men are inclined to the belief that in business at any rate possibilities are only limited by the will power and resourcefulness of those who are in command.

The business of a retailer in a back country store in Ontario had reached a stage beyond which the proprietor was beginning to wonder whether or not further growth was possible. He had not reached the point at which he had abandoned hope. He wasn't made of that kind of stuff. But during his meditations he felt that even if there was further growth it could scarcely be material, particularly as the town in which he did business appeared to have reached the stand-still stage.

One day, however, in the midst of his meditations, a newspaper friend dropped in to see him. And the thing that was on his mind became the subject of discussion, during which the newspaper man suggested that he get out a small illustrated catalogue, placing one in the home of every family in the town and surrounding country.

The dealer, who was never known to turn down a suggestion, gave this one much consideration. After some deliberation he decided to make the venture. He sought and secured the co-operation of a number of manufacturers and jobbers whose goods he handled, and from them he obtained the use of a number of engravings.

When mailed the catalogue was accompanied by a short and nicely worded circular letter.

It is about a year since the venture was made, and not only has the dealer secured business from homes which had not hitherto dealt with him, but the general turnover of goods in his store has materially increased.

He does not now depend wholly upon his catalogue as an advertising medium. He has been encouraged to use the columns of the local newspapers to tell the news of his store.

That he is no longer perturbed about the future of his business may be taken for granted. He feels that his business has taken a new lease of life, and he intends to take all the advantage of it that he can.

Even a little advertising will help remind forgetful customers that you are still doing business at the old stand.

A Good Scheme. Heads of departments of a number of mercantile and financial concerns in New York are brought together every two weeks to listen to addresses on efficiency and to discuss business problems.

The idea is an exceedingly good one. If properly conducted its possibilities are great. No one person possesses a monopoly of either ideas or experiences, and when a group of practical men are brought together for free and open discussion great benefit to all participating must result.

It is a scheme which might be undertaken by business men everywhere. Those in small towns may not have at hand the facilities for employing it that large cities have, but even if the place was so small that only half a dozen business men, heads of departments and clerks could be got together it would be a good thing. Not only would those who participated benefit, but better business conditions generally in the locality would naturally follow.

He who has a narrow mind is never sharp enough to cut much of a figure in business.

Interest Clerks in Business. Are your clerks merely putting in the time, or are they interested in the business? It must be admitted that there are many clerks that take little interest in making sales, and that it is frequently a difficult problem to get them interested. The merchant should at least make an attempt to arouse real effort, and he can often do much to arouse their enthusiasm by taking them into his confidence as to how much business he wants to do each week or month, and asking for their views on how it is best to go after that amount of business.

It is not luck, but successful methods, that bring success in business ventures.

Death Roll of Consumers. Twelve hundred and twenty industrial workers were killed in Canada last year while engaged in their regular vocations.

This is of more than passing interest to business men. Every life lost destroyed at least a consumer if not a customer direct.

As a consumer of various forms of merchandise each victim may be estimated to be worth $500 a year to the country. If this estimate is approximately correct it means that by the death of these 1,220 persons, $610,000 was lost to the business men during the year. On the same basis $6,100,000 would be lost in ten years.

But this is not all, for by the serious accidents which befell 5,780 other persons, there was a further decrease in purchasing power.

It is quite evident that business men should have more than a passing interest in the "safety first" movement which is now becoming so general in Canada as well as in other civilized countries.

There is an economic as well as a humanitarian aspect to the subject.

It may take ambition to start a man developing his ability, but simple common sense will keep him at it.

System in Business System introduced into business works for greater profit because it guards against losses, and keeps the merchant acquainted with the standing of different departments of his business. This refers to system used in connection with book-keeping, and in keeping track of sales, stock, book accounts, etc.

System in delivery, in looking after stock and orders, in handling of customers, packaging up of goods, and similar work, lessens the amount of labor in connection with it, and this, of course, has a bearing on profit, because it allows the maximum amount of business to be done at a minimum cost.

The business of the best families in town is mighty nice trade to have, but it isn't worth getting at the expense of the trade of the rest of the public.

Retailers and the Church and School Furniture Trade

By WILLIAM E. LEWIS

A FRIEND asked me recently why such a small proportion of the orders for church and school furniture went through the retail dealer. The question set me thinking, and thinking finally led me to enquiry among manufacturers and others. In the process of enquiry I have discovered a few things. And these meditations have led me to some conclusions about which I would like to speak somewhat candidly.

A Reason Why.

In the first place, the dealer is himself in part to blame. Note that I say in part to blame. His blame, in certain instances at least, is that he does not take enough interest to land the business when an order for either school or church furniture is to be given out in his locality. Here is one instance which will serve as an illustration:

A dealer in a Western Ontario town had discovered that a supply of furniture was to be put into one of the schools in his town. Thinking there was a possibility of his getting a little rake-off he notified one of the manufacturers and asked if he could get a commission if the order fell to that particular manufacturer. Although he obtained an affirmative answer that is where the matter ended as far as he was concerned. He never lifted a finger to get the business.

He Wouldn't Co-operate.

Having, however, learned by experience that it was well to have a representative on the spot, the manufacturer sent one of his salesmen to the town in the course of a few days. When the latter arrived he found that the dealer had not even taken the trouble to ascertain the names of the trustees of the local board. And when the salesman suggested that he go out with him and endeavor to round-up the school trustees, he refused to move from his store, even though the plea was advanced that he might be able to pick up some selling points in regard to school furniture.

The salesman eventually got the members of the school board together and landed the order; but it can hardly be said that the dealer did anything to earn his commission.

This is no doubt an unusual instance of inaction on the part of a retailer, but unfortunately it is an example of what others have done in a modified way.

A Discouraged Manufacturer.

"After about twenty years' experience in trying to sell school and church furniture through the retail trade," said a manufacturer to me, "I abandoned it four or five years ago for the simple reason that I could not awaken in the retailer sufficient interest to induce him to get after his local trade. Instead of getting after the school trade when it is in season, they hold off, fearing they will be intruding. At least that is too often the case. The average dealer is, therefore, no help to the manufacturer. If retailers would get a share of this business they must get after it early."

Still another manufacturer says that as the selling of church and school furniture is a special business, it is necessary for the traveler of the manufacturer to appear before church and school boards and demonstrate the quality of his line. He also maintains that the margin of profit is too small for the manufacturer to put the sale through the local retailer.

One manufacturer with whom I had some correspondence takes a somewhat different view. He maintains that every effort should be made to induce the retailer to take a lively interest in this line of business. "Speaking for ourselves," he continued, "we are confident we would rather deal through the retail store than direct with churches and schools, and furthermore, we would be glad to assist in making this a general principle."

No one will deny that selling school and church furniture is a different proposition altogether from selling ordinary furniture. Knowledge, therefore, which is useful for selling the one is altogether different from that which must be possessed in selling the other.

The Retailer's Possibilities.

It by no means follows that he who knows how to sell ordinary household furniture cannot acquire the knowledge necessary to making himself a fairly good salesman of church and school furniture. All retailers, however they may apply themselves, may not become experts. The opportunity is lacking. But if they really do apply themselves to the task they will soon be able to figure out at least approximately the seating capacity of a school or church building.

There is one thing, however, that every retailer can do, and that is keep on the alert for news regarding schools and churches which are to be erected. And then, as soon as information has been secured, get into touch with the trustees or officials as the case may be. The next step is to get into touch with one of the manufacturers and make arrangements to secure his co-operation in landing the business.

Manufacturers are, as a rule, willing to co-operate with the retailer who is alert and businesslike. Where they draw the line is at the dealer who aims to secure a share in the profits without doing a "hand's turn" to get the business.

The advertisements running in the trade papers will give him a line on the manufacturers who make a specialty of church and school furniture.

Getting Transient Business

There is still another reason why dealers should keep in close touch with church officials and school trustees, and that is for the purpose of securing the transient business in desks, chairs and other lines of furniture. Much of this business, particularly for church supplies, now goes to department stores, and often because no effort has been made by local dealers to get it. Quite recently I came across a couple of concrete instances of this.

Even if the dealer does not stand much chance of landing orders for the furnishing of new churches and schools he is certainly the logical medium through which transient orders should come. An occasional letter to church and school boards would help him to get the business. So would an occasional advertisement in his local paper.

THE value of a man from his chin down to his feet averages about $1.00 a day. The difference in the value of men is from the chin up to the top of the head; in fact, the real value in earning power is from the nose up to the top of the head; for so many use the space between the chin and nose overtime.

Getting the Most Out of Summer Furniture

By A. B. LEVER

THAT dealers generally are year by year giving more attention to what is termed summer furniture there can be no doubt.

Having more money to spend than they had in the years gone by, Canadians naturally are ambitious to place in their homes a greater variety as well as a better variety of furniture.

Under favorable circumstances like these, summer furniture naturally "catches on." It is quite in order to put in a stock of summer furniture suitable for the requirements of their locality.

Emphasize Quality Goods.

But in putting in a stock of summer furniture, it is well not to undervalue the buying capacity of their customers as far as quality is concerned.

The cheaper lines it would, of course, be unwise to leave out, but it would be equally unwise to presume that the better quality goods should be eliminated. A good many dealers have discovered this in regard to furniture in general, and some may possibly yet have to learn the lesson in regard to summer lines.

The Power of Salesmanship.

Business men in all lines of merchandising have learned that, through the art of salesmanship it is possible to educate the public to purchase higher quality goods than was at one time in their history deemed possible. Furniture exhibitions have probably done as much as any other influence, backed by the trade papers, to inspire the retail furniture dealer to systematically undertake the education of the public along this line.

That the success a dealer obtains from handling summer furniture is chiefly determined by the selling methods he employs goes without saying.

Make Surroundings Seasonable.

One thing that all experienced and intelligent dealers appreciate is the importance of surrounding displays of summer furniture with that which is suggestive of the season.

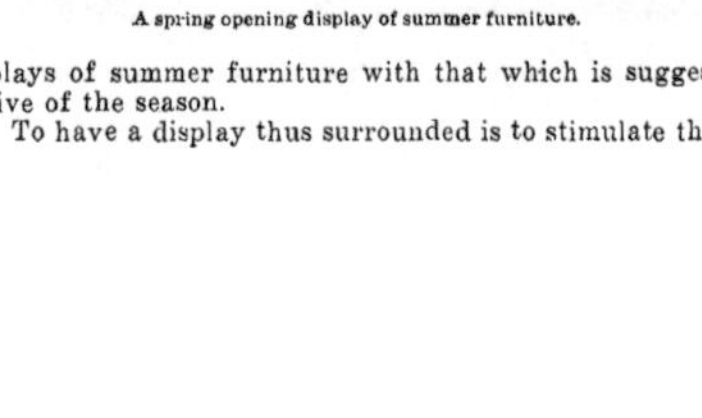

An attractive set-out of summer furniture by a large U. S. house. The columns were enclosed in lattice work decorated with flowering vines. At the tops were masses of preserved natural oak foliage. In the background was a large painting of a summer landscape.

that it should. It is attractive in style, in comfort the acme of perfection, and in price within the reach of people of moderate means.

Another thing is that much of the so-called summer furniture is adaptable for all-the-year round use as well as during the warm weather.

Psychological Time For Specializing.

While this is quite true, the psychological time for specializing on summer furniture is during the "good old summer," from the very fact that people are more inclined to buy it then than at any other time, even though it may be used in midwinter as well as in midsummer.

Most dealers, being thoroughly alive to this fact, make a special effort to bring summer furniture to the front as soon as the warm weather begins to show signs of asserting itself.

By carefully studying the advertisements which appear in the trade journals and consulting the travelers that call upon them, it is a comparatively easy matter

A spring opening display of summer furniture.

To have a display thus surrounded is to stimulate the

desire to purchase on the part of those whose attention has been arrested.

While the larger stores may have an advantage in this respect, because of the greater facilities at their disposal, yet they by no means possess a monopoly of facilities. To an ingenious dealer, whether he be large or small, a way will always be found for exhibiting his skill for making attractive and timely displays.

Displays in which the setting suggests pergolas, verandahs, porches, sunrooms, sleeping porches, and garden scenes, are sure to attract and please. Real and artificial flowers, vines and shrubs readily lend themselves to displays of this kind.

Night Illuminations.

At night, after the store is closed, the window should be kept illuminated until such time as people retire from the streets. Otherwise there are many people who would probably never see the displays.

The illustrations given in the accompanying engravings will no doubt assist many dealers in arranging their displays.

During the early part of the season a display of summer cottage furniture would undoubtedly attract a great deal of attention.

Make a liberal use of window cards. The course of lessons that is running in the Furniture World will help you if you have not already mastered the art.

Importance of Advertising.

A summer furniture campaign without advertising would be almost as unthinkable as one without window and interior displays. For this reason I am reproducing a few advertisements which progressive dealers have in times past run in their local newspapers during the summer season. From these, too, helpful suggestions may be obtained.

If you have not already done so, get your clerks together and talk over with them the plan of campaign. A good place at which to foregather will be around the dining room table at your home. Ideas loosen up around the festive board.

Advertise in busy times, because the iron must be struck while it is hot, and advertise in dull times to heat the iron.

Letters of incorporation have been issued to The Fischman Mattress Co., Ltd., Toronto. A new patented feature is being added to the mattress. H. Levy is general manager, and J. A. McLaughlin, until recently of McLaughlin & Scott, one of the best known furniture travelers in Ontario, is sales manager.

Summer furniture ads. No. 1 Hudson Bay Co., Calgary. An artistic ad; original 6¼ x 18 inches. No. 2 Baldwin, Robinson, Ltd. St. Thomas. A striking ad. Note lines top and bottom referring to delivering goods to Port Stanley. Original 10 x 9 inches. No. 3 Murray-Kay, Toronto. A well written and artistic ad; original 8½ x 8½. No. 4 Blowey Henry Co., Edmonton. A good all round ad. Original 4½ x 7. No. 5 Standard Furniture Co., Vancouver. An all round good ad; original 4¼ x 5¼. No. 6 J. O. Mitchell, St. Mary's. An attractive ad, but it would have been stronger had prices been named.

Collins' Course in Show Card Writing

Seventh of a series of articles specially prepared for this journal.

There is a very common error, with many who have not been shown differently, that the spacing of letters resolves itself into equal parts, like one inch for the letter and a half inch for the spacing. This is absolutely incorrect. In the first place, all letters are not the same width. There are various mathematical rules for determining the relative widths of letters, but, as in shading, no card writer can afford the time to measure letters with a rule. However, it is well to know the relative widths in order that correct sizes may be adhered to as much as possible when measuring with the eye. The following letters will be found to be about the same width: E, F, H, I, L, N, P, S, T, U, and Z.

The following will be found to be about the same width each, but will be a little wider than the line above: A, B, C, D, G, K, O, Q, R, V, X, and Y. A and Y may be even a little extra in width. Some set a rule that A and Y should be about one-fifth wider and the others about a half of a fifth. This can be determined if the space is divided into squares and give five squares to each of the letters in the first line mentioned above. The letter J can be a little narrower than the first line above, and the letter M a little wider than the second line, and the W widest of all.

The above rules apply to the capital letters. The small letter, or lower case, will divide themselves about

LAWYER
MILTON
Fig. 11—Example of good spacing.

as follows. These of the same width will be the following: a, b, c, d, e, g, h, k, n, o, p, q, u, v, x, y. Those a little narrower will be f, j, r, s, t. The s will not be much narrower. i and l will be the width of the stroke. w will be wider than any mentioned above, and m is the widest of all the lower case letters. Close

observation and practice will soon familiarize yourself with these sizes, so that no measuring will be necessary except a glance of the eye.

The same rule which applies to the width of letters will apply to the spacing between the letters. It cannot be measured by an equal distance from the point of one letter to the point of another. The correct spacing is to have about an equal area of space between each letter. The great difference in the shape of the various letters will show at a glance that the spacing

CLOTHING
CLOTHING
Fig. 10—Example of correct and incorrect spacing.

can only be measured or gauged with the eye. Where straight-sided letters, like H, N, M, and others come together, the letters must be farther apart than when open-sided letters like L, T, and others come together. The word LAWYER, Fig. 11, is a notable example. The L and A being open, must be placed close together. The angles of the A and W are such that if placed as near each other as the L and A, the space would be very much less in area. Therefore, the W must be much farther from the A. On the same principle the Y and W must be close together. The E may be farther away and the E and R still farther apart.

The word CLOTHING is another good example of spacing. If all the letters are measured the same distance apart the spacing will appear very uneven and the I will look as if it had been forgotten and crowded in afterwards. See Fig. 10. All the letters except H, I, N are open letters. The straight, solid sides of these letters necessitates their being farther apart than the others. When correctly spaced, as in the lower line of Fig. 10, the L and T are almost in line with the sides of the O. On the other side, the T is quite close to the

ABCDEFGHI
JKLMNOPQR
STUVWXYZ &
1234567890

Plate 27—Full block Roman (heavy).

abcdefghijklmn opqrstuvwxyz

Plate 28—Full block Roman (heavy).

11, but the l is away from it, and the N equally as far from the I. The upper line, Fig. 10, is an example of incorrect spacing, while the lower line is correctly done.

Where the letters L and T come together, as in Hamilton, belting, malt, Milton, etc., the points of these two letters may actually overlap each other. The word MILTON, Fig. 11, is another good example of spacing. Note how far apart the letters M and I and L are, while the L and T lap each other.

With practice and experience you will be able to do spacing correctly, almost involuntarily. Always bear in mind to arrange the word as a whole and not as individual letters. The word MILTON, in Fig. 11, looks like one word, whereas if spaced with the L and T as far apart as the O and N it would look like two words, MIL and TON.

The alphabets this month are excellent for practice work, and every student should do plenty of hard practice. Especially learn how to finish the corners neat and sharp and to do it quickly. Plates 27 and 28 are full block Roman (heavy). We have mentioned before that letters of this type are too slow to make to be of general use on a card. As illustration of how much longer it will take to make "blocked" letters, the M has six more corners than the M of the Egyptian style. As it is the corners that take so much time in making letters, it will be seen how much time blocked letters will consume. They are very suitable, however, for one word or a line that requires to be accentuated, while the balance of the letters on the card may be smaller. The figures shown in the same plate correspond with the style of letters.

Plates 29 and 30 can be used for small brush or pen work. They are not good for general use, as they are too hard to read. But for a small card with some announcement, motto, or crisp saying, cards that can be used to hang in an office with some short notice on them, they will answer admirably.

Sample Cards.

June is the month for weddings. From a trade point of view, it is the bride who must be considered this month. Feature your gifts. It matters not whether you have hardware, clothing, furniture, groceries, or any other line, there will be in your stock something that will make a wedding gift. Then think it out and offer some suggestion along the gift line and dress your windows accordingly. Place an attractive card in the window, calling attention to the lines you have. The $5 card is a fitting example of what might attract attention. The bells may be in gilt and the ribbon in some attractive shade of violet or blue. The lettering can be in black or red and shaded in a subdued color to match the ribbon. The old shoes are very appropriate, and may be in a dull grey color.

The June bride card is done on a plain card set behind a pebbled mat. The color of the think of large letters may be red or some bright color. The shading is in some subdued color. The small letters are in black.

ABCDEFGHIJKLM NOPQRSTUVWXYZ

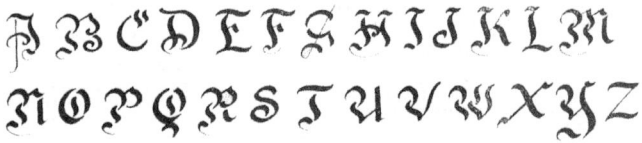

Plate 29—Upper case suitable for pen or small brush.

abcdefghijklmn opqrstuvwxyz &

Plate 30—Lower case suitable for pen or small brush.

This card may be used as the other one, to attract attention to some lines that will make suitable presents.

The fancy card may be used the same way. If desired, prices may be put on the cards the same as the $5 sample. But this can only be done where the articles are all one price, or where it is one article.

HOME-MAKING FURNITURE MEN.
By Albert Leon

We represent one of the most important branches of the retail business. We are home makers. We are engaged in enterprises that mean homes for the wage-earner, in which he can spend his leisure hours in ease and comfort.

Thirty years' experience in all the branches of the furniture and carpet business have convinced me further that the most serious evil of our business is the excessive competition which prevails generally throughout the trade. It is obvious that reasonable competition is desirable and a most necessary condition to keep us wide awake. Likewise, it is understood that excessive competition cannot always be avoided, yet I am free to confess my belief that the curse of the furniture business of to-day, is unnecessary excessive competition. We all know of numerous towns and cities where only three or four, or perhaps a half dozen dealers are located. The owners of these stores have in many instances, gone on year after year trying to outdo each other. Of course, if a new competitor comes into one's field and goes after business, it may be necessary to increase expense to hold the business.

I do not think, however, that it is ever necessary or desirable to meet competition with cutting prices advertising furniture without deposit, free premiums, free life insurance and trading stamps, and all the other baits which are thrown out to turn the tide of trade their way. This is the rock upon which so many of our furniture dealers shatter their hopes of success. How much better would competition be met with an argument for sound business methods, legitimate advertising, the kind that tells a true story in every line. In other words, not how cheap, not how little the terms, not free premiums, not free life insurance—but more salesmanship and less order taking.

WIPING OUT THE WHITE SPOTS.

If a customer should complain about white spots appearing on some furniture you sold him, you will find on investigation that the trouble was caused by the piece being exposed to either heat or water, and through no fault of the finish.

Instead of disputing about the cause of the damage, it is always better to adjust matters quietly to the satisfaction of the customer. At the same time you can make a very favorable impression on him by giving his family a practical demonstration on the care of furniture, by doing the job right in the home instead of taking the piece to your store.

Take alcohol and moisten the white spot, then rub over it boiled oil; continue these changes till the spot is entirely removed. On tops where there is a fine polished finish, it is better to apply the alcohol with a camel's-hair brush; when this is dry, follow up with the oil. After the oil has thoroughly hardened, polish in the usual way.

If properly done, this will ensure a complete renovation, and by doing the work right under the eyes of the customer, you are imparting useful information on the care of furniture and incidentally avoiding future complaints, by showing him in a practical way that while the trouble was caused by carelessness, it is really not a very serious matter, and that while such things should not be allowed to happen, they can be easily remedied.

Cash in on the possible business in seasonable lines before the other fellow has secured the cream of the trade.

There is nothing like advertising to keep the eyes of June brides focused on the retailer's stock.

A timely window card.

A Charming Wedding Gift $5

Following Up the Newlyweds for Business

Some suggestions for utilizing lists of married couples who have taken up housekeeping—The importance of thinking out plans and securing the co-operation of employes.

By W. L. EDMONDS

ALL the business arising out of June weddings does not cease when the bride is led to the altar. In fact, it is only the first stage in its possibilities. To obtain a share of the purchases that are made by the bride and groom before they are married, and by the friends in the shape of gifts, is, of course, of great importance. But what is also of great importance is the making of the new home-builders permanent customers.

No married couple start off so well equipped with house furnishings that when they have settled down in their new home they find it so equipped from top to bottom that there is no need of even further immediate purchasings. For many a day Mr. Newlywed will receive instructions from Mrs. Newlywed to purchase this and that article.

But even if there is no immediate necessity for purchasing house furnishings there are the possibilities of the future to consider.

That future implies a generation, and the possibilities of a generation no one can compute. But while no one can compute it everyone recognizes the greatness of its possibilities.

The importance, therefore, of the retailer forming a permanent business relationship with Mr. and Mrs. Newlywed cannot be gainsaid.

All these newlyweds no one dealer can link up to his store as permanent customers, or even as occasional customers. He can, however, make an effort to so link them up. And one thing is certain, he who exhibits the most enterprise and employs the most intelligent and systematic methods will have his efforts crowned with the greater success.

As in farming, so in business, those who sow well reap well. And yet there are business men, as well as farmers, the world over, who ascribe their want of success to the partiality of Providence instead of to their own inadequate methods of cultivation.

Of course, the first essential in order to hold business after it has tentatively been secured is service.

It is a comparatively easy matter, through good advertising, for the dealer to attract people to his store, but good advertising will not, in itself, hold customers. Service, and nothing but service, will do this.

It may, however, be presumed that every dealer who has the enterprise and energy to make a strong effort to secure the business of Mr. and Mrs. Newlywed, is in a position to render good service when he once gets them inside the front door of his store.

The purpose, therefore, of this article, is to discuss ways and means of getting them into his store and linking them up as permanent customers.

It is naturally presumed that every dealer who has made preparations for the June bride trade has a carefully compiled list of the persons immediately concerned. It may also be presumed that the list has, in most instances, been compiled upon the card index principle. Those who may not have done so are strongly advised to do so. The card index system is much more convenient than any other can possibly be.

As the list was originally compiled for prospective brides and bridegrooms, it naturally follows that it can no longer serve its original purpose after the couples enumerated become man and wife. But they can be made of great possible further use if, after the marriage service, the cards are transferred to what might be termed the housekeepers' list, particularly if, when compiling the original list of prospective brides and bridegrooms, the precaution has been taken to procure the location of the dwelling the young people will occupy after they have returned from their honeymoon.

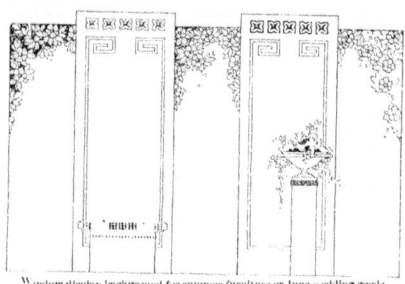

This being taken for granted, I would suggest that a nicely worded typewritten letter be sent to Mr. and Mrs. Newlywed tendering congratulations. It might also be pointed out that should Mrs. Newlywed have discovered that she needed any articles in order to complete the furnishing of her home they would be forwarded at once on receipt of a telephone message. A neatly printed booklet containing a list of articles as required in the home might also be enclosed. If this list is departmentalized, so much the better. But whether departmentalized or not, the list will nine times out of ten remind the new housewife of certain necessary articles which have been overlooked in the furnishing of the home. The selling value of the list would be enhanced if prices were also given.

A list printed in good clear type might also be hung in different parts of the store.

Toward the latter part of June the dealer will find it advantageous to set apart a day or so, or even a week, for a special sale for newlyweds.

During such special sale sections of the store should,

THE JUNE BRIDE

AFTER the wedding comes the problem of furnishing the young bride's home—what to buy? Where to buy? Her home should be furnished in such a manner that she will be proud of it. Proud to invite her friends to visit her, and at the same time, comfort and cost must be taken into consideration. The newly married couple will find that they are called upon to spend money for numerous articles that they had not taken into consideration, but articles that are necessary. In many cases they will find that the means they possess are entirely inadequate to furnish their home in the manner they would like. To such, our liberal credit system will prove a friend in need. You can *furnish your new home here on a small cash payment*. At no other store can you find furniture of better quality, a larger stock to select from or lower prices. We have furnished and made happy hundreds of "newly weds" at this store, and we feel confident that you will be more than satisfied with all your dealings with us. Remember, we are the largest credit furniture store in the west. Our prices are the lowest and our stock as large as any, and all of the stock is of one quality—*the best*. Your home will be comfortable and you will have no worry if you patronize us. Let us explain our system of selling and show you around the store.

$1.00 Per Week

The Home Furniture Co.
130 Seventh Avenue East
Between First Street East and Centre Street

A Western dealer's method of getting after the newlyweds

as far as possible, be fixed up to represent corresponding rooms in the home.

While the larger stores would naturally be in a position to carry this idea out in greater detail than the smaller ones, that should not deter any dealer from at least making an effort along this line. No matter how small the store may be, it will bring him some additional business.

In certain instances demonstrations might be made and refreshments served.

During the campaign the store windows will, of course, be dressed specially for the occasion. The advertising, too, will have a specific bearing on the campaign. And the advertising will have double potency if an invitation to visit the store during the period set apart for the special sale is sent out. This invitation, which should be sent out on the regulation card, should be mailed not only to the newlyweds and the prospective brides, but to a selected list of housewives in general, for interest in occasions of this kind lasts with women as long as life lasts.

Resourcefulness is one of the most important of factors in bringing to a successful issue special campaigns of this kind; in fact, campaigns of all kinds for that matter.

The resourceful man is a thinking man. It, therefore, naturally follows that the dealer who gives much thought to the subject under review will develop the most business-getting ideas.

No two men will develop ideas alike in every detail,

but all may at the same time be productive of good results. The doing of the same thing in a little different way is rather an evidence of originality than of imitation.

It does not follow that in carrying on a campaign for securing the business of prospective brides and newlyweds that the dealer should ignore the experiences of others. Experiences of others it is well to study, for he who does so develops his own ideas by the process.

Some, for example, have by experience learned that during a campaign such as that here suggested, the offer of a paid-up fire insurance policy to every newly married couple who purchase goods up to a certain amount has been productive of good results.

While if all dealers did this particular thing it would no longer possess uniqueness, which is the desideratum sought, yet the knowedge that one dealer had found it successful would naturally be an incentive to other resourceful dealers to set themselves to the task of working out one that would suit the requirements of their own business.

The possibility of attaining success in this or any other campaign will be increased if the dealer will take into his confidence every employe on his staff; for in the counsel of numbers there is wisdom. The promise of an honorarium for the best suggestion would probably act as a stimulus to ideas.

SOME GOOD RESOLUTIONS

Resolve:

That you will keep so busy boosting that you won't have time to knock.

That you will vote, talk, and work for a bigger, better, brighter town.

That you will help to make this a good town so the town can make good.

That you will increase the value of your property by improving its appearance.

LET US FURNISH YOUR HOME

Special Sale for Summer Brides.

The first home of the summer bride will be a happy one if it is furnished by us. Special terms are offered here for the youthful couple entering the bonds of matrimony.

Of course other people besides brides can take advantage of the terms and we want them to do so, but our main interest just now is to furnish the homes of "newly weds" in their first housekeeping venture. We sure can please.

Our terms is a simple system, the payments of which are so adjusted as to fit your income and to make home building a pleasure and not a burden.

We want to show you something smart in Davenports that are turned with one motion into a luxurious bed with cool springs and thick felt mattress. It adds a room to the house and you are always provided with the means to care for the unexpected guest. Really the "last word" in bed-davenports.

Moncton Carpet & Furniture Co., 562 566 Main St., Opposite Post Office

Eastern dealer's idea of inducing sales from summer brides

That you will say something good about this town every time you write a letter.

That you will invest your money here where you made it and where you can watch it.

That you will never buy a thing outside of town until the local merchants have been given a chance to sell it to you.

That you will keep your premises pinked up and your buildings repaired as a matter of both pride and profit.

Selling Methods in the Furniture Store

Some Experiences and Suggestions

NOVEL MOVING DOOR SIGN

HERE is a novel and inexpensive plan for calling attention to special lines of goods. For lack of a better name, we will call it the moving door sign, for it bobs up and down before the eyes of each customer as he or she comes into your store.

Measure off the distance on the frame above your door entrance until you find the point just above the centre of the glass panel in the door. Mark this point and then fasten two small screw eyes, one three inches to the left of this mark and one three inches to the right. You will

How the Burroughes Furniture Co., Toronto, are advertising their 3-room outfits.

then have the centre six inches of the glass panel measured off. Close the door, and directly under these two screw eyes, fasten two more as near the very top of the door as possible.

Sign Runs Up to Meet Customer's Eye

Take two pieces of fish line, or strong, fine string, long enough to reach from the top screw eye to a point four and one-half feet from the floor. Fasten to each one of the top screw eyes one of the pieces of string. After putting both strings through the eyes on the door which are just below the eyes to which they are fastened, place a sign card on the ends of the string. In placing the cards on the string, connect the strings so that they will continue to run parallel, six inches apart.

Now if you will open the door, you'll find that the sign will run up the glass panel to meet the eye of the customer as he opens the door to come in.

Can Place New Card in It Each Day

This is bound to attract much attention, and our suggestion would be to fasten a small frame here and slip in a new card every day, calling attention to some one article. If your signs are brief, they'll be read by most of the people, and if this is accomplished then you can call it good advertising.

Should the frame have a tendency to go up and down in an uncertain, zigzag manner, this may be overcome by two strings running through eyes, fastened to each outside end corner of the frame and secured at the top and bottom of the glass panel. This, you see, provides a track for the sign to run up and down on.

We think this idea will bring in extra business, but even if it does not, it will surely create favorable comment on your store and aggressive methods, and that's the best kind of advertising.

TURNS PICTURE UPSIDE DOWN.

"Excuse me, please, I know I am upside down, but my prices are right side up," writes E. G. Seaman, in charge of the Vancouver Furniture Co.'s store, in their ad. He runs his photo upside down in his copy, thus drawing attention to his story. He is thus doing a stunt similar to Tom Murray, of Chicago, who uses his bald pate as an advertising stunt.

WAITING ON MORE THAN ONE CUSTOMER.

Many of the large retail stores have the rule "Do not try to wait on two customers at the same time." This is all right where there is a big selling force. Suppose we laid down this rule in the medium-sized furniture store. How would it work? It might be all right for the beginner, but for the experienced salesman it might prove costly. For example, if a man comes in and asks for a wardrobe, you take him over to the display and he looks them over, at the same time telling you the kind he likes and what he expects to pay. While he is doing this, in comes a woman who wants two cheap kitchen chairs; but you stick to the man and the wardrobe. The woman is in a hurry to get home; so, not wishing to wait, she goes out, and $3.50 or so sails into the other fellow's pocket. While this is going on, in steps an elderly man, who stands back and waits a few minutes. You saw the woman go out of the store and you did not worry, but when the old man goes out, you call to him and ask if there was something he wanted. He replies, "No, never mind; I'll call again." Now, if the old gentleman wanted to buy a chamber suite for his daughter, it would certainly cost your concern a lot to sell that wardrobe. Could you have held all three customers? Most certainly you could. The woman knew what she wanted, and it would have been a matter of only one or two minutes to make the sale, and at the same time you could have easily kept the wardrobe man interested by telling him to look over the other wardrobes and examine their construction. When the old man stepped in you could

The Calgary Furniture Store before removing to their splendid new premises conducted a "Removal Sale." All the goods were bluesticketed, the top of each ticket being illustrated as above, showing the new store, with the prices in white figures.

have addressed him at once. Not that you should have entirely neglected the wardrobe man. He, too, might be thinking of buying other furniture later, and thus be just as valuable to you later as the other customer, but you could excuse yourself a minute, tell him to look at the way the better kind of chiffo-robes were arranged, and keep him interested. That's the golden rule, and the only rule you can lay down for the fair-sized furniture store. The salesman must, just as soon as the door is opened, be on the alert, and be prepared not only to sell, but be ready to entertain and make people feel at home, and, above all, keep them interested. As long as a customer is interested, and kept that way, your business will grow, and you will find that you can make and keep many friends—which is the great secret of the business of retailing.

A GOOD FURNITURE TICKET.

Customers are often lost by clerks having to take time to refer to catalogues. Salesmen can tell essential facts at a glance with the aid of a ticket which the Upholsterer describes as follows:

"A good scheme for keeping track of prices in furniture stock was introduced some months ago by Mr. Williams when he was buyer for Lord & Taylor. It consisted of a special form of price ticket to be used in connection with grouped suites. On one side of the ticket was contained all of the particulars referring to the entire suite, its number, description, and price, while on the reverse side was given a separate price for each individual piece. This enabled the salesman to tell the customer at once how much any part of the suite would be and avoided constant reference to catalogues, price lists, etc., before the customer, which is invariably disconcerting and lessens the possibility of a sale."

The new tag is exceeding simple, but is the result of years of experience. It should be widely used.

HAVE YOU MISSED MANY OF THESE SALES?

In a furniture store in Iowa four sales were lost in one day recently because the dealer did not have the goods the customers wanted, and was unable to locate the catalogues showing them while the parties were in the store. After the first "misfire," a salesman started to look up the catalogues, and finally found the exact goods required, illustrated and described in two of them, published by two different manufacturers. This was small satisfaction, however, as the people had left the store. Had these catalogues been kept in a handy place and a card index made showing who manufactured specific lines, the pictures could have been presented and the goods ordered. Some other dealer in that city, better prepared for emergencies of this kind, doubtless got one or more of those orders.

A dealer cannot keep all kinds of furniture. But the least he can do is to have the information about their origin at his fingers' ends. Some people have a vague, half-formed idea of what they want and go from store to store groping for something new—something stylish and inexpensive. Of course, the intelligent salesman will do everything possible to help them select from his present stock, but if he sees they are determined to go elsewhere, he ought to impress on his parties the fact that he can get them exactly what they want in a reasonable time. Then, if he has his catalogue file in proper shape, he can quickly show them just what they want and secure the order.

This sequence of events does not always follow that way, but it is admitted by experienced dealers that the inability to locate catalogues for the purpose of rescuing a sale, has lost much profitable business to dealers who can ill afford to lose it.

No matter how you do it, get a filing system for your catalogues, and in addition compile a list of sorts and kinds of furniture, and who makes them.—Northern Furniture.

SIMPLE AND FULL REFUND CHECK.

A representative of this paper while on a recent visit to Boston went into Chandler & Barber's store to make a small purchase and note any special method they have of facilitating business. The accompanying illustration gives a good idea of their refund check. Every clerk in the store has a number of these check forms on a file in his department. When a refund is to be made, all the entries are filled in by the clerk who made the sale. The salesman then signs his name, and the department manager's O. K. is necessary before payment is made. A distinctive color is used for the various store forms, the refund check being salmon color. A carbon duplicate can also be made with this check for verification purposes.

PROUD OF HIS FATHER

Little Tommy had a very smart father, and was arguing with a playmate about his abilities. "My daddy," he cried, "can do most anything. He keeps a furniture store, an' he's a notary public, an' he can pull teeth, an' he can mend chairs and wagons an' things, an' he can play the fiddle, an' he's a regular jackass at all trades."—Northern Furniture.

Beds and Bedding

PENNSYLVANIA ENACTS BEDDING LAW

The State of Pennsylvania, on the 1st of January last, put into force a new law regulating the making, remaking, and sale of mattresses; also prohibiting the use of insanitary and unhealthy materials therein. The Installment Dealers' Protective Assn. of Pennsylvania advocated the passage of the measure, which met with the approval of both the Senate and House of Representatives of that State.

However, since its enactment, the president of the Installment Dealers' Association, J. S. Lowengard, Harrisburg, Pa., in a letter to The Canadian Furniture World, says that he has found that there are several things which impose a hardship on the legitimate dealer. One of these is that there is no provision in the Act for cases where possibly a mattress is out one or two days and the customer wishes it exchanged. Under the new Act such a mattress would be classed as second-hand, and to dispose of such a mattress would entail inconvenience, not to say loss, to the dealer. All told, however, the Act is regarded as advanced legislation.

The wording of the Act is as follows:

The term "mattress," as used in this Act, shall be construed to mean any quilted pad, mattress pad, bunk, quilt, or cushion, stuffed or filled with wool, hair, or other soft material, except feathers, to be used on a couch or other bed for sleeping or reclining purposes.

No person or corporation, by himself or by his agents, servants, or employes, shall employ or use in the making, remaking, or renovating of any mattress,

(a) Any material of any kind that has been used in, or has formed a part of, any mattress used in or about any public or private hospital or institution for the treatment of persons suffering from disease, or for or about any person having any infectious or contagious disease.

(b) Any material known as 'shoddy," and made in whole or in part from old or worn clothing, carpets, or other fabric or material previously used, or any other fabric or material from which shoddy is constructed.

(c) Any material not otherwise prohibited by this Act, of which prior use has been made, unless the said material has been thoroughly process-approved by the Commissioner of Health of this Commonwealth.

No person or corporation, by himself or by his agents, servants, or employes, shall sell, offer to sell, deliver, or consign, or have in his possession with intent to sell, deliver or consign, any mattress made, remade or renovated in violation of subsection one of this section.

Descriptive Statements Upon Mattresses

No person or corporation, by himself or his agents, servants, or employes, shall, directly or indirectly, at wholesale or retail or otherwise, sell, offer for sale, deliver, or consign, or have in his possession with intent to sell, deliver or consign, any mattress that shall not have plainly and indelibly written or printed thereon or upon a muslin or linen tag securely sewed to the covering thereof, a statement in the English language setting forth the kind or kinds of materials used in filling the said mattress, and whether the same are in whole or in part new, or old or second-hand, and the name and address of the manufacturer thereof.

Whenever any kind of hair has been used in the making, remaking, or renovating of any mattress, the said statement shall designate and describe the kind, grade and quality of hair used by standard trade terms and not otherwise, and where two or more kinds, grades or qualities have been used, the statement shall also set forth that the material used is "Mixed Hair."

It shall be unlawful to use in the said statement concerning any mattress the word "felt," or word of like import, if there has been used in filling said mattress, any materials which are not felted and filled in layers, unless the said statement shall plainly set forth all the different materials so used.

Misleading Description Prohibited

It shall be unlawful to use in any way in the description in the said statement any misleading term or designation, or term or designation likely to mislead.

The statement required under section three of this Act shall be in the following form:

Materials Used in Filling:
....
....
Made by
Address

This article is made in compliance with the Act of Assembly of Pennsylvania, approved the   day of   1913.

Any person who shall remove, deface, alter, or in any manner attempt the same, or shall cause to be removed, defaced or altered, any mark or statement placed upon any mattress under the provisions of this Act, shall be guilty of a violation of this Act.

The unit for a separate and distinct offense in violation of this Act shall be each and every mattress made, remade, renovated, sold, offered for sale, delivered, consigned, or possessed with intent to sell, deliver, or consign, contrary to the provisions hereof.

Any person or corporation violating the provisions of this Act shall be guilty of misdemeanor, and upon conviction thereof, before a magistrate or justice of the peace, shall be punished by a fine of not less than twenty-five dollars and not more than fifty dollars for each offense.

Within sixty days after any process of sterilization and disinfection shall have been submitted to the Commissioner of Health of this Commonwealth, under sub-section 1 (c) of section two of this Act, the said commissioner shall approve or disapprove the same, and, if he disapproves, shall state his reasons therefor.

All places where mattresses are made, remade or renovated, or materials for mattresses prepared, or where mattresses are offered for sale, or are in the possession of any person or corporation with intent to sell, deliver or consign them, shall be subject to inspection by the Chief Factory Inspector, whose duty it shall be, in case he has reason to believe any person or corporation is violating this Act, to prosecute such person or corporation therefor.

Information and Enforcement by Individuals

Any individual who has reason to believe that this Act has been or is being violated, may present the relevant facts to the chief factory inspector or any of his deputies, in which case it shall be the duty of the chief factory inspector to make an investigation of such

BED-MAKING PLANT AT GALT.

Arrangements have been completed for the incorporation of the Maple Leaf Bedding Company, Limited, at Galt, Ont., with the following officers: President, J. C. Dietrich, Galt; vice-president, C. C. Osborne, Toronto; treasurer and managing director, Roy Torrance, Galt; secretary, G. Gordon Plaxton, Toronto; J. W. Daw, Hamilton, director.

The company will manufacture beds, springs and mattresses, and already have chosen a site. Of the $30,000 to be invested in the establishment of the company, $12,000 is asked as a loan from the town, to be paid back with interest in ten annual instalments, covering a period of ten years.

The whole proposition has been carefully considered by the Board of Trade and the result of their investigation is that they unqualifiedly stand behind it. A large delegation of the members of the board appeared before the council recently to support the request of the company.

Mr. Plaxton explained to the council that the company will take over the bed business formerly conducted by the Shurly-Dietrich Co. At least $30,000 would be needed to put the concern on a firm basis. Of this amount it was asked that the town contribute $12,000 as a loan on the usual terms. J. C. Dietrich would be the president of the company and would hold part of the stock. Mr. Plaxton stated who the other gentlemen to be associated with the company would be and said the loan would be secured for the town by a mortgage on the plant of the company.

Ald. Willard said he thought the proposition a good one. It was a business that would grow and expand. There was no doubt that it would be a going concern from the start, and be a good addition to the industries of the town.

Secretary J. H. Hancock, of the Board of Trade, suggested that the matter be taken up at once by the industrial committee and that it receive consideration with as little delay as possible.

Joseph Stauffer said the Board of Trade had gone into the proposition from every aspect, and it looked to be a clear cut business deal. The firm wanted to get started at once, so as to be ready for the fall trade. The granting of the loan would cost the town nothing and would be the means of adding another to the list of industries.

Reeve McIrvine stated his conviction that the industrial committee would give the matter favorable consideration.

Mayor Buchanan expressed his entire satisfaction with the proposition.

It is expected that the council will prepare the necessary by-law for submission to the people. General opinion is that the proposal will appeal to the ratepayers as one of sound business and one that will result advantageously to the town.

SAFETY FIRST IN BED MAKING

Conforming to the general rule of "safety first"—which has recently become almost a national slogan—the Ideal Bedding Co., Ltd., Toronto, has given the utmost regard to this up-to-date practice. Once one enters the factory it is noticeable what a number of precautions have been taken to protect the employes from danger of accidents. The white-painted truck aisle marks along the floor in all departments ensure at all times clear spaces between the stocks, machines, and supplies. The machines are all enclosed in themselves, or are placed in enclosed spaces, with all wheels, cogs, and other seemingly dangerous parts covered. Nor is this all, the company is aiming to eliminate all belting and shafting in the plant, and have nearly succeeded, many of the machines being run by individual motors.

In the basement, where are located the heavy presses, these machines and surroundings are painted white. In fact, white seems to be the "safety first" color of the plant. It has the added advantage of making the working places brighter, and this in the long run means a saving in the light bill.

The adoption of "safety first" has led to the introduction of improvements in other respects and in other divisions of work in the plant—improvements which have made the Ideal Bedding Co.'s factory a model industrial establishment.

BEDDING NOTES

The Stoddard Bedding Co., Montreal, has been registered.

A. S. Carr's mattress factory at Red Deer, Alta., was damaged to the extent of $1,200 by fire recently.

A license has been granted Geo. Gale & Sons, Ltd., to do business in Ontario under a capital of $40,000.

J. A. McLaughlin, recently a partner of McLaughlin & Scott, and a well-known furniture traveler, is now sales manager of the Fischmann Mattress Co., Toronto.

T. J. Moore is removing his cot, spring, bedstead, and stretcher manufacturing plant from Oliphant to Wiarton, where he contemplates employing twenty-five men.

It is expected that a new bedstead and mattress factory is soon to be erected in East Angus, Que., a lot of land having been purchased on the north side of the river for that purpose. When completed this factory will give employment to about thirty men.

A small fire occurred some days ago in the newly-completed building of the Quality Mattress Company, of Waterloo, Ont. The cause of the fire was from some flying molten metal lodging in cotton bales. The smoke was dense, and the firemen for a while had great difficulty in locating the actual blaze. No time will be lost, however, and orders will not be delayed, as all the employes were back at work the following morning.

STRATFORD GIVES POINTERS TO U. S.

M. J. Murphy, the head of the Murphy Chair Company, Detroit, Mich., one of the largest manufacturers of chairs in the United States, was a recent visitor at Stratford, the guest of H. W. Strudley, of the Imperial Rattan Co. He paid Stratford a visit to get some pointers on rattan work, he having heard that the Imperial was turning out superior designs.

It may seem strange for Americans to come to Canada for pointers in manufacturing, but the incident shows what advances furniture making has made in the Dominion in recent years in producing the goods that warrant such enquiry. Mr. Murphy expressed himself as pleased with what he saw, and, rattan work being one of his lines, will doubtless carry back with him some good ideas.

---

facts as on his own initiative, and, if he is of opinion that the Act has been or is being violated, to prosecute the person or corporation guilty thereof. Any individual may institute proceedings to enforce this Act and to punish violations of its provisions.

Floor Coverings

GETTING RUGS TO THE FRONT
By Bessie L. Putnam

We see the rug growing in popularity every year. And yet there are many homes in which it should be given a place where it has not yet gained entrance. This may be due, in the home of moderate means—and this is the home of the masses— through lack of finances to give the floors a suitable finish. Some of these homes, if the owners but realized the fact, have the basis for an excellent hardwood finish which, with proper treatment, would be much preferable to fancy veneers. Just waken the general public up to the fact that they can treat their own floors, and the demand for the rug will grow. Whether you realize it or not, as a rule the luke-warm reception of rugs is largely due in any community to the unwillingness to employ the professional. Once get the common people to understand that they can prepare their floors themselves and the proposition is received in an entirely different manner.

Keep your eyes open for possibilities. The problems are different in every community, and, to a certain extent, in every home. It may be that your neighbor has a hardwood floor which would respond beautifully to some finish you keep in stock. Just make the suggestion. Tell him how to prepare it properly. What if you are giving away a bit of professional knowledge. It will be profitable in the end. After he has done the finishing in an approved style he will be so enthusiastic over results that his neighbors will take the matter up and do likewise.

Or if paints, or stains, or matting are preferable, advise carefully and conscientiously. Work up a reputation as a specialist on this very subject—how to treat old floors. It is a large one, and highly important. Hunt about until you find the best finishings to solve the various problems of your own vicinity and then give your knowledge and you will find a growing sale for the finishing materials and the rugs.—Bessie L. Putnam.

HARPING ON HARMONY

Some salesmen in the drapery and carpet departments strongly feature "harmonious effects," so-called. If a customer calls for certain designs for colorings, these salesmen must know, at once, the general decorative effects of the room. If it is a Queene Anne room, or mission den, just what the wall decorations are, and the color schemes. Then follows a long and strong argument on "harmony," blending of colors and effects. Every detail of drapery, floor covering and furniture must harmonize. This is well enough for some customers, but it is a wise salesman who will not overdo the "advice" end of the business. If customers seem to have "clashing" tastes, if you see they are insistent on purchasing what has struck their eye, a simple word of advice, a casual display of some more harmonious combinations may be safely made, and often you can guide the purchaser in the right channels. But we cannot all be artistic, folks are privileged to have opinions of their own, so do not harp on "harmony" to the extent that you carry your point, but have forever after a dissatisfied patron.

BUYING A RUG.

Study of the figures used for most rugs, whether the expensive imported kind from the hand looms of the East or the frankly American manufactured rugs and carpets really shows very little that is essentially beautiful. The most expensive rugs from abroad are often very lovely, especially in colors. But even in these the designs are often irrelevant and awkward with little trace of real charm. One lately shopped for a rug of moderate price. One wanted blue, though this is not a very satisfactory color for the floor, it is said, as it shows dust and foot marks more than reds and browns and greens do. The search was very long before the shopper found a rug that in pattern and color was really pleasing. It would seem as if here were an excellent field for new enterprise, in making inexpensive floor coverings that shall be really artistic. It appears that the cheaper grades of rugs and carpets are the uglier. One pays not for the material or the expense of making but for the happy thought that produced an attractive design and a good color. But it would seem as if it is just as easy to make a pretty design as an ugly one and as if soft and warm colors should cost no more to produce than the cold, harsh colors. Perhaps the best solution of floor covering is a plain surface. This to be sure shows every mark and bit of dust with tell-tale frankness; but an everyday sortie of the carpet sweeper should keep even such a rug tidy. In the search just mentioned the rug finally chosen had a plain dull blue body with a border where a pale blue figure of indefinite outline and dull tint lay between borders of deeper blue. This was chosen in preference to a rug where figures in pale blues ran all over the surface. It was decided that one would tire of the figured surface sooner, especially as there was something jarring between these two shades of blue. The usual idea for a rug seems to be a figure so mixed that it resembles a careful hash. If one wishes to use furniture of various periods of purchase and consequent different colors the indefinite mixed carpet or rug is useful. But in all forms of stuffs, whether chair covers or table scarfs or wall paper or whatever it be, the simple, plain figure that is easily deciphered is for many people more restful than the confused mixtures. The covering of the ground, with its uniform green, is a very good example of how to do it. There was once a lady who said that she distrusted her own taste, so whenever she had a rug to buy she chose plain green because that was like nature. The excuse for the old-time flowered carpet used to be that the flowers grow on the ground; but with the exception perhaps of some daisied fields one does not often walk on flowers. A conventional design as simple and beautiful as some of the ancient tiles seen in the wonderful glaze of the Moors in the Alhambra is most desirable for floors.—The Furniture Journal.

Whatever I have tried to do in my life, I have tried with all my heart to do well. What I have devoted myself to, I have devoted myself to completely. Never to put my hand to anything on which I could not throw my whole self, and never affected depreciation of my work, whatever it was, I find now to have been golden rules.—Charles Dickens.

THE SELLING OF STOVES.

One of the first things which the prospective buyer of a heater asks is, "How large a room will it heat?" Your figures are for the largest possible space when run at its extreme capacity. If you quote these dimensions with no application you are bound to be censured. This is not a practical application of the terms of the question and the average patron, finding that it falls short of the desirable, will feel that there has been misrepresentation in reality if not in words. Tell plainly just what it will do in an emergency; but also explain that economy in both fuel and lasting qualities of the stove demands one of a larger size, which does not require crowding save in the most extreme cold weather.

A superabundance of nickel trimmings looks nicely in the shop, but it does not take the busy housewife long to find out that there can be too much even of a good thing. If ornament is the main thing, you may safely emphasize the fact that there are elaborate trimmings. But if the stove is a general utility one, impress the fact that while it is neat and tasteful in design and trimmings, there is not the elaborate work which requires so much rubbing and polishing to keep in order.

Those not familiar with hard coal will appreciate helpful hints in the care of such a stove. Safety from asphyxiation demands that the mica be kept free from leaks. If the draughts are all opened for a few minutes after filling the magazine the gas will form freely and then pass up the chimney, thus saving danger of trouble later. At other times the large stove with dampers closed or nearly closed will ensure a more even temperature and requires less fuel. If the hard coal fire becomes low, a very little shaking and opening up will permit the fire to re-kindle itself, when a new supply of coal on the already dying coals would be but to extinguish it entirely. Cheap coal is dear at any price; that of good quality lasts longer, and contains fewer impurities of all sorts.—Ex.

ESSENTIALS IN STOVE SELLING.
Location.
Adequate display.
Proper line.
Efficient sales organization.
Advertising plan.
Demonstration.
Enthusiastic knitting together of all.

SELLING STOVES IN THE SPRING.

It has been wisely said that the stove trade comes to the dealer in the fall, but that he must go after it at other seasons. The stove should not be classed, however, as a one season article, for the trade can be made steady all the year round if suitable methods are adopted for the different seasons. It is a general habit for people to buy stoves when the cold weather is approaching or is upon them as they do not give the matter attention until the actual necessity for buying arises. It is this "putting off" attitude that makes the fall trade in stoves invariably brisk at the expense of the other seasons.

A buyer of stoves is more likely to receive better attention from the dealer during the slack periods and will have more time to make a careful selection. In many cases this purchase can be looked after during the spring or winter seasons of the year. It is always within the power of the hardware and stove dealer to stir up new business during the winter season, although such requires energetic handling. There are always with us those who for economic reasons can be induced to buy outside the regular seasons.

ELORA FURNITURE CO. INCORPORATED.

Letters patent have been issued by the Ontario Government constituting Joseph E. Walser, Ferdinand Daub, Otto C. Schmidt, Peter Daub, and Sylvain B. Jeanneret, all of Elora, Ont., shareholders in the Elora Furniture Co., Limited, to take over as a going concern the partnership business at present being carried on by the Elora Furniture Company. The capital of the company is set at $40,000.

Mr. Jeanneret, one of the four partners in the original firm, and who has acted as financial manager, is said to be retiring and his place is being taken by D. H. Bell, of Bell Bros.

This and above rocker are two new items made by J. P. Albrough & Co., Ingersoll

Why Furniture Men Should Take Stock and How to Do It

Every dealer who wishes to keep in touch with all particulars of his business should take an annual inventory—Hints and suggestions on how to do it with accuracy and least interference with business

Editor's Foreword.—The benefits to be had from the subject of stock taking to a business man are so great that there should be a place for it on the calendar of every dealer who is aiming to be successful. It unearths many particulars of his business that are of the utmost importance, and could not be otherwise ascertained.

We advise dealers to read carefully the following hints on inventory taking. If there are any points in the work on which any reader is not quite clear, we invite him to write in. We believe stock taking is of so much value that we want to help the dealer in any way possible in carrying it out.

* * *

EVERY merchant, no matter how large or small his business may be, should take stock at least once a year. If he can arrange to do so oftener, so much the better, but at least one inventory should be taken annually. Those dealers who make a practice of taking stock regularly are generally loud in their praise of its value in bringing to light those particulars of the business which are essential in order to ascertain the progress that is being made. In every well-conducted establishment, the dealer always has a method of finding out from time to time if the progress being made is satisfactory.

No Room for Guesswork in Business

The writer has heard certain dealers say that they know well enough how their business is getting on, without going to all the trouble of stock-taking—for there is indeed considerable work connected with taking stock properly and accurately, but it must be remembered that the best things in this life are secured only by some effort. The man who thinks he knows well enough how he is getting on—who "guesses" that he is making satisfactory headway, is likely to find out in the end that he has guessed wrong. In these days of increasing expenses and decreasing margins of profit, there is no room for guesswork in business. Stock-taking allows the dealer to gauge his actual progress in the matter of profits with an accuracy that would in no other way be possible.

The Value of Stock-Taking

Here is a thought worth deep consideration—the majority of real successful men make a practice of regular stock-taking. It is not meant to imply that stock-taking will make a dealer successful, but it has a tendency in that direction, because it shows him that important thing—how much money he is or is not making. If satisfactory headway is not being made, the merchant, knowing this, will at once begin an examination into the cause, and aim to remove it. If he does not take stock, he will not be aware of the fact that profits are not what they should be, and therefore he continues on, all unconscious that he is not sailing in the direction of Port Success.

A Factor in Fire Insurance

The matter of fire insurance is another incentive for taking an inventory. Every dealer knows full well the necessity of being fully insured, and of course, stock-taking shows him whether the stock on hand is well enough insured. In addition, the rules of fire insurance companies make it necessary, in case of fire, for the dealer to establish the fact that he had the amount of stock in his store, that he asks remuneration for. The yearly stock-taking records prove a material help in quickly and accurately proving loss.

Stock-taking is the business man's X-ray, enabling him to examine closely into the important details of his business, and to judge if profits are what they should be.

CARE IN TAKING INVENTORY

A common blunder in inventory-taking is that of giving the departments of stock, respectively, to those persons who are in charge of them, or who much be expected from daily habit to know most about the particular lines. This often leads in inaccurate reports.

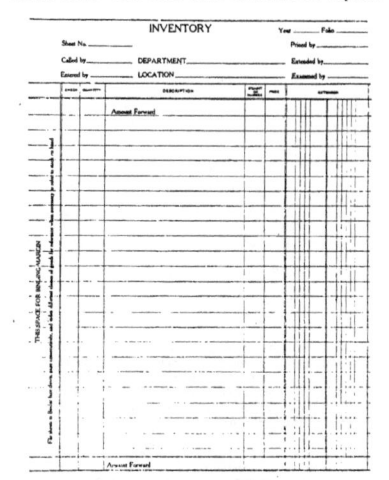

Form of loose leaf inventory sheet on which goods are listed in taking stock.

Many such stock-takers rely upon their knowledge of a line, its quantity, condition, etc., instead of investigating in detail. A surer plan is to deliberately give each department to a squad of men whose very lack of acquaintance with the quantities of stock will compel them to inspect and tabulate it with care. Each such squad should have a captain, or leader, who may be held responsible for the results. Too many inventories are merely expert guesses as to quantity and condition. An organized search is necessary for reliable results.

> Unless the best of ideas are backed by persistent effort the best of them will run to seed.

The Salesman

SALARY OR COMMISSION FOR THE SALESMAN
By William Talbott Childs

Vitally important to the retail dealer is the basis upon which he pays his house salesmen, whether salary or commission. Is it best for the dealer to pay his house salesmen—

1st.—A regular, stipulated weekly or monthly salary?

or

2nd.—An agreed percentage on the actual gross sales and no regular, stipulated weekly or monthly salary?

or

3rd.—A combination of the two—that is, a regular, stipulated weekly or monthly salary, and in addition an agreed percentage on all sales exceeding a stated amount?

That there is much to say on all phases of the question is apparent. There will be exponents of each of the three systems, and the dealer who has for years been pursuing one system will not change to another instanter; he thinks his present system is the best for his own individual interest, and he will tell you that it does not concern him what systems are practised by his competitors. And yet there is a proviso to this last statement, which if not expressed, is nevertheless implied, and that is, provided the systems of his competitors do not interfere with his individual profits. When he begins to feel the effects of his competitors' systems, he will sit up and take notice. No sensible man, however self-satisfied he may be, will refuse to heed the call for change or reform when he becomes convinced that such change or reform will bring him ultimate gain.

An advocate of the system of paying the house salesman a regular, stipulated weekly or monthly salary argued that such method enables him to know for a certainty what his total expense for selling goods will be; that if he agrees to pay a salesman a salary of $20 per week, for instance, he knows that he must count upon a certain fixed expense of $1,040 a year for selling goods, and that this certain knowledge, together with the certain knowledge of other fixed charges, such as rental, cost, insurance, drayage, breakage and depreciation, serves his individual purposes far better than the knowledge that he must pay his salesman on the basis of a certain percentage on the total amount such salesman sells during the year.

Another retailer said: "The commission basis puts too much power in the hands of the salesman, for a good salesman always can personally control more or less trade, and when he leaves one house for another, he can take with him much business which otherwise would have remained with his previous employer."

Another argued in favor of the straight salary basis, claiming that the commission basis tempted the salesman to force sales, than which there was nothing more detrimental to a retail dealer. A woman, to illustrate, might be persuaded into buying a piece of furniture by the glibness of a salesman, and she might actually be made to believe, at the time of the purchasing, that she needed the article; but when she gets home and fully considers the cost, she resents the influence the salesman had over her in persuading her to make the purchase. The result is that she keeps away from that salesman in the future, and consequently the dealer who employs him pays the penalty.

A salesman himself, one who has worked on all three basis—straight salary, straight commission and a combination of salary and commission—preferred the straight commission basis.

One salesman who worked on the combination plan argued thus: "I prefer to work at this place because in addition to the general agreeableness of my employers, I think their plan of paying is the best—at least for me, and perhaps for the employers as well. In addition to paying their salesmen fair salaries, according to the individual ability of the salesmen—and I do not believe in the principle of paying every member of a profession the same salary simply because he is a member of that profession, and regardless of that profession, and of individual ability—they offer an incentive to each salesman, in the way of a commission, at the end of each year, being a certain percentage on all sales he has made during the year aggregating a previously stated amount. Now, the salesman who has his heart in his work will do his level best at all times, to be sure; but a salesman is made of flesh and blood, just as is his employers, and he is as anxious to increase their profits. Therefore, when the salesman has some incentive for doing a little more than his level best, he will make extra, unusual exertions to excel his past records. An extra commission at the end of the year of 1 per cent. on all sales, if the aggregate is $20,000 or over, for instance, or an extra commission at the end of the year of a certain percentage on all sales exceeding $20,000, means in the first case $200 bonus, and in the latter case perhaps as much for the salesman who

Two recent productions
of the
Geo. McLagan, Co.,
Stratford

succeeds—and the right sort of hustling salesman who knows his business will get that bonus of $200 if his health and strength hold out, unless the bottom falls out of business."

"There is a little couplet which runs something like this—

"'Some men paint hope
As an angel in flowing clothes,
But 'tis not so,
'Tis the hay
That's tied o'er a donkey's nose
To make him go.'

"Salesmen need something to make them go, just as donkeys," concluded the salesman; "and there is decidedly more to be had out of a donkey or a salesman by placing the incentive in front rather than the whip in the rear."

"Speaking of the commission basis," said an old salesman, "I used to work with one of the largest retail houses in the East, and the proprietors had every item of expense figured to the dollar. The cost of a piece of merchandise was first considered; then the expense of hauling, unpacking, fixing up, interest on the money invested, selling, delivering to the customer, and, in fact, every item from the time of purchase from the manufacturer until it was delivered to and paid for by the customer. All these items being considered the desired profit was added, and the article was marked to sell at a certain figure.

"And there was a scheme of disposing of articles that remained unduly long in the store," continued the old salesman. "After an article was displayed for six months a red tag would be placed on it, which meant that the salesman who sold the article would be allowed an extra commission of 5 per cent. If the article did not go at the end of another period of six months a yellow tag was placed on it, which meant that an additional commission of 5 per cent. would be allowed the salesman who sold it. Of course, with 10 per cent. commission on an article, or even with an extra commission of 5 per cent., extra efforts were made by all the salesmen to sell the article, with the result that the house was never overstocked."

One more salesman interviewed advocated the commission basis, saying: "I prefer all commission, and I hope I may never have to return to the salary basis, although before I changed from salary to commission I was quite doubtful. When on a salary basis I never gave any thought to the business, after leaving the store in the evening, and yet I always wished I had the opportunity to make some extra money in my spare time. Now whenever I learn of friends, acquaintances or strangers who contemplate purchasing furniture, or even when I call on interested parties in my own spare time, after hours, and there is very good reason for doing so, for, while I sell my employers' good, I derive compensation for such work in my commissions."

The Andrew Malcolm Furniture Co., Kincardine, will supply the furnishings of the new wing at the Banff Springs Hotel, Banff, Alta.; refurnish the Vancouver Hotel, Vancouver, and the new wing of the Alexandria Hotel, Winnipeg.

The Canadian Baby Car Company, Limited, has been incorporated under the Dominion Companies Act to manufacture automobiles, motorcycles, aeroplanes, etc., with a capital stock of $300,000. The company's headquarters will be at Montreal.

SPLENDID FURNITURE CATALOGUE

"Twins" is the short but comprehensive title of the new catalogue just published by the Chesley Furniture Co., Limited, Chesley, Ont., descriptive of their twin pedestal extension dining tables and other table lines. The catalogue gives a very fair idea of the advances which have been made during the past year in the extension line, the illustrations showing in detail the construction of this patented pedestal. All the twin tables are made duostyle in construction, permitting the insertion of several fillers without dividing the base. The table is always perfect and secure, whether extended or closed. It has no locks and no unfinished surfaces when extended. The tables come in a variety of designs and finishes.

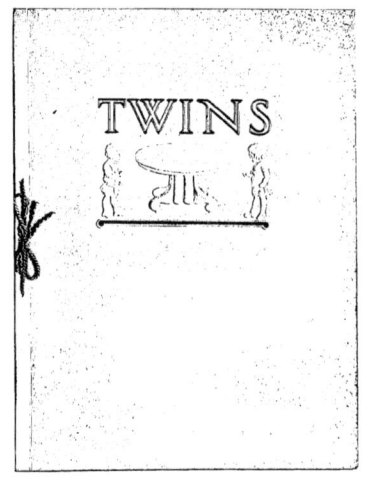

Library, club, bedroom, kitchen, folding, fall-leaf, centre, and other tables; jardinieres, hall trees, and mirrors are also described in the catalogue, which is well worth having.

DEVELOP YOUR SALESMANSHIP

THE clerk who can sell the most goods is the one who is the most valuable to his employer in most instances. It is on his ability to make sales that his wages are generally set. Therefore, the need of every man behind the counter giving study and effort to the increasing of his daily sales.

It is wonderful, too, what the clerk can do in the way of developing his salesmanship ability when he makes a real earnest effort to do so. Demand for goods is by no means a set quantity, and the clerk who would be a real salesman must first realize this. Then he must give study to the ways of increasing demand for goods by tactful and intelligent suggestions to customers whenever the opportunity is presented. He must, in addition, seize the opportunities for making these suggestions. That is the way to increase his sales.

Meeting of the Dominion Board of the R. M. A.

A special meeting of the Board was held in Toronto at which various questions of general interest were dealt with.

A special meeting of the Dominion Board of the Retail Merchants' Association of Canada was held at the head office of the association, Toronto, on Tuesday and Wednesday, April 28 and 29. President B. W. Ziemann, of Preston, Ont., presided at the various sessions. At the morning session on Tuesday an address of welcome was delivered to the delegates by J. C. Van Camp, president of the Toronto branch.

Making Preparations for Extended Campaign.

The principal business of the meeting was to prepare plans for an extended campaign, so as to take in all the other provinces that are not yet organized under the Dominion Board. The desire of the members of the board is to have every province united, so that a uniform expression of opinion can be secured from the retail merchants of all the various provinces of Canada.

Those in Attendance.

The Dominion Board meeting is a delegate body, with representatives from all the organized provinces. Those present were as follows:
B. W. Ziemann, Preston, Ont.; A. M. Patterson, Brockville, Ont.; G. A. Maybee, Moose Jaw, Sask.; J. G. Watson, Montreal; J. A. Beaudry, Montreal; J. D. O. Picard, Quebec; O. H. Piche, Drummondville, Que.; J. A. Bucknall, Calgary, Alta.; E. M. Trowern, Toronto; A. Weseloh, Berlin, Ont.; R. D. Cameron, Lucknow, Ont.; J. C. Van Camp, E. C. Matthews, and F. C. Higgins, of Toronto.

Resolutions Considered by the Board.

Among the various resolutions, the following were considered by the board:

"That the convention consider the advisability of securing inter-provincial judgment that will be operative in every province, so as to facilitate the collection of small debts."

"That this board consider the advisability of having the words 'or voting contest' added to the Criminal Code for the prevention of 'trading stamps,' after the words 'premium ticket.'"

Considering an "Across Canada" Excursion.

"That this convention consider the advisability of inaugurating a retail merchants' excursion, starting at Halifax and going through Canada to the Pacific Coast, some time during the coming summer."

"That whereas farmers' co-operative movements are being advocated by provincial Governments, and they are gradually being put into operation, that this meeting take some steps to form a policy to deal with the same."

"That this convention formulate some policy to protect our members against account collecting companies and persons who are promoting credit rating companies, and which are not based on fair business principles."

"The Provincial Board of Saskatchewan desires this convention to consider if it would not assist our association work to extend the time for the holding of provincial conventions from the present date to not later than June 1st."

On Wednesday evening a banquet was tendered to the officers of the Dominion Board at McConkey's, when many interesting and eloquent addresses were delivered. J. A. Bucknall, secretary of the Alberta Retail Merchants' Association, and G. A. Maybee, president of the Saskatchewan Association, were among those who spoke, and told of the work being done by these two new provincial associations in the West. J. A. Beaudry, of Montreal, spoke on behalf of the Quebec Association.

Eloquent Addresses on Canada.

J. C. Van Camp, president of the Toronto branch, emphasized the outstanding and attractive features of Canada in an elaborate manner in his opening address. Those present certainly must have gone up with even greater pride in their country because W. B. Ziemann, of Preston, and R. D. Cameron, of Lucknow, followed with eloquent addresses on the extensiveness, growth, and advantages of our great Dominion. F. C. Higgins, of Toronto, treasurer of the Ontario Board, proposed the toast to "Our Guests."

1,500 Members in Saskatchewan.

Mr. Maybee, of Moose Jaw, in responding, after a humorous introduction, told of what the association in Saskatchewan, which now has 1,500 members, is doing. He felt sure that nothing would be put on the statute books of the province of a detrimental character if the merchants can prevent it. "We are well satisfied with results," he said, "and you can depend on the Western provinces to stand behind the association." He pointed out that one of the great values of organization was the establishment of a great brotherhood between the merchants of the country.

Alberta Has Heard the Call.

"The merchants of Alberta are keen on the work of the association," stated J. A. Bucknall, of Calgary. "The West has heard the call, and are ready to back you to a finish in any work you may undertake." The Alberta association is just holding its first annual convention. It is represented in 102 towns in Alberta.

Among those who spoke during the evening were Jno. Caslor, of Toronto, treasurer of the Ontario Retail Hardware and Stove Dealers' Association, and F. M. Tobin, secretary of the Canadian Hardware Manufacturers' Exhibition Association.

BUNGALOW FURNITURE.

Under this suggestive title, Baetz Bros. & Co., Berlin, Ont., have just published a neat catalogue illustrative and descriptive of their new "bungalow" line. Somewhat similar in style to mission furniture, the bungalow line in that it has that style's strength, it differs in being lighter in make, appearance, and color. It comes in all kinds of articles and sets, upholstered and plain—tables, chairs, davenports, and fancy pieces. Cane paneling has a prominent part in its make-up, and various shades of grey are the more popular colorings. An idea of the line is given in the catalogue, which itself is printed to harmonize in color with the line it describes. The catalogue is worth writing for.

Ontario Provincial Board of R. M. A. Meets

At the close of the special meeting of the Dominion Board of the Retail Merchants' Association, the executive officers of the Ontario Provincial Board held a meeting to receive the report from the Finance Committee, which was appointed at the last Ontario provincial convention, and to take action upon its recommendations.

The report from the finance committee—which consists of Messrs. J. A. McCrea, chairman, Guelph; J. C. Van Camp and T. Bartrem, of Toronto—was received and adopted, and the secretary was requested to have the same printed and sent to the officers of the various branches throughout the province.

Organizing Field Secretary for Each District.

They took immediate action on the proposal to divide Ontario into districts and appoint an organizing field secretary in each district, who will keep in constant touch with all the merchants in each district, and thus overcome a difficulty which the association has had to encounter for some time, which was that as soon as an organization was formed it was left without anyone whose duty it was to see that the work taken up by the local association was continued. These organizers will be engaged on salary and paid out of the general fund of the Ontario Provincial Board.

All the officers were present, as follows: B. W. Ziemann, president, Preston. Ont.; A. M. Patterson, first vice-president, Brockville, Ont.; R. D. Cameron, second vice-president, Lucknow, Ont.; F. C. Higgins, treasurer, Toronto, Ont.; E. M. Trowern, secretary, 21 Richmond street west, Toronto.

The officers will meet each month, so that great progress should be noted in the work of the association by the end of the year.

Amalgamation of Grocers.

At the close of the meeting the officers and executive committee of the Ontario Retail Grocers' Association waited upon the board and announced that they had decided to unite with them and become members of the Grocers' Section of the association.

A special committee was appointed to complete arrangements whereby the officers elected at the last convention of the Ontario Retail Grocers' Association would become the officers of the Grocers' Section for the province for the coming year.

What's What in Furniture Industry

HELPING TO BUILD BERLIN'S FURNITURE INDUSTRY

Berlin's proud position as a Canadian centre of the important furniture industry is in some large measure due to the D. Hibner Furniture Co. Founded over thirty years ago and in business continuously from that time to this, it has gained and maintained a reputation that is enviable, and a business career that is remarkable for its great success and generally acknowledged prestige in its line. The company occupies a large four-storey building, modern in all its appointments, and the last word in mechanical perfection, adjoining the G. T. R. tracks.

The eighty employes of the concern are all expert furniture men, whose ability to turn out work that is a credit to their employers and to Berlin is everywhere recognized, while the high-grade furniture of all kinds made by them is considered the best examples of the cabinetmaker's art. These elegant and useful pieces may be found in thousands of homes all over Canada, wherever good furniture is appreciated; they are good to look at, strongly made, and reasonably priced—three great factors that have brought success to the company. A half dozen travelers are employed to market the product, covering the entire Dominion, and the large force of men in the factory is kept working the whole year to meet the demands of the Canadian public for good furniture. Dealers everywhere handle the product, and many of the customers of the Hibner Company have been placing their orders with that concern for many years, for they have learned the value of dealing with a reliable and responsible firm, whose word is as good as its bond.

The officers of this company are all well known for their civic activities, while the guiding genius of the Hibner factory has been Mayor of Berlin, chairman of the parks commission, and has been a member of the city council for over fifteen years. To him is due the responsibility for the purchase of the beautiful Victoria Park, that splendid recreation ground for young and old alike. He is a valued member of the board of trade.

GLOBE FURNITURE BY-LAW PASSED.

The ratepayers of Waterloo, Ont., decided to loan the Globe Furniture Company the sum of $50,000 for twenty years and to grant it exemption from taxation for ten years, on condition that a large addition, costing $125,000, is erected to the present plant. The vote was 510 to 175 in favor of the by-law, a majority of 53 over the necessary two-thirds of the vote polled.

The contracts for the erection of the big addition to the plant have been awarded as follows: Excavation and foundation, to Paul Bergmann; carpenter work to Henry J. Jacobi; and brick and mason work to Ellis Bros., all of Waterloo.

Work has been commenced on the addition to the present factory at the north end of the building, and will be pushed rapidly. It is expected that this part of the addition will be completed by the middle of July. Plans for the separate building to be erected at the west end of the present factory are being drawn, and specifications called for. This building will be ready for operations by fall.

ENLARGING GALT FURNITURE BUSINESS.

W. F. Allen and D. Y. Ray have purchased the furniture and undertaking business at Galt of J. Anderson. Both the new men are Galtonians and well known in business. Mr. Allen was connected with T. Little & Son's furniture and undertaking business for the past eleven years.

Plans to entirely remodel the Anderson building, making it one of the finest furniture stores in the province, are being prepared. The store front will be altered so as to provide two large display windows with a large centre entrance. The partition which now divides the block into two stores will be removed and both stores devoted to show rooms. A staircase to the second floor will lead from the centre of the main floor.

The new firm has purchased an up-to-date undertaking outfit funeral car, call buggy, furniture wagon, horse, etc., and an entire new stock of furniture is now on order.

Knobs of News

H. V. Bernier, Montreal, has registered his furniture business.

Durocher & Chatillon, furniture dealers, Montreal, have dissolved partnership.

Gernthal & Gordon have opened a furniture and hardware store at Winnipeg.

Bisson & Cote, furniture dealers, Outremont, Montreal, have dissolved partnership.

Richard Winter has opened an upholstering and furniture repair shop at Seaforth.

The furniture stock of the estate of W. H. Davis, at Crystal City, Man., has been sold to Robert Gorrell.

The reed workers of the American Furniture Co., Walkerton, Ont., held their second annual ball last month.

David E. Turner, of the Globe Furniture Co., Limited, Waterloo, was in Toronto a few days recently on business.

Rapid progress is being made with the new building being finished for a furniture store for J. R. Hicks, at Smithfield, Ont.

J. D. Corning, formerly of the D. A. Smith Co., Vancouver, is opening with a line of furniture in South Fort George, B. C.

The erection of a furniture store at Sarnia is being considered by Baldwin, Robinson, Ltd., 402 Talbot St., St. Thomas, at an estimated cost of $20,000.

The Bedell housefurnishing store, on Yonge Street, Toronto, is to be closed. The company are conducting a clearing sale, offering all goods at a low figure for cash only.

R. H. Pillar has recently taken charge of the furniture department of W. R. King Co., of Penticton, B.C. He was for several years with the Standard Furniture Co., Ltd., of Vancouver.

The Standard Furniture Co., Ltd., Nelson, B.C., state that business is steady. Last year their turnover slightly exceeded 1912; and this year it is in excess of last year, the trade being steady.

Dalgleish & Harding, Kelowna, B.C., have installed a house and office furniture department. The opening orders were placed with the following firms: Preston Furniture Co., Preston; Krug Bros., Chesley; Crown Furniture Co., Preston; Bell Furniture Co., Southampton; John C. Mundell & Co., Elora; Ham & Knot (Springs), Brantford; Durham Furniture Co., Durham; Lippert Furniture Co., Berlin. The firm also have a store at Kamloops.

An industry opened in Peterboro recently is the Peterboro Novelty Co., which has taken over the cabinet making factory at the rear of Belleghem's furniture store, on Hunter Street. The company will manufacture everything in the line of cabinet work, making a specialty of moulders' bellows and kitchen tables. The factory has been thoroughly equipped and is to be under the management of W. A. Weese. B. Weese is the business manager.

A petition of the Peterboro retail furniture dealers, asking that a by-law be passed, requiring all retail furniture stores to be closed each day at 7 p.m., Saturdays and days preceding holidays excepted, was sanctioned by the city council recently. The petitioners were: E. B. Clegg and Co., J. D. Craig, McFadden and Son, Empire Furniture Co., A. Comstock, Cressman Co., Ltd., D. Belleghem, Lane and Eano, R. Begley, W. T. Butcher, Zacks Bros., R. C. Braund.

James Young, manager of the furniture department of the Hudson Bay Co., at Macleod, Alta., wants to receive catalogues from our advertisers, as they intend greatly to increase the size of the furniture department. At present they carry only kitchen utensils, etc.

The T. F. Harrison Co., Ltd., Kingston, has received an Ontario charter to carry on the business of wholesale and retail merchants and dealers in furniture and furnishings of all kinds and descriptions, including carpets, curtains, linoleum, draperies, rugs, crockery, china, earthenware, woodenware, stoves, and tinware; to carry on the business of upholsterers, manufacturers, and repairers of all of the aforesaid articles; to carry on the business of storing any or all of the aforesaid articles; to carry on the business of beating, cleaning, repairing, and delivering carpets, mattings, rugs, and articles of a similar description. The capital is set at $50,000.

PRIZE WINDOW—Winner of 1st prize during Edmonton's Horse Show. Blowey-Henry were highly complimented by the judges on the simplicity and good taste exhibited in the arrangement of the display. The color scheme was blue and gold (official colors of the horse show), and it made a very effective window, though the striking contrast is not shown in the illustration.

FURNITURE GATHERING AT CLINTON.

Wes. Walker, of Hoover & Walker, Guelph and Clinton, entertained a number of his friends in those two towns in his home at Clinton recently. A number of furniture travelers were there also, among them Walter Bateman, W. White, Thos. Armstrong, Mat Brown, James Dore, W. Dalby, and Otto Thies.

From Guelph came J. B. Hoover, Ald. Gemmell, Joe Henry, Geo. Richardson, Art Watson, Ed. Stewart, L.

Mr. Walker's home at Clinton.

Watts, Norman McDonald, Rollie Hoover, Jas. Hillis, R. Weatherstone, G. T. R. district freight agent, and J. Knight, G. T. R. Guelph agent. The Clintonites were represented by Mayor Fred Jackson, Jno. Ransford, Don McPherson, Dr. Shaw, B. J. Gibbings, C. Whitmore, Nels Bell, Gal. Holliway, H. B. Combe, Jos. Ford, W. Stevenson, and Jos. Sterling.

The catering was attended to by Harry Bartlett, of Clinton, and he surpassed himself in providing the good things. The dinner brought on speeches, and the

Mr. Walker, his wife, and children.

speeches songs, the travelers taking a foremost part in the latter, with the exception of Tommy Armstrong, who insisted on speaking in favor of woman suffrage. The Mayor was obliged to call Tommy to order and tell him such radical expressions were not allowed to be mentioned in Clinton. Cards filled in a goodly part of the evening, and the party returned to their homes enthusiastic about Mr. Walker's hospitality. A finishing touch was put on the proceedings by the arrival of a case of liquid veneer.

PUNCTUALITY ESSENTIAL TO SUCCESS IN LIFE.

By J. Wilheim, Salesman, T. Eaton Co., Toronto.

Punctuality is one of the distinguishing characteristics, not only of a successful salesperson, but of any person, no matter with what business activities he may be interested or connected. It is one of the marks of personal reliability and worth. Any salesman or business person who is looking for success must either possess it or cultivate it, as it is a virtue of vital importance to his influence and usefulness. President Lincoln once said: "Punctuality is the mother of confidence." It is one of the marked degrees by which a person inspires confidence with his fellowmen in business circles, no matter what relation he may hold. One of the Presidents of the United States found that his private secretary one morning came into his office ten minutes late, when the President told him that he would either have to get a new watch or he would get a new secretary. The application was clear to the secretary, and thereafter was always at his desk a few minutes ahead of time. The writer of this article can speak with authority in this respect, as he has been identified as a salesman for the last ten years in the largest retail store in Canada, and he has, with few exceptions, always been at his place for business from twenty to forty minutes before the opening of the store. If punctuality and promptness has become a principle as well as a practice with salespersons, it will prove an incentive for the day's work, and instead of descending in their relation with a firm, they, on the contrary, are always in the ascend.

Habitual tardiness, or just to arrive at the last minute the door closes, tends to make one's personality and influence as a moth-eaten garment. It savors of carelessness. Business houses all over the world to-day are becoming more and more intolerant to the disposition of carelessness and tardiness. Whatever good qualities and qualifications a person may have or possess, if he is careless in meeting his engagements, and habitually indifferent as to his promises, and in carrying out his appointments, in society, in business, or any other interest or activity with which he may be connected, he reduces his effectiveness far below par, and seriously disqualifies himself for any important position. One who has so little interest in his work as not to apply the principle of punctuality in its performance, is unworthy of the lowest station in business life. Many failures are in a large part due to a want of punctuality and of earnest endeavor. They forget that the man who succeeds in this world is the man who knows how to use time, and that punctuality is a valuable asset in the career of any individual.

Fire damaged Laing & Mackie's furniture store, North Bay, Ont., recently, as also did fire in Mrs. Lake's stove and furniture store at Brantford.

NEW MANAGER FOR SASKATOON STORE

Robt. McJannett has been appointed manager and buyer for the furniture department of the R. F. Macmillan store at Saskatoon. Mr. McJannett is an experienced furniture man, both in the West and East. Up to two years ago he was a member of the furniture sales staff of Murray-Kay, Ltd., Toronto. The past two years he has been with the Cope, Fletcher Furniture Co., Saskatoon. Now he is going up the ladder another step.

NEW FURNITURE STORE AT ST. KITTS.

A new store of large dimensions and displaying a valuable stock of furniture, rugs, curtains, draperies, etc., was opened on May 1 at 41 Ontario street, St. Catharines, by Veale Bros., who have the advantage of long experience in the various branches of the trade, having spent many years with the Toronto Carpet Mfg., T. Eaton Co., Robert Simpson Co., Toronto, and the Thos. C. Watkins, Ltd., of Hamilton. They have brought together a stock that bespeaks their acquaintanceship with the best manufacturers.

Among the stock is a limited number of real Turkish and Persian pieces. A strong feature will be made of Persian and Kermin Shah patterns in Wilton quality, as well as power loom tufted squares made from the very finest wools and worsteds. There are also the cheaper makes of heavy Brussels and Axminsters, seven, eight and nine-wire tapestry squares.

A full line of draperies of all kinds is shown, including curtains, yardage goods, silk and linen shadow cloths, velours, German twills, cretonnes, chintz, window shades, etc.

In the furniture department, a strong attraction is being made in den goods and in Circassian walnut suites, with gold thread coverings, Jacobin, colonial, and Sheraton suites of rich finish. The eye is also drawn to the newest in bedroom suites, including white enamel, mahogany, kyonyx, and all grades of iron, brass, and wood beds. The dining room makes are in the various up-to-date finishes and designs.

FURNITURE TRADE NEWS

Durocher & Chatillon, furniture dealers, Montreal, have dissolved partnership.

A. E. Hollings, picture frame dealer at Maple Creek, Sask., is succeeded in business by W. Woods.

The Hudson's Bay Co. at Kamloops now have three furniture showrooms, and are showing an extensive line of high-class furniture.

A $100,000 woodworking factory will be built at Orillia, Ont., by J. R. Eaton & Sons, Ltd. A loan of $50,000 is asked of the town.

The Blowey-Henry Co., of Edmonton, who are developing a large wholesale trade in addition to their retail business, state they find trade particularly active in the wholesale department, and they are looking forward to a good turnover this year. The firm represents the Canada Furniture Manufacturers, Ltd., in Northern Alberta.

J. Wilder, of J. Wilder & Sons, furniture dealers, 239 Queen Street West, Toronto, is retiring from that firm after twenty years in business. His sons will continue the business under the name of Wilder Furniture Co., and in larger premises.

TWIN PEDESTAL EXTENSION TABLE

The patented twin pedestal extension table, made by The Chesley Furniture Co., Ltd., Chesley, Ont., has a number of features which commend the table both as an attractive piece of furniture and as a useful one as well. The pedestals are crossbanded veneer; the chamfers on the corners are likewise, and so are the feet. Altogether it is a strictly high-class production. The twin pedestal is not a novelty, though its construction is on novel lines; it is a dining table which stands in a class by itself.

> Ask for what you want. We are likely to have it; but if we haven't we'll get it.

Suggestion for a window or interior card.

TURNING SAWDUST INTO FUSEL OIL

A large English company has recently commenced the commercially successful production of acetone and fusel oil from sawdust by a simple process of fermentation. From these two products isoprene can be derived, which latter can be changed into rubber, merely by allowing it to lie in contact with a small quantity of the metal sodium. This synthetical rubber vulcanizes readily and compares favorably with the natural product in resilience, durability and price.

Acetone is used in the manufacture of cordite, and fusel oil is used in the manufacture of artificial leather cloth. Previously it was chiefly obtained as a by-product in the manufacture of whisky, brandy and vodka, but by this new process it can now be extracted much more cheaply, making possible a large profit. It is calculated that these by-products of sawdust are worth almost $400 a ton. As it takes only ten tons of sawdust to yield a ton of these valuable constituents, the resultant profit is obvious.

In Europe, with its densely populated regions contiguous to the forests, the elimination of wood-waste is an economic essentiality, and hence methods have been evolved which, in some cases, utilize even the leaves and roots of trees. While this is not essential in America at present, it is desirable to reduce the waste which takes place in the different processes of transforming the standing timber into finished product, which amounts to something like fifty per cent. of the total volume of the tree. To this end, the Canadian Government is establishing a fully equipped Wood Products Laboratory at McGill University in charge of Mr. A. G. McIntyre, B.A., B.Sc., under whose direction experiments will be conducted to discover new uses for common Canadian trees and for the enormous quantities of sawdust and other forms of waste wood which now represent a money loss to the country of millions of dollars annually.

SAWDUST AS A FIRE EXTINGUISHER

A considerable number of experiments were conducted by the inspection department of the Associated Factory Mutual Fire Insurance Companies, Boston, in extinguishing fires in lacquer and gasoline in tanks with sawdust. The results, which were satisfactory, showed that sawdust is an excellent extinguishing agent for certain volatile liquids, especially those of a viscous nature, and were presented in a paper read at the recent annual meeting of the American Society of Mechanical Engineers by Edward A. Barrier, Boston, who is identified with the inspection department.

The efficiency of the sawdust for this purpose, he explained, is undoubtedly due to its blanketing action in floating for a time upon the surface of the liquid and excluding the oxygen of the air. For that reason its efficiency is greater on viscous liquids than on thin ones, as it floats more readily on the former than on the latter. The sawdust itself is not easily ignited, but if it does it burns without flame and the temperature of the burning embers is not sufficiently high to reignite the liquid.

In making tests, the liquids were placed in three tanks of different sizes, all having the same depth, 16 in. The sawdust was applied with a snow shovel having a large blade and in every case the fires were extinguished readily, especially in the two smaller tanks, which were about the same size as those ordinarily employed for lacquer in manufacturing establishments. It was found that the character of the sawdust, whether from soft or hard wood, was not important and the amount of moisture contained in it was not a factor also, so that the drying out of sawdust when kept in manufacturing establishments for a time would not affect the efficiency.

It was also found that adding of bicarbonate of soda increased the efficiency of the sawdust by shortening the length of time and decreasing the amount of material required to extinguish the fires. A further advantage of the addition of bicarbonate of soda is that it decreases the possible danger resulting from the presence of sawdust in manufacturing plants, as it would be difficult, if not, impossible, to ignite the mixture by a carelessly thrown match or any other ready source of ignition. While the efficiency of the sawdust is greatest on viscous liquids, such as lacquers, heavy oils, japan, waxes, etc., in the tests referred to, fires were extinguished in gasoline contained in the smallest of the three tanks, measuring 12 x 30 ins., and also when spread upon the ground. In the larger tanks it was found that the sawdust or the mixture of sawdust and bicarbonate did not work as well, as the sawdust sunk before the entire surface could be covered and the exposed liquid reignited.

SERVICEABLE BRACKET OF ANGLE IRONS

The angle iron bracket shown in the accompanying illustration is in one of the departments of the Lufkin Rule Co., Windsor, and supports the motor which operates the machinery in that department. It is of very

Motor bracket built of angle iron attached to wall, thus removing any vibration of the floor.

rigid construction and rests on the foundation wall, being fastened to the side wall of the factory. It thus takes up no valuable space, but most important, it eliminates any chance of vibration from the floors. This is essential for the fine and accurate work necessary in the manufacture and graduation of rules.

Similar brackets are also used in other departments. In one instance a small air compressor is set up on one of these angle iron brackets, near the second floor in one department, and interferes in no way with the operation of the department, nor does it occupy any valuable space.

SHELLACS

If you are in the market for first-class Shellac we believe it would be to your advantage to get in touch with us.

HIGH GRADE VARNISHES
FILLERS and GRAINING INKS

THE AULT & WIBORG CO. OF CANADA, LIMITED

MONTREAL   TORONTO   WINNIPEG

ROBERTSON SOCKET HEAD
Wood Screws

See That Square Hole

Pat. Feb. 2, 1909

THIS IS A REAL WOOD SCREW

It is driven by a simple square bit, and is the only one of its type on the market.

Driver fits snugly into the square hole and positively cannot slip and cut the fingers, or disfigure costly furniture or woodwork. It is driven with less exertion. No ragged slots after driving. Saves time, labor, money and material. We make the drivers in all suitable styles.

Drivers sent free with first order. Write for catalogue and prices.

P. L. Robertson Mfg. Co., Limited

We also manufacture Wire Nails, Rivets, Wire and Washers

MILTON :: ONTARIO

The gathering of the clans

"On to Toronto"

YOU have doubtless noted with gratification the great movement for honesty and square dealing which is revolutionizing American and Canadian business methods. Our goods, our salesmanship and our advertising are being cleansed and vitalized by the spirit of truth and sincerity.

As a result we see a growing public confidence in manufactured products and their advertising—a confidence which if preserved and fostered, will decrease our costs, increase our profits, and become a business asset of incalculable value.

Foremost in the fight which has brought about this revolution stand the Associated Advertising Clubs of America, whose emblem is shown above. If you are a business man, interested in the manufacture, distribution, or selling of commodities of any nature, you should attend the Tenth Annual Convention of the A. A. C. of A. at

TORONTO
JUNE 21-25, 1914

At this Convention you will hear the inspiring story of the manner in which these tremendous reforms are being effected. More than this, you will hear the problems of distribution, merchandising, salesmanship, and advertising discussed by able and successful business men, in a series of open meetings.

These meetings will cover the questions of chief interest to the 10,000 business men comprising the 140 clubs of the A. A. C. of A.—your own problems included.

EDWARD MOTT WOOLLEY, the famous writer on business topics, has written a booklet entitled "The Story of Toronto." This booklet describes in a forceful, intensely interesting manner, the wonderful work the A. A. C. of A. are doing for clean advertising and square business methods, and the significance and importance of the Toronto Convention. This booklet will be sent free to all business men asking for it on their business stationery—together with detailed facts as to the convention programme and rates for accommodations.

Address Convention Bureau
ASSOCIATED ADVERTISING CLUBS OF AMERICA
TORONTO   CANADA

BUYER'S DIRECTORY

When writing to advertisers kindly mention the Canadian Furniture World and the Undertaker

ARTS AND CRAFTS FURNITURE
Geo. McLagan Furniture Co., Stratford.
John C. Mundell & Co., Elora.

ASBESTOS TABLE COVERS.
Canadian H. W. Johns-Manville Co., Toronto.

BABY CARRIAGES.
Gendron Mfg. Co., Toronto.

AWNINGS
Stamco, Limited, Saskatoon, Sask.

BENT WOOD FURNITURE.
John C. Mundell & Co., Elora.
J. & J. Kohn, Toronto (W. Craig).

BOOKCASES.
Knechtel Furniture Co., Hanover.
Globe Wernicke Co., Stratford.
Geo. McLagan Furniture Co., Stratford.
Meaford Mfg. Co., Meaford, Ont.

BUFFETS
Bell Furniture Co., Southampton, Ontario.
Knechtel Furniture Co., Hanover.
Geo. McLagan Furniture Co., Stratford.
Meaford Mfg. Co., Meaford, Ont.
Peppler Bros., Hanover.
Stratford Chair Co., Stratford.
Victoriaville Furniture Co., Victoriaville, Que.

BEDS (Brass and Iron).
Canada Beds, Ltd., Chesley.
Ideal Bedding Co., Toronto.
Geo. Gale & Son, Waterville Que.
Ives Modern Bedstead Co., Cornwall Ont.
Ontario Spring Bed & Mattress Co., London, Ont.
Standard Bedstead Co., Victoriaville, Que.
Stamco, Limited, Saskatoon, Sask.
Stratford Bed Co., Stratford, Ont.
S. Weisglass, Ltd., Montreal, Que.

BEDS (Modern Wood).
Elora Furniture Co., Elora.
Knechtel Furniture Co., Hanover.

BED SPRINGS.
Colleran Spring Mattress Co., Toronto.
Knechtel Furniture Co., Hanover.
Frame and Hay Fence Co., Stratford.
Gold Medal Furniture Co., Toronto
Leggett & Platt Spring Bed Co., Windsor.
Ideal Bedding Co., Toronto.
Ontario Spring Bed & Mattress Co., London, Ont.
Stamco, Limited, Saskatoon, Sask.
S. Weisglass, Ltd., Montreal, Que.

BED ROOM CHAIRS.
Baetz Bros., Berlin.
Bell Furniture Co., Southampton, Ontario.
Elmira Furniture Co., Elmira, Ont.
Lippert Furniture Co., Berlin.

BEDROOM ROCKERS
Lippert Furniture Co., Berlin, Ont.

BED ROOM SUITES.
Bell Furniture Co., Southampton, Ontario.
Knechtel Furniture Co., Hanover
Meaford Mfg. Co., Meaford.
Victoriaville Furniture Co., Victoriaville, Que.

BUNGALOW CHAIRS & SUITES
Baetz Bros. & Co., Berlin, Ont.

CARD AND DEN TABLES.
Geo. McLagan Furniture Co., Stratford.
John C. Mundell & Co., Elora, Ont.

CARPET RACKS
Steel Furnishing Co., New Glasgow, N. S.

CAMP FURNITURE.
Stratford Mfg. Co., Stratford.
Ideal Bedding Co., Toronto.

CEDAR BOXES
D. L. Shafer, St. Thomas, Ont.

CELLARETTES.
John C. Mundell & Co., Elora, Ont.

CHAIRS AND ROCKERS.
Bell Furniture Co., Southampton.
J. P. Albrough & Co., Ingersoll.
Baetz Bros., Berlin.
Knechtel Furniture Co., Hanover.
John C. Mundell & Co., Elora.

Stratford Chair Co., Stratford.
Waterloo Furniture Co., Waterloo.
Canadian Rattan Chair Co., Victoriaville.
Gold Medal Furniture Co., Toronto.
Elmira Furniture Co, Elmira, Ont.
Imperial Furniture Co., Toronto.
Lippert Furniture Co., Berlin.
Victoriaville Chair Mfg. Co., Victoriaville.

CHESTERFIELDS.
Imperial Furniture Co., Toronto.

CHIFFONIERS.
Bell Furniture Co., Southampton.
Knechtel Furniture Co., Hanover.
Meaford Mfg. Co., Meaford, Ont.
Stratford Chair Co., Stratford.
Victoriaville Furniture Co., Victoriaville, Que.

CHILDRENS' SULKIES
Jennings Co., St. Thomas

CHINA CABINETS.
Bell Furniture Co., Southampton, Ontario
Peppler Bros., Hanover.
Knechtel Furniture Co., Hanover.
Geo. McLagan Furniture Co., Stratford.
Meaford Mfg. Co., Meaford, Ont.

CLOCK CASES
Elmira Interior Woodwork Co., Elmira, Ont.

COMFORTERS.
Toronto Feather & Down Co., Toronto.
Stamco, Limited, Saskatoon, Sask.

COTS
Ideal Bedding Co., Toronto.
Ontario Spring Bed and Mattress Co., London.

COSTUMIERS
Elmira Interior Woodwork Co., Elmira, Ont.

COUCHES.
J. P. Albrough & Co., Ingersoll.
Ellis Furniture Co., Ingersoll.
Gold Medal Furniture Co., Toronto.
Kindel Bed Co., Toronto.
Imperial Furniture Co., Toronto.
John C. Mundell & Co., Elora, Ont.
Montreal Upholstering Co., Montreal.
Steel Furnishing Co., New Glasgow, N. S.
S. Weisglass, Ltd., Montreal, Que.

COUCHES (Sliding).
Ideal Bedding Co., Toronto.
Farquharson-Gifford Co., Stratford.
Ontario Spring Bed & Mattress Co., London, Ont.
Stamco, Limited, Saskatoon, Sask.
Gold Medal Furniture Co., Toronto.

CRIBS (Brass and Iron)
Ideal Bedding Co., Toronto.
Ontario Spring Bed & Mattress Co., London, Ont.
Stamco, Limited, Saskatoon, Sask.
S. Weisglass, Ltd., Montreal, Que.

CUSHIONS.
Stamco, Limited, Saskatoon, Sask.

DAVENPORT BEDS.
Farquharson-Gifford Co., Stratford.
Kindel Bed Co., Toronto.
Lippert Furniture Co., Berlin, Ont.
Montreal Upholstering Co., Montreal, Que.
Imperial Rattan Co., Stratford.
John C. Mundell & Co., Elora.

DAVENPORT FRAMES
Elmira Interior Woodwork Co., Elmira, Ont.

DEN FURNITURE
Elmira Furniture Co, Elmira, Ont.
Farquharson-Gifford Co., Stratford.
John C. Mundell & Co., Elora, Ont.

DIVANETTES.
Lippert Furniture Co., Berlin.

DESKS.
Bell Furniture Co., Southampton.
Elmira Interior Woodwork Co., Elmira.

Knechtel Furniture Co., Hanover.
Geo. McLagan Furniture Co., Stratford.
John C. Mundell & Co., Elora.
Stratford Desk Co., Stratford, Ont.

DINING-ROOM FURNITURE
Crown Furniture Co., Preston.
Farquharson-Gifford Co., Stratford.
Lippert Furniture Co., Berlin, Ont.

DINING SUITES.
Bell Furniture Co., Southampton.
Knechtel Furniture Co., Hanover.
Geo. McLagan Furniture Co., Stratford.
John C. Mundell & Co., Elora.
Peppler Bros., Hanover.
Stratford Chair Co., Stratford.

DINERS
Lippert Furniture Co., Berlin, Ont.

DINNER WAGONS.
Geo. McLagan Furniture Co., Stratford.
Peppler Bros., Hanover.

DRESSERS.
Bell Furniture Co., Southampton.
Knechtel Furniture Co., Hanover.
Stratford Chair Co., Stratford.
Victoriaville Furniture Co., Victoriaville, Que.
Meaford Mfg. Co., Meaford, Ont.

EXTENSION TABLES.
Bell Furniture Co., Southampton.
Peppler Bros., Hanover.
Berlin Table Mfg. Co., Berlin.
Meaford Mfg. Co., Meaford, Ont.

FILING DEVICES.
Elmira Interior Woodwork Co., Elmira.
Globe Wernicke Co., Stratford.
Knechtel Furniture Co., Hanover.
Geo. McLagan Furniture Co., Stratford

FILING CABINETS
Globe Wernicke Co., Stratford, Ont.

FOLDING CHAIRS.
Stratford Mfg. Co., Stratford.
Ideal Bedding Co., Toronto.

FOLDING TABLES.
Hourd & Co., London.
Stratford Mfg. Co., Stratford

FOOTSTOOLS
Elmira Furniture Co, Elmira, Ont.

GRASS FURNITURE (Chinese)
Jennings Co., St. Thomas

HALL RACKS
Lippert Furniture Co., Berlin, Ont.

HALL SEATS AND MIRRORS.
Geo. McLagan Furniture Co., Stratford.
Lippert Furniture Co., Berlin, Ont.
Meaford Mfg. Co., Meaford, Ont.

HALL TREES.
Geo. McLagan Furniture Co., Stratford

HAMMOCKS
Dominion Hammock Mfg. Co., Dunnville, Ont.

HAMMO-COUCHES.
Ideal Bedding Co., Toronto.

INVALID CHAIRS.
Gendron Mfg. Co., Toledo, Ohio.
Victoriaville Chair Mfg. Co., Victoriaville, Que.

IRONING BOARDS AND DRYERS.
Stratford Mfg. Co., Stratford.

JARDINIERE STANDS.
Elmira Furniture Co, Elmira, Ont.
Elora Furniture Co., Elora.
Geo. McLagan Furniture Co., Stratford
Meaford Mfg. Co., Meaford, Ont.

KITCHEN CABINETS.
H. E. Furniture Co., Milverton.
Nagrella Mfg. Co., Hamilton.
Knechtel Kitchen Cabinet Co., Ltd., Hanover, Ont.

KITCHEN TABLES.
Knechtel Furniture Co., Hanover.
Victoriaville Furniture Co., Victoriaville.

LADIES' DESKS
Meaford Mfg. Co., Meaford, Ont.

LAWN SEATS AND SWINGS.
Stratford Mfg. Co., Stratford.

LIBRARY TABLES.
Bell Furniture Co., Southampton.
Peppler Bros., Hanover.
Elmira Interior Woodwork Co., Elmira, Ont.
Geo. McLagan Furniture Co., Stratford.
Meaford Mfg. Co., Meaford, Ont.
John C. Mundell & Co., Elora.

LIVING-ROOM FURNITURE
Lippert Furniture Co., Berlin, Ont.

LOUNGES
J. P. Albrough & Co., Ingersoll.

LUXURY CHAIRS.
Lippert Furniture Co., Berlin.

MAGAZINE RACKS AND STANDS.
Geo. McLagan Furniture Co., Stratford.

MATTRESSES.
Berlin Bedding Co., Toronto.
Canada Mattress Co., Victoriaville, Que.
Gold Medal Furniture Co., Toronto.
McKellar Bedding Co., Fort William, Ont.
Ontario Spring Bed & Mattress Co., London, Ont.
Stamco, Limited, Saskatoon, Sask.
Standard Bedding Co., Toronto.
Antiseptic Bedding Co., Toronto.
Ideal Bedding Co., Toronto.
Fischman Mattress Co., Toronto.

MANTELS—Wood, Tile
Elmira Interior Woodwork Co., Elmira, Ont.

MANTELS—Electric
Elmira Interior Woodwork Co., Elmira, Ont.

MEDICINE CABINETS.
Meaford Mfg. Co., Meaford, Ont.

MORRIS CHAIRS.
Ellis Furniture Co., Ingersoll.
Imperial Rattan Co., Stratford.
Knechtel Furniture Co., Hanover.
Lippert Furniture Co., Berlin, Ont.
John C. Mundell & Co., Elora.
Waterloo Furniture Co., Waterloo.

MUSIC CABINETS.
Geo. McLagan Furniture Co., Stratford

ODD CHAIRS
Lippert Furniture Co., Berlin, Ont.

OFFICE CHAIRS.
Bell Furniture Co., Southampton.
Elmira Furniture Co, Elmira, Ont.
Knechtel Furniture Co., Hanover.
H. Krug Furniture Co., Berlin.
Stratford Chair Co., Stratford.
J. & J. Kohn, Toronto (W. Craig).
John C. Mundell & Co., Elora, Ont.

OFFICE TABLES
Stratford Desk Co., Stratford, Ont.

PARK SEATS.
Stratford Mfg. Co., Stratford.

PARLOR CHAIRS and ROCKERS
Ellis Furniture Co., Ingersoll.
Elmira Interior Woodwork Co., Elmira.
John C. Mundell & Co., Elora, Ont.
Waterloo Furniture Co., Waterloo.

PARLOR FRAMES
Elmira Interior Woodwork Co., Elmira, Ont.

PARLOR SUITES.
Elmira Interior Woodwork Co., Elmira.
Ellis Furniture Co., Ingersoll.
Knechtel Furniture Co., Hanover.
Waterloo Furniture Co., Waterloo.
Gold Medal Furniture Co., Toronto.
Lippert Furniture Co., Berlin, Ont.

PARLOR TABLES.
Geo. McLagan Furniture Co., Stratford.
Meaford Mfg. Co., Meaford, Ont.
Elora Furniture Co., Elora.
Elmira Furniture Co., Elmira, Ont.
Knechtel Furniture Co., Hanover.
Peppler Bros., Hanover.

PEDESTALS
Lippert Furniture Co., Berlin, Ont.
Geo. McLagan Furniture Co., Stratford.
Peppler Bros., Hanover.

PILLOWS.
Ontario Spring Bed & Mattress Co., London, Ont.
Stamco, Limited, Saskatoon, Sask.
Toronto Feather & Down Co., Toronto.
Ideal Bedding Co., Toronto.

PILLOW SHAM HOLDERS.
Tarbox Mfg. Co., Toronto.

RATTAN FURNITURE.
Imperial Rattan Co., Stratford.
Canadian Rattan Chair Co., Victoriaville, Que.
Gendron Mfg. Co., Toronto.

RECLINING CHAIRS.
Ellis Furniture Co., Ingersoll.
Knechtel Furniture Co., Hanover.
Lippert Furniture Co., Berlin, Ont.
John C. Mundell & Co., Elora.

RUG RACKS
Steel Furnishing Co., New Glasgow, N. S.

SECTIONAL BOOKCASES
Knechtel Furniture Co., Hanover.
Globe Wernicke Co., Stratford.

MATTHEWS' QUALITY SERVING TRAYS

MOULDINGS, PICTURE FRAMES, MIRRORS, GLASS, MATBOARD, PICTURE BACKING

Ask for our new catalogue just out

for wedding presents. The June weddings are near at hand and all the ladies want Trays. All our Trays have glass set in with waterproof cement and are non leakable and have felt bottoms. All our latest Trays are fixed with simple screw fastener allowing the back to be readily removed for replacing with owner's own fancy work, chintz or tapestry. Mail us an order for immediate shipment and we will send you a sample dozen assorted kinds and sizes that will not average more than $12.00 per doz. net and will retail at a good profit.

Matthews Bros. Ltd., 788 Dundas St. Toronto

Canadian School of Embalming
Instruction in Practical Embalming and Funeral Directing
PREPARATION FOR EXAMINATIONS
ENTER AT ANY TIME
R. U. STONE, Principal — 32 Carlton Street, Toronto

For Sale / Wanted

TERMS FOR INSERTION
25 Cents per line, one insertion
Four lines once for $1.00, three times for $2.00.
Cash must accompany the order
No accounts booked.
MINIMUM 50 CENTS

SCHOOL FURNITURE.
Bell Furniture Co., Southampton.
SIDEBOARDS.
Knechtel Furniture Co., Hanover.
Meaford Mfg. Co., Meaford, Ont.
Stratford Chair Co., Stratford.
STORE FRONTS
Kawneer Mfg. Co., Toronto.
TABLES.
Berlin Table Mfg. Co., Berlin, Ont.
Bell Furniture Co., Southampton, Ontario.
Elora Furniture Co., Elora.
Knechtel Furniture Co., Hanover.
John C. Mundell & Co., Elora.
Orillia Furniture Co., Orillia.
Peppler Bros., Hanover.
Stratford Chair Co., Stratford.
Victoriaville Furniture Co., Victoriaville, Que.
TABOURETTES.
Elora Furniture Co., Elora.
Kensington Furniture Co., Goderich.
TAPESTRY CURTAINS
Dominion Hammock Mfg. Co., Dunnville, Ont.
TELEPHONE STANDS.
John C. Mundell & Co., Elora, Ont.
TYPEWRITER DESKS.
Elmira Interior Woodwork Co., Elmira.
Stratford Desk Co., Stratford, Ont.
UPHOLSTERERS' SUPPLIES
Ellis Furniture Co., Ingersoll.
Gold Medal Furniture Co., Toronto.
UPHOLSTERED FURNITURE
Bartz Bros., Berlin.
Ellis Furniture Co., Ingersoll.
Farquharson-Gifford Co., Stratford, Ont.
Imperial Rattan Co., Stratford.
Imperial Furniture Co., Toronto.
John C. Mundell & Co., Elora.
Knechtel Furniture Co., Hanover.
Waterloo Furniture Co., Waterloo.
Gold Medal Furniture Co., Toronto.
Quality Furniture Makers, Welland.
A. J. Scafe & Co., Berlin.
VACUUM CLEANERS.
Onward Mfg. Co., Berlin.
VERANDAH FURNITURE.
Imperial Rattan Co., Stratford.
Stratford Mfg. Co., Stratford.
WARDROBES.
Knechtel Furniture Co., Hanover.
Meaford Mfg. Co., Meaford, Ont.
Stratford Chair Co., Stratford.

FACTORY SUPPLIES

BRASS TRIMMINGS
Stratford Brass Co., Stratford.
CLAMPS.
Batavia Clamp Co., Batavia, N.Y.
FURNITURE SHOES.
Onward Mfg. Co., Berlin.
DRY KILNS.
Morton Dry Kiln Co., Chicago.
FURNITURE HARDWARE
Stratford Brass Co., Stratford, Ont.
GLUE JOINTING MACHINES.
Canadian Linderman Co., Wood stock.
NAILS
P. L. Robertson Mfg. Co., Milton.

PLATING
P. L. Robertson Mfg. Co., Milton, Ontario.
RIVETS AND SCREWS
P. L. Robertson Mfg. Co., Milton.
SPRINGS.
James Steele, Guelph.
Ideal Bedding Co., Toronto.
SPANISH LEATHER.
Lackawanna Leather Co., Hackettstown, N. J.
STERILIZED HAIR.
Griffin Curled Hair Co., Toronto.
TABLE SLIDES
B. Walter & Co., Wabash, Ind.
TRUCKS.
W. I. Kemp Co., Ltd., Stratford.
VARNISHES.
R. C. Jamieson & Co., Montreal.
Ault & Wiborg, Toronto.
VENEERS.
Adams & Raymond Veneer Co., Indianapolis, Ind.
VENEER PRESSES.
Wm. R. Perrin & Co., Toronto.
WASHERS
P. L. Robertson Mfg. Co., Milton.

UNDERTAKERS' SUPPLIES

AMBULANCES.
Mitchell & Co., Ingersoll.
BURIAL ROBES.
James S. Elliott & Son, Prescott.
Evel Casket Co., Hamilton.
Globe Casket Co., London.
Semmens & Evel Casket Co., Hamilton.
CLOTH CASKETS
Michigan Casket Co., Detroit, Mich.
CEMENT CASKETS
Canadian Cement Casket Co., Prescott.
CEMETERY SUPPLIES
Frigid Fluid Co., Chicago, Ill.
CASKETS AND COFFINS.
Dominion Casket Co., Guelph.
Evel Casket Co., Hamilton.
Globe Casket Co., London.
Semmens & Evel Casket Co., Hamilton.
Western Casket Co., Winnipeg.
EMBALMING FLUIDS.
Egyptian Chemical Co., Boston.
Frigid Fluid Co., Chicago, Ill.
Michigan Casket Co., Detroit, Mich.
H. S. Eckels Co., Philadelphia
EMBALMERS' SUPPLIES
Frigid Fluid Co., Chicago, Ill.
HEARSES.
Mitchell & Co., Ingersoll.
LOWERING DEVICES
Frigid Fluid Co., Chicago, Ill.
SCHOOLS OF EMBALMING.
Canadian School of Embalming, Toronto.
STEEL GRAVE VAULTS
St. Thomas Metallic Vault Co., St. Thomas, Ont.
Michigan Casket Co., Detroit, Mich.
UNDERTAKER'S CHAIRS.
Stratford Mfg. Co., Stratford
UNDERTAKERS' SUNDRIES
Frigid Fluid Co., Chicago, Ill.

WANTED—to hear from owner of good furniture store for sale. D. F. Bush, Minneapolis, Minn. 14/5/2

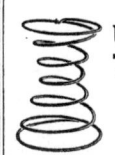

BUY Upholstery Springs That "Stand Up"

Our Tempered Furniture Springs will outlast almost any piece of upholstered furniture. They are built to "stand up" indefinitely.

JAMES STEELE, LIMITED
GUELPH :: :: ONTARIO

Invalid Chairs and Tricycles of every description.

This has been our study for thirty-five years. We build chairs that suit the requirements of any case. Write us for catalogue No. 20 and prices, if interested.

Gendron Wheel Co., Toledo, O. U.S.A.

"STORE MANAGEMENT COMPLETE"

272 Pages — ONLY ONE DOLLAR — 13 Chapters

Tells all about the management of a Store, so that not only the greatest sales but the largest profit may be realized.—By FRANK FARRINGTON.

COMMERCIAL PRESS, Ltd., 32 Colborne St., Toronto

IF YOU WANT TO BUY OR SELL

A Furniture or Undertaking Business, try our Classified Pages. The Canadian Furniture World and The Undertaker is read by practically every furniture merchant and undertaker in Canada every month.

Dominion Casket Co., Limited

Telephones: Day No. 1020. Nights, Sundays and Holidays Nos. 1069-1101

Guelph, Ont.

RUSH ORDERS SOLICITED

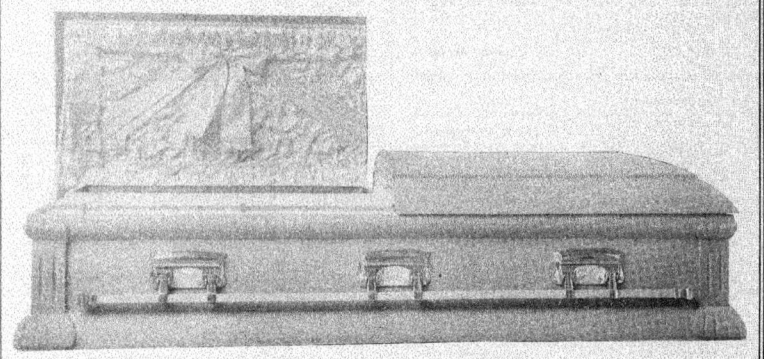

No. 365. "TONCON" STEEL CASKET

REMEMBER the hot sultry days will be here in a short time. The Combination Metallic Casket furnishes a heavy metal receptacle for burial or shipment, that is hermetically sealed. Insuring absolute safety under all circumstances, eliminating all chance of embarrassing situations.

The metal used in the casket is especially adapted to the use, as its rust resisting qualities are much greater than other metals of this class. These goods are made in Canada and are the only metallic caskets manufactured in the Dominion.

We guarantee perfect workmanship and high quality materials in all goods we place on the market. The

Combination Metallic Casket

can be furnished in any style or design with the different panel effects in appearance, the same as our wood caskets. Covered with black or colored broadcloth and embossed or silk plush of any shade. Children's cases in sizes from 3-0 to 5-0 inclusive.

Try one of these cases and be convinced that your trade will demand more

Undertakers' Department

Problems affecting the Undertaking Profession are here discussed and readers are invited to send letters expressing their views on any of the subjects dealt with—News of the profession throughout Canada.

Hints and Helps for Embalmers

By H.S. Eckels, Ph. G., Dean of Eckels College of Embalming, Philadelphia, Pa.

We are just at the beginning of the season when the embalmer must keep a close lookout for danger signals. He always SHOULD keep such a lookout, but during the summer season he MUST. A few hours of hot and sultry weather will work disastrous changes in a body which has been carelessly or faultily embalmed. Summer is the season for certainty, and the undertaker's vigilance must, of necessity, be doubled.

It is exceedingly difficult in print to describe the exact appearance the skin takes on when the embalming fluid reaches it, but it is, after all, too well-known to every embalmer to need description. What many of us really need is repeated caution and warning to make a careful examination of every body to see that the signs of embalming are everywhere present. If the embalmer is at all uncertain as to whether or not he has injected sufficient fluid, he need only examine the surface tissue across the abdomen. If sufficient signs of fluid are present here, he may know that the total quantity of fluid used has been sufficient. There remains then only the probability as to whether circulation has been complete to each of the extremities.

Strange as it may seem, it takes fluid much longer to travel the apparently short distance from the left axillary, let us say, to the navel than it does to travel from the left axillary to the toes on the right foot. The last place the fluid would reach in the natural course of events would be the tissue over the abdomen. The reason for this is that the main trunk arteries which supply this tissue lie to the back of the body, and the branches and laterals extending from them are the longest in the human body, reaching half-way around the body. Circulation in life through this tissue is sluggish, a tendency which is greatly exaggerated after death. If, therefore, signs of embalming are present around the navel, you may be sure that sufficient fluid has been injected to properly embalm the body. Examination should, however, be made of each of the extremities to see that no obstruction has shut off or diminished the flow. No body is safe, however, especially in hot weather, unless these signs are quite marked.

Flushing or regurgitation of blood may be produced by the injection of fluid into the veins. Former authorities assumed that this was the cause of flushing, and the consequent discolorations in almost every instance, and it is a fact that fluid injected into the vein when mistaken for the artery, carries the blood with it into the superior vena cava. Then the blood in the innominate and jugular veins is usually forced back into the face tissues. This condition, therefore, was thought to be produced only when the veins were injected. This, however, is not always the case, for the rapid injection of the artery in some cases where the veins are not properly drained has very frequently produced regurgitation of the blood through the veins, which in those cases causes the flushing of the blood to the face and ears.

In cases of sudden death an abundance of blood is occupying the tissue in the neck and face. This is due to the corpse having been laid flat on the bed. We find, however, that after the body has been properly elevated on the embalmer's board that this fluid circulation is improved, and the first quart or two of fluid injected into the arteries, aided by gravitation, forces the blood away from the face, and if further assisted by manipulation of the embalmer, by the time that this quart or two of fluid is injected the face tissue is entirely cleared.

But if it is a large body, warm weather and a shipping case, the embalmer knowing that two quarts of fluid are not sufficient to reach the extremities of the body, and therefore wishing to continue the injection, frequently finds that by the time three quarts of fluid are injected into the arteries a backing up of the blood and fluid through the veins from the superior vena cava occurs, producing a decidedly pinkish color of the face. If this is allowed to remain there, it would grow darker and would result in either a putty, lead, or brownish hue in the course of a day or so.

This condition is not rare, and when thoroughly understood seems quite natural, even in the normal body. A study of the circulation from the arteries, through the capillaries, into the veins, shows us how this regurgitation occurs from the veins back to the tissue of the face and neck during the time that the arteries are being injected. The fluid naturally flows most freely through the largest branches of the aorta first and supplies the capillaries throughout that portion of the tissue which lies closest to the centre of the circulation, such as the lungs, the heart, the liver, and other organs of the abdominal cavity which lie closest to the aorta. Therefore, the blood would first be forced from these capillaries and enter the superior vena cava. When this large vein is filled further pressure of blood in the veins naturally would be directed towards its largest branches, the jugular veins.

These jugular veins have two pairs of valves, but, owing to their position in the neck, which always is at an incline above the rest of the body, these valves are not fully enough developed to restrain the flow of blood, as are the valves in the veins elsewhere, which are exercised to a greater extent, and as the jugular veins are surrounded by soft tissue, such as the blood and thyroid platysma myoides, as well as the mastoid muscles, the veins may easily stretch beyond the controlling influence of their valves. Therefore regurgitation of the blood is quite natural to occur through them.

As an example: Should you hold your hand straight down for any length of time, there is no backing up of the blood from the veins into the capillary tissue,

IT *will* pay *you* to *drop us a card* if you have not received our catalogue. ¶ *It will furnish you with an intimate knowledge* of the largest line of *cloth and plush covered Caskets in Western Canada* at right prices and terms.

Our Motto:---Dispatch With Utmost Promptness.

Open Day and Night. Phone Garry 4657.

The Western Casket Co.,
Limited
Winnipeg, Manitoba

but they remain about the same color as though you hold it above your head or on a level with it, showing the circulation of the blood from the arteries to the tissues is carried away by the veins, and the valves in these veins do not collapse nor are they stretched apart so that the blood can flow back through the valves to the tissues of the hands, as it does through the valves in the veins of the neck to the tissues of the face.

Should a person who is not practised in athletics stand on his head for only a few moments, congestion occurs there, a headache immediately follows, and flushing of the face and neck occurs, so that they become a dark purple and also swell considerably. Should he remain in this position for a long period of time, death would likely ensue. Therefore, where there is an excess of blood in the body, which is evidenced first by the swelling of the superficial veins, which proves that the larger veins into which they should empty are already filled, there is abundant evidence that these veins need to be relieved of blood.

If you are embalming cases where sudden death has not depleted the blood supply of the body, and you are using a vein tube, it is perfectly safe and proper to allow the drainage of the blood to commence about the time you begin to inject the fluid into the artery, and continue during the entire time you are injecting. This is really one of the most scientific and satisfactory methods of injecting a body. Draining blood from the venous system in this way allows you to tie up the vein after removing the tube, leaving your circulation without any rupture or break, and should you desire to reinject your body on the next day, or even a day later, you will be sure to find the circulation intact. Therefore you will be able to distribute fluid to all parts of the body through the general arterial circulation.

When draining the blood in that manner there is no danger of flushing or regurgitation of the blood to the face while injecting arterially, particularly if you have the head and shoulders at an incline. Too much care cannot be given to this operation to produce a natural color or complexion. When this blood flushing occurs while the injection of fluid is being made, the blood should be drained either as above described by the vein tube or by the puncture of a trocar between the second and third rib, one or two inches from the right side of the sternum bone (breast bone), puncturing the vena cava, which lays on the right side of the spinal column (backbone). This large vein collects all of the blood from the jugular veins and head, as well as that from the subclavian veins, which drain the veins of the arms and hands. Its location may easily be determined by the position of the vertebrae. The insertion of your cardiac needle from this position can be accomplished with less fear of puncturing the arteries than to insert it at any other place. However, the vein tube in the axillary vein is always the safest of these two operations. After the blood commences to flow freely, your continued injection through the artery, with manipulation, should entirely clear up this tissue. Indeed, it should be continued until it does.

In some very rare and obstinate cases it is occasionally necessary to inject a little fluid directly up through each of the carotid arteries, massaging the face tissue during the time. To the inexperienced this may seem like a very difficult task, but I want now to show you the importance of knowing how to use the carotid arteries and to call attention to the fact that they lead to the most important part of the body which is exposed at the time of the funeral. This face tissue should be cleared up properly at the time of the first injection, no matter how much trouble you may think it might be, because this blood, mixed with fluid, would naturally grow dark as the body would lie. After it has stained the tissue it is indeed difficult—almost impossible—to get rid of it by any means. Discoloration may not make its appearance during the first injection, and occasionally the embalming of such body may seem to be perfect without the draining of the blood at the time of the injection, but the embalmer finds every once in a while that such cases become somewhat darker around the ears and neck, and, indeed, up over the cheeks, and wonders why this should be when he left the body only ten or twelve hours before in such perfect condition.

Blood is described as a viscid opaque liquid of a characteristic red color, which is a bright scarlet in the arteries and a purplish or brownish hue in the veins. Its average specific gravity is about 1055, being lower in women than in men, and still lower in children.

When examined under the microscope, blood is found to consist of a transparent and faintly yellow liquid known as Plasma, in which are suspended a very large number of minute bodies, known as blood corpuscles. These are what interest the embalmer mostly. They are two kinds, red and white.

The contents of the red corpuscles confer upon the blood its red color. They comprise about fifty per cent. of the bulk of the blood. These red blood corpuscles are very small, although individual bodies. A single drop of human blood contains about three hundred and twenty-five millions of them. Under the microscope we find that these red corpuscles remain round and perfect in the blood in its pure state, but when mixed with any other liquid, the walls are soon broken, and thus coloring matter is liberated and stains and discolors the tissues. When mixed with fluid in any proportion, the stains become fixed in a few hours and cannot be cleared up by even a further injection of fluid.

It is, therefore, apparent that to have a natural color this blood should be washed completely from the tissue and kept therefrom. This best may be done by the injection of the arteries with clear fluid and draining the veins of their blood. This will not only insure the best preservation, but also the most desirable conditions.

Where there is an interference with the normal circulation, and where the fluid that is injected into the axillary artery does not pass freely through the carotid arteries and up into the face sufficiently to wash the blood out of the capillaries in this region, as it should do, but instead is divided through the branches of the aorta towards the lower extremities and into the organs of the trunk of the body, or perhaps leaking from some of them into the cavities, then it is advisable to raise both of the carotid arteries and inject a small quantity of fluid through each of them, manipulating during the time.

This direct and specific injection of fluid will wash the blood from the tissue and leave it clear and of a natural complexion. In this treatment, the injection of the carotid arteries towards the face, care need only

Dominion Manufacturers
Limited

MANUFACTURERS OF

Fine Funeral Requisites

We guarantee

The Highest Quality

and the

Quickest Possible Service

*Night or Day Orders
given Prompt Attention*

BRANCHES

The Globe Casket Co., and Branches	London, Ontario
The Semmons & Evel Casket Co., and Branches	Hamilton, Ontario
The National Casket Co.	Toronto, Ontario
Jas. S. Elliot & Son	Prescott, Ontario
Girard & Godin and Branches	Three Rivers, Quebec
Christie Bros. & Co,	Amherst, N. S.

FRED W. COLES 　　　　　　　　　　　　D. M. ANDREWS
General Manager 　　　　　　　　　　　*Secretary Treasurer*

HEAD OFFICE

468 King Street W., Toronto

to be observed that the fluid shall not be injected in sufficient quantity to swell up the tissue of the face and eyes and thus change the expression. Reasonable care and attention will prevent the operator from causing this annoying condition.

A little swelling is readily noticed by the embalmer and is not a serious matter, as the tissues will contract and reduce to a natural size within twenty-four hours, so that a small amount of swelling would not be noticed. With this discoloration all removed and the complexion clear and white, the body will present the most favorable impression of the embalmer's skill and be the occasion of your receiving the gratitude of your patrons.

PULMOTOR AS UNDERTAKER'S ASSISTANT.

An American journal recently conducted a prize question competition on the topic of "What is a pulmotor, and in what way can undertakers best profit by its use?" The third prize was won by a Canadian, Sidney C. Richardson, of Port Arthur. His answer was as follows:

A pulmotor is a machine to give respiration, or help the continuance of same, to any human being that has been nearly overcome by fumes, gas, electric shock, smoke, or similar causes, if there still is life in the person affected. Oxygen is used to give respiration, it being contained in a steel cylinder inside the pulmotor cabinet.

The person is placed on his back, the mouth opened and tongue drawn out, same being held that way with tools provided, so as to give free access for the air. Next there is a rubber mask placed over the mouth and nose and strapped on tightly with four straps around the back of the head, so as to make it airtight in fitting against the face. The air tube is then attached to the mask; the inhalation valve on the pulmotor opened and the machine works at once.

Oxygen is forced into the lungs by its pressure from the cylinder, and as it works automatically, it is only possible for the lungs to fill to their normal capacity, when they at once empty again. The machine works steadily until the person comes back to his own normal breathing, dies, or the machine is shut down by the operator.

As for an undertaker benefiting by its use—well, that is a question not easily solved! But I would suggest as a large majority of undertakers have an ambulance service in connection with their business, why not equip same with pulmotors along with the first aid cabinets that progressive men have their ambulances equipped with? The room and weight of same would make very little difference, and it would show that the undertaker is equipped for all emergencies, no matter of what kind, that would be apt to happen in his own locality.

Take, for instance, an emergency call. If you were equipped with a pulmotor, and saved a person's life thereby, look what that would mean in that locality as an advertisement. It would be on every person's lips that Mr. ——— saved a person's life by being equipped with the pulmotor.

Or, for instance, an undertaker, called to a death, on arriving might not be just sure that death had occurred. Sooner than wait for a doctor, if he had a pulmotor close at hand, he could attach same and revive the person in a few minutes if the body were still living.

Look again what that would mean as an advertisement, if a case of that kind really did appear. But some men that were heartless, I suppose, would say, "Do you think I would lose the price of a good casket by using that machine?"

Then, again, if undertakers getting through dirty cases in hovels and slums of big cities where the smell was anything but desirable, could just hold the mask of the pulmotor against their nose and mouth and take a few whiffs of pure oxygen into their lungs, look what that would mean to guard them against disease; refresh them and make them feel more like working in the stench. As a fire chief told me the other day, it is good just to be able to take a few whiffs of the pure oxygen after coming out of a fire where the smoke has been bad.

A CAPTAIN OF INDUSTRY

Jacob Chas. Siemon, president of the recently-formed Canada Casket Co., Ltd., Wiarton, Ont., while perhaps a new figure in the casket-making world, is not a stranger to the furniture field, as many years ago he entered that business. He is a Canadian, and was born of German parentage, at Walkerton, Ont., in 1864. Educated in the public school of his town, he soon entered on a business career, and at 21 was a partner of McIlveen & Siemon, contractors and architects. Three years later, in 1888, he entered the furniture manufacturing business at Wiarton, being senior member of Siemon & Hill.

In 1894 he formed Siemon & Bros. Mfg. Co., Wiarton, furniture makers and lumber dealers. This concern was in 1905 incorporated as a hardware, flooring and sawmill firm under the name of Siemon Bros., Ltd. The Siemon Co., Ltd., Toronto and Wiarton, followed in 1907, and last year Mr. Siemon organized the Canada Casket Co., of which he is president.

For ten years past Mr. Siemon has given a good part of his time to securing control of timber lands, and as a result has some billion acres of these tracts. He also has taken great interest in the development of the northern part of Bruce county, and has helped build up the town of Wiarton. He was councillor of the town from 1890 to 1894, and declined nomination for the House of Commons in 1900.

Besides being head of the new Canada Casket Co., Mr. Siemon is president of the National Securities Corporation; president of The Siemon Co., Ltd., and a director of The Siemon Bros., Ltd. He is unmarried. His recreation is fishing, and he is also a lover of travel. He is a well-known figure in philanthropic work. At present Mr. Siemon is making his home in Toronto.

Burglar Proof and Water Tight

"The St. Thomas"

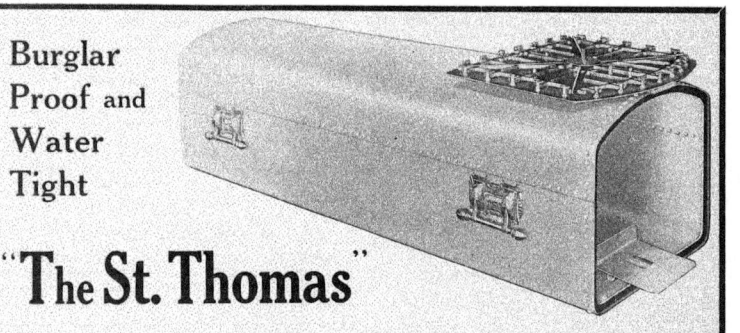

Original, Quick Closing End Vault

MANUFACTURED BY

The St. Thomas Metallic Vault Company, Limited
ST. THOMAS, ONTARIO

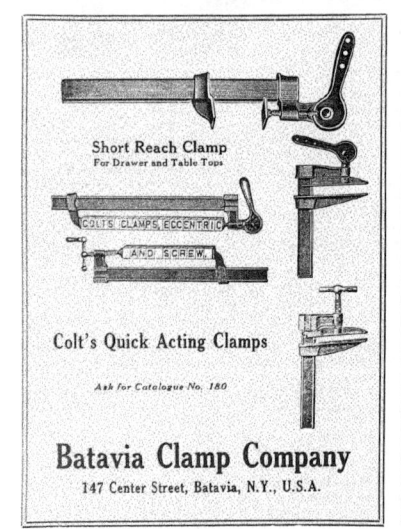

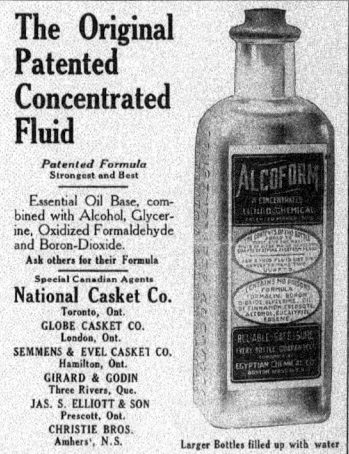

Short Reach Clamp
For Drawer and Table Tops

COLT'S CLAMPS, ECCENTRIC AND SCREW

Colt's Quick Acting Clamps

Ask for Catalogue No. 180

Batavia Clamp Company
147 Center Street, Batavia, N.Y., U.S.A.

The Original Patented Concentrated Fluid

Patented Formula
Strongest and Best

Essential Oil Base, combined with Alcohol, Glycerine, Oxidized Formaldehyde and Boron-Dioxide.

Ask others for their Formula

Special Canadian Agents

National Casket Co.
Toronto, Ont.
GLOBE CASKET CO.
London, Ont.
SEMMENS & EVEL CASKET CO.
Hamilton, Ont.
GIRARD & GODIN
Three Rivers, Que.
JAS. S. ELLIOTT & SON
Prescott, Ont.
CHRISTIE BROS.
Amherst, N.S.

Larger Bottles filled up with water

Egyptian Chemical Co. Boston, U.S.A.

Alberta Directors' Annual Meeting

The secretary of the Alberta funeral directors and embalmers has sent out the following circular letter to the profession in the Province of Alberta, calling attention to the annual meeting of that body and enclosing a return card, on which the recipient states whether or not he can attend:

Red Deer, Alta., May 1st, 1914.

To the Members of the Alberta Funeral Directors' and Embalmers' Association:

Owing to the fact that we have been able to make our arrangements for a demonstrator and lecturer so much earlier this year, we expect to be able to hold our annual convention on or about the 23rd of July and the two days following.

We will more than likely hold it in the same place as last year, viz., Nolan's Hall, Calgary.

Our lecturer and demonstrator will be our old friend, Prof. Hohenschuh, whom many of you will remember, he having been with us in 1910 and 1911. The professor needs no boosting from your secretary. You all have heard him or of him; he is so well known that it's a waste of time and ink to say more.

Try your best to be with us this year, for we are going to give you the best time you have ever had at any of our conventions. This is to be the banner year for us, so be sure that you make your arrangements early, and do not forget the ladies, they will be looked after.

With Messrs. Armstrong and Foster on our entertainment committee, right on the spot to make all arrangements, you may be sure that you will get your money's worth, and we want you with us. Will you not drop us a post card, saying that you will be one of the bunch?

I want to get in touch with you all in time to mail you full particulars, etc., so be sure and send me the enclosed card; it will only cost you one cent. Won't you do it?

If you have any suggestions to make, I will be pleased to receive them any time before the convention.

Let everyone try to do some little thing that will be a help towards making this year's convention the best of all the conventions yet held. What say you?

If you have anything on your chest in the way of a grouch, come, and we will help you to get rid of it; it only grows larger by keeping it, and inward growths are dangerous sometimes.

You will get some more letters from me before the convention, but they will not be like this.

Trusting that you take enough interest in the work of the association to keep the ball rolling.

I remain, yours truly,
H. G. STONE,
Secretary-Treasurer.

SASKATCHEWAN DIRECTORS MEET

The first convention of the Saskatchewan funeral directors and embalmers was held in Regina on April 18, at which a provincial association was formed. It was decided to hold a school of instruction for undertakers and embalmers some time this summer, about the end of May or the first of June. A matter of great importance to the profession was the decision of the convention to appoint an examining board consisting of five members, three appointed by the Government and two by the association.

Funeral directors and embalmers from all over the province were in Regina for the convention. In the morning the delegates met Dr. Seymour, commissioner of the health department of Saskatchewan, at the legislative buildings, and talked over the matter of the formation of an association, and following lunch the meeting was continued at the Clayton Hotel, when organization was effected. The new association is to be known as "The Saskatchewan Funeral Directors' and Embalmers' Association, Limited," to be capitalized at $5,000. This will be provided for by the levying of 500 ten-dollar shares.

A resolution was passed and put on record thanking Dr. Seymour for the earnest effort made by him to bring about the organization of this association. A code of by-laws will be prepared by the officers and directors, to be submitted at the first general meeting, which will be held about the end of May or the first of June in Regina.

School of Instruction.

At that time also the school of instruction will be held for undertakers and embalmers who wish to obtain diplomas, and to improve their knowledge and standing in the art of embalming. Dr. Seymour is making arrangements to obtain for this school a professor who will lecture and demonstrate on the science of embalming to the students who attend.

At the close of the school examinations will be conducted, at which all who wish to obtain diplomas may write. The association appointed as its representatives on the examining board J. Droppo and A. Broadfoot, both of Moose Jaw.

The fee for joining the association was fixed at ten dollars, which includes the first year's assessment, and five dollars per year hereafter, paid annually.

A resolution was passed granting the commercial travelers representing houses for undertaking supplies membership in the association as social members.

Officers Elected.

Officers and provisional directors were appointed as follows: Hon. president, A. Broadfoot, Moose Jaw; president, A. E. Young, Saskatoon; first vice-president, George Speers, Regina; second vice-president, M. S. Popplewell, Davidson; sergeant-at-arms, G. H. McKague, Saskatoon; secretary-treasurer, A. C. Howard, Prince Albert; executive committee, G. E. Bowker, Regina; J. B. Hill, Rouleau; and James McGurri, Moosomin.

AN OUTRAGE AGAINST CHRISTIANITY.

The Saskatoon Star recently took up the case of the burial of indigents in that city. Their comment on the situation is as follows:

"The rate for burying indigents for the city has gone up. Some time ago tenders were called from two local undertakers, and the contract was awarded to W. A. Edwards at the rate of fifty cents per burial. This action was taken up by the local undertakers then, and, in fact, was made the subject of comment in undertaking journals all over Canada and the United States. A short time ago Mr. Edwards announced that he was not prepared to go ahead any further with this idea, and as another undertaker had since located in this city, all three were called upon. Mr. McKague, representing the newest firm, told the city what he thought of burying any Christian at fifty cents per case. He said it was a disgrace to Christianity. He believed in giving Christian burial to every one, and he

To Canadian Funeral Directors

THE CENTRAL LINE

Mahogany, Oak, Plush and Cloth Covered Caskets

WE SHIP PROMPTLY

We can also supply anything desired in Casket Linings, Burial Robes, and a general line of Undertakers' Supplies

Orders given our Canadian representative, or sent to our factory at Bridgeburg by mail, telegraph or telephone will be shipped promptly.

CENTRAL CASKET COMPANY

Bridgeburg, Ont.
Telephone 126

R. S. Flint   Canadian Representative: 241 Fern Ave., Toronto
Telephone Parkdale 3257

No Undertaker Should Overlook

the fact that he can make a full gallon of fluid of standard strength from each sixteen-ounce bottle of RE-Concentrated Dioxin. Re-Concentrated Dioxin costs no more per bottle than any standard concentrated fluid, but it is twice as strong—in other words, there are twice as many ounces of preservation in a bottle of RE-Concentrated Dioxin as there are in any bottle of merely concentrated fluid.

If economy were the only recommendation for RE-Concentrated Dioxin, however, we should not urge it upon our patrons.

As a matter of fact, it is easy to explain and equally easy to demonstrate the fact that the fluid thus produced gives a far better cosmetic effect and produces a far more life-like body than possibly could be produced by any raw formaldehyde concentrated fluid.

This is because RE-Concentrated Dioxin has a double base. When diluted to make a full gallon of fluid to the bottle, its main base is peroxide, with a secondary base of purified formaldehyde (formochloral).

Every funeral director knows that peroxide of hydrogen is the best bleacher known to chemical science. Not everyone realizes, however, that peroxide of hydrogen has blood solvent qualities far in excess of any other chemical yet discovered which is suitable for use in embalming fluid.

Peroxide of hydrogen is composed of two atoms of oxygen and two atoms of hydrogen. Since oxygen is fifteen times heavier than hydrogen, fifteen-sixteenths of the atomic weight of peroxide of hydrogen, therefore, is oxygen.

Every embalmer knows that venous blood is much darker in color, is much more sluggish and much heavier than arterial blood.

What is the difference between the two?

Arterial blood is merely venous blood, which has been purified in the lungs, which has been lightened in color and rendered vastly more fluid by the oxygen which the lungs have extracted from the air we breathe.

Since fifteen-sixteenths of the atomic weight of peroxide of hydrogen is oxygen, it must be apparent, therefore, that the oxygen in the extra rich peroxide in Dioxin has a tendency to exercise the same purifying and solvent qualities upon the dark, discolored venous blood after death as the oxygen which the lungs extract from the air we breathe has upon the venous blood in life.

The result is that much more blood can be drained from a body in which RE-Concentrated Dioxin is injected than is possible from a body in which raw formaldehyde is used and in which the astringent qualities of the formaldehyde have sealed up the discolored blood corpuscles in the capillaries.

Putty color is caused by raw formaldehyde fluid seating up the discolored corpuscles of the blood in the capillaries. It is inevitable where raw formaldehyde fluids are used unless exceeding care is used to drain blood. And even then there is great danger.

RE-Concentrated Dioxin is distinctly the most modern and the most scientific embalming fluid on the market, as well as the most economical. The progressive funeral director will not hesitate, but will order a trial shipment.

RE-Concentrated DIOXIN

H. S. ECKELS & CO.

1922 Arch St., Philadelphia, Pa.
241 Fern Ave., Toronto, Ont., Can.

would do so, if he was out of pocket. We have interviewed the undertakers in the city, and recommend that a new arrangement be made whereby the undertakers will in future bury all indigent persons at the following rates, viz.: $15 for adults and $10 for juveniles, and that the superintendent of the hospital be requested to see that the undertakers get the bodies in rotation.''

Gossip of the Profession

F. J. Martyne's undertaking parlors at North Bay were damaged by fire recently.

Daniel Genge, undertaker, Alvinston, Ont., is dead.

R. A. Currie, Wingham, has added a new rubber-tired casket wagon to his undertaking equipment. The wagon is of the very latest type manufactured and up-to-date in every particular.

Tickell & Sons Co., of Belleville, Ont., purchased at auction at Montreal recently, the stock of the defunct Poirer-Casket Co., Roxton Falls, Que., about six carloads in all, and shipped it to their headquarters at Belleville.

V. H. Wetmore, undertaker, has taken up residence in Melville, Sask., where he will engage in business.

Plans for undertaking parlors and an apartment block on Brodie street, Vancouver, have been drawn for L. H. Cameron, 711 Victoria avenue, by R. E. Mason, architect, at an estimated cost of $50,000.

A by-law granting a loan of $25,000 to the Canada Casket Co. was carried by a sweeping majority, 325 votes for and 40 against, in Wiarton last month.

Charles R. Woodburn, an experienced director and embalmer, who holds diplomas from the most advanced schools in Canada and the United States, has opened new and up-to-date undertaking parlors at 586 Bank street, Ottawa.

The Terrace Lawn Cemetery Co., Ltd., North Bay, Ont., has obtained a charter.

J. R. Reid, undertaker at Banff, Alta., has been spending several days at Lethbridge on business.

William Williams has removed his funeral and undertaking estblishment into his new premises on Carlton street, Thorold, Ont.

Question Box

We have been requested to open a Question Box, wherein the newer men in the profession might ask for the opinions of those who have been longer operating, and so help disseminate the views and methods of others that have met with success in the past. A Western correspondent states there are many undertakers in Canada who do not know too much about many cases that are likely to be brought to them, and instancing one case, he asks the following question, which we will be pleased to have our readers answer when this paper comes to hand:

"What is the best way to preserve a drowned body from stench?"

UNDERTAKERS SHOULD BE READY.

When a sudden death occurs in a community the undertaker should be as ready and well prepared to look after the case as the physician, and is quite as likely to be called to attend the person. He is prepared to make the necessary tests for life, and should be posted as to what should be required for restoring a person to consciousness who has fallen in a faint or is temporarily unconscious from heart failure or other similar cause. Many undertakers are supplied with ambulance and other means of transporting disabled persons to the hospital, and that would very naturally bring to him the call for assistance. He is thoroughly posted as to first aids to the injured, and understands the applying of bandages, etc. There is one item in the preparation of the undertaker for such cases that has recently been invented, and that is the pulmotor, not the instrument for testing the capacity of the lungs, but the one for the filling of the lungs with oxygen, so that respiration may be aided and restored. The machine is comparatively inexpensive; it is an easy matter to learn how to operate it, and there is little danger from the use of it, even to a person in full health. Many of the instruments are being introduced in the larger cities, and many lives have already been saved by their prompt use. The instruments should be in the establishment of every undertaker.—Western Undertaker.

COMRADES LEFT BEHIND.

"Talking about omens," said the ex-Canadian soldier. "a queer thing happened in the Boer war.

"A troop of mounted rifles were returning after a hard day's scouting to our camp near Middleburg, in the eastern part of the Transvaal. On our way back we had to pass the town cemetery, which was on the side of a hill. Near the gate of the cemetery stood a shed in which was kept the town hearse.

"The doors of this building were open as we were riding past, and in some manner the blocks which were usually kept under the wheels of the hearse must have become dislodged, for the hearse slowly moved out of the shed and rolled down the hill into the middle of our party, who scattered in all directions.

"The officer in charge of the troop ordered four men to dismount and take the hearse back. Now comes the queer part. Soon after this we went to Cape Town and took ship for home. Every one of that scouting party returned alive and well to Canada except the four men who handled that hearse. Not a man of that four returned.''

The former warrior paused and heaved a sigh.

"Good men, true comrades, they were," he said.

"Have another drink," said the bartender, "and tell us how the poor fellows died."

Silently the soldier drank to the memory of his comrades, set down the empty glass, and edged toward the door.

"The reason they did not come back was because two of them got jobs in Cape Town; the other two married Boer widows and settled down on farms," he said.—New York Sun.

MARITIME DIRECTORS' CONVENTION

The Maritime Funeral Directors' Association will hold their annual convention this year on August 11, 12, and 13. The executive of that body will issue an invitation to all the funeral directors of Canada to be present at their meetings.

TRAVELLERS WANTED For the Maritime Provinces, Manitoba and Northwest, and Pacific Coast to represent the Fischman Patent Mattress. Sell by photograph. Liberal commission. Fischman Mattress Co., 331 Adelaide St. W., Toronto.

Index to Advertisements

A
Anbrough & Co., J. P. 22
Antiseptic Bedding Co. .... i.f.c.
Associated Ad. Club 55
Ault & Wiborg Co. 54

B
Baetz Bros. & Co. 8
Batavia Clamp Co. 64

C
Canadian Linoleum Co. 23
Canadian School of Embalming. 57
Can. H. W. Johns-Manville Co. .. 25
Central Casket Co. 66
Chesley Furniture Co. 19
Colleran Patent Spring Mat. Co. 12

D
Dominion Casket Co. 58
Dominion Hammock Mfg. Co. .. 25
Dominion Mfrs., Limited 62

E
Eckels & Co., H. S. 66
Egyptian Chemical Co. 64
Elmira Interior Woodwork Co. .. 21

F
Farquharson-Gifford Co. 7
Fleshman Mattress Co. 8
Frame & Hay Fence Co. 11

G
Gale & Son, Geo. 14-15
Globe-Wernicke 9
Gold Medal Furniture Mfg. Co. . 13
Gendron Wheel Co. 57

H
Hourd & Co. 10

I
Ideal Bedding Co. 28
Imperial Furniture Co. 22
Imperial Rattan Co. 5

K
Kawneer Mfg. Co. 12
Kindel Bed Co., Limited 12
Knechtel Furniture Co. 20-21
Kuhn, J. & J. 10

L
Lippert Furniture Co. 26

M
Manufacturers' Exhibition Building .... o.b.c.
Matthews Bros. 57
Menford Mfg. Co. 6
McLagan Furniture Co., Geo. 3
McKellar Bedding Co. 27
Montreal Upholstering Co. 4
Mundell, J. C., & Co. .... i.f.c.

N
N. A. Bent Chair Co. 34

O
Onward Mfg. Co. 25
Ontario Spring Bed 4

R
Robertson, P. L., Mfg. Co. 54

S
Shafer, D. L. & Co. 22
Steele, James, Limited 57
Stratford Brass Co. 10
Stratford Chair Co. .... o.f.c.
Stratford Mfg. Co. 11
St. Thomas Metallic Vault Co. ... 64

V
Victoriaville Bedding Co. 16-17

W
Walker & Co., B. 25
Western Casket Co. 60
Weisglass, S., Limited 13

Undertakers Shipping Directory

ONTARIO
Aurora—
   Dunham, Charles.
Barrie—
   Smith, G. G. & Co.
Brockville—
   Quirmbach, Geo. R., 162 King St.
Brooklin—
   Disney, R. S.
Campbellford—
   Irwin, James.
Campden—
   Hausel, Albion.
Clinton—
   Walker, Wesley.
Coboconk—
   Greenley, A.
Copper Cliff—
   Boyd, W. C.
Dungannon—
   Sproul, William
Dutton—
   Schultz, B. L.
Elmira—
   Dreisinger, Chris.

Fenelon Falls—
   Deyman, L. & Son.
Fenwick—
   H. A. Metler.
Fergus—
   Armstrong, M. F.
   Thomson, John & Son.
Fort William—
   Cameron & Co., 711 Victoria.
   Morris, A.
Haileybury—
   Thorpe Bros.
Galt—
   Anderson, J. & Son.
Hamilton—
   Green Bros., 124 King St. E.
   Robinson, J. H. & Co., 19-21 John St. N.
Hanover—
   Wunnenberg, Norman.
Hastings—
   Howard, P. N.
Hepworth—
   Downs, E. J.
Inwood—
   Lorriman, E. S.
Kemptville—
   McCaughey, Geo. A.

Kenora—
   Horn & Taylor.
Kingston—
   Corbett, S. S.
Lakefield—
   Hendren, Geo. G.
Little Current—
   Sims, J. G.
Markdale—
   Oliver, M.
Newmarket—
   Millard, J. H.
North Augusta—
   Wilson, J. R.
North Bay—
   St. Pierre, E.
Oakwood—(Mariposa Station G.T.R.) Wilmot F. Webster.
Ohsweken—
   Johnson, F. L.
Oshawa—
   Disney Bros.
   Luke Bros.
Ottawa—
   Rogers, Geo. H., 128 Bank
Petrolia—
   Steadman Bros.
Port Arthur—
   Collin Wood, 36 Arthur St.
   Morris, A.
Prescott—
   Rankin, H. & Son.
Renfrew—
   O'Connor, Wm.
St. Mary's—
   N. L. Brandon.
St. Thomas—
   Williams, P. R. & Sons, 519 Talbot St.
Seaforth, Ont.
   W. T. Box & Co.
Scotland—
   Vaughan, Jos. H. M.
Sudbury—
   Henry, J. G.
Toronto—
   Cobbledick, N. B., 2068 Queen St. East and 1508 Danford Ave. Private Ambulance.
   Humphrey, E. J. Burial Co. Head Office, 359 Yonge St.; Branch, 407 Queen St. W. Private ambulance.
   Stone, Daniel (formerly H. Stone & Son), 82 Bloor St. West.
   Vancamp, J. C., 30 Bloor St. West.
Waterloo—
   Klipper Undertaking Co.
Welland—
   Sutherland, G. W.
Woodstock—
   Meadows, T. & Sons.
   Mack, Paul.

QUEBEC
Buckingham—
   Paquet, Jos.

Cowansville—
   Judson, M. B.
Montreal—
   Tees & Co., 912 St. Catherine St. West.
St. Hyacinthe—
   Cadorette, Mongeau & Leary.
St. Laurent—
   Gougeon, Jos.

NEW BRUNSWICK
Petitcodiac—
   Jonah, D. Allison.
Welland—
   Sutherland, G. W.
Woodstock—
   Van Wart, Jacob.

NOVA SCOTIA
Ferrona—
   Fraser, D. & Co.
Halifax—
   Snow & Co., 90 Argyle St.
Sydney, C.B.—
   Beaton, A. J. & Son, 374-384 George St.

MANITOBA
Brandon—
   Campbell & Campbell.
   Vincent & McPherson.
Souris—
   McCulloch, Wm.
Swan River—
   Paull, Geo.
Winnipeg—
   Bardal, A. S., 834 Sherbrooke
   Thompson, J. C., 501 Main
   Clark-Leatherdale Co., Ltd., 232 Kennedy St.

SASKATCHEWAN
Gull Lake—
   Morrow, Fred. A.
Saskatoon—
   Young, A. E.
Kamsack—
   Russell, G. E. I.
Lanigan—
   Robertson, Wm.
Moose Jaw—
   The Bellamy Co.
   Broadfoot Bros.
Rush Lake—
   Friesen, John M.
Prince Albert—
   Howard, A. C.
   Hadley, C. L.
Regina—
   Speers, George.
Semans—
   Haygarth, Jas.
Welwyn—
   LeAvens, Merritt.
Wolseley—
   Barber, B.

ALBERTA
Calgary—
   Graham & Buscomb, 611 Centre St.
Castor—
   Winter, W. G.

BRITISH COLUMBIA
Hosmer—
   Cornett, T. A.
Victoria—
   Hana & Thompson, 827 Pandora Ave.

Every Furniture Manufacturer

installs new equipment in his plant from time to time—the old must go! There is a way to dispose of it—economically and effectively. Let's tell you!

Canadian Furniture World, 32 COLBORNE ST. TORONTO

Leisure reading that means more dollars when you work

A knowledge of the big problems of business, put into a very comprehensive and readable style, helps you in finding easier and quicker ways of overcoming them. That's what Frank Farrington does in these two books. You will like the way his mind works. The wide scope of his experience, the accuracy of his statements, and his knowledge of human nature all combine to make them volumes that will be read not only for the entertainment they afford, but for their practical worth in the conduct of a retail store. The busy man will appreciate these books for another reason; they are written in concise form and he may start reading anywhere and find that particular chapter complete in itself, and depending in no wise upon those which precede or follow. Although if he fails to read every one of them he is depriving himself of a privilege.

Retail Advertising

"Retail Advertising Complete" covers with a comprehensive grasp such subjects as newspaper advertising, how to get up the ads, many representative samples being presented. A chapter is given to window advertising, and the subject of novelties is thoroughly discussed; that important part of advertising which is done inside the store is in no manner overlooked, while equal attention is given to outside advertising, such as bill posting and other means of reaching outlying districts; advertising direct by mail and mail order opportunities and advantages are gone into carefully; special sales as business getters, and some features that make them successful, are presented in a convincing manner. In short, this book is the common sense psychology of advertising.

266 Pages, 5 x 7 inches, Cloth
Price $1.00 Delivered

Store Management

In "Store Management Complete," which is well illustrated, the author gives a clear and concise picture of the kind of man, physically and mentally, that the successful merchant should be; the writer's experience has taught him that one kind of personality is most desirable, and he tells you about this. In a chapter on "Where to Start" the advantages of various locations are discussed; how to make the most of a poor one, and the desirable side of the street. "Store Arrangement" dips to the bottom in such subjects as making entrance easy, best arrangement of windows; how to plan the lighting, heat, and ventilation; utilizing waste space, and systems of storing extra stock.

An interesting chapter on "Clerk Management" brings out the advantage of knowing people and how to handle them. The other chapters deal with the buying end; the store policy; leaks; the store's neighbors; working hours; expenses; the credit business; what to sell; premium giving. The man and the business; their relation and success, that's the book.

252 Pages, 5 x 7 inches, Cloth
Price $1.00 Delivered

Both Volumes $1.90 Postpaid

The Commercial Press, Limited

Publishers of
Canadian Hardware Journal
The Retail Grocer
Canadian Furniture World
Retail Druggist of Canada
The Canadian Provisioner
The Canadian Nurse
Recreation in Canada

32 Colborne Street
Toronto, Canada

Publishers of
The Canadian Manufacturer
The Canadian Builder and Carpenter
The Canadian Clay-Worker
The Electrical Railway Journal
The Machine Shop
Motoring
Good Roads of Canada

THIRTEEN-NINETEEN-CHICAGO
OPPORTUNITY KNOCKS-ONCE AT EVERY-MAN'S-DOOR
BUT-IN-JULY SHE-WILL-AWAIT-YOU WITH-OPEN-ARMS AT "1319"
OPPORTUNITY
MANUFACTURERS EXHIBITION BUILDING COMPANY.
THIRTEEN-NINETEEN THE BIG BUILDING THE CHICAGO EXHIBITION OPEN ALL YEAR FOR DEALERS ONLY
MANUFACTURERS EXHIBITION BUILDING COMPANY.
1319 MICHIGAN AVE. ENTRANCE TO THE BIG BUILDING
C.E.R.
MANY LEADING FURNITURE DEALERS OF TO DAY CAN TRACE THEIR RISE TO SUCCESS FROM THE TIME OF THEIR FIRST VISIT TO THIS WONDERFUL MARKET.
THE SUCCESS OF YOUR SELLING PLANS - AND IN FACT, THE VERY LIFE OF YOUR BUSINESS - DEPENDS UPON YOUR DISCRIMINATION IN BUYING. GOOD SALESMEN HELP A GREAT DEAL BUT THEIR ABILITY CANNOT MAKE UP FOR GOODS THAT ARE NOT BOUGHT RIGHT.
WHAT YOU ARE LOOKING FOR IS THE FURNITURE THAT SELLS - AND THAT STAYS SOLD. WELL HERE IS WHERE YOU CAN FIND IT. THERE IS HERE THE GREATEST AGGREGATION OF THE FOREMOST SELLING LINES OF THE COUNTRY THAT COULD POSSIBLY BE GATHERED UNDER ONE ROOF. IT IS AN EDUCATION IN ITSELF JUST TO LOOK THEM OVER.
MORE THAN 2800 LIVE FURNITURE DEALERS VISITED THIS BUILDING LAST JANUARY AND THERE IS NOT ONE OF THEM WHO FEELS THAT HE CAN AFFORD TO STAY AT HOME IN JULY, NO MATTER HOW GOOD HIS BUSINESS MIGHT BE.
COME TO "1319" IN JULY AND MEET THE REAL BIG MEN OF THE FURNITURE INDUSTRY. CHICAGO'S SPLENDID HOTELS AND UNLIMITED FIELD FOR AMUSEMENT WILL MAKE YOUR BUYING TRIP A REAL VACATION INSTEAD OF A PAINFUL DUTY.
1319 MICHIGAN AVE. CHICAGO.

Vol. 4 No. 7   JULY, 1914

Canadian Furniture World
AND THE UNDERTAKER

Published by the Commercial Press, Limited, 32 Colborne Street, Toronto

The Selection *of* Tasteful Buyers

McLagan Furniture is always the selection of **tasteful** buyers, because McLagan Furniture is always **good taste**.

The present popularity of *Jacobean Furniture* assures the creation of much admiration and many profitable sales when such beautiful suites as this shown are included in your store display.

The Geo. McLagan Furniture Co., Limited
Stratford   Ontario

MISSION FURNITURE

THE MUNDELL MAKE

WHAT strikes you about our Mission Furniture is the variety. We make Davenports and Footstools and everything between that you can think of in Mission Goods,—all grades, all descriptions.

For Spring business these Mission Lines are indispensable. Furniture for halls, dens, living rooms, libraries, dining rooms, smoking rooms—frequently more than one half of many dwellings is furnished in Mission Style, and the demand goes on increasing.

You will be pleased with our new designs in this furniture—Heavy Oak Frames, Rich Spanish Leather Upholstering, all in dark tints as if centuries old,—simple lines, heavy, substantial, rich looking, there is no doubt that this class of furniture is one of the dealer's most attractive and profitable lines.

You will find all the varieties, all grades, all prices, in the Mundell line. Let us mail you blue prints.

JOHN C. MUNDELL & CO., LIMITED
ELORA :: ONTARIO

The Fischman Mattress

THE FISCHMAN PATENT MATTRESS

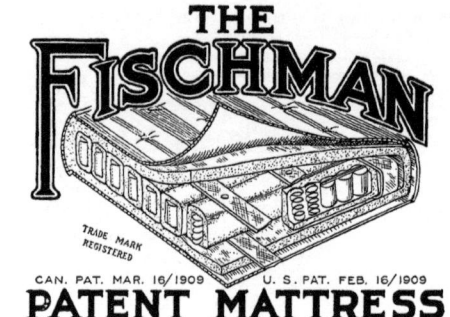

CAN. PAT. MAR. 16/1909   U. S. PAT. FEB. 16/1909

TRADE MARK REGISTERED

Is the *only* Spring Mattress made that can be rolled up—proof of its flexibility and greater wearing qualities, besides being easier for the user to handle.

We guarantee the Fischman Mattress for Five Years' good service.

The Fischman Patent Mattress can be secured in either felt or hair construction.

The Fischman Patent Mattress is so constructed that sagging or stretching is an impossibility.

The Fischman Mattress Co., Limited
333 Adelaide St. W.   Toronto

STRATFORD

There is an Ever-Widening Market for

¶ Upholstered Reed Chairs, Rockers and Suites, Verandah and Living Room Tables, Work Baskets, Jardiniere Stands, Palm Stands, Magazine Stands, etc. in great variety.

¶ Does your stock include a selection from our Davenport Beds and Leather and Imitation Upholstered Chairs and Rockers?

Attractive values every one.

Built right, finished right and sold to you at right price to make a good profit.

WRITE FOR PARTICULARS

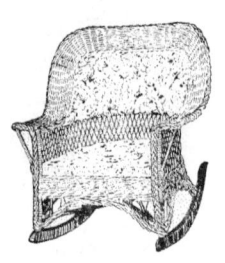

Stratford   Ontario

Camping Out Time is Here

Now is the season to stock up with Canvas Stretchers, Wire Cots, Upholstered Cots, and Verandah Sliding Couches.

We make them in various styles and widths from the cheapest wood frames to the more expensive steel and we can ship promptly.

Show these goods now---when people are interested. Don't wait for the rush--- order to-day and be prepared.

We also make a complete line of Brass Beds, Iron Beds, Springs, Mattresses and Pillows. Send for new complete catalog. It will interest you.

Victor Steel Sliding Couch. A couch by day and a 4 ft. bed at night.

The all steel "Wit Edge" Divan Cot.

The Ontario Spring Bed & Mattress Company, Limited
The Largest Bedding House in Canada
London - Ontario

For Small Living Rooms or Parlors

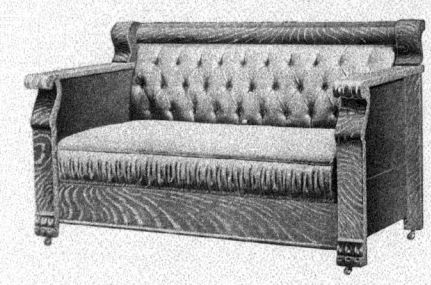

THE DUOFOLD BED is the latest product of a Bed. It supplies the demand for a handsome, practical Bed and Sofa Davenport combined in one piece of furniture. It is particularly designed for use in

**Small Apartments
Flats
Bungalows, Etc.**

where it is important that all furniture shall provide the maximum amount of comfort and serviceability, yet occupy as little space as possible. Size, when closed as sofa, only 50 inches between arms.

We have Duofolds to suit every customer, rich or poor. Prices from $24.50 to $59.00 net. We will sell them with mattresses complete. Try a sample

The Montreal Upholstering Company
1611-1613 Clarke St., MONTREAL, Can.

July, 1914   CANADIAN FURNITURE WORLD AND THE UNDERTAKER   5

STRATFORD

"Yes, Madam, They're as
Good as They Look —They're

There's no better foundation for a good selling argument than to *know* that you have the *right goods* to sell. Dealers can, with confidence, recommend Stratford Chairs to the limit because the materials, designing and construction are not surpassed in their class.

QUARTERED OAK
BOX SEAT DINERS
A SPECIALTY

Stratford   Ontario

Fashionable Furniture That Wears

Jacob & Josef Kohn
(The First Austrian Bentwood Furniture Mfg., Co., Ltd. of Vienna, Austria)

Manufacturers and Importers of

Genuine Austrian Bentwood Furniture

Especially designed to meet the needs of department stores—colors and patterns to match any scheme of decoration—specially adapted to the needs of confectioners and soda fountains. In fact, in all places where fine up-to-date appearance and long, rugged wear are economical necessities.

Special finishes in unusual colors made of selected Austrian Beechwood to your order. Remarkably rigid and durable. Write for catalog.

Inexpensive, Lightweight, Noiseless

Jacob & Josef Kohn
Vienna

110-112 West 27th St., New York
1414-18 So. Wabash Ave.   418 Maritime Bldg.
Chicago   Seattle, Wash.
215-19 Victoria St., Toronto, Canada

July, 1914   CANADIAN FURNITURE WORLD AND THE UNDERTAKER

STRATFORD

Every F.-G. Design is an

Our showing of carefully made Living Room Furniture includes only designs that will *hold* the admiration of the customer—no faddish effects that " go out " in a season or two.

Then these *sensible* designs are backed by sensible construction— the very strongest, with the greatest comfort-giving qualities that can be produced at a price the average customer will pay.

Davenport Beds Couches and Living Room Furniture

We are enthusiastic about these lines that are becoming so popular throughout the country. Let us send you details for comparison. We believe that you will like our proposition. Write us to-day.

Stratford   Ontario

BAETZ BROTHERS AND COMPANY
BERLIN :: ONTARIO.

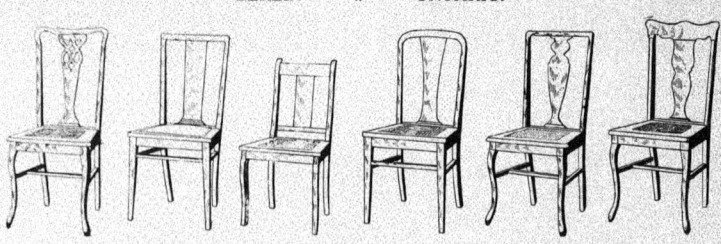

BEDROOM CHAIRS

These are some of the designs we make. They are made in many finishes:—*White, Grey and Ivory Enamel; Golden, Fumed and Silver Grey Oak; Standard, Tuna and old English Mahogany; Circassian Walnut, Satin Walnut and Kyonyx.*

Summer Days are "Peerless" Days

THE "Peerless" Folding Table

THIS Folding Table is very attractive, light in weight and exceptionally strong. It serves many purposes on the Verandah, in the garden and at the summer camp. Folds in the smallest possible space, making it the handiest table to carry about.

Our price will prove another big inducement to stock up at once. Write to-day.

HOURD & COMPANY, LIMITED
Wholesale Furniture Manufacturers
LONDON, - - CANADA
Sole Canadian Licensees and Manufacturers

Fine Grade Brass Furniture Trimmings

WRITE for prices and samples of our designs and finishes before placing your next order.

Exclusive Furniture demands *Exclusive Trimmings*. We can help you.

Special designs made up on the shortest notice.

Stratford Brass Co.
Limited
Stratford   Ontario

STRATFORD

No Better Time to Stock Up With

Made in all Woods, Designs and Finishes to Match Other Furniture Styles

WE manufacture **Globe-Wernicke** Sectional Bookcases and Office Filing Devices exclusively. Our factories at Stratford are entirely modern in every respect and are well equipped to maintain the high standard of excellence that has always been associated with **Globe-Wernicke**.

Hundreds of thousands of dollars have, and are now being spent in advertising to popularize the **Globe-Wernicke** product—to make it *the finishing touch to the furnishing of every home* and *the equipment of every office*.

Can you invest your money in any line of furniture that will sell so quickly and profitably?

WRITE FOR OUR CATALOG AND PRICES

Stratford   Ontario

The Kindel — Two Separate
Extremely Useful Articles at the Price of One.

Kindel Convertible Parlor Beds offer your customers added convenience, a saving in space and a money saving in the original purchase and in the reduction of rent.

Three types—The Somersaultic, Divanette and Parlor bed, all intended for separate and definite purposes. You'll find the prices *right* and the advertising that backs them up an added incentive to buy.

Write for our selling plan of "The Bed That Makes Itself."

The Kindel Bed Co. Ltd.
Toronto - Ontario

Authentic Store Front Book

Our eight years' experience in helping to design and build more than 30,000 KAWNEER STORE FRONTS has enabled us to compile and publish an authentic book on Store Fronts. This book contains photographs as well as drawings of many of the best paying Store Fronts in the country and if you are interested in Store Fronts don't take another step until you have seen "Boosting Business No. 2." Let us help you build a new Store Front that will pay for itself by increasing your business.

Just a Card for "Boosting Business No. 2" will bring it without obligation

Kawneer Manufacturing Co., Ltd.
Francis J. Plym, President
Dept. S.   1197 Bathurst Street
Toronto, Ontario

Colleran's Lock Weave Spring

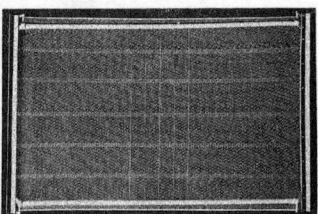

Restful because it is flexible. Good value because its strength makes it last a lifetime. Guaranteed not to sag.

This spring is interlocked with coppered steel wire and reinforced with heavy welded end cross wires. Made in wood or steel frame. Write for our prices.

Colleran Patent Spring Mattress Co.
Toronto, Ont.

July, 1914   CANADIAN FURNITURE WORLD AND THE UNDERTAKER   11

STRATFORD

Keep Your Stocks Complete

You can't afford to lose sales by not having what your customers ask for in Outside Furniture. Keep a full line of Stratford goods on your floors and you'll be money ahead.

Our Summer Furniture Lines include all kinds of Garden, Lawn, Verandah, Park and Camp goods. Write for our prices and get after the Summer trade at once.

Stratford Manufacturing Company, Limited
Stratford   Ontario

The "Classic Queen" is Well Made

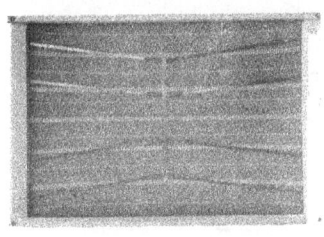

SINGLE weave with extra heavy ribs every eight inches. Exceptionally strong iron support. Tin over key-way. Absolutely vermin proof.

All Classic Woven Wire Bed Springs are made of the very best materials for the popular priced trade. Every spring we turn out is fully guaranteed, and each sale affords you a generous profit.

Classic Springs Pay the Dealer

The Frame & Hay Fence Co., Limited - STRATFORD ONTARIO

KELLARIC MATTRESSES

"Makes Sleeptime Sleepfull"

—They are Already Introduced to Your Customers

WHEN you start to describe the principle of the McKellar Mattress your customer immediately remarks, "Oh yes, I've seen them advertised." Then she looks for the laced opening and feels the soft cotton felt---so firm, resilient and sanitary. She **knows** a good mattress when she **sees** one.

If you have Kellaric Mattresses in stock you can sell them quickly, and every sale made helps to sell more.

Let us get together. It will be good business for both of us for you to write for our prices to-day.

The McKellar Bedding Co., Ltd.
Fort William   Ontario

The Berlin Bedding Company, Limited, 31-33 Front St. E., Toronto, Ont.

**Let the "Chesley Twins"
Build Up Your Trade**

No Gaping Pedestal
in the

"Twin" Pedestal Extension Table

¶ Once the dealer places two or three designs of the "Chesley Twins" on his floors he begins to notice the trend of public opinion in favor of the **twin pedestal** idea.

¶ "Twin" Extension Tables are made with a pair of pedestals, each complete in itself. They always present a completely finished appearance whether opened or closed, showing no unfinished surfaces when extended. The three-point support of each pedestal gives the table unequalled supporting strength.

¶ In our range of designs and finishes you'll find just those qualities that appeal to those of average and better means---the trade that you find most profitable.

¶ Our new catalog will enable you to determine the advantages of the "Twin Pedestal Extension Table." Why not write for it.

*lso Parlor
nd Library
ables and
pecialties.*

The Chesley Furniture Co., Limited
Chesley, - Ontario

That New Home Should Have An

"Elmira" Electric Grate Mantel

THE Bride, as she steps into her new home, will be pleased with the cosiness and finished appearance of her living room fitted with an "Elmira" Electric Mantel.

No trouble to install---No chimney or tiling necessary---No smoke, dust or dirt---no danger of anything catching fire. Just steady, even heat at small cost. If she moves, she can take the mantel along just as conveniently as the piano.

Let us show you our new designs, Mr. Dealer. There's big profit awaiting you in Elmira Electric Mantels.

The Elmira Interior Woodwork Co., Limited
C.P.R.   Elmira, Ontario   G.T.R.

Our No. 10H Chair For Ice Cream Parlors

Hot weather opens up new avenues of profit. This attractive chair is made especially for Ice Cream Parlors and for every purpose where a serviceable light-weight chair at a moderate price is required. Furnished without the tray if desired. **Your order will be shipped at once.**

Our catalog shows a great variety of chairs and rockers for bedroom and living-room; chairs for dining-room, kitchen, kindergarten and office; folding chairs, restaurant and assembly hall seating. Have you a copy?

The
North American Bent Chair Co.
Limited
Owen Sound   -   Ontario

An appeal to the Taste as Well as the Purse

A Meaford Effect in
Surface Mahogany and Surface Oak

¶ This suite is a big drawing card wherever it is shown. It is a good example of the exclusive lines that have *increased* our trade despite depression periods.

¶ The true color and graining of the highest priced mahogany and oak are produced so perfectly that even good judges of woods frequently admit their inability to determine its genuineness. Both color and finish are permanent and will not crack nor chip.

¶ We are bringing out many more suites equally attractive, affording you choosing possibilities unequalled in Canada in popular-priced furniture.

¶ Your customers will appreciate the real value in Meaford Furniture. Why not stock up now?

The
Meaford Manufacturing Co.
Limited
Meaford, Ontario

Textileather

If you have not seen the above brand of **artificial leather,** then get acquainted, ask for samples.

It is the most satisfactory furniture covering ever made anywhere.

Textileather Co., 212 Fifth Ave., New York, N.Y.
WRITE DIRECT OR TO
Frank Schmidt - Berlin, Ontario

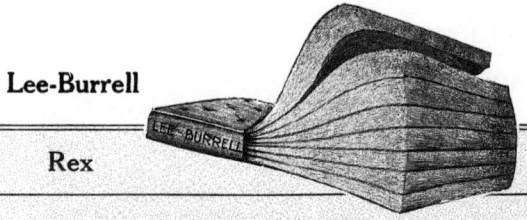

Lee-Burrell   Regent

Rex   Invictus

Mattresses of Proven Quality

The **appearance** of a mattress does not finally determine its worth. ¶ Its real value doesn't show up in the "looks." ¶ Neither is it "selling talk" that makes a commodity serviceable--- it is the **real worth in the construction.**

The Standard lines are built for exceptional service, every one of them, and they have fulfilled, in actual use, the many claims we have made for them. ¶ That's the **Standard** guarantee for both you and your customer.

The Standard Bedding Company
27-29 Davies Ave. - Toronto, Ontario

WEISGLASS

Trade Marks that ensure Satisfaction

Confidence between manufacturer and dealer is essential to successful trading. S. Weisglass, Limited, have established a most satisfactory connection based on careful attention to all orders—large or small. The same critical appreciation of details—perfect construction—enduring finish, obtained with "ACID PROOF" Lacquer—shipment on time—all these features are considered. In this manner confidence has been established between us and our dealers. We at all times endeavor to promote the most friendly relations, coupled with businesslike attention.

LOOK AT THIS BED!

The one design wanting on your floor

S. WEISGLASS, LIMITED
TORONTO   MONTREAL

Beds
Springs
Couches

Davenports
Costumers
Wall Racks

Right to the Minute

are these new effects we have brought out in

Leather Covered Lounge Chairs

Good value in sight from every angle, with the necessary toughness in frame and upholstering to keep it so.

Write for our prices. You can use the Imperial make to increase your profits every month in the year.

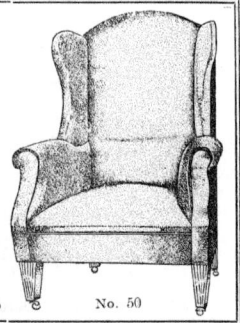

No. 62

No. 50

Imperial Furniture Co., 585-591 Queen St. W., Toronto

Give Your Salesmen Increased Efficiency

Install the "TWENTIETH CENTURY" RUG RACK and make selling rugs a pleasant, easy task. The old, laborious "rug pile" method is a time waster and a severe tax upon the patience of both salesmen and customers.

By displaying your rugs on the "TWENTIETH CENTURY" RUG RACK, several customers can be waited upon at once and a demonstration is easily affected. Send us the height of your ceiling and specify the number of rugs you wish to put on rack and we will give you full particulars as to space taken up, etc.

No matter how large or small your business, we have a rug rack to just suit your purpose at a price that is speedily repaid by the additional business obtained. Write for Catalog.

The Steel Furnishing Co., Ltd.
New Glasgow, N.S.

Manufacturers of Rug Racks, Linoleum Racks, Hearth Rug Racks and Clothing Racks.

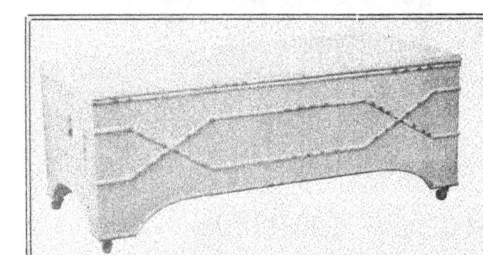

Three large Rug Racks holding 120 rugs each

AN ATTRACTIVE Bedroom Box

¶ Made of ¾ in. B.C. Red Cedar covered with Japanese matting and trimmed with rattan. Bent brass hinges and casters. Top panelled and nicely padded. Made in three sizes.

Catalog of other attractive designs sent on request.

D. L. Shafer & Co.
ST. THOMAS · ONTARIO

Do you know of any Furniture Dealer or Funeral Director, anywhere in Canada, who is not a subscriber to the Canadian Furniture World and The Undertaker? If so, you will be doing him a favor by sending us his name and address so that we can send him a sample copy and subscription order blank.

Victoriaville Furniture

is made to last. Our designs are up-to-date and neat in every respect,—designs that go a long way towards making a sale.

This is the class of furniture that appeals to the majority of your customers and our prices allow the Furniture Dealers who handle our goods to make a good substantial profit.

Send for our catalogue and see all the new and pleasing designs we have to offer.

The Victoriaville Furniture Company
Victoriaville, Que.

"Iron Chairs"

Made of wood; otherwise, chairs that wear like iron.

That is what you get from our factory, which is devoted exclusively to the manufacture of chairs.

Our prices are ridiculously low when you consider the quality, and our catalogue will show you our different lines. Will you send for it?

The Victoriaville Chair Manufacturing Company
Victoriaville, Que.

Rattan Chairs

are the most popular class of furniture for the hot summer months, especially for verandah and porch use as well as inside the house.

Canadian Rattan Chairs

are manufactured from the best selected reeds, and the designs are so attractive that they almost sell themselves especially when the reasonable price at which we are able to produce them is also taken into consideration.

The Canadian Rattan Chair Company, Limited
Victoriaville, Que.

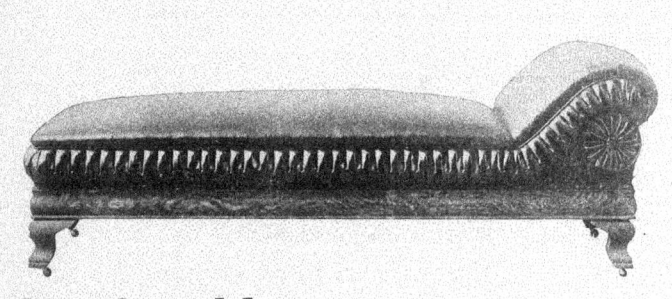

Comfortable Upholstered Furniture and Brass Bedsteads

are our specialties. Our upholstered furniture is made to give the greatest possible value and comfort at the least possible cost to your customers.

Our Brass Bedsteads are made in new and pleasing designs and a stock of these on your floors will boost your business and profits. They are made so that they may be cleaned with gasolene.

The Victoriaville Bedding Company
Limited

Victoriaville, Que.

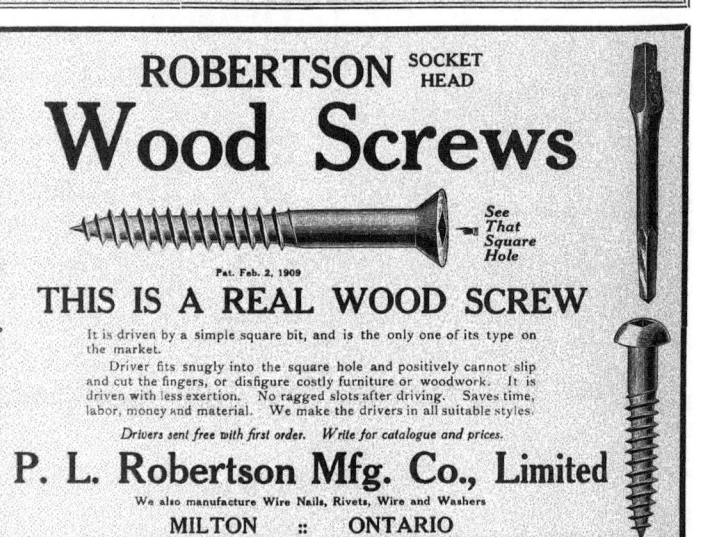

SHELLACS

If you are in the market for first-class Shellac we believe it would be to your advantage to get in touch with us.

HIGH GRADE VARNISHES
FILLERS and GRAINING INKS

THE AULT & WIBORG CO. OF CANADA
LIMITED

MONTREAL   TORONTO   WINNIPEG

ROBERTSON SOCKET HEAD
Wood Screws

See That Square Hole

Pat. Feb. 2, 1909

THIS IS A REAL WOOD SCREW

It is driven by a simple square bit, and is the only one of its type on the market.

Driver fits snugly into the square hole and positively cannot slip and cut the fingers, or disfigure costly furniture or woodwork. It is driven with less exertion. No ragged slots after driving. Saves time, labor, money and material. We make the drivers in all suitable styles.

Drivers sent free with first order. Write for catalogue and prices.

P. L. Robertson Mfg. Co., Limited
We also manufacture Wire Nails, Rivets, Wire and Washers

MILTON :: ONTARIO

KNECHTEL

Our New House Desk is Large and Roomy—

and is built to accommodate

"Weis - Knechtel" Receding Door Bookcases

Bound to be Big Sellers

No. 36

Thousands of Dollars Spent in Advertising "WEIS" Bookcases

The leading American magazines with enormous circulations in Canada are telling their Canadian readers about the "Weis" sectional bookcases, thereby creating a demand that every furniture dealer should capitalize.

Weis-Knechtel Bookcases have more genuine talking points than any other on the market, and are therefore easily sold.

You—Mr. Dealer, have our new catalogue showing these bookcases. Mail us a trial order right now for at least a sample stack.

No. 36

THE KNECHTEL FURNITURE CO., LIMITED
HANOVER   ONTARIO

"L & P" Construction
Prevents Sagging

¶ Leggett & Platt Single Cone Spring Beds conform to the weight of every part of the body it supports, insuring the most refreshing sleep.

¶ In construction, material and workmanship, the "L" Metal Tag Trade Mark guarantees fidelity in every detail.

¶ The influence of the ultimate purchaser is always to be reckoned with. One "L" MetalTag sale invariably leads to another.

¶ An order for "L" Trade Marked Spring Beds puts you in the "no competitors" class. They are the best paying line to which you can devote your attention.

Our complete catalogue is ready for you

The Leggett & Platt
Spring Bed Company, Ltd.
Windsor, Ont.

This Metal Tag — on Every Spring

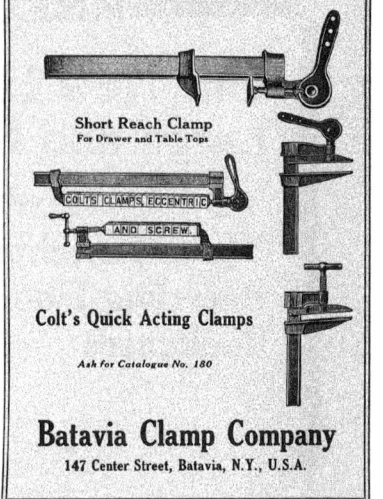

Short Reach Clamp
For Drawer and Table Tops

COLT'S CLAMPS, ECCENTRIC AND SCREW

Colt's Quick Acting Clamps

Ask for Catalogue No. 180

Batavia Clamp Company
147 Center Street, Batavia, N.Y., U.S.A.

Is Yours a Growing Store?

Here are ideas which will help it grow faster. Here are suggestions for the young man starting in business in Northwest Canada, as well as for the dealer with an established trade.

BUILDING A FURNITURE BUSINESS

is a cloth bound book of 205 pages, every one of which contains helpful hints for the furniture dealer. Though written in easy narrative style as the story of "Bobby Burton, Successful Furniture Dealer," the book is neither fiction, theory or dry preachment. The incidents, plans and experiences are woven together from actual practice in widely separated localities.

If your trade is in a rut you will find here a suggestion for a new sales plan, a new advertisement or something to start people talking about your store.

Every man who is looking for new ideas in furniture merchandise and methods will find something worth while in this book.

Postpaid, $1.00.

The Commercial Press, Ltd.
Publishers of The Canadian Furniture World and The Undertaker

The Lightest Mattress Ever Made

The Celebrated "DIXIE" Compartment Mattress
Stuffed with "Java Kapok"
The Finest Mattress Material Known

Unlike any other mattress now on the market in every particular—and far superior in every detail.

"Java Kapok" has long been recognised as the finest mattress material available. But on account of its extreme lightness it could not be used in the ordinary tufted mattress. In the DIXIE'S "compartments" it is held in position.

Regular 4' 6" DIXIE stuffed with "Java Kapok" weighs only 30 lbs., as compared with the 45 to 47 lbs. weight of the finest cotton felt mattresses. Could you have a better selling argument?

"Java Kapok" is a vegetable product, perfectly pure and clean, and wonderfully light, buoyant and elastic. It is also perfectly non-absorbent.

Get one examine it and you'll realize it is the big-selling mattress of the future.

Geo. Gale & Sons, Limited
Waterville, Quebec
MONTREAL   TORONTO   WINNIPEG

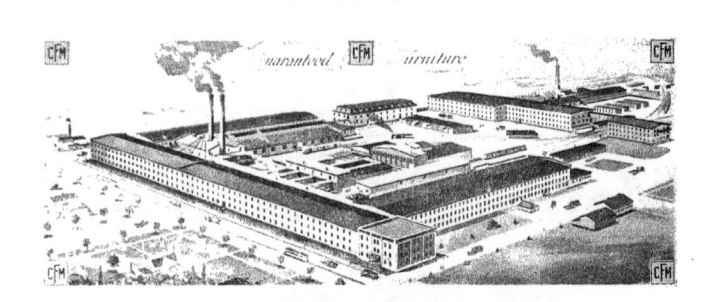

CANADA FURNITURE MANUFACTURERS
LIMITED

GENERAL OFFICES
WOODSTOCK, ONTARIO.

June 10, 1914.

Messrs. CANADIAN LINDERMAN CO.,
Woodstock, Ont.

Gentlemen,

With reference to the Linderman Dovetail Glue Jointer, which we have had in operation for the past two years, would say that at the outset there were some handicaps to the most successful results from the Linderman, but these have been removed and we can conscientiously say that the Linderman Process is a signal success for those who will intelligently handle the proposition. We find there is quite a saving in lumber, time and glue, and there is no question of the superiority of this tapered wedged joint over all others.

We will be pleased at any time to show prospective purchasers this Machine in operation at our Woodstock Factory.

Yours truly,

CANADIAN FURNITURE MANUFACTURERS, Limited.

A. H. Watson
General Superintendent.

Making TABLE-SLIDES is a Specialty Business

For more than TWENTY-FIVE YEARS we have made TABLE SLIDES exclusively. Our Factory is equipped with Special Machinery which enables us to make SLIDES,—BETTER and CHEAPER than the furniture manufacturer.

Canadian Table makers are rapidly adopting WABASH SLIDES

Because { They ELIMINATE SLIDE TROUBLES
{ Are CHEAPER and BETTER

Reduced Costs
Increased Out-put } BY USING **WABASH SLIDES**

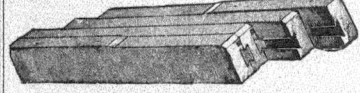

Made by
B. WALTER & CO.
Wabash, Ind.

The Largest EXCLUSIVE TABLE-SLIDE Manufacturers in America
ESTABLISHED 1887

J-M ASBESTOS TABLE COVERS AND MATS
ARE BIG MONEY-MAKERS

Hundreds of dealers are reaping a neat harvest of dollars every year from the sale of these goods.

You can do the same if you will display them to advantage in your store. Every up-to-date housewife in your community is a prospect for J-M Asbestos Table Covers and Mats.

Being manufacturers we can sell at prices that enable you to undersell your competitors at a better profit than they make—and at the same time give your customers better goods.

Don't ignore this opportunity to increase your revenue. *Write to-day for our interesting Dealer Proposition.*

THE CANADIAN H. W. JOHNS-MANVILLE CO., Limited

Manufacturers of Show-Case, Show-Window and General Illuminating Systems; Pipe Coverings; Dry Batteries; Fire Extinguishers, Etc.

TORONTO MONTREAL VANCOUVER WINNIPEG

Sell Berlin Tables With the Automatic Top

BERLIN Tables are made with non-dividing pedestals. Our Positive Extension Controller opens both sides by a gentle pull on one side, the top always being centered. ¶ Combined with rare beauty of design and finish and reliable workmanship, Berlin Tables offer you a real advantage in sale making.

Write for reproductions of our newest designs and prices. The popularity of of Berlin Tables warrants you in placing a stock on your floors at once.

The Berlin Table Manufacturing Co., Limited
BERLIN :: ONTARIO

This Beautiful Alabastine Statuary
Makes a Profitable Side Line for the Live Furniture Dealer

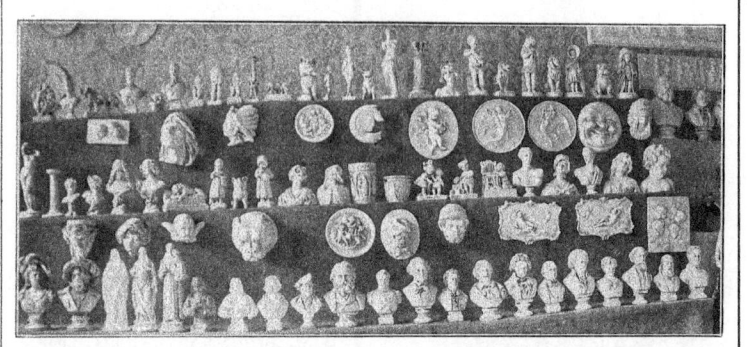

$20.00 buys this assortment of attractive **ALABASTINE STATUARY**. 100 different pieces up to 12 inches in size, all artistically finished. Statuary is greatly in demand, and these pieces retail as high as $1.00 each. We can give you any quantity of any subject.

All the most popular subjects from the leading art galleries are included in our showing. $150.00 for this assortment—the most beautifully finished goods on the market. The very best selection of sellers suitable for home, club, den, and hall. Get our new proposition.

We also manufacture a profitable line of beautiful **FRAMED PICTURES** and **MIRRORS**, especially for the furniture trade. It consists of **OIL PAINTINGS, ENGRAVINGS, PASTELS, WATER COLORS, ETC.**, at prices that are the very lowest in Canada for the quality. We make up an admirable line of 75 Framed Pictures at $50.00.

Write for Our Complete Catalogs

G. L. IRISH, 499 Queen St. West, Toronto

Canadian Furniture World and the Undertaker

PUBLISHED THE 1ST OF EACH MONTH BY

THE COMMERCIAL PRESS, LIMITED
32 COLBORNE STREET, TORONTO
Phone Main 4978

D. O. McKinnon	- - -	President
W. L. Edmonds	- - -	Vice-President
Weston Wrigley	-	Vice-President and Manager of Trade Papers
J. C. Armer	-	Vice-President and Manager of Technical Papers
James O'Hagan	- - -	Editor
John A. Fullerton		Associate Editor
Wm. J. Bryans	"	"

Staff Representatives

Geo. H. Honsberger, Advertising Manager - - - Toronto
F. C. D. Wilkes, Eastern Manager, 704 Unity Bldg. - Montreal
R. C. Howson, Western Representative - - Winnipeg
E. J. MacIntyre, Room 1155, 122 South Michigan Avenue - Chicago
C. G. Brandt, *Circulation Manager*, Toronto

Subscriptions
Canada, $1.00 a year. Other Countries, $2.00 a year

Publishers' Statement.—2000 copies of this issue of the Canadian Furniture World are printed for circulation. Itemized statement, showing distribution according to provinces, will be furnished on request.

Vol. 4   JULY, 1914   No. 7

Business Still Adjusting Itself. Business is still going through the process of adjustment; and in the process it is gradually getting into better shape.

It will, no doubt, be some months before normal conditions will again obtain, but the fact should not be overlooked that the general quiet condition of trade to-day was preceded by a period of abnormal trade activity such as the country had never in its history experienced. In other words, we are measuring the trade conditions of to-day by the abnormal trade conditions of a year or two ago.

With the manufacturers business is somewhat irregular. It takes a spurt some weeks and then possibly takes a rest other weeks, but practically all agree that the net result is a step forward.

The fact that the demand for merchandise, as experienced by the manufacturers, is good in fits and starts, proves that which has time and again been asserted, namely, that stocks in retailers' hands are light and require to be frequently replenished in order to meet the everyday demand. That is a healthy sign.

Until, however, the current year's crop is assured, we cannot expect to see confidence fully restored, and particularly in the Western Provinces.

So far conditions for the crop of 1914 are favorable. In the Prairie Provinces the area under cultivation is larger than last year. Last Autumn the climatic conditions were favorable to plowing and this Spring they have been favorable for seeding.

If the best is not any too good for yourself it should not be any too good for your customers.

Canada's Wealth-Creating Powers. But whether or not good crops are gathered in the Dominion as a whole during the current year, there can be no doubt about the future of the country.

There undoubtedly was a great deal of wild speculation in the West, but that no longer exists. It has been smothered.

So far as the wealth-producing resources of the country are concerned, there can be no doubt in regard to the greatness of their possibilities. They are as real as the fact of our existence. All authorities abroad as well as at home agree upon this point.

Our agricultural, manufacturing, mining, fishing and forestry industries are all told creating new wealth at the aggregate rate of approximately three billion dollars annually. And in this estimate no consideration is given to the wealth-producing potentialities of the immigrant.

A country that is creating wealth at this rate— $250,000,000 monthly—has no need to put on crape when a period of rest and recuperation settles down upon it.

It is a wise man who knows his own business, and a wiser one who thoroughly attends to it.

Is Any of the Money Yours? There are lying in the banks of Canada unclaimed balances to the amount of $775,164.97, and unpaid dividends to the amount of $2,921.97.

The surprising part of it is the small amount of unpaid dividends. People who have dividends coming due are evidently less forgetful than people who have money on deposit. But forgetfulness is not the only cause of balances being unclaimed. Among the known causes is death, which incidentally reminds one it is us and not our money that the Grim Reaper wants when he beckons us over the border.

The Blue Book doesn't tell how much of the unclaimed balances is the property of business men. But it is safe betting that very little of it belongs to retailers. Very few of them have so much money that they forget about it.

Should you have any doubt about your having any unclaimed balances or dividends, just glance over the Blue Book. It only contains about eleven hundred pages.

It would be interesting to know how many people ever open its pages. In all probability the number is even smaller than that which opens the Greek Testament.

But the law says the book must be printed. Thank goodness the law doesn't say it must be read.

Don't leave your store in charge of one who has not a practical knowledge of the goods; any customer wants and expects intelligent attention.

The Furniture Man as a Stockholder. Every furniture man has a certain amount invested in his business, and should receive a certain return on that investment over and above his own salary and other expenses. He is the stockholder in his business, and like the stockholder in any other enterprise, should receive a certain dividend upon his capital.

Many furniture men have not a proper conception of business. They seem to hold the opinion that as long as they get a living, and put away a few dollars for a rainy day, that they are successful business men. They should, however, give themselves a certain salary. This should be possible, as well as all other expenses, and still leave something for revenue from capital. The dealer, if he was not in business, could draw a certain salary elsewhere, and invest his capital where it would bring some return.

It is time that every furniture man got down to a business basis in the conduct of his store. In every well-conducted establishment, the manager, superintendent and other officers, receive a salary. So should the furniture man.

Profits are only made after all legitimate expenses in the conduct of a business have been met.

No man ever got nervous prostration pushing his business; you get it only when the business pushes you.

Canada's Magnificent Distances. Canada is a great country, at any rate as far as magnificent distances are concerned. It took the member of the House of Commons from the Yukon nineteen days to reach the capital. Mr. D. B. Hanna, of the Canadian Northern Railway, has figured out that had he journeyed westward, crossed the Behring Sea, taken the Siberian railway at Vladivostock for Europe and crossed to Canada it would only have taken the member for the Yukon six days more to reach Ottawa than by the more direct route.

If some of the members of the House of Commons were so far away that they never reached the capital it is improbable the country would be the loser thereby. This of course does not apply to the member for the Yukon.

Do you know what per cent. of your sales it costs you to do business? If you do not, you should get busy at once and install some simple method that will give you this vital information

Cater to the Masses. The trade of the well-to-do is certainly valuable, and is to be sought after by the merchant, but the dealer in the country will find it unwise to cater especially to this class of trade, and neglect the masses. It is this latter class that the merchant in the country has to depend on principally for the building up of big sales. It may be nicer to serve the person who comes in attired in costly clothes, but it should not be forgotten that the fellow in the overalls or the woman in the print dress, frequently have considerable money to spend, and are generally easier to please and satisfy.

Make a little more effort and a little more business will come to you.

A Record In Exports. While the manufacturers of Canada have experienced a diminution in business in the home market, the opposite has been the case in the export trade.

This is quite apparent from the preliminary statement just issued for the fiscal year ending March 31, 1914.

This statement is gratifying in two ways. It shows not only an increase in the total, but in the proportion of manufactured goods to the total exports of Canadian products generally.

The value of the manufactured goods exported was $57,443,452. This is the largest on record, being an increase of 24.10 per cent. over 1913, and of 37.80 per cent. over 1912.

Putting it another way, the increase over 1913 in the exports of manufactured goods was larger by two million dollars than the total exported fifteen years ago, while the increase over 1912 was about half a million dollars larger than the total of nine years ago.

For example, in 1899 the value of the manufactured goods exported was $11,706,000; the increase for the fiscal year 1914 over 1913 was $13,749,000. In 1905 the total value of the manufactured goods exported was $21,191,000; the increase for 1914 over 1912 was $21,607,000.

Now in regard to the proportion of the exports of manufactured goods to the total exports of all kinds of Canadian products. In 1914 the proportion was 13.30 per cent.; in 1913, 12.56 per cent.; and in 1912, 12.34 per cent.

It will thus be seen that the Canadian manufacturers are more than holding their own in the export trade with other branches of industry.

While the home market is, and always will be our most important market, the experience of the past year has taught more clearly than ever before that the manufacturers of this country must, if their factories are to run to full capacity in dull seasons as well as in active ones, pay greater attention to the export trade than many of them have been disposed to do in the past.

If it had not been for the large export trade which certain manufacturers had developed, they would have been compelled to run their factories on short time during the past year, on account of the decline in the home trade. One of them, at least, exported nearly 70 per cent. of its output and kept its plant going at full blast.

The home market is the manufacturer's right hand, but the foreign market is his left, and it is a good thing to cultivate its use.

SHORT NOTES FROM THE EDITOR'S PEN.

Signs of better business are evident everywhere.

* * * *

This is the season of renewed life. Put new life into your business.

* * * *

Keep busy and you will be happy. And you remember that phrase about the devil finding mischief for idle hands to do?

* * * *

The dealer who first catches on to a new need of the public will be the first to reap the advantages of the business in that line.

* * * *

Practical demonstration begets sales, except in the case of a clerk demonstrating the jaw-exercising qualities of chewing gum.

* * * *

The number of hours devoted to work is not a gauge of value. Some clerks can sell more goods in an hour than others can in a day.

* * * *

There are only two ways you can increase your business—you must either get new customers, or get more business from old customers.

* * * *

Shake hands as if you meant to extend a welcome, not as if you were afraid the other fellow would bite you before you let go of him.

* * * *

One set of manners for the store, and another set for the street will not make the merchant popular with the rank and file of his patrons.

Furniture for the Porch

Pergola erected in large Western furniture store to display summer porch furniture items. It does the trick splendidly.

NEARLY all the houses being built to-day as family homes have porches or verandahs added, making very nearly an extra room. This extra room should come in for considerable attention at this season by furniture dealers, and in the larger centres it does so. In Halifax, Montreal, Toronto, Winnipeg, Vancouver, and the many cities and towns in between the large furniture stores are devoting more attention to summer verandah and porch furniture, but there is still plenty of opportunity for more business in the large centres and new business in the smaller towns.

In Europe full advantage is taken of the porch and verandah as a living room, while here in the New World we are just beginning to realize these advantages. Eldon Thompson and Mary W. Mount bring out this in an article in a recent number of The House Beautiful. We are now beginning to covet sequestered verandahs and outdoor living rooms, say they, and it is almost needless to say that the furniture of these places should be appropriate in form and contour, built very substantially, so that it may be able to stand the test of inclement weather and the more rugged outdoor use.

Grass rugs are much used for floor coverings, and there are also beautiful Indian rugs to be had. If fortunate enough to possess a Navajo blanket use it by all means, for the simple crude colors and primitive designs are very effective, and its wearing capacity is endless. An air of coziness and more seclusion may also be gotten by using the rolling shades of split bamboo; they are so deftly made and so good in color, that they always add to rather than detract from a piazza.

Wicker and Chintz Combinations.

There are also many attractive accessories that impart a home-like quality and add a sense of exquisite comfort—beautiful objects made of wicker and willow combined with bright colored chintzes and cretonnes of simple designs that harmonize so well with green trees, cool-toned vines, and the open sky.

Porch chairs there are in variety, but something new are those imported from China made of Indian cane whose luxury is not to be gauged on a hot summer's day. One of these has the back arranged like a Morris chair, where one can either sit erect or recline by means of adjusting a willow rod. It has broad arms containing deep cane pockets for books and magazines, and fitting beneath its ample seat is a wicker bench which can be drawn out to form a semi-couch for lounging. Another Chinese chair is merely broad and deep and comfortable and substantially woven, defying the ravages of the elements.

Almost all piazzas have hanging baskets filled with flowers and trailing vines, and willow flower stands have come into vogue which are shown either in their natural color or they may be stained to tone in with the porch furniture. There are wicker work stands, too, whose tops, made of chintz covered with glass, may be utilized as a tray, or the stand itself may be used as a fit substitute for a serving table. The small folding wicker work stands are also very practical and can be carried from place to place. And then there is the new porch screen, whose frame is wicker with a broad frieze of cretonne at the top. It is light enough to be portable and possesses not only decorative possibilities, but is a serviceable contrivance for protection from wind and sun.

A cellarette and serving-table combined made of willow is circular in shape, with a large metal tank in the centre for keeping the various drinks, etc., chilled; the removable tray on top can be used for serving, and the compartments surrounding the tank keep in place the bottles and glasses. This may be easily removed when not in use or it may be converted into a convenient device for holding serving or writing materials.

Portable tea tables are used more and more. Perhaps the most practical are those on wheels—carts made of light wicker and cretonne, with a shelf beneath for holding toasted muffins and cakes. Another popular model is composed of two tiers, two large round cretonne-covered trays resting upon a wicker framework, having a firm handle on each side by which it is carried. Muffin stands of wicker or plaited grass are also useful, and they are generally a necessary part of the tea-serving outfit.

For Afternoon Refreshments

If sandwiches and cakes and beer or ginger ale are to be preferred as refreshments, there are an endless array of fascinating wicker and cretonne novelties that are just the thing for informal use. The sandwich basket, for instance, of wicker, is long and narrow and shallow, with two strong handles that cross in the centre, and the bottom is of glass or a bright-colored plaque of porcelain, which is easily kept clean. This is a far more interesting and convenient way of serving than the more conventional fashion of former days. The basket idea is again carried out in the form of a

When we bought this furniture we had in mind the sweltering hot days of midsummer. We knew you would want comfortable chairs into which to sink your weary and overheated body. Come in an see. what we have. It makes you long to rest even to look at them.

We would like everyone to see our line of Porch and Lawn Furniture made from Japanese ea Weed. These goods are extra g oodvalue.

W. H. HEATH & SON.
Wallaceburg and Sombra

Advertising outdoor furniture in the small town.

beer or ginger ale moat, which is circular in shape, having a tank in the centre for holding ice, and the surrounding compartments used for glasses and bottles. This basket has also strong handles that can stand the strain of weight.

Another receptacle that includes all the conveniences, is an Apollinaris and ginger ale tray, with compartments for various sized glasses, with an ice chamber in the centre. The whole thing is of willow with a solid bottom, and the coasters have centres of flounced cretonne, covered with glass.

These various accessories have an unusual value, too, when used for serving refreshments for any outdoor occasion. In the free and easy hospitality of a summer home, these trays may be arranged and then placed upon the piazza, or brought out under the trees, or beside the tennis court, and the guests may then help themselves to refreshing drinks at their pleasure.

The warm summer evenings spent in an outdoor living room in easy chair or hammock are perhaps the most luxurious of all hours, and if one wants the added comfort of reading there is no better light than that cast by softly glowing wicker lamps. Those that have electric attachments, of course are much cooler and more convenient than those which depend upon oil. They come in various shapes and sizes—some are round, others again are oblong and square, having wicker shades that conform with the general scheme of the lamp. They have metal turrets and compartments for holding cut flowers, which is a novelty this season, and they are not only practical, but very beautiful and decorative. There are myriad other lamps of wicker, too, which are very attractive without the flower receptacles, and how much more suitable they are to country needs than those of metal or china of former days, which were overloaded with ornament and too glaring decoration! Lanterns for porch and outdoor use with electric attachments are also shown with wicker frames lined with bright-colored cretonnes that give a light subdued and beautiful.

Make the Verandah the Summer Room

With these many possibilities that are suggested here, the piazza should vie in comfort and attractiveness with any of the most carefully furnished rooms in the house. Many of the articles suggested are well suited for the interior. Another style of furnishing an inexpensive porch is to use for a wooden house blue and white as the scheme for the decoration. Japanese cotton rugs are the prettiest and least expensive for this purpose, and Delft jars and bowls can be beautifully introduced for flowers. The cushions would be best covered with English block chintz in Delft blue and white, while the furniture might be hickory or wood painted blue, with natural colored woven seats and backs. The awnings for such a porch should be blue and white, unless vines are planted about the porch for shade. To add to the attractiveness of this scheme of decoration, blue and white flowers would be very lovely, outlining the porch in boxes, although a blue furnished porch is sometimes particularly beautiful when edged with golden nasturtiums.

Birch furniture has many attractions. It is made of the limbs and straight, slender trunks of the yellow birch in their natural state. The beautiful, yellowish gray coloring and satiny surface of the bark of this most beautiful of the trees give it a peculiar attractiveness. It is always suitable for porch furnishing, and if it is desired to give a sort of rough-and ready aspect, a touch of the unconventional to the house or to a single room, it is especially for bungalows in the woods, at once pleasing and appropriate.

Seats for Porch and Lawn.

For porch and lawn use there are wooden benches, seating four people, and folding chairs of painted wood. There is also a variety of plain and serviceable chairs, useful for porch, hall or living room, with maple or fumed or green oak frames and cane seats and backs. Weatherproof willow armchairs, roomy and comfortable, made on the simplest lines, in the natural color, are a nice line.

The Tilbury tea cart, for serving tea or refreshments on the porch or the lawn, is a unique bit of mechanism in willow. It runs on two castered legs and two wheels, has shelves across the lower part for refuse bowls, and a glass tray on the top for serving. The wheels have rubber tires, and the casters are on ball bearings, so that it obeys the directing hand easily and quickly. A willow muffin rack, or stand, with four shelves, for serving muffins, sandwiches, toast, at afternoon tea, or at the bedside, is a novelty. Large willow trays, with three coasters in the centre for holding bottles, are nice features. Still another cheap class of porch furniture is the white wood Dutch variety, which one sees a great deal of just now, but which has little to recommend it for outdoor use except its cheapness, as no all-wood furniture made with glue or nails lasts well when exposed to all sorts of weather conditions.

NEW WICKER FURNITURE

This spring shows a tendency away from the long popular greens to browns and greys for willow furniture. Of course, green will always be immensely popular with some people, and it is full of summery suggestion, especially in its olive tones. The best wicker furniture is absolutely simple in weave, the shapes more often square than curved, and the dimensions of chairs and settles very generous indeed. In fact, and this is a point to be considered always in buying chairs, the seats of many pieces are too deep to be comfortable for a short person.

Much of the willow furniture shown is intended for piazza use, and some pieces have been specially devised for use in narrow spaces, like the long, very narrow tables, with end pockets for papers, books, or work. There are triangular tables, which fit into corners, and are sold in twos, to be fitted together to make a square table, at need. Beside the always popular muffin stands, "curate's assistants," as the English call them, there are portable work tables supplied with a handle.

By no means cheap, but a most desirable possession, is the hooded chair, in which an old or delicate person is perfectly protected from sun and wind while enjoying the out-of-doors. Such a chair is often very useful in the house for the unfortunate individual who is susceptible to draughts. Then there are willow beds for the sleeping porch, which can be had in single or double width, and some very good-looking willow window and porch boxes, which have the advantage of being much lighter than the wooden ones.

GARDEN FURNITURE

Every year sees marked advancement along the lines of out-of-door life and recreation, and surely an attractive garden is a distinct asset, a beauty spot where one may be in seclusion from the outside world and enjoy nature to the utmost.

In order to derive all the enjoyment possible from an attractive and well-laid-out garden, it must have the necessary adjunct of harmonious and artistic garden furniture. And not only must it satisfy all the aesthetic senses, but it must combine beauty with practicability and durability.

There are many styles of wicker, reed, rattan, and rustic chairs and settees on the market, some chairs and benches are modeled colonial or Old English designs, with the backs of slats or latticework, which are able to withstand the ravages of sun and rain. Children's swings in dull green or brown are better than the bright red ones so often sold.

AN IMPORTANT BERLIN INDUSTRY

At Louisa corner Ahrens Streets, Berlin, is one of the best known manufacturing plants in that city. It is known from coast to coast as the place where are made parlor frames, diners, hall racks, rockers, fancy and odd chairs, and other specialties in high-grade furniture. The Lippert Furniture Company, Limited, was established in 1899, in a small factory, but in a few years the business had grown to such proportions that a larger building became an absolute necessity. Accordingly, in 1903, an extensive addition was created, that afforded the company twice the floor space of their original plant. To-day there are over one hundred hands employed in the factory, and it is one of the busiest in the city. George Lippert, the founder and manager of the company, is one of the best known furniture men in the Dominion, and superintends all manufacturing operations. He makes it a point to have nothing but the very best in his respective lines, with the result that the Lippert line of furniture has a reputation, and is upholding it among the dealers of the country, with a high standard of excellence. The very newest type of machinery is installed to facilitate manufacturing, and the lumber that is used is of the best grades only, and carefully selected by the firm. The president of the company is a well-known citizen of the community, George Lippert, Sr., who is considered one of Berlin's public-spirited citizens. He has held a number of important posts in the city administration, and at the present time is the chairman of the light commission, which post he is filling with much profit to the people, for, during his term he has been instrumental in inaugurating improvements that have brought the light commission to a high state of efficiency and brought him the thanks of the city. He is a member of the board of trade, and is ever on the alert to do his share in the upbuilding of the city. His able assistant in the Lippert Furniture Company is Herbert Lippert, a young man of exceptional ability, who is a wide-awake, progressive business man, with the respect of his business associates and all who come in contact with him.

FURNITURE CLUB IN NEW YORK.

"The Furniture Club," an organization to promote sociability among furniture men, and to be composed of furniture commercial men, dealers, or their accredited buyers, has been formed in New York. At a first meeting of the club the following temporary officers were elected: Isidor I. Gans, temporary chairman; Ed. Saunders, temporary treasurer; and Geo. Snyder, temporary secretary.

It is generally conceded a mistake for a girl to marry a man to reform him. It is about the same kind of a mistake to hire a man to reform him.

Collins' Course in Show Card Writing

Eighth of a series of articles specially prepared for this journal.

PRACTICE WORK. With card writing, as with music or painting or any other line of human endeavor, the average person does not appreciate practising. Practice is the humdrum part of the accomplishment that sometimes becomes drudgery. But proficiency in card writing, the same as in other branches of art, can only be obtained by exercise and practice.

It is generally understood that to be a successful card writer one must have a very steady hand. But many card writers have "shaky" hands. This is overcome by practice and the various ways of resting the hand while at work. Some whose hands shake perceptibly while holding the brush free from the work will have a perfectly steady "nerve" the moment the brush is applied to the card. This condition is obtained only by practice.

Fig. 12 contains excellent examples for practice that should be made by the hundred. They are all one-stroke lines, and can be applied to any class of lettering. Take any one of the examples and make it a hundred times or more. This will accustom your hand to the work. Follow this until you have done the entire number. The arrows indicate the direction of the stroke. These examples cover almost every kind of stroke in the making of the various styles of alphabets met with in card writing. Nos. 26 and 27 are examples of "sharpening" the corners of a letter; 26 is the

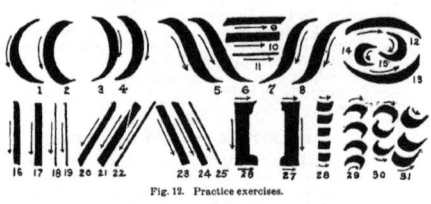

Fig. 12. Practice exercises.

Fig. 13. Righting an error.

left-hand corner and 27 is the right-hand corner. After making the vertical strokes, as indicated by the arrows, the corners are finished with a cross or horizontal stroke.

ERRORS.—It is easy to make errors in writing cards. One may be writing a word and mentally spelling it

ABCDEFG
HIJKLMN
OPQRSTU
VWXYZ &

Plate 31.—Full Block Roman (heavy).

abcdefgh
ijklmnopq
rstuvwxyz

Plate 32.—Lower case of Full Block Roman (heavy).

as he proceeds with the work. For example, he may be writing the word "Right." While working at the letter "G" he mentally says the next letter, "H." By the time he has finished the letter G, having said in mind "H," he may go on and write the letter "T," and leave the letter "H" out. There are various ways

Sample of "spatter" work.

of correcting errors. If it be a small card with little work on it, and you are not far advanced with it, it may be well to throw the whole card away and make another. Where the error is slight, as a slip of the brush or a drop of color, these may be erased with a sharp knife, and then sandpaper the place with a very fine grade of sandpaper. If the card is large and you are well advanced with the work and should leave out a letter, as in Fig. 13, you may be able to overcome the mistake by panelling the word and changing the color of the letters. This is only expedient in a card on which you have spent considerable time, and where the lay-out will permit it. On white cards it is often possible to correct errors by painting over them with white.

ALPHABETS.—The two styles of alphabets this month will furnish good material for practice. Plates 31 and 33 are upper and lower case Full Block Roman (heavy). Such letters are very suitable for words needing special emphasis on a card. They are not suitable for general use, as all block letters take too much time to execute. Plate 33 is an eccentric style of letter suitable for special words, etc. The card writer has much liberty in making letters of this character, but it is well to adhere to a general line of conformity throughout. Notice the first stroke in B, P, D, and A are straight, while E, F, K, L, H, I, etc., are crooked. The former letters may have been crooked also, but they do not seem out of place as they are. A similar divergence is noticeable in the small letters. The outlining of these letters adds a finish to them that is very effective.

SAMPLE CARDS.—The card suggestions this month are adaptable to almost any line of trade. During July business usually falls off a little on account of the hot weather and people going a-holidaying. At such a time many merchants run a special sale to clear out the odds and ends of the spring and early summer stocks. For such a sale the "July Sale" card will be very appropriate. It will do admirably for hardware, furniture, music, groceries, drugs, clothing, and many other lines. The goods on display in the window should be well price-ticketed. The words "July Sale" on the card is a good example of letters in Plate 31. These should be in red and shaded in

Example of use of letters in plate 31.

grey or green. The small lettering should be in black, with border in grey or green.

Every line of business will have something for the holiday-seeker. The "Summer Outing" card is an example of one for the summer cottagers' needs. The picture is in the natural colors, or you may paste a picture on to the card and work the border around it. The letters are good examples of the eccentric style shown in Plate 33. The large letters should be in red with the outline in black.

The $5 card is made with "spatter work," which is almost as fine as air brush work. This card is a sug-

Example of use of eccentric letters.

gestion any store may adopt. Hardware, furniture, drugs, music, groceries, clothing, boots and shoes, and plenty of other things are all needed at the camp or summer cottage. The price may be changed to suit the article. The background, or spatter work, should be in red or green with a dark red ribbon, and $5 in red, and balance in black and shaded in grey.

STOP THE STORE LEAKS.

It is one thing to mark goods at a certain price which should show a neat profit at the end of the year, but it is quite another thing to cash in on this basis!

Too many stores carry over from year to year a large percentage of stock that becomes out-of-date, shop-worn or damaged in some slight manner. Herein profits are seriously eaten into.

Clearance sales should be held twice a year. Interest on investment is costing money every day. Depreciation is costing money every day. Keep the goods moving. Turn your money over often, each time at a profit means successful merchandising.

Clearance sales mean money in the hand. Cash discounts make up the largest part of many department stores' profits. Ready money makes cash discounts possible.

Carelessness in buying is responsible for many serious leaks. The mail order houses are keen buyers—get all the cash discounts, ship many of their goods direct from the factory and thereby save handling, buy in large quantities and get this additional discount. These houses are your real competitors. Careful buying, know-how buying, is imperative. Do not blame others for your own carelessness. The farmer is a great student of catalogues and is generally a careful buyer.

BUSINESS PHILOSOPHY.

Just because you have pulled off a good advertising stunt, don't expect its momentum to last forever.

The man who stops advertising because times are dull will never see good times again for his business.

The merchant who makes good is not he who has the most capital or the best location. It is he who has the most ambition.

When business is rotten shut up about it. Don't advertise the fact for the benefit of competitors and the disgust of customers.

No matter how hot your competition may be, there are always plenty of lines that are not well sold, lines that you can sell better than anybody else sells them.

Don't have any quarrel with your competitor. If your disposition is such that you must quarrel with someone, quarrel with the railroad company or your lawyer.

Don't fall into a pessimistic attitude about your business. Pessimism is based more on what you are afraid may happen than on what has happened, or what is really apt to happen.

LIFE ETERNAL.

"The elm lives for 200 years, the linden for 300, the oak for 500 years—"

"And the chestnut," interrupted the other half of the sketch, "lives forever."

Plate 33.—An eccentric style of letters.

Selling Methods in the Furniture Store

Some Experiences and Suggestions

EVERY dealer should have a desk pad or a book of the proper kind for making notes of things that he should do or intends to do on certain days. How often is it the case that a dealer makes a mental note of something he must do on a certain day—perhaps a week, month or even farther ahead. The day comes and goes without that thing being done, because the mental note has failed to remind him. Here is where a note pad or book can be made of value. Properly conducted the merchant will get in the habit of looking over it each morning to see what should be done that day—or he may have his bookkeeper keep tab on the book and draw these things to his attention.

FURNISHING TWO ROOMS FOR A DOLLAR.

Gordon & Keith, "the premier housefurnishers," of Halifax, N.S., during June conducted a "one dollar furniture sale," for articles regularly sold from $2 to $125. Their announcement of the event reads as follows:

STARTING MONDAY And until not less than 2,500 people have visited our store to secure these marvellously wonderful offerings. That's what we want— More people to know us,—and where we are,—we are in the Big Red Brick Keith Building,—and that's where you will find strictly guaranteed, highest quality, newest and latest 1914 styles and designs of Furniture, Carpets, Lanoleums, Stoves, Curtains, Linens, etc. And you will also have the opportunity of a **Free** choice and selection from any article in the house for $1.00, paying in full for the selection you make. Don't forget that statement,—whatever you select from the special ONE DOLLAR SALE, will cost you not a cent more than ONE DOLLAR, no matter its value, you get it for ONE DOLLAR.

For Example: --- You purchase $25.00 worth of any kind of goods and it gives you a FREE and unrestricted choice of any $5.00 article in the store for $1.00 or a total of $26.00 for all, other amounts as follows:—

PUSH THIS BUTTON AND SEE OUR STORE.

A dealer is using a novel way of making talk about his store, and in a cheap and practical way. He has wired his store lights to a push button switch located at the entrance of his store, and placed underneath the switch a sign which reads: "Push this button and see our store." Passers-by in the evening are attracted to the show window, and observing the odd sign, comply with its request, when the entire establishment is brilliantly illuminated. All this happens, of course, after the store has been closed at night. The switch is of a type that releases as soon as the pressure is removed from the button, and consequently only a small amount of current is consumed. Persons who have seen the result of the contrivance have mentioned it to their friends, and brought them to witness the scene. The amount of oral advertising received has been very extensive. The one drawback that occurs to us is that the children might use it as a source of amusement.

SOLICIT SUGGESTIONS FROM CUSTOMERS

The Regina Trading Co., Regina, Sask., solicit customers to make suggestions to the managers as to how their service may be bettered or the efficiency of the organization increased. A suggestion box has been

---

OUR SUGGESTION BOX

Being ever on the lookout for suggestions and ideas which will better our service and increase the efficiency of our organization we have placed a suggestion box in the centre of the store on the ground floor, on the door beside our time clock. We will be pleased to have our patrons and friends drop in any suggestions which they think will better our service or efficiency. And these will receive our prompt consideration. You as a purchaser will no doubt notice lots of little things which we overlook and which should be remedied. Let us have your ideas and views. We thank you.

Announcement of suggestion box made by Regina Trading Co. in their ad.

placed on the main floor for this purpose. In a recent ad. they drew customers' attention to this feature. The section of the ad. in question is reproduced here. It has a marked value in getting the goodwill of customers, and inspiring greater confidence in the store.

GAVE AWAY MAIL BOXES

The American Paint and Oil Dealer tells of a Nebraska dealer who recently gave away metal mail-boxes to people on the rural routes, each box bearing his advertisement. He sent out postals telling each farmer to present the card and get his box. Then each signed a receipt, which prevented anyone getting more than one box, brought desirable people to his store, got their correct names for his mailing list—and made many friends among people who had never been in the store before. A special sale that week showed the people calling for their boxes that this dealer was onto his job. Here's hoping that none of these boxes carried much mail to or from the catalogue houses.

NOVEL ADVERTISING STUNT.

The F. C. Burroughes Furniture Co., Toronto, during the hot days of June, filled their three big windows with large sunshade umbrellas such as are used by drivers of express wagons. Cards announcing a special sale of these for 48 cents each to drivers brought buyers from all sections of the city, and the result is seen to-day, and will be seen until the end of the summer, in a lot of free advertising for the Burroughes Co., as the umbrellas are panelled with advertising matter printed on the outside.

A VALUE GUARANTEE SALE.

Some time ago the Home Furniture Company, Limited, Calgary, ran what they termed "A Value Guarantee Sale."

During this, as well as all other campaigns, they backed up their advertising with good window displays, and the sale was a successful one.

When advertising they give prices, and take every precaution in regard to supply the goods at the figures given.

The Home Furniture Co. have been in business about two years, and they do not hesitate to say that a great deal of their growth is due to their insistent advertising.

"Advertising," they say, "invariably brings us good results."

The accompanying engraving is a reproduction of one of the ads they ran during the "Value Guarantee Sale." The original, which was 11 by 10 inches, was an all-round good ad.

PROFIT FROM ADVERSITY

A motor-omnibus in London recently ran on the sidewalk in Tottenham-court-road, and found its ultimate destination in the plate glass window of a furnishing store. A notice was promptly pasted on the window, the Westminster Gazette states, announcing: "The most attractive window in London to-day. Even draws motor-buses."

DOES COMPETITION HELP OR HINDER?

Here is an actual happening that shows the benefits of competition: In a small town not a thousand miles from Toronto, two merchants were doing a fair business. It was nip and tuck between them, when one suddenly died. The other merchant then sat back and began to take things easy, feeling that he could afford to do it. His stocks gradually became depleted, he bought carelessly, and grew indifferent to the wants of his customers. In less than a year his business was barely paying expenses, the mail order houses flourishing at his expense. Then, along came a young man who opened up in the store left vacant by the merchant who died. The newly painted front, the clean appearance and fresh stocks of the new merchant attracted trade from the start. This close competition aroused the other merchant to the necessity of doing something to save his business. The rivalry between the two merchants became spirited, and the new life in both stores won back the local trade. Within a year both merchants were prospering, a result due entirely to close competition.

ONE PRICE SALES.

Many firms conduct one price sales with considerable success. In many communities it is new and therefore this form of advertising proves interesting to customers. The dealer lists a number of lines that can be sold singly or grouped at a certain price. If it is intended to make the one price sale a big feature, the advertising can be supplemented by window and interior display showing goods at that certain price. In this way, a number of lines can be advertised or displayed in a way to sell, and yet only take up the minimum amount of space.

AN INTERIOR DISPLAY.

In a large metropolitan furniture store an entire floor was converted into a garden and verandah, approximately seventy-five feet long and built along the wall. Between the columns were painted river scenes, while the columns were made to imitate brick with clinging vines and nasturtiums. The top was built with rafters and intertwined with imported German province roses. On the verandah were suspended Japanese lanterns. On the newel posts of the balustrade were placed large jardinieres holding plants and creepers. The floor was covered with matting. The whole floor served the double purpose of making customers comfortable and showing them goods in natural surroundings at the same time.

PRICE CARDS AND THEIR VALUE.

Many dealers fail to realize the tremendous value of price cards in their windows. To show goods without prices kills more than fifty per cent. of the value or effectiveness of the display. The average person, even

This corner of a restroom in a Canadian factory suggests another outlet for the live furniture dealer. This room is furnished with wicker furniture and a player piano.

though he is attracted to an article in a window, will pass it by, and not inquire about it or go in to buy, if the price is not shown on it. If he has seen the price on the article in the window, and then comes into the store and asks to see the goods, the sale can be made with little trouble.

Attractive Display Fronts for Furniture Stores

BY W. S. FRENCH
Publicity Manager of the Kawneer Mfg. Co., Ltd., Toronto

The only thing on earth that justifies the purchase of a store front is sales. Mere protection to the merchandise on display never justified the expenditure of the amount of money it takes to put in a modern store front. The money a good store front saves pays very little interest on what is invested—the thing that counts is the money it makes.

To display furniture it requires a furniture store front—to display jewelry, the jeweler must have a front designed and built in accordance with his requirements—the butcher needs a butcher store front. In fact, right down the line you will find that each retail establishment requires its own individual and representative store front if the retailer would push his sales to the limit.

To boil the whole thing down, we might say that the modern store front is a part of the business with which it is associated, and not simply a part of the building in which it is installed.

The lack of consideration and belief in this fact has caused the misapplication of thousands and thousands of dollars in store fronts.

Too many merchants are prone to hand the entire matter over to the local contractor—to one who is incompetent to put in store fronts that will do the work expected of them. You wouldn't entrust your business with a carpenter—still, on the other hand, if you were to build a new store front, you would be very liable, according to the custom, to call in your local carpenter and ask him to design a store front to fit your business. What does he know about the furniture business—what does he know about your display requirements? He can take care of your structural requirements in good shape, but he is not qualified and not competent to tell you what you need in the way of a commercial store front.

You will grant that your big money is made in the sale of complete suits of furniture, not merely because of the increased profit per sale but because of the increased volume and because of the increased satisfaction on the part of your customer. All this is not true with the sale of single pieces of furniture. And in order to sell complete suits, it is absolutely necessary to show complete suits and not simply single pieces of furniture. True, there are many single articles in the retail furniture store that are not a part of complete suits, so their display is easily taken care of.

In order to show complete suits of furniture in the show windows, large space is necessary, and in the case of a narrow building oftentimes this presents difficult obstacles to overcome.

The accompanying illustration is a treatment of a comparatively narrow furniture store, and while it is very simple in design it enables the display of furniture in the proper way. This constitutes but one department, so but one complete suit can be shown at a time. The minor, single pieces can be placed in the rear of the show window near the door, and will not complicate the display as a whole.

This particular illustration shows the show window floor on a line with the top of the bulkhead, but in most cases that should be changed. The bulkhead of a furniture store should not be over 12 in. in height, and in many instances it is advisable to eliminate the false floor and to extend the store floor throughout the front. Such a treatment facilitates the handling of heavy pieces of furniture, and at the same time allows the passers-by to view the furniture in a normal way. Tops of such articles as tables and desks can be easily seen.

Show your furniture as it will appear in the home or office—make it appear natural—that's the way to build up your sales.

One furniture dealer states that his modern store front is paying a big interest on the investment, simply because he is able to sell what he wants to sell, not what the people want to buy, also because it keeps his stock up-to-date, not allowing any particular style of furniture to become antiquated.

If you were to build a home you would take into consideration your own requirements, then why not do

A window that meets the requirements of the furniture trade. Plenty of display space, lots of light, and simple attractive background.

the same when you build a store front? Your prosperity depends absolutely upon your ability to cause the people to enter your store, and there is not a more logical means of doing that than by a good, made-to-fit, representative store front.

A GOOD RESOLUTION.

The merchants in Colborne have signed a petition pledging themselves not to buy tickets from ticket sellers for concerts, socials, teas, etc.

The Vancouver Furniture Co. has removed to North Vancouver.

Keeping the traveling salesman waiting all morning and then at noon rushing off to dinner doesn't win the confidence of the traveler or anybody else.

GET INTERESTED IN WINDOW TRIMMING

WE urge upon furniture clerks that they interest themselves in, and give some study to, the matter of window trimming. The importance of good window display as a means of attracting business to the store is becoming recognized more and more every day. It therefore stands to reason that the furniture clerk who, in addition to possessing selling ability, is a good window trimmer, will meet with the greater success and will secure a larger salary than if he knows nothing in regard to arranging good displays.

Good Window Trimmer Receives Larger Wages

It has to be admitted that some other lines of business are more advanced in window trimming. This is just because they recognized the value of window dis-

Attractive front of a London, Eng., store.

play sooner. Clerks in these other lines, as for instance drygoods, receive a bigger wage when they know something about window trimming. The same thing is true in the furniture trade, and will become more so as time advances, and every clerk should be looking to the future. If a clerk expects to go into business for himself, it is equally as important that he study window trimming.

In addition to reading as much as possible on the question of window trimming, the clerk should give some study to it himself, and put forth an effort to turn out as attractive and as great selling displays as possible. Time spent at this work is well spent.

Window trimming, when it is gone into in the right way, is one of the most interesting parts of the clerk's work. Where is the clerk who does not take interest and pride in turning out a display that attracts people, brings forth favorable comments from them, and sells goods for the store?

Another line of endeavor that the ambitious clerk would do well to take up is show card writing. A good show card writer can always command a higher salary than the ordinary clerk. In this connection we would draw the reader's attention to the splendid series of articles on show card writing that are being run in the Furniture World. They are prepared by a competent card writer, and should be a great value to the clerk interested in increasing sales by means of show cards.

SUMMER WINDOW DISPLAY SUGGESTIONS

As to the character of the goods which are to be shown in a window devoted to summer specialties dependence must be placed upon whatever is in stock, but if the window is large enough and sufficient goods are on hand it ought to include all articles of hot weather furniture that could be supposedly used in a porch, a garden, a summer cottage or a seaside bungalow, not forgetting such things as swinging benches and hammocks. It is not well to crowd the space nor to set the various pieces in any stiff or angular arrangement. They must be placed in an easy, natural way, just as if they were in actual use by human beings. Finally the tableau or picture idea must be always kept prominent so that no one piece obstructs the view of another; all alike must be given an equal chance to be seen.

SHOWING SUMMER SPECIALTIES

Planning for a pleasing display of summer furniture specialties is a fascinating pursuit, because this is one of the very rare occasions when decorative accessories can be consistently used in showing the goods. As a general rule, the wisest window trimmers having to do with furniture, omit all those elaborate details that are properly employed with other lines. Everyone concedes that furniture is too substantial, permanent and solid a commodity to be treated lightly or fantastically as to the surroundings in which it is shown. Summer specialties, however, present a different opportunity, and the prevailing rule can be advantageously broken in this case. The plan which has been studied up for recommendation at this time is to indicate, as far as possible, a well-furnished porch, largely because it can be made adaptable for either a small window or one of large proportions. One of the first points of pertinent interest that comes to mind is that of correct lighting, and a series of experiments were accordingly made in this field. In the same way that no store is too small to have its show window given watchful care, in just the same way is no store too obscurely located to have its windows well lighted at night, regardless of whether or not the establishment is kept open after dark.

WINDOWS THAT STAY CLEAN

Once a window is properly cleaned and polished (don't forget the polish), it will stay clean a long time, unless rain and dust come on it together.

Let the one person clean your windows all the time. It is not everybody's job; and if you try to make it so, your windows will be no better than anybody else's. The inside windows should be washed with tepid water and chamois leather—no soap or powder of any kind. Wipe this off dry with chamois, and polish with cheesecloth. The outside is cleaned with the following mixture:

1 oz. pulverized whiting,
1 oz. grain alcohol,
1 oz. liquid ammonia,
1 pint water.

Apply with a soft cloth, after having sprayed the window to remove surface dirt. When this preparation is allowed to dry, and is then rubbed off with a polishing motion, the surface of the window will be extremely brilliant, and it will remain so far longer than when washed in the ordinary way.

If the window has become badly scratched, a filler should be applied, consisting of an ounce of white wax dissolved in a pint of pure turpentine. This fills the cracks or scratches, and prevents dirt lodging there.

Getting After the Refrigerator Trade

BY A. B. LEVER

AS the weather increases in warmth the thoughts of the housewife naturally turn more and more to the necessity of buying a refrigerator. It is equally natural that in satisfying her wants she should be most influenced in purchasing from the dealer whose stock has been brought to her attention by the advertisements which have consistently appeared in the local newspapers.

Refrigerators, like all other articles, sell all the more freely for being advertised.

There are a great many dealers throughout the country who recognize this, but there are all too many who do not appear to have yet learned this fact.

I have selected and grouped for reproduction in this issue a number of advertisements of refrigerators.

The advertisement of Renaud, King & Patterson, Montreal, is in more ways than one a good ad. It not only looks well, but its reading matter is excellent, appealing as it does to the commonsense of every housekeeper. Every housekeeper knows that to keep food in a wholesome, sanitary, clean, and sweet condition is a good thing, and when she is told that a certain refrigerator is just the one to secure this desired end she is naturally interested. The original was 4¼ by 7 inches.

The advertisement of B. E. Smith, Moncton, is also strong in both reading matter and appearance. It catches the eye, and in plain and simple language describes the merits of the refrigerator offered for sale. Original 4½ by 5¾.

The advertisement of Wright's, Limited, Sydney, being 6⅜ by 9 inches, naturally affords more scope than any of the other ads. And the firm have made good use of it, both in the layout and in the reading matter. The introduction is well worded and the description under each of the illustrations is a good idea. There is a variety of refrigerators at a variety of prices to suit the necessities of different classes of housekeepers.

The advertisement without firm name is from a department store announcement, and may well serve as a model. The same may be said of the small, single-column ad. which adjoins it.

Although without an engraving the advertisement of the Blowey-Henry Co. is nevertheless a good one. It shows that good results can be obtained, even when there is the absence of an illustration. Original 4⅜ by 5.

The last ad. in the group is another of Wright's, Sydney. It is an attractive ad., although I think I would prefer to have used the whole of the space in advertising refrigerators or something more akin to them than mops and sweepers. If, however, it sold the goods, there cannot be much room for criticism. The original was 4⅜ by 8 inches.

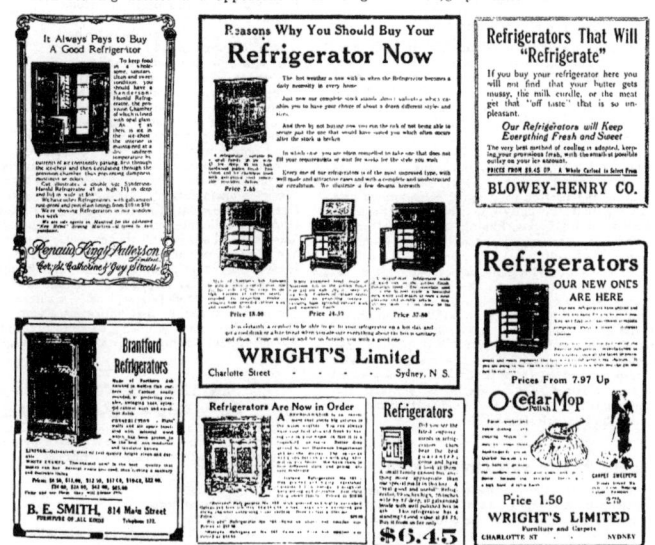

RETAIL FURNITURE ADVERTISING

The character of the ads. for exploiting summer furniture is commendably good this season, and it is encouraging to thus recognize the fact that selling furniture at retail is becoming imbued with the best principles of effective merchandising. The ads. thus referred to are those printed in the daily newspapers of the country, which, coming to the editor's desk, present so much in the way of good furniture advertising that they make interesting reading.

It is becoming more apparent as one notes the current advertising efforts that the principles of proper publicity are more generally realized than they were two years ago. Furniture advertising constantly grows better, but there are many good merchandisers who should study more deeply the basic methods which are common to all good advertising. One of the most important is the proper use of display type and the correct arrangement of matter to be displayed. Of course, it is a truism that the copy has been well prepared with a strong, forceful talk about the articles to be exploited. Their selling points should be fully understood and well phrased in clear-cut, incisive language, and then the copy must be studied so that the most salient points are put into the sizes of type best suited for them, in accordance with the relative importance of the statements and the space at disposal. If this matter is neglected, even the best copy may be glanced over hastily without a full understanding of the merits of the article. It is best to set off these statements by themselves in type that attracts and holds the eye, carrying conviction by the force of the words used and not wasting space by exaggeration.

Using Too Much Description

Many advertisers make a great mistake in endeavoring to crowd too much reading matter into the space purchased by them. They seem to have an idea that every atom of space must be covered with type or pictures. This is decidedly bad policy, since it detracts from the effect of the advertisement in general and renders the announcement less forceful. This impression is largely to blame for the ineffectiveness of many advertisements for which, too often, the paper is blamed. The principal value of plenty of white space lies in making the matter used more conspicuous and readable. Whether the body of the advertisement should be set solid (that is, having the lines close together) or leaded (having a space between them) is largely a matter of individual taste, but the best advertisers prefer it leaded, which makes it more legible. If plenty of space is left around the matter otherwise, the body matter may be set solid, or what is termed "two-point leaded," that is, with a two-point space between the lines. Where the matter is too open, it is apt to weaken the contrast between the displayed lines and the body of the advertisement. The reader may also gain the impression that there is not much to say about the articles advertised. There should be a sharp contrast between the type used in the display lines and the body of the advertisement.

SLACK TRADE AND ADVERTISING.

One of the most peculiar manifestations of psychological phenomena is the disposition of a certain class of business man to cut down his advertising appropriation when his business slackens so that he feels the necessity of economizing. He seems to feel that the habit of advertising is something akin to a vice, and as advertising is one of the easiest of vices to conquer, he makes drastic cuts in his advertising outlay whenever his income lessens.

A man of this calibre ordinarily does a small business and is desperately in need of attracting custom. When his business is poor he is much more desperately in need of attracting attention to the goods he has to sell. He does not realize that judgment is needed in the selection of his mediums and that if his advertisements do not "draw" it is probably because he does not know how to prepare his "copy."

If he advertises spasmodically and does not make it pay him an immediate profit, he is prone to condemn the medium and decide that advertising is a delusion and a snare. And he is among the first to blame his troubles upon politics and the administration. Here is an instance of the effectiveness of advertising in "bad" times.

When at the close of 1907 a firm which manufactures a household necessity found that it was losing business because of the financial stringency, it did not follow the example of one of its most prominent competitors. Instead, it increased its advertising appropriation for 1908 from $250,000 to $400,000.—American Metal Market.

SHOWCARD AND ADVERTISING PHRASES.

For the convenience of the dealer, we here give some advertising phrases for use in the store's ads., as well as for show cards:

Good reasons for selling good goods.
Take your time and study our stock.
Tell us your wants—we can suit you.
We handle only one grade—the best.
Bright bargains for the bright buyer.
This is a new line—at a standard price.
We've stated our case—now state yours.
Tempting bargains throughout the store.
All our offerings mean something to you.
You can open an account here—any time.
Every article you buy here is guaranteed.
Good points in these goods are abundant.
Here is the right store—with the right prices.
We purchased them knowing you'd like them.
We keep customers by keeping the best goods.
Here are a few bargains for these bright days.
Here is a full line—and they need no apology.
We want to help you all we can—ask questions.
We're here for your benefit—and also our own.
Here are a few price hints for the thrifty buyer.
A purchase to-day means contentment to-morrow.
No finer stock at so fair a price. Examine them.
Trade with the store that appreciates your custom.
Don't be backward in telling us your buying troubles.
An occasional purchase will make you a regular customer.

AN ADVERTISING RHYME

Roy E. Harris, Ontario representative of the Stratford Manufacturing Company, Limited, while musing in the train one day recently was struck by an inspiration, during which he coined this phrase:

"A sprained arm is bad.
A break is worse.
Sell Stratford ladders.
Then safety first."

Mr. Harris thinks this may ultimately be worked into some of the firm's advertisements.

Floor Coverings

CARE OF ORIENTAL RUGS

Suggestions as to the care of Oriental rugs should interest retail dealers as well as housekeepers. There is constant complaint on the part of the purchasers of authenticated antique rugs because of the unsatisfactory wear they give in the modern home. They last for a century or two in the Far East, but oftentimes do not stand up under two years of strenuous American use.

"It is first necessary to explain to the customer," suggests The Upholsterer, "that the rug she is buying for use on her floors has been used as a couch or wall covering, perhaps, and certainly has not been subjected to the hard wear and tear that it will now receive. She must understand that the clear air of the Mediterranean countries is vastly different from that of a manufacturing city, and that in the East there is little of the dampness that soaks our atmosphere even in the cleanest of towns, and is so fatal to rugs. She must realize that in the Orient sandals are worn, heels on shoes are an exception and bare feet are common.

"A rug should be inspected once in every two years at least, by an expert, who will see little flaws that may be just starting, when they are much easier and cheaper to remedy than when they have reached the stage where they are obvious even to the layman.

"The greatest danger that menaces a rug is the presence of moths. These insect pests will find entry wherever there is the slightest opportunity, and they favor dark spots. Those parts of rugs covered for long periods by furniture are veritable incubators for the moth, and the only way to keep them away is to expose such rugs—indeed, all rugs—at frequent intervals to sunshine and fresh air, say once or twice a month, according to conditions.

"Rugs should not be left in a house when empty during the summer, but should be carefully cleaned and packed and deposited in cold storage. The low temperature has a toning effect on the fabric which counteracts the effects of the hot dry air so common in our homes in winter.

"Damp is almost as dangerous an enemy as moths are, and a rug should be reversed and exposed face down at frequent intervals to free the warp from the effect of continued dampness, and an airing will help here as well."

The Upholsterer quotes S. Kent-Costikyan, an authority on rugs, to say that the portable vacuum cleaner, by its simplification of the removal of sediment from rugs, undoubtedly tends greatly to prolong the life of good rugs. The most important factors which contribute to the longevity of rugs are cleanliness, freedom from dampness, and freedom from moths.

RUGS CURE NOISE IN BUILDING

With buildings of concrete construction used for office purposes noise is often a very annoying feature, more especially so on floors devoted to general offices where large unbroken rooms occur, often sparsely furnished, and having relatively a few people working in them compared with the size of the room.

Under such conditions the sounds produced by people walking about, or shuffling their feet on the concrete floor, by typewriters, or even from talking, are greatly enhanced and echo very badly.

In a four-storey building of reinforced concrete construction throughout, erected recently by an industrial corporation for use exclusively as an administration building, the noise, particularly on one of the floors, was the greatest nuisance, it being at all times well nigh an impossibility to hear what anyone said when talking over the telephone, and various expedients were tried during several months in an effort to remedy the trouble, without success.

Notices were posted prohibiting whistling, loud talking, slamming doors, etc., which of course reduced the noise from these causes, but still left a good deal that was unavoidable. Finally, after various other experiments had been tried, a professor from one of the leading universities, who is an authority on acoustics, was consulted. He advised putting down a square of carpet or a rug in the centre of each of the private offices, and one or two in various spots in the main office. The result in each case was a great surprise. The echo from the voice in talking has entirely disappeared, the office force no longer seems to be perpetually shuffling its feet at the desks, and the clicking from eight or ten

Carpet and rug schowroom in H. Buckley's store at Niagara Falls

typewriters, although they are situated on an uncarpeted part of the floor, is markedly subdued.

It would seem that here lies one simple solution of the noise problem that is often advanced as one of the drawbacks to concrete construction for office buildings, and it contains a suggestion for furniture men to increase their rug and carpet business, especially in the larger centres.

THE "DEN" DEFINED IN VERSE

What is a den?
A den is when
The broken chairs,
The rugs with tears,
The pictures cracked,
The table hacked,
A tickless clock,
Desk that won't lock
Are gathered in a heap by Ma
And put into a room for Pa.

Judicious buying is buying often, to keep down the investment. It is buying many lines in one bill to keep up the variety. It is buying enough at a time to get minimum freight rates.

Beds and Bedding

Ohio's Sanitary Bedding Law

N. K. Billow, Columbus, Ohio, president of the Ohio Bedding Manufacturers Association, in writing to the Furniture World concerning sanitary bedding conditions in his locality says:

conditions in his locality says:

"I can only say that conditions in the mattress business in this State were very bad. The use of secondhand unsanitary materials was prevalent to some extent. Also considerable deception was practised as to the quantities of materials used by the manufacturer. It seemed that it was was absolutely necessary to inaugurate some reforms of some kind. The mattress manufacturers of this State, therefore, got together and concluded that they were going to let the consuming public know just exactly what was in their mattresses and the weights of the different kinds of materials, and to get the matter started we framed up a bill which soon became a law. This law absolutely prohibits the use of bedding or any other materials which have been discarded by public or private hospitals, or which have been in or around any person having infectious or contagious diseases. This law further provides that every mattress offered for sale shall bear a label, and on the label must be a statement of the materials used and the kind and quantity of the materials used. The law is very carefully observed, and its requirements are rigidly enforced; it has been the means of toning up the mattress business of the State, and in the end we all hope it will mean better financial returns to the manufacturer. While it is still possible for the manufacturer of mattresses of this State to make up a mattress of clean, sound, sanitary materials. I am pleased to say that the use of second-hand materials of every description went out automatically with the passage of the bill. I enclose herewith a copy of the Act."

Wording of the Act.

Be it enacted by the General Assembly of the State of Ohio:

Section 1.—Whoever manufactures for sale, offers for sale, sells, delivers, or has in his possession with intent to sell or deliver any mattress which is not properly branded or labeled as hereinafter provided, or which is falsely branded or labeled, or whoever uses, either in whole or in part, in the manufacture of mattresses any cotton or other material which has been used or has formed a part of any mattress, pillow, or bedding, used in or about any public or private hospital, or in or about any person having infectious or contagious diseases, or whoever dealing in mattresses has a mattress in his possession for the purpose of sale or offers it for sale without a brand or label as herein required, or removes, conceals, or defaces the brand or label thereon, shall be fined not less than $25.00 nor more than $500.00, or be imprisoned in the county jail not more than six months or both.

Section 2.—The brand or label required by the next preceding section shall contain in plain print in the English language a statement of the material used in the manufacture of such mattress, whether such materials are in whole or in part new or second-hand, and the quantities and qualities of the material used. When it is necessary to use a label, it shall be in the shape of a paper or cloth tag to be sewed or otherwise securely attached to each article; and a label of this description shall in all cases be placed upon the outside of each bale, box, or crate in which such mattresses are packed, shipped, or exposed for sale.

Section 3.—A mattress within the meaning of this Act shall include any quilted pad, stuffed with hair, wool, or other soft material, except feathers, to be used on a bed for sleeping or reclining purposes.

Section 4.—When the Commissioner of Labor statistics has reason to believe that any of the provisions of this Act are being violated, he shall advise the Attorney-General thereof, giving the information in support of such belief, and the Attorney-General, or under his direction, the prosecuting Attorney of any county in which the violation occurs, shall forthwith institute the proper legal proceedings for the enforcement of its provisions, and for the punishment of all violations thereof.

Section 5.—This Act shall take effect and be in force on and after September 1, 1911.

S. J. VINING,
Speaker of the House of Representatives.

HUGH L. NICHOLS,
President of the Senate.

Passed May 31, 1911.
Approved June 6, 1911.

JUDSON HARMON, Governor.

MAPLE LEAF CO. BUILDING

The ratepayers of Galt authorized a loan of $12,000 to the Maple Leaf Bedding Co., a by-law for this purpose receiving 558 votes in favor and only 84 being polled against. Already the contractors have started on the erection of a building, and the firm expects to be ready to meet the demands of the fall trade.

The officers of the Maple Leaf Bedding Co., Galt, successors to Shurly-Dietrich Co., Ltd., are: J. C. Dietrich, Galt, president; C. Osborne, Toronto, vice-president; G. Gordon Plaxton, Toronto, secretary; Roy Torrance, Galt, managing director and treasurer; J. W. Dore, Hamilton, director. These men are well-known financial men, and form a strong company. The new company have purchased a site, and now that the by-law is passed will immediately proceed with the erection of an up-to-date brick plant, 80 ft. by 200 ft., with additions later. They will manufacture a line of high-grade iron beds, springs, and mattresses of superior quality and finish, and will be in a position to handle fall business.

The Shurly-Dietrich company have always had the confidence of the trade, and a splendid reputation for the quality and finish of their goods. They claim to always originate their designs and give to the trade something different from that obtained elsewhere.

MATTRESSES AS LIFE RAFTS.

A mattress stuffed with ten pounds of kapok will support in the water a two-hundred-pound man lying on it, says the Scientific American. Kapok is a fibrous silky material which grows in the seed pods of a tropical tree. The tree grows in the East Indies, India, West Indies, and other tropical lands, but it is only that which comes from the island of Java that has this remarkable property of buoyancy to a satisfactory and reliable degree.

It is a remarkable material for filling mattresses and cushions, and for that use it comes into the market. The mass of fibres keeps the water out because its own surface tension restrains it from penetrating the interstices of the mass. Java kapok will support in water twenty times its own weight; and if the kapok is in a leather or artificial leather casing it will continuously support this weight for two months or more before the water does finally penetrate the mass sufficiently to make it sink.

The United States Navy is beginning to use kapok, and the Scientific American urges the steamboat inspectors to accept mattresses stuffed with it in lieu of cork life preservers and life rafts.

BEDDING NOTES.

Geo. Gale & Sons state that in their "Dixie" compartment mattress they have made about the lightest mattress ever made. This is because of their use of Java kapok as filling. This Java kapok is a vegetable product, pure, clean, light, buoyant and elastic, making it one of the finest mattress materials known. On account of its extreme lightness, however, it could not be used in the ordinary tufted mattress until the Dixie compartments made it possible to be held in place. The regular 4 ft. 6 in. Dixie mattress stuffed with kapok weighs only 30 pounds. Besides its other qualities kapok is non-absorbent and sanitary.

A small fire a month ago occurred in the Antiseptic Bedding Co.'s factory at Toronto.

The Ideal Bedding Co., Toronto, issued during the latter part of June a supplementary catalogue showing about 60 new Ideal lines, including 30 brass beds, 13 chilled and chilless steel beds, and a dozen or more Ideal specialties, such as the "Neverspred" mattress, duplex springs, foldaway cot, and new Ideal hammocouch. The company also announce that they have cut out making some 22 numbers in their iron bed line.

SCRUTINIZE YOUR FREIGHT BILLS?

How many retailers scrutinize freight bills carefully? The question is asked by an American trade journal, which points out the large losses to retailers arising from this negligence.

"It is well known that the tariffs of the railroads and other transportation companies are complicated affairs," says this paper, "and that the average railroad billing clerk is far from knowing all the details which affect the method of classification alone is probably no overstatement. Yet in the classification a large difference in the rate may be involved. Usually, moreover, when the clerk is in doubt he decides the question in favor of his employers—by charging the higher rate. We have heard it stated that in order to encourage such action transportation companies compel their clerks to pay out of their own salaries any losses which the company may suffer from undercharges.

"The difficulty with the average merchant is that his own employes are not fully posted in the details of routing, classification, rates, etc. And the dealer may well ask, 'What are we going to do when we have not such facilities?'

"For one thing, when the dealer is a member of a local merchants' association, he can induce his fellow members to join in providing facilities for the examination of freight bills and the detection of overcharges."

Every man in business will find it profitable to develop his salesmanship ability.

WHEN you do anything or give anything, do it whole-heartedly. There are many things on the "free list" in the store, but when a person asks for the directory, or a glass of water, or a match, give it to them and throw in a smile to put them at their ease, for perhaps they did not like to ask. It is good sense and good judgment, when you are going to do a thing, to do it right.

Strong window showing of many "Ideal" lines by Jas. Irwin, Campbellford.

For the Office Man

DON'T FOOL YOURSELF ON PROFITS

THE writer has before him a booklet sent out to retailers by a wholesale firm, in which they set forth that the dealer can make 40 per cent. profit on one of their lines. According to the booklet, the dealer buys a quantity of this line at $5.00 and sells it at $7.00. making $2.00 on the transaction. This is figured out as giving the dealer 40 per cent.

Figuring on the cost price, this is of course, 40 per cent., but if we figure it on the selling price—the basis on which every merchant figures his expenses—we find it is only $2.00 made on a sale of $7.00, or 28 4-7 per cent. For argument's sake, we will say that a dealer's expenses are 22 per cent.—of course, on selling price, because they are always figured that way. He would imagine, according to this booklet, that this line would net him 18 per cent., while in truth it would only net him some 6 4-7 per cent.—which it must be admitted is considerable of a difference.

Many dealers are being fooled, and are fooling themselves by the incorrect figuring of profits. They don't seem to recognize the difference between profit on cost price and profit on selling price. Let us suppose, for example, that a dealer's expenses figured out at 18 per cent. He might think that if he got an average profit of 20½ per cent. on the cost price of goods that he would be making money. That is just where he would be fooling himself, and fooling himself badly, for 20½ per cent. on cost price would only mean 17 per cent. on selling price. If his expenses figured out at 18 per cent. he would be losing 1 per cent. on all business done, instead of making a profit as he supposed. Surely, there is much need of examining thoroughly into this question of profit. There are not a few dealers who think they are making a profit on certain lines when they are not.

Frequently, travellers in putting before retailers the profit to be made on the line they sell, figure their percentage of profit on the cost price, and not on the selling price. Such a traveller will tell the dealer that the line will pay them a profit of 25 per cent.—but that is on the cost, and only means 20 per cent. on selling price. In the same way, 33 1-3 per cent. quoted on cost only means 25 per cent. on selling price—38.9 per cent. on cost only means 28 per cent. on selling price—and so on.

The dealer who courts success must concern himself with profits. He must realize that advance on cost does not mean the same percentage on sales. He must remember that expenses are always figured on selling price. He would do well to always figure his profits on selling price. Then he will be safe—and it is better to be safe than sorry.

COST BOOK KEEPS USEFUL RECORDS

The progressive dealer who is aiming to conduct his business along systematic lines, will find a cost book giving in concise form a record of stock purchased and the price paid, a valuable help in his business. Probably the chief value of the cost book is that it acquaints the dealer with the quantity of each variety of goods purchased with the price paid, and this information is of a good deal of assistance in placing other orders. Travellers will tell you that when many dealers wish to find out the quantity of a certain line he has disposed of in a certain time, it is necessary to ransack the invoice files in order to get this information. When a cost book is conducted, this information is always at hand.

Dealers are coming more and more to recognize the value and necessity of a cost book. There are many systems in use, but many do not give as much information as it is well that the dealer should have to conduct his business to the best advantage.

With the cost book, there is little danger of goods being sold at too low a price. In addition this system shows the retail selling price, and is a great aid to clerks if the proprietor is absent, and the selling price of an article is desired. Then again, a quantity price on many lines is only asked for occasionally, and the salesman finds it difficult to keep it in his mind. This cost book gives it to him without delay.

Useful in Detecting Errors in Invoices.

This book is also useful in detecting errors in prices on invoices. In some cases the merchant will want to use his own private cost mark, especially when junior clerks, whom he does not want to acquaint with the selling price of goods, have access to it to look up selling prices. Then again, a customer may be around when you are looking up the retail price, and having cost price in private mark will prevent them from becoming acquainted with it.

If you are not using a cost book in your business, you should start now. The advantages of having one are so great that the dealer will be well repaid for any work necessary in conducting it.

UNINTENDED HELP.

A commercial man who has gained a valuable list of customers for his firm, was told by one of the best of these how he came to get his account: "Do you remember the first time you called on me?" asked the customer. "Well, now," was the reply, "I cannot recollect my first meeting with you."

"I was very busy and very tired when you entered my store that day," said the customer; "I was taking stock, and I told you I had no order for you for that reason. You said quietly that you would be glad to help me, as you had some spare time that day, and though you were a stranger I took your offer and asked you to make a list of some shelves of goods. You did so, and, what is more, you came back with me in the evening and helped me to finish up my stock-taking, and went away without asking me again for an order.

"I liked your way of taking a refusal, and your unselfish kindness, and now after many years of dealing with you, I esteem it a privilege to call you my friend. Every time you come here you help me in some unintended way. Your firm's goods are quite satisfactory, but your helpful character is what commands my patronage of your house."—The Gimlet.

AMEND JOINT STOCK COMPANY ACT.

Legislation along the lines of an amendment to the Joint Stock Act is proposed to be introduced in the Manitoba Legislature next session covering points such as untrue statements made in prospectuses; adding the English practice of making retiring members of companies liable for debts for one year after disposition of stock; and proper requirements of a guarantee by a debtor.

Who's Who in the Furniture Trade
BY W. L. EDMONDS

Study of a man who is a leader in developing Canada's industrial life.

JAMES HENRY SHERRARD.

AMONG the many passengers that stepped off a train in Montreal on a certain day twenty-three years ago was a young man of medium height and sprightly appearance. He had come from the "Land of the Blue Noses." He had been a clerk in a general store at Shediac, New Brunswick, where he had been both born and educated. Like most of the passengers, he carried a "grip," but, unlike most of them, he carried something which, though invisible, was greater than either "grip" or trunk. That something was a Purpose.

The dictionary gives a slight variation to the meaning of the word "purpose," but the definition which is given of the word as applied to the purpose this young "blue nose" carried with him is "the idea or ideal kept before the mind as an end of effort or action."

His Purpose in Life to Create a Bigger Business.

As by instinct, as well as by training, this young "blue nose" was a business man, his purpose was to create a business bigger and broader than he conceived to be possible in the little town of Shediac.

How this young man succeeded in working out his purpose may be gathered from the fact that he is to-day the president of the Alaska Feather and Down Co., Limited, Montreal, and the vice-president of the subsidiary companies scattered over this country which have since sprung from its loins.

It is almost needless for me to say that the name of the young man is James Henry Sherrard, who was the other day unanimously elected to the office of first vice-president of the Canadian Manufacturers' Association, an office which means a stepping-stone to the presidency itself.

This is not, of course, the first time he has been in the eye of the C. M. A. Three years ago he was chairman of the Montreal branch, and last year at Halifax, although unable to be present in person, he was elected second vice-president of the central organization.

If there is a busy business man in Montreal, it is Henry Sherrard. He is on the job day in and day out. And his working day is not a short one, either. But, in spite of this, he is not unmindful of his duty as a citizen. He has served the suburban town of Westmount as alderman and Montreal as chairman of the parks committee.

His philanthropic spirit is manifested in the interest he takes in hospital work. For this spirit he has been honored with the vice-presidency of the Victorian Order of Nurses and a seat at the board of management of the Montreal General Hospital.

His Purpose Brought to a Successful Issue.

That Mr. Sherrard has accomplished much since his advent in Montreal twenty-three years ago, there can be no gainsaying. But to those who know him best his success is no secret. Success is the effect of a cause. Combine certain qualities in business and you'll produce certain results.

The world is full of men who conceive a Purpose, but who lack either the Will Power or the Ability necessary to the bringing of it to a successful issue.

When Mr. Sherrard landed in Montreal with his Purpose, he also possessed the Will Power to force it along. Ask anyone who is intimate with him as to what is his outstanding characteristic as a business man, and he'll nine chances to one tell you that it is forcefulness.

But forcefulness is not his only quality. He also possesses in a marked degree the quality of organization, a quality which will stand him in good stead when a year hence he steps into the presidential chair of the C. M. A.

Sincerity is another of his outstanding qualities. This, in turn, creates in those who are brought into contact with him confidence in his integrity and in the bona fides of his propositions.

Men strong in sincerity of purpose and forceful in carrying it to an issue are not always ready to take the time to carefully weigh the pros and cons of their proposition. By jumping to conclusions they some

JAMES HENRY SHERRARD
the new First Vice-President of the C.M.A. and President of the Alaska Feather & Down Co., Limited, Montreal.

International Press Photo.

times find themselves in the fire. Whether it is because of his Presbyterian training or not, I cannot say, but whatever the source of it may be, one thing is certain, you do not, as a rule at any rate, find Mr. Sherrard jumping to conclusions. But while he has been taught to be cautious, it by no means follows that he dilly-dallies with a proposition. He merely takes time to weigh and gauge it. This done, the matter is settled, and settled promptly. This is, I suppose, another way of saying, as one of his intimates in the C. M. A. did the other day, that he is a man "chock full of common sense." And, of course, the object of all education is to create common sense, for he who possesses it is an All-Round Man.

But plus his all-roundedness as a business man and a public-spirited citizen, is his personality. Courtesy he possesses to a high degree. And it isn't a courtesy which, like certain people's religion, is practised on certain occasions and days. It is good for every hour in every day in every week. He practises it, not only toward his fellow businessmen and those he meets in social intercourse, but towards his employes as well.

"Towards his employes he is one of the most courteous of men," remarked a former employe. "He is also a most considerate employer," added the same ex-employe.

At conventions of the C. M. A. Mr. Sherrard does not rise to his feet with frequency to speak, but when he does he has something to say, and to say it with such force and clearness that he immediately demands attention. In a coming president this is an excellent quality.

In his political affiliations Mr. Sherrard is a Conservative: in his economic belief a protectionist. But he not only is an advocate of the tariff as an aid to the development of Canadian industries. He believes also in the aid which comes of individual buying of Canadian-made goods. He not only believes in it, but he practises it. And whenever he can get an opportunity he preaches it.

Scheme Used to Urge Employes to Purchase Made-in-Canada Goods.

Among his employes he has a method of preaching it that other manufacturers might well imitate. His particular method is to drop into the pay envelope a printed slip of paper on which is set forth in brief and concise form a statement in regard to the advantages which accrue to the country as a whole from purchasing, whenever possible, goods of Canadian production.

Great and all as are the exactions which business makes upon his time, Mr. Sherrard has discovered that one of the secrets of health is a diversity of interests. Consequently, during the summer time he steals away week-ends to his country club to enjoy a game of golf. And if not to play golf, to a spot where he knows he can catch a few good fish. In the winter he is a keen snowshoer. His friends say he is a good one. And his build would indicate he is. He is clean-cut in limbs and features, and in appearance reminds one somewhat of Woodrow Wilson, although he has one advantage over the President of the United States—he was born in Canada.

To sum up in a sentence my estimate of the new first vice-president of the C. M. A., I would say he is esteemed for his personality and admired for his business ability.

STEEL FURNITURE IN INDIA.

U. S. Consul Henry D. Baker, of Bombay, India, in a letter to Washington, says: "India appears to be a good field for the sale of steel office equipment, such as tables, desks, chairs, cabinets, bookcases, etc. At first such goods when introduced here were considered merely as an interesting novelty, but now their real usefulness and peculiar adaptability to conditions in India are becoming well realized, so that sales are constantly increasing.

"Ordinary wooden office equipment in India quickly depreciates as a result of adverse climatic influences. Not only does wooden furniture tend to warp and to lose all finish and pleasing exterior appearance, and drawers and doors cease to fit, but such furniture is also peculiarly subject to the ravages of white ants and other insects and is difficult to keep clean, so that it does not harbor vermin. Steel furniture, on the other hand, as sold in this market, retains its appearance and utility through all seasons of the year, and is easy to keep free of vermin. It has been well demonstrated that it has particular advantages in affording proper protection for books and valuable papers. It is not at all uncommon to notice in a Bombay office an army of white ants invading the premises from windows or small holes in walls and flooring, and attacking the wooden furniture and the contents of desks and cabinets. In a very short time a great deal of damage can be caused before the presence of these white ants is noticed. Steel office equipment, however, offers a sure resistance to these insect marauders.

"The greater part of the office equipment at the American Consulate at Bombay is of steel, supplied from the United States by the Department of State, and its pleasing appearance and obvious utility is often favorably commented upon by visitors to this office. This equipment has been at this office during several monsoon periods, and yet it looks as fresh and is in as good order as when it came, in decided contrast to wooden furniture also in the office, which every now and then needs some special attention in the way of carpentry work, cleansing, and varnishing, in order to look presentable. Furthermore, in the latter kind of furniture the office has not infrequently met with damage to books and papers from white ants and mice which have entered them."

NEW COMMERCIAL TRAVELERS' OFFICERS.

At the convention of the United Commercial Travelers grand council for Manitoba, Saskatchewan and Alberta, held in Brandon last month, the following officers for the ensuing year were elected:

Grand Councillor, T. A. Colquhon, Brandon; grand junior councillor, S. S. Savage, of Calgary; grand past councillor, R. M. McGowan, Winnipeg; grand secretary, F. C. Smith, Regina; grand treasurer, J. J. Murphy, Winnipeg; grand conductor, W. C. Bell, Regina; grand page, W. S. Clay, Edmonton; grand sentinel, James Gillespie, Moose Jaw.

Grand executive committee: F. H. Agnew, Winnipeg; V. W. Libby, Calgary; H. W. Laird, Regina; A. A. Williams, Saskatoon.

Representatives to supreme council at Columbus, Ohio: F. J. C. Cox, Winnipeg; O. S. Chapin, Calgary; R. M. McGowan, Winnipeg.

The next convention will be held at Saskatoon, Sask.

How does your clerk know you appreciate the work he is doing for you? He is no mind reader.

ENGLISH BUNGALOW FURNITURE.

English bungalow furniture is the product of a new school of designers. It is, however, not the result of a localized endeavor to overthrow the traditions of furniture designing, but the same ideas seem to have grown simultaneously in the fancy of furniture designers in Germany and Austria, as well as in England. This style follows somewhat closely the mission lines, having the appearance of strength and durability, as well as comfort, but it is lighter in weight and appearance, due to the liberal use of cane in most of the pieces. The main difference between the English and German and Austrian designs is that the Germans and Austrians adhere strictly to straight lines, whereas the English designers are not entirely bound by this rule.

The vogue is for Bulgarian colorings. The return of old-fashioned chintzes and cretonnes, with their riot of colors; the revival of tapestry coverings, have all had their effect on the new style of furniture, these being the coverings used. Thus the Bungalow style has all the quaint effects of mission furniture, but in a livelier mood, giving rein to one's own taste in the matters of decoration. Thus English bungalow furniture is the legitimate successor of mission furniture, which has had, and still has, such a hold on people who demand comfort in their furniture, and the ability of that furniture to withstand the wear of every-day use. It is a style that strongly appeals to people with individuality of taste; people who build bungalows and summer cottages, sun rooms, wide porches, breakfast rooms, and dens and living rooms.

The wood used in its construction is the solid, close-grained quartered white oak of the middle Southern States, finished in a beautiful soft grey, or in a deep brown, fumed finish.

Two bungalow chairs made by Baetz Bros., Berlin.

COURTESY AS AN ASSET.

To the Editor of Canadian Furniture World:

Since your magazine is having a decided increase of circulation among the salesmen and employes of the retail furniture trade, I think it would perhaps be instructive and interesting to them to learn and practise what is undoubtedly one of the, if not the chief, assets of successful salesmanship, an asset that one cannot help noticing is glaringly deficient in many cases, but without which no man however anxious or ambitated, and, consequently, more critical class of customers or efficient in other respects can possibly become a really first-class and successful salesman—I refer to that indispensable asset of courtesy. So absolutely necessary to success is courtesy that I would strongly advise every man to cultivate the art and to start right now. Do this seriously and earnestly and you will soon acknowledge it is your greatest and proudest asset—one that will serve you profitably in every stage of your life.

What is courtesy? It is simply the art of pure politeness, carrying with it an irresistible charm that never fails to attract; it is an indispensable acquisition to successful salesmanship, adding tone and sincerity to your conversation.

Never in the history of the furniture trade in Western Canada was courtesy more necessary or desirable than it is to-day, and it will certainly become more and more so when we take into consideration the growing demand for a much higher grade of furniture than has ever been introduced into this country before, the demand of course being created by the settling in our large cities, especially, of a more enlightened, cultivated, with whom courtesy will alone enable you successfully to deal.

When we take into consideration the fact that high-grade furniture of all periods is now to be found on the floor of every up-to-date furniture store in the West, it naturally follows the buyers of such departments are looking for the most cultured and experienced salesmen they can find. Realising the best are none too good for the successful handling of the customers we now have to deal with, they are willing to pay the price that will retain their services.

Remember then that courtesy must shine in your character, it tells at every step, it tells and carries great weight especially on your first approaching a customer, and will at all times open the door to a conversation generally leading to good business.

I have in my mind the furniture department of a large store out West where a big staff of men is employed who have the very enviable reputation of being, on the whole, the most courteous and obliging salesmen in the store. I have no doubt their manager is fully alive to their unusual qualifications and appreciates their services in the most tangible manner.

Yours very truly,
B. Cautious.

New Ideas in Fireless Cookers
BY AGNES ATHOL

The great appeal of the fireless cooker, no matter what its construction, is in the economies it makes possible. To the dullest woman it must be obvious that the application of the "hay box" principle to cookery means a great saving of fuel, whether gas, coal, wood, oil, alcohol, gasoline, or electricity. Every maker of a cooker can claim this and several other important savings. Next to fuel, and of almost equal importance, is the cutting down of food cost. This is accomplished by the double benefit of conserving all the juices and nutriment contained in any article of diet, allowing no escape by evaporation, and of making palatable those cheaper cuts of meat which, cooked in the ordinary way, equal the cost of high-priced foods because of the immense amount of fuel required to make them edible and digestible.

The economy of time and labor, owing to the elimination of watching over food in a fireless cooker, is a valuable point for busy women to keep in mind. The final saving in health, due to the release of the housewife from some of her tasks, and the benefit received because the cooker yields slowly cooked and therefore more digestible foods to the family, is difficult to estimate, but none the less real.

While it is possible that some of these advantages may have escaped the woman who has given the subject of fireless cookery but little attention, on the whole these are the main arguments for using any fireless device. The discriminating housekeeper must inquire further before she decides upon the purchase of one brand rather than another. Certain features and improvements may suit her particular needs better than others.

Lest the underlying principle by which fireless cookers work be not clearly understood by some reader, let me explain here that the idea in every one of them, as in the thermos bottle, is to heat the food to the boiling point over a fire, and then, by sealing it inside the cooker, to allow it to continue cooking by its own heat, which cannot escape. Heat of some description is essential to start the cooking process; the economy lies in the small amount required.

The most interesting innovation on the market is the electric fireless stove. It is simplicity itself. The food is put into aluminum utensils, which come in cylindrical shape to fit the wells into which they are to be packed. The cover of the cooker is tightly closed, the electric current turned on for twenty minutes, and then shut off, while the food continues to cook for two or three hours.

The use of electricity in the kitchen has the same advantages that it has in lighting—it is clean, safe, simple, and efficient. If there are two compartments in the cooker each may be separately attached to a switch in a wall socket. Furthermore, the heat can be regulated according to the article to be cooked. Four marks—"high," "low," "high-low" and "off"—indicate the amount of current obtained at each turn of the key. The economy of fuel attainable by such regulation is at once apparent, and the possibility of variation is one that no other device seems to permit. For example, oatmeal and other cereals are best started and cooked by low heat; but steaks, potatoes and biscuits should be started by high heat, no matter what form of stove the housewife uses.

The fact that in many small towns and suburban settlements electricity, rather than gas, is used for lighting, should induce any thoughtful woman to consider how electricity can be applied to her cooking problem. In the past, the great trouble has been the prohibitive cost of electrically operated stoves; and although the nearby trolley plant could supply the power, the frugal housewife felt obliged to continue the drudgery of handling coal, wood, or oil stoves. She did not approve either of the dirt or the fire danger necessitated by the limitations of her purse. But it was not until the cost of using electricity was minimized by conjunction with the fireless cooker principle, that she could escape them.

The city mother, satisfied with the convenience of her gas range, very often leaves the possibilities of fireless cookery unexplored. If she is one of the mothers who must stop work entirely to go to market or to take the baby out for a certain number of hours a day, it would be an inestimable boon to her to be able to put the lunch or dinner into a box before starting out, and to remove it entirely cooked upon her return. And yet I have known many city women who not only had never seen or experimented with a fireless cooker, but who looked upon it merely as an overnight method for cooking cereals, in which they were not interested!

Housekeepers who have limited time for getting meals, and who often come home in the evening too tired to do more than sit down to a meal, should examine the valuable claim of the fireless cookers.

There are many practical, co-operating households in New York where the fireless cooker would be a boon. Teachers and stenographers who are managing a sort of home life in a little bachelor flat, and women who do light housekeeping because they go to business would find that it would relieve them of a heavy burden.

The fireless cooker really proves worth while, and its value is recognized by every user of one. Its experimental stage is passed. It is now a permanent and well-established utility, the general use of which will doubtless be widespread in far less time than was the case with gas and electricity for cooking. Even those who use the imperfect hay box fireless cooker concede to all its economical and advantageous features, and the few complaints to be heard in any direction arise from a lack of knowledge as to the proper length of time required for the various foods. This, of course, should be considered, and some information on the subject obtained before undertaking an experiment.

Put concisely, these are the principles and results in fireless cookery: radiation and conduction are overcome; a steady application of heat is obtained; foods retain all their juices; moist and dry heat are both available. The economies effected are at least five: fuel, food, time, labor, and health. Where is the woman who does not consider these savings worth her study?
—Abridged from Pictorial Review.

BELL CHAIRS AND TABLES.

"Chimes from the Bell line" is the attractive title of a catalogue booklet of neat design issued by the Bell Furniture Co., Southampton. These goods—"the line with the tone"—are nicely illustrated by half-tones on calendered paper, which set off the beauties of the tables, chairs, and rockers to good effect. The booklet will be sent on request.

Knobs of News

D. W. Lundy has opened a furniture store at Hanna, Alberta.

The Ideal Furniture Co. have opened a store at Outlook, Sask.

J. C. Robinson has started a retail furniture business at Edmonton.

Alex. Thompson's furniture store at Hamilton was damaged by fire recently.

The Hammond Furniture Mfg. Co., Vancouver, suffered a fire loss recently.

Wesley Walker, of Clinton, has sold his furniture business to Jas. Dunford.

Benjamin Glove has registered the Glove Furniture Co. at Maisonneuve, Montreal.

The Star Furniture Co., Dundas, recently conducted an auction sale of special bargains.

W. L. Kiel & Co., hardware men and furniture dealers at Brock, Sask., are succeeded by W. L. Kiel.

A big fire at Portage du Fort, Que., damaged the stock and store of A. J. Rougier, furniture dealer there.

A. A. McLean, furniture dealer and undertaker at Moose Creek, Ont., suffered a loss through fire in his premises recently.

The wife of W. H. Dobson, furniture dealer and undertaker at North Augusta, Ont., died recently at her home, aged 34 years.

The Berlin Interior Hardwood Co. are building an addition to their office and show rooms, and will have considerable increased accommodation when completed. They will use the new wing largely for display purposes.

The Berlin Plate Glass and Mirror Co. are erecting a new building on Victoria street. Its dimensions are 75 x 78 ft., and will be one storey, built of reinforced concrete. It will be ready for occupation in about two months.

The Berlin Office and Fixture Co., Ltd., has been incorporated with a capital of $60,000, to take over S. Binbacher's planing mill and to manufacture office furniture and fixtures. S. Binbacher, J. M. Woolner, J. Rudy, H. Rogge, and E. Klein are provisional directors.

The Hoover Electric Cleaning and Service Co., Ltd., Toronto, has been incorporated, with a capital of $40,000, to clean, repair, and make furniture, carpets, and household equipment. The provisional directors are: W. H. C. Burnett, Detroit; J. Skelton and H. S. Colebrook.

The Minneapolis police were puzzled by new tactics of thieves recently when a moving van of the Flour City Transfer Co., laden with furniture, was stolen from one of the principal streets. The big wagon vanished with the household goods of Mrs. R. Eaton, and the police could not find them.

G. W. Bard, an old Guelph boy, who has been engaged in the furniture business in Woodstock for a number of years, has returned to his native city, and has opened a shop at 194 Norfolk street. Mr. Bard will make a specialty of upholstering, packing furniture, and retiring baby carriages. He is also carrying a new stock of goods.

Harper Bros. have purchased the furniture and undertaking business of W. C. Browne & Son, at Watford, Ont., and will offer the entire stock for sale at a big reduction from the regular prices. They rented the Browne stand and will dispose of the stock in that place. Bills will be issued in a day or two giving list of goods that will be sold at cut rates.

The Knechtel Furniture Factory employes put on a monster Victoria Day celebration in Walkerton on Monday, May 25th, when the Lucknow pipe band and dancers and the Hanover brass band were present. Amongst the items on the programme were a football match between the league teams of Mildmay and Walkerton and a baseball match between Clifford and the Walkerton Red Sox. There were also foot races and Highland dancing on the platform.

ADAMS FURNITURE CO. TO BUILD.

It is rumored that the Adams Furniture Co. is to erect a new building on Yonge street, Toronto, which will cost between $300.000 and $400,000. The site takes in Nos. 211 to 217 Yonge street, part of which is occupied by the Russell House. This property, which was purchased some time ago by C. S. Coryell, president of the company, has about 87 feet frontage by a depth of about 122 feet. The Yonge street frontage is assessed at $3,500 a foot.

FAVOR ANNUAL EXHIBITION ONLY.

The National Association of Metal and Spring Bed Manufactures of the United States, at its recent Chicago conference, passed a resolution endorsing the plan for one furniture exhibition a year and one line a year. This action was taken following an exhaustive discussion of the question, in which every member present took part. Commissioner Wulpi was directed to obtain the views of the members who were not present at the meeting and the bed manufacturers not affiliated with the association.

FILLING A BIG ORDER.

Some interesting facts have come out regarding the recent order for park seats made by the Stratford Mfg. Co., Stratford, Ont. Four weeks from the time the first car of steel was set on the company's tracks they had the entire lot finished. When set end to end in a line, the seats reach 2¼ miles. There were 33 miles of slats on the seats, 9¾ miles of steel, 126,025 holes punched, 95,779 rivets used. There were, all told, 13 large furniture and automobile carloads. Among other large orders filled by the Stratford Mfg. Co. were the Toronto Exhibition and a number of the larger public parks throughout the Dominion.

VENEERED TABLES

Enterprising advertisers of furniture have lately taken up a new idea and instead of striving to conceal the fact that a product is a veneered one, they are proudly announcing this and making capital out of it. They point to their table tops, for example, as being better than the regular sawed lumber, because they are made of reinforced or built-up lumber, with the plies crossing so as to give greater strength and to reduce the tendency to shrink and warp. Reinforced construction is the latest advertising phrase for veneered tables.

The Furniture Manufacturer

A Department of News and Ideas

Suggestions for Sanders
By C. J. Townsley

Sanding is such an important part of the process of finishing off veneer and cabinet work that it really deserves as much thought and study, also as much in the way of experimenting with a view of obtaining improvements, as the process of cutting or gluing up veneer. Also, the man whose sander work is not giving full satisfaction cannot spend a little time to better advantage than visiting around other places to see what is being done by other machines. By doing this, and by talking with manufacturers of sanding machines, he can get a lot of new light on the subject of sanding that should help him out considerably.

Take drum sanders, for example, and there are roll feeds and endless-bed feeds, sanders with rolls to finish on one side, and sanders to finish both sides at once. Then there are different methods of putting the paper on the rolls. Some put it on square around the roll and some wind it spirally, and the chances are that one of these will prove better for one kind of work, while the other may be better for another kind.

For work that is being fed straight through, as with a hopper feed, or even by hand, the spiral drum would seem to offer advantages, while for some other kinds of work one may find advantages in the straight opening drum; for instance, for ease of adjustment or tightening up of the paper if it gets a little loose. The best thing to do before buying anything in this line is to not only study the new offerings in relation to the work you have to do, but make it a point to go see some of them at work and see just what they are doing.

There is no question in any thinking man's mind but what it pays to put on new sandpaper as soon as that on the drum is worn so that it will no longer do good work freely. The important point here is to know just when and how often the paper should be changed on the drums of your sanding machine. This depends some, of course, on the kind of work being done, as well as on the grade of the sandpaper. The way to get at real facts and figures on when to change sandpaper, and how often, is to keep a record of the work, not only the number of hours the machine is actually at work, but also the quantity of stock handled, giving both the linear feet and the widths. Pretty soon you will be able to establish a pretty good schedule and to know in advance just about when your sandpaper should be changed. If it requires changing on an average of once a day, why not manage it to have the change made at night, and start in each morning with fresh paper on the drums. Generally more pains will be taken to get the paper on well if the change is made at some regular time than if it becomes necessary to stop right in the midst of the busy part of the day and make these changes.

By keeping a record of the hours of work and of the exact quantity and nature of the stock handled through the sander, and also of the quality of paper used, as well as the number, you not only get to know the exact cost of your sanding work and what to expect of it, but you are in a position to judge intelligently between the different offerings in sandpaper and to know which you are getting the most out of for your money. This itself is worth the time and trouble it takes to keep the record.

In sanding short lengths with a hopper feed on an endless-bed drum sander, there is some good argument in favor of the idea of using the spiral drum, but what you want is facts, not argument, so if you have work of this kind to do, make it your business to see the different machines at work and study the results.

For sanding several lots of panels of veneered work of different thicknesses, with a limited number of each thickness, the belt sander should offer advantages, because you may often be able to finish off a lot in the time it would take you to adjust a drum sander. It depends, of course, and it is merely a suggestion to beget experiments. Also, if there are a number of panels, presumably the same thickness, but which have been made in different lots and made varying somewhat in their actual thickness, one should be able to get better results with a belt sander, especially if the face veneer is thin.

No sanding room really seems complete without both drum and belt sanders, because while one may beat the other at certain kinds of work, the work of finishing off cabinet work varies so that one can hardly get along without a variety of machines—not only machines to sand various shapes, but some variety in the machines used for sanding straight surfaces.

For sanding core bodies off before putting on thin face veneer, if you are using a three-drum sander, a good plan is to drop the two back rolls out of commission and use coarse paper, say No. 2, 2½, or 3, without oscillation. This will size the work down to an even face and give a tooth-planed effect which will make the core body take and hold glue.

If you have some work that has been through the drum sander, and yet is not quite as smoothly finished as you think it should be, work that will requite too much time to finish off by hand, you have a nice job for the sand belt, provided there is one at hand to do the work. If not, and you think it will improve it by running it a second time through the drum sander, don't have all the rolls cut, but put the first and second rolls out of commission and simply use the finishing roll. Or should there be lots of the stock, and you want to do an extra fine job, repaper all the rolls with fine paper and try an experiment that way.

Experienced sander men say that if you have two lots of stock to sand, one of pine and one of oak, you should sand the oak first, because if the pine is sanded first it gums up the paper so that it will not cut freely on the oak. This is good argument in a way, but, on the other hand, if the oak is sanded first it gives you comparatively smooth paper to work the pine with, whereas pine or soft wood of any kind works best with a sharp sandpaper, just as it works best with sharp tools in the cabinet shop.

Wood having pronounced streaks of hard and soft grain, like oak, chestnut, and edge-grain pine and fir, should be fed through a drum sander with more angle than woods of even grain, because it is necessary to

TO PREVENT IDLE MACHINES RUSTING

To prevent machines and tools rusting when a plant shuts down for a time, or where they are used only occasionally, either one of the following will be found very useful:

Dissolve ½ oz. camphor in 1 lb. lard, or in that proportion, according to the quantity used, and before it cools enough to be hard, mix in enough black lead to give it the color of iron (gray). This should be well and thoroughly applied all over the metal, being careful to not miss any spots, and let it remain over night. The next day rub off clean with rags. If kept dry, metal treated in this way will keep free from rust all winter.

Olmstead's varnish, another rust preventive, is made by melting 2 ozs. resin in 1 lb. of fresh, sweet lard, melting the resin first and then adding the lard, mixing thoroughly. This is applied to the metal, which should be warm, if possible, and perfectly clean, afterwards rubbing off the mixture.

RELATION OF FIRES TO WORK

A wise employer put up in his factory a sign reading thus:

> FIRE WARNING!
> If The Plant Burns You Will Be Out of Work
> Safeguard The Factory And Protect Your Job

More and more factory owners are installing fire preventive and protective systems in their plants, and more and more they are winning the employes, by their own interest, to active and friendly co-operation in the work of fire control.

NEW DRAWER SLIDE

A well known Wisconsin furniture merchant has demonstrated the fact that it is the man who handles the goods and sells to the customer who is most likely to discover the wants of his customer. He is the fellow who is in the best position to discern new features that will prove a big selling point with the articles in his stock. Robert H. Kroos, of Sheboygan, Wis., has met with the same difficulty in drawers that refuse to work, especially in unseasonable weather, as all other furniture salesmen have some time during their experience. These difficulties set him thinking, and the result is a slick little device known as The Kroos Ball Bearing Drawer Slide. The slide is so simple that any average furniture repair man can put them in. All that is necessary is to bevel off the bottom edge of the drawer and tack the slide in on the runner on which the drawer rests.

FOR A FACTORY FLOOR

A mixture of two and one-half parts of clean sawdust, two parts sand, and one part of cement, used instead of concrete for floors, is said to be especially adapted for factory floorings. Men often go lame from working upon a cement floor, and it is very fatiguing if no worse evil results. The sawdust floor also is elastic and does not result in such damage to tools or fragile objects falling upon it. It can be laid for less than one-half the cost of concrete, and will stand hard wear, but is not adapted for outdoor use. Such floors are warmer and less noisy than concrete floors, and it is probable that they will be widely used in the future.

FASTENING MACHINERY TO CONCRETE FLOOR

The sketch represents a small section of concrete floor and shows two ways of placing fastenings. The first is a plank embedded in the concrete. Sometimes the plank is made narrower at the top than at the bottom, to increase the holding power of the concrete.

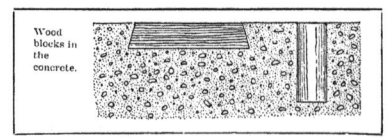

The planks must be set when the floor is laid. A method of placing a fastening when the floor is already laid is shown by the plug, which is of hardwood and driven into a hole drilled in the concrete. Lag screws are turned into the plug.—Popular Mechanics.

EFFICIENCY OF WIRE GLASS IN CASE OF FIRE

The amazing efficiency of wire glass is due largely to the difference in expansion between the glass and the steel. When the two are molded together at the melting point of glass and allowed to cool, the wire contracts more rapidly than the glass, and when a crack occurs the tension of the wire tends to draw the broken pieces together and maintain them in position. This is why a broken skylight does not fall or leak, and is why a window, cracked into innumerable pieces by the attack of fire, does not give way, but maintains its position up to the very melting point of the material itself.

A USEFUL TRESTLE

The accompanying illustration shows the construction of an adjustable trestle which Mr. A. W. Betsar finds very useful in connection with a woodworking machine.

The trestle is placed at such a distance as to catch and support the lumber as it leaves the end of the saw table. In this way it is possible to avoid the inconvenience of a very long saw table in a place where space may be at a premium, and still keep the work from tipping up while it is being sawn.

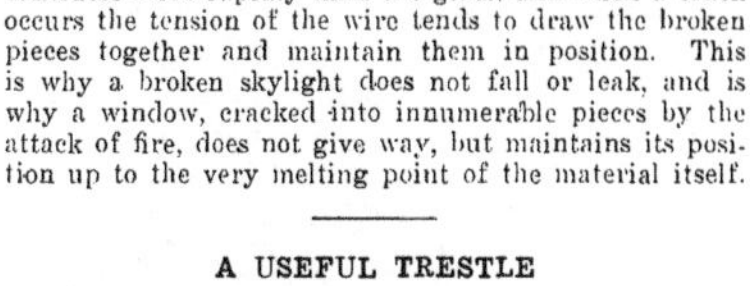

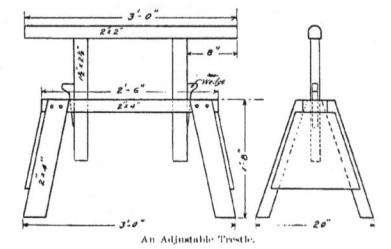

By means of the wedges the height may be adjusted exactly to suit the height at which the saw-table is set.

BUYER'S DIRECTORY

When writing to advertisers kindly mention the Canadian Furniture World and the Undertaker

ARTS AND CRAFTS FURNITURE
Geo. McLagan Furniture Co., Stratford.
John C. Mundell & Co., Elora.
ASBESTOS TABLE COVERS.
Canadian H. W. Johns-Manville Co., Toronto.
BABY CARRIAGES.
Gendron Mfg. Co., Toronto.
AWNINGS
Stamco, Limited, Saskatoon, Sask.
BENT WOOD FURNITURE.
John C. Mundell & Co., Elora.
J. & J. Kohn, Toronto (W. Craig).
BOOKCASES.
Knechtel Furniture Co., Hanover.
Globe Wernicke Co., Stratford.
Geo. McLagan Furniture Co., Stratford.
Meaford Mfg. Co., Meaford, Ont.
BUFFETS.
Bell Furniture Co., Southampton, Ontario.
Knechtel Furniture Co., Hanover.
Geo. McLagan Furniture Co., Stratford.
Peppler Bros., Hanover.
Stratford Chair Co., Stratford.
Victoriaville Furniture Co., Victoriaville, Que.
BEDS (Brass and Iron).
Canada Beds, Ltd., Chesley.
Ideal Bedding Co., Toronto.
Geo. Gale & Son, Waterville, Que.
Ives Modern Bedstead Co., Cornwall, Ont.
Ontario Spring Bed & Mattress Co., London, Ont.
Standard Bedstead Co., Victoriaville, Que.
Stamco, Limited, Saskatoon, Sask.
Stratford Bed Co., Stratford, Ont.
S. Weisglass, Ltd., Montreal, Que.
BEDS (Modern Wood).
Elora Furniture Co., Elora.
Knechtel Furniture Co., Hanover.
BED SPRINGS.
Colleran Spring Mattress Co., Toronto.
Knechtel Furniture Co., Hanover.
Frame and Hay Fence Co., Stratford.
Gold Medal Furniture Co., Toronto.
Leggett & Platt Spring Bed Co., Windsor.
Ideal Bedding Co., Toronto.
Ontario Spring Bed & Mattress Co., London, Ont.
Stamco, Limited, Saskatoon, Sask.
S. Weisglass, Ltd., Montreal, Que.
BED ROOM CHAIRS.
Baetz Bros., Berlin.
Bell Furniture Co., Southampton, Ontario.
Elmira Furniture Co, Elmira, Ont.
Lippert Furniture Co., Berlin.
BEDROOM ROCKERS
Lippert Furniture Co., Berlin, Ont.
BED ROOM SUITES.
Bell Furniture Co., Southampton, Ontario.
Knechtel Furniture Co., Hanover.
Meaford Mfg. Co., Meaford.
Victoriaville Furniture Co., Victoriaville, Que.
BEDROOM TABLES.
Chesley Furniture Co., Chesley, Ontario.
BUNGALOW CHAIRS & SUITES
Baetz Bros. & Co., Berlin, Ont.
CARD AND DEN TABLES.
Chesley Furniture Co., Chesley, Ontario.
Geo. McLagan Furniture Co., Stratford.
John C. Mundell & Co., Elora, Ont.
CARPET RACKS
Steel Furnishing Co., New Glasgow, N. S.
CAMP FURNITURE.
Southampton Seating Co., Southampton, Ont.
Stratford Mfg. Co., Stratford.
Ideal Bedding Co., Toronto.
CEDAR BOXES
D. L. Shafer, St. Thomas, Ont.
CELLARETTES.
John C. Mundell & Co., Elora, Ont.
CHAIRS AND ROCKERS.
Bell Furniture Co., Southampton,

J. P. Albrough & Co., Ingersoll.
Baetz Bros., Berlin.
Knechtel Furniture Co., Hanover.
John C. Mundell & Co., Elora.
Stratford Chair Co., Stratford.
Waterloo Furniture Co., Waterloo.
Canadian Rattan Chair Co., Victoriaville.
Gold Medal Furniture Co., Toronto.
Elmira Furniture Co, Elmira, Ont.
Imperial Furniture Co., Toronto.
Lippert Furniture Co., Berlin.
Victoriaville Chair Mfg. Co., Victoriaville.
CHESTERFIELDS.
Imperial Furniture Co., Toronto.
CHIFFONIERS.
Bell Furniture Co., Southampton, Ontario.
Knechtel Furniture Co., Hanover.
Meaford Mfg. Co., Meaford, Ont.
Stratford Chair Co., Stratford.
Victoriaville Furniture Co., Victoriaville, Que.
CHILDRENS' SULKIES
Jennings Co., St. Thomas
CHINA CABINETS.
Bell Furniture Co., Southampton, Ontario.
Peppler Bros., Hanover.
Knechtel Furniture Co., Hanover.
Geo. McLagan Furniture Co., Stratford.
Meaford Mfg. Co., Meaford, Ont.
CLOCK CASES
Elmira Interior Woodwork Co., Elmira, Ont.
COMFORTERS.
Toronto Feather & Down Co., Toronto.
Stamco, Limited, Saskatoon, Sask.
COTS
Ideal Bedding Co., Toronto.
Ontario Spring Bed and Mattress Co., London.
Elmira Interior Woodwork Co., Elmira, Ont.
COSTUMIERS
Elmira Interior Woodwork Co., Elmira, Ont.
COUCHES.
J. P. Albrough & Co., Ingersoll.
Ellis Furniture Co., Ingersoll.
Gold Medal Furniture Co., Toronto.
Kindel Bed Co., Toronto.
Imperial Furniture Co., Toronto.
John C. Mundell & Co., Elora, Ont.
Montreal Upholstering Co., Montreal.
Steel Furnishing Co., New Glasgow, N. S.
S. Weisglass, Ltd., Montreal, Que.
COUCHES (Sliding).
Ideal Bedding Co., Toronto.
Farquharson-Gifford Co., Stratford.
Ontario Spring Bed & Mattress Co., London, Ont.
Stamco, Limited, Saskatoon, Sask.
Gold Medal Furniture Co., Toronto.
COUCH FRAMES.
Southampton Seating Co., Southampton, Ont.
CRADLES.
Knechtel Furniture Co., Hanover.
CRIBS (Brass and Iron)
Ideal Bedding Co., Toronto.
Ontario Spring Bed & Mattress Co., London, Ont.
Stamco, Limited, Saskatoon, Sask.
S. Weisglass, Ltd., Montreal, Que.
CUSHIONS.
Stamco, Limited, Saskatoon, Sask.
DAVENPORT BEDS.
Farquharson-Gifford Co., Stratford.
Kindel Bed Co., Toronto.
Lippert Furniture Co., Berlin, Ont.
Montreal Upholstering Co., Montreal, Que.
Imperial Rattan Co., Stratford.
John C. Mundell & Co., Elora.
DAVENPORT FRAMES
Elmira Interior Woodwork Co., Elmira, Ont.
DEN FURNITURE
Elmira Furniture Co., Elmira, Ont.
Farquharson-Gifford Co., Stratford.
John C. Mundell & Co., Elora, Ont.
DIVANETTES.
Lippert Furniture Co., Berlin.
DESKS.
Bell Furniture Co., Southampton,

Elmira Interior Woodwork Co., Elmira.
Knechtel Furniture Co., Hanover.
Geo. McLagan Furniture Co., Stratford.
John C. Mundell & Co., Elora.
Stratford Desk Co., Stratford, Ont.
DINING-ROOM FURNITURE
Crown Furniture Co., Preston.
Farquharson-Gifford Co., Stratford.
Lippert Furniture Co., Berlin, Ont.
DINING SUITES.
Bell Furniture Co., Southampton, Ontario.
Knechtel Furniture Co., Hanover.
Geo. McLagan Furniture Co., Stratford.
John C. Mundell & Co., Elora, Ont.
Peppler Bros., Hanover.
Stratford Chair Co., Stratford.
DINERS
Lippert Furniture Co., Berlin, Ont.
DINNER WAGONS.
Geo. McLagan Furniture Co., Stratford.
Peppler Bros., Hanover.
DRESSERS.
Bell Furniture Co., Southampton, Ontario.
Knechtel Furniture Co., Hanover.
Stratford Chair Co., Stratford.
Victoriaville Furniture Co., Victoriaville, Que.
Meaford Mfg. Co., Meaford, Ont.
EXTENSION TABLES.
Bell Furniture Co., Southampton, Ontario.
Berlin Table Mfg. Co., Berlin.
Chesley Furniture Co., Chesley, Ontario.
Peppler Bros., Hanover.
Meaford Mfg. Co., Meaford, Ont.
FILING DEVICES.
Elmira Interior Woodwork Co., Elmira.
Globe Wernicke Co., Stratford.
Knechtel Furniture Co., Hanover.
Geo. McLagan Furniture Co., Stratford
FILING CABINETS
Globe Wernicke Co., Stratford, Ont.
FOLDING CHAIRS.
Ideal Bedding Co., Toronto.
Southampton Seating Co., Southampton, Ont.
Stratford Mfg. Co., Stratford.
FOLDING TABLES.
Chesley Furniture Co., Chesley, Ontario.
Hourd & Co., London.
Stratford Mfg. Co., Stratford.
FOOTSTOOLS
Elmira Furniture Co. Elmira, Ont.
GRASS FURNITURE (Chinese)
Jennings Co., St. Thomas
HALL RACKS
Chesley Furniture Co., Chesley, Ontario.
Lippert Furniture Co., Berlin, Ont.
HALL SEATS AND MIRRORS.
Chesley Furniture Co., Chesley, Ontario.
Geo. McLagan Furniture Co., Stratford.
Lippert Furniture Co., Berlin, Ont.
Meaford Mfg. Co., Meaford, Ont.
HALL TREES.
Chesley Furniture Co., Chesley, Ontario.
Geo. McLagan Furniture Co., Stratford.
HAMMOCKS
Dominion Hammock Mfg. Co., Dunnville, Ont.
HAMMO-COUCHES.
Ideal Bedding Co., Toronto.
INVALID CHAIRS.
Gendron Mfg. Co., Toledo, Ohio.
Victoriaville Chair Mfg. Co., Victoriaville, Que.
IRONING BOARDS AND DRYERS.
Chesley Furniture Co., Chesley, Ontario.
Stratford Mfg. Co., Stratford.
JARDINIERE STANDS.
Chesley Furniture Co., Chesley, Ontario.
Elmira Furniture Co, Elmira, Ont.
Elora Furniture Co., Elora.
Geo. McLagan Furniture Co., Stratford.
Meaford Mfg. Co., Meaford, Ont.
KITCHEN CABINETS.
H. E. Furniture Co., Milverton.
Nagrella Mfg. Co., Hamilton.
Knechtel Kitchen Cabinet Co., Ltd., Hanover, Ont.
KITCHEN TABLES.
Chesley Furniture Co., Chesley, Ontario.
Knechtel Furniture Co., Hanover.
Victoriaville Furniture Co., Victoriaville.
LADIES' DESKS
Meaford Mfg. Co., Meaford, Ont.

LAWN SEATS AND SWINGS.
Southampton Seating Co., Southampton, Ont.
Stratford Mfg. Co., Stratford.
LIBRARY TABLES.
Bell Furniture Co., Southampton, Ontario.
Chesley Furniture Co., Chesley, Ontario.
Peppler Bros., Hanover.
Elmira Furniture Co. Elmira, Ont.
Elmira Interior Woodwork Co., Elmira, Ont.
Geo. McLagan Furniture Co., Stratford.
Meaford Mfg. Co., Meaford, Ont.
John C. Mundell & Co., Elora, Ont.
LIVING-ROOM FURNITURE
Lippert Furniture Co., Berlin, Ont.
LOUNGES
J. P. Albrough & Co., Ingersoll.
LUXURY CHAIRS.
Lippert Furniture Co., Berlin
MAGAZINE RACKS AND STANDS.
Chesley Furniture Co., Chesley, Ontario.
Geo. McLagan Furniture Co., Stratford.
MATTRESSES.
Berlin Bedding Co., Toronto.
Canada Mattress Co., Victoriaville, Que.
Gold Medal Furniture Co., Toronto.
McKellar Bedding Co., Fort William, Ont.
Ontario Spring Bed & Mattress Co., London, Ont.
Stamco, Limited, Saskatoon, Sask.
Standard Bedding Co., Toronto.
Antiseptic Bedding Co., Toronto.
Ideal Bedding Co., Toronto.
Fischman Mattress Co., Toronto.
MANTELS—Wood, Tile
Elmira Interior Woodwork Co., Elmira, Ont.
MANTELS—Electric
Elmira Interior Woodwork Co., Elmira, Ont.
MEDICINE CABINETS.
Chesley Furniture Co., Chesley, Ontario.
Meaford Mfg. Co., Meaford, Ont.
MORRIS CHAIRS.
Ellis Furniture Co., Ingersoll.
Imperial Rattan Co., Stratford.
Knechtel Furniture Co., Hanover.
Lippert Furniture Co., Berlin.
John C. Mundell & Co., Elora.
Waterloo Furniture Co., Waterloo.
MUSIC CABINETS.
Geo. McLagan Furniture Co., Stratford.
Knechtel Kitchen Cabinet Co., Ltd., Hanover, Ont.
ODD CHAIRS
Lippert Furniture Co., Berlin, Ont.
OFFICE CHAIRS.
Bell Furniture Co., Southampton
Elmira Furniture Co., Elmira, Ont
Knechtel Furniture Co., Hanover.
H. Krug Furniture Co., Berlin.
Stratford Chair Co., Stratford.
J. & J. Kohn, Toronto (W. Craig).
John C. Mundell & Co., Elora, Ont.
OFFICE TABLES
Stratford Desk Co., Stratford, Ont.
PARK SEATS.
Southampton Seating Co., Southampton, Ont.
Stratford Mfg. Co., Stratford.
PARLOR CHAIRS and ROCKERS
Ellis Furniture Co., Ingersoll.
Elmira Interior Woodwork Co., Elmira.
John C. Mundell & Co., Elora, Ont.
Waterloo Furniture Co., Waterloo.
PARLOR FRAMES
Elmira Interior Woodwork Co., Elmira, Ont.
PARLOR SUITES.
Ellis Furniture Co., Ingersoll.
Knechtel Furniture Co., Hanover.
Waterloo Furniture Co., Waterloo.
Gold Medal Furniture Co., Toronto.
Lippert Furniture Co., Berlin
PARLOR TABLES.
Chesley Furniture Co., Chesley, Ontario.
Geo. McLagan Furniture Co., Stratford
Meaford Mfg. Co., Meaford, Ont.
Elora Furniture Co., Elora.
Elmira Furniture Co., Elmira, Ont.
Knechtel Furniture Co., Hanover.
Peppler Bros., Hanover.
PEDESTALS
Lippert Furniture Co., Berlin, Ont.
Geo. McLagan Furniture Co., Stratford.
Peppler Bros., Hanover.

MOULDINGS PICTURE FRAMES MIRRORS GLASS MATBOARD PICTURE BACKING	**MATTHEWS' QUALITY SERVING TRAYS** *Ask for our new catalogue just out*	for wedding presents. The June weddings are near at hand and all the ladies want Trays. All our Trays have glass set in with waterproof cement and are non leakable and have felt bottoms. All our latest Trays are fixed with simple screw fasteners allowing the back to be easily removed for replacing with owner's own fancy work, chintz or tapestry. Mail us an order for immediate shipment and we will send you a sample dozen assorted kinds and sizes that will not average more than $12.00 per doz. net and will retail at a good profit. **Matthews Bros. Ltd., 788 Dundas St. Toronto**

PILLOWS.
Ontario Spring Bed & Mattress Co., London, Ont.
Stamco, Limited, Saskatoon, Sask.
Toronto Feather & Down Co., Toronto.
Ideal Bedding Co., Toronto.

PILLOW SHAM HOLDERS.
Tarbox Mfg. Co., Toronto.

RATTAN FURNITURE.
Imperial Rattan Co., Stratford.
Canadian Rattan Chair Co., Victoriaville, Que.
Gendron Mfg. Co., Toronto.

RECLINING CHAIRS.
Ellis Furniture Co., Ingersoll.
Knechtel Furniture Co., Hanover
Lippert Furniture Co., Berlin, Ont.
John C. Mundell & Co., Elora, Ont.

RUG RACKS
Steel Furnishing Co., New Glasgow, N. S.

SECTIONAL BOOKCASES
Knechtel Furniture Co., Hanover.
Globe Wernicke Co., Stratford.

SCHOOL FURNITURE.
Bell Furniture Co., Southampton.

SIDEBOARDS.
Knechtel Furniture Co., Hanover.
Meaford Mfg. Co., Meaford, Ont.
Stratford Chair Co., Stratford.

STORE FRONTS
Kawneer Mfg. Co., Toronto.

TABLES.
Berlin Table Mfg. Co., Berlin, Ont.
Bell Furniture Co., Southampton, Ontario.
Elora Furniture Co., Elora.
Knechtel Furniture Co., Hanover.
John C. Mundell & Co., Elora.
Orillia Furniture Co., Orillia.
Peppler Bros., Hanover.
Stratford Chair Co., Stratford.
Victoriaville Furniture Co., Victoriaville, Que.

TABOURETTES.
Elora Furniture Co., Elora.
Kensington Furniture Co., Goderich.

TAPESTRY CURTAINS
Dominion Hammock Mfg. Co., Dunnville, Ont.

TELEPHONE STANDS.
John C. Mundell & Co., Elora, Ont.

TYPEWRITER DESKS.
Elmira Interior Woodwork Co., Elmira.
Stratford Desk Co., Stratford, Ont.

UPHOLSTERERS' SUPPLIES
Ellis Furniture Co., Ingersoll.
Gold Medal Furniture Co., Toronto.

UPHOLSTERED FURNITURE
Basts Bros., Berlin.
Ellis Furniture Co., Ingersoll.
Varquharson-Gifford Co., Stratford, Ont.

Imperial Rattan Co., Stratford.
Imperial Furniture Co., Toronto.
John C. Mundell & Co., Elora.
Knechtel Furniture Co., Hanover.
Waterloo Furniture Co., Waterloo
Gold Medal Furniture Co., Toronto.
Quality Furniture Makers, Welland.
A. J. Scafe & Co., Berlin.

VACUUM CLEANERS.
Onward Mfg. Co., Berlin.

VERANDAH FURNITURE.
Imperial Rattan Co., Stratford
Southampton Seating Co., Southampton, Ont.
Stratford Mfg. Co., Stratford.

WARDROBES.
Knechtel Furniture Co., Hanover
Meaford Mfg. Co., Meaford, Ont
Stratford Chair Co., Stratford.

FACTORY SUPPLIES
BRASS TRIMMINGS
Stratford Brass Co., Stratford.

CLAMPS.
Batavia Clamp Co., Batavia, N.Y.

FURNITURE SHOES.
Onward Mfg. Co., Berlin.

DRY KILNS.
Morton Dry Kiln Co., Chicago

FURNITURE HARDWARE
Stratford Brass Co., Stratford, Ont.

GLUE JOINTING MACHINES.
Canadian Linderman Co., Wood stock.

NAILS
P. L. Robertson Mfg. Co., Milton.

PLATING
P. L. Robertson Mfg. Co., Milton, Ontario.

RIVETS AND SCREWS
P. L. Robertson Mfg. Co., Milton.

SPRINGS.
James Steele, Guelph.
Ideal Bedding Co., Toronto.

SPANISH LEATHER.
Lackawanna Leather Co., Hackettstown, N. J.

STERILIZED HAIR.
Griffin Curled Hair Co., Toronto.

TABLE SLIDES
B. Walter & Co., Wabash., Ind.

TRUCKS.
W. I. Kemp Co., Ltd., Stratford.

VARNISHES.
R. C. Jamieson & Co., Montreal.
Ault & Wiborg, Toronto.

VENEERS.
Adams & Raymond Veneer Co., Indianapolis, Ind.

VENEER PRESSES.
Wm. R. Perrin & Co., Toronto.

WASHERS
P. L. Robertson Mfg. Co., Milton.

BUY
Upholstery Springs
That "Stand Up"

Our Tempered Furniture Springs will outlast almost any piece of upholstered furniture. They are built to "stand up" indefinitely.

JAMES STEELE, LIMITED
GUELPH :: :: ONTARIO

Invalid Chairs and Tricycles of every description.

This has been our study for thirty-five years. We build chairs that suit the requirements of any case. Write us for catalogue No. 20 and prices, if interested.

Gendron Wheel Co., Toledo, O. U.S.A.

"STORE MANAGEMENT COMPLETE"

272 Pages   **ONLY ONE DOLLAR**   13 Chapters

Tells all about the management of a Store, so that not only the greatest sales but the largest profit may be realized.—By FRANK FARRINGTON.

COMMERCIAL PRESS, Ltd., 32 Colborne St., Toronto

For Sale **Wanted**	**TERMS FOR INSERTION** 25 Cents per line, one insertion Four lines once for $1.00, three times for $2.00. Cash must accompany the order No accounts booked. **MINIMUM 50 CENTS**

FOR SALE—Good Furniture and Undertaking business in thriving town. No opposition. Large country trade. Prospective buyers will do well to look after this at once. Easy terms for quick sale. Box 127, Canadian Furniture World and The Undertaker, 32 Colborne street, Toronto, Ont.   11 7-1.

FOR SALE—Furniture and Undertaking business in Western Canada. For particulars write at once to Mrs. A. Metcalf, Treherne, Man.   11 7-3

TRAVELLERS—Wanted for Eastern and Northern Ontario, to handle a side line of upholstered goods in couches, davenports, divanettes, etc., on a commission. Apply to Montreal Upholstering Co., 1611-1613 Clark St., Montreal, Can.   11/7/1

IF YOU WANT TO BUY OR SELL

A Furniture or Undertaking Business, try our Classified Pages. The Canadian Furniture World and The Undertaker is read by practically every furniture merchant and undertaker in Canada every month.

Every Furniture Manufacturer installs new equipment in his plant from time to time the old must go! There is a way to dispose of it economically and effectively. Let's tell you

Canadian Furniture World, 32 COLBORNE ST. TORONTO

Dominion Casket Co., Limited

Telephones: { Day No. 1020. Nights, Sundays and Holidays Nos. 1069-1101 } **Guelph, Ont.** RUSH ORDERS SOLICITED

No. 314

No. 314 is a design that is very popular at present. Made with the "K" panel effect and trimmed with fine silk "Bosco." The mechanical workings of this casket are perfect, and we solicit your inquiries for this and any other styles upon the market.

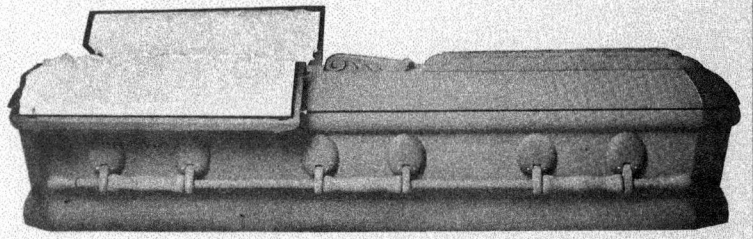

No. 152

No. 152 is especially made for the trade that requires a class of goods that is without fuss or feathers, but just plain and conservative with the right amount of richness which denotes quality.

NOTICE TO THE FUNERAL DIRECTOR

If you do not receive one of our new catalogs within the next few days, upon application we will gladly furnish same.

Undertakers' Department

Problems affecting the Undertaking Profession are here discussed and readers are invited to send letters expressing their views on any of the subjects dealt with—News of the profession throughout Canada.

Physical Agents in Disinfection

By Professor H. S. Eckels
Dean of Eckels' College of Embalming, Philadelphia, Pa.

CIVILIZATION grants an ever-increasing protection to the individual in return for his surrender of his natural rights. In the primitive state, man is restricted in his conduct only by his own inclinations and the fear that should he disregard the rights of others that in turn his own rights will be ignored by his fellows. All religions preach morality, but back of this lies the vast intangible fact that morality pays—pays if only in the example we set to others in their conduct towards us.

As man grows nearer and nearer to a state of civilization, he surrenders more and more of his individual rights to the government, whether that government be local, state or national. These rights thus acquired by the ruling powers are known as police rights, in which the individual turns over to the community at large his own inherent right to defend himself and those who naturally look to him for protection. These police rights, these protective powers, are constantly widening. They vary greatly in different nations, in different states and in different communities.

In Germany, for instance, the personal privileges of the citizen are almost entirely submerged into government regulation. In the Eastern States of our own country, these rights are more largely taken up by the community than in the West. Of late years there has been, however, a widespread demand that our national government take over from the various local and state authorities many powers hitherto held by the several communities, thus enacting uniform laws throughout the various commonwealths that comprise the American nation. If only the dead human body were to be considered, no state would have the inherent right to prohibit any man from becoming an undertaker.

What rights the state has acquired to regulate undertaking, embalming and especially sanitary science, are held by these police powers for the protection of the living. Not all undertakers realize this—that the protection of the living is the only valid excuse by which the state can license some men and refuse licenses to others. Sanitary science is, therefore, the basis of the undertaker's license and its protection from unrestricted competition. When undertakers begin to realize this unquestionable truth, doubtless much more attention will be paid to disinfection than heretofore has been the case.

Disinfection Should be Considered.

The license laws have been broken down in a number of states because this point has been neglected or overlooked. If the license laws are to continue, if the undertaker of the future is to receive the protection of the governing authorities, he must give a greater consideration to the subject of disinfection than is now the case. Every undertaker knows that there are certain chemical compounds which are disease-destroying in their effects. Not all realize, however, that there are also physical agents which work to the same end and, in many cases, even more efficiently. It is to a consideration of these physical agents that this paper is devoted, describing as it does the best uses that can be made of the available means of destroying infective bacteria with the physical agents that Nature has provided. In this list we will find steam, dry heat, burning, boiling, electricity and sunlight. Each of these has its different application (for different circumstances as well as material) and should be used and advised when and wherever practical.

The physical agents should be applied as aids or assistants to other measures of disinfection. Used by themselves, they would seldom give satisfactory results, but are invaluable in some instances when used along with other methods and with knowledge as to their effects on both the bacteria and the article to be disinfected. In such cases, where the destruction of the germs and not of the object itself is desired; for instance, in clothing, mattresses, bedding, carpets and such like objects, it has been found to be practically impossible to satisfactorily penetrate and disinfect by formaldehyde gas.

Steam will be found to be the only trustworthy agent to be employed in thoroughly penetrating to the centre of very large and cumbersome articles. Such disinfection, however, requires special and expensive apparatus, and until the undertaker is prepared to take up disinfection on a large scale, he is not likely to have much practical experience in this work nor find it desirable to keep such elaborate apparatus.

For ordinary household disinfection of fabrics and clothing which the undertaker needs to disinfect with steam, they should be hung up in a box or small space, to which steam from a boiler can be conveyed by means of a tubing inserted at the top of the enclosure, and the streaming steam continued for about fifteen minutes, when the articles will be found to be disinfected. Great care should be taken in selecting the articles to be submitted to this kind of disinfection, for steam is very apt to shrink woolens, and is injurious to silk fabrics. It also is injurious to leather goods of all kinds, furs, rubber and mackintoshes, etc., and it really finds its best uses in disinfecting clothing of a cheaper grade, the heavier kinds of bedding, mattresses, etc.

Carpets from an infected room may also be disinfected with steam, especially in cases where they have become soiled with infected discharges, and after they have already been subjected to gaseous disinfection. Streaming steam with two hours' exposure is necessary for the disinfection in spore-bearing diseases, such as anthrax, tetanus, glanders, actinomycosis, dengue, etc. Those articles which can be steamed without danger of injury to their fabric should receive steam disinfection in all cases of the above-named diseases, but these

A Most Hearty Invitation

is extended to the Funeral Directors to make their headquarters with us during their visit to the City to attend the Annual Convention.

Your Comfort our Pleasure.

Have your correspondence addressed, care of the Western Casket Co.

Take the Arlington Car at City Hall running West on William Ave. Ask Conductor to let you off at Emily St.

The Western Casket Co.,
Limited
Winnipeg   Cor. Emily St., & Bannatyne Ave.   Manitoba

require at least two hours' exposure to a temperature of 212 Fahr.

Practical Disinfection.

A practical method of steaming and thus disinfecting small objects, hangings, rugs, etc., that the undertaker may find desirable to submit to steam disinfection, is carried out by placing a large pot or wash boiler on the fire, having previously arranged the articles to be disinfected over the top and the whole covered with a sheet or cloth to retain the heat. After one hour's exposure the articles will be found to be thoroughly disinfected. A little salt added to the water will raise the boiling point, and the steam will, therefore, be given off at a higher temperature than 212 Fahr., which is a distinct advantage. Some of the small steam sterilizers are inexpensive and instill more confidence of your work into the mind of the family, than if disinfection is done by rough and ready means. However, at some time the undertaker will find himself in a position where it may be desirable to immediately disinfect, and in these cases an explanation can be given for the improvised measures that are used.

Steam with formaldehyde is the method that finds favor among disinfectors who have great quantities and much of this work to do. It may be used in a great many different ways, but is likely to be more used by city boards of health officers in places where they have a large amount of disinfecting to do, and where the undertaker is the director and adviser of disinfection on a large scale or perhaps is desirous of passing an examination in his district as disinfecting officer, he will find further information on this subject to be of great interest and value to him. Steam is such an important agent for disinfection that it is to be regretted that its action is so injurious on many materials, in fact, more injurious than most any other method. Its action on bacteria is immediate, as it kills them at once. The most resistant spores are killed after two hours' exposure, and, therefore, there is no restriction on the use of steam beyond that of the possible injurious effect it may have on materials. This the disinfector must consider before calling this agent into use.

Boiling water is another agent that is certain in its effects and only limited in its application to those articles on which the deleterious effect of boiling a considerable time is not noticeable. There is no better agent for the disinfection of bed linens, body linens, towels, kitchen and tableware, cuspidors, and a great variety of objects. It is sometimes the best, in fact, the only method to be applied with some articles. Boiling kills the bacterial life in all the contagious and infectious diseases immediately. Exposure to boiling water at 212 Fahr., continued for half an hour, will destroy the living principles in all the known infectious diseases, even the most resistant spores. A little corrosive sublimate added to boiling water adds very much to its efficiency, while carbolic acid and soap are also two substances that can be used in connection with boiling water to advantage. As is well known, strong alkaline solutions such as lye soap, added to boiling water, used with energy on the part of the disinfector, will penetrate any surface soiled with organic or oleaginous matter and greasy surfaces.

(Concluded in next issue.)

W. C. Browne & Son, of Watford, who have purchased the furniture and undertaking business of the late Dan Genge, have sold their business in Watford to Harper Bros., of that place.

AFTER TWENTY-SEVEN YEARS.

Mr. Daniel Stone, the well-known Toronto undertaker, with Mrs. Stone, is home after a delightful two months' trip to the coast. This is the first real holiday Mr. Stone has taken in twenty-seven years, and the good results as to improved health, has decided him that it will not be so long before he takes another trip. Going via Sante Fe route gave them an opportunity to visit the beautiful southern California country, and while there Mr. Stone made a short dash into Mexican territory, but escaped capture. The return trip was up the coast to British Columbia and C.P.R. home.

Mr. Stone is now in his new home directly opposite Earl street. The opening of this street to Jarvis will give a clear view through to Yonge street. The extension we understand is to be made this year, and will be a great improvement and convenience. Mr. Stone is to be complimented on the very quiet home atmosphere of his well appointed establishment; anything that suggests death or bereavement is not observable. A funeral service held in these parlors gives a person the feeling that it is from a private house parlor.

CHANGE IN OWNERSHIP AT ST. MARY'S

J. O. Mitchell has disposed of his furniture and undertaking business at St. Mary's to L. A. Ball, of Aylmer, a man who has spent his whole life in the furniture and undertaking business. Mr. Ball is no stranger in St. Mary's, being already well and favorably known by many Stone Town residents. In 1901 he graduated from the Chicago School of Embalming, and has since followed this business successfully. On his leaving Aylmer recently, the Methodist Church presented him with a chain and locket in appreciation of his services as superintendent for the past three years, while the Epworth League showed their appreciation of his services as president by giving him a handsome gold-headed cane. In connection with the change of business, it has been arranged to have the building extensively altered and re-arranged with the idea of making it one of the finest and most up-to-date furniture establishments in Western Ontario. Mr. Ball has secured the assistance of the retiring proprietor, Mr. Mitchell, whose services will be available in connection with the undertaking department.

NEW PARLORS AT BELLEVILLE

The third undertaking establishment in Belleville has just been opened by the Hogan Burial Company at 189 Front street, with Frank L. Hogan as manager. He received his technical education in Syracuse, is a graduate of the American College of Anatomy, Philadelphia, and is licensed in New York, Michigan and Ontario. All his life he has been in the undertaking, practising in the larger cities in the States. This establishment will be open day and night. There are waiting room and office at the front, back of this is a private funeral chapel. In the showroom are caskets displayed on trucks. Behind the trimming room is the private morgue, finished in white enamel. The most of the establishment except the front is decorated in peacock blue. The fittings and equipment are declared to be the best between Toronto and Montreal.

800 COFFINS IN TRANSPORTS.

Eight hundred coffins were taken aboard the U. S. army transports from Galveston, Texas. These will be sent with the Fifth Brigade of the United States army to Mexico if the War Department so orders.

Dominion Manufacturers
Limited

MANUFACTURERS OF

Fine Funeral Requisites

We guarantee

The Highest Quality

and the

Quickest Possible Service

*Night or Day Orders
given Prompt Attention*

BRANCHES

The Globe Casket Co., and Branches	London, Ontario
The Semmons & Evel Casket Co., and Branches,	Hamilton, Ontario
The National Casket Co.	Toronto, Ontario
Jas. S. Elliot & Son	Prescott, Ontario
Girard & Godin and Branches	Three Rivers, Quebec
Christie Bros. & Co,	Amherst, N. S.

FRED W. COLES   D. M. ANDREWS
General Manager   *Secretary Treasurer*

HEAD OFFICE

468 King Street W., Toronto

Ontario Appoints Examining Board

The long mooted question of an examining board for undertakers and embalmers in the Province of Ontario has been settled by the selection by the Ontario Government of T. Simpson, Mayor of Sault Ste. Marie; W. G. Burrows, Chatham; J. Tickell, Belleville; J. V. Van Camp, Toronto; and J. Torrance, M.P.P., Milverton, as members of the board.

The announcement was made by J. G. Henry, Sudbury, president of the Canadian Embalmers' Association, who was active in trying to persuade the Government to create the board.

The members of the board are recognized as thoroughly capable men in the profession, and are expected to add dignity and weight to the examining board, and help raise the profession in Ontario to a higher standard of excellence.

Under the law which has created this board, and which was passed by the Ontario Legislature, embalmers will now have to obtain a license before they can carry on their business, this, of course, applying to new members of the profession. Present embalmers throughout Ontario practising their profession will obtain a permit to continue, after complying with some necessary requirements. New men entering the profession will, after complying with a term of probation, be required to take the examination before being allowed to practise.

A local undertaker and embalmer considers that the working of the new law will be the best possible thing that could happen, as the public health will be safe guarded. Up to the present undertakers have been allowed to carry on embalming, but in future they will have to have two years' experience before they are allowed to take out a license, and therefore this law will be the means of assuring the public that they can place their confidence in the embalmers. The public will also now know that the embalmers can deal with contagious diseases when they have become qualified.

At a meeting of the board on May 28 the members elected T. Simpson as chairman; J. Tickell, treasurer; and J. Torrance, secretary. The latter only will be allowed a salary of something like $1,800 a year, though traveling expenses will also be allowed the members who attend meetings of the board. It is understood that a license fee of $10 a year will provide the fund for sustaining the board. Incidentally, the courses of study which the Canadian Embalmers' Association have been conducting for several years past will obtain greater worth as a result of the appointment of the board of embalmers' examiners for the Province of Ontario.

Joseph L. Tickell, treasurer of the new board, is a member of Tickell & Sons Co., furniture and casket manufacturers, a firm which was established in Belleville since 1858. He was born in that city in 1866, and for 30 years has been a member of the undertaking profession. He is a member of a great many societies, and was for a while a representative on the Belleville Board of Education. Travelers in all sections of older Canada know him, for Mr. Tickell has been a member of the Dominion Commercial Travelers' Association for 25 years. He also stands well with the profession, and will add weight to the board of examiners to which he has just been appointed.

FUNERAL DRAPERIES CONDEMNED.

The St. Louis (Mo.) board of health recently authorized the health commissioner to eliminate the use of cloth coverings and other cloth articles of ornament used by undertakers for funerals, except when such articles are fumigated. It was claimed that undertakers sometimes neglected to fumigate such articles after using them in homes where death was caused by a contagious disease.

J. C. VAN CAMP, Toronto, appointed a member of board. He is well-known throughout the province, having been secretary of Canadian Embalmers Association in the past.

JOSEPH L. TICKELL,
Treasurer of Ontario Embalmers Board of Examiners.

Burglar Proof and Water Tight

"The St. Thomas"

Original, Quick Closing End Vault

MANUFACTURED BY

The St. Thomas Metallic Vault Company, Limited
ST. THOMAS, ONTARIO

The Original Patented Concentrated Fluid

Patented Formula
Strongest and Best

Essential Oil Base, combined with Alcohol, Glycerine, Oxidized Formaldehyde and Boron-Dioxide.

Ask others for their Formula

Special Canadian Agents
National Casket Co.
Toronto, Ont.
GLOBE CASKET CO.
London, Ont.
SEMMENS & EVEL CASKET CO.
Hamilton, Ont.
GIRARD & GODIN
Three Rivers, Que.
JAS. S. ELLIOTT & SON
Prescott, Ont.
CHRISTIE BROS.
Amherst, N.S.

Larger Bottles filled up with water

Egyptian Chemical Co. Boston, U.S.A

FOR SALE

Second-hand, single horse, rubber tired, leather lined, Undertaker's coupe for personal use. Price $160.00. Also one Bomgardner lowering device. Price $40.00.

Blachford & Son
57 King Street West   Hamilton, Canada

Convention Meetings

President J. G. Henry, of the Canadian Embalmers' Association, says he expects to see a bumper crowd at the convention in Toronto in September. Arrangements for the meeting are in progress.

Manitoba Directors Call Meeting

The Western Canada Funeral Directors' and Embalmers' Association announce that their next annual convention will be held at Winnipeg, July 14, 15, and 16, during the week of the Canadian Industrial Exhibition. It has been decided to make this meeting, which is the tenth anniversary of the organization, the biggest, best, and most enthusiastic meeting in its history. In pursuance of this plan, the services of Prof. W. P. Hohenschuh, of Iowa City, have been secured. The professor is famed as an author, lecturer, embalmer and funeral director.

The programme, as in former years, will be of an instructive and educational character, covering the following subjects: Anatomy of the Organs, Cavity Preservation, the Circulation, Arterial Embalming, Bacteriology for Embalmers, Decomposition, Communicable Diseases, Blood and Discolorations, Mutilated and Post-mortem Cases, Cosmetics and Demi-surgery. The meetings will be held at Oddfellows Hall, and Manitoba Medical College, where fine accommodation is offered for the sessions.

The Maritime Convention

The twelfth annual meeting of the Maritime Funeral Directors' Association will be held at the old railroad city of Moncton, N.B., Tuesday, Wednesday, and Thursday, August 11, 12, and 13. The dates have been selected to enable members from the Upper Provinces to attend the Maritime meetings, also to give members from Eastern Canada an opportunity to visit Toronto during the thirty-first annual meeting of the Canadian Embalmers' Association, in September. The Moncton meeting should be one of the largest and best meetings ever held by the Maritime Association. The city is most central, having railway connections with every part of Eastern Canada.

Tuttle Brothers have just completed a model and up-to-date establishment, where everything is carried on in funeral management. This should attract everyone who is engaged in funeral directing and embalming. There will be many new features introduced this year, both in entertainment and in an educational way.

Alberta Convention Dates

Secretary H. G. Stone, of the Alberta Funeral Directors' and Embalmers' Association, writes to alter slightly the dates given out last month as those on which the Alberta association will meet. The convention will open on Tuesday morning, July 21, and will continue for the next two days July 22 and 23.

CREMATION ASSOCIATION TO MEET.

The second annual convention of the Cremation Association of America will be held at 320 North Illinois street, Indianapolis, Ind., September 3 and 4. The Montreal crematorium, thus far, is the only Canadian member, but Hugo Erichsen, M.D., of Detroit, president of the association, writes the Furniture World and The Undertaker to say that any of our readers who may happen to be in Indianapolis at the time mentioned will be welcomed.

MORTUARY CHAPEL AT GUELPH.

A well-attended meeting of those interested in the proposal to build a mortuary chapel and mausoleum at the Union Cemetery was held at the Y. M. C. A. in Guelph recently. Several plans for such a structure were considered, and it was found that a handsome building can be erected for between $6,000 and $7,000. If it is decided to go ahead with the matter, St. George's Cemetery board are willing to assist. The Trades and Labor Council are also very interested in the matter. The proposal that met with the most favor was that the cemetery board give $1,000, the churches $1,000, the ladies to raise $1,000, the combined lodges to give $1,000, and with these donations there would not be a very large sum to be raised by general subscription.

Mayor Carter stated that he thought it was up to the combined lodges of the city to take a more active interest in the matter, as the cause was a worthy one. The following committee was appointed to see what could be done regarding the matter: Ven. Archdeacon Thos. Davidson, Ald. W. T. Doughty, Thos. Hall, James Laidlaw, and Mayor Carter.

DOMINION CASKET COMPANY ENLARGE.

The Dominion Casket Company, Guelph, have been making considerable enlargement to their factory, as business has been far beyond their expectations. They also have just issued their first catalogue, which contains a good selection in all grades of goods including their famous combination metallic caskets, and also the finished oak and mahogany cases, which are something new to the undertakers. The company expects to exhibit at the convention of funeral directors in Toronto this year goods which they say will "revolutionize the casket trade."

NEW WESTERN FUNERAL DIRECTORS.

New undertakers' parlors have been opened in the West by Luke & Ross, at Assiniboia, Sask.; Wilson Bros., Ramsey, Alta.; Dan Woodrow, Kincaid, Sask.; Scott & Saunderson, Domremy, Sask.; Fort George Undertaking Co., Fort George, B.C.; Rantz & Co., McBride, B.C.; J. M. Courtney, Many Berries, Alta.; G. R. Binkley, Shaunavon, Sask.; and W. R. Merrill & Co., Antler, Sask. The opening orders in all cases were supplied by the Winnipeg Casket Co.

Question Box

Replying to the question put by a correspondent in the last number of Canadian Furniture World and The Undertaker as to "What is the best way to preserve a drowned body from stench," we have received from a correspondent the following reply: "A charcoal bed is a good way, and was for a time considered the only way, but a cotton vest of formaldehyde fluid is perhaps a better method."

George Goheen has bought out an undertaking business in Campbellford.

To Canadian Funeral Directors

THE CENTRAL LINE

Mahogany, Oak, Plush and Cloth Covered Caskets

WE SHIP PROMPTLY

We can also supply anything desired in Casket Linings, Burial Robes, and a general line of Undertakers' Supplies

Orders given our Canadian representative, or sent to our factory at Bridgeburg by mail, telegraph or telephone will be shipped promptly.

CENTRAL CASKET COMPANY

Bridgeburg, Ont.
Telephone 126

R. S. Flint — Canadian Representative: 241 Fern Ave., Toronto
Telephone Parkdale 3257

No Undertaker Should Overlook

the fact that he can make a full gallon of fluid of standard strength from each sixteen-ounce bottle of RE-Concentrated Dioxin. Re-Concentrated Dioxin costs no more per bottle than any standard concentrated fluid, but it is twice as strong—in other words, there are twice as many ounces of preservation in a bottle of RE-Concentrated Dioxin as there are in any bottle of merely concentrated fluid.

If economy were the only recommendation for RE-Concentrated Dioxin, however, we should not urge it upon our patrons.

As a matter of fact, it is easy to explain and equally easy to demonstrate the fact that the fluid thus produced gives a far better cosmetic effect and produces a far more life-like body than possibly could be produced by any raw formaldehyde concentrated fluid.

This is because RE-Concentrated Dioxin has a double base. When diluted to make a full gallon of fluid to the bottle, its main base is peroxide, with a secondary base of purified formaldehyde (formochloral).

Every funeral director knows that peroxide of hydrogen is the best bleacher known to chemical science. Not everyone realizes, however, that peroxide of hydrogen has blood solvent qualities far in excess of any other chemical yet discovered which is suitable for use in embalming fluid. Peroxide of hydrogen is composed of two atoms of oxygen and two atoms of hydrogen. Since oxygen is fifteen times heavier than hydrogen, fifteen-sixteenths of the atomic weight of peroxide of hydrogen, therefore, is oxygen.

Every embalmer knows that venous blood is much darker in color, is much more sluggish and much heavier than arterial blood. What is the difference between the two? Arterial blood is merely venous blood, which has been purified in the lungs, which has been lightened in color and rendered vastly more fluid by the oxygen which the lungs have extracted from the air we breathe.

Since fifteen-sixteenths of the atomic weight of peroxide of hydrogen is oxygen, it must be apparent, therefore, that the oxygen in the extra rich peroxide in Dioxin has a tendency to exercise the same purifying and solvent qualities upon the dark, discolored venous blood after death as the oxygen which the lungs extract from the air we breathe has upon the venous blood in life.

The result is that much more blood can be drained from a body in which RE-Concentrated Dioxin is injected than is possible from a body in which raw formaldehyde is used and in which the astringent qualities of the formaldehyde have sealed up the discolored blood corpuscles in the capillaries.

Putty color is caused by raw formaldehyde fluid sealing up the discolored corpuscles of the blood in the capillaries. It is inevitable where raw formaldehyde fluids are used unless exceeding care is used to drain blood. And even then there is great danger.

RE-Concentrated Dioxin is distinctly the most modern and the most scientific embalming fluid on the market, as well as the most economical. The progressive funeral director will not hesitate, but will order a trial shipment.

RE-Concentrated DIOXIN

H. S. ECKELS & CO.   1922 Arch St., Philadelphia, Pa.
241 Fern Ave., Toronto, Ont., Can.

Making Obituaries Pay

Written for Canadian Furniture World and The Undertaker
by Chas. Fulton Oursler

Upon the undertaker falls usually the task of inserting the advertised death notices in the newspapers. Most undertakers are familiar with the check system by which such notices are copied and forwarded to the editorial rooms, so that reporters may be sent to the houses and obituary notices secured. Right there is an excellent opportunity to secure legitimate publicity in a way that is sure to attract business.

All the display advertising in the world, carried in heavy black type, such as some members of the profession delight to pay for, does not give one hundredth the prestige that attaches to a modest little notice in the news columns that Mr. Anybody Soandso had charge of the funeral arrangements. Such notices, ordinarily, are hard to get, for it is the aim of the editor to keep anything that smacks of advertising out of his columns. Yet, in a considerable experience in an editor's chair, I have seen undertakers do it, and win the goodwill of the city editor as well.

It is this man, the chief of the reporters, the real brains of the local room, who must be conciliated. Let it be understood, first and foremost, that there was never a city editor who really had enough reporters. He might reject applicants every day, but it is not because he doesn't need them. The payroll has to be kept as short as possible. Therefore it is up to the city editor to get the best results out of his staff, no matter how small it may be. No easy job it proves sometimes, and when ten or twelve death memoranda come to his desk, each meriting an investigation, he sometimes wonders where he is going to come out. Right there is the undertaker's chance. Let him save a reporter a trip out to the house, and he will earn the benediction of the city editor and a line in the obituary notice thrown in.

The objection may be interposed that an undertaker is an undertaker, not a reporter; that he knows nothing about writing for newspapers. That is an easy matter. Every day a newspaper publishes a number of death notices, all patterned more or less after a conventional model, and with one of them before him, the undertaker should find it easy to write the notice in proper form. Regard the facts to be secured, I am appending here a copy of slip which I once had prepared for my reporters:—

DEATHS.

Name of Deceased ....
Address .... Occupation ....
Age .... Date of Death .... Cause ....
Time Ill .... Where Born ....
Name of Wife or Husband ....
Names of Parents ....
Names of Children ....
....
....
No. Grandchildren ...... Great Grandchildren ......
Lodges or Societies ....
....
Date of Funeral .... Time ....
Place ....
Pastor .... Church ....
Undertaker ....
Cemetery ....
Pallbearers and Miscellaneous ....
....
....

Then, when he inserts the advertisement, he can go to the editorial rooms and introduce himself to the city editor. He will receive a gentlemanly welcome, and his relations will grow more cordial with each succeeding visit.

His energies should not stop there, however. Every once in a while some feature crops out in a death that is peculiar enough to make interesting reading. For instance, a woman may die, one day, and the next her husband will fall heir to a large fortune. Or a man may die while telling a joke or boasting of his good health. These and a thousand other such coincidences are news, in the strict sense of the term, and a city editor will exert every effort to get the facts. When a reporter goes to the house, the family are often so grief-stricken that they are unable to talk to strangers. How welcome, then, is the undertaker who walks into the newspaper office with all the facts, and requests, as a reward, simply that his name be used as the man who had the funeral arrangements in charge.

A parting word of advice: Treat all papers alike, showing partiality to none, unless one has left your name out of a notice and you want to bring them to terms by giving good items to its rival. And keep everlastingly out. It's worth while, and builds a reputation better than all the paid ads. in the world.

Gossip of the Profession

I. C. Beattcay, undertaker at St. John, N.B., has sold his business to N. L. Brenan.

Mr. Black, of Beaverton, has taken over the undertaking business of W. J. Barker at Brechin.

Kathleen, youngest daughter of Mr. and Mrs. J. C. Van Camp, Toronto, was married in June to Dr. Wm. J. Defries at a very pretty house wedding.

A meeting was held at Tinkham, Sask., recently, for the purpose of selecting a site for a cemetery. A committee was appointed to secure sufficient land at once.

Kerr & Company, undertakers, who recently bought out J. W. Young, have removed to the premises formerly occupied by Mr. Young at 386 Talbot street, St. Thomas.

Kingston undertakers are experiencing difficulties in answering ambulance calls on account of Princess street being dug up in front of their places of business. Some boards have been placed across the track at Sydenham street to allow them to cross.

V. S. Sweeney, funeral director, Yarmouth, N.S., lost a valuable automobile by fire recently. Mr. Sweeney had his car stored in the front shop of the garage, where it was being repaired for summer use. Fire destroyed the building, and with it his car. We understand there was no insurance.

Ben D. Humphrey, the well-known Yonge street (Toronto) undertaker, who has been dangerously ill at the Wellesley Hospital there, is reported to be improving. Mr. Humphrey, who was taken suddenly ill some few weeks ago as a result of an internal ailment, underwent a serious operation.

F. L. Hogan, M.C., has opened an undertaking establishment on Front street, Belleville. A mortuary chapel and a private funeral chapel have been provided, something the city heretofore lacked. Mr. Hogan is an experienced undertaker, having served in every capacity in connection with the business, both in Canada and the United States.

CANADIAN FURNITURE WORLD AND THE UNDERTAKER.   July, 1914

Index to Advertisements

A
Ault & Wiborg Co 22

B
Baets Bros. & Co..................8
Batavia Clamp Co..................21
Berlin Table Mfg. Co..............27
Blachford & Son...................62

C
Canadian Linoleum Co.............26
Canadian School of Embalming....55
Can. H. W. Johns-Manville Co....27
Can. Rattan Chair Co.............21
Central Casket Co................64
Chesley Furniture Co.............13
Colleran Patent Spring Mat. Co..10

D
Dominion Casket Co...............56
Dominion Mfrs., Limited..........60

E
Eckels & Co., H. S...............64
Egyptian Chemical Co.............62
Elmira Interior Woodwork Co.....14

F
Farquharson-Gifford Co............7
Fleshman Mattress Co...........i.f.c.
Frame & Hay Fence Co............11

G
Gale & Son, Geo..................25
Globe-Wernicke Co.................9
Gold Medal Furniture Mfg. Co. o.b.c.
Gendron Wheel Co.................55

H
Hourd & Co........................8

I
Imperial Furniture Co............18
Imperial Rattan Co................3
Irish, G. L......................28

K
Kawneer Mfg. Co..................10
Kindel Bed Co., Limited..........10
Knechtel Furniture Co............23
Kohn, J. & J......................6

L
Leggatt & Platt Spring Bed Co...24

M
Matthews Bros....................55
Menford Mfg. Co..................15
McLagan Furniture Co., Geo..o.f.c.
McKellar Bedding Co..............12
Montreal Upholstering Co..........4
Mundell, J. C., & Co...........i.f.c.

N
N. A. Bent Chair Co..............14

O
Ontario Spring Bed................4

R
Robertson, P. L., Mfg. Co........22

S
Shafer, D. L. & Co...............18
Standard Bedding Co..............16
Steele, James, Limited...........55
Steel Furnishing Co..............13
Stratford Brass Co................8
Stratford Chair Co................6
Stratford Mfg. Co................11
St. Thomas Metallic Vault Co....62

T
Textile ather Co.................16

V
Victoriaville Bedding Co.........21
Victoriaville Chair Co...........20
Victoriaville Furniture Co......19

W
Walter & Co., B..................27
Western Casket Co................58
Weisglass, S., Limited...........17

Undertakers Shipping Directory

ONTARIO

Aurora—
  Dunham, Charles.
Barrie—
  Smith, G. G. & Co.
Brockville—
  Quirmbach, Geo. R., 162 King St.
Brooklin
  Disney, R. S.
Campbellford—
  Irwin, James.
Campden—
  Hausel, Albion.
Clinton—
  Walker, Wesley.
Coboconk—
  Greenley, A.
Copper Cliff—
  Boyd, W. C.
Dungannon—
  Sproul, William
Dutton—
  Schultz, B. L.
Elmira—
  Dreisinger, Chris.
Fenelon Falls—
  Deyman, L. & Son.
Fenwick—
  H. A. Metler.
Fergus—
  Armstrong, M. F.
  Thomson, John & Son.
Fort William—
  Cameron & Co., 711 Victoria.
  Morris, A.
Haileybury—
  Thorpe Bros.
Galt—
  Anderson, J. & Son.
Hamilton—
  Green Bros., 124 King St. E.
  Robinson, J. H. & Co., 19-21 John St. N.
Hanover—
  Wunnenberg, Norman.
Hastings—
  Howard, P. N.
Hepworth—
  Downs, E. J.
Inwood—
  Lorriman, E. S.
Kemptville—
  McCaughey, Geo. A.

Kenora—
  Horn & Taylor.
Kingston—
  Corbett, S. S.
Lakefield—
  Hendren, Geo. G.
Little Current—
  Sims, J. G.
Markdale—
  Oliver, M.
Newmarket—
  Millard, J. H.
North Augusta—
  Wilson, J. R.
North Bay—
  St. Pierre, E.
Oakwood—(Mariposa Station G.T.R.) Wilmot F. Webster.
Ohsweken—
  Johnson, F. L.
Oshawa—
  Disney Bros.
  Luke Bros.
Ottawa—
  Rogers, Geo. H., 128 Bank
Petrolia—
  Steadman Bros.
Port Arthur—
  Collin Wood, 36 Arthur St.
  Morris, A.
Prescott—
  Rankin, H. & Son.
Renfrew—
  O'Connor, Wm.
St. Mary's—
  N. L. Brandon.
St. Thomas—
  Williams, P. R. & Sons, 519 Talbot St.
Seaforth, Ont.
  W. T. Box & Co.
Scotland—
  Vaughan, Jos. H. M.
Sudbury—
  Henry, J. G.
Toronto—
  Cobbledick, N. B., 2068 Queen St. East and 1508 Danforth Ave. Private Ambulance.
  Humphrey, E. J. Burial Co. Head Office, 359 Yonge St.; Branch, 407 Queen St. W. Private ambulance.
  Stone, Daniel (formerly H. Stone & Son), 82 Bloor St. West.
  Vancamp, J. C., 30 Bloor St. West.
Waterloo—
  Klipper Undertaking Co.
Welland—
  Sutherland, G. W.
Woodstock—
  Meadows, T. & Sons.
  Mack, Paul.

QUEBEC

Buckingham—
  Paquet, Jos.

Cowansville—
  Judson, M. B.
Montreal—
  Tees & Co., 912 St. Catherine St. West.
St. Hyacinthe—
  Cadôrette, Mongeau & Leary.
St. Laurent—
  Gougeon, Jos.

NEW BRUNSWICK

Petitcodiac—
  Jonah, D. Allison.
Welland—
  Sutherland, G. W.
Woodstock—
  Van Wart, Jacob.

NOVA SCOTIA

Ferrona—
  Fraser, D. & Co.
Halifax—
  Snow & Co., 90 Argyle St.
Sydney, C.B.—
  Beaton, A. J. & Son, 374-384 George St.

MANITOBA

Brandon—
  Campbell & Campbell.
  Vincent & McPherson.
Souris—
  McCulloch, Wm.
Swan River—
  Paull, Geo.
Winnipeg—
  Bardal, A. S., 834 Sherbrooke
  Thompson, J. C., 501 Main
  Clark-Leatherdale Co., Ltd., 232 Kennedy St.

SASKATCHEWAN

Gull Lake—
  Morrow, Fred. A.
Saskatoon—
  Young, A. E.
Kamsack—
  Russell, G. E. I.
Lanigan—
  Robertson, Wm.
Moose Jaw—
  The Bellamy Co.
  Broadfoot Bros.
Rush Lake—
  Friesen, John M.
Prince Albert—
  Howard, A. C.
  Hadley, C. L.
Regina—
  Speers, George.
Semans—
  Haygarth, Jas.
Welwyn—
  Leavens, Merritt.
Wolseley—
  Barber, B.

ALBERTA

Calgary—
  Graham & Buscomb, 611 Centre St.
Castor—
  Winter, W. G.

BRITISH COLUMBIA

Hosmer—
  Cornett, T. A.
Victoria—
  Hana & Thompson, 827 Pandora Ave.

Canadian School of Embalming

Instruction in Practical Embalming and Funeral Directing
PREPARATION FOR EXAMINATIONS
ENTER AT ANY TIME

R. U. STONE   **32 Carlton Street**
Principal   Toronto

Leisure reading that means more dollars when you work

A knowledge of the big problems of business, put into a very comprehensive and readable style, helps you in finding easier and quicker ways of overcoming them. That's what Frank Farrington does in these two books. You will like the way his mind works. The wide scope of his experience, the accuracy of his statements, and his knowledge of human nature all combine to make them volumes that will be read not only for the entertainment they afford, but for their practical worth in the conduct of a retail store. The busy man will appreciate these books for another reason; they are written in concise form and he may start reading anywhere and find that particular chapter complete in itself, and depending in no wise upon those which precede or follow. Although if he fails to read every one of them he is depriving himself of a privilege.

Retail Advertising

"Retail Advertising Complete" covers with a comprehensive grasp such subjects as newspaper advertising, how to get up the ads., many representative samples being presented. A chapter is given to window advertising, and the subject of novelties is thoroughly discussed; that important part of advertising which is done inside the store is in no manner overlooked, while equal attention is given to outside advertising, such as bill posting and other means of reaching outlying districts; advertising direct by mail and mail order opportunities and advantages are gone into carefully; special sales as business getters, and some features that make them successful, are presented in a convincing manner. In short, this book is the common sense psychology of advertising.

266 Pages, 5 x 7 inches, Cloth
Price $1.00 Delivered

Store Management

In "Store Management Complete," which is well illustrated, the author gives a clear and concise picture of the kind of man, physically and mentally, that the successful merchant should be; the writer's experience has taught him that one kind of personality is most desirable, and he tells you about this. In a chapter on "Where to Start" the advantages of various locations are discussed; how to make the most of a poor one, and the desirable side of the street. "Store Arrangement" dips to the bottom in such subjects as making entrance easy, best arrangement of windows; how to plan the lighting, heat, and ventilation; utilizing waste space, and systems of storing extra stock.

An interesting chapter on "Clerk Management" brings out the advantage of knowing people and how to handle them. The other chapters deal with the buying end; the store policy; leaks; the store's neighbors; working hours; expenses; the credit business; what to sell; premium giving. The man and the business; their relation and success, that's the book.

252 Pages, 5 x 7 inches, Cloth
Price $1.00 Delivered

Both Volumes $1.90 Postpaid

The Commercial Press, Limited

Publishers of
Canadian Hardware Journal
The Retail Grocer
Canadian Furniture World
Retail Druggist of Canada
The Canadian Furnisher
The Canadian Nurse

32 Colborne Street
Toronto, Canada

Publishers of
The Canadian Manufacturer
The Canadian Builder and Carpenter
The Canadian Clay Worker
The Machine Shop
Motoring
Good Roads of Canada

DIRECTORS	THE	Montreal Factory
W. J. McMURTRY, President and General Manager	**GOLD MEDAL**	C. A. HART, Vice-Pres. and Mgr.
W. R. DALBY		Winnipeg Factory
G. C. EMMERSON		W. J. RIMMINGTON, Manager
H. B. SHORTT, Secretary	**LINE**	Uxbridge Factory
G. HUGHES, Assistant Manager		GEO. WILSON, General Supt.

Davenports and Divanettes

No. 714—One of our Twenty Designs

Our factories at Toronto and Uxbridge are the most perfectly equipped in Canada for the manufacture of Davenports and Divanettes. In addition to making our wood frames and other parts, we make all our own interior steel frame work for operating Bed constructions, which are fitted with the best National Steel fabric Springs.

The principal features of our Davenports and Divanettes are:

Perfection and Simplicity of Operation
More Bedding Space than any other make
Spring Edge Fronts and Ruffle Borders
Elegant Designs and well made and finished frames
Prices Lower than any other makes.

Patent Locking Device for Divanettes
A Good Mattress on a Good Spring Bed
Indestructible Patent Truss Construction for Springs

Ready Now for Prompt Shipment

The Gold Medal Furniture Mfg. Co.
Limited

TORONTO   MONTREAL   WINNIPEG   and UXBRIDGE

Vol. 4 No. 8   AUGUST, 1914

Canadian
FURNITURE WORLD
AND THE UNDERTAKER

Published by the Commercial Press, Limited, 32 Colborne Street, Toronto

For *the* Sun Parlor, Porch *and* Living Room

Decorative effects and practical usefulness can be obtained in reed furniture. You will find copies of some of our pieces that we have made for many years being brought out as new goods by imitators. Others can copy our designs on paper, but can't give you the service and variety that has always been our aim.

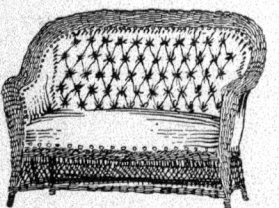

Imperial Reed Furniture for any room in the house, in a grade to suit the most fastidious, and at an honest price.

The Stratford Davenport Bed

The Stratford Davenport Bed is the REAL leader in convertible furniture. Soft upholstering and simplicity are features that put it ahead of all other beds.

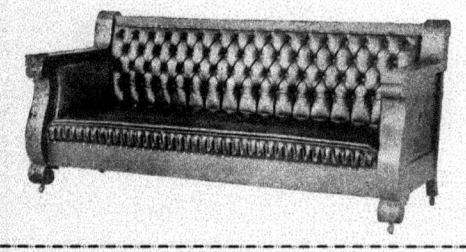

The Imperial Rattan Co., Ltd.
Stratford, Ont.

MUNDELL-MADE-FURNITURE

Rockers *Library Tables*
 Arm Chairs *Sewing Tables*
  Side Chairs *Taborettes*
   Settees *Stools*
    Telephone Stands
Couches *Davenports* *Jardiniere Stands*

Are you selling your share of the above lines?

It is not difficult to do if you carry a full line of the Mundell Made Furniture. The material and construction are of the best, and most of the designs are fully equal to those found in the highest priced lines

We specialize on furnishings for Public Buildings, Colleges, Hotels, etc.

JOHN C. MUNDELL & CO., LIMITED, ELORA, ONT.

Antiseptic Mattresses

Antiseptic Pillows

Made from sheets and sheets of downy white cotton felt, scientifically treated to ensure perfect sanitation; and strong, well finished coverings to give great wearing service, Antiseptic Mattresses constitute the best kind of foundation for sound, profitable merchandising.

Get in touch with our line of first quality pillows. They please those customers who want things "right."

THE ANTISEPTIC BEDDING CO.
187-189 Parliament Street - Toronto, Ontario

August, 1914   CANADIAN FURNITURE WORLD AND THE UNDERTAKER   3

STRATFORD

You can rely upon every piece of Stratford Furniture being the very best in its class. Stratford service is quick, and the goods will open up RIGHT

An Admirable Example *of* Colonial Designing

Mr. Western Dealer! Write for particulars of th Stratford Shipping Combination. It will save you many dollars on your freight bill.

ABOVE-the-ordinary designing in furniture is not accomplished off-hand. The present-day effects in McLagan Furniture which are so prized by people of culture and discrimination, have only been produced after years of study and specialization in our line. McLagan designing will give an impetus to your sales, Mr. Dealer-in-Good-Furniture, that will make future choosing from our lines a real pleasure. Write for the price of the elegant matched suite shown above.

agan urniture o., imite
Stratford   Ontario

BETTER BRASS BEDS

Go where you will, search every brass bed factory, and you will not find a single one that pays as much attention to designs, the quality of the brass used, and the application of the lacquer as we do.

That's why you, as a progressive dealer, should send us your order for this matchless pattern No. 1020 knowing that in so doing you are providing your customers with the best bed modern ingenuity and methods can conceive and construct.

We also make a complete line of Iron Beds, Spiral and Woven Wire Springs, Steel Couches, Mattresses and Pillows.

Our new catalog just off the press shows our full line. Write for your copy—to-day.

Ontario Brass Bed No. 1020—Pillars, 2 ins. Head, 69 ins. Top Rods, 1¼ in. Foot, 55 ins. Fitting, ½ in. square and 1 in. round. Sizes, 3-0, 3-6, 4-0, 4-6. Finish—Satin, Bright or Polot. List Price $44.00.

The Ontario Spring Bed & Mattress Company, Limited
The Largest Bedding House in Canada

London - Ontario

The Largest Line of Couches in Canada
AT THE LOWEST PRICES

Here we are showing you another of our quick selling lines. Quick SELLING because you can BUY them at Rock Bottom Prices. When placing your fall orders in Couches, don't overlook our line. Our prices are the lowest on the market.

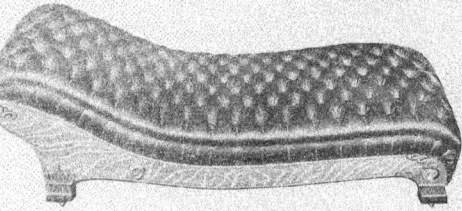

Frames Quartered Cut Oak, Golden or Fumed Oak Finish.

Upholstered in different coverings.

Try a Sample Order.

No. 43 COUCH

The Montreal Upholstering Company
1611-1613 Clarke St., MONTREAL, Can.

STRATFORD

You can rely upon every piece of Stratford Furniture being the very best in its class. Stratford service is quick and the goods will open up RIGHT.

The "Backbone" of Your Chair Business—

¶ The line which you can place all confidence—from a quick sale standpoint as well as in wearing qualities—can only be a line that has *made good* in the broadest sense.

¶ That's the focus point of all Stratford Chair arguments — they have been *making good* for so long that *you* simply can't help but come out on top on a Stratford order.

Mr. Western Dealer!
Write for particulars of the Stratford Shipping Combination. It will save you many dollars on your freight bill.

New designs coming out continually. Keep in touch with the Stratford Chair Line.

The Stratford Chair Co., Limited
Stratford - Ontario

Kohn's Imported Bentwood Furniture

Exclusive Designs   Staple Styles

Kohn's imported Bentwood Furniture may be had in all grades for all classes of trade.

Imported to order in exclusive designs and finishes to fit all requirements. Supplied in certain selling styles at the lowest prices consistent with good quality.

Send for Catalog for Comparison

Write for our catalog and price list. See how artistic in outline each design really is. Kohn's Imported Bentwood Furniture is made of tough Austrian Beechwood, bent by a special strength retaining process and fastened with steel screw leg joints.

Department Stores, Hotels, Clubs, Theatres, and other "hard service" public places have tested its durability.

The variety offered for selection provides designs specially suited to all demands.

Jacob & Josef Kohn of Vienna

215-219 Victoria Street   Toronto, Canada

NEW YORK	CHICAGO	GRAND RAPIDS
110-112 W. 27 Street	1410-1418 So. Wabash Ave.	2nd Floor, Keeler Building

---

A Sturdily Designed Rocker in Oak

This comfortable, roomy Rocker, No. 1044, will give exceptionally good service. It is made in Golden or Fumed finish, and presents a very attractive appearance considering its low price.

Have you seen the photos of our line of Hardwood Rockers? Better write for them—N. A. Chairs will please those customers who want popular priced goods.

The
North American Bent Chair Co.
Limited
Owen Sound - Ontario

August, 1914   CANADIAN FURNITURE WORLD AND THE UNDERTAKER

STRATFORD

You can rely upon every piece of Stratford Furniture being the very best in its class. Stratford service is quick, and the goods will open up RIGHT

New Designs *for* *the* Living Room

WITH the coming of the Fall Season comes renewed interest in furniture for the Living Room. This Chair must be replaced—a Couch is needed here—limited space necessitates the purchase of a Davenport Bed. On every hand are sales possibilities — opportunities to make *new customers* and *new profits*. The demand is here, what you need now is the *right goods*.

Our lines for Fall include a host of pleasing effects for the family of average means — Davenport Beds, Couches, Upholstered Chairs and Rockers, made with the purpose of giving such good value that the first sale will create many others. Wait for our traveller to call with photos. The goodness of our lines will surprise you.

Mr. Western Dealer! *Write for particulars of the Stratford Shipping Combination. It will save you many dollars on your freight bill.*

rson-

Stratford   Ontario

The "Imperial" Line
of Fine Upholstered Furniture

IS LARGE ENOUGH TO AFFORD YOU excellent choosing possibilities. "Imperial" designed furniture is very popular, and while the attractive designing does not add anything to the price, it goes a long way towards making the sale.

There is big value for every dollar invested in Imperial goods.

Write for details and prices

Imperial Furniture Company
584-591 Queen St. West, Toronto

Tennessee Cedar Chests

Absolutely moth-proof. Made in three popular sizes. Best copper trimmings used throughout. We can make immediate shipment.

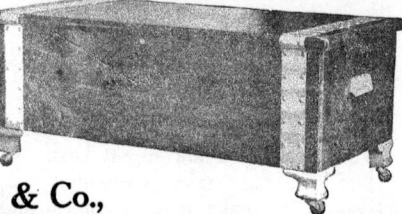

Every Woman Wants One

Their handsome appearance and great utility make them favorites with all. The price will enable you to make a good profit.

D. L. Shafer & Co.,   St. Thomas, Ont.

Stratford Brass Co.
Limited
Stratford   Ontario

Guaranteed Brass Furniture Trimmings in Period, Colonial and Modern Designs. Quality uniform. Finish unequalled in Canada.

Let us quote you our prices on special designs. Our equipment enables us to make quick delivery on all orders.

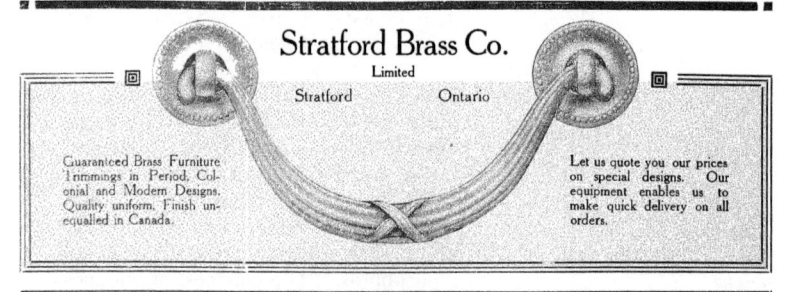

"Matthews" Mouldings and Frames
Matthews Bros., Limited, 788 Dundas Street Toronto, Can.

Do you know of any Furniture Dealer or Funeral Director, anywhere in Canada, who is not a subscriber to the Canadian Furniture World and The Undertaker? If so, you will be doing him a favor by sending us his name and address so that we can send him a sample copy and subscription order blank.

STRATFORD

You can reply upon every piece of Stratford Furniture being the very best in its class. Stratford service is quick and the goods will open up RIGHT.

The Globe-Wernicke Agency
Carries *Prestige* That Increases Sales

GLOBE-WERNICKE goods have a reputation because of quality, Reasonable Price and Extensive Advertising that will influence people to buy Globe-Wernicke Bookcases at *your* store just as soon as you put out the *Globe-Wernicke Sign*.

Mr. Western Dealer! Write for particulars of the Stratford Shipping Combination. It will save you many dollars on your freight bill.

Globe-Wernicke Sectional Bookcases are made in so many designs and can be made up in so many combinations of units that they are within the reach of those who buy medium grade of furniture. Your store will better serve your community if you display the unequalled advantages of Globe-Wernicke Sectional Bookcases.

Write To-day For Our Catalogs and Prices

Stratford - Ontario

BAETZ BROTHERS AND COMPANY
BERLIN :: ONTARIO

"Specializing in Chairs"

No. 150—DINERS

Made of Solid Quartered White Oak in Golden and Fumed Finishes.

This is one of the large line of BETTER DINERS we make. We do not make cheap diners, but we do claim to give value for value in every chair we make.

Our chairs are designed by experienced chair designers, and made by chair makers —specialists in every branch.

"Peerless" Folding Tables

The Best for Scores of Purposes

"PEERLESS" Folding Tables are made in round and square styles, in 24, 30 and 36-inch sizes, weighing 9, 10 and 12 lbs. respectively. 12 tables folded occupy about the same space as one standing. A 12 lb. "Peerless" table will support 1,000 lbs.

Made in fumed oak, early English and golden oak with polished or green felt tops.

Write for our Catalog and Price List

HOURD & COMPANY, LIMITED
Wholesale Furniture Manufacturers
LONDON, - - CANADA
Sole Canadian Licensees and Manufacturers

Colleran's Higher Grade Lock Weave Springs

¶ To those of your customers who want the **best** Springs, it will be to your best interests to show the **Colleran line**.

This Lock Weave Spring is very flexible, exceptionally strong, and we guarantee it not to sag. Interlocked with coppered steel wire and reinforced with heavy welded end cross wires. Wood or steel frame.

Prices of our complete range on request

Colleran Patent Spring Mattress Co.
TORONTO, ONT.

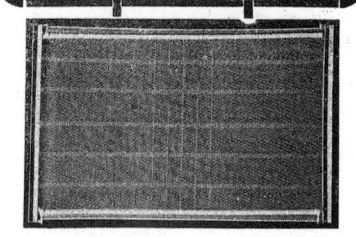

STRATFORD

You *can get* Assembly Seating Business

You can rely upon every piece of Stratford Furniture being the very best in its class. Stratford Service is quick, and the goods will open up RIGHT.

AN average order for "Stratford" Assembly Seating makes one of the very top notch profits you can make on any sale in your business. Use your influence to have the public halls, lecture rooms, etc., fitted with the "Stratford" reliable make when they require new seating.

This Style, No. 21, is made of serviceable hardwood, 5-ply quick curve, Birch or Oak veneer seat and back. Wood supports, rests on rubber bumpers, making the chair perfectly noiseless. Made single and in sections of 2, 3 and 4. Finished in natural or golden oak. The most comfortable, convenient and economical seat made.

Stratford Manufacturing Co., Limited

Mr.
Write for particulars of the Stratford Hospital **Combination. It will save** you many dollars in your **freight bill.**

KINDEL advertising will play a very important part in boosting your sales when you feature the KINDEL KIND in your store. In many cases the sale has been consummated in the prospect's mind by our advertising before the goods reach you. The Kindel Bed is so simply constructed that a child can operate it. First grade materials only are used, and they are put together by the most skilled artisans and mechanics.

Ordering time is NOW. Don't let another week pass without writing for particulars and prices.

Our new catalog is now in press and will be ready for distribution August 1st.
BE SURE YOU GET A COPY

The Kindel Bed
Co., Limited
Toronto - Ontario

The Kindel
"The Bed that Makes Itself" is The Bed that Sells Itself

Will Your New Store Front be a SALES POWER or Simply a Combination of Building Materials

When you contract for a new Store Front make sure of one thing above all others—that it will add a *sales power* to your business, not merely a "partition" to keep out the cold and rain. Store Fronts should *sell*, not simply protect the merchandise on display.

During 1914 thousands of new Fronts will be installed—some will increase the sales of the Stores with which they are associated and others will do nothing more than insulate the store room from the street. Today competition among retail stores demands that the leaders be attractive. Attraction through show windows is the power that sells more merchandise than any other Store element. One Merchant tells us that 60% of his entire business is created by his KAWNEER FRONT —another says his Front is worth $5,000 a year (and it's only 20 feet wide)—another increased his business 40% by installing a KAWNEER FRONT. One Merchant said, "Our old Front was fair but it takes KAWNEER to increase business.—Ours jumped 30%.

Kawneer Fronts Pay for Themselves

When you buy a KAWNEER FRONT you don't expend its cost—you simply loan it to your business because it will all come back to you in a few months, then for years and years the profits on the constantly increasing business will be yours—net—won't even have to paint or repair the Front as KAWNEER is built permanently—only solid copper, brass, bronze or aluminum is used. A KAWNEER FRONT can pay for itself in your Store.

Show Window Ventilation

Just think of the thousands of sales lost every winter day by frost or sweat on show windows. One Merchant wrote, "Have been in business 42 years, had 41 winters of frosted windows—placed a KAWNEER FRONT in last fall—have had one winter of clear windows." KAWNEER FRONTS give constant service.

Just think what 365-day-and-night show window service would mean to your business.

Nearly Eight Years Experience

Since 1906 we have worked with Merchants, Architects and Contractors in the construction of over 30,000 Store Fronts—not alone in big cities but in towns even as small as 150 people. Among this long list of users you will not find one Merchant who regrets the money spent—you will never hear even one say, "I wish I had the old Front." KAWNEER FRONTS have been developed around *your* requirements and we can help you increase sales, just as we have helped the Merchants behind the 30,000 KAWNEER FRONTS that now stand.

A Store Front Book

Naturally during these years of specialization we have learned a great deal about Store Fronts that cannot be learned in any other way—information that cannot be bought, and to be of greater service to you who contemplate the erection of new Store Fronts, we have compiled a book "Boosting Business No. 2" which is without a doubt the most instructive and most interesting Store Front book ever published. This book we will gladly send to you free — yours in an envelope, stamped with a 5c stamp, and all ready for your name and address. Just send along this coupon and see the book that contains photographs and drawings of many of the best paying, big and little Store Fronts in the country. Don't risk the amount of money you will invest in a new Front when you get the most complete Store Front book for a 2c stamp. Send Coupon today.

Kawneer Manufacturing Company

Francis J. Plym, President
Dept. S
1197 Bathurst Street
TORONTO, CAN.

COUPON

Kawneer Mfg. Co.
Dept. S
1197 Bathurst Street
Toronto, Can.

Kindly send "Boosting Business No. 2" without obligations

Name..

St. and No. ....

City or town ....

Business......................................

Compare this Suite with *real* Mahogany—

Then you will understand why "Meaford" *Popular Priced* Surface Mahogany Furniture is taking such a strong hold on the popular price, and the *better than popular price trade.* There is even a substantial percentage of "high class" trade who see the wisdom of utilizing such handsome suites as this when the price is so low and the quality so high.

The process we employ is Stain, Shellac and Varnish. It can't fade, chip or wear off because the stain has penetrated the wood, and the shellac and varnish hold it there, and take any wear the piece may be subject to.

Put it up to us to *prove* that *you* can handle the "Meaford" Line at a better than ordinary profit.

Write us for some interesting facts on "Meaford" trade conditions that we can show you

Meaford Manufacturing Co.
Limited
Meaford　　　　　Ontario

The St. Lawrence Furniture Co.

WHOLESALE Furniture Manufacturers

RIVIERE-DU-LOUP, QUE.
CANADA.

April 16th, 1914.

The Canadian Linderman Co., Ltd.
Woodstock, Ont.

Gentlemen:

After having used one of your Linderman 6' Dovetail Glueing machines for over 20 months, we are pleased to say that it has given the best of results. We are satisfied we save the purchase price of the machine each year; saving about 7% on the lumber; two men's time, and considerable glue. The upkeep of the machine has been very small taking into consideration the amount of work it does.

Were we without one and knowing all we know about it we would order one without delay.

Yours very truly,

St. Lawrence Furniture Co.
Per .... MANAGER.

The above expression is only one of forty-five satisfied purchasers of Linderman Dovetailers in Canada. We can save you money—let us tell you how much.

Canadian Linderman Co., Limited

FACTORIES:

Woodstock, Ont.   Muskegon, Mich.

Compare this Pedestal with the "Twin" Below

Twin Pedestals are finished all the way round. Whether open or closed, they always look "Finished" and complete.

"Twin" Pedestal Extension Tables Have Exclusive Features

YOUR customers will appreciate the many desirable features of Twin Pedestal Extension Tables.

The extend to eight feet and over, and show no gaping pedestals. Each pedestal is complete in itself, and looks neat all the time. Even should a child attempt to climb on one end when the table is extended, it will not upset. "Twin" Tables are easily opened—they will not "stick."

The designs are strictly up-to-the-minute, and the workmanship throughout is exceptionally fine.

The **"Twin" Pedestal Extension Tables** range in price from $12.00 up. Made in plain and quarter cut oak, and in mission and colonial patterns.

Get in on this profitable "Twin" business at once, Mr. Dealer, you'll find it really worth while.

Our New Catalog of "Twins" will be mailed on receipt of your name and address.

Chesley Furniture Co.
Limited
Chesley   Ontario

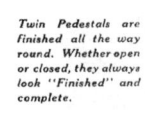

Textileather

If you have not seen the above brand of **artificial leather,** then get acquainted, ask for samples.

It is the most satisfactory furniture covering ever made anywhere.

Textileather Co., 212 Fifth Ave., New York, N.Y.
WRITE DIRECT OR TO
Frank Schmidt - Berlin, Ontario

Leggett & Platt
Single Cone Bed Springs

Our "L" Metal Tag Trade Mark

No. 8, designed especially for metal beds. Weight 50 lbs. Guaranteed in every way.

It is the only spring so constructed as to allow each coil to act independently. This feature makes this spring, without exception, the most comfortable on the market.

Our "L" Metal Tag Trade Mark

L. & P. Bed Springs *will not* sag. They will give the best of service for years.

L. & P. goods defy competition. Write for catalog and order early.

Leggett & Platt Spring Bed Co.
Limited
Windsor   Ontario

The Beauty of

GALE — GUARANTEED BEDS AND BEDDING — WATERVILLE, QUE.

Brass Beds

proves irresistible to the prospective bed-buyer

Many's the customer who will say: "I'll take that one!" when they see this new Gale design in Square Brass Beds. Compare it with the best-selling designs you have, and we are confident you will decide to feature this in your Fall display.

Solid brass castings at the corners; 1½ inch pillars; ⅝ inch fillers; ⅞ inch bottom rod—made in all sizes. List price $65.00. At the price it's a sale-winner. Get particulars.

GEO. GALE & SONS Limited
Waterville - Quebec

MONTREAL   TORONTO   WINNIPEG

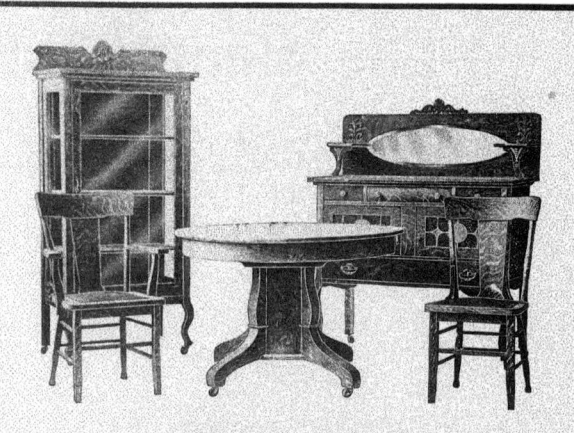

$32.50
For this Dining Room Set

Can you beat that? This set (No. 103) comprises 1 Buffet, B. B. Mirror, leaded glass; 1 China Cabinet; 1 Pedestal Table; 5 Diners, upholstered seats; and 1 Arm Chair.

Victoriaville Furniture is made to last, our designs are new and up-to-date and our prices are the lowest (quality considered) that can be found anywhere.

Send for our Catalog and Prices and see for yourself.

The Victoriaville Furniture Co.
Victoriaville
Quebec

The Big Five Mixed Carload Center

"Victoriaville" Upholstered Furniture

will greatly improve the appearance of your furniture display and attract customers to your store.

After you have told them the price and they have experienced the comfort and admired the pleasing designs from which our furniture is made up, the sale is practically closed.

1272

Victoriaville Brass Beds

Have you a good stock of bedsteads on your floors? The cut below shows one of our many different designs, they sell at a price that will interest the majority of your customers.

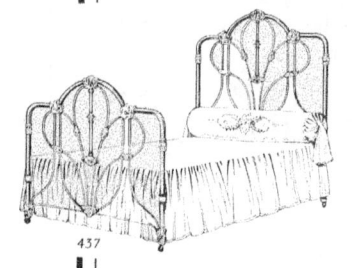

The Victoriaville Bedding Co., Limited

Victoriaville
Que.

437

Victoriaville Chairs
for every purpose

We manufacture a line of hardwood chairs for any requirements, and the fact that we confine ourselves to the manufacture of chairs only, enables us to produce a high quality product at a very low price to you.

Our Catalog will show where you can save money when buying wooden chairs

The Victoriaville Chair Manufacturing Co.

Victoriaville   **Quebec**

SHELLACS

If you are in the market for first-class Shellac we believe it would be to your advantage to get in touch with us.

HIGH GRADE VARNISHES
FILLERS and GRAINING INKS

THE AULT & WIBORG CO. OF CANADA
LIMITED

MONTREAL   TORONTO   WINNIPEG

WEISGLASS

Trade Marks that ensure Satisfaction

Confidence between manufacturer and dealer is essential to successful trading. S. Weisglass, Limited, have established a most satisfactory connection based on careful attention to all orders—large or small. The same critical appreciation of details—perfect construction—enduring finish, obtained with "ACID PROOF" Lacquer—shipment on time—all these features are considered. In this manner confidence has been established between us and our dealers. We at all times endeavor to promote the most friendly relations, coupled with businesslike attention.

LOOK AT THIS BED!

1297
The one design wanting on your floor

S. WEISGLASS, LIMITED

TORONTO   MONTREAL

Beds   Davenports
Springs   Costumers
Couches   Wall Racks

The "Gold Medal" Line
Davenports and Divanettes

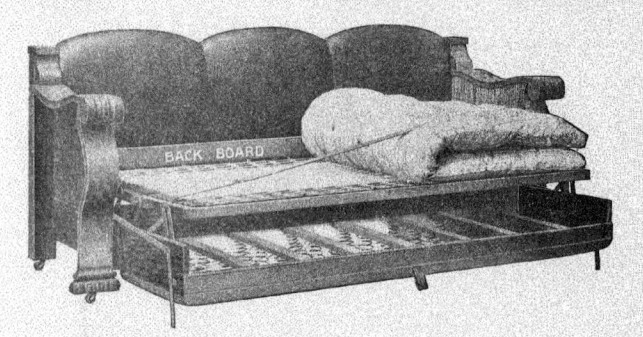

No. 717.—One of Our Twenty Designs

Our factories at Toronto and Uxbridge are the most perfectly equipped in Canada for the manufacture of Davenports and Divanettes. In addition to making our wood frames and other parts, we make all our own interior steel frame work for operating Bed constructions, which are fitted with the best National Steel fabric Springs.

THE GOLD MEDAL LINE

DIRECTORS:
W. J. McMURTRY, President and General Manager
W. R. DALBY
G. C. EMMERSON
H. B. SHORTT, Secretary
G. HUGHES, Ass. Manager

FACTORIES:
MONTREAL FACTORY
C. A. Hart, Vice-Pres. and Mgr.
WINNIPEG FACTORY
W. J. Rimmington, Mgr.
UXBRIDGE FACTORY
Geo. Wilson, Gen. Supt.

The Principal Features of our Davenports and Divanettes are:

- Perfection and Simplicity of Operation
- More Bedding Space than any other make
- Spring Edge Fronts and Ruffle Borders
- Elegant Designs and well made and finished frames
- Prices Lower than any other makes
- Patent Locking Device for Divanettes
- A Good Mattress on a Good Spring Bed
- Indestructible Patent Truss Construction for Springs

READY NOW FOR PROMPT SHIPMENT

The Gold Medal Manufacturing Co.
Limited
Toronto   Montreal   Winnipeg   and Uxbridge

This Electric Mantel

offers advantages in selling to you, and utility to the user, never found in mantels burning ordinary fuel.

No chimney or tiling is necessary in the installation of an Elmira Electric Grate Mantel. It is set up against the wall as easily and as quickly as a bookcase. Just connect the electric wiring at the back, and there is no more work attached to it.

Dealers can sell "Elmira" mantels with **little effort and big profit.**

New designs ready. Write for descriptive literature and prices

The Elmira Interior Woodwork Co., Limited
ELMIRA ONTARIO

A Display that Never Fails to Bring in the Dollars

WHEREVER J-M Asbestos Table Covers and Mats are shown, it means quick sales. Women simply can't pass them by. And in most cases a hint from the saleslady at the "psychological moment" clinches the sale.

You actually realize a better profit on J-M Asbestos Table Covers than other dealers make on inferior goods. Being the largest manufacturers of asbestos goods in the world, we can sell at a price that enables you to undersell your would-be competitor.

On account of their superior quality, J-M Asbestos Table Covers never fail to give satisfaction. And one satisfied customer makes another.

You don't have to carry a large stock, as we fill hurry-up orders promptly. Write our nearest Branch for interesting dealer proposition.

THE CANADIAN
H. W. JOHNS-MANVILLE CO., Limited

Manufacturers of Show-Case, Show-Window and General Illuminating Systems; Pipe Coverings; Dry Batteries; Fire Extinguishers, Etc.

TORONTO MONTREAL WINNIPEG VANCOUVER

Making TABLE-SLIDES is a Specialty Business

For more than TWENTY-FIVE YEARS we have made TABLE SLIDES exclusively.

Our Factory is equipped with Special Machinery which enables us to make SLIDES—BETTER and CHEAPER than the furniture manufacturer.

Canadian Table makers are rapidly adopting WABASH SLIDES

Because They ELIMINATE SLIDE TROUBLES
Are CHEAPER and BETTER

Reduced Costs
Increased Out-put

BY USING
WABASH SLIDES

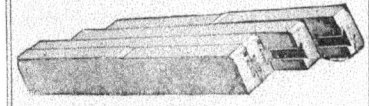

Made by
B. WALTER & CO.
Wabash, Ind.

The Largest EXCLUSIVE TABLE-SLIDE Manufacturers in America

ESTABLISHED 1887

Full of New Suggestions this New "Elmira Line" Catalog

Your Fall ordering will be made easier and productive of more profitable sales if you have this catalog to assist you. Dictate a letter for your copy now.

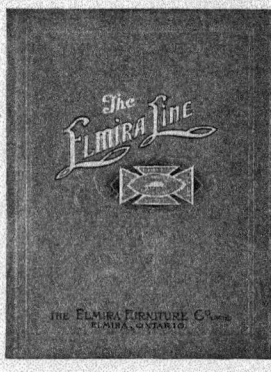

Our Latest Productions

linked up with our well known high quality, first-class workmanship and finish and fair prices, make the "Elmira Line" better and stronger than ever.

This index gives the various lines we manufacture and the number of pages devoted to each line.

INDEX

Diners	3-22	Library and Card Tables	42-45
Hall and Desk Chairs	23	Parlor Tables	46-48
Bedroom Chairs and Rockers	24-25	Umbrella Stands	49
Parlor Chairs and Rockers	26-29	Jardiniere Stands	50
Den and Library Furniture	30-38	Footstools	51
Office Chairs and Tilters	39-41	Important Notice	52

We have just installed a new Grand Rapids Dry Kiln. Every furniture man knows what this means in the science of drying lumber. It first steams the board, taking out the sap, thereby opening up the pores, which allows the stock to dry from the heart of the board. This is the only method of drying lumber so that it will not swell or warp but remain its actual dimensions as the life of the wood is taken out. This is the strongest guarantee any factory can have against open joints, warped tops, raised grain, etc.

Push the "Elmira Line" for Better Profits

Elmira Furniture Company, Limited
Elmira :: Canada

Canadian Furniture World and the Undertaker

D. O. McKINNON, President
W. L. EDMONDS, Vice-President and Contributing Editor
J. C. ARMER, Vice-President and Manager of Technical Papers

Published about the Twenty-First of Preceding Month by

The Commercial Press, Limited
32 Colborne Street, Toronto
(Next King Edward Hotel)

WESTON WRIGLEY, Vice-President and Manager of Trade Papers
JAMES O'HAGAN, Editor
WM. J. BRYANS, Associate Editor
GEO. H. HONSBERGER, Advertising Manager

F. C. D. WILKES, 704 Unity Building, Montreal
C. G. BRANDT, Circulation Manager, Toronto
E. J. MACINTYRE, Room 1155, 122 S. Michigan Ave., Chicago
N. D. WEBSTER, 95 Liberty Street, New York

Subscription rate, Canada and Great Britain, $1.00 per year; United States, $1.50 per year.
A minimum circulation of 2,000 copies is guaranteed each month.

VOLUME FOUR   TORONTO, AUGUST, 1914   NUMBER EIGHT

Value of an Attractive Store. That the neat, clean, bright and otherwise attractive store has an appreciable value in the promotion of trade is a fact that no dealer will deny. In the face of this generally acknowledged truth, it is surprising that many dealers do not give more attention to this particular. They believe, apparently, but do not act on their belief.

A store is judged by its appearance. If you set out to buy an article, you pick out an establishment that is bright and clean because you believe that you are likely to find goods of quality in such a store. The good appearing store attracts customers to it.

Then again the more goods are sold where they are presented to advantage, and this cannot be done in a dark, untidy or unclean store. Presented in the proper way, goods will to a considerable extent sell themselves. This is where the store with attractive display facilities wins out.

Recognizing this fact, the merchant should give some study to ways and means by which the appearance of the store may be enhanced. It will mean more trade.

Business consistency requires no costly setting either to enhance its beauty or keep it from being lost.

Sacrificing Profits for Volume. Not a few merchants in aiming for volume of business forget about profits, that important and needful factor in every successful business. They seem to think that as long as they secure the volume, that profits will look after themselves. Here they fool themselves.

Not only are they doing a great deal of work for a small or perhaps no return, but they are taking trade which their brother dealers could and would handle with profit. A recent visitor to our office complained of such a dealer in his town, following this dog-in-the-manger policy. Just for the mere satisfaction of taking the trade away from the other dealers, this dealer seemed willing to handle it without a sufficient profit. He was not making any money himself, and he was preventing the other dealers from making any.

This craze for a big volume of business has been the downfall of not a few merchants, and the curse of many others. The man who would put his money into a farm and go out and dig just for the mere pleasure of digging would be looked upon as a fool. What is to be said of the merchant who does business just for the sake of doing it?

It is a commendable thing to aim for big business, and every ambitious merchant should, but in accomplishing his aim, profits should not be sacrificed. A man is in business to make money, so what does he profit if he secures more trade than any other dealer in town, but makes nothing on it?

Business is a good companion for the daytime; but it is a bad bed-fellow. Keep business out of your bed if you desire to live long and die happy.

Realize Value of Good Window Display. Furniture window trimming is gradually advancing to a high standard, and this is the result of dealers recognizing the great value of the well-kept display window in interesting customers in such a way as to attract them into the store and make sales.

More and more dealers are realizing the sales value of the window, and are giving greater attention to this part of their business. As a help in this direction, a special department is devoted to window trimming in this issue, that is well worth the careful perusal of every dealer and clerk, because of the practical hints and suggestions on window trimming it contains.

The show window is one of the cheapest and best advertising mediums the dealer has, and should be cashed in on to the fullest extent.

Commonsense is more frequently found in commonplace business men than in professional men with initials affixed as well as prefixed to their surname.

Teach the Clerk. Greater interest in their clerks is something that is badly needed on the part of many furniture men to-day. In some instances, the clerk is not exactly getting a square deal. When he hires with a merchant, he does not receive a very princely salary on the start, but this is supposed to be made up for by the training which he expects to receive from the merchant, which will make him a more valuable employe, and enable him to command and be worth a better wage.

Yet it is frequently the case that a dealer will engage a young man, green in the business, put him behind the counter, and expect him to work out his own salvation with practically no training beyond a few hints and suggestions the first morning he starts in.

The clerk will perhaps in the course of events acquire a certain knowledge of himself, but it comes slowly in this way, and experience is always a dear teacher. This experience is paid for, not only by the clerk, but by the employer as well, as it comes out of his pocket in the smaller profits than would be the case if the clerk were more efficient.

The clerk requires to be taught, and it is the merchant's duty to teach him. It is sometimes argued by the dealer that the clerk is apparently not interested in the business—that he is merely putting in the time. Then, the best way to get him interested is to give him a greater knowledge of the business. No one is very much in love with anything that they don't understand. The clerk as he becomes better acquainted with the ways of doing things properly in the store, and is given an insight into some of the details of the business, will take a deeper interest in it.

Teach the clerk—especially the younger clerk. Treat him as if you expected him to stay with you and make good—not as if he might get bounced any minute.

It is a peculiarity of slow-going merchants that the slower trade gets the further they get behind it.

Store Service. The best of advertising campaigns will be greatly minimized in effectiveness unless accompanied by effective service in the store.

The absence of this service is the explanation of many an unsatisfactory advertising campaign.

There are business men of all kinds who seem to think that all they need do is to insert an advertisement in the newspapers and then sit down and wait for customers to flock into their store in droves.

No dreamer ever had a worse delusion.

Service is the right hand of advertising. And business without either is crippled.

Time and again merchants have been known to advertise special prices for certain articles and leave their clerks entirely in ignorance of the fact. This is certainly not conducive to service. There is one thing to which it certainly does tend, and that is disorganization. This is the very antithesis of co-operation.

To make the window displays co-operate with the advertisement is to greatly enhance the value of the latter. The practice of the leading department stores and that of many retailers is a proof of this.

The one tells the story in print. The other gives an ocular demonstration.

Service implies a bright, clean and attractive store, one that will prove attractive to women as well as to men.

Good service creates confidence. That quality cannot, however, be created in a day. It comes through a process of evolution. Here a little and there a little. A little courtesy to-day. A little attention to-morrow. Goods never being other than they are represented to be, and goods delivered when it was promised they should be.

Service does not come from the right performance of one or two things. It is in the performance of many things, with the whole tenor of the store and its organization being bent in the direction of satisfying and pleasing customers.

Economy prevents leakage in the store; penuriousness prevents customers coming into the store.

Manufacturing and Agricultural Industries. While to all intents and purposes farming must for a long time to come be considered the basic industry of Canada, yet there are a great many people who fail to recognize the important place which our manufacturing industries occupy in the development of our national life and wealth.

Canada cannot do without her farms; but neither can she do without her manufacturing industries. Poor indeed would she be if she undertook to do so.

As a matter of fact, the products of the factories in Canada exceed in value by about 100 per cent. the field products of the Canadian farms.

Last year, according to the estimate of the Census Bureau, the value of the field crops of Canada was slightly less than $600,000,000, while three years ago the same bureau placed the value of factory products of Canada at $1,165,822,639. Of course the products of the farm are not confined to field crops. There is the live stock and poultry to be taken into consideration. But as the census returns governing these have not yet been made public, they cannot be given. At any rate there can be no doubt as to the relative value of the products of the factories and farms of Canada. Nor can there be any doubt as to the relative number of persons employed and the wages and salaries paid by the two branches of industry. The figures relating to the agricultural industry are not obtainable, but according to the last census the manufacturers of Canada paid out in salaries and wages over $241,000,000 in 1910.

The deadbeat was born of roguery and cradled by careless credit.

SHORT NOTES FROM THE EDITOR'S PEN.

The sale that you almost made will not add to your profits or increase your bank account.

* * * *

If 1914 is to do more for you than 1913 did, you will find that you must do more for yourself.

* * * *

It would be a good thing if some dealers could see their stores as their customers see them.

* * * *

The retailer to-day who would forge to the front, must use brains in the conduct of his business.

* * * *

Get people talking about your store. The wagging tongue of a pleased customer is the best advertisement a dealer can have.

* * * *

Repeat orders are essential to the success of any mercantile enterprise. The profitable sale is the one which brings another and repeated sales.

* * * *

An editorial note in a daily newspaper says that a man never gets all the credit he deserves. The merchant with a long list of past due accounts; will probably say that a good many get more than they deserve.

Standards of Practice for Business Papers

Adopted by the publishers of Trade and Technical Papers at the Associated Ad. Clubs' Convention in Toronto, June 21 to 25, 1914.

THE publisher of a business paper should dedicate his best efforts to the cause of Business and Social Service, and to this end should pledge himself:

1. To consider, first, the interests of the subscriber.
2. To subscribe to and work for truth and honesty in all departments.
3. To eliminate, in so far as possible, his personal opinions from his news columns, but to be a leader of thought in his editorial columns, and to make his criticisms constructive.
4. To refuse to publish "puffs," free reading notices or paid "write-ups"; to keep his reading columns independent of of advertising considerations, and to measure all news by this standard: "Is it real news?"
5. To decline any advertisement which has a tendency to mislead or which does not conform to business integrity.
6. To solicit subscriptions and advertising solely upon the merits of the publication.
7. To supply advertisers with full information regarding character and extent of circulation, including detailed circulation statements subject to proper and authentic verification.
8. To co-operate with all organizations and individuals engaged in creative advertising work.
9. To avoid unfair competition.
10. To determine what is the highest and largest function of the field which he serves, and then to strive in every legitimate way to promote that function.

Collins' Course in Show Card Writing

Ninth of a series of articles specially prepared for this journal.

EVERY show card writer should keep an "Idea Box." This does not necessarily need to be a literal box, but it should be some sort of receptacle, scrap book, box, basket, drawer, or similar place into which he may place clippings, prints, photos, illustrations and designs that will be of assistance to him in giving ideas for work. Magazines, newspapers, and other periodicals furnish excellent articles of this character that should be preserved for future use. Arrange these clippings methodically, either by subject or alphabetically. A carefully arranged collection of these will be of the very greatest assistance to the practical card writer.

Spatter Work.

Many of the cards shown in previous lessons have been in "spatter work" designs. This work, if done properly, can be executed almost as finely as air-brush work. Very simple tools are needed to do the work. These consist of a small frame of window screen wire and an old tooth brush. The latter should be fairly stiff in the hair. From a piece of thin wood, like picture backing, cut an opening about 4 ins. long by 2 ins. wide. Leave one end sufficiently long for a handle. Leave about an inch and a half of wood on the ends and an inch on the sides to tack the wire to. See Fig. 14. Across the ends of the frame it will be well to nail a thin, narrow strip to keep it from cracking. If you can procure heavy millboard to make the frame of it will answer better than wood, for it will not crack.

Having made your tools, you will find that very effective cards can be made with a little care and thought. After you have your desired pattern cut out lay it on the card and fasten with weights, or if too fine a pattern, fasten with pins. Use your regular colors. Dip the tooth brush very lightly into the color and rub it on the wire over a piece of waste paper, to get the excessive color out of it. If there is too much color it will make too big blotches or spots. Should you find the color froths or foams when rubbed on the wire, put

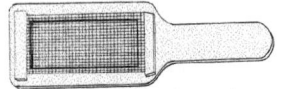

Hand-made wire frame for doing "spatter work."

Examples of simple "spatter work."

a little gasoline into it, which will immediately remedy the trouble. After ridding your brush of the extra amount of color, try it on your waste paper, and when you are able to get a very fine "spatter" it is ready to work on your pattern. Hold the wire as close as you can to the pattern, and rub the brush just over the edges of your pattern. Very attractive cards can be made with simple patterns. Ovals, circles, squares, and oblongs can be used, and with the addition of strips of paper and other simple patterns very gratifying results are obtainable. Initial letters can also be made with this process. These will add very materially to the attractiveness of a card. A fine pattern of lace laid over a card and spattered will give a very unique result. We give a number of simple pattern designs to illustrate the operation of "spatter work." See Fig. 15.

The Alphabets.

The two alphabets shown this month differ very

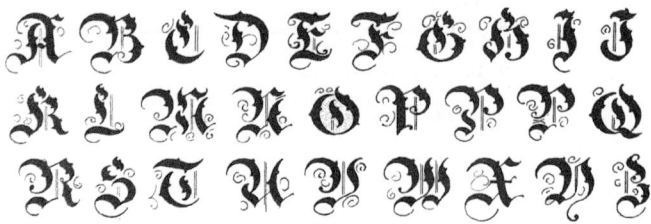

Plate 34.—Example of fancy Old English capitals.

a b c d e f g h k i j k l m m n
o p q r s t u v w x y z 1234

Plate 35.—Lower case alphabet fancy Old English.

materially in the character and formation of the letters. Plates 34 and 35 are excellent examples of fancy Old English. These, like other fancy letters, are suitable for one work or line that needs bringing out prominently. This style of letter is used extensively for pen work or engrossing. The letters are easily made when one has mastered the principle of the curves.

Plates 36 and 37 are full block heavy Roman with a touch of ornamentation added to take away the effect of the severe plainness. This style is suitable only for a word or line that needs to be brought out

Finished samples of "spatter work."

with emphasis. It is not practical for general use, as it takes too long to make it. Both alphabets will be excellent for practice.

Sample Cards.

During the month of August business seems unable to shake off the effects of hot weather. The sultry days have a tendency to make buyer and seller feel lax and spiritless. The average merchant feels like "lying down" on the job and letting things go by default. But if the dog days of August make business dull, then

Example of double shading.

it is the merchant's place to put on some extra spurts to counterbalance these hot-day effects. If you can arrange a special sale of a few lines that are a little out of season, but which are fairly saleable, you will be surprised at the results. Let the list be wide in range and sufficiently reduced in price to make the sale attractive. The hardware merchant could arrange a line of paint in one color only that would attract attention, and being in one color only many would buy other colors to trim up with. Graniteware, step ladders, and

A B C D E F G H I
J K L M N O P Q R
S T U V W X Y Z &
1 2 3 4 5 6 7 8 9 0

Plate 36.—Alphabet of full block heavy Roman caps with touch of ornamentation.

abcdefghijklmn
opqrstuvwxyz

Plate 37.—Full block, heavy Roman alphabet, lower case.

many other articles will fill all the requirements of this sale. The grocer could run a line of canned goods of one particular fruit or vegetable. Also the various house cleaning needs that are now a little out of the regular season. The furniture dealer will find abundance to unload at this particular time. He could run a special on pillows, or if he handles wall papers and window shades, run these as a special. The main feature is to have the price sufficiently low to attract trade.

Two of the sample cards are in spatter work design. The 39c. card may be priced to suit any line of articles. The spatter work is in dark brown with the figures in black. The lettering is in dark brown to harmonize with the spatter work. The shading is in grey.

The $4.65 card is the same pattern as the 39c. card, only it is reversed. The 39c. card had an oval laid on it, while the "spatter work" was being done. This was not used on the other card. These cards should be about 12 by 20 ins., or in that proportion.

The dark card is an example of double shading. Note how the letters have that "stand-out" effect. The lettering is all done in black and the shading in grey and white.

Who's Who in Furniture Making

No review of Berlin's industrial activities would be complete without a history and description of that sterling manufacturing concern, Baetz Brothers & Company. For many years the business of Pommer Cowan Co. was established in an old iron-clad building on Victoria street, and met with but ordinary success. In January, 1908, Baetz Brothers & Company was founded to take over the business, and now, after four years of operation by them, the concern is one of the largest in the furniture line in that big furniture centre in Western Ontario, guided by men whose energy and ability knew no obstacle. To-day this concern is known far and wide wherever good furniture is appreciated, carrying the name of Berlin throughout the Dominion to add to its prestige and advertise the city and its products to the people of Canada.

In July, 1910, the company was visited by a disastrous fire that wiped out the plant, but with characteristic energy and progressiveness a new and modern structure was planned. The following fall building was started, and in the spring of 1911 manufacturing operations were commenced in the new quarters, one of the finest manufacturing buildings in Berlin. The plant is a brick, mill-constructed building, 330 ft. long and 66 ft. wide, and is one and two storeys high, giving the company in all about 33,000 square feet of space. Only the very best is turned out there, comprising especially chairs and parlor suites, in all the fashionable styles, while the materials that enter into these products are of the best obtainable, only selected grades of oak, birch and mahogany being used.

Sixty expert mechanics are employed, and they possess a high degree of skill and excellence, turning out pieces of furniture that are handsome and durable. Seven travelers cover the Dominion from coast to coast. The concern has been eminently successful and is daily adding to its reputation as a firm that carries out its promises, shipping orders as required, and seeing that none but the right kind of goods are sent out from the factory.

The firm is composed of Jacob Baetz, Sr., one of Berlin's best known contractors and builders, and one who is interested in a number of other industries in Berlin. He has held public office on several occasions, serving a term as alderman, as well as being chairman of the board of works. Charles Baetz, the factory manager, has made a lifelong study of the furniture trade, both in Canada and in the United States, and is considered one of the best informed men in the trade. Jacob H. Baetz is the other remaining member of the firm and takes an active interest in the company's affairs.

Of Jacob H. Baetz it can be said that few men are better known to the furniture trade throughout the Dominion, yet his experience in this industry has all been gained in the course of six years. Previous to that time he had been a member of the Berlin Rubber Co. staff, but when an opportunity offered to enter the furniture business, he saw its possibilities, and so well has his energy and ability been rewarded that to-day the plant over which he presides is one of the largest in the furniture colony of the "Grand Rapids of Canada."

Mr. Baetz, coming as he does of a family of builders, is a worthy son of a worthy sire. He is a member of the board of trade, the Canadian Club and the Lutheran Club, and devotes a great portion of his time to church work. In regard to the furniture outlook he expects to see trade revive shortly, as it is already taking on a normal aspect, and, instead of buying in small quantities, he thinks the trade will stock more liberally for future selling.

JACOB H. BAETZ, of Baetz Bros. & Co.

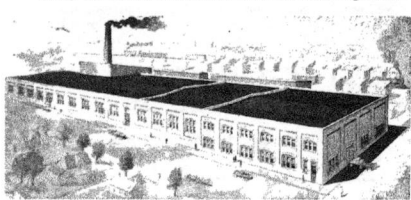

Baetz Bros. & Co's. Berlin factory.

Some of the Problems of the Small Retailer[*]

By Harvey R. Young
Advertising Manager of the Columbus Dispatch, Columbus, Ohio.

Bradstreet says: "More small retailers fail because of incompetency than lack of capital." I am sure that most every man who has given the subject much study believes Bradstreet's statement to be correct.

Incompetency in retailing covers a multitude of sins, but the worst is generally conceded to be that of

Over-Buying.

Statistics prove that over 30 per cent. of the failures among retailers in Canada and the United States during 1913 were due to over-buying.

Months before the selling season starts, many injudicious merchants are persuaded by the smooth, experienced traveling salesman into believing that his particular line of merchandise is going to sell like "hot cakes." He names certain stores in other towns which placed big orders, and adds that there is doubt about future orders being filled, thus persuading the retailer into over-buying.

I have known unscrupulous manufacturers and jobbers to over-load retailers with small capital to the extent of jeopardizing their credit with other houses, thus practically placing these retailers in their clutches.

When the traveling salesman from one of these houses calls, the retailer feels obligated to give him an order, whether he needs the goods or not, fearing if he doesn't, the house may demand a settlement which he could not make. Hence, the retailer continues to over-buy, paying the long price, too, because he is not in a position to dictate terms.

If the retailer of changeable styles would take his previous year's business as a basis when buying for the season and order no more than one-third of his needs, then later on as styles change buy as his sales require, he will find at the end of the season that he has operated at a profit.

Every stock should be turned at retail from three to twelve times a year (according to the stability of the merchandise). In specifying retail price, it means if the merchant has an average stock through the season of $10,000 at retail selling price, then he should do, if his stock calls for a four-time a year turn, a $40,000 business.

The large, successful retailer figures how often he can turn his stock and buys carefully as sales require. This has put him where he is to-day, while the reverse has kept down the small retailer.

I once heard a successful merchant say in giving instructions to his buyers: "I much prefer to see ten invoices of $100 each come in than one of $500."

Even when the injudicious retailers discover they have bought unwisely, they are slow or sometimes lack the nerve to take what sooner or later must become a necessary loss. They are "hangers-on" of out-of-date styles or poor sellers, hoping eventually to get the original sale price, while the successful retailers, big and small, act quickly in turning stock, thereby getting the cash with which to purchase what the trade is demanding.

Another big financial error many small retailers make is their failure to take cash discounts. Very few realize

[*]Address delivered before the Associated Advertising Clubs of the World at recent Toronto Convention.

what a high price they pay for the privilege of taking full time on their invoices. For instance, 1 per cent. in 10 days on a 30-day bill, means 18 per cent. per annum. Example: Invoice $1,000, 30 days net, 1 per cent. for cash in 10 days. If the merchant pays in 10 days, he receives $10 cash discount, which, in effect, is the interest the wholesale house pays him for the use of $1,000 for the 20 days unexpired time. This is at the rate of 18 per cent. per annum. Proof: The interest on $1,000 for 20 days, at 18 per cent., is $10.

The value of discounting one's bills does not lie only in the amount thus saved, though this is considerable in view of the fact that the discount rate is so much above the banker's rate for money that it would be a good investment to discount even if the money had to be borrowed for the purpose. The prestige which comes with gaining a reputation as the firms who discount their bills is worth a great deal. The manufacturer and wholesaler generally save their special offerings for the gilt-edge accounts of this kind.

First Cost is Not the Whole Cost.

Some retailers neglect to figure selling or overhead expense on top of first cost. I venture to say that many of them, if asked what an article cost, will say, for instance, $18 a dozen, $1.50 apiece, neglecting to add their per cent. of overhead expense, which for safety should be based on the selling price.

For example: If a retailer is doing a gross business of $50,000 a year at an expense of $10,000, then he is doing business at a cost of 20 per cent. on his gross sales.

If he pays the manufacturer or jobber $1 a yard for silk, he must sell it at $1.25 to recover his net cost of doing business, and the retailer who figures otherwise is a loser.

The Small Merchant Loses Valuable Time

I know of a lot of retailers who are laboring under the false impression that in order to make a success, they must personally do the so-called chores about the store—everything from opening up to sweeping out, dusting off, keeping stock, etc.—work which a $10 a week employe properly instructed might do. These merchants had far better be taxing their brains estimating with care possible sales, making sure that expenses are reasonable, thus resulting in a profit making stock turn.

The Importance of the Show Windows

Years ago, large, successful retail merchants learned that display windows and cases were a big asset, while even to-day many small merchants and a few incompetent large merchants overlook or neglect this important feature of their business.

I have known retailers to let window displays stand one to four weeks without a change until the merchandise became dusty and fly specked—their window displays and advertising seldom harmonized, whereas the properly conducted store makes frequent changes in keeping with its advertising.

The retailer who is neglecting his display windows should stop to do a little figuring for himself and he will discover that he would not agree to pay $3,000 for his $10,000 store room without show windows or front excepting the entrance, consequently, he must be paying $7,000 a year rent for the show window space, and if he is—it's commercial suicide to neglect this valuable space.

Again, many retailers change their show window displays during the busiest hours of the day, when the streets are crowded with shoppers, while the rightly conducted store engages experienced window trimmers to make these changes over night, having the displays ready for business in the morning. Changing show window displays during shopping hours is much like taking the highest priced salespeople off duty when the store is full of customers.

Of course I realize that many stores are not large enough to justify the engaging of an experienced window trimmer. In these cases I would suggest the proprietor or manager giving this work personal attention. If he watches the trade papers in his particular line he will secure many valuable ideas of how to successfully advertise and display his merchandise.

The Advertising

Out of 11,143 small retailers in the United States who closed their doors in 1913, it is claimed over half of them did not realize the necessity of proper advertising and many of those who did were at times careless in the preparation of their copy, and they scattered their appropriation by going into every publication, program or scheme presented, thus destroying the possible and profitable effects.

Some small retailers advertise just because their competitors do—considering it a necessary evil. They buy space and prepare copy with just about as much pleasure as a child takes castor oil. It seems drudgery for them to furnish copy or even make suggestions to the advertising solicitor, who, I believe in many cases, would gladly assist in preparation of copy if requested to do so. Why, some retailers when called upon for copy (according to contract) look up in disgust, saying, "I have been busy buying goods, taking care of correspondence. I haven't had time to write an ad., I have so many other things more important to do." The result is the solicitor finally gets an order to repeat any old ad. and possibly a slurring remark, "I may as well throw my money in the sewer," yet these selfsame merchants wonder why advertising doesn't always pay.

Advertising under such adverse circumstances cannot possibly produce a satisfactory measure of results for any merchant, be he large or small.

When over ten million women in this country shop daily, 90 p.c. of whom are influenced through advertising to buy a certain article or go to a certain store, it behooves the small as well as the big merchants to wake up and give this part of their business proper attention.

The big successful store is simply a result of organization made possible by concentration of capital, backed up by good and continuous advertising. The large successful merchant not only buys advertising judiciously but engages the best talent to prepare the right copy about the right merchandise at the right time.

Nationally Advertised Brands

The competent, experienced merchant, whether large or small, is also shrewd in taking advantage of the advertising done by manufacturers of trade marked goods. He makes attractive show window and interior displays, especially at the time certain trade marked goods are to be advertised in the newspapers or magazines. He also calls attention in his own advertising that his store sells nationally advertised articles. The incompetent or thoughtless merchant not only overlooks these opportunities but goes so far as to offer patrons a substitute, thereby losing all the effects of a national advertising campaign.

The competent merchant and his sales organization work in harmony. Every salesperson is informed of what has or is going to be advertised and how to properly present the goods to the shopper. Nine times out of ten the incompetent merchant even fails to notify the salespeople about the advertising—this brings us to the last and one of the most difficult problems of the small retailer to-day.

His Sales Organization

Dr. Stanley Krebs, of Philadelphia, in a recent talk said, "World progress, world peace, depend upon the retailer passing the goods across the counter. You may buy what you please, advertise in any manner you like, the final result rests with the salesman. Thousands have been spent to promote every part of retailing except to educate salespeople. The day is past when anybody can be a clerk in a store. Education of salespeople must be buckled onto business. When the merchant properly educates his salespeople, he will find that five star salesmen will sell as much as fifteen ordinary clerks."

A shoe manufacturer tells me that out of his 65 traveling salesmen, the 15 stars sell as much as the other 50. The small retailer must learn how to make two sales grow where one grew before. This he can only accomplish by training his salespeople to be courteous, willing, honest, clean and competent. If the employes in any one store are below the standard of personnel shown in competitive stores the former business will suffer. The fight to hold its customers and secure more customers will be just that much harder and less productive.

Frequently we hear it said that the small retailer has had his best day. I most emphatically disagree with anyone making such a statement because I think the small retailer is going to be more necessary than ever, consequently more prosperous and more successful. But, he will have to concentrate—by that I mean concentration of personal service, closer friendly relations with customers.

Just recently a merchant for whose opinion I have the highest regard said, "Why, there are not three stores in our city having a salesforce that is thoroughly courteous and obliging." It is said that the tone of the average American store's salesman sounds like steel when compared to that of the English salesman. It might be well for our retailers to take this as a cue. Mr. M. P. Gould, in his interesting book, "Where Have My Profits Gone," says, "The human heart is the same everywhere and always will be. It likes company, sympathy, personal attention. The merchant who takes this fact into consideration, making his store in all its dealings reflect his friendship, his appreciation of his customers' trade, and his sincere desire to be of real service, is bound to be just as prosperous and I am sure more so in the future than he has been in the past."

Personally I believe it isn't because a store is big or small that it succeeds. Is it the personnel behind it—there isn't any magical formula that makes any business a success. Willing, courageous humans plentifully mixed with energy and briskly stirred with ambition—that is the recipe.

The Development of the Sliding Couch in Canada

Whether or not the term "sliding couch" is a good one, embracing as it does all that class of furniture grouped under the general heads of folding beds, bed-davenports, etc., the development and growth of the line here in Canada during the past few years have been remarkable. On enquiring of some of the large Canadian furniture-makers, the term "sliding couch" seemed to be somewhat ambiguous. "We don't know what you mean," say they; but when on further enquiry the point was explained, almost all of them expressed themselves as believing the line to be one of the most important in the furniture line.

Necessity is the mother of invention, and because of this the folding bed and couch have been brought into requisition. Many people whose homes are small, (and houses are built on the small size these days), and whose means are limited, are on the lookout for something that can be put to more than one use, and thus economize space, and at the same time save money. This demand of late years has led to the evolution of the folding bed, sliding couch, kitchen cabinet, and other kindred articles of household utility. The humble man would enjoy a small house to himself and family.

These conditions have created a demand for such articles of furniture as can be most conveniently folded away when not in use or converted to another purpose during the daytime. This is where the sliding couch slides in. Having a good resilient top or bed of woven wire or other fabric and a folding mattress or cushion, it makes a very comfortable couch at daytime and is easily changed to a bed at night by pulling out the lower section and opening the mattress.

The Gold Medal Furniture Company were one of the first manufacturers of the folding wood mantel bed in Canada, and they enjoyed almost a monopoly of this article of furniture for many years, but the sale of these was insignificant compared to the present sliding couch. Then followed the bed lounge, and, finally, the various styles of davenport beds and steel couches.

The type of temporary bed and couch combined is one of the most popular of bed couches on account of its adaptability for different uses, and comparatively low cost, and it is now responsible for an industry which gives employment to hundreds of workmen in factories

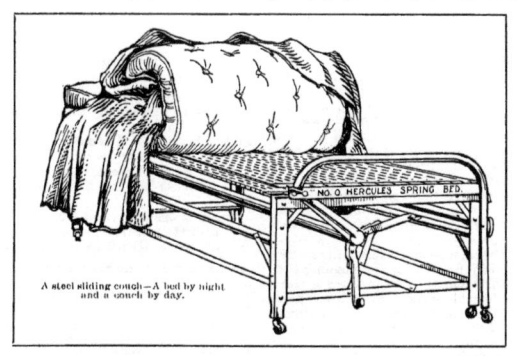

A steel sliding couch—A bed by night and a couch by day.

housewife may not be able to afford a couch and a bed, too, for certain of her rooms, and often the living room has to be converted into a bedroom by night. Here it is that the sliding couch comes to her rescue and solves the problem she has been trying to solve. The steel, or the wood, sliding couch can be converted from a very respectable looking and cosy couch into a comfortable bed of double width by the addition of a few bedclothes and the necessary pillows, which may be removed in the morning and the bed re-converted into a couch for the day.

One of the most striking developments in this class of goods is the advent of the steel sliding couch. A few years ago such a piece of furniture would have met with a poor reception by the trade and general public, but the marvelous growth of the large cities, and the equally marvelous growth of the cost of living, and consequent high rents, have compelled many families to share residences, where formerly an ordinary working which a few years ago were hardly dreamed of, and the sales of this article have exceeded the most sanguine expectations. To produce steel sliding couches at a popular price, means a very considerable outlay on the part of the manufacturer for the various machines required for its production. A visit to the plant of the Gold Medal Furniture Company, where complete and up-to-date equipment is to be seen, would convince any one of the optimistic view taken for the future of these very useful articles of furniture, the trade for which is already spread to almost every small town from the Atlantic to the Pacific. It is predicted that the sliding steel couch, being already a staple article, has a long future before it, ere something can be produced to oust it from the public favor.

The folding beds or couches may be had in a great variety of styles to suit a variety of purses, and to suit a variety of rooms and uses. The Imperial Rattan Company, to mention but one of a number of makers of this class of goods, have a davenport bed called the "Stratford," which is a perfect davenport with soft, comfortable seat by day and a perfect bed by night, having a substantial box spring to sleep on, with separate box to put bedding in. So simple is it in operation from bed to davenport or davenport to bed that it can be operated by one hand. The call for these bed-davenports, says the manager of the company, is mostly in larger cities, where rooms are small and a sleeping apartment has to be converted into a living apartment also, where only an occasional extra person needs sleeping accommodations.

We manufacture two styles of sliding couches, say the Ontario Spring Bed and Mattress Co., a medium-priced one called the Victor and a better one, the Canadian Davenport. Both are made of steel angle bars, and have a very strong, yet resilient, spring attached to the angle bars by means of oil-tempered helical springs of strength and elasticity. The mattress for the Victor is made in two pieces, with a valance, and, when the couch is extended into bed form, the mattress opens out so as to cover the entire spring. This couch has no back, but is intended to go against the wall when used as a couch. It is supplied with casters and is finished in bronze or oxidized. It is a very popular seller, and may be used on the verandah as well as inside the house. The Canadian Davenport has a back, and the mattress is made in three pieces. When the couch is converted into a bed the mattress covers the full width of the spring. It can be used also as a bed of single width as well as double.

The Alaska Bedding Co. say these bed-davenports are popular sellers, not only in the cities, but in small country towns as well. They first placed sliding couches on the Western market six years ago, and have developed a large business in them since. Owing to the climatic and economic conditions common to nearly the whole of Canada, there is a tendency to economize space in houses and apartment buildings, and the sliding couch is welcomed in many homes as a useful and attractive piece of furniture, that can serve the double purpose of a couch in the daytime and a full-sized, comfortable bedstead at night, at a price within the reach of the most modest purse.

The combination of a lounge and bedstead is no new thing, of course, but it remained for the bedding companies, says the Alaska manager, to produce a clean, attractive, and comfortable article at a low price. Sliding couches of their manufacture, he continued, have no mechanism whatever to get out of order; in fact, the two halves of the couch can be separated and used separately if desired, by simply lifting one out of the other. While the sliding couch is an apparently simple proposition to manufacture, a good deal of experimenting had to be done before a satisfactory article was produced, and many improvements have been, and are being made, both in the frame and the fabric of the sliding couch. One of these, for instance, is that it has always been quite a problem as to how to dispose of the bedclothes, where a person uses a couch regularly as a bed by night and a couch by day, so a couch with a box underneath was designed, so that the bedding could be stored away when not in use.

In addition to the sliding type of steel couch, there is made the style of couch with the back which lets down to form a double bed, and some with a double seat and back, providing a place to store the bedding in between.

The Max Englander Spring Bed Co., Brooklyn, N.Y., have decided to establish a plant in Canada.

DON'T BE A HABIT MAN
By Everett R. Roeder

Do you know what a habit man is? He is a man who does a thing to-day because he did the same thing yesterday. Repeating is easier than thinking—so Mr. Habit Man repeats.

His name is legion. We find him everywhere.

There he is now—that bookkeeper. He has been holding the same job for the last ten years. He has been putting the same figures in the same books all that time. His horizon ends at the top of the page. That is the reason the other fellow who is five years his junior and has been with the firm only two years is now secretary at twice the bookkeeper's pay. The younger man thought. He grew. He found better ways of doing things. He became worth more to the firm and they paid him more. Just a simple commercial transaction, that's all.

A Habit Man is a machine. A machine, you know, does not improve with age. It usually wears out. So does the Habit Man.

Repetition is rust. Doing the same thing in the same way day after day wears a rut that finally penetrates down to the very depths of stagnation.

Cudgel that brain of yours or it will surely lapse into a lifetime sleep.

Think—Dig! Make every day a day of improvement. No man is doomed save the Habit Man. And no chains of habit can bind tight red-blooded thinking effort.

BUSINESS PHILOSOPHY.

A man may have a legal right to waste as much of his own time as he will, but it is another matter when it comes to wasting the time of someone else.

It pays to carry the interests of your employer close at the heart, for it is said that loyal service makes a generous paymaster.

Store windows are to allow those outside to look in. Who wants to look into a window where there is nothing to see?

There is one important item that ought not to be forgotten in the construction of an advertisement, and that is white space. Don't be afraid to use plenty of it.

SMILES—SOME TO BE AVOIDED

THE attitude of the dealer and his clerks to the public, is an important factor in success. Geniality, obligingness, cheerfulness, are vastly appreciated. The smile is an asset—but there are smiles and smiles. Here are a half-dozen to avoid:

1. The pitying smile, when the customer signifies a desire to look at a cheaper article than the one first shown.
2. The sarcastic smile, when the customer intimates she is a more competent judge of her own needs than the clerk.
3. The knowing smile, when the customer says she is buying an electric shaving mug for her "brother."
4. The idiotic or meaningless, vacant, perpetual smile of the clerk who considers a smirk his stock-in-trade.
5. The bored smile, when the customer speaks pridefully of the exceptional cleverness of her sister-in-law's second cousin's children.
6. The "Heaven-help-me" smile, exchanged with a fellow employe, when the customer finds difficulty in deciding between two patterns.

This list may seem mere pleasantry, but many a sensitive buyer has been driven away from a store by just such slight and covert insolences as these.

The Importance of Good Buying

What it Involves and What it Means to a Business

One of the most interesting problems in commercial affairs is why so small a percentage of retail merchants succeed even to the extent of remaining in business and meeting in full their obligations, though they go into business presumably expecting to do better than make both ends meet.

The answer to this problem is that men rush into business ventures with an idea that it is a very simple matter to run a business, and that the only elements that really enter into it are buying and selling. They have no idea how involved and intricate are the elements that go into the making of a generally successful business.

We would not entrust a machine for motive or productive power to an unskilled laborer if safety and success are to be assured, and so it is that the business machine breaks down and brings disappointment to the unskilled and unfitted operator.

In this country there is too much reliance upon native shrewdness. Men confuse shrewdness with skill, thinking they are identical, but they are not, for while shrewdness may be a source of reliance in time of emergency, it is skill—or honest, energetic application of common sense, knowledge, and experience to the task in hand—that builds substantially and makes for successful operation.

Buying is the fuel of the business machine, and should be the first subject for the exercise of skill upon the part of the retail merchant. If good judgment is not used as to quality or quantity the business machine will be deficient in profit-producing power. There is a homely but pertinent maxim, "Goods well bought are half sold." It takes skill, with all that that word implies, to compass this first requisite of profitable business. Present-day competition calls for such skill as men never had to exercise before to satisfy rapidly changing tastes and needs of the consumer, and create new demands which the merchants must arrange to satisfy.

This leads us to consider the relation of buying to the important feature of creating a debt, for the meeting of which provision must be constantly made. A debt contracted, known commercially as a credit, has two terminals—that when the debt is contracted or the credit extended, and that when the credit is redeemed or the debt extinguished—and there can be no safe and successful start from the first terminal without having the second distinctly in view.

Dependence cannot be placed upon Providence or chance to extinguish the debt. Retail merchants fail and are unsuccessful because they overbuy or lack the skill properly to adjust purchases to the selling power of their business or to their available capital, which eventually brings about embarrassment due to disproportion of matured obligations to likely or available assets. Overbuying or inflation of stock is the danger against which every merchant must constantly struggle.

Therefore the merchant must first determine the safe purchasing power of his capital—must know how often it is necessary for the stock or capital to be turned over each year, so that his credit obligations may be properly provided for, the largest discounts availed of, and the expense of depreciation for undesirable and out-of-date goods kept at a minimum.

In illustration—a merchant starts with $5,000 capital and at the end of the year has carried an average stock of $10,000, had total sales of $15,000, with a gross profit of 25 per cent., and an expense of 19 per cent. His payments for merchandise had averaged 30 to 60 days' slow, with the assistance of a small bank credit. The result would approximate the following:

Year's gross profits $3,750 00
Deduct—
Operating expenses $2,850 00
Six per cent. on capital 300 00
Interest on overdue accounts 150 00
Interest on bank loan 60 00
Depreciation on stock 300 00
————$3,660 00

Net profit ....$ 90 00

Should this merchant have carried an average stock through the year of $5,000, sold for the year $15,000, on a cash basis his turn-over of capital would have been three times during the year and he could have taken advantage of discounts with the following approximate results:

Gross profits $3,750 00
Discount on merchandise purchases 350 00
                                         ————
Total $4,100 00

Deduct—
Operating expenses $2,700 00
Six per cent. on capital 300 00
Depreciation on stock 200 00
————$3,200 00

Net profit ....$ 900 00

Skillful buying as exemplified in these two illustrations would have spelled success and earned a difference of over 16 per cent. on the capital invested by this merchant, and given to the business machine its fuel on a profit-producing basis.

These two illustrations prove that it is not the extent of gross profit that assures success, but the skillful and discreet handling of purchases which have eliminated some of the charges against gross profit and added to the net result which is the real test of profit-earning power.

As a final word, for it cannot be too frequently dwelt upon, success in retail merchandising is in proportion to good buying, for upon it depends the rapid turn-over of capital, the securing of best discounts, and a reasonable net profit.

What signifies wishing and hoping for better times? We may make these times better, if we bestir ourselves.—Benjamin Franklin.

Guard Against Running Out of Goods

Value of a Want Book

"We're just out!"

How often have these words turned a customer away from a store in disgust, and with rather an ill feeling towards the dealer and the store. It is greatly to the detriment of business, too, for a person who receives this answer is inclined to patronize some other establishment where the stock is kept complete.

Big Stores Aim to Supply all Wants

The big departmental stores recognize the bad features of being out of goods that customers inquire for and put forth their best effort to maintain complete stocks. In fact, it is their aim to impress upon the people that they can supply their every want. Of

GOODS ASKED FOR TO-DAY THAT ARE NOT IN STOCK				
DEPARTMENT		CIRCLE.		DATE........
Full Description of Goods, Size, Color, Number, etc.			Sales Number	Signature
	Signature of Head of Circle.................			

Reproduction of want sheet used by T. Eaton Co. on which clerks list all goods asked for during the day that are not in stock.

course it takes a system to guard against running out of goods and they have one, as every well managed store should have. The T. Eaton Co., of Toronto, have a want sheet in each department, on which clerks list all goods that are asked for during the day that are not in stock. This serves the double purpose of keeping the stock complete and also bringing to notice any lines that customers may want and which are not in stock.

Want Sheet of T. Eaton Co.

The sheet in question is reproduced on this page. The instructions to the sales force on the stub reads, "Clerks are to list any goods here which are asked for and which are not in stock, even though they may have been previously listed." It may seem a waste of time to list goods each time they are asked for, but the number of times an article is listed serves as a gauge as to whether it should be stocked or not. At the end of the day the head of the circle looks over the sheet and sends it on to the order department.

Simple Want Book will do small Dealer

A similar system should be used in every store, no matter what its size may be. In the small store it is just as necessary, for on account of small stocks close stock-keeping is essential. It is not necessary to have any complicated system. A small book kept in a convenient part of the store in which to list wants will serve the purpose of the small dealer admirably. The important thing is that it be made use of. Get in the habit of jotting down those articles that are getting short and instruct your clerks to do the same.

It does not do to rely on memory. One case of forgetfulness may mean the loss of a customer. It means at any rate unpleasantness, and this should be avoided. Guard against having to tell a customer, "We're just out."

MAKING COLLECTIONS EASIER WHERE CREDIT IS EXTENDED.

There are many people who seem to respect a promissory note more than they do other kinds of "promises to pay." Many merchants, therefore, find it good business when a customer is tardy in paying, if it is likely to be some time before the money is forthcoming, to get a note for the amount from him. People seem to respect the note more, and in addition, it is an acknowledgment of debt, and is not open to dispute by the customer in case of suit or garnishee as with an ordinary account.

Coupon Book Given for Promissory Note.

This same idea is being carried out by some merchants to make collections easier by means of coupon books. Instead of allowing a customer to run a straight account, when he wishes credit, he signs a promissory note for $5 and gets a book of coupons good for that amount in merchandise.

The dealer can purchase these coupon books in form already for use. On the front is a space for the name of the merchant issuing, as well as the person issued to. The first page is a promissory note for $5, which is signed by the customer, detached and kept by the dealer. The balance of the book is made up of sheets of detachable coupons worth 5, 10 and 25 cents in merchandise.

It is claimed by the manufacturers of these coupon books that they make easier the collection of accounts. The customer signs a note setting a definite time when the $5 is to be paid, while with ordinary accounts, the understanding as to time of payment is frequently rather indefinite. Then again, the customer knows exactly at all times how much he owes the merchant, while it is also claimed that the plan keeps the customer dealing at the one store.

The writer has one of these coupon books before him. The front cover reads "The coupons in this coupon book are good for merchandise only if not detached, and bearing the same number as cover." A notice on the back reads, "Always bring this book with you. Do not lose this as it is the same as cash. Do not tear the coupons off. Hand it to the clerk and he will detach the amount you have purchased."

It is dust that makes shopworn goods. One of the most important steps toward economical management is doing away with dust.

WHEN SYSTEM DRIVES

Sometimes a merchant, after a tiresome day's work, feels like letting the compiling of the records of the day's business go. It is then that system seems a burden. But the wise man knows that it will pay him to keep these records so that he can tell at all times how his business stands and how it compares with other years.

Making Out Financial Statement After Stock Taking

How to prepare the statement that will allow dealer to compare standing of business with previous year—Resources and liabilities account

THE listing of the stock does not complete the inventory. The dealer does not only want to know the amount of his stock, but also the exact standing of his business, so as to make possible a comparison with previous years to ascertain what progress is being made. This is the annual financial statement—a statement of resources and liabilities for the entire business.

Summarizing of Stock Sheets

In the preparation of this, the summarizing of the stock sheets is first necessary. The extensions first have to be made. Where the cost price has been taken from the article as called off, this is an easy matter; if not, it will be necessary to refer to the cost book. Some of the most common articles will be known offhand by the dealer. The work of summarizing may be carried on at leisure, although most dealers are impatient to ascertain the results of the year's labors.

Other Figures That are Necessary

In order to make out a financial statement, other particulars are required to be taken at the same time as the stock. These include book accounts, fixtures and equipment, cash on hand and in bank, notes receivable and payable, as well as the amount due by the dealer for goods. Book accounts should be put in at their actual collectable value. Different methods are used in listing fixtures. Some dealers deduct a certain percentage each year for deterioration in fixtures. The percentage of reduction is based on the life of the fixture. For instance, if the life of a fixture is estimated at seven years, 14 per cent. plus would be deducted off the cost yearly. Say, if a fixture cost $100, then the dealer, operating on this plan, would reduce the value of it in his inventory $14.30 each year.

All dealers do not favor this plan, some arguing that a fixture may be worth as much to-day as it was a year ago, and that therefore the dealer should use his own judgment in setting the value of his fixtures. They at least should not be listed at the cost price,

because a used article cannot be sold for its cost, even though it may be practically as good as new.

Making Out the Statement

When all these particulars are at hand, the dealer is ready to make out his yearly statement, showing the exact standing of the business. The resources will include amount of stock on hand, accounts on the books, fixtures and equipment, cash on hand and bills receivable. On the other side will be the amount due on stock, bills payable any any other liabilities of the firm.

Herewith is reproduced a sample financial statement. In this case the resources of the business amount to $5,300 and liabilities to $1,500, leaving a difference of $3,800. This dealer when he took inventory in January of the previous year had a balance of $2,100, so that the net profit of the business for the year amounts to $1,900. When this inventory is carried on from year to year, it allows of an excellent comparison of progress.

In Case Dealer Owns Building

In case the dealer owns the building he occupies and wishes to include it in the statement, if there has been any advance in the value of the building, the amount of advance should be deducted from the net profits of the year to show the exact amount of money made by the business itself. The advance in the value of the building should have nothing whatever to do with the profits of the business. If, however, any improvements have been made in the building during the year, and the cost has been borne by the business, it is then only right that the advance in value should be allowed in the net profits.

A correct yearly statement is of immense value to a dealer, and special care should be taken in its preparation to get it accurate.

Don't leave your store in charge of one who has not a practical knowledge of the goods; any customer wants and expects intelligent attention.

Resources		Liabilities	
Amt. of stock on hand	2500	Amt due on stock	1200
Accounts on books	1500	Drafts signed but not due	300
Fixtures & Equipment	500		
Cash in Bank	300		
Cash on hand	100		
Notes - Bills Receivable	400	Resources over Liabilities	3800
	$5300		$5300
		Resources over Liab - this year	3800
		Resources over Liab - last year	2100
		Net Profit for year	1900

Sample financial statement made out after stock-taking, showing dealer's liabilities and assets. Explained in accompanying article.

System is Needed in Collection of Accounts

The dealer who conducts his collections in a systematic manner will secure the best results -- Sending out follow-up letters according to a system

TO secure the best results, system is as essential in the collection of accounts as in other phases of business. It should commence when the account is first opened. At this time, arrangements should be made as to when the customer shall pay. If the dealer has more credit customers than allows these particulars to be remembered conveniently, he should have a system of filing away the time of payment of each customer. At any rate, it is well to keep a record of this information, so that it will be available at all times.

The Need of System in Collections.

The need of system is apparent to anyone who has made any study of the method of collection of accounts used by some dealers. For instance. it is not an infrequent thing for a dealer to send a letter in regard to an overdue account, declaring that the debtor must do something within a certain length of time, or action will be taken by the dealer. But the stipulated time is allowed to pass and the dealer takes no action, because he has no system to remind him when the stipulated time is up.

Simple System Will Do the Work.

A simple system by which notes can be made that will serve as a reminder to the dealer is all that is necessary. A desk date pad will serve the purpose admirably or any kind of a book properly divided into divisions for each day can be made. This will serve to remind the dealer of days when certain collection letters should be sent—of days when debtors receive their pay and on which he should make an effort to collect their accounts—of days on which they promised to pay, and which should be followed up—of dates on which legal proceedings against delinquents should be instituted.

How Dealer Lost by Lack of System.

The need of some such a system is shown by a case recently related by a retailer. A man who was in the town for only a short time and who was unknown to the merchant, asked for credit. His appearance did not impress the dealer as to his reliability, but he decided to take a chance, as the man told him the date he was drawing his pay for his work—and he decided to be on hand when he was drawing his pay, and collect the amount due him. The merchant, however, had no system to remind him, and being busy, the pay day slipped by without him thinking of it. Two days later when he did think of it, he found the man had drawn his pay and left town, and that he was out the amount of the bill. System would have avoided this loss.

Send Follow-up Letters Systematically.

The dealer should also send his collection letters out in a systematic manner. For instance, if a dealer sends one letter demanding payment in an emphatic manner, if the one following asks for payment in a meek manner, the customer thinks that the dealer was just trying to scare him into line in the first letter, and seeing that he could not do that, has changed his tactics. This is often the case because the dealer, not knowing what he said in the first letter, is not in a position to follow it up in just the manner that it should be. This gives the debtor the idea that the dealer's collection notices are just "talk," and so he gives little or no attention to them.

Make Collection Letters Gradually Stronger.

When an account becomes overdue, the dealer should at once start in to collect it—going about it in a systematic manner. The first effort should be a gentle reminder of their indebtedness, and the letters following should gradually become stronger. The dealer should have a system so that he will know how strong he made his last letter, so that he can follow it up by one a little stronger.

Many merchants have a number of accounts on their books that are overdue. The dealer should list these and start in to collect them, the system way. This is not possible by a mere reminder, but requires a strong campaign, and this the dealer should undertake. The initial reminder needs to be followed up by more strenuous methods until results are secured.

CASH DISCOUNTS AND INVOICE PRICE

By an Old Retailer

Cash discounts should not be deducted from invoice price before applying the cost of doing business; to do this would cause the dealer to lose the cash discount—provided he add the same net profit. If the dealer's expense account includes all the real expense of his business, then interest is charged in this account for all money invested and all money borrowed, and it is this money that enables the dealer to secure the cash discounts. The fact that the dealer creates an expense to secure money to take his discounts is proof that the cash discount should protect this expense, and the dealer who deducts the cash discount before applying the cost of doing business loses the discount. The cost of doing business cannot be measured entirely by the total amount of the expense account. Many times dealers do certain things in business that do not cause them to add anything to their expense account in dollars and cents; the dealer who does not study the line of goods he sells; the dealer who does not place quality above price; the dealer who is continually changing, selling one make of goods this year and another next; the dealer who sacrifices his profit to secure a greater volume of business; the dealer who sells goods all year without checking his sales and stock against goods on hand and from inventory and goods delivered without settlement; the dealer who neglects to take his cash discounts, even if he has to borrow the money; the dealer who neglects to make a demand for settlement of note and account when due; the dealer who is not able to meet his customers with a smile, no matter what his own troubles may be, all add to their cost of doing business.

If some of your stock looks better in one light and some in another, get each line, as far as possible, in the most favorable light.

Selling Methods in the Furniture Store

Some Experiences and Suggestions

NOVEL FURNITURE SALES PLAN.

Newspaper advertising by an Ohio furniture firm reveals an unusual and novel scheme for drumming up business in furniture lines. The offer was that on specified days every child between seven and eleven years calling at the store would be given a jumping rope free. At the same time the child was told how it could get a welfare sand table free. The welfare sand table is an indoor seashore box, which gives the children an opportunity of playing in the sand inside the house without littering up the room with sand. It includes tools for handling, and is featured as furnishing a compact playground for the very best sort of creative play. An option was given of a pair of nickel-plated roller skates or a child's dinner set if the latter were preferred to the welfare sand table.

As the children gave their names and addressses to the store, these were registered and formed a part of a new mailing list. They were also given a mailing card to take home with them, on which were blanks which the children's parents were expected to fill in with names and addresses of prospective furniture purchasers. The children were registered under a number, which number also appeared on the mail cards which they took home. Thus it was unnecessary for the parents to sign the mail card. In addition to the space provided for the names and addresses of prospects, there was a column in which could be checked the class of furniture, etc., which the prospects would require.

The company had its salesmen follow these prospects, and immediately as they became customers and bought goods amounting to $25 or more a welfare box or a pair of roller skates or a child's dinner set was delivered to the child responsible for the tip leading to the business. Within twelve days from the appearance of the advertisement the company had already acquired enough new business to pay all the expenses of the plan and "then some."

In addition to this work, the company is following up the published lists of newly-born children with mail cards. The card offers a premium of a gold baby ring when it is presented at the store. These lists are also turned over to the manufacturers of go-carts and baby carriages, for which it is exclusive agent. This plan has boosted go-cart business as well as crib sales.

AUTO DELIVERY SAVED SALES.

"We'll deliver it to-day," is the slogan of an enterprising Western dealer, which is said to have been productive of immediate profits. Full publicity advantage was taken of the purchase of a new motor truck, which supplanted several teams of horses formerly used for delivering purposes. The slogan was repeated in newspaper advertising, in show windows, on the truck itself, and in connection with street car advertising. The exploitation of the increased service and the ready accomplishment made possible by the new truck, is declared to have rectified one of the weakest points in the owner's business. "Many sales had been lost because of the necessary rule that no promise of delivery the same day be made to customers making purchases in the afternoon," reports our correspondent. "With the truck service, delivery of articles bought before 4 o'clock p.m. can be assured, and our former losses have been retrieved. This is due to some extent to the impression of enterprise and prosperity conveyed by our delivery system."

THE PUBLIC BE ——.

From Texas comes the aluminum dollar suggestion and the store slogan, "The Public be Pleased." To encourage sales, a Waco firm distributed silver dollars encased in a thin, open aluminum case as change to its customers. The case on one side bears the stamp, "Good for $1.10 in —— Furniture Department." On the other side of the case appears the expressive slogan of the Waco store. The additional dime has been the means of many a "return" sale.

INCREASING REFRIGERATOR SALES.

If local conditions have retarded the sale of your refrigerators this season, says the Furniture Record, and the prospect of a heavy "carry-over" clouds the midsummer horizon, the offer of an Indianapolis furniture house may be adaptable to the situation. This big Indiana payment house, which is one of a chain of some sixteen furniture stores in large communities, has advertised 500 pounds of ice free with each refrigerator sold. Particularly fortunate are the Indianapolis dealers in being able to co-operate with a local ice service corporation which serves the entire city. Unless the service of the company with which the contract is arranged is general, some difficulty may be experienced in actual performance. The ice was given with "boxes" ranging for from $7.75 to $21.50. According to the text of the firm's advertisement: "Ninety tons of ice have been secured for free distribution. With each refrigerator we sell we will give free a book of ice coupons. Each of these books is worth $1.75, and calls for 500 lbs. of ice in any quantity from five cents' worth up, delivered to your door, anywhere in Indianapolis."

MAGAZINE PICTURES FOR SHOW CARDS.

Pictures cut out of magazines and mounted on plain white cardboard, together with some message regarding merchandise, make distinct additions to a store's interior decorating plan. If you are skilled at all in card-writing, you can make decidedly attractive cards by use of these pictures. You can use them anyway, skillful or no.

The Hudson Bay Co.'s store at Kamloops, B.C., rents furniture to the theatrical companies playing that town, and besides getting a cash rental return, also gets some free advertising in the theatre programme and in the local paper.

Creating of Sales Should be Aim of Trimmer

BY C. WHITEHOUSE, CALGARY, ALTA.

Editor's Note—The point brought out by Mr. Whitehouse—that the window trimmer should keep selling power in mind in arranging his displays—is one that is well worthy of emphasis. Altogether too many dealers and clerks seem to think that as long as the window is filled up with goods arranged with some degree of order, that it is fulfilling its mission. This is not so, for the purpose of the window is to sell goods, and this should ever be kept in mind in arranging displays. As pointed out here, a window may even appeal to the eye and yet fail to sell goods. Of course, an attractive window has always a general advertising value, but the aim should be to not only make it appear attractive, but also create as many direct sales as possible. The question is worth thinking over.

THE main thing to be aimed at in trimming a window, in my estimation, is selling power. A window may look good to the eye and yet fail in its real object—that of creating sales. It was selling force that I had in mind in arranging this display.

Another point I consider should be remembered, is the use of price tickets. These should have an appearance pleasing and attractive to the eye, and should be placed so as to attract attention to each particular line and in such a manner that there will be no mistake as to the line of goods for which they are intended.

Fixtures for Trimmer in Small Store.

The trimmer in the small store sometimes thinks he has not the window fixtures at the disposal of the trimmer in the large establishment. There are always plenty of boxes around every store. These can be brought into use by placing some for supports and breaking up others and using them for shelves. By this means, the trimmer in the smallest store can have fixtures at practically no cost.

DO NOT UNDERRATE SHOW WINDOWS

This is a straight talk to retailers in towns and villages, though much of the matter herein set down applies with almost the same force to many city merchants. Time and again the fact has been forced upon the attention of the writer, both by observation and

Seasonable background for summer furniture display.

conversation, that the average merchant in such places is not alive to the realization of what his windows might mean to him, provided they were used intelligently.

No keen business man disputes the fact that careful window dressing "pulls" new custom into the store, and is often instrumental in holding the old. When a man is ready to argue on this point, he is standing in his own light. Why does such an immense retail concern as the United Cigar Stores Company pay men to stand at different business corners in large cities with automatic counting machines, to keep tally of the number of men passing that corner within certain hours? The answer is obvious. Simply to see how many possible customers would be within the scope of

Window background imitating a room interior designed for a showing of furniture draperies, rugs, etc., by Geo. J. Cowan, Chicago.

appeal of a strong window display, backed by A1 service at that point. But the show window is counted on to turn possibilities into actualities, hence it must have the material to work on.

The Possible Field

Now, it is not necessary to be on a city street to realize on the possibilities of good window displays. Did you ever try to estimate, no matter how roughly, the number of people passing your door in a week? A little offhand calculation would be surprising. This is especially the case when one considers market days, Saturdays, and other occasions when the farmers and their families are wont to flock into town. Human nature is the same the world over.

Every man, woman and child that passes your store front daily is a possible customer. That is beyond dispute. Perhaps many of them are actual customers. If so, do you reason that they can always be suited by you, that they know your stock without any such frills, that you hold them because of personal reasons, and so on? Well, perhaps. But you can count on these facts operating in your favor, just so long as all your competitors look on things from the same standpoint as yourself. The minute some one of them suddenly comes alive to the opportunities he has been missing, and starts in to make up for lost time by employing modern methods, the human nature in your supposedly steadfast circle of customers will begin to assert itself, and your trade will be cut in upon here, there, and elsewhere.

This explains the reason why the mail order houses have made big inroads upon the country trade. There is altogether too much of a tendency to "let things slide" among retail merchants to-day—that is generally at the root of the "dull business" trouble.

How it Works Out

As a possible example, do any of your farmer customers know that you are carrying a high class hardware stock? They will know, if they see the goods in your window carefully displayed with a neat show card, giving the main selling points in a brief, snappy manner. Yes, and they will buy as well, if they are likely to need such an article in the near future. If not needed at once, they will remember where they saw it, when next they want it. The impression sinks in, and this is what is of importance to you.

As to expense, do you ever consider your windows in the light of a by-product? When you use space in the newspapers or other mediums to acquaint the public with your goods, you pay extra for the privilege. But the use of your windows is covered by store rent, consequently all the business that is secured from such a source is net profit. If the merchant would look at the matter from this point of view, more active interest would be taken in window dressing.

Objection is frequently made to the statement that the return from window dressing is net profit. Time, trouble and material are supposed to weigh heavily on the debit side. Why? The time used is also a by-product—the odd minutes snatched between sales or in dull periods, that might be spent in talking politics. As for trouble, it is a pleasure to the man on the keen lookout for anything that will make his business more productive. The material used is a negligible quantity. Elaborate and costly backgrounds are not needed, nor desired, in the smaller places, as their very novelty detracts attention from the goods on display. It is well to remember that window displays are primarily for the purpose of selling goods, not to cause comment.

Why not determine to give your windows a thorough trial? Put your best ideas into the arrangement of specimens of your best stock; use in your displays attractive show cards and price tickets, and the result cannot be long in doubt.

PHOTOS OF WINDOW DISPLAYS

The Furniture World would like photographs of your windows.

Whenever you make a window you think is good, let us have a photograph of it. We expect to use a number of these windows in The Furniture World and will make comments on the same for the benefit of all concerned.

The photograph should be taken at night or the window should be covered on the outside if taken in the day time.

At night if the window is well lighted the photographer can make a long exposure of perhaps 25 minutes and thus get a good strong picture.

For daytime photographs arrange your window like this: Get two poles, each a little longer than the height of the window. Then get strips of black cloth a trifle longer than the window is wide, sew them together and tack upon the poles. This acts as a large black screen to cut off all reflections from across the street. Cut a hole in the cloth for the camera and you will be ready for the picture.

Have all the lights in your windows well shaded and as high up and as near the pane as possible. This will bring out the contrast and the high lights.

WHAT THE SHOW WINDOW IS.

Of all mediums and phases of general advertising, the show window display must be acknowledged as one of the most direct and promising of results. There have been periods of advertising, even as there have been geological periods and ages of civilization—the period of announcement, the informative period, and the period of the poster—but through them all the element of display has lost none of its importance. Ancient peddlers displayed their goods before the gates of the city, merchandise was shown in booths in the market place of old Bagdad; the commodities of Cheapside were shown on hooks before stalls; Colonial America had its shops, and modern business establishments are incomplete without proper facilities for display attained most satisfactorily through the big plate glass window. The modern show window is a development of each of these older methods and has come to be a merchant's closest affiliation with the purchasing public. The show window is the peep-hole through which the public looks into an establishment and many stand or fall accordingly as the show window attracts or repels customers.

WINDOW EYE-PULLERS

Why do so many window dressers of furniture stores neglect a method of support which is extremely easy to use and which produces a very telling effect? This is the method of suspension, by means of fine cord or fine wires, of the various articles from the ceiling of the window. A number of small screw-eyes could be quickly inserted by means of a screw-eye holder and the wire or cords dropped down from these and cut at various lengths. These wires could be used to hold the lighter articles in the hardware store. This would admit of bringing special sales goods close to the front and on a level with the eye of the passerby.

Beds and Bedding

WESTERN BEDDING STORE OPENING.

Under the heading "Edmonton's Business Houses," the Daily Bulletin of that city tells of the grand opening of the Reliable Bed Outfit Company's store, which drew crowds throughout the whole of the opening day. As early as ten o'clock there was already the nucleus of a crowd, and from that hour onward to the evening the stream of visitors never ceased. The opening had been widely advertised, and the results could not have been surpassed. Interest in the store had also been greatly stimulated by the brilliantly lit windows on the evening before, in which the most dramatic episode in the history of Red Riding Hood and a "Now I lay me down to rest" scene were cleverly depicted.

It was a morning of roses. Every man in the store had a perfumed buttonhole, which had been pinned upon him personally by one of the genial proprietors. And the roses had an aim. The back leaf of each had been stamped with a horsehide and the words "The Reliable." It was a pretty gift, and gave the store quite a garden air. And by means of the roses the name of the Reliable company was carried to the four quarters of the city. Roses abounded throughout the day on Jasper avenue, and in nine cases out of ten the back leaf was inscribed with the magic words "The Reliable."

Did Not Forget the Ladies.

But it must not be supposed that the ladies had been forgotten. Every wise firm knows that to prosper it must please the ladies. Of the fortune of a furniture store woman is the supreme arbitress. Man's demand for furniture would be limited to small dimensions if woman had ceased her existence. A camp bed, a strip of carpet in his bedroom, a wardrobe to put his clothes in, a sitting room furnished with a Turkey carpet, some easy chairs, a sofa, a pier glass, some choice pictures— this would satisfy the majority of men for living quarters.

It is safe to say that Adam never troubled about the furniture in the Garden of Eden until the arrival of Eve. And then for the first time in the history of the world was born the art of making a house attractive.

"Give me a couch in leafy bowers,
Where myrtle breathes 'mid lotus flowers."

So sang Anacreon, the Greek poet. A perfumed bed of leaves would suit few people where mosquitoes are thick. The beds sold by the Reliable Bed Company are far better adapted to ordinary climates, and especially to Alberta, whose boast it is that no matter how hot the day, the nights are nearly always cool. All kinds of beds are to be found at the Reliable store, from the handsome brass bedstead to the interchangeable bed and couch, which the rooming house landlady finds so useful to multiply the number of her sitting rooms.

After some thousands of roses had been distributed as souvenirs to men, the doors were closed for the lunch hour, with the notice that the souvenirs for ladies would be distributed on the re-opening at two o'clock. Some of the fair sex were so eager for their souvenirs that they waited beside the door for about an hour in order to be first on hand. From the time that the doors opened till six o'clock the line of lady visitors kept passing through the store. General admiration was expressed for the spaciousness of the store, which measures 150 by 25, the admirable lighting arrangements, there being two skylights, and the appointments of the store as a whole. For souvenirs, one thousand beautiful German caster sets had been secured, and one of these was presented to each lady. The success of the day was enhanced by musical selections by an orchestra from three to six.

Have Strategic Position.

Success in business, it is generally acknowledged, depends to a great degree upon what is termed the strategy of location. So the Reliable Bed Outfit is fortunate in this respect. The store is next door to the Monarch Theatre, on Jasper avenue east, on the south side, quite near the corner of First street. It is a location passed by thousands of people every day. To attract the notice of these thousands by clever window displays, which will be frequently changed, will be the aim of the proprietors. To judge by the "Red Riding tableau," their window displays will be marked by novelty and power to appeal. The proprietors are men of wide experience in the furniture business.

To those who wish to furnish their houses with beds, couches, etc., on the credit system by small weekly or monthly payments, the Reliable Bed Outfit Company makes a special appeal. "Your credit is good" is one of the mottoes of the store.

NEW BEDDING CATALOGUE.

The Ontario Spring Bed and Mattress Co., Limited, have just issued their new catalogue E, descriptive of their "Ontario Line" of sanitary beds, cribs, springs, mattresses, steel couches, davenports, pillows, and bolsters. The booklet contains close on to a hundred pages of reading matter, and illustrations, printed on coated paper and encased in a golden brown cover with the title embossed. The catalogue, which is a splendid one, will be mailed to any legitimate furniture dealer.

COST OF DOING BUSINESS.

System, of Chicago, has made a nation-wide investition of the costs of doing a retail business. It seems to run from 16 per cent. for groceries, 20 per cent. for hardware stores, 25 per cent. for drug stores, 26 per cent. for jewelers, and 23 per cent. for dry goods. The furniture store runs to almost 24 per cent.

Furniture Store Costs.

	Per cent.
Rent	3.44
Salaries	8.73
Advertising	2.72
Heat and light	.92
Delivery	.94
Supplies	.41
Insurance and taxes	1.57
General expenses	1.10
Depreciation and shrinkage	2.14
Bad debts	1.94
Total percentage of expenses to sales	23.91

These figures, it will be observed, are percentages of the selling price. They speak eloquently of the advantages of rapid turnover.

STOVES AND HOUSE FURNISHINGS

How Demonstrations Sell Stoves

There is nothing in the world that sells goods so readily as demonstration. Buyers want to see what they are going to buy before buying it. This holds good in any business, and the retailer who has an eye for business will not overlook such things. For instance, if your wife is thinking of buying a new washing machine for her washwoman or a gas or oil stove, one that is being put on the market through a systematic advertising campaign, she first wants to see how it works. Advertising, no matter how brilliant and how convincing, doesn't show her what she is getting. She merely has the word of the maker or the dealer as to its superior qualities. Show her, however, that it is all that it is advertised to be, and she'll buy it, for it means money to her.

The need of demonstration holds good in all retail businesses. Especially is this so when a dealer has to transact business with a number of women, and the progressive furniture man always has quite a list of women customers. I have found that store and window demonstrations bring in big returns. Several months ago I inaugurated the idea, and on each Wednesday and Saturday I have a young man working in my two big windows demonstrating my goods.

Both in Canada and the United States the idea that stove demonstrations pay holds good. In one of the smaller class a hardware concern I have in mind finds that stove demonstrations are very profitable. It has been the custom of this concern to set aside a week each year in which stoves receive attention almost to the exclusion of other considerations.

A portion of the store is set aside as a sort of lunch room, tables being immaculately set for the purpose of serving hot coffee and cakes to women visitors. Women, many times accompanied by their husbands, drive in from miles around to attend these demonstrations. The stove sales of the company amount to several thousand dollars annually, and it is by demonstrations that a large part of this business has been built up.

Another concern in a town in a rural community, to draw attention to their summer stove line, held a demonstration and a drawing, and on the day set for awarding the prize it is estimated that 2,500 people were in the crowd before the store when the lucky winner drew the prize number. Everybody in that crowd went home to talk of the dealer's stove line. These people were reached in a way hard to do through other methods, and the gathering of the crowd more than repaid all that had been spent in advertising the event.

Furniture dealers, especially in small towns, who handle their stove demonstrations properly, are always successful in creating interest and frequently successful in making sales. The one great reason that more are not successful is because they do not co-operate with the manufacturer to direct attention to the demonstration which is going to be held. Most of the Canadian stove-makers are willing and anxious to lend their help, and the accompanying illustrations of demonstrations of summer stoves show what one at least of them has been doing in this respect in Ontario towns.

With the plan of publicity for the stove campaign fully mapped out by experts, with the posters prepared at the expense of the manufacturer, it is astonishing to find the number of people who wait almost until the factory representative is in their store before doing anything towards creating public interest. When the opening day of the demonstration is at hand they wonder at the few people who visit the store and begin to lose interest at the beginning.

In the store mentioned in the above incident different tactics were pursued. A month before the demonstration the firm began distributing the tickets. The customer retained the stub of the ticket, while the remainder, bearing the number, was placed in a box provided for the purpose. Two weeks before the demonstration the range to be given away was placed in the show window with suitable cards, announcing that it was to be given away. This, together with the newspaper advertising which was done, served to create interest among prospective buyers before the demonstration was begun.

Quite naturally, everyone was interested in the outcome, so that the beginning of the stove week, with the customary distribution of coffee and biscuit, was well attended. Excitement reached the highest pitch when, on the day of the drawing, the stove was taken out in the open in a wagon and fired up. A stove in operation in the open without flue connection created additional interest, and gave an opportunity for a talk on the merits of the goods before the drawing took place.

HANDY OIL STOVES
ENSURE SUMMER COMFORT

CAMP STOVES

David Spencer Limited

How a Vancouver firm draws attention to its summer stove line.

The wagon was driven underneath a large advertising banner that had been stretched across the street in front of the store, and the box containing the tickets placed on it. A disinterested party was called upon to draw a ticket from the box, and the number appearing thereon was announced. The customer holding the duplicate of the first number called was awarded the stove.

A Western house furnisher held a successful exhibit and demonstration at a fair in their town recently. Coffee and biscuit were served to 2,800 people during the exhibit. Methods similar to those of the demonstration idea were used to advantage.

The merchant who is not doing everything in his power to create the maximum interest in his summer and winter stove demonstrations will never secure the maximum results. The examples mentioned merely go to show that co-operation with the manufacturer along these lines will bring excellent results.

FIRST PAYMENT ON LEASED GOODS
By A. E. Yont
Secretary Massachusetts Home Furnishers' Association

"Probably the most important question in the lease business is the initial or down payment. This question has troubled the instalment business for years and the failure to observe proper safeguards has cost the dealers heavily. The lease business has some very peculiar features.

"It differs radically from any other line of credits. The ordinary method of investigating a purchaser seeking credit is to find out the financial responsibility, and the dealer depends almost entirely on his investigation on this point. In the lease business, however, the question to be investigated is not so much the financial responsibility as the moral responsibility. Theoretically, the goods themselves are security. As a matter of fact, however, no dealer would sell a customer if he had the slightest expectation of being compelled to depend on the goods themselves to satisfy the claim. The fact that he can retake the goods under the lease is a moral inducement to the lessee to fulfill the terms of his or her agreement, and this is the peculiar feature of the instalment business. When this moral responsibility is lacking the instalment system is defective. Now let us see what brings about the moral obligation. There is little question but that this is governed largely on the first down payment.

"This payment constitutes what may be called the investment of the lessee. Suppose the purchaser obtains goods to the value of $300 and pays $30 down. This is on a 10 per cent. basis and some dealers are willing to do this. The purchaser has invested $30 as against $270 belonging to the dealer. Perhaps one or two payments are made and then there is a default. Possibly the lessor obtains a situation some distance away. The cost of moving the goods would be as much as his investment and the question arises as to whether it is worth while for him to keep the goods.

"In many cases he will voluntarily give them up and it is easy to see that the dealer has suffered a heavy loss. It is the general experience of the trade that two-thirds of the cases where goods are taken back are due to the fact that the first down payment was too small. If this lessee had been compelled to pay at least 20 per cent to 25 per cent. down, as most of the reputable dealers require, he would probably have kept the goods. Such an occurrence is not uncommon and the dealer who suffers has only himself to blame.

"There have been a number of discussions among the councils of the association as to a uniform first payment. It is the general feeling among not only the representative dealers but among heads of philanthropic organizations that the first payment should not be too small. It is liable to bring on lax business methods on the part of the lessee and induce him to assume a larger burden than he can carry. Selling goods is easy, but collecting is a fine art."

SENSIBLE ADVICE
By F. L. Brittain

I am sure that merchants spend too much time bemoaning the fate of dealers in general and themselves in particular. They abuse the mail order houses in print and say unkind things of those who order, some of which must surely reach the ears of those talked of. Here is about the best thing I ever saw in the way of an advertisement in defence of trading at home. Run it in every one of your ads. and give it a little time to soak in, and you will see its effect. Notice how little it says about the mail order habit—but it hits the point:

WHY BUY AT HOME?

I buy at home —

Because my interests are here.

Because the community that is good enough for me to live in is good enough for me to buy in.

Because I believe in transacting business with my friends.

Because I want to see the goods I am buying.

Because I want to get what I buy when I pay for it.

Because my home dealer "carries" me when I run short of cash.

Because some part of every dollar I spend at home stays at home and helps work for the welfare of the city and county.

Because the home man I buy from stands back of the goods, thus always giving value received.

Because I sell what I produce to my home people, be it labor or goods.

Because the man I buy from pays his share of the county and city taxes.

Because the man I buy from helps support our poor and needy, our schools, our churches, our lodges and our homes.

Because if ill luck, misfortune, or bereavement comes, the man I buy from is here with his kindly expressions of greeting, his words of cheer and, if needs be, his pocketbook.

Here I live and here I buy

Let us make — and — County a good place in which to work and live.

It's easy and certain if every one will contribute his share.

NEW METHOD DRY KILN.

The Elmira Furniture Co., Elmira, Ont., have just installed a new Grand Rapids dry kiln—a new machine in the science of lumber drying. It first steams the board, taking out the sap, thereby opening up the pores, which allows the stock to dry from the heart of the board. This is the only method of drying lumber so that it will not swell or warp, but remain its actual dimensions as the life of the wood is taken out. This is one of the strongest guarantees any factory can have against open joints, warped tops, raised grain, or any other defect.

SALESPEOPLE

ETHICS OF SALESMANSHIP.

We were asked the other day, "What do you mean by a good clerk?" Now to answer this question there are a good many elements to be considered. There must be his appearance, his ability as a seller of goods, his relations with his customers, with the "boss" and with his fellow employes, and last of all his relations with himself.

Let us consider the first of these. Personal appearance is perhaps to be placed first because it is almost the first thing that impresses a customer when the salesman approaches. An opinion is almost always formed by the customer, oftentimes unconsciously, and it is most desirable that the impression be favorable. Not but what sometimes an unfavorable first impression may be later overcome and be overbalanced by other qualities, but at least it is strongly in the salesman's favor that the impression be pleasing. In bringing up the question of personal appearance it must not be supposed that the writer means that the salesman should be a fashion plate sort of a man, by any means, or that he be anything except absolutely neatly and tidily dressed. The principal essential is clean linen and well polished shoes and a clean, wholesome personality, the kind that soap and water gives, and we regret to say the kind that we have noticed to be lacking in some clerks in retail stores. A salesman must be confident, that is he must know his goods and his stock absolutely and he must be able to convey this impression of confidence which he has in himself, to his customer, and yet do it in a way that will not appear to be suggestive of a "swelled head." If a salesman can impress himself and his knowledge of his goods upon the customer in a favorable way it is then possible, or at any rate more possible, for him to sell the customer what he ought to have rather than, perhaps, what he wants, and according to one of the greatest retail shoe managers in this country that is what every salesman should try to do. He must be beyond all things, tactful, he must use that knowledge that he possesses carefully and for the best results. He must not be a bluffer, for while such an one gets by sometimes, when he falls, which is more often the case, it is a bad fall. A salesman should be persuasive without forcing his customer, that is the customer should never be pushed but should rather be led. A salesman should be one who can tell his story and know when to stop without boring his customer. He should tell his story so impressively the first time that he need not repeat it.

As we have said, another strong thing to consider in measuring up a salesman is his relationship with his fellow salesmen, and with the head of the house and the other executives of the store, that is, he is a part of the store machinery that fits in harmoniously with the rest of the organization, and the store organization as a whole is the most important thing for a merchant's consideration. Many a good salesman individually has proven a bad investment as a part of what should be a perfectly smooth running business machine.

The man who is in constant state of unrest through petty disagreements with his fellows, or the man who is a disturber of peace through his constant talk to other employes of his real or imagined wrongs can do more harm in this way than he ever could good through a selling ability above the ordinary. The man who is afraid that he may do some bit of work that belongs to somebody else is not the kind of salesman that would be picked as the long run winner.

Now, as to the man's relations with himself we would refer to the way that he conducts himself out of business hours. Many a man has said that outside of his business hours he may do as he pleases. We grant this, but he must also realize that while he does as he pleases and it concerns him alone, yet if what he does so affects his personality that it has effect upon his value when in the store, why right there the rights of his employer becomes encroached upon. A man should so take care of himself that physically and mentally he be able to give to his work the best that there is in him, and only by doing so is he giving value received. The man who goes out at night and so behaves that he arrives at the store in the morning nursing a dark brown taste and a sixty horse-power grouch, has encroached upon his employer's rights the night before and he can neither do justice to himself nor to his firm in his treatment of customers. These we think are some of the elements that constitute a good salesman.

ALL CLERKS CAN PROFIT BY THESE RULES

When the late H. M. Sampson, general manager of Rothschild & Company, one of Chicago's big department stores, once was asked how he worked himself up from a retail clerk to the general managership, he produced a typewritten set of rules by which he had guided his career and with which every clerk in the big store is familiar. The rules are applicable to salespeople in wholesale and retail paint stores, and they are given herewith because they point a lesson:

1. Take as much interest in your work as if you were the proprietor himself.
2. Acquire a thorough knowledge of the goods you are selling.
3. Cultivate a pleasing personality. Pleased customers mean increased sales, and increased sales mean successful salesmen.
4. Don't be content to simply fill orders. Anyone can be an order-taker, but it requires salesmanship to sell goods.
5. Constantly study your stock. More sales are lost through lack of knowledge concerning the goods than from any other cause.
6. Experience is the best teacher a salesman can have, and the same is true of any business.
7. The salesman who has brains, perseverance and initiative is certain to succeed.
8. Learn to judge human nature. This is the application of practical psychology to business.

DO YOU READ THE TRADE PAPERS?

The majority of dealers read the trade papers—that is, those papers that refer to his lines of business—because he realizes that the time is well spent, as there are always some new ideas worth having and lots of hints that help him keep up to date and alert to adopt suggestions in reaching out for business.

We sometimes wonder, however, if the boss realizes what a good thing it would be to make sure that his clerks read them as well.

EVERYDAY LIFE OF TRAVELERS
By J. C. Darcy

To begin with, what is a traveling man? A traveling man is the live wire which conveys the message of quality from the manufacturer to the dealer. There are two kinds of traveling men, first, the successful traveling man, or salesman; second, the unsuccessful traveling man, or order-taker. The successful traveling man, or salesman, is the man who goes out and gets orders by convincing the trade that he has the quality and value received, and is always on the job. The unsuccessful traveling man, or order-taker, is the one who takes what he can get, uses no argument to get more and always wants the price to sell the goods, and gives more time and attention to his personal pleasures than he does to selling goods.

The successful traveling man is envied because it is human nature to envy success. The unsuccessful traveling man is envied because from all appearances he has a life of ease and as they say "lives on the fat of the land." The successful traveling man performs the same function relative to the business he represents that the human heart does relative to the circulation. Consequently the successful traveling man is the heart and life of any successful mercantile enterprise, and it might not be amiss to set forth some of the necessary qualifications which a successful traveling man must have:

Honesty and integrity in all of his business transactions, thereby winning the confidence of his customers. He must be a good judge of human nature, better enabling him to approach with the least possible chance of offense. He must be quick to catch a customer's requirements and offer intelligent suggestions. He must be courteous to all at all times—he must be moral, he must be liberal—but not a spendthrift. He must not betray his customer's confidence, for he who carries tales is liable to lose business. He must not knock, as it centers attention on the other fellow and advertises him, or his goods. He must be more pleasant, if it were possible, when he does not get an order than he is when he gets one. He must get up early and hustle and make time count. Rest on Saturday, if he must, rather than any other week-day. Cover his territory systematically, keep his appointments promptly, let well enough alone, as "he who lets well enough alone never gets anything better."

A traveling man's environments while on the road are not always enviable. The road to success is not a smooth one. A traveling man's life is by no means enviable, and if he wins success, it is by constant and faithful application of time to duty.

The traveling man's life is a long and venturesome journey, away from friends and home. If he is deserving, treat him kindly and make him feel at home when he calls. The traveling man needs your friendship and you need his. Should the traveling man be called off the road you would have to revert to the catalogue house system of doing business, that is, buying "unsight and unseen," as we used to say when we were boys and traded knives when every boy was trying to get the poorest knife possible so as to stick the other fellow. The traveling man's life, as a whole, is not an enviable one.

HIS NOTEBOOK GOT HIM A RAISE

"Harris," said the boss as the junior clerk entered his private office, "do you ever think of any suggestions or ideas for the betterment of the business?"

"Once in a while," the junior clerk replied.

"Got any now?"

The junior clerk took a small notebook from his pocket and began to turn the pages. Now and then he would stop to ruminate a moment, then go on.

"About the best thing I can offer is this," he said at last. "Our lobby downstairs is too small. We do a business that brings a lot of people from the country who know nothing about the working of the store and how to get to the various departments. They stand around and get in each other's way and often become embarrassed and leave the place without even looking around and giving an order. Now what we should have would be a set of guides, something in the order of bellboys in a hotel, who would take these people to the departments to which they desire to go. When a man comes here to buy he usually expects to buy enough for us to afford spending a little money on him, and I think the guides would more than pay for themselves."

The boss jotted down the notation on a piece of paper. "Anything else?" he asked.

Harris turned the pages of his notebook and soon had given another idea. He turned a few more pages and then came forth with another. The boss smiled to himself and waved his hand.

"You have given some mighty good suggestions," he said, "but the best one hasn't come yet. Whatever put that idea of carrying a notebook into you head?"

Harris laughed in an embarrassed manner.

"Well," he began, "when it first became known that you wanted ideas for the betterment of the business I found that they did not come to me down here, but that they arrived after I got home in the evening and when my mind was free from other things. I tried to remember the ideas and invariably found I forgot them by the next morning, and so I just got this notebook to jot them down in that I might have them at hand when you asked me for them."

"That is the big idea I was talking about," said the boss. "If every one in this establishment carried a notebook and jotted down the ideas as they came to them business would jump $10,000 in a month. I am going to give orders this morning for seventy-five notebooks to be distributed to the entire office force, and, by the way, you remember that I said I would pay a bonus for ideas that helped? Yours will be a raise of $5 a week, beginning next Saturday."

"WHAT CAN I DO FOR YOU?"

A writer in Collier's recently made a psychological study of the many reasons why the inquiry, "What can I do for you?" is an extremely unfortunate, unsatisfactory and antique expression. We have not the space to reproduce the psychology of the matter, but suffice it to say that there are ample reasons why it gives many persons a mighty uncomfortable feeling to be greeted by this inane inquiry. In the first place, it is not the empty-headed salesman who simply repeats the formula, "What can I do for you?" who is rendering a service. The customer who comes into the store ready to lay down hard cash for stock is the one who is rendering the service. Let the salesman give a cordial greeting or an inquiry based upon some real thought. "Can I show you something?" is infinitely better than "What can I do for you?" Some of the little dubs who use the latter expression must get very much on the nerves of customers. Our suggestion is: Cut out this inquiry entirely in the retail store—or anywhere else—and get nearer the attitude of the visiting customer. Don't insult him, anyhow. A young salesman cannot be a tremendous benefactor to him in any event.

Knobs of News

The Helbert House Furnishing Co. has been registered at Montreal.

A. J. Bell & Co., Newcastle, N.B., have built a new furniture warehouse.

The furniture factories at Wingham, Ont., shut down during July for stock-taking.

Ruben Herscovitz has retired from the Dominion House Furnishing Co., Montreal.

The Globe Furniture Co., wholesale and retail dealers, Montreal, have been registered.

J. M. Gibson, lumber dealer and furniture man at Saltcoats, Sask., has sold his lumber yard.

R. K. McCammon has purchased the furniture and undertaking business of C. F. Edwards at Phoenix, B.C.

W. J. Mather, Wroxeter, Ont., has sold his furniture and undertaking business there to Robert Stocks, of Mindemoya.

A. A. McPherson, of Armstrong, B.C., has purchased the furniture and undertaking business of English & Blanchard, of that place.

Walker & McKay, dealers in furniture and carpets, Seaforth, Ont., have dissolved partnership, and the business is now conducted by Walker & Whitely.

J. C. McNabb & Co., house furnishers at Cobalt, Ont., have sold their Porcupine branch to Barton & Easton, who will continue the business along the same lines that have made the store successful in the past.

At the recent convention in Toronto of the Associated Ad. Clubs of the World, C. B. Hamilton, advertising manager of the Berkey & Gay Co., Grand Rapids, Mich., occupied the pulpit in Broadway Methodist Tabernacle the first night of the meeting.

The Reliance Moulding Co., Toronto, has been incorporated with a capital of $100,000, to take over the business of the Reliance Moulding Co. F. R. Phillips, W. H. Martin, and S. C. Spangenberg are provisional directors. Mouldings and picture frames will continue to be made.

W. Muldoon has opened a new furniture and furnishing store at 202 North May street, corner Leith, Fort William, Ont., under the name of Furnishers, Limited, with a full line of household necessities. Mr. Muldoon is by no means a stranger to the people of the Twin Cities, as he has been connected with the house furnishings business there for the last six or seven years.

One thousand dollars' damage was done by fire recently to the furniture store occupied by H. Sapiro & Co., 545 Barton street east, Hamilton, Ont. The fire evidently started in the rear, where mattresses are stored, and before the reels arrived the flames had got a firm hold, and it was with great difficulty that the fire was eventually got under control.

There is one town in Ontario that has no complaint to make about hard times. Elmira at present is experiencing a period of unusual prosperity. Buildings worth over $100,000 are now in course of construction, and improvements to the same value are being undertaken to buildings already erected. All the factories are running, the board of trade, with over 100 members, is active, and citizens generally are boosting the town. General satisfaction is expressed with conditions. Among the new buildings is an addition being put to the Elmira Furniture Factory.

NATIONAL HOME FURNISHERS' CONVENTION.

The third annual convention of the National Home Furnishers' Association was held in the Grand Central Palace, New York, on July 22, 23, and 24. The convention was called to order by the president, Henry L. Kincaide, and after the presentation of officers' reports, a number of addresses were delivered on interesting business topics. Among them were these subjects:

"Amalgamation of the Retail Furniture Trade," Raphael Levy, ex-president National Home Furnishers' Association, Philadelphia; "Fraudulent Advertising." Chas. A. Smith, president Mass. Home Furnishers' Association, Boston; "Organization and What It Means to the Trade," Paul F. Treanor, treasurer National Home Furnishers' Association, Saginaw, Mich.; "Factories Selling Direct," Alexander I. Lawson, president Jamestown, N.Y., Retail Furniture Dealers' Association, Jamestown, N.Y.; "Relation between Manufacturer and Retailer," John Trounstine, president New York Wholesale Furniture Association, Brooklyn; "Retailing From Manufacturers' Exhibits," John Buys, secretary, Grand Rapids Retail Dealers' Association, Grand Rapids; "One Line a Year," Chas. E. Spratt, New York Furniture Exchange.

WINNIPEG FIRM HAS WINNING BALL TEAM.

Banfield & Co., home furnishers, located on Main street, Winnipeg, believe in the old adage that "all work and no play makes Jack a dull boy." They believe that it is well for employes to forget business occasionally and indulge in some good healthy exercise, and as a means towards this end they give their

Banfield's Baseball Team.
Top row—Kellock, 3 b., Rigall, l.f., Tanney, 1 b., and captain, Smith, c. f., Bateson, s.s. Kneeling—Glendinning, r.f., Atkinson, 2 b. Sitting—Tackaberry, c., Neil, p. Mascots—Chas. Tanney and Jack Smith.

support and co-operation each year towards the formation of a baseball club among the employes of the store. Last year, with A. M. Tanney, manager of the store, as captain of the team, they got together a "nine" that was successful in winning the championship of the House Furnishing League. This year they entered in the Commercial League of Winnipeg, which is composed of the following teams:

Banfield & Co., John Leslie, furniture dealers; the Alaska Bedding Co., John Deere Plow Co., Carter, Hall & Elinger, Dingle & Stewart, Polin Chambers, and the McClary Mfg. Co.

In addition to affording a means of recreation for

the employes, the baseball team proves an excellent way for the members of the staff to become better acquainted.

FURNITURE MEN AT PLAY

The furniture travelers residing in Toronto, Hamilton, and Peterborough have organized a baseball club, and according to Jack McLaughlin, an authority on the game, "they are some team, believe me." If you don't think so, look at their "pitchures." Will H. Beney is captain of the team, and at their first game a month ago at Island Park, Toronto, they took into camp the Adams Furniture Co.'s sluggers to the tune of 25 to 19 or thereabouts.

The Adams team was made up of Coutie, Montgomery, Henderson, Coryell, Lebrun, Mitchell, McHattie, Jenner, and McDonough. While Coryell pitched a fine brand of ball, the sluggers on the other side connected at telling points. E. Bagshaw and W. Pearson were the battery for the winners. Griffin and Souter were the umpires and scorers, exchanging positions when they got tired shouting decisions.

The other members of the winning team were: Montgomery, Byron, Mackie, Lippert, Dunke, and Menzie.

The winners journeyed to Hamilton on July 8 and played the furniture retailers there at the ball grounds in Victoria Park before a couple of hundred spectators. The travelers brought along a number of rooters, too,

The Travellers' Winning Team.
Top row—L. Cohen, J. A. McLaughlin, B. Byron, A. Dunke, Ed. Lippert, W. Pearson. Middle row—J. Montgomery, Will H. Beney, E. Bagshaw, B. Menzie. Bottom row—J. Griffin and F. J. Mackie.

but the Hamilton boys put one over, defeating the travelers' aggregation 16 to 14. There is, however, some doubt about the score being correct, and there is still some controversy about it. The above result, however, seemed to please Louie Yolles, as he immediately issued a challenge to the travelers to play them a game and so wipe out the stain on Toronto's escutcheon.

Griffin pitched for the travelers and Pearson caught. The rest of the team was made up of Dunke, Montgomery, Mackie, Beney, Armstrong, Menzie, and Bateman. Bert Burroughes was umpire, and his decisions were ———. J. Montgomery and Billy Beney were captains of the losers.

Murray Souter pitched for the winners, the rest of the team being made up of P. Thompson, Goodman, Sterns, Kelly, Thompson, Nash, Stevenson, and R. Green. Dave Souter and Billy Sterns captained the winners.

The winning of the game was due chiefly to the efforts of George Falconer, who, despite all rules, persisted in doing the coaching. Bunches of lead pencils were offered as prizes to the home run getters, and souvenir bottles of jam were given to all hands. To salve the losers, a burlesque game was pulled off after the big event, in which Tom Inglis featured. Tom is some batter, but he will have to train in running if he wants to play baseball.

And, talking about Tom's running, the feature of the day's sports was a foot race between Bert Menzie and Tom Inglis for a prize of $2. They insisted on putting the money in an old lady's hand. Tom Inglis won, and when he went to collect the money the old lady had disappeared, and did not return.

After the game, Jim Doer took the players and visitors over to Dundurn Park, where refreshments were served and some more races run off.

FURNITURE OPENING AT GALT.

The newly-renovated furniture store of Allen & Ray at Galt, Ont., was the scene of a busy throng of visitors on the recent occasion of the opening of the new premises. The store donned holiday attire, and looked most attractive to the visitors. The large, bright windows were nicely illuminated with samples of the stock within, tastefully displayed.

The two floors were stocked with every style of new furniture, and the constant flow of complimentary comment must have been very gratifying to the proprietors. Cut flowers, palms, and ferns gave a festive air to the store, and as the visitors passed along the aisles inspecting the furniture the scene appeared very pleasing and bright indeed. The proprietors, W. F. Allen and D. Y. Ray, very courteously received their visitors, and with the aid of several assistants piloted the guests through the store, and, incidentally, made some sales. Nearly seven hundred visitors in all passed through the store during the afternoon and evening.

While all the furniture was admired, some suites or pieces came in for special attention. Among these were the beautiful Jacobean dining room and living room pieces. There are also bedroom suites in the lovely Circassian style. The gum wood furniture, with the Kyonyx finish, attracted considerable attention for its novelty.

The lovely summer furniture for the bungalow, the sun room, living room, or verandah, were shown upstairs, and admiring groups gathered about that section continually. The tanned fumed oak with tapestry coverings were shown for drawing room furniture, and a new style was introduced with the caned backs. The living room and den suites were shown in the latest styles, besides an array of brass beds, and the Ostermoor mattresses. Other articles that young brides would view with pleasure were the sectional book cases, kitchen cabinets, and the pretty complete ladies' secretaries.

Gave Away Prizes.

Three prize drawings were offered, and the tickets were very eagerly sought. The first prize was a handsome secretary, the second a music cabinet, and the third a pretty jardiniere stand. The lucky numbers were 441, 550, and 194. The second has been claimed by Mrs. Hugh Fayden, of Galt, and the others are to be claimed.

Messrs. Allen & Ray are receiving the hearty congratulations of their many friends on their successful opening, and every wish for a continuance of their prosperous beginning is expressed.

Furniture Exhibits at Panama-Pacific Exposition
By H. M. Wright

One may read much of the culture and civilization of a people in the architecture and adornment of the home. And, correspondingly, in proving its appearance and comforts must tend to the elevation of society and the refinement of the individual. To gather together in one place at one time the various styles and makes of furniture in use throughout the world must afford opportunities for comparison by visitors that will have an important educational result. Seeds of information

Samples of parlor tables from The George McLagan Furniture Co's. range.

sown by reason of these worldwide displays will bear fruit in foreign lands and for the welfare of many peoples. All this may be seen at the Panama-Pacific Exposition next year at San Francisco.

In one great group in the Department of Manufactures and Varied Industries will be displayed office and household furniture and utilities. In a single class will be exhibited sideboards, bookcases, tables, stands, beds, mirrors, desks, files, filing systems, cabinets, wardrobes, chiffoniers, chairs, settees, couches and lounges, billiard tables, vacuum cleaners, washing machines, etc.

It is perhaps a matter of interest to business men to consider aesthetic values as a part of business assets. The wide range of exhibits possible under the above classification not only forms a means for the extension of trade, but it constitutes an appeal to the better side of life, the love of the beautiful. We live in the home. In a way, the environment of nature is changed for that of art. The four walls of a room come to constitute the boundaries of the world. To make this "world" brighter is to make it better. So that in the business of selling furniture there is unlimited opportunity for placing before possible buyers not only replicas of historic styles, but new creations of artistic worth. This, then, is a distinctive business asset to all dealers, and the advantages of the exposition as an advertising medium by manufacturers in a rapidly growing country of the extent of Canada are great.

The whole Canadian exhibit will be a notable one. The first installment has arrived on the grounds, and the palaces are ready. As all the world knows, the Panama-Pacific Exposition is a national celebration of the construction and opening of the Panama Canal. And Canada has a stake in the canal. Canadian lumber and grain are to find readier egress to the east and west ports of the world through the new waterway. And there is to be a corresponding influence on trade and territorial development.

Coming back to furniture displays at the exposition, in whatever direction their advertising value may be considered, whether they indicate new fields to the buyer or the seller, the fact remains that Canadian business interests in this industry have an immense and rapidly developing country—a country filling with homes, in which to exploit furniture. And they can push the better makes of furniture as well as the more utilitarian, because, where immigration centres, there wealth concentrates. The exposition is the place to learn where to buy and what to sell, as well as how and where to sell. Moreover, the old and populous cities of Eastern Canada are legitimate grounds for pushing into the market the changing styles and new designs.

SPLENDID FURNITURE CATALOGUE.

The Charles Rogers & Sons Co., Limited, Toronto, manufacturers of high-grade furniture, have just issued a catalogue of their goods. It is a splendid example of the printers' art, run off as it is on calendered paper, which sets the illustrations up to advantage. Dining tables, buffets, china cabinets, side tables, arm chairs, diners, butlers' trays, tea curates, tea tables and trays, parlor and music cabinets, desks and writing tables, bookcases, rockers, davenports, pedestals, hall seats, umbrella stands, and similar articles are embraced in the line made by Rogers & Sons, and a very good idea of their worth is to be obtained by a glance through this catalogue, and the purchaser has the company's guarantee that every confidence may be placed in the construction and finish of the goods.

ELMIRA QUALITY FURNITURE.

"The Elmira Line" is the striking title of the Elmira Furniture Co.'s new 1914-1915 catalogue, just issued. This company makes diners, hall, and desk chairs, bedroom and parlor chairs and rockers, den and library furniture, office chairs and tilters, library, parlor, and card tables, umbrella and jardiniere stands, and footstools. All these goods are illustrated and described in this new catalogue, and many of them are new items. So comprehensive is the Elmira line, that over fifty pages are necessary to give an idea of their range. The catalogue is printed on coated paper and covered in green with gold and black letterpress. The illustration gives an idea of its artistic qualities.

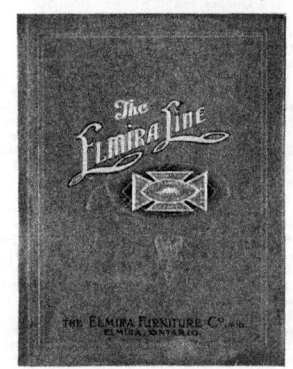

A New Town in West Every Week

By Norman S. Rankin

By no means the least important work of a great railway like the Canadian Pacific Railway is the establishment of new cities, towns, and villages along its lines. The development of the agricultural resources of Western Canada necessitates a continuous programme of railroad construction, and new lines are being rapidly carried into districts not hitherto served, and, at the same time, there is just as strong a necessity for these new towns, which arise almost automatically when there is sufficient demand for them.

The Canadian Pacific Railway, through its department of natural resources, is now engaged in locating these towns along its system in Western Canada wherever they are required. The great influx of immigration and the settlement of hitherto unpopulated farm lands, makes it essential to open up new townsites to correspond. The Canadian Pacific Railway has on its Western system, which extends from Fort William, Ont., at the head of the Great Lakes, to the Pacific coast, a total mileage of about 7,800, extending from the international boundary north, the most northerly point being Edmonton, which is about 315 miles from the boundary. This mileage is that in Canada only, and does not include the lines controlled by the company in the western parts of the United States. About 1,650 miles are in the Province of British Columbia, and about 350 miles in the western portion of Ontario, between Fort William and Lake of the Woods, leaving about 5,800 miles in the three prairie provinces of Manitoba, Saskatchewan, and Alberta, the wonderful agricultural district which the C. P. R. is now engaged in colonizing.

On this Western system there are nearly 1,200 cities, towns, and villages, ranging in size from big industrial centres, like Winnipeg, Vancouver, and Calgary, down to the smallest hamlets of a score or so of souls. Twenty-four out of these have a population of over five thousand, sixteen of over ten thousand, nine of over twenty thousand, five of over fifty thousand, two of over 100,000, and one (Winnipeg) of 260,000. The company's programme this year calls for the placing on the market of an average of one new townsite every week. These are mostly along the new railway lines, the most important of which in progress are the completion of the Weyburn to Lethbridge cut-off, which will tap the very rich agricultural districts of extreme Southern Saskatchewan and Alberta, the Bassano to Swift Current cut-off, which will provide for an alternative main line route, and the extension of the central Alberta branch, which runs from Lacombe, from its present terminus at Monitor, Alta., to Kerrobert, Sask., on the north main line branch from Winnipeg to Edmonton. Approximately five hundred miles of new line will be ready for operation or in operation by the end of 1914.

In placing new townsites upon the market, the Canadian Pacific Railway endeavors as much as possible to eliminate the element of speculation. The speculator's operations have not always conduced to the best interests of a new country like Western Canada, but have, on the contrary, sometimes had the effect of retarding its development by creating inflated values; and just as the company withdrew its six million acres of farm lands from sale to speculators, by imposing the conditions that all such lands bought must be occupied and developed, so in the case of townsites it tries to have those why buy town lots improve them instead of holding them out of use pending a rise in values. To that end, it has practically abolished the once popular system of auctioning town lots, and now sells only by list prices on the principle of first come first served, and by fixing a limit to the number of lots which can be acquired by one man; and in some cases it has granted a rebate where buildings to a stipulated value have been built within a stated time after the purchase.

There is often a tendency to underrate the importance of the small town, and to exalt the big city at its expense; but the small town has its own very definite place in the scheme of things, and plays a very useful part in the life of the community. It is the mart and business hub for the farmer. The volume of trade that passes through some unpretentious little Western town is sometimes amazing; in fact, it is a commonplace that a country store is often a very much more profitable proposition than one in a big city. The small town serves as the social centre of the surrounding district. To it the farmer comes to church, to dances, and to other happenings, as well as to sell his wheat or to buy his household commodities; and, while it is small, it is generally quietly prosperous, and its prosperity reflects the success of those who are tributary to it.

DAVENPORT FACTORY FOR STRATFORD.

The Stratford Davenport Co., Ltd., has been incorporated at Stratford, Ont., with a capital of $25,000, by Ernest William Forsberg, Adolph Alfred Leipold, Samuel Bell Kind, Gustav Adolph Wenzel, John Paul Reder, Joseph Oimak, Michael Reder, W. C. August Leipold, Louis Andrew Schuler, and W. C. F. Leipold, all of Chicago, to make and sell furniture, especially davenports.

MISSING AN OPPORTUNITY.

The tenth annual convention of the Associated Advertising Clubs of America, held in Toronto last month, was, from the point of the retail dealer, whether furniture man or not, one of the best conventions ever held in Canada. One whole section was devoted to the question of "Retail Advertising," and in that department were given the views, opinions, and experiences of men from various parts of the United States and Canada—men who have devoted their whole lives to the problems affecting their business—men who began at the bottom of the ladder and worked to the top through sheer force of energy and ability—and they gave their views freely to those who are themselves passing through these stages, and who cared to listen and question.

Retail dealers who had an opportunity of listening to the papers and subsequent discussions and neglected the opportunity missed many valuable helps to bring success to their business.

From time to time during the next few months Canadian Furniture World will endeavor to give summaries of some of the important papers, so that some at least of the helps and hints may be placed at the disposal of our readers.

The Furniture Manufacturer

A Department of News and Ideas

Furniture Factory Short-Cuts

The further manufacturers and consumers of dimension stock go with the proposition, the more numerous do its advantages become. The general, basic arguments in favor of using lumber cut to size have long been familiar to the trade; but the detailed benefits appear only with actual trial of the proposition.

Experience is beginning to accumulate, and the results are the more impressive by reason of the improvements brought about, from every angle. In a word, dimension stock has not only made good, but it has made good in more ways than it had been expected to do, and the latter features furnish a strong argument in favor of the more general use of the plan.

For example, it was pointed out not long ago that consumers are insisting more than ever before on carrying small stocks, and on getting just enough lumber to ensure a sufficient supply at all times. The dimension stock plan fits into this mode of operation as though designed for it, and the experience of a number of furniture factories in this connection is enlightening.

When ordinary lumber is purchased, it is necessary to kiln-dry it, of course, before putting it through the factory. It is next to impossible to arrange receipts of lumber on so exact a schedule to keep the kiln filled and to ensure an ample supply of dry lumber constantly being available. The result is that, whether the consumer wants to or not, he is compelled to carry a surplus of considerable extent, and the rehandling of this lumber, from the car to the yard and from the yard to the kiln, is an added expense which an ideal operation of the system would get away from.

This is accomplished by means of the dimension system. The manufacturer of lumber cut to size kiln-dries his lumber before cutting it up, and as a matter of course keeps a considerable quantity of dry stock on hand. When he gets an order for dimension lumber, all that is necessary is to cut the stock to size and ship. Thus the consumer is nearer to his supply of material by the length of time required to dry under ordinary conditions, and is consequently that much better off when it comes to planning his purchases and arranging his manufacturing operations.

In fact, experience has shown that the plan of having a steady supply of lumber move from the manufacturer to the factory consumer can be handled more conveniently when dimension lumber is used than when ordinary stock is shipped. If the plan of the consumer has been to carry a considerable stock of lumber, and have enough kiln-dried stock on hand to keep the machine room supplied at all times, the use of the facilities of the lumberman enables him to reduce his investment in stock and to have shipments made against his actual requirements and not against his future needs.

In this connection another advantage has been discovered. The manufacturer who heretofore has carried a considerable amount of lumber on his yard, in order to have plenty of stock ready for the kiln, or who has had a good deal of money tied up in dry stock, awaiting the needs of the cutting department, is now able to take the same money, put it into dimension stock, and be ready to surface the material, and send it to the cabinet room at a moment's notice.

In other words, the furniture manufacturer has heretofore been "up against it" on the matter of deliveries, in a good many cases, because of the difficulty of getting out special lots in less than sixty days. In fact, many furniture men assert that it is impossible to do justice to the work and put a piece of furniture through, from the kiln to the car door, in less than two months.

The peculiar trade conditions in this business emphasize the disadvantage of not being able to ship quickly. Usually the retailer does not order until the last minute, and when he wants a piece of furniture or a carload of it, he usually wants it in a hurry to take care of demand which is developing at that time. Delay in getting the goods to him is frequently fatal, and interferes with the success of the manufacturer. But since he is not in a position to anticipate the demand, except in the case of staples which can be depended upon, he is compelled to wait for orders, and then must rush in order to get them out in time for use by the retailer.

That makes the big advantage of being several important steps in advance of the usual procedure all the more desirable. If, instead of putting the lumber through the kiln and then having it cut to size in his own machine room, he can take the dimension lumber from stock, where it was carried for just such an emergency, he can save from three to four weeks in getting out the goods. And that much time is often the difference between holding a customer by good service and losing him because of slow deliveries.

The flour miller seldom carries the finished goods in stock. The chief reason is that flour values are much greater than wheat, and interest, insurance, and other carrying charges mount up too high to make it profitable or practicable to have a very large supply of flour ahead. But the miller does carry wheat in stock—all he can afford to buy when the market is right. He wants to have his material where he can get it at short notice, and in such shape that he will not be delayed in beginning the important work of converting grain into flour.

The furniture manufacturers have learned that they can play the same sort of game in connection with dimension stock. Instead of manufacturing their furniture complete, and carrying it in stock, a procedure which is difficult and dangerous, from the standpoint of policy, because of the absence of exact knowledge on the subject of demand, they work up their raw material as far as possible, under the restrictions necessarily imposed, and are thus ready, at any time the demand for a given item develops, to begin its manufacture at a point much further along than would ordinarily be the case. Even in the case of numbers which are doubtful sellers, standard parts can be provided, so that only the odd items need to be made up when the order comes in.

"We make a wide and constantly changing range of styles," said a furniture man not long ago, "but we have found it to be a considerable advantage to put in a big stock of standard parts, such as legs, tops, etc. We order these for practically the entire season's requirements, as we see them, and then specify deliveries from time to time in sufficient quantity to give us a big stock of this material. The process of manufacturing, when orders are received, is considerably shortened. We have much of the material, even on the numbers regarding the demand for which we are not certain, already made up, and the work of getting it out is therefore greatly expedited. This, we believe, is one of the greatest advantages of using dimension stock, from the standpoint of the consumer."

A point which dimension men have been quick to take note of is that the cost of handling a great number of small pieces is much larger than the expense involved in taking care of the same footage of lumber of standard lengths. Consequently, in order to meet this objection, furniture material is now shipped in bundles, secured with wire, so that a car can be unloaded quickly and economically.

In the same connection it is worth noting that the dimension men are performing a service not unlike that of the veneer manufacturers, some of whom match and tape veneers so that they are ready to lay when received at the factory. That is, in many cases the dimension manufacturer matches up lumber that is to be joined, rips it to size, and keeps the various pieces together in the bundle, so that each top is an unit, and the consumer is assured of having uniformity as to color and figure. This is a real service to the factory man, who ordinarily makes many blunders in setting out solid tops through being unable to secure uniformity in these respects.

These and many other practical advantages, which are developed only by actual operation of the system, have served to win many permanent customers for dimension stock manufacturers, and to increase the business of those mills which provide the right kind of service regarding such things as matching up, inspection, etc.—Hardwood Record.

CHIPPENDALE CHAIR MODEL

Designers and manufacturers are continually searching the museums and by-ways of the antiquities for specimens of pure period styles. The Chippendale chair illustrated herewith is an accurate reproduction of an original now in possession of the Metropolitan Museum of Art, New York, and for purity of design, accuracy of detail workmanship, it is as near perfect as is possible. The chair is the work of John Helmsky, New York, who has secured permission to make copies of any other pieces now in the Museum.

LOCATION AFFECTS MACHINERY EFFICIENCY

A man who owns a woodworking establishment was having trouble with his exhaust fan. This fan would work all right for most of the day, but at five o'clock, or just before quitting time, it would get stuffed and have to be cleaned out. The boss thought he would have to get a new machine. One day, however, a friend who, by the way, was a competitor in the same line, was going through the plant, and the manager complained to him about the fan and asked if a new one was needed. Right there the friend pointed out that the fan in question was all right, and that all it needed was a change of location.

At the time, the heavy machinery in the factory was placed on the ground floor and the rest on the second floor, while the boiler and the exhaust blower were in the basement. With this arrangement, the shavings dropped right into the fan and had to be moved but a short distance to the shavings bin. Just before closing time, however, with the blocks and shavings coming down in bunches, the fan soon got clogged, owing to the fact that the pulling power of any exhaust fan is limited.

The friend suggested that the fan be placed on the ground floor or on the second storey, and the suction pipes arranged so that the air must lift the refuse into the pipes. This was done and there has been no trouble since.

DOUBLING DUTIES OF SPRINKLER SYSTEM

"Why not connect the sprinkler equipment with the hot water heating system and so gain this much additional radiating surface"? thought the Gray & Davis Company when they put up their new reinforced concrete factory building. A difficulty presented itself with regard to the effect of the hot water upon the sprinkler heads which open at 155 deg. Fahrenheit. This was overcome by attaching the heads on extensions of small piping, the effect of which is to cool below the danger point the water that collects in these dead ends. The circulation is thus confined to the main pipes only. The adoption of the beam-and-girderless type of construction was an aid to this double functioning of the sprinkler piping, since there are no projections from the ceiling to form heat pockets and obstruct the free movement of the air along the ceiling. This type of construction also assists the natural illumination which in this case is seen to be remarkably good. Adequate general illumination is furnished at night and on dark days by tungsten lamps with deep reflectors. Additional lamps similarly equipped are provided over benches.—Factory.

Authentic Model Chippendale Chair.

Above Illustration Represents one of our Toronto Buildings. We are also Erecting Buildings in a Number of Other Parts of Canada.

INTERNATIONAL MAUSOLEUM COMPANY
LIMITED

OFFICES: 14, 15 and 16 FIRST FLOOR NATIONAL TRUST BLDG.

20 EAST KING STREET
(Right close to corner of King and Yonge Streets)

TORONTO, ONT., CANADA

THIS is to inform you that A. J. H. Eckardt, late proprietor of National Casket Company and National Silver Plate Company, of Toronto, Ont., has accepted the Presidency and General Management of the International Mausoleum Company, and would be glad to correspond or receive interviews with parties in all parts of Canada as regards erecting these beautiful patent Mausoleums, which are thoroughly sanitary and much superior in every way to Cemetery Grave form of burial, and again not only much superior but much more reasonable when taking into consideration the cost of grave plots and monuments also; again the cost and worry of keeping these plots in order annually is entirely done away with by the adoption of mausoleum burial. These beautiful buildings are PERPETUAL, whereas cemeteries are not and are so often disturbed in the way of being moved, etc. Another agreeable feature in connection with the Mausoleum is that when people are in deep trouble and do not care just at the time about selecting a family group of crypts, arrangements can be made to purchase one crypt only and then can decide later on as regards the selection of a family section, and if so can arrange a credit for the previous purchase. When arranging with parties as regards building a mausoleum in your town, if you write us we will gladly have someone call and talk matters over with you, and also forward you a lot of very important literature bearing upon the beautiful mausoleum burial proposition.

As Toronto Exposition is now near at hand A. J. H. Eckardt would be glad to see any of the Funeral Directors and their friends and talk matters over generally as regards old times and also the erection of mausoleums in different parts of the country.

INTERNATIONAL MAUSOLEUM COMPANY, LIMITED
TORONTO, ONT., CANADA

BUYER'S DIRECTORY

When writing to advertisers kindly mention the
Canadian Furniture World and the Undertaker

ARTS AND CRAFTS FURNITURE
Geo. McLagan Furniture Co., Stratford.
John C. Mundell & Co., Elora.

ASBESTOS TABLE COVERS
Canadian H. W. Johns-Manville Co., Toronto.

BABY CARRIAGES
Gendron Mfg. Co., Toronto.

AWNINGS
Stamco, Limited, Saskatoon, Sask.

BENT WOOD FURNITURE
John C. Mundell & Co., Elora.
J. & J. Kohn, Toronto (W. Craig).

BOOKCASES
Knechtel Furniture Co., Hanover.
Globe Wernicke Co., Stratford.
Geo. McLagan Furniture Co., Stratford.
Meaford Mfg. Co., Meaford, Ont.

BUFFETS
Bell Furniture Co., Southampton, Ontario.
Knechtel Furniture Co., Hanover.
Geo. McLagan Furniture Co., Stratford.
Meaford Mfg. Co., Meaford, Ont.
Peppler Bros., Hanover.
Stratford Chair Co., Stratford.
Victoriaville Furniture Co., Victoriaville, Que.

BEDS (Brass and Iron)
Canada Beds, Ltd., Chesley.
Ideal Bedding Co., Toronto.
Geo. Gale & Son, Waterville, Que.
Ives Modern Bedstead Co., Cornwall Ont.
Ontario Spring Bed & Mattress Co., London, Ont.
Standard Bedstead Co., Victoriaville, Que.
Stamco, Limited, Saskatoon, Sask.
Stratford Bed Co., Stratford, Ont.
S. Weisglass, Ltd., Montreal, Que.

BEDS (Modern Wood)
Elora Furniture Co., Elora.
Knechtel Furniture Co., Hanover.

BED SPRINGS
Colleran Spring Mattress Co., Toronto.
Knechtel Furniture Co., Hanover.
Frame and Hay Fence Co., Stratford.
Gold Medal Furniture Co., Toronto
Leggett & Platt Spring Bed Co., Windsor.
Ideal Bedding Co., Toronto.
Ontario Spring Bed & Mattress Co., London, Ont.
Stamco, Limited, Saskatoon, Sask.
S. Weisglass, Ltd, Montreal, Que.

BED ROOM CHAIRS
Baetz Bros., Berlin.
Bell Furniture Co., Southampton, Ontario.
Elmira Furniture Co, Elmira, Ont.
Lippert Furniture Co., Berlin.

BEDROOM ROCKERS
Lippert Furniture Co., Berlin, Ont.

BED ROOM SUITES
Bell Furniture Co., Southampton, Ontario.
Knechtel Furniture Co., Hanover.
Meaford Mfg. Co., Meaford.
Victoriaville Furniture Co., Victoriaville, Que.

BEDROOM TABLES
Chesley Furniture Co., Chesley, Ontario.

BUNGALOW CHAIRS & SUITES
Baetz Bros. & Co., Berlin, Ont.

CARD AND DEN TABLES
Chesley Furniture Co., Chesley, Ontario.
Geo. McLagan Furniture Co., Stratford.
John C. Mundell & Co., Elora, Ont.

CARPET RACKS
Steel Furnishing Co., New Glasgow, N. S.

CAMP FURNITURE
Southampton Seating Co., Southampton, Ont.
Stratford Mfg. Co., Stratford.
Ideal Bedding Co., Toronto.

CEDAR BOXES
D. L. Shafer, St. Thomas, Ont.

CELLARETTES
John C. Mundell & Co., Elora, Ont.

CHAIRS AND ROCKERS
Bell Furniture Co., Southampton,
J. P. Albrough & Co., Ingersoll.
Baetz Bros., Berlin.
Knechtel Furniture Co., Hanover.
John C. Mundell & Co., Elora.
Stratford Chair Co., Stratford.
Waterloo Furniture Co., Waterloo.
Canadian Rattan Chair Co., Victoriaville.
Gold Medal Furniture Co., Toronto.
Elmira Furniture Co, Elmira, Ont.
Imperial Furniture Co., Toronto.
Lippert Furniture Co., Berlin.
Victoriaville Chair Mfg. Co., Victoriaville.

CHESTERFIELDS
Imperial Furniture Co., Toronto.

CHIFFONIERS
Bell Furniture Co., Southampton, Ont.
Knechtel Furniture Co., Hanover.
Meaford Mfg. Co., Meaford, Ont.
Stratford Chair Co., Stratford.
Victoriaville Furniture Co., Victoriaville, Que.

CHILDRENS' SULKIES
Jennings Co., St. Thomas

CHINA CABINETS
Bell Furniture Co., Southampton, Ontario.
Peppler Bros., Hanover.
Knechtel Furniture Co., Hanover.
Geo. McLagan Furniture Co., Stratford.
Meaford Mfg. Co., Meaford, Ont.

CLOCK CASES
Elmira Interior Woodwork Co., Elmira, Ont.

COMFORTERS
Toronto Feather & Down Co., Toronto.
Stamco, Limited, Saskatoon, Sask.

COTS
Ideal Bedding Co., Toronto.
Ontario Spring Bed and Mattress Co., London.

COSTUMIERS
Elmira Interior Woodwork Co., Elmira, Ont.

COUCHES
J. P. Albrough & Co., Ingersoll.
Ellis Furniture Co., Ingersoll.
Gold Medal Furniture Co., Toronto.
Kindel Bed Co., Toronto.
Imperial Furniture Co., Toronto.
John C. Mundell & Co., Elora, Ont.
Montreal Upholstering Co., Montreal.
Steel Furnishing Co., New Glasgow, N. S.
S. Weisglass, Ltd., Montreal, Que.

COUCHES (Sliding)
Ideal Bedding Co., Toronto.
Farquharson-Gifford Co., Stratford.
Ontario Spring Bed & Mattress Co., London, Ont.
Stamco, Limited, Saskatoon, Sask.
Gold Medal Furniture Co., Toronto.

COUCH FRAMES
Southampton Seating Co., Southampton, Ont.

CRADLES
Knechtel Furniture Co., Hanover.

CRIBS (Brass and Iron)
Ideal Bedding Co., Toronto.
Ontario Spring Bed & Mattress Co., London, Ont.
Stamco, Limited, Saskatoon, Sask.
S. Weisglass, Ltd., Montreal, Que.

CUSHIONS
Stamco, Limited, Saskatoon, Sask.

DAVENPORT BEDS
Farquharson-Gifford Co., Stratford,
Kindel Bed Co., Toronto.
Lippert Furniture Co., Berlin, Ont.
Montreal Upholstering Co., Montreal, Que.
Imperial Rattan Co., Stratford.
John C. Mundell & Co., Elora.

DAVENPORT FRAMES
Elmira Interior Woodwork Co., Elmira, Ont.

DEN FURNITURE
Elmira Furniture Co., Elmira, Ont.
Farquharson-Gifford Co., Stratford.
John C. Mundell & Co., Elora, Ont.

DIVANETTES
Lippert Furniture Co., Berlin.

DESKS
Bell Furniture Co., Southampton,
Elmira Interior Woodwork Co., Elmira.
Knechtel Furniture Co., Hanover.
Geo. McLagan Furniture Co., Stratford.
John C. Mundell & Co., Elora.
Stratford Desk Co., Stratford, Ont.

DINING-ROOM FURNITURE
Crown Furniture Co., Preston.
Farquharson-Gifford Co., Stratford.
Lippert Furniture Co., Berlin, Ont.

DINING SUITES
Bell Furniture Co., Southampton,
Knechtel Furniture Co., Hanover.
Geo. McLagan Furniture Co., Stratford.
John C. Mundell & Co., Elora.
Peppler Bros., Hanover.
Stratford Chair Co., Stratford.

DINERS
Lippert Furniture Co., Berlin, Ont.

DINNER WAGONS
Geo. McLagan Furniture Co., Stratford.
Peppler Bros., Hanover.

DRESSERS
Bell Furniture Co., Southampton,
Knechtel Furniture Co., Hanover.
Stratford Chair Co., Stratford.
Victoriaville Furniture Co., Victoriaville, Que.
Meaford Mfg. Co., Meaford, Ont.

EXTENSION TABLES
Bell Furniture Co., Southampton,
Berlin Table Mfg. Co., Berlin.
Chesley Furniture Co., Chesley, Ontario.
Peppler Bros., Hanover.
Meaford Mfg. Co., Meaford, Ont.

FILING DEVICES
Elmira Interior Woodwork Co., Elmira.
Globe Wernicke Co., Stratford.
Knechtel Furniture Co., Hanover.
Geo. McLagan Furniture Co., Stratford.

FILING CABINETS
Globe Wernicke Co., Stratford, Ont.

FOLDING CHAIRS
Ideal Bedding Co., Toronto.
Southampton Seating Co., Southampton, Ont.
Stratford Mfg. Co., Stratford.

FOLDING TABLES
Chesley Furniture Co., Chesley, Ontario.
Hoord & Co., London.
Stratford Mfg. Co., Stratford.

FOOTSTOOLS
Elmira Furniture Co., Elmira, Ont.

GRASS FURNITURE (Chinese)
Jennings Co., St. Thomas

HALL RACKS
Lippert Furniture Co., Berlin, Ont.
Chesley Furniture Co., Chesley, Ontario.

HALL SEATS AND MIRRORS
Chesley Furniture Co., Chesley, Ontario.
Geo. McLagan Furniture Co., Stratford.
Lippert Furniture Co., Berlin, Ont.
Meaford Mfg. Co., Meaford, Ont.

HALL TREES
Chesley Furniture Co., Chesley, Ontario.
Geo. McLagan Furniture Co., Stratford.

HAMMOCKS
Dominion Hammock Mfg. Co., Dunnville, Ont.

HAMMO-COUCHES
Ideal Bedding Co., Toronto.

INVALID CHAIRS
Gendron Mfg. Co., Toledo, Ohio.
Victoriaville Chair Mfg. Co., Victoriaville, Que.

IRONING BOARDS AND DRYERS
Chesley Furniture Co., Chesley, Ontario.
Stratford Mfg. Co., Stratford.

JARDINIERE STANDS
Chesley Furniture Co., Chesley, Ontario.
Elmira Furniture Co, Elmira, Ont.
Elora Furniture Co., Elora.
Geo. McLagan Furniture Co., Stratford.
Meaford Mfg. Co., Meaford, Ont.

KITCHEN CABINETS
H. E. Furniture Co., Milverton,
Nagrella Mfg. Co., Hamilton.
Knechtel Kitchen Cabinet Co. Ltd., Hanover, Ont.

KITCHEN TABLES
Chesley Furniture Co., Chesley, Ontario.
Knechtel Furniture Co., Hanover.
Victoriaville Furniture Co., Victoriaville.

LADIES' DESKS
Meaford Mfg. Co., Meaford, Ont.

LAWN SEATS AND SWINGS
Southampton Seating Co., Southampton, Ont.
Stratford Mfg. Co., Stratford.

LIBRARY TABLES
Bell Furniture Co., Southampton,
Chesley Furniture Co., Chesley, Ontario.
Peppler Bros., Hanover.
Elmira Furniture Co., Elmira, Ont.
Elmira Interior Woodwork Co., Elmira, Ont.
Geo. McLagan Furniture Co., Stratford.
Meaford Mfg. Co., Meaford, Ont.
John C. Mundell & Co., Elora, Ont.

LIVING-ROOM FURNITURE
Lippert Furniture Co., Berlin, Ont.

LOUNGES
J. P. Albrough & Co., Ingersoll.

LUXURY CHAIRS
Lippert Furniture Co., Berlin.

MAGAZINE RACKS AND STANDS
Chesley Furniture Co., Chesley, Ontario.
Geo. McLagan Furniture Co., Stratford.

MATTRESSES
Berlin Bedding Co., Toronto.
Canada Mattress Co., Victoriaville, Que.
Gold Medal Bedding Co., Toronto.
McKellar Bedding Co., Port William, Ont.
Ontario Spring Bed & Mattress Co., London, Ont.
Stamco, Limited, Saskatoon, Sask.
Standard Bedding Co., Toronto.
Antiseptic Bedding Co., Toronto.
Ideal Bedding Co., Toronto.
Fischman Mattress Co., Toronto.

MANTELS—Wood, Tile
Elmira Interior Woodwork Co., Elmira, Ont.

MANTELS—Electric
Elmira Interior Woodwork Co., Elmira, Ont.

MEDICINE CABINETS
Chesley Furniture Co., Chesley, Ontario.
Meaford Mfg. Co., Meaford, Ont.

MORRIS CHAIRS
Ellis Furniture Co., Ingersoll.
Imperial Rattan Co., Stratford.
Knechtel Furniture Co., Hanover.
Lippert Furniture Co., Berlin, Ont.
John C. Mundell & Co., Elora.
Waterloo Furniture Co., Waterloo.

MUSIC CABINETS
Geo. McLagan Furniture Co., Stratford.
Knechtel Kitchen Cabinet Co., Ltd., Hanover, Ont.

ODD CHAIRS
Lippert Furniture Co., Berlin, Ont.

OFFICE CHAIRS
Bell Furniture Co., Southampton,
Elmira Furniture Co., Elmira, Ont.
Knechtel Furniture Co., Hanover.
H. Krug Furniture Co., Berlin.
Stratford Chair Co., Stratford.
J. & J. Kohn, Toronto (W. Craig).
John C. Mundell & Co., Elora, Ont.

OFFICE TABLES
Stratford Desk Co., Stratford, Ont.

PARK SEATS
Southampton Seating Co., Southampton, Ont.
Stratford Mfg. Co., Stratford.

PARLOR CHAIRS and ROCKERS
Ellis Furniture Co., Ingersoll.
Elmira Interior Woodwork Co., Elmira.
John C. Mundell & Co., Elora, Ont.
Waterloo Furniture Co., Waterloo.

PARLOR FRAMES
Elmira Interior Woodwork Co., Elmira.

PARLOR SUITES
Ellis Furniture Co., Ingersoll.
Knechtel Furniture Co., Hanover.
Waterloo Furniture Co., Waterloo.
Gold Medal Furniture Co., Toronto.
Lippert Furniture Co., Berlin.

PARLOR TABLES
Chesley Furniture Co., Chesley, Ontario.
Geo. McLagan Furniture Co., Stratford.
Meaford Mfg. Co., Meaford, Ont.
Elora Furniture Co., Elora.
Elmira Furniture Co., Elmira, Ont.
Knechtel Furniture Co., Hanover.
Peppler Bros., Hanover.

PEDESTALS
Lippert Furniture Co., Berlin, Ont.
Geo. McLagan Furniture Co., Stratford.
Peppler Bros., Hanover.

PILLOWS
Ontario Spring Bed & Mattress Co., London, Ont.
Stamco, Limited, Saskatoon, Sask.
Toronto Feather & Down Co., Toronto.
Ideal Bedding Co., Toronto.

PILLOW SHAM HOLDERS
Tarbox Mfg. Co., Toronto.

RATTAN FURNITURE
Imperial Rattan Co., Stratford.
Canadian Rattan Chair Co., Victoriaville, Que.
Gendron Mfg. Co., Toronto.

RECLINING CHAIRS
Ellis Furniture Co., Ingersoll.
Knechtel Furniture Co., Hanover.
Lippert Furniture Co., Berlin, Ont.
John C. Mundell & Co., Elora, Ont.

RUG RACKS
Steel Furnishing Co., New Glasgow, N. S.

SECTIONAL BOOKCASES
Knetchel Furniture Co., Hanover.
Globe Wernicke Co., Stratford.

SCHOOL FURNITURE
Bell Furniture Co., Southampton.

SIDEBOARDS
Knechtel Furniture Co., Hanover.
Meaford Mfg. Co., Meaford, Ont.
Stratford Chair Co., Stratford.

STORE FRONTS
Kawneer Mfg. Co., Toronto.

TABLES
Berlin Table Mfg. Co., Berlin, Ont.
Bell Furniture Co., Southampton, Ontario.
Elora Furniture Co., Elora.
Knechtel Furniture Co., Hanover.
John C. Mundell & Co., Elora.
Orillia Furniture Co., Orillia.
Peppler Bros., Hanover.
Stratford Chair Co., Stratford.
Victoriaville Furniture Co., Victoriaville, Que.

TABOURETTES
Elora Furniture Co., Elora.
Kensington Furniture Co., Goderich.

TAPESTRY CURTAINS
Dominion Hammock Mfg. Co., Dunnville, Ont.

TELEPHONE STANDS
John C. Mundell & Co., Elora, Ont.

TYPEWRITER DESKS
Elmira Interior Woodwork Co., Elmira.
Stratford Desk Co., Stratford, Ont.

UPHOLSTERERS' SUPPLIES
Ellis Furniture Co., Ingersoll.
Gold Medal Furniture Co., Toronto.

UPHOLSTERED FURNITURE
Baetz Bros., Berlin.
Ellis Furniture Co., Ingersoll.
Farquharson-Gifford Co., Stratford, Ont.

Imperial Rattan Co., Stratford.
Imperial Furniture Co., Elora.
John C. Mundell & Co., Elora.
Knechtel Furniture Co., Hanover.
Waterloo Furniture Co., Waterloo.
Gold Medal Furniture Co., Toronto.

QUALITY FURNITURE
Quality Furniture Makers, Welland.
A. J. Scafe & Co., Berlin.

VACUUM CLEANERS
Onward Mfg. Co., Berlin.

VERANDAH FURNITURE
Imperial Rattan Co., Stratford.
Southampton Seating Co., Southampton, Ont.
Stratford Mfg. Co., Stratford.

WARDROBES
Knechtel Furniture Co., Hanover
Meaford Mfg. Co., Meaford, Ont.
Stratford Chair Co., Stratford.

FACTORY SUPPLIES

BRASS TRIMMINGS
Stratford Brass Co., Stratford.

CLAMPS
Batavia Clamp Co., Batavia, N.Y.

FURNITURE SHOES
Onward Mfg. Co., Berlin.

DRY KILNS
Morton Dry Kiln Co., Chicago

FURNITURE HARDWARE
Stratford Brass Co., Stratford, Ont.

GLUE JOINTING MACHINES
Canadian Linderman Co., Woodstock.

NAILS
P. L. Robertson Mfg. Co., Milton.

PLATING
P. L. Robertson Mfg. Co., Milton, Ontario.

RIVETS AND SCREWS
P. L. Robertson Mfg. Co., Milton.

SPRINGS
James Steele, Guelph.
Ideal Bedding Co., Toronto.

SPANISH LEATHER
Lackawanna Leather Co., Hackettstown, N. J.

STERILIZED HAIR
Griffin Curled Hair Co., Toronto.

TABLE SLIDES
B. Walter & Co., Wabash, Ind.

TRUCKS
W. I. Kemp Co., Ltd., Stratford.

VARNISHES
R. C. Jamieson & Co., Montreal.
Ault & Wiborg, Toronto.

VENEERS
Adams & Raymond Veneer Co., Indianapolis, Ind.

VENEER PRESSES
Wm. R. Perrin & Co., Toronto.

WASHERS
P. L. Robertson Mfg. Co., Milton.

"20TH CENTURY" RUG RACKS AND LINOLEUM RACKS

SAVE LABOR. MAKE QUICK SALES. PAY PERPETUAL DIVIDENDS.

THE GREATEST SILENT SALESMAN ON EARTH. THOUSANDS IN USE TODAY.

ASK FOR CATALOGUE

THE STEEL FURNISHING CO., LIMITED
NEW GLASGOW, N.S.

STEELE'S STANDARD SOFA SPRINGS

If you are a maker of high grade Upholstered Furniture you should use our Springs. We positively guarantee that our Springs will never set, and the prices will please you too.

Makers of Sofa Springs since 1886

JAMES STEELE, Limited, Guelph, Ont.

Invalid Chairs and Tricycles of every description.

This has been our study for thirty-five years. We build chairs that suit the requirements of any cases. Write us for catalogue No. 20 and prices, if interested.

Gendron Wheel Co., Toledo, O. U.S.A.

READ THIS ISSUE FROM COVER TO COVER

Then you will agree that this Paper is worth ten times the price.

$1.00 per Year
Send Your Subscription in to-day.

THE COMMERCIAL PRESS, LIMITED
32 Colborne Street, Toronto.

For Sale — Wanted

TERMS FOR INSERTION
25 Cents per line, one insertion
Four lines once for $1.00, three times for $2.00.
Cash must accompany the order
No accounts booked.

MINIMUM 50 CENTS

FURNITURE and House Furnishing business for sale. Good town. Surrounding country in British Columbia. Reasons for selling, failing health. For full particulars apply Box 128, Canadian Furniture World and The Undertaker, 32 Colborne St., Toronto. 11-8-3

FOR SALE—Undertaking business in an excellent town in Ontario, with large country trade. A golden opportunity and a bargain for quick sale. Best reasons for selling. Box 641, Canadian Furniture World and The Undertaker, 32 Colborne St., Toronto. 11-8-3

FOR SALE—Furniture and Undertaking business in Western Canada. For particulars write at once to Mrs. A. Metcalf, Treherne, Man. 11-7-3

FOR SALE—Double deck casket wagon, built by Cunningham, Rochester; cost $800.00; very little used; cheap for quick sale. Photo on application. Box 129, Canadian Furniture World and The Undertaker, 32 Colborne St., Toronto. 11-8-1

FOR SALE—Furniture and Undertaking in town of Staynor; established twenty years. Forced to give up business on account of getting disabled. Act quick — low rent. Address D. Mathers, Staynor, Ont. 11-8-1

VENEER PRESSES WANTED—Several second hand veneer presses wanted. Send full particulars to Brantford Piano Case Co., Brantford, Ont.

FOR SALE Four hearses, sell at half price, going out of the hearse business. Our hearses are made of the very best stock, English College axles and best workmanship. Also wagonettes and three seated carriages. Write for particulars. W. J. Thompson & Son, London, Ont. 14-8-3

Dominion Casket Co., Limited

Telephones: { Day No. 1020. Nights, Sundays and Holidays Nos. 1069-1101 }

Guelph, Ont.

WE SOLICIT YOUR
EXPRESS WORK

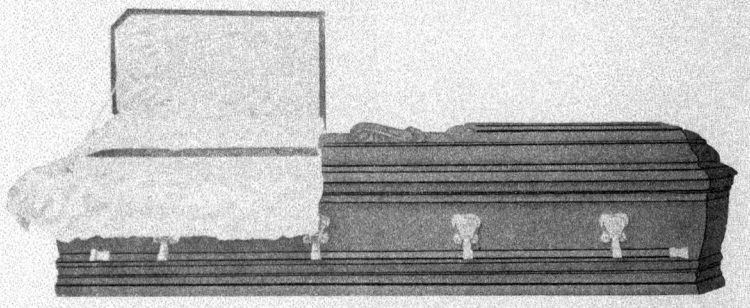

No. 132

Combination Metallic Casket, sealed inner top, made in "K" panel and trimmed throughout with fine Bosco Silk or Satin, non-corrosive handles put on. This makes a very complete outfit manufactured only by us.

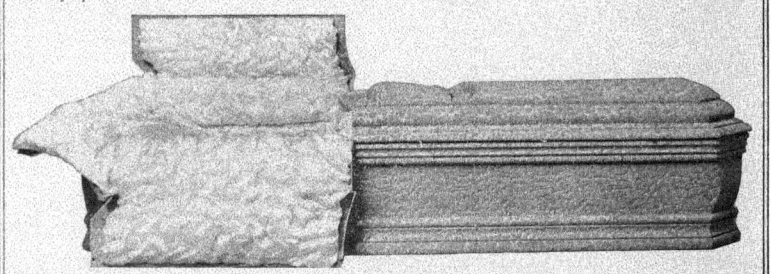

No. 168

Massive Octagon Casket, swell corner, one and one-half inch plates, made with "C" panel, Bosco or Satin crushed trimming, covered with fine black broadcloth or any shade of embossed plush. In using goods made by the Dominion Casket Co., the dealers obtain a pleasure by assuring their customers entire satisfaction. A thoroughly pleased customer will do more for your business than any other form of advertisement.

Watch for our Exhibit at Toronto, during Canadian Embalmers' Convention at 126 King Street West.

Undertakers' Department

Problems affecting the Undertaking Profession are here discussed and readers are invited to send letters expressing their views on any of the subjects dealt with—News of the profession throughout Canada.

Physical Agents in Disinfection—II.

By Professor H. S. Eckels
Dean of Eckels' College of Embalming, Philadelphia, Pa.

Dry vs. Moist Heat.

Dry heat is not as satisfactory a disinfectant as moist heat, especially as it lacks penetration, and is injurious to clothing, fabrics, etc. The temperature needed to destroy most pathogenic bacteria will scorch many articles, and the over-drying renders them very brittle, and also fixes stains, if any, so that they will not wash out. Albuminous materials coagulate with heat and, therefore, dry heat should not be used for the disinfection of fabrics containing bloodstains, sputum, excreta or similar substances. It may, therefore, be practically disregarded by the disinfector, as he will find other methods more practical and of greater value. Burning is mostly confined to the destruction of those articles that are known to be contaminated with infectious matter, and as it is instantly fatal in its action, it should certainly be used in the destruction of cloths and articles of little value, together with mattresses, old upholstered furniture, carpets, etc., that are known to be laden with disease germs. In cases of tuberculosis, where the patient has lived many months, probably years, in the one room and is naturally supposed to have contaminated the entire room and contents, should the draperies and carpet not be of sufficient value to pay for disinfection, they should be burned without delay, for in no other disease, as in tuberculosis, does the germ lurk in like manner in furnishing, and wait favorable opportunity for its development.

The burning of garbage and refuse is also the safest method of disposing of these substances from a sanitary standpoint, and the disinfector can feel safe in his work when he knows he has finally disposed of by burning any questionable substance that may convey disease. Caution should be taken to see that an infected room is not swept until after it has been thoroughly disinfected, both with gases and solutions. The sweeping stirs up the dust ladened with bacteria or disease germs that have settled into it and are protected by the dust covering them for the time being, and sweeping would be the surest means of distributing these minute organisms into the atmosphere throughout the entire house, and be the cause of communicating a further spread of the disease.

Instead of sweeping, the floor should be treated with a solution of bichloride of mercury, or sprayed with formaldehyde and thoroughly scrubbed and cleansed. A case that has come to my notice within the last few days proved that by such carelessness scarlet fever was spread among an entire family. One of the children was taken sick with scarlet fever and these precautions were not properly observed, resulting in the death of the child, a girl of twelve years, with the possibility of more deaths occurring in the family later on.

Electricity, another of the physical agents, is one that will be found to be of little practical value to the disinfector. For the purification of water, it has considerable merit, but it is an agent that the disinfector will have little occasion to use and, therefore, need not be gone into further here.

Value of Sunlight.

Sunlight is a physical agent whose disinfecting action is of the greatest assistance, and the benefit to be derived from its application cannot be sufficiently impressed upon the notice of the disinfector. Disease germs cannot live long where the direct rays of the sun can reach and have full power to destroy, and its' importance in preventing and destroying micro-organisms in Nature cannot be overestimated. Neither can its purifying and life-giving propensities. Sunlight (so essential to the growth of human, animal and vegetable life) is fatal to bacteria in any form, and observations prove that the most deadly of the spore-bearing diseases resist the direct action of the sun's rays in no case longer than forty-four hours.

The disinfector should always use the sunlight in supplementing his other methods whenever possible. Rooms and objects may always be sunned and aired to advantage after disinfection, especially carpets, curtains and other hangings which can be removed from the room. These should be exposed to the direct rays of the sun for a day or two at least. The disinfector should not be confused by the apparent contradiction regarding the efficacy of the sun's rays as a physical disinfecting agent. It has direct and positive powers, and the more direct the rays, the greater its power.

The seeming contradiction of this would be that in Cuba, India, and near the equator, where the sun's rays are the strongest, there are to be found the most deadly epidemic diseases known to man, namely: Asiatic cholera, bubonic plague, and yellow fever. The reason why these are so prevalent there is on account of the warm climate and moist atmosphere. These conditions aid the development of bacteria, and when the bacteria are protected from the rays of the sun, they develop in an alarming degree and in epidemic form.

In the transportation rules which have received the endorsement of the National Funeral Directors' Association, provincial boards of health, and the Association of the American Baggage Agents, a layer of dry cotton, not less than one inch thick, is used to envelop a body prepared for transportation when dead of some contagious disease, for the purpose of preventing the spread of any disease germ which may not have been destroyed, and thus give further protection to those who are compelled to handle such cases. This rule should receive the hearty co-operation and support of every intelligent and conscientious embalmer, for while there is a possibility of any such germs not being destroyed by the previous treatment, this dry cotton one inch thick will prevent the germs of any disease penetrating through it.

For germs to multiply it is necessary for them to have moisture, and this dry cotton, absorbing all of this

Mr. Funeral Director

_We_ carry a complete line of Funeral Supplies.

_We_ are open Day and Night.

_We_ have sent you our Catalogue, if not, a post card will bring it.

_We_ would ask you for a trial order.

Always at your service

The Western Casket Co.,
Limited

Winnipeg   Cor. Emily St., & Bannatyne Ave.   Manitoba

Day and Night Calls   Phone Garry 4657

moisture, deprives them of their power of reproduction and effectually prohibits their further dissemination. While discussing the subject of physical agents, I believe it will be of interest for you to know the various ways they are used in the different countries for the destruction of the dead. For instance, the Parsees, of India, who represent the highest type of civilization and culture in the East, use burning for the destruction of their dead bodies, and undoubtedly this is the most cleanly and healthful method in that particular country.

Customs of India.

India is well-known as the hot-bed of the most deadly diseases known to man, namely: Asiatic cholera and bubonic plague, and were the rest of the various denominations of India to destroy their dead bodies in a like manner, there would undoubtedly be an elimination of these diseases in a short space of time, but the custom for centuries has been for each particular caste to use their own methods of burial, with the result that the lower caste of Hindoos insist on burying their dead at night in the Ganges, thus contaminating that river and doing much to accomplish the continuation of these diseases.

On the "Tower of Silence," outside the city of Delhi, in India, the dead are carried and left for the vultures to consume. In a short space of time after the body has been placed there, there is nothing left but a few bones which are afterwards gathered by the relatives and buried. Although this method is revolting to contemplate, yet in practice it is known to be effective against the spread of disease, especially as the dead are not kept for any length of time, but are carried there within a few hours after their decease.

Certain tribes in Central America, also in Central Africa, have a custom of placing their dead high in the air on poles or scaffolds and allowing the air to decompose, dry and finally disintegrate them. This generally takes place in those higher altitudes where the air is rarefied, and the increased oxygen in the air, acting as a preservative on the body, arrests the processes of decay, dries and mummifies the body, so that it is free from obnoxious odors, and is as well preserved (except for a dried, leathery appearance) as if it had been embalmed. In these cases the action of the sun and air serves to thoroughly dry out all the element known as H_2O, or water, this being quickly absorbed by the preponderance of oxygen present in the air, while the rarefied air effectually preserves them until the body finally disintegrates and returns to dust.

In ascending high mountains, such as Pike's Peak, the peculiar effect which is felt is due to the decreased pressure to the extracardiac atmosphere, and is known as cardiac failure. It is caused by the expansion of the heart, which, lying as it does between the lungs, prevents their full expansion, resulting in bleeding from the nose and mouth, dizziness and eventually complete heart failure. For your better guidance and instruction as to the temperature needed for the complete destruction of the best known of the communicable diseases, I append herewith a table showing the temperature, the time of exposure necessary to destroy these organisms under favorable conditions.

I may add that these tests were applied without any protection to the germs whatever, i.e., in laboratory tests, and that in actual practice, with the added protecting substance to be considered, a higher degree of heat or a longer exposure is necessary.

The thermal death point of the various bacteria have been ascertained to be as follows:

Name of Organism.	Fahrenheit.	Min. Exposure.
Anthrax Bacillus	132.8 Deg.	4
Anthrax Spores	212 Water	20
Anthrax Spores	212 Steam	80
Cholera Spirillum	160 Steam	20
Diphtheria Bacillus	160 Steam	15
Diplococcus of Pneumonia	125.6	10
Streptococcus of Erys'las	129.2	10
Glanders Bacillus	131	10
Bacillus Tuberculosis	212	4
Typhoid Bacillus	132.8	4
Smallpox (Virus of Vac.)	125	15

FIRST ELECTRIC AMBULANCE.

Probably the first electric car for ambulance work to be used in Canada is that now put into service by Rogers & Burney, of Ottawa. It was built by the Tate Electric Co., of Walkerville, Ont.

It is constructed in limousine style, and finished with an aluminum body. It is also fitted with the latest and largest type of batteries, which are charged at Rogers & Burney's own plant. The tires are Motz, of cushion variety, and car is electrically lighted through-

Rogers & Burney's electric ambulance

out, also electrically heated. It has a guaranteed speed of 25 miles per hour, and can run 60 miles without recharging.

Rogers & Burney's idea in getting an electric car is that they are easier to start and smoother to ride in; also there is no odor as from a gasoline car. No extra insurance is required on the building for storing an electric car, as is the case with a gasoline car.

AMBULANCES NOT SPECIALLY CONSIDERED

Only the fire reels and the police ambulance have right-of-way on the streets of Toronto. It has apparently been established that private ambulance-owners are not entitled to special consideration when they are carrying emergency cases to the hospital, although a person's life may be hanging in the balance, and every minute counts. William Speers, a West Toronto undertaker, was fined $5 and costs, amounting to about $7.50 in all, by Magistrate Brunton in the County Police Court, for exceeding the speed limit along the Lake Shore road. Mr. Speers was coming from Port Credit with a man named Switzer in his private ambulance, who had been seriously injured when a wall fell on him. The doctors told Mr. Speers that Switzer must get to the hospital as quickly as it could be done, so Speers instructed the driver to get to the said hospital as fast as he might. However, the magistrate, having heard the circumstances, decided Mr. Speers was not entitled to any consideration.

Dominion Manufacturers
Limited

MANUFACTURERS OF

Fine Funeral Requisites

We guarantee

The Highest Quality

and the

Quickest Possible Service

*Night or Day Orders
given Prompt Attention*

BRANCHES

The Globe Casket Co., and Branches	London, Ontario
The Semmons & Evel Casket Co., and Branches	Hamilton, Ontario
The National Casket Co.	Toronto, Ontario
Jas. S. Elliot & Son	Prescott, Ontario
Girard & Godin and Branches	Three Rivers, Quebec
Christie Bros. & Co,	Amherst, N. S.

FRED W. COLES   D. M. ANDREWS
General Manager   *Secretary Treasurer*

HEAD OFFICE

468 King Street W., Toronto

Convention Meetings

CANADIAN EMBALMERS MEET IN SEPTEMBER.

The 31st annual convention of the Canadian Embalmers' Association will be held in the anatomical building of Toronto University during the second week of the Toronto Exhibition. The convention will be called to order at ten o'clock on Tuesday, September 8, and will continue for the three following days.

*Jos. Torrance, Milverton,
Secretary of the Ontario Board of Embalmers' Examiners.*

Secretary F. W. Matthews is at present busy arranging the details of the convention programme, which will be both interesting and profitable to those who attend this year's gathering.

The school of embalming will be held during the whole of the previous week, and will be in charge of Horace Moll, Ph.G., of the International School of Embalming, Chicago, who will also be the lecturer and demonstrator during the convention. The board of examiners recently appointed by the Provincial Government will have their first opportunity to show their worth, and because of the fact that it is now necessary for newcomers in the profession to take and pass an examination before being allowed to practice in Ontario, should make the school enroll a class larger this year than ever before in its history.

* * * *

Saskatchewan's First Convention.

The first convention of the Saskatchewan Funeral Directors' and Embalmers' Association was held at Regina College, Regina, July 27 and 28, and the course of lectures by Prof. W. P. Hohenschuh was given concurrent with the convention, from July 27 to 30. The professor was engaged by the health department of Saskatchewan on the recommendation of the association. His programme of subjects was interesting, practical, and educational. The subjects treated of were: Anatomy of the Organs; Cavity Preservation; The Circulation; Arterial Embalming; Bacteriology for Embalmers; Decomposition; Communicable Diseases; Blood and Discolorations; Mutilated and Post-Mortem Cases; and Cosmetics and Demi-Surgery.

Much of the success of the convention is due to the hard work of Secretary A. C. Howard, of Prince Albert.

Saskatchewan health department has legislated that all railway agents receiving bodies from shipping undertakers must see that the license number of the funeral director is entered in the shipping form.

* * * *

Convention at the Coast.

The third annual convention of the B. C. Funeral Directors' and Embalmers' Association will be held in Vancouver from September 7 to 12, the convention proper being held on September 10, 11, and 12, preceded by a three-day school of instruction. The lecturer and demonstrator will be Prof. W. P. Hohenschuh, of Iowa City, Iowa, who is also to act in the same capacity for the Manitoba and Alberta conventions.

The B. C. officers intend to make their 1914 convention the best they have ever held, and they are asking the attendance of every funeral director in the Pacific province. Details are being worked out in programme form, and suggestions are invited from members as to what they consider their greatest need. The enter-

*W. G. Bemows, Chatham
Member of Ontario Embalmers' Examiners' Board*

tainment side will not be neglected, and Secretary-Treasurer G. M. Williamson, the live wire of the association, is planning to have something doing all the time.

* * * *

Maritime Directors' Convention.

The annual meeting of the Maritime Funeral Directors' Association will be held in the undertaking parlors of Tuttle Bros., Moncton, N.B., on August, 11, 12, and 13. Prof. L. R. Simmons, of Syracuse, N.Y., is to lecture and conduct the demonstrations.

Burglar Proof and Water Tight

"The St. Thomas"

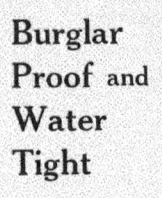

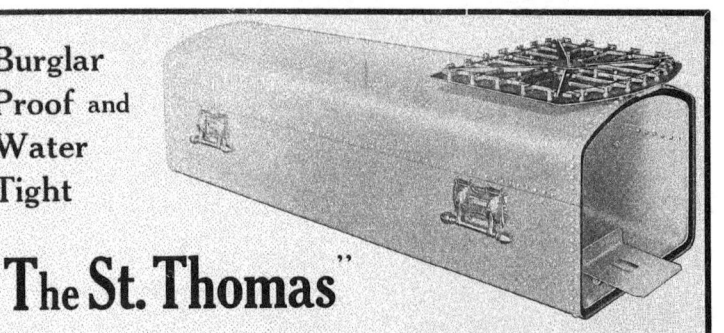

Original, Quick Closing End Vault

MANUFACTURED BY

The St. Thomas Metallic Vault Company, Limited
ST. THOMAS, ONTARIO

The Original Patented Concentrated Fluid

Patented Formula
Strongest and Best

Essential Oil Base, combined with Alcohol, Glycerine, Oxidized Formaldehyde and Boron-Dioxide.

Ask others for their Formula

Special Canadian Agents
National Casket Co.
Toronto, Ont.
GLOBE CASKET CO.
London, Ont.
SEMMENS & EVEL CASKET CO.
Hamilton, Ont.
GIRARD & GODIN
Three Rivers, Que.
JAS. S. ELLIOTT & SON
Prescott, Ont.
CHRISTIE BROS.
Amherst, N.S.

Larger Bottles filled up with water

Egyptian Chemical Co. Boston, U.S.A

FOR SALE

Second-hand, single horse, rubber tired, leather lined, Undertaker's coupe for personal use. Price $160.00.

Blachford & Son
57 King Street West   Hamilton, Canada

3,000-MILE FUNERAL JOURNEY.

A widow's careful instructions for keeping her husband's memory green in Canada are set out in the will of Mary, Baroness de Longueuil, of Rochampton, England, which was published recently. She was the wife of Vice-Admiral Samuel Arthur Johnson, R.N., and widow of Charles Colmore Grant, seventh Baron de Longueuil, and left estate in the United Kingdom valued at £43,200 14s. 11d. gross. She expressed a desire to be buried in the cemetery at Montreal, Canada, with her husband. She requested that her body should be embalmed, and the trustees are to arrange with some person to convey her body to Montreal and see it buried there in accordance with her directions. She left £500 to such person for such services, and directed that her wedding ring and the gold locket with the name "Charlie" shall be buried with her, and the said locket shall not be opened after her death, and she left £15 per annum for the upkeep of her grave.

SILVER WEDDING ANNIVERSARY.

Mr. and Mrs. Ritchie Macpherson celebrated their silver wedding anniversary at the home, Netherhill Farm, on July 4. Mr. Macpherson is a member of the Vincent & Macpherson firm of funeral directors and embalmers, Brandon, Man., and members of the staff motored out from the city to present a handsome mahogany clock to the happy couple. Those members were: Mr. and Mrs. A. P. Frost, Mr. and Mrs. G. G. McKay, Mr. and Mrs. James Sprague, Mr. and Mrs. H. B. Bedford, Mr. and Mrs. Gilchrist, Mr. and Mrs. James Scott, Miss Olive Bedford, of Winnipeg; J. W. Stranks, and G. Brockie. The lane in front of Netherhill Farm was gaily decorated with Chinese lanterns, forming a very effective scene in the evening, and showing to some distance in the country. A delightful time was spent by the party in the evening, refreshments being served by the host and hostess, the return journey being made in the wee sma' hours.

Gossip of the Profession

R. Minns has opened in the undertaking business at Kelowna, B.C.

Ben Priest, of Merritt, B.C., has purchased the undertaking business of Stewart & Syer, at Penticton, B.C.

George Trickett & Son, of New Denver, B.C., have purchased the undertaking business of Murdock McLean in that town.

Mrs. John McCrea, wife of the well-known undertaker at Omemee, Ont., died recently at her home. The funeral took place at Omemee.

Will J. Hodginson, a Toronto boy, well known to the profession, has accepted a position as head man with Green-Guernsey, of Hamilton.

Mrs. M. S. Cross has disposed of her furniture business at Wiarton, Ont., to Levine Bros., but she is still carrying on the undertaking business.

The Harriston Casket Co., Harriston, Ont., have recently added to the equipment of their factory a number of new machines of the most recent construction, which will largely increase the capacity of the concern.

A. W. Robinson, of the Western Casket Co., Ltd., Winnipeg, Man., has returned home after an extended trip through Alberta and British Columbia' and reports having a most successful trip in the interests of his firm.

The Embalmers' Act of Ontario, under which the examining board was recently appointed by the Provincial Government, was signed by the Lieutenant-Governor in March, 1911, but to make the Act effective and give it force it was necessary to appoint the examining board.

A new east end Toronto firm of undertakers have opened offices at 742 Broadview avenue, that city, under the style of Booth & Trull. One of the principals, Dan T. Booth, has been acting as manager for the H. Ellis firm, and is well known in the east end, being a member of a number of societies, while his colleague, Lorne W. Trull, has had several years' experience in the business in Oshawa as well as in Toronto.

L. and T. E. Sleeman, of Toronto, have decided to locate in Weburn, Sask., and open up undertaking parlors in the building directly opposite the Herald office, formerly occupied by the Royal Bank. The building is undergoing extensive improvements to fit it up for the special line of business the new tenants desire to carry on. L. Sleeman will manage the business, and his attention will be devoted to the one line. He is a graduate of the Canadian School of Embalming, and has had considerable experience in his special line of work.

QUESTIONABLE PLACE

Mr. Simpson was reading the newspaper.

"Here's a man got into a drunken brawl and was stabbed to death," he said aloud.

His wife glanced up from her knitting, and commented:

"In some low drinking den, I suppose?"

"No; th' paper says he got stabbed in th' thoracic cavity."

"Same thing; you'd think th' police'd close such a place up."—Exchange.

ACCORDING TO HIS WAY

While travelling in Africa, William Bernard, now stage director of the Baker players, once arrived in a small town shortly before time for the curtain to go up. He needed a shave and asked the hotel clerk to direct him to a barber shop. "The shops all close at 6 o'clock," said the clerk. "Well, I must get shaved some place," said Billy, who was playing a smooth-faced juvenile part. "Don't you know of someone who might be induced to help me out?"

The clerk directed him to a place down the street.

A man standing in the doorway said he would fix him. Bill was told to lie down on a couch, and after a painful series of scrapings and raspings, was shorn of the troublesome brush. "That's the first time I have ever been shaved lying down. Do you always do it that way?" asked Bernard.

"Oh, yes," said the man. "You are the first live person I ever have shaved. You see I am the undertaker."—Portland Journal.

WANT ADS. BRING RESULTS.

"Discontinue advertising the Bomgardner device we offered for sale in the July issue of your paper. We have sold it.

"We still have a coupe for sale.

"BLACHFORD & SON.

"Hamilton, July 9, 1914."

To Canadian Funeral Directors

THE CENTRAL LINE

Mahogany, Oak, Plush and Cloth Covered Caskets

WE SHIP PROMPTLY

We can also supply anything desired in Casket Linings, Burial Robes, and a general line of Undertakers' Supplies

Orders given our Canadian representative, or sent to our factory at Bridgeburg by mail, telegraph or telephone will be shipped promptly.

CENTRAL CASKET COMPANY

Bridgeburg, Ont.
Telephone 126

R. S. Flint Canadian Representative: 241 Fern Ave., Toronto
Telephone Parkdale 3257

No Undertaker Should Overlook

the fact that he can make a full gallon of fluid of standard strength from each sixteen-ounce bottle of RE-Concentrated Dioxin. Re-Concentrated Dioxin costs no more per bottle than any standard concentrated fluid, but it is twice as strong—in other words, there are twice as many ounces of preservation in a bottle of RE-Concentrated Dioxin as there are in any bottle of merely concentrated fluid.

If economy were the only recommendation for RE-Concentrated Dioxin, however, we should not urge it upon our patrons.

As a matter of fact, it is easy to explain and equally easy to demonstrate the fact that the fluid thus produced gives a far better cosmetic effect and produces a far more life-like body than possibly could be produced by any raw formaldehyde concentrated fluid.

This is because RE-Concentrated Dioxin has a double base. When diluted to make a full gallon of fluid to the bottle, its main base is peroxide, with a secondary base of purified formaldehyde (formochloral).

Every funeral director knows that peroxide of hydrogen is the best bleacher known to chemical science. Not everyone realizes, however, that peroxide of hydrogen has blood solvent qualities far in excess of any other chemical yet discovered which is suitable for use in embalming fluid.

Peroxide of hydrogen is composed of two atoms of oxygen and two atoms of hydrogen. Since oxygen is fifteen times heavier than hydrogen, fifteen-sixteenths of the atomic weight of peroxide of hydrogen, therefore, is oxygen.

Every embalmer knows that venous blood is much darker in color, is much more sluggish and much heavier than arterial blood.

What is the difference between the two?

Arterial blood is merely venous blood, which has been purified in the lungs, which has been lightened in color and rendered vastly more fluid by the oxygen which the lungs have extracted from the air we breathe.

Since fifteen-sixteenths of the atomic weight of peroxide of hydrogen is oxygen, it must be apparent, therefore, that the oxygen in the extra rich peroxide in Dioxin has a tendency to exercise the same purifying and solvent qualities upon the dark, discolored venous blood after death as the oxygen which the lungs extract from the air we breathe has upon the venous blood in life.

The result is that much more blood can be drained from a body in which RE-Concentrated Dioxin is injected than is possible from a body in which raw formaldehyde is used and in which the astringent qualities of the formaldehyde have sealed up the discolored blood corpuscles in the capillaries.

Putty color is caused by raw formaldehyde fluid sealing up the discolored corpuscles of the blood in the capillaries. It is inevitable where raw formaldehyde fluids are used unless exceeding care is used to drain blood. And even then there is great danger.

RE-Concentrated Dioxin is distinctly the most modern and the most scientific embalming fluid on the market, as well as the most economical. The progressive funeral director will not hesitate, but will order a trial shipment.

RE-Concentrated DIOXIN

H. S. ECKELS & CO. 1922 Arch St., Philadelphia, Pa.
241 Fern Ave., Toronto, Ont., Can.

ECKARDT FINANCIAL REALTY, CONSULTING AND INVESTIGATING COMPANY

Offices: 14, 15 & 16 First Floor, National Trust Building.
20 East King St., Toronto, Ont., Canada, close to cor. King & Yonge Sts.

A. J. H. ECKARDT, late proprietor of the National Casket Company and National Silver Plate Company, Toronto, Ont., has had 33 years of successful general business career.

ALL COMMUNICATIONS STRICTLY CONFIDENTIAL

This is the first and only business of its kind in Canada. Opportunity is offered of consultation with a man who has been a successful large manufacturer, and one who has had all-round business success, who has also had a large experience in connection with all kinds of business matters. A. J. H. Eckardt will give all matters his personal attention. Some of the objects and purposes of this company are to save you money and to help you to make money.

1. **NUMBER ONE BANKING.** Banking arrangements negotiated for different kinds of businesses in Toronto and elsewhere.
2. **LOANS.** Loans arranged on real estate and all kinds of securities.
3. **REAL ESTATE.** Our specialty, manufacturing and business properties generally. Mr. Eckardt, with his experience, should know something about what you require after receiving particulars, with his long experience as a successful business man. Another of our specialties is COCHRANE, ONT., PROPERTIES the coming great railroad junction and terminal, and great distributing centre for the great agricultural clay belt in Northern Ontario in latitude much south of Winnipeg, and tempered by a large body of salt water, known as James Bay, with ten times the resources of the prairies.
4. **ARBITRATION.** Services of this firm are available also in connection with matters of arbitration and adjustments.
5. **INSURANCE.** Fire and life, of all kinds, also insurance adjustments in case of fire, etc. Valuations made of all kinds of securities, businesses and properties.
6. **BUSINESS ARRANGEMENTS.** Business consultations offered as to testamentary dispositions and as to all other business matters, personal or partnership.
7. **CONSULTATIONS** offered on all kinds of business, manufacturing, wholesale or retail, real estate, bonds, debentures, stocks, mining interests, etc., and personal subjects.
8. **REPORTS AND INVESTIGATIONS.** Reports and investigations obtained on parties in all parts of the world as regards financial standing, business reputation, character, etc.
9. **SYSTEMS AND AUDITS**, books and accounts, office, factory and warehouse, commercial, municipal and financial.
10. **MERCHANT SALESMEN.** Traveling salesmen selected and recommended for all kinds of businesses. Think for a minute how many star salesmen there are representing Canadian firms in Canada to-day. Not many. This is a very important matter to every firm. As you readily know, the expenses of a poor salesman are very much greater than those of a star salesman, as the latter is a good business man and knows how to handle money.
11. **REORGANIZATION. TRAVELING SALESMEN.** Reorganization of traveling staffs for all kinds of businesses under the route sheet, daily report sheet, monthly and annual bonus systems, so as to get the best possible results.
12. **CONSULTING.** How to purchase and how to sell goods so as to get the best sure possible results. There is a real knack in this. Try us on this matter.
13. **CONSULT** with us on how to get out of trouble and how to keep out of trouble.
14. **CORRESPONDENCE.** Correspondence solicited and undertaken on any and all subjects. When corresponding be sure and give full particulars and details as far as possible.
15. **A. J. H. ECKARDT**, of our firm, has had thirty-three years of successful business experience in different classes of wholesale and manufacturing business, all on a large scale, and is still largely interested in manufacturing, but has retired from active mercantile life in his prime.
16. **IMPORTANT.** After reading above, don't you think it would be profitable to write or see our Mr. Eckardt?

ECKARDT FINANCIAL REALTY, CONSULTING AND INVESTIGATING COMPANY

Offices: 14, 15 & 16 First Floor, National Trust Company Building
20 East King St., Toronto, Ont., Canada, Close to cor. King & Yonge Sts.

AGAIN IN TOUCH WITH THE PROFESSION

A. J. H. Eckardt is again going into business which will bring him in touch with the profession throughout Canada. After a number of months of continual pressure brought to bear on him by the directors, among whom are some of Toronto's most prominent capitalists, he has been persuaded to take the presidency and general management of the International Mausoleum Co., Ltd., Toronto. He is also entering into the practice of consultor on business and financial subjects, for which his successful experience of 33 years past should qualify and fit him. He is opening centrally located offices on the first floor of the National Trust Building, 14 King street east, and is having them fitted up in a sumptuous manner.

INTERESTING HEAVYWEIGHT CASE.

A casket three times the size required for a man of average stature, and a grave three times as large as the one in which the average-sized man is buried, were required for John B. Lynch, 48 years old, a widower, who died at his home, 2339½ Clark Avenue, St. Louis, of fatty degeneration of the heart.

Lynch weighed 692 pounds, wore a No. 6 shoe, had a hand like a woman's, and was 3 inches short of being 6 feet tall.

Lynch's body was removed to the undertaking establishment of Hickey & Stephens, 1325 Market Street, where a special casket was built for it. The casket is 5 feet wide, 4 feet deep, and is reinforced and braced with steel. In each side of the casket are five handles for the use of pall-bearers, with one handle at each end for the use of the undertaker and his assistant, so that twelve men will be required to handle the casket.

IT WOULD BE OBVIOUS THEN.

"I confess," said the old doctor, "I can not make out your case."

"Well, but what are you going to do?" asked the forlorn patient.

"Oh!" said the doctor, as he brightened up, "We'll wait and ti...

CANADIAN FURNITURE WORLD AND THE UNDERTAKER   August, 1914

Index to Advertisements

A
Antiseptic Bedding Co. .... i.f.c.
Ault & Wiborg Co. 20

B
Baetz Bros. & Co. 10
Batavia Clamp Co. .... i.b.c.
Blachford & Son 62

C
Canadian Linderman Co. 14
Canadian School of Embalming ... 66
Can. H. W. Johns-Manville Co. .. 23
Central Casket Co. 64
Chesley Furniture Co. 15
Colleran Patent Spring Mat. Co. . 10

D
Dominion Casket Co. 56
Dominion Mfrs., Limited 60

E
Eckels & Co., H. S. 64
Egyptian Chemical Co. 62
Elmira Furniture Co. 21
Elmira Interior Woodwork Co. ... 23

F
Farquharson-Gifford Co. 7

G
Gnie & Son, Geo. 17
Globe-Wernicke Co. 9
Gold Medal Furniture Mfg. Co. .. 22
Gendron Wheel Co. 55

H
Hourd & Co. 10

I
Imperial Furniture Co. 8
Imperial Rattan Co. .... o.f.c.

K
Kawneer Mfg. Co. 12
Kindel Bed Co., Limited 11
Knechtel Furniture Co. .... o.b.c.
Kohn, J. & J. 6

L
Leggatt & Platt Spring Bed Co. . 16

M
Matthews Bros. 8
Menford Mfg. Co. 13
McLagan Furniture Co., Geo. 3
Montreal Upholstering Co. 4
Mundell, J. C., & Co. .... i.f.c.

N
N. A. Bent Chair Co. 6

O
Ontario Spring Bed 4

R
Robertson, P. L., Mfg. Co. .. i.b.c.

S
Shafer, D. L. & Co. 8
Steele, James, Limited 55
Steel Furnishing Co. 65
Stratford Chair Co. 5
Stratford Brass Co. 8
Stratford Mfg. Co. 11
St. Thomas Metallic Vault Co. .. 62

T
Textleather Co. 18

V
Victoriaville Bedding Co. 19
Victoriaville Chair Co. 20
Victoriaville Furniture Co. 13

W
Walter & Co., B. 23
Western Casket Co. 58
Weisglass, S., Limited. 21

Undertakers Shipping Directory

ONTARIO

Aurora—
  Dunham, Charles.
Barrie—
  Smith, G. G. & Co.
Brockville—
  Quirmbach, Geo. R., 162 King St.
Brooklin—
  Disney, R. S.
Campbellford—
  Irwin, James.
Campden —
  Hansel, Albion.
Clinton—
  Walker, Wesley.
Coboconk—
  Greenley, A.
Copper Cliff—
  Boyd, W. C.
Dungannon—
  Sproul, William
Dutton—
  Schultz, B. L.
Elmira—
  Dreisinger, Chris.
Fenelon Falls—
  Deyman, L. & Son.
Fenwick—
  H. A. Metler.
Fergus—
  Armstrong, M. F.
  Thomson, John & Son.
Fort William—
  Cameron & Co., 711 Victoria.
  Morris, A.
Haileybury—
  Thorpe Bros.
Galt—
  Anderson, J. & Son.
Hamilton—
  Green Bros., 124 King St. E.
  Robinson, J. H. & Co., 19-21 John St. N.
Hanover—
  Wunnenberg, Norman.
Hastings—
  Howard, P. N.
Hepworth—
  Downs, E. J.
Inwood—
  Lorriman, E. S.
Kemptville—
  McCaughey, Geo. A.
Kenora—
  Horn & Taylor.
Kingston—
  Corbett, S. S.
Lakefield—
  Hendren, Geo. G.
Little Current—
  Sims, J. G.
Markdale—
  Oliver, M.
Newmarket—
  Millard, J. H.
North Augusta—
  Wilson, J. R.
North Bay—
  St. Pierre, E.
Oakwood—(Mariposa Station G.T.R.) Wilmot F. Webster.
Ohsweken—
  Johnson, F. L.
Oshawa—
  Disney Bros.
  Luke Bros.
Ottawa—
  Rogers & Burney, 283 Laurier Ave. W.
  Chas. R. Woodburn, 586 Bank St. Tel. Carling 600 and 1009.
Petrolia—
  Steadman Bros.
Port Arthur —
  Collin Wood, 36 Arthur St.
  Morris, A.
Prescott—
  Rankin, H. & Son.
Renfrew—
  O'Connor, Wm.
St. Mary's—
  N. L. Brandon.
St. Thomas—
  Williams, P. R. & Sons, 519 Talbot St.
Seaforth, Ont.
  W. T. Box & Co.
Scotland—
  Vaughan, Jos. H. M.
Sudbury—
  Henry, J. G.
Toronto—
  Cobbledick, N. B., 2068 Queen St. East and 1508 Danford Ave. Private Ambulance.
  Humphrey, E. J. Burial Co. Head Office, 359 Yonge St.; Branch, 407 Queen St. W. Private ambulance.
  Stone, Daniel (formerly H. Stone & Son), 82 Bloor St. West.
  Vancamp, J. C., 30 Bloor St. West.
Waterloo—
  Klipper Undertaking Co.
Welland—
  Sutherland, G. W.
Woodstock—
  Meadows, T. & Sons.
  Mack, Paul.

QUEBEC

Buckingham—
  Paquet, Jos.
Cowansville—
  Judson, M. B.
Montreal—
  Tees & Co., 912 St. Catherine St. West.
St. Hyacinthe—
  Cadórette, Mongeau & Leary.
St. Laurent—
  Gougeon, Jos.

NEW BRUNSWICK

Petitcodiac—
  Jonah, D. Allison.
Welland—
  Sutherland, G. W.
Woodstock—
  Van Wart, Jacob.

NOVA SCOTIA

Perrona—
  Fraser, D. & Co.
Halifax—
  Snow & Co., 90 Argyle St.
Sydney, C.B.—
  Beaton, A. J. & Son, 374-384 George St.

MANITOBA

Brandon—
  Campbell & Campbell.
  Vincent & McPherson.
Souris—
  McCulloch, Wm.
Swan River—
  Paull, Geo.
Winnipeg—
  Bardal, A. S., 834 Sherbrooke
  Thompson, J. C., 501 Main
  Clark-Leatherdale Co., Ltd., 232 Kennedy St.

SASKATCHEWAN

Gull Lake—
  Morrow, Fred. A.
Saskatoon—
  Young, A. E.
Kamsack—
  Russell, G. E. I.
Lanigan—
  Robertson, Wm.
Moose Jaw—
  The Bellamy Co.
  Broadfoot Bros.
Rush Lake—
  Friesen, John M.
Prince Albert—
  Howard, A. C.
  Hadley, C. L.
Regina—
  Speers, George.
Semans—
  Haygarth, Jas.
Welwyn —
  Leavens, Merritt.
Wolseley —
  Barber, B.

ALBERTA

Calgary—
  Graham & Buscomb, 611 Centre St.
Castor—
  Winter, W. G.

BRITISH COLUMBIA

Hosmer—
  Cornett, T. A.
Victoria—
  Hana & Thompson, 827 Pandora Ave.

Canadian School of Embalming
Instruction in Practical Embalming and Funeral Directing
PREPARATION FOR EXAMINATIONS
ENTER AT ANY TIME
R. U. STONE   **32 Carlton Street**
Principal   Toronto

ROBERTSON SOCKET HEAD Wood Screws

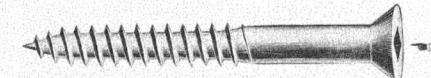

See That Square Hole

Pat. Feb. 2, 1909

THIS IS A REAL WOOD SCREW

It is driven by a simple square bit, and is the only one of its type on the market.

Driver fits snugly into the square hole and positively cannot slip and cut the fingers, or disfigure costly furniture or woodwork. It is driven with less exertion. No ragged slots after driving. Saves time, labor, money and material. We make the drivers in all suitable styles.

Drivers sent free with first order. Write for catalogue and prices.

P. L. Robertson Mfg. Co., Limited

We also manufacture Wire Nails, Rivets, Wire and Washers

MILTON :: ONTARIO

For Every Furniture Man

A Helpful, Thoroughly Practical Book, Written by an Authority—

HOW TO KNOW PERIOD STYLES IN FURNITURE

150 Pages　317 Illustrations

Price, $1.50

Designers will find illustrations of the work of celebrated designers of history. Examples are taken from the recognized collections and museums of the world.
Buyers—The book is arranged for easy reference with the distinguishing features of each period clearly shown.
Salesmen—The information in "How to Know Period Styles" will enable you to talk authoritatively on the subject.
Students—The confusing element has been eliminated, but all necessary information is included.

Send us $1.50. Keep the book 10 days, and if it isn't worth the price, return it and get your money back.

The Commercial Press
Publishers The Canadian Furniture World and The Undertaker
32 Colborne Street, Toronto

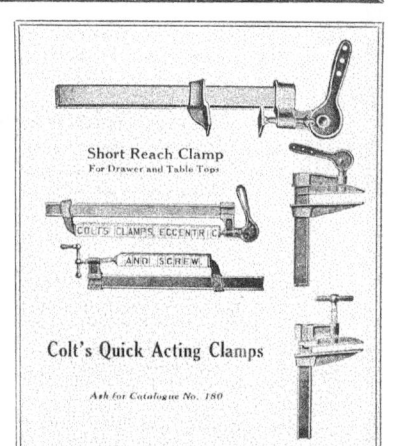

Short Reach Clamp
For Drawer and Table Tops

COLT'S CLAMPS, ECCENTRIC AND SCREW

Colt's Quick Acting Clamps

Ask for Catalogue No. 180

Batavia Clamp Company
147 Center Street, Batavia, N.Y., U.S.A.

Mr. Dealer—Here is a live Prospect

The stationer, druggist, tobacconist, sporting goods dealer and many others must have shelves to store and display their stocks—sell them the

Weis-Knechtel Sliding Door Bookcase
Here are reasons "why it is the best display shelf."

1. The sliding door permits quicker and easier access to contents than any other style door.
2. Contents are fully displayed and protected from dust.
3. If he moves---ordinary shelves are worth only ten cents on the dollar---W.-K. cases are worth one hundred---and they fold flat.
4. Goods look better in W.-K. sliding door cases, than in any other sectional case because there is no wood around the glass to obstruct a complete view of the contents.

There are other good reasons---you are hustling for business---get out and get some of this---It's dead easy.

THE KNECHTEL FURNITURE CO. LIMITED
HANOVER   ONTARIO

Vol. 4 No. 9　　　Furniture Buyers' Directory, Pages 3 to 14　　　SEPTEMBER, 1914

Canadian Furniture World
AND THE UNDERTAKER

Published by the Commercial Press, Limited, 32 Colborne Street, Toronto

Who also Publish: The Retail Grocer, The Canadian Provisioner, The Retail Druggist, Canadian Hardware Journal, Canadian Manufacturer, Canadian Builder and Carpenter, The Canadian Clay-Worker, Motoring and Motor Trade, Good Roads of Canada, The Railway Journal of Canada, The Canadian Nurse.

From McLagan's

Comes the Most Charming of Jacobean Designed Furniture

DESIGNS SUCH AS THESE APPEAL TO THOSE OF *TASTE* AND *POSITION* WHO MAKE THE MORE DESIRABLE CUSTOMERS

TURN YOUR THOUGHTS TO McLAGAN'S FOR THE BETTER GRADES OF FURNITURE THAT WIN THE POPULAR FANCY.

MAY WE SEND YOU REPRODUCTIONS OF THE MANY OTHER NEW EFFECTS WE HAVE BROUGHT OUT FOR THE FALL SEASON?

The Geo. McLagan Furniture Co.
Limited
Stratford　-　Ontario

Exhibition of Mundell-Made-Furniture

August 29th to September 14th

69 King Street West - Toronto, Ontario

Living Room Furniture will be especially featured, with examples of the best in Arts and Crafts designs, besides a complete showing of Fancy Rockers, Arm Chairs, Library Tables, Couches, Settees and Davenports, etc.

Make your headquarters **69 King West** *while in the city*

JOHN C. MUNDELL & CO., LIMITED, ELORA, ONT.

Well Made and Shows It

While "N. A." Chairs are low in price, no detail of construction that will add to their serviceability has been omitted. The design shown is made in oak only, fumed or golden gloss finish, leather pad seat. Same style made with wood seat. Let us send you reproductions or our many new, better profit designs for an immediate selection.

The
North American Bent Chair Co.
Limited
Owen Sound - Ontario

No. 1700U

First Annual
CANADIAN FURNITURE WORLD BUYERS' DIRECTORY

Containing the Most Extensive and Most Conveniently arranged Buyers' Guide ever compiled for Canadian Furniture Dealers and Manufacturers.

¶ In January the publishers of the Canadian Furniture World announced that a Buyer's Directory Number of the Furniture World would be published during 1914. The announcement was followed by the hasty publication of two "Buyers' Guides" by a competitor. Imitation is the sincerest form of flattery.

¶ This Directory Number has not been hastily compiled. Every furniture manufacturer in Canada has been written to several times for information, and months have been spent in making the Directory complete. If the Directory is incomplete in any way it is the fault of the manufacturers who failed to supply information in answer to our requests.

¶ The Directory is published as an editorial service to the Furniture Dealers of Canada. Manufacturers from whom the Furniture World has never received a dollar for advertising—and some from whom it probably never will—have their lines listed as completely as other manufacturers who are more progressive and recognize the advertising value to be obtained in the pages of a trade newspaper which subscribers pay real money for.

¶ Being an editorial service to readers, and not part of any advertising proposition, the names of advertisers and non-advertisers are given in the same style of type. The Directory is intended to be a real Directory.

¶ Practically every furniture retailer in Canada will receive a copy of the Directory Number, and to enable them to more conveniently preserve the Directory for reference during the coming year, each copy is perforated and corded to hang up like a telephone directory.

¶ The Furniture World has a monthly circulation of 2,000 copies, but 2,500 are printed this month, the extra copies being mailed to furniture manufacturers and to non-subscribers.

¶ Compare this Directory Number with other publications, and consider the broad policy of service followed by the Furniture World, and the reason for the rapid growth of this paper in circulation and popularity will be recognized. The publishers express appreciation for the liberal support given the Furniture World by the furniture trade in Canada during the past three years, and will further appreciate suggestions as to how next year's Directory Number, and the Furniture World every month, can be made of greater service to the trade.

THE COMMERCIAL PRESS, LIMITED

Publishers
Trade Papers:
Canadian Furniture World
Canadian Hardware Journal
The Retail Grocer
The Canadian Provisioner
The Retail Druggist of Canada

32 COLBORNE STREET
TORONTO   CANADA

Magazines:
Motoring and Motor Trade of Canada
The Canadian Nurse

Publishers
Technical Papers:
The Canadian Manufacturer
The Railway Journal of Canada
The Canadian Builder and Carpenter
The Canadian Clay-Worker
Good Roads of Canada

Bedroom Furniture

BEDS—Brass only
Canadian Mercereau Co., Toronto.
Stratford Bed Co., Stratford.

BEDS—Brass and Iron
Alaska Bedding Co., Winnipeg.
Alaska B.C. Bedding Co., Vancouver.
Alaska Feather and Down Co., Montreal.
Canada Furniture Mfrs., Woodstock.
Geo. Gale & Son, Waterville, Que.
Ideal Bedding Co., Toronto.
Ives Modern Bedstead Co., Cornwall.
Moffat Stove Co., Winnipeg.
Ontario Spring Bed and Mattress Co., London.
S. Weisglass, Ltd., Montreal, Que.
Victoriaville Bedding Co., Victoriaville, Que.

BEDS—Iron only
Canada Beds, Ltd., Chesley.
Maple Leaf Bedding Co., Galt.
Reliable Bedding Co., Weston.
Stamco, Ltd., Saskatoon.

BEDS—Davenports
See Davenports (upholstered furniture).

BEDS—Folding
Alaska Bedding Co., Winnipeg.
Alaska B.C. Bedding Co., Vancouver.
Alaska Feather and Down Co., Montreal.
Canada Furniture Mfrs., Woodstock.
Farquharson-Gifford Co., Stratford.
G. Gale & Sons, Waterville, Que.
Gold Medal Furniture Mfg. Co., Toronto.
G. H. Hachborn & Co., Berlin.
Ideal Bedding Co., Toronto.
Imperial Rattan Co., Stratford.
Ives Modern Bedstead Co., Cornwall.
Kindel Bed Co., Toronto.
Maple Leaf Bedding Co., Galt.
Montreal Upholstering Co., Montreal.
Ontario Spring Bed and Mattress Co., London.
Otterville Mfg. Co., Otterville.
Owen Daveno Co., Hespeler.
Snyder Bros., Upholstering Co., Waterloo.
Stamco Limited, Saskatoon.
S. Weisglass, Ltd., Montreal.

BEDS—Institution
Alaska Bedding Co., Winnipeg.
Alaska B.C. Bedding Co., Vancouver.
Alaska Feather and Down Co., Montreal.
Canada Beds, Ltd., Chesley.
Canada Furniture Manufacturers, Woodstock.
Geo. Gale & Sons, Waterville, Que.
Ideal Bedding Co., Toronto.
Ives Modern Bedstead Co., Cornwall.
Maple Leaf Bedding Co., Galt.
Ontario Spring Bed and Mattress Co., London.
Stamco Limited, Saskatoon.
Victoriaville Bedding Co., Victoriaville, Que.

BEDS—Sofa
Alaska B.C. Bedding Co., Vancouver.
Gold Medal Furniture Co., Toronto.
Ideal Bedding Co., Toronto.
Kindel Bed Co., Ltd., Toronto.
Montreal Upholstering Co., Montreal.
Owen Daveno Bed Co., Hespeler.
Snyder Bros. Upholstering Co., Waterloo.

BEDS—Wooden
Alaska B.C. Bedding Co., Vancouver.
Anthes Furniture Co., Berlin.
Beach Furniture Co., Cornwall.
M. F. Beach Co., Winchester.
Bell Furniture Co., Southampton.
Berlin Furniture Co., Berlin.
Canada Furniture Manufacturers, Woodstock.
Classic Furniture Co., Stratford.
Crown Furniture Co., Preston.
Durham Furniture Co., Durham.
Dymond Colonial Co., Strathroy.
Elora Furniture Co., Elora.
Gibbard Furniture Co., Napanee.
Gold Medal Furniture Mfg. Co., Toronto.
Hepworth Mfg. Co., Hepworth.
Hespeler Furniture Co., Hespeler.
Kilgour & Bros., Beauharnois, Que.
Knechtel Furniture Co., Hanover.
Krug Bros. & Co., Chesley.
A. Malcolm Furniture Co., Kincardine.
Malcolm & Souter Furniture Co., Hamilton.
Meaford Mfg. Co., Meaford.
North American Furniture Co., Owen Sound.
Spiesz Furniture Co., Hanover.
St. Lawrence Furniture Co., Riviere du Loup, Que.
Tickell Sons & Co., Belleville.
Toronto Furniture Co., Toronto.
Victoriaville Furniture Co., Victoriaville, Que.
Windsor Furniture Co., Windsor, N.S.

BEDROOM CHAIRS
Also see Upholstered Chairs.
Alaska B.C. Bedding Co., Vancouver.
Baetz Bros. & Co., Berlin.
Ball Furniture Co., Hanover.
Bell Furniture Co., Southampton.
Canada Furniture Manufacturers, Woodstock.
Classic Furniture Co., Stratford.
F. E. Coombe Furniture Co., Kincardine.
Dymond-Colonial Co.'s, Strathroy.
Elmira Furniture Co., Elmira.
Fraserville Chair Co., Riviere du Loup, Quebec.
Giddings, Ltd., Granby, Que.
Glaeser & Leinberger, Hanover.
Hespeler Furniture Co., Hespeler.
Hibner Furniture Co., Berlin.
Knechtel Furniture Co., Hanover.
H. Krug Furniture Co., Berlin.
Lippert Furniture Co., Berlin.
A. Malcolm Furniture Co., Kincardine.
Malcolm & Souter Furniture Co., Hamilton.
J. C. Mundell & Co., Elora.
North American Bent Chair Co., Owen Sound.
Owen Sound Chair Co., Owen Sound.
Preston Chair Co., Preston.
Snyder Bros. Upholstering Co., Waterloo.
Stanfold Chair Mfg. Co., Stanfold, Quebec.
Stratford Chair Co., Stratford.
Schierholtz Furniture Co., New Hamburg.
Toronto Furniture Co., Toronto.
Woeller Bolduc Co., Waterloo.

BEDROOM TABLES
Alaska B.C. Bedding Co., Vancouver.
Anthes Furniture Co., Berlin.
Beach Furniture Co., Cornwall.
Bell Furniture Co., Southampton.
Berlin Furniture Co., Berlin.
Canada Furniture Mfrs., Woodstock.
Chesley Furniture Co., Chesley.
Durham Furniture Co., Durham.
Elmira Furniture Co., Elmira.
Elora Furniture Co., Elora.
Knechtel Furniture Co., Hanover.
G. J. Lippert Table Co., Berlin.
Lucknow Table Co., Lucknow.
Malcolm & Souter Furniture Co., Hamilton.
Markdale Furniture Co., Markdale.
Meaford Mfg. Co., Meaford.
G. McLagan Furniture Co., Stratford.
Moffat Stove Co., Winnipeg.
J. C. Mundell & Co., Elora.
National Table Co., Owen Sound.
North American Bent Chair Co., Owen Sound.
North American Furniture Co., Owen Sound.
J. Oliver & Sons, Ottawa.
Spiesz Furniture Co., Hanover.
St. Lawrence Furniture Co., Riviere du Loup, Quebec.
Stratford Chair Co., Stratford.
Strathroy Furniture Co., Strathroy.
Toronto Furniture Co., Toronto.
Windsor Furniture Co., Windsor, N.S.
Victoriaville Furniture Co., Victoriaville, Que.
Woeller-Bolduc & Co., Waterloo.

BED SPRINGS
Alaska Bedding Co., Winnipeg.
Alaska B.C. Bedding Co., Vancouver.
Alaska Feather & Down Co., Montreal.
Canada Beds, Chesley.
Canada Furniture Manufacturers, Woodstock.
Canadian Feather and Mattress Co., Toronto.
Canadian Mercereau Co., Toronto.
Colleran Patent Spring Mattress Co., Toronto.
Frame and Hay Fence Co., Stratford.
G. Gale & Sons, Waterville, Que.
Gold Medal Furniture Co., Toronto.
Ham & Nott Co., Brantford.
Ideal Bedding Co., Toronto.
Ives Modern Bedstead Co., Cornwall.
Kilgour & Bro., Beauharnois, Que.
Krug Bros. & Co., Chesley.
Leggett and Platt Spring Bed Co., Windsor.
Maple Leaf Bedding Co., Galt.
Moffat Stove Co., Winnipeg.
Maydwell Mfg. Co., Toronto.
J. Oliver & Sons, Ottawa.
Ontario Spring Bed and Mattress Co., London.
J. C. Sloane, Owen Sound.
St. Lawrence Furniture Co., Riviere du Loup, Quebec.
Stamco, Ltd., Saskatoon, Sask.
The Steel Furnishing Co., New Glasgow.
Victoriaville Bedding Co., Victoriaville.
S. Weisglass, Ltd., Montreal, Que.
Whitworth & Restall, Toronto.

BOX SPRINGS
Alaska B.C. Bedding Co., Vancouver.
Canada Furniture Manufacturers, Woodstock.
Canadian Feather and Mattress Co., Toronto.
Dymond-Colonial Co.'s, Strathroy.
G. Gale & Sons, Waterville, Que.
Gold Medal Furniture Co., Toronto.
Ideal Bedding Co., Toronto.
Ives Modern Bedstead Co., Cornwall.
McKellar Bedding Co., Fort William.
Quality Mattress Co., Waterloo.
Shurly-Dietrich Co., Galt.
Stamco Limited, Saskatoon.
Standard Bedding Co., Toronto.

BOLSTER ROLLS
Dymond Colonial Co., Strathroy.
Ideal Bedding Co., Toronto.
Ontario Bed & Mattress Co., London.
Quality Mattress Co., Waterloo.

CHIFFONIERS (Odd or to match Dressers and Stands)—
Alaska B.C. Bedding Co., Vancouver.
M. F. Beach Co., Winchester.
Beach Furniture Co., Cornwall.
Bell Furniture Co., Southampton.
Berlin Furniture Co., Berlin.
Canada Furniture Manufacturers, Woodstock.
Crown Furniture Co., Preston.
Dominion Furniture Mfg. Co., St. Therese, Que.
Durham Furniture Co., Durham.
Dymond Colonial Co., Strathroy.
Hepworth Mfg. Co., Hepworth.
Hespeler Furniture Co., Hespeler.
Knechtel Furniture Co., Hanover.
Malcolm & Souter Furniture Co., Hamilton.
Markdale Furniture Co., Markdale.
Meaford Mfg. Co., Meaford.
Moffat Stove Co., Winnipeg.
J. Oliver & Sons, Ottawa.
Spiesz Furniture, Ltd., Hanover.
Stratford Chair Co., Stratford.
St. Lawrence Furniture Co., Riviere du Loup, Quebec.
Windsor Furniture Co., Windsor, N.S.

COMBINATION STANDS
Alaska B.C. Bedding Co., Vancouver.
Berlin Furniture Co., Berlin.
Chesley Furniture Co., Chesley.
Durham Furniture Co., Durham.
Knechtel Furniture Co., Hanover.

COMFORTERS
Alaska Feather and Down Co., Montreal.
Canada Feather and Mattress Co., Toronto.
Stamco, Ltd., Saskatoon, Sask.
Toronto Feather and Down Co., Toronto.

COSTUMERS
Alaska Bedding Co., Winnipeg.
Alaska B.C. Bedding Co., Vancouver.
Alaska Feather and Down Co., Montreal.
Beach Furniture Co., Cornwall.
Bell Furniture Co., Southampton.
Berlin Furniture Co., Berlin.
Canada Furniture Mfrs., Woodstock.
Collie-Cockerill Mfg. Co., Aurora.
Dymond-Colonial Co.'s, Strathroy.
Elmira Interior Woodwork Co., Elmira.
Hespeler Furniture Co., Hespeler.
Ideal Bedding Co., Toronto.
J. & J. Kohn, Toronto.
Knechtel Furniture Co., Hanover.
A. Malcolm Furniture Co., Kincardine.
Malcolm & Souter Furniture Co., Hamilton.
Meaford Mfg. Co., Meaford.
J. C. Mundell & Co., Elora.
North American Furniture Co., Owen Sound.
Ontario Spring Bed & Mattress Co., London.
Snyder Bros. Upholstering Co., Waterloo.
Toronto Furniture Co., Toronto.
S. Weisglass, Montreal.
Woeller Boldue & Co., Waterloo.
Wunder Furniture Mfg. Co., Berlin.

COTS
Alaska Bedding Co., Winnipeg.
Alaska B.C. Bedding Co., Vancouver.
Alaska Feather and Down Co., Montreal.
Canada Beds, Ltd., Chesley.
Canada Furniture Mfrs., Woodstock.
Frame and Hay Fence Co., Stratford.
G. Gale & Sons, Waterville, Que.
Gold Medal Furniture Co., Toronto.
Ham & Nott Co., Brantford.

Ideal Bedding Co., Toronto.
Ives Modern Bedstead Co., Cornwall.
Knechtel Furniture Co., Hanover.
Krug Bros. & Co., Chesley.
Maple Leaf Bedding Co., Galt.
Maydwell Mfg. Co., Toronto.
Munro Steel and Wire Works, Winnipeg.
Ontario Spring Bed and Mattress Co., London.
Otterville Mfg. Co., Otterville.
Stamco Limited, Saskatoon.
St. Lawrence Furniture Co., Riviere du Loup, Quebec.
Victoriaville Bedding Co., Victoriaville.
S. Weisglass, Ltd., Montreal.

CRADLES.
(See also Iron and Brass Beds).
Canada Furniture Mfrs., Woodstock.
Durham Furniture Co., Durham.
Gendron Mfg. Co., Toronto.
Kilgour & Bros., Beauharnois, Que.
Knechtel Furniture Co., Hanover.
Krug Bros. & Co., Chesley.
Moffat Stove Co., Winnipeg.
North American Bent Chair Co., Owen Sound.
J. Oliver & Sons, Ottawa.
Progress Spring Bed Mfg. Co., Montreal.
Roxton Mill & Chair Co., Waterloo, Quebec.
St. Lawrence Furniture Co., Riviere du Loup, Quebec.

CRIBS
See Beds (brass and iron).
(See also Cradles).

DRESSERS.
Anthes Furniture Co., Berlin.
Beach Furniture Co., Cornwall.
Crown Furniture Co., Preston.
Knechtel Furniture Co., Hanover.
Malcolm & Souter Furniture Co., Hamilton.
Moffat Stove Co., Winnipeg.
J. Oliver & Sons, Ottawa.
Alaska Bedding Co., Winnipeg.

DRESSERS, CHIFFONIERS, CHEVALS, WASHSTANDS, SOMNOES, DRESSING TABLES, ETC.
Alaska B.C. Bedding Co., Vancouver.
Anthes Furniture Co., Berlin.
Beach Furniture Co., Cornwall.
Bell Furniture Co., Southampton.
Berlin Furniture Co., Berlin.
Canada Furniture Manufacturers, Woodstock.
Classic Furniture Co., Stratford.
Durham Furniture Co., Durham.
Dymond-Colonial Co.'s, Strathroy.
Gibbard Furniture Co., Napanee.
Hepworth Mfg. Co., Hepworth.
Hespeler Furniture Co., Hespeler.
Kilgour & Bros., Beauharnois, Que.
Knechtel Furniture Co., Hanover.
Krug Bros. & Co., Chesley.
Malcolm & Souter, Hamilton.
A. Malcolm Furniture Co., Kincardine.
Meaford Mfg. Co., Meaford.
North American Furniture Co., Owen Sound.
Orillia Furniture Mfrs., Orillia.
Spiesz Furniture Co., Hanover.
Stratford Chair Co., Stratford.
St. Lawrence Furniture Co., Riviere du Loup, Que.
Toronto Furniture Co., Toronto.
Victoriaville Furniture Co., Victoriaville, Que.
Windsor Furniture Co., Windsor, N.S.

DRESSERS AND WASHSTANDS (Odd)
Alaska B.C. Bedding Co., Vancouver.
M. F. Beach Co., Winchester.
Bell Furniture Co., Southampton.
Berlin Furniture Co., Berlin.
Canada Furniture Manufacturers, Woodstock.
Crown Furniture Co., Preston.
Dominion Furniture Mfg. Co., St. Therese, Que.
Durham Furniture Co., Durham.
Eastern Townships Furniture Mfg. Co., Arthabaska, Que.
Harriston Furniture Mfg. Co., Harriston.
Hepworth Mfg. Co., Hepworth.
Knechtel Furniture Co., Hanover.
Malcolm & Souter Furniture Co., Hamilton.
Markdale Furniture Co., Markdale.
McGill Chair Co., Cornwall.
J. Oliver & Son, Ottawa.
Spiesz Furniture, Ltd., Hanover.
St. Lawrence Furniture Co., Riviere du Loup, Quebec.
Windsor Furniture Co., Windsor, N.S.

DRESSING TABLE DESKS
Berlin Furniture Co., Berlin.
Canada Furniture Manufacturers, Woodstock.
Dymond Colonial Co., Strathroy.
Knechtel Furniture Co., Hanover.
St. Lawrence Furniture Co., Riviere du Loup, Quebec.

HAMPERS
Alaska B.C. Bedding Co., Vancouver.
Canada Furniture Manufacturers, Woodstock.

IRON BUNKS
Alaska Bedding Co., Winnipeg.
Alaska B.C. Bedding Co., Vancouver.
Alaska Feather and Down Co., Montreal.
Geo. Gale & Sons, Waterville, Que.
Ideal Bedding Co., Toronto.
Ives Modern Bedstead Co., Cornwall.

LADIES' DRESSING TABLES (Odd or to match Dressers and Stands)
M. F. Beach Co., Winchester.
Beach Furniture Co., Cornwall.
Bell Furniture Co., Southampton.
Berlin Furniture Co., Berlin.
Canada Furniture Manufacturers, Woodstock.
Classic Furniture Co., Stratford.
Crown Furniture Co., Preston.
Durham Furniture Co., Durham.
Dymond Colonial Co., Strathroy.
Knechtel Furniture Co., Hanover.
Malcolm & Souter Furniture Co., Hamilton.
Markdale Furniture Co., Markdale.
Meaford Mfg. Co., Meaford.
Spiesz Furniture Co., Hanover.

MATTRESSES
Alaska Bedding Co., Winnipeg.
Alaska B.C. Bedding Co., Vancouver.
Alaska Feather and Down Co., Montreal.
Antiseptic Bedding Co., Toronto.
Berlin Bedding Co., Toronto.
Bothwell Mfg. Co., Bothwell.
Canada Furniture Mfrs., Woodstock.
Canadian Feather and Mattress Co., Toronto.
Clark Mattress Co., Toronto.
Dymond-Colonial Co.'s, Strathroy.
Edmonton Tent and Mattress Co., Edmonton.
Fischman Mattress Co., Toronto.
G. Gale & Sons, Waterville, Que.
Gold Medal Furniture Co., Toronto.
Golden Fleece Bedding Co., Toronto.

Ham & Nott Co., Brantford.
Ideal Bedding Co., Toronto.
Ives Modern Bedstead Co., Cornwall.
Kilgour & Bro., Beauharnois, Que.
Knechtel Furniture Co., Hanover.
Krug Bros. & Co., Chesley.
J. R. Larose, Hull, Que.
McKellar Bedding Co., Fort William.
F. W. & S. Mason, St. Andrews, N.B.
Moffat Stove Co., Winnipeg.
Ontario Spring Bed and Mattress Co., London.
Peterboro Mattress Co., Peterboro.
Quality Mattress Co., Waterloo.
Quebec Mattress Co., Quebec.
Restmore Mfg. Co., Vancouver.
Stamco, Ltd., Saskatoon, Sask.
Standard Bedding Co., Toronto.
Schreiter & Co., Berlin.
Standard Bedding Co., Toronto.
St. Lawrence Furniture Co., Riviere du Loup, Que.
Spiesz Furniture Co., Hanover.
Thomson Mattress Co., Montreal.
Victoriaville Bedding Co., Victoriaville.
Whitworth & Restall, Toronto.

PILLOWS
Alaska Bedding Co., Winnipeg.
Alaska B.C. Bedding Co., Vancouver.
Alaska Feather and Down Co., Montreal.
Antiseptic Bedding Co., Toronto.
Berlin Bedding Co., Berlin.
Canada Furniture Mfrs., Woodstock.
Canadian Feather and Mattress Co., Toronto.
G. Gale & Sons, Waterville.
Ideal Bedding Co., Toronto.
Ives Modern Bedstead Co., Cornwall.
Kilgour & Bro., Beauharnois, Que.
Krug Bros. & Co., Chesley.
Ontario Spring Bed and Mattress Co., London.
Quality Mattress Co., Berlin.
Restmore Mfg. Co., Vancouver.
Stamco, Ltd., Saskatoon, Sask.
Standard Bedding Co., Toronto.
Spiesz Furniture Co., Hanover.
Toronto Feather and Down Co., Toronto.
Victoriaville Bedding Co., Victoriaville, Que.
Whitworth & Restall, Toronto.

WARDROBES
Alaska B.C. Bedding Co., Vancouver.
Berlin Interior Hardwood Co., Berlin.
M. F. Beach Co., Winchester.
Canada Furniture Manufacturers, Woodstock.
Collie-Cockerill Mfg. Co., Aurora.
Crown Furniture Co., Preston.
Dominion Furniture Mfg. Co., St. Therese, Que.
Eastern Townships Furniture Co., Arthabaska, Que.
Elmira Interior Woodwork Co., Elmira.
Hepworth Mfg. Co., Hepworth.
Hespeler Furniture Co., Hespeler.
Knechtel Furniture Co., Hanover.
Krug Bros. & Co., Chesley.
Lindsay Library and Office Fitting Co., Lindsay.
Malcolm & Souter Furniture Co., Hamilton.
Markdale Furniture Co., Markdale.
Meaford Mfg. Co., Meaford.
Moffat Stove Co., Winnipeg.
J. Oliver & Sons, Ottawa.
Peppler Bros., Hanover.
Spiesz Furniture Co., Hanover.
Stratford Chair Co., Stratford.
St. Lawrence Furniture Co., Riviere du Loup, Que.

Dining Room Furniture

BUFFETS, SIDEBOARDS, EXTENSION TABLES, SIDE TABLES, CHINA CABINETS, DINERS.
Alaska B.C. Bedding Co., Vancouver.
Anthes Furniture Co., Berlin.
M. F. Beach Co., Winchester.
Bench Furniture Co., Cornwall.
Bell Furniture Co., Southampton.
Canada Furniture Mfrs., Woodstock.
Crown Furniture Co., Preston.
Durham Furniture Co., Durham.
Gibbard Furniture Co., Napanee.
Hepworth Mfg. Co., Hepworth.
Hespeler Furniture Co., Hespeler.
Hibner Furniture Co., Berlin.
Knechtel Furniture Co., Hanover.
Krug Bros. & Co., Chesley.
H. Krug Furniture Co., Berlin.
A. Malcolm Furniture Co., Kincardine.
Malcolm & Souter Furniture Co., Hamilton.
Geo. McLagan Furniture Co., Stratford.
Meaford Mfg. Co., Meaford.
Moffat Stove Co., Winnipeg.
North American Furniture Co., Owen Sound.
J. Oliver & Sons, Ottawa.
Peppler Bros., Hanover.
Charles Rogers & Sons Co., Toronto.
Stratford Furniture Co., Stratford.
Strathroy Furniture Co., Strathroy.
St. Lawrence Furniture Co., Riviere du Loup, Quebec.
Tickell Sons & Co., Belleville.
Toronto Furniture Co., Toronto.
Victoriaville Furniture Co., Victoriaville, Que.
Windsor Furniture Co., Windsor, N.S.

BUFFETS AND SIDEBOARDS (only)
(Also see Buffets, etc.).
Bell Furniture Co., Southampton.
Dominion Furniture Mfg. Co., St. Therese, Que.
Durham Furniture Co., Durham.
Eastern Townships Furniture Mfg. Co., Arthabaska, Que.
Harriston Furniture Mfg. Co., Harriston.
Hepworth Mfg. Co., Hepworth.
Kilgour & Bros., Beauharnois, Que.
D. H. Langlois & Co., St. John, Que.
Markdale Furniture Co., Markdale.
Megantic Furniture Co., Megantic, Que.
J. Oliver & Sons, Ottawa.
Orillia Furniture Co., Orillia.
Paquet & Godbout, St. Hyacinthe, Que.
Spiesz Furniture, Ltd., Hanover.

CHINA CABINETS (odd, or to match Sideboards and Buffets)
Berlin Furniture Co., Berlin.
Chesley Furniture Co., Chesley.
Crown Furniture Co., Preston.
Dominion Furniture Mfg. Co., St. Therese, Que.
Durham Furniture Co., Durham.
Knechtel Furniture Co., Hanover.
G. McLagan Furniture Co., Stratford.

CURATES
Canada Furniture Mfrs., Woodstock.
Gendron Mfg. Co., Toronto.
Toronto Furniture Co., Toronto.

DINERS (only)
(Also see Buffets, etc.).
Baetz Bros. & Co., Berlin.
Ball Furniture Co., Hanover.
Chesley Chair Co., Chesley.
Chesley Furniture Co., Chesley.
F. E. Coombe Furniture Co., Kincardine.
Durham Furniture Co., Durham.
Elmira Furniture Co., Elmira.
Fraserville Chair Co., Riviere du Loup, Quebec.
J. Ferguson & Sons, London.
Giddings, Ltd., Granby, Que.
Glaeser & Leinberger, Hanover.
Gold Medal Furniture Co., Toronto.
Lippert Furniture Co., Berlin.
John C. Mundell & Co., Elora.
National Furniture Co., Berlin.
Neustadt Mfg. Co., Neustadt.
North American Bent Chair Co., Owen Sound.
Owen Sound Chair Co., Owen Sound.
Preston Chair Co., Preston.
Schierholtz Furniture Co., New Hamburg.
Stanfold Chair Mfg. Co., Stanfold, Quebec.
Victoriaville Chair Co., Victoriaville.
Woeller Bolduc & Co., Waterloo.
Wunder Furniture Mfg. Co., Berlin.

DINING ROOM TABLES (not adjustable)
Elora Furniture Co., Elora.
Glaeser & Leinberger, Hanover.
National Table Co., Owen Sound.

EXTENSION TABLES (odd)
(Also see Buffets, etc.).
Alaska B.C. Bedding Co., Vancouver.
Baird Bros., Plattsville.
Berlin Table Mfg. Co., Berlin.
Chesley Furniture Co., Chesley.
Dominion Furniture Mfg. Co., St. Therese, Que.
Durham Furniture Co., Durham.
Eastern Townships Furniture Co., Arthabaska, Que.
Harriston Furniture Co., Harriston.
Kilgour & Bro., Beauharnois, Que.
Geo. J. Lippert Table Co., Berlin.
Lucknow Table Co., Lucknow.
G. McLagan Furniture Co., Stratford.
National Table Co., Owen Sound.
Orillia Furniture Co., Orillia.
Spiesz Furniture Co., Hanover.

Parlor and Living Room

FOR SPECIAL LINES, SUCH AS PEDESTALS, TELEPHONE STANDS, ETC., SUITABLE FOR VARIOUS ROOMS, SEE NOVELTIES.

CHESTERFIELDS
See upholstered furniture.

DAVENPORTS
See upholstered furniture.

MUSIC CABINETS
Beach Furniture Co., Cornwall.
Bell Furniture Co., Southampton.
Canada Furniture Mfrs., Woodstock.
Chesley Furniture Co., Chesley.
Collie-Cockerill Mfg. Co., Aurora.
Dominion Furniture Mfg. Co., St. Therese, Que.
Dymond-Colonial Co., Strathroy.
Hespeler Furniture Co., Hespeler.
Knechtel Furniture Co., Hanover.
Malcolm & Souter Furniture Co., Hamilton.
A. Malcolm Furniture Co., Kincardine.
Geo. McLagan Furniture Co., Stratford.
Meaford Mfg. Co., Meaford.
Peppler Bros., Hanover.
Charles Rogers & Sons Co., Toronto.

PARLOR CHAIRS
See reed and upholstered furniture.

PARLOR SUITES
See upholstered furniture.

September, 1914   CANADIAN FURNITURE WORLD AND THE UNDERTAKER   7

PARLOR TABLES
Alaska B.C. Bedding Co., Vancouver.
Anthes Furniture Co., Berlin.
Beach Furniture Co., Cornwall.
Canada Furniture Manufacturers Woodstock.
Chesley Furniture Co., Chesley.
Durham Furniture Co., Durham.
Elmira Furniture Co., Elmira, Ont.
Elora Furniture Co., Elora.
Gendron Mfg. Co., Toronto.
Harriston Furniture Mfg. Co., Harriston.
Hespeler Furniture Co., Hespeler.
Hibner Furniture Co., Berlin.
Kilgour & Bro., Beauharnois, Que.
Knechtel Furniture Co., Hanover.
J. Kreiner & Co., Berlin.
H. Krug Furniture Co., Berlin.
Geo. J. Lippert Table Co., Berlin.
Malcolm & Souter Furniture Co., Hamilton.
Markdale Furniture Co., Markdale.
Meaford Mfg. Co., Meaford.
Moffat Stove Co., Winnipeg.
Geo. McLagan Furniture Co., Stratford.
National Table Co., Owen Sound.
North American Bent Chair Co., Owen Sound.
J. Oliver & Sons, Ottawa.
Orillia Furniture Co., Orillia.
Peppler Bros., Hanover.
Strathroy Furniture Co., Strathroy.
Stratford Chair Co., Stratford.
St. Lawrence Furniture Co., Riviere du loup, Que.
Toronto Furniture Co., Toronto.
Woeller, Bolduc & Co., Waterloo.

PEDESTALS
Beach Furniture Co., Cornwall.
Canada Furniture Mfrs., Woodstock.
Chesley Furniture Co., Chesley.
Elmira Furniture Co., Elmira.
Elora Furniture Co., Elora.
Glaeser & Leinberger, Hanover.
Globe Furniture Co., Waterloo.
Gold Medal Furniture Co., Toronto.
D. Hibner Furniture Co., Berlin.
Knechtel Furniture Co., Hanover.
J. Kreiner & Co., Berlin.
Krug Bros. and Co., Chesley.
G. J. Lippert Table Co., Berlin.
Lippert Furniture Co., Berlin, Ont.
Malcolm & Souter Furniture Co., Hamilton.
Geo. McLagan Furniture Co., Stratford.
Meaford Mfg. Co., Meaford.
J. C. Mundell & Co., Elora.
National Table Co., Owen Sound.
Peppler Bros., Hanover.
Charles Rogers & Sons Co., Toronto.
Strathroy Furniture Co., Strathroy.
Toronto Furniture Co., Toronto.
Wunder Furniture Mfg. Co., Berlin.
Woeller Bolduc & Co., Waterloo.

Library and Den Furniture

BOOKCASES
Alaska B.C. Bedding Co., Vancouver.
Berlin Furniture Co., Berlin.
Canada Furniture Mfrs., Woodstock.
Collie-Cockerill Mfg. Co., Aurora.
F. E. Coombe Furniture Co., Kincardine.
Dominion Furniture Co., St. Therese, Que.
Elmira Interior Woodwork Co., Elmira.
Gibbard Furniture Co., Napanee.
Glaeser & Leinberger, Hanover.
Globe Furniture Co., Waterloo.
Kilgour & Bro., Beauharnois, Que.

Knechtel Furniture Co., Hanover.
J. Kreiner & Co., Berlin.
Krug Bros. & Co., Chesley.
A. Malcolm Furn. Co., Kincardine.
Markdale Furn. Co., Markdale.
G. McLagan Furn. Co., Stratford.
Meaford Mfg. Co., Meaford.
North American Furniture Co., Owen Sound.
Charles Rogers & Sons Co., Toronto.
Strathroy Furniture Co., Strathroy.
St. Lawrence Furniture Co., Riviere du Loup, Quebec.
Spiesz Furniture Co., Hanover.
Toronto Furniture Co., Toronto.
Windsor Furniture Co., Windsor, N.S.

BOOK STANDS
(See Magazine Racks).

BOOKCASES (Sectional)
Canada Furniture Mfrs., Woodstock.
Collie-Cockerill Mfg. Co., Aurora.
Elmira Interior Woodwork Co., Elmira.
Globe-Wernicke Co., Stratford.
Hibner Furniture Co., Berlin.
Knechtel Furniture Co., Hanover.
Lindsay Library & Office Fitting Co., Lindsay.
George McLagan Furniture Co., Stratford.

CARD AND DEN TABLES
Alaska B.C. Bedding Co., Vancouver.
Buetz Bros., Berlin.
Bell Furniture Co., Southampton.
Canada Furniture Mfrs., Woodstock.
Chesley Furniture Co., Chesley.
F. E. Coombe Furniture Co., Kincardine.
Elmira Furniture Co., Elmira.
Gendron Mfg. Co., Toronto.
Glaeser & Leinberger, Hanover.
Hespeler Furniture Co., Hespeler.
Hourd & Co., London.
Knechtel Furniture Co., Hanover.
J. Kreiner & Co., Berlin.
H. Krug Furniture Co., Berlin.
G. J. Lippert Table Co., Berlin.
Malcolm & Souter Furniture Co., Hamilton.
Geo. McLagan Furn. Co., Stratford.
Meaford Mfg. Co., Meaford.
Montreal Upholstering Co., Montreal.
J. C. Mundell & Co., Elora.
National Table Co., Owen Sound.
North American Bent Chair Co., Owen Sound.
Preston Chair Co., Preston.
Snyder Bros., Upholstering Co., Waterloo.
Stratford Mfg. Co., Stratford.
Strathroy Furniture Co., Strathroy.
Walker & Clegg, Wingham.
Westport Woodworking Co., Westport, Ont.
Woeller Bolduc & Co., Waterloo.

CELLARETTES
Canada Furniture Mfrs., Woodstock.
Dymond-Colonial Co.'s, Strathroy.
Hespeler Furniture Co., Hespeler.
J. Kreiner & Co., Berlin.
A. Malcolm Furn. Co., Kincardine.
Geo. McLagan Furniture Co., Stratford.
J. C. Mundell & Co., Elora.
North American Furniture Co., Owen Sound.
Toronto Furniture Co., Toronto.

CHAIRS
See upholstered furniture.

COUCIES
See upholstered furniture.

DAVENPORTS
See upholstered furniture.

DESKS, LIBRARY
Anthes Furniture Co., Berlin.
Baird Bros., Plattsville.
Canada Furniture Mfrs., Woodstock.
F. E. Coombe Furniture Co., Kincardine.
Dominion Furniture Co., St. Therese, Que.
Dymond Colonial Co., Strathroy.
Elmira Interior Woodwork Co., Elmira.
Globe-Wernicke Co., Stratford.
Knechtel Furniture Co., Hanover.
Lindsay Library & Office Fittings, Lindsay.
Markdale Furniture Co., Markdale.
Meaford Mfg. Co., Meaford.
Geo. McLagan Furniture Co., Stratford.
J. C. Mundell & Co., Elora.
National Table Co., Owen Sound.
Strathroy Furniture Co., Strathroy.

LIBRARY TABLES
Alaska B.C. Bedding Co., Vancouver.
Anthes Furniture Co., Berlin.
Beach Furniture Co., Cornwall.
Bell Furniture Co., Southampton.
Berlin Furniture Co., Berlin.
Canada Furniture Mfrs., Woodstock.
Chesley Furniture Co., Chesley.
Collie-Cockerill Mfg. Co., Aurora.
F. E. Coombe Furniture Co., Kincardine.
Dominion Furniture Mfg. Co., St. Therese, Que.
Durham Furniture Co., Durham.
Dymond-Colonial Co.'s, Strathroy.
Elmira Furniture Co., Elmira.
Elmira Interior Woodwork Co., Elmira.
J. Ferguson & Sons, London.
Hespeler Furniture Co., Hespeler.
Hibner Furniture Co., Berlin.
Kilgour & Bros., Ltd., Beauharnois, Que.
Knechtel Furniture Co., Hanover.
J. Kreiner & Co., Berlin.
H. Krug Furniture Co., Berlin.
Lindsay Library & Office Fittings, Lindsay.
G. J. Lippert Table Co., Berlin.
A. Malcolm Furniture Co., Kincardine.
Malcolm & Souter Furniture Co., Hamilton.
Geo. McLagan Furn. Co., Stratford.
Meaford Mfg. Co., Meaford.
John C. Mundell & Co., Elora.
National Table Co., Owen Sound.
North American Furniture Co., Owen Sound.
Peppler Bros., Hanover.
Preston Chair Co., Preston.
C. Rogers & Sons Co., Toronto.
Spiesz Furniture, Ltd., Hanover.
Snyder Bros. Upholstering Co., Waterloo.
Stratford Chair Co., Stratford.
Strathroy Furniture Co., Strathroy.
Toronto Furniture Co., Toronto.
Walker & Clegg, Wingham.
Waterloo Furniture Co., Waterloo.
Woeller Bolduc & Co., Waterloo.

MAGAZINE RACKS AND STANDS
Buetz Bros., Berlin.
Canada Furniture Mfrs., Woodstock.
Chesley Furniture Co., Chesley.
Collie-Cockerill Mfg. Co., Aurora.
Dymond Colonial Co.'s, Strathroy.
Elmira Interior Woodwork Co., Elmira.
Glaeser & Leinberger, New Hamburg.
Gold Medal Furniture Co., Toronto.
J. Kreiner & Co., Berlin.
H. Krug Furniture Co., Berlin.
A. Malcolm Furniture Co., Kincardine.

Malcolm & Souter Furniture Co., Hamilton.
Geo. McLagan Furn. Co., Stratford.
John C. Mundell & Co., Elora.
Lindsay Library & Office Fittings, Lindsay.
National Table Co., Owen Sound.
Preston Chair Co., Preston.
Snyder Bros. Upholstering Co., Waterloo.
Strathroy Furniture Co., Strathroy.
Walker & Clegg, Wingham.

MORRIS CHAIRS
Alaska B.C. Bedding Co., Vancouver.
J. P. Albrough & Co., Ingersoll.
Canada Furniture Mfrs., Woolstock.
F. E. Coombe Furn. Co., Kincardine.
Dominion Furniture Mfg. Co., St. Therese, Que.
Ellis Furniture Co., Ingersoll.
Farquharson, Gifford & Co., Stratford.
Glaeser & Leinberger, Hanover.
Gold Medal Furniture Co., Toronto.
G. H. Hachborn & Co., Berlin.
Imperial Rattan Co., Stratford.
Knechtel Furniture Co., Hanover.
Krug Bros. & Co., Chesley.
H. Krug Furniture Co., Berlin.
Lippert Furniture Co., Berlin.
Walter Mead & Co., Hanover.
Morlock Bros., Hanover.
John C. Mundell & Co., Elora.
Moffat Stove Co., Winnipeg.
Owen Daveno Bed Co., Hespeler.
Charles Rogers & Sons Co., Toronto.
Schierholtz Furn. Co., New Hamburg.
Snyder Bros. Upholstering Co., Waterloo.
Victoriaville Bedding Co., Victoriaville.
Walker & Clegg, Wingham.
Waterloo Furniture Co., Waterloo.
Woeller Bolduc & Co., Waterloo.

SMOKERS' SETS
A. Malcolm Furniture Co., Kincardine.

WRITING TABLES AND SECRETARIES
Alaska B.C. Bedding Co., Vancouver.
Canada Furniture Manufacturers, Woodstock.
Chesley Furniture Co., Chesley.
Durham Furniture Co., Durham.
Elmira Interior Woodwork Co., Elmira.
Kilgour & Bro., Beauharnois, Que.
Knechtel Furniture Co., Hanover.
Krug Bros. & Co., Chesley.
H. Krug Furniture Co., Berlin.
Lindsay Library & Office Fittings, Lindsay.
G. J. Lippert Table Co., Berlin.
A. Malcolm Furniture Co., Kincardine.
Malcolm & Souter Furniture Co., Hamilton.
Meaford Mfg. Co., Meaford.
A. Malcolm Furniture Co., Kincardine.
J. C. Mundell & Co., Elora.
G. McLagan Furniture Co., Stratford.
National Table Co., Owen Sound.
North American Furniture Co., Owen Sound.
Snyder Bros. Upholstering Co., Waterloo.
Spiesz Furniture Co., Hanover.
Stratford Chair Co., Stratford.
Strathroy Furniture Co., Strathroy.
St. Lawrence Furniture Co., Riviere du Loup, Quebec.
Toronto Furniture Co., Toronto.
Windsor Furniture Co., Windsor, N.S.

Hall Furniture

CONSOLE TABLES AND MIRRORS
A. Malcolm Furniture Co., Kincardine.

HALL CHAIRS
Elmira Furniture Co., Elmira.
H. Krug Furniture Co., Berlin.
G. McLagan Furniture Co., Stratford.
North American Bent Chair Co., Owen Sound.
Preston Chair Co., Preston.
Wunder Furniture Co., Berlin.

HALL CLOCKS
Berlin Furniture Co., Berlin, Ont.
Elmira Interior Woodwork Co., Elmira.
John C. Mundell & Co., Elora.

HALL SEATS AND MIRRORS
Anthes Furniture Co., Berlin.
Canada Furniture Mfrs., Woodstock.
Chesley Furniture Co., Chesley.
D. Hibner Furniture Co., Berlin.
H. Krug Furniture Co., Berlin.
Lippert Furniture Co., Berlin.
Geo. McLagan Furn. Co., Stratford.
Meaford Mfg. Co., Meaford.
Markdale Furniture Co., Markdale.
Peppler Bros., Hanover.
Charles Rogers & Sons Co., Toronto.
Wunder Furniture Mfg. Co., Berlin.

HALL TREES
Canada Furniture Mfrs., Woodstock.
Chesley Furniture Co., Chesley.
Collie-Cockerill Mfg. Co., Aurora.
Hespeler Furniture Co., Hespeler.
Ideal Bedding Co., Toronto.
Lindsay Library & Office Fittings, Lindsay.
Geo. McLagan Furn. Co., Stratford.
Meaford Mfg. Co., Meaford.
Peppler Bros., Hanover.
Snyder Bros. Upholstering Co., Waterloo.
Woeller Bolduc & Co., Waterloo.
Wunder Furniture Mfg. Co., Berlin.

HALL RACKS
Anthes Furniture Co., Berlin.
Chesley Furniture Co., Chesley.
Canada Furniture Manufacturers, Woodstock.
Dominion Furniture Mfg. Co., St. Therese, Que.
Dymond-Colonial Co.'s, Strathroy.
Hibner Furniture Co., Berlin.
Kilgour Bros. & Co., Beauharnois, Que.
Lippert Furniture Co., Berlin.
Meaford Mfg. Co., Meaford.
G. McLagan Furniture Co., Stratford.
Peppler Bros., Hanover.
St. Lawrence Furniture Co., Riviere du Loup, Quebec.
Wunder Furniture Co., Berlin.

UMBRELLA STANDS
Berlin Interior Hardwood Co., Berlin.
Canada Furniture Manufacturers, Woodstock.
Chesley Furniture Co., Chesley.
F. E. Coombe Furniture Co., Kincardine.
Dominion Furniture Mfg. Co., St. Therese, Que.
Dymond-Colonial Co.'s, Strathroy.
Elmira Furniture Co., Elmira.
Elmira Interior Woodwork Co., Elmira.
Elora Furniture Co., Elora.
Glaeser & Leinberger, Hanover.
J. Kreiner & Co., Berlin.
H. Krug Furniture Co., Berlin.

Malcolm & Souter Furniture Co., Hamilton.
Geo. McLagan Furn. Co., Stratford.
Meaford Mfg. Co., Meaford.
North American Furniture Co., Owen Sound.
Peppler Bros., Hanover.
Snyder Bros. Upholstering Co., Waterloo.
St. Lawrence Furniture Co., Riviere du Loup, Quebec.
Wunder Furniture Mfg. Co., Berlin.

Kitchen and Laundry

BAKE, AND IRONING BOARDS
Chesley Furniture Co., Chesley.
Stratford Mfg. Co., Stratford.

CHAIRS
Ball Furniture Co., Limited, The, Hanover.
Canada Furniture Mfrs., Limited, Woodstock.
Chesley Chair Co., Limited, Chesley.
Danville Chair & Specialty Co., Danville, Que.
Dominion Chair Co., Limited, Bass River, N.S.
Durham Furniture Co., Durham.
Fraserville Chair Company, Fraserville, Que.
Giddings, Limited, Granby, Que.
D. Hibner Furniture Co., Berlin.
Kilgour Bros. & Co., Beauharnois, Que.
Knechtel Furniture Co., Hanover.
Moffat Stove Co., Winnipeg.
North American Bent Chair Co., Owen Sound.
Neustadt Furniture Co., Neustadt.
Stanfold Chair Mfg. Co., Stanfold, Quebec.
George Valliere, Quebec, Que.
Victoriaville Chair Co., Limited, Victoriaville, Que.

CUPBOARDS
Canada Furniture Manufacturers, Woodstock.
Durham Furniture Co., Durham.
Hepworth Mfg. Co., Hepworth.
Kilgour & Bro., Beauharnois, Que.
Knechtel Furniture Co., Hanover.
Meaford Mfg. Co., Meaford.
St. Lawrence Furniture Co., Riviere du Loup, Quebec.
J. Oliver & Sons, Ottawa.

KITCHEN CABINETS
Alaska B.C. Bedding Co., Vancouver.
Canada Furniture Mfrs., Woodstock.
Eastern Townships Furniture Co., Arthabaska, Que.
J. Ferguson & Sons, London.
Hepworth Mfg. Co., Hepworth.
Hourd & Co., London.
H. E. Furniture Co., Milverton.
Knechtel Kitchen Cabinet Co., Hanover.
Krug Bros. & Co., Chesley.
Lee Mfg. Co., Pembroke.
Markdale Furniture Co., Markdale.
Meaford Mfg. Co., Meaford.
Moffat Stove Co., Winnipeg.
National Mfg. Co., Ottawa.
Nagrella Mfg. Co., Hamilton.
J. Oliver & Sons, Ottawa.
Stratford Chair Co., Stratford.
Thompson Kanuck Kitchen Cabinet Company, Belleville.
Universal Cabinet Co., Chatham.

SAFES
Canada Furniture Manufacturers, Woodstock.

STOVES AND RANGES
Beach Foundry Co., Ottawa.
Burrow, Stewart & Milne, Hamilton.
Canadian Heating & Ventilating Co., Owen Sound.
Clare Bros., Preston, Ont.
Galt Stove & Furnace Co., Galt.
Enterprise Foundry Co., Sackville, N.B.
Findlay Bros., Carleton Place.
Gurney Foundry Co., Toronto.
Hall-Zryd Foundry Co., Hespeler.
Hamilton Stove & Heater Co., Hamilton.
Kir-Ben, Limited, Almonte, Ont.
McClary Mfg. Co., London.
Moffat Stove Co., Weston.
D. Moore Co., Hamilton.
Jas. Smart Mfg. Co., Brockville.
Jas. Stewart Mfg. Co., Woodstock.
Supreme Heating Co., Welland.

TABLES
Alaska B.C. Bedding Co., Vancouver.
Canada Furniture Mfrs., Woodstock.
Chesley Furniture Co., Chesley.
Cushing Bros., Calgary.
Czerwinski Box Co., Winnipeg, Man.
Durham Furniture Co., Durham.
Eastern Townships Furniture Mfg. Co., Arthabaska, Que.
Kilgour & Bros., Ltd., Beauharnois.
Knechtel Furniture Co., Hanover.
Krug Bros. & Co., Chesley.
H. Krug Furniture Co., Berlin.
Lucknow Table Co., Lucknow.
Hepworth Mfg. Co., Hepworth.
D. Hibner Furniture Co., Berlin.
G. J. Lippert Table Co., Berlin.
Meaford Mfg. Co., Meaford.
Moffat Stove Co., Winnipeg.
National Table Co., Owen Sound.
J. Oliver & Sons, Ottawa.
Peppler Bros., Hanover.
Spiesz Furniture, Hanover.
St. Lawrence Furniture Co., Riviere du Loup, Que.
Strathroy Furniture Co., Strathroy.
Victoriaville Furniture Co., Victoriaville, Que.
Windsor Furniture Co., Windsor, N.S.
Weiler Bros., Victoria, B.C.

REFRIGERATORS
Eureka Refrigerator Co., Toronto.
Ham & Nott, Brantford.
McCray Refrigerator Co., Kendallville, Ind.
John Hillock & Co., Toronto.
Sanderson, Harold, Co., Paris.
James Smart Mfg. Co., Brockville.

WASHING MACHINES
E. H. Briggs Co., Winnipeg.
J. H. Connor & Sons, Ottawa.
Cummer-Dowswell, Hamilton.
Excello Motor Washer Co., Berlin.
Geo. C. Kaitting & Son., Galt.
Lee Mfg. Co., Pembroke.
D. Maxwell & Sons, St. Mary's.
One Minute Washer Co., Toronto.

Bathroom Furniture

MEDICINE CABINETS
Alaska B.C. Bedding Co., Vancouver.
Canada Furniture Mfrs., Woodstock.
Chesley Furniture Co., Chesley.
Dymond-Colonial Co., Strathroy.
Dominion Furniture Mfg. Co., St. Therese, Que.
Durham Furniture Co., Durham.
Gendron Mfg. Co., Toronto.
Knechtel Furniture Co., Hanover.
Meaford Mfg. Co., Meaford.
Markdale Furn. Co., Markdale.
Matthews Bros., Toronto.

Maydwell Mfg. Co., Toronto.
J. Oliver & Sons, Ottawa.
St. Lawrence Furniture Co., Riviere du Loup, Quebec.

MIRRORS
See Novelties.

STOOLS
See Novelties.

Verandah, Lawn and Camp

AWNINGS AND WINDOW SHADES
Geo. H. Hees & Sons Co., Toronto.
Fred G. Soper Co., Toronto.
Stameo, Ltd., Saskatoon, Sask.

CAMP STOOLS
Stratford Mfg. Co., Stratford.
Southampton Seating Co., Southampton.

CAMP BEDS
(See Iron and Brass Beds).
Colieran Patent Spring Mattress Co., Toronto.
Gold Medal Furniture Co., Toronto.
J. Oliver & Sons, Ottawa.
Progress Spring Bed Co., Montreal.

CHAIRS, ROCKERS AND SETTEES
Baetz Bros., Berlin.
F. Bibby & Co., Dundas.
Canada Furniture Mfrs., Woodstock.
Canadian Rattan Chair Co., Victoriaville, Que.
Chesley Chair Co., Chesley.
Danville Chair Co., Danville, Que.
Fraserville Chair Co., Fraserville, Que.
Gendron Mfg. Co., Toronto.
Imperial Rattan Co., Stratford.
W. B. Jennings, St. Thomas.
Krug Bros. & Co., Chesley.
Malcolm Co., Limited, Vancouver.
Royal Chair Co., Quebec, Que.
Snyder Bros. Upholstering Co., Waterloo.
Southampton Seating Co., Southampton.
Stanfold Chair Mfg. Co., Stanfold, Quebec.
Stratford Mfg. Co., Stratford.

COUCH HAMMOCKS
Alaska B.C. Bedding Co., Vancouver.
Alaska Feather & Down Co., Montreal.
Alaska Bedding Co., Winnipeg, Calgary and Vancouver.
G. Gale & Sons, Waterville, Que.
Galt Robe Co., Galt.
Ideal Bedding Co., Toronto.
Steel Furnishing Co., New Glasgow, N.S.

FOLDING CHAIRS
Alaska B.C. Bedding Co., Vancouver.
Berlin Interior Hardwood Co., Berlin.
Canada Furniture Mfrs., Woodstock.
Canadian Rattan Chair Co., Victoriaville, Que.
Chesley Chair Co., Chesley.
J. Ferguson & Sons, London.
Ideal Bedding Co., Toronto.
Krug Bros. & Co., Chesley.
North American Bent Chair Co., Owen Sound.
Otterville Mfg. Co., Otterville.
Roxton Mill & Chair Co., Waterloo, Que.
Southampton Seating Co., Southampton.
Stratford Mfg. Co., Stratford.
Valley City Seating Co., Dundas.

FOLDING TABLES
Alaska B.C. Bedding Co., Vancouver.
Canada Furniture Mfrs., Woodstock.
Chesley Furniture Co., Chesley.
Dominion Hammock Co., Dunnville.
Durham Furniture Co., Durham.
J. Ferguson & Sons, London.
Hourd & Co., London.
National Table Co., Owen Sound.
J. Oliver & Sons, Ottawa.
Strathroy Furniture Co., Strathroy.
Stratford Mfg. Co., Stratford.

HAMMOCKS
Dominion Hammock Co., Dunnville.
Galt Robe Co., Galt.

LADDERS
Stratford Mfg. Co., Stratford.

LAWN SEATS AND SWINGS
Canadian Buffalo Sled Co., Preston.
Canadian Rattan Co., Victoriaville, Que.
Danville Chair & Specialty Co., Danville, Que.
Malcolm Co., Limited, Vancouver.
J. C. Mundell & Co., Elora.
Stratford Mfg. Co., Stratford.
Southampton Seating Co., Southampton.
W. F. Vilas, Cowansville, Que.
John Watson Mfg. Co., Ayr.

PARK SEATS
Stratford Mfg. Co., Stratford.
Southampton Seating Co., Southampton.

REED AND RATTAN FURNITURE
Canada Furniture Mfrs., Woodstock.
Canadian Rattan Chair Co., Victoriaville, Que.
Gendron Mfg. Co., Toronto.
Imperial Rattan Co., Stratford.
Kilgour & Bro., Beauharnois, Que.

SEAGRASS FURNITURE
W. B. Jennings Co., St. Thomas.
The Malcolm Co., Vancouver, B.C.

WILLOW FURNITURE
F. Bibby & Co., Dundas.
Brantford Willow Works, Brantford.
Malcolm Co., Limited, Vancouver.

Office Furniture

BOARDROOM TABLES
Alaska B.C. Bedding Co., Vancouver.
Berlin Interior Hardwood Co., Berlin.
Canada Furniture Mfrs., Woodstock.
Chesley Furniture Co., Chesley.
Collie-Cockerill Mfg. Co., Aurora.
F. E. Coombe Furn. Co., Kincardine.
Elmira Interior Woodwork Co., Elmira.
Glaeser & Leinberger, Hanover.
Globe Furniture Co., Waterloo.
Knechtel Furniture Co., Hanover.
H. Krug Furniture Co., Berlin.
Krug Bros. & Co., Chesley.
Lindsay Library & Office Fittings, Lindsay.
Meaford Mfg. Co., Meaford.
National Table Co., Owen Sound.
John B. Snider, Waterloo.
St. Lawrence Furniture Co., Riviere du Loup, Quebec.
Toronto Furniture Co., Toronto.

BOOKCASES
Canada Furniture Mfrs., Woodstock.
Collie-Cockerill Mfg. Co., Aurora.
Globe Furniture Co., Waterloo.
Globe-Wernicke Co., Stratford.
D. Hibner Co., Berlin.
Knechtel Furniture Co., Hanover.
Lindsay Library & Office Fittings, Lindsay.
Geo. McLagnan Furn. Co., Stratford.
Meaford Mfg. Co., Meaford.
St. Lawrence Furniture Co., Riviere du Loup, Quebec.

CHAIRS

Ball Furniture Co., Hanover.
Bell Furniture Co., Southampton.
Berlin Interior Hardwood Co., Berlin.
Canadian Office & School Furniture Co., Preston.
Canada Furn. Manufacturers, Woodstock.
Chesley Chair Co., Chesley.
Collie-Cockerill Co., Aurora.
F. E. Coombe Furniture Co., Kincardine.
Danville Chair & Specialty Co., Danville, Que.
Elmira Interior Woodwork Co., Elmira.
Elmira Furniture Co., Elmira.
Fraserville Chair Co., Riviere du Loup, Quebec.
Glaeser & Leinberger, Hanover.
Globe Furniture Co., Waterloo.
D. Hibner Furniture Co., Berlin.
Knechtel Furniture Co., Hanover.
J. & J. Kohn, Toronto (W. Craig).
H. Krug Furniture Co., Berlin.
Krug Bros. & Co., Chesley.
Lindsay Library & Office Fittings, Lindsay.
McGill Chair Co., Cornwall.
Moffat Stove Co., Winnipeg.
John C. Mundell & Co., Elora.
North American Bent Chair Co., Owen Sound.
Owen Sound Chair Co., Owen Sound.
Preston Chair Co., Preston.
Stanfold Chair Mfg. Co., Stanfold, Quebec.
Stratford Chair Co., Stratford.
John B. Snyder, Waterloo.
Woeller Boldue & Co., Waterloo.

DESKS—FLAT AND ROLL-TOP

Baird Bros., Plattsville.
Beach Furniture Co., Cornwall.
Berlin Interior Hardwood Co., Berlin.
Canada Furniture Mfrs., Woodstock.
Canadian Office & School Furniture Co., Preston.
Collie-Cockerill Mfg. Co., Aurora.
Dominion Furniture Mfg. Co., St. Therese, Que.
Elmira Interior Woodwork Co., Elmira.
Krug Bros. & Co., Chesley.
Kilgour & Bros., Beauharnois, Que.
Knechtel Furniture Co., Hanover.
Lindsay Library & Office Fittings, Lindsay.
A. Malcolm Furniture Co., Kincardine.
Markdale Furniture Co., Markdale.
Meaford Mfg. Co., Meaford.
National Table Co., Owen Sound.
North American Furniture Co., Owen Sound.
J. Oliver & Sons, Ottawa.
Paquet & Godbout, St. Hyacinthe, Que.
Preston Furniture Co., Preston.
Charles Rogers & Sons Co., Toronto.
Strathroy Furniture Co., Strathroy
Stratford Desk Co., Stratford.
John B. Snider, Waterloo.
St. Lawrence Furniture Co., Riviere du Loup, Que.
Steel Equipment Co., Ottawa.
Windsor Furniture Co., Windsor, N.S.

DESKS—STANDING

Berlin Interior Hardwood Co., Berlin.
Canada Furniture Mfrs., Woodstock.
Canadian Office & School Furniture Co., Preston.
Collie-Cockerill Mfg. Co., Aurora.
Elmira Interior Woodwork Co., Elmira.
Globe Furniture Co., Waterloo.
Knechtel Furniture Co., Hanover.
Lindsay Library & Office Fittings, Lindsay.
John B. Snider, Waterloo.
Stratford Desks, Stratford.

FILING CABINETS AND SUPPLIES

Canada Furniture Manufacturers, Woodstock.
Collie-Cockerill Mfg. Co., Aurora.
Elmira Interior Woodwork Co., Elmira.
Globe-Wernicke Co., Stratford.
Knechtel Furniture Co., Hanover.
Lindsay Library & Office Fittings, Lindsay.
Geo. McLagan Furniture Co., Stratford.
Steel Equipment Co., Ottawa.

OFFICE TRUCKS

Collie-Cockerill Mfg. Co., Aurora.
Elmira Interior Woodwork Co., Elmira.
Hespeler Furniture Co., Hespeler.
Lindsay Library & Office Fittings, Lindsay.

SETTEES

Berlin Interior Hardwood Co., Berlin.
Canadian Rattan Chair Co., Victoriaville, Que.
Collie-Cockerill Mfg. Co., Aurora.
Elmira Interior Woodwork Co., Elmira.
Glaeser & Leinberger, Hanover.
Globe Furniture Co., Waterloo.
Imperial Rattan Co., Stratford.
H. Krug Furniture Co., Berlin.
James Smart Mfg. Co., Brockville.
Snyder Bros. Upholstering Co., Waterloo.
Walker & Clegg, Wingham.

STOOLS

Ball Furniture Co., Hanover.
Bell Furniture Co., Southampton.
Berlin Interior Hardwood Co., Berlin.
Canadian Office & School Furniture Co., Preston.
Canada Furniture Mfrs., Woodstock.
Chesley Chair Co., Chesley.
F. E. Coombe Furniture Co., Kincardine.
Danville Chair Co., Danville, Que.
Elmira Furniture Co., Elmira.
Elmira Interior Woodwork Co., Elmira.
Glaeser & Leinberger, Hanover.
Globe Furniture Co., Waterloo.
Gold Medal Furniture Co., Toronto.
Knechtel Furniture Co., Hanover.
H. Krug Furniture Co., Berlin.
North American Bent Chair Co., Owen Sound.
Otterville Mfg. Co., Otterville.
Snyder Bros. Upholstering Co., Waterloo.
Stratford Chair Co., Stratford.
St. Lawrence Furniture Co., Riviere du Loup, Quebec.

TABLES

Alaska B.C. Bedding Co., Vancouver.
Bell Furniture Co., Southampton.
Berlin Interior Hardwood Co., Berlin.
Canada Furniture Mfrs., Woodstock.
Canadian Office & School Furniture Co., Preston.
Chesley Furniture Co., Chesley.
Collie-Cockerill Mfg. Co., Aurora.
Elmira Furniture Co., Elmira.
Elmira Interior Woodwork Co., Elmira.
Glaeser & Leinberger, Hanover.
Globe Furniture Co., Waterloo.
Knechtel Furniture Co., Hanover.
H. Krug Furniture Co., Berlin.
Krug Bros. & Co., Chesley.
Lindsay Library & Office Fittings, Lindsay.
G. J. Lippert Table Co., Berlin.
A. Malcolm Furniture Co., Kincardine.
Meaford Mfg. Co., Meaford.
Moffat Stove Co., Winnipeg.
J. C. Mundell & Co., Elora.
Peppler Bros., Hanover.
Strathroy Furniture Co., Strathroy.
Stratford Desk Co., Stratford.
John B. Snider, Waterloo.
Stratford Desks, Ltd., Stratford.
St. Lawrence Furniture Co., Riviere du Loup, Quebec.
Snyder Bros. Upholstering Co., Waterloo.
Windsor Furniture Co., Windsor, N.S.

TYPEWRITER DESKS

Alaska B.C. Bedding Co., Vancouver.
Baird Bros., Plattsville.
Berlin Interior Hardwood Co., Berlin.
Canada Furniture Mfrs., Woodstock.
Canadian Office & School Furniture Co., Preston.
Collie-Cockerill Mfg. Co., Aurora.
Dominion Furniture Mfg. Co., St. Therese, Que.
Elmira Interior Woodwork Co., Elmira.
Globe-Wernicke Co., Stratford.
Knechtel Furniture Co., Hanover.
Lindsay Library & Office Fittings, Lindsay.
A. Malcolm Furniture Co., Kincardine.
Preston Furniture Co., Preston.
John B. Snider, Waterloo.
Stratford Desk Co., Stratford.

WARDROBES

Canada Furniture Mfrs., Woodstock.
Collie-Cockerill Mfg. Co., Aurora.
Knechtel Furniture Co., Hanover.
Meaford Mfg. Co., Meaford.
Peppler Bros., Hanover.

WASTE BASKETS

See Novelties.
Elmira Interior Woodwork Co., Elmira.

Church and School Furniture

ASSEMBLY, HALL AND THEATRE

Berlin Interior Hardwood Co., Berlin.
Canadian Office & School Furniture Co., Preston.
Canada Furniture Mfrs., Woodstock.
Chesley Chair Co., Chesley.
Danville Chair & Specialty Co., Danville, Que.
Dominion Chair Co., Bass River, N.S.
Fraserville Chair Co., Fraserville.
Globe Furniture Co., Waterloo.
Ideal Bedding Co., Toronto.
North American Bent Chair Co., Owen Sound.
J. Oliver & Sons, Ottawa.
Owen Sound Chair Co., Owen Sound.
Otterville Mfg. Co., Otterville.
Royal Chair Co., Quebec.
Stratford Mfg. Co., Stratford.
Stanfold Chair Mfg. Co., Stanfold.
Southampton Seating Co., Southampton.
Valley City Seating Co., Dundas.

BLACKBOARDS
Globe Furniture Co., Waterloo.

CHURCH, SCHOOL AND LODGE
Berlin Interior Hardwood Co., Berlin.
Canada Furniture Manufacturers, Woodstock.
Canadian Office & School Furniture Co., Preston.
Globe Furniture Co., Waterloo.
North American Bent Chair Co., Owen Sound.
J. C. Mundell & Co., Elora.
J. Oliver & Sons, Ottawa.
James Smart Mfg. Co., Brockville.
John B. Snider, Waterloo.
St. Lawrence Furniture Co., Riviere du Loup, Quebec.
Valley City Seating Co., Dundas.
W. F. Vilas, Cowansville, Que.
Westport School Furniture Co., Westport.
Walker & Clegg, Wingham.

LODGE SETTEES, PEDESTALS, ALTARS, ETC.
Walker & Clegg, Wingham.

Upholstered Furniture

CHESTERFIELDS
Alaska B.C. Bedding Co., Vancouver.
J. P. Aibrough & Co., Ingersoll.
Baetz Bros. & Co., Berlin.
Canada Furniture Mfrs., Woodstock.
F. E. Coombe Furniture Co., Kincardine.
Gold Medal Furniture Co., Toronto.
Imperial Furniture Co., Toronto.
Imperial Rattan Co., Stratford.
H. Krug Furniture Co., Berlin.
Quality Furniture Makers, Welland.
Snyder Bros. Upholstering Co., Waterloo.
Walker & Clegg, Wingham.

COUCHES
Alaska B.C. Bedding Co., Vancouver.
J. P. Aibrough & Co., Ingersoll.
Alaska Bedding Co., Winnipeg, Calgary and Vancouver.
Alaska Feather & Down Co., Montreal.
Canada Furniture Mfrs., Woodstock.
Continental Upholstered Furniture Co., Montreal.
F. E. Coombe Furniture Co., Kincardine.
Dominion Furniture Mfg. Co., St. Therese, Que.
Dymond-Colonial Co.'s, Strathroy.
Ellis Furniture Co., Ingersoll.
Farquharson-Gifford Co., Stratford.
Gold Medal Furniture Co., Toronto.
G. H. Hachborn & Co., Berlin.
Hibner Furniture Co., Berlin.
Imperial Furniture Co., Toronto.
Imperial Rattan Co., Stratford.
Ideal Bedding Co., Toronto.
Kindel Bed Co., Toronto.
Kilgour & Bros., Beauharnois, Que.
Knechtel Furniture Co., Hanover.
Krug Bros. & Co., Chesley.
H. Krug Furniture Co., Berlin.
Walter Meads Upholstering Co., Hanover.
Maple Leaf Couch Co., Toronto.
Moffat Stove Co., Winnipeg.
Montreal Upholstering Co., Montreal.
Morlock Bros., Hanover.
John C. Mundell & Co., Elora.
Ontario Spring Bed & Mattress Co., London.
Quality Furniture Makers, Welland.
Stamen, Ltd., Saskatoon, Sask.

Schierholtz Furniture Co., New Hamburg.
Snyder Bros. Upholstering Co., Waterloo.
Steel Furnishing Co., New Glasgow, N.S.
Victoriaville Bedding Co., Victoriaville, Que.
Walker & Clegg, Wingham.
Waterloo Furniture Co., Waterloo.
S. Weisglass, Ltd., Montreal, Que.
Woeller Boldue & Co., Waterloo.

COUCH FRAMES
Elmira Interior Woodwork Co., Elmira.
Gold Medal Furniture Co., Toronto.
Southampton Seating Co., Southampton.
James Steele & Co., Guelph.

DAVENPORTS
Alaska B.C. Bedding Co., Vancouver.
Baetz Bros. & Co., Berlin.
Canada Furniture Mfrs., Woodstock.
F E. Coombe Furniture Co., Kincardine.
Continental Upholstering & Furniture Co., Montreal.
Dymond-Colonial Co.'s, Strathroy.
Elmira Furniture Co., Elmira.
Gold Medal Furniture Mfg. Co., Toronto.
G. H. Hachborn & Co., Berlin.
H. Krug Furniture Co., Berlin.
Lippert Furniture Co., Berlin.
Maple Leaf Couch Co., Toronto.
Montreal Upholstering Co., Montreal.
J. C. Mundell & Co., Elora.
Owen Daveno Bed Co., Hespeler.
Preston Chair Co., Preston.
Quality Furniture Makers, Welland.
Schierholtz Furniture Co., New Hamburg.
Snyder Bros. Upholstering Co., Waterloo.
Walker & Clegg, Wingham.
Waterloo Furniture Co., Waterloo.

DAVENPORT BEDS
(See also Iron and Brass Beds).
Alaska B.C. Bedding Co., Vancouver.
Canada Furniture Mfrs., Woodstock.
Continental Upholstering Co., Montreal.
Dymond Colonial Co., Strathroy.
Farquharson-Gifford Co., Stratford.
Gold Medal Furniture Co., Toronto.
Hachborn & Co., Berlin.
Ideal Bedding Co., Toronto.
Imperial Furniture Co., Toronto.
Imperial Rattan Co., Stratford.
Kindel Bed Co., Toronto.
Lippert Furniture Co., Berlin.
Montreal Upholstering Co., Montreal.
John C. Mundell & Co., Elora.
Owen Daveno Bed Co., Hespeler.
Progress Spring Bed Mfg. Co., Montreal.
Quality Furniture Makers, Welland.
Schierholtz Furniture Co., New Hamburg.
Snyder Bros. Upholstering Co., Waterloo.
Stratford Davenport Bed Co., Stratford.
Waterloo Furniture Co., Waterloo.
Walker & Clegg, Wingham.

DAVENPORT FRAMES
Elmira Interior Woodwork Co., Elmira.
Gold Medal Furniture Co., Toronto.
J. C. Mundell & Co., Elora.
Snyder Bros. Upholstering Co., Waterloo.
Walker & Clegg, Wingham.

DEN CHAIRS
J. P. Aibrough & Co., Ingersoll.
Baetz Bros. & Co., Berlin.
Canada Furniture Mfrs., Woodstock.
F. E. Coombe Furniture Co., Kincardine.
Elmira Furniture Co., Elmira.
Gendron Mfg. Co., Toronto.
Glaeser & Leinherger, Hanover.
Gold Medal Furniture Co., Toronto.
G. H. Hachborn & Co., Berlin.
Knechtel Furniture Co., Berlin.
H. Krug Furniture Co., Berlin.
Lippert Furniture Co., Berlin.
A. Malcolm Furniture Co., Kincardine.
Maple Leaf Couch Co., Toronto.
Walter Meads Upholstering Co., Hanover.
Menford Mfg. Co., Meaford.
Morlock Bros., Hanover.
J. C. Mundell & Co., Elora.
Owen Daveno Bed Co., Hespeler.
Preston Chair Co., Preston.
Quality Furniture Makers, Welland.
Charles Rogers & Sons Co., Toronto.
Snyder Bros. Upholstering Co., Waterloo.
Strathroy Furniture Co., Strathroy.
Waterloo Furniture Co., Waterloo.
Woeller & Boldue & Co., Waterloo.

DIVANS
Alaska B.C. Bedding Co., Vancouver.
Canada Furniture Manufacturers, Woodstock.
Dymond-Colonial Co.'s, Strathroy.
Gold Medal Furniture Co., Toronto.
Ideal Bedding Co., Toronto.
Snyder Bros. Upholstering Co., Waterloo.
Woeller Boldue & Co., Waterloo.
Wunder Furniture Mfg. Co., Berlin.

DIVANETTES
Gold Medal Furniture Mfg. Co., Toronto.
Kindel Bed Co., Toronto.
Lippert Furniture Co., Berlin.
Montreal Upholstering Co., Montreal.
J. C. Mundell & Co., Elora.
Owen Daveno Bed Co., Hespeler.
Snyder Bros. Upholstering Co., Waterloo.
Wunder Furniture Mfg. Co., Berlin.

LIVING ROOM FURNITURE AND SUITES
J. P. Aibrough & Co., Ingersoll.
Baetz Bros., Berlin.
Canada Furniture Manufacturers, Woodstock.
F. E. Coombe Furniture Co., Kincardine.
Dymond Colonial Co., Strathroy.
Ellis Furniture Co., Ingersoll.
Elmira Furniture Co., Elmira.
Farquharson-Gifford Co., Stratford.
Gendron Mfg. Co., Toronto.
Gheser & Leinberger, Hanover.
Gold Medal Furniture Co., Toronto.
Imperial Rattan Co., Stratford.
Imperial Furniture Co., Toronto.
Knechtel Furniture Co., Hanover.
Lippert Furniture Co., Berlin.
A. Malcolm Furniture Co., Kincardine.
Morlock Bros., Hanover.
John C. Mundell & Co., Elora.
National Table Co., Owen Sound.
Owen Sound Chair Co., Owen Sound.
Quality Furniture Makers, Welland.
Schierholtz Furniture Co., New Hamburg.
Walker & Clegg, Wingham.
Waterloo Furniture Co., Waterloo.
Woeller Boldue & Co., Waterloo.

LOUNGES

Alaska B.C. Bedding Co., Vancouver.
J. P. Albrough & Co., Ingersoll.
Canada Furniture Manufacturers, Woodstock.
Gold Medal Furniture Co., Toronto.
Kilgour & Bro., Beauharnois, Que.
Owen DaVeno Bed Co., Hespeler.
Snyder Bros. Upholstering Co., Waterloo.

MORRIS CHAIRS

See Library and Den Furniture.

PARLOR FRAMES

Baetz Bros. & Co., Berlin.
Berlin Specialty Furniture Co., Berlin.
Canada Furniture Mfrs., Woodstock.
Ellis Furniture Co., Ingersoll.
Elmira Furniture Co., Elmira.
Elmira Interior Woodwork Co., Elmira.
Elora Furniture Co., Elora.
Glaeser & Leinberger, Hanover.
Gold Medal Furniture Co., Toronto.
J. Kreiner & Co., Berlin.
Lippert Furniture Co., Berlin.
Snyder Bros. Upholstering Co., Waterloo.
Walker & Clegg, Wingham.
Waterloo Furniture Co., Waterloo.
Woeller, Bolduc & Co., Waterloo.
Wunder Furniture Mfg. Co., Berlin.

PARLOR, RECEPTION AND DRAWING ROOM CHAIRS AND ROCKERS.

J. P. Albrough & Co., Ingersoll.
Baetz Bros. & Co., Berlin.
Canada Furniture Mfrs., Woodstock.
Canadian Rattan Chair Co., Victoriaville, Que.
F. E. Coombe Furniture Co., Kincardine.
Dominion Furniture Mfg. Co., St. Therese. Que.
Danville Chair & Specialty Co., Danville, Que.
Dymond-Colonial Co.'s, Strathroy.
Ellis Furniture Co., Ingersoll.
Elmira Furniture Co., Elmira.
Farquharson-Gifford Co., Stratford.
Fraserville Chair Co., Riviere du Loup, Quebec.
Gendron Mfg. Co., Toronto.
Glaeser & Leinberger, Hanover.
Gold Medal Furniture Co., Toronto.
Geo. H. Hachborn & Co., Berlin.
D. Hibner Furniture Co., Berlin.
Imperial Furniture Co., Toronto.
Imperial Rattan Co., Stratford.
Knechtel Furniture Co., Hanover.
H. Krug Furniture Co., Berlin.
Krug Bros. & Co., Chesley.
Lippert Furniture Co., Berlin.
The Malcolm Co., Vancouver, B.C.
Montreal Upholstering Co., Montreal.
Morlock Bros., Hanover.
John C. Mundell & Co., Elora.
Quality Furniture Makers, Welland.
Snyder Bros. Upholstering Co., Waterloo.
Schierholtz Furniture Co., New Hamburg.
Stanfold Chair Mfg. Co., Stanfold, Quebec.
Victoriaville Bedding Co., Victoriaville, Que.
Walker & Clegg, Wingham.
Waterloo Furniture Co., Waterloo.
Woeller, Bolduc, Waterloo.
Wunder Furniture Mfg. Co., Berlin.

PARLOR SUITES

J. P. Albrough & Co., Ingersoll.
Baetz Bros. & Co., Berlin.
F. Bibby & Co., Dundas.
Canada Furniture Mfrs., Woodstock.
Dymond-Colonial Co.'s, Strathroy.
Danville Chair & Specialty Co., Danville, Que.
Ellis Furniture Co., Ingersoll.
Elmira Furniture Co., Elmira.
Farquharson-Gifford Co., Stratford.
Glaeser & Leinberger, Hanover.
Gold Medal Furniture Co., Toronto.
G. H. Hachborn & Co., Berlin.
Kilgour & Bro., Beauharnois, Que.
Knechtel Furniture Co., Hanover.
Krug Bros. & Co., Chesley.
H. Krug Furniture Co., Berlin.
Lippert Furniture Co., Berlin.
McGill Chair Co., Cornwall.
Walter Meads Upholstering Co., Hanover.
Moffat Stove Co., Winnipeg.
Morlock Bros., Hanover.
J. C. Mundell & Co., Elora.
Quality Furniture Makers, Welland.
Schierholtz Furniture Co., New Hamburg.
Snyder Bros. Upholstering Co., Waterloo.
St. Lawrence Furniture Co., Riviere du Loup, Que.
Victoriaville Bedding Co., Victoriaville, Que.
Woeller, Bolduc & Co., Waterloo.
Walker & Clegg, Wingham.
Waterloo Furniture Co., Waterloo.
Wunder Furniture Mfg. Co., Berlin.

Reed and Rattan Furniture

LIVING ROOM SUITES — CHAIRS, ROCKERS, SETTEES, COUCHES, FOOTSTOOLS, TABLES, DESKS, BOOK STANDS, FLOWER STANDS, TEA TABLES, TEA TRAYS, WORK BASKETS, CURATES, WASTE BASKETS, CRADLES.

Alaska B.C. Bedding Co., Vancouver.
Canada Furniture Mfrs., Woodstock.
Canadian Rattan Chair Co., Victoriaville, Que.
Gendron Mfg. Co., Toronto.
Giddings, Ltd., Granby, Que.
Imperial Rattan Co., Stratford.
W. B. Jennings, St. Thomas.
Kilgour Bros., Beauharnois, Que.
Malcolm Co., Limited, Vancouver.

Novelties and Sundry Lines

ARTS & CRAFTS FURNITURE

Canada Furniture Mfrs., Woodstock.
F. E. Coombe Furniture Co., Kincardine.
Elmira Interior Woodwork Co., Elmira.
Glaeser & Leinberger, Hanover.
Knechtel Furniture Co., Hanover.
H. Krug Furniture Co., Berlin.
Geo. McLagan Furniture Co., Stratford.
John C. Mundell & Co., Elora.
National Table Co., Owen Sound.
Snyder Bros. Upholstering Co., Waterloo.
Strathroy Furniture Co., Strathroy.
Toronto Furniture Co., Toronto.

ASBESTOS TABLE COVERS

Canadian H. W. Johns-Manville Co., Toronto.

BABY CARRIAGES

Canada Furniture Mfrs., Woodstock.
Gendron Mfg. Co., Toronto.
Giddings & Co., Granby, Que.
J. W. Kilgour & Bro., Beauharnois, Que.

Sidway Mercantile Co., Goderich.
J. E. Smith & Co., Windsor, N.S.

BABY GATES

Rock Island Mfg. Co., Rock Island, Que.

BENT WOOD FURNITURE

Canada Furniture Manufacturers, Woodstock.
J. & J. Kohn, Toronto (W. Craig).
John C. Mundell & Co., Elora.
North American Bent Chair Co., Owen Sound.

BUNGALOW CHAIRS AND SUITES

Baetz Bros. & Co., Berlin.
Canada Furniture Mfrs., Woodstock.
Elmira Furniture Co., Elmira.
J. C. Mundell & Co., Elora.
Walker & Clegg, Wingham.
Waterloo Furniture Co., Waterloo.

CAMP FURNITURE

Ideal Bedding Co., Toronto.
Southampton Seating Co., Southampton.
Stratford Mfg. Co., Stratford.

CARPETS AND RUGS

Brinton Carpet Co., Peterboro.
Canadian Carpet Co., Milton.
Canadian Carpet & Comforter Mfg. Co., Toronto.
Dominion Axminster Co., Toronto.
Guelph Carpet Mills Co., Guelph.
Otto Veit & Co., Toronto.
Perth Carpet Co., Perth.
Toronto Carpet Mfg. Co., Toronto.

CEDAR BOXES

Czerwinski Box Co., Winnipeg.
Keenan Bros., Owen Sound.
J. C. Mundell & Co., Elora.
National Table Co., Owen Sound.
D. L. Shafer, St. Thomas.
Tickell, Sons & Co., Belleville.
Widespread Implement Co., Port Dover.

CHAIRS AND ROCKERS

J. P. Albrough & Co., Ingersoll.
Baetz Bros. & Co., Berlin.
Ball Furniture Co., Hanover.
Bell Furniture Co., Southampton.
F. Bibby & Co., Dundas.
Canada Furniture Mfrs., Woodstock.
Chesley Chair Co., Chesley.
Continental Upholstering & Furniture Co., Montreal.
F. E. Coombe Furn. Co., Kincardine.
Danville Chair & Specialty Co., Danville, Que.
Durham Furniture Co., Durham.
Dymond-Colonial Co.'s, Strathroy.
Ellis Furniture Co., Ingersoll.
Elmira Furniture Co., Elmira.
Fraserville Chair Co., Riviere du Loup, Quebec.
Glaeser & Leinberger, Hanover.
Gold Medal Furniture Co., Toronto.
Geo. H. Hachborn & Co., Berlin.
D. Hibner Furniture Co., Berlin.
Hespeler Furniture Co., Hespeler.
Imperial Rattan Co., Stratford.
Imperial Furniture Co., Toronto.
Knechtel Furniture Co., Hanover.
Krug Bros. & Co., Chesley.
H. Krug Furniture Co., Berlin.
Lippert Furniture Co., Berlin.
A. Malcolm Furniture Co., Kincardine.
Moffat Stove Co., Winnipeg.
Morlock Bros., Hanover.
J. C. Mundell & Co., Elora.
North American Bent Chair Co., Owen Sound.
Neustadt Mfg. Co., Neustadt.
Owen Sound Chair Co., Owen Sound.
Preston Chair Co., Preston.
Quality Furniture Makers, Welland.
Roxton Mill & Chair Co., Waterloo, Que.

Charles Rogers & Sons Co., Toronto.
Schierholtz Furniture Co., New Hamburg.
Snyder Bros. Upholstering Co., Waterloo.
Stanfold Chair Mfg. Co., Stanfold, Quebec.
Stratford Chair Co., Stratford.
Victoriaville Chair Co., Victoriaville, Que.
Walker & Clegg, Wingham.
Woeller Boiduc & Co., Waterloo.
Wunder Furniture Mfg. Co., Berlin.

CHAIRS—Children's
Bail Furniture Co., Hanover.
Canada Furniture Mfrs., Woodstock.
Chesley Chair Co., Chesley.
Danville Chair Specialty Co., Danville, Que.
Durham Furniture Co., Durham.
Fraserville Chair Co., Riviere du Loup, Quebec.
C. P. Gelinas & Frere, Three Rivers, Quebec.
Gendron Mfg. Co., Toronto.
Knechtel Furniture Co., Hanover.
Moffat Stove Co., Winnipeg.
Neustadt Mfg. Co., Neustadt.
North American Bent Chair Co., Owen Sound.
Stanfold Chair Mfg. Co., Stanfold, Quebec.
Stratford Chair Co., Stratford.
S. Weisglass, Ltd., Montreal.

CHILDREN'S HIGH CHAIRS
Bell Furniture Co., Southampton.
Canada Furniture Mfrs., Woodstock.
Chesley Chair Co., Chesley.
D. Hibner Furniture Co., Berlin.
Knechtel Furniture Co., Hanover.
North American Bent Chair Co., Owen Sound.
Stanfold Chair Mfg. Co., Stanfold, Quebec.

CLOCK CASES
Berlin Furniture Co., Berlin.
Elmira Interior Woodwork Co., Elmira.

CROKINOLE BOARDS
Canadian Buffalo Sled Co., Preston.

CUSHIONS
Canadian Feather & Mattress Co., Toronto.
Canada Furniture Mfrs., Woodstock.
Ideal Bedding Co., Toronto.
Stamen, Limited, Saskatoon, Sask.
Toronto Feather & Down Co., Toronto.
Whitworth & Restall, Toronto.

DESK TRAYS
Canada Furniture Mfrs., Woodstock.
Collie-Cockerill Mfg. Co., Aurora.
Elmira Interior Woodwork Co., Elmira.
Lindsay Library & Office Fittings, Lindsay.

DRAPERIES
Daly & Morin, Lachine, Montreal.
Dominion Hammock Mfg. Co., Dunnville.

FOLDING TABLES
(See Card and Den Tables).

FOOTSTOOLS
Canada Furniture Mfrs., Woodstock.
F. E. Coombe Furniture Co., Kincardine.
Dymond-Colonial Co.'s, Strathroy.
Elmira Furniture Co., Elmira.
Glauser & Leinberger, Hanover.
Gold Medal Furniture Co., Toronto.
H. Krug Furniture Co., Berlin.
J. C. Mundell & Co., Elora.

North American Bent Chair Co., Owen Sound.
Schierholtz Furniture Co., New Hamburg.
Snyder Bros. Upholstering Co., Waterloo.
Woeller Boiduc & Co., Waterloo.

FURNITURE POLISH
Domestic Specialty Co., Hamilton.
Ronuk, Ltd., Toronto.
St. Lawrence Furniture Co., Riviere du Loup, Quebec.

GO-CARTS
Beilstein & Kranz, Berlin.
Canada Furniture Mfrs., Woodstock.
Gendron Mfg. Co., Toronto.
Sidway Mercantile Co., Goderich.

ICE CREAM TABLES
Canada Furniture Manufacturers, Woodstock.
Chesley Furniture Co., Chesley.
Elmira Furniture Co., Elmira.
Knechtel Furniture Co., Hanover.
J. & J. Kohn, Toronto (W. Craig).
Meaford Mfg. Co., Meaford.
National Table Co., Owen Sound.
North American Bent Chair Co., Owen Sound.
J. Oliver & Sons, Ottawa.
St. Lawrence Furniture Co., Riviere du Loup, Quebec.

INVALID CHAIRS
Canada Furniture Mfrs., Woodstock.
Gendron Mfg. Co., Toronto.
Gendron Wheel Co., Toledo, Ohio.
Victoriaville Chair Mfg. Co., Victoriaville, Que.

INVALID TABLES
Maple Leaf Bedding Co., Galt.
National Table Co., Owen Sound.
J. Watson Mfg. Co., Ayr.

INVALID TRAYS
Canada Furniture Manufacturers, Woodstock.
Malcolm & Souter Furniture Co., Hamilton.

JARDINIERE STANDS
Beach Furniture Co., Cornwall.
Canada Furniture Mfrs., Woodstock.
Chesley Furniture Co., Chesley.
Dominion Furniture Mfg. Co., St. Therese, Que.
Dymond-Colonial Co.'s, Strathroy.
Elmira Furniture Co., Elmira.
Flora Furniture Co., Elora.
Gendron Mfg. Co., Toronto.
Glaeser & Leinberger, Hanover.
G. J. Lippert Table Co., Berlin.
Andrew Malcolm Furniture Co., Kincardine.
Markdale Furniture Co., Markdale.
Geo. McLagan Furniture Co., Stratford.
Meaford Mfg. Co., Meaford.
J. C. Mundell & Co., Elora.
National Table Co., Owen Sound.
J. Oliver & Sons, Ottawa.
Popular Bros., Hanover.
Snyder Bros. Upholstering Co., Waterloo.
Strathroy Furniture Co., Strathroy.
Windsor Furniture Co., Windsor, N.S.
Woeller Boiduc & Co., Waterloo.
Wunder Furniture Mfg. Co., Berlin.

KINDERGARTEN SETS
Canada Furniture Manufacturers, Woodstock.
Canadian Rattan Chair Co., Victoriaville, Que.
Chesley Chair Co., Chesley.
Danville Chair & Specialty Co., Danville, Que.
Durham Furniture Co., Durham.
Gendron Mfg. Co., Toronto.
J. Oliver & Sons, Ottawa.

LADIES' DESKS
Baird Bros., Plattsville.
Beach Furniture Co., Cornwall.
Berlin Furniture Co., Berlin.
Canada Furniture Mfrs., Woodstock.
Crown Furniture Co., Preston.
D. Hibner Furniture Co., Berlin.
Knechtel Furniture Co., Hanover.
J. Kreiner & Co., Berlin.
A. Malcolm Furniture Co., Kincardine.
Malcolm & Souter Furniture Co., Hamilton.
Geo. McLagan Mfg. Co., Stratford.
Meaford Mfg. Co., Meaford.
J. C. Mundell & Co., Elora.
National Table Co., Owen Sound.
Strathroy Furniture Co., Strathroy.
Windsor Furniture Co., Windsor, N.S.

LAMPS, PORTABLES AND CHANDELIERS
Gendron Mfg. Co., Toronto.
J. C. Mundell & Co., Elora.

MANTELS—WOOD, TILE, ELECTRIC
Elmira Interior Woodwork Co., Elmira.

MIRRORS
Matthews Bros., Toronto.
Phillips Mfg. Co., Toronto.

MOULDINGS & PICTURE FRAMES
G. L. Irish, Toronto.
S. Knechtel Wood Turning Co., Southampton.
Matthews Bros., Toronto.
Phillips Mfg. Co., Toronto.
Reliance Moulding Co., Toronto.

ORIENTAL MATS AND RUGS
Malcolm Co., Limited, Vancouver.

PICTURES
G. L. Irish & Co., Toronto.
Matthews Bros., Toronto.
Phillips Mfg. Co., Toronto.

PILLOW SHAM HOLDERS
Tarbox Bros., Toronto.

SEWING TABLES
Canada Furniture Mfrs., Woodstock.
J. C. Mundell & Co., Elora.
North American Bent Chair Co., Owen Sound.
Stratford Mfg. Co., Stratford.

SHIRT WAIST BOXES
D. L. Shafer & Co., St. Thomas.

SMOKING CABINETS
Bell Furniture Co., Southampton.
Canada Furniture Mfrs., Woodstock.
F. E. Coombe Furniture Co., Kincardine.
Dymond-Colonial Co.'s, Strathroy.
J. Kreiner & Co., Berlin.
A. Malcolm Furniture Co., Kincardine.
Geo. McLagan Furniture Co., Ltd., Woodstock.
John C. Mundell & Co., Elora.

STATUARY
G. L. Irish & Co., Toronto.

TABOURETTES
Canada Furniture Mfrs., Woodstock.
Chesley Furniture Co., Chesley.
Dymond-Colonial Co.'s, Strathroy.
Elmira Furniture Co., Elmira.
Elora Furniture Co., Elora.
Glaeser & Leinberger, Hanover.
Knechtel Furniture Co., Hanover.
G. J. Lippert Table Co., Berlin.
Andrew Malcolm Furniture Co., Kincardine.
Geo. McLagan Furniture Co., Stratford.
Meaford Mfg. Co., Meaford.
J. C. Mundell & Co., Elora.
North American Furniture Co., Owen Sound.

Peppler Bros., Hanover.
Strathroy Furniture Co., Strathroy.
Woeller Boldue & Co., Waterloo.
Wunder Furniture Mfg. Co., Berlin.

TAPESTRY CURTAINS
Dominion Hammock Mfg. Co., Dunnville.

TEA TRAYS
See also Reed and Rattan Furniture.
Berlin Furniture Co., Berlin.
Canada Furniture Mfrs., Woodstock.
Malcolm & Souter Furniture Co., Hamilton.
Toronto Furniture Co., Toronto.

TEA TABLES
(See Card and Den Tables).
Canada Furniture Mfrs., Woodstock.
Gendron Mfg. Co., Toronto.
Malcolm & Souter Furniture Co., Hamilton.
G. McLagan Furniture Co., Stratford.
Charles Rogers & Sons Co., Toronto.
Woeller Boldue & Co., Waterloo.

TELEPHONE CABINETS
Berlin Interior Hardwood Co., Berlin.
Collie-Cockerill Mfg. Co., Aurora.

TELEPHONE STANDS
Canada Furniture Mfrs., Woodstock.
Collie-Cockerill Mfg. Co., Aurora.
F. E. Coombe Furniture Co., Kincardine.
Dymond-Colonial Co.'s, Strathroy.
Elmira Furniture Co., Elmira.
Glaeser & Leinberger, Hanover.
D. Hibner Furniture Co., Berlin.
Lindsay Library & Office Fittings, Lindsay.
J. C. Mundell & Co., Elora.
National Table Co., Owen Sound.
North American Furniture Co., Owen Sound.

TRAYS
Canada Furniture Manufacturers, Woodstock.
Matthews Bros., Toronto.

TOY SETS
Canada Furniture Manufacturers, Woodstock.
Canadian Rattan Chair Co., Victoriaville, Que.
Chesley Furniture Co., Chesley.
Gendron Mfg. Co., Toronto.
Kilgour & Bro., Beauharnois, Que.
J. Oliver & Sons, Ottawa.

VACUUM SWEEPERS
J. H. Connor & Sons, Ottawa.
Clements Mfg. Co., Toronto.
Onward Mfg. Co., Berlin.

WAGONS AND SLEDS (Children's)
Canadian Buffalo Sled Co., Preston.
Canada Furniture Mfrs., Woodstock.
Gendron Mfg. Co., Toronto.

WASTE PAPER BASKETS
Canada Furniture Mfrs., Woodstock.
Dymond-Colonial Co.'s, Strathroy.
Elmira Interior Woodwork Co., Elmira.
Gendron Mfg. Co., Toronto.
Knechtel Furniture Co., Hanover.
H. Krug Furniture Co., Berlin.
North American Bent Chair Co., Owen Sound.
Snyder Bros. Upholstering Co., Waterloo.

Factory Supplies

ALUMINUM CAULS
British Aluminum Co., Toronto.

ART WOOD STAINS
Adams & Elting Co., Chicago.
Marietta Paint & Color Co., Marietta, Ohio.

BRASS TRIMMINGS
Canadian Saddlery & Hdw. Mfg. Co., Walkerton.
Hahn Brass Co., New Hamburg.
Stratford Brass Co., Stratford.

CASTERS
John Duer & Sons, Baltimore, Md.
James Smart Mfg. Co., Brockville.
Universal Castor & Foundry Co., New York.

HOUSE FURNISHING FABRICS
Richard Haworth Co., Ltd., Manchester, England.
Stonards, Ltd., Paternoster Bldgs., London, E.C., England.

CLAMPS
Batavia Clamp Co., Batavia, N.Y.
James Smart Mfg. Co., Brockville.

CURLED HAIR
Griffin Curled Hair Co., Toronto.

DOWELS AND DOWEL PINS
S. Knechtel Wood-turning Co., Southampton.

DRY KILNS
Grand Rapids Dry Kiln Co., Grand Rapids, Mich.
Morton Dry Kiln Co., Chicago.

FURNITURE HARDWARE
Hahn Brass Co., New Hamburg.
John Duer & Sons, Baltimore, Md.
James Smart Mfg. Co., Brockville.
Stratford Brass Co., Stratford.

FURNITURE SHOES
Onward Mfg. Co., Berlin.
Stratford Brass Co., Stratford.

GLASS AND MIRRORS
Berlin Plate Glass & Mirror Co., Berlin.
Consolidated Plate Glass Co., Toronto.
Hobb Mfg. Co., London.
Matthews Bros., Toronto.
Phillips Mfg. Co., Toronto.
Toronto Plate Glass Co., Toronto.

GLUE
Canada Glue Co., Brantford.
Delaney & Pettit, Toronto.
Snap Co., Montreal.

GLUE JOINTING MACHINES
Canadian Linderman Co., Woodstock.

KITCHEN CABINET ACCESSORIES
American Can Co., Hamilton.
American Nikeloid Co., Peru, Ind.
Northern Aluminum Co., Toronto.
Sheet Metal Products Co., Toronto.
E. T. Wright Co., Hamilton.

LADDERS
Stratford Mfg. Co., Stratford.

LEATHER SUBSTITUTES
British Leather Cloth Mfg. Co., Manchester, Eng.
Dupont Fabrikoid Co., Toronto.
Lackawanna Leather Co., Hackettstown, N.J.
Marlatt & Armstrong, Oakville.
Peerless Leather Co., Berlin.
Textileather Co., New York, N.Y.

MIRRORS AND GLASS
Berlin Plate Glass Co., Berlin.
Consolidated Plate Glass Co., Toronto.
Excelsior Plate Glass Co., Toronto.
Hobbs Mfg. Co., London.

WIRE NAILS
P. L. Robertson Mfg. Co., Milton.

WOODWORKING MACHINERY
Canadian Linderman Co., Woodstock.
Berlin Machine Works, Hamilton.

PLATING
P. L. Robertson Mfg. Co., Milton.

RIVETS (Iron, Copper, Brass, Aluminum) AND SCREWS (Wood)
P. L. Robertson Mfg. Co., Milton.

SANDPAPER
Delaney & Pettit, Toronto.

SPRINGS
Ideal Bedding Co., Toronto.
National Spring Co., Windsor.
James Steele, Guelph.
Waterloo Spring Co., Waterloo.

TABLE SLIDES
B. Walter & Co., Wabash, Ind.

TRUCKS
James Smart Mfg. Co., Brockville.
J. Watson Mfg. Co., Ayr.

UPHOLSTERERS' SUPPLIES
Gold Medal Furniture Co., Toronto.
G. H. Hees & Son, Toronto.
Snyder Bros. Upholstering Co., Waterloo.

VARNISHES
Adams & Elting, Chicago.
Ault & Wiborg, Toronto.
Dougall Varnish Co., Montreal.
Glidden Varnish Co., Toronto.
Imperial Varnish & Color Co., Toronto
International Varnish Co., Toronto.
R. C. Jamieson & Co., Montreal.
Scarfe & Co., Brantford.
Sherwin-Williams Co., Montreal.
Standard Paint & Varnish Co., Windsor.

VENEERS
Adams & Raymond Veneer Co., Indianapolis, Ind.

VENEERED PANELS
Hay & Co., Woodstock.

VENEER PRESSES
Wm. R. Perrin & Co., Toronto.

WASHERS
P. L. Robertson Mfg. Co., Milton.

VENEERS, PANELS AND LUMBER
Des Arc Veneer & Lumber Co., Des Arc, Arkansas.
Grand Rapids Veneer Works, Grand Rapids, Mich.
Henry S. Holden, Grand Rapids, Mich.
Geo. W. Hartzell, Piqua, Ohio.
Indiana Veneer & Lumber Co., Indianapolis, Ind.
J. J. Nartzik, Chicago, Ill.
Underwood Veneer Co., Wausau, Wis.
Wisconsin Timber & Land Co., Matoon, Wis.

WIRE (BRIGHT OR ANNEALED)
P. L. Robertson Mfg. Co., Milton.

WOOD DRAWER KNOBS
S. Knechtel Wood-turning Co., Southampton.

Store Equipment

BANK, OFFICE & STORE FITTINGS
Berlin Interior Hardwood Co., Berlin.
Collie-Cockerill Mfg. Co., Aurora.
Walker Bin & Store Fixture Co., Berlin.

CARPET AND RUG RACKS
Steel Furnishing Co., New Glasgow, N.S.

COUNTER STOOLS
Canada Furniture Manufacturers, Woodstock.
North American Bent Chair Co., Owen Sound.

RUG DISPLAY RACKS
Steel Furnishing Co., New Glasgow, N.S.
John H. Best, Galva, Ill.

SHOW CASES & SILENT SALESMEN
Berlin Interior Hardwood Co., Berlin.
Kent McClain Co., Ltd., Toronto.
Knechtel Furniture Co., Hanover.

STORE FRONTS
Kawneer Mfg. Co., Toronto.

TABLE DISPLAY RACK
Strathroy Furniture Co., Strathroy.

September, 1914   CANADIAN FURNITURE WORLD AND THE UNDERTAKER   15

STRATFORD

No. 1   THE FURNITURE CITY   Sept. '14

Dealers who base their success on "satisfied customers" will find the thoroughness of Stratford Chair construction the most valuable ally they can employ.

Stratford Chairs sell to the class of people who buy despite the times. An order for Stratford Chairs is the best guarantee of sales — and *profitable* sales.

We give such careful attention to the packing and loading of Stratford Chairs that dissatisfaction caused by damage in transit is almost unknown. This is a service feature worth the money to you, Mr. Dealer.

Buy "Stratford-Made" Furniture for better quality, better service and the most consistent pricing. Mixed car loads shipped to Western Buyers.

No. 1028 Brass Bed. List Price, $34.00

No. 914—Iron Bed. List Price, $20.00

No. 15—Safety Crib. List Price, $13.00

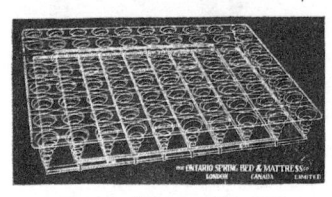

No. 1— Spiral Spring. List Price, $6.00

"ONTARIO"
Brass and Iron Beds, Springs Pillows, Cots and Mattresses

Ontario Goods are made up to a standard that stands for pleased customers.

Ontario Goods and good service go hand in hand. That's a very important feature, Mr. Dealer.

Ontario Goods are priced to allow you a profit that will keep you on our books.

Ontario Goods will keep more customers coming to your store. An order now will be good business for both of us.

Ask for a copy of our new catalog

The Ontario Spring Bed & Mattress Co., Limited
The Largest Bedding House in Canada

London   -   Ontario

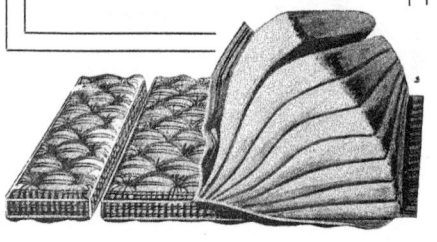

STRATFORD

No. 1. THE FURNITURE CITY Sept. '14

THE *Imperial Rattan* Line is recognized by the majority of our competitors, dealers and the buying public as the criteron of all that is new and desirable in Reed Furniture.

Keep in touch with "Imperial" ideas for profitable buying.

The largest and most select stock of Tapestry, Chintz, denim, imitation leather and solid leather coverings in Canada is carried in the Imperial Rattan factories a great feature is filling orders to *your* taste.

No dealer ever has a "kick" against "Stratford-Made" goods.
He gets the kind of quality and good service that makes friends.

Long Service---Great Comfort---Perfect Sanitation---Consistent Price ---every feature that makes a line of Bed Springs desirable, both for the dealer and the user, is developed in multiplied form in

Leggett & Platt
Single Cone Bed Springs

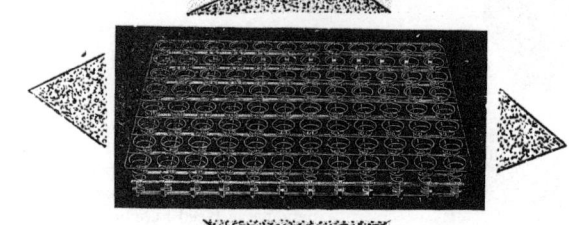

Leggett & Platt Single Cone Bed Springs have the "natural" spring--- **up and down**---not from sides and ends as is the case with woven wire springs. The weight is absorbed where the weight rests by the individual coils.

The Leggett & Platt Springs are the only springs so constructed so as to allow each coil to act independently.

No. 8 shown above is designed especially for metal beds. Weight only 50 lbs.

Leggett & Platt Springs, backed by our broad guarantee, will convince **your** customers.

Write for our illustrated catalog

The Leggett & Platt Spring Bed Co., Ltd.
Windsor   Ontario

September, 1914   CANADIAN FURNITURE WORLD AND THE UNDERTAKER   19

STRATFORD

No. 1   THE FURNITURE CITY   Sept. '14

Charm and Adaptability are Salable Features in

Globe-Wernicke Art Mission Bookcase
With Desk Unit

Globe-Wernicke Bookcases are made in designs to harmonize with the furnishings of any room, and in combinations to suit any desired space.

¶ Globe-Wernicke Sectional Bookcases are exceedingly profitable to the dealer. Coupled with a very attractive profit obtainable on every sale made, there is that national reputation behind them that makes the Globe-Wernicke make the **first thought of** and the **first bought** by the vast majority of possible customers.

Put "Stratford-Made" Furniture on your floors and insure the building of that prestige that comes from the sale of **reliable** goods.

Nothing Like 'Imperial' Quality for Brisk Business

There is room in **every** good furniture store for the profitable displaying of a certain number of selected pieces from the "Imperial" Line of Fine Upholstered Furniture.

"Imperial" Chairs, Rockers, Suites, Couches, etc., embody the artistic touch in style with a tone of goodness in the making that invariably sells to the careful buyer at a fair price.

Visit our Exhibition of
Fine Upholstered Furniture
at 585-591 Queen St. W., Toronto
(near Queen and Bathurst), during

The Canadian National Exhibition

We are featuring many new effects that should interest every wide-awake Furniture Dealer.

If you haven't as yet looked into the merits of the "Imperial" line, let us send you photos with the prices that will convince you of their **profitable** saleability.

No. 62

Imperial Furniture Company

Best Copper Trimmings

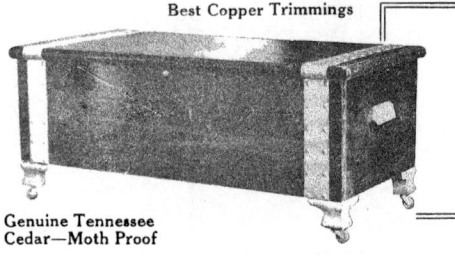

Genuine Tennessee Cedar—Moth Proof

Try Out This
Big Profit Maker

This Shafer Cedar Chest is a live seller because it combines attractiveness, fashion and utility with moderate price—An appeal the modern woman can't resist. Write for prices.

D. L. Shafer & Co.
St. Thomas - Ontario

Best Quality

Large range of Period and Modern Designs carried in stock.

Stratford Brass Co.
Limited
Stratford   Ontario
Write for Prices

Fine Finish

Special Designs to specifications on the shortest notice.

STRATFORD

No. 1   THE FURNITURE CITY   Sept. '14

for Quality embrace many absolutely original features that mean additional profits to our dealers.

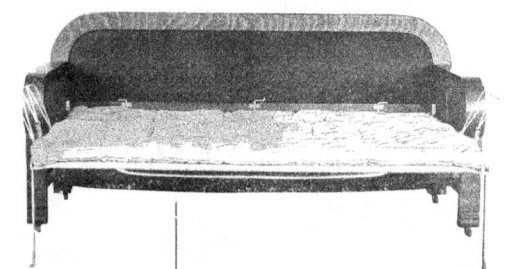

They are wonderfully easy to operate; they cannot possibly bind or get out of order, and they possess that style and finish necessary to attract the customers from the first glance.

The Davenport Bed season is right on us. Order a few designs in the "F.G." make and be prepared to obtain the greatest returns from your stock.

Living-Room Furniture is our Specialty.

Write for our Attractive Prices.

All Western Buyers should know about the Stratford Shipping Combination. Let us give you the details.

BAETZ BROTHERS AND COMPANY
BERLIN :: ONTARIO

Specializing in Chairs

This illustrates our No. 142 Diner

Made of quartered White Oak, Golden or Fumed

"Acme" and "Peerless" Folding Tables

can be used for so many purposes, yet cost so little, that they are good "live" sellers ALL the time.

The "Acme" weighs only 10 lbs. Folds into one-twelfth its standing space. Conceded to be the strongest and most durable table of its kind made. All finishes. Tops covered with green felt or leatherette.

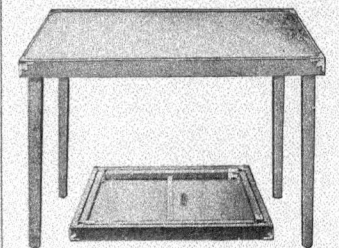

The "Peerless" possesses symmetry and beauty of design as well as utility. An ordinary "Peerless" table will support 1,000 lbs.

Order a crate of 12 for the biggest Folding Table business you've ever experienced.

If you have not received our new catalogue say the word and we will do the rest

HOURD & COMPANY, LIMITED
Wholesale Furniture Manufacturers
LONDON, - - CANADA
Sole Canadian Licensees and Manufacturers

September, 1914   CANADIAN FURNITURE WORLD AND THE UNDERTAKER   23

STRATFORD

No. 1   THE FURNITURE CITY   Sept. '14

Net Price, $9.00 Per Doz.

A new "Stratford" Folding Chair that beats anything else on the market for strength, stability, convenience in handling and appearance.

The illustration shows a man weighing 290 lbs. standing on the front rail. Besides being the strongest chair of its weight made, it will not tip when the occupant leans forward. This is an exclusive feature of "Stratford" Folding Chairs.

Posts are made of select, straight grained stock, steam bent. The construction ensures ease in folding and freedom from binding when opening.

At $9.00 per doz. you can make a splendid profit. Order now for the busy season. The number is 10A.

"Stratford-Made" Goods are built right and sold right. You can place all confidence in the reliability of every piece of Stratford furniture you buy.

Profit and Prestige—

The Dealer best serves his own business interests by marketing a make of furniture that will reflect credit on his good judgment after years of hard service in actual use. Such a reputation is to be gained by featuring

The "Orillia" Line of Buffets Extension and Parlor Tables

Buffet No. 750 shown here is made in fine quartered oak, any finish. Note its appealing style and large, roomy construction. A real winner at its price.

Write for our catalog and price list

The Orillia Furniture Company, Limited
Orillia   Ontario

"Make the 'Orillia' Line Your Line"

In Demand *by* *the* Majority

ISN'T it so, Mr. Average Dealer, that the bulk of your trade want plenty of style, even individuality; the very best kind of long-wearing service; and, above all, the lowest price they can find?

You'll find all these qualifications in

The "Meaford" Make of Surface Oak and Mahogany also White Enamel Furniture

Made of select maple, stained, shellaced and varnished or enamelled by our own process, there is more service and better appearance in the Meaford make than in any other line at the same prices.

Let us give you full particulars and prices on Sideboards, Buffets, China Cabinets, Extension Tables, Hall Racks, Hall Seats, Mirrors, Library Tables, Desks and Bookcases, Jardiniere Stands, Centre Tables, Dressers, Chiffoniers, Dressing Tables, Wardrobes, Bedroom Tables and Medicine Cabinets.

The Meaford Mfg. Co.
Limited

Meaford   Ontario

KNECHTEL

New Designs in Plain Oak
That are selling well because designs and prices are right

No. 216 CHINA CABINET. An excellent design, perfect proportions and a seller. Plain Oak, Fumed or Golden. Height, 61 inches. List, **$36.00**.

No. 216 BUFFET. The big 52 inch case, inset panels, and fine proportions make this Buffet a leader, and the price is right. List, **$55.50**.

No. 94 DINER. Solid plain oak, with genuine leather covered pad seat and back. A first-class design at a low price. List, **$6.75**.

No. 103 EXTENSION TABLE. This fine fumed oak design needs no introduction. Plain oak, Golden, or fumed finish. Top, 45 by 45 inches. List, 6 ft. Extension, **$36.00**.

No. 95 DINER. Your stock is not complete without this suite. Solid oak arm chair. List, **$9.75**.

THE KNECHTEL FURNITURE CO., Limited, Hanover, Ont.

KNECHTEL
Perfect White Enamel Finish and Design
account for the popularity of our enamelled goods

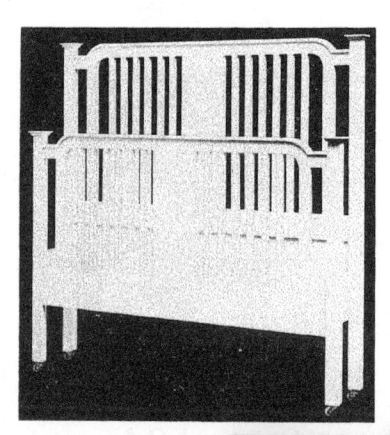

No. 410E BED. This is one of "those new KNECHTEL designs" in enamel. Made in 4 ft. 6 in. and 3 ft. 3 in. widths. List, **$37.50.**

No. 410E DRESSER. The design is simple, but full of character, and takes well. White Enamel. Top, 20 by 40. Mirror, 22 by 28 B.B. List, **$39.75.**

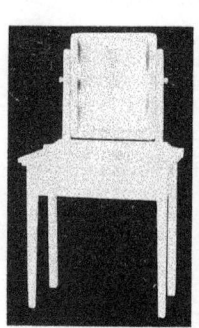

No. 110E DRESSING TABLE. The suite is not complete without this piece. It also sells well as an odd dress table. Top, 19 by 30. Mirror, 16 by 20 B.B. List, **$23.25**

No. 110E CHIFFONIER. Besides completing the No. 110 suite, this piece sells well as an odd Chiffonier. Top, 19 by 30. Mirror, 16 by 20 B.B. List, **$36.75.**

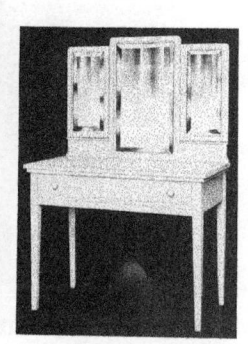

No. 110 E DRESSING TABLE. Has the "wing" mirrors and is doubly attractive. Top, 20 by 38. Mirrors, one 11 by 21 and two 8 by 18. List, **$32.25.**

THE KNECHTEL FURNITURE CO., Limited, Hanover, Ont.

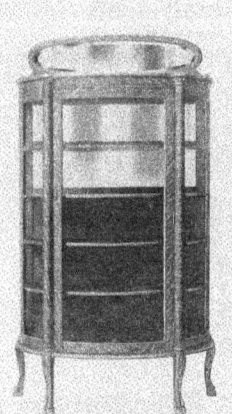

Nos. 22-365. 40 in. wide, 74 in. high

Nos. 14-374. 37 in. wide, 70 in. high

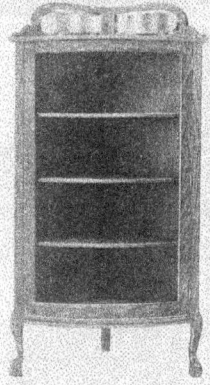

No. 14-369. 23 in. long on the side, 66 in. high

Quartered Oak
China Cabinets
at Medium Prices

NO line offers better sales opportunities than the Gibbard make. The materials are selected with a view to rich appearance and great serviceability, while the cabinet-making is thoroughly reliable.

The low prices of these fine quartered oak Cabinets will convince you of their salability. Why not write for our special China Cabinet Catalogue now.

The Gibbard Furniture Co. of Napanee, Limited
Napanee   Ontario

The **Kindel** Kind

Partly Sold Before They Reach You!

Some of the Best Canadian Magazines are Making Kindel Sales for You

THE THREE TYPES

Taken by themselves, Kindel Beds present the very limit in retail sales possibilities. They comprise the one and only line in which there are three distinct types of convertible beds—each of them designed to meet some actual desire and requirement. And together meeting every possible need.

With these three Kindel types—the Somersaultie, the De Luxe, and the Divanette—every customer can be satisfied. For all of them are perfect davenport beds—simple, luxurious, and convenient. All three types come in a good variety of designs, including a number of brand new patterns in Periods which are being shown for the first time.

THE SALES PROPOSITION

The order you place this month will be partly marketed even before the goods leave our factories—partly sold through the Magazine advertising that is reaching out and creating desire for the comfort and convenience of the Kindel.

Six fine publications—four of them Canadian—that are conceded to be real merchandisers have been carrying this message—your message if you'll let it be that—since the first of the year.

And during that time a big, elaborate Retail Sales Plan has backed them up, cashing in the value of this work. Centring around the demonstration and including all sorts of good helps, this plan is almost a wonder-worker.

See the KINDEL DEMONSTRATION
at the
TORONTO EXHIBITION

The
Kindel Bed Company
Toronto   Ontario

DAY & NIGHT SERVICE   **DAY & NIGHT SERVICE**

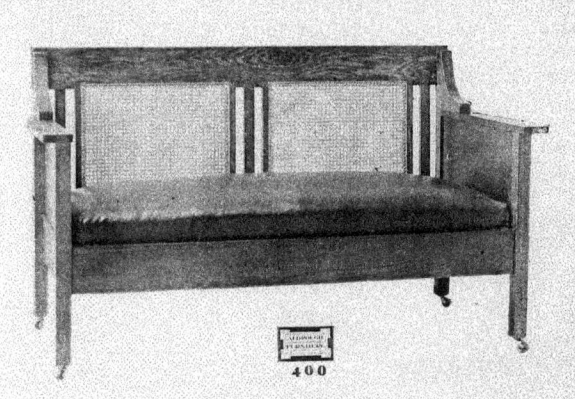

QUALITY

We uphold our high standard of quality in every piece we make. *A fact that is being proven by the increasing demand for—*

Albrough Furniture

Notice the high-grade appearance—*solid comfort and solid construction* of these pieces—a feature that convinces the customer and makes sales. Our photos and prices will convince you of the wisdom of displaying ALBROUGH FURNITURE on your floors this fall.

Better let us supply you with the facts at once

J. P. ALBROUGH & COMPANY

Makers of Quality Couches and Easy Chairs

INGERSOLL   CANADA

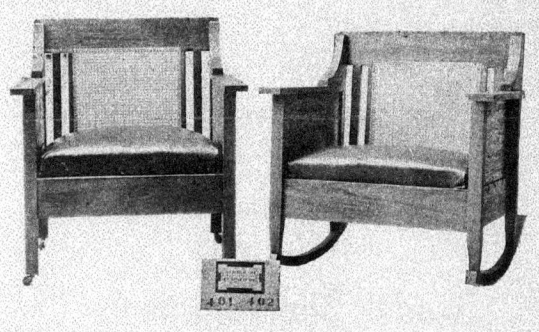

Are you keeping up your stock of Rattan Chairs

with a good profitable line?

Canadian Rattan Chairs

are entirely hand made by expert reed workers, and nothing but the best class of reed is used in our chairs. Our prices are very reasonable, and our catalog will show you our different designs. Do you want one?

The Canadian Rattan Chair Company, Limited.

VICTORIAVILLE, QUEBEC.

An Old Store with a New Front

54 years the Appeldoorns did business behind this old Front—always did a good business and made money—but when they installed their KAWNEER FRONT their business was increased 40%. The new Front actually paid for itself in eight months. Now and for years to come the profits on the increased business will go straight to the profit column. Think of the sales this one Store lost because of the old Store Front—and if yours is an old Front you are losing sales just as the Appeldoorns did. Let their experience together with the experience of thousands of other Merchants behind KAWNEER FRONTS help you to increase your business.

Within three doors of the Appeldoorn Store, a KAWNEER FRONT is making money for Max Livingston. In a letter he said, "We are very much pleased with our new Front that we have installed for us, are only sorry that we did not have it done years ago as we can now see it is the best asset a Merchant can have—it is better advertising than a newspaper."

Never before could a KAWNEER STORE FRONT do you so much good as now—never before could one pay such big returns on the investment. The success of every commodity is dependent upon its outlook—in the case of Store Fronts it's sales. If you intend to install a new Store Front, let the experience of 50,000 KAWNEER users help you. Don't let sentiment move you—guide yourself by the paid-for experience of other Merchants.

Store Front Book

For eight years we've specialized in the designing, manufacturing and installing of modern KAWNEER STORE FRONTS—our experience has been the experience of Merchants and by this we believe we are competent to help you with your new Front. Don't risk the amount of money you will necessarily spend for any kind of Store Front when you can secure "Boosting Business No. 2" for a mere post-card. "Boosting Business No. 2" is compiled expressly for you Merchants—it contains photographs and drawings of many of the best paying Store Fronts in the country—both big and little. See what other Merchants have done in erecting decided paying Store Fronts. Just a post-card for "Boosting Business No. 2" will bring it to you by return mail. No obligation.

Kawneer Manufacturing Company

Francis J. Plym, President
Dept. S
1197 Bathurst Street
TORONTO, CAN.

r'aville
of Quality

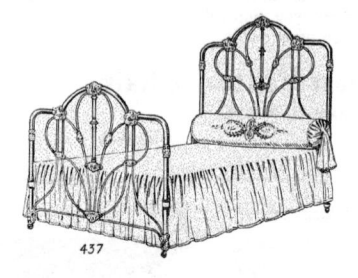

457

Victoriaville bedsteads are noted for their good selling qualities, viz:—
Neat and attractive designs, and the advantage of new and up-to-date equipment which enables us to produce beds of first class quality at a medium price.

Another advantage you gain when dealing with us is our facilities for shipping in mixed carload lots, which reduces your freight bills considerably.

Send us a small trial order and we are sure you will be a regular customer of ours in future.

i toriaville Bedding Company, Limited
Victoriaville
Quebec

The Big Five Mixed Carload Center

A

for Furniture Dealers is our line of upholstered furniture. It is designed and made for comfort as well as beauty (note the two cuts) and the material and workmanship cannot be beaten.

Drop us a line for our prices and see for yourself the profit you can make after retailing at a reasonable price, or, a small order will prove the truth of our claim:—"A Profitable Proposition for the Furniture Dealer."

Victoriaville
Quebec

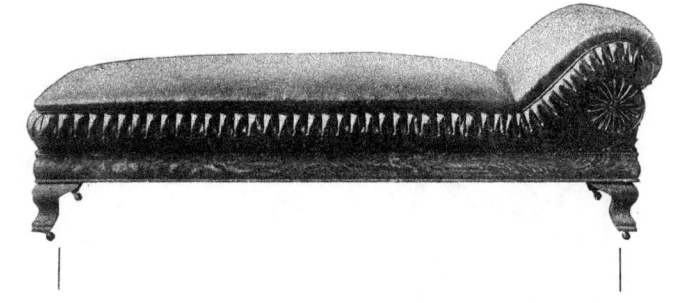

Some More Victoriaville Bargains

These bureaus are finished in the same way as the buffets shown on the opposite page and we offer them at a price which is ridiculously low when you consider the quality of the lumber, and the class of workmanship and finish which we put into them.

Victoriaville Furniture

is a medium grade furniture, made more for utility rather than show although our designs are all neat and up-to-date.

May we send you our Catalogue

The Victoriaville Furniture Company

Victoriaville, Que.

finished in Quartered Oak

These Buffets are finished in imitation quartered oak and the designs are the very latest.

They are soundly constructed and will last as long and look as well as the genuine quartered oak goods, while the price is 50 per cent. less. This big difference in price will go a long way towards closing sales with the majority of your customers.

Drop us a line for further particulars and prices

The Big Five Mixed Carload Center

Victoriaville
Quebec

Handle

aville

it's

and you will come to the conclusion that you have lost money by not doing so before.

Our factory is equipped with up-to-date machinery and is devoted exclusively to the manufacture of wooden chairs. These facts alone enable us to produce a better class of chairs than factories who manufacture a general line of furniture and therefore cannot give as much attention as we do to any one line.

Send us a post card for our catalog

or av'lle Chair Mfg. Co.
Victoriaville
Quebec

Chairs
That are made to wear

and give full value to your customers for the money they spend.

These are the kind of chairs that are most in demand by your customers and, owing to the facts given on the preceding page, we are able to produce them at a very low cost to you.

Our facilities for shipping in mixed carload lots at a low rate is another advantage you gain by dealing with us.

Won't you give us a trial?

The Victoriaville Chair Manufacturing Company
Victoriaville
Que.

None better made!
None easier to sell!
None surer to satisfy!

THAT'S the experience of hundreds of 'GALE' customers in all parts of Canada.

THAT'S why the 'GALE' business continues to grow year after year.

'GALE' good are always a 'good buy.' Write for our catalogue and newest designs.

E . GALE & SONS LIMITED

Waterville, Quebec

Montreal   Toronto   Winnipeg

GUARANTEED GALE — WATERVILLE, QUE.

Iron and Brass
Bedsteads
Institution Beds

Cribs and Cots
Steel Couches
and Davenports

DIXIE
NoTuft Mattress
Kapok Mattress

Astoria
Box Spring and
Other Specialties

Cuban Spring
Iron Frame Springs
Spiral Springs

A Popular "Bell" Production

One that is regarded by the trade everywhere as a real winner. Distinctly classic in design, yet not "fussy"; joints tight as a drum; finish exceptionally rich; price really attractive this suite presents a good example of the scope for profit offered in

"The Bell Line
The Line With the Tone"

Included in the "Bell" make are matched Dining-room Suites, Bed-room Suites, Library Tables, Parlor Tables, Diners, Living-room and Office Chairs.

Write for our latest catalog and Price List.

The Bell Furniture Co., Ltd.
Southampton   Ontario

Our Positive Extension Controller

Means
Greatest Ease in Opening
Top Always Centered

Did you ever hear of an extension Table, other than the "Berlin" make, that opens both sides at once by a gentle pull on one side?

Our Positive Extension Controller does the trick.

BERLIN TABLES

Berlin Tables are made in a wide range of attention drawing designs. Select quartered oak, beautifully finished. You can **back up** the most convincing sales arguments when you show a **Berlin Table.**

Get our prices and details of our line. You can't put *better sellers* on your floors than *Berlin Tables.*

The Berlin Table Manufacturing Co., Limited
BERLIN :: ONTARIO

The Chair Craft Proposition

"REST-FEST" and "REX-RECLINER" Chairs hold first place in the lounge chair world because they have more really worth while comfort features than any other line in their class.

Come in and get your share of the immense profits they offer. Chair Craft's new Sales Plan includes pulling Newspaper Ads, Consumer Booklets, interest compelling Window Trim, Demonstration Cards, handsome Window Posters—everything to boost the sale of Rest-Fest and Rex-Recliner Chairs.

"Rex-Recliner" Chairs

You sit and rest or recline and rest. "Rex-Recliners" are self-adjusting. The body is supported perfectly in any position.

UPHOLSTERED IN ANY MATERIAL DESIRED.

"Rest-Fest" Chairs

A slight pressure on the floor immediately puts occupant into reclining position with all parts of body supported.

LARGE RANGE OF ATTRACTIVE PATTERNS.

No. 4. 308

May We Hear from You To-Day?

THE CHAIR CRAFT COMPANY
Traverse City   Michigan

We manufacture a cheap and medium line of

DRESSERS & STANDS
Finished in Surface Oak, Golden Elm, Mahogany, White Enamel

WARDROBES
In Surface Oak, Mahogany, Golden Elm, White Enamel

SIDEBOARDS
In Surface Oak and Golden Ash

TABLES
Extension
Centre and Folding
Finished in Golden Ash or Surface Oak

KITCHEN CABINETS
Cupboards and Tables

Prompt Shipments Guaranteed

J. Oliver & Sons, Limited :: Ottawa, Canada

Elmira
Electric Grate
Mantels

can be sold, profitably, by any dealer. The ease with which they can be installed, no tiling or chimney required—the absence of dust, dirt or smoke—their handsome appearance and low costs for electric power, make them popular with both tenants and owners.

Elmira Interior Woodwork Company, Ltd.
C. P. R. Elmira, Ontario G. T. R.

Look for our Display at The Toronto Exhibition

These trade-marks protect both you and your customers

No. 2268

With Us it's "SERVICE First"

Only by co-operating with the dealer in every possible way, can we hope to establish a permanent state of confidence between him and ourselves. We have a well-established reputation for satisfactory service from coast to coast.

This is the result of our endeavor to be prompt in shipment—careful study of the dealer's requirements, and the high grade materials and expert workmanship embodied in our goods.

You'll find that linking up with Weisglass service is something more than it appears on the surface.

S. WEISGLASS, Limited

TORONTO   MONTREAL

Beds
Springs
Couches

Davenports
Costumers
Wall Racks

HIGH-GRADE DINING ROOM AND BED ROOM FURNITURE

That we manufacture **good furniture** is evidenced in this exquisite Dining Suite No. 1470. Wouldn't it attract the artistically inclined in **your** locality?

"Hespeler" Furniture is popular because it offers the **best** and **most exclusive designs**, while the prices are within the reach of the average better class customer.

You can use the "Hespeler" make to good advantage in **your** business.

Write for our catalog if you haven't one on file.

HESPELER FURNITURE CO., Limited,   -   Hespeler, Ontario

What Your Trade Has Been Looking For—
A New Queen Anne Suite in Bird's Eye Maple

No. 117

No. 117

No. 117

THE above Suite is one of our latest productions and is made in American Black Walnut and Genuine Mahogany, as well as Bird's Eye Maple. It is a high-grade suite throughout and is correct in detail and finish.

Bird's Eye Maple

Unlike many other Manufacturers we have not dropped this wood because we could not handle it, but have mastered its peculiarities. We can give you goods that are perfectly figured and beautifully finished.

Let our Representative show you the new line

The Andrew Malcolm Furniture Company, Limited
Kincardine and Listowel, Ontario

Fast Service to Western Dealers

Moffat's Wholesale Furniture Department
Winnipeg

WE can supply you with furniture of all kinds at attractive prices and on short notice. Large stocks carried in Winnipeg.

We also represent some of the best Ontario Furniture Manufacturers, and can sell you direct from factories in cars to points in Manitoba and Saskatchewan.

Mail orders given careful attention.

The Moffat Stove Co., Limited
137 Bannatine Avenue   -   Winnipeg

Textileather

If you have not seen the above brand of **artificial leather**, then get acquainted, ask for samples.

It is the most satisfactory furniture covering ever made anywhere.

Textileather Co., 212 Fifth Ave., New York, N.Y.
WRITE DIRECT OR TO

Frank Schmidt   -   Berlin, Ontario

Avoid that Gaping Pedestal—

The "Twin" Pedestal Extension Table **cannot** break away, showing an unsightly gap. It is the most practically constructed table made.

"TWIN" Tables extend to eight feet and over, yet they always present a well-balanced appearance.

Made in a wide range of attractive designs in all finishes.

Let us send you a copy of our new book, "TWINS."

Write us to-day

THE dividing pedestal table has a way of developing an annoying V shaped gap after a few weeks' use that locks and extra casters fail to overcome.

A table that is so defective is sure to cause dissatisfaction. Can your business afford such a handicap?

Dealers everywhere are devoting more and more floor space to the line of tables that is proof against ordinary extension table troubles—

Twin Pedestal Extension Tables

The Chesley Furniture Co., Limited
Chesley, - Ontario

"COLLERAN'S" ALL-STEEL LINE

"COLLERAN" SPRINGS

are constructed on "Life-time Service" principles. Our guarantee covers every phase of satisfaction to the user.

Colleran Patent Divan No. 10.

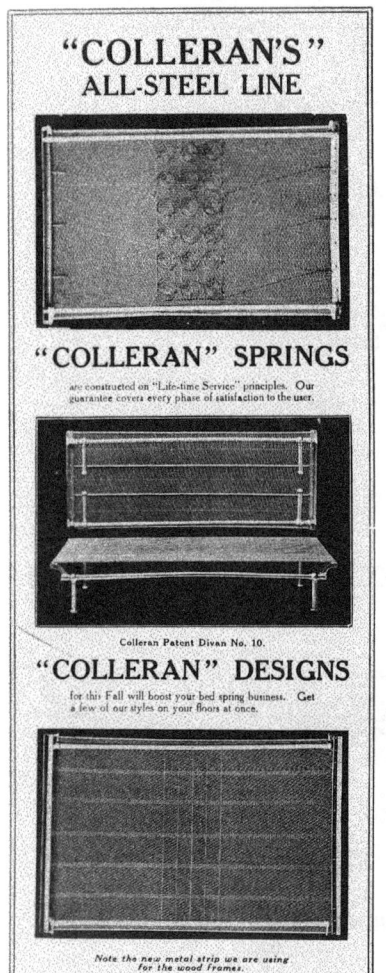

"COLLERAN" DESIGNS

for this Fall will boost your bed spring business. Get a few of our styles on your floors at once.

Note the new metal strip we are using for the wood frames.

Cuts loaned to Dealers for advertisements on request.

Colleran Patent Spring Mattress Co.
TORONTO, ONT.

Mr. Dealer! The Lee-Burrell is—

the most profitable high grade Cotton Felt Mattress you can handle.

THE LEE-BURRELL is no experiment to the dealer who sells, or who *wants* to sell, a mattress that is above "cheap" goods, and yet is not so high priced that its sale will be restricted to well-to-do trade only. The Lee-Burrell never fails to justify our claim as a leading profit maker.

Our other well known lines of Mattresses are the Rex, Regent and Invictus.

May we send you our Price List

The Standard Bedding Company

Toronto   Ontario

Making TABLE-SLIDES is a Specialty Business

For more than TWENTY-FIVE YEARS we have made TABLE SLIDES exclusively. Our Factory is equipped with Special Machinery which enables us to make SLIDES,—BETTER and CHEAPER than the furniture manufacturer.

Canadian Table makers are rapidly adopting WABASH SLIDES

Because They ELIMINATE SLIDE TROUBLES
Are CHEAPER and BETTER

Reduced Costs
Increased Out-put
BY USING
WABASH SLIDES

Made by
B. WALTER & CO.
Wabash, Ind.

The Largest EXCLUSIVE TABLE-SLIDE Manufacturers in America
ESTABLISHED 1887

Table Top Profits

J-M ASBESTOS
Table Covers and Mats

will produce greater profits for you than any other articles of a similar nature.
Why? Because we are the OLDEST and LARGEST miners and manufacturers of Asbestos in the world, and make J-M Asbestos Table Covers and Mats in OUR OWN FACTORIES from Asbestos taken from OUR OWN MINES. Therefore we can offer you LOWER PRICES, so that you can undersell ALL competitors and still clear BIGGER PROFITS and give your customers BETTER GOODS.
A SMALL STOCK is all you need, as we can supply you quickly from any of our numerous Branches. More styles and sizes and wider range of prices than any other line made.

Write our nearest Branch NOW for Special Dealer Proposition and Booklet.

THE CANADIAN
H. W. JOHNS-MANVILLE CO., LIMITED
TORONTO   MONTREAL   WINNIPEG   VANCOUVER

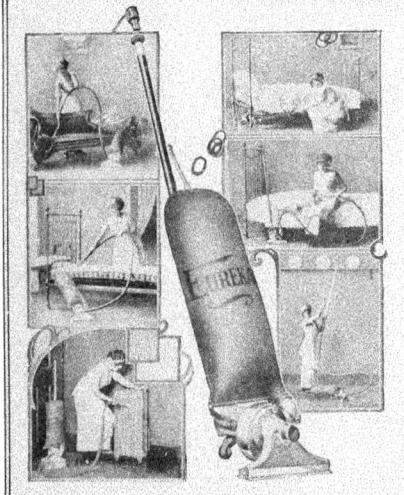

BIG REDUCTION

EUREKA
Electric Vacuum Cleaner

Now $39.50

Nothing changed in the Eureka but the PRICE

The same high quality—the same guarantee—the same $45.00 machine in every detail at a reduction of $5.50 after September 1st, 1914.

The enormous increase in our business during the past year has made this big reduction possible. It places the most durable and efficient electric cleaner within the means of every Canadian family.

Extra attachments Complete $10.

Price Winnipeg and West add $5.00. We Want Dealers Everywhere

Write for trade prices

Onward Manufacturing Company
Berlin, Ontario

FACTORIES:
MONTREAL FACTORY
   C. A. Hart, Vice-Pres. and Mgr.
WINNIPEG FACTORY
   W. J. Rumberger, Mgr.
UXBRIDGE FACTORY
   Geo. Wilson, Gen. Supt.

DIRECTORS:
W. J. McMURTRY, President and General Manager
W. R. DALBY
C. C. EMMERSON
H. B. SHORTT, Secretary
G. HUGHES, Ass. Manager

The "Gold Medal" Line
Davenports and Divanettes

Our factories at Toronto and Uxbridge are the most perfectly equipped in Canada for the manufacture of Davenports and Divanettes. In addition to making our own wood frames and other parts, we make all our own interior steel frame work for operating Bed constructions, which are fitted with the best National Steel fabric Springs.

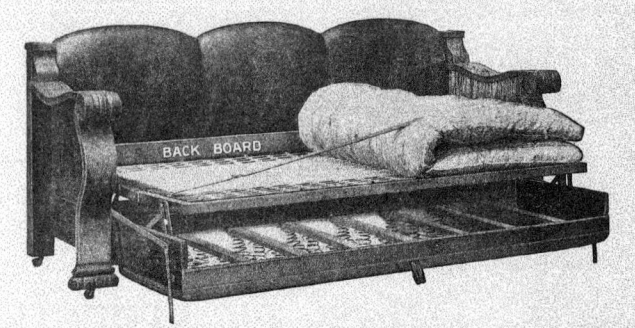

No. 717.—One of Our Twenty Designs

The Principal Features of our Davenports and Divanettes are:

- Perfection and Simplicity of Operation
- More Bedding Space than any other make
- Spring Edge Fronts and Ruffle Borders
- Elegant Designs and well made and finished frames
- Prices Lower than any other makes
- Patent Locking Device for Divanettes
- A Good Mattress on a Good Spring Bed
- Indestructible Patent Truss Construction for Springs

READY NOW FOR PROMPT SHIPMENT

See our exhibits at the Toronto and Ottawa Exhibitions

The Gold Medal Manufacturing Co.
Limited
Toronto   Montreal   Winnipeg   and Uxbridge

"Lippert" Handy Leaf and Equalizer Tables

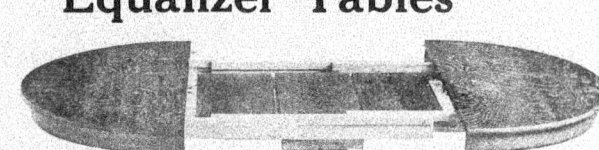

THE extra leaves are hinged for folding, and stored out of sight in a well under the top of the table.

The top of the table is always centred or "equalized" over the pedestal. The equalizer does not interfere with the slides. Nothing to get out of order and make the slides bind.

Patented Dec. '13

Centre Pedestal is made in both round and square patterns.

Made in attractive designs and all finished.

The "Comp-Rite"

The New Table Drawer Writing Desk that can be used in Dressing Table, Library Table or Desk

A NEW INVENTION that can be used in almost any table fitted for a drawer. It works **without disturbing any article resting on the table,** being absolutely independent of the table top.

The "Comp-rite" contains inkstand, penholders and stationery holders which rise automatically when the drawer opens.

Made in all finishes.

Patent Applied For

Write for Particulars and Prices

Geo. J. Lippert Table Company, Limited
Berlin :: Ontario

"On the Job" 24 Hours in Every Day

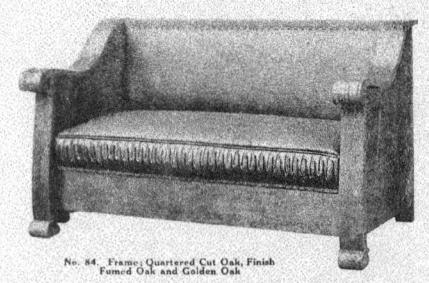

Our Famous
Duofold

THERE is always a place and a use in every home, large or small, rich or poor, for either a Revolving Bed or a Duofold, and every wise dealer, who wants to buy better value for less money and make a large profit for himself, ought to send his orders to the Montreal Upholstering Co., where style and prices are made to suit everybody.

TRY A SAMPLE ORDER

No. 84. Frame: Quartered Cut Oak, Finish Fumed Oak and Golden Oak

Special Discount on Car Lots

Prices: Genuine Leather, $71.00 List; Genuine Spanish, $74.00 List

Above prices with Cotton Felt Mattresses Complete

The Montreal Upholstering Company
1611-1613 Clarke St., MONTREAL, Can.

The Most Practical Truck for Furniture Factories

In the Stratford Furniture Factories alone there are several hundred WATSON Trucks in use. They are considered to be the most efficient and economical made.

WATSON TRUCKS

are made in nearly 200 styles and sizes—a truck for every purpose. Write for catalog and prices to-day. We can make prompt delivery.

John Watson Mfg. Co., Limited
Ayr, Ontario   Winnipeg, Man

Get Our Catalogue
MATTHEWS BROS. LIMITED
788 Dundas Street   -   TORONTO

QUALITY and PRICE the same.

THE FAMOUS
OSTERMOOR MATTRESS

Sold By The Leading Furniture Dealer In Nearly Every Canadian Town at The Following Retail Prices

4'6" Wide 45 Lbs.	4'0" Wide 40 Lbs.	3'6" Wide 35 Lbs.	3'0" Wide 30 Lbs.
$15.00	$14.00	$12.50	$11.00

All 6 Feet 3 Inches in Length.   Standard 4 Inch Band.   Best A.C.A. or Fancy Striped Tickings

We Want An Ostermoor Agent in Every Town in Canada

Exclusive Selling Rights Given to One Dealer.   Write Us To-day
For Agents' Discounts and Particulars

IT MEANS MONEY FOR YOU

MANUFACTURED EXCLUSIVELY IN CANADA BY

The ALASKA FEATHER & DOWN CO., Limited — Montreal
The ALASKA BEDDING CO., Limited — Winnipeg
The ALASKA B. C. BEDDING CO., Limited — Vancouver

Kohn's Imported Bentwood Furniture

The Right Grade for All Classes of Trade

Rich enough in appearance for the homes of the wealthy, so inexpensive in many styles that even the most economical may buy.

Sure to Satisfy in Service

Made of tough Austrian beechwood, specially seasoned to prevent warping or splitting, bent by a patented strength-retaining process, the leg joints rigidly fastened with steel bolts mortised into the wood.

KEEP THE KOHN CATALOG ON YOUR DESK

Write for a free copy to-day. Keep it on your desk for reference or for placing special orders. Special styles and finishes will be made according to your specifications.

No. 48-45 Saddle Seat

No. 119/B Cane seat

Jacob & Josef Kohn of Vienna
215-219 Victoria Street, Toronto, Canada

NEW YORK—110-112 W. 27 Street   CHICAGO—1410-1418 So. Wabash Ave.

Sterilized Curled Hair

We make the best grades suitable for all classes of work. When using Griffin's make, satisfaction is guaranteed—

Mattress and Upholsterers' Supplies

Prompt delivery of all orders. Let us quote you prices on your requirements.

Write us to-day

The Griffin Curled Hair Co., Limited

Head Office and Factory
Bloor St. and St. Helen's Ave., Toronto

Branch Office and Warehouse
252 St. James St., Montreal

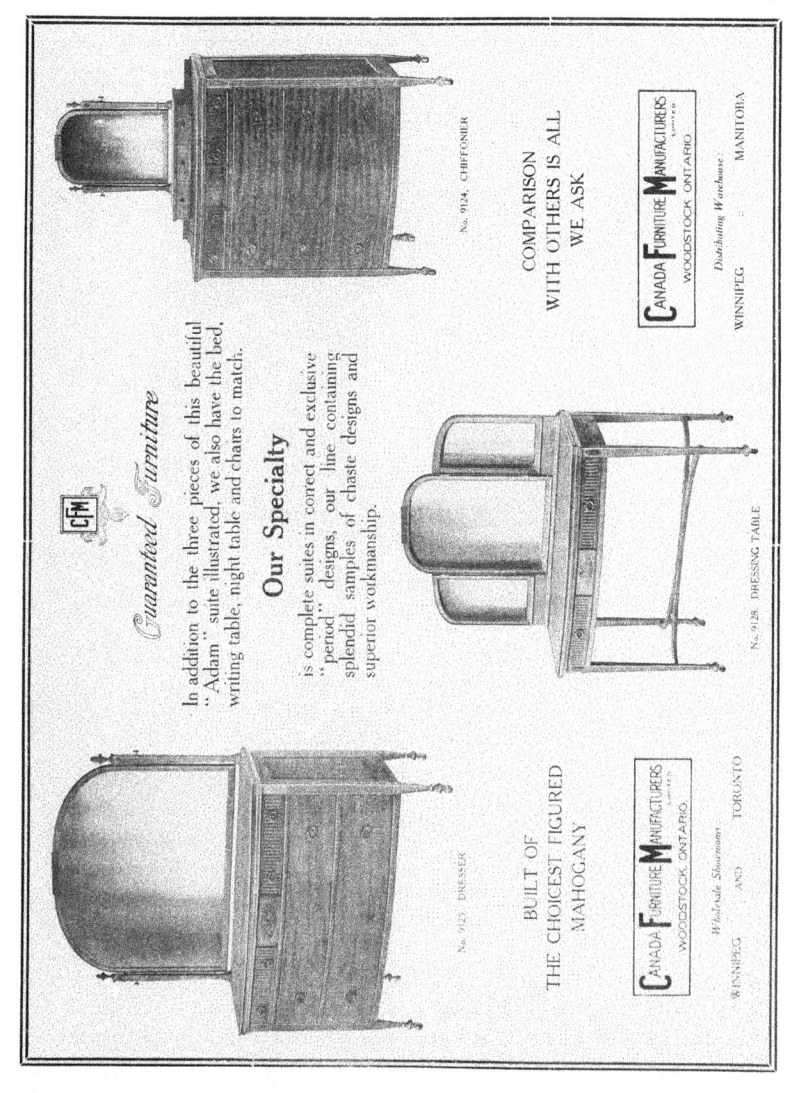

September, 1914   CANADIAN FURNITURE WORLD AND THE UNDERTAKER.   55

No. 9124, CHIFFONIER

Guaranteed Furniture

In addition to the three pieces of this beautiful "Adam" suite illustrated, we also have the bed, writing table, night table and chairs to match.

Our Specialty

is complete suites in correct and exclusive "period" designs, our line containing splendid samples of chaste designs and superior workmanship.

No. 9128, DRESSING TABLE

COMPARISON WITH OTHERS IS ALL WE ASK

Canada Furniture Manufacturers
WOODSTOCK, ONTARIO
Distributing Warehouse:
WINNIPEG   MANITOBA

No. 9127, DRESSER

BUILT OF THE CHOICEST FIGURED MAHOGANY

Canada Furniture Manufacturers
WOODSTOCK, ONTARIO
Wholesale Showroom:
WINNIPEG   AND   TORONTO

CANADIAN FURNITURE WORLD AND THE UNDERTAKER. September, 1914

The "Ideal" Motto is Quality First

B. 91—BRASS BEDSTEAD

Pillars 2 ins. sq.   Fillets 1 in. sq.   Top Rod 1½ in. sq.   Btm. Rod 1 in. sq.   Cast Brass Vases and Trimmings.
Head 55 ins.   Foot 38 ins.   Sizes—4-6 4-0 3-6 3-0.   Shipping Weight 165 pounds.

*"Commerce hath its Victories
No less renowned than War"*

The commercial supremacy of Ideal Brass Beds has been won by steadfast campaigning,
Campaigning that has involved keen judgment in buying raw materials.
Fine sensing of the public taste in originating new designs.
Splendid organization of factory forces.
Infinite capacity for employing most up-to-date methods and machinery.
And---sincere regard for the dealers' profit in handling the line.
To-day, Quality for Price considered, we believe IDEAL BRASS BEDS ARE SUPREME.
You dealers who sell them know it.

IDEAL BEDDING CO. LIMITED
2-64 JEFFERSON AVENUE · TORONTO

Canadian Furniture World and the Undertaker

Published about the twenty-first of preceding month by

The Commercial Press, Limited
32 Colborne Street, Toronto
(Next King Edward Hotel)

D. O. McKINNON, President
W. L. EDMONDS, Vice President and Contributing Editor
J. C. ARMER, Vice President and Manager of Technical Papers
WESTON WRIGLEY, Vice-President and Manager of Trade Papers
JAMES O'HAGAN, Editor
WM. J. BRYANS, Associate Editor
GEO. H. HONSBERGER, Advertising Manager

F. C. D. WILKES, 784 Unity Building, Montreal
C. G. BRANDT, Circulation Manager, Toronto
E. J. MacINTYRE, Room 1155, 122 S. Michigan Ave., Chicago
N. D. WEBSTER, 95 Liberty Street, New York

Subscription rate, Canada and Great Britain, $1.00 per year; United States, $1.50 per year. A minimum circulation of 2,000 copies is guaranteed each month.

VOLUME FOUR   TORONTO, SEPTEMBER, 1914   NUMBER NINE

Don't Diminish Your Exports. Although the outbreak of war somewhat dims the prospects for fall trade, business will by no means come to a standstill.

Furniture may be bought and sold in smaller quantities than would have been the case had financial conditions been normal.

But, as in times of activity, so in times of depression, the larger share of the business that is to be had will go to manufacturers and retailers who make the best use of the possibilities that are at their command.

It would be a decidedly unwise thing for any business man, manufacturer or retailer, to crowd on more sail than he ordinarily carries, but it would be equally unwise to take in more sail than is necessary. That will only hinder instead of help matters.

Should the war be a prolonged one Canada will undoubtedly share in the world-wide evils which it will work in regard to trade and commerce.

But it must also be remembered that the situation is not without its compensating factors. For Canada's food products there will unquestionably be an export demand, and at prices which will yield a revenue even larger than that for the crop of 1913, in spite of the smaller yield. And what applies to farm products also applies, although in a lesser degree, to factory products.

It must also be remembered that, being a part of the British Empire, we shall probably find that we shall derive greater advantage relatively from the British marine service than any other country. That to our export and import trade will be a matter of enormous advantage.

When one comes to calmly consider the situation one must conclude that in spite of the undoubted adverse influences attendant upon the war now being waged that we in Canada have much to inspire us to keep the wheels of commerce revolving.

By keeping this thought before us, and putting our best efforts forward, we shall at least minimize the adverse influence of the war upon the business interests of the country.

Keep up your courage and keep up your advertising, for advertising is one of the outward and visible signs of the faith that is in you. To discontinue advertising, on the other hand, is an outward and visible sign that your confidence has vanished. And that, in turn, will diminish the confidence of your customers and cause them to curtail their purchases. That is a fact of psychology.

Take advantage of the war to work the war spirit into your window display. It will attract attention.

The Value of Trade Associations. The value and worth of trade associations have been discussed and emphasized time and time again in the trade press of Canada, and the English-speaking world generally, and the wonder of it all is that no move has as yet been made by many Canadian merchants to get, through co-operation, better conditions for the protection of their own particular business and lines of trade, and more satisfactory arrangements for the carrying on of their everyday avocations.

If there is one line of business that has been lacking in this co-operation it is the furniture trade. With the exception of one or two local associations, formed for social purposes among some few dealers and clerks here and there throughout the country, there is not in the length and breadth of Canada any association among the furniture dealers that is built on broad, firm, commercial or educational lines—lines that are beneficial to the dealer himself and to the trade generally.

With the social associations no complaint at all can be made. They are a beginning, at least, and because of this fact are a good thing; but what is wanted is a good strong organization of Canadian furniture dealers, banded together on an educational basis, for the upbuilding of the trade. A beginning might be made with associations spread across the country, similar to those obtaining across the border in the many States of the Union.

There are two nation-wide furniture associations in the United States: one, the National Home Furnishers' Association, and the other, the National Retail Furniture Dealers' Association. Both of them act in co-operation with the various State associations, and thus are able to be of assistance to the trade in different parts of the country.

Business Men's Savings.

There are doubtless a good many men in business to-day who wish they had saved more money when they were clerks in order that they might to-day have had more capital at their command. And there are clerks who, after many years' experience behind the counter, would be merchants to-day where it not for the fact that they had not cultivated the habit of saving in their early days.

Most of us would like to have our days over again. But we cannot eat our cake and have it. What is past is past. And it is easier to foretell the future than to bring back the past. But the experiences of others can serve as warnings to others.

There is no clerk whose salary is so small that he cannot set aside a certain amount each week on savings bank account. The habit of saving a certain fixed amount weekly does not of necessity become a penurious habit.

Penuriousness is more to be avoided than even an extravagant habit, for to be penurious is to narrow and warp one's life. And while a life that is narrow and warped may amass money, it cannot, in its truest sense, be termed successful.

To be a successful merchant in its widest and best sense is to be a successful man.

Money makes money. And the best thing a young man can do when he has a hundred or so dollars at his command is to invest it in some security that will yield him a fair and reasonably sure return.

That which is a gamble he should avoid, at any rate until he has amassed such a large sum of money that he can afford to take a chance without seriously impairing his financial standing.

No man should run the risk of losing his all in a speculative venture, no matter how attractive it may be.

Avoid those sure things that industrious promoters are so zealously offering to their friends.

There are so many tried and trusted things in which the man with small savings can invest that there is no excuse for him to place his money in those which are chimerical.

While we are at war with our enemies it is better that we should be at peace with our competitors.

Get Out After New Ideas.

There is always danger of the merchant getting into a rut—of sticking to old and laborious methods of doing business, when more modern and more profitable ones might be employed. This is especially so with the man who sticks everlastingly to his business, never getting out to see just how other dealers in his particular line conduct their stores.

Just as the merchant who would progress and expand must get out after new business, so must the dealer who would succeed get out after new and up-to-date ideas for conducting and increasing his business.

The writer knows of a dealer in a comparatively small town who makes a practice of regularly visiting larger centres in order to secure new ideas and methods. He makes the round of the stores, and from each trip brings back many ideas on window trimming, display, etc., that he is able to work into his business to advantage.

He considers such trips profitable and charges them up to the expense account of the store. They do not cost him much either, for a person can do a lot of looking around in a day. He also generally plans to make his trips around holidays when reduced rates can be obtained on the railroads.

If more dealers would follow this plan of getting out in search of modern and progressive ideas, they would become better merchants and their business would be benefited. No dealer has a monopoly on the creating of all the good merchandising plans. Even the cleverest dealer must admit that he can frequently learn from the other fellow.

SHORT NOTES FROM THE EDITOR'S PEN.

Good intentions are the paving-stones on which many a man slips.

* * *

The merchant who would succeed must concern himself with profits.

* * *

No employe is apt to be rated higher by his employer than he rates himself.

* * *

Almost every merchant has a customer whom, when his back is turned he calls "Old tightwad."

* * *

Being funny at someone else's expense will in the end prove most expensive for yourself.

* * *

Just because you have pulled off one good merchandising scheme, don't expect its momentum to last forever.

* * *

Lack of ambition is more responsible for the summer quietness some merchants complain about than lack of opportunity.

* * *

There are two sides to every offer and oftentimes the Something-for-nothing offer carries its most important features on the under side.

* * *

The man who is considering going into a new store should give a good deal of thought to the selection of his location. It often makes or breaks a business.

* * *

Bad as a fault may be, it often happens that the effort to conceal it develops something worse than the fault. It is better to eliminate a fault than to cover it up.

* * *

Don't get the idea that the more things you mention in one advertisement, the more things it will sell. In the crowded ad., as in the crowded window display, the attention is not concentrated on any one line, and therefore the interest of customers is not aroused.

* * *

Are you keeping pace with the schedule you mapped out at the beginning of the year? The engineer in charge of a train does not wait until the end of his run to see if he is on time, but keeps timing himself at each station as he goes along. The dealer who hopes to attain a certain ideal for the year, should do the same thing—should keep comparing his progress with his schedule as he goes along.

Be Not Dismayed—Keep Up Your Courage :
BY W. L. EDMONDS

That the outbreak of a war in which all the world's first-class powers but one are engaged should cause a worldwide unsettling of trade and commerce is only what is to be expected.

But for Canadians to develop a state of "blue funk" is not justified by conditions, and will only make matters worse.

When an individual is ill of a fever you do not feed him with the germs that cause the disease. You give him medicine.

The war upon which the British Empire and half a dozen other countries have embarked has undoubtedly debilitated trade and commerce.

But do not let us add to the patient's troubles by stampeding at the first blast of the trumpet of war.

We are undoubtedly beset by possibilities grave and uncertain. Both our national existence and our trade are menaced.

But it is the uncertainties, and not the actualities, that are the occasion of the "blue funk" that is possessing altogether too many people in Canada at the moment.

At the time of writing (the second week in August) neither has the British fleet been swept from the sea nor the allied armies annihilated.

Until either one or the other of these unexpected things happen, there is no earthly reason why we should allow our confidence, either in the existence of the British Empire or in the trade and commerce of the Dominion to go by the board.

Uncertainty there doubtless is, but there is less reason for it to-day than there was a week ago.

The highways of the ocean are again open, with the result that our export and import trade is resuming its accustomed channels, while its further development has been facilitated by the arrangement entered into by the Minister of Finance and the Bank of England, whereby gold is being deposited by the latter with the former at the rate of a million dollars a day, in order that the machinery of exchange, so essential to the working of international trade, may again go into operation.

The action of the Minister of Finance in authorizing the banks to issue emergency currency and to secure legal tender notes from the Receiver-General on depositing securities instead of gold, is a provision designed to relieve the financial strain at home, and consequently expedite the movement of merchandise.

But these are not the only factors whose tendency should be to strengthen rather than to weaken the confidence of business men in the trade situation in Canada. There is another and a very important one. And that is the export demand which is certain to be experienced for the products of our farms and factories.

Food products, particularly, will be in demand, and the only thing that can prevent Canada's contributing to that demand will be the sealing up of the highways of the Atlantic by the warships of a hostile power. That is, however, something on which we do not reckon as even an eventuality.

The cereal crops are smaller than last year, but the appreciation in value will compensate for the depreciation in quantity, while the strides which have been made in the West in the direction of mixed farming will prove an additional compensating factor.

There is no exhibition of "blue funk" in England. The restoration of the bank rate to what is practically a normal status is proof of this. And if their confidence is strong, there is certainly no reason why ours should be weak. In the meantime, let us keep down expenses and keep up our courage.

Local Dealer Gets Church and School Fittings Trade

Wright & Hepburn, retail furniture dealers, Port Arthur, Ont., have secured several good-sized contracts from local institutions — An interview with them on the subject.

BY A STAFF EDITOR

ONE Canadian furniture firm that believes that the local dealer is the one who should and can get the business in furniture and fittings for local churches, schools, and other institutions is Wright & Hepburn, of Port Arthur, Ont. Not only do they believe this, but they are proving the possibility of it in a convincing manner by actually securing a good deal of business of this character. Some interesting points in regard to this particular question were brought out in an interview which an editorial representative of the Canadian Furniture World had with the manager.

Not Handed to Dealer on Silver Platter.

"I read an article in a trade paper not long ago," said Mr. Wright, "stating that it was difficult for the local furniture dealer to get this class of business, on account of the competition of larger outside firms that make a specialty of this business. I do not agree with that view at all, because I think the local dealer is in a position to get a good deal of this trade if he only makes a bid for it. It is not to be expected that it will be handed to the dealer on a silver platter. Very little is secured in this world without effort, and accordingly the dealer who desires this trade must go after it in an aggressive and businesslike manner. Our experience, however, has demonstrated that it can be got."

Contracts Amounting to $18,000.

Contracts amounting in all to a total of $18,000 have been secured in a comparatively short space of time from local institutions for fittings by Wright & Hepburn. One contract was for fittings for a church, including seats, carpets, etc. Bids for this piece of work were entered by a number of outside concerns, but Wright & Hepburn were successful in landing it.

"The very fact that we are on the job and can look after the work in a competent manner as it proceeds, is no doubt a factor in getting us this business," points out Mr. Wright. "Those who let the contract prefer to have it in charge of some local man with whom they may easily discuss any questions that arise rather than in the hands of some distant firm, with whom it is difficult to take up any questions pertaining to the work."

Kindly Feeling Towards Home Merchant.

"There is also generally a kindly feeling towards the home business man. It is local people who support local institutions, and it is only right that the local merchant, other things being equal, should be given the preference by these institutions when they have any contracts of this nature to let."

Backing this up, however, must be aggressiveness on the part of the dealer. Wright & Hepburn keep a line on all local institutions that are erecting new buildings which will require new fittings, and at once make an appeal for this business. Some of the contracts and their size that they have filled recently include:

Church fittings $8,000
Masonic Hall 4,000
Club house furnishings 4,000
Seats for new school 2,000

Here is a total of $18,000, showing that it is worth while going after this trade. In addition, it is good advertising for a firm when it becomes known to the public that they supply fittings for such large institutions. The public rather reason that a firm that can satisfy in regard to quality and price in such big work as this, is good enough for them to patronize. Recognizing the advertising value of these big contracts, Wright & Hepburn intend having photographs taken of the places that they have fitted for to use in advertising.

Believe in Good Display.

Good display is recognized by Wright & Hepburn as a valuable method of inducing sales. To give greater display they have had a gallery erected around the sides of their store, fitted with a glass front. The double window thus secured gives them much larger display to the passing public, the upper window being especially valuable in attracting the attention of people on the opposite side of the street. They find it valuable, too, quite frequently finding customers come in as a result of the display in the upper section.

A second storey to the building provides space for rugs, but shows them up better to customers, and thus being used for storage purposes.

Carpets and Linoleum.

It is their intention to enlarge the carpet department, because it is realized that being able to show this line to advantage helps materially in its sale. The plan of showing rugs on swinging racks is utilized in this department to good advantage. The rack arrangement not only saves space and facilitates the handling of rugs and additional furniture display, the rear portion helps in sales.

For the handling of long rolls of linoleum, iron rods are run through them and they are suspended in a rack at the side of the wall. In order to make it easy to turn the rolls when it is desired to unroll them, a crank that fits on to the end of the rod is made use of.

WATCH THE BUYING END.

Mistakes in buying lead to overstocks and lost profits.

There are two kinds of mistakes in buying: The mistake of buying the wrong thing, and the mistake of buying too much of the right thing. Both are equally dangerous. Either can bring disaster.

The kind of buying that leads to these mistakes is done on a chance—a gamble. It wins, once in a while. All gambling does. But the other times—!

Safe buying is the kind that eliminates all gambling possibilities. It is the kind that insures a fair deal to all parties in the transaction. It is the kind that does not thrive either on the misfortune of the seller or the ignorance of the buyer. It is the kind that provides several profits on a moderate investment rather than one profit on a larger investment that means buying in quantities to take a discount.

Western Canada: Past Progress, Present Conditions and Future Prospects

By WM. J. BRYANS

IN TWO PARTS—Part I

Some facts regarding the progress that has been made by the West in the past— Features of present business conditions — Looking forward to the future with the highest degree of confidence — A staff article from first-hand observations in the Western Provinces.

FOR a number of years now, Western Canada has been very much in the spotlight, not only in regard to the Dominion itself, but in a world-wide way. The grain fields that are so extensive and yield such bountiful harvests have won for the Western provinces a no uncertain place in the supplying of the world's grain—so great a position in this regard as to win for it that appropriate appellation: "Bread basket of the world." Producing, as it does now, over two hundred million bushels of wheat alone, and a total of about half a billion bushels of grain nearly, there is no wonder that it has been brought prominently before the eyes of the entire world, and recognized as an important factor in the world's grain supply.

Western Conditions Reflected in East.

For one thing, everyone will agree that the Western provinces form an exceedingly important part of the Dominion. This is recognized by the Eastern business man as well as the Western, and probably never so much before as during the past year or so. It has been shown that good or bad times in Western Canada reflect themselves to no little extent in the degree of activity and prosperity in the East. The greater purchasing power the West has, the greater is the demand from that direction for products manufactured in the East. This is felt not only by the manufacturer, but right down the line, for if manufacturing plants are busy, the laboring man will have more money to purchase goods from the local retailer. Thus, the situation in the West reflects itself in the general state of prosperity of the country.

Great Interest in West at Crop Time.

All Canada is interested all the time in the progress and business conditions in Western Canada, but just at this time when the harvest is again looming up as an important factor in the general and commercial life of the country for the twelve months ahead, there is a keener interest in that great stretch of country which lies west of the Great Lakes. As the West turns out its yearly crop, manufacturers, wholesalers, retailers, and the public in general, become much more interested in it, not only as to the probable size of the current year's crop, but also as to the progress that has been made in the past as well as what the future may hold forth for a country that has made remarkable—yes, more than remarkable—progress in the past ten years.

"Booming" of Certain Centres Proved Bad Feature.

Some say that the West has grown too fast, but that is not the case. There have merely been some circum-

---

Good Prices Will Be Received For Grain

A FACTOR of a great deal of importance in sizing up the Western situation is the good prices which the Canadian farmer will receive for his grain this year. The outlook for fair prices was favorable all along, but with the opening of a world's war this became assured. The reason for this is obvious. Not only will grain and its products be needed by the warring nations while hostilities are being carried on, but harvesting of the crop in the European countries will be seriously interfered with, and there will naturally be a greater demand on this continent for grain. This will assure the Canadian farmer a good price for his crops.

Thus, although there have been reports of damage to the grain crops of Western Canada through drought, the farmer will have the advantage of higher prices for the grain he does harvest and also the advantage of a larger supply of labor, at less cost, than has been the case in past years. Every person who gives the subject consideration will realize the important bearing which these factors will have on the general situation.

There is no doubt that the Western crop is not as promising as earlier in the season, on account of lack of sufficient rain in certain sections. The average yield will be below last year, and how far that will be made up by the increased acreage remains to be seen. However, it is realized that the higher prices of this year are the big factor in the situation.

stances connected with its growth that might have been better otherwise, and which would be avoided if it was to be done over again, and which will be eliminated to a large extent in the development of those portions of the country which still remain to be opened up. One of these things was the "booming" of certain towns, and the inflation of real estate values in certain sections to figures that meant reaction should a period of financial stringency strike the country. Led on by the big profits that had been made by many people by increases in their real estate holdings, people in every walk of life began putting their surplus cash into real estate. In many instances they incurred liabilities for large amounts, believing from the past experiences of themselves or other people that they would be able to sell before called upon for payment, or that they would be able to borrow on the property sufficient to meet payments.

Bankers Call Halt in Speculation.

With heavy buying of real estate, values at some centres were naturally inflated. This was helped along by "wildcat" speculation in subdivided lands in and near cities, towns, and possible—and in some cases, impossible—commercial centres. Then came a period of depression. This was not alone confined to the West nor to Canada, but was a worldwide financial stringency, but it has probably been felt more in Western Canada than elsewhere, for the reasons already set forth, and because it is only natural in a new and necessarily a borrowing country. In addition, the bankers who saw that there was need of curbing the wild speculation that was taking place in the West, made the worldwide money tightness an excuse for shutting down on real estate loans.

"Screws" Applied Effectively.

The halt thus called in over-speculation in land and the floating of subdivisions near towns and cities was certainly a good thing, because the longer delayed, the greater would have been the ill effects on the country. The "screws" have certainly been applied in an effective manner—some say with a vengeance. At any rate, the real estate business all over Western Canada is certainly quiet. Prices in many instances have fallen off materially, and sales of property are exceedingly few as compared with the wild rush of a few years ago. The floating of "wildcat" propositions in subdivisions many miles removed from cities is an impossibility. Hundreds of men who were engaged in the real estate business during the flowery period have been forced to seek other means of earning a livelihood.

Credit Was Extended Too Recklessly.

While the curbing of over-speculation is a commendable thing, and could probably only be brought about by the curtailing of loans, it is contended that in some cases bankers have been too strict in the matter of extension of loans, and that in many cases legitimate business concerns have been materially handicapped by the refusal of the banks to advance money even on the very best of security. There is no doubt that many business concerns have a real grievance in this regard, but there is no denying that the curtailment of loans by the bankers has done much to cut down the reckless extension of credit that was taking place in the West. The several years of marked activity and prosperity in the West had caused manufacturers and wholesalers to be very liberal in extending credit to retailers, many of whom were trying to operate big businesses on little or no capital. The retailers in turn gave easy credit to farmers, and so all down the line was a reckless extension of credit that was bound to have its evil effects when the day of reckoning came.

Not Taking Any Chances Now.

This day did come with the general financial stringency and the tightening up by the bankers. Manufacturers and wholesalers found it necessary to press for payments on the demand of their bankers, and retailers in turn were confronted with the problem of collecting outstanding accounts—this being a difficult problem because everyone had their funds tied up in real estate. Profiting by their experiences, business men are giving

A view of the wholesale district in Edmonton. Note how the walk for pedestrians is laid down the centre of the street, allowing the wagons to be driven up to the doors of the warehouses without interfering with traffic.

much greater care to the matter of credit—are being forced to, in fact, on account of the present scarcity of funds. Many orders are being turned down daily by manufacturers and wholesalers. because they are unwilling to take chances on any long-term accounts or on unreliable purchasers. Some houses are requiring their travelers to collect all money due from the retailers on whom they call before taking any more orders from them. Two years ago, such firms would never have thought of turning their travelers into collection men. Their work then was to sell each man just as large a quantity of goods as possible.

Looking Forward to Future With Confidence.

During the past year the West generally has felt the business depression to no little extent. That is generally agreed. Business men, while realizing the value of giving out optimistic reports, admit that business has been quiet. There are exceptions, of course, but in most businesses the past year has not been so rosy as the couple of years preceding. But out of the reports of quiet times, one fact stands out prominently—the business men of the country are looking forward to the future with confidence, and believe that as soon as the present financial stringency is past and trade blossoms forth again, that it will be upon a much steadier and more solid basis. Men are now looking forward to the time when the tide will turn and conditions will begin to swing back to normal. They feel that the West will not be long getting back into its old stride, and that it will soon regain its old activity and prosperity.

New Crop Big Factor in Immediate Future.

"What is the outlook as to the immediate future?" is naturally an expected question at this time. As to this, the outcome of the present crop in Western Canada will prove an important factor. It will decide to what extent conditions will immediately begin to swing back to normal. The importance of a good crop lies mainly in the probability that, if a failure, the depression will not be relieved. If a success, the depression should gradually lift. Business men are apt to make the mistake of thinking that a good crop will lead to an instant revival of business on the large scale of past years. It is probably more accurate to estimate that a good crop will be the first step in a gradual but sure improvement that should gain force as it proceeds. With the stimulus of a good crop will come a certain amount of expenditure on the part of the railroad companies, and this will be valuable in overcoming the inertia of the industrial machine. Once started, the momentum of the machine in motion tends to carry it forward.

Much Depends on Price Received.

With regard to the effect that this year's crop will have on existing commercial conditions in this country, it must be patent to every student of economics that the prices that the agricultural section receives for its products will play a very important part. If good prices are received, it will mean a much larger aggregate sum in the pockets of the farmers. It is contended that the present condition of affairs is, to a large extent, the result of the strict economy which the farming population has been practising, whether voluntarily or involuntarily, during the past nine months. The reference here is to the West particularly.

If, then, this fall, the farmers receive what they consider to be profitable prices for their offerings of grain and other commodities, they will no doubt relax to a greater or less degree the stern frugality which has marked their attitude during the period of depression. With this relaxation will come a better demand for goods in all lines of manufactures. It is only a sufficient quantity of ready money that can restore the West to anything of its old-time activity.

Larger Acreage This Year.

The estimate of the Census and Statistical Department of the Dominion Government for the three North-West Provinces of Manitoba, Saskatchewan, and Alberta gives the wheat acreage as 10,063,500 acres, as

View of the Winnipeg Industrial Bureau where a permanent exposition of local manufactured products and natural resources of the Canadian West is maintained.

for the three crops is: Wheat, 27,500; oats, 314,000; and barley, 13,000 acres; a total of 354,500 acres for the three crops. The largest increase of area in the three provinces is for oats, 314,000 acres, which apparently compared with 10,036,000 acres last year, an increase being shown in Saskatchewan and Alberta, but a decrease in Manitoba. Oats in the three provinces occupy 6,106,000 acres, as compared with 5,792,000 acres in 1913, and barley 1,038,000 acres, as compared with 1,025,000 acres. The net increase in the three provinces ently shows that increased attention is being given to mixed farming.

The acreages under the later sown cereal crops of 1914 are estimated as follows: Buckwheat, 354,000, as against 380,700 in 1913; flax, 1,163,000, as against 1,552,500; corn for husking, 256,000, against 473,500; turnips, etc., 175,000, against 186,400; sugar beet, 15,500, against 17,000; and corn for fodder, 317,000, against 303,650. It will be noted that the area under flaxseed is 389,800 acres less than last year, the decrease being principally in Saskatchewan, where the area sown to flax is 1,030,000 acres, or 356,000 less than in 1913.

Revival Leading to Years of Prosperity.

In connection with the country's crops, some interesting estimates have been made by the Department of Trade and Commerce as to our future capacity in agricultural production. Of the total land in the Dominion of Canada, amounting to about a billion and a half acres, the possible farm land is estimated at 440,000,000 acres, or about one-third. Of this all that is occupied at the present time is about 109,000,000 acres, or about one-quarter. Of the land occupied, only about 35,000,000 acres, or one-third, is under cultivation. In other words, there is twelve times as much land capable of producing crops in this country as is now under cultivation.

These estimates have been very carefully made, and, considering that only 31 per cent. of the total area is estimated to be possible farm land, must be considered highly conservative. No account has been taken of forests and swamp lands, which may ultimately be tilled, nor of northern areas of which the agricultural possibilities are at present unknown, because unexplored and unsurveyed.

The facts as to Canada's position towards the rest of the nations, so far as the world's food supply is concerned, were set forth in an analysis made by the Tenth International Congress of Agriculture at Ghent. At this congress it was stated that the world's supply of grain was not keeping pace with the demand, and that in years to come the world would look mainly to Canada for their supply of wheat. In other words, we still have eleven-twelfths of our agricultural development ahead of us, and we are sure of a market for all that it may produce. And agricultural development is first and always the basis of other development and enduring prosperity.

The Development in Grain-Growing.

Although the farmers of Western Canada are fast taking up mixed farming, grain is, and for some time will be, the crop that is raised to the greatest money value each year. Figures in regard to Western Canada, by comparison with the average yields of the leading grain-producing States of the American Union, establish the claim of Western Canada to be classed as the finest grain-producing section of the continent, if not of the whole world.

Some idea of the increase in grain production in the three Prairie Provinces may be gained from the following approximate figures for the year 1903 and 1913, showing the development in a ten-year period. Figures shown are bushels:

Year.	Wheat.	Oats.	Barley.	Flax.
1903	56,146,021	47,215,479	10,448,461	884,000
1913	188,018,000	244,125,000	28,156,000	15,056,000

The second part of this article on Western Canada will appear in the next issue of The Furniture World.

The new hotel which the Grand Trunk Pacific is erecting at Regina, Sask. It is being built near their station in that city and close to the Provincial Government Buildings.

FINE STORES IN THE WEST

There are some fine retail establishments in Western Canada, and many of them are the outcome of a comparatively short period of endeavor by the owners. Those who have been fortunate enough to locate in the right centres at the right time have in many cases experienced a rapidity of growth that those in the more settled districts of Canada would never even expect. The West has demonstrated itself as a country where big things are done in short order, and thus, although a young country, it has many fine retail stores.

Being newly erected, the majority of them are built on modern principles and extensive use made of the latest fixtures and appliances that assist in giving the store an attractive appearance, showing goods up to the best advantage, and allowing the work in the store to be carried on with the greatest rapidity and efficiency.

Not only is this true with the departmental stores, of which all the larger centres have their full share, but there are also many creditable smaller establishments.

Collins' Course in Show Card Writing

Tenth of a series of articles specially prepared for this journal.

AMONG the various accessories a card writer needs is a card rack for holding finished cards while they are drying. Cards laid on a table to dry take up too much space, as they cannot be laid on top of each other while the color is wet.

There are various ways of making racks suitable for holding cards. The illustrations in Fig. 16 show two simple methods that are very satisfactory. The one at the left (a) is made with a 1½ in. x ¾ in. strip, and may be any convenient length you desire. The pegs for holding the cards are ½ or ⅝ in. dowels, with a saw-cut down the centre, into which the card is placed. This saw-cut should be widened a little or made a V shape at the end of the peg, so the cards may be inserted easily. The pegs should be 3½ or 4 ins. long outside the standard. Ordinary clothes pegs will serve very nicely. Note that the pegs are slanted upward to prevent the cards from coming out. This style of rack is made to screw on to the wall.

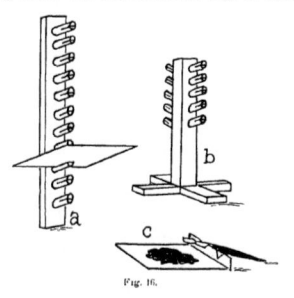

In the event of your not being able to fasten this holder to a wall, we show another design (b), arranged to stand on a flat surface, like a table or the floor. It is similar in arrangement to design "a." In this design two sides are shown with pegs, but four sides may be utilized if you take care to have the pegs alternate with the spaces, so the cards will clear each other when placed in position. This rack may be made any desired height, but the higher the rack the larger the bottom will need to be to prevent the rack from tipping over.

Even simpler devices may be arranged with a little thought and the exercise of a little ingenuity. Four-inch nails may be driven into a strip of wood at regular intervals to support the cards. They should be slanted upwards the same as the pegs. It will require two nails about one or two inches apart horizontally to support the cards. They will require to be driven close enough together (about a quarter of an inch), vertically, so that the card will rest on the top and the edge of the card press up against the bottom of the nails above. Finishing nails are best for this, as they have very small heads.

Still another device may be easily constructed by taking a strip of wood three inches by seven-eighths and running saw-cuts in it at regular intervals to receive the cards. The cuts should be slanted about the same angle as the pegs. This device is not a good one, however, as the saw-cuts cannot be put close enough together to conserve the space. If put close together the pieces will break out on account of the short grain of the wood.

You will find a rack a very great convenience, as a great number of cards may be drying at once in a very small space.

Another device, shown in Fig. 16, is a card palette and brush-holder. The name sounds much more artistic than the article really is. It is simply a waste piece of cardboard with two or three V's cut in one end of it, and that end turned up about three-quarters of an inch to rest your brushes on when not in use. The flat portion of the card is used to flatten your brushes out on when wiping out the surplus color. This is the "palette" part of the card.

How to Make an Oval

Not every one is conversant with the method of making or laying out an oval. Ovals can be utilized very much in card writing, therefore it will be found very convenient to know how to lay them out. The rule is very simple, and an oval of any dimensions can be made accurately without any guesswork. Suppose you want an oval three inches wide and four inches long.

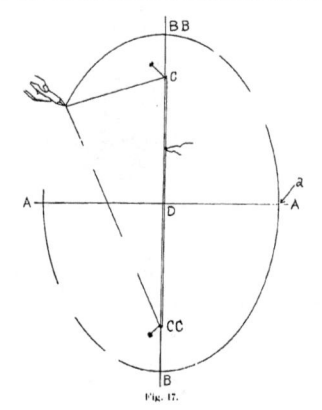

Draw two diameters at right angles. See lines BB, B, and AA in Fig. 17. Mark a point on AA one and a half inches from the centre, where line BB, B intersects AA. Next mark a point on line B two inches from the centre. This makes the diameter of line B

ABCDEFGHIJK MNOPQRSTUV WXYZ 1234578

Plate 38—Fancy design, upper case.

four inches and the diameter of line A three inches. The rule is as follows: Set your compasses or dividers the radius of your greater diameter, in this case two inches. Next, place one point of your compasses at point "a" and "sweep" line B, BB. At the points of intersection on line B, BB drive in two tacks or pins at C, CC. Next, make a loop or band with a piece of string by looping it around one of the tacks at C and tying it at B. This loop should reach from C to B or from CC to BB. Insert a pencil in this band and mark on the paper, pulling the band out taut. Run the pencil around the band, and you will make the oval the desired size. The string must be left over the two tacks at C and CC. This rule will apply to ovals of any dimensions.

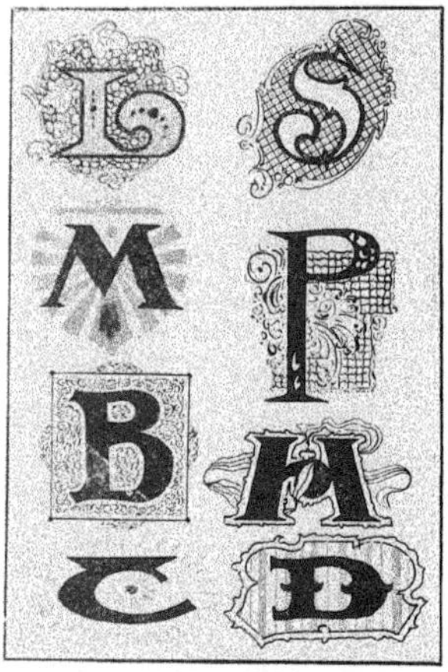

Alphabets.

The style of alphabets shown in plates 38 and 39 is a fancy design that may be utilized for a display word or line on a card. The design, though quite fancy, is easily read, and is very attractive if done neatly and in colors. Care should be taken to have the points all equal and on a line with each other in the various letters forming a word. This style can be used very well in engrossing. With a little study and practice, you will soon become familiar with the formation of the letters. Note that the figures shown adhere to the general formation of the letters.

Plates 40 and 41 show a condensed letter. By "condensed" we mean that the letters are high in proportion to their width. The design is one midway between the Roman and Egyptian, and is very suitable for general use.

Fancy Initials.

Fancy initials, or capitals, may be used with great effect on show cards. One must guard against making them too fancy, for you cannot afford to spend too much time on your work, for you must always remember that "time is money," and this is particularly true in card writing. In using fancy capitals the strongest colors should be used for the letters and the backgrounds should be in subdued or weaker colors. The letter is the main feature, and the background is secondary. The examples in Fig. 18 will give you some idea of the latitude you have in the use of fancy initials. The backgrounds are all interminably interchangeable. That is, any letter may be adapted to any background. The letter L has a red body and black outline, with a pale green background.

S may be in open white, with brown outline and pink background.

M may be in dark blue, with a pale blue back.

P may be in purple or violet, with the back in a lighter shade of these colors.

B may be solid black, with a grey or pale blue back.

H may be dark green, with a pale green back.

C may be in bright color, and the rays in gold or silver.

Fig. 18—Fancy initials.

abcdefghijklmnop qrstuvwxyz

Plate 39.—Fancy design, lower case.

ABCDEFGHIJKLM
NOPQRSTUVWXYZ

Plate 40—Spurred Roman, upper case.

D may be black or gold, with black edge. Background in silver or grey, with a black border.

Sample Cards.

The sample cards this month are suitable for almost any business, and will give suggestions for you in working out other designs. They are both half sheets cut from full sized cards, 22 x 28. You will observe one is cut the long way, while the other is cut crosswise. They are both "spatter work" designs, as explained last month. The fall goods card is made by cutting a circle and laying it on to the card. Also two strips and two rectangular pieces are laid on the card, and the spatter work done around these. The colors used for the spatter are, first, a coat of yellow, then red, then blue. The edge around the circle is made by cutting a smaller circle and placing on the white space after spattering the background and spattering around this smaller circle lightly. The small letters are in black and the fall goods in red and black, and shaded with grey. Cards of this character should be supplemented with price tickets.

The long card can be adapted to any trade, but in this case it is for a furniture window. The design is made exactly the same as the other card, and the lettering is in black with grey shading. This type of card can be utilized to fill vacant wall spaces.

ADDING TO THEIR UPHOLSTERED LINE.

While not exactly a new line, a particularly strong line at present with Walker & Clegg, Wingham, Ont., is their upholstered English living room furniture items. These in davenports and Chesterfields have been selling splendidly. The firm brought out experienced men from the Old Country specially to make this English line, and the result is a high grade production. There are no medium or low-priced, though for the quality of the furniture the price is reasonable.

The upholstered coverings are in the latest designs and colors, and the seats come tufted and plain. Frames are of selected quartered oak or mahogany, and finishes are in golden oak, early English, fumed and mahogany. As an adjunct to Walker & Clegg's upholstered furniture these new English living room items are meeting with much favor.

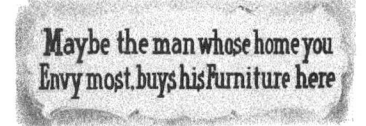

Sample of "spatter work" designing.

Maybe the man whose home you Envy most, buys his Furniture here

Timely "spatter work" card.

New Arrivals in FALL GOODS Exceptional Values

abcdefghijkmnopqrs
1234 tuvwxyyz · 56789

Plate 41—Spurred Roman, lower case.

Selling Methods in the Furniture Store

Some Experiences and Suggestions

THERE is plenty of business to be secured just now by the furniture dealer who is prepared to go after it in an aggressive manner. The cool weather brings with it many opportunities, and the dealer should reap as richly as possible by going after business now strongly.

Value in Letting Clerk Take Charge.

It might be pointed out here that causing a head clerk to take charge for a time is frequently a good thing for the business. Having to shoulder the responsibility while the proprietor is absent, he not only be-

---

BRINGING BACK CUSTOMERS.

Perhaps it is a little brightening up that the store needs. Unless watched carefully the interior of the store will become shabby and more or less forbidding. No one likes to purchase goods at a mussy or dirty store. Keep everything clean. Keep it bright. Keep it arranged in an attractive way. The extra effort required doesn't amount to much, and the effect is almost incalculable. Customers will return again and again to a clean, well-kept and attractively arranged store, when they will never go back to one that presents the opposite appearance. The influence of this particular business is more far-reaching than seems possible, and for many years never had any attention devoted to it.

---

comes capable of taking more responsibility at regular times, but he quite often develops an interest in the business while the proprietor is away that continues after he returns, and thus makes him a much more valuable man.

The dealer in the country can at least arrange to take a day now and again. The writer knows of a furniture dealer who takes a day off regularly each week during the summer, when he hies away to a nearby lake and forgets business cares in the sport of fishing. That is the way he takes his holidays, and I don't think his business suffers in the least.

SELLING KITCHEN CABINETS.

A popular appeal of definite value is exerted by the co-operative retail sales plan of a well-known manufacturer of kitchen cabinets. Previous to the sale opening and during its progress, "twenty-four familiar grocery articles" were advertised free with each $18.50 kitchen cabinet. The cabinet itself, fully equipped with the two dozen articles of household supply, all of which were of nationally advertised brands, offered material for window displays of instant attraction. A list of the groceries offered, which included a ten-pound sack of flour, was published, and it was announced that no increase in price had been made to cover the cost of the generous premium. Cabinet and premium entered many homes long in need of better culinary equipment, at liberal terms of one dollar down and one dollar a week. Many women, unapproachable through the medium of stereotyped sales plan, are made live prospects by trade inducements of this nature.

KEEP THE CATALOGUE HANDY.

The furniture merchant who doesn't sell anything but what he has right in the store, is almost unknown.

Every dealer is willing to take orders for other goods than those in stock, and most merchants are looking for such orders.

Most dealers take special orders only when a customer comes in and asks for something not in stock. Under these conditions the dealer says: "We haven't got a dresser exactly like that, but we can easily get it for you." This is good, but not good enough.

Your catalogue file should be so handy, so well indexed and cross-indexed by name, subject and kind, that you can show your party a picture of the thing he wants, and get the order.

There should be no delay in finding the book and the illustration. You have it in front of your customer before he has time to say, "Well—I'll see."

A catalogue in a customer's hands acts as a display of goods might act in developing and making sales.

WEEK-END SALES.

"Week-end" has come to mean a holiday and time of relaxation in every part of the country. Week-ends are the play time of thousands, the time when men get a chance to associate with their families and to get better acquainted with their own sons and daughters. In hundreds of homes, Saturday afternoon is the time when "Father brings home something"; in hundreds of homes, Sunday is the time when this "something" is

---

CASH REGISTER USED AS ADDING MACHINE.

BEVERLY McDONALD, of Picton, Ont., finds his cash register, which is a total adding one, useful and valuable in many ways. He frequently uses it as an adding machine. The sums that it is required to add are punched on the register, which keeps track of the totals as it goes along. The register may be set for this purpose, so that it is not necessary for the cash drawer to go in and out each time an amount is punched.

The register, of course, has to be used for this purpose after the day's business is over, and the day's business, in so far as the cash register is concerned, has been totalled up. It is found of immense value in making up totals of cash or credit sales, amount received on account, etc., for any period, and especially because it can be depended on as to accuracy. It is extremely useful in making up totals in stocktaking, and in other additions of figures that are tedious, or where accuracy is demanded.

---

especially enjoyed by the younger members of the family. It pays to take advantage of a popular whim. Advertise a week-end sale and let the special merchandise be something that will fill a vacant place in the home. Furniture for the den, the play room and the sewing room finds a ready demand through this appeal. If you favor the premium plan, give a box of candy with each week-end sale. There is nothing that will more quickly gain you the support of the children.

Maintained Valuable Entrance in Enlarging Store

How Campbell & Campbell, of Brandon, Man., solved the problem of securing larger premises and yet maintaining old-established location — Some features of the new building.

BY A STAFF EDITOR

THE firm of Campbell & Campbell, furniture dealers, of Brandon, Man., were confronted with a difficult problem when they found it necessary, on account of the increase in business, to find larger premises than those occupied for many years on Rosser avenue, of that city. Naturally, when a firm has been located in the one place for a long period, their location becomes a valuable factor in the securing of business, and they are loath to give it up because of the possible loss in business that may be experienced as a result of the change.

Did Not Wish to Give Up Valuable Location.

This was the situation in which Campbell & Campbell found themselves, and it was for just this reason that they remained in smaller premises than their trade warranted for a considerable length of time. They recognized in their long establishment in the one location on Rosser avenue, a business advantage not to be given up on the spur of the moment. In addition, Rosser avenue, being the principal thoroughfare of the city, it would be giving up another valuable advantage to move to a less frequented street. And still there was no opportunity for to enlarge the cramped premises occupied. What was to be done?

How Problem Was Solved.

Eventually, the problem was solved by acquiring on another street property that butted on the premises already occupied. On this property they erected a new store, still maintaining their old stand on Rosser avenue, and connecting it up with the new building. Thus they were given an "L" shaped store, with a frontage on two streets. The outstanding feature was the fact that they were enabled to maintain their old-established entrance, and the value of this is demonstrated by the fact that the majority of customers enter the store by the Rosser avenue entrance, although the other entrance is the most spacious and the frontage on the other street the largest and best appearing. Nevertheless, the street on which the new building fronts is becoming a more frequented one, and is expected to become more so as time goes on.

New Building Spacious and Well Arranged.

The new building erected is large, spacious, and well arranged. It gives them five floors, including basement, each one measuring 51 by 120 ft. In addition, they have the Rosser avenue section, with a floor space of 75 by 25 ft. Altogether, they have space for carrying on a large business, and yet plenty of room for the proper display of goods.

The first floor is devoted to heavy case goods, dining room furniture, and linoleum and rugs. On the second floor are bedroom furniture, bedding, and associated lines. The third floor shows office furniture and living and drawing room furniture. The fourth floor is used for odd pieces and storage purposes. In the basement are the repair and workshop.

The first floor forms an attractive-looking show room. The walls are nicely finished, a metallic ceiling adds to the brightness, while the two rows of pillars, which extend down the centre, are fitted with mirrors that enhance the general appearance of the floor.

A section of the front of the main floor is divided off and used for undertaking parlors. There is a separate entrance to this department, which is nicely furnished. To the rear of this section quite a large space has been given over to linoleums, there being plenty of room for display as well as for the cutting of stock. To the rear are the offices in a raised position. There are windows at the rear which, with the spacious front, give plenty of light for the interior.

A Big Trade in Leather Chairs.

The Rosser avenue section, which is 25 ft. wide, is divided up into several rooms, each of which is devoted to a separate line. For instance, one is completely given over to picture framing and another to rugs.

Interior of Campbell & Campbell's store. Note the economical and tasty arrangement of stock.

A line that this store makes a feature of is leather chairs, in which they have been successful in working up a large trade. In making a bid for this business, they got out a special catalogue, showing samples of the different leather chairs carried in stock. This was distributed quite widely, and as a result orders are received from all over Canada, while one order came all the way across the ocean, from the Old Country. Doctors, lawyers, and other professional men prove good prospects for this class of chair, and their trade is especially appealed for.

Features of Store and Business.

The members of the firm have a private office at the rear of the store.

Catalogues are filed away, being properly indexed according to the name of the firm issuing the catalogue. If it is desired to look up information on any particular line of furniture, it is much easier when the catalogues are properly indexed.

The windows of the new section of the store are large, and allow excellent displays to be made.

Good use is made of bill boards throughout the country in all directions for advertising purposes.

To impress the passerby with the fact that linoleum

is sold, samples are stood on end at one side of the entrance.

Twenty Years in Business.

The members of the firm are A. F. Campbell and R. J. Campbell, and although their names are similar, they are no relation to one another. They have both been residents of Brandon for a long time—the latter for 32 years, and the former for 26 years. Twenty years ago they joined forces in the furniture business. Since then Brandon has made some remarkable progress, but Campbell & Campbell have also been experiencing their share of success. They now have a large and well arranged store, and a trade that is well in keeping with their premises.

DOLLAR DAY IN WEST.

Moose Jaw has had its first "Dollar Day" recently, and from all reports from the merchants participating in the event, it proved as great a success as it has been in the other cities where it already has been tried out. The Morning News introduced "Dollar Day" in Moose Jaw. During the first few weeks, G. H. Tyndall, the advertising manager of that newspaper, had been gathering data on the way "Dollar Day" has been handled in various eastern Canada and United States cities; and after conferring with several of the leading merchants in the city, announced, about ten days in advance, that Moose Jaw's first "Dollar Day" would be held on Thursday, July 30. Thursday was purposely selected as it is the dullest day of the whole week for most of the merchants, and the last week of July because it is ordinarily one of the dullest weeks of the whole year.

The papers gave the event plenty of advance publicity and for the windows of the stores the News furnished yellow paper pennants free of charge. It was a splendid sight on the morning of dollar day to see the transformation in the business section of the city. Practically every important store in the city was displaying the yellow pennants and the general aspect of the windows gave one the idea of a gala day.

Farmers in the surrounding country were well informed in advance of the event so that they, as well as the shoppers from the towns on the railroads nearby came into the city in large numbers to participate in the savings offered by the dollar day bargains. All the stores displaying dollar day signs report having done wonderful business. Many of them duplicated their record of such days as Christmas Eve shopping, and one prominent merchant, who has been doing business in the city for the past seven years, states that it was the best day he ever had.

BIG SALES THROUGH GOOD ADVERTISING.

It has remained for a Pacific coast dealer to prove the worth of advertising. This dealer made up his mind to move out $100,000 worth of stock, and this is the method he used. He issued a four-page sheet—each page the size of the page in a daily newspaper. The first page bore simply the words, in very large, bold type: "Quick Action. Everybody in Stockton will have Quick Action Now." The two inside pages were filled with illustrations of furniture which was offered, with the prices given. No attempt was made to give the figures at which the goods had been previously listed, and the prices at which the goods were offered; simply the price at which the goods were to be sold. But the introductory matter carried the information that the goods were to be sold at a sacrifice, which was the case. The method of the sale was further described on the fourth page of the sheet. This fourth page told this story: "We must get Quick Action on $100,000. 100 handsome articles of furniture to be given away absolutely free. We have hung pink tags on the door knobs throughout the city. They are duplicates of the Quick Action sale tags throughout the store ———. These tags are all numbered—bring yours in the opening morning (Thursday, 9 a.m.) of this Quick Action Sale, and if you find the duplicate of number on your tag on any article in this stock, you get that article absolutely free—no matter what it's priced at. If they missed your door knob, phone 3,600."

People began to gather an hour before the store opened on the morning of the commencement of the sale, and five minutes after the doors were opened the store was crowded. Among those who were waiting were women who have brought with them the numbered tags which they expected to be able to match up with the like number on some piece of furniture in the store. The dealer writes that the sale was a big success—this, too, in spite of the fact that his chief competitor opened a sale the day before his sale.

THE EVILS OF OVERBUYING

Why do many of the large business houses employ a man to buy goods exclusively? asks an exchange. First, it requires all of one man's time to keep up the stock; second, because they realize the importance of buying at the right price and of not buying too much of any one article.

If the man with a large capital realizes the importance of not overbuying, why shouldn't the man with a small capital do the same thing?

It is not my intention in this short talk to make you so conservative about buying that half the time you will not have in stock what your customers want, but it is my desire to impress you with the fact that to have in stock $150 to $200 worth of whips, and not have enough good team collars in stock to fit an ordinary team, is a flagrant case of the "Evil of Overbuying."

This is an extreme case, but there are such instances actually existing; and while the majority of us don't go to the extreme, we certainly do many times overbuying in one class of goods or another.

Overbuying not only accumulates a lot of stock that gets shop-worn and depreciates in value, but it ties up your cash and renders the discounting of your bills difficult, and many times makes it impossible.

You should strive to discount every bill of goods you buy. It is the easiest and cleanest profit in any business, and will surprise anybody who has never been in the habit of taking discounts to see what it will total up in the course of a year.

The other advantage of discounting your bills is, it gives you a financial rating that is almost worth the amount you actually save on discounting.

A 2-cent stamp will take an order to any house in the country, and nine times out of ten your trade is not so urgent but that you can better afford to wait ten or twelve days to get the goods than to have a lot of surplus stock getting shop-worn, and which will not be sightly or easily sold, even if customers were coming in thick and fast.

Consequently only buy a reasonable amount of stock—enough to fill the demands of your trade. Conserve your capital and endeavor to discount as many bills as you can—the more, the better, and you will be pleased with yourself and satisfied with your business.

The Art of Display

Suggestions for Window and Interior Arrangements.

GOOD window displays should not be confined to any one season of the year. They should be maintained all the year round. Some trimmers put forth a big effort to turn out an attractive and sales creating display on special occasions such as Easter and Christmas, and although they find that the extra effort is well worth while in increased business and publicity for the store, they allow their attention to their windows to dwindle to an unfortunate extent as soon as the special occasion is over. This should not be. Good window display should be maintained during every season and will be found profitable. A special window at ordinary times of the year, when many dealers are inclined to neglect their displays, will make your store stand out prominently—more prominently, in fact, than on special occasions when everyone is going in for something extra in this direction. The trimmer who gives any thought to this point will realize the value of frequently working up something special in window display at all seasons of the year.

WINDOWS SHOW CHARACTER OF STORE.
By Marsh K. Powers

In general, there are three main classes of people whom you cannot reach by live window displays—the invalid who is bedridden, the child too young to understand, and the people who never pass your store. The first two classes never buy furniture, and the third class for the most part is almost altogether out of your reach. All the rest can be, and are being, reached every day by live window displays.

Buys Not on Price Alone.

Live customers like live dealers. No one has confidence in a dead one—no one cares to do business with him, for the purchaser cannot put faith either in his advice or in his merchandise. Remember, too, that it is the live customer that means real money for you. He is the man who has money to spend, and he is the man who spends it when you go after him in the right way. His money is never glued to his pocket. He does not buy on price alone. Best of all, he is the man who is always on the lookout for new things to buy.

"On the lookout" means that when he sees an attractive, interesting window display, he stops to examine it. Nine chances out of ten, he does not come in and buy at once. Instead he thinks to himself, "That man is a live merchant—his stock is up-to-date—he knows his business."

I do not mean to say that he actually repeats these things to himself, but I do mean that he gains real confidence in your store, because through your windows you have proven yourself a live dealer. Then when the time arrives that he needs something in the hardware line, he comes to you to ask your advice, and he buys according to your recommendation because you have already gained his confidence. Your window displays have made him your customer.

Take an actual case out of the writer's own experience. Two miles from my home there is a retail store which has built an enviable reputation for the careful displays in its show windows. As it is in a neighborhood which I frequently visit, I long ago learned to watch for its new displays.

One of the most popular bed and bedding windows ever put in by a dealer is this one here illustrated. It has been seen in many of the U.S. cities, and recently attracted a good deal of attention when shown in Toronto. The wax figure is lifelike and, to give added effect, through the use of a small electric motor, is made to "breathe." The furniture and furnishings come, of course, from the dealer's stock.

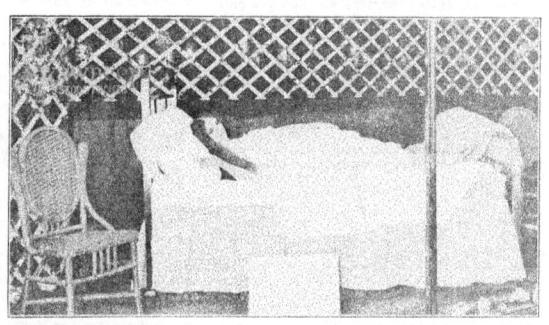

Frequently I go actually out of my way in order to pass this store, and have often advised other people to be sure to see special displays. Not only do I thus advertise this store for its owner, but two-thirds of my ordinary purchases are made at this inconvenient place, merely because no other store in my neighborhood has yet caught my eye.

No—I will withdraw that last phrase. There is another store three blocks from my home which I pass several times a week. Its window is always carelessly filled. Needless to add, I have never entered that store.

When a salesman comes into my office, I judge him first by his face. Is he clean? Is he shaved? Is he smiling or gloomy? Does he look trustworthy? Before I know who he is or what he sells, I have a definite impression of some sort about him.

Your show window is the "face" of your store—keep it clean and smiling. A dull, uninteresting face is never a good introduction either for a salesman or a store. As long as I have not entered your store, I can judge it only by what I see of its windows as I pass. If this fails to attract and interest me, only the force of urgent necessity will make me investigate further.

Compare the policies of the two stores that I have mentioned. One is the natural, handy, and convenient place for me to trade, yet I have never stepped inside its door or even paused to study its windows. It has lost my trade to a store over two miles away. How many more possible customers is it losing each day by this policy of "It's-too-much-trouble-to-fix-up the windows, and-it-doesn't-pay-anyway"?

On the other hand, the store that does use its windows to attract trade, succeeds in securing customers from neighborhoods two miles away. If it does that, you can be sure that it does not feel much competition in its immediate neighborhood.

Your Windows the Introduction.

In closing, notice one thing: I have not even mentioned that window displays sell the goods on display. That is an additional feature that often makes them return big profits on a small investment. Wholly outside of this valuable feature, however, is the undeniable fact that live customers like live dealers—and the easiest way for myself and my friends to judge a store from the outside is by its windows.

Until we actually enter your store, we know you only through your window displays. Is yours a favorable introduction?

WINDOW DISPLAYS AND ADVERTISEMENTS.

To attend to the requirements of the display window, the trimmer sprang up to conceive the arrangement and execute the designs that look out upon the sidewalks night and day. His art is to draw the buyer and to make profit to the merchantman. Windows were used long before there were newspapers or newspaper advertising, and they are to-day the strong forte of the small dealer to whom newspaper advertising rates are prohibitive. Even to the large retail dealers the show window is the more necessary if either had to be dispensed with. The window is indispensable to the live merchant. He may cut down the selling force and curtail expenses, but the window must go on and the trimmer who is onto his job will receive as much as ever. Marshall Field's establishment spent last year on window display more than $80,000. The store window is an ever-changing panorama of beauty and style, the wedge that opens all purses.

The advertisement in the paper tells what we have to sell and brings people to the store. The window displays the goods. One seeks confidence of the buyer, the other compels it. The one speaks of fashions, the other produces them. The windows are used in general advertising, as are the newspapers, such as featuring events, as fairs and corn shows. Even National events may be profitably used in featuring the window arrangements. No other medium of advertising is quite so good as the window, properly done.

The merchant to-day is advertising-mad. He nibbles at every scheme. He is what is called "easy money," and throws away many a dollar that never comes back. To the young man starting in business with a small amount for advertising, after his store and stock are ready, the window is to be the first consideration, for it speaks by day and works overtime by night, and is never silent.

CHALK TALK WINDOWS.

A Buffalo retailer attracts considerable attention by his unique windows. He has a local cartoonist work out a cartoon in chalk or whiting, right on the glass, changing the subject each week. Sometimes these subjects are devoted to certain goods. At other times they are of historic interest or appropriate to coming holidays. If you can make a suitable arrangement with a cartoonist or good sign painter you might find this a good suggestion to follow.

GIVE PRAISE WHERE PRAISE IS DUE

"If window trimmers in many stores received more encouragement from the merchant in their work," remarked a Calgary dealer recently, "they would put forth more effort in this direction. Some merchants withhold praise even for an exceptional good trim, fearing that the clerk may form an exalted opinion of his work. I know from experience that when a trimmer receives some recognition of his good work, he puts more brain work into the details next time in an effort to turn out an even better display. If he finds that the boss pays no attention to it, whether it be good or bad, he naturally begins to lose interest in his work also.

"Window display is a valuable selling agent, and every druggist should encourage his window trimmer to make it sell as much goods as possible."

SHOW WINDOW BACKGROUNDS

The American Architect has printed the following as to the amount of light given by different colored show window backgrounds:

Dark blue reflects 6½ per cent. of the light falling upon it.
Dark green, about 10 per cent.
Pale red, a little more than 6 per cent.
Dark yellow, 20 per cent.
Pale blue, 30 per cent.
Pale yellow, 40 per cent.
Pale green, 46½ per cent.
Pale orange, nearly 55 per cent.
And pale white, 70 per cent.

A window finished in light oak can be lighted with much less wastage than a window finished in dark mahogany; likewise, a window in which white goods are displayed can be lighted much more economically than a window for a display of dark clothing, furniture or hardware, such as stoves, tools and goods of a like nature.

SEND THEM ALONG

Whenever you have a good display, have a photograph taken and send it along to us for reproduction. We will appreciate it and so will your brother dealers and clerks all over Canada. This is one way in which you can contribute to the general welfare of the business in which you are interested. When you put in your next good window display keep us in mind.

Selling Beds and Bedding Through Advertising
By A. B. LEVER

Just as in time of peace nations prepare for war, so business men before one season has expired are of necessity compelled to prepare for that which follows.

Housekeepers may not at the moment be much concerned about beds and bedding for the fall and winter, but it will not be a great while before they will be giving some thought to the matter. People may be sweltering just now, but in another two or three months they will probably be shivering. Then they will be thinking seriously of their bed and bedding necessities.

The furniture dealer is, of course, quite aware of this fact. But he does not wait until the "shivering days" have arrived before reminding the public of their necessities. He undertakes that task long before the advent of cool weather. To catch the eye of the passer-by he carefully dresses his window and, in order to reach a still wider field he uses advertising space in his local newspapers.

The advertisements which I have selected for reproduction in this issue of the Furniture World are such that have been used by retailers in different parts of the Dominion. They are of various types and every retailer should be able to glean something from them which will assist him in the preparation of his own advertising copy.

The advertisement of Wilders, Limited, Montreal, is a striking one, and in a few words explains the convenience of sofa beds. I think, however, that the ad. would have been strengthened had the line "Davenport Sofa Beds" been given first place. The purpose of the ad. was to advertise sofa beds, not that "Wilder's will furnish the home on credit." If used at all the latter phrase should have been given a subordinate position. The heading of an advertisement, like the heading of an article, should give an indication of its contents. The original was 6¼ by 7.

An advertisement which tends to excite desire is influential. This is the outstanding characteristic of the advertisement of the Hastings Furniture Co., Vancouver. "Draw it (the eiderdown quilt) up close and snug and sleep warm and tight," certainly appeals to the average man or woman. And on top of this the ad. goes on to point out the merits of the particular kind of quilt which is being offered to the public. Typographically the ad. is also commendable. The original was 4½ by 6⅞ inches.

Although less than 2 inches deep by 4½ wide, the advertisement of the Lord Furniture Co., Ottawa, is a good example of how small space can be used to advantage. It stands out well and no words have been wasted in describing the bed advertised.

The narrow mattress ad. is from the announcement of a department store. It is "newsy" and may well serve as the basis of a similar advertisement. It was 2 inches wide by 6 inches deep.

Freiman's is, of course, the outstanding ad. in the group. The original was 11 by 16½ inches, and this naturally afforded ample space for making such an an-

How some Canadian furniture dealers sell their bed and bedding lines through advertising.

nouncement. Not only is the advertisement well written, but it is arranged with artistic skill. As a selling force there can scarcely be any question as to its potency. Taking it all round, it is one of the best ads. of the kind I have seen for some time.

Lemont & Sons, Fredericton, usually turn out good ads., and the one reproduced in the group is no exception to the rule. It is striking in appearance and in pointed and terse language points out the merits of the couch bed advertised. But would it not have been strengthened had some reference to prices been made? In my opinion it would. The original was 4½ by 6½ inches.

The advertisement of Wright's, Sydney, is a good bargain announcement. It is strong in both arrangement and manner of display and other dealers will find it a good basis to work upon in the construction of their announcements. Original was 4½ by 6.

By reminding customers that they spend one-third of their time in bed, and that the bed and mattress they advertised were conducive to comfort, the Thompson Co., Belleville, made a strong point. The ad. was unfortunately rather overcrowded, but even had the line above the firm's name been left out a little more white space would have been obtained. Another defect, and one for which the publishers are wholly to blame, was the defective border. Such worn out rules as those used in this instance detract from the appearance of the ad. and advertisers should insist on better service in this respect. The original was 4½ by 3.

PERSONALITY OF ADVERTISING.
By M. J. Reid

Advertising is like folks.

Some advertising you "warm up" to the minute your eyes light upon it.

There are no harsh color tones to offend—no shouting statements— no commands that you mentally refuse to obey.

It just "makes friends" with you right away.

You feel a sense akin to gratitude that someone has taken all this trouble, time and labor, to present this article to your notice with such nicety, such courtesy, with so much regard for your feelings, making its purchase so convenient, saving you endless worry and search.

Of course, you don't actually think this all out. You just feel it without really thinking about it at all. Your mind is centred upon the good points of the article presented, and the benefit you will derive from owning it.

This must be the advertisement of a considerate, enterprising merchant, or manufacturer, who has a thought and care for his customers beyond sordid money-making; who knows that his product is right, and that its purchase means a good and an advantage to mankind.

You do not want to look long at an advertisement which seems to have an x-ray eye glued to your pocketbook, as if to search out the very last farthing. You, being a natural creature, and obeying a natural law, are considering your own comforts and needs, and resent the mercenary glint in an advertisement as much as you do in the merchant's eye.

The courteous ad., ever mindful of the other fellow's feelings, is constantly endeavoring to benefit. It is not in a hurry; it carries dignity, certainty, and delivers its message in a pleasant manner—conveying the confidence of its master, the man who created it and who also produced the article which it is offering you.

Your advertisement is a reflection of yourself—of your business; you are judged by it.

There is no need for megaphone copy with harsh, strident tones for the man who knows he is right all through.

True it is that with the multi-millions of articles placed upon the market by different advertising methods, there must be something distinctive about your copy to attract notice. But let that something be inviting, harmonious, and welcome to the senses.

There, also, are millions of people. During a week you may meet thousands—each produces an impression of some sort. The one from whom you get the lasting, pleasing impression, and of whom you think many times afterwards, is the cheerful, confident, successful man who knows that he knows and is big enough to be kind.

He needn't din it into your ear that he is a gentleman. You can't just say how you know it, yet you know. There is that indefinable something. Here is a man worth while. No extremes in appearance announce this fact. He does not wear a bright red vest, a grotesque hat—yet you are attracted, and you know the man is right; he is a leader, he is worthy.

Your advertisement may possess a personality just as effective. It may carry the same success, leadership note; the same impressiveness, the same conviction of honest, earnest, simple truth which makes you know—just how you can't say—that the article presented is worthy.

A DEFINITION OF ADVERTISING.

In an address on advertising E. D. Gibbs, President of the Sphinx Club, New York, recalled to his hearers that some years ago a certain magazine offered a prize for the best definition of advertising, and that the award was made to the contestant who sent in the best definition, "Advertising is the voice of supply and the ear of demand."

"Without discussing the merits of this definition of advertising," said Mr. Gibbs, "I would suggest something broader, and would say that advertising is 'Causing another to know,' and still further, 'Causing another to remember,' and after that 'Causing another to do.'"

"Summing up, my definition of advertising is 'Causing another to know, to remember, and to do.'"

REAL ADVERTISING

Random advertising, like random shooting in the woods, fails to bring down the game. Advertising—the real kind—is a continuous campaign closely related to salesmanship, and no business house would hire salesmen just for a day or a week.

Advertising is a steady drive for business. How to do it most intelligently is an important subject of consideration in every successful business.

Suggestions of great value often come from most unexpected sources. The man who prepares copy must ever be on the lookout for new ideas or his efforts will be commonplace or obsolete. The clever salesman is constantly looking for good points about his goods or new and attractive ways of presenting them, while the advertiser, who prepares the "salesmanship on paper," must do likewise.

Beds and Bedding

DEVELOPMENT OF THE SLIDING COUCH
By V. C. Lowell
Assistant Manager, Ideal Bedding Co., Ltd., Toronto.

The sliding couch was probably first developed in the United States, more especially in eastern centres of dense population, and its success there as filling a real need in house furnishings was probably largely due to the small houses with few rooms, a condition that became necessary in a modern eastern city.

Regular beds required special bedrooms, and in addition occupied during the day time more space than any other piece of furniture, and, where room was limited, this was a disadvantage. Naturally, attention was given towards some improvement of the situation, and as a result a number of folding beds were brought out, built to close and give the appearance of a wardrobe or other piece of furniture, in this way turning the bedroom into a sitting room or living room for the daytime.

These articles were both costly and in the end unsatisfactory, because they were cumbersome and unhealthy. For a time it would appear that the enamelled iron beds and brass beds would relieve the situation, but the demand was increasing for some article compact, sanitary, convenient, and low-priced. The result was the introduction of a steel frame cot, and a little later a double-frame sliding couch supplied with a hinge mattress and covered in various tapestries and velours, the whole made to give the appearance of a comfortable couch during the daytime and capable of being opened out to form a double bed at night.

For families of small means renting houses of from three to five rooms this article met an immediate demand, as an article of convenience, being sanitary, likely in appearance, durable and at a comparatively low price. Several designs were developed with added features, such as a foot arrangement for opening the couches, special attachment for throwing the mattress back, and storage boxes for pillows and extra clothing.

As the apartment house idea developed, both in the United States and Canada, the demand grew for a better article, and as a result the heavy wood davenport with arrangement for converting into a bed, has been developed. An interesting feature in this connection is our own experience in Montreal, where, while the demand for a sliding couch already existed, no one had seen the need until in 1907 we placed a number of accepted designs on the market. The demand was instantaneous, and Montreal became the centre for a big output of this class of article from our factory.

During the summer months of the last few years there has been an increasing demand for this item from campers and cottagers at summer resorts, etc. It is a convenience built to meet the present requirements of people forced to live in small houses. It by no means can be said to replace a real bed, spring and mattress, and perhaps for the best interest of all people it would be better could they live under conditions that would discourage the folding couch rather than encourage it. There is no doubt people are the worse for sleeping at night and living during the day in the same rooms, and a large bedroom, with a really comfortable bed, is conducive to the best interests of all people, both mental and physical.

ALASKA BEDDING CONVENTION.

The sales force of the Alaska Bedding Co., Ltd., had a very interesting and instructive convention at the head office of the company at Winnipeg on July 29, 30, and 31, A. W. Johnson, better known as "Budd" Johnson, the sales manager, who conducted the various meetings, not only made the visit a most beneficial one in a business way, but a most enjoyable one for the boys socially. The visitors were: E. J. Brownlee, C. W. Crawford, G. W. Acton, R. B. McClennon, E. C. Bromley, and A. E. Pearson.

Many new and distinctive features were discussed, and added to their already extensive range of bedding knowledge, and the boys are so enthused and refilled with Alaska "ginger" that they departed for their various territories on the first, fully convinced that this fall's business would be a record-breaker, and that they have "the goods" to bring about this result. There is a great deal of pleasant rivalry between the boys on an Ostermoor competition, which was launched. The salesman who sells the greatest number of this mattress by December 15 is to be given a free trip to New York at Christmas. Each and every one of the boys is out to win, and is looking forward to the loyal support of his good customers.

J. H. Parkhill, president, and F. J. Baker, manager, addressed the convention, and expressed satisfaction

This is how Logan's furniture store, St. Catharines, featured their bedding line in the recent Dominion Day celebration in that city. The little colored boy in the bed attracted a deal of attention to the float.

at the latent possibilities which were exhibited by the salesmen in connection with their business, and A. W. Johnson has arranged to have these conventions held at stated intervals, as it has been demonstrated this time that it is certainly very advantageous, not only to the firm and salesmen, but to the public as a whole.

MAPLE LEAF COMPANY INCORPORATED.

Letters patent have been issued by the secretary of the Province of Ontario, to Jerome Colwell Dietrich, Roy Charles Torrance, Edward Mullins Worth, and Charles Frederick Mielke, all of Galt, and James Wm. Dore, of Hamilton, a corporation to carry on the trade of manufacturing all kinds of beds, bedding, springs, hammocks and hammock frames, mattresses, and also all kinds of hospital equipment. The corporate name of the company is to be The Maple Leaf Bedding Company, Ltd.; the capital to be $40,000; the head office to be at Galt, and the provisional directors of the company to be J. C. Dietrich, Roy C. Torrance, J. W. Dore, E. M. Worth, and C. F. Mielke.

NEW IDEAL BED GOODS.

"Ideal Beds" is the title of the Ideal Bedding Co.'s supplement to their catalogue "A," just published. Since the complete catalogue was issued, the Ideal Company have produced 30 new designs in brass beds, five new steel beds, ten new model chilless beds, the "Neverspread" mattress, Ideal foldaway cot, two duplex springs, a woven wire and a Simmons link fabric, Perth spring, new No. 88 coil spring, a double-deck bunk, two hat racks, and a new design in the Ideal hammo-couch. All of these new goods are illustrated in this supplement; in fact, describing these new items is the object of getting out the supplementary catalogue. It is of such size that it can readily be slipped inside the regular catalogue without danger of splitting the binding.

The same care and attention to detail is noticeable in the printing and coloring of the supplement as in the big book itself, and a net price list is a good index for both books.

THE FISCHMAN MATTRESS.

The Fischman Mattress Co., Ltd., have just issued a catalogue for the trade, explaining the construction of the Fischman patent spring mattress, and exemplifying its merits. It has taken years of careful consideration and study to perfect the mattress and bring it to its present state of efficiency, the machines used in making the mattress being invented specially for the purpose by Mr. Fischman.

First, there is the automatic pocket sewing machine—a labor-saving device which automatically sews and divides the pockets ready to receive the steel coil springs—requiring no attention from an operator. Next, there is the Fischman spring machine. By a special contrivance this machine manufactures the springs in such manner as to have no sharp points, and automatically, by the use of a patented plunger, also invented by Mr. Fischman, to insert the springs in individual pockets.

Specially tempered steel wire, which ensures resiliency, is used in the springs, and each individual coil is surrounded by felt to ensure independent action of each spring. The mattress is tufted through the felt and to top and bottom of each spring. This helps to make the action of the spring respond readily to any pressure placed on it. In shipping the Fischman mattress is rolled. This is done without injury to the construction. Every mattress is numbered and dated from time of delivery, and is guaranteed for five years.

METAL BEDS IN SIAM.

Metal beds are not manufactured in Siam, but are imported ready-made, complete. Statistics of imports are not available. However, from information furnished by the leading importers of this class of goods it appears that there is a steady demand for the cheaper grades of metal beds.

English-made metal beds, 3½ feet wide, 6½ feet long, with extended pillars for holding mosquito nets, japanned black, and brass tops, retail in the local bazaars at $7. This style seems to be the most popular with the Siamese.

One of the leading European retail firms of Bangkok advertises metal beds as follows: Four-post metal beds, 1¼ in. pillars, 6½ ft., extended foot rail, brass tops, japanned black, 3½ ft. wide, $17.02; 4 ft. wide, $17.76; 4½ ft. wide, $18.50; 5 ft. wide, $19.24; 5½ ft. wide, $20.35. All-brass, four-post beds, 1½ in. pillars, 6½ ft. long, 5 ft. wide, $43; 5½ ft. wide, $44.

The import duty on all kinds of metal beds is 3 per cent. ad valorem, including freight, packing, and all other charges.

BEDDING NOTES

The Ideal Bedding Co. will exhibit this year at the exhibitions to be held in London, Ottawa, and Toronto.

E. Baker, late of Buffalo, has become superintendent of the Stratford Bed Company's plant at Stratford, Ontario.

A. A. Leipold, late superintendent of the Pullman Davenport Bed Co., Chicago, and E. W. Foisburg, late office manager of the same company, are the men behind the Stratford Davenport Bed Co.

The five "Alaska" Canadian bedding factories give a floor space of 376,500 square feet, and they manufacture annually 270,000 steel beds, 30,000 brass beds; 515,000 mattresses, 370,000 springs, 100,000 couches, and 180,000 pairs pillows.

Cope & Son, Ltd., Vancouver, makers of brass beds, have moved into their new warehouse and factory building. The business was started fourteen years ago. The new building is a seven-storey concrete structure, which gives 40,000 square feet of floor space.

The Reliable Bed Outfit Company, of Edmonton, recently organized by Adolph Nachman, of New York, and N. Jerlaw, of Chicago, reports that its business during the first 30 days was much larger than expected. The company specializes in beds, davenports, and couches and bedding. It is the only concern of its kind in Alberta.

"I'm glad the world is full of sunshine," said the fat man.

"You are an optimist," remarked the thin man.

"No," replied the fat man, "I am an awning salesman."

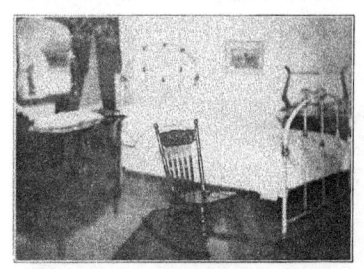

The bedroom in the window.—How C. J. Learight, Norwood, Ont., featured his bedroom furniture and furnishings. The display for a small town was splendidly arranged. It had a natural set-off and was well thought out, pincushion, comb and brush on the dresser showed that the smallest detail was not neglected.

STOVES AND HOUSE FURNISHINGS

GOING AFTER THE STOVE BUSINESS.

Did you ever stop to consider the reason why, of two dealers selling practically the same line of stoves, one will be successful while the other is a failure? Did it ever occur to you that there must be some strong reason for this difference in results? On one hand, we see a dealer dragging along and making only a bare living, while a few blocks down the street another one with the same sort of competition and with practically the same line of goods to sell is doing a good business and making satisfactory profits.

When we analyze the situation, we find that the reason for the discrepancy is due, in most instances, to the men themselves. In selling stoves, no matter how high-grade the line carried, nor how well-known the manufacturer of these stoves is, if the merchant selling them does not do his part, the results will not be satisfactory.

Better Results From One Line.

There is no question but that in selling stoves to-day it pays to handle and sell one high-grade line only. Enough dealers have been successful by sticking to one line only to prove the truth of this assertion. No dealer can sell two lines of stoves profitably any more than he can serve two masters. Many merchants, even to-day, are making the mistake of trying to push several lines of stoves, leaving it to the customer as to just what stove he will select. That is the reason that so many times dealers lose customers after they have practically clinched sales. The stove buyer goes into the store with the idea of purchasing a stove. The clerk gets an idea of the kind of stove he is interested in, takes him over to the display floor, and shows him the stove he believes he will like best. He explains its merits and tells the customer it is the best stove he can buy for the money, and that there is no doubt it will prove satisfactory in his home.

The customer agrees, and is about to place his order when, in looking about the store, his eye rests on another stove of a different make, but with practically the same trimmings and pattern. What is the result? He walks over to this stove and sees something which impresses him more favorably than the one just examined. What is the clerk to do? He cannot back up on his former arguments and say the latter stove will serve the purpose best. He must leave it to the judgment of the customer. The customer is undecided and leaves the store, saying he will perhaps call later. Nine times out of ten such a customer is lost to this store because his confidence is shaken in the merchant who tries to use the same arguments on two different lines of stoves.

Take the instance of the dealer selling one stove line only. This merchant knows his stove line from top to bottom. He shows the customer the kind of stove he is interested in, and makes his talk on this particular line. There is no opportunity for the customer to hesitate between this and some other make of stove, for the reason that the dealer sells no other. The result is, if he is a good salesman, the sale is closed then and there. There is no argument on this point; dealer after dealer has found out that the handicap which comes from trying to sell several different makes of stoves is not overcome by the few extra sales made.

Cheap Stoves Proved Costly.

A dealer told the writer the other day that he had built up an excellent business by selling a high-grade line of stoves, advertising them and securing a reputation for selling high quality stoves only. He was doing business in a locality where a certain number of foreigners resided. He had had some calls for cheap stoves, and, acting on the assumption that he could sell

A splendidly arranged stock of kitchen and household utensils.

anything, he decided to place a stock of cheap stoves on his floor. After a few months the result was costly. To use the dealer's own words, "I almost killed my stove business. The cheap stoves did not give satisfaction, and in order to protect my reputation, I had to make good on the sales. The result was that I not only lost profits on the stoves, but a great many of these purchasers were dissatisfied and took the balance of their trade elsewhere. It will take me years to overcome the mistake I made of trying to sell cheaply-made stoves." This merchant found that price is forgotten soon after the article is purchased, but the quality remains and makes its presence felt for years to come.

In selling stoves nowadays, mail order house and range peddler competition make it necessary to use aggressive methods. A dealer cannot expect to display a line of stoves on his floor, advertise once or twice during the season in his local papers, and then sit back and wait for buyers to come in. He must not only get out after stove business, but he must also keep in touch with the local situation and find out from time to time who, of the people in his locality, are in the market for stoves.

One dealer in a medium-sized town makes a point of watching all the marriage announcements. He then calls in person upon the bride and groom, presents his card, and states that he will be glad to talk with them further regarding their stove purchase at their convenience. This dealer also sends their names to the stove manufacturers whose line he sells, and they in turn write personal letters congratulating them upon their marriage and asking them to step into the store of the dealer, whose name is mentioned in the letter, for the purpose of picking out just the stove needed in the new home.

Some years ago it was not considered essential for a dealer to make any special display in the stove department. A great many dealers did not even go to the trouble of having a special stove department. They figured that the person interested in purchasing a stove would be willing to wait until they had pulled off the piles of rope and other junk that covered the stoves so that the purchaser could examine the line.

To-day the live merchant realizes that just in proportion to the time he gives to the stove department, just so will his sales increase. He has found it is good business to have his stoves well blackened, the nickel polished, and provision made for a separate department where the stoves can be shown. He uses attractive cards to call attention to special features of the line he is selling, the salesmen on the floor have been posted on the merits of the stoves, and when a stove buyer comes in salesmen can talk intelligently.

IDEAS THAT HAVE SOLD STOVES.

One of our dealers told us that he gets a list, every four or five days of the marriage licenses and then follows these up. This enables him to sell many a range and an outfit of kitchen utensils and the hundred and one other things needed to start housekeeping. It further means that if your service and goods please the man and his wife that you have secured another permanent customer.

This is a plan well worth following up.

GAVE RANGE AS ADVERTISEMENT.

A year ago a dealer in the United States secured the agency for a well-known line of ranges that had been sold in that city for a number of years by another concern.

In order to acquaint the public fully with the fact that they had secured this agency, the proprietors advertised that they would give a $65 range of the make advertised free to the person who could show she had been using one of these ranges for the greatest length of time. These advertisements were made part of the regular advertising of the firm, and a comparatively small amount of money expended. Answers were received from 1,164 persons giving the length of time they had used this range, the oldest being 41 years.

A selected number of letters, highly commendatory in their nature, were saved and pasted in a scrap book which this firm keeps convenient to the display of ranges. Prospects are invited to look through this book and secure the expressions of citizens of Memphis as to this make of goods, and these testimonials assist in closing many sales.

CANVASSING FOR STOVE SALES.

Have you ever given any thought to this method of securing business in your district? If not, is it not worth while considering?

When one considers to what extent this is being done in all lines of business, and, further, when we see the efforts being made by mail order houses, who make such attractive appeals through their catalogues, it is worth while considering whether more aggressive methods, on the part of the local dealer, are not necessary in order to offset this.

Personally, we believe that a great deal of business can be secured and many more sales made by more aggressive methods and by bringing to the attention of the customers the advantages you have to offer. Many who have been thinking of buying a new stove, but have put it off (buying something else instead), can be made immediate buyers. Consider how many times you yourself have purchased goods solely because you were canvassed by an energetic salesman.

Again, many ranges are sold by peddlers at very high prices, and the goods, as a rule, are quite inferior; but from the fact that peddlers can sell inferior stoves at their high prices is very conclusive evidence that there are a lot of people ready to buy through personal solicitation.

STOVE SELLING POINTERS.

A little stove polish and elbow grease applied to stoves on display will not come amiss.

Different points appeal to different purchasers of stoves. Women like a stove that has a good appearance and is yet not hard to keep clean. Too much nickel work is an objection for that reason. A stove from which the ashes can be easily taken also appeals to a woman, as she dislikes the dust accompanying this operation. Naturally, a woman also likes a cook or range that is a good baker, that has a large oven, warming closet, and other useful appliances. With a man economy in fuel is a strong consideration. He also will take the lighter stove on account of ease in handling, if he is assured that it is as good as the heavier one. A heating stove that is easily supplied with fuel is also a favorite with the men. These points should be borne in mind when showing a prospective customer a stove.

Are you keeping up to your schedule? The dealer who wishes to do a certain amount of business during 1914 must secure a certain percentage of the total each month. He has a certain schedule which he must keep pace with in order to achieve his desire. Look up the timetable that you mapped out at the beginning of the year, and see if your business train is on time. Like the engineer on a long run, keep timing yourself as you go along.

These photos show tasty arrangements of gas stove and refrigerator lines in a large shopping centre. They suggest valuable hints to less ambitious dealers worth their while adopting.

SALESPEOPLE

The Lazy Bug a Highly-Paid Worker

Banish It from your Store

ONE of the highest paid workers in many stores is the lazy bug. It does not receive direct wages, but if the merchant could get down to its exact cost to him, the figures in some cases would startle him.

The lazy bug, despite its name, is a hard worker. The trouble is, though, that when it works on a man, the clerk won't work. When the lazy bug has a good job in a store, the clerk is liable to lose his job, or if it happens to be the merchant himself who is affected, the right principles of merchandising are strangers there.

How You Can Tell the Bug is Present.

Good housekeeping and the lazy bug won't mix. In a store dominated by the lazy bug you don't see price tickets; you look in vain for proper display; you are offended by the makeshifts for window trims; you see a poorly balanced stock; you see merchandise old enough to have whiskers; you see plain dirt; you see on every hand evidence of things not done.

If you are lazy yourself—well, come on, wake up! Work some. It will make you feel like a real man. Get some dirt on your hands. It will look better there than on the merchandise. While you are on the job, be there. When you're through, be through.

Big Reward for Faithful Work.

There is hope for the lazy man, too, if he is O.K. in other ways. A man is not necessarily lazy because he doesn't like work. A lazy man is one who won't work. Therefore, if you determine to work and really do work, you are not lazy, no matter whether you like work or not. Before you know it, work and you will be good friends. You'll see the good returns. You'll be healthier, happier and more prosperous.

Old Man Work is a mighty square fellow. There's absolutely no limit to the reward he gives when you do the fair thing by him. It's up to you. You get all you earn. And he always is ready and able to pay, whether it's a nickel or ten million dollars.

Get Interested in Your Work

Speaking of work, isn't it a tragedy to see a fellow, merely to get a living, drilling away at some job he despises with all his heart?

When a man isn't interested in his work, when he can not get up real enthusiasm, when he does not take pride in the things he creates—then work to him is bondage. He may as well be in jail or trying to make bricks without straw.

But when he finds real joy in the things he does, when he loves his work—well, he can give the best of them lessons in how to be happy though working.

Everybody Has to Work

Everybody has to work. Killing time is working. Even the princes know that. I used to think I'd like a job as prince. Being a royal pie-eater was to my untutored mind the very acme of earthly felicity. But I've seen so many lazy people since then that my mind is changed. Now my ideal, my hero, is the man who has an all-consuming love for his work. My feeling to him is the same whether he is the biggest business man in America or the lowest clerk in a small store.

THE ART OF DEMONSTRATING

The clerk who can demonstrate as well as talk the merits of an article is the valuable man. This is not merely another way of saying he must know the stock to sell it. It is one thing to know—and quite another to impart. Many a salesman whose mind is a logical inventory of the goods on the shelves behind him, fails in the crucial test of demonstrating those goods to a customer. He may be a good talker—and a poor explainer. The knack of resultful demonstrating is an art in itself. It demands not only understanding of the product, but a quick eye and instinct for the method which best suits the mind of the individual buyer. With a captious customer it may be a matter of self-defense—like the trained judgment of the pitcher who learns to put the ball in the only place where the batter can't possibly hit it. With the average reasonable buyer, however, it is merely a matter of fitting the goods to the man—salesmanship in the concrete and raised to the ninth power. The article, well demonstrated, is more than half sold—and often resold as well.

Not the Thing for Him.

Furniture Dealer—Here's a folding article you might like, sir; a comfortable settee in the daytime and a bed at night.

Customer—No use to me; I do night work. Show me something that I can use as a settee at night and a bed in the daytime.

SALESMANSHIP PHILOSOPHY.

By A. F. Sheldon

Business philosophy is the science of effect by its causes.

Salesmanship is the power to persuade people to buy your product at a profit.

A house is known by the customers it keeps.

Quality, quantity and mode make for satisfaction.

Take care of cause and effect will take care of itself.

Millions of men are eating their graves with their teeth, and millions of men are breathing backward.

There are three essentials necessary before beginning a sale—thinking, remembering, imagining.

Thinking is a science to-day and can be taught as easily as mathematics.

The best ability is reli-ability.

Ethics in business pays and pays mightily.

The cheapest man on the pay-roll is ofttimes the most expensive in the organization; and the highest-salaried is not infrequently the cheapest in the end.

Bring life into harmony with God's law of efficiency.

Do not get into a rut. The difference between a rut and a grave is one is wider and deeper than the other.

Knobs of News

The Home Furniture Co., Montreal, has been registered.

Brisebois & Amyot Furniture Co., manufacturers, Montreal, have been incorporated.

Shulman Harris' furniture and mattress store at Toronto was damaged by fire recently.

Jacobean hall seat and mirror made by The Geo. McLagan Furniture Co., Ltd.

Disney Bros., furniture dealers and undertakers, Oshawa, Ont., have dissolved, the business being sold to L. V. Disney.

Nordquist Bros. & Anderson, furniture and hardware dealers at Halbrite, Sask., have opened a branch store at Talmage, Sask.

The Bell factory of the Canada Furniture Company, at Wingham, Ont., is at present undergoing repairs, parts which were decaying being replaced in cement.

D. A. Smith, president of the D. A. Smith Furniture Co., Vancouver, is interested, along with others, in establishing the B.C. Steel Works, on Lulu Island, B.C.

The Colonial Furniture Factory, Strathroy, Ont., which shut down for a couple of weeks, while a water system was being installed, has commenced operations again.

Furniture stores are wanted in the Canadian West in Saskatchewan at Allan, Cudworth, Grandora, Leney, Meacham, Talmage, Wakaw, Young; in Alberta at Holden, Wabamun, and in British Columbia at New Hazelton, Smithers.

Furniture factories are wanted in Ontario at Fort William; in Saskatchewan at Darmody, Forgray, Linstrom, Melville, Regina, Rowletta, Stoney Beach; in Alberta at Edmonton, Tofield; in British Columbia at Port Edward, Prince Rupert.

Brisebois & Amyot, furniture dealers, Montreal, have formed their firm into a limited liability company under the name of the Brisebois & Amyot Furniture Co., Ltd.

The Montreal Mattress Mfg. Co. has been registered at Montreal.

J. O. Mitchell, of St. Mary's, has sold his furniture business to L. A. Ball, formerly of Aylmer, who comes with ripe experience in the furniture business and will, no doubt, try to outdo even his predecessor, if possible, in meeting the demands of the people in St. Mary's and its surrounding country. Merchants throughout the country towns are waking up to the fact that higher efficiency in trade management is the keynote, and that trade methods must meet the rapid advancement of the times.

IMPROVEMENTS AT ALBROUGH PLANT.

Owing to the increasing demand for Albrough furniture, J. P. Albrough & Co., Ingersoll, Ont., have found their present upholstery room too small, and have moved it to the east wing of the factory. The old upholstery room will be converted into a showroom, where samples of the full line will be on display at all times.

FURNITURE FIRE AT WINNIPEG.

During an electrical storm in Winnipeg recently the electric wires in the building occupied by the Knechtel Furniture Co., Ltd., were struck by lightning and a blaze started on the second floor of the building. A number of roller-top desks covered by heavy paper were ignited. The flames gradually spread until the greater part of the furniture on the floor was ablaze. The goods were of the more expensive class, being of mahogany and oak veneer, and where the flames did not actually reach the goods, the excessive heat effected considerable damage. A quantity of furniture on the first floor was also damaged by water, but this was of the less expensive kind. The total loss was estimated

Some of the furniture travelers who recently journeyed to Hamilton to play ball, and were defeated by retailers of the Ambitious City. Dunke, Pearson, Ingles, Mackie and Menzies in characteristic poses.

Some of the victims of the Hamilt.... catastrophe. Will Beney, umpire; Herb. Burroughes, "Matty" Gifford, Frank Walker, and another snap of Gifford. "They did their best, but their best was not good enough."

at between $25,000 and $30,000, and is covered by insurance.

The Ives Modern Bedstead Company, occupying the other part of the building, also sustained damage by smoke. A fire wall about 18 inches thick, however, protected the goods from the blaze.

NEW FURNITURE FACTORY AT GODERICH.

A special meeting of the Goderich, Ont., town council was held recently to consider a proposition for a furniture factory in connection with the new sawmill being erected by J. E. Baechler, which would call for an expenditure of from $45,000 to $50,000. A loan of $25,000 is asked for this, a by-law for which will be submitted to the ratepayers.

AUGUST FURNITURE SALES STUNTS.

The August furniture sales throughout Canada brought forward the usual methods for increasing sales and in addition some new ones. The F. C. Burroughes Co., Toronto, gave a cabinet of silver to every purchaser of $100 worth of goods. The Adams Furniture Co. organized another of their kitchen cabinet clubs whereby members on payment of $1 down and a promise to pay $1 a week were allowed to have one of these step savers sent into their homes.

FIRE IN WALKERTON SAWMILL.

The sawmill in connection with the Knechtel Furniture Company's factory at Walkerton, Ont., was burned on August 13. All that remains of the building is standing timbers. The fire is supposed to have originated with a hot box in the machinery, and the mill was in flames before the hands were aware of it. The company's own fire company, with the south ward company, was quickly on the spot, and the full town brigade arrived soon after, but could not save the building. The main factory was not damaged. The building was insured, but the loss will be heavy.

STRATFORD CHAIR TO DOUBLE PLANT.

At a recent special meeting of the Stratford, Ont., city council, a letter was read from the Stratford Chair Company, asking permission to build a siding on High street, also for piling space on High street for lumber. The company proposes, if their request is granted, to materially enlarge its present plant, in which is manufactured a high grade class of chairs and seats.

Mayor Stevenson pointed out that the new addition would take up, with the present building, the entire block of the company, and this was the reason for asking piling space for their lumber on High street. "The addition will be as large as their present plant, which is good news under present conditions," added His Worship. The matter was referred to the railway and industrial committee.

COMBINED LIBRARY AND WRITING TABLE.

The Geo. J. Lippert Table Co., Berlin, Ont., have just put on the market a new drawer attachment which they may put on most of their table lines, at least, those of them that are fitted for a drawer. For the present they are attaching it to their library table, making it suitable for the hall, bedroom, or in fact any room in the house. The contrivance makes the table a writing desk by simply pulling open the drawer. When extended its length the stationery holder automatically jumps up with paper, envelopes, ink and pens. For closing, a spring is touched which lowers the holder and allows the drawer to be closed. The top of the drawer is a

The new "Comp Rite" writing table.

writing desk, and this may be lifted to insert articles, as in an ordinary drawer. The drawer is independent of the top, so there is no necessity for interference with articles that may be on the table should a person wish to write. For hotels this combination table should fill

CANADIAN FURNITURE WORLD AND THE UNDERTAKER — September, 1914

a long-felt want, and for small houses or homes where economy must be practised by tasty people, this table should prove a boon.

FURNITURE PEOPLE DISPORT THEMSELVES.

The enterprising Yolles Furniture Co., at 363-5 Queen street west, Toronto, and their employes, devoted their energies to picnic pastimes on Wednesday, Aug. 5, when they held high holiday at Island Park. The company numbered about 100. The travelers were the guests of the afternoon, and a feature of the picnic was a baseball game, in which the store beat the travelers 15 to 13. Montgomery's fine play at first base, and the good work of the drummers' battery, kept the score down. The travelers' team showed a big improvement over their last appearance, due, in a great measure, to the transference of Menzies from the outfield to the hot corner. Great team work distinguished the store's play, a feature of which was also Barnum's home run drive over the lagoon which somewhat unnerved pitcher "Jeanne" Bagshaw. James Dore's circus catch in centre field, with the bases occupied, must also be mentioned. This is the way the teams lined up:

Store.	Travelers.
Joe Cohn ....1st Base........	Montgomery
Barnum ....Catcher.........	Pearson
Canfield (Mgr. & Cap.). Pitcher...........	Bagshaw
Jud Cohn ....3rd Base	Menzies
Geo Cast ....2nd Base..........	Dunke
Weinstein ....Centre Field.........	Dore
S. Yolles ....Shortstop...........	Mackie
C. Brown ....Right Field.........	Morlock
E. Brown ....Left Field.	Beney (Mgr. & Cap.)

After an enjoyable lunch came more sporting events. Miss Horn won the ladies' race. It was a keen contest. Mrs. Beney and Mrs. Menzies surprised everyone by their sprinting powers. The fat man's race (handicap) was won by W. H. Beney, but Menzies (280 lbs.) declared he was only beaten by a "tongue," which the winner shot out as he neared the post. A great tug-of-war contest between store and travelers was the last, but not the least, event on the programme. The first pull was decided in the drummers' favor by the end man simply sitting on the ground. The second, and as it proved, final pull, also went to the travelers, after they had "broken" the rope.

In the course of the afternoon the travelers presented Mr. and Mrs. Yolles with umbrellas.

Louie Yolles and his merry crowd at Island Park making the welkin ring. Beney and Menzies, in "borrowed plumes," are the end men, and a number of other traveling salesmen may be seen in the chorus forming the background.

TRYING OUT SUITE SALES.

The Robert Simpson Co., Toronto, have of late been developing their sales in upholstered furniture, and particularly in parlor suites. Recently they conducted a special sale for one day of this line, setting aside 40 parlor suites for the purpose. While they did not in the one day sell the 40 suites, the sales, according to the company's representatives, were eminently satisfactory. The special sale was the culmination of a "feel-out" as to whether there was an opening for the sale of any particular line or lines of furniture, and the result is that there are opportunities if salesmen plan and go after the business along original lines.

In conversation, it developed that an opening order was placed by the firm in May for 60 suites; so well did they sell that the order was duplicated the month following, and increased by 105 suites some six or seven weeks later. Then came the special sale—and all the sales were successful.

AN EARLY FURNITURE ORDER.

One of the oldest and most successful furniture businesses in Carleton Place recently changed hands, when Geo. E. Leslie, who succeeded his father in 1879, sold out to W. M. Mathews, who will put new life into the concern, and who hopes to improve even on the success of his predecessor.

The business was started by Jacob Leslie in 1852, who made his own furniture by hand. He continued in this way, and made a fair living, which was considered in those days the height of success. When his son George took it over, he wished to go a little faster than his father, but having been trained by his careful parent, and as he had no money, he was afraid to buy anything on credit, for fear he could not meet the bills when they came due. In consequence, he depended on his own hard work to earn some money before he would buy any stock.

His first purchase was a dozen of common chairs, which he ordered from Bowmanville, and which came C.O.D. Soon after that a traveler called on him and offered to take his order for some furniture and give him four months' time to pay for it, and even had to promise that if he could not pay it then he would extend the time. On these conditions, he gave his first order, and when it was summed up it amounted to $75. After the traveler had gone, he began to think over the matter, and the amount looked so big to him that he decided to cancel the order. The firm, however, insisted that he should take the goods and that they would give him all the time he needed to pay for

---

AMERICAN MANFACTURERS SUPPORT BRITAIN.

Canadian Furniture World, Toronto:

Gentlemen,—We regret that our plans do not yet permit us to undertake a peaceful invasion of Canada at this time. A little later we are hoping to have our spring placed on the market in your country, and so take this occasion to offer our heartiest and most genuine good will and wishes to your Mother Country in her present troubles. Her loyalty to sense of duty and obligation invokes the admiration of every American.

WAY SAGLESS SPRING CO.,
Per J. M. Anderson,
Vice-President.

Minneapolis, Minn., Aug. 8, 1914.

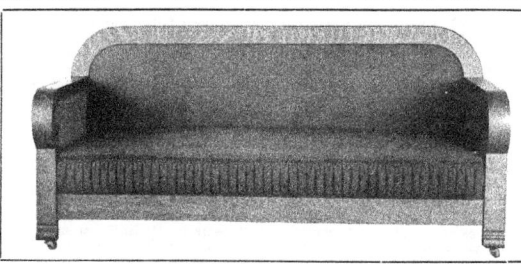

One of the new designs of davenport beds being shown by Farquharson-Gifford Co., Stratford.

them. He had them sold and the money ready long before any bill came due. This gave him courage, and from then on his business prospered.

Mr. Mathews, who succeeds him, is well and favorably known in the town and its surroundings, has splendid business qualifications, and will likely reap a good harvest.

NATIONAL HOME FURNISHERS MEET.

The third annual convention of the National Home Furnishers' Association was called to order by President Henry L. Kincaide, in the New York Furniture Exchange on July 22. President Kincaide presented to the convention C. Ludwig Baumann, who welcomed the visiting dealers, and told them of the splendid results accomplished by the New York Retail Furniture Association, of which he is president. Upon motion duly made, seconded and carried, a rising vote of thanks was tendered to Mr. Baumann.

The report of the president was read, as also was the report of the treasurer, which was approved and accepted.

James A. Gilmore then explained to the convention the operation and benefits derived from the bureau maintained by the Birmingham Retail Furniture Dealers' Association, where a record is kept of all removals. Mr. Richardson, of Baltimore, told of the difficulty they are having in attempting to have a removal ordinance passed in Baltimore. Campbell M. Voorhees was next introduced and delivered a most interesting address on Association matters in Ohio. Raphael Levy spoke on "Amalgamation of the Retail Furniture Trade," and Paul F. Treanor on "Organization and What it Means to the Trade."

Interesting addresses were also delivered by Charles A. Smith, on "Fraudulent Advertising," and by Alexander I. Lawson on "Factories Selling Direct."

BED AND DINING ROOM FURNITURE.

The Gibbard Furniture Co., of Napanee, Ltd., makers of bedroom furniture in oak and mahogany, and buffets and china cabinets in quartered oak, have just issued a supplementary catalogue of their products. Printed on coated stock, the illustrations are well set off, and give a splendid idea of the goods; especially is this true of the fine line of china cabinets, samples of which are illustrated. These cabinets have all wood panels in the back. The buffets, too, are well represented, as also are bedroom bureaus, dressing tables, chiffoniers, and dressers.

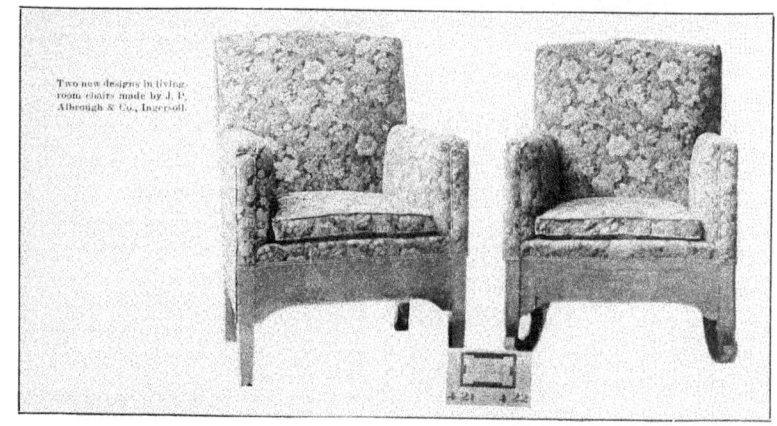

Two new designs in living-room chairs made by J. P. Albrough & Co., Ingersoll.

Making Your Job Pay Big Returns

By Edward Dreier

There is only one way to make anything pay, and that is by giving. The only way large businesses succeed is by spending money. To make your job succeed, you must give, not money, but yourself. And you will get back from your job just what you put into it.

I saw two clerks develop in a store a few years ago. One was a nephew of the Old Man, and the other was one of the town boys, who needed the job. The nephew was in the store over a year before the other boy came in, and knew the line handled in a fair sort of a way. Of course, when the other chap came in, this nephew knew it all, and showed it. He saw to it that

On the highway to failure

the young chap opened all the boxes and did all the rough work around the store, while he sat back and did the easy things.

The boy didn't seem to mind; in fact, he liked the jobs which were given to him. He studied everything that came into the store. He learned the uses of each article. He found out how and why they were made. He talked with the salesmen who came in, and learned all he could from them. He studied the furniture journals, and found out how the other fellows were doing things. He read the advertisements, and got selling talks from them. He used the brains of these thousands of big advertising men to make himself big. He used their talks in every sale he made—he made money out of other people's brains—and he developed his own at the same time. He took combinations of talks and worked them up into talks of his own. He worked the combinations of many ideas into ideas of his own.

Then the Old Man died, and the store went to the nephew. He took the business over and made many radical changes. They were changes which hurt the business, and when the clerk told him so he was fired.

One year later the business failed, and the old clerk bought it for a song. He started in, and if you should go into a certain Western Ontario town to-day someone would be sure to take you to the furniture store and relate with pride that it is one of the finest in the country.

Here was a boy who, in a very few years, worked up from a clerk to be proprietor of the store. Maybe it is something out of the ordinary—I believe it is—for there is a very small percentage of the clerks who really see and grasp their opportunity.

A boy, to succeed, must study hard. He must go out into the highways and the byways to find out things about his business. He should talk with the salesmen when they come in. It isn't just enough to know that a stove is a stove to be able to sell it. One must know why this particular stove is better than some other make. One must know what materials are used in the make-up of the stove—why a damper is here instead of some other place—why the oven is built thicker in some parts than in some other, and why the firepot is made deep instead of shallow.

It isn't enough to know that a piece of silverware is triple-coated—one should know why it is coated that way, and how it is coated. Most customers don't know these things, and it is the wise clerk who knows them and tells them that gets the orders.

I know a man who made a study of fountain pens—he made a specialty of that one article. He started in as a salesman in a drug store at five dollars per week. He made such a sale of pens for that store that the manufacturers of the pens became interested in him, and he is to-day getting $6,000 a year teaching their salesmen how to sell pens.

A clerk must have an open mind and be able to take in a lot of things. He must know how to serve people. He should study the needs of every customer. This is an easy thing in the average town. If a woman should run in for some clothespins, the clerk should try to sell her some clothesline or some other thing which has just come in. Perhaps she needs a cookie-cutter or a paring-knife. It really isn't a good selling talk to ask: "Can I do something else for you to-day?" Why not say: "We have just received some very handy kitchen knives, and I am sure that you will want one of them to help you in your work down home." You have shown some interest in her, and she will appreciate it. Women appreciate the little attentions—I know.

I could sit here and talk to you all day on this question of giving service, but the editors only allow me so much space each month, so I will just have to wait until next month to tell you other things which will be of help to you.

TWO VIEWPOINTS.

Frank Farrington, a successful merchant, recently said: "No business can grow unless you have ideas behind it—new ideas. One good business idea, showing how to make or save money in your store, will be worth to you in a year from ten to a thousand times what you pay for trade paper subscriptions."

E. Nichols, late of the F. C. Watkins, Ltd., Hamilton, and now with J. F. Cairns department store at Saskatoon, recently wrote: "I have found the Canadian Furniture World and The Undertaker to be an A1 journal for the furniture trade, full of suggestions, the editorials on profits, modes of selling, window displays, floor arranging, etc., always being of a helpful nature both to dealers and clerks, and I wish you every success."

The Furniture Manufacturer

A Department of News and Ideas

Modern Methods of Finishing Hardwoods

By C. J. La Vallee
Vice-president and Secretary of the Marietta Paint and Color Company, Marietta, Ohio.

Wood finishing is in this day and age taking its place among the highest of the recognized arts. This may sound like an extravagant statement, but nevertheless it is truer to-day than it ever was in the world's history. The marvelous development of the furniture business is, to a great extent, directly responsible for the advances made by man in the finishing of the native and imported woods used largely in that line of manufacturing. Some of the finest examples of furniture design that we have to-day are products of the master craftsmen of centuries ago, and where we see designers copying the ideas of these old masters, we also see the finishing end of the business vastly improved over the old days, and processes used to beautify, preserve, and protect the woods, that Chippendale and his contemporaries never dreamed of. I do not wish to convey the impression that finishing is on a higher plane than formerly, because that would not be true. The old-time finisher filled the pores of the wood with coat after coat of varnish, scraping down each coat until, after a long space of time, the surface was level; thus ensuring a very fine finish and an exceedingly durable one. The point I do wish to make prominent, however, is that where in the case of the old style workman he consumed months in putting out a finished job, to-day the length of time may be measured in days—a condition absolutely necessary in this utilitarian age, where size of production is the paramount issue, and where the dollar reigns supreme. Later day methods have accomplished all this, and it may possibly be that it has been done at the expense of quality and durability.

It has been truthfully said that there is nothing new under the sun, and the staining and finishing line is no exception to the rule. Looking back over the cycle of years, we see numberless inventions which astounded and amazed the world. The application and working out of the idea might be new, but in nine cases out of ten the idea itself was not new. So in the finishing line. We claim to have made great discoveries and improvements, and it's true we have, but where did the underlying idea come from? It came from nature, and all that we can do is to imitate the effects of the sun, the rain, and the years. The old masters must have realized that their main difficulty lay in properly finishing their work in order to protect and beautify it. Hence, in order to avoid filling and its attendant troubles, they used, in most cases, close-grained woods. The finishing on this consisted of painting and varnishing. Some of the old pieces made by Sheraton had the panels painted by Angelica Kaufman, a German woman, whose long residence in England anglicized her to a great extent. Her medallions are exquisite examples of the art of that period, and most of her subjects are taken from Greek mythology. It is curious in observing the trend of those times, to notice how fast they changed from the thin, spindly designs to the heavier massive creations made out of harder and more open-grained woods. To the student of evolution it presents an interesting study. He can look around him to-day and readily pick out shades and designs upon which the past has put its stamp.

One of the artistic and most popular finishes we have to-day is the mission, and we can directly trace its origin to the mission period of certain parts of our country. The term "mission" formerly meant a style, but nowadays it signifies a finish as well as a design. This period has had a tremendous influence upon the shades and finishes in vogue to-day. How long it will last, time alone can tell, and even at this time, in the height of mission popularity, the painted furniture and woodwork of long ago is creeping back into popular favor.

Denninger, of Mayence, Germany, was one of the earliest to devise processes for the staining of wood. He confined his attention almost entirely to alcoholic mixtures, because at that time to stain a piece of wood was a matter of a week or more duration, and where water stains were used the pores of the wood were opened so widely, and the grain raised so badly that a good finish was almost an impossibility; hence, his attempts were all confined to a stain of a spirit nature. His efforts, contrasted with the customs in vogue today, were very crude, and depended to a great extent upon reactions which took place upon the wood itself. For instance, if a golden yellow were wanted, he would saturate the wood with a solution of tin chloride, and then place in a tight room where it would come into contact with the fumes of sulphide of hydrogen. A reaction would, of course, take place, on the wood, and a golden yellow compound be formed known as tin sulphide. Others of his processes called for boiling the wood for as long as a day in one bath and then an equally long time in another before the staining was complete. He was strongly opposed to the use of violent acids, like hydrochloric, sulphuric, etc., as, in his estimation, they had a deteriorating effect upon the materials used in finishing the wood. Denninger is but one of a number, during his time and after, who worked upon stains for wood with more or less success. The wood dyes came in about this time. They were an improvement on the metal solutions, and for many years were considered standard. However, no great strides were made until the discovery of the coal tar derivatives, from which time is dated the birth of the wood stain business. The history of the discovery of the various colors reads like a romance. Many of them were accidentally made by some old German chemist who was hunting for something else; others were worked out systematically. At any rate, we are indebted to the German chemists for practically all of the advances which their work has made possible, and the end is not yet. They are still working on it, and coal tar has proved so prolific that no prophet can say how far they will develop it.

I believe you will agree with me when I say that until about the year 1890 wood finishing had been going along the even tenor of its way, with but few radical changes. Oak was beginning to be appreciated as a cabinet and building wood, but its possibilities had hardly been dreamed of. It was then mostly finished natural by filling with a paste filler. About that time the 16th century fad came into favor, but it did not last long, and the antique followed, which was produced by coloring the filler. I might say that the real awakening began about 1898, when, through an accident, that most beautiful and effective finish, golden oak, was born. There never was a finish that brought out to such an advantage the king of our native wood, the white oak of Indiana and northern Ohio. It is still popular, and the fact that it is being imitated on all the cheaper woods proves my assertion. This finish, or effect, has remained in favor longer than any other special finish since oak has been used in furniture. It was at that period that I entered the ring as a manufacturer, and, if modesty did not forbid, I might say that the keystone in the arch of our success is golden oak. This required so much research work in the laboratory that it has since been comparatively easy to meet the issues, as one after the other the different effects on oak have been evolved. Let use take as an example

Weathered Oak—The Mission Period.

The original of this finish was not a finish at all, in the ordinary sense of the word, but rather an effect produced by long years of service, which accounts for the soft indescribable mixture of grey, green, and brown, which has been so aptly called "weathered." In the early stages of this fad, we attempted to reproduce this effect, and succeeded, but, as it could be done only with an acid or water stain, and on account of the great amount of labor necessary to effect a correct finish, it could not be used on but the finest examples of this design. The maker of a medium grade of mission furniture soon discovered that a more economical method of finishing must be devised, so he came to us with his problem, and we solved it with our Spartan process, enabling him to reduce this finishing cost about 50 per cent. without materially affecting the quality or the artistic effect of the result. I firmly believe that weathered oak would have retained its popularity if the original idea of adhering to the mission design had not been lost sight of. The artistic merit of this finish brought out weathered oak on all kinds of furniture of no particular design, making it so commonplace that people of refined tastes soon demanded a more exclusive effect, and from the ashes of the weathered arose the early English, erroneously called a mission finish. The true mission, as you well know, shows an open pore, and depends entirely upon the depth and beauty of tint for its effect; while early English is a solid finish—the pore being filled to produce a smooth, level surface. It shows the beauty of the oak by contrast, accentuating the high lights in the same manner as the golden oak, but much more subdued. Early English has also been very popular, and still retains some hold upon the people, but for the same cause that marked the decadence of the weathered, it is being displaced by that most beautiful and artistic effect, the fumed oak. This effect, as its name implies, was first obtained, and still is, to a certain extent, by exposing the oak to the fumes of ammonia, then coating over with shellac and rubbing dull. On some pieces the result was most beautiful. Fumed oak was at once favorably received by the trade, and promised to become very popular, but on account of the great difficulty in producing a uniform effect on the various kinds of oak entering into the manufacture of the cabinet work, it was soon seen that it was not as simple an operation as had at first appeared, and the great majority eliminated it from their lines for the time being, so that not much was done about it for several years. However, as has been the case with nearly all new finishes that have real merit, fumed oak did not die out. A few of the more persevering ones kept experimenting until a process was found that enabled them to produce a reasonably uniform color effect on nearly all species of oak, but here again it was an expensive operation. We had been watching developments all this time, however, and as soon as the demand for this finish forced the trade to add it to their lines, we were ready to offer our acid stain, enabling them to compete successfully with as high-grade a finish and effect as the original, but at a much lower cost. The trade was quick to see the merit in this process, and fumed oak jumped into favor at once, so that there is now scarcely a manufacturer of woodwork that does not offer a fumed oak line. This is a fair expose of the birth and growth of all the popular fads and fancies in the finishing world. If these several finishes remained true to the name, so that a standard could be established, the manufacture of stains would be a simple operation, but we have no sooner mastered a certain shade, or tint, than we are asked for something more on the brown or green or grey—or a little darker or lighter, until out of the maze we usually manage to evolve a medium shade, which is used as a standard, and after a time it becomes so in fact. As I have said in the beginning, many of these effects (some of them most artistic) are named after some Old World master designer, and not the particular shade or color used in his day to bring out the best in that design. As, for instance, we are suddenly requested to furnish a stain to produce a Flanders effect on oak. We know that the name implies a design only, but, being familiar with the period when this design was brought out, we soon evolve a stain that produces the required effect. The same can be said of the Flemish, the Baronial, the Sheraton, the Chippendale, the Cathedral, etc. There is this to be said, however, of the Cathedral: It conveys more meaning to the mind of one familiar with the subject than any of the other above mentioned, because, while it denotes a special design, one can readily picture the effect of the light shining through the beautiful art windows in one of the mammoth temples of the Old World, blending the ambers, greens, blues, yellows, and reds in one harmonious golden brown tint. Silver grey, formerly produced only by boiling the veneers in a solution of sulphate of iron, is now satisfactorily made with an acid stain applied with a brush, making it possible to get the effect on all kinds of cabinet work. It is usually correct only on maple, however—a special stain being necessary on other woods.

Mahogany Finishing.

We now come to mahogany. For many years an acid or water stain has been used with good results on all kinds of woods, but, like all successes, it has its drawbacks, and one of the most serious of these is the raising of the grain of the wood. On built-up furniture it is especially objectionable, on account of the water swelling the wood and breaking the joints. Then, again, the veneers used in many instances are so thin that when soaked with water they blister badly, and often have to be removed and replaced at great expense. With these points in mind, it is not difficult to appreciate the demand for a so-called oil mahogany stain. The first question that arises is, what are the chief claims for or against an oil stain? If I were asked that question (speaking of a genuine oil stain), I would say that for a surface exposed to the elements an oil stain is the best, from the fact that being made by reducing pigment colors with oil, turpentine, etc., it covers and protects the surface as would a thin paint (which, in fact, it is). It naturally retains its color longer, but for interior finish, where a real wood tint is desired, my answer would be, the day of the oil stain is passed, because it is necessarily made from pigment colors. and lacks altogether the depth and brilliancy of the acid or water stain. We must, then, look elsewhere for a material which possesses these qualities, and at the same time be entirely soluble in the proper vehicles. This we find in the coal tar dyes, known as the oil soluble group. In this group can be found almost every color of the rainbow, and by blending intelligently most of the effects obtained with acid colors can be duplicated quite satisfactorily. There is this exception, however, that these stains do not possess the mordant properties of an acid, and are, therefore much more transparent; hence their clearness and great brilliancy. In some instances this is considered an advantage, but owing to the fact that most of the stains are made to match a water stain, it was necessary that some way be found to overcome and diminish what at first seemed to be its chief claim. This demanded another long series of experiments in the laboratory, and after many attempts the solution was found to rest in the proper mixture of the several coal tar solvents and specially prepared alcohols. As to whether these experiments were successful, I leave it to you to judge, as most of you are familiar with the stains manufactured by my company with flattering success. You will better appreciate the difficulty when you consider the number of delicate points which had to be kept in mind.

First—The combination of ingredients must be correct in shade.

Second—The vehicles must be so well balanced that the whole will be in perfect solution.

Third—It must penetrate deeply into the fibre of the wood.

Fourth—It must not raise the grain.

Fifth—It must evaporate absolutely, and yet leave the stain properly bound, and, lastly, it should hold its color reasonably well. I say reasonably, because we know that the best of these colors are more or less fugitive, and unless some care is taken to protect them, when they are exposed to a strong light, the results are sometimes unsatisfactory. Naturally, the stain is blamed, and with some show of reason.

We had already passed some of the milestones on the road to success, but as the demand for a mahogany stain—correct in every detail—was on the increase, and we could see the vast magnitude of that demand, we inaugurated a long series of laboratory experiments with all the known reagents, following our motto of looking backward, only that we may more surely move forward and avoid past mistakes. The result was a glaze or toner—permanent in color—absolutely transparent and perfectly practical for application. This removed the last objection. We now offer these stains to the world with confidence and without apology. This is a brief outline of the working out of a principle, and it applies to this entire group of stains.

Paste Filler.

Before closing, I want to say a little more about paste fillers. I will be brief, realizing that you are quite familiar with that material, but there are two points that I want to bring out which I consider very important; the first is the close relation that paste filler bears to stains. It is a well-known fact that in many cases the color of the filler is as important as the stain itself in producing a certain effect or tone. the second is the difference in the quality of the filler. I have many times marveled at the indifference manifested by users of paste fillers in general. Some select the filler for the color effect, others simply to fill the pore, both seeming to forget that both qualities should be found in a well-balanced filler. But there is one point that is being insisted upon by the discriminating buyer after he has been shown the advantage of it. and that is—the filler, in addition to all the requisites mentioned above, must dry so hard that one coat of finish can be omitted without impairing the beauty or durability of the work; to anyone familiar with this subject, the logic will be obvious. To you, gentlemen, who use large quantities of this material, a word of caution—remember that when dealing with a reliable house, a fair price ensures a high quality. In the brief time that is allotted to me, I have endeavored to give you some idea of the history of wood finishing—its evolution through various stages of development—its position to-day. There are large books that could be written on this subject to cover it thoroughly, but it will have to suffice to touch upon a bare outline. I have seen many of the developments in this line that I have told you about to-day, and it has been my good fortune to have been able to work out the application of many of these discoveries to a practical purpose in my laboratory. My experience has taught me that stains are still in their infancy—their field is the whole world. With such a condition at present, and with so glowing a future, who among use will dare define a limit?

THE GLUE ROOM FLOOR.

Cleanliness in the glue room is even more imperative in summer than during the winter months, and the order of cleanliness should extend even to the glue room floor. "How can we keep the glue room floor clean?" was asked recently. The first answer is, to keep the waste glue and drippings cleaned off. When that is countered by the statement that the glue drippings stick tight to the floor and cannot be cleaned off by scraping, then it becomes a matter of putting the floor in such shape that the glue will not stick so tightly it cannot be cleaned off by scraping. If on the ground floor, and one can use concrete, it is comparatively easy to scrape the waste glue up. If it must be a wooden floor, though, stop a minute and think about the things one does to keep glue from sticking to cauls, and he may find the answer to the trouble. Glue will not stick to an oily substance, therefore, if one has a smooth floor and oil it, he may easily keep the glue cleaned off. Or a hard varnish might serve the same purpose. Also, we know that wax will keep glue from sticking. In fact, when we come to looking over the matter carefully, there are a number of things that will keep glue from sticking, including that of covering the drippy spots with tin or zinc. The main thing is to think about it, figure out which is the most practical in each case, and then make it a point to keep the glue room floor clean. It makes it a better and more wholesome place to work, and also makes for quality in the glue work.

Just because one kind of advertising has helped your business, don't eliminate all other kinds. You can use them all.

THE FISCHMAN PATENT MATTRESS

Can. Pat. Mar. 16, 1909   U.S. Pat., Feb. 16, 1909

VISIT OUR DISPLAY
AT
TORONTO EXHIBITION
ALSO AT THE LONDON AND OTTAWA FAIRS

Send for a copy of our New Catalogue and see why the Fischman Mattress is in a class by itself and the fastest seller you can offer to your trade.

THE FISCHMAN MATTRESS CO., LIMITED
333 Adelaide St. West   Toronto

GLOBE FURNITURE EMPLOYES MAKE MERRY.

The employes of the Globe Furniture Co., Waterloo, and their families, made gay when they held their annual picnic a short time ago at the beautiful Waterloo Park. It was a joyous occasion for the employes. The factory closed at 11.30 o'clock. About 1.30 o'clock a parade was formed at the corner of William and King streets, headed by the Waterloo Band, and marched to the park. At the park some good races were pulled off, and the winners awarded valuable prizes. A close and exciting baseball game also added much interest to the afternoon's sport.

EUREKA VACUUM CLEANERS REDUCED.

The Onward Mfg. Co., Berlin, Ont., announce that commencing September 1, their "Eureka" electric vacuum cleaner, which up to now has been selling for $45, was reduced in price to $39.50. This means that a saving of $5.50 will be effected to buyers of this machine, which will continue to be of the same high quality, with the same guarantee as in the past. The enormous increase in the company's business during the past year has made this big reduction possible. The extra attachments complete show a reduction as well, from $11.50 to $10. This makes the machine, complete with attachments, $49.50 instead of $56.50, as in the past.

The Reliable Bedding Co., Weston, Ont., are this summer building a large three-storey brick addition to their plant.

SHELLACS

If you are in the market for first-class Shellac we believe it would be to your advantage to get in touch with us.

HIGH GRADE VARNISHES
FILLERS and GRAINING INKS

THE AULT & WIBORG CO. OF CANADA
LIMITED
MONTREAL   TORONTO   WINNIPEG

THE HOME OF

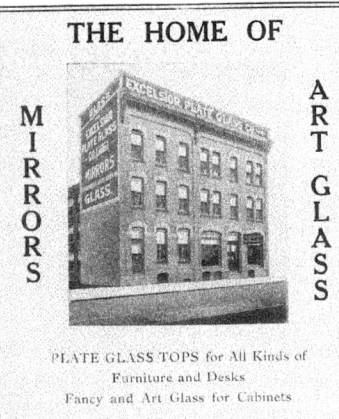

MIRRORS   **ART GLASS**

PLATE GLASS TOPS for All Kinds of Furniture and Desks
Fancy and Art Glass for Cabinets

Excelsior Plate Glass Co., Limited
189-191 Queen Street East
TORONTO, ONT.

"20TH CENTURY" RUG RACKS AND LINOLEUM RACKS

SAVE LABOR. MAKE QUICK SALES. PAY PERPETUAL DIVIDENDS.

THE GREATEST SILENT SALESMAN ON EARTH. THOUSANDS IN USE TODAY.

ASK FOR CATALOGUE

THE STEEL FURNISHING CO., LIMITED
NEW GLASGOW, N.S.

STEELE'S STANDARD SOFA SPRINGS

Did you ever test the Springs you put in your Upholstered Furniture? Our Springs will stand the most severe test. Write for prices, it will pay you.

Makers of Sofa Springs since 1886

JAMES STEELE, Limited, Guelph, Ont.

For Sale / Wanted

TERMS FOR INSERTION
25 Cents per line, one insertion
Four lines once for $1.00, three times for $2.00.
Cash must accompany the order
No accounts booked.
MINIMUM 50 CENTS

FURNITURE and House Furnishing business for sale. Good town. Surrounding country in British Columbia. Reasons for selling, failing health. For full particulars apply Box 128, Canadian Furniture World and The Undertaker, 32 Colborne St., Toronto. 14-8-3

FOR SALE—Undertaking business in an excellent town in Ontario, with large country trade. A golden opportunity and a bargain for quick sale. Best reasons for selling. Box 681, Canadian Furniture World and The Undertaker, 32 Colborne St., Toronto. 14-8-3

FOR SALE—Furniture and Undertaking business in Western Canada. For particulars write at once to Mrs. A. Metcalf, Treherne, Man.

FOR SALE—Four hearses, sell at half price, going out of the hearse business. Our hearses are made of the very best stock. English Collonge axles and best workmanship. Also wagonettes and three-seated carriages. Write for particulars, W. J. Thompson & Son, London, Ont.

Invalid Chairs and Tricycles of every description.

This has been our study for thirty-five years. We build chairs that suit the requirements of any case. Write us for catalogue No. 20 and prices, if interested.

Gendron Wheel Co., Toledo, O. U.S.A.

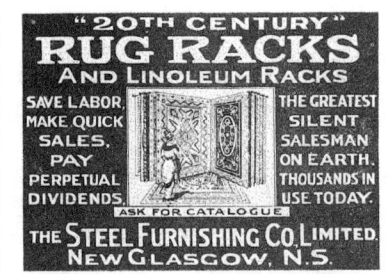

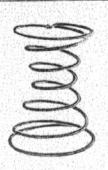

"W & R" Mattresses, Woven Wire Beds, Pillows

and Sofa Cushions—made in the qualities that bring reputation.
We also deal in Feathers, Mattress Supplies, Twine, Jute and Cotton Felts, Fibre, Seagrass, Ticking, Bed Lace, Hair, etc.

WRITE FOR OUR PRICES

Whitworth & Restall
Rear of 112 Adelaide Street, W. Toronto

WHEN YOU WANT TO SELL YOUR BUSINESS

You want to get the best possible offer. The more possible buyers you get in touch with the better chance you have of making a good sale. The "For Sale" and "Want" ads. in the CANADIAN FURNITURE WORLD are read every month by over two thousand manufacturers, travellers, retail dealers and store salesmen.

Four Cents a Word   **Ten Cents a Word**
One Insertion   Three Insertions

Dominion Casket Co., Limited

Telephones { Day No. 1020. Nights, Sundays and Holidays Nos. 1069-1101 }

Guelph, Ont.

RUSH ORDERS SOLICITED

No. 532

Solid quartered oak polished. Our oaks have an individuality that stamp our goods as being in a class by themselves, quality and good designs being the predominant features. The above style can be furnished in oak, mahogany or Circassian walnut. The mere fact of carrying our cases in your display room insures a sale of satisfactory proportions.

No. 522

This solid oak with quartered lids, made in mahogany or walnut if desired. Compare these styles with any others on the market, and your own common sense will tell you where to buy.

DO NOT FAIL TO EXAMINE THESE GOODS AT 126 KING STREET WEST DURING THE ANNUAL CONVENTION OF THE CANADIAN EMBALMERS' ASSOCIATION, 1914.

Undertakers' Department

Problems affecting the Undertaking Profession are here discussed and readers are invited to send letters expressing their views on any of the subjects dealt with—News of the profession throughout Canada.

Back to First Principles—Part I.

Professor Eckels Reviews the Underlying Elements of Good Embalming

Every once in a while it pays us to cast our mind's eye over the past as an index to guide us in the future. In our school days, the weekly review was a feature which had a strong bearing upon our grasp of our studies. Four days would we delve and dig, and on the fifth conscientiously have the rough spots smoothed out and the hollows between our bumps of knowledge filled in.

In this short review I wish, therefore, to say a good many things which have been said before, and yet which many have lost sight of in the following of specialties and in the thirst for research along individual lines.

To begin at the beginning, "What is Embalming?" The question is familiar to everyone, yet the answer oft is forgotten. "Embalming is the chemical disinfection of the dead human body."

And the chemical disinfection of the dead human body requires what? No other answer is possible than "The chemical saturation of the dead human body. If there is no saturation of the tissue, obviously that tissue cannot be disinfected, because disinfection is accomplished by the actual contact of the chemicals with the bacteria present throughout the flesh and fibrin."

What is more utterly futile, then, than to have some embalmer tell you that he can properly embalm a two hundred-pound body with two quarts of fluid? He cannot do it, because it can't be done. Of course, it is possible for him to place two quarts of fluid so that, with luck, the decomposition which is certain to follow will not be observable on the day of the funeral. That is, of course, within the range of possibility, but that body is not embalmed any more than the body in which only trocar work is done is embalmed.

The only practical method so far discovered of doing good work is by utilizing the arterial circulation for the complete dissemination of the fluid to all portions of the body, and through that arterial system enough fluid must be injected so that no portion of the flesh or fibrin is left untouched by the purifying action of the chemicals. When this is done, the body is embalmed, and until it is done, it is not embalmed in the true sense of the term.

As to the best method for injecting fluid, there are many opinions. I have tested most of them, and so has almost every embalmer. Indeed, I recommend to every other embalmer, test every method presented to try to discover what good, if any, there is in it.

Embalming is an exact science, but embalming must be done in an exact manner, and is not fool-proof. Much depends upon the experience and judgment of the embalmer. Much depends upon his choice of fluid. Much depends upon the way he mixes it and how he injects it.

Personally, I inject fluid slowly, because I wish to secure the complete saturation, and I find no other way will give me the same assurance of success. I continue to inject until signs of embalming everywhere are present. When I see the peculiar mottled appearance which denotes that the fluid has completed its circulation and has reached the capillaries, then I know that I have injected a sufficient quantity, and I never stop until I observe this appearance. Perhaps, I would better say, I never stop permanently, because during the injection I stop frequently.

When the signs of embalming everywhere are present and any of the standard embalming fluids have been used, the undertaker may feel reasonably assured that in nine hundred and ninety-nine cases out of one thousand preservation is absolutely accomplished. Especially at this season of the year, however, there are two or three complications which should be carefully guarded against.

The first of these is in sudden death cases, due either to heart disease, the heat, alcoholism, or a combination of the three. Another cause of death in which the complications are much the same is in those "drowned" cases which really are not drowned at all, but in which death is caused by heart failure, due to shock. In all of these cases, the body will be heavily gorged with blood, and if heat has a large part in bringing about death, the blood will be very badly congested, especially in the head and face.

Fluid Should Go Where Intended.

In such cases, the embalmer must not be content with having injected the customary amount of fluid; he must see that the fluid goes where it is intended. He never is safe, especially in warm weather, unless the fluid shows its presence over the abdomen. Unless it is there in plentiful quantity, he should continue his injections until the mottled signs appear. The reason for this is that the branch arteries feeding the tissue over the abdomen are the longest and the furthest from a main trunk artery of any in the body. If, therefore, he fills these small branch arteries which lead around the surface of the body from the trunk arteries near the spine clear around the surface over the abdomen, he may feel reasonably assured that he has injected a sufficient quantity of fluid at least to have reached every extremity.

To avoid the possibility of something having clogged the circulation, however, it would be wise to assure himself that each extremity has been reached. Many of the sudden deaths in hot weather are caused by the weakening of the mitral valve of the heart, resulting in regurgitation of the blood through the heart and literally drowning and smothering the victim in his own blood. In such cases, the injection of one, or even two gallons of fluid in the customary way is no guarantee at all that the body is embalmed.

Let us again go back to first principles for the cause of this: In arterial embalming, we do not as a rule inject the fluid into the arteries which we design it

CANADIAN FURNITURE WORLD AND THE UNDERTAKER September, 1914

We will Exhibit a complete Line of

Undertakers' Supplies

At the Annual Convention of

The Canadian Embalmers' Association

Toronto, September 8-11

Fast Service

THE EVEL CASKET Co.
TRADE MARK

Reasonable Prices

The Evel "Quality" Line

Polished Oak and Mahogany Caskets. Cloth and Plush covered Caskets. Exclusive designs in the latest fashions in Ladies Dresses, Gentlemen's Suits and Casket Linings. Wesfield Plate Hardware.

Meet us in Toronto and inspect the newest ideas offered the trade.

Evel Casket Company, Limited
Hamilton   Ontario

Has no affiliation with any other firm in the Trade

eventually to travel. Instead, by the use of our flexible arterial tube, we pour the fluid directly into the aorta. If the valves of the heart be closed, as they are in normal cases, we soon fill the aorta, and by continuing to force in fluid, either with our pump or by gravitation, we secure sufficient pressure to send the fluid through nature's own channels, and with the same relative pressure as nature provides in life. In this way, each main and branch artery, down to the smallest capillary, receives fluid in proportion to the amount of blood it received during life.

In sudden death cases, in which the heart valves are affected, our fluid, however, does not fill the aorta, much less create pressure there. If the valves be weak and open, the fluid flows through the heart into the pulmonary circulation and on into the lungs, which are capable of absorbing almost as much fluid as we normally would inject to ensure preservation.

The fluid is in the body to be sure, but it is not so distributed as to ensure preservation. The failure to observe this is responsible for a very great proportion of the failures which fall to the lot of the undertaker. It, therefore, should be especially carefully guarded against, and he who does not thoroughly understand what I have just written should read and reread it until he does.

In sudden death cases, as I have said, the fluid in the head especially is apt to be congested and thickened to such an extent that it will not at first flow easily from the capillaries.

How often we hear an embalmer say: "I injected a gallon of fluid, but could not clean up all the face discolorations." In all such cases, especially where a raw formaldehyde fluid was used, the embalmer is lucky to escape with nothing worse than a puttied face. He is in danger of leaving it badly discolored, and the face grows darker each day between the time of embalming and the time of funeral.

It is quite possible to drain this blood at the first operation. It is almost impossible to secure any later. The bulb syringe should be attached to the vein tube and a sufficient amount of solvent fluid injected to dissolve the blood, when it will start the flow of blood. This will come out at first slowly, but if sufficient fluid is then injected in the arteries it will come out. After a few moments, if this be persisted in, it will begin to flow more naturally, until finally almost as good drainage can be secured as in the normal case.

This is a hot weather precaution which never should be overlooked. When necessary, get drainage by all means, no matter how great the difficulty. The blood furnishes the worst liability to trouble, and especially at this season of the year should be gotten rid of at all hazards.

(To be Continued.)

Prof. A. Johnston Dodge, of Boston, Mass., who lectured last year at the Canadian Embalmers' Association convention at Toronto, is seriously ill at his home.

DOES ADVERTISING SELL?

In the August issue of Canadian Furniture World and The Undertaker, F. Rosar, Toronto, used a condensed ad. to tell of a $800 Cunningham casket wagon he had for sale. After one insertion, Mr. Rosar 'phoned to say he wished the ad. discontinued, as he had sold the wagon. This single insertion was the only advertising he had placed to sell the wagon.

Program of 31st Annual Convention of the Canadian Embalmers' Association and the 4th Annual School of Embalming, Anatomical Building of the Toronto University

School will open on Tuesday, September 1st, at 10.00 a.m., and continue one week.

The convention will open Tuesday, September 8th, at 10.00 a.m., and continue on 9th, 10th and 11th.

MONDAY EVENING, SEPTEMBER 7th

The Financial Secretary will be at the University Building to meet those who wish to pay fees and dues.

TUESDAY, SEPTEMBER 8th

The Officers will receive members at 9 a.m. to 10.30 a.m.

10.30 a.m.—Professor Moll will talk to those present for a short time.

11 a.m.—Reading minutes of last Convention. Appointment of Committees by President. A short address—T. E. Simpson.

Afternoon Session

Secretary and Financial Secretary will be present at 1.30 p.m. to receive dues.

2.00 p.m.—Invocation and address by Rev. Byron Stauffer. Response—Wm. Edwards, Vice-President. Address of welcome by Mayor Hocken. Response—J. H. Robinson, of Hamilton, Ont. President's address.

3.00 to 4.30 p.m.—Lecture by Prof. Horace Moll: Blood Drainage, Methods. Purging. Skin Slip, etc. The Chemistry of Embalming. Septic Infection, and its Treatment.

WEDNESDAY, SEPTEMBER 9th

9.00 a.m.—Report by the Secretary. Report by the Treasurer.

9.30 a.m.—Lecture by Prof. Horace Moll: Practical Demonstrations on the Cadaver. Cavities of the Body and Contents. Anatomical Divisions. Vascular System and Heart. Aorta and Branches. The Blood. Circulation and its Systems. Arteries used in Embalming: Location, Anatomical and Linear Guides. Veins used in Blood Drainage: Location and Guides. Practical Embalming of all kinds of Cases. Relative Value of the Different Arteries. Conditions Encountered. Rigor Mortis, Ante and Post Mortem Discolorations and Stains, Putrefaction and Fermentation. Embalming Difficult Cases. Dropsy, Drowning, Mutilated Bodies, etc. Embalming: All Methods Considered and Discussed. Sanitation, Disinfection, Operation, Chemicals and Methods.

Wednesday Afternoon

2.00 p.m.—Lecture by Prof. Moll. (Continuation of this morning's subjects.)

4.30 p.m.—Reports of Committees.

THURSDAY, SEPTEMBER 10th

9.00 a.m.—Reports and Unfinished Business.

10.00 a.m.—Prof. Moll. Demonstration on Cadaver. Contagious and Infectious Diseases, and their Exciting Causes. Bacteria— Their Relations to Disease and Changes in the Morbid Body. Muscles. Skin and Nervous System. Pathology. Disease, Death, and Signs of Death. Hints on Restoring Bodies, and Practical Suggestions.

11.00 a.m.—Election of Officers. General Business. Dinner.

2.00 p.m.—Dr. John McCullough.

3.00 p.m.—Installation of Officers by the Retiring President. Unfinished Business.

3.30 p.m.—Lecture by Prof. Moll: Visceral Anatomy of the Organs of the Chest. Visceral Anatomy of the Abdomen and Pelvis. Alimentary Canal. Question Box.

Proceedings of the Tenth Annual Convention of the Western Canada Funeral Directors' and Embalmers' Association

The tenth annual convention of the Western Canada Funeral Directors' and Embalmers' Association, held at Winnipeg on July 14, 15, and 16, was called to order and formally opened by President Alex. Broadfoot, of Moose Jaw, who welcomed the delegates, and wished them a most enjoyable and profitable meeting. Rev. J. Irvine Walker offered the invocation, and Controller J. W. Cockburn, in the absence of Mayor Deacon, delivered a very warm welcome to the visitors, and extended the freedom of the city.

W. D. Dunbar, of Napinka, responded on behalf of the delegates, and expressed extreme pleasure at the controller's gracious and hearty greeting.

Rev. Mr. Walker delivered a splendid address on "The Modern Funeral Director." He displayed keen sympathy with all that stood for the uplifting and betterment of all things pertaining to the calling of the undertaker. He stood for high ideals, suggesting even an academic course of two years covering the subject of embalming, sanitation, and funeral conduct. He also expressed the hope that in the near future the calling might be raised to the rank of a profession. He discouraged the custom of Sunday funerals, and asked the assistance and co-operation of the delegates in the discontinuance of this custom. He also deprecated the practice of lavish display of flowers. The address was most keenly appreciated, and on motion of Messrs. Gardiner and Kerr, a vote of thanks was tendered Rev. Mr. Walker.

The president addressed the members briefly, touching on the good work done by the association during the year, and suggesting a National Canadian Association.

Secretary's Report.

The report of the Secretary-Treasurer was presented, as follows:

To the Officers and Members of the Western Canada Funeral Directors' Association:

I herewith submit my report as your secretary-treasurer for the year ending July 10th, 1914.

After our meeting last year at Brandon, I mailed synoptic reports on our deliberations to the various trade journals, and immediately arranged for the publication of the ninth report, the first step of which being to secure advertisements from the supply houses of the trade. From this quarter, as usual, we received a loyal and ready response.

Diplomas of proficiency were also prepared and forwarded to all applicants fortunate enough to secure this certificate of proficiency furnished by our association.

Copies of proceedings were mailed to all dealers handling funeral goods, not only in Manitoba, but also in Saskatchewan.

The executive committee met in Winnipeg, February 18, to arrange details and dates for this convention. At this meeting much optimism was exhibited, and it was unanimously decided to make our tenth anniversary the most interesting and profitable convention in the history of the association. We feel proud of the fact that Prof. W. P. Hohenschuh has consented to again appear before us as lecturer and demonstrator. We have always considered him not only as a benefactor of undertakers everywhere, but a friend of the members of our association in particular, and I am sure we extend to him our most cordial greetings.

During the past year the Province of Saskatchewan has formed an association, and a number of our members are assisting the good work in that province by lending their support to the efforts of that organization. While we are sorry to lose a number of our membership, it is only another indication of the development and expansion of our fair Dominion, and I am sure we one and all extend to them our heartiest best wishes for a splendid association, and will be only too delighted to extend the glad hand to any of the members of Canada's baby association in the Province of Saskatchewan, and we shall always feel, as their parent organization, a warm and kindly interest in all their undertakings.

Treasurer's Statement.

Our finances are still in a healthy condition, of which the following is a brief summary:

RECEIPTS.

Balance on hand, July 10th, 1913 ..$	767 16
Receipts from dues	300 00
Receipts from memberships	100 00
Miscellaneous	112 69
	———$1,279 85

EXPENDITURE.

As per statement and vouchers attached ....$	505 91
Balance July 10th, 1914, N. C. Bank	773 94
	———$1,279 85

Respectfully submitted,
(Signed) A. B. GARDINER,
Secretary-Treasurer.

On motion of Messrs. Kerr and Dunbar, the secretary-treasurer's report was referred to the resolution committee, as also was a letter from R. J. Campbell, suggesting that the name of the association be changed to "The Manitoba Funeral Directors' and Embalmers' Association."

Communications Read.

The following letter was read from J. C. Van Camp, of Toronto:

30 Bloor Street West,
Toronto, Ont., March 30th, 1914.
Mr. A. B. Gardiner,
Winnipeg, Man.:

Dear Sir,—You will see by the accompanying letter that A. J. H. Eckardt has placed in my hands 1,500 shares of the Dominion Manufacturers, Limited, to be passed over to your association. The conditions are that your association will appoint trustees, or a trustee, who will take charge of these shares, and hold them in trust for your association, to be devoted to educational work, as is being done year by year. The dividends only to be used.

The trustee, or trustees, to give bonds to association for the faithful performance of their duties. When this is done and the name of the trustee sent to me, I will forward the shares.

May I suggest that the president and secretary should communicate with the other members of the executive, and receive their consent to appoint the trustees? If, when the association meets in convention, they decide not to accept the shares, they could be returned; but, of course, we would very much regret if they should so determine.

We would appreciate an early reply.

I am, sincerely yours,
(Signed) J. C. VAN CAMP.

On motion of Messrs. Kerr and Clark, this letter was referred to the resolution committee.

Committees Appointed.

The sessional committees were then appointed:
Committee on Membership—J. R. Burland, J. Kerr, W. D. Dunbar, W. T. Clark, J. Thomson.
Committee on Resolutions—W. D. Dunbar, James Nicol, J. W. Neill, R. Macpherson, J. R. Burland.
Committee on Examination—J. Thomson, J. Kerr, A. B. Gardiner, A. Broadfoot, D. J. Clark, Jas. Nicol.

Prof. Hohenschuh, of Iowa City, was introduced and delivered his opening address, which took up the rest of the time that morning.

TUESDAY AFTERNOON, JULY 14.

The afternoon session was opened by an address by Prof. Hohenschuh on "Anatomy of the Organs." At its conclusion and in the absence of R. Macpherson, of Brandon, the secretary read the following paper on "How I Became an Undertaker."

How I Became an Undertaker.

"'How I Became an Undertaker' is the subject I selected from a number of subjects submitted to me by our worthy secretary. During all the time I have been connected with the profession I cannot remember ever having heard of anyone choosing the profession of an undertaker because he had an idea that he would like the work. An aversion to death is, I think, an instinct not only in man but in nearly all the animal world. A cow or a horse displays a great deal of fear at the sight of a dead animal of their own kind, and I have no doubt but that you have noticed on many occasions the great aversion some people have to looking at or touching any dead body.

"I think I was no exception to this myself, and until I had reached the age of 30 years I could have counted on one hand all the bodies of dead people I had seen. Among all the daydreams that I, as a young man, had ever indulged in, I have no recollection of ever having dreamt of being an undertaker. Seven years ago this summer I went home to Scotland to see my mother, whom I had not seen for 26 years, and one of the first questions she asked me after our first greetings, was, 'How did you ever come to be an undertaker?'

"The year 1886, the year following the Riel Rebellion, found a brother and myself homesteading in what was then known as Assiniboia. This year turned out to be one of the hottest and dryest that it has ever been my misfortune to encounter. When the fall came and I expected a crop, there was no crop there. I had to make a living, and my money was all gone. I was broke and pretty well disgusted of farming. So my brother and I sold everything that we had left to any of our neighbors who were willing to purchase, and I am sure they all ought to have jumped at the chance, for very few of them ever paid any of those bills, and I started out to look for a job.

"I landed back in Brandon in May, 1888 (it was from this point I had started out to homestead in 1882). I got work, and started as a carpenter. In the same boarding house with myself was a gentleman well known to most of you. I refer to D. McKillop, of Portage la Prairie, one of our past presidents of the association. He was then working for the old firm of Wilson & Smyth, of Brandon, furniture dealers and undertakers. He was just about to start in business for himself at Rapid City, and Wilson & Smyth were in need of a man to take his place. He prevailed on me to apply for the position, which I did, and was accepted. From that day until the present I have been connected with the same stock, a period of 26 years.

Crude Undertaking.

"For the first year I had no connection with the undertaking. This was looked after by an upholsterer. He was pretty well imbued with the idea that in order to bring up one's nerves and protect one's system it was absolutely necessary to "gin up" every time he had a case. The undertaking done was of the crudest kind. If, at the time I speak of, there was any embalming ever done, it must have been in Winnipeg alone. About a year and a half after starting with the firm mentioned above our undertaker got drinking so badly that his services were anything but satisfactory. Whether he left or was dismissed I do not know, but, at any rate, they asked me to take charge of this part of the work. I did this with a great deal of fear and trembling. Any time now when I am called to attend to a person who has perhaps been dead for some little time before I have been called, and the odor is anything but pleasant, it always recalls my first experiences in the art.

"The first interment I made at the cemetery was in a

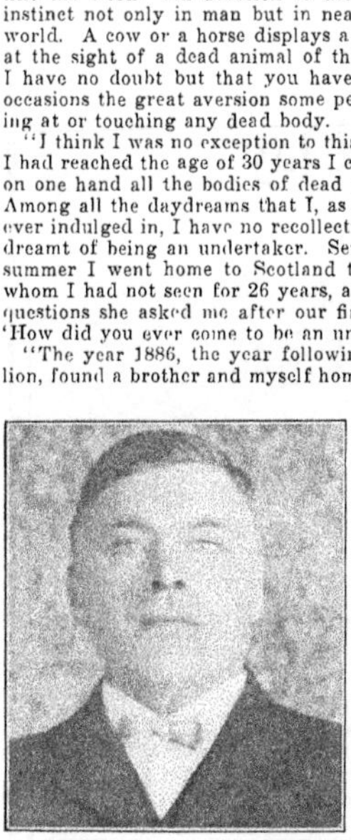

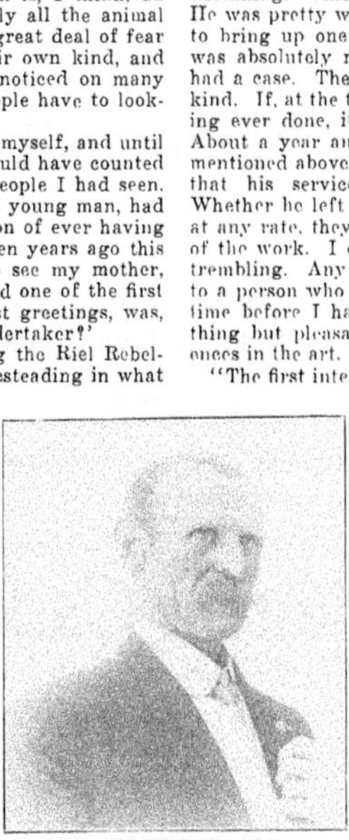

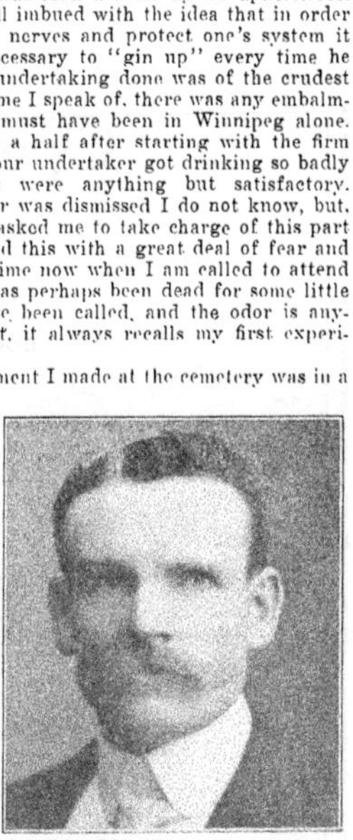

J. R. BURLAND, Rapid City, 1st Vice-President   W. D. DUNBAR, Napinka, President   S. H. ROFF, Emerson, 2nd Vice-President
OFFICERS FOR 1914-15 WESTERN CANADA FUNERAL DIRECTORS' AND EMBALMERS' ASSOCIATION.

Get it at the Western

A Safe, Profitable Place to Buy

All Kinds of Undertakers' Supplies

Open Night and Day

Our Catalogue is with you, if not, a Post Card will bring it.

Give us a trial express order.   Phone Garry 4657.

The Western Casket Co.,
Limited
Winnipeg   Cor. Emily St., & Bannatyne Ave.   Manitoba

No. 22 casket, and I got so flustered when we got to the cemetery that I buried the man with his feet to the West and his head to the East. However, I doubt if there was anyone but myself who discovered the mistake. If they did so, they kept quiet about it, and so did I. Two years ago in order to get a road through an old part of the cemetery they had to disinter some bodies, and our caretaker said to me, "Do you know we found one man buried with his feet to the West?" I at once said, 'I can tell you his name,' and I was correct. After over twenty years my mistake was brought to light again.

"I think it was in the year 1890 that I made my first attempt at embalming and shipping a case to the East with any reasonable expectation of its reaching its destination in a fit state to be viewed by friends. I procured the assistance of a medical student, and asked him to lift the femoral artery, and I injected from this point.

"What I often wonder at now is the amount of success we met with in our early efforts at the art of embalming, as we knew next to nothing about the arterial systems. Often in hunting for an artery we were prepared to swear that we had discovered something out of the common, and that the artery we were trying to locate was minus. We made very little, if any, attempt at trying to withdraw blood. Our first instructors taught that the arteries were empty of blood after death. Probably fortunately for ourselves quite a few of our first cases were in this state, but we soon began to run across cases in which there was blood in the arteries, and plenty of it, and it gave us lots of trouble.

"I have no intention of following out a history of the strides that have been made in embalming since my first attempt. Our association has done a splendid work in putting it easily within the reach of every undertaker in Manitoba to become efficient in his business. Aside from any monetary gain that may come from the practice of embalming I certainly would not want to be an undertaker unless I could care for the dead in a more efficient and practical way than we practised 25 years ago."

Membership Committee Report.

The report of the membership committee was read as follows:

"We, the members of your membership committee, having examined the applications presented to us, recommend the following be received into membership:

"Associate—Albert Edward Treasure, Winnipeg; C. J. Hentgen, Winnipeg; H. S. Tower, Winnipeg; Wesley D. Campbell, Winnipeg.

"Active—A. J. Taylor, Kenora, Ont.; D. Sutherland, Canora, Sask.; Albert F. Farrell, Dauphin; F. Blankstin, Minnedosa.

"Respectfully submitted, J. R. Burland, chairman; W. D. Dunbar, J. Kerr, W. T. Clark, J. Thomson."

President Broadfoot, in a few well chosen words, in his own genial way received the new members into the association.

Some discussion next took place as to the inactivity of the Government in respect to the Embalmers' Act, and a committee composed of R. J. Campbell, A. B. Gardiner and D. J. Clark was appointed on motion of Messrs. Kerr and McKague, to wait on the Board of Health and see what assistance could be secured in bettering conditions in general.

Professor Hohenschuh continued his lecture on anatomy.

WEDNESDAY MORNING, JULY 15,

Professor Hohenschuh delivered a lecture on the circulation.

The following paper on "The Conduct of the Country Funeral" was read by James Nicol, of Shoal Lake.

Conduct of the Country Funeral.

Where you have to go ten or twenty miles to a funeral, always remember to be on time. If the roads are bad, you must make due allowances for that. Of course, if you have been out and prepared the body you will know what to do, but sometimes it happens that you have not been to the house before the day of the funeral and you will have to make your arrangements then. Find out from the family their wishes. Get the pall bearers together at the door where the casket is to come through. Place them in their positions. Put on the arm drapes, give them their gloves and tell them this is their position all the way through. When you come to tak-

"The man behind the gun"
A. B. GARDINER, Winnipeg, re-elected Secy-Treas.
W.C.F.D. & E.A.

ing out the casket, have the bearer at the head assist you in carrying it out, you take the foot, then you are in the lead and when the other bearers take hold you can go to the hearse.

In good weather gather up the pall bearers' hats and put them in the rig they are to ride in. If the weather is cold have them keep their hats on.

When you are ready to start have all the drivers know where they are to be. There is never any need for words, just a little sign with the hand is all that is needed. After the casket is in the hearse have it drive ahead a little so as to give room for the mourners' carriages. See that the mourners are all comfortable in their carriages, then start, leaving the rest of the people to form in the procession as they wish by driving slowly for a while till all have started. (I always ride on the hearse and leave my hat there until ready to start.)

At the grave have your straps divided evenly, so there will be no trouble lowering.

A few words about your personal appearance, and of your hearse. Have your hearse clean. Dress neatly. Have your drivers dress respectably. Always act like a gentleman in your profession and out of it and there will be no trouble keeping your business.

About two years ago I had been out 10 miles with a casket and I was preparing a body. When I came home

Dominion Manufacturers
Limited

MANUFACTURERS OF

Fine Funeral Requisites

We guarantee

The Highest Quality

and the

Quickest Possible Service

*Night or Day Orders
given Prompt Attention*

BRANCHES

The Globe Casket Co., and Branches	London, Ontario
The Semmons & Evel Casket Co., and Branches	Hamilton, Ontario
The National Casket Co.	Toronto, Ontario
Jas. S. Elliot & Son	Prescott, Ontario
Girard & Godin and Branches	Three Rivers, Quebec
Christie Bros. & Co,	Amherst, N. S.

FRED W. COLES   D. M. ANDREWS
General Manager   *Secretary Treasurer*

HEAD OFFICE

468 King Street W., Toronto

in the evening there were some Galicians around. A Galician woman had come, for a coffin for her father, who had died that morning, she said. My wife sold the coffin, had it trimmed and was all ready when I came home. The next day the doctor was called to see the old gentleman and made several visits afterwards. The doctor told me they were using the coffin for a cupboard.

The morning session was concluded with a lecture by Professor Hohenschuh on "Arterial Embalming."

AFTERNOON SESSION, JULY 15.

The afternoon session was opened by Prof. Hohenschuh with the continuation of the morning lecture, coupled with demonstration on the cadaver.

J. Kerr read a paper on "Details of Funeral Conduct."

The professor concluded the afternoon with a lecture on "Cavity Embalming."

During the evening the delegates visited the exhibition as guests of the local funeral supply houses, and enjoyed a most delightful evening.

THURSDAY MORNING, JULY 16.

Prof. Hohenschuh opened with a lecture on "Blood and Discolorations," after which the resolutions committee reported. After discussing their report clause by clause, the following amended report was adopted on motion of Messrs. Dunbar and McKillop:

Resolutions Report.

"We, your resolutions committee, having considered the correspondence and matters left to us for our consideration, beg leave to report as follows:

"In reference to the communication received from J. C. Van Camp re granting stock of the Dominion Manufacturers, Limited, to the number of 1,500 shares, we are strongly of the opinion that it should be left in the hands of the executive for further consideration.

"Your committee would recommend that a hearty vote of thanks be tendered to Controller Cockburn for his address of welcome, and extending to the members of this association the freedom of the City of Winnipeg.

"That this association do extend to the Rev. Mr. Walker their hearty appreciation for his able and instructive address at the opening of our meeting.

"We furthermore move that congratulations be extended to our president for the enthusiastic and able manner in which he has conducted the affairs of this association during the past year.

"That this association extend to our worthy secretary, Brother A. B. Gardiner, a hearty vote of thanks for his able and proficient services during the past year.

"That a resolution be passed thanking Prof. W. H. Hohenschuh for the very able and instructive manner in which he has conducted the lectures and demonstration during our session. We feel that those who have heard him will carry away with them instructions that will be of great assistance to them.

"That a vote of thanks be passed to the several casket companies for the very kind manner in which they entertained the members and their friends of this convention.

"That a resolution be passed thanking all those who have made an effort to make the meetings such a great success.

"Resolved, That the time has arrived when this association should plan a campaign of education among the dealers who have not affiliated, and, therefore, are not licensed embalmers.

"That influence should be brought to bear on the medical health department to have a list of licensed embalmers sent to all health officers.

"That a committee should be appointed to have representatives throughout the province in different districts to be responsible for the directors who are not members, thereby securing, if possible, every director in this province for this association.

(Signed) "W. D. DUNBAR.
"JAMES NICOL.
"D. McKILLOP.
"J. R. BURLAND."

Funds All Right.

The auditors' report was presented, as follows:

"We, your committee appointed to examine the books and vouchers of the secretary-treasurer, beg to report that we have examined same and find them correct, and we wish to compliment our secretary-treasurer on the splendid way in which the proceedings of this association are kept.

"We find the funds of the association in good condition, with $773.94 in the Northern Crown Bank.

"JAMES NICOL.
"JOHN W. NEILL.
"Auditors."

On motion of Messrs. Neill and Clark, the report was adopted.

Greetings From East.

The following letter was then read by the secretary:

"37 Glengarry Avenue,
"Windsor, Ont., July 13, 1914.

"To the Western Canada Funeral Directors' and Embalmers' Association in Convention, Winnipeg:

"Mr. President and Fellow-Members:

"Although unable to be present with you in person, I desire to extend to you all greetings and the sincere hope that you have enjoyed an instructive and interesting series of sessions. In fact, it may be taken as an assured success, if the presence of our old-time friend and co-worker, Prof. Hohenschuh, counts for anything.

"It would have given me the greatest of pleasure to have had the opportunity of renewing old acquaintances, and I wish to tender to all our association my heartfelt thanks and appreciation of their kind remembrances and expressions of good-will so kindly sent me through our worthy secretary.

"I trust the association has advanced in members, influence, and prestige, and is making itself felt as a power in the furthering of the profession in Western Canada.

"Wishing you every success in your endeavors, and again thanking you for your kindness in remembering me.

"Believe me to be, always, fraternally,

(Signed) "GEO. B. BURGESS."

On motion of Messrs. Burland and McKague, the secretary was instructed to suitably acknowledge this kind remembrance of our convention.

Prof. Hohenschuh then addressed the convention on

"The St. Thomas"

Burglar Proof and Water Tight

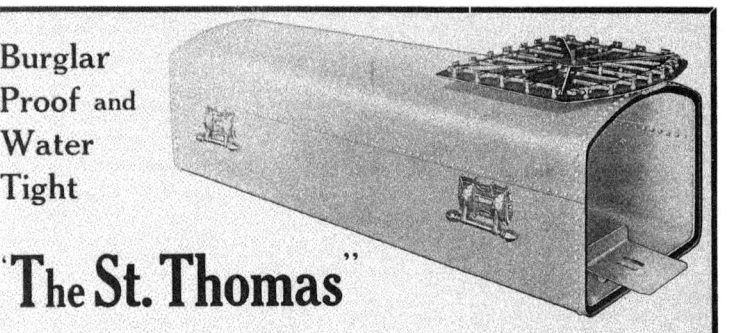

Original, Quick Closing End Vault

MANUFACTURED BY

The St. Thomas Metallic Vault Company, Limited

ST. THOMAS, ONTARIO

The Original Patented Concentrated Fluid

Patented Formula
Strongest and Best

Essential Oil Base, combined with Alcohol, Glycerine, Oxidized Formaldehyde and Boron-Dioxide.

Ask others for their Formula

Special Canadian Agents

National Casket Co.
Toronto, Ont.
GLOBE CASKET CO.
London, Ont.
SEMMENS & EVEL CASKET CO.
Hamilton, Ont.
GIRARD & GODIN
Three Rivers, Que.
JAS. S. ELLIOTT & SON
Prescott, Ont.
CHRISTIE BROS.
Amherst, N.S.

Larger Bottles filled up with water

Egyptian Chemical Co. Boston, U.S.A

Is Yours a Growing Store?

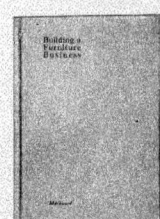

Here are ideas which will help it grow faster. Here are suggestions for the young man starting in business in Northwest Canada, as well as for the dealer with an established trade.

BUILDING A FURNITURE BUSINESS

is a cloth bound book of 205 pages, every one of which contains helpful hints for the furniture dealer. Though written in easy narrative style as the story of "Bobby Burton, Successful Furniture Dealer," the book is neither fiction, theory or dry preachment. The incidents, plans and experiences are woven together from actual practice in widely separated localities.

If your trade is in a rut you will find here a suggestion for a new sales plan, a new advertisement or something to start people talking about your store.

Every man who is looking for new ideas in furniture merchandise and methods will find something worth while in this book.

Postpaid, $1.00.

The Commercial Press, Ltd.
Publishers of The Canadian Furniture World and The Undertaker

"Demi-Surgery," giving in conclusion a fifteen minutes' talk on "Bacteriology and Disinfection."

THURSDAY AFTERNOON, JULY 16.

The afternoon session opened at 2 p.m., with an address by the professor on "Post Mortem Cases."
The election of officers resulted as follows:
Hon. President—A. Broadfoot, Moose Jaw.
President—W. D. Dunbar, Napinka.
First Vice-President—J. R. Burland, Rapid City.
Second Vice-President—S. R. Rott, Emerson.
Secretary-Treasurer—A. B. Gardiner, 531 Main street, Winnipeg.
Sergeant-at-Arms—G. H. McKague, Saskatoon.
On motion of Messrs. Dunbar and McKague, the next convention was settled on for Winnipeg.
On motion of Messrs. Dunbar and Clark, the secretary was authorized to settle all unpaid accounts, and meet all bills until the next convention.
The professor concluded his talks by opening up the Question Box. His able answers proved very valuable and instructive to all.
Examinations were also held for those desiring to secure diplomas. The examination committee later reported as follows:
We, the undersigned members of your examining committee, having examined the papers submitted, beg to advise the granting of diplomas of proficiency to A. E. Treasure, Winnipeg, and H. Reid, Selkirk, they having made the required 75 per cent.

(Signed) J. KERR.
J. THOMSON.
A. BROADFOOT.
D. J. CLARK.
J. NICOL.
A. B. GARDINER.

Convention adjourned.

Saskatchewan's First Conventions

The officers chosen to look after the interests of the Saskatchewan Funeral Directors' and Embalmers' Association during the coming year, who were elected at the first convention of that body, held at Regina on July 27-30, were as follows: Honorary president, A. Broadfoot, Moose Jaw; president, A. E. Young, Saskatoon; first vice-president, George Speers, Regina; second vice-president, M. S. Popplewell, Davidson; sergeant-at-arms, G. H. McKague, Saskatoon; secretary-treasurer, A. C. Howard, Prince Albert; all of them re-elected.
Saskatoon was selected as the place for holding the second annual convention.
Dr. M. M. Seymour, Superintendent of Public Health for Saskatchewan, was largely instrumental in bringing about the successful organization of this association, and the health authorities of the province further showed their interest in the movement by engaging and paying for W. P. Hohenschuh's services as lecturer and demonstrator of the convention. Besides the professor interesting papers were read by James McQuirl, of Moosomin, on "Funeral Management," and A. B. Purdy, on "A Code of Ethics," in which he brought out forcibly the necessity of treating a cheap funeral as conscientiously as an expensive one. This, he said, was the best advertising for the funeral director.
The financial committee reported that the books were in good condition, and well kept and that they showed a balance of $108.

On Thursday morning the examinations were held and twelve out of the thirteen who handed in papers passed successfully. Six of these had a percentage over 90, and one paper, that of H. F. McCallum, of Saskatoon, was found perfect. In the afternoon, at the Clayton Hotel, Honorary President Broadfoot, in behalf of the association, presented Secretary-Treasurer Howard with a handsome gold watch as a token of appreciation of his persistent efforts in promoting the success of the convention. To Mr. Broadfoot's complimentary address Mr. Howard responded gratefully, modestly asserting, however, that he had not done as much as he might have done.
The other successful candidates who passed their examinations were Geo. Bowker, Regina; A. Ross, Assiniboia; J. W. McLean, Moose Jaw; W. E. Everest, Yellow Grass; R. Cantley, Regina; V. H. Wetmore, Yellow Grass; F. T. Durant, Whitewood; Rae, of Rae Bros., Goyan; Ross, of Ross & Luke, Assiniboia; W. J. Nichol, Viscount; P. McKague, Saskatoon; Webb, of Webb & Salmon, Broadview.

Alberta Association's Convention

The eighth annual convention of the Alberta Funeral Directors' Association was held in Nolan Hall, Calgary, July 21 to 23, and will undoubtedly result in much good to the cause of organization and co-operation and the upbuilding of the profession in Canada. W. P. Hohenschuh was the lecturer.
Officers for the ensuing year were elected as follows: President, B. H. Armstrong, Calgary; first vice-president, R. C. Foster, Calgary; second vice-president, J. A. Reid, Banff; secretary and treasurer, H. G. Stone, Red Deer; sergeant-at-arms, C. W. Chase, Strathmore. Executive committee: Mr. Gooder, Olds; Mr. Connelly, Edmonton; Mr. J. Wilson, Okotoks.
The entertainment committee, composed of B. H. Armstrong, chairman; R. C. Foster and Mr. Millard, all of Calgary, gave entertainments in the form of card parties at the houses of Mr. Armstrong and Mr. Millard, which were much enjoyed.

Professional Notes

J. A. Kenny's undertaking establishment at Barrington, N.S., was burned recently.
Openings for undertakers are said to exist in Saskatchewan at Grandora; in Alberta at Edson, Holden, Mirror, and in British Columbia at New Hazelton, Smithers.
A. J. Beaton & Son, Sydney, C.B., have thoroughly overhauled their undertaking establishment and made it up-to-date in every particular, having added funeral parlors, toilet rooms and made their morgue most sanitary and convenient.
James Ross & Son, New Glasgow, N.S., recently added an up-to-date covered delivery wagon to their equipment. They have also made many improvements about their establishment. They have also recently associated with them C. E. Nichols, who is also throwing his energies in the interests of the firm.
An interesting building project is that of the Western Mausoleum Company, Winnipeg, who have obtained from the city of Calgary a cemetery site for the erection of a mausoleum with a capacity for 600 crypts. The building will be of reinforced concrete construction with stone facings. The crypts will be lined with marble.

We Invite the Trade to Visit us at
The Prince George Hotel

During the 31st Annual Convention of the
Canadian Embalmers Association
Toronto, Sept. 8 to 11

We shall have on display at the Prince George, a new CRYSTAL CASKET possessing features with which you should be acquainted. Let us explain it to you.

Make OUR headquarters YOUR headquarters

CENTRAL CASKET COMPANY

Bridgeburg, Ont. R. S. Flint — Canadian Representative: 241 Fern Ave., Toronto
Telephone 126 Telephone Parkdale 3257

No Undertaker Should Overlook

the fact that he can make a full gallon of fluid of standard strength from each sixteen-ounce bottle of RE-Concentrated Dioxin. Re-Concentrated Dioxin costs no more per bottle than any standard concentrated fluid, but it is twice as strong—in other words, there are twice as many ounces of preservation in a bottle of RE-Concentrated Dioxin as there are in any bottle of merely concentrated fluid.

If economy were the only recommendation for RE-Concentrated Dioxin, however, we should not urge it upon our patrons.

As a matter of fact, it is easy to explain and equally easy to demonstrate the fact that the fluid thus produced gives a far better cosmetic effect and produces a far more life-like body than possibly could be produced by any raw formaldehyde concentrated fluid.

This is because RE-Concentrated Dioxin has a double base. When diluted to make a full gallon of fluid to the bottle, its main base is peroxide, with a secondary base of purified formaldehyde (formochloral).

Every funeral director knows that peroxide of hydrogen is the best bleacher known to chemical science. Not everyone realizes, however, that peroxide of hydrogen has blood solvent qualities far in excess of any other chemical yet discovered which is suitable for use in embalming fluid.

Peroxide of hydrogen is composed of two atoms of oxygen and two atoms of hydrogen. Since oxygen is fifteen times heavier than hydrogen, fifteen-sixteenths of the atomic weight of peroxide of hydrogen, therefore, is oxygen.

Every embalmer knows that venous blood is much darker in color, is much more sluggish and much heavier than arterial blood.

What is the difference between the two?

Arterial blood is merely venous blood, which has been purified in the lungs, which has been lightened in color and rendered vastly more fluid by the oxygen which the lungs have extracted from the air we breathe.

Since fifteen-sixteenths of the atomic weight of peroxide of hydrogen is oxygen, it must be apparent, therefore, that the oxygen in the extra rich peroxide in Dioxin has a tendency to exercise the same purifying and solvent qualities upon the dark, discolored venous blood after death as the oxygen which the lungs extract from the air we breathe has upon the venous blood in life.

The result is that much more blood can be drained from a body in which RE-Concentrated Dioxin is injected than is possible from a body in which raw formaldehyde is used and in which the astringent qualities of the formaldehyde have sealed up the discolored blood corpuscles in the capillaries.

Putty color is caused by raw formaldehyde fluid sealing up the discolored corpuscles of the blood in the capillaries. It is inevitable where raw formaldehyde fluids are used unless exceeding care is used to drain blood. And even then there is great danger.

RE-Concentrated Dioxin is distinctly the most modern and the most scientific embalming fluid on the market, as well as the most economical. The progressive funeral director will not hesitate, but will order a trial shipment.

RE-Concentrated DIOXIN

H. S. ECKELS & CO. 1922 Arch St., Philadelphia, Pa.
241 Fern Ave., Toronto, Ont., Can.

Important to Ontario Embalmers

The Ontario Board of Embalmers' Examiners met on the 10th, 11th and 12th of August in the Parliament Buildings at Toronto, at which Secretary James Torrance presented over 160 applications, which were carefully considered and passed upon by the Board.

Preliminary preparations were made for holding examinations on the 11th of September, and the secretary was instructed to send a copy of the accompanying circular to every undertaker or embalmer, who had not complied with the first circular sent out in the early part of July.

The Furniture World and The Undertaker is advised to counsel all undertakers and embalmers in the province that it is very important that every embalmer wishing to secure a certificate of qualification should attend to this matter before the next meeting of the board, which will be on Wednesday, September 9th.

Nearly 800 circulars were sent out in July and less than 200 replies were returned. As the full measure of the Act will come into force on October 1, it is essential that every embalmer in Ontario be possessed either of a license or permit by that date, also he will incur a penalty of $50 for any case he handles after that date.

The following is the circular sent out by the board:

The Board of Examiners,
Milverton, Ont., August 15th, 1914.

Dear Sir:—

Early in July I mailed you a circular letter, together with a list of questions and form of application, requesting that you fill in the answers to these questions as well as the application and return to me with the necessary fee before August 1st. Several of the embalmers have complied with this request, and their applications are now being considered by the Board, but up to the present time I have not received yours, and thinking, perhaps, you have laid it aside or overlooked it, I desire to remind you of the necessity of filling it in carefully and mailing it to me at once, as no person can be permitted under the Act to carry on the business of embalming without a license or permit from the Provincial Board of Examiners. The Board are not desirous of dealing harshly with any embalmer, and will certainly deal in a very generous manner with those now engaged in the business, but you cannot expect to get a license if you do not supply the information asked for and forward your application and fee.

I also desire to inform you that all those carrying on the business of embalming in Ontario prior to May 6th, 1914, and who have the necessary qualifications, will be granted a certificate or permit, but that all assistants whose experience did not extend back prior to May 6th, 1912, will have to go before the board for examination before they will be entitled to receive a certificate of qualification and license.

If you have an assistant, whose experience dates back prior to May 6th, 1912, and who may be desirous of obtaining a certificate of qualification, have him write me for an application form and, if the Board finds him well qualified, he will receive his license and certificate.

There appears to be some confusion as to the fees and, in order to make it clear, I will explain the matter fully.

1st. For those who are engaged in the business of embalming and owned the business prior to May 6th, 1914, and all experienced assistants engaged in the business prior to May 6th, 1912, the fee for certificate of qualification or permit (as the Board may determine) will be ten dollars ($10).

2nd. For all assistants whose experience does not date back past May 6th, 1912, and all new applicants, the fee will be twenty dollars ($20).

These fees will entitle the applicants to a certificate of qualification and a license. The certificate will be nicely lithographed and it is expected the applicant will have it framed and displayed in his place of business. The license will hold good for one year, and must be renewed yearly, the annual renewal fee will not exceed $4. (This license is in addition to the license required by the Provincial Board of Health.)

I would also draw your attention particularly to this fact, that this Board has been appointed by the Government, and has no connection with the Canadian Embalmers' Association, and believe that you have received value for any fees which you may have paid to that association, but wish to make it clear that any fees which you have paid to the association have no bearing whatever on the fee which we now ask for a provincial license. We heartily approve of the work of the association, and hope the undertakers of the province will loyally support it.

The Canadian Embalmers' Association are conducting a school on embalming this year in the anatomical section of the Toronto University building, commencing Tuesday, September 1st, and continuing for one week. The convention follows on September 8th, 9th and 10th. The school will be under the direction of Prof. Horace Moll, president International College of Embalming and Sanitation, Chicago, Ill., who will also lecture and demonstrate before the convention, and I would advise all who purpose writing on the examination to attend this school and convention. The Canadian Embalmers' Association will not conduct an examination of candidates this year, but the Government Board of Examiners will conduct an examination in the same building in which the convention is held on Friday, September 11th, commencing at 9 o'clock in the morning, for all those who wish to take an examination for the Government license, and I would ask all those who desire to take this examination to write me enclosing the prescribed fee at as early a date as possible.

For the convenience of those who may wish to see me in connection with any matter pertaining to the Board, I may say that I will be at my temporary office in the Parliament Buildings, on Wednesday, Thursday and Friday of convention week, and will be pleased to have you call.

Kindly forward your application and fee promptly, and oblige,

Yours truly,
JAMES TORRANCE, Secretary.

Geo. B. Thomson, son of John Thomson, the well-known funeral director of Fergus, Ont., has purchased the undertaking business of Thomson & Morrison, of Fernie, B.C. Among the changes to be made at once by Mr. Thomson is the erection of a modern funeral chapel. This chapel will have cathedral art stained glass windows; drop concealed lights will also be used, and when completed it will be one of the finest in Western Canada.

T. A. Cornett, of Hosmer, B.C., has decided to discontinue the undertaking business. He has sold his stock of goods and equipment to G. B. Thomson, of Fernie, B.C.

CANADIAN FURNITURE WORLD AND THE UNDERTAKER   September, 1914

Index to Advertisements

A
Alaska Feather & Down Co. ...53
Albrough, J. P. ...30
Ault & Wiborg Co. ...88

B
Baetz Bros. & Co. ...22
Batavia Clamp Co. ...i.b.c.
Bell Furniture Co. ...26
Berlin Table Mfg. Co. ...10

C
Canada Furn. Mfg. ...55
Can. Rattan Chair Co. ...31
Canadian School of Embalming ...104
Can. H. W. Johns-Manville Co. ...19
Central Casket Co. ...102
Chesley Furniture Co. ...47
Chair Craft Co. ...11
Colleran Patent Spring Mat. Co. ...48

D
Dominion Casket Co. ...101
Dominion Mfrs., Limited ...98

E
Eckels & Co., H. S. ...102
Egyptian Chemical Co. ...100
Elmira Interior Woodwork Co. ...12
Eyet Casket Co. ...92
Excelsior Plate Glass ...88

F
Farquharson-Gifford Co. ...21
Fischman Mattress Co. ...88

G
Gale & Son, Geo. ...38
Globe-Wernicke Co. ...19
Gold Medal Furniture Mfg. Co. ...50
Gendron Wheel Co. ...89
Gibbard Furniture Co. ...23
Griffin Curled Hair Co. ...51

H
Hespeler Furn. Co. ...44
Hourd & Co. ...22

I
Ideal Bedding Co. ...56
Imperial Furniture Co. ...20
Imperial Rattan Co. ...17
Ives Modern Bedstead Co. ...o.b.c.

K
Kawneer Mfg. Co. ...31

Kindel Bed Co., Limited ...29
Knechtel Furniture Co. ...26-27
Kohn, J. & J. ...54

L
Leggett & Platt Spring Bed Co. ...18
Lippert Table Co., Geo. J ...54

M
Malcolm Furniture Co., Andrew ...45
Matthews Bros. ...50
Menford Mfg. Co. ...25
Melagan Furniture Co., Geo. o.f.c.
Montreal Upholstering Co. ...52
Mundell, J. C., & Co. ...i.f.c.
Moffat Stove Co. ...46

N
N. A. Bent Chair Co. ...i.f.c.

O
Ontario Spring Bed ...16
Onward Mfg. Co. ...50
Oliver & Sons, J. ...42
Orillia Furniture Co. ...24

R
Robertson, P. L., Mfg. Co. ...i.b.c.

S
Shafer, D. L. & Co. ...20
Steele, James, Limited ...89
Steel Furnishing Co. ...88
Stratford Brass Co. ...20
Stratford Chair Co. ...15
Stratford Mfg. Co. ...23
St. Thomas Metallic Vault Co. ...100
Standard Bedding Co. ...48

T
Textileather Co. ...46

V
Victoriaville Bedding Co. ...32-33
Victoriaville Chair Co. ...36-37
Victoriaville Furniture Co. ...34-35

W
Watson Mfg. Co., John ...52
Walker & Co., B. ...49
Western Casket Co. ...99
Weisglass, S., Limited ...43
Whitworth & Restall ...89

Undertakers Shipping Directory

ONTARIO

Aurora—
  Dunham, Charles.
Barrie—
  Smith, G. G. & Co.
Brockville—
  Quirmbach, Geo. R., 162 King St.
Brooklin
  Disney, R. S.
Campbellford—
  Irwin, James.
Campden —
  Hansel, Albion.
Clinton—
  Walker, Wesley.
Coboconk—
  Greenley, A.
Copper Cliff—
  Boyd, W. C.
Dungannon—
  Sproul, William
Dutton—
  Schultz, B. L.
Elmira—
  Dreisinger, Chris.

Fenelon Falls—
  Deyman, L. & Son.
Fenwick—
  H. A. Metler.
Fergus—
  Armstrong, M. F.
  Thomson, John & Son.
Fort William—
  Cameron & Co., 711 Victoria.
  Morris, A.
Haileybury—
  Thorpe Bros.
Galt—
  Anderson, J. & Son.
Hamilton—
  Green Bros., 124 King St. E.
  Robinson, J. H. & Co., 19-21 John St. N.
Hanover—
  Wunnenberg, Norman.
Hastings—
  Howard, P. N.
Hepworth—
  Downs, E. J.
Inwood—
  Lorriman, E. S.
Kemptville—
  McCaughey, Geo. A.

Kenora—
  Horn & Taylor.
Kingston—
  Corbett, S. S.
Lakefield—
  Hendren, Geo. G.
Little Current—
  Sims, J. G.
Markdale—
  Oliver, M.
Newmarket—
  Millard, J. H.
North Augusta—
  Wilson, J. R.
North Bay—
  St. Pierre, E.
Oakwood—(Mariposa Station G.T.R.) Wilmot F. Webster.
Ohsweken—
  Johnson, F. L.
Oshawa—
  Disney Bros.
  Luke Bros.
Ottawa—
  Ch. R. Woodburn, 586 Bank St. Tel. Carling 600 and 1009.
  Rogers & Burney, 283 Laurier Ave. W.
Petrolia—
  Steadman Bros.
Port Arthur —
  Collin Wood, 36 Arthur St.
  Morris, A.
Prescott—
  Runkin, H. & Son.
Renfrew—
  O'Connor, Wm.
St. Mary's—
  N. L. Brandon.
St. Thomas—
  Williams, P. R. & Sons, 519 Talbot St.
Seaforth, Ont.
  W. T. Box & Co.
Scotland—
  Vaughan, Jos. H. M.
Sudbury—
  Henry, J. G.
Toronto—
  Cobbledick, N. B., 2068 Queen St. East and 1508 Danforth Ave. Private Ambulance.
  Stone, Daniel (formerly H. Stone & Son), 525 Sherbourne St.
  Vancamp, J. C., 30 Bloor St. West.
Waterloo—
  Klipper Undertaking Co.
Welland—
  Sutherland, G. W.
Woodstock—
  Meadows, T. & Sons.
  Mack, Paul.

QUEBEC

Buckingham—
  Paquet, Jos.

Cowansville—
  Judson, M. B.
Montreal—
  Tees & Co., 912 St. Catherine St. West.
St. Hyacinthe—
  Cadorette, Mongeau & Leary.
St. Laurent—
  Gougeon, Jos.

NEW BRUNSWICK

Petitcodiac—
  Jonah, D. Allison.
Woodstock—
  Van Wart, Jacob.

NOVA SCOTIA

Ferrona—
  Fraser, D. & Co.
Halifax—
  Snow & Co., 90 Argyle St.
Sydney, C.B.—
  Beaton, A. J. & Son, 374-384 George St.

MANITOBA

Brandon—
  Campbell & Campbell.
  Vincent & McPherson.
Souris—
  McCulloch, Wm.
Swan River—
  Paull, Geo.
Winnipeg—
  Bardal, A. S., 834 Sherbrooke
  Thompson, J. C., 501 Main
  Clark-Leatherdale Co., Ltd., 232 Kennedy St.

SASKATCHEWAN

Gull Lake—
  Morrow, Fred. A.
Saskatoon—
  Young, A. E.
Kamsack—
  Russell, G. E. I.
Lanigan—
  Robertson, Wm.
Moose Jaw—
  The Bellamy Co.
  Broadfoot Bros.
Rush Lake—
  Friesen, John M.
Prince Albert—
  Howard, A. C.
  Hadley, C. L.
Regina—
  Speers, George.
Semans—
  Haygarth, Jas.
Welwyn—
  Leavens, Merritt.
Wolseley —
  Barber, B.

ALBERTA

Calgary—
  Graham & Buscomb, 611 Centre St.
Castor—
  Winter, W. G.

BRITISH COLUMBIA

Hosmer—
  Cornett, T. A.
Victoria—
  Hana & Thompson, 827 Pandora Ave.

Canadian School of Embalming
Instruction in Practical Embalming and Funeral Directing
PREPARATION FOR EXAMINATIONS
ENTER AT ANY TIME
R. U. STONE   32 Carlton Street
Principal   Toronto

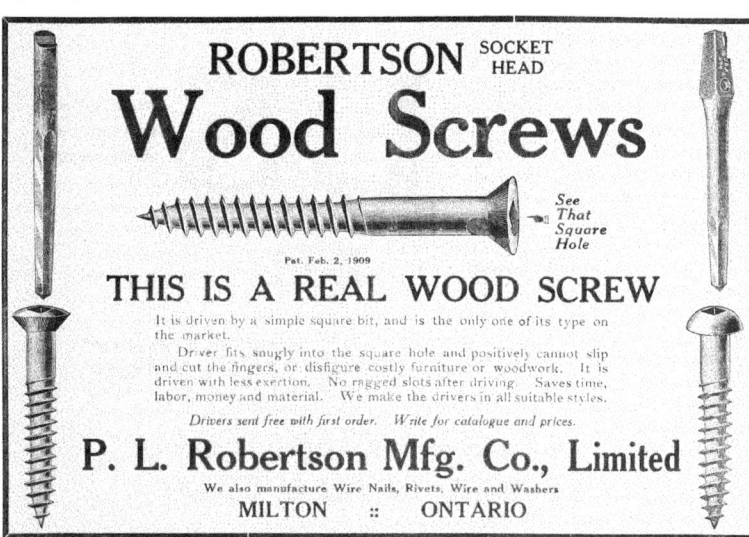

September, 1914   CANADIAN FURNITURE WORLD AND THE UNDERTAKER

ROBERTSON SOCKET HEAD Wood Screws

See That Square Hole

Pat. Feb. 2, 1909

THIS IS A REAL WOOD SCREW

It is driven by a simple square bit, and is the only one of its type on the market.

Driver fits snugly into the square hole and positively cannot slip and cut the fingers, or disfigure costly furniture or woodwork. It is driven with less exertion. No ragged slots after driving. Saves time, labor, money and material. We make the drivers in all suitable styles.

Drivers sent free with first order. Write for catalogue and prices.

P. L. Robertson Mfg. Co., Limited

We also manufacture Wire Nails, Rivets, Wire and Washers

MILTON :: ONTARIO

For Every Furniture Man

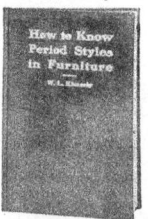

A Helpful, Thoroughly Practical Book, Written by an Authority—

HOW TO KNOW PERIOD STYLES IN FURNITURE

150 Pages   317 Illustrations

Price, $1.50

Designers will find illustrations of the work of celebrated designers of history. Examples are taken from the recognized collections and museums of the world.
Buyers—The book is arranged for easy reference with the distinguishing features of each period clearly shown.
Salesmen—The information in "How to Know Period Styles" will enable you to talk authoritatively on the subject.
Students—The confusing element has been eliminated, but all necessary information is included.

Send us $1.50. Keep the book 10 days, and if it isn't worth the price, return it and get your money back.

The Commercial Press

Publishers The Canadian Furniture World and The Undertaker
32 Colborne Street, Toronto

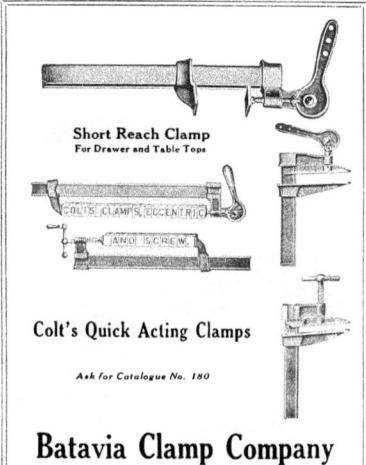

Short Reach Clamp
For Drawer and Table Tops

Colt's Quick Acting Clamps

Ask for Catalogue No. 180

Batavia Clamp Company

147 Center Street, Batavia, N.Y., U.S.A.

ES

"Regal" Beds
right, regal SERVICE

form an unbeatable combination, standing out pre-eminently the best in Canada

ves Modern Bedstead Co., Limited
Montreal   Cornwall   Winnipeg

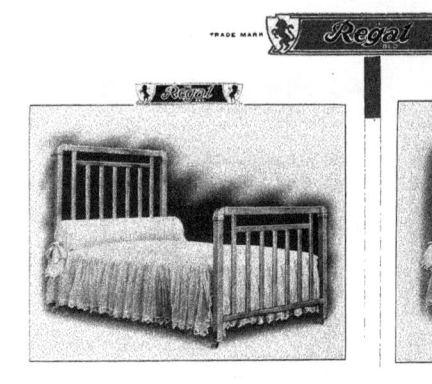

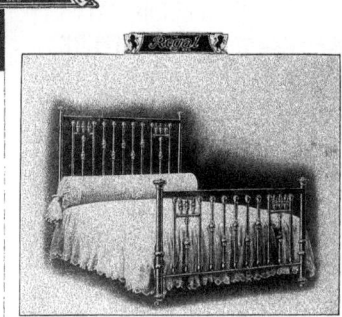

Vol. 4 No. 10   OCTOBER, 1914

Canadian Furniture World
AND THE UNDERTAKER

Published by the Commercial Press, Limited, 32 Colborne Street, Toronto

Who also Publish: The Retail Grocer and Provisioner, The Retail Druggist, Canadian Hardware Journal, Canadian Manufacturer, Canadian Builder and Carpenter, The Canadian Clay-Worker, Motoring and Motor Trade, Good Roads of Canada, The Railway Journal of Canada, The Canadian Nurse.

No Let-up in "Stratford Chair" Progressiveness

STRATFORD Chairs have, for years, been made as well as brains and painstaking effort could make them. They are the same to-day, with greater variety, and more artistic beauty in designing. They will be the same in selling value years from now, and will continue to sell and make good profits for dealers who retain the progressive spirit.

"Energize" your business this season by stocking **more** "Stratford" Chairs.

Made in
Stratford, Ont.
the Furniture
City.

Mr. Furniture Dealer:

Are you making the most of your opportunity of selling the householders the indoor furniture they now need?

NOW is the time to feature Living Room Furniture. WE HAVE IT, in either standard Mission designs, or the newer Jacobean, in cheap and higher-priced grades. Besides this is our regular line of fancy chairs and rockers, couches, davenports and novelties.

Write for illustrations and prices. We lend electro cuts free of charge, with descriptive matter, for advertising.

JOHN C. MUNDELL & CO., Limited
Elora, Ontario

Stand by the Red Cross

Antiseptic Line

The bedding that is doing so much for the comfort of those Canadians who are still enjoying the privilege of their homes.

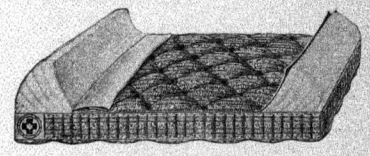

The Antiseptic Bedding Company
187-189 Parliament St., Toronto, Ontario

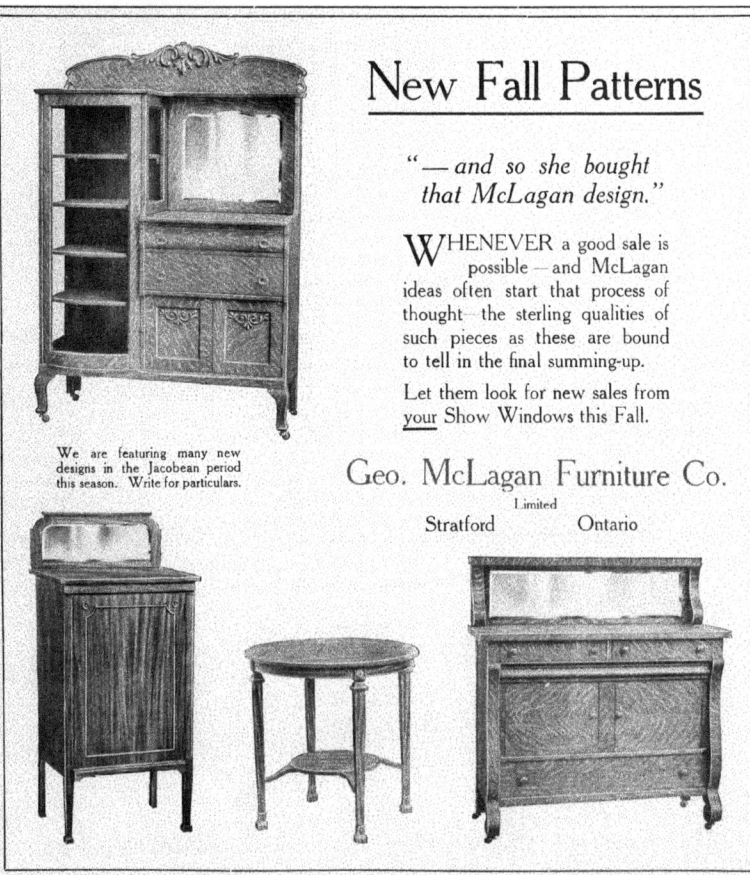

STRATFORD

New Fall Patterns

"— and so she bought that McLagan design."

WHENEVER a good sale is possible — and McLagan ideas often start that process of thought — the sterling qualities of such pieces as these are bound to tell in the final summing-up.

Let them look for new sales from your Show Windows this Fall.

We are featuring many new designs in the Jacobean period this season. Write for particulars.

Geo. McLagan Furniture Co.
Limited
Stratford   Ontario

"Ontario" Beds are Staple Sellers

THIS sturdy design embodies plenty of quiet, lasting style, richness of appearance and excellent value for the money---that "Ontario" quality which makes the line so popular everywhere.

No. 1038 Illustrated. Pillars, 2½ inches; bottom rod, 2 inches; fillers, 2 inches; head, 58 inches; foot, 37 inches. A very massive ornamental brass bed. Sizes made: 3 ft., 3 ft. 6 in., 4 ft., 4 ft. 6 in.

All Ontario Beds are lacquered by a new process which ensures a permanent finish.

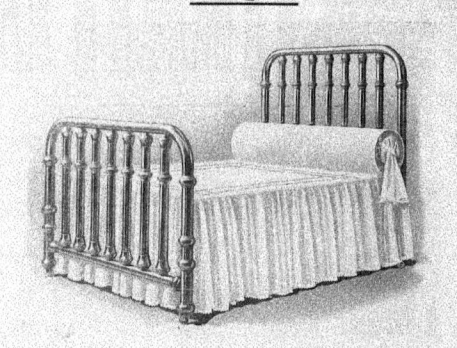

The Ontario Spring Bed & Mattress Company, Limited
LONDON   *The Largest Bedding House in Canada*   ONTARIO

Made in Canada

Why buy Duofolds and Revolving Davenports in the United States, when you could buy the same goods from us, manufactured in Canada, for the same prices. Our new line of Duofolds consists of 40 different designs and also 10 new Duofold Suites, with chairs to match. Our goods are guaranteed. They also have a much more superior finish than the goods from the United States.

We are manufacturing Duofolds from $19.50 up to $50.00

Frame: Quartered Cut Oak or Mahogany

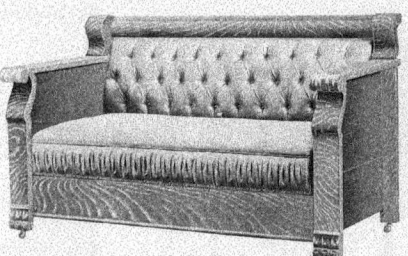

Finish; F.O. Golden or Mahogany, RUBBED and POLISHED

No. 80. Duofold

The Montreal Upholstering Co.   1611-1613 Clarke Street   Montreal, Can.

October, 1914   CANADIAN FURNITURE WORLD AND THE UNDERTAKER

STRATFORD

Canada's *Only* "Imperial" Battery
of Original Designs in Rattan Furniture

Elegance, strength, lightness of weight, durability and economy make Imperial Rattan Furniture adaptable for use at any time or place, in perfect harmony with any furnishings or color scheme.

The demand for furniture that possesses all the desirable features in appearance and quality, with lowness in price, will be particularly pronounced this Fall. Try out the "Imperial" Line.

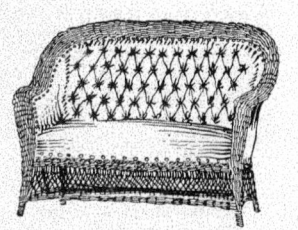

See that it's made in Stratford

Imperial Rattan Company, Limited
Stratford   Ontario

Here's a Bed Spring that Will Not Sag

The study of the spring construction shown below will explain **why** L. & P. Springs will not sag. There is no side pull---no strain to wear out the wire. The resistance is natural, up and down, and the weight is supported where it rests without affecting the entire spring.

Leggett & Platt Single Cone Bed Springs

have a pliable mattress surface which is obtained by our method of fastening at the bottom of each coil. This is fully covered by patents.

Get our prices and stock this reliable and profitable line.

The Leggett & Platt Spring Bed Co., Limited

Windsor - Ontario

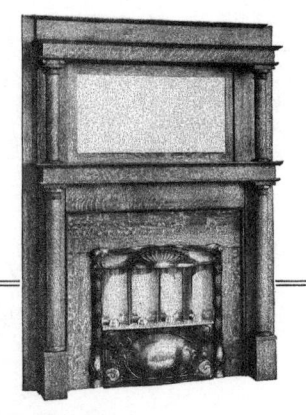

This Mantel is Really Inexpensive

CONSIDER this from a sales standpoint, Mr. Dealer :

Elmira Electric Grate Mantels are all ready to set up and connect with the wiring in the room. They are handsome in appearance and are constructed as coal fuel mantels, but do not require a chimney or tiling. The user saves this initial expense and again saves on the low cost of electric power. You'll like the "Elmira" proposition when you know the details. May we send them?

We also manufacture Tables, Office Furniture, Bookcases, and Special Goods in Oak, Mahogany and Birch.

Elmira Interior Woodwork Co., Limited

Elmira - Ontario

STRATFORD

The Renewed Interest in the Home Surroundings, is Your *"Globe-Wernicke"* Opportunity

ALL the folks are back from their vacation. With the long evenings and a cheerful fire burning, most people will spend their "after suppers" reading and enjoying home comforts.

Certainly no better time to demonstrate the utility, adaptability and beauty of Globe-Wernicke Sectional Bookcases.

A window display of two or three combinations of this world-known make now, should greatly increase your Fall and Holiday trade.

You'll like the Globe-Wernicke proposition all through.

Just ask for a copy of our well illustrated catalog and get busy.

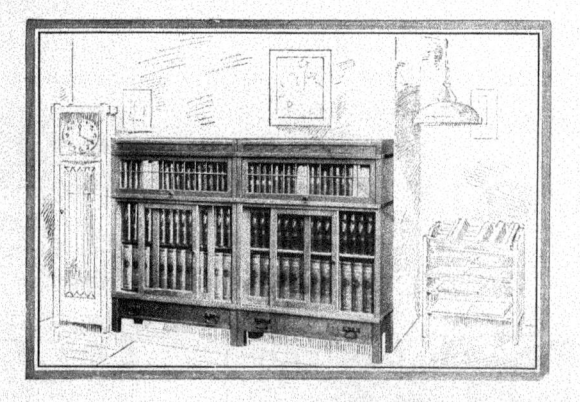

The Globe-Wernicke Co., Ltd.

None better made!
None easier to sell!
None surer to satisfy!

THAT'S the experience of hundreds of 'GALE' customers in all parts of Canada.

THAT'S why the 'GALE' business continues to grow year after year.

'GALE' goods are always a 'good buy.' Write for our catalogue and newest designs.

GEO. GALE & SONS
LIMITED

Waterville, Quebec

Montreal   Toronto   Winnipeg

Iron and Brass Bedsteads
Institution Beds

Cribs and Cots
Steel Couches and Davenports

DIXIE
NoTuft Mattress
Kapok Mattress

Astoria Box Spring and Other Specialties

The Cuban Spring
Iron Frame Springs
Spiral Springs

STRATFORD

A Farquharson-Gifford Design

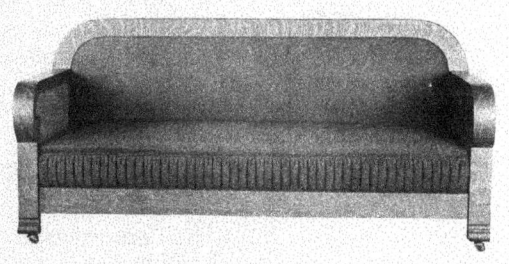

THE weak points in most Davenport Beds are in the mechanical features and the upholstering. Not so with the "F-G." Line. The spring and mattress turn out with one motion—no tugging or heavy lifting, no sharp sag in the middle of the mattress—the bed is soft and restful at night, and converts into the most inviting davenport for use during the day.

Every "F-G." Davenport Bed is *scientifically* upholstered. We employ materials and workmanship that ensure a finished product of exceptional wearing powers.

We specialize on Davenport Beds, Couches, and Living-room Furniture

When ordering Davenport Beds from Stratford, Remember to order "F-G."

The Farquharson-Gifford Co., Limited
Stratford   Ontario

Textileather

looks like real leather and gives better service than any other furniture covering made

We'll Send You Samples

Judge Textileather first hand. A card will bring you liberal samples of this tough, richly-grained artificial leather. **Send it to-day.**

Textileather Co., 212 Fifth Ave., New York

Write Direct, or to   **Frank Schmidt**   Berlin, Ontario

Quality and Exclusiveness in Brass Furniture Trimmings

ORDER "Stratford" Brass Trimmings because they are absolutely exclusive in design.

Because we carry a large range of period and modern effects for immediate delivery.

Because the prices are always consistent.

Because we stock, or can make to order, **anything** you require.

Write for Particulars

The Stratford Brass Co.
Limited
Stratford   -   Ontario

The Four Aces in Folding Card Tables
are held by the
"Peerless"

1. Lightness of weight and ease of handling.
2. Small space required when folded—twelve folded occupy the same space as one standing.
3. Great strength and durability and finished appearance.
4. The lowest price for the best quality.
5. Stock up now for the card playing season. Orders shipped immediately.

Hourd & Co., Limited
Wholesale Furniture Manufacturers
London, Canada
Sole Canadian Licensees and Manufacturers

"Peerless" Folding Tables

STRATFORD

Most Used Portable Seating in Canada
The *Stratford* Make

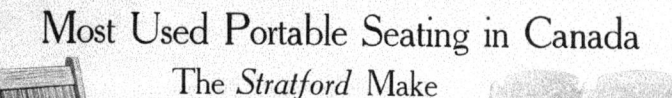

WITH such a reputation behind this line, many dealers find it an easy matter to obtain contracts for the furnishing of Portable Seating for various institutions in their towns, many sales bringing upwards of $100 net profit.

Write to-day and let us tell you how Furniture Dealers are getting this profitable business.

Stratford Manufacturing Co., Limited

Genuine Tennessee Cedar   Moth Proof

A good moth-proof Cedar Chest is a very practical convenience — one that every family should possess. A **Shafer** design displayed in the show window with a card explaining its advantages, usually results in profitable sales.

Prices for the asking

D. L. Shafer & Co.
St. Thomas · Ontario

IF you know a Furniture Dealer or Funeral Director in Canada who is not receiving the Canadian Furniture World and The Undertaker as a subscriber you will favor the publishers by sending the address to 32 Colborne St., Toronto.

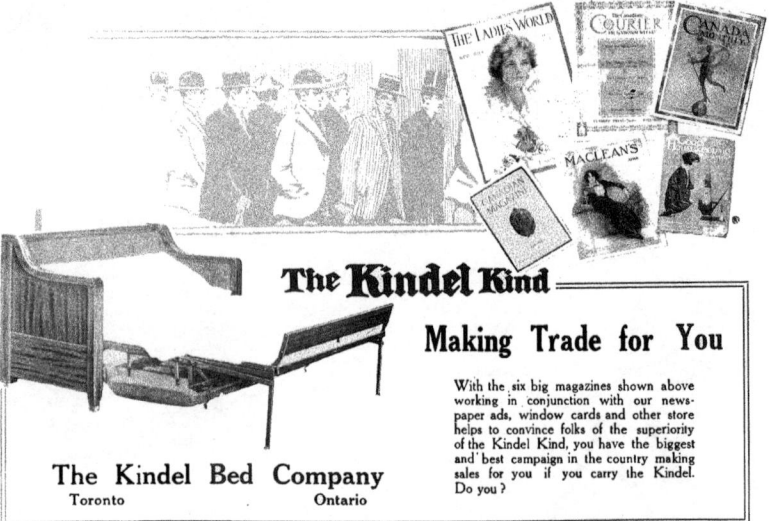

The Kindel Kind

Making Trade for You

With the six big magazines shown above working in conjunction with our newspaper ads, window cards and other store helps to convince folks of the superiority of the Kindel Kind, you have the biggest and best campaign in the country making sales for you if you carry the Kindel. Do you?

The Kindel Bed Company
Toronto   Ontario

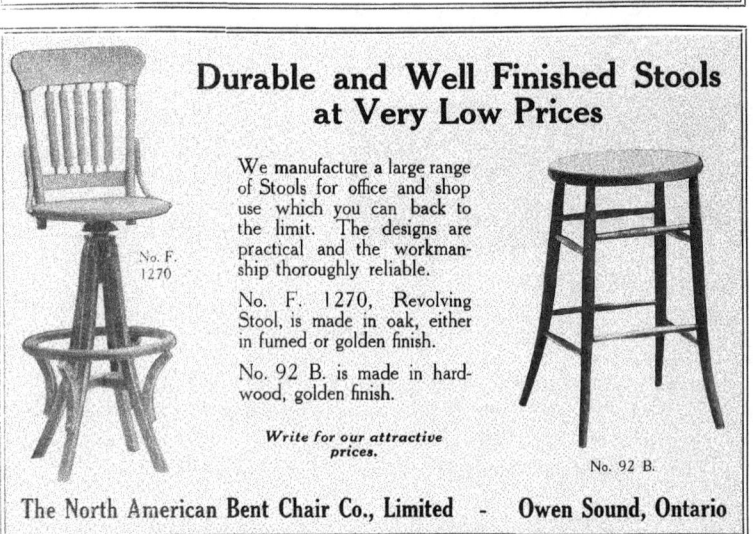

Durable and Well Finished Stools at Very Low Prices

We manufacture a large range of Stools for office and shop use which you can back to the limit. The designs are practical and the workmanship thoroughly reliable.

No. F. 1270, Revolving Stool, is made in oak, either in fumed or golden finish.

No. 92 B. is made in hardwood, golden finish.

Write for our attractive prices.

No. F. 1270

No. 92 B.

The North American Bent Chair Co., Limited - Owen Sound, Ontario

The Most Salable of
Fall and Holiday Goods

THE best of the less expensive lines of Furniture---those that pass the final quality tests---will be by far the biggest sellers this season.

This condition will accentuate the demand for Meaford goods---the line that breaks sales records every season despite the times.

When a customer sizes up a piece of Meaford Surface Oak or Surface Mahogany, the exquisite graining, rich tone, non-crackable and non-chippable finish are the factors that invariably close the sale.

We are featuring for this month, many new designs in *Music Cabinets, Desks and Bookcases, Jardiniere Stands, Pedestals, Centre Tables, Bookracks, Smoking Sets, Etc., Etc.*

Prices gladly sent on request

The Meaford Manufacturing Company, Limited
Meaford, Ontario

BAETZ BROTHERS AND COMPANY
BERLIN :: ONTARIO

"Adam Brothers" Period
Drawing Room Suite

Made of solid Cuban Mahogany, finished in old English brown mahogany.

Other suites in Elizabethan and Chippendale periods.

Makers of Diners, Bed Room Chairs, Parlor Suites, Living Room Suites and English Bungalow Furniture

---

Price Reduced

EUREKA
Electric Vacuum Cleaner

The same high quality—the same guarantee — the same $45.00 Machine now **$39.50**

Price Winnipeg and West $44.50

Canadian housewives showed their unstinted appreciation of the *Eureka* during the past year by increasing our sales quite beyond our expectations. Dealers everywhere met with the greatest success.

With a reduction of $5.50 in the retail price, made possible by our increased production, the *Eureka* is now way beyond competition as a profit-maker.

Write for our trade offer

Onward Manufacturing Company
Berlin, Ontario

"COLLERAN'S"
ALL-STEEL LINE

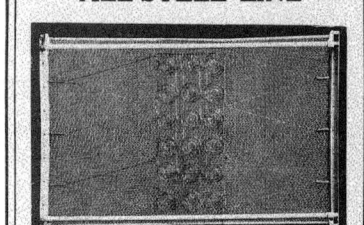

The Line of Better Profit

Colleran Spring Mattresses are more than a Bed "Spring," they perform half the service of the mattress also. A demonstration of the **Colleran** invariably makes the sale. Why not show them on your floor, Mr. Dealer?

Write for prices. Electros furnished dealers free

Colleran Patent Spring Mattress Co.
TORONTO, ONT.

KNECHTEL

No. 615

Another New One

Never before have we had such a large number of new patterns for the Fall trade, and almost without exception suggested or selected by our travellers—the men who have to sell them—they are surely what you want.

No. 615 is a Winner

We have selected this dresser to show you, because it is big, bold, handsome and low priced—made entirely of plain oak—good Knechtel quality of construction throughout. The case measures 42 x 21 inches and the mirror 30 x 24 inches. List price, golden varnish or fumed finish, **$44.25**; polish finish, **$47.25**. Chiffonier, dressing table and commode to match.

THE KNECHTEL FURNITURE CO., LIMITED
HANOVER - ONTARIO

A Good Display

of

Victoriaville Upholstered Furniture

in your windows will attract customers to your store

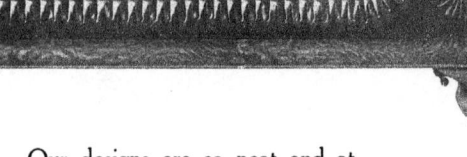

Our designs are so neat and attractive that they attract attention wherever they are displayed.

Comfort,—This is another very important factor in upholstered furniture and we have not forgotten this in making up our designs. Our prices are very reasonable and enable our customers to make a good profit on our furniture.

Write for further information and prices

The Victoriaville Bedding Company

Victoriaville
Que.

Limited

More Chair Comfort and More Sales—

REX-RECLINER and REST-FEST Chairs have a positive effect in creating new sales among the friends of those who already enjoy the comforts of these better made chairs. The original mechanical features, the body conforming construction and the soft, serviceable upholstering make an appeal that cannot be resisted. Every Chair Craft sale is a boost for future business.

This Rest-Fest Chair fits the body at every angle. A slight pressure on the floor instantly puts the occupant in a reclining position with all parts of the body evenly supported. The price is very reasonable. Write for details.

No mechanism to get out of order in this Rex-Recliner Chair. Gives solid comfort for years and years. Foot rest is cleverly concealed and slides out the moment you wish to use it. Made in all styles, all grades of upholstering, all prices.

Our New Sales Plan

Our new sales plan includes newspaper ads., consumer booklets, interest compelling window trims, demonstration cards, handsome window posters.

Why not get in on this profitable business at once?

CATALOG ON REQUEST

The
Chair Craft Company
Traverse City   Michigan

Goods that help to create a demand

and make easy sales. One of the latest Lippert designs in new den and livingroom furniture. You will make a good investment by ordering now and having some of these leaders on your floor for the fall trade. *They are repeaters.*

No. 842 set
Quartered Oak
Cane Back
with Automobile
Spring Seat
Any Covering

If you have not received a copy of our new catalogue, write for yours to-day.

The Lippert Furniture Company, Limited
Berlin - Ontario

Here's one for war-times!

List
$34.00

Made in all sizes. Weight, Crated, 125 lbs.

No. 878. Pillars 2", Top Rod, Sq. 1¼, Height of Head 58", Fillers ⅝", Cross Rod 1", Height of Foot 34"

You must buy more carefully in war-time

THE secret of retail success when things are disturbed by war or unusual conditions of any kind, is in *buying carefully.* You want goods that will sell quickly — popular goods that you can sell at reasonable prices with good profit to yourself. And you must be more careful than ever in your buying, because competition gets keener in such times and customers are not so easily satisfied.

We help our customers to buy carefully by offering them the biggest range of brass bedsteads made by any manufacturer in Canada

No matter what styles of bed your customers prefer, you can satisfy every one of them from the big new Weisglass Catalogue — and from it you can select a stock assortment that will put you ahead of all competition, mail-order or local.

On all beds we place our *Special Guarantee*

S. Weisglass Limited
Head Office: Montreal

Manufacturers of Weisglass Acid-proof Brass Bedsteads, Springs, Couches, Mattresses and Specialties

THE "GOLD MEDAL" LINE

DIRECTORS:
W. J. McMURTRY, President and General Manager
W. B. DALBY
G. C. EMMERSON
H. B. SHORTT, Secretary
G. HUGHES, Ass. Manager

Our factories are all running and we are prepared to make prompt shipments in all departments—

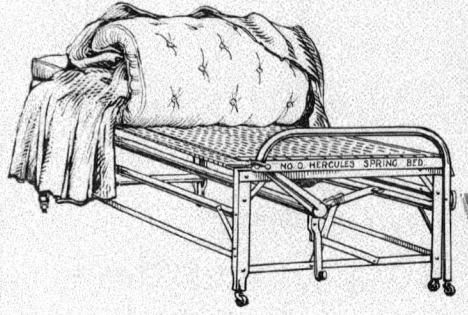

FACTORIES:
MONTREAL FACTORY
C. A. Hart, Vice-Pres. and Mgr.
WINNIPEG FACTORY
W. J. Rimmington, Mgr.
UXBRIDGE FACTORY
Geo. Wilson, Gen. Supt.

STEEL SLIDING COUCH   No. 694.—ROCKER

Davenports and Divanettes

Upholstered Furniture
Living Room Chairs
Steel Couches
Hercules Bed Springs
Gold Medal
Felt Mattresses

No. 679. DAVENPORT

The Gold Medal Furniture Mfg. Co., Limited
Toronto   Uxbridge   Montreal   Winnipeg

Authentic Store Front Book

Our eight years' experience in helping to design and build more than 30,000 KAWNEER STORE FRONTS has enabled us to compile and publish an authentic book on Store Fronts. This book contains photographs as well as drawings of many of the best paying Store Fronts in the country and if you are interested in Store Fronts don't take another step until you have seen "Boosting Business No. 2." Let us help you build a new Store Front that will pay for itself by increasing your business.

kawneer STORE FRONTS

Just a Card for "Boosting Business No. 2" will bring it without obligation

Kawneer Manufacturing Co., Ltd.
Francis J. Plym, President
Dept. S.
Guelph - Ontario

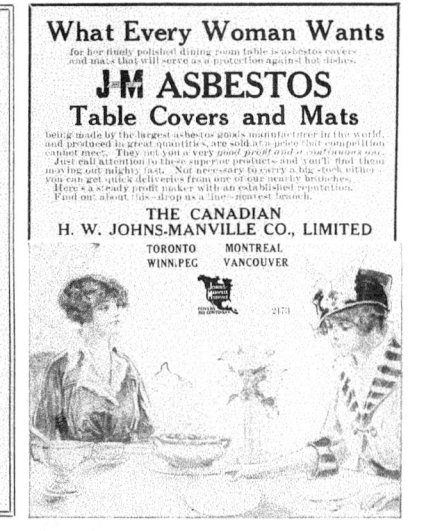

What Every Woman Wants
for her finely polished dining room table is asbestos covers and mats that will serve as a protection against hot dishes.

J-M ASBESTOS
Table Covers and Mats

being made by the largest asbestos goods manufacturer in the world, and produced in great quantities, are sold at a price that competition cannot meet. They net you a very *good profit and a continuous one*. Just call attention to these superior products and you'll find them moving out mighty fast. Not necessary to carry a big stock either, you can get quick deliveries from one of our nearby branches. Here's a steady profit maker with an established reputation. Find out about this — drop us a line — nearest branch.

THE CANADIAN
H. W. JOHNS-MANVILLE CO., LIMITED
TORONTO   MONTREAL
WINNIPEG   VANCOUVER

About the Upholstering of Imperial Furniture—

NO rough, cracked surface on the leathers. No wearing away on the sharp edges of the frame; no bulging seat showing the outline of the springs. Imperial leather upholstered furniture stands up under years and years of continual service because it's made *right*.

Details of our newest lines sent on request

Imperial Furniture Company
585-591 Queen St. W., Toronto

BETTER FINISH.
BETTER MAKE.
A VERY MUCH
BETTER PRICE.

MADE IN CANADA

MOULDINGS
AND FRAMES

Matthews Bros. Ltd., 788 Dundas St. Toronto

Duplex No. 1
Guaranteed 20 Years

"The Spring With a Backbone"
The
"Ideal" Duplex Woven Wire Fabric Spring

Companion to the Ideal Duplex Woven Wire Fabric Spring. Notice its construction. To an 1⅜ in. centre steel band twenty-six strong, oil tempered steel helical springs are attached. This overcomes all tendency to sag at the centre. A man could lie on one side with a baby on the other without their rolling together.

There is a special copper wire rope edging at the outer sides.

Each spring has The New "Ideal" oxidized finish that for beauty and appearance cannot be excelled, and carries our twenty-year ironclad guarantee.

Order one: It will pull business for your Bed Spring Department.

THE IDEAL BEDDING CO. LIMITED
2-24 JEFFERSON AVE. - - - - TORONTO

Canadian Furniture World AND THE Undertaker

The Commercial Press, Limited
32 Colborne Street, Toronto
(Next King Edward Hotel)

D. O. McKINNON, PRESIDENT
W. L. EDMONDS, VICE-PRESIDENT AND CONTRIBUTING EDITOR
J. C. ARMER, VICE-PRESIDENT AND MANAGER OF TECHNICAL PAPERS
WESTON WRIGLEY, VICE-PRESIDENT AND MANAGER OF TRADE PAPERS
JAMES O'HAGAN, EDITOR
WM. J. BRYANS, ASSOCIATE EDITOR
GEO. H. HONSBERGER, ADVERTISING MANAGER

F. C. D. WILKES, 794 UNITY BUILDING, MONTREAL
C. G. BRANDT, CIRCULATION MANAGER, TORONTO
E. J. MACINTYRE, ROOM 1155, 122 S. MICHIGAN AVE., CHICAGO
N. D. WEBSTER, 95 LIBERTY STREET, NEW YORK

Subscription rate, Canada and Great Britain, $1.50 per year; United States, $1.50 per year. A minimum circulation of 2,000 copies is guaranteed each month.

VOLUME FOUR　　　TORONTO, OCTOBER, 1914　　　NUMBER TEN

Important Change in Dumping Clause.

The change in the dumping clause of the Customs tariff, which went into effect on September 1, is of considerable importance to importers.

Under the Customs tariff of 1907, importers were permitted to purchase merchandise abroad at as low as 7½ per cent. below the price ruling in the market where purchased, without being penalized by the dumping clause. This margin, under the change of September 1, has been reduced to 5 per cent.

By way of illustration, the effect of the change is this: Under the old regulation, if an importer in Canada could persuade a manufacturer or jobber abroad to sell him an article at $92.50 whose regular selling price was $100, no penalty was imposed. Should, however, he find the foreign seller magnanimous enough to accept, say, 10 per cent. off, he would not only be compelled to pay the regular rate of, say, 30 per cent. when making entry at the Canadian Customs, on not only the valuation of $100, but an additional 10 per cent., besides. In other words, he would be assessed, in addition to the regular duty, an amount equal to the reduction that had been made in the price.

Now, no matter how magnanimous the foreign seller of an article may be, the Canadian importer cannot accept a reduction of less than 5 per cent. If he gets a cut of even 6 per cent., the rate of duty will be the regular rate plus that 6 per cent.

The regulation, as in that which formerly obtained, also applies to free goods when of a kind made in Canada; but in the case of round rolled wire rods, no margin is allowed for a cut in the price below that obtaining in the country of production.

When the dumping clause was first inserted in the Customs tariff, the margin allowed was 2½ per cent. Later it was fixed at 5 per cent., and, as already pointed out, was raised to 7½ per cent. in 1907. It is now, therefore, back to where it was prior to 1907.

In the United States the dumping clause only allows a margin of 1 per cent. below the regular market price, so it will be seen at a glance that the Canadian regulations are much more liberal to the importer than those obtaining across the border.

All's Well With the Banks.

The Government's report for July regarding the condition of the chartered banks of Canada is reassuring rather than otherwise.

While the effect of the war upon the standing of the banks cannot be gauged by the report, as hostilities did not break out until August, yet the outlook was sufficiently threatening during the third week in July to exercise at least some adverse influence on the financial situation.

Although demand deposits show a reduction of no less than $81,000,000, as compared with June, yet savings deposits increased $7,500,000 in the month and $49,866,000 in the year. Taking deposits as a whole, they were over $40,000,000 in excess of a year ago.

Commercial loans to Canadian business houses, while smaller by $18,000,000 than a year ago, were larger by $1,922,000 than they were at the end of June. It will be with some interest that we shall await the August returns in order to ascertain what effect the war has had upon loans of this character. Commercial loans outside Canada also increased, being $1,826,000 larger than in June.

That the banks have been strengthening their position is evident from the fact that there has been a decline in deposits abroad of $7,188,000, and in call loans abroad of $11,574,000.

While in both assets and liabilities there was a decline in value of over $7,000,000 for the month, yet the former is larger by $48,657,000 than a year ago. The increase in liabilities for the twelve months was $47,955,000.

It is quite apparent that the banks still have a good grip on the situation. It is also apparent that they are in a position where it is possible for them to lend assistance to the commercial enterprises of the country.

Keep up your courage if you would retain a grasp on your business.

Prosperity of Ontario Farmers.

Ontario's Minister of Finance has been gathering statistics during the past year regarding the financial condition of the farmers of the province.

Furniture men, like other classes of business men, will be interested in the data gathered, particularly in view of its optimistic nature.

There are a good many people in Canada who are quite pessimistic in regard to the financial standing of the farmers of this country. They will not, however, find much consolation in the data which has been gathered by the Government of the Province of Ontario, whatever the conditions may be in the other provinces.

We are told, for example, that mortgages against farm property in the province represent only 15 per cent. of its value.

But conditions even better than that are revealed by the bank deposits of the farmers. During the last few years these deposits, we are told, have increased 20 to 30 per cent., while in some counties the amounts standing to the credit of individual farmers run all the way from $700 to $12,000.

Taking farmers' deposits for the whole of rural Ontario, the aggregate amount is estimated to be $100,000,000. Even this does not represent the cash surplus of the farmers of Ontario when the fact is taken into consideration that there are a good many farmers in the province who still prefer to hide their cash in a stocking rather than deposit it in a bank.

But these figures do not, of course, reveal all the wealth possessed by the farmers of the province. There are the land, buildings, implements, and live stock, not including the potentialities of the vigorous sons and daughters to be taken into consideration. The last report of the Ontario Bureau of Industries shows the value of these to be about $1,406,000,000.

And it is a great source of satisfaction to know that, because of better methods of cultivation, the farmers of Ontario, as well as those of Canada in general, are yearly increasing their productiveness. Of the ten million dollars which the Federal Government has set aside for agricultural instruction, Ontario last year received $195,000, and this amount will be increased annually until the share of this province will be $363,319.

Cut down your advertising if necessary, but don't cut it out. The purpose of advertising is to get more business.

Big Profits Clog Business. He who to-day bases his hope for success in business on big profits is building on a rather sandy foundation.

It is on quick turn overs, not big profits, that the modern merchant relies.

In this day and generation to exact big profits is not good policy. High prices tend to reduce consumption. And the dealer who essays to exact them drives customers to the stores of competitors who aim at quick turn overs and moderate profits.

It is in the interests of all that it should be so.

To turn over a line of goods only once a year, even at a large profit, is not as good for the dealer as to turn it over three or four times a year at a moderate profit. And it certainly is not as good for the consumer, whose rights have also to be taken into account.

The machinery for expediting the turning over of merchandise was never as efficient and never as intelligently worked as it is to-day.

There was a time, not so many years ago, when very little thought was given to such business-getting machinery as window dressing, advertising and good service. This is now all changed. Retailers realize that the more attention they give to window dressing, advertising, and methods of keeping as well as attracting customers, the more quickly are their stocks of merchandise turned over.

To exact big profits is to clog the machinery of the selling organization.

SHORT NOTES FROM THE EDITOR'S PEN

Get your stock in shape for the fall trade.

* * *

Now is a good time to decide to attempt extra sales by suggestion.

* * *

With the bases full and none out, it isn't taking it easy that gets the pitcher out of the hole. It's determination. It is the same with getting a business man out of a hole.

* * *

Do you anticipate trade and order goods in plenty of time to meet the demand when it comes? Do not wait until the special season arrives before looking to requirements.

* * *

Peterborough, Ont., merchants found that over half the amount collected by a canvasser for colored church work went into her own pockets. Naturally, they refused to donate.

* * *

This advertising business is a good deal like irrigation. The farmer would probably be able to raise a little by depending upon the scanty rain, but he raises a whole lot more by irrigating.

* * *

Do you attempt to increase sales by suggestion? If not, you are passing up an opportunity for considerable increased business. Anyone can hand over the counter the goods asked for, but it takes a salesman to sell goods over and above actual demand.

* * *

It is proposed by a town in the western part of the United States to make one certain day in the year pay-up day, when all bills must be squared away and no one owe a dollar. What a beautiful scheme. We suggest that it be made universal.

* * *

"Some one has said, "It is just as easy to catch big fish as little fish. There are but two rules to follow. One is to fish where big fish are, and the other is to use bait that catches big fish. Some men devote their entire lives to fishing in washtubs, where there aren't any fish." In selecting a location **for a business,** always figure on the size of the fish in the neighborhood and the kind of bait that is necessary.

"A SMILE."

NOTHING on earth can smile but man. Gems may flash reflected light, but what is a diamond flash compared to an eye flash and a mirth flash? Flowers cannot smile; this is a charm that even they cannot claim. It is the prerogative of man; it is the color which love wears, and cheerfulness and joy; these three. It is a light in the windows of the face, by which the heart signifies it is at home and waiting. A face that cannot smile is like a bud that cannot blossom, and dries up on the stalk. Laughter is day, and sobriety is night, and a smile is the twilight that hovers gently between both—more bewitching than either.—Henry Ward Beecher.

Developing the Furniture Trade in Time of War
BY W. L. EDMONDS

OF such housefurnishings as are to be found in the modern complete furniture store, Canada imports something like ten and a half million dollars' worth annually.

True, by far the largest part of this is composed of carpets, mats, and rugs of various kinds. Furniture itself contributes $3,187,780 to the total. The countries from which this principally came were: United States, $2,761,190; Great Britain, $264,351; Hong Kong, $65,279; France, $26,441; Japan, $25,716; Austria, $23,442; Italy, $11,042; Germany, $8,232. All told, we imported from twenty-one countries.

The accompanying table gives with some detail our imports from the countries that are at war, and also from Holland and Switzerland, the export trade of these two countries naturally being affected by the hostilities in which their neighbors are engaged. The sum total of the imports described in this table is a little over $6,500,000, of which $4,487,000 are carpets, mats, and rugs. The imports from the United States under the same classifications that are given in the table covering our purchases from the eight countries therein referred to, were as follows:

part of dealers to place orders at the present stage of the war.

Chief interest, of course, centres around the imports from Austria and Germany, the two nations with which we are at war. Our imports of furniture and housefurnishings from these two countries last year were valued at $159,000. This trade is now a thing of the past, and will necessarily continue to be so as long as the war lasts. In the meantime, therefore, it is as dead as if it never existed.

The chair manufacturers of Canada will scarcely object if the import trade with Austria is never restored, the bent chairs from that country having of late years been a decidedly disturbing factor to the home manufacturer.

While Canadian manufacturers of furniture, carpets,

CANADA'S IMPORTS OF FURNITURE AND FURNISHINGS FROM COUNTRIES AFFECTED BY WAR.

	Gt. Britain	Austria	Belgium	France	Germany	Holland	Japan	Switl'd
Curtains	$ 569,653	$ 1,322	$ 856	$33,231	$ 757	$ 71	$ 123	$36,720
Bedding, quilts, etc.	960,533	1,488	581	4,935	44,017	5	16,320	812
Children's carriages, go-carts, etc.	4,870	.....	.....	.....	30	.....	.....	.....
Carpet lining and stair pads	670	.....	.....	.....	.....	.....	.....	.....
Carpet sweepers	8	.....	.....	.....	.....	.....	.....	.....
Carpets, rugs, mats, oilcloths	4,286,640	12,725	9,769	25,873	65,875	3,479	82,220	744
Furniture	264,351	23,442	871	26,441	8,232	373	25,716	761
Railway Rugs	61,957	131	52	.....	845	.....	.....	.....
	$6,148,682	$39,123	$12,133	$90,470	$119,756	$3,928	$114,179	$39,037

Imports of Housefurnishings From United States.

Curtains	$ 92,752
Bedding, quilts, etc.	87,750
Children's carriages, etc.	311,243
Carpet linings and stair pads	1,148
Carpet sweepers	16,071
Carpets, mats, rugs, oilcloths	247,927
Furniture	2,761,190
Railway rugs	470
Total	$3,359,451

As to how the import furniture trade in particular, and that of housefurnishings in general, may be affected by the war cannot, of course, be definitely stated. At the best, it can only be premised; but for the undertaking of that task we are not altogether traveling in the dark.

One thing is certain: the manufacturers in Great Britain intend neither to slumber nor sleep in regard to their export trade, while the soldiers of the Empire are engaged with vigor in fighting the enemies of the nation. The want of men to man the factories and the want of ships may curtail their export trade, but any decrease that may take place will not be for lack of enterprise. We may, therefore, take it for granted that, as far as imports from the Mother Country are concerned, there is not likely to be any very great decline, and although there is some hesitancy on the

and housefurnishings generally will to some extent be inconvenienced through having their supply of certain raw materials disturbed by the war, yet the net result is likely to be beneficial rather than otherwise. Competition from Europe in finished products will, for the time being at any rate, be much modified. That is one favorable probability.

Another is the sentiment which the war has stimulated in favor of Canadian-made goods. Nothing that has previously transpired in the history of the country has been such a factor in stimulating this sentiment. As a result, greater progress has been made in this respect in weeks than was previously made in years.

People are beginning to realize to a greater extent than ever before that to purchase on every possible occasion that which is made in the country is a phase of patriotism. Both manufacturers and dealers should take advantage of this favorable condition of affairs to further impress upon their respective customers the importance and reasonableness of this sentiment.

Furniture is being made in Canada to-day which compares favorably with that of any other country. But there are still altogether too many people in Canada who do not appear to be aware of this fact. It is time they were educated. And this is the psychological moment for undertaking the task. As a matter of fact, one enterprising Canadian manufacturer has since the beginning of the year even undertaken the task of educating the American trade by opening a showroom in New York, and is already doing a nice business there.

Many manufacturers are fully alive to the opportunity that the situation presents for securing a larger proportion of the home trade. And they are setting themselves to the task with vigor, in spite of the somewhat unsettled condition of the financial situation, by making lines that are designed to replace those imported or that are likely to prove attractive sellers. What they are doing in the way of special efforts in manufacturing they are backing up by special efforts in selling. This is enterprise.

Some are carrying their enterprise still further. They are at least going to make an effort to capture a part of the foreign trade that went to Germany, and particularly in Central and South American countries. As far as I have been able to ascertain, the number who are making any new and special effort along this line is small. The fact that the lines are manufactured for the home market are unsuitable for the foreign, doubtless deters others from embarking in new foreign enterprise. The unsatisfactory financial conditions obtaining in South America probably cause hesitation on the part of others. Others, again, have lost too heavily on previous export enterprises to make any further ventures into the field. "We'll never touch it again," remarked one furniture manufacturer to me a few days ago. Still others appear to have not yet made up their mind what they will do. They are in the meantime sitting tight and studying the pros and cons of the export situation.

One thing that characterizes the South American trade, according to those who have given some study to the matter, is that while the ruling demand in Canada is for simplicity in style, patterns, and trimmings, in that part of the world it is for furniture of the opposite characteristics.

The Argentine Republic imports about $2,600,000 worth of furniture, of which over $300,000 worth is from Germany. Mexico imports from all countries about $1,750,000. These two countries, the one in Southern and the other in Central America, import between them approximately $4,500,000 worth of furniture. I have been unable to procure the figures regarding the furniture imports of other Central and South American countries.

Canada's exports of furniture last year to all countries in those two parts of the world were valued at a little less than twenty-five hundred dollars. Her total to all countries in the world was $381,506, of which about 38 per cent. went to Australia, our largest market. These were made up as follows:

Canada's Exports of Furniture.

United Kingdom..	$ 23,746	New Zealand ...	$ 52,188
Australia	144,074	Argentina	1,077
Bermuda	6,365	Brazil	15
Brit. E. Africa...	253	China	1,132
Brit. S. Africa...	69,126	Cuba	175
Brit. W. Africa..	1,349	France	2,988
British Guiana ..	1,123	Japan	446
British India	392	Mexico	1,344
British W. Indies	11,611	Miquelon and St.	
British Oceanic.		Pierre	23
other	18	United States ...	26,111
Fiji	235		
Newfoundland ..	37,715	Total	$381,506

With Germany and Austria out of the way, and the demands of the home market less exacting, it is possible we may see a development in our export trade in furniture. At any rate, it is gratifying to know that some of the manufacturers are making an effort to bring it about.

As far as carpets are concerned, the Canadian import trade is not likely to be influenced to any great extent by the war. By referring to the table dealing with our imports from Europe, it will be noticed that our purchases of carpets from both Austria and Germany only total about $78,000. As a matter of fact, the lines manufactured in those countries are in styles and qualities not altogether suitable for the Canadian market.

Manufacturers of such lines as doll carriages may feel the effect of the war, because most of the reed they use is imported from Germany, the article produced in that country being of better quality than that brought from China. The manufacturers of reed furniture may be similarly affected, for the same reason. In anticipation of what may happen, the price of reed has advanced 25 to 50 per cent. In children's and dolls' carriages, go-carts, etc., nearly all our imports are from the United States. The German-made article, which is of cheaper construction and material than the Canadian-made article, does not compete with the latter to any extent.

One gratifying feature of the situation is the improvement which has developed during the last week or two in the trade and financial situation in Canada. It is true trade is on the whole still dull, particularly in the manufacturing centres. But that confidence which is the basis of credit, is gradually strengthening there can be no doubt, and in most of what may be termed the farming towns business is fairly good.

A well-known author once wrote: "Most failures lie in not going on long enough."

In times like these to go on demands courage and perseverance, whether it be in regard to the home or the export trade. The thing to do is to summon these qualities to our aid, and go on and keep going.

FURNITURE MEN CAUGHT IN WAR ZONE

Mr. and Mrs. F. C. Burroughes, of the Burroughes Furniture Co., Toronto, who recently returned from England, had intended visiting Holland and Germany, but cancelled their trip when the European trouble broke out. Mr. and Mrs. Burroughes were among those to feel the pinch when the banks closed in London, and they could not cash their travelers' checks.

They had been motoring through rural England, and when they arrived in London all the coin of the realm they had was two pennies. Mr. Burroughes went into a barber's and got a shave, but was unable to pay for it, as the barber could not change the note he had. Then when luncheon time came, they found themselves in the predicament of not having sufficient cash to get something to eat. Fortunately, however, Mrs. Burroughes espied a friend, and found that he had a supply of gold and was able to accommodate his friends, so that Mr. Burroughes could pay the barber and the waiter.

Mr. Harry Struthers, of London, a nephew of Mr. Burroughes, was compelled to return steerage.

J. J. Marks, of the Dominion House Furnishing Company, Ottawa, is another man who has arrived home after a most exciting trip through Germany and France after the declaration of war. Mr. Marks was visiting relatives in a town near the German and Russian frontier when the first alarms of war were heard, and he immediately left for Berlin. War was declared on Russia the day he arrived there. The general feeling in the east being intense fear of the Russians, Mr. Marks made England his objective, and for several days he had a most exciting time, passing through refugees and scenes of mobilization till he reached France, and then to England, taking the first boat home to Canada.

Selling Methods in the Furniture Store

Some Experiences and Suggestions

EXHIBIT AT FALL FAIRS

Marceau & Fils, furniture dealers, St. Joseph Street, Quebec, take advantage of the advertising to be had from showing at the Quebec Provincial Fair. The manager, Mr. Amyot, is a firm believer in these exhibits, particularly in Quebec, where there is so much contributory territory. They also use quarter and half pages in daily newspapers about twice a week.

In seven years they have grown from a small store to a large building of three storeys and with two extra warehouses in other parts of the city. They use the whole three storeys for display, and carry complete lines of furniture, carpets, lamps, and office furniture.

They keep a woman doing nothing else but cleaning

Bedding display made at Quebec Fair by Marceau & Fils.

and polishing furniture on display, and it certainly shows the result. Each floor, or part of floor, is given over to certain groups, but on ground floor, instead of as in so many stores, parallel lines of chairs, dressers, tables, etc., they have a pleasing display of goods as if in actual use.

They do not go in for special sales, except a big February sale; but they believe in a strict money back policy to dissatisfied customers, and carry only such lines as they feel they can conscientiously recommend to their patrons.

WINDOW SELLS GOODS FOR WINNIPEG FIRM.

A. H. Banfield & Co., furniture dealers, Main street, Winnipeg, find their display windows a valuable factor in attracting trade to the store.

"Window display probably puts you in touch with more customers at less cost than any other medium at the disposal of the retailer," was the opinion expressed by the manager, A. M. Tanney, to the Canadian Furniture World.

"Just as an instance of their value," he continued, "we put two 3-piece walnut parlor suites, retailing at $170 and $210, in the window on a Monday and on Wednesday we sold them both, and to customers who had never been in the store before. There was a double value in this sale for which the window was responsible. We got a good profit on the two suites and also got in touch with two entirely new customers."

Printer's Ink Brings Good Returns.

"We do not depend on window advertising, however," he states. "We spend a large sum of money every year in printer's ink and find it an excellent investment. We believe that it pays because we can see it bringing in business for us every day. Not infrequently do people come into the store and state that they were induced to come by our ad. in the local paper."

This firm does an extensive credit business. Asked as to their experience in competing with departmental stores which sell strictly for cash, Mr. Tanney stated that they do not mind the competition of the departmental stores as long as it is legitimate. "We can compete with them on cash business," he stated.

COLLECTING FREIGHT CLAIMS RAPIDLY

T. B. Cramp, of Orillia, Ont., who has had 15 years' experience in business in that town, is of the opinion that it is frequently the merchants' own fault if they don't secure payment for freight claims in proper time. This was pointed out by him at a recent convention of merchants when he emphasized the necessity of merchants putting in their claims in the proper form if they wish to secure quick settlement.

He points out that it is first necessary to get a notation of short or damaged goods made on the freight bill. The bill of lading has also to be attached to the claim. This generally comes along with the invoice of goods, or a copy may be secured from the wholesale house that shipped the goods.

He points out that the merchant should not forget to add to his claim the freight on goods that have been lost. The dealer should not be out this amount, and Mr. Cramp always adds it to his claim.

A SCHOOL CHILDREN'S CONTEST

Now that the school season is with us again, furniture men might stir up some interest among the young people through popular contests. Children are natural born advertisers. Once they get scent of a premium

Furniture display of Hespeler dining suite made at Hamilton Industrial Exposition by Hoodless Furniture Co. W. Nash and Bernard Hoodless are the men in booth. The latter has since gone to the war

plan, guessing contest or anything which has a prize in connection they will spread the news like wildfire. The following is a good plan.

Advertise that to every child who comes into your

store and registers, you will give a small tag showing a certain number. Tell them that duplicates of these numbers will be placed in a large box and that every day, three numbers will be drawn and written on a large blackboard in the rear of your store.

The children who have the numbers drawn are entitled to any ten-cent article in your store, provided

	1	2	3	4	5	6	7	8
WRIGHT & HEPBURN	9	10	11	12	13	14	15	16
	17	18	19	20	21	22	23	24
	25	26	27	28	29	30	31	32
No. _____	33	34	35	In Stock		36	37	38
	39	40	41			42	43	44
Maker _____	45	46	47	48	49	50	51	52
Finish _____	53	54	55	56	57	58	59	60
Cost _____	61	62	63	64	65	66	67	68
	69	70	71	72	73	74	75	76
S. Price _____	77	78	79	80	81	82	83	84

Front and back of stock card attached to articles on floor of Wright & Hepburn. Port Arthur, Ont. The number of articles purchased is written in centre blank and the number sold are crossed off from time to time, so there is always a record of stock on hand. The back of card gives information in regard to make, price, etc.

they bring one of their parents with them when choosing the article.

The card should read something like this:

"Get in the School Children's
Contest at
Jones' Furniture Store
Number 25."

Each youngster should be required to wear the card continuously during the contest and present it when prize is claimed. Save the names and addresses obtained and you have a splendid mailing list of school children. If you wish you could have them register parents' names also.

FREE TRIAL STOVES TO ABOUT-TO-BE-WEDS.

One of the methods pursued by A. Welch & Son, stove dealers, Toronto, to induce sales and bring their line before those who are about to take up the cares of housekeeping is to send out a typewritten letter similar to the following to those whose names are inserted in the "engaged" columns of the local press. The form letter is the outcome of a competition held among the employes as to the best composition, and the one thought most provocative of salesmanship. One of the clerks in the office keeps watch of the engagements as they are announced, and then this letter is sent:

Dear Madam:

We notice that you are about to assume the responsibilities of keeping house, and feel sure that you, like every bride, will take pride in showing your friends through your new home, which we know will be furnished in the best of taste.

No woman likes to feel less proud of her kitchen than the rest of her house; therefore, to make sure that YOUR friends will appreciate your good judgment and taste, let us suggest that you permit us to install one of our guaranteed Detroit Jewel gas stoves in your kitchen on our 30-day FREE trial offer.

You will find more Detroit Jewel gas stoves in the homes of particular people in Toronto than any other make. You are sure to be complimented on your selection, and at the same time may feel that it is impossible for any of your friends to have any better stove.

Later on you may require a refrigerator. If you find the Detroit Jewel gas stove satisfactory (as we know you will), you are sure to want a Jewel refrigerator. Like Jewel gas stoves, Jewel refrigerators represent the very best in construction, efficiency, and economy.

We also take the liberty of reminding you of our gas water heaters and electric fixtures. We feel sure that we can do better for you in these lines than anyone else.

Just to show our good faith in the matter, we will give a special 10 per cent. discount to every newly married couple presenting this letter or sending it in when paying their account.

Please remember that in coming to our store to see our display of stoves, ranges, water heaters, fixtures, etc., you are under absolutely no obligation to buy, and whether we have the honor of your patronage or not, we wish you every success in life and many returns of the anniversary of your wedding day.

Yours faithfully,
A. WELCH & SON.

MOVING THE STICKERS.

The way a manager handles the stickers is often a good way to judge his ability. It doesn't take long to see that a certain item is going to move slowly. Get after it right away. The longer they stick the harder they stick, until it is almost impossible to get rid of them. The stickers help eat up the profits made on the

The W. W. Chown Co., Limited
FOR TELEPHONE ORDERS ONLY

From Mr. ....
Address ....
Phone No. ....
Date ....

Telephone orders should be FILLED PROMPTLY and CAREFULLY
Copy this order onto a sales slip and then hand it to the manager for filling.

....
....
....
....
....

Time received .... Time order was filled ....
Order received by ....
Order put up by ....
Delivered by ....

How an Edmonton firm takes care of phone orders. A special form is used, copy of which is sent to sales manager.

quicker moving goods. They also kill the appearance of fresh, clean stock. Use the stickers as leaders, feature them prominently, run specials on them; if you only get cost out of them be happy that they are not eating up interest and valuable shelf room. Use them to bring the customers into your store and the better numbers will take care of themselves.

The Art of Display

Suggestions for Window and Interior Arrangements.

The window trimmer at this season of the year is afforded rich opportunity for artistic and effective Autumn displays, there is a royal chance to use autumn leaves, rich colorings, the boughs and branches of the trees, with golden rod and fall flowers, which are mostly quite lasting, with draperies and cloth backings of bright colors are all applicable at this season. Then there are the great varieties of artificial leaves, moss, grass, fruits and real pumpkins and corn stalks—the choice of accessories is practically unlimited.

An arch covered with bright leaves, and with bunches of flowers at the base gives a frame for various pieces that is always effective. Thanksgiving Day brings its own suggestions of good trims, the dining-room, the kitchen—how varied an arrangement can be produced, at this time. It has a human interest that clings close.

Then there is the football season. College pennants should be used, and may be purchased at moderate prices. The local school or college colors should predominate. A veritable riot of colors may be used in this regard, and the room scene may depict the college "den," or the library, or study.

Use plenty of price tickets. No one buys an article unless they first ask the price, and naturally the prospective customer before your windows is instinctively wondering "How much?" Answer this universal query by using price cards. These may be as plain or elaborate as your resources will permit. Many fine stock designs are on the market and easily adapted to use. Most anyone can draw in the figures desired. In some instances where artistic effect only is aimed at, a window made for attracting general attention, price cards may be cut out—but it will be found wise to use them as often as possible, together with timely window cards stating briefly what the goods are, their use, or some good store mottos or slogans.

One store in mind has a Saturday special sale, all come-backs, odd lots, small wares, etc., are gathered together and placed in one of the large windows, which is on the sidewalk level. The window is filled to the limit—and every piece has a huge price card on it. This has paid well, but the idea is just what it is intended for—the idea of "bargains" and low prices. It does not pay to crowd the regular displays, a more moderate arrangement is less confusing and more artistic and conventional.

MAKING GOOD USE OF SHOW WINDOW.

Authorities agree on two general principles of decoration—to plan and design the display before undertaking it, or to build as the work progresses. Many

The furnished room in the window.—Splendid finish of background and furnishings set off to advantage this display of parlor furniture in a Toronto furniture store window.

working plans fail because they fail to look as well in practice as on paper. Then, again, it is useless to undertake the decoration of a window without some idea of what is to be done. The best results are frequently brought about by a combination of the two plans—by deciding upon a scheme and by altering it to meet the requirement of the display. In arranging a window, a good background is of first necessity, since it is the setting of the picture to be presented. Many articles, desirable in themselves, need a background to bring them out effectively. Practical decorators devote no little time to the arrangement of backgrounds, often relying entirely upon them to arrest the notice of the passer-by and to bring to his attention the goods them-

Background for harvest sale, autumn or Thanksgiving window.

selves. No matter how artistic a window display may be, it loses more than half its attractiveness if not suitably backed. The background affords relief to the trim, and is as necessary as scenery to a stage setting or as the sky is to a landscape. Different goods require different backgrounds, as different pictures require different frames.

In selecting goods for the show window, two considerations are of importance. The newest and most up-to-date lines, of which there is a large stock, should be exhibited. The purpose of the window is not to display unsalable goods, but to sell goods, and the more attractive the window is made to appear, the more rapidly will the lines illustrated sell. Naturally, the latest styles are the most interesting. Then, when a window has created the desired impression—a desire for ownership—there must be a sufficient stock to back it. Frequently, however, it is necessary to display old goods in order to move the stock. In this case, in order to interest passers, it is necessary to create prices.

Tie up your window display and newspaper advertising. Both are used for the same purpose, both are intended to bring results. It is certainly undesirable to have a window display made up of freak propositions which have no direct bearing upon that which the merchant is trying to impress upon the public. Prominent advertisers interested in the production or sale of more than one article believe that the value of an advertisement is depreciated where more than one article is displayed at one time in the same space, since the mind of the observer is not concentrated and, therefore, not so greatly influenced by the advertisement or window display showing many wares, as by the advertisement or display picturing and describing but one thing. If much is to be gained through concentration of effort in copy or display, how much more is possible when the united effort of both is concentrated toward a single end. The possible customer—the whole public is made up of possible customers—has perhaps seen a newspaper advertisement of a certain sale. Later passing the window, he is reminded of what he read and invariably stops. The sale is then half made. Your show window and your ads. are your salesmen.

BLACK BACKGROUNDS

The latest note in decoration, straight from Paris, and said to be extraordinarily effective, is for black and white rooms. It seems that we have gloried sufficiently in color, and the very newest thing decrees not only black carpets but black and white striped walls, chintzes with a bold black pattern on a parchment-colored ground, lamp-shades and cushions to harmonize, and even lace curtains having a white design applique on black net, while the inner draperies are of moire silk. It sounds sombre, but in reality is charming. Probably the modern woman has devised it for her special benefit. As a background black is superb. Flowers, books, and ornaments take on a peculiar distinction in such monochrome surroundings.

This idea is daringly carried into the decoration of bedrooms with a still greater effectiveness. An oxidized or white enameled bedstead with black silk sheets and pillowcases, and a black taffeta eiderdown with white fal-lals at one corner, is probably the most original development in bedroom furniture that there has been since the first giant four-poster appeared. In this case the chintzes will have a black ground to contrast with a string-colored carpet, and the dressing-table silver will gleam as never before against the sheen of black satin. It is very modern and sophisticated. Already the feeling for rooms in this fashion is extremely marked.

BOUND TO DRAW ATTENTION.

A novel idea of connecting up the sidewalk with the window display which will attract the attention of every passerby, is to draw a line of paint—red or other color—from the curb across the walk to the window and up the glass to about the height of the eye. Inside the leaving-off point can be connected with ribbons of the same color, running to individual furniture items on display. This scheme has been tried with other lines of goods, and should prove equally satisfactory with furniture.

PRICE TICKETS IN WINDOW.

Some window dressings of housefurnishing articles look as if the man responsible was trying to run an exhibit of all the kitchen appliances used since Eve first fried potatoes in a cocoanut shell, and in all the maze not a single price can be discovered. Suppose some patient woman finally found something that looked good to her do you expect her passing interest to be sufficient to induce her to come in just to ask you the price? Well, she won't. Stick price tags on everything in sight. If the article is of use and the price looks right she will come in and buy; if there is no price displayed she may feel that the price might be more than she cares to pay, and rather than risk embarrassment she will wait until another time.

Make a new noise with your selling talk—introduce something new, and you will keep your prospect awake (to his opportunities).

Advertising Bargains in Furniture and Furnishings
By A. B. LEVER

These are days when many furniture dealers put bargain prices on goods in stock which it is desirable should be cleaned out at this particular season. The advertisements which are appearing in the newspapers all over the Dominion show that the practice is quite common just now. Many of the advertisements are creditable, indeed. A few of them I have selected for reproduction in this issue of the Furniture World.

The advertisement of the T. H. Pratt Company, Hamilton, is a good example of simple, yet effective, advertising. It occupied a space of 4¾ by 10½ inches, and good use has been made of the space by embodying within it a lot of information regarding quality and price of floor coverings. A gratifying feature of the ad. is the emphasis which the introduction lays upon the fact that the different lines dealt with in the announcement are Canadian made. The desire to purchase home-made goods was never so strong as it is to-day, and he is a wise business man who writes his ads. and displays his windows with a view to catering to that sentiment.

The Nova Scotia Furnishing Co. usually make good use of their 4¼ by 6¼ inch space. This is because they take pride in their advertising. When a man takes pride in doing a thing he usually does it well. At any rate he will do it as well as he possibly can, and whatever defects he may have will be corrected as time goes on. The advertisement herewith reproduced is no exception to the rule. It is well written, well balanced and well displayed, and somehow one feels that there is no attempt to "put one over" on the public. An advertiser has gained a strong point when the public, from experience, have learned that there is no exaggeration in his advertising methods.

The advertisement of the Neilson Furniture Company, Calgary, is a good one from nearly all points of view. The space, 8½ by 9½ inches, gave ample opportunity for both the ad. writer and the printer to dis-

Some furniture bargain advertisements of Canadian dealers.

play their ability. The information conveyed in regard to carpets and bed comforters is particularly well done, being brief and to the point. If there is one point that I would venture to criticize it is in regard to the bottom of the ad. Through the absence of a display line one looks a second time at the ad. to see whether or not it has been concluded. Had, for example, the line devoted to the name of the firm been placed at the bottom instead of at the top, this deficiency would have been corrected. While the ad. is a good one, it would, from a typographical standpoint, have been still better had this been done, because it would have been more evenly balanced.

The advertisement of McLaren & Co., St. Catharines, is also a good one, although I would suggest that in future in ads. of this size and description, the firm name at the top should be left out, allowing precedence to be given to the line which carries the main thought of the advertisement. It also allows more room for either additional matter or more white space. "Speeding Out the Furniture" is good, and particularly because it is a phrase which is a little out of the ordinary, while the subject matter of the ad. is put in simple and readable language. The original was 6⅝ by 8¼ inches.

Wright's, Limited, of Sydney, have made good use of their space—4¾ by 9¼. The ad. is well balanced and striking, and a list of prices is furnished which are calculated to interest all sorts and conditions of people.

Storey's (Ottawa) is a straight-to-the-point ad. The writer of the ad. had something to say and he said it without any waste of words, and in a way that both described the couch and tended to excite the interest of those who possibly had not been thinking of buying a steel couch. From a typographical standpoint the ad. is artistic and striking. The original was 2⅛ by 7 inches.

The bed advertisement without firm name attached is from a department store announcement, and is merely reproduced for illustrating how a small ad. of this description can be made effective. It was 2⅛ by 5½ inches.

The advertisement of the Dominion Furniture Co., Moose Jaw, is reproduced for a similar purpose. It was only 2⅛ by 2⅞ inches, but it caught the eye just the same. The space is smaller than I would recommend using as a rule, but this particular ad. shows that even small space can be made to stand out when an engraving is used and too much reading matter is not crowded in.

RETAIL ADVERTISING PROBLEMS.

By Hugh King Harris

Probably no other line of products is sold so little through the medium of jobbers and wholesalers as furniture and kindred lines. The larger per cent. of goods sold along these lines is bought direct from the factories, or direct factory representatives, either on the road, or through means of the various exhibitions. Very often manufacturers advertise heavily in trade journals and back up their dealers with national and local ads. In some instances these manufacturers use few if any salesmen.

It is, therefore, apparent that the retailer is, in house furnishing lines practically the middle man, he is the source of supply to the consumer, the source of outlet for the manufacturer. Business logic dictates a policy of handling goods which are first, adapted to the locality in which the retailer is located, and secondly in selecting lines which will be backed by proper publicity on the part of the maker.

The middleman, so-called, has been criticized and condemned in many cases, but though the middle man is not a producer, he is necessary in the conduct of business, in the disposal of the product of the makers and it is an erroneous idea to think he is the dictator of prices, or taking unfair advantages in handling trade. The middle man, in the present instance, the retailer, must be given credit for many things; it is he who studies local conditions and keeps in touch with public demand, thus allowing the manufacturer safety in the production of that which will prove salable and profitable. The retailer assumes the risks and burdens of distribution, he incurs personal risks and liabilities in stocking and disposing of the wares purchased for conducting his business.

Under the circumstances the retailer has a moral and legal right to demand from the manufacturer articles of real quality. He has a right to demand that prices be protected, that the maker does not sell to mail order concerns or to vicious trade combines who will develop unfair competition locally.

Dealers sometimes abuse their privilege by using advertised goods as leaders at a cut price. This is a grave mistake, while it may be considered good advertising up to a certain point, it means a loss at the best, and eventually that dealer will become known to makers and the trade generally as undesirable and the right lines will be difficult to procure. If the line is ever discontinued in that locality by the price cutter, other dealers will avoid taking it on at a loss, and so the manufacturers' right in the matter must be considered.

The successful home furnisher to-day should pursue a course of real co-operation with the manufacturer. The trade journals should be studied, the sales force educated to act in harmony with the publicity department, the staple, nationally advertised goods should be featured, at the regular prices, leaders may be made along lines which are not "standard," and the sales helps furnished by the makers in the way of window trims, newspaper cuts, street car cards, etc., should be utilized to the utmost. Many dealers lose good money every year by their lack of appreciation of such sales service.

Where mail order competition is felt, it is well to secure the catalogues of the mail order folks and by window displays of their goods and your own, by actual price comparisons and by the use of the MAILS and parcel post, booklets and store catalogues fight the battle in a way which has won and which will win if logically and persistently carried out on the right basis. And always demand of the manufacturer that he does not sell to this class of trade. If he does, buy elsewhere.

GOOD AD. COPY

By Arthur Brisbane

Writing a successful advertisement is the most difficult thing in the business of writing. You can write an interesting story about noses and every man will feel of his nose and look in a glass. It concerns something which is his. But in writing an advertisement you must first overcome his reluctance to read it.

The trouble with the average man is that he will advertise a heater only when it is cold. He should pick the hottest day of summer and say: "It is hot as the devil to-day. Next winter will be just as cold." Then when winter comes the consumer is familiar with that particular heater.

Collins' Course in Show Card Writing

Eleventh of a series of articles specially prepared for this journal.

The Fountain Air Brush.

IT will be remembered that several of the sample cards given in previous lessons have been "Fountain air brush" designs. This instrument is a very desirable and valuable acquisition to a card writer's outfit as it is capable of a very wide range of use, extending from the ordinary shading of plain letters to the most elaborate designs and ornamentations in all colors and shades. Engravers, portrait artists, photographers and other commercial artists utilize it with economical results. Originally it was designed for portrait work, and for years its usefulness did not extend beyond this field, but later improvements in its construction greatly widened its utility, which now seems almost illimitable. It is of special use to the card writer for its wonderful and effective results are easily and quickly obtained.

The illustration shows the exact size of the brush. It derives its name from the fact that it does the work of a brush but is operated with compressed air. The color cups hold enough color to suggest the idea of a "fountain" or reservoir. The necessary air pressure may be supplied with a foot pump and small storage tank, or with a carbonic gas tank the same as used in soda fountains. Of course, power pumps may be used for the purpose if desired. It requires about 20 or 25 pounds pressure to assure good work. After the connections are made with the tank by means of a small rubber tube, air is forced into the brush by opening a valve, which is done by pressing down the top lever with the index finger. This air passes out at the point of the brush around a small pointed needle. This arrangement of having the air pass out all around the needle assures an equal pressure and evener work, and also requires much less air than if the air pressure were obtained from one side of the needle. As the compressed air passes out it forms a suction which draws the color from the cup either in large or small quantities and distributes it in a fine spray all under the control and at the will of the operator.

Various colors may be used and must be free from grit, dust or dirt to prevent clogging the brush. The amount of color you wish to use is regulated by pressing down the lever which opens the valve sufficient to admit a fine spray to emit, and by pulling the lever back the amount of spray will be increased. The color cup may be adjusted to any angle so that you may work on cards lying flat on a table, or standing in a perpendicular position on a wall or easel, or if necessary the brush may be used on a ceiling with the color cup tipped to accommodate that position. This is a very important feature.

Care should be taken to always clean the brush after each using by blowing clean water through it, and then drying thoroughly by blowing with air from the tank after disconnecting the brush. With care this instrument should last a lifetime.

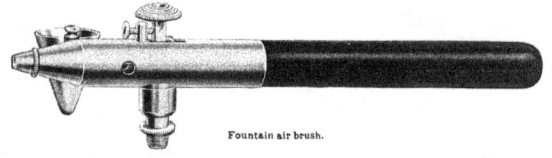

Designs Effective and Varied.

Simple and effective designs may be created and executed with the fountain air brush. By simply laying a smaller card on the one you wish to work and spraying around the edges you can obtain a very pretty and effective border design. The sample "Turkey" card shown in this lesson is made by cutting the pattern out of a fairly heavy manilla paper and laying it on to the card and air brushing around it. The outside mat of the same design may be used if desired, but in this case the spraying with the air brush will be done on the inside of the pattern. This is a very simple form of design.

Alphabets.

Plates 42 and 43 are fancy alphabets that are not hard to execute. Like all fancy alphabets they are suitable for one word or a line that needs accentuating. They are capable of taking much color. For example, the upper part may be in bright red or blue and the bottom and upper outline and fancy over-lay may be in black. Or the tops may be in light blue and the bottom and outlines and overlay may be in dark blue. And

Fountain air brush.

abcdefghijklmn
opqrstuvwxyz&

Plate 43. Fancy design, well spurred, lower case.

in a similar way other combinations may be utilized. This style of letters is excellent for practice work.

Initials.

We give a number of sample initials this month that will furnish a foundation for an inexhaustible supply of these very effective embellishments.

Seasonable autumn card.

A may be made in black or any strong color with the outline in black, and the background striped in some subdued color.

E may be in black or brown and the spray in a blue or yellow color and the foliage in green.

F is an unique ribbon design in blue, purple or any bright color.

G has a heavy and light outline with a clouded centre of any bright color. This makes a very effective design.

H has a background of bright red, blue or yellow and dotted with black. The letter may be in black or dark blue, according to the harmonizing effect of the background.

I is a plain black letter with a fancy outline. Of course, it can be worked in any other color.

J may be done in black or red or brown or blue, with a subdued ornamental back in harmonious color.

K may be done with a wall paper effect or some other fancy back, and the letter in black or some other dark color.

O is a simple outlined letter with side embellishments and fancy overlaid work.

Any of the letters may be interchanged, that is, the different ideas may be worked with any letter.

Sample Card.

We show only one sample card this month. It is a design suitable for Thanksgiving, which is the only holiday October offers. All merchants should take advantage of every holiday and make it an advertising feature. The colors to use are those in keeping with the season, browns, dark reds, yellows, etc. This design is made by cutting the shape of the turkey out of a piece of heavy paper and laying it on to the card and air brushing around it with a light spray of brown. The lettering is done in dark brown and shaded with grey and the figures are in red and shaded with grey.

Some specimen initial letters.

Plate 42.—Fancy design, well spurred, upper case.

Beds and Bedding

TWO NEW IDEAL LINES.

The Ideal Bedding Co., Ltd., Toronto, have just brought out a new patented wire mattress in their "Duplex," the U. S. rights of which have been sold to an American house. Across the line these mattresses are said to be selling in thousands. The illustration herewith gives some idea of the appearance of the "Duplex" in a woven wire weave. It is also made in the Ideal twin-link twisted fabric.

The mattress, or rather double mattress, is connected by springs to the centre divider, and also by springs to top and bottom. The mattress frame is colored in

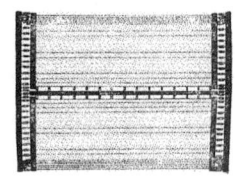

New Ideal "Duplex" patented wire mattress.

the new oxydized finish, which keeps the "Duplex" always clean and neat-looking, and it carries a guarantee from the company for 20 years stamped on the frame.

The Ideal Co. are also getting out a new trundle bed with twin-lock twisted wire fabric mattress. The whole frame and mattress are in one. Head and foot fold, so that it is possible when not in use to shove it under the bed. This makes an additional bed at low cost, which is quite a consideration in city houses, where space and price are to be reckoned with. The bedclothes need not be removed, as they remain on the cot, and are kept in place and folded away with the trundle bed itself.

Half a dozen new designs of chill-less iron beds have also been added.

BEDSTEADS FOR SOLDIERS

The Ives Modern Bedstead Co., Cornwall, have secured an order for a considerable number of bedsteads for barracks, hospitals and ambulance work, which will keep them busy for several weeks and possibly longer. The season promised to be fairly good for this company, and there was a fair supply of orders, but the uncertainty caused by the war has changed the views of buyers, and they are taking less bedsteads than they would otherwise have done. However, this order for military use will help a good deal, and there maye be a difference in the aspect of affairs when they are completed.

The Pacific Wall Bed Company, Ltd., Winnipeg, has been incorporated for the purpose of manufacturing, contracting, installing, buying, selling, trading and dealing in beds, bedding, furniture and furnishings, wire and wire products, etc., with a capital of $60,000. The incorporators are: George Earl Betts, accountant; Frederick Goodwill Rumble, commission merchant; John Wood Gibson, accountant; Thomas Joseph Coyle, manufacturing agent, and Edwin Loftus, barrister, all of Winnipeg.

ADVERTISING A MATTRESS.

A new window advertising stunt is being put on by the Ideal Bedding Co., Ltd., this fall. In their booth at the Toronto Exhibition were a number of electric "canteen" lamps, frosted, showing a picture of an Ideal "Neverspred" mattress, which alternately lighted and went out. They drew much attention to the display. For the rest of the season the company's representatives on the road will have a number of these lamps for loan among their customers. All that is necessary is to place the lamp in the window and connect it to the nearest electric light socket and turn on the power.

BEDDING NOTES.

Percy Brown, lately representative for the Gale bedding line, is now connected with the Canadian Mersereau Co., Ltd., selling this new line in Western Ontario. It is a long time since Percy began to sell beds, almost as long as the time he began to ride and sell bicycles. Even to-day Percy sees the connection between beds and bicycles, due no doubt to the similarity of frames of new brass tube bed and the old-time bicycle, and longs for those days when he rode so often to victory the Gendron wheel of happy memory.

The Montreal factory of the Alaska Bedding Co. covers a total floor space of 182,000 square feet, and the annual manufacturing capacity of the plant is 90,000 steel beds, 30,000 brass beds, 180,000 mattresses, 150,000 springs, 40,000 couches, and 360,000 pillows.

LETTER BOX

The Editor, Canadian Furniture World:

Will you kindly give us a list of names of manufacturers of school desks?
Barrie.   DOUGALL BROS.

Berlin Interior Hardwood Co., Berlin; Canadian Office and School Furniture Co., Preston; Globe Furniture Co., Waterloo; James Smart Mfg. Co., Brockville; John B. Snider, Waterloo; Valley City Seating Co., Dundas; W. F. Vilas, Cowansville, Que.; Westport School Furniture Co., Westport, are among the makers of this class of goods. —Editor.

In the good old summer time. McLaughlin, Bingerman, Pres. Fischman, Cohen and Bell of the Fischman Mattress Co.

Knobs of News

The Stratford Chair Co. proposes to double its plant.

The Great West Furniture Co. has been incorporated at Regina, Sask.

The Markdale, Ont., furniture factory was struck by lightning during a recent storm, and sustained a slight damage.

The Westminster Furniture Store has moved to new premises at New Westminster, B.C.

R. P. Newton has leased the premises formerly occupied by Mr. Killingsworth, corner of Wellington and Ross Streets, St. Thomas, Ont., and will start up an upholstery and furniture store.

S. M. Wilder's furniture store, at Toronto, was damaged by fire recently.

Lepage & Co., stove dealers, etc., Quebec, have been registered.

A by-law to loan $25,000 to the newly-organized Goderich Furniture Co., Ltd., and to give a fixed assessment of $10,000 for a period of 20 years was carried by a majority of 558 to 58 recently. The company will start building operations at once.

Lieut. C. A. James, who is in charge of the 22nd Oxford Rifles, Woodstock, Ont., now at Valcartier, is a member of the general-office staff of the Canada Furniture Manufacturers, at Woodstock.

The furniture and hardware stock belonging to the estate of Irwin & Bryant, Balcarres, Sask., has been sold to H. E. Chaplin.

Torey & Bush, Reg., have been registered at Montreal as chair frame and cabinet makers.

F. W. Smith's department store, at Weyburn, Sask., will erect a new store next spring, and add a furniture department on its completion.

B. Haram & Co.'s furniture store at Ottawa, Ont., was burned recently, as also was the furniture store of J. B. Roy.

The general contract for the construction of the front for the furniture store for J. M. Farthing, Talbot Street, Aylmer, Ont., has been awarded to H. J. St. Clair Co., Limited.

D. Reider, of the Leader Store, at Estevan, Man., is determined that the service of his establishment must keep pace with the growth of the town. To that end he has opened a new addition to his store devoted entirely to furniture and house furnishings. On his recent visit to Winnipeg Mr. Reider made extensive purchases of furniture, stoves, and all lines of house furnishings to the amount of several carlots. These goods are now arriving and are being assembled for display in the new salerooms. Mr. Reider is one of the business men of the West who have not been disturbed by war's alarms. He is satisfied that whatever may be the influence of the war in other lands, it should in no way work damage to the trade or commerce of Canada.

An Ontario license has been granted to Jacob & Josef Kohn, Inc., New York, to purchase, acquire, import, and deal in furniture and upholstery of all kinds, and to use $40,000 capital. Wm. J. Craig has been appointed agent.

A. B. Purdy, late of Prince Albert, is opening up a furniture business at Melfort, Sask.

Stewart & Co., of the "Palace Furniture Store," Ottawa, made a rich showing of modern and antique furniture at the recent Central Canada Exhibition. Among the curios displayed was a table said to be the one on which was signed the peace treaty which brought the Franco-Prussian war to a close.

The Gold Medal Furniture Co. made a display of their davenports and divanettes at the recent Ottawa Exhibition. L. G. Fournier, of Ottawa, was in charge of the exhibit.

Wm. G. Colgate has been appointed advertising manager of the Toronto Furniture Co., Ltd. Mr. Colgate is a tried newspaper man who has always had a bent towards the furniture industry. For several years he handled the Toronto company's advertising as a member of the Gagnier Advertising Service, and before that was a member of the Maclean Publishing Co.'s staff. He seems to have struck his gait in making a combination of the furniture business with his journalistic experience.

Walter Wrench, designer with the Toronto Furniture Company, is at present on a two months' trip to the Old Country, where it is his intention to visit the principal museums and antique shops, with a view to securing fresh ideas from a close, first-hand study of the work of the famous old-time craftsmen and designers.

A rush order for several thousand tables designed for field hospital or Red Cross work was recently given to the Toronto Furniture Company. Instructions were received on September 15, and the last delivery was made to Ottawa on the 19th, thus constituting something of a record for this class of work. The rush was such, however, that the shops were forced to run day and night.

The Dominion Furniture Co., Moose Jaw, is now under new management. F. M. Brock and T. F. Hutchinson, both favorably known in Moose Jaw, have taken entire charge. Many improvements have been made, not only in the stock, but in the arrangement of the store. The firm has built up a large business in Moose Jaw and throughout Saskatchewan. Shipments are being continually made to outside points. A wholesale as well as retail business is done, and the firm has recently started to manufacture several popular lines. This department is in charge of an expert workman. Pedestals, jardiniere stands, and tables of all kinds are being made right on the premises. The firm also manufactures store fixtures, including showcases.

NEW ADDITIONS TO LIPPERT LINE.

The Lippert Furniture Co., Ltd., Berlin, have issued a supplementary catalogue of the new additions to their line. These include bedroom chairs and rockers in solid mahogany and Circassian walnut in varied styles, some with cane panel backs. Armchairs and diners, too, in solid mahogany and quartered oak are new. Some have plain wood and others upholstered backs. The seats are all upholstered, some of them with leather slip seats.

The Lippert Heinco chairs are described and illustrated. These automatic reclining chairs work on a balanced roller-bearing, yet are simple in operation and as free from mecharism as a plain rocker. They are made in quartered oak in any oak finish, have nine styles of leather upholstered backs, all of them interchangeable, and supplied with any frame. They may be had also in any cloth covering.

Living room and den furniture have nearly two dozen items added in chairs, rockers, sofas, and settees, and the Lippert davenports and divanettes have several new designs. By having springs in the back, as well as in the seat, these revolving beds give all the comfort of a davenport without sacrificing the efficiency of the bed.

LIGHT AND COLOR IN THE WINDOW.

Dark blue reflects 6½ per cent. of the light falling upon it. Dark green, about 10 per cent. Pale red, more than 16 per cent. Dark yellow, 20 per cent. Pale blue, 30 per cent. Pale yellow, 40 per cent. Pale green, 46½ per cent. Pale orange, nearly 55 per cent. White, 70 per cent.

SIDWAY MERCANTILE CO. IN CANADA

C. A. Coryell, lately of the Bedell's Furniture Co., Ltd., Toronto, has become connected with the Sidway Mercantile Co., of Elkhart, Ind., and Goderich, Ont., and will represent that company in Ontario during 1915. The company will also be represented in Quebec and the East, travelers covering that territory regularly.

The Sidway Mercantile Co. make collapsible carts, baby carriages with reed and wood sides, also sulkies. They have met with success in the United States, and expect to duplicate that success in Canada.

NEW RECLINING CHAIRS.

While furniture manufacturers making reclining chairs pride themselves on some one particular design or pattern, The Chair Craft Co., of Traverse City, Mich., are making two reclining chairs which are in a class by themselves. Their "Rest-Fest" or "Sleepy Hollow" design is unlike anything else in the chair line that is made, and so is in a class by itself. The "Rex-Recliner" is similar to other makes in general outline, but it is different in operation in that the back will recline perfectly flat, forming a bed. Both these designs are copyrighted and patented in Canada and the United States.

Two new furniture items—One of the latest divanette designs made by The Lippert Furniture Co., Berlin, Ont., and a "Rex—Recliner" chair, made by The Chair Craft Co., Traverse City, Mich.

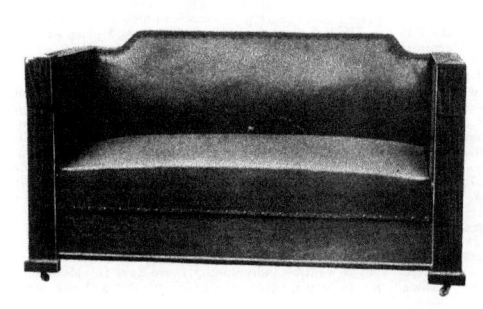

MANUFACTURERS' BUILDING AT CANADIAN NATIONAL EXHIBITON GROUNDS, TORONTO.

Furniture Exhibits at the Canadian National Exhibition

BIGGER and better than ever is a term which is exclusively the property of the Canadian National Exhibition, which, annually held at Toronto, increases its influence and its usefulness with the public, whether they be, in a trade sense, consumers, dealers, or manufacturers. It serves the good purpose of showing the advances made in industrial art from year to year, and so is a valuable aid for the manufacturer to display and demonstrate his wares; for the dealer to note their effect on the public, and for the consumer to see, not only the new things, but, more important, their practical application to the needs of everyday life.

Among the many and varied exhibits none claimed a greater share of attention than did those of the makers and dealers of furniture, beds, stoves and housefurnishings. A number of booths were looked after by several Toronto retail furniture dealers, who act as district agents for the various lines exhibited. For instance, the Adams Furniture Co. had charge of the exhibits of "Hoosier" kitchen cabinets, "White" sewing machines, the Pullman Couch Co.'s davenport beds and the D. Moore Co.'s stoves.

Louis Yolles had the "Napanee" kitchen cabinet booth, where his salesmen explained and gave demonstrations on this step-saver.

S. Levinter looked after the Hamilton Stove & Heater Co.'s "Souvenir" stoves and ranges.

The F. C. Burroughes Furniture Co.'s salesmen handled both the Harriston Stove Co.'s exhibit of "Royal" stoves and ranges and the A-B Stove Co.'s gas range display.

Furniture Displays.

In the downtown district, on King street, near Bay street, John C. Mundell & Co., The Elora Furniture Co. and the H. E. Furniture Co., held a joint exhibition of their various productions. The Mundell line of living room, dining room, library and den all-wood chairs ran pretty much to fumed oak, many of them of Jacobean design. Particularly was this true of diners. A number of new library tables with cane ends looked very attractive, as also did a three-piece living room suite, the backs of the chairs being set with cane panels. Other items shown were large and comfortable luxurious living room chairs in leather, and some new bedroom chairs in Adam and colonial designs made up in mahogany, oak and enamels. Morris chairs, roll seat and cobbler rockers seem to be as popular as ever, and some imitation leather rockers, smokers' tables, cellarettes, telephone and magazine stands, and card tables in odd designs were standard novelty lines shown.

Couches in leather and tapestry filled out the display, which looked exceedingly well. John C. Mundell was at the exhibit a couple of days, and J. Smith was in charge.

The Elora Furniture Co.'s display ran principally to wood beds in enamel, mahogany, and fumed oak, a three-in. continuous post bed in mahogany being a particular feature. Parlor tables, jardiniere stands, pedestals, umbrella stands, in all woods, finishes and designs, were perhaps the most numerous items in the display, but every one of them deserved some special mention.

The H. E. Furniture Co., of Milverton, Ont., displayed eight patterns of their better grade kitchen cabinets in gum wood and oak. One of these was particularly nice, showing as it did for the first time the new roller curtain across the whole front. It was finished in valspar varnish and had a white porcelain top, making it easy to keep clean, sanitary and decidedly attractive in appearance. Mr. H. Honderick was in charge of both the Elora and H. E. Furniture displays.

Everything in Furniture.

Also in the downtown district, at 136-140 King street east, the Canada Furniture Manufacturers, Ltd., kept open house. The whole four floors of the building were given over to a showing of their many and varied lines. This company in their many factories make practically everything in the line of furniture, and include in this also a big department of baby carriages and go-carts. Period furniture and modern styles for every room in the house were shown in large and tasty variety, and enamel items and suites in white ivory and French grey specially appealed to the ladies. Besides the high class period suites there were shown a number of miscellaneous lines for ordinary use in medium and cheap grades, all of them, however, of first-class workmanship.

Period Furniture.

The Toronto Furniture Co. made a special exhibition of their lines in their factory show rooms on Dufferin street, and as this was on the way to the Exhibition grounds, many of the trade visiting Toronto stepped in to see the new goods. Being makers of dining room, library and chamber suites, the showing of these goods of course was very extensive. The company specializes in period styles, and exquisite suites in various woods and finishes were shown. Each suite occupied a compartment, or room, of its own, thus the beauties of any particular suite were set off to advantage. Many of the suites were constructed along original lines, so that a buyer wanting individuality could have it. Many odd pieces in mahogany, Circassian walnut and oak were also displayed in modern and period styles. Some of these pieces were made up in furniture items not now usually seen on the floor of a furniture store. As showing the progress of the trade, the display was an excellent one.

In the Industrial Building.

Snyder Bros. Upholstering Co., Ltd., Waterloo, Ont., made an exhibit and gave demonstrations of their "Thorobed" davenports. It is only some few months ago now that the company introduced this "Thorobed" to the Canadian market. It is made in two sizes—divanette and davenport—both of them fitted with "Simmons" steel fabric, and supported by oil-tempered helical springs to carry a 35-pound mattress. In the back is a dust-proof wardrobe for storing all the bedding. The foot rail on the divanette allows of sleeping at either end, as well as being a convenient place for the spare comforter. To show how easily the "Thorobed" is operated, a boy gave demonstrations in opening and closing the various exhibits. The davenports and divanettes come in a great many designs, all woods, and over 200 coverings, in denims, velours, tapestries, silks, imitation leathers and genuine leather.

In this same building the Gendron Mfg. Co., Toronto, carried an exhibit of baby carriages, children's wagons and reed furniture. The latter were shown in fancy parlor and verandah chairs, also invalids' chairs. Thos. Chadwick and W. Brady looked after the display.

How Many Hides Has a Cow?

The above heading was used as a centrepiece motto in the Du Pont Fabrikoid Co.'s booth, where they displayed innumerable samples of their imitation leather coverings for upholstered goods used by furniture and automobile factories, makers of baby carriages and trunks and bags. Two-thirds of the leather to-day is "coated split." A real cowhide is split into three sheets and the splits are coated and embossed in imitation of grain leather. The makers of "Fabrikoid" claim that these splits being really artificial leather, are inferior in quality to their scientifically made artificial leather, based on a woven fabric much stronger and more uniform than the fleshy split hide, but coated and embossed in the same way. "Fabrikoid" is not affected by water, heat or cold, and sells at a medium and a low price. It gives good service; it can be washed, and does not scratch. The company have just completed this summer a new $25,000 wing to their Toronto factory, which speaks well for the progress of the company during the present cry of "hard times." W. A. Cotton, manager, and A. W. Purtle, looked after the display.

Iron and Brass Beds.

The Ideal Bedding Co. made a very large display of their productions in two booths in the Industrial Building. In the first booth they showed their folding beds, the improved Hammo-couch, the "Foldaway" and a number of "clear porcelain white enamel" beds. A special feature of the exhibit was the demonstration made with the Ideal Duplex Spring No. 1 mattress. From the commencement of the Exhibition until its close, one of these mattresses sustained a weight of 1,300 pounds of iron pipe without any noticeable stretching, the mattress returning to its original position when the weight was removed. The Duplex carries a 20-year guarantee. It created quite an amount of interest.

Also in this exhibit were shown samples of folding wood chairs for assembly halls and theatres, and a novelty was the vest pocket folding stool for autos. As its name suggests, this stool folds up in a very small space and is decidedly useful for an extra seat in the auto when such is required. Some brass costumiers were also shown.

In booth No. 2 displays were made of made up brass and enamel beds, cribs, stuffed mattresses, etc. Some of the brass beds were exceedingly tasty, several of them showing brass panels imitating cane in appearance, set in head and foot, which were not only novel but very pretty as well. The "Neverspred" mattress was used on the made-up beds, and one of them was shown in sections, so that visitors could see how sanitary and good they were made up. The new safety crib with noiseless side—being fitted with felt washers drew a great deal of attention.

The appearance of the booth was well set off by the fences made of small woven mattresses, and the top pieces made of sample iron bed frames in white enamel. V. C. Lowell, T. J. Mackie and B. W. Woon were in charge of the displays.

The Dixie Mattress.

Geo. Gale & Sons, Ltd., featured in their exhibit their "best on earth," no-tufted Dixie mattress, a mattress that is sanitary, will not spread, and that has no dirt pockets. It is a comfortable mattress, with plenty of elasticity and resiliency; has a neat appearance, and is durable. The mattress has ten compartments, and a sample Dixie was dissected to show the various sections and the method of construction.

Some of the newer lines of Gale brass beds were also displayed. The company has an exceptionally wide range of choice, and the patterns bristle with new features.

Acid-proof Brass Beds.

S. Weisglass, Ltd., Montreal, made a showing of some 40 new designs of brass beds. These beds are guaranteed both for construction and finish. Being proof against acids, they will not tarnish under the use of any acids, alcohol, salts, or solutions. Though showing but 40 samples, the company's range of patterns and designs number about 200. The exhibits were arranged to show the various finishes—bright, satin, and velvet. This latter finish was striking, the brass taking on a shining finish like a mirror. Several brass costumiers were also shown. R. W. Menzie was in charge of the booth.

The Stove Display.

The present year is bringing out a number of improvements to standard and popular stove and range lines, and, in addition, is pulling forward many new stoves with distinctive features. In decoration and finish almost every stove-maker is going back to simple lines and plain trimmings.

U.S. FURNITURE IN CANADA.

The value of imports of furniture into Canada from the United States in 1912 was $1,092,809; in 1913, $1,877,478, and so far this year, $1,479,310.

"When business is good, advertise some to get more."
"When business is bad, advertise more to get some."

The Furniture Manufacturer

A Department of News and Ideas

FINISHING GOLDEN OAK.

By Rudolph Kilbourne

A correspondent asks for information on how to finish quarter-cut golden oak so as to leave the flakes white. He says: "Some flakes will appear almost the color of the natural wood and look dingy." I do not know just what he means by that, because the natural wood is never dingy; but if he means that the flake under his present method of finishing takes the stain almost as dark as the porous part of the wood, and looks dirty and murky, then probably I can give him the cause and tell him how to remedy it.

At the outset, let us not forget that the way quartered oak is cleaned up when finished golden has a lot to do with the clearness of the finish, also, that the oak itself has much to do with the color of the flake. Remember that oak never gets lighter in color during the process of finishing. If it is "blue" oak, or is not a nice, light sample of either white or red oak, you cannot get that nice white flake that is such a distinguishing feature of some furniture.

As a rule, in the cleaning up of wood for the finish, anything that savors of a polish is not of advantage to the finish, but the preparation of quarter-cut oak to be finished golden is an exception to that rule. Where a clear flake is desired the surface of the wood cannot be made too fine and smooth. The grade of paper should be gradually reduced until the very finest is used for the final sanding. This will insure the removal of sandpaper scratches. If these are not removed the stain will get into the minute fibres along the scratch and show dark, and if there are many of them the result will be a "dingy" appearance.

A good, clear finish is not made with a combination stain and filler. The clearest finishes are always made by staining first, then filling. There are a number of stains on the market that will produce the desired result, but if one wishes to make his own stain he can use the following formula as a basis from which to work, changing the proportions to make whatever shade is desired. There is a standard shade of golden oak, known as the "Grand Rapids shade," and all the large wood-finishing supply houses handle a stain to produce this shade. But frequently the finisher finds himself in difficulty because this stain produces different results on different woods. If one makes his own stain he can change it to suit the wood, provided, of course, he is not given too many different kinds to finish.

The principal ingredients entering into the composition of a golden oak stain are oil yellow, oil black, and asphaltum. A good turpentine asphaltum should be used. The oil black should be jet black, and the oil yellow should be the pale lemon shade. This is very important.

Dissolve 1 oz. of the oil yellow in 1 pint of turpentine, and dissolve 4 ounces of oil black in 2 quarts of turpentine. If one has a hot water vat, dissolution may be hastened and made more complete by the use of heat. For obvious reasons it would not be safe to use these materials near a fire.

After the oil yellow and oil black have been thoroughly dissolved, pour them into 1 gal. of the asphaltum. This will produce a beautiful, rich shade of golden oak stain of about the consistency usually supplied by stain manufacturers. This may be reduced to the desired depth of color by the use of a reducer made of equal parts turpentine and benzine.

This stain may be applied either with a rag or a brush, but it should be applied evenly and not very heavily. On flat surfaces a better and more even job can be made with a rag than with a brush. If the stain is not put on with something that will let it off evenly, it is liable to be taken up too rapidly by the soft, absorbing parts, will not dry properly, and will ooze out after the goods are filled and varnished.

A properly applied coat of stain will dry sufficiently in from thirty minutes to an hour to allow of filling. The filler is an important item in the making of a nice, clear, clean golden oak. If one wishes a real, light-colored flake, the oil in the filler must not contain any coloring matter. Where a colored filler is used the coloring matter must be in the pigment. Some finishers use a white filler, depending on the stain that is raised to give sufficient color; but one ought not to put the stain on heavy enough for that. The better way is to color the pigment when the filler is made. The best filler is made of silex. The more finely it is ground the better. Silica also makes a good pigment for oak filler.

Filler should be made 24 hours before using, but it is not well to have it made too far ahead. Filler works hard and stiff when it becomes old, especially filler containing japan. For this reason one should not make more than enough to last about ten days. The proportions given in the following formula may be used for any quantity desired: 4 qts. pure boiled linseed oil, 4 qts. pale brown japan, 2 lbs. vandyke brown ground in oil. Stir the above together and add sufficient silex to make a stiff dough. Keep the filler in the dough state until required for use. Such quantities as are required for immediate use may be reduced with benzine to the proper consistency. Paste filler may be reduced to the fluid state much more easily and quickly if but a small quantity of benzine is added at the start. With this break up the thick paste, and when this is done the balance of the benzine may be added.

Oak filler should be well brushed into the pores of the wood. Unless it is worked well into the deep pores it will pull out during the process of cleaning off. Allow the filler to stand until it has dried flat all over, then remove with excelsior or seamoss or other suitable material. Rub crosswise the grain to remove filler; there is less danger of pulling it out that way. Work stained and filled in the manner here described will have a rich brown background to a nice white flake.

The next thing is, how to preserve this clearness during the balance of the finishing process. White shellac may be used for a surfacer, or a pale pigment surface may be used. Use a pale varnish for the "bodying up" and the clearness of the color will be maintained throughout.—The Wood-Worker.

NEW SYSTEM OF DRY KILNS.

An unduly large proportion of the fires in woodworking plants start in connection with the dry kilns, so that any fire protection improvements in this feature of the plant are of special importance. Twelve per cent. of the woodworker fires start in the dry kilns, and statistics show that the common type of steam heating dry kilns has averaged a fire life of only a little over five years.

A new type of dry kiln is being installed, which shows a marked reduction in the fire hazard and equal superiority in the quality of lumber turned out. Its distinctive feature is in the manipulation of the moist air in drying the lumber. The moisture aids the processes by keeping the pores at the outer surfaces of the wood open, so that the sap and moisture inside can pass freely to the outside, where it can be removed in such quantities as is desired. The principle follows that of the natural drying out of doors, where rain and dew alternate with the sun and wind to thoroughly season the lumber.

The improved moist air dry kilns are based on the principle that high temperatures can support large amounts of moisture. Air is taken from the lumber compartment at 175 degrees, for instance, bearing all the moisture it can contain, but when cooled to a temperature of 150 degrees it drops half its moisture. This 150 degrees air when returned through the kiln carries its moisture to the wood to keep it open and soft, but in passing the steam coils its temperature is again raised to 175 degrees, reducing its relative humidity from 100 per cent. to 50 per cent., so that in passing through the lumber it is again capable of absorbing moisture until 100 per cent. humidity is again reached.

The system is based upon a continued repetition of this process. The new kilns are usually well built from a fire protection standpoint, and the fire hazard is materially reduced by the fact that there is a gentle circulation of very moist air in place of the baking process of old-style kilns, or the strong draught used in the blower kilns. This reduces the danger of carbonization of the woodwork. Fire protection engineers urge that kilns should be sprinklered, 212 or other high degree heads being used, or equipped with steam jets. Wood construction should be discouraged, and location inside the factory should be permitted only where it is absolutely necessary.

CIRCASSIAN WALNUT.

The high cost of Circassian walnut is due to the scarcity of the beautifully figured variety demanded for furniture and interior finish, for the tree itself is more widely distributed than almost any other of commercial importance. The demand for the best wood, however, has always outrun the supply.

Even in the eighteenth century, when wars in Europe were frequent, so much Circassian walnut was used for gunstocks that the supply was seriously depleted. Early in the nineteenth century the wood of 12,000 trees was used for this purpose alone. Single trees, containing choice burls or fine birdseye figures, have sold for more than $3,000.

The United States is probably the largest consumer of Circassian walnut, one of the world's best known and most expensive cabinet woods.

The tree is native to the eastern slopes of the Caucasus and ranges eastward to the foothills of the Himalaya Mountains, from which it extends southward to northern India and the mountains of upper Burma. It has been widely planted in Europe and the United States, in this country under the name of English walnut. The wood grown here, however, has not the qualities demanded by the cabinet and furniture maker. Much of the Circassian walnut now used comes from the Black Sea and from other parts of Asia.

According to a circular just issued by the Forest Service the demand for Circassian walnut has resulted in the substitution of other woods, our own red gum is often sold as Circassian walnut, and butternut is also similar in general appearance to the less highly figured grades. Many good African, Asian and South American woods resemble Circassian walnut, though none possess the magnificent figure, delicate tones and velvety texture of the latter. The circular discusses the supply and uses of Circassian walnut, and those who wish to know how possible substitutes may be distinguished can thus learn from the Government's experts the distinctive marks of the true and the false woods.

CIRCASSIAN WALNUT AND SATINWOOD.

The furniture papers are predicting a decline in the call for Circassian walnut soon, and that it will likely be followed by an enlarged call for satinwood. Maybe the call for Circassian will wane a little by-and-by, for it has been unusually strong, but, like mahogany, it will always find a favored place. Then if a change is desired from the extreme flashiness of the prominent figure, why not more gum? Indeed, gum should come in two ways here: the figured and the red, as softer tones than the Circassian, yet in the same order, and the white gum for the white or satinwood effects. We have some white gum that, when carefully dried and finished, makes a mighty beautiful white wood, and it works well in the form of veneer. The predictions as to furniture changes, if they are well founded, should indicate a good opening ahead for figured and white gum for face work.

OPPORTUNITY FOR FURNITURE DEALER

Just now, when the furniture business is slightly off color and sales are a little slower than usual, should be a good time to look about for new lines that will fit in with the trade. One of these is the graphophone. With the long evenings at hand and outdoor amusements curtailed, there should be profitable sales in store for the dealer live enough to go after the business. Graphophones are becoming a necessity, and they are becoming the vogue in the home. For winter evenings, to entertain company, to amuse the children, and at house parties to take the place of the professional piano player for dancing, the graphophone seems to be the thing needed. No doubt dealers can get sales ideas from customers as to how buyers are best interested but the dealer himself should have some ideas of his own as to how to begin a graphophone department.

NEW YORK ESTABLISHES CREDIT BUREAU.

The New York Retail Furniture Association have organized a credit bureau with a permanent office, to which all members report their delinquent debtors, skips and general bad accounts, so that when any of them sell a new applicant on credit they can immediately refer to this office to see if the applicant's name is listed. If it is, it is a simple matter to find out from the member who reported the name, as to the trouble he had with this applicant.

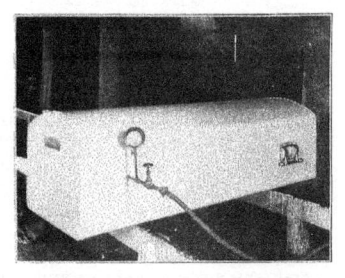

"Purity"

The "Safest Vault on Earth"

Made from Purity Metal. 50 year guarantee against effects of corrosion—most durable vault made. Practically indestructible. Acid tests show a ratio of 22 to 1 compared with common steel.

Burglar, Vermin and Water Proof

DOMINION MANUFACTURERS, LTD., Canadian Distributors
Head Office : TORONTO, Ont.

WRITE ANY BRANCH FOR ILLUSTRATED DESCRIPTIVE CIRCULAR

We Help You to Sell "Purity" Vaults

BY supplying small mailing cards and large, beautiful photo engraved wall hangers, 11 x 14 inches, illustrating the greater service and longer life of "Purity" Vaults as compared with the ordinary caskets.

Purity Vaults are all thoroughly tested before leaving the factory

---

National Grave Vault Company
Galion - Ohio

Undertakers' Department

Problems affecting the Undertaking Profession are here discussed and readers are invited to send letters expressing their views on any of the subjects dealt with—News of the profession throughout Canada.

Canadian Embalmers' Convention

Thirty-first annual meeting of oldest Funeral Directors' Association in the Dominion—Old officers promoted—Result of examinations.

THE 31st annual convention of the Canadian Embalmers' Association was held in the Anatomical Building of the University of Toronto, on Tuesday, Wednesday and Thursday, September 8, 9 and 10, with a registered attendance of 151.

In the absence of J. G. Henry, the president, who was prevented from being present because of illness, the second vice-president, N. B. Cobbledick, opened the convention formally at 10.30 on the morning of the first day by calling on the secretary, F. W. Matthews, to read the minutes of the last convention.

Because of the length, and also because the majority of the members had already read the report of last year's convention in the Furniture World and The Undertaker, it was, on motion of N. J. Boyd and F. Scott, moved that the minutes be considered as having been read and adopted, which motion was unanimously carried.

The chairman then suggested if there was anything in the minutes which the secretary wished to bring particularly before the convention, that he do so, but Mr. Matthews stated the minutes would be dealt with in the committees' report, and he invited any member who wished information to ask any questions he wished. None being forthcoming, the chairman went on to the next item on the programme, calling on Professor Moll to take the floor.

This lecture of Professor Moll on the "Draining of Blood" will be published in the next issue of Canadian Furniture World and The Undertaker.

TUESDAY AFTERNOON.

The convention was called to order at 2 o'clock by First Vice-President Edwards, who acted as chairman for the rest of the convention. He introduced Rev. Byron Stauffer to the meeting, who spoke in a jocular vein, at the same time dropping many words of wisdom and much good common sense.

REV. BYRON STAUFFER'S ADDRESS.

"To think of addressing undertakers twice in two or three years is what I suppose you folks would call a 'stiff' job," said Mr. Stauffer by way of introduction. "It was one of the biggest jobs in the world to find out what I had not said to you three years ago, and to make it worth while, because your business and mine are alike pretty serious kinds of businesses, and I thought perhaps I ought to say to you men, and especially the younger men, that one thing the undertaker requires above anything else is a cool head. The advantage of a Britisher behind one of the guns in our dreadnoughts is that he does not get flustered. You men should never get flustered. I remember that when I first went to the city my church way in a very poor part of the town. There was one undertaker I will never forget, and I think if I had been as old then as I am now, there would either have been a dead undertaker or a dead preacher. He rushed out to the carriages waving his hands at the mourners, and calling out, 'Come around this way with the carriages!' so loud that sometimes the mourners might hear it.

"Now, I think I made the remark to you when I was here three years ago that the best undertaker is the invisible undertaker, the man who goes around with gum shoes so easily that you hardly know he is there. I think I said something then that the undertaker should be like the man used by a photographer to hold up your head while you are

COMMENDING THE FURNITURE WORLD

I COULD not let this occasion go by without commending the Canadian Furniture World and The Undertaker to the members of this association, its columns being devoted to our interests and its articles both helpful and instructive. I would recommend every member to be loyal in its support and a paid-up subscriber."—From President J. G. Henry's address.

Born in Gananoque some forty years ago, and is now carrying on business in both the furniture and undertaking lines, in succession to his father, Wm. Edwards, Sr., who retired some years ago, having spent over 25 years in the business, and in which he is still able to take a keen interest. Wm. Edwards, Jr., having thus been born into the line of business which he has always followed, has seen a great many changes, from the days of the coffin maker to the present embalmer and funeral director. He has also spent several years in connection with the manufacturing end of the furnishing business, in different parts of the Dominion. For many years the business has held membership in the Canadian Embalmers' Association and whatever advances have been made in sanitation, lines are attributable to the instruction and inspiration furnished by attendance at the conventions and demonstrations given by the Association.

WM. EDWARDS
The new President of the Canadian Embalmers' Association.

having your picture taken; it ought to be out of sight and yet do the job. For one thing, when the undertaker is too much in evidence it takes the attention off the preacher, and that is always unfortunate. (Laughter.) The next thing is that the folks, while they may not know why they do not like that particular man as an undertaker, are unusually affected by him fiddling about.

As a preacher, I believe thoroughly in shaking hands with everybody on the right occasion. If I were an undertaker, especially in the small town, yes, and in a big town, I would be the most cordial fellow in the whole town, as most of you are, I think. I would join every lodge within fifty miles, and I would send flowers to the sick and everybody else, doing it carefully, though. And to most of us it goes perfectly natural to shake hands; but there is one time when a preacher should not rest everybody, and that is when he is in the pulpit. And somehow meeting the undertaker at the door of a friend's house where there is a corpse inside, I like him to greet me, and yet as quietly and gently and almost solemnly as the occasion demands. We had a preacher in Buffalo. He was a great handshaker, and it did not matter if it was in the home where he conducted a funeral service or in the church or any where else, he would eternally shake hands and squeeze your hands, and hold it and shake it again. He had a nice way of going to the front door of the church. I don't see how he did it, but he would while out after the benediction, and before you could say 'Jack Robinson' he would be out in front of the church shaking hands with the people, and, of course, they just had to go past him in procession, and he had to make his hand a pump handle. But finally a Swedish girl came down the aisle and was very much embarrassed and she would have given ten dollars if

The Globe Casket Company
London   Ontario

Manufacturers of
Fine Burial Caskets, Casket Hardware, Burial Robes and Linings

Our solid Oak and Mahogany Caskets and Casket Hardware meet every demand in design, quality and finish.

All orders executed promptly, and every care is used in packing and shipping to ensure safe delivery.

We extend our thanks to those who made our showing at the Convention such a marked success.

Telephones: Factory, 169—Mr. Watson, 1654—Shipper, 1020

Did You See
The D. W. Thompson Co., Ltd. Exhibit

At Toronto during the Convention of The Canadian Embalmers' Association?

If you did you appreciate the superior quality of our lines, and if you didn't we'll be glad to send you our literature and prices.

We manufacture a complete line of
High Grade Undertakers' Supplies
and our service is prompt and reliable.

The D. W. Thompson Co., Limited
93-109 Niagara Street   Toronto, Ontario

Telephones: Adelaide 454 and Main 5085.

The "National" Display Pleased Convention Visitors

ONCE again, during the Annual Convention, our Funeral Director friends turned out in full strength to inspect the new ideas in Undertakers' Supplies offered in the "National" make.

As in previous years, the results of our efforts were far from disappointing, and we appreciate the interest shown by our many visitors.

To those who have not been in touch with "National" goods, we suggest that you write for particulars and prices. Being located in Toronto, our service is unequalled. Prices always the most reasonable.

Telephones: Adelaide 454
Adelaide 455 and North 5085

The National Casket Company, Limited
93-109 Niagara St.   Toronto

Fine Burial Robes and Linings

were featured in our exhibit at the Annual Convention of The Canadian Embalmers' Association. The fine quality of our lines was never so forcibly emphasized nor so greatly admired. Many Funeral Directors took advantage of the opportunity to connect up with this reliable line. We specialize on

Everything in Undertakers' Furnishings

S. & E. QUALITY ALWAYS PLEASES. S PERIOR DESIGN AND ELEGANT FINISH

Service is best in every way

"WE NEVER MISS A TRAIN"

The Semmens & Evel Casket Co., Limited
Hamilton, Ontario

Nights and Sundays call: Phone 517   Winnipeg, Man., 470 Ross Ave.
Nos. 517, 3319 or 3353   Chas. Crossland, Manager

she could have avoided the preacher's handshake, but she came on until finally the minister reached her. He held out his hand to her. 'And how do you do sister?' 'And how do you do!' she answered. 'Are you a stranger here, my dear sister?' 'Yes.' 'What is your name?' 'My name is Hilda Anne.' 'And where do you live?' 'At 95 Bird avenue.' 'Now tell me what afternoon you will be in so that I can call to see you.' And timorously she got away from him as she said, 'I tank you, but I have a fellow already.'

Quiet and Unostentatious Funerals.

"Now, this matter of being quiet at funerals and doing things in an unostentatious manner may not be recognized in its importance by some of the younger undertakers. I have sometimes asked undertakers. 'Is it possible to change the thought of people so that they themselves will not

N. B. COBBLEDICK,
Promoted First Vice-President.

want emotional funerals?' and often the undertaker has responded that he does not want it, but that some people want an emotional, spectacular funeral, with loud accompaniments of mourning and weeping, etc. Now, I want to put this right to you this afternoon that it is not that kind of folk that make you a popular undertaker any more than it is the folks who constantly want to go to church to vent their tears make the preacher a popular preacher. In fact, this sort of thing wears out a church very quickly. The kind of folks who make you a successful and popular undertaker in a community are the small minority of folks who like a plain, quiet funeral. The very folks who you think are going to get you because you will give them an emotional funeral are the very folks who, if they find out that one or two of the leading folks of the community are hiring you because you are a quiet fellow, are going to hire you because they want to follow in the footsteps of the leaders of the community. Therefore, I want to suggest to you that what the best class of people want in a community in this 20th century is a funeral where the mourners do not mean to go through the proud pillory of viewing their dead in the presence of everybody. They are the people who make you popular or unpopular in a community, and those folks don't want that sort of thing. I know how hard it is to change people in that matter. For instance, in my own town of Berlin we had a funeral in my wife's family some years ago, and I suggested to the widow and the dead man's sister that they view the remains before the public arrived at the house or the church, and then not look at him again—to let that finish it. I could not accomplish my purpose. The undertaker could not have done it. They wanted to view the remains while the people were looking on. So I grant you there are a good many things in cases where you want to change people's ways about funerals, and yet it is coming very fast, the time when it will be considered an outrage on the feelings of bereaved people to have them gaze on the face of friends for the last time while the public surrounds them, and every Tom, Dick, and Harry are gazing on. So that I think it is the nicer way to have friends in a retreat near the parlor where the remains are, and then to keep the women there afterwards, for they are apt to be emotional.

"Now, I want to tell you another thing, and you have felt this wherever your place of business, whether it is out in the country or in the town. I think that all of you who have been in business ten or twenty years realize that the day of the long funeral is past. The two-hour or two-hour-and-a-half funeral is gone, and you can discuss it as you may, and you can say that it is cold-blooded. We are busier folks than we used to be, and it is a hard thing to get a business man to leave his office at all to attend a funeral. The German philosopher Kant, who used to draw his students from all over the world to hear his lectures, was so cold-blooded that he never would go to visit a sick friend. He would never go to a funeral, and never mentioned that friend after death. I grant you that is pretty cold-blooded. Now, the longer the funeral, the harder we will find it to get a business man to attend, so that we must allow something to the busy age. The short funeral is the thing. The punctual funeral is the thing. I was a few minutes late to-day because the carriage was a few minutes late. When Mr. Matthews called me up, I told him I wanted an automobile to go out to my house instead of to the church downtown. Mr. Matthews told me it was not going to be an automobile, but a carriage. I reminded Mr. Matthews that we lived in the twentieth century, and that horses and carriages are out-of-date—the automobile is the thing. He gave me as the reason that the horse and cab belonged to a livery man who advertised with them a good deal in their programmes, etc. That shut me up. I am not finding any fault. Mr. Matthews said, 'You know you will have a speedy pair of horses,' as though a livery man's horses ever could be speedy. My experience with a livery man's horse is that you never could hurry it up, and, thank heaven, you never could slow them down. They go the same pace, ratty-tat-tat, ratty-tat-tat. Now, I was going to use this to make a prophecy to you, that in ten years from now, in the larger towns and cities of Ontario, you will not have a single horse hearse nor a horse carriage go to a cemetery.

Don't Get in a Rut.

"But that was not what I was going to say. I was going to say that that livery horse teaches me that we can get in a rut, and we will never be able to hurry or change our gait. And undertakers and preachers alike get into that rut. Sombody showed me a race horse and then showed me a grocer's delivery horse, and said there is all the difference in these two horses in blood, heredity, etc. It is true, there is a difference in blood, but there is one thing more, there is a difference in the trainers who trained the delivery horse and who trained the race horse. You can take a son of 'Maud S.' or 'Dexter,' and you could take that young race horse and put him into the same grocery delivery under the delivery boy, and in ten years that horse would go ratty-tat-tar, ratty-tat-tat, about the same as the delivery horse. What I want to say to you is that, that we can combine speed with quietness, promptness, and punctuality.

"I said I was a few minutes late this afternoon. I pride myself on punctuality. I like to open a church so promptly that folks can always set their clocks by the time I enter the pulpit. I believe that your average undertaker is a model in that regard. There are some folks who always will be late. They will come late to the funeral of their friends; they come late to weddings. I have even known folks to telephone to the bride to ask to have the wedding postponed fifteen minutes so that they could get there on time, and they are decidedly selfish people. The thing to do is to hold the funeral punctually at the time appointed. Somebody said regarding this that the train that is on time is helped along by every switch, but that semaphores will always be up against the train that is late. Switches are set for the man that is on time; semaphores are turned against the man who is late. Now, I want to say this one more thing to the young undertaker, be generous—generous as regards money matters. Somebody said that a stingy preacher was of no earthly account, and it is I think, about the same with you. The undertaker is expected to be a pretty open-hearted sort of a fellow. If God has been good to you, be liberal in the community, hold up your end. I went into a drug store the other day, and I was buying a box of cigars. The clerk asked me what I usually got them for. I said, 'I usually get them for $1.40.' 'Are you sure?' he said, 'that it is not $1.45?' 'No, I am not. Five cents one way or another does not count much.' 'Well,' he said, 'we will make it $1.40. We will get it out of you some other way, anyhow. Pretty good advice to all you fellows; hold your end up.

"Be generous also with your rival. Don't brag too much, and don't run down the other fellow. Some of the most delightful visits I have had were with an undertaker in a carriage, on the way to the cemetery. But sometimes when you get around to the fellow who says, 'We had a dozen funerals last week; we had 29 funerals week before last,' the visits are not so delightful. Let me illustrate: A man went out to a trout farm to fish, and when he was shown the roe of the trout he said, 'It is a wonderful providence that made the fish without a voice.' 'Without a voice!' said his host. 'Why, yes,' said the man; 'the fish lays a thousand eggs all at once, and what an awful thing it would be if the fish cackled every time it laid an egg, as does the hen.'

Be Generous to Rivals.

"They say that doctors are very jealous of each other; they say that preachers are just as jealous of each other. I have known some preachers who on the least encouragement will jab the bayonets into their brother preachers as hard as do the Russians. It is a nasty thing to hate another man in the same town. It is a nasty thing to have a man in the same town to whom you cannot say, 'Good day.' It does not matter if that town is as big as Toronto, you will meet that sinner oftener than your preacher, and it is a fine thing to be so friendly with your rival that you can always shake hands with him.

"You know Smith and Jones lived side by side on adjoining lots, and Mrs. Jones was a bit quarrelsome. Mrs. Jones had a great big black cat, and Mrs. Smith said that Mrs. Jones' cat had upset her flower pot on her porch, and run across the lot and dug up the whole business; so the two women quarrelled. Well, Smith did not like it because he and Jones had been good friends, visiting with each other at night and spending many pleasant hours together. Mrs. Jones said she had a right to have a cat, and Mrs. Smith could keep her flowers where the cat could not get at them. By-and-by, Mrs. Jones did not speak to Mrs. Smith, and Mr. Smith, as befitted a good husband, had, of course, to discontinue his visits to Jones' house. By-and-by the big black cat died, and Mr. Jones, rejoicing that the cause of the trouble was removed, wrote to Smith and said, 'You will be glad to know, Brother Smith, that the old black cat has died.' But Smith had the hatchet unburied, and he wrote back, saying, 'Very sorry to hear of your bereavement. I had not even heard that Mrs. Jones was sick.'

"Be generous. You can't have all the funerals in your community. I often wish I could have all the folks in my neighborhood come to Bond street church. But some of them go to the Metropolitan church, some go to Cooke's church, and some even go up to the Jewish synagogue. I can't have all the folks. There are always some that will go to the smallest store and to the poorest preacher and to the poorest undertaker.

"Old Dr. Shaw, the pastor of the Brick Presbyterian church, of Rochester, for fifty years, when he was asked for the secret of his long pastorate, said, 'It is my ability for swallowing things.' If the Ladies' Aid got into a tangle with the choir, he swallowed it. If we want to be successful, whether undertaker or preacher, merchant, or lawyer, we have to have a throat as big as a cobra. Swallow and wait until by-and-by the man who does not like you will come around to almost apologize for not liking you. I am thinking of an old friend of mine, a Methodist preacher from New York State, who in his later years was one of the most careful and sincere men in doing his work. He was constantly busy with the sick, the dying, and the bereaved, but there was a family on his appointment that loved his predecessor so well that they felt it would not be loyal to him not to hate the next man who came, so that family had a funeral in the house. Though my friend had visited that poor daughter that was dying over and over again, when the time came for conducting that funeral the family sent far over the hills for the former pastor at much expense, and they did not even know enough to send a little note to the present pastor. But Brother Nicholson was a good ran, and went to the funeral. He ever sat in the back pew of his own church, and afterwards he went and visited the bereaved family over and over again, and finally, after some months, their mushroom affection for the former pastor sort of wore off, and they found out that they had made a big mistake, made fools of themselves, so that when he called again they said, 'Dear Brother Nicholson, were you offended when we sent for dear Brother Gray to come to bury our dear daughter?' 'No, no,' says Brother Nicholson, 'I was not offended. I would not mind if he came and buried the whole lot of you.'

Worker Worthy of His Hire.

"I sincerely hope that you will have a prosperous convention. It ought to mean something for us to meet with one another and compare methods. It ought to send us back to our vicinity and be worth more money to the folks in our community, and the only money that we have any right to have is that which we are worth. There is a big mill somewhere out in the country away from the city that employed two or three hundred men. They had a breakdown in some of the electrical machinery, and nobody knew how to repair it. The hands were lying around on the grass resting when they ought to have been working. They telephoned to the city, only to find that it would take another day and a half to repair the damage. An employee who had been around only three or four days, a sort of a tramp, came to the manager and said, 'I think I can fix that thing for you.' 'Why,' said the manager, 'I would be very glad to have you do so,' and he took his down to where the break was and had three or four men waiting on him. And by-and-by the wheels were revolving, the machinery was going, and the men started to work, and they gained a day or two in a busy time of the year. The boss finally went down to the tramp and said, 'How much do I owe you?' He said, 'Twenty-five dollars.' 'Twenty-five dollars!' said the boss. 'You give me an itemized bill for such a charge.' The fellow came back with a bill reading something like this:

"'Sich and Such Factory,
"'Debtor to John Dough.
"'By 2½ hours at 25c. an hour .... $ .63
"'By knowing how 24.37
"'Total .... $25.00'

"I hope you will all get paid better for knowing how."

The Civic Welcome.

Mr. Edwards expressed to Rev. Mr. Stauffer, on behalf of the association, his hearty thanks for the interesting address delivered to the convention, which had been unusually enjoyed. He also introduced to the members Ald. Ryding, who welcomed the delegates on behalf of Mayor Hocken.

Ald. Ryding in his remarks said he didn't know why his Worship suggested his welcoming them, as he was a trifle nervous about appearing before so many undertakers, but when he heard that Rev. Byron Stauffer was present he felt a trifle safer. "I extend to you, one and all," said Mr. Ryding, "on behalf of His Worship and all my colleagues, a hearty welcome to our city, and I trust that you will go away perfectly satisfied, having enjoyed yourselves and derived at least some benefit from your visit to our city. I consider that you are a very important body of men. Your profession is something that you ought to be proud of. I think if I had to start business over again I would go into the undertaking business.

"Your business has undergone an immense change in a very few years. I well remember the time when we used to have a carpenter measure the corpse and take three or four days to make the coffin. Now you invite people into your place of business and they can choose what they want. A friend of mine some time ago had the misfortune to lose his wife in Germany, and he was taxed $150 for embalment. He told me, however, he would willingly have paid $1,500 when he saw the body after the ten days' journey. He was surprised to see the good condition it was in.

"I hope your stay will be instructive and I hope each and all of you will enjoy yourselves. Again I thank you for coming here, and I hope this will not be the last time that I may have the pleasure of seeing you. Go wherever you like, take whatever you like in our city, and I will stand responsible for each and all of you. I thank you, Mr. President, and wish you and all of you every success."

J. B. McIntyre responded, saying: "I speak for and on behalf of this assembly, we appreciate the kind words of welcome which Mr. Ryding has spoken to us.

I was very much pleased with that portion of his welcome where he spoke of the funeral directors and embalmers of the present day making comparisons with those in the early days of our organization and before. I speak as one who has spent 54 years in the burial of the dead. As one of the oldest members of this organization I may say to you this is the thirty-first time that I have had the pleasure of being present and hearing the words of welcome extended to this organization by the Mayor of Toronto or his representative, and while the attendance this afternoon is not as large as it will be later on during the session, you see before you representative citizens, men who stand high in the districts in which they are located. I can well remember in the early days, away back in 1860, when I entered my father's establishment, how crude the work of funeral management was conducted. I am pleased to-day to be informed that we have made such progress that we stand second to no other organization on the continent of America. I say this advisedly, as it has been my privilege of visiting 28 of the embalming colleges throughout different states of the Union.

"I was very much pleased to see that Toronto is in the forefront, not only in funeral management, but also in the magnificent send-off they have given to your citizens, your soldier citizens, whom you have sent to the front to fight under that flag which has for so many years withstood the storms of war. It pleases me more to see that you have in this grand old city citi-

ROBT. NUGENT.
Elected Second Vice-President.

zens who have assisted with their means and words of encouragement, and I would say to Professor Moll, who is with us for the first time, that quite independent of the neighboring relations, that both the citizens of the United States and Canada, are engaged in a work of worldwide importance, that of lifting the standard of humanity, and let us hope that we will work in harmony and that we will join forces and try and convert this great Northern American Continent into a vast paradise of international peace and commercial prosperity. Between two nations thus occupied nothing but the most cordial relations should prevail. We know, as Canadians, as citizens, that we have a duty at

Dominion Casket Co., Limited

Telephones: Day No. 1020. Nights, Sundays and Holidays Nos. 1069-1101

Guelph, Ont.

RUSH ORDERS SOLICITED

No. 184

The two caskets on this page are styles without which a Funeral Director's show rooms would not be complete. They are designs brought out to fill a long-felt want and without forcing the trade to purchase same outside of Canada. A card mailed to us will bring you quotations of prices of these goods or anything that you may require.

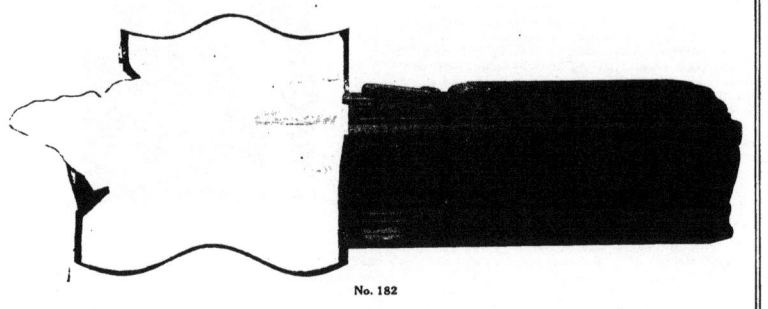

No. 182

Massive Casket, deep mouldings, heavy panels, scroll name plate, "Serpentine" "C" panel. Interior of triple shirred embossed silk.

WRITE FOR PRICES

this time, to build up a nation that will command the respect of the people of the civilized world."

The Presidential Address.

Mr. Edwards, the chairman, expressing regret that the president was unable to be at the convention, read Mr. Henry's presidential address as follows:

PRESIDENT'S ADDRESS.

"I am pleased to welcome you to this, the 31st annual convention of the Canadian Embalmers' Association. I am sorry that so many of the funeral directors throughout the province do not attend these gatherings, and do not take any part or interest in the work of the association. They are not fair to themselves or their friends, or they would by their attendance and counsel try to help along our good work. We are pleased, however, to see so many new members coming in every year and taking an interest in the work. I trust the older ones will see the error of their ways and the benefits to be derived by becoming active.

"Since our last convention many matters of importance have been considered and dealt with by your officers, a great deal of the work being done by correspondence. Your executive only held three official meetings, one immediately after last year's convention, another the 2nd of July of this year, and the last since coming to the city. Although some of the officers have made several trips to Toronto in the interests of the association at their own expense, I wish to apologize for not holding more meetings, to consult with my colleagues. My only reason for not doing so was a financial one, as the funds in hand after paying expenses of last year were low and we were anxious not to show a deficit at the end of our term.

"In 1911, as you all know, the association, through its officers and members, succeeded in having what is known as the Embalmers' Act passed by the Legislature. The accomplishment of this had occupied the attention of officers and members for many years, and the result was very gratifying, being a step in the right direction, Ontario being the first province in the Dominion to have a law of this kind, looking to the safety of the public health and advancement of our profession, making it necessary for men in the profession and going into the undertaking business to know something in regard to sanitation, disinfection, etc.

"The Government at that time for some cause did not see fit to appoint the board of examiners in accordance with the Act. I believe the reason for this not being done was a good deal the fault of our own organization. To try and have this appointment made was one of the most important matters that was before us, and we are pleased to say that the board was named and appointed at the last session of the Legislature. We believe the selection of the men was a wise one, and we wish to congratulate the members upon their appointment to such an important office. We believe the duties required of them will be well and promptly done. We would also congratulate the association upon the appointment of men whom we know will have our interests at heart.

"Some amendments to our by-laws will be necessary at this session. I believe it would be wise, if the by-laws committee would take up this work as early as possible, so as to be able to report before the close of the convention.

"I could not let this occasion go by without commending the Canadian Furniture World and The Undertaker to the members of this association, its columns being devoted to our interests, and its articles being both helpful and instructive. I would recommend every member to be loyal in its support and a paid-up subscriber.

"Since we last met, one of our most esteemed and prominent members, Mr. E. J. Humphries, has passed away. In his death we have lost one who always had the interests of our association at heart. I would ask that a motion be passed at this convention, conveying our most sincere sympathy to his family in their bereavement.

"Your executive, knowing that there were many undertakers throughout the province who lacked the experience required to secure a Government license, felt that it was our duty to arrange for a school on embalming and sanitary science, so that those who desired might take advantage of this opportunity. We accordingly arranged with Prof. Horace Moll, of Chicago, to conduct the school for us.

"The association has accomplished a great work in the past, thanks to the untiring efforts of such men as J. B. McIntyre, A. R. Colfart, A. Dodds, T. E. Simpson, J. C. Van Camp, W. Greenwood, J. Marsh, H. B. Beckett, and others, who have been active workers for years, and there is still a great work to be done. I would strongly advise that the executive committee keep in close touch with the examining board and assist them in their endeavors in a satisfactory way to carry out the provisions of the Act. The examining board, with Mayor Simpson, of the Soo, as chairman, and J. Torrance as secretary, are to be congratulated on the amount of work they have been able to accomplish since their appointment. I had the privilege of being present at one or two of their sittings, and I believe that their work to date will meet with the approval and support of the majority of the members of this association and the undertakers generally throughout the province.

"I cannot close my address without referring to the work and efforts of our worthy secretary, Mr. Matthews. He has always been on the job, and has been a tower of strength to your president. Credit must be given him for the splendid programme in your possession, which is not only a credit to him, but also the association. I, for one, will agree with me when I say he is the right man in the right place, and I am sure you will want to keep him there. I have not only been blessed with a good secretary, but I have had the support and assistance of the most active and efficient committee, who have been most faithful in the performance of every duty given them.

"In conclusion, gentlemen, there are a few things I would ask you to keep in mind: First, loyal support to our association, our code of ethics, and our creed. By doing this we will bring honor to ourselves and credit to our calling. I thank you for the honor you have given me in making me your president. It has been my aim to treat all matters that have come before me in a fair and a fearless manner, and I ask for my successor as loyal support as you have given me.

(Signed) "J. G. HENRY."

The president's address was, on motion of N. J. Boyd, seconded by W. G. Burrows, referred to the committee on the president's address.

Prof. Moll continued his lecture of the morning, and at its conclusion T. E. Simpson addressed the convention.

MR. SIMPSON'S ADDRESS

"I can assure you that I will not keep you here very long. I know that you have been sitting patiently to what has been going on now for some little time and listening to Prof. Moll I think would be much more instructive than listening to me.

"I am glad to have the pleasure of speaking a few words to this convention. I have been a regular attendant of the Canadian Embalmers' Association for a number of years. I was, unfortunately, unable to be with you last year. I missed it. I enjoy being here with my fellow-undertakers at the convention, and go home fitted better for my work after listening to the addresses, seeing the demonstrations, and meeting with my fellows. I am sorry, Mr. Chairman, that our president is detained through illness. Our president is one of the most industrious workers of this association that we have in the Province of Ontario. He lives not a great distance from me (up in the northern part of the province we don't consider 175 or 180 miles very far apart). He has paid visits here to the City of Toronto on at least two or three occasions when the board of examiners met here—he felt it, I presume, his duty as president of the association to come down and see what we were doing. He met with us on the last occasion, and his counsel and advice were appreciated by the members of the board.

"I feel that the officers and the committee are to be congratulated on securing the services of Prof. Moll if I have read of him in the trade journals, of the manner in which he conducted himself in the Winnipeg convention). I was a little disappointed that there are not a greater number present. I feel that if we are going to raise the standard of our profession, there is only one way of doing it, and that is to educate

J. G. HENRY, Retiring President.

the individual member of the association. What means has he of becoming educated? This is the best means in his power of securing education, and the man who does not take advantage of this opportunity is the greater loser.

"But the whole profession is the loser as well, because the failure of some of the members will cast a black mark in a measure against even those who are trying to do their work right, and it is the duty of each and every member of this association to try to get to these conventions annually. Our aim should be to belong, to become members, and to band ourselves together with one another in view, and that is the elevation of the undertaking business, until it is recognized as a profession.

"I have heard it said on several occasions that the Embalmers' Association will be extinguished now that the Government Board of Examiners has been appointed. The function of the board is entirely separate and distinct from the function of the association. The function of the association will be not only to improve their education, but to provide a means such as we are doing now, a means for those who want to come in and become members of the association, a means of becoming educated in and prepare themselves for the profession, that is one of the main functions of this association, and I think it will always remain necessary for this association to remain in business, and I think it should do a flourishing business.

"I have been asked to speak for a moment or two this afternoon in connection with the Act that has been passed a short time ago and what the board of examiners propose to do. Now, I have no prepared speech, and anything I may say will be absolutely of an informal nature, and when I get through if I have not made matters clear, I will answer any questions. You know that the members of this association have been striving for nearly twenty years to get the Government of this province to recognize their association. Mr. Colfart, who has been a member for a very long time, states that it is probably upwards of twenty years that we have been striving year after year, but the Government would not listen to what we considered the very reasonable demands we were making. Arguments were advanced along these lines, that they would get an interview with some of the members of the cabinet and explain the whole condition.

"The situation formerly was something as if a blacksmith from Smiths Falls would come up and fit up a nice undertaking establishment in Hamilton. Who would know the difference, and who would know that he was not fully qualified? There is only one means of people finding out whether he is qualified or not, and that was by way of experiment. This is rather an expensive method of finding out. That was one of the arguments that was advanced. But the strong argument that was advanced was along the lines of sanitation, saying that those who were engaged in the embalming and undertaking business should be most familiar with the laws and methods of sanitation, so that not only the body would be thoroughly disinfected, but the room in which the

Reliability and Quality in Funeral Conveyances

Motor Funeral Cars, Motor Ambulances and Motor Delivery Wagons a Specialty

WE have had forty years' experience in the building of first-class Funeral Cars, Coaches, etc., and for forty years we have been pleasing particular buyers. That is our warranty of quality.

The large range of designs we offer you, together with the most efficient and prompt service, is deserving of your consideration.

We shall be pleased to send you our catalog and quotations. Write us concerning your requirements.

A. B. GREER
101 York Street
London   Ontario

Funeral Cars

Landaus

Pall Bearers' Coaches

Ambulances

Undertakers' Wagons

Embalmers' Buggies

Carriages

Traps

Buggies, etc.

"Standard Canadian Made Goods."

death occurred, and even the house should be thoroughly disinfected, so as to protect the living.

"In 1911 we succeeded in getting the Government to admit that there was something in our claim, and owing to the fact that we had laid particular stress on the principle of health and of sanitation, the matter was referred to the Provincial Board of Health to get their opinion as to the advisability of enacting such legislation. The bill as we had it drafted did not meet entirely with their approval, and the bill was redrafted, and the Provincial Board of Health, not at the request of this association, not at the request of the undertakers of the province, added two clauses which dealt solely with the burial of the dead. These two clauses had nothing to do with the embalment of bodies.

"As I say, this association is not responsible for those last two clauses. You have all had to take out your licenses, I presume. The object of the Provincial Board of Health was this: They have to compile the vital statistics of this province. They had not been very successful in getting an accurate account, in getting all the deaths, and here they saw an opportunity. They said, 'Now, if these fellows are going to get legislation we will make them responsible for reporting to us every burial of which they have charge.' They provide each and every one of us with the form on which to make that return, and they say immediately after you have interred a body, you must fill out that report and drop it into the mail. There is no postage required on such report. In that way they have an accurate return of the deaths, and are able to compile the vital statistics, and I am informed that they have succeeded better than ever before.

"The other portion of the Act is that dealing with embalmers, and I presume that you are all familiar with it, and all know what the conditions are. At any rate, that portion of the Act did not become operative until the board was appointed. The Act was passed by the Legislature, as I said, in 1911. The board naturally should have been appointed in that year, and the Act would become operative on January 1st, 1912. And I tell you right here that you don't want to blame the Legislature that the board was not appointed. There was certain pull by undertakers in certain portions of the province. The undertakers were to blame themselves; it is not the Government. However, that has been cleared away, and the board was appointed on the 6th of May of this year. I have the honor of being chairman of that board, and Mr. Torrance, of Milverton, is secretary. We have held two meetings, and we have tried to get organized, and to get into shape so that we could meet you here at this convention and conduct an examination for any who wished to take that examination at the close of this convention, but I am free to admit that there are a good many things that are not in shape yet. It takes some time to get these things worked out on a satisfactory basis, but we have entered into this thing, and we are going to get it working, and working satisfactorily.

"Now, we have heard considerable objection from one source and another in connection with some of the provisions made by this board. In the first place, the board considered that all those who were engaged in the business prior to the 6th day of May, 1914, should be granted a certificate of qualifications, and that the fee should be $10. If he does not satisfy the board that he is an embalmer, he gets a permit, for which he pays the same fee as for the certificate, but the permit runs out in time.

"Then as to the assistant. We figured that there might be some of the assistants who had started in business, probably the beginning of this year, and all those who had been engaged in the business prior to May 6th, 1914, would be given the certificate, but that would not be fair to the man in business. Consequently the assistant who was engaged in business prior to May 6th, 1912, would be placed on the same basis as the man who was engaged in the business prior to May 6th, 1914. The board has not yet determined the length of service that an assistant must render to a licensed or experienced embalmer before he will be granted his certificate of qualification. I think in the majority of the States of the Union the term is two years. But all assistants who have started in business since the 6th of May, 1912, will be required to take an examination, and the fee for them will be $20, and the fee for all newcomers who will want to start in business after the 6th of May, 1914, will be $20. We feel that it is only fair to those who are engaged in business that the new man coming in must stand his share of the expense. I find that some States of the Union charge more than this but I think probably the majority of them charge less.

"Now, the question is, how long does this certificate of qualification hold good? The certificate of qualification is just simply like a diploma to hang up, showing that you have been recognized by the board to carry on this business of embalming. In addition to that you require a license, which is renewed each year. There is no additional fee required for the first year for this license, and it runs until the 1st of October, 1915, but after that it must be renewed year by year, and that renewal fee will not be more than $4. I don't think it will be $4. This board is not anxious to pile up any money in the bank that is not required for their own operations. The board propose that they should be paid for their time spent in working out the operation of this Act at a reasonable amount, and the Government sanction that. Now, the fees, as stated, are thus: Each member of the board will receive $15 per day for every day that he is away from his business engaged in the work of the board, and he will receive his travelling and hotel expenses in addition. Now, $15 per day may seem possibly a little large, but so far as I am concerned, I would rather spend my time at home with my business. There is a meeting called for a certain day, you have got to be there, no matter what conditions are, and you have to answer the call.

"Now, as to the secretary, with the amount of work he has to do it will take all of his time. I just had a letter from him the other day. He was away from home for the other day. He was away from home for three days and on his return he found that 101 letters had come in those three days. Forty-three were applications and the rest were asking questions, which he had to answer. The secretary's salary is fixed at $1,000 per year. Now, I have been asked this question: What are you fellows going to do with the money? You get possibly 800 undertakers; at $10 apiece that would be $8,000. Have you ever stopped to think how much it is going t cost between the 6th of May and the 1st of October of next year, for the salary of the secretary, railway fares, engraving, printing, licenses, postage, and other incidental expenses? It will run about $4,500.

"The first year, of course, is the heaviest year. We have no guarantee that these 800 men will take out a license. They have not all applied for one yet. Then, in the course of the board going to be. If this board is going to do its part in bringing the association up to the standard that the professor so well showed us this morning was necessary for us to reach to be successful embalmers, they are going to insist on the man who simply ignores circulars, to insist on that man coming across, and we are simply trying to provide for certain funds to enforce the Act for that man.

"Another question that is asked. Here is a man, he does embalming. He does not advertise, he does not charge for it. If that is absolutely true, if he does not advertise it in any shape or form, he goes ahead and makes no charge directly or indirectly, there would be very little to be done. Now, undertakers may be as philanthropic as any other class of people. But I venture to say that the man who refuses to put up $10 for his application will hesitate to spend his money in embalming fluid without being paid for his work. You have to show me that that man is not going to be paid for that directly or indirectly, and I think we will have no trouble in demonstrating beyond the shadow of a doubt that every man who is doing embalming is being paid for it directly or indirectly, and consequently comes under the provisions of the Act. As I stated before, we are going to be absolutely fair and absolutely lenient with the men who are in business. It is not the desire of the board or of the Government that any man who is practising embalming be legislated out of business. If a man can fill out a certificate of qualification, certainly he will receive his certificate."

WEDNESDAY MORNING.

The convention met at 9 o'clock, and Mr. Edwards immediately called upon Secretary Matthews for his report for the year.

Secretary's Report.

"In giving you my report for the year ending September 1st, 1914, I am pleased to state that everything pertaining to our association has been running along very smoothly. As you have already been told of the outcome of some of the endeavors of the executive board, I will not take up your time by going into it again, and although we have some members who have taken exception to what has been done, I am personally of the opinion that it has been a work of importance, and we hop look for more and better things in the near future.

"Your executive met on July 4th, 1914, and recommended the following:

"The acceptance of fifteen $100 shares of preferred stock bearing 7 per cent and five $100 shares of common stock of the Dominion Manufacturers, Limited. This allotment has been very kindly tendered by Mr. Eckardt, formerly proprietor of the National Casket Co.

"We also recommend that trustees be appointed by the association as custodians; and that a letter be drafted by the secretary, tendering thanks to Mr. Eckardt for his kindness in the matter.

"Again I would like to thank you for the confidence you have placed in me in electing me your secretary. A few of the communications received throughout the year, I will read to you. I have received the following letter from the C. F. R.:

"'I understand that your association will meet in Toronto some time next month, and would be pleased if you would draw its attention to the fact that the rule on Canadian and United States railway lines pertaining to the shipment of dead bodies is that where the casket and body weighs more than 500 lbs. excess weight charges at current express baggage rates must be paid. Some of the modern caskets weigh more than 500 lbs.; in fact, I believe that they run as as high as 700 and 800 lbs., and it occurred to me that it would be a good idea for you to notify the association of the fact, so that they may advise passengers purchasing caskets for shipments of dead bodies.'

"The financial report is as follows:
Cash on hand in the Bank of Toronto $858.85
Sundry expense (this is only a petty account covering the year) 20.06"

Mr. Matthews also read to the convention various other letters covering thanks for flowers sent to bereaved families of dead members, etc.

It was moved by W. N. Knechtel, seconded by W. O. Dixon, of Chesterville, that Mr. Matthews' report be received and handed to the Committee on the Secretary's Report. Carried.

Mr. Edwards called on Mr. Coltart, the treasurer, for his report.

Mr. Coltart was greeted with loud applause. He said: "It is not necessary to occupy a lot of time with this report. As you are all aware, this report is composed of receipts and expenditures, and as going over each individual item would take a great deal of time,

F. W. MATTHEWS, re-elected secretary.

Get it at the Western

A Safe, Profitable Place to Buy

All Kinds of Undertakers' Supplies

Open Night and Day

Our Catalogue is with you, if not, a Post Card will bring it.

Give us a trial express order.   Phone Garry 4657.

The Western Casket Co.,
Limited

Winnipeg   Cor. Emily St., & Bannatyne Ave.   Manitoba

which is quite unnecessary, I will merely give you the standing of the finances of the association.

"After paying all the accounts during the year we have a balance in the Merchants Bank to the credit of the Association of $1,453.43, which represents a gain over any previous year. Last year it was $1,347.98."

Moved by W. N. Knechtel, seconded by S. Leatherland, of Schomberg, that Mr. Coltart's report be received and handed to the Committee on the Treasurer's Report. Carried.

Chairman Edwards then announced the committee appointments as follows:

Committee on By-laws—C. N. Greenwood, Stratford; T. H. McKillop, Brampton; H. Ellis, Toronto.

Committee on Finance—N. Boyd, Mitchell; Arch. D. McRae, Vankleek Hill; Mr. Nugent, Lindsay.

President's Address Committee—R. U. Stone, Toronto; Frederick Arthur, Cobalt; Frederick Fisher, Elora.

Committee on Secretary's Report—W. A. Wright, Richmond Hill; S. Leatherland, Schomberg; B. Wright, Chesley.

Committee on Treasurer's Report—W. N. Knechtel, Toronto; W. O. Dixon, Chesterville; E. Miller, Kincardine.

Professor Moll then gave a demonstration on a cadaver.

WEDNESDAY AFTERNOON.

The convention met at 2 o'clock, and Prof. Moll immediately proceeded with his lecture on "Sanitation," after which Mr. Edwards called for the reports of committees, and further announced that Mr. Greenwood, as chairman of the by-laws committee, in company with Mr. McKillop, of Brampton, and Mr. Ellis of Toronto, would take up this work during the year, so as to be able to thoroughly revise them and submit them at the next meeting.

Mr. Curry, the chairman of the committee on the secretary's report, gave his finding as follows:

"We your committee, appointed to report on secretary's address, beg to report as follows: That we have examined the secretary's report, and would recommend that it be adopted. We would also recommend that Mr. Eckardt's offer of stock in the Dominion Manufacturers, Ltd., be accepted, and that the thanks of the association be extended to Mr. Eckardt for same, and also would wish to express our appreciation of the manner the secretary has conducted the business of the association for the past year.

(Signed) "R. A. CURRIE,
"S. LEATHERLAND,
"BART WRIGHT."

The report was adopted.

It was moved by Mr. Cobbledick, seconded by Mr. Nugent, that two trustees be appointed to care for the Eckardt stock, and to see that the association get the full benefit of it. Carried.

Report on Treasurer's Statement

W. N. Knechtel presented the report of his committee on the treasurer's report, as follows:

"We, your committee to report on the treasurer's books, beg to report as follows: That we find them to be in good shape and would recommend that the books be handed to the auditors, and would express our hearty approval of the condition in which we find the books, and sincerely hope that he may long be spared to fill this office for us.

"All of which is respectfully submitted.

(Signed) "WM. N. KNECHTEL,
"E. MILLER,
"W. O. DIXON."

The report was adopted on motion of W. O. Dixon and E. Miller.

Mr. Greenwood, of Stratford, addressed the convention on timely topics, as follows:

MR. GREENWOOD'S ADDRESS

In regard to the Embalmers' Act, as far as the undertaking business of this province is concerned, it is a step in the right direction and will be a great elevation to the undertaking business in this country. I think every undertaker, if he carefully considers his business, will say that the $10 will be well spent and will place him on a standing of which he has been very neglectful in the past. This first step will put his business on a professional footing. Out of that $10, which he is paying to the Government, he should gain at least $200 in a year, and it seems to me we can make a professional charge, and we can do it conscientiously and without fear of criticism by anyone. I think we have come to a time when the undertaking profession is going ahead with leaps and bounds. There is no profession in the Province of Ontario or the Dominion of Canada that has advanced as rapidly as

A. R. COLTART.
Re-elected Treasurer for the twentieth time.

the undertaking business. Where would you stand if you were to conduct a funeral or prepare a body as you did ten years ago? I am sure that that is convincing enough to see that we are only starting now on the way to where we shall be in the next ten or fifteen years, and we will have to thank the gentlemen who have represented us on this board. Mr. Coltart and our president and some of the men who are not here to-day, these are the men who have worked from year to year until we are on the basis we are to-day, and we little appreciate what they have done. These are the men who have placed before the Provincial Government our cause in such a way that they have seen fit to place this law on the statute book, and to-day you are professional men, as soon as you have taken out your license with the Ontario Government. I say to-day it is an important thing for us that we as undertakers throughout the province are recognized as professional men. I am very sorry indeed to see so many of the old faces not present to-day. I was looking for our good friend Mr Simpson. I would just like to make the suggestion, Mr. Chairman, that in this convention we have been looking more after the interests of the younger men, and in studying the interests of the young man who joins our association we have been neglectful of the interests of the older undertakers of Ontario, the man who has been in business for years. That man has been neglected because we have come down here and we have spent the whole four days with the professor's lectures to us on anatomy. Now, there are a great many things, Mr. Chairman, that we should consider in the way of the business side of our profession. If Mr. So and So is making a greater success of his business than I, I say this is one of the best places for me to come and get some ideas from the men who are making a greater success than I am. I think we should meet here for at least one day to discuss the practical business side of our profession. We have been spending our money here every year listening to the lectures on anatomy. That is all very good, but we want to get down to the real root of where we are going to make dollars. You know, Mr. Chairman, there are hundreds who go out and embalm a body quite as well as you or I and don't charge a cent for it. Such men are afraid to charge $15 for embalming a body. If this convention were to meet and discuss questions of this kind, if we were taught by the men who have figured it out, how to make money, it would be of recommended benefit to us all. I think we should have some schedule rate for embalming. If we are going to lose some business by making that charge, all right, but we will gain in the long run. The time has come when we as a convention must step aside and look after the business side of our affairs. Let us see if we cannot set aside one day to mix together here and apply some practical common sense, and see where the other fellow has the advantage over us.

I am very skeptical to listen to the man who says he is afraid to charge for his services. The best satisfaction is when your customer comes along after you have made a reasonable charge and says that he is satisfied with your services and with your bill.

Commercial Aspect of Embalming

Mr. Edwards: I am sure that the time taken up by Mr. Greenwood was well spent by his listeners. I think we lose sight of some things that he has suggested. We come here and meet one another. While

Fast Service

Fair Prices

THE EVEL CASKET CO.
TRADE MARK

"Quality" Line

The Newest and Best in

Polished Oak and Mahogany Caskets. Cloth and Plush covered Caskets. Exclusive designs in the latest fashions in Ladies' Dresses, Gentlemen's Suits and Casket Linings. Wesfield Plate Hardware.

No less a feature than the well known "Evel" Quality is our prompt and efficient service. Write for our prices and concentrate on the "Evel" line.

The Evel Casket Company, Ltd.
Hamilton   Ontario

Has no affiliation with any other firm in the Trade

we may know one another by sight, we do not exchange ideas, and I think it would be a very good idea to follow out Mr. Greenwood's suggestion.

Prof. Moll again took up his demonstration, and in his opening remarks seconded Mr. Greenwood in his suggestion that the commercial aspect of embalming should not be forgotten. He said that the embalming profession was a dangerous one. There was always the danger of blood poisoning, the embalmer may have a slight cut or bruise, and in this there is danger to the embalmer. A charge of $25 is not too much to be asked for embalming, and certainly where an embalmer is afraid to make this charge he should at least charge $10 for professional services.

After the demonstration, Mr. Edwards called for the balance of the committee reports.

R. U. Stone presented to the convention the report of the committee on the president's address, as follows:

COMMITTEE ON PRESIDENT'S REPORT

The Committee on the President's Address feel with you the absence of our good leader, but as all are aware it was entirely unavoidable.

We have carefully considered all the clauses therein, and would impress upon the members the president's reminder that the matter of attracting new members should not devolve on your executive, but it should be the bounden duty of each and every member of this association to shoulder that part of the work.

We feel that the executive has been working in the interests of our association in conserving the funds by not calling numerous meetings, but we would caution that this exercise of economy be not the dominant thought.

Speaking of our president's reference to the "Embalmers' Act" and the appointment of the Provincial Board of Embalming Examiners, he went into that most fully, and we know that his words will have your entire commendation.

Too much cannot be said for the "Canadian Furniture World and Undertaker." The interest that paper is taking in our work is highly commendable. Should we not, therefore, show our appreciation by each and every one of us becoming a subscriber?

It is with feeling of regret that we refer to the passing of two of our members in the persons of E. J. Humphrey and George E. Bodson, of Toronto, earnest workers in the good cause. We trust you will express yourselves in accordance with the wishes of our president.

We look with a great deal of favor on the choice of your executive in the selection of Professor Horace Moll, of Chicago, Ill., as our lecturer and demonstrator at this convention. His work has been of a very high order, and in the expounding of his theories he has been most explicit.

We would refer with a good measure of satisfaction to the pioneers whose names were mentioned by the president, and trust that as the harness of office falls to the shoulders of others, their untiring efforts will stand out as an incentive to high ideals and unceasing toil.

There is no doubt but that the president and his executive have carried on the labors of the year in a manner that reflects credit to our pilot and his crew, and it is with confidence we hope for a strong set of officers for the incoming year, and we would solicit your most earnest support, that they may be enabled to administer the affairs of our association, so may we look forward to even greater accomplishments than have been gained in the past.

All of which is respectfully submitted

(Signed) F. J. McArthur,
Fred Fischer,
R. U. Stone, (Chairman.)

The report was adopted.

Letters of Condolence

It was moved by F. J. McArthur, Cobourg, seconded by R. U. Stone, Toronto, that letters of condolence be sent from this association to the families of the late E. J. Humphrey and George E. Bodson. Carried.

Moved by Fred Fischer, Elora, seconded by F. J. McArthur, Cobourg, that a letter be sent to our president, expressing the hope of this association for his speedy recovery. Carried.

J. H. Robinson, Hamilton, asked Prof. Moll if there was anything which would restore the lifelike appearance to a dead body. Prof. Moll replied that where there is a chemical change, he could do nothing. Somebody higher must do that. He could arrest decomposition, but could not restore the lifelike properties to parts that have decomposed.

The professor went on with his demonstration. Speaking on the eye, he said that seven eighths of the eye is composed of liquid, and in order to restore the natural appearance he sometimes inserted the hypodermic needle in the eye-cap, thus allowing the fluid to run down the eye and hold it in its natural shape. This is also done with the nose.

The professor again impressed upon the convention the importance of using enough fluid and distributing it freely through circulatory system.

THURSDAY MORNING.

The convention was called to order at 9.20.

A change being made in the programme, the election of officers was taken up.

On motion of N. J. Boyd and H. B. Beckett, W. Edwards, of Gananoque, was unanimously elected president for the ensuing year.

Mr. Edwards thanked the association for the honor conferred upon him, and assured the members that he would do all in his power to further the interests of the association.

N. B. Cobbledick was nominated first vice-president for the ensuing year by H. B. Beckett and F. J. McArthur. Unanimously carried.

Robert Nugent, of Lindsay, was nominated second vice-president for the ensuing year. Unanimously carried.

F. W. Matthews was re-appointed secretary for the ensuing year, on motion of N. J. Boyd and C. R. Bolton.

A. R. Coltart was reappointed treasurer for the ensuing year by unanimous choice.

Messrs. Green (three years), R. U. Stone (two years), and N. J. Boyd (one year) were selected as the board of trustees of the Eckardt stock on behalf of the association.

Mr. Greenwood again spoke of the lack of interest of old members due to no discussion of business at these conventions and entirely of affairs relating to the profession. He stated further that they had had splendid lectures and demonstrations by various professors during the past twenty years that he had attended the conventions, and it is well worth while attending these conventions to get the benefit of these lectures, but a great many of the members are interested in the dollars and cents side of our profession. Therefore, he thought at least some time be set aside at further conventions for the discussion of business matters affecting everyday dealings, and because of this he moved "that the incoming executive be asked to endeavor to set aside a day at the next convention whereby all the members of the association in Ontario may come together and discuss association and business topics."

The motion was seconded by Bart Wright, Chesley.

Mr. Cobbledick stated that he had attended conventions across the line, where business was discussed, and he believed Mr. Greenwood's words were true. "What we want is more business matters and experiences discussed at our conventions." He thought the motion a good one.

N. J. Boyd thought the motion might be altered so as to be devote one-half day, as there was a great deal of work for the executive and convention to do.

Mr. Edwards thought the matter should be left with

SHOWING APPRECIATION

"TOO much cannot be said for the Canadian Furniture World and The Undertaker. The interest that paper is taking in our work is highly commendable. Should we not, therefore, show our appreciation by each and every one of us becoming a subscriber?" Report of Committee on President's Address.

the executive as a suggestion for them to do with as they thought best.

Mr. Coltart stated the difficulty would be easily overcome if the half-day were specified in the programme, that this would solve the matter.

Mr. Greenwood said he thought it would be better to have two days rather than the half-day. The professor gave the members many little tips which it would be well for us to discuss among ourselves—how does the man in the little town solve some of his difficulties? The demonstrations given us show how things are done in large cities and towns, where many of the instruments are at hand, but when a man is in a small place, away from his home, how is he going to solve his difficulties. However, if half a day was thought sufficient he would not object.

Mr. Cobbledick suggested leaving to the executive whether it would be half or a whole day.

Mr. Beckett stated that he was not a pessimist, but that in the past the trouble had been that many attended the conventions to see and learn all they possibly could, and when the business affecting the association came up they leave the room to let the other fellow settle the business. When they know of something good they will not tell the other fellow, and he did not see how the members could get them to tell. Mr. Cobbledick told us of the United States association giving a day or two to association work. He did not say that these American associations come together for three or four days for the sake of having a good time. If we have something like this, we could do the same.

A Voice in the Hall: Let Harry Ellis sing.

Another member said he thought it would be well to have a little banquet as a feature of the annual convention, and another speaker said it would be well if members brought their wives to these gatherings.

The chairman then put the motion, and it was carried.

THURSDAY AFTERNOON.

Prof. Moll conducted for the benefit of the members an autopsy, again speaking on sanitation, and impressing very forcibly with the necessity of thoroughness in disinfecting. He further advocated the use of raw cotton in closing orifices of the body.

He answered the questions in the quiz box, there being but two, one on a sanitary question, the answer to which appeared in the professor's lecture on sanitation; the other being for an embalming fluid formula, which the professor said he regretted being unable to give because of business reasons.

At the conclusion of the address it was moved by N. B. Cobbledick, seconded by Robert Nugent, that the very best thanks of this association be tendered Prof. Moll for the very able manner in which he conducted the demonstrations in this convention and for his very excellent work in the school. Carried unanimously.

Prof. Moll: Members of the Canadian Embalmers' Association: I am afraid I scarcely deserve it, but I accept it most gratefully.

Mr. Edwards then announced that the association had with them Prof. Eckels, and with the permission of the audience he would be granted a few moments to express his good will towards the association.

Mr. Edwards: We will try to have our law as up-to-date as any law that is in effect in the American States, and we are glad to have had Mr. Eckels give us his personal felicitations and greetings for the American association. He then called for installations of officers, and asked Past President N. J. Boyd to conduct the ceremony.

Before doing so, Mr. Boyd said it had been the custom of the association for years to make a presentation to the retiring president. "Unfortunately," said he, "our president has been detained on account of sickness; consequently, we are going to ask Mr. Simpson, of the 'Soo,' to act as proxy for Mr. Henry."

He said it had been a source of satisfaction to have Mr. Henry on the executive board, particularly as he had been such a valuable member of the association. "It had been a pleasure to meet him. His counsel and judgment at all times have been such that our admiration for him has been raised, and," continued Mr. Boyd, "we are here to-day to do an honor that we hope, not for the intrinsic value it represents, but for the spirit in which we are giving, will remain fresh in his mind for many a year." He then asked Mr. Simpson to accept, on behalf of Mr. and Mrs. Henry, a beautiful cabinet of silver.

Mr. Simpson, as proxy for Mr. Henry, replying, said: "I have possibly two regrets to express. In the beginning, one is that your worthy president is not present to hear the glowing tributes that Mr. Boyd has just paid, and, secondly, that I am acting as proxy." He said the association had no stronger friend than Mr. Henry. He was greatly interested in its work. "The reason, I presume, that he is so desirous for the success of the association is because he is that kind of a man, that no matter what he undertakes, he wants to make it a genuine success, and I have no doubt that he appreciates this fact, that there is only one way of reaching the high standard in the undertaking profession that we all hope to reach, that we are all going to strive to reach, that is, the means of education, and what other means of education have we got other than studying books at home? We have no regular schools here in Ontario; the annual school and the annual meeting of the association is practically the only method of education that we have, and I think I am quite safe in saying that is one of the strongest reasons that induced your retiring president to take such an active interest in this association. I can assure you that it will afford me the very greatest pleasure to accept this present on behalf of Mr. Henry, and to take it home and present it to him in his own house on your behalf, and I will see that Mrs. Henry is right there when the presentation is made. I feel that you can count on the attendance and assistance of your retiring president for years to come if his health is spared, and he is at all able to get away to be with you. I feel that he will not allow his interest to lag in the association after passing through the chairs and receiving the honors that the association can confer on him."

Mr. Greenwood gave his committee's report as follows: "Your committee on by-laws reports that clause six of our present by-laws be struck out, and that your committee be allowed to stand for one year, and the president be authorized to call the committee to convene when your executive is in session and prepare our present by-laws to conform with the new law as laid down by the Government and present same for your approval at our next annual meeting.

(Signed) "C. N. GREENWOOD.
"HARRY ELLIS.
"J. McKILLOP."

Mr. Boyd then proceeded to install the officers for

the ensuing year, assisted by Past President Greenwood.

After the installation, there being no further business, the convention was declared closed.

REGISTERED AT CONVENTION

Furniture Gallery 15
N. J. Boyd, Mitchell.
N. B. Cobbledick, Toronto.
Samuel Leatherland, Schomberg
F. A. Wunder Frankford.
Fred Scott, Woodbridge.
Chas. S. Clarke, Ottawa.
F. W. Matthews, Toronto.
C. M. G. Smith, Barrie
G. G. Smith, Barrie.
P. C. Lloyd, Barrie.
W. R. Egan, Bolton.
T. E. Simpson, Sault Ste. Marie.
T. Henderson, Drayton.
T. H. Speers, Drayton.
J. A. Cummings, Hazeldean.
Patterson Bros., Carleton Place.
R. B. Gohesn, Campbellford.
E. Palmer Whiteley, Seaforth.
G. A. Dixon, Winchester.
W. O. Dixon, Chesterville.
J. A. Campbell, Dutton.
W. G. Burrows, Chatham.
C. R. Scott, Almonte.
Arch. D. McRae, Vankleek Hill.
G. H. Rogers, Ottawa.
Jno. P. McCammon, Paris.
Max MacPherson, Delhi.
Pen. G. Walker, Brussels.
F. L. D. Bell, Thessalon.
N. D. Brontmire, Cardinal.
H. C. Box, Seaforth.
A. R. Coltart, Chatham.
W. N. Knechtel, Toronto.
F. J. McArthur, Cobourg.
A. S. Preston, Toronto.
Chas. R. Bolton, Toronto.
Anderson, Nugent & Co., Lindsay.
Adam Klippert, Waterloo.
Herb. Klippert, Waterloo.
Geo. H. Honsberger, Toronto.
Jas. O'Hagan, Toronto.
J. M. Usher, Sudbury.
J. C. McNiven, Dorchester.
W. A. Hunt, Belmont.
J. N. Burkholder, Stouffville.
Jno. Hammer, Neustadt.
Chas. Miller, Ayton.
Geo. Botherington, Langton.
Colin McMillan, Dromore.
R. U. Stone, Toronto.
J. O. Reid, Princeton.
J. Werlich, Preston.
E. I. Stonehouse, Toronto.
Frank Kelkenny, Bradford.
C. J. Hasslin, Hagersville.
Wm. Speer, Toronto.
Harry Hugill, Woodbridge.
Dorman A. Craig. Toronto.
J. Paul, Feversham.
Herb. K. Levell, Guelph.
Alf. Lovell, Guelph.
Wm. J. Osborne, Warkworth.
A. E. Maynes, Toronto.
J. B. McIntyre, St. Catharines.
E. Miller, Kincardine.
M. Moore & Son, Niagara Falls.
Chris Droininger, Elmira.
Geo. Droininger, Elmira.
Jet. Bartlett, Toronto.
Ald. Ryding, Toronto.
T. H. McKillip, Brampton.
Hugh Walker, Port Hope.
D. Louis Brown, Dundas.
Geo. W. Stitt, Buffalo, N.Y.
J. A. Donaldson, Caledon East.
Roger Wilson, Chatsworth.

Fred Fischer, Elora.
Harry Ellis, Toronto.
Jas. H. Nicholson, Whitby.
Fd. Strasler, Queensville.
J. Runge, Clifford.
Bart Wright, Chesley.
Chas. Dunham, Aurora.
W. Edwards, Gananoque.
N. M. Steinman, Baden.
S. Flanano, Baden.
G. W. Lawris, Maple.
R. S. Fleischauer, Wellesley.
John Leach, St. Thomas.
Wm. H. Bunt, Flesherton.
Joseph Brophey, Goderich.
F. T. Morris, Bowmanville.
C. L. Forster, Park Hill.
Thos. Porter, Toronto.
Geo. S. Wilson, Norwich.
Chas. Hackett, Lucan.
L. A. Taylor, Singhampton.
A. J. Phelan, Arthur.
R. Moffatt, Toronto.
Ernest E. Bolton, Toronto.
John Rozer, Atwood.
Robt. A. Currie, Wingham
G. H. Linklater, Teeswater.
Geo. C. Graham, Toronto.
P. M. Howard, Hastings.
J. M. Taylor, Tillsonburg.
A. L. Oatman, Tillsonburg.
M. S. Bedford, Toronto.
Jos. A. Krug, Tavistock.
P. R. Williams, St. Thomas.
E. C. Williams, St. Thomas.
W. Pattison, Port Elgin.
Jas. McFarquhar, Toronto.
Alexander Logan, Parry Sound
James M. Logan, Parry Sound.
Fred Ausay, Montreal.
Geo. C. Byng, Bobcaygeon.
Jas. Beverley, Exeter.
Tickell Sons Co. (J. L. Tickell).
Belleville.
Wm. Finlayson, Paris
H. R. Marston, per W. F., Paris.
Thos. L. Puffer, Norwood.
A. M. McDonald, Stayner.
J. J. Ryan, Toronto.
A. M. Mitchell, Guelph
Fred W. Keeler, Ingersoll.
S. F. L. McMurtry, Midland.
H. B. Beckett, Brantford.
R. A. Breckenridge, Owen Sound.
Greenwood & Vivian, Ltd., Stratford.
G. A. Winterstein, Zephyr.
John A. Stewart, Strathroy.
C. R. Turner, Milton.
Frederick Skinner, Schomberg.
John H Summerfeldt, Unionville.
Norman C. Rundle, Toronto
J. H. Robinson Hamilton.
J. A. Robinson, Hamilton.
N. A. Johnson, Seeley's Bay.
G. W. Sutherland, Welland.
E. W. Williamson, Burlington.
Sam Avery, Clemondin.
A. H. Hermleson, Listowel.
Ed. W. Morris, Walkerville.
W. A. Britton, Grand Valley.
J. B. Martin, Ripley.
K. F. Best, Simcoe.
Robt. McMane, Milverton.
W. & J. Comstock, Peterboro.
W. A. Wright, Richmond Hill.

EMBALMING BOARD OF EXAMINERS MEET

The provincial board of embalming examiners appointed under the Act relating to Embalmers and Undertakers, held their third meeting since their appointment in the Parliament Buildings, Queen's Park, Toronto, commencing on Wednesday, September the 9th. All the members were present. Secretary James Torrance, of Milverton, placed before the board a large number of applications from embalmers in all parts of Ontario, between four and five hundred, who have applied for certificates or permits.

It has come to the knowledge of the board that many of the embalmers have been laboring under some misunderstanding. The existence of the Canadian Embalmers' Association, which has been doing an educational work for over thirty years in Ontario, has been taken in connection with the examining board appointed by the Provincial Legislature of the Province of Ontario. The new board is doing what it can to get the embalmers to understand the difference, and to understand the importance of complying with the request to make application to the secretary of the board at an early date, so that all the embalmers in Ontario will be qualified to carry on the business and practice embalming in Ontario under the conditions and requirements of the new Act, which means that all persons in the business of embalming must apply to the board of examiners, as per the request sent them.

On Friday, September 11, a class of fifteen students applied to the board to write on examination. These students, who had attended the C. E. A. school the previous week, proved to be quite proficient, as eight out of the fifteen took honors, making over 90 per cent. on a fairly difficult paper. The following are the names of the students who passed, the first eight of whom received honors in merit as their names appear. Only one of the fifteen failed to reach the required percentage: John Clarke, Caledonia; Chas. A. Butler, St. Catharines; N. D. Brontmire, Cardinal; E. Palmer Whitely, Seaforth; E. F. Best, Simcoe; James Chapman, Paris; John A. Robinson, Hamilton; J. M. Usher, Sudbury; A. McNiven, Guelph; Wm. Gormley, Columbian; W. R. Egon, Bolton; Ray Bailey Gohen, Campbellford; Benj. Walker, Brussels; H. C. Box, Seaforth.

GLENCOE UNDERTAKER DEAD.

Donald McAlpine, one of Glencoe's most prominent citizens and one who was highly esteemed by a large circle of friends and acquaintances, died recently at that place. Mr. McAlpine was ill about three weeks with typhoid fever. Pneumonia and other complications shortly afterwards set in.

Mr. McAlpine was born in Ekfrid Township on February 12, 1856, and was the youngest son of the late Malcolm and Ann McAlpine, who were among the early pioneers of Western Ontario. After spending several years at farming, he moved to Glencoe. In 1911 he took over the furniture and undertaking business formerly carried on by R. F. Howard & Son, which he continued up to the time of his death. He was married on April 29th, 1903, to Miss Mary McNabb, of Glencoe, who survives him, with a family of two boys and three girls. He also leaves two brothers and two sisters—Dr. John, of Lindsay; Duncan, of Ekfrid; Mrs. Arch. McAlpine, of Aberfeldy; and Margaret, of St. Thomas. Two brothers and one sister predeceased him. These were Hugh, of Ekfrid; Peter, of Kansas; and Mrs. Malcolm Galbraith, of Ekfrid.

The funeral was one of the largest ever held in that section, and was conducted by the Sons of Scotland, of which society he was a member. Mr. Percy of the National Casket Co., Toronto, went to Glencoe to take charge of the funeral.

The business will be continued by the widow and family.

TORONTO ESTABLISHMENT CHANGES HANDS.

Colin E. Burgess, who represented the Semmens & Evel Casket Co., Hamilton, for seven years, covering Eastern Ontario and Quebec, and Manitoba for two years, has purchased the undertaking establishment of the E. Hopkins Burial Co., at 529 Yonge street, Toronto. Mr. Burgess is a practical undertaker and em-

Burglar Proof and Water Tight

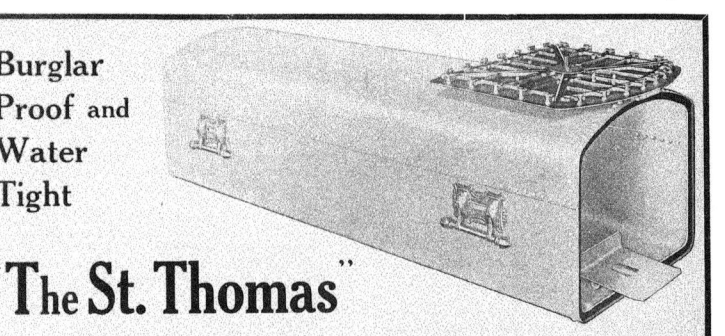

"The St. Thomas"

Original, Quick Closing End Vault

MANUFACTURED BY

The St. Thomas Metallic Vault Company, Limited
ST. THOMAS, ONTARIO

IMPERIAL CASKET COMPANY
ROBERT A. AVES

CASKETS AND FUNERAL SUPPLIES

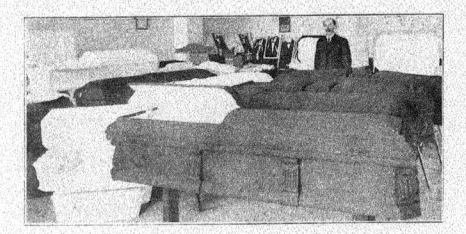

WIRE AND LONG DISTANCE TELEPHONE ORDERS RECEIVE PROMPT ATTENTION

1100 Eighth Ave. East.   Phones { DAY FAIRMONT 1612 / NIGHT " 770R. }   Vancouver

balmer, having been manager for leading undertakers of Toronto and Chicago in years past.

Mr. Hopkins, who is retiring, will take a trip to the Old Country for a short time.

INTERNATIONAL MAUSOLEUM CO. ENLARGING

A. J. H. Eckardt, having assumed the presidency of the International Mausoleum Co., Ltd., has moved the offices to new quarters, at 20 King Street East, Toronto. These new offices are amongst the most sumptuous in Canada. The rooms are en suite. Mr. Eckardt's private office being in mahogany with luxurious Chesterfield furniture, and lighted with the latest electric devices. Mr. Eckardt entertained many of the visiting members who attended the embalmers' convention in his new quarters.

A new booklet has been issued descriptive of the Toronto mausoleum. Another building will be erected shortly on the International Co.'s property in North Toronto—a two-storey structure, the upper one to be finished in white marble and the lower in imitation marble.

Mr. Eckardt is interested in Cochrane property, which he hopes to see one of the largest cities in the North, and he believes that when the clay belt is opened up there will be opportunities for furniture dealers and undertakers to commence business. He is still giving away his money. Mr. Eckardt's latest donation being a $3,000 mahogany organ to the Lutheran Church at Unionville, in memory of his own and his family's forefathers who immigrated into Canada from the United States in 1792.

PROFESSIONAL NOTES

John T. Leak, furniture dealer at Squamish, B.C., is entering the undertaking business.

The Etormamic Valley Cemetery Co., Astwood, Sask., has been incorporated.

J. A. Wright has opened an undertaking establishment in Parry Sound, Ont., and will have an up-to-date outfit.

Thomson and Morrison, undertakers, Fernie, B.C., have dissolved partnership.

After a serious illness which kept him confined to bed for nine weeks, Ben D. Humphrey, the well-known Toronto undertaker, is well again, and attending to business.

The F. W. Matthews Co., Toronto, contemplate moving from 235 to 665 Spadina avenue about October 1.

Disney Bros., furniture dealers and undertakers, at Oshawa, Ont., are succeeded by L. V. Disney, though the firm name will remain unchanged.

The establishment of James A. Kinney, undertaker, Barrington, N.S. together with a number of caskets,

was totally burned by lightning recently. The estimated loss is one thousand dollars, insurance about four hundred.

TO OUR READERS

We are compelled, through lack of space, to withhold much matter of interest to the profession in various parts of Canada at this time. There are the reports of the conventions in British Columbia and the Maritime Provinces, Prof. Mall's lectures at Toronto, Prof. Eckels' interesting embalming article, and notes and incidents from various parts of the Dominion. These we hope to publish in our next issue.— Editor.

The Original Patented Concentrated Fluid

Patented Formula
Strongest and Best

Essential Oil Base, combined with Alcohol, Glycerine, Oxidized Formaldehyde and Boron-Dioxide.

Ask others for their Formula

Special Canadian Agents
National Casket Co.
Toronto, Ont.
GLOBE CASKET CO.
London, Ont.
SEMMENS & EVEL CASKET CO.
Hamilton, Ont.
GIRARD & GODIN
Three Rivers, Que.
JAS. S. ELLIOTT & SON
Prescott, Ont.
CHRISTIE BROS.
Amherst, N.S.

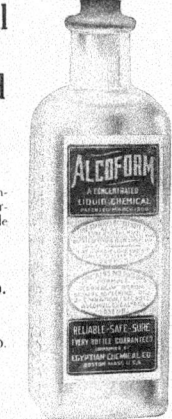

Larger Bottles filled up with water

Egyptian Chemical Co. Boston, U.S.A

Invalid Chairs and Tricycles of every description.

This has been our study for thirty-five years. We build chairs that suit the requirements of any case. Write us for catalogue No. 20 and prices, if interested.

Gendron Wheel Co., Toledo, O. U.S.A.

For Sale / Wanted

TERMS FOR INSERTION
25 Cents per line, one insertion
Four lines once for $1.00, three times for $2.00.
Cash must accompany the order
No accounts booked.
MINIMUM 50 CENTS

FURNITURE and House Furnishing business for sale. Good town. Surrounding country in British Columbia. Reasons for selling, failing health. For full particulars apply Box 128, Canadian Furniture World and The Undertaker, 32 Colborne St., Toronto.

FOR SALE—Undertaking business in an excellent town in Ontario, with large country trade. A golden opportunity and a bargain for quick sale. Best reasons for selling. Box 681, Canadian Furniture World and The Undertaker, Colborne St., Toronto.

FOR SALE - Four hearses, sell at half price, going out of the hearse business. Our hearses are made of the very best stock, English Collonge axles and best workmanship. Also wagon ettes and three seated carriages. Write for particulars, W. J. Thompson & Son, London, Ont.

Patronize The Line of "Established Quality"

The features of the Central Line are features that make good business everywhere—honest quality, fair prices and efficient, prompt service. We specialize on

Mahogany, Oak, Plush and Cloth Covered Caskets

We can also supply anything desired in Casket Linings, Burial Robes, and a general line of Undertakers' Supplies.

Orders given our Canadian Representative, or sent to our factory at Bridgeburg by mail, telegraph or telephone will receive prompt attention.

CENTRAL CASKET COMPANY

Bridgeburg, Ont. R. S. Flint, Canadian Representative: 241 Fern Ave., Toronto
Telephone 126 Telephone Parkdale 3257

No Undertaker Should Overlook

the fact that he can make a full gallon of fluid of standard strength from each sixteen-ounce bottle of RE-Concentrated Dioxin. Re-Concentrated Dioxin costs no more per bottle than any standard concentrated fluid, but it is twice as strong—in other words, there are twice as many ounces of preservation in a bottle of RE-Concentrated Dioxin as there are in any bottle of merely concentrated fluid.

If economy were the only recommendation for RE-Concentrated Dioxin, however, we should not urge it upon our patrons.

As a matter of fact, it is easy to explain and equally easy to demonstrate the fact that the fluid thus produced gives a far better cosmetic effect and produces a far more life-like body than possibly could be produced by any raw formaldehyde concentrated fluid.

This is because RE-Concentrated Dioxin has a double base. When diluted to make a full gallon of fluid to the bottle, its main base is peroxide, with a secondary base of purified formaldehyde (formochloral).

Every funeral director knows that peroxide of hydrogen is the best bleacher known to chemical science. Not everyone realizes, however, that peroxide of hydrogen has blood solvent qualities far in excess of any other chemical yet discovered which is suitable for use in embalming fluid.

Peroxide of hydrogen is composed of two atoms of oxygen and two atoms of hydrogen. Since oxygen is fifteen times heavier than hydrogen, fifteen-sixteenths of the atomic weight of peroxide of hydrogen, therefore, is oxygen.

Every embalmer knows that venous blood is much darker in color, is much more sluggish and much heavier than arterial blood.

What is the difference between the two?

Arterial blood is merely venous blood, which has been purified in the lungs, which has been lightened in color and rendered vastly more fluid by the oxygen which the lungs have extracted from the air we breathe.

Since fifteen-sixteenths of the atomic weight of peroxide of hydrogen is oxygen, it must be apparent, therefore, that the oxygen in the extra rich peroxide in Dioxin has a tendency to exercise the same purifying and solvent qualities upon the dark, discolored venous blood after death as the oxygen which the lungs extract from the air we breathe has upon the venous blood in life.

The result is that much more blood can be drained from a body in which RE-Concentrated Dioxin is injected than is possible from a body in which raw formaldehyde is used and in which the astringent qualities of the formaldehyde have sealed up the discolored blood corpuscles in the capillaries.

Putty color is caused by raw formaldehyde fluid sealing up the discolored corpuscles of the blood in the capillaries. It is inevitable where raw formaldehyde fluids are used unless exceeding care is used to drain blood. And even then there is great danger.

RE-Concentrated Dioxin is distinctly the most modern and the most scientific embalming fluid on the market, as well as the most economical. The progressive funeral director will not hesitate, but will order a trial shipment.

RE-Concentrated DIOXIN

H. S. ECKELS & CO. 1922 Arch St., Philadelphia, Pa.
241 Fern Ave., Toronto, Canada.

Undertakers Shipping Directory

ONTARIO

Aurora—
 Dunham, Charles.
Barrie—
 Smith, G. G. & Co.
Brockville—
 Quirmbach, Geo. R., 162 King St.
Brooklin—
 Disney, R. S.
Campbellford—
 Irwin, James.
Campden—
 Hansel, Albion.
Clinton—
 Walker, Wesley.
Coboconk—
 Greenley, A.
Copper Cliff—
 Boyd, W. C.
Dungannon—
 Sproul, William
Dutton—
 Schultz, B. L.
Elmira—
 Dreisinger, Chris.
Fenelon Falls—
 Deyman, L. & Son.
Fenwick—
 H. A. Metler.
Fergus—
 Armstrong, M. F.
 Thomson, John & Son.
Fort William—
 Cameron & Co., 711 Victoria.
 Morris, A.
Haileybury—
 Thorpe Bros.
Galt—
 Anderson, J. & Son.
Hamilton—
 Green Bros., 124 King St. E.
 Robinson, J. H. & Co., 19-21 John St. N.
Hanover—
 Wunnenberg, Norman.
Hastings—
 Howard, P. N.
Hepworth—
 Downs, E. J.
Inwood—
 Lorriman, E. S.
Kemptville—
 McCaughey, Geo. A.
Kenora—
 Horn & Taylor.
Kingston—
 Corbett, S. S.
Lakefield—
 Hendren, Geo. G.
Little Current—
 Sims, J. G.
Markdale—
 Oliver, M.
Newmarket—
 Millard, J. H.
North Augusta—
 Wilson, J. R.
North Bay—
 St. Pierre, E.
Oakwood—(Mariposa Station G.T.R.) Wilmot F. Webster.
Ohsweken—
 Johnson, F. L.
Oshawa—
 Disney Bros.
 Luke Bros.
Ottawa—
 Ch. R. Woodburn, 586 Bank St. Tel. Carling 600 and 1009.
 Rogers & Burney, 283 Laurier Ave. W.
Petrolia—
 Steadman Bros.
Port Arthur —
 Collin Wood, 36 Arthur St.
 Morris, A.
Prescott—
 Rankin, H. & Son.
Renfrew—
 O'Connor, Wm.
St. Mary's—
 N. L. Brandon.
St. Thomas—
 Williams, P. R. & Sons, 519 Talbot St.
Seaforth, Ont.
 W. T. Box & Co.
Scotland—
 Vaughan, Jos. H. M.
Sudbury—
 Henry, J. G.
Toronto—
 Cobbledick, N. B., 2068 Queen St. East and 1508 Danforth Ave. Private Ambulance.
 Stone, Daniel (formerly H. Stone & Son), 525 Sherbourne St.
 Vancamp, J. C., 30 Bloor St. West.
Waterloo—
 Klipper Undertaking Co.
Welland—
 Sutherland, G. W.
Woodstock—
 Meadows, T. & Sons.
 Mack, Paul.

QUEBEC

Buckingham—
 Paquet, Jos.
Cowansville—
 Judson, M. B.
Montreal—
 Tees & Co., 912 St. Catherine St. West.
St. Hyacinthe—
 Cadorette, Mongeau & Leary.
St. Laurent—
 Gougeon, Jos.

NEW BRUNSWICK

Petitcodiac—
 Jonah, D. Allison.
Woodstock—
 Van Wart, Jacob.

NOVA SCOTIA

Perrona—
 Fraser, D. & Co.
Halifax—
 Snow & Co., 90 Argyle St.
Sydney, C.B.—
 Beaton, A. J. & Son, 374-384 George St.

MANITOBA

Brandon—
 Campbell & Campbell.
 Vincent & McPherson.
Souris—
 McCulloch, Wm.
Swan River—
 Paull, Geo.
Winnipeg—
 Bardal, A. S., 834 Sherbrooke
 Thompson, J. C., 501 Main
 Clark-Leatherdale Co., Ltd., 232 Kennedy St.

SASKATCHEWAN

Gull Lake—
 Morrow, Fred. A.
Saskatoon—
 Young, A. E.
Kamsack—
 Russell, G. E. I.
Lanigan—
 Robertson, Wm.
Moose Jaw—
 The Bellamy Co.
 Broadfoot Bros.
Rush Lake—
 Friesen, John M.
Prince Albert—
 Howard, A. C.
 Hadley, C. L.
Regina—
 Speers, George.
Semans—
 Haygarth, Jas.
Welwyn—
 LeaVeus, Merritt.
Wolseley —
 Barber, B.

ALBERTA

Calgary—
 Graham & Buscomb, 611 Centre St.
Castor—
 Winter, W. G.

BRITISH COLUMBIA

Hosmer—
 Cornett, T. A.
Victoria—
 Hanna & Thompson, 827 Pandora Ave.

Colt's Quick Acting Clamps

Short Reach Clamp
For Drawer and Table Tops

COLTS CLAMPS, ECCENTRIC AND SCREW.

Ask for Catalogue No. 180

Batavia Clamp Company
147 Center Street, Batavia, N.Y., U.S.A.

Canadian School of Embalming
Instruction in Practical Embalming and Funeral Directing
PREPARATION FOR EXAMINATIONS
ENTER AT ANY TIME

R. U. STONE   32 Carlton Street
 Principal   Toronto

Index to Advertisements

A
Antiseptic Bedding Co. ... i.f.c.
Ault & Wiborg Co ... 62

B
Baetz Bros. & Co. ... 11
Batavia Clamp Co ... 61

C
Canadian School of Embalming. III
Can. H. W. Johns Manville Co. ... 21
Central Casket Co ... 60
Chair Craft Co ... 17
Colleran Patent Spring Mat. Co. 11
Columbia Grafonola Co. ... o.b.c.

D
Dominion Casket Co. ... 48
Dominion Mfrs., Limited ... 14-15

E
Kokels & Co., H. S. ... 10
Egyptian Chemical Co ... 30
Elmira Interior Woodwork Co. ... 6
Evel Casket Co. ... 51

F
Farquhar-on-Gifford Co. ... 11

G
Gale & Son, Geo. ... 8
Gendron Wheel Co. ... 39
Globe-Wernicke Co. ... 7
Gold Medal Furn. Mfg. Co. ... i.b.c.-20
Greer, A. H. ... 50

H
Hourd & Co. ... 10

I
Ideal Bedding Co. ... 22
Imperial Casket Co. ... 38
Imperial Furniture Co ... 21
Imperial Rattan Co ... 5

K
Knowneye Mfg. Co. ... 21
Kindel Bed Co., Limited ... 12
Knechtel Furniture Co. ... 13

L
Leggett & Platt Spring Bed Co ... 6
Lippert Furniture Co. ... 18

M
Matthews Bros. ... 21
Menford Mfg. Co. ... 13
McLagan Furniture Co., Geo. ... 3
Montreal Upholstering Co. ... 4
Mundell, J. C., & Co. ... i.f.c.

N
N. A. Bent Chair Co. ... 12
National Grave Vault Co. ... 62

O
Ontario Spring Bed ... 4
Onward Mfg. Co ... 14

S
Shafer, D. L. & Co. ... 11
Sidway Mercantile Co. ... 41
Stratford Brass Co ... 10
Stratford Chair Co. ... o.f.c.
Stratford Mfg. Co. ... 11
St. Thomas Metallic Vault Co. ... 58

T
Textileather Co. ... 10

V
Victoriaville Bedding Co. ... 16

W
Walter & Co., B. ... 62
Western Casket Co. ... 52
Weisglass, S., Limited ... 19

Making TABLE-SLIDES is a Specialty Business

For more than TWENTY-FIVE YEARS we have made TABLE SLIDES exclusively. Our Factory is equipped with Special Machinery which enables us to make SLIDES,—BETTER and CHEAPER than the furniture manufacturer.

Canadian Table makers are rapidly adopting WABASH SLIDES

Because { They ELIMINATE SLIDE TROUBLES Are CHEAPER and BETTER }

Reduced Costs
Increased Out-put } **BY USING WABASH SLIDES**

Made by
B. WALTER & CO.
Wabash, Ind.
The Largest EXCLUSIVE TABLE-SLIDE Manufacturers in America
ESTABLISHED 1887

SHELLACS

If you are in the market for first-class Shellac we believe it would be to your advantage to get in touch with us.

HIGH GRADE VARNISHES FILLERS and GRAINING INKS

THE AULT & WIBORG CO. OF CANADA
LIMITED
MONTREAL   TORONTO   WINNIPEG

The Furniture Trade Outlook

To the Editor of the Furniture World:

For some months past, and up to the time of the outbreak of the war, the furniture trade, while recording a good steady business, could not be considered brisk, and no one seemed to know exactly where to locate the cause of the apathetic buying among dealers and public alike, but conditions have been generally ascribed to the tightness of the money market. This leads the average person at the present time to pause and reflect that this very condition has probably presaged the advent of the present great but inevitable conflict.

Now that the conflict is on, it would be well for the furniture men to consider the best means of keeping up a good average volume of business. In Canada, while we deeply deplore the human sacrifice which such a war entails, this closing up of much European productiveness, both of merchandise and agricultural produce, should be the means of greatly stimulating Canadian manufactures and incidentally lead to the establishment of new industries, which, if energetically pursued while the trade door is open, cannot but prove of lasting benefit to our country.

With the vast agricultural and mineral resources at hand, and also with vast tracts of fertile soil still untilled, Canada at the present time should occupy the most enviable of positions among nations. In a land of plenty and to spare, with wheat at more than a dollar a bushel, where is the pessimist who would dare predict hard times ahead?

One way of silencing the pessimist is for everyone to take the view that what is the other fellow's loss is our gain, and more especially does this apply to the populations of the rural districts. The farmers of Canada have absolutely no grounds for retrenchment at this time. They are producing the very articles of food most in demand, and getting big prices. It is, therefore, the evident duty of the merchant to be buoyant in spirit and infuse a feeling of "good times ahead" in all parts of Canada.

This might be done in several ways. One of which I would suggest is that all stocks should be kept up to the limit, and the newest and brightest of furniture be displayed in the stores. The better the assortment the greater is the inducement to buy, and I firmly believe that if country dealers kept larger and better stocks that much of the business that now goes to the big cities would be done locally.

The Gold Medal Furniture Co. is doing its best to keep its various factories running with full pay for employes. Although most of the raw materials used have advanced in price, no increase has been made in the selling prices, and having full confidence in the future, we look forward to renewed activity in the furniture trade as a direct result of the prosperity of the farming community of the Dominion.

A song once popular used as its theme, "War is a bountiful jade." May it prove true for Canada and the Empire.

THE GOLD MEDAL FURNITURE CO., LTD.,
Per George Hughes, Assistant Manager.

Toronto, September 25, 1914.

Are You Satisfied With Your Business?

HAVE you carefully considered if your store is yielding all the profits your labor, expenses and investment deserve?

If you want to increase your profits, you should investigate our special proposition to furniture stores.

Will you let us tell you how to double your profits this year?

Write to the undersigned for confidential letter and book "Music Money," something every merchant ought to read. It is yours for the asking.

General Sales Manager

Columbia Graphophone Company
Toronto
Ontario

Columbia Double-Disc Records are made in Canada

Vol. 4 No. 11   NOVEMBER, 1914

Canadian
Furniture World
AND THE Undertaker

Published by the Commercial Press, Limited, 32 Colborne Street, Toronto

Who also Publish: The Retail Grocer and Provisioner, The Retail Druggist, Canadian Hardware Journal, Canadian Manufacturer, Canadian Builder and Carpenter, The Canadian Clay-Worker, Motoring and Motor Trade of Canada, Good Roads of Canada, The Machine Shop, The Canadian Nurse.

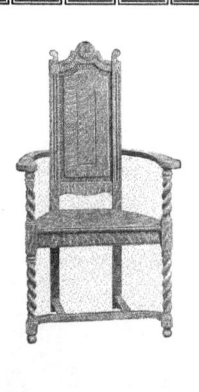

The McLagan Line

Excels in Pieces for Sensible Gifts

We are especially well prepared for the Holiday trade this season. Our new designs include a great variety of prices, which make excellent gifts. With the name McLagan behind them, their sale-making qualities are well assured. Why not look into their possibilities at once?

STRATFORD MADE

MIXED CAR LOTS

Mr. Furniture Dealer:

Are you making the most of your opportunity of selling the householders the indoor furniture they now need?

NOW is the time to feature Living Room Furniture. WE HAVE IT, in either standard Mission designs, or the newer Jacobean, in cheap and higher-priced grades. Besides this is our regular line of fancy chairs and rockers, couches, davenports and novelties.

Write for illustrations and prices. We lend electro cuts free of charge, with descriptive matter, for advertising.

JOHN C. MUNDELL & CO., Limited
Elora, Ontario

The Kindel Kind

Leaders of Thought—and Sales

PEOPLE were first taught the advantage of real Davenport-Bed utility through the national advertising of the Kindel Bed Company. That first good and lasting impression has been added to in thousands and thousands of Canadian homes since the first campaign was carried out.

To-day, the public are thoroughly familiar with the superior features of the Kindel Kind, and their good-will need only be focused on a certain point to enable the dealer to obtain full returns from our vast advertising expenditures. That focus point can be **your store** if you choose.

Why not make it so?

Let us send you full particulars of the new designs in Kindel convertible beds and our great retail selling plan. Get in touch with us at once.

The Kindel Bed Company, Limited
Toronto   -   Ontario

DAY & NIGHT SERVICE

November, 1914   CANADIAN FURNITURE WORLD AND THE UNDERTAKER   3

STRATFORD

The People's Decree is

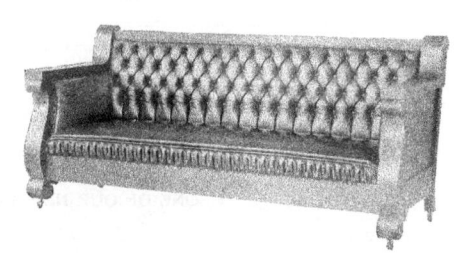

*"Originators of Designs—
Not copies of the other fellow's."*

THOUGH "hard times" exponents have not been hard to find during the past year, and especially since August 1st, there is still the brisk demand for "Imperial Rattan" goods that has characterized our lines for a long, long time.

You must meet the people's requirements. The "Imperial Rattan" line has *proven* its adaptability and saleability under present conditions. Make your holiday trade a "good times" success by featuring "Imperial Rattan" goods.

Stratford   Ontario

This Design is Decidedly Popular

LOOK to the "Ontario" Line for those designs that meet the popular fancy. Our showing of Iron and Brass Beds is particularly attractive just now. Write that order **to-day** for your Holiday stock.

No. 910. A massive, cleancut, chill-less Iron. Pillars, 2 ins., continuous. Fillers, ⅝ in.; height of head, 55 ins.; height of foot, 34 ins. Sizes made, 4 ft. 0 ins. and 4 ft. 6 ins. Finished in white porcelain enamel. An excellent seller.

The Ontario Spring Bed & Mattress Company, Limited
LONDON   *The Largest Bedding House in Canada*   **ONTARIO**

Made in Canada

We are the only Manufacturers in Canada who manufacture the famous Duofold Divan Beds. We manufacture the largest line of Divanettes and Davenports in Canada. Our line of Divanettes consists of 50 different designs, and by buying from us we could supply you Divanettes from the cheapest priced to the highest priced.

ONE OF OUR NEW DESIGNS

Specializing on Davenports and Couches only

Specializing on Davenports and Couches only

Frame: Quartered Cut Oak

Finish: Fumed Oak, Golden Oak, Rubbed and Polished.

No. 94

The Montreal Upholstering Co.   1611-1613 Clarke Street   Montreal, Can.

STRATFORD

Nothing More Appropriate—
Nothing More Appreciated, than

as the Gift to "Mother"

AND judging from our ever increasing Holiday business, **nothing easier to sell** than "Stratford" Chairs. Our lines are replete with practical suggestions for the Holiday Season.

Make the **quality** of "Stratford" Chairs boost **your** sales next month. **Order now.**

"Stratford-Made Increases trade."

Stratford   Ontario

No Holiday Stock will be Complete Without

"Elmira"
Electric Grate Mantels

YOU will want a few Elmira Mantels for your windows to attract trade—many of your *customers* will want them for the Xmas stocking "display" and for the comfort they will give on cold winter nights.

No chimney or tiling necessary—just set it against the wall and connect with electric wiring. A money saver in first cost and in fuel consumption.

Write for Our Proposition

Elmira Interior Woodwork Co., Ltd.
Elmira - Ontario

For Winter 'Sociables'—
'Acme' and 'Peerless' Tables

The lightest, strongest, most attractive and most inexpensive folding tables on the Canadian market. They fold into one-twelfth their standing space.

Any woman who entertains can use a number of "Acme" or "Peerless" folding tables to advantage. Write for prices and order a few dozen to meet the demand this Fall and Winter.

Made in Canada

"PEERLESS" Folding Tables. Square or round styles. Made in fumed oak, early English or golden oak. Polished top. Also green felt covered top.

Hourd & Company, Limited
Wholesale Furniture Manufacturers
London - Canada
Sole Canadian Licensees and Manufacturers

"ACME" Folding Table. Square style only. Made in early English, fumed oak and invitation mahogany. Tops covered with green felt or leatherette. 30-in. size weighs only 10 lbs.

November, 1914   CANADIAN FURNITURE WORLD AND THE UNDERTAKER

STRATFORD

Many of Your Customers *Will Start* *Globe-Wernicke* Combinations this 'Xmas

BY reason of the elasticity of Globe-Wernicke Sectional Bookcases, it is an easy matter for almost anyone to start with a few sections, adding to them from time to time as desired.

The many designs and finishes offer a style to harmonize with any scheme of decoration and furnishings. ¶ Get in the Globe-Wernicke spot-light. Our advertising will link up your store with the best paying proposition of its kind. ¶ Decide **now** to show the Globe-Wernicke line on your floors next month.

OUR LITERATURE WILL EXPLAIN ALL THE DETAILS. WRITE US TO-DAY

Stratford   Ontario

THE "GOLD MEDAL" LINE

DIRECTORS:
W. J. McMURTRY,
President and General Manager
W. R. DALBY
G. C. EMBERSON
H. B. SHORTT, Secretary
G. HUGHES, Ass. Manager

FACTORIES:
MONTREAL FACTORY
C. A. Hart, Vice-Pres. and Mgr.
WINNIPEG FACTORY
W. J. Rimmington, Mgr.
UXBRIDGE FACTORY
Geo. Wilson, Gen. Supt.

Parlor and
Living Room
Furniture

Morris
Chairs

Couches
Chairs
Rockers
Davenports
Divanettes

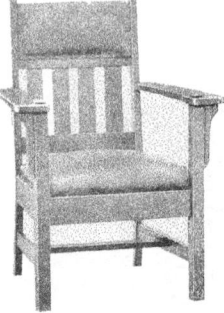

We have several other good designs in Den or Living Room Sets.

NO. 697 THREE PIECE LIVING ROOM SET

Hercules Bed Springs, Steel
Couches *and* Mattresses

The Gold Medal Furniture Mfg. Co., Limited
Toronto   Uxbridge   Montreal   Winnipeg

November, 1914 CANADIAN FURNITURE WORLD AND THE UNDERTAKER

STRATFORD

This *Design* is Making *Many* Sales —

Is It Displayed in *Your* Stock?

AN F-G. DESIGN that reaches the very highest standards of first grade *Davenport Bed* making. Richly finished and upholstered in serviceable tapestry of attractive pattern, it makes an appeal to the artistic taste that cannot be resisted.

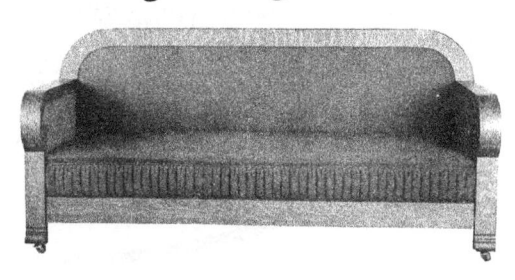

"Stratford Made Increases Trade"

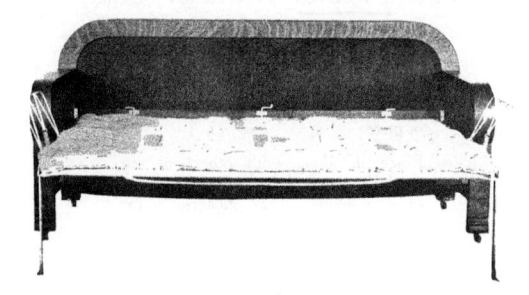

INCLUDE a few Davenport Beds and Couches and two or three Suites of Living-room furniture from the F-G. showing for your Holiday trade. They will give the kind of satisfaction that builds future business.

WHEN ORDERING DAVENPORT
BEDS FROM STRATFORD
REMEMBER TO ORDER F-G

Stratford   Ontario

Why Not Buy a Self-Paying Store Front?

The Merchant next door may have just installed a new Store Front—it looks new and may be a great improvement over his old Front, so far as appearance is concerned. But what about the design? Does it truly represent him—is it individual or are there others in town just like it—is he able to show every line, every day and is his Front *paying for itself*. Mere newness does not spell the success of any Store Front, nor does permanency or stability pay big profits. *Sales* is the thing you, as a Merchant, should be most interested in. *Your* business—*your* Store requires its particular type of KAWNEER STORE FRONT. The only way in which a new Store Front would pay you, or any other Merchant, is to increase the business with which it is associated.

Count the number of people who pass your Store uninterested—then think how a good Front would make them *your* customers.

Kawneer STORE FRONTS

For eight years we have worked with Merchants, Architects and Contractors, in the designing and building of modern Store Fronts and today KAWNEER stands in 30,000 Stores—each one *making sales*. Let us help you—we feel competent by our specialized experience.

If you haven't seen the most interesting Store Front book ever published, "Boosting Business No. 2," send for your copy today. It shows photographs and drawings of many of the best-paying Store Fronts in the country—both in big cities and small towns. This will not obligate you in the least, as we want to show you proofs.

Kawneer Manufacturing Company
Limited
Francis J. Plym, President
Dept. S
Guelph, Ont.

Roomy and Comfortable—
This *Popular* Windsor Chair

MADE in nicely finished hardwood with solid seat, well braced, it is very durable yet surprisingly low in price.

Place it, along with others of our staple lines, on your floors for a brisk season's selling. No "stickers" in the N.A. make.

1340

North American Bent Chair Co.
Limited
Owen Sound   Ontario

STRATFORD

Show this *Folding Chair* for Card Parties, Socials--

and for any purpose that requires a strong, light-weight, inexpensive chair. Absolutely the strongest of its weight made. Constructed so that it will not tip when the occupant leans forward.

Net Price $9.00 a doz. Order at once by the number, 10a.

Made of select, straight grained stock. Posts steam bent.

Note how compactly the "Stratford" folds

Stratford Manufacturing Co.
Stratford - Ontario

SHELLACS

If you are in the market for first-class Shellac we believe it would be to your advantage to get in touch with us.

HIGH GRADE VARNISHES
FILLERS and GRAINING INKS

THE AULT & WIBORG CO. OF CANADA
LIMITED
MONTREAL　　TORONTO　　WINNIPEG

BAETZ BROTHERS & COMPANY
BERLIN :: ONTARIO

Pretty Parlor Pieces

Stock "Phillips" Framed Pictures for 'Xmas Gifts

Sensible, useful things will capture the big bulk of the Holiday Gift trade this year. What more appreciable than a beautiful pastelle, colorgraph, photogravure or painting?

No. 10-2178. Framed Pastel

Our Holiday range includes a host of subjects of all kinds, framed and unframed. ¶ Choice line of Toilet and Bathroom Mirrors in fine White Enamel with new Waterproof Copper-plated backs. Framed Mirrors in all sizes and designs. ¶ Quick delivery for Christmas trade guaranteed. Catalogue on request.

The "Phillips" plant is the largest of its kind in Canada

Phillips Mfg. Co., Limited
Carlaw Ave. Toronto

No. 10-3089. Framed Photogravure

Meet those Calls for Gift Chairs with Chair Crafts---They'll Please

DURING the Holiday Season there is nothing more worthy of first place in your list of gift suggestions than Rest-Fest or Rex-Recliner Chairs. "Chair Craft" is essentially a line that has "stepped ahead" in good lounge chair making. Check up the many desirable features exclusive in Chair Craft designs and the result will at once show you their great sale-making possibilities. In the advertising helps that come along with your trial order are newspaper ads., mailing folders, window posters, window cards, etc.—the kind that are bound to bring you many profitable sales.

Better have a showing of Chair Crafts on your floors and be *sure* of a big season.

A trial order for a few patterns in either Rest-Fest or Rex-Recliner styles will include our complete sales plan. May we send them?

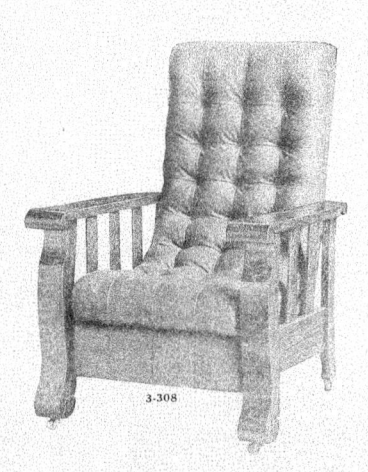

3-308

No need to push buttons or bother with rods and brackets in this Rest-Fest Chair. It adjusts itself simultaneously with the movements of the body. All styles of upholstering, all prices.

The Chair Craft Company
Traverse City :: Michigan

"Victoriaville" Gift Suggestions

JUST the sort a great percentage of your customers will favor this season—something practical and useful for the home.

These pieces are made in imitation quartered oak, attractively designed and well constructed.

At the prices we quote you will be able to make a splendid turnover next month.

WRITE US TO-DAY

The Victoriaville Furniture Company
Victoriaville   Quebec

Push on the *Paying* End—

"Victoriaville"

BRASS BEDS
TO PLEASE *ALL* TASTES

"Victoriaville" Brass Beds present a rare combination of style, quality and lowness of price that makes them worth while featuring prominently at all seasons.

Let us send you details. You can make *more* sales and *more* profit on "Victoriaville" lines.

1272

UPHOLSTERED GOODS
FOR *GIFTS*

The kind that are just filled with soft resilient springs—real comfort-giving qualities—and retain it to a good old age. Attractive designs all, and the price invariably means business. Stock up now for the Holiday trade.

437
ONE OF OUR LEADING POPULAR PRICED DESIGNS

The Victoriaville Bedding Company, Limited
Victoriaville   Quebec

"Hemco" Chairs

for XMAS TRADE

THE "Hemco" makes satisfied customers and brings new sales.

It is the only absolutely automatic reclining chair on the market, and the only one that is actually trouble-proof. There are no push buttons, rods or levers to operate or get out of order. You simply lean back in the chair and rest.

As the back drops at the will of the occupant, the seat rises forming a perfectly flat bed with foot rest in natural position.

Every "Hemco" Sale

means a satisfied customer and a boost for increased business.

Now is the time to get a line of sample *Hemcos* on your floor and increase your Xmas sales.

WRITE FOR PRICES TO-DAY

The Lippert Furniture Co.
Limited

Berlin - Ontario

November, 1914   CANADIAN FURNITURE WORLD AND THE UNDERTAKER   17

Macey Inter-Inter Desks

The two illustrations show the great adaptability of the "Macey Inter-Inter Desks." They can be fitted with any of the approved filing devices used in modern office practice, and have proved themselves to be the greatest time and trouble savers ever put in an office.

The Units can be put either in the top or bottom of Pedestals and are interchangeable, thereby allowing an entire change of equipment to meet any changed conditions that may arise without the necessity of changing the Desk itself.

THEY GET THE BUSINESS

Because they make a strong and direct appeal to the man that uses a desk, he can see at a glance the great advantages they have over ordinary desks.

ANY STYLE YOU WISH

Can be supplied, either Roll Top, or Flat Top, Single or Double. We control the patent rights and are sole Manufacturers for Canada.

CANADA FURNITURE MANUFACTURERS LIMITED

GENERAL OFFICES   WHOLESALE SHOWROOMS   DISTRIBUTING WAREHOUSE
Woodstock, Ontario   Toronto, Winnipeg   Winnipeg, Man.

Two Big Selling Specialties!

"Emperor" Box Lounge

An elegant-looking, splendidly upholstered lounge that serves a double purpose. Substantially made and nicely finished in every particular, covered with green denim, operated by patent spring hinge, adjusted on inside.
A great many of these combination arrangements are being sold just now. Get an "Emperor"—show it—and it will sell itself.

List Price $24.00

"Galex" Extension Couch

The illustration tells the story of its simple, sturdy construction—a strong selling point, considering the complicated construction of many such couches.
Makes a handsome-looking couch by day and, when required, is quickly transformed into a **comfortable** double bed. There are others—oh, yes—but do they equal the "Galex" in simplicity and value?
Fitted with either "Dominion" or "Kinney Fabric" Spring, and an unusually well-made, green-denim-covered mattress. Shall we ship you a couple?

List Price $15.00

Geo. Gale & Sons Limited
Waterville, Quebec

November, 1914   CANADIAN FURNITURE WORLD AND THE UNDERTAKER   19

No. 104    No. 112    No. 430

THE
"Meaford" Line
Abounds in
XMAS GOODS

THE holiday trade in furniture this season will be exceptionally good in the lower priced lines. People, generally, will be more economical than usual, and then attention will turn to goods like the "Meaford" make.

We have endeavored to meet this condition, and have produced a range of designs in Desks, Bookcases, Library Tables, Centre Tables, Jardiniere Stands, Music Cabinets and Hall Furniture that will please anyone.

Correct in style, well built, and possessing the non-crackable and non-chippable finish so pronounced a feature of all "Meaford" Imitation Oak and Mahogany Furniture, you will have no difficulty in disposing of a much larger stock than the ordinary.

Let us get together at once — you should have your displays arranged as soon as possible.

Write Us To-day

No. 439

The Meaford Manufacturing Company, Limited
Meaford   -   Ontario

This New Design is a Great *Seller*

BESIDES possessing new and exclusive features of great importance to the housewife, this **"Knechtel"** design is being advertised extensively in the leading home papers and magazines of the country.

We also provide dealers with a complete set of explanatory show cards for window displays. Line up with the **"Knechtel"** line and make next month a record breaker.

The above trade-mark stands for **"the best cabinet in America for Canadians."**

No. 63. Oak. Open.

No. 63. Closed.

The 14 Features that make the Sales—

1. Improved cylindrical flour bin (patented) with sifter attached. Tilts forward for filling and has heavy bent glass front 6 ins. by 12 ins. to show contents. Is removable for cleaning. Has no corners for flour to stick and become mouldy.
2. Disappearing slide shutters allowing of access to the interior at any time without disturbing the contents on the work table. (A feature that every housewife will be interested in, and one that will make a mighty strong talking point on your sales floor.)
3. Mirror in centre door 8 ins. by 16 ins. by ¼ B. Bevel.
4. Glass sugar bin in swinging bracket.
5. Crystal glass Coffee, Tea and five spice jars with nickel plated screw covers.
6. Extra heavy glass salt Jar with cover.
7. Handy spice Jar shelf with nickel border. "Looks very attractive."
8. Daily Reminder and Order Form Pad.
9. Metal Bread Drawer with tight fitting lid. Draws out on a slide.
10. Nickeloid sliding extension top. Has a gutter at the back to drain off any liquids accidentally spilled, thus preventing same from entering inside of cabinet.
11. Nickel plated towel or linen holder on left hand gable.
12. Handy rack on large door for holding pie plates, etc. and packages.
13. Movable shelf in base cupboard.
14. Bottom sliding tray allowing contents to be drawn within easy reach.

Write for Prices at Once
Knechtel Furniture Co., Ltd
Selling Agents, Hanover

Knechtel Kitchen Cabinet Co. Limited, Hanover, Ontario

NO. 223 BUFFET. LIST 71.25

Here is Your "Leader"

THE biggest buffet that we ever made at the price —54 inches long —all solid plain oak, and as bold as we could make it, consistent with good proportions. The china cabinet and side tables are in like proportions. Put this suite in your window with a price on it and you will agree with us that it is a real leader. Fumed or golden finish. The *China Cabinet* is, list— 43.50 *Side Table*, list—23.25.

Our Travellers Will Show You

the biggest and strongest lines of new Diningroom Suites that we have ever had. Popular prices, popular designs and good Knechtel workmanship are responsible.

THE KNECHTEL FURNITURE CO.
LIMITED
HANOVER - ONTARIO

Feature the *Malcolm* Holiday Gift Line—

NOTHING is more acceptable as a present than an article of household furniture, on account of its lasting value.

Selections made from the comprehensive "Malcolm" line are sure to win the enthusiastic admiration that increases your immediate profits and makes valuable friends for your store.

Besides the pieces shown we have produced many other exquisite designs in Parlor Lamps, Book Racks, Smokers' Stands, Pedestals, Console Tables, Ladies' Work Tables, Music Cabinets, Ladies' Desks, Cellarettes and Magazine Racks.

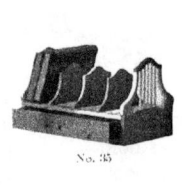

Andrew Malcolm Furniture Company
Limited
Kincardine and Listowel

Boost "Made-in-Canada Presents this Season"

YOU haven't a day to spare if you would obtain the very best results from your displays.

Write for a copy of the new 1915 gift line we have just issued. A card will bring it by return mail. Get busy!

Many more of your customers will buy furniture — Canadian-Made-Goods — this Christmas, if you show the "Malcolm" Gift line. The materials, workmanship and finish of our lines are the best obtainable, and all goods are sold under a guarantee of quality.

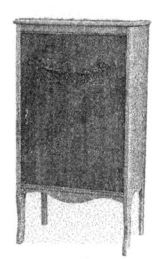

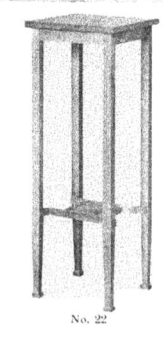

Andrew Malcolm Furniture Company
Limited

Kincardine and Listowel

A Quiet, Dignified Design *from* Canada's Newest Brass Bed Plant

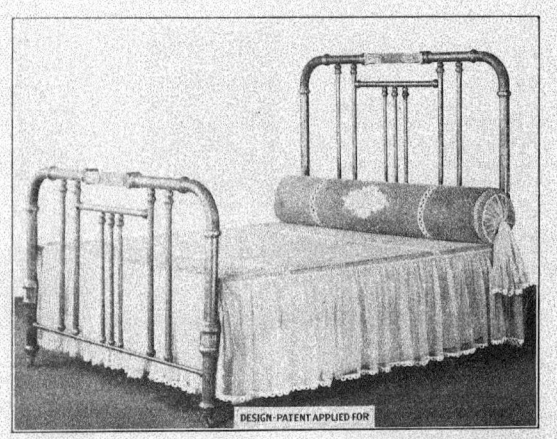

No. 8006. The newest design on the market—one of our own special patterns. Made with square brass tubing centres and inlaid copper trimming.

Mersereau Brass Beds

ARE made of the finest grade materials only. They are the most durable known, and have been on the American market longer than any other make. We are showing a good range of *new designs* for all classes of trade.

Write for Illustrations and Prices at Once

Canadian Mersereau Company, Ltd.
119 Brock Avenue   Toronto, Ontario

Fine Quality Brass Furniture Trimmings

THE finish of our goods is the equal of any obtained anywhere.

Great variety of modern and period designs carried in stock.

Special designs made to order on the shortest notice.

Prices Reasonable

The Stratford Brass Co.
Limited
Stratford   Ontario

J-M Asbestos Mats and Table Covers

Attract Every Woman Who Sees Them

PROMINENTLY displayed, they practically sell themselves. They tell their own story—suggest the money and trouble they save by preventing hot dishes from marring the polish of the dining room table.

As we are the largest manufacturers of asbestos goods in the world we can manufacture J-M Asbestos Table Covers and Mats at a price so low that you can sell them below all competition and still make a handsome profit.

Here are staples for the fall trade. Needed in every home.

Write nearest branch to-day for our special dealer proposition

**THE CANADIAN
H. W. JOHNS-MANVILLE CO., LTD.**
Toronto   Montreal   Winnipeg   Vancouver

This Guarantee Sells Beds for You!

SPECIAL GUARANTEE
This bedstead is guaranteed for construction and finish, and will not tarnish under the use of alcohol, salts, solutions or acids.
S. WEISGLASS, LIMITED

When a customer has admired the design, examined the construction, and noted the lustrous finish of a Weisglass Brass Bed, you have only to show her the Special Guarantee to close the sale right there. It absolutely protects her against faulty construction, and guarantees that the brass is untarnishable. She will find the price right because you can make a good profit in Weisglass beds and still beat your competitors' prices.

If you have not received our new catalogue, showing the largest range of Brass Beds in Canada, advise us and we will gladly send you one

S. WEISGLASS, LIMITED - MONTREAL

THE IDEAL
NEVERSPRED
MATTRESS

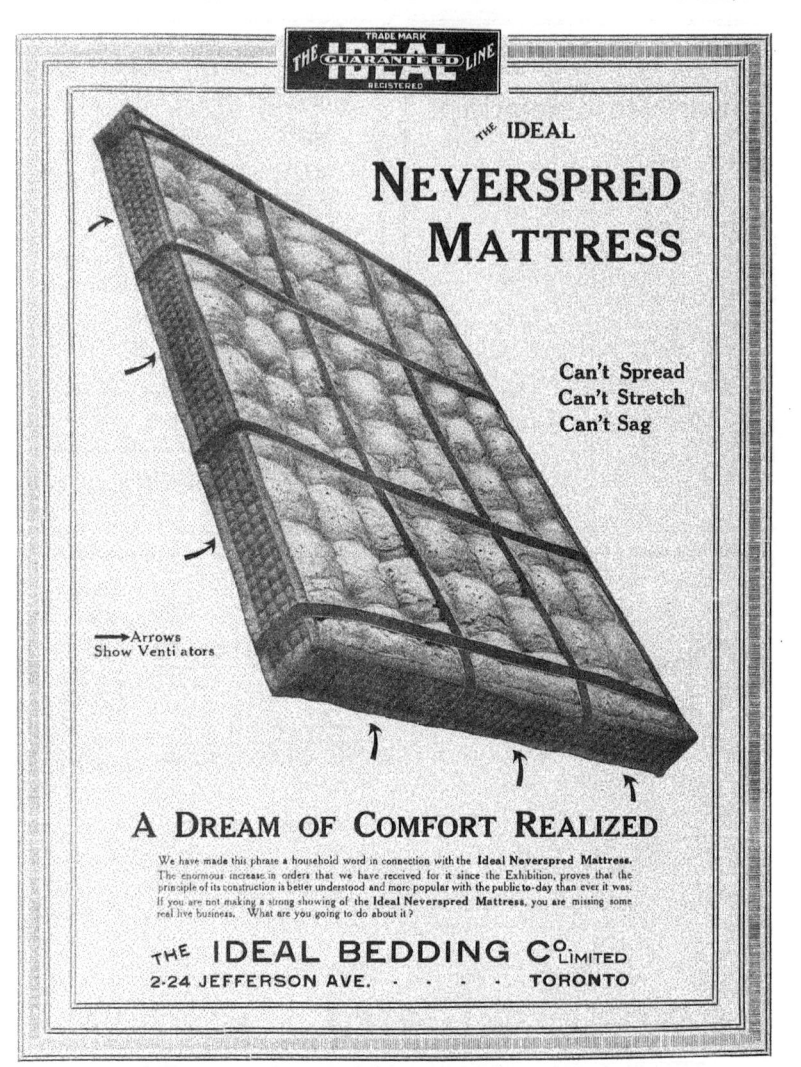

Can't Spread
Can't Stretch
Can't Sag

→ Arrows Show Ventilators

A DREAM OF COMFORT REALIZED

We have made this phrase a household word in connection with the **Ideal Neverspred Mattress**. The enormous increase in orders that we have received for it since the Exhibition, proves that the principle of its construction is better understood and more popular with the public to-day than ever it was. If you are not making a strong showing of the **Ideal Neverspred Mattress**, you are missing some real live business. What are you going to do about it?

THE IDEAL BEDDING CO. LIMITED
2-24 JEFFERSON AVE. - - - - TORONTO

Canadian Furniture World and the Undertaker

Published by The Commercial Press, Limited
32 Colborne Street, Toronto
(Next King Edward Hotel)

D. O. McKINNON, President
W. L. EDMONDS, Vice-President and Contributing Editor
J. C. ARMER, Vice-President and Manager of Technical Papers
WESTON WRIGLEY, Vice-President and Manager of Trade Papers
JAMES O'HAGAN, Editor
WM. J. BRYANS, Associate Editor
GEO. H. HONSBERGER, Advertising Manager
F. C. D. WILKES, 794 Unity Building, Montreal
C. G. BRANDT, Circulation Manager, Toronto
E. J. MacINTYRE, Room 1155, 122 S. Michigan Ave., Chicago
Canadian Advertising Service Co., New York

Subscription rate, Canada and Great Britain, $1.00 per year; United States, $1.50 per year.
Circulation has averaged over 2,000 copies monthly for nearly two years.

Volume Four   TORONTO, NOVEMBER, 1914   Number Eleven

The Returning Confidence. Keep up your courage. Those who are deficient in courage are lacking a quality which is particularly essential at this particular time.

The slump that business experienced when hostilities broke out was not due to a destruction of the buying possibilities of the people. It was because there was a temporary wavering in the courage of financial and commercial interests. And when they lost courage confidence was blown to the four winds like leaves on an autumn day.

This fit of temporary aberration is now a thing of the past. A quiet consideration of the situation revealed the fact that there was no need of our taking to the woods. On the contrary, there was every reason why we should stay in the open and fight for business as if, in the words of Sir George Paish, "no great eventualities were pending." And as they buckled up their courage their confidence returned. The result is that business conditions are gradually becoming more normal. In some respects they are even better than they were before the war broke out.

Last year the field crops of all kinds yielded a value of over $700,000,000. This year, owing to the higher prices obtaining, they will yield even a greater value. This spells added prosperity for the farmers, and, in turn, better conditions for the retailers and manufacturers of the country. Plus this are the large orders which many manufacturers in Canada are receiving from the Imperial and Dominion Governments for equipments and outfits of various kinds, and for food supplies for the troops.

As Sir George Foster told the Toronto Board of Trade the other day, Canada holds a better position today, commercially, than any country in the world. We are thousands of miles from the scene of hostilities and the demand for our products will be for many a month greater than we have ever before experienced.

We have, therefore, a real basis for confidence. Let us make the best possible use of it.

You can't saw wood with a hammer.

A Sign of Improvement. While both bank clearings and railway earnings are smaller than they were a year ago, the statements issued the first week in October show that the decreases are not as marked as they were. This is gratifying, being as it is a reflection of the improvement in business generally.

The decrease in the bank clearings during the week ending October 8 was 13.7, for the whole of Canada, while for the Eastern group of nine cities it was only 11 per cent. When we take into consideration the fact that the stock exchanges are transacting no business it is rather remarkable that the decrease is not more marked.

Then again there is the movement of grain. Last year grain shipments were being rushed out from the West as fast as the railways could make them. This Fall there is not the same impetuosity. On account of the war the farmers are holding on to a good part of their grain in anticipation of higher prices later on. It is estimated that only about 25 per cent. of the wheat crop has so far gone forward to the elevators at Fort William and Port Arthur.

This, to some extent, would be reflected in the bank clearings when comparison is made with the figures of a year ago. The same influence would also be reflected in the railway earnings. But, after all, it is better for all concerned that shipments of grain should be spread over a more extended period than in previous years.

People are possessed of the buying spirit during the Christmas holiday season, but this spirit will not take them to the store that doesn't advertise.

A Good Sign. The business men of Calgary have embarked upon an ambitious scheme. They propose to obtain money from the banks on their own guarantee, and purchase therewith live stock of different kinds and place them with farmers of known integrity, who will pay for them in installments. The object is, of course, the development of the live stock industry.

The object is a commendable one, and it is to be hoped it will be crowned with success.

Alberta was once a great cattle raising province, but its relative importance has dwindled of late years, on account of the wheat-growing purposes to which much of the land has been put. By experience it has been learned that much land which has been put to raising wheat might have been more profitably employed in mixed farming. It is for the purpose of expediting this that the business men of Calgary are undertaking their present scheme, which, if successful, will be beneficial to them indirectly, as well as to the farmers directly.

This incident shows that the business men of Calgary recognize how closely the mercantile and agricultural interests are inter-related. And not only that they recognize it, but that they are willing to co-operate in solving the financial problem which now hinders many of the local farmers in their effort to develop an important and necessary industry.

It is a good sign.

He who gets the viewpoint of his customer obtains a grip upon him that competitors will find difficulty in breaking.

Importance of the Country Town. The Right Honourable Arthur Balfour recently addressed a public meeting in England on the subject of the importance of the country town.

"I should say there is no element in the common life of our country which we could less afford to lose than the life of the country towns," was one of the trite things he said.

What he said about the importance of the country towns to the Mother Country might be said with equal force in regard to their importance to the life and well-being of Canada.

It is unfortunate that we have not in public life in Canada a few Arthur Balfours to impress this fact upon us. It would mean much to us.

The daily newspapers in the metropolitan cities sometimes dilate upon the subject of "back to the farm." But upon the building up of our country towns they are silent.

Their silence can scarcely be born of ignorance. They probably realize the importance to the country of a chain of prosperous and healthy villages and towns in the midst of agricultural surroundings. If they think at all they cannot help realizing it. And that their publishers often have their thoughts turned toward the rural towns is evident from the zeal they display for securing subscribers in them at rates below the cost of the white paper on which their publications are printed.

One, however, has only to turn to their advertising pages to discover the cause of their silence in regard to the building up of the country towns. The advertisements of the department and mail order houses therein to be found is the explanation.

One can scarcely dilate upon the importance of the country town to the life of Canada without emphasizing the importance of patronizing the merchants that do business in the town. With their columns crowded with the advertisements of the department stores this is something the daily newspapers cannot emphasize. At any rate, it is something which it would not be good policy for them to emphasize. In fact, with some of them in part owned by department stores, it is something they would not be permitted to do.

And yet the decadence of many a village and country town in Canada can be traced to the failure of local merchants through the competition of the large department stores of the metropolitan cities.

Every time the store in a country town is driven out of business by department store competition the potency of that town as a factor in the life of the nation has been diminished. And yet this diminishing process is steadily going on.

The Brunt of the Battle But— In most battles there is usually a certain arm of the service upon which falls the brunt of battle.

The same thing happens in regard to difficulties that crop up from time to time in business affairs.

And the one branch of the complex business army upon which the brunt of the battle falls is almost invariably the retail dealer.

We do not for one moment mean to infer that neither the manufacturer nor the wholesaler never suffer. On the contrary they often do suffer. In fact, that which affects the retailer must in turn, to some extent at least, affect both the wholesaler and the manufacturer as well. The three branches of trade are too closely interwoven for it to be otherwise. There is a trinity of business factors, but an interest which, in the final analysis, is one.

The disturbances which have arisen in business circles as a result of the advent of the modern mail order house, are certainly bearing more heavily on retail trade than on any other branch of business. To say this is merely to utter a truism. Everybody recognizes the fact. But everybody does not recognize that each one in the business trinity also suffers, or is even ever likely to suffer.

This is particularly true of the manufacturing interest. It is quite obvious, to most people at least, that the wholesale dealer may or can suffer from the inroads of the mail order house upon the field of the retailer. But as the manufacturer can sell in many instances larger quantities to a mail order house than he can to a wholesale house they cannot see how a possible ebbing in the retail trade can lower the water where the manufacturer sails his ship. The fallacy of this is apparent when one views the situation from all standpoints.

It is to the interest of the manufacturer as well as to that of the country as a whole that the smaller towns and villages throughout the land should grow and multiply. No one will gainsay this. It, therefore, follows as the day the night that anything which tends to prevent this consummation is no more in the interest of the manufacturer than it is of the country. Yet this is the ultimate effects of the competition of the mail order houses.

The backbone of every town is its business interests. When this backbone is impaired or destroyed it naturally follows that the town is either unhealthy or dead.

When manufacturers give mail order houses special prices for quantity purchases, thus allowing them to undersell the local dealer, they are contributing to the downfall of both the dealer and the town in which he does business.

The brunt of the battle may be upon the retailer, but the manufacturer does not get off "Scot free." There are some manufacturers who do not see it that way. But it is a fact nevertheless.

The way to meet the competition of the mail order houses is to offer better furniture than the mail order houses offer, at a price as good or better. This can be done by any live dealer who will show his goods right, advertise them right, and talk quality instead of price.

> **E**VERY patriotic man ought now to stay on his job until the crisis is passed, and ought to stay where his job can best be done.—Woodrow Wilson.

How to Get After the Christmas Gift Trade

BY W. L. EDMONDS

NOTHING worth while can be done except when preceded by preparation. In a few weeks' time furniture dealers, like all other dealers, will be in the midst of the Christmas holiday trade.

The measure of success with which they meet will be largely in proportion to the preparations they make.

That furniture will play an important part in the Christmas gift trade there can be no doubt. There was a time when, relatively speaking, it did not play an important part. But that time has gone by.

People are realizing that the greater an article's utility the greater is its suitability as a Christmas gift. And as there is scarcely any article of merchandise that possesses greater utility than furniture it is naturally benefiting by this latter-day tendency.

During the coming Christmas holiday season this tendency will be more marked than at any time in the history of the furniture trade.

Owing to the world-wide conditions which have been created by the war in Europe, articles of a flimsy and a luxurious description will receive less attention than usual. The preference will be for things possessing utility.

In view of the undoubted utility of furniture, the conditions will naturally be opportune for the furniture dealer who makes preparation to take advantage of them.

The manufacturers have certainly done their part in anticipating the goods that will be required for the holiday gift trade. Never before have they made such excellent preparations. Some of those manufacturing such lines as baby carriages, doll cabs, folding go-carts, are turning out special cheap lines to take the place of those hitherto imported from Germany and other countries.

The experiences of the past have taught them that there are practically unlimited possibilities for the furniture trade during the Christmas season, with the result that they have this year a wider and more varied assortment of goods from which retailers can assort their stocks than ever before.

A study of the advertising columns of The Furniture World, and of the excellent special catalogues which some of the manufacturers in Canada have prepared, will convince one of this.

The furniture dealer has, therefore, the goods at his command as well as the opportunity before him for getting his share of the holiday gift trade.

It is now up to him to get the machinery at work which will reap the holiday gift business crop.

The opportunity is within the reach of the small as well as of the large furniture dealer. The latter has, of course, the greater opportunity. But the difference is only one of degree.

It would be a mistake, of course, for any dealer to attempt to bite off more than he could chew. Let him first of all carefully study the possibilities. If he employs salesmen, let him call them in for consultation. The more counsellors there are the better. It might also be advisable to consult a few outsiders, particularly society women, as to what lines would prove the best sellers. Advertising, as well as advice, would be secured by this latter course. At all such conferences it would be well to have the advertising pages of the trade journals and the catalogues of the manufacturers for reference and study.

Certain expensive suites it may not be advisable for any but the largest dealers to put in stock, but even in many of the expensive lines there are possibilities for the moderate-sized dealers. The most of them can, at least, buy one or two pieces which can be regarded as opportunity affords. Customers can, of course, be acquainted with this fact, and knowing they can complete suites by this gradual process many of them would, no doubt, be induced to make the initial purchase.

In these days of quick delivery the opportunity to the resourceful and enterprising dealer is very great.

It is only when one begins to consider the variety of lines directly and indirectly connected with the furniture trade that one gets a conception of the possibilities there are in store for the dealer who

---

Christmas Gift Furniture

Tea trays	Cribs Cradles
Book cases	Dressing tables
Book racks	Mattresses
Book stands	Comforters
Waste paper baskets	Chiffoniers
Work tables	Bedroom chairs
Work baskets	Beds Pillows
Card tables	Wardrobes
Folding breakfast table	Couches and sofas
Den tables	China cabinets
Library tables	Buffets and sideboards
Tea tables	Hall racks
Odd parlor chairs	Umbrella stands
Smokers' stands	Hall clocks
Candlesticks	Hall seats
Lamps	Hall mirrors
Foot stools	Hall trees
Pedestals	Bake and ironing boards
Writing desks	Cupboards
Muffin stands	Stoves and ranges
Magazine stands	Camp stools
Desks	Washing machines
Wicker flower stands	Divans
Wicker tables	Folding chairs
Wicker chairs	Divanettes
Jardiniere stands	Baby carriages
Music cabinets	Cedar boxes
Doll cabs	Children's high chairs
Doll beds	Invalid tables
Morris chairs	Invalid trays
Couch beds	Cushions
Parlor suites	Casters
Bedroom suites	Vacuum cleaners
Dining room suites	Ladies' writing desks
Kitchen cabinets	Sectional book cases
Parlor tables	Statues
Pictures	Bric-a-brac
Curtains and draperies	Jardinieres
Carpets	Costumiers
Rugs	Sewing machines
Children's Tricycles	Chinaware
Oilcloths	Candlesticks
Linoleums	Talking Machines
Go-carts	Period Furniture
Children's sleighs	Bathroom Mirrors
Console tables	Chess and checker tables

Dealers should paste or hang this panel in their store where customers can read it.

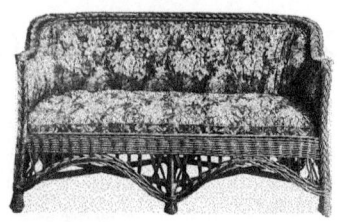

A page of illustrations of furniture items suitable for Christmas gifts.

Upholstered reed rocker, settee and chair by Imperial Rattan Co., Stratford.

Brass or enamelled iron bed by Ideal Bedding Co., Toronto.

Secretary-bookcase, built to accommodate Weis-Knechtel receding door bookcases by The Knechtel Furniture Co., Hanover.

Rocker by Stratford Chair Co., Stratford.

Grafonola by Columbia Graphophone Co'y Toronto.

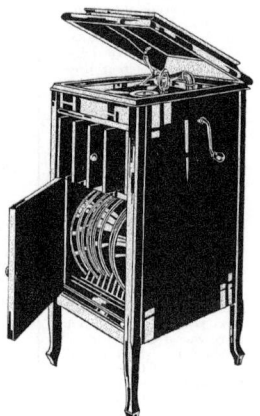

wisely and well prepares his plans for the gift trade.

The duty of the dealer is to impress two things at least upon the public. The first is as to the suitability of furniture and furnishings as Christmas gifts. The other is his ability to supply them.

The advertisement and the window and interior displays are the factors which are at his command for educating the public regarding furniture as Christmas

Suitable gifts for Christmas—A Sheraton music cabinet and a Martha Washington sewing table—by The Toronto Furniture Co., Toronto.

gifts. And one great advantage during the Christmas holiday is that the people court education. They want to buy, but in many instances they do not know what to buy. The dealer, therefore, who, through his advertisements and window displays can suggest articles suitable for the occasion, has a sympathetic audience.

Everybody except a fool knows that furniture possesses both beauty and utility. But it isn't everybody that recognizes either the suitability of furniture for Christmas gifts or the variety of lines that are to be found in the average well appointed store.

As a matter of fact, furniture manufacturing has developed to such an extent in Canada of late years that there are few people outside the trade who possess anything like a grasp of its variety and quality, for even the furniture exhibitions are visited by but comparatively few consumers.

The Christmas holiday season affords the opportunity for driving home some of these facts, while the recognized necessity for developing Canadian trade in this time of crisis is a particularly favorable time to urge customers to purchase furniture which has been made in the factories of the Dominion.

Canadian furniture for Canadian homes will be a taking slogan.

In their advertising campaign retailers will find that many of the manufacturers are ready to co-operate by lending engravings for illustrating purposes. It would be well, therefore, to plan advertising campaigns well ahead in order that all the facilities may be at hand when the season arrives.

Of one thing the dealer may be assured: The more he advertises and displays furniture and furnishings for Christmas gifts the greater will be the demand.

Lists of articles suitable for gifts inserted in the advertisements and also printed on cards or sheets of paper and displayed in the store will help customers in making their selections, as well as save the time of dealers and clerks. The list to be found in the panel accompanying this article may either be pasted on cardboard and hung up in a conspicuous place in the store or serve as a basis for a new list. This list might also remind dealers of lines they should put in stock.

Another thing that dealers might with advantage do is to cut out the illustrations of articles from the advertisements and reading matter which appear in this issue of The Furniture World and paste them on cardboard, either separately or in groups, and write in prices at which they can be purchased. It would facilitate business and bring grist to the mill. One handy with the pen or brush could make up a number of attractive and artistic cards in this way.

In arranging and displaying the stock in the store a good many dealers have met with success in grouping articles of a similar character. Others have experienced success in creating a gift department. As to the benefit which comes from specializing, there cannot be any doubt. It pays to specialize.

In regard to window displays, I would suggest that a plan be determined upon that will provide for a change at least once a week. Twice a week would, as a rule, be better still, although a display that has made a particularly good hit might be allowed to run a full week.

By carefully watching the effect of a display some idea can be obtained as to the length of time it should be maintained. Window space is so valuable that it should be used at all times to the very best advantage.

As to the character of the displays, they should be made as closely in keeping with the Christmas season as it is possible to make them. Their drawing power will be less effective if this feature is neglected.

A figure of Santa Claus should be used, occasionally, at any rate. The use of wax figures representing men, women and children will also increase the effectiveness

Christmas gift furniture—folding table and folding chair—shown by The Stratford Mfg. Co., Stratford.

of a display. For example, in a display of children's furniture, what would take better than a few figures representing children at play? Then take a scene representing a bachelor's den, an interesting display could very easily be made up that would show a bachelor comfortably seated in an easy chair before a grate fire. Dealers who have no wax figures in their possession can

(Continued on page 43)

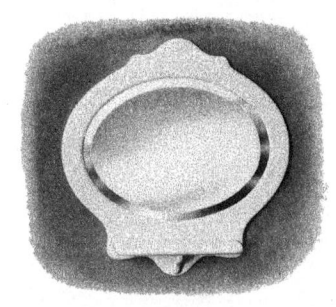

SUITABLE CHRISTMAS GIFT FURNITURE.—Medicine cabinets in white enamel and quartered oak by The Knechtel Furniture Co., Hanover. Bathroom mirror in centre by Phillips Mfg. Co., Toronto. Two willow chairs by Brantford Willow Works, Brantford, and rocker by Stratford Chair Co., Stratford. Adaptable china cabinet and Jacobean library table by The George McLagan Furniture Co., Stratford, and a quartered white oak umbrella stand by The Elmira Furniture Co., Elmira.

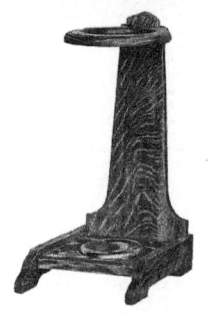

Selling Methods in the Furniture Store

Some Experiences and Suggestions

DEALERS' ADVANTAGE OVER MAIL ORDERS.

That there is nothing to be saved, but much to be lost, to the purchaser who buys a stove through a mail order house, should be emphasized by stove dealers all over the country to prospective customers; as when the drawbacks are pointed out the dealer should be able to hold his own. Some of these disadvantages are:

First, in dealing with a mail order house, the cash must be sent in advance.

The risk of breakage or damage in transit, especially on an article like a stove, as everyone knows, is very

Article	Cost	
	Freight	
	Cost Laid Down	
ON HAND	RECEIVED	SOLD

How a Calgary dealer keeps track of his stock by card system in his office.

great, and the annoyance and worry consequent upon loss or damage from this cause is a serious drawback.

Again, if, for any reason, the stove does not work properly, there is no dealer or anyone interested near at hand to look after it, explain it, or make it right.

And, worst of all, when repairs are needed there is no one to look after and order them; and sending to the mail order house in that case is apt to be full of vexation and expense.

NOVEL DISPLAY METHODS.

The Adams Furniture Co., Toronto, have put on several good stunts during the past month in the nature of window dressing.

They had a red cross nurse making bandages for military hospital purposes for a couple of days, incidentally showing sewing machines.

They had a harvest window—fall furniture embellished with fall vegetables and produce.

They had a window depicting by sample the gifts making up the Dominion, provincial and other colonial donations in cash and kind to the Empire during the present war.

CRANBERRIES AS PREMIUMS TO SELL STOVES

A furniture dealer who wanted to call special attention to his store, and, particularly, to a new line of stoves and ranges for which he had just secured the agency, did so in an indirect way, which turned out to be a great success. He picked out a lot of stew pans—graniteware seconds—which he was able to buy in quantities at about 75 cents per dozen, and laid in a supply of cranberries, costing him between $7 and $9 per barrel, running seventy-five quarts of berries to the barrel. The regular retail price of the two-quart graniteware stew pan in that town was 25 cents, but he advertised that he would sell them at 22 cents apiece, and give as a premium with each a quart of cranberries. He advertised the sale heavily, and sold 150 stew pans, which used up two barrels of berries. His profit on each sale was only three cents.

The sale was talked of all over the country, and brought a great many women into the store who had never been there before. He was able to give his new lines of stoves and ranges an excellent start. The day preceding the sale his principal show window was full of stew pans, while one corner was taken up with a barrel of cranberries lying on its side with the lid knocked off and the berries pouring out in a luscious torrent. In the centre of the window he placed a large range with cooking utensils arranged on top. An imitation turkey, made of paper composition, lay exposed in the oven of the range, the door being open. On the front of the store windows he pasted copies of his newspaper advertisements of the sale.

Here is a seasonable suggestion for other furniture men at the commencement of the winter season, when enquiry begins to be made for stoves and heating goods. Christmas is just ahead, and the cranberry season in sight. A slight variation would make the plan timely just now.

THERMOMETERS ADVERTISE STORE.

Thermometers bearing an advertisement of the store have been found an effective form of advertising by a retail furniture dealer in one of the suburbs of a large American city. Fifty thermometers were put out, each bearing the name of the store and the slogan: "Furniture Store of Merit." The thermometers were

How Marceau & Fils advertise their bed and bedding line at the annual fair.

placed in prominent positions in buildings and on corners, where a large number of people were in the habit of passing daily. The 50 thermometers cost $27, and the proprietor of the store feels that the expenditure was a wise one.

CARPET SHOWROOM IN THE BLOWEY-HENRY CO'S STORE AT EDMONTON.

Edmonton Firm Believes in Quoting Special Prices

THE Blowey-Henry Company, of Edmonton, Alberta, are quite extensive advertisers in the local papers, and follow the practice in their advertising of quoting occasional special prices, and find that it is a valuable method of attracting customers to the store, when an opportunity is presented of selling them additional goods.

"We frequently have instances illustrating to us the part that special prices play in putting us in touch with customers and in helping business generally," stated F. P. Newson, manager of the retail department of the store, to a representative of the Canadian Furniture World. "At least," he continued, "the fact that an advertised article is first on a big list of goods would seem to indicate that such is true.

"Quite often I notice that a $4 or $5 article that has been advertised in the local paper is first on a sales slip, and perhaps the total bill may run up to $70 or $80. No doubt they would have bought the goods anyway, but it is a question whether we would have got the business."

Work Windows and Ads. Together

The display windows are found valuable sales creators and play nearly as important a part in attracting customers to the store as newspaper advertising. "We make a practice of working the windows and newspaper advertising together," says Mr. Newson, "and find this plan of co-operation productive of the best results. Not infrequently do we find direct results coming in from each." A good deal of attention is given to the arrangement of windows and some attractive and sales-producing displays are turned out.

Big Store and Well Arranged

The retail store of the Blowey-Henry Co. is a large one, with the various departments well arranged. The basement is given over to baby carriages, iron and brass beds, springs and mattresses, kitchen furniture, cheap chairs and rockers.

The main floor is used for the display of lines it is desired to feature, and the character of displays is frequently changed. This is the floor that customers see when they enter the store, and thus the value of having varied displays that will attract attention and arouse interest. The lines that are generally shown on this floor are library and den furniture, parlor goods, music cabinets, ladies' desks, bookcases, and similar lines.

Show Furnished Suite of Rooms

The second floor is used for the display of dining room furniture, parlor furniture and tables. A feature of this floor is that one side is devoted to sample furnished rooms, showing a complete suite of rooms furnished. This is found to be of a good deal of advantage in making sales. Many customers don't seem able to size up the requirements for a room or a house and this method of display assists them materially. It also tends to increase sales, for people will frequently buy additional lines when they see how well they work in with the articles they had decided on. This is shown by the fact that one man who came in to select furnish-

(Continued on page 43)

Window Displays the Best Advertising for any Merchant
By R. D. BALDWIN

One of the questions most often found in the question boxes which are run at the various retail furniture dealers' conventions is, "What form of local advertising pays best?"

In the majority of cases, the consensus of opinion is that window display advertising is the best form that a furniture dealer can do, and that if he is limited to one medium only his efforts should be directed towards attractive windows rather than toward any other form of advertising.

Buying centres are formed by attractive store windows. Take any city of moderate size and group in the same block three or four stores noted for their individual and interesting window displays, and you will find that there is a buying centre. The public want to be shown, and they will go any place where there is enough for them to see. If, in the neighborhood of your store, there are not several other interesting windows, it is all the more necessary for you to provide one yourself. You will find that gradually the quality of your neighbors' windows improves and thereby influences just so much more trade to come to that particular centre.

Window a Miniature Theatre.

A window is really a miniature theatre. There must be something about it which attracts the crowd, and something which holds its attention. Get a clear conception of what that quality is that interests the public and then work on various phases of it through your window, and people will continue to talk—favorably—about your store.

It is easy to prove the interest of the street audience, especially so by contrast. Consider the monotony of walking through a street with nothing whatever of interest to look at. Consider a city street on Sunday when the curtains of the shop window are all closely drawn, or take a wholesale district of any large city where the windows, if there are any, are filled with boxes instead of attractive displays. In such places that feeling of lively interest in things about you is absent. Your sole desire is to get through the street to your destination. But given, on the other hand, a series of especially prepared windows, you will find yourself loitering and looking and thoroughly enjoying the walk.

Not only that. You will find yourself in a receptive frame of mind. You will find an item in this window or that one which interests you and appeals to your desire for possession. It is just this feeling which your windows must arouse in the people you want for your customers.

The Cheapest Advertising.

Window display advertising is, from the standpoint of cost, the cheapest advertising you can do, because for a given amount of expenditure it is the most effective. However, don't expect your windows to be effective without any expenditure of money or effort. Don't hesitate to put a little money into window equipment when necessary. Such things as boards, fixtures, paper, cloth, and lights must be provided, and the expense of a man to work with these things while the windows are being arranged. Charge these items up to your advertising, as it is all money well spent.

Remember, the first essential of a window display is to attract attention; then to interest, and finally to create a desire of ownership. This last, however, is least, since to a large extent your windows are expected only to attract attention and to interest, as many purchases are made months after a display, simply because the person saw such a thing on display and was interested in the display in your window, but the need or the desire to buy did not arise until the later date.

Sales the Ultimate Purpose.

The ultimate purpose in every case is, of course, to sell, so your window must attract favorable attention by a distinctive hardware display and aim toward a sale. You may not be following this policy, but one of the methods most successful in helping along the window sale is a good, plain price tag on every article in the window. Price tags add a touch of reality to the display. The spectator in looking at something of interest to him can correctly place it in his scale of relative values.

Take your own case when you are looking at a shoe display or at a men's furnishing store display. Aren't you always just as well satisfied to see a price tag on the collars and shirts exhibited, as to be left in the dark regarding their selling price? Doesn't the price tag sometimes lead you into the store when otherwise you would not go in?

Don't overcrowd a window, or, rather, don't crowd. One thing or one line at a time, with very frequent changes, is the best working plan.

Demonstrations Always Good.

Window demonstrations are almost always good. Use all you can get of them. If a manufacturer wants to put somebody in the windows to attract attention to your store, let him do it, and assist in all ways you can, since at best yours is usually the short end of the expense. Circular advertising or a little advertising in your local newspaper in connection with demonstrations is usually advisable.

Many furniture dealers use circulars and newspaper advertising in connection with special displays which they make and in which demonstrations take place. These displays usually have some unique features which make them worth while and call forth extra public attention.

A regular schedule for your window is necessary. The busy mind of the passer-by will not long find interest in what you keep before it, day after day, without change, because that mind is too intent on looking for new things each day. How would you like to receive every day for three weeks exactly the same kind of a letter from a man who was trying to interest you in some proposition? At the end of the three weeks you would not pay much attention to that letter. Each store must work out for itself the best schedule for changes of displays, and, once worked out, the schedule must be held to rigidly. In some cases this will be twice a week, in the majority once a week, and still a few others every ten days or two weeks, while in very few cases is it ever desirable to keep a display longer than three weeks.

Do you live in a live city? If so, an occasional afternoon spent in the best retail district will be a revelation to you. Make it your object to study window displays and nothing else. Don't look for the furniture stores, but find interest rather in any kind of a store which has an attractive window.

BACKGROUND SUGGESTION FOR FALL

The accompanying illustration shows just one-half of the suggested background. The plain part of the background is of fawn color. The top border is made of three rows of ribbon in different shades of brown and the darkest one at the top. The bottom edge of the border is finished with a light brown ribbon, and the bottom of the background with a wide piece of dark brown ribbon. The loops are made of wheat laced with dark brown ribbon, which is also used for the lover's knot at the top of each loop, from which point ears of corn are hung.

BRIGHTEN UP THE WINDOWS

Do you illuminate your windows and the front of your store at night; that is, after the closing hour and until ten or eleven o'clock or until such time as people retire from the streets? To the man who doesn't, let him know that most merchants think it a mighty effective method of getting publicity. The cost of lighting is incomparable with the benefits derived. You might say that your particular locality is not frequented by passersby after closing hours; but did it occur to you that light acts as a magnet and that you can literally drag the people past your store? Take the customary darkened street in any town, where there are few pedestrians after dark; light up one store well and notice the transformation. It's a good thing to know that light attracts humanity.

And then, again, many men who have been confined to shop or office all day, very often take a stroll with their wives and families after dark, for a bit of air, we'll say. Such a man with a full meal under his belt feels very kindly toward the world, far more so than he did prior to his arrival home for his evening dinner. He no longer looks at your window as if it were something to be shunned. He takes a kindly interest in all things. Even though he may be on his way to some particular place, he'll have time to stop and glance over your offerings. It's the psychological moment. It is now that the good window display proves its worth. The man is interested at the right time; very often the result will be an order from his wife the following day for a new chair, a rocker, or some other useful piece of merchandise.

VALUE OF INTERIOR DISPLAYS.

Many furniture merchants overlook the advantages in profits and advertising to be gained from the well-arranged displays of merchandise inside the store. There are merchants who will give proper attention to their show windows, but will neglect opportunities for interior display that would net them good returns on the investment.

REMOVING SCRATCHES FROM PLATE GLASS

Surface scratches on plate glass may be removed or polished out by rubbing the surface with a soft leather pad and rouge. Make the rouge into a paste and apply to the glass and well polish.

"THE Canadian Furniture World is a very well edited trade magazine, and the work throughout is well executed, both in the advertising and the general information pertaining to the trade. The Canadian Furniture World should be of untold value to any man who is interested in the furniture trade, either manufacturing or selling."
Signed by: Richard Potter, Manufacturers' Agent, Vancouver, B. C.

Background suggestion for Fall or Harvest window display.

Advertising Furniture for the Christmas Trade
BY A. B. LEVER

ADVERTISING is becoming more and more a feature of the Christmas holiday trade. This year should see a further development of the idea. The economic conditions should help, rather than retard, this development.

If ever there was a time when it was opportune for the retailer to drive home arguments regarding the suitability of furniture, rugs, lamps and other lines of house furnishings for Christmas presents, it will be this year, for while things trashy and useless will be less wanted, things substantial will be in greater demand than ever. And of all things substantial there is nothing, generally speaking, that approximates more closely to this classification than furniture.

This fact retail furniture dealers would do well to "hammer home" in their advertisements during the holiday trade season.

In order that retailers may have some examples of holiday furniture advertising before them, I have selected for reproduction this month a number of good advertisements which were used a year ago by dealers in different parts of the Dominion. From a study of these, dealers will doubtless be able to unearth suggestions which will assist them in the preparation of their advertisements during the ensuing holiday season.

* * * *

Strictly speaking, the advertisement of Lemont & Sons is not a Christmas one, but I have included it in the group because of the suitableness of lamps as holiday presents. The ad. is a decidedly good one, and with a few minor changes could be made to apply directly to the holiday trade. The subject matter makes an appeal to both people who read and people who sew, and it makes it in a way that is unanswerable. In other words, it gives a strong selling talk. In typographical appearance the ad. is also good. The original was 4¼ by 6½ inches.

* * * *

The advertisement of T. F. Harrison Co., Kingston, hits the nail on the head regarding the place of furniture in the Christmas holiday trade.

"Christmas cheer will be more cheerier if good, sensible presents are given. Among these, none better than furniture, rugs or curtains, chairs, tables, parlor or kitchen cabinets, desks, couches, divans, sofas, fancy rush or rattan chairs." That these sentences are to the point no one will dispute. Original was 4¼ by 9½ inches.

* * * *

The advertisement of the Robert Simpson Co., Toronto, is, of course, the most striking one in the group. This was what might be termed a preliminary ad. early in the holiday trade season, and was an invitation to the public to visit what they suitably called their "Furniture Gift Shop." This is an ad. which can be adapt-

How Canadian furniture dealers advertised for Christmas trade.

ed to the needs of many a retailer throughout the country. The ad. is an all-round good one, and was 15½ by 10³⁄₄ inches.

* * * *

Gordon & Keith, Halifax, made a happy hit in their advertisement. No one forgets children during the Christmas holiday season, but there are a good many people who might overlook the furniture store as a place in which to buy serviceable toys. Gordon & Keith's ad. obviates this possibility—at any rate as far as the readers of Halifax papers are concerned. No doubt there were many children who saw that their parents did not overlook this particular ad. I think the ad. would have been improved typographically had the main line on the top been devoted to the subject of the ad. instead of the name of the firm. The latter should have gone below. This defect, if I may be permitted to call it so, was not, however, sufficient to affect the selling qualities of the ad; it merely affected its typographical appearance. Original 4⅜ by 6 inches.

* * * *

Although the advertisement of the Moncton Carpet & Furniture Company did not go into details in regard to any particular lines or name prices, yet it is made interesting by the selling talk which it gives on the subject of "Christmas Gifts That Last." That is a good line of talk for any year, but it is a particularly good one for the ensuing holiday season, when gifts of substantial articles like furniture will be particularly acceptable to a good many people. The original was 8⅞ by 7⅜ inches. A plainer border would have improved the ad. So would have better type, but these defects are the fault of the printers, and not the advertisers.

* * * *

D. A. Smith, Limited, Vancouver, have an all round good ad. "Are you spending your money to best advantage for Christmas gifts?" and "There are few things just as good as furniture for Christmas giving. This year we are well stocked with all the useful, pretty pieces that are inexpensive and yet are very much admired," are two decidedly apt sentences with which to introduce the subject of furniture as Christmas gifts. The list of goods, with their prices, which follows, is also particularly apt. The original was 6½ by 9¾ inches.

* * * *

The advertisement of Wright's, Limited, Sydney, is an artistic and striking announcement. They might have crowded a lot of other matter into the ad., but they wisely preferred to confine their announcement to one line, and to surround it with plenty of white space in order that its psychological effect may be the greater. It is a style of advertising that is worth emulating. The original was 6½ by 7½ inches.

* * * *

Although the Christmas holiday season is some weeks away it is none too early to prepare plans for the advertising campaign. Advertising that is prepared in the eleventh hour can scarcely be as effective as that which is prepared at high noon.

Another thing I would suggest is: Push and advertise Canadian-made furniture, and furnishings. The hearts of the Canadian people are inclined that way at present. And the furniture dealer will be wise who bends his efforts in the direction that will meet this inclination.

ADVERTISED FURNITURE

In a recent issue of Printers' Ink, (New York), S. Karpen & Bros. explain how they have met the problem of convincing the larger dealer that if he handled their advertised furniture they would not, later, sell direct and get for themselves all the good of the popularity it had won largely by his efforts.

"In the first place, we gave the dealer a fair profit. In the second place, we did no business direct, but turned all orders, no matter how large they were or how they came to us, over to a dealer.

"Again, we gave dealers in towns and small cities exclusive rights. This could not be done in the large cities.

"Then we took pains to show the dealer that the advertising we were doing was really in the nature of dealer help, that it advertised furniture as much as it did the name of Karpen and that he could profit by it by establishing a connection between it and his own store; both by local advertising, by the distribution of our literature and by proper window and store display.

"We showed him that the improvement of the public taste in respect to furniture, which would tend to be the result of our advertising, meant a steadying influence and a larger volume of sales.

"The average dealer cannot afford to carry a heavy stock of furniture. The more expensive it is, the fewer pieces he can afford. To meet this condition, we made our catalogue very comprehensive and elaborate, with large illustrations in detail, showing all features of the furniture. This served the double purpose of permitting patrons to see exactly what they might be getting and of allowing dealers to order at need and secure in short order. It is not an advantage to carry a large stock at the factory, but it is practically unavoidable, and the dealer appreciates any improvement in catalogue service and deliveries. We have, in consequence, paid more than ordinary attention to the development of our correspondence department, which handles this phase of the business.

"We supplied booklets for distribution to the dealers' customers or for the circularization of his mailing list. Lastly, we sent out furniture experts to assist local dealers in closing important orders. They went out with books and photographs and such other matter as the local dealer would hardly carry, and afforded the fullest possible information. This encouraged the dealers to stir up new business on their own account.

"We travel nine men through the United States, and find that the advertising has made their task much easier than before.

"Through these means, which we are continuing and seeking to improve, we have been fortunate in building our business up. In one sense, it is in the hands of our dealers. In another sense it is in our own hands; we have put ourselves in a position where we can take the initiative and assist the dealer to become an active and creative selling force, to go after business, instead of waiting for it to come to him."

It might be wise to exploit a sale of furniture at present-day standard prices—prices which it is possible to still make, but which it is not at all likely it will be possible to make six months hence.

How to Display Mattresses

By R. H. Browne
Ideal Bedding Co., Ltd., Toronto

THIS question has engaged the attention of thoughtful men of the trade for many years, and while some have devised fairly satisfactory methods of displaying their beds and bedding, it is unfortunately too true that a great majority of dealers, especially in the smaller places, don't seem to have the slightest conception of how to show their beds and bedding to advantage.

The writer has gone into many stores not only in small towns, but in some of the largest cities in Canada, and found beautiful displays of mahogany and Circassian walnut bedroom and dining-room furniture arranged on the main floor, and in inquiring for metal beds and bedding was directed to the basement, where these goods were displayed amidst unattractive surroundings, poorly lighted and poorly decorated. In some cases whitewashed walls, beds covered with dust and dirt, small samples of springs and mattresses under beds or lying on top of or under stoves, filthy, dirty and dusty, and altogether about as unattractive as they could possibly be. Yet customers are expected to select goods from samples kept in this unsanitary condition, and dealers sometimes wonder why they don't sell more of this class of goods; in fact, many furniture dealers seem to regard metal beds and bedding as a side line, quite apart from the balance of their stock, and give them the poorest space, either in some dark corner or in the basement, instead of being the most staple article in their stock, the easiest sold and handled, and the one yielding the greatest percentage of profit for the space occupied. In fact, metal beds and bedding in a furniture store are as staple as sugar in a grocery store.

Goods well displayed are half sold, and in the display of metal beds and bedding the first requisite is a clean, well-lighted space, beds grouped according to design and size, and kept scrupulously clean and free of dust.

Springs and mattresses should be displayed on a rack, where full length samples can be shown and are easily accessible at all times. I have seen various styles of both spring and mattress racks, but the most complete and perfect that has come to my notice is one recently built and erected by the Ideal Bedding Co., Ltd., for the T. Eaton Co., Toronto, which is illustrated on this page.

This rack is made entirely of heavy steel tubing, all the uprights and frame work of 2 in. stock attached by solid malleable iron corner castings. This is the overhead trolley style of rack, the springs and mattresses being suspended lengthwise from steel rollers running on heavy tracks. This allows any spring or mattress to be pulled out beyond the balance of the springs or mattresses, giving an unobstructed view of each article. A customer can be shown both the upper and lower sides of a spring. All samples are swung clear of the floor, and are easily kept clean and free from dust. Samples can be shown in any width desired—3 ft. 0 in., 3 ft. 6 in., or 4 ft. 6 in., according to the amount of space at disposal.

The actual floor space occupied by this rack is only three feet, the upper portion of the rack being an overhang, and allowing free and uninterrupted passage of trucks, etc., underneath.

Many dealers raise the point that they have not the space to devote to a rack, but it will be readily seen that the argument does not apply in this case, as a rack of this description will not occupy one-fifth the space of a rug rack, and will soon pay for itself in increased business.

How bed springs are displayed in Eaton store at Toronto. A similar section is used to show mattresses. Where space is a consideration these can be combined. Similar display racks were made by the Ideal Bedding Company for Adams, Burroughes, and Simpson, Toronto; Home Furniture Co., Hamilton, and other dealers in Canada.

KAPOK PRICES GOING UP.

Kapok is selling at an advance of 25 per cent. in the United States, and those who deal in it say that it will be higher. Mattress manufacturers who laid in a stock at the old prices are congratulating themselves, and those who bought Kapok at 16 cents have a golden opportunity now to make a little money on silk floss mattresses. Heavy insurance rates prevail now on account of war risks, and this adds materially to the cost of Kapok, the raw material. Kapok comes from Java. The Dutch control Java, ship Kapok from there in their own bottoms, and usually tranship from Holland to the United States and Canada.

TWO BARGAIN OFFERS.

The Ideal Bedding Co. are making two special offers to the trade to introduce their "Canuck" link fabric spring. The first offer is a bungalow style "Ideal" chill-less steel bed, a "Canuck" spring and a Paragon cotton felt mattress for $10; the second offer is an "Ideal" chill-less steel bed, a "Canuck" spring, and a paragon mattress for $15. The "Canuck" fabric is composed of double twisted wire links running longitudinally every two inches. There are no sharp points to snap or break, and the cross links are securely locked. The fabric is attached to the steel frame by 58 fine quality oil-tempered steel helical springs, which not only assure comfort and resiliency, but prevent sagging or stretching. The spring is reinforced on each side with a strong copper wire edging, and is guaranteed for 20 years. Without extra charge this spring may be had in either oxydized or bronze finish, but oxydized finish will be sent unless otherwise specified.

BEDDING AT THE EXHIBITIONS

At the recent exhibitions at Toronto, London and Ottawa, The Fischman Mattress Co. made displays of their products, and both J. McLaughlin and J. Cohen looked after the exhibits at these fairs. The Fischman

Making the Fischman mattress.—Automatic spring making and filling machine, so finished that no sharp points are left to pierce cotton. Invented by M. Fischman.

patent mattress is a spring mattress tufted between the felt and the top and bottom of each spring. This helps to make the action of the spring respond readily to any pressure placed upon it. While the springs are placed in rows, each spring is independent of the others, and so the action of each is independent.

The mattress is made with either a high quality of layer felt or a good quality of black curled hair, is made under hygienic conditions and is entirely sanitary. The displays brought much favorable comment and many inquiries.

QUICK WORK ON BED ORDER.

The Ives Modern Bedstead Company, of Cornwall, received a rush order for 1,000 beds from the Militia Department some time ago, to be delivered at Quebec at a given time, and all hands were set at work to fill the order. By working the entire staff overtime, the beds were made and shipped, and will be sent to Europe for use in the field hospitals. The beds are constructed entirely of iron and are very substantial.

BIG BEDDING OUTPUT

With a total floor space of 105,000 square feet, the manufacturing capacity of the Winnipeg plant of the Alaska Bedding Co. is 90,000 steel beds, 150,000 mattresses, 90,000 springs and 30,000 couches, annually.

There should be room in the furniture store for a department of furniture for the babies and for the children.

CHANGE IN IDEAL BEDS.

The News-Bulletin, published by The Ideal Bedding Co., contains notices stating that their brass beds, B No. 1 and B No. 9, have been changed in height. The former now has a head 58 inches high and a foot 34 inches high; the latter has a head 61½ inches high and a foot of 37½ inches.

An error in their July price list makes out that their steel bed No. 740 has been discontinued. This is not so. Steel bed No. 742 is the one that has been discontinued.

TEN DEMANDMENTS.
By the Boss

Rule 1. Don't lie—it wastes my time and yours. I'm sure to catch you in the end, and that's the wrong end.

Rule 2. Watch your work, not the clock. A long day's work makes a long day short, and a short day's work makes my face long.

Rule 3. Give me more than I expect and I'll pay you more than you expect. I can afford to increase your pay if you increase my profit.

Rule 4. You owe so much to yourself that you can't afford to owe anybody else. Keep out of debt or keep out of my shop.

Rule 5. Dishonesty is never an accident. Good men, like good women, can see temptation when they meet it.

Rule 6. Mind your own business, and in time you'll have a business of your own to mind.

Rule 7. Don't do anything which hurts your self-respect. The employe who is willing to steal for me is capable of stealing from me.

Rule 8. It's none of my business what you do at night. But if dissipation affects what you do the next day, and you do half as much as I demand, you'll last half as long as you hoped.

Rule 9. Don't tell me what I'd like to hear, but

Making the Fischman mattress.—Automatic pocket sewing machine, which sews and divides the pockets ready to receive the steel coil springs. Invented by M. Fischman.

what I ought to hear. I don't want a valet to my vanity, but I need one for my money.

Rule 10. Don't kick if I kick—if you're worth while correcting you're worth while keeping. I don't waste time cutting specks out of rotten apples.

November, 1914   CANADIAN FURNITURE WORLD AND THE UNDERTAKER   41

Collins' Course in Show Card Writing

Twelfth of a series of articles specially prepared for this journal.

THE securing of patterns for fountain air brush designs is not so difficult as one would first imagine. A glance over the advertising pages of various magazines will often bring to your notice suggestions for designs that you can readily adapt to card use. Or by keeping your eyes open you may often obtain ideas from show bills, street posters and billboards that can be turned to use in card work. By using your

Maybe the man whose home you Envy most, buys his Furniture here

Fig. 19.—Completed.

own ingenuity you may take one part of a design and work it into some other part of another design and evolve something new of your own.

The sketching of patterns is quite simple. We have chosen for illustration the card shown in Fig. 19. This is a uniform design. That is the four quarters of the design are all the same. To make the pattern, take a piece of paper that is not too heavy. Ordinary plain white news paper or wrapping paper will do. Fold it twice as shown in Fig. A. The folds shown in the drawings are exaggerated to show how they should go. Of course, when you are working them they will lie perfectly flat. The dotted lines in Fig. B show where the folds should go. After folding the paper, take sufficient carbon paper and place inside so the carbon side will cover the entire surface of the paper. This may be better understood by a glance at Fig. B. The carbon surface should be sufficient to cover the entire design. After inserting the carbon paper, lay the folded paper on a smooth, flat surface and trace one-fourth of the design as in Fig. A. Then open the paper and you will have the four quarters or the entire design traced out complete as in Fig. B.

Secure a heavy piece of manilla paper, or, if you have many of the same design to do, take a piece of thin sheet lead, and lay the pattern on it and trace with carbon paper. With a sharp knife cut the design out, being careful to preserve the outside mat. Make an other pattern of the inner line cutting it the same way, but you need not be careful of the mat in this one.

Working the Design With the Fountain Air Brush.

It is a very simple matter now to operate the fountain air brush with this design. Lay the larger pattern on the card and air brush around it. It is always well to spray lightly and go over it several times as the effect is much better than a larger spray put on quickly. Use whatever color you desire for the card you have to do. Remove the pattern and place the smaller or inside pattern on the card, and air brush around the edges lightly. This will give a bevelled effect to the design. Leave this inside pattern in place and lay the outside mat on. This will permit only the bevel part or edge of the design to show. Next hold a piece of straight edged card at the various corners of the design and with air brush darken as shown in Fig. 19. It will be necessary in do-

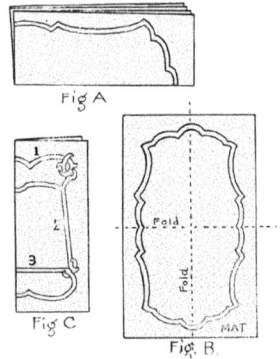

Fig. 19.—How to make.

ing this to assume that the light comes from the upper left-hand corner. This will throw the darker shades on the lower and right-hand sides. Remove your patterns and your design is completed.

The design of Fig. 20 is more difficult to execute. The

ABCDEFGHIJKLM
NOPQRSTUVWXYZ

Plate 45.—Fancy spurred Roman, upper case.

tracing is done the same as described above with the exception that there is only one fold instead of two. A glance at Fig. C will show how to lay it out. In this design the three parts, 1, 2, 3, should be cut separately. These should be hooked together just as shown in the pattern and turned upside down on the card to be worked. This will bring the "hooked" parts just the reverse of the way you want them. This is done because when one pattern is laid over or on top of the other it is raised a little from the card. This permits a little spray from the air brush to go underneath and which will bring the spray to the right places under the card. After spraying with the air brush all around the pattern, remove the patterns and hold one of them in place and spray carefully around the different parts to give the effect of overlapping as shown in the finished card. You will need to exercise a little care at first to get this just right. After finishing all the corners spray all the edges all the way around the design to give it the rounded effect.

In Fig. 21 you have a different design from either of the other two. It is quite irregular, which will not permit it to be drawn like the others. None of the four corners are the same. Cut the design from the same kind of pattern material. Lay it on to the card and air brush the background with any dark color you desire. The oval is cut out of the pattern and air brushed on the inside edge. The panels are made by cutting strips of cardboard and laying them on as shown in the design and air brushing around them. The top will need two curved pieces cut the proper size and shape and laid on

Fig. 20.—A little more difficult example.

and air brushed at the lower edges. This is a very effective card.

Treatment of Fancy Initials.

Q may be in any dark color, red, blue or even black, with the background in pale colors that will harmonize.

R. Black outline, white centre and subdued color in the background.

T. This is an old English design that may be done very effectively with red or green and blue outline.

U. Will look well in red with black outline and pale blue or green ornamentation.

V. In blue, red or black, with pale blue, pink or red back, will be quite effective.

W. In solid black or red with a yellow back ornamentation.

X. Black outline, red or blue filling and subdued harmonizing color for the back.

Fig. 21.—Sample of an air brush design.

Y. Red or black, with a blue and black scroll.

Z. Black outline, open white centre, and subdued color ornamentation.

Alphabets.

The alphabets this month are a practical design suitable for one or two lines or a word that needs to be accentuated on a card. They are fancy spurred Roman upper and lower case.

Plate 44.—Fancy spurred Roman, lower case.

Mahogany piano lamp with silk shade, equipped with electric fixtures and silk cord.

Odd book rack.

Solid mahogany ladies' work table, Queen Anne style.

Another style of mahogany piano lamp.

Smokers' stand.

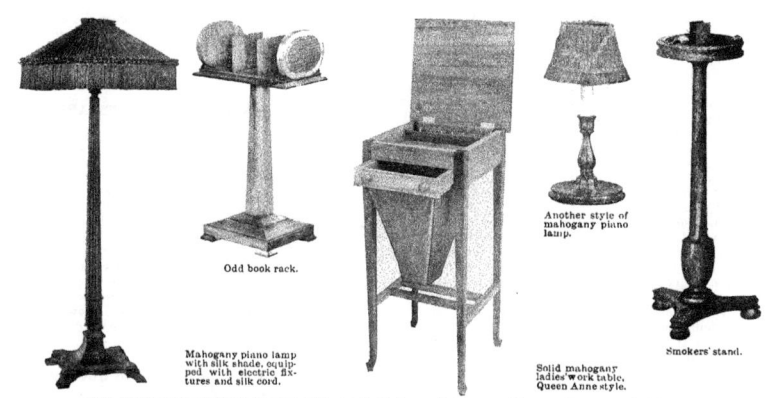

SOME EXAMPLES OF THE MANY CHRISTMAS HOLIDAY GIFTS AMONG THE ANDREW MALCOLM FURNITURE CO.'S LINE.

HOW TO GET AFTER CHRISTMAS GIFT TRADE

(Continued from page 31.)

usually borrow them from dry goods and men's furnishing stores.

A manufacturer who takes an interest in the subject of window dressing suggests a divided window arranged something after the following manner: In the one part he would depict an outside winter scene, and in the other a well furnished bedroom, den or sitting room, emphasizing comfort and illustrating articles of furniture which would make suitable gifts.

In display of living room furniture it would be well to occasionally work in a talking machine with wax figures arranged in comfortable attitudes listening to the music. Talking machines should be a part of every furniture dealer's stock, and displays made during the Christmas holiday season would show the public that the furniture store was the place in which to buy them.

A display that would show an afternoon tea scene would take particularly well with the ladies, and would afford the dealer an excellent opportunity to display tea trays, muffin holders, tea wagons, tea tables, lamps, screens, etc.

One or more displays should be devoted to novelties such as book racks, book ends, lamps, etc., and staple articles which can be obtained at moderate prices.

In window displays and in advertisements emphasize as much as possible Canadian-made goods. It will help to make sales.

MALCOLM GIFT LINE.

Under the title "Holiday Gifts," The Andrew Malcolm Furniture Co., Ltd., Kincardine and Listowel, Ont., have just published a splendidly printed and illustrated booklet of ideal Christmas gifts, which the up-to-date furniture store is carrying these days. Nothing is more acceptable than an article of household furniture, because of its lasting value, and if these articles can be placed in the nature of presentation goods, the furniture dealer should command a very large share of the gift trade.

The articles illustrated and described in the booklet include parlor lamps, book racks, smokers' stands, pedestals, console tables, ladies' work tables, music cabinets, ladies' desks, cellarettes and magazine racks—all of them in odd and individual shapes and styles, and all of them suitable for presents.

A novel feature of this "Holiday Gifts" catalogue is that a number of them may be had by dealers handling

Collins' course in showcard writing. Some fancy initials.

the Malcolm line with the dealer's own name and address on them for distribution among his customers in his community, as if the catalogue was gotten out specially by the dealer.

GRAPHOPHONES IN FURNITURE STORES

A number of furniture dealers appear to be letting a golden opportunity pass by in the way they have been neglecting the line of graphophones and talking machines. Not all of them, of course, but most of them. And even in a number of cases where this line, with their records are handled, too frequently is it regarded as a sideline. This, no doubt, is the reason why the best possible has not been made with sales of graphophones. So much is this true that music houses making a feature of this line are now adding music cabinets and furniture items to their record and music box departments.

One such dealer remarks that his sales of music cabinets this past year would astonish many of his competitors in the furniture trade. To those who buy talking machines or records he introduces his cabinet line, and in a number of instances he has been successful in making sales.

If ever an opportunity to introduce the line of graphophones and records presented itself to a furniture dealer it is now, right at the commencement of the Christmas gift buying season. That there will be an active trade goes almost without the saying. These machines have been very popular at this time in years past, and despite the pessimistic tone in business due to war talk, there will be a great many of these machines sold this season.

For one thing, the small cost of this style of music box appeals to the majority of patrons desiring a musical instrument in the home. Their newness, too, is another appealing feature, which, with the patriotism in the air, and the possibility of obtaining so many of the songs on records of the human voice, should prove a strong inducement to buy if the furniture dealer lets the public know he has the line, and makes them know the worth of the instruments.

WAR'S EFFECT ON WILLOW AND RATTAN.

Next summer's furniture business may bump up against some problems if the war continues for any length of time. Most of our willow comes from Germany and France, but it can also be had in the Madeira Islands and Portugal, both neutral countries, so far.

Singapore is one of the principal markets for rattan, and if a reasonable amount of peace is maintained on the Pacific Ocean it ought to be possible for the manufacturers of rattan furniture in this country to get their supply direct instead of having it shipped to the European ports and then to America. Singapore is about half way round the world and, if measured by time, a little shorter across the Pacific than across the Atlantic.

ANNUAL TORONTO FURNITURE EXHIBITION.

There is a movement on foot to make the furniture exhibition at Toronto a permanent annual institution, and arrangements are under way to get a suitable building to properly and adequately house the exhibits. The second annual exhibition is proposed to be held next January, and plans for this will be discussed by the committee in charge at an early date.

BISSELL'S MAKE A VACUUM CLEANER.

The Bissell Carpet Sweeper Co. announce to the trade that they are to make a Bissell Vacuum Cleaner. Two models have been perfected, both hand-propelled—one with a brush and one without. They will be known respectively as Bissell's Vacuum Sweeper and Bissell's Vacuum Cleaner. From their description it appears that their first offerings will be as full-fledged machines of unusual merit, both mechanically and in general appearance. Their Christmas announcement, just issued, is a handsome specimen of the printer's art, and contains a very attractive proposition to the trade. A special advertising feature is a free motion window display that should interest merchants from the viewpoint of the general interest it will create in their window space.

EDMONTON FIRM BELIEVES IN QUOTING SPECIAL PRICES.

(Continued from page 34.)

ings for a house looked over the arrangement of the entire five rooms, and found they appealed to him, so he gave an order for the entire five to be duplicated in his own house. If he had been picking out the goods one at a time, it is probable that he would not have purchased near as much.

Extensive Display of Rugs and Carpets

Carpets, linoleum, drapery goods and bedding are shown on the third floor, a photograph of which is reproduced here. It will be noted that the department is artistically laid out. Rugs and carpets are draped in an attractive manner in the foreground. Along one side extends shelving for carpets, while displays of linoleum extend down the other, with the drapery department at the rear. The floor is large and well lighted and allows of the advantageous display of the various lines.

On the fourth floor are shown office furniture, bedroom and hall furniture.

A fine catalogue of 132 pages is gotten out by the firm, being sent principally to people outside the city, this being the method used of reaching out for trade. It is printed on heavy coated paper and contains many fine cuts, it being felt that illustrations assist to no little extent in interesting people in a piece of furniture.

Turner & Farrell, furniture dealers and undertakers at Dauphin, Man., have dissolved partnership, and the business will be carried on by Wm. C. Turner, who will give his personal attention to the furniture end. N. R. Henderson, of Moose Jaw, has been engaged as undertaker and embalmer.

Have you framed the pictures of our **WAR HEROES** Kitchener, French, Jellicoe, Beatty
There are also boys from your locality.
SEE THAT THEIR PICTURES GET FRAMED.

MATTHEWS BROS., LIMITED, 788 DUNDAS ST., TORONTO

Knobs of News

The Great Western Furniture Co., Ltd., with a capital of $50,000, has been incorporated at Regina.

The Western Wood Works, furniture manufacturers, have moved to larger premises at 860 Hornby street, Vancouver.

Jas. McArthur, furniture dealer at Powassan, Ont., is going to handle hardware too, and has started a department for that purpose.

Frank Gibson, former superintendent of the Canadian Furniture Manufacturers, Ltd., Woodstock, died last month at Meredith, N.H.

J. W. Pennington has opened a new furniture store at 30 Park Street, Niagara Falls, Ont. "Cheap in price, but not cheap in quality," is his trade slogan.

His Master's Voice, Ltd., Toronto, has received an Ontario charter to deal in gramophones, talking machines, records, etc. The provisional directors are J. S. Lovell, W. Bain and R. Gowans. The capital is set at $100,000.

The Calgary Furniture Store Co., on First Street W., Calgary, Alta., have awarded a contract to McDougall & Forster, for $3,500, for altering portion of store into offices. It will be of mill and frame construction, with electric lighting and spruce and fir floors.

D. Hamilton has bought the furniture business of J. F. Nevile, in Wapella, Sask., and will continue the business in the same premises. A large range of new goods has been added to the stock, and picture framing and repairing will be made a special feature in connection with the business.

FURNITURE MAN MENTIONED IN DISPATCHES.

Lieut. John Niquet, at present at the front serving with the 258th regiment of reservist infantry of the French army, has been mentioned for bravery in dispatches. He is a partner with C. J. Forte, in the Quebec Furniture Co., at 293 St. Paul street, Montreal, and for nine years previous was with N. G. Valliquet.

When the call came for French reservists to join the colors, Lieut. Niquet responded at once, sailing for Liverpool on August 7. The last letter received from Lieut. Niquet was dated August 28, and announced that he was leaving for the front to take the place of the captain of his company, who had been wounded.

PIANO AGENCY WANTED IN SOUTH AFRICA

Editor Canadian Furniture World, Toronto:

Dear Sir,—I have been connected with the pianoforte trade for the last five years, and would like to get into communication with Canadian manufacturers of pianos and organs with a view to opening up a new business. The prospects are good.

OCCUPIER, P.O. Box 3336, Johannesburg.
Transvaal, South Africa.

"BLACK HAND" BURNS FURNITURE STORE

J. A. Banfield's wholesale warehouse on Young street, Winnipeg, was burned on October 8th, with a loss of $40,000. He had been threatened in Black Hand letters for several days that his warehouse would be burned if $500 was not produced. The police arrested Alex. Stewart, who confessed, and was sentenced to five years to-day.

NEW ONWARD DISPLAY STAND

The Onward Mfg. Co., Berlin, Ont., have had a quantity of very handsome display stands made for the display of their "Onward" sliding furniture shoes. These display stands are equipped with one sample of each size shoe they manufacture, of which there are nineteen sizes in all. They are furnishing the stand complete, free of charge, with an order for $15 or over. To dealers who are already handling their shoes they will supply them with one of the display stands upon receipt of their application.

WHO'S WHO IN FURNITURE WORLD.

J. Bernard Hoodless, president of the J. Hoodless Furniture Co., Ltd., Hamilton, Ont., has been connected with the company about six years. After graduating from the Ontario Agricultural College, he held an important position in the management of a great estate in New York, but resigning that, he identified himself with the furniture business established about sixty years ago by his grandfather, the late Joseph Hoodless.

About a year ago, young Mr. Hoodless took a course of instruction at the Military College, Kingston, passed with distinction, and on the formation of the Thirty-third Howitzer Battery at Hamilton, he was gazetted a lieutenant in that corps. On the breaking out of the present war, when the Imperial Government asked Canada for aid, Mr. Hoodless immediately volunteered for active service. He was accepted, and after a month of hard work at Valcartier camp, he is now with the Canadian division as lieutenant of the right half divisional ammunition column on its way to the front to assist in defending the honor and the integrity of the Empire.

LIEUTENANT HOODLESS.

We can at least show our sympathy with England by continuing to sell furniture after the patterns of the English masters of design.

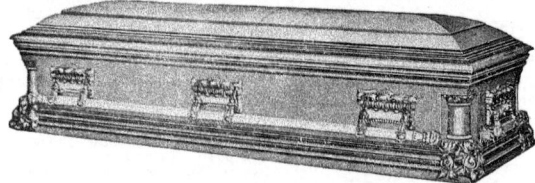

No. 54 F. Connaught Cloth Covered Casket

A New Plant and a New Line of
Undertakers' Supplies

WITH one of the largest, most modern and best equipped plants in the country we are prepared to give Canadian undertakers a standard of quality and service that cannot be equalled.

We manufacture the better grades of **Caskets, Robes, Linings, Casket Hardware, etc.**, our designs being entirely new and original.

Prompt service day and night will be a pronounced feature of our business.

Write for new Calendar Booklet at once

Canada Casket Company, Limited
Wiarton
Toronto Office:
311 Confederation Life Building
Ontario

Undertakers' Department

Problems affecting the Undertaking Profession are here discussed and readers are invited to send letters expressing their views on any of the subjects dealt with—News of the profession throughout Canada.

Back to First Principles—Part II.

Professor Eckels Reviews the Underlying Elements of Good Embalming.

IN our review of the general embalming situation and our return to first principles, we must remember that complete saturation of the tissue is necessary to secure preservation. This is far from being as simple as it seems. If we content ourselves with inserting our arterial tubes, injecting a given quantity of fluid and "letting it go at that," we have no assurance at all that our saturation will be as complete as is necessary for either preservation or for cosmetic effect—which, by the way, I will take up a little later on in this article.

In life the blood makes a complete circuit of the arterial system in something less than a minute. After death, however, we find conditions greatly changed, especially if embalming be delayed until a considerable time has elapsed after death. The arteries, especially the minor branches, and the capillaries will contract and in many cases collapse. Putrefaction will set in and either weaken or swell the walls, until the actual passage is very much smaller and much less stable than even in the hours which immediately preceded death. Even then the circulation usually is extremely tardy, due to the enfeebled condition of the patient. In many cases this feebleness of the circulation was the secondary cause of death. A hasty injection, therefore, will suffice only to fill the trunk arteries and their larger branches. This is especially the case if a strong, raw formaldehyde fluid be used, since its astringency will seal up many of the smaller sub-branches long before the fluid has had a chance to reach the capillaries, much less penetrate them. Unless as much blood as possible has been drained from the body, both before and during the process of embalming, it is pretty certain to be sealed in the capillaries, where it first will cause putty color and later discoloration.

Not infrequently I hear undertakers say that it is absolutely impossible to secure cosmetic effect merely by the injection of embalming fluid. They declare that they are quite satisfied to attain preservation; that the cosmetic effect can be secured later by paints, powders and pigments of various kinds. There never was a greater error. It IS possible to secure cosmetic effect with a properly compounded embalming fluid, and it is possible for the careful, conscientious and studious worker to give a life-like color to practically every body which comes to his hands. It must be realized, however, that this cannot be done without great care, attention and time. The use of extremely weakened fluid for the earlier stages of injection, gradually increasing its potency, is being recognized to-day as the one best method of securing not only preservation, but cosmetic effect.

Use Mild Fluid First.

The embalmer who uses about two ounces of his first bottle of RE-Concentrated fluid to a quart of water, who mixes three ounces with his next quart, and the remainder of the bottle for the next half-gallon will secure results and an effect which could not be attained by making a half-gallon of fluid or even a gallon from a bottle. The milder and more bland fluid will act as a lubricant, a wash and a pathfinder for the more powerful fluid. It will cleanse the arteries, assist the flow of blood, clear out the capillaries and by its chemical action restore the walls of these blood vessels as nearly as possible to their normal state. It will have sufficient astringency to hold them firm, but not enough to contract them unduly. In the moments which elapse while the embalmer is mixing his second or his third batch of fluid, the milder fluid will have done its work, so that practically no intermission of his injection is necessary. It is, however, desirable sometimes to allow about ten minutes between injections.

Not long ago one of my students, for whom I had secured a position, came to me and said that he was going to quit, and asked my assistance in locating him elsewhere.

"You were well treated where you are?" I inquired.

"Splendidly," he replied.

"Paid a sufficient amount?"

"As much as I am worth."

"Then, why do you want to make a change?"

"Because," he said, "when I am sent out to embalm a case in some poor family, I am allowed to take all the time necessary to do the kind of work that you have taught me to do. In these cases, on which little depends, I spend time and take trouble and produce bodies of which I am proud. When I am sent into a home of position and refinement—one where a good body means increased business—then I am limited to a half hour in the house. My employer insists that this kind of people don't want the embalmer around. 'Get in, do the best you can, and get out as quickly as possible.' This is his motto. 'We can't afford to annoy that kind of people,' he says."

He sincerely had my sympathy. I know his employer to be one of the very best embalmers in the country. As a business man he has proven his ability, yet his patronage has been, and under this practice, will continue to be, among the poorer classes. He has turned the real principles of embalming upside down. He has formed the idea that the better class of people are annoyed by the presence of the embalmer. He is wrong; dead wrong. Everyone in the whole length and breadth of the land wishes the best work that is possible for the amount charged, and I ask you, my readers, what possible justification he can have for charging $25.00 or even $10.00 for embalming a body, when the family realize that it was done too hurriedly.

Proper Embalming Takes Time

Perfect embalming cannot be done within a limited space of time. The best body which it is possible to produce cannot be given due care and attention in a half hour. If you can preserve a body in thirty min-

Dominion Casket Co., Limited
Guelph, Ont.

Telephones { Day No. 1020. Nights, Sundays and Holidays Nos. 1069-1101 }

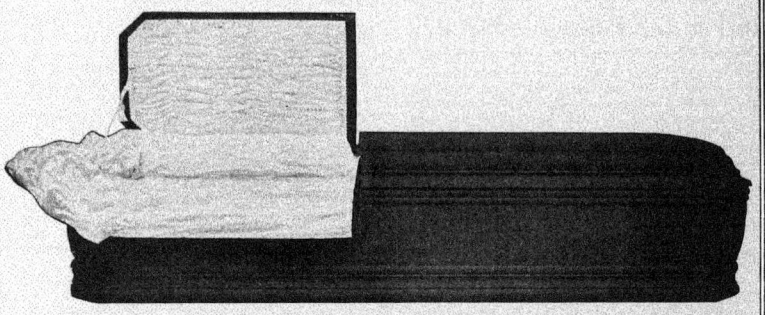

RUSH ORDERS SOLICITED

No. 184

The two caskets on this page are styles without which a Funeral Director's show rooms would not be complete. They are designs brought out to fill a long-felt want and without forcing the trade to purchase same outside of Canada. A card mailed to us will bring you quotations of prices of these goods or anything that you may require.

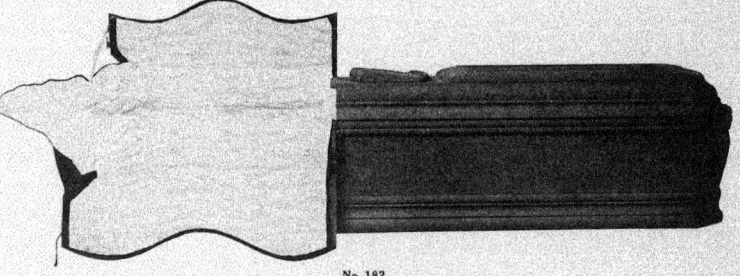

No. 182

Massive Casket, deep mouldings, heavy panels, scroll name plate, "Serpentine" "C" panel. Interior of triple shirred embossed silk.

WRITE FOR PRICES

utes, take sixty, and the cosmetic results will justify your time. Take two hours and they will begin to justify your price.

The average undertaker has no commodity which he sells that is more plentiful than time, and there is no commodity which he buys less expensive than embalming fluid. Of all of his expenses in connection with the funeral, his fluid forms the least part. The handles for the casket cost more; even the simplest lining is more expensive. The very varnishing of the casket itself or the manual labor of putting on the cloth cover in the factory, the use of the team to drive to the house, the time of the man who does the embalming—all of these cost him more than the fluid he uses. Why then, since all depends upon the efficiency, potency and quantity of the fluid used, should he attempt to economize at the spigot while his expense barrel is leaking, not only from the bung hole, but around every stave?

During the summer season, especially and particularly during the humid weather, quantity as well as quality of fluid is the embalmer's only salvation. By this I do not mean large quantities of strong fluid. But what I do want to impress upon my readers is the fact that large quantities of mild fluid are far to be preferred to small quantities of strong fluid. I will carry this to the extreme and say that I believe that better embalming can be done and that preservation can be more effectually secured by making a gallon or even a gallon and a half of fluid from one RE-Concentrated bottle, than by making a gallon of fluid from two bottles.

When the embalming fluid manufacturer urges that an increased quantity of fluid be used, he often is accused of having selfish motives. If this were true, he surely would be acting under shortsighted motives. Every manufacturer desires that his customers have the greatest possible satisfaction in the use of his product. This is the only way in which he can depend upon having his continued patronage. Nine-tenths of all the complaints that come not only to myself but to the other standard embalming fluid manufacturers, are based upon either failure to realize that the mitral valves of the heart, if open, admit the fluid to the lungs instead of distributing it throughout the body, or to the fact that unless a good circulation be developed the blood cannot be driven from the capillaries in certain types of cases, or to the fact that an insufficient quantity of too strong a fluid was used.

One of these three causes lie at the bottom of practically every complaint—and in none of these cases is the fluid to blame.

Echoes From Canadian Embalmers' Convention

One of the most interesting and entertaining addresses delivered at the recent Toronto convention of the Canadian Embalmers' Association, was given by Professor H. S. Eckels. Addressing the members, he said:

Mr. President, and members of the Canadian Association, I came here to-day to enjoy the pleasure of hearing your lecturer. Needless to say, my visit was gratified, and I listened to one of the most interesting and instructive expositions of the art of embalming that I have had the pleasure of hearing in a long while. My apology to you for taking any of your valuable time is that I cannot come here and see you in this splendid meeting without wishing you well—each and every one of you. It seems to me that we, on our side of the line, are peculiarly close to you, and that we both are doing all we can to make progress for our profession, and it is through your association that you are making such splendid headway.

I first came to you as your demonstrator, if I recall correctly, ten years ago, then again five years later; and was also with you the year before last. Even you, yourselves, cannot realize the progress I have seen you make within that time. But the most splendid advance which you have made was when you influenced the Legislature to enact the new law which becomes effective on the first of October. It is a splendid law and must prove of lasting benefit.

Perhaps some of the embalmers have not yet fully realized that this new law does not supersede any of the rules and regulations of the association and make them any the less necessary nor deserving of your support. It is through your association that you have obtained recognition of the profession to which you belong. Your association won for you the same standing in the eyes of your Government as the profession of law or medicine or of the ministry. It is, therefore, only fair that you should continue to support the association, because of its past success and the results which it has already achieved are but indications of yet greater things which they will accomplish in the future.

It should be a source of great satisfaction to you that at last you are legally recognized as of professional standing, but while you do receive such recognition and do enjoy the rights, privileges and immunities afforded by the law, you should always have in mind the thought that each and every one of you owes this, not to the endeavors of one individual, or of a small group, but to the united efforts of this association which created the demand for this law and upon whom it will devolve, with your united support, to uphold, protect and perfect it. It is a magnificent law, and it deserves your support. Remember, it is the law which you are supporting, and not the men who are to administer it. You do not refuse to obey, nor do you ignore the ordinances of your city council because you are not in thorough harmony with the individuals who compose that council. Individuals may change; administrations may change; but the law is mighty and eternal. It must be obeyed.

The embalming law needs your support as much as you need its protection. Lord Kitchener and his staff alone could not fight the Germans successfully, but through the courage of not only each individual in the British army, and in the contingents from beyond the seas, he has been accorded a support not of and for himself, but by reason of the fact that he represents the Law—which is the Empire. It is through the endeavors of each individual connected with our profession, individually and collectively, that the embalming law will be made effective. How, therefore, can this be done better than through your association?

On our own side of the line, the enactment of restrictive laws has strengthened, instead of weakened, the association. The laws were enacted through the efforts of the association and through the co-operation and support of the undertakers who were members of the association. Of what value is a license unless it is productive of benefit to the Commonwealth? It is a protection to each one in the province, as well as to the profession at large. Self preservation is the first law of nature. The embalming law is valuable because if there was no other good to be obtained from it, it has the protective features which would alone justify its existence on the statute books. This protection would be sufficient to encourage every undertaker to be a member of the association.

One protection which has been highly developed in some of our States is the fact that it is through the association that examining boards obtain their information as to the character, good repute and length of apprenticeship of applicants for examination for license. It is manifestly impossible for the examining boards to obtain unbiased and truthful reports from each and every applicant who comes before them for examination. What the boards in many of our States is to apply to the state association for data regarding the applicants who come before the examining boards for examination and the secretary of the association in turn inquires of the members of the association in the neighborhood from which the applicant comes or in which he claims to have worked. It is, therefore, almost impossible for an applicant to be successful in obtaining a license unless he is the type of man who will be a credit to the profession, and unless he first has served the apprenticeship which the law requires. False affidavits by an applicant—and many have been tendered examining boards—will not avail when the board has at its service the cream of the profession, as exemplified in the association, watchful and alert to protect the profession and their own interests from unfair and incompetent competition. This development will doubtless come to your own association, and when it does, will extend the usefulness of not only the association, but of the examining board itself. But in order fully to protect himself, a man must be a member of the association.

I hope that these considerations alone will be sufficient to urge the undertakers in this province to realize the advantages to be obtained through organization. I wish success to each of you and to all of you, especially to Mr. Edwards in his new office of president of the association. I do not believe that this success can be more quickly obtained in any other way than by allying yourselves and urging that your examining board ally itself with the American Conference of Examining Boards which meets from year to year, not only to exchange greetings, but to confer with each one and to exchange ideas. I hope that your examining board will see its way clear to join this association and send at least one representative to the coming meeting of the National Funeral Directors' Association in New Orleans. Half of the programme of these meetings, which are held jointly, is given over to the conference of these boards. It is universally recognized that nothing connected with the association work is more valuable than the interpretation of the law and the bringing into harmony the regulations of the various states and provinces. We would hail with great joy your representation at the conference, and I would recommend that this association as a body urge that your board join. I am sure that I can guarantee that we shall always greet with joy and consideration any representation from the Province of Ontario.

READ FROM COVER TO COVER.

We receive The World regularly, and are perfectly satisfied with it. We read it from cover to cover each edition.

SNOW & CO., LTD.,

Halifax, N.S.   per John Snow.

Manufacturers' Exhibition of Supplies

The Central Casket Co., of Bridgeburg, Ont., and Buffalo, N.Y., made a display of their goods in a suite of rooms in the Prince George Hotel, under the supervision of E. A. Chandler and R. S. Flint. One room was given over to a showing of robes and ladies' costumes, put up in patented wood reinforced boxes. Noticeable in the men's suits was the fact that many of them are getting away from the plain black cloths and adopting more neat, quiet colors as worn by business men.

In caskets, the Central Company have a decidedly new thing in their crystal casket. It is a glass cylinder blown in one piece, with glass ends, airtight when closed. In the bottom of the cylinder is the bed rest for the body, which slides out to receive the body, is then returned, and the ends closed up. The body is then wholly encased in glass. The company have experimented with this casket for twelve years before reaching what they regarded as a good casket. So good is it that the Buffalo Department of Health consider it the proper thing for shipment of bodies. This crystal casket for burial is enclosed in a lined wooden case, whose sides and ends may be folded flat.

Other caskets in walnut, Circassian and mahogany were shown in solid wood, and covered with black and colored broadcloth. A davenport casket, lined and hand tufted in royal purple, was the centrepiece of the casket room. The new hardware colors are Circassian silver, Yeddo bronze and statuary bronze.

Hand-painted door drapes, waterproofed, in all colors, were novelties, and a "Gibraltar" folding and interlocking pedestal for supporting caskets looked like a wantable article.

Eckels' Embalming Outfits.

In connection with the Central Co.'s display, H. S. Eckels & Co., Philadelphia, made an exhibition of a great many of their embalming outfits, supplies and accessories. These embrace so many articles that it is not possible even to enumerate them. Among the new things shown, however, were dermasurgical cases, containing everything that could be thought of to help the embalmer in fixing up accident cases. Colon tubes for stomach work are particularly new. With them it is possible to do cavity embalming without using a trocar.

Other new goods were post mortem outfits, gravity system embalming outfits, and many new tools helpful and useful to the embalmer. The new waxing outfits, too, proved attractive to visitors. A telescoping flower-stand—one that folds up into the minutest space—was the newest thing in accessories. A new waterproof shipping envelope for attaching to boxes was so good that it is strange no person thought of bringing one like it out before. On the outside is space for the undertaker's advertisement, while inside are inserted the shipping instructions. Mr. Eckels was present for a couple of days, and Mr. Flint looked after the display.

Dominion Metallic Caskets.

The Dominion Casket Co., of Guelph, made their exhibition in a King street store. They showed a great range of samples of both wood and patented steel caskets, made into a variety of styles of cases. Some of the wooden cases had steel linings, others had copper, with airtight glass tops. The caskets ran to all shapes—square, round and octagon—and were covered with an immense variety of colors and in all cloths. Plush covered, solid mahogany, Circassian, and oak sample caskets drew much favorable comment.

Some children's cases in new designs and with the tiniest linings were particularly new. But it is perhaps in their patented all-steel caskets that the Dominion Casket Co. have a line all to themselves, and a popular selling line, too. It makes a splendid shipping case.

The hardware the Dominion line has a number of distinctive features, and the same may be said of their robes and linings. Messrs. Drake and McMurray looked after the exhibition, and Messrs. Arnold and Whitehead, of the head office, were in for a few days.

The Champion Chemical Co., of Springfield, Ohio, had a stand in the exhibit, where they displayed some of Dr. Ferguson's embalming fluid.

Semmens and Evel Caskets.

The Semmens & Evel Casket Co., Ltd., Hamilton, made a display of their goods in connection with the Globe Casket Co., of London. The whole exhibit was sold, some of the caskets several times over. They had a new feature in an all-copper (polished) casket. They showed, as well, two new solid mahogany caskets; and one of these—the King—was about the best in the whole exhibition. It had a copper metallic lining, the cloth lining being hand tufted, with the covering a soft broadcloth.

In hardware they showed some of the newest designs in steel in many finishes and colors, silver, copper and brass being leaders, and as well there was shown an immense range of dry goods and some embalming outfits.

In connection with the display there was shown J. J. Blachford's "Magnum" embalming fluid, and the new Wellman device for lowering caskets into the grave, and a new Maxwell copper alloy non-corrosive vault. F. W. Elliott, manager; Jos. McMurray, J. R. Tupper, Walter J. Singleton, and J. McClaren, representatives of the company, were in attendance.

Globe Casket Co.

The Globe and National Companies made a combined display, although the latter made a more elaborate showing of their completed lines at the Niagara street factory.

In caskets the Globe's range of samples included seven quarter-sawn oaks and seven mahoganies. In design they were plain, but massive. Several shown, too, were set out, as were also a number of cloth-covered caskets.

The hardware line of the Globe Company is a very extensive one, and took almost the whole length of one wall to show off. This line included practically every design and color that could be imagined, and many new finishes which they have added during the year.

Metallic Grave Vaults.

Included in the exhibit were displays of the St. Thomas grave vault and vaults of the National Vault Co., of Galion, Ohio. This latter is made from "purity" metal and carries a 50-year guarantee against the effects of corrosion. The vault is practically indestructible, and acid tests show a ratio of 22 to 1 compared with common steel. It is burglar, vermin and water proof. Dominion Manufacturers, Ltd., Toronto, are the Canadian distributors.

St. Thomas Grave Vault.

The St. Thomas is, as well, a metallic vault, burglar proof and watertight. It also carries a guarantee. It is the original quick closing end vault, a special device enabling this to be done. It is made in Canada by the St. Thomas Metallic Vault Co., Ltd., St. Thomas, Ont.

The Globe and National Casket Co.'s display was in charge of F. W. Coles, Watson, Fred Coles and Messrs. Percy, Bartlett, Raymond, Me-Cully, Henderson and Caulfield.

National Casket Co.

Besides the samples shown in the King street exhibition hall the National Casket Co. made a full display of their caskets in the Niagara street factory showrooms. An extensive exhibit was made of solid hardwood caskets in high grade oak and mahogany. Samples from the entire range of couch caskets were as well displayed, some of the colorings of the cloth-covered cases being very rich.

The hardware and dry goods were displayed in a separate section of the exhibition and they were up-to-date, rich and extensive.

The D. W. Thompson Co.

This company exhibited in connection with the National. They, too, showed a big range of all wood, cloth-covered and couch caskets. The copper interior shell with heavy plate glass top, making the casket entirely airtight, was a big feature.

The hardware and costume lines were neat and rich. Mr. Black looked after the callers.

Greer's Carriage Exhibit.

A. B. Greer, London, Ont., made a display of their funeral cars, hearses, undertaker's wagons, etc., at the National factory on Niagara street. Making these carriages for nearly half a century Mr. Greer should know something about their manufacture, and this was abundantly shown in this year's showing of landaus, pall-bearers' coaches, ambulances and buggies.

Evel Casket Co.

The Evel Casket Co., Hamilton, made an elaborate showing of all their lines at 71 King street, occupying two floors to set off their goods. On the lower floor were solid hardwood caskets, in which Mr. Evel. Sr., took especial pride showing. The solid mahogany and solid oak caskets were certainly fine. Fitted with copper linings, and heavy plate glass tops, they are airtight. The linings, too, correspond with the richness of the wood and all the details of manufacture are carefully looked after. On the second floor were set out the cloth-covered caskets in a great many colorings and a great many cloths.

The hardware had a section to itself. Here were shown samples of an almost innumerable line of design and some 45 different finishes. The costumes had a room to themselves. Women's robes, which have been increasing in range and design for several years, now have company in that men's suits are this year being made up in fashionable cloths of quiet designs in tweeds, cheviots and diagonals. Besides Mr. Evel, Sr., there were present to look after visitors, W. G. and H. B. Evel and W. Braithwaite.

The Dominion Mausoleum Co., Ltd., has, by Ontario charter, increased its capital from $40,000 to $1,000,000, and changed its head office from Brantford to Toronto.

The Washington Burial Co., Ltd., Toronto, has been incorporated with a capital of $40,000. Jas. Robt. Fleury, B. R. Rapier, Lottie L. Washington, Geo. T. Walsh and Jennie C. Derrett are interested.

On every side there is a call on British undertakers to surrender their horses to the army. Leading undertakers everywhere are under contract to do so. The demand, however, came with terrible suddenness, and has terribly upset many a business throughout England. So great has been, and still is, the demand for horses, that there have been some strange funerals. A day or two ago a coster's barrow took the place of honor.

THANKS FROM PAST PRESIDENT

Canadian Furniture World and The Undertaker:

I would ask you to kindly allow me space in your valuable journal to thank the Canadian Embalmers' Association for the beautiful cabinet of silver presented to me at convention.

It is needless for me to say how highly myself and family appreciate this splendid gift. It is highly gratifying to know that the work done and efforts put forth by the executive during our term of office was approved of and acknowledged in such a splendid manner.

It was a great disappointment to me, not being able to attend convention on account of illness. I assure you the progress and welfare of the association will always be one of my chief interests.

Yours sincerely,
J. G. HENRY,
Past President C.E.A.

First Quality   **Dominion Manufacturers**   Prompt Service
Limited

Unequalled Facilities
for Quick *and* Efficient Delivery

YOU, Mr. Funeral Director, realize the advantage of having the goods you "rush order" arrive as expected.

Our location—near the Union Depot, Toronto, the hub of Canadian Railways; our large well-equipped plant ; our staff of experienced men who specialize in packing and shipping, and the well known high quality and thorough construction of our lines are features that are invaluable to the particular undertaker.

Complete line of Undertakers' Supplies

Telephones
Adelaide 454
Adelaide 455
North - 5085

Attentive Service Day and Night

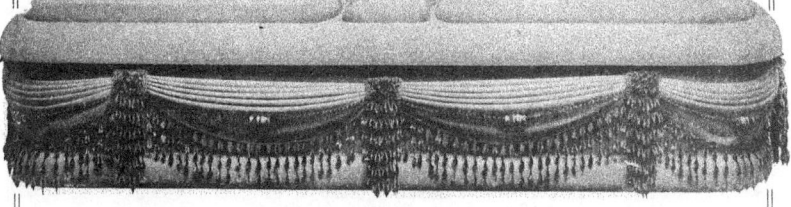

No. 640

The National Casket Company, Limited
93-109 Niagara Street   Toronto, Ontario

First Quality — **Dominion Manufacturers** Limited — Prompt Service

We *Excel* in the Manufacture of *Fine* Solid Oak and Mahogany Caskets and Casket Hardware

THE tasteful, dignified designing and rich finish of our *Caskets* and *Casket Hardware* merit your consideration. All styles carried in large quantities.

No. 537

Let us have your orders for first train delivery. You'll appreciate this perfect feature of our business

Telephones
Factory - 169
Mr Watson, 1654
Shipper - 1020

THE GLOBE CASKET COMPANY
LONDON   ONTARIO

First Quality **Dominion Manufacturers** Prompt Service
=============== Limited ===============

No. 325

SUPERIOR QUALITY

in the better grades of Caskets, Coffins and Funeral Furnishings. Fine Covered Caskets, Piano Polished Oak and Mahogany Caskets.

Investigate our Ebonet Finished Hardware.

Experienced salesmen in our factory and offices night and day capable of taking and executing all orders promptly.

"We Never Miss a Train"

The Semmens & Evel Casket Co., Limited

Hamilton   Winnipeg

Telephones: 517, 3316. Nights and Sundays, 517, 3319, and 3353   470 Ross Avenue
Chas. Crosland, Manager

First Quality — **Dominion Manufacturers** — Prompt Service
===== Limited =====

High Grade Undertakers' Supplies

Get in touch with the D.W.T. Line for reliable goods and efficient service.

The newest in everything for the undertaker.

Telephones:
ADELAIDE 454
and NORTH 5085

The
D. W. Thompson Co.
Limited
93-109 Niagara St., Toronto

Caskets, Robes and Linings

The best for every purpose. Our excellent shipping facilities enable us to deliver promptly.

Write or phone us next time.

James S. Elliott & Son
Prescott   Ontario

Unequalled Service to Eastern Undertakers

The location of our plant ensures the most satisfactory service to the Eastern Undertaker.

We manufacture all kinds of **Undertakers' Supplies.** Satisfaction guaranteed.

GIRARD & GODIN
Three Rivers, Que.

Complete Line of Caskets, Hardware
ETC., ETC.

The best quality possible for the money. All styles and finishes.

We Fill Orders "Right" Always

We solicit your orders by letter, telegram, or telephone

CHRISTIE BROS. & CO.
Amherst, N.S.

Blood Drainage

Lecture delivered at Canadian Embalmers' Convention at Toronto, by Prof. H. Moll, Chicago.

It affords me an unusual amount of pleasure to be with you. I feel highly honored, in fact, because I consider this a very auspicious time for the embalmers of Canada, at any rate, for the embalmers of the Province of Ontario. Your civil authorities, the Government of the Province have seen fit to recognize you, or at least to open the portals of a profession, to you. Heretofore you have scarcely been professional men, at least, you have not had the opportunity to call yourselves professional men, because the civil authorities failed to recognize you, but when the civil authorities place their stamp on your work as legal, when they recognize it, then they open the gates of professionalism.

PROF. HORACE MOLL
Chicago.

Now then, it is up to you, as we say in the States (and I trust you will pardon the expression) to create that profession. Your Government has not created the profession, but they have given their consent to recognize you as professional men. Becoming professional men rests with you. You all know that this is a serious profession, at any rate, we should regard it as such. The duties of the embalmer or the undertaker come directly to the home, and you perform one of the most sacred functions that anyone in life is called on—to care for those who are near and dear to someone. That increases your responsibilities greatly. In the professions of law and medicine men and women rank high. You have the same opportunities, the same privileges to make your profession rank at least next to the physician, and I am more than pleased that your Goverument has seen fit to place the stamp of professionalism on your work.

In the States we have for a number of years licensed our people, in fact, it is compulsory before a man is allowed to touch a body as an embalmer, that he procure a certain standard of education and show the ability to carry out his work. True, we have many men who are still inferior, they do not all rank in the first class, but we have some very able and brilliant men, and in all professions, in all lines of work, some men reach the top of the ladder and some remain at the foot.

It is your own personal effort that counts. The Government of this province will not make you professional men. It rests with you to gain the esteem, the respect of your clients, of the people whom you serve, and in that way we become professional men. We make ourselves just what we are. Occasionally someone to the detriment of others, or in some unaccountable way, will rise for the hour, but the true, honest scientific requirements are due to yourselves—to be observant, to do your work conscientiously, thoroughly, always to bring those things home to yourselves, and the golden rule is an excellent one to work by in this line, "Do unto others as you would have them do unto you." When you are called into the home, treat the remains of the one who is dear to the whole family just as you would expect a professional man to come into your home and care for them, were they your own. It is the only way to gain the esteem of the people whom you serve.

Still a Student.

I come to you, not with the idea that I know it all. I am still a student, and study every day. I expect to be a student as long as I am in this work, and I have yet a lot to learn. Now, to get the best out of anything is to consult with one another. If you have an idea that clashes with mine, tell it. Don't hesitate to antagonize me. I like an argument, in fact, I love it, and I may not always have the correct idea. I still have a lot to learn, and by exchanging ideas, we get new ones; we create new ones. A little friction in an argument will sometimes bring out a point that is intensely valuable, and which redounds to the benefit of all, so that in our work this week I want you to feel that you have the privilege of asking questions, to make suggestions; in fact, the closer we get together the more benefit we will derive from this meeting.

Friction of ideas creates new thoughts, and in that way we learn. We also learn by our mistakes. They are the greatest educators, and do us the most good. The philosopher tells us that a man who makes a mistake is a wise man, but the man who makes the same mistake twice is a fool. The merest accident has sometimes caused the greatest invention, has brought out the greatest ideas. Gentlemen, the way to accomplish this in my estimation is for you to become anatomists. We need to study anatomy. The knowledge of anatomy is the foundation of our work for success. The man who does not know anatomy never becomes a successful embalmer in my estimation. The idea of just knowing the location of an artery, how to raise it and to force the disinfectant material into that artery and await results is not scientific work. If you do not realize where that material goes, you will never become a proficient embalmer.

Do you suppose that an engineer could build a bridge without knowing mathematics? I doubt it. It always has been a puzzle to me how a man could successfully embalm a body without knowing anatomy. I know you will take me to task for making this statement, because some men who really do not know anything about this subject have a reasonable amount of success in their work, but what we must accomplish is not to do work in a hit-and-miss sort of way, but to go to a body, study it like a physician does. When he is called to your bedside he feels your pulse, takes your temperature, asks you questions until he arrives at a conclusion, and then he prescribes for you. The treatment of the disease is not difficult when he succeeds in making an exact diagnosis. Now, that is your point. When you are called to the home, and you have had your interview with the family, you view the body and you notice the conditions. It may be a bad dropsical case; it may be a typhoid fever case; it may be pneumonia; it may be meningitis, or some contagious disease. You can't treat all bodies alike, and be successful. You may have to study conditions.

Different Cases, Different Treatment.

If it is a typhoid case you will realize that the seat of the trouble is in the abdomen, that the tissue that is diseased is filled with congested blood. Then you will also realize that when that condition exists, you will be unable to distribute the embalming fluid or the disinfectant material into those vessels that contain blood that does not circulate, and would have to, by cavity injection, distribute fluid into the portion of the body that requires the greatest amount of care. If you fail to realize that, you will not be properly disinfecting the body, and the consequence will be the formation of gas, a condition that is totally unsatisfactory on the day of the funeral. You may, of course, have some plausible excuse, and the family may be satisfied, but you cannot tell that to your neighbor who is engaged in the same kind of work that you are.

But if you know the conditions, study them and carry out your disinfecting work carefully, there is no reason why you should fail. I grant you, however, that there are some conditions in our work that we have not solved. The time will come when we will solve them. There are some conditions in the dead human body that are baffling even to the expert, but we are making progress, and by close study, and especially the exact study of anatomy, we are enabled to conquer many conditions that have heretofore baffled all attempts at solution. The knowledge of the location of the organs of the body is extremely important and the comprehensive study of anatomy necessary to make you successful embalmers. That gives you a general idea of what we are going to do this week. I shall try to cover the entire subject with your aid and tell you all I can, which probably is not very much, but I will let you be the judge when I finish.

I want you to be entirely free, we will throw away all formality. I try to be dignified, but not any more so than is necessary to further our interests, and you have the privilege of asking questions, of making suggestions, open up an argument; in fact this will not be entirely a demonstration, but it will be a consultation—that is the way I desire it. In conclusion, I will just say that I want to again thank you for giving me the privilege of appearing before you. I had the pleasure three years ago of delivering a course of lectures to the Manitoba Association at Winnipeg, and had a most delightful and charming time. I don't want to flatter you, but I think highly of the Canadian people; they are universally pleasant and agreeable, and I have a very warm spot in my heart for you as neighbors. There is, after all, just an imaginary line that separates us, and we are largely of the same stock, originate from the same people, and for that particular reason I was anxious to come here, to meet the people of Eastern Canada, and I expect to have a most pleasant time with you.

Lecture on Blood Drainage

Blood drainage is the first subject, and that interests everybody as a rule. There are, however, a few men who say it is totally unnecessary to drain blood from the dead human body, but up to the present time I have seen no reason to change my opinion and I still drain blood. When you study blood chemically and scientifically you find it is a very peculiar compound. It is a loosely associated mixture of four different ingredients. It contains red corpuscles, white corpuscles, blood liquor and salts. Blood always reminds me of a combination like this: If you take a pound of white lead, a pint of linseed oil, a pint of turpentine, some lampblack, and mix all together, you have black paint. That is how blood is mixed in the human body, just loosely a general mixture. The red corpuscles originate in the red marrow of the flat bones. They are formed in the cavities of the bones and then carried to the liver, which gives them their red color, and then they go on in their mission as oxygen carriers.

The air you breathe is carried into the lungs and there is absorbed in the red corpuscles. The combination of iron and albumin absorbs the oxygen and then carries it to the tissues of the body, and there performs the function of burning that tissue. The oxygen burns the tissue and keeps you warm. The red coloring of the blood has the power of absorbing oxygen freely and also of releasing it freely. It also has the power of absorbing waste matter and of releasing it. This goes on continually—it absorbs oxygen and expels carbon.

The other ingredient is the white corpuscle. The word corpuscle means a small body. They are, of course, too small to be seen by the naked eye, and it is necessary to magnify them 200 and 300 times and sometimes as many as 800 times to see them. These originate in the spleen. The function of the spleen for a long time was in dispute, but it has been agreed that the spleen gives forth the white corpuscles. The spleen is a ductless gland—it has no channel—and the white corpuscles go directly into the blood stream, where they perform their function.

The red corpuscles flow with the blood always. The white corpuscles can travel against the blood stream or in any direction that they please, and their function is to follow and destroy the germs of disease or any foreign matter that is carried into the blood. The blood stream carries what is needed for the purpose of nourishing the body, and the white corpuscles perform the function of protecting the body against disease. If it was not thus we would be eaten up by germs, but the white corpuscles act as the police system of the human body and succeed in arresting these germs.

The third is the blood liquor; it has a very important function in the blood. The corpuscles float in this liquid stream—just the same as if you wanted to transport logs, you would perhaps throw them into the river or stream, which would carry them along without any more effort, and the blood liquor is the corpuscle-carrying medium. It is composed of a substance which is called lymph. The blood liquor also contains the nutriment from the blood after it is properly digested and absorbed, conveying it into the blood stream through the thoracic duct into the left subclavian vein and then into the pulmonary circulation. After it enters the pulmonary circulation it is delivered by the aorta and its branches to all parts of the body. It is necessary after the process of burning is carried out in the body for the waste to be carried off, and this consists of carbon dioxide and water, the blood becoming a dark blue color. That is the function of the blood liquor—the work it performs is nutrition. This process of waste and repair, as carried out by the blood, goes on forever. The temperature of the body must be maintained at a certain point in order that the organs may carry out their functions.

Salts in the Blood

The fourth constituent of the blood is salts. The blood liquor, as you know, contains 90 per cent water. The salts perform the function of keeping some of the substances in solution. The living substance in the human body is albumin or protoplasm. It is almost identical with the white of an egg, and is the principle that maintains life. This must be constantly renewed and kept in solution. The most abundant of these salts is common table salt. We all eat more or less salt and require it to keep the different ingredients that enter the blood in a condition to be absorbable.

(To be continued.)

Get it at the Western

A Safe, Profitable Place to Buy

All Kinds of Undertakers' Supplies

Open Night and Day

Our Catalogue is with you, if not, a Post Card will bring it.

Give us a trial express order.   Phone Garry 4657.

The Western Casket Co.,
Limited

Winnipeg   Cor. Emily St., & Bannatyne Ave.   Manitoba

Third Annual Convention B. C. Funeral Directors

Delegates at Closing Banquet.

The third annual convention of the British Columbia Funeral Directors' and Embalmers'' Association met in Vancouver on Sept. 10, 11 and 12, and was fairly well attended. Practically nothing but the ordinary routine business was transacted.

Prof. W. P. Hohenschuh, of Iowa City, Iowa, was the lecturer and demonstrator, and his lectures and demonstrations were highly appreciated by all in attendance.

The officers elected for the following year were: J. A. Green, Vancouver, president; J. C. Gillies, Huntingdon, 1st vice-president; I. Lehman, Ashcroft, 2nd vice-president; G. M. Williamson, Vancouver, secretary-treasurer, re-elected; J. H. Jones, Mission, sergeant-at-arms; and O. McPherson, Armstrong; D. J. Jenkins, Nanaimo, and T. Edwards, Vancouver, an executive committee along with the regular officers.

The place of meeting of the next annual convention was left in the hands of the executive committee. On Friday evening, Sept. 11, a banquet was tendered to the visiting members by the funeral directors of Vancouver in the banquet room of the Dunsmuir Hotel.

On Monday, Tuesday and Wednesday, of the same week, a school of instruction was held under the direction of Prof. Hohenschuh, open to members of the association only. Ten members took advantage of this school, and they all pronounced it one of the best features of the convention.

The Maritime Convention

The twelfth annual convention of the Maritime Funeral Directors' Association opened at Moncton, N.B., on the afternoon of Tuesday, August 11th. President F. W. Wallace, of Sussex, N.B., called the meeting to order, and Rev. Edward Sewage, of St. Bernard's church, offered invocation. A cordial address of welcome was delivered by Mayor W. K. Gross, and Joseph Spencer, of Halifax, N.S., responded.

Professor Lena R. Simmons, of Syracuse, N.Y., was introduced by President Wallace, and made an address that contained much information of prime interest to her hearers.

The minutes of the last convention were read, and adopted after slight correction. The secretary-treasurer's report was also read and adopted. The report showed $275.59 receipts and $243.18 disbursements, giving a credit balance of $32.41.

President Wallace, in his annual address, paid fitting tribute to the memory of the late Abraham A. Tuttle, of Moncton, and the late A. J. Beaton, of Sidney. He outlined the work upon which he had been occupied during his term of office, and explained how difficult it had been to arrange for a convention owing to the war situation.

"I wish to make a few recommendations to the profession at large in Canada," he said, concluding his address. "Unite in having a national association for Canada. Unite on one independent funeral directors' journal for Canada. Select with great care your presidents and secretaries. If they are not progressive your work will lag. If association work goes back, the profession will not progress. Let every man who accepts office bear in mind he has a great responsibility to give account for. May our funeral directors, like our Canadian military officers and men, stand shoulder to shoulder as in one common cause—a worthy one."

The president read a number of letters of regret from absent members, and the meeting was adjourned.

Wednesday morning's session opened at 9.30, by Rev. G. A. Lawson, of the Baptist church, who delivered an address. The president also introduced Rev. H. A. Goodwin, who represented the Methodist denomination. Both clergymen made suggestions concerning Sunday funerals, and also service at the grave and funerals in general, and their remarks were heard with much interest.

The election of officers for the ensuing year resulted as follows:

Joseph Spencer, Halifax, N.B., president; D. A. Jonah, Petitcodiac, N.B., vice-president; A. W. Murray, Nova Scotia, vice-president; D. L. McKinnon, Prince Edward Island, vice-president; E. C. McKinnon, Prince Edward Island, secretary-treasurer; A. W. Maher, sergeant-at-arms; H. T. Stevens, chaplain; Mrs. F. W. Wallace, Sussex, N.B., chaperon.

After the election a letter was read from A. J. H. Eckardt, formerly proprietor of the Canadian National Casket Co., offering a quantity of preferred stock to the association. After some debate the stock was accepted and a vote of thanks was tendered Mr. Eckardt.

The afternoon session opened with an address by Rev. Canon Sisam, of the Church of England, who spoke interestingly on 'Funerals in Different Countries.' He was followed by Prof. Simmons, who continued her series of lectures.

The deaths of John Acorn and A. G. Jenkins, both of Prince Edward Island, were reported by the president, and a motion was carried that a letter of sympathy be sent to both families.

At the opening of the evening session Chaplain David A. Jonah offered prayer, and President Wallace called upon Mrs. Simmons to speak to the funeral directors concerning the helpfulness of good trained nurses. Mrs. Simmons spoke at some length on this subject, after which the meeting took the form of a round table talk, many present giving their experiences in personal

"Purity Vaults"
The Vaults that are Guaranteed
Against Effects of Corrosion for a Period of 50 Years

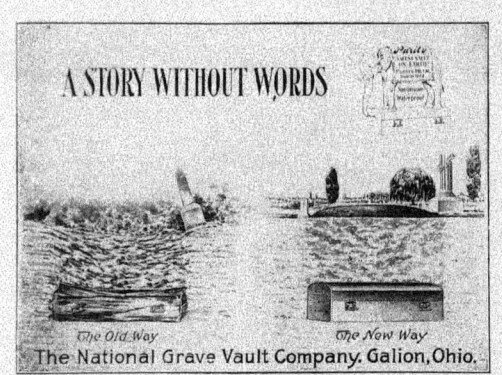

A STORY WITHOUT WORDS

The Old Way   The New Way
The National Grave Vault Company, Galion, Ohio.

Practically indestructible. Acid tests show a ratio of 22 to 1 compared with common steel vaults.

Burglar, Vermin and Waterproof

Dominion Manufacturers, Limited
Canadian   Head Office
Distributors   Toronto
National Casket Co., Limited   Toronto
Globe Casket Co., Limited   London
Semmens & Evel Casket Co. Ltd. Hamilton
J. S. Elliott & Son   Prescott
Girard & Godin   Three Rivers, Que.
Christie Bros. & Co.   Amherst, N.S.

Write for descriptive circular and how we help you sell "PURITY VAULTS"

Burglar Proof and Water Tight

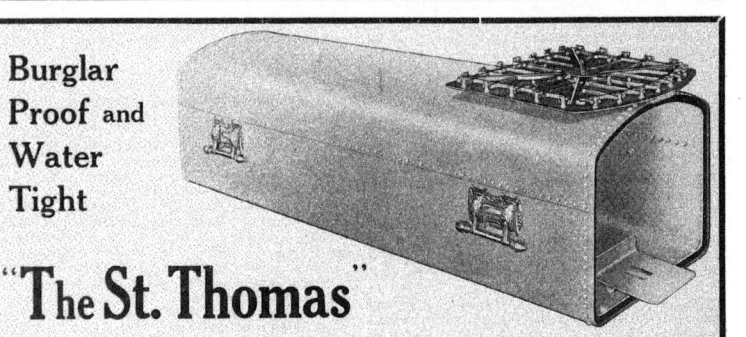

"The St. Thomas"
Original, Quick Closing End Vault
MANUFACTURED BY

The St. Thomas Metallic Vault Company, Limited
ST. THOMAS, ONTARIO

cases. The committee on president's address and secretary-treasurer's report then submitted their report, which was adopted.

W. G. Smith spoke of the great results of annual gatherings as he saw them in his rounds as a traveling man. He spoke highly of the fine funeral home of Tuttle Bros., and of the good work of the late A. A. Tuttle.

The Thursday morning session was given over largely to the disposal of various business matters, after which Mrs. Simmons delivered her closing lecture. After the singing of "God Save the King," Chaplain Jonah pronounced the benediction and the convention adjourned, to meet at the call of the executive.

During the convention the New Brunswick Association also proceeded with their routine business, electing their officers as follows: President. F. L. Tuttle; first vice-president, W. E. Brenan; second vice-president. D. L. McKenna, of P.E.I.; secretary-treasurer, W. S. Chapman; chaplain. D. A. Jonah; sergeant-at-arms, W. E. Campbell.

The following are the officers of the Nova Scotia Funeral Directors' Association for 1914-15: President, J. F. Rice; vice-president, John Pickard; secretary-treasurer, Joseph Spencer; chaplain, A. W. Murray; sergeant-at-arms, A. H. Brown.

Both the New Brunswick and the Nova Scotia Associations will meet next year conjointly with the Maritime F.D.A.

BIG NEW CANADIAN CASKET COMPANY

The Canada Casket Company, Ltd., Wiarton, Ont., whose incorporation was noted in these columns a couple of months ago, are putting through the press at present a calendar booklet intended for distribution among the undertakers of Canada. This is the means they are adopting to introduce Siemon Brothers at one time a well known and foremost furniture manufacturing concern to their former customers, under the new company's name, the Canada Casket Co., Ltd.

Since selling their plant and interest in the furniture manufacturing business, some years ago, Siemon Brothers have greatly developed their other lumber industries, and of late years have acquired large tracts of some of the finest timber in the world, which will give them an abundant supply of raw material at first cost for making caskets in their new plant. This new casket factory is one of the largest plants in Canada; has up-to-date equipment; and the superintendent, J. C. Brumfield, is one of the foremost men in casket manufacturing on the continent, having been connected with some of the largest concerns in the United States for over twenty years.

The whole organization of the various Siemon companies' interests is behind the Canada Casket Co., Ltd., and there is no dead weight of over-capitalization, their own financial corporation taking care of the capital. The capital of the company is $300,000; they have no taxes to pay; overhead charges are low; cost of management is not heavy; and being under their own direct supervision the output should be placed on the market at the lowest possible cost. Besides this, they have splendid shipping facilities by rail and water.

The aim of the Canada Casket Co. is to turn out only high class goods, with a guarantee of 30 years' manufacturing experience on a large scale at their back. The company, in addition to caskets, will make their own robes and linings, as well as casket hardware. The president of the company is J. C. Siemon; vice-presidents, J. L. Siemon and A. Siemon; secretary, Chas. L. Forster; assistant secretary, B. A. Bulyea; and directors, D. Widmeyer, F. Widmeyer, C. Weltz, and J. Weltz. Their Toronto office is located at 309-311 Confederation Life Building.

Invalid Chairs and Tricycles of every description.

This has been our study for thirty-five years. We build chairs that suit the requirements of any case. Write us for catalogue No. 20 and prices, if interested.

Gendron Wheel Co., Toledo, O. U.S.A.

Patronize The Line of "Established Quality"

The features of the Central Line are features that make good business everywhere—honest quality, fair prices and efficient, prompt service. We specialize on

Mahogany, Oak, Plush and Cloth Covered Caskets

We can also supply anything desired in Casket Linings, Burial Robes, and a general line of Undertakers' Supplies.

Orders given our Canadian Representative, or sent to our factory at Bridgeburg by mail, telegraph or telephone will receive prompt attention.

CENTRAL CASKET COMPANY

Bridgeburg, Ont.   R. S. Flint, Canadian Representative: 241 Fern Ave., Toronto
Telephone 126   Telephone Parkdale 3257

No Undertaker Should Overlook

the fact that he can make a full gallon of fluid of standard strength from each sixteen-ounce bottle of RE-Concentrated Dioxin. Re-Concentrated Dioxin costs no more per bottle than any standard concentrated fluid, but it is twice as strong—in other words, there are twice as many ounces of preservation in a bottle of RE-Concentrated Dioxin as there are in any bottle of merely concentrated fluid.

If economy were the only recommendation for RE-Concentrated Dioxin, however, we should not urge it upon our patrons.

As a matter of fact, it is easy to explain and equally easy to demonstrate the fact that the fluid thus produced gives a far better cosmetic effect and produces a far more life-like body than possibly could be produced by any raw formaldehyde concentrated fluid.

This is because RE-Concentrated Dioxin has a double base. When diluted to make a full gallon of fluid to the bottle, its main base is peroxide, with a secondary base of purified formaldehyde (formochloral).

Every funeral director knows that peroxide of hydrogen is the best bleacher known to chemical science. Not everyone realizes, however, that peroxide of hydrogen has blood solvent qualities far in excess of any other chemical yet discovered which is suitable for use in embalming fluid.

Peroxide of hydrogen is composed of two atoms of oxygen and two atoms of hydrogen. Since oxygen is fifteen times heavier than hydrogen, fifteen-sixteenths of the atomic weight of peroxide of hydrogen, therefore, is oxygen.

Every embalmer knows that venous blood is much darker in color, is much more sluggish and much heavier than arterial blood.

What is the difference between the two?

Arterial blood is merely venous blood, which has been purified in the lungs, which has been lightened in color and rendered vastly more fluid by the oxygen which the lungs have extracted from the air we breathe.

Since fifteen-sixteenths of the atomic weight of peroxide of hydrogen is oxygen, it must be apparent, therefore, that the oxygen in the extra rich peroxide in Dioxin has a tendency to exercise the same purifying and solvent qualities upon the dark, discolored venous blood after death as the oxygen which the lungs extract from the air we breathe has upon the venous blood in life.

The result is that much more blood can be drained from a body in which RE-Concentrated Dioxin is injected than is possible from a body in which raw formaldehyde is used and in which the astringent qualities of the formaldehyde have sealed up the discolored blood corpuscles in the capillaries.

Putty color is caused by raw formaldehyde fluid sealing up the discolored corpuscles of the blood in the capillaries. It is inevitable where raw formaldehyde fluids are used unless exceeding care is used to drain blood. And even then there is great danger.

RE-Concentrated Dioxin is distinctly the most modern and the most scientific embalming fluid on the market, as well as the most economical. The progressive funeral director will not hesitate, but will order a trial shipment.

RE-Concentrated DIOXIN

H. S. ECKELS & CO.   1922 Arch St., Philadelphia, Pa.
241 Fern Ave., Toronto, Canada.

Undertakers Shipping Directory

ONTARIO
Aurora—
 Dunham, Charles.
Barrie—
 Smith, G. G. & Co.
Brockville—
 Quirmbach, Geo. R., 162 King St.
Brooklin—
 Disney, R. S.
Campbellford—
 Irwin, James.
Campden—
 Hansel, Albion.
Clinton—
 Walker, Wesley.
Coboconk—
 Greenley, A.
Copper Cliff—
 Boyd, W. C.
Dungannon—
 Sproul, William
Dutton—
 Schultz, B. L.
Elmira—
 Dreisinger, Chris.
Fenelon Falls—
 Deyman, L. & Son.
Fenwick—
 H. A. Metler.
Fergus—
 Armstrong, M. F.
 Thomson, John & Son.
Fort William—
 Cameron & Co., 711 Victoria.
 Morris, A.
Haileybury—
 Thorpe Bros.
Galt—
 Anderson, J. & Son.
Hamilton—
 Green Bros., 124 King St. E.
 Robinson, J. H. & Co., 19-21 John St. N.
Hanover—
 Wunnenberg, Norman.
Hastings—
 Howard, P. N.
Hepworth—
 Downs, E. J.
Inwood—
 Lorriman, E. S.
Kemptville—
 McCaughey, Geo. A.
Kenora—
 Horn & Taylor.
Kingston—
 Corbett, S. S.
Lakefield—
 Hendren, Geo. G.
Little Current—
 Sims, J. G.
Markdale—
 Oliver, M.
Newmarket—
 Millard, J. H.
North Augusta—
 Wilson, J. R.
North Bay—
 St. Pierre, E.
Oakwood—(Mariposa Station G.T.R.) Wilmot F. Webster.
Ohsweken—
 Johnson, F. L.
Oshawa—
 Disney Bros.
 Luke Bros.
Ottawa—
 Ch. R. Woodburn, 586 Bank St. Tel. Carling 600 and 1009.
 Rogers & Burney, 283 Laurier Ave. W.
Petrolia—
 Steadman Bros.
Port Arthur —
 Collin Wood, 36 Arthur St.
 Morris, A.
Prescott—
 Rankin, H. & Son.
Renfrew—
 O'Connor, Wm.
St. Mary's—
 N. L. Brandon.
St. Thomas—
 Williams, P. R. & Sons, 519 Talbot St.
Seaforth, Ont.
 W. T. Box & Co.
Scotland—
 Vaughan, Jos. H. M.
Sudbury—
 Henry, J. G.
Toronto—
 Cobbledick, N. B., 2068 Queen St. East and 1508 Danforth Ave. Private Ambulance.
 Stone, Daniel (formerly H. Stone & Son), 525 Sherbourne St.
 Vancamp, J. C., 30 Bloor St. West.
Waterloo—
 Klipper Undertaking Co.
Welland—
 Sutherland, G. W.
Woodstock—
 Meadows, T. & Sons.
 Mack, Paul.

QUEBEC
Buckingham—
 l'aquet, Jos.
Cowansville—
 Judson, M. B.
Montreal—
 Tees & Co., 912 St. Catherine St. West.
St. Hyacinthe—
 Cadorette, Mongeau & Leary.
St. Laurent—
 Gougeon, Jos.

NEW BRUNSWICK
Petitcodiac—
 Jonah, D. Allison.
Woodstock—
 Van Wart, Jacob.

NOVA SCOTIA
Ferrona—
 Fraser, D. & Co.
Halifax—
 Snow & Co., 90 Argyle St.
Sydney Mines—
 D. A. McRae, Clyde Ave.
Sydney, C.B.—
 Beaton, A. J. & Son, 374-384 George St.

MANITOBA
Brandon—
 Campbell & Campbell.
 Vincent & McPherson.
Souris—
 McCulloch, Wm.
Swan River—
 Paull, Geo.
Winnipeg—
 Bardal, A. S., 834 Sherbrooke
 Thompson, J. C., 501 Main
 Clark-Leatherdale Co., Ltd., 232 Kennedy St.

SASKATCHEWAN
Gull Lake—
 Morrow, Fred. A.
Saskatoon—
 Young, A. E.
Kamsack—
 Russell, G. E. I.
Lanigan—
 Robertson, Wm.
Moose Jaw—
 The Bellamy Co.
 Broadfoot Bros.
Rush Lake—
 Friesen, John M.
Prince Albert—
 Howard, A. C.
 Hadley, C. L.
Regina—
 Speers, George.
Semans—
 Haygarth, Jas.
Welwyn—
 Leavens, Merritt.
Wolseley —
 Barber, B.

ALBERTA
Calgary—
 Graham & Buscomb, 611 Centre St.
Castor—
 Winter, W. G.

BRITISH COLUMBIA
Hosmer—
 Cornett, T. A.
Prince Rupert
 Haynes, S.
Victoria—
 Hann & Thompson, 827 Pandora Ave.

The Original Patented Concentrated Fluid

Patented Formula
Strongest and Best

Essential Oil Base, combined with Alcohol, Glycerine, Oxidized Formaldehyde and Boron-Dioxide.

Ask others for their Formula

Special Canadian Agents

National Casket Co.
Toronto, Ont.

GLOBE CASKET CO.
London, Ont.

SEMMENS & EVEL CASKET CO.
Hamilton, Ont.

GIRARD & GODIN
Three Rivers, Que.

JAS. S. ELLIOTT & SON
Prescott, Ont.

CHRISTIE BROS.
Amherst, N.S.

Larger Bottles filled up with water

Egyptian Chemical Co. Boston, U.S.A

Canadian School of Embalming
Instruction in Practical Embalming and Funeral Directing
PREPARATION FOR EXAMINATIONS
ENTER AT ANY TIME

R. U. STONE   32 Carlton Street
Principal   Toronto

Index to Advertisements

A
Ault & Wiborg Co 11

B
Baets Bros. & Co. 12
Batavia Clamp Co. 62

C
Canada Casket Co. 16
Canada Furn. Mfrs. Ltd. 17
Can. Morsereau Co. 21
Canadian School of Embalming 61
Can. H. W. Johns-Manville Co. Ltd. 25
Central Casket Co. 60
Chair Craft Co 13
Columbia Graphophone Co. ...o.b.c.

D
Dominion Casket Co. 48
Dominion Mfrs. Limited ..51-52-53-54

E
Eckels & Co., H. S. 60
Egyptian Chemical Co. 61
Elmira Interior Woodwork Co... 6

F
Farquharson-Gifford Co 9

G
Gale & Son, Geo. 18
Gendron Wheel Co. 59
Globe-Wernicke Co. 7
Gold Medal Furn. Mfg. Co 8

H
Hourd & Co. 8

I
Ideal Bedding Co. 26
Imperial Rattan Co. 3

K
Kawneer Mfg. Co. 10

Kindel Bed Co., Limited ..... i.f.c.
Knechtel Furniture Co. 21
Knechtel Kitchen Cabinet Co. .. 20

L
Lippert Furniture Co. 16

M
Malcolm Furn. Co., Andrew ..22-23
Matthews Bros. 44
Menford Mfg. Co. 19
McLagan Furniture Co., Geo .o.f.c.
Montreal Upholstering Co. 4
Mundell, J. G. & Co. .... i.f.c.

N
N. A. Bent Chair Co. 10
National Grave Vault Co. 58

O
Ontario Spring Bed 4

P
Phillips Mfg. Co. 12

S
Shafer, D. L. & Co. .... i.b.c.
Stratford Brass Co. 25
Stratford Chair Co. 5
Stratford Mfg. Co. 11
St. Thomas Metallic Vault Co. .58

T
Textileather Co. .... i.b.c.

V
Victoriaville Bedding Co. 15
Victoriaville Furn. Co. 14

W
Walter & Co., B. 62
Western Casket Co. 56
Weisglass, S., Limited. 25

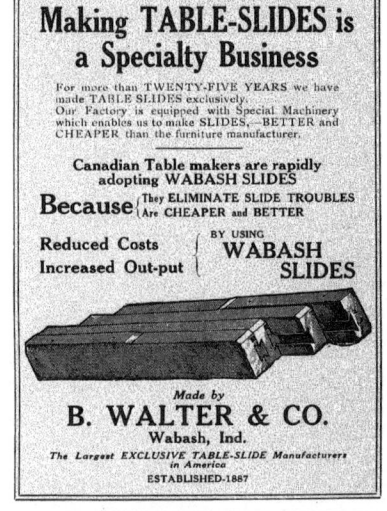

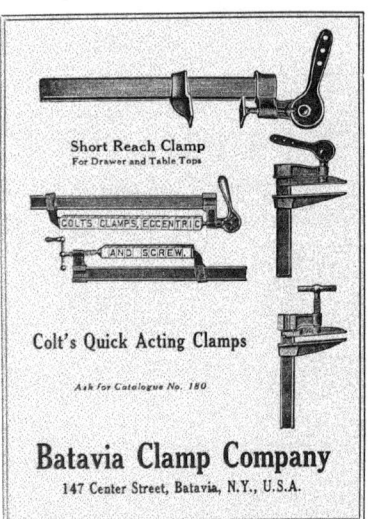

Making TABLE-SLIDES is a Specialty Business

For more than TWENTY-FIVE YEARS we have made TABLE SLIDES exclusively. Our Factory is equipped with Special Machinery which enables us to make SLIDES,—BETTER and CHEAPER than the furniture manufacturer.

Canadian Table makers are rapidly adopting WABASH SLIDES

Because { They ELIMINATE SLIDE TROUBLES Are CHEAPER and BETTER

Reduced Costs
Increased Out-put

BY USING
WABASH SLIDES

Made by
B. WALTER & CO.
Wabash, Ind.

The Largest EXCLUSIVE TABLE-SLIDE Manufacturers in America
ESTABLISHED 1887

Short Reach Clamp
For Drawer and Table Tops

COLT'S CLAMPS, ECCENTRIC AND SCREW.

Colt's Quick Acting Clamps
Ask for Catalogue No. 180

Batavia Clamp Company
147 Center Street, Batavia, N.Y., U.S.A.

For Every Furniture Man

A Helpful, Thoroughly Practical Book, Written by an Authority—

HOW TO KNOW PERIOD STYLES IN FURNITURE

How to Know Period Styles in Furniture — W. L. Kimerly

150 Pages   317 Illustrations

Price, $1.50

Designers will find illustrations of the work of celebrated designers of history. Examples are taken from the recognized collections and museums of the world.
Buyers—The book is arranged for easy reference with the distinguishing features of each period clearly shown.
Salesmen—The information in "How to Know Period Styles" will enable you to talk authoritatively on the subject.
Students—The confusing element has been eliminated, but all necessary information is included.

Send us $1.50. Keep the book 10 days, and if it isn't worth the price, return it and get your money back.

The Commercial Press
Publishers The Canadian Furniture World and The Undertaker
32 Colborne Street, Toronto

Textileather—

An artificial leather that gives better service than any other furniture covering made. All shades.

Textileather

Possesses all the characteristics of genuine solid leather, wears longer and costs much less.

Write for a sample of Textileather and put it to the test. Address:

Textileather Co. 212 Fifth Avenue
New York City
or Frank Schmidt, Berlin, Ontario

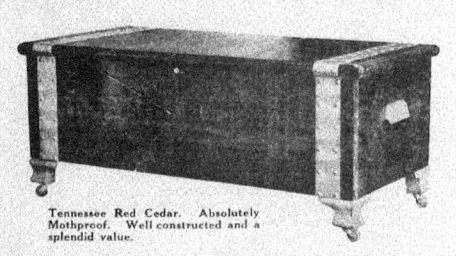

Tennessee Red Cedar. Absolutely Mothproof. Well constructed and a splendid value.

Something "Different" for the Xmas Gift—

A Shafer Chest

A great many of your customers would undoubtedly appreciate such a suggestion. Shafer Cedar Boxes and Chests give genuine service, are handsome in appearance and are priced low enough to attract the majority of people.

Feature Shafer Chests in Your Windows

The sooner you do it the better. Get the suggestion working at once and you are sure to reap the benefit. Send for prices on the next mail.

D. L. Shafer & Co.
St. Thomas, Ontario

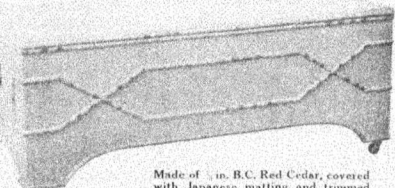

Made of ⅜ in. B.C. Red Cedar, covered with Japanese matting and trimmed with rattan. Tops padded.

An Open Letter to Readers of the "Furniture World"

The biggest furniture dealers in Canada are putting in Grafonola departments.

Why? Because a well-managed Columbia Grafonola department not only is a big source of profit by itself, but it attracts a host of people into the store.

Now, the furniture dealer's store is one of two logical places where a Columbia Grafonola should be bought.

The first place admittedly is the music store. But even as well-equipped furniture dealers have agencies for pianos, so are they taking on agencies for Columbia Grafonolas. In fact, Columbia Grafonolas and records have in many cases displaced the piano field, because sales of Grafonolas are much more frequent and a turnover of records at a good profit is a daily occurrence.

The seven months from November to May is the big season for selling Columbia Grafonolas and records. The months of November and December may well be said to be the harvest time, and if you are equipped to handle an agency of this kind at once, we can make you a most interesting proposition.

Frankly, we don't want to place a Columbia agency in a store that isn't properly equipped to take care of it. Our agency is too valuable for that.

But if you think that you have the organization and facilities to work a department of this kind, let us hear from you.

When we tell you that in Toronto alone such big stores as The T. Eaton Co., Murray-Kay, Ltd., Adams Furniture Co., all have strong prosperous Columbia departments and that the Columbia proposition is a protected price agency, you will readily appreciate that there must be something in it.

If you think that way about it, and are equipped to take hold of a Columbia agency and really work it, write to us for our agency offer to furniture dealers and free book "Music Money," something every merchant ought to read.

Columbia Graphophone Company

365 Sorauren Avenue

Toronto

Vol. 4 No. 12   eaturing Christmas an   o Y   DECEMBER, 1914

Canadian
FURNITURE WORLD
AND THE UNDERTAKER

Published by the Commercial Press, Limited, 32 Colborne Street, Toronto

Who also Publish: The Retail Grocer and Provisioner, The Retail Druggist, Canadian Hardware Journal, Canadian Manufacturer, Canadian Builder and Carpenter, The Canadian Clay-Worker, The Electrical Dealer and Contractor Good Roads of Canada, The Machine Shop, The Canadian Nurse, Motoring

---

"Imperial Rattan"
FOR LAST MINUTE ORDERING

MOST any piece selected from the "Imperial Rattan" Line will delight the recipient on Christmas morning.

Keep a good showing on your floors. We can make deliveries in good time for the Holiday shopper.

A Merry Xmas

The Season's Greetings and a Right Prosperous 1915 to our friends and customers. And may the year ending have brought you as much good cheer as your appreciation of our efforts has given us.

IMPERIAL RATTAN COMPANY
LIMITED
STRATFORD   ONTARIO

To Increase YOUR Christmas Sales:

Buy MUNDELL-MADE Christmas Specials. Smokers' Stands, Sewing Tables, Telephone Stands, Tabourettes, Waste Baskets, Magazine Stands, etc., will be big sellers this season.

¶ See our Special Circular showing these articles among others, and take advantage of the unusual values offered. Quick shipment.

JOHN C. MUNDELL & CO., LIMITED
ELORA   ONTARIO

A Red Cross Service That Puts New Life in Bedding Business

The Antiseptic Bedding Company
187-189 Parliament St., Toronto

December, 1914   CANADIAN FURNITURE WORLD AND THE UNDERTAKER

STRATFORD

Sincere Wishes for every Joy of the Yuletide Season from the Stratford Manufacturers

For Aristocratic Gift Pieces — The McLagan Line

Furniture of true artistic beauty and grace, yet consistent with the demands of the middle class trade.

"Stratford Made Increases Trade"

Orders received for McLagan Gift Pieces can be promptly executed.

Christmas novelties are a feature of our line.

The Geo. McLagan Furniture Co., Limited
Stratford   Ontario

Special Announcement

WE ARE IN A SPLENDID POSITION TO TAKE ON LINES WHICH HAVE HITHERTO BEEN IMPORTED, SUCH AS COSTUMIERS, DESKS, FILING CABINETS, TABLES, CHAIRS, CLOCK CASES AND OTHER MANUFACTURES OF WOOD

THERE IS NO REASON ON TOP OF THE EARTH THAT CANADIAN DEALERS NEED TO GO OUTSIDE OF OUR COUNTRY TO PURCHASE LINES IN THESE DAYS, INDEED IT WOULD BE UNPATRIOTIC AND UNJUST TO DO SO

WE WANT YOUR ENQUIRIES FOR LINES KNOWN AS SPECIAL. OUR WELL KNOWN LINES OF MANTELS, DESKS AND PARLOR FRAMES ARE STILL UP TO THEIR USUAL STANDARD, BUT OWING TO CONDITIONS WE SHALL BE GLAD TO TAKE ON OTHER SPECIAL LINES AS WELL

The Elmira Interior Woodwork Co. Limited
Elmira   Ontario

OUR FACTORY RUNS FULL TIME AND WE WANT TO KEEP
"BUSINESS AS USUAL"

Ontario Brass Beds
Are Built for a Lifetime of Satisfying Service

We guarantee for our beds that the finish is protected by the best lacquer on the market and that our improved methods of construction insure absolute and permanent rigidity.

Ontario Goods give continued satisfaction. This means that your customers come back.

ASK FOR COPY OF OUR
NEW CATALOGUE

The Ontario Spring Bed & Mattress Co., Limited
The Largest Bedding House in Canada
LONDON - ONTARIO

Brass Bed No. 1012. Pillars 2-inch, Filling ½-inch, Top Rod 2 inch x 1 inch, Head 60-inch, Foot 36-inch. Finish Bright, Satin or Polet

STRATFORD

Sincere Wishes for every Joy of the Yuletide Season from the Stratford Chair Makers

Wouldn't She be Pleased with this Superb Set of "Stratford Chairs"

Made of beautifully grained quartered oak with box slip seats in genuine leather. This new design should prove an exceptionally fast seller.

Stratford
Made
Increases
Trade

Rush in that *Stratford Chair Order Now* and we will have the goods delivered in plenty of time for you to close up many profitable sales before Christmas. Attend to it while you think of it.

The Stratford Chair Company, Limited
Stratford   Ontario

CANADIAN FURNITURE WORLD AND THE UNDERTAKER   December, 1914

FREE
DISPLAY CASE

We have now ready for Onward dealers a number of these handsome stands for

Onward Sliding Furniture Shoes and Onward Slides
(MADE IN CANADA)

These cases cost us $2.50 apiece, but we'll send one to you with an order for $25.00 worth of shoes and slides. If you bought no more than the first order, we'd lose money, but we know from experience that once you get started with this line you will find it very profitable and will re-order regularly.

Do you want one? The case is small and compact, just large enough to hold nicely a sample of each size. Each week new names are being added to our list of dealers who take pleasure and profit selling to their customers these modern inventions which do away with the old fashioned casters and prevent ruin to carpets and floors.

ONWARD MFG. CO. - BERLIN, ONT.
WESTERN REPRESENTATIVES
MONCRIEFF & ENDRESS, LIMITED, GALT BUILDING, WINNIPEG, MAN.

Stylish Chairs
at
Reasonable Prices

In getting up our new design we have endeavored to turn out a neat and up-to-date chair at a price which will appeal to the greater number of your customers.

No. 1362 and No. 1360 shown here, is the result.

These chairs are made of Oak, with Cane Panel in back, and Leather Slip Seat, and are of exceptionally good workmanship and finish.

Write for full information about this line

North American Bent Chair Co., Limited
Owen Sound   Ontario

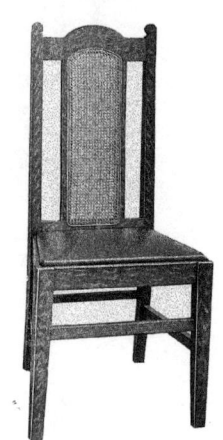

No. 1362   No. 1360

STRATFORD

Sincere Wishes for every Joy of the Yuletide Season from the Stratford Manufacturers

A Handsome, Useful Gift at *Anyone's* Price — This Art-Mission Desk-Bookcase

COMPLETE in itself in every way, this combination is suitable for even the smallest of living rooms. With the addition of other units, it is in keeping with the most pretentious and best of libraries and living rooms. This feature alone makes the Globe-Wernicke line particularly strong in sales possibilities. ¶ We can make deliveries at once. Write for particulars.

Have you copies of our Catalogs?

The Globe-Wernicke Co., Ltd.
Stratford   Ontario

Mattresses that Make Good

Can you afford to sell Mattresses whose wearing qualities you are not sure of?

Our Mattresses
Lee-Burrell, Regent, Rex and Invictus

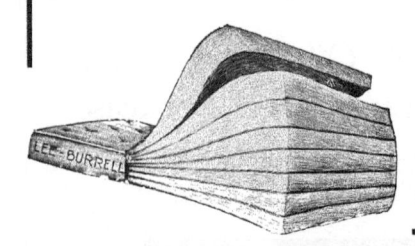

Have the honest construction which enables you to recommend them with every assurance that they will give perfect satisfaction.

For a high-grade Cotton Felt Mattress at a reasonable price, you can't the Lee-Burrell.

Let us send your our Price List.

The Standard Bedding Co.
27-29 Davies Ave. Toronto, Ont.

Use Textileather Because

—it possesses QUALITY—wears longer than any other furniture covering made.
—it has all the rich graining and fine appearance of genuine solid leather.
—it is priced low enough to enable you to use it on the cheaper, as well as on the best lines.

Write for samples of Textileather and convince yourself. Let us have your name at once.

Textileather Co., 212 Fifth Ave., New York, N.Y.
Write Direct, or to Frank Schmidt, Berlin, Ontario

STRATFORD

Sincere Wishes for every Joy of the Yuletide Season from the Stratford Manufacturers

Are You Looking to the Future of Your Business? *Then—*

You will include Farquharson-Gifford Furniture in Your Christmas Stock.

F.-G. Furniture not only combines all the characteristics desired for a gift, such as beauty, permanence and utility, but gives that lasting satisfaction that builds up future business.

A selection from the F.-G. line of Davenport Beds, Couches and Living Room Furniture will enable you to obtain the greatest returns from your stock.

When ordering Davenport Beds from Stratford, remember to order
F.-G.

Farquharson-Gifford Company, Limited
Stratford   Ontario

Colleran Improved Steel Clamping Bar

For fastening spring fabric on Wood Frames

The Strongest and Neatest Bar on the Market

Rigid Construction

One edge of the polished steel bar is bent at right angles forming a flange which fits into the groove in frame. The other edge is turned over making a round edge which **cannot cut the wire**. The end of the fabric fits snugly against the flange.

No ends sticking up to tear mattress.

Vermin Proof

The bar fastens down tight on the frame leaving no cracks or crevices.

The Colleran Improved Steel Clamping Bar is used on all the Colleran wood frame springs.

You should have the Best

Colleran Patent Spring Mattress Co.
Toronto — Ontario

Authentic Store Front Book

Our eight years' experience in helping to design and build more than 30,000 KAWNEER STORE FRONTS has enabled us to compile and publish an authentic book on Store Fronts. This book contains photographs as well as drawings of many of the best paying Store Fronts in the country and if you are interested in Store Fronts don't take another step until you have seen "Boosting Business No. 2." Let us help you build a new Store Front that will pay for itself by increasing your business.

Kawneer STORE FRONTS

Just a Card for "Boosting Business No. 2" will bring it without obligation

Kawneer Manufacturing Co., Ltd.
Francis J. Plym, President
Dept. S.
Guelph - Ontario

Exclusive Effects in Furniture Trimmings

USE the "Stratford" make of attractive Furniture Trimmings in Brass and you can rest assured that the quality will always stand out in your favor.

Let us quote you prices on your specially designed trimmings.

The Stratford Brass Co.
Limited
Stratford — Ontario

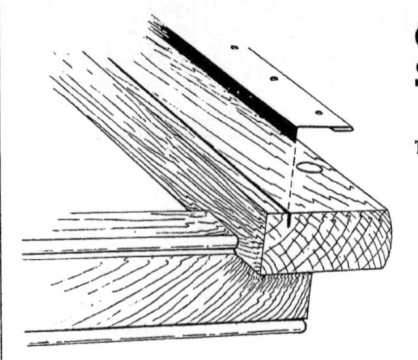

STRATFORD

Sincere Wishes for every Joy of the Yuletide Season from the Stratford Manufacturers

The Demand for Extra Chairs and Tables

at this season of social functions and entertainments will afford you an opportunity of working up a brisk trade in Stratford folding tables and chairs.

The "**Stratford**" **Chair** is absolutely the strongest of its weight made. Constructed so that it cannot tip forward.

"**Stratford**" **Folding Table** is of strong, light construction. Folds compactly. Steel leg supports hold table firmly in position when in use.

A stock of chairs and tables to rent out to customers would be a good investment.

WRITE US

No. 10A
Made of select straight grained stock. Prests steam bent. Net price, $9.00 per dozen.

No. 50. Folding Card or Lunch Table. Height, 30 inches. Top, 24 x 36 inches. Finish, Natural. Put up 6 in a crate. Net price, $18.00.

The Stratford Manufacturing Company, Limited
STRATFORD — ONTARIO

Genuine Tennessee Cedar — Moth Proof

Shafer Chests for 'Xmas Gifts

B.C. and Tennessee Red Cedar Chests in a wide range of popular designs. Quality and finish of the best.

Send us a trial order for the Holiday trade

D. L. Shafer & Co.
St. Thomas — Ontario

MADE-IN-CANADA
MATTHEWS BROS., LIMITED
788 DUNDAS ST., TORONTO, Can.

OVAL FRAMES
for CONVEX and FLAT GLASS
A VERY MUCH BETTER PRICE — BETTER FINISH
BETTER MAKE.

"Business as Usual"

After a temporary cessation of activity our factory is again running and we are supplying for quick delivery our increasingly popular—

Twin Pedestal Tables

What More Practical Christmas Gift

can you offer your customers.

"Twin" Extension tables are supported by a pair of pedestals, each complete in itself. These pedestals present a completely finished appearence whether open or closed and give greatest support at all times.

In our wide range of designs and finish you will be able to suit any of your customers. They will all like the Twin idea.

Our new catalogue will give you further information about our Twin Pedestal Extension Table and also our extensive line of Parlor and Library Tables and Specialties.

The Chesley Furniture Co., Limited

Geo. Durst, Pres
Wm. Damm, Vice-Pres.

Chesley, Ont.

W. G. Durst, Manager
J. Hauser, Executive Officer

1915

1915

JANUARY 11th to 16th

This year's Exhibition will afford the careful buyer an unequalled opportunity for selecting his stock and enable him to keep in touch with all the new features and designs being brought out by Canada's leading furniture manufacturers.

THE EXHIBITION WILL BE HELD IN THE

Furniture Exhibition Building
Queen Street South, Berlin

Outside Exhibitors may secure space at very reasonable rates
26,000 SQUARE FEET OF FLOOR SPACE
For Full Information write J. P. SCULLY, Secretary, Berlin, Ont.

We will endeavor to make the trip profitable for all visiting retailers.

Factories and Permanent Show Rooms will be thrown open to visiting furniture dealers, allowing them to obtain a greater technical knowledge of the furniture manufactured in Canada's greatest furniture centre. Full list of exhibitors will appear in next issue of the *Canadian Furniture World.*

Keep the dates open and spend a few days with us

YOUR CHRISTMAS & The S·P·U·G IDEA·

The universal tendency during the past few years toward the selection of more useful Christmas Gifts took a definite outward form last year in such demonstrations as the S-P-U-G advertising, which translated, means Society Promoting Useful Giving.

Chair Craft Chairs offer you an unusual opportunity to cash-in on this idea for never were Christmas Gifts as thoughtful, useful, and lasting as Chair Craft Chairs.

Then there are the Christmas Sales Helps that are included with every order *free*, which will work for your store as only Chair Craft helps can work. Send in your order now. It will bring Chair Craft Chairs to your floor in plenty of time for your early Christmas shoppers.

Join the S-P-U-G Movement—exploit the idea in your vicinity around Chair Craft Chairs. With *such* Comfort Chairs as the Chair Craft kind it means bigger Christmas Profits with quicker Sales than ever before.

TRY IT

The Chair Craft Company
Traverse City, Michigan

Something Useful will be Acceptable this Xmas

Peerless and Acme
FOLDING TABLES

are just the thing to meet the demand for this class of present

The Many Uses of the Peerless
Make It Popular Everywhere.

The Peerless is made of selected oak, weighs 12 pounds, but by actual test will support half a ton. Legs fold within the table rim. Made with square top in 24 inch and 30 inch sizes. Round tops in 30 inch and 36 inch, polish finish or covered with green felt. Get particulars re our new 42 inch round felt top table.

Get both on your floor

They will sell themselves

The ACME is lighter in weight than the Peerless but will stand any amount of ordinary usage. Made in E.E. Fumed Oak or Imitation Mahogany. Top covered with Green Felt. 30 inches square.

THE ACME

Hourd & Company, Limited
London   *Sole Licensees and Manufacturers*   Ontario

No. 445

No. 151

No. 441

Christmas Goods
that are
Quick Sellers

The store which will show PROFIT as the result of the Christmas trade is the one which has a large variety of attractive, moderately priced furniture suitable for Christmas gifts.

That is the store which handles

The Meaford Line

In preparing our Christmas stock we have kept this thought in view, and the result is a line of Desks, Bookcases, Library Tables, Parlor Tables, Music Cabinets, Jardiniere Stands, Smokers' Sets, etc., possessing that finish for which the Meaford Line of Surface Oak and Surface Mahogany is famous, at prices which place it within the means of even the more economical.

Write us At Once—Every Day Counts

The Meaford Manufacturing Company, Limited
MEAFORD - ONTARIO

THIRTEEN-NINETEEN · CHICAGO

January 1915   Twenty-Seventh Season

The reason why "1319" has become the headquarters for America's Furniture Buyers is because the best selling and greatest profit producing lines are shown there.

If you fail to attend the January Exhibition here you are jeopardizing the best Interests of your Business.

MANUFACTURERS' EXHIBITION BUILDING COMPANY, 1319 MICHIGAN AVE., CHICAGO

The Beauty
Comfort
and
Strength
of
"Victoriaville"
*Upholstered
Furniture*

1272

VICTORIAVILLE BRASS BEDS

Are made in a variety of styles which will please all tastes.

They are the kind for which there is a steady demand at all seasons.

Have established a reputation which makes it the best business getting line you can have on your floor.

If you have not already done so, you should send in your order at once to be ready for the Christmas rush.

"Victoriaville" Lines stand for
Bigger Sales and Bigger Profits

The Victoriaville Bedding Co., Limited
Victoriaville, Quebec

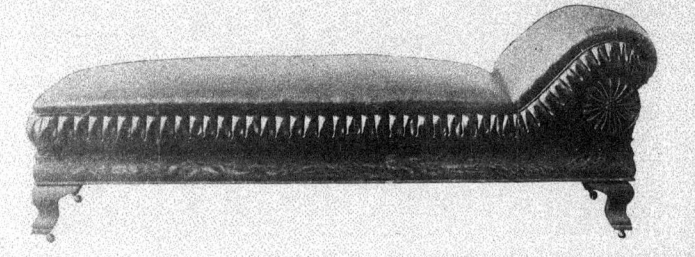

THE "GOLD MEDAL" LINE

DIRECTORS:
W. J. McMURTRY, President and General Manager
W. R. DALBY
G. C. EMMERSON
H. B. SHORTT, Secretary
G. HUGHES, Ass. Manager

Seasonable
Living Room Furniture

FACTORIES:
MONTREAL FACTORY
C. A. Hart, Vice-Pres. and Mgr.
WINNIPEG FACTORY
W. J. Rimmington, Mgr.
UXBRIDGE FACTORY
Geo. Wilson, Gen. Supt.

Upholstered in

Tapestries
and
Leathers

No. 654½   No. 691

No. 152   No. 687

Quarter Cut Oak Smoker's Morris Chair.   Quarter Cut Oak Rocker and Chair to match.

The Gold Medal Furniture Mfg. Co., Limited
Toronto   Uxbridge   Montreal   Winnipeg

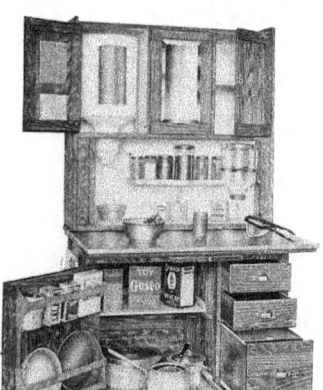

The Great
Cabinet Success
of the Year

¶ This, the new Knechtel No. 63, is recognized as the Cabinet of more really worth while features than any other on the Canadian market.

¶ With our big consumer advertising campaign, window cards, etc., to assist you, this invaluable Kitchen Cabinet presents unequalled sales possibilities.

No. 63. Oak. Open

KNECHTEL KITCHEN CABINET

Order this design at once for Xmas Trade

¶ With 13 other special features, this design has disappearing slide shutters which allow of access to the interior at any time without disturbing the contents on the work table—a mighty big selling point, Mr. Dealer.

Get in touch with our Proposition at Once
Knechtel Furniture Co. Ltd.
Selling Agents, Hanover

Knechtel Kitchen Cabinet Co.
Limited
Hanover   Ontario

No. 63. Closed

December, 1914   CANADIAN FURNITURE WORLD AND THE UNDERTAKER   21

BE PREPARED!

It stands to reason that Christmas buying this year will be largely confined to practical, useful articles, such as furniture. It is clear, also, that the furniture dealer who has a good assortment of gift furniture will attract a lot of business that would otherwise go elsewhere. *Be prepared* with a good stock of Knechtel's new ones.

No. 33—List—47.25. A Secretary-Bookcase that is not new, but certainly deserving of a place on your floor—made of quartered oak, polished golden or fumed, 75 inches in height and 36 inches wide, leaded glass bookcase doors.

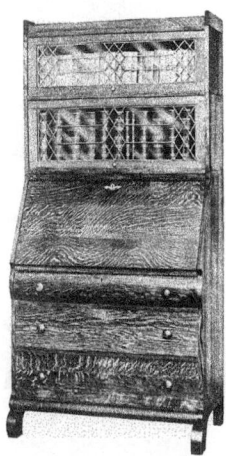

No. 37¼—List—65.55. This one is comparatively new, and is fitted with two sections of our Weis-Knechtel receding door bookcase. Solid quartered oak, 73 inches in height, 34 inches wide. No. 37 (without bookcase) List. 40.50.

Don't Talk War! Talk Business!

We are talking too much war. We have met the first shock of the big surprise. We have passed throug's it and found ourselves alive. Let's act like live men. Let's put some good Knechtel Christmas Novelties in our stores and make some money.

THE KNECHTEL FURNITURE CO.
HANOVER - ONTARIO
LIMITED

BAETZ BROTHERS & COMPANY
BERLIN :: ONTARIO

Bed Room Chairs

in white Enamel and all Standard Finishes.

See our exhibit at the

Berlin-Waterloo Furniture Exhibition

Central Building

This Guarantee
Sells Beds for You!

SPECIAL GUARANTEE
This bedstead is guaranteed for construction and finish, and will not tarnish under the use of alcohol, salts, solutions or acids.
S. WEISGLASS, LIMITED.

When a customer has admired the design, examined the construction, and noted the lustrous finish of a Weisglass Brass Bed, you have only to show her the Special Guarantee to close the sale right there. It absolutely protects her against faulty construction, and guarantees that the brass is untarnishable. She will find the price right—because you can make a good profit in Weisglass beds and still beat your competitors' prices.

If you have not received our new catalogue, showing the largest range of Brass Beds in Canada, advise us and we will gladly send you one

S. WEISGLASS, LIMITED - MONTREAL

December, 1914   CANADIAN FURNITURE WORLD AND THE UNDERTAKER   23

We bring you Greetings for a Merry Xmas and a Prosperous and Happy New Year

Parlor   Bedroom   Den, Living-Room

THE ELMIRA LINE
is Full of Attractive Pieces for Xmas Gifts

Made in Canada

Chairs will appeal to many of your customers as appropriate Christmas gifts. The selections which we show here are typical of our line.

A comfortable arm rocker for the parlor. A dainty rocker for the bedroom. A sturdy leather upholstered spring seated rocker for the den or living room. For every room where a chair is used there are many Elmira designs at prices which make it worth your while.

Made in Canada

Make Your Selections To-day

THE ELMIRA FURNITURE CO., LIMITED
ELMIRA   ONTARIO

Quality Service   Quick Delivery

GUARANTEED GALE WATERVILLE, QUE. BEDS AND BEDDING

Triplex Spring

Will save you money in freight charges.
Will save keeping stock of side rails.
Will always sell spring with the bed.

Will stimulate spring bed business.
Will be largest selling spring in Canada.
Will give satisfaction in every particular.

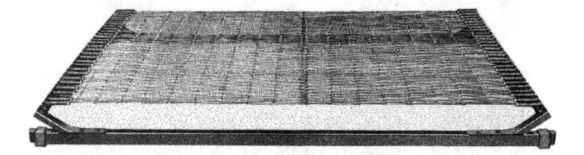

Specially tempered angle-iron frame.
Dovetailed ends to fit any bed of GALE make.
Fabric elevated 4 in. from side-rail by angle-iron 1½ x 1½.
Fabric made of the best "Dominion" wire.

Shipped to you "knock-down"—packed either in cases or bales. Economizes your store-space. Weight 58 pounds. *May we send you a few?*

Geo. Gale & Sons Limited
Waterville, Quebec

Montreal   Toronto   Winnipeg

Making TABLE-SLIDES is a Specialty Business

For more than TWENTY-FIVE YEARS we have made TABLE SLIDES exclusively. Our Factory is equipped with Special Machinery which enables us to make SLIDES,—BETTER and CHEAPER than the furniture manufacturer.

Canadian Table makers are rapidly adopting WABASH SLIDES

Because They ELIMINATE SLIDE TROUBLES Are CHEAPER and BETTER

Reduced Costs | BY USING
Increased Out-put | **WABASH SLIDES**

Made by
B. WALTER & CO.
Wabash, Ind.

The Largest EXCLUSIVE TABLE-SLIDE Manufacturers in America
ESTABLISHED-1887

A Suggestion Means a Sale

A suggestion from your salesman, when a woman is purchasing articles for her household, will almost invariably convince her of the need of preserving the beauty and brilliance of her dining table or buffet with

J-M ASBESTOS
Table Covers and Mats

Hot dishes cannot mar their shining surfaces when protected in this way.

Dealers make an especially attractive profit from J-M Asbestos Table Covers and Mats, because of the low prices we can give. We secure Asbestos from our own mines and manufacture these products in our own factories; thus greatly lowering the cost of their production. Large stocks are unnecessary as we can fill rush orders from any of our numerous branches.

Write our nearest branch for the special dealer proposition we are now offering.

THE CANADIAN
H. W. JOHNS-MANVILLE CO., LTD.
Toronto   Montreal   Winnipeg   Vancouver

The Kindel Kind
for Profitable Xmas Displays

WHEN you consider the practicability of Kindel Convertible Beds, together with the large margin of profit obtainable and the almost universal acceptance of the fact that nothing better can be had—you have the best reasons for pushing the Kindel kind.

Many more families in your neighborhood will awaken on Xmas morning to find new Kindel Beds in their homes.

Display a couple of designs in your windows with our window cards, posters, etc. and see that you get your share.

Christmas Orders Will be Filled at Once

The Kindel Bed Company, Limited
Toronto - Ontario

DAY & NIGHT SERVICE

Quality Service   Quick Delivery

GALE GUARANTEED BEDS AND BEDDING WATERVILLE, QUE.

Triplex Spring

Will save you money in freight charges.
Will save keeping stock of side rails.
Will always sell spring with the bed.

Will stimulate spring bed business.
Will be largest selling spring in Canada.
Will give satisfaction in every particular.

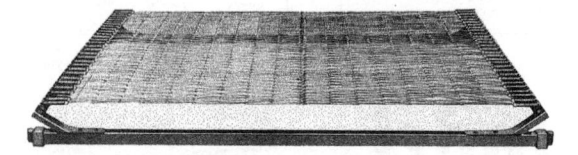

Specially tempered angle-iron frame.
Dovetailed ends to fit any bed of GALE make.
Fabric elevated 4 in. from side-rail by angle-iron 1½ x 1½.
Fabric made of the best "Dominion" wire.

Shipped to you "knock-down"---packed either in cases or bales. Economizes your store-space. Weight 58 pounds. *May we send you a few?*

Geo. Gale & Sons Limited
Waterville, Quebec

Montreal   Toronto   Winnipeg

Making TABLE-SLIDES is a Specialty Business

For more than TWENTY-FIVE YEARS we have made TABLE SLIDES exclusively. Our Factory is equipped with Special Machinery which enables us to make SLIDES,—BETTER and CHEAPER than the furniture manufacturer.

Canadian Table makers are rapidly adopting WABASH SLIDES

Because They ELIMINATE SLIDE TROUBLES Are CHEAPER and BETTER

Reduced Costs
Increased Out-put
BY USING
WABASH SLIDES

Made by
B. WALTER & CO.
Wabash, Ind.
The Largest EXCLUSIVE TABLE-SLIDE Manufacturers in America
ESTABLISHED 1887

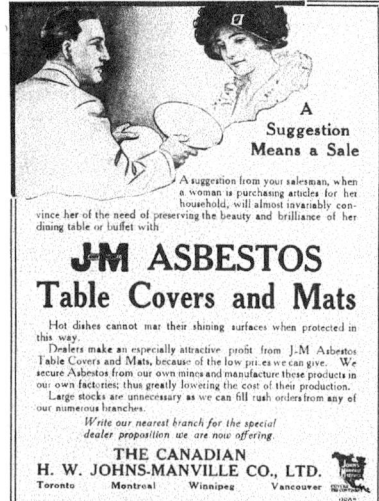

A Suggestion Means a Sale

A suggestion from your salesman, when a woman is purchasing articles for her household, will almost invariably convince her of the need of preserving the beauty and brilliance of her dining table or buffet with

J-M ASBESTOS Table Covers and Mats

Hot dishes cannot mar their shining surfaces when protected in this way.

Dealers make an especially attractive profit from J-M Asbestos Table Covers and Mats, because of the low prices we can give. We secure Asbestos from our own mines and manufacture these products in our own factories; thus greatly lowering the cost of their production. Large stocks are unnecessary as we can fill rush orders from any of our numerous branches.

Write our nearest branch for the special dealer proposition we are now offering.

**THE CANADIAN
H. W. JOHNS-MANVILLE CO., LTD.**
Toronto   Montreal   Winnipeg   Vancouver

The Kindel Kind
for Profitable Xmas Displays

WHEN you consider the practicability of Kindel Convertible Beds, together with the large margin of profit obtainable and the almost universal acceptance of the fact that nothing better can be had—you have the best reasons for pushing the *Kindel* kind.

Many more families in your neighborhood will awaken on Xmas morning to find new *Kindel* Beds in their homes.

Display a couple of designs in your windows with our window cards, posters, etc. and see that *you* get your share.

Christmas Orders Will be Filled at Once

The Kindel Bed Company, Limited
Toronto   -   Ontario

DAY & NIGHT SERVICE

A Real "Christmas Box" For You

THE IDEAL
SOFT NAP
(Patented Inner Spring)
MATTRESS

Noiseless
Comfortable
Sanitary
Ventilated
Handled Easily
Ten-Year
Ironclad
Guarantee

This new Ideal production is the last word in inner spring mattress construction. The centre consists of a very large number of highly tempered steel coil springs covered on both sides with extra heavy burlap, each spring being sewn into a separate pocket, giving an individual action on every spring. On each side of these springs we place fifteen pounds of pure snow-white cotton felt, or thirty pounds in all. The elasticity of the felt combined with the highly tempered coil springs, produces a mattress delightfully soft and pliable.

The workmanship is the very best that we can produce, the cover being of the very highest grade of ticking made with imperial edge, and in the box are inserted brass ventilators, which permit the circulation of air into the interior of the mattress.

We feel so sure that this mattress is absolutely satisfactory in every respect, that we are placing on it an ironclad guarantee for ten years.

THE IDEAL BEDDING CO. LIMITED
2-24 JEFFERSON AVE. - - - - TORONTO

TRADE MARK — THE IDEAL LINE — GUARANTEED — REGISTERED

Canadian FURNITURE WORLD AND THE UNDERTAKER

D. O. McKINNON, PRESIDENT
W. L. EDMONDS, VICE-PRESIDENT AND CONTRIBUTING EDITOR
J. C. ARMER, VICE-PRESIDENT AND MANAGER OF TECHNICAL PAPERS

PUBLISHED ABOUT THE TWENTY-FIFTH OF PRECEDING MONTH BY

The Commercial Press, Limited
32 Colborne Street, Toronto
(Next King Edward Hotel)

WESTON WRIGLEY, VICE-PRESIDENT AND MANAGER OF TRADE PAPERS
JAMES O'HAGAN, EDITOR
WM. J. BRYANS, ASSOCIATE EDITOR
GEO. H. HONSBERGER, ADVERTISING MANAGER

F. C. D. WILKES, 794 Unity Building, Montreal
C. G. BRANDT, Circulation Manager, Toronto
E. J. MacINTYRE, Room 1155, 122 S. Michigan Ave., Chicago
CANADIAN ADVERTISING SERVICE CO., New York

Subscription rate, Canada and Great Britain, $1.00 per year; United States, $1.50 per year.
Circulation has averaged over 2,000 copies monthly for nearly two years.

VOLUME FOUR   TORONTO, DECEMBER, 1914   NUMBER TWELVE

Preaching and Practising.

A furniture dealer in an Eastern Ontario town recently expressed indignation because a local merchant in another line of business had bought a dining-room suite from a department store in Toronto.

That he had ground for his indignation there can be no doubt, for he could have supplied similar goods just as cheap and just as good.

But much of his indignation fell upon dull and unsympathetic ears, for this particular furniture dealer himself often resorted to the mail order houses for articles which he could have obtained in his home town.

Those who preach should practise their own doctrines if they hope to gain disciples.

The measure of the share of the Christmas holiday trade he gets is usually in proportion to the effort he puts forth to get it.

He Retaliated and Won.

A furniture dealer in a small town was somewhat perturbed because a local merchant was giving away furniture as a premium for groceries purchased.

Being an Irishman, he decided, after the practice had been going on some weeks, to retaliate in kind.

Through a merchant in another town he secured a few lines of staple groceries. These he displayed in his window, announcing on show cards and in his advertisements in the local paper that purchasers of furniture at certain prices would be presented with certain groceries.

It was now the turn of the offending merchant to be perturbed, particularly as his store was next door. When a week had passed by he hoisted the white flag, and through the mediation of a third party offered terms of capitulation. To these terms the furniture dealer readily consented, and each, like the cobbler, is now "sticking to his last."

As a rule, retaliation is not to be commended, but that in exceptional cases it may be justified this particular incident would seem to prove. But suppose the merchant who was the offender in the first instance had been Irish too? Well, then, we fear there would have been "war to the knife."

The Dealer Who Hides Behind Himself.

The dealer who says that he has been so long in business that he does not need to advertise is hiding behind himself. He may not realize the fact, but it is true, nevertheless. And the more persistently he hides behind himself the greater will be the number of people who will forget him.

If all dealers were to agree to refrain from publicity all would, of course, be on an equal footing. But the trouble is no really progressive dealer would agree to conform to any such reactionary policy.

Once upon a time a group of manufacturers in Canada agreed to discontinue all advertising. There were only three or four in the group, but they were the only manufacturers of the kind in the country. Even they, however, soon found that their policy was an unwise one.

Like a good many other business men, they thought that money paid out in advertising was an expenditure. Their experience, however, taught them that it was an investment. They are now all consistent advertisers.

The question naturally arises: If a group of manufacturers who monopolize the manufacture of an article find that it is an unsound business practice not to advertise, what must be the case when a retailer, who has to meet the keenest kind of competition, decides that he will not use the columns of his local newspaper? The answer is easy—he is handicapped.

Some business men have been heard to remark that if they knew how to prepare copy they would advertise.

Writing an advertisement is merely putting on paper the substance of what they would say to a customer who entered their store to buy a certain article.

True, some can do this better than others; but just as there is no one in business who is such a poor salesman that he becomes dumb when a customer enters his store, so there is no one so inefficient that he cannot put on paper the selling points of an article that he wishes to advertise.

Where there's a will there's a way. But the trouble is that some do not appear to have the will as far as advertising is concerned.

Give the Young Blood a Chance. Too frequently it is the case that merchants who belong to the old school will not give the younger men in the store a chance to put some of their modern ideas into practice in the store—much to the detriment of sales.

The writer encountered an instance, illustrating the point, just the other day. A young fellow, who had been head clerk in a certain store for a considerable length of time, had a good many live merchandising ideas that he would liked to have tried out in the business, but the proprietor, a staid and sober merchant of the old school, at once squelched any proposals by the clerk of live and modern methods of going after business.

However, the proprietor, on account of ill health, was forced to go on a holiday, and left the clerk in charge of the business. The clerk at once began to introduce a number of modern ideas and methods into the business. They were not expensive ones, but just small things that helped trade in various departments, and impressed customers with the fact that the establishment was a live—not a decaying one. As a result, the sales in that store are averaging $12 per day more than when the proprietor went south and the clerk took charge, and the store is only a comparatively small one. The increased sales are about paying the clerk's salary.

There is a moral in this story that not a few merchants need to heed. Too often, it is the case that business getting ideas in the young men are nipped in the bud by the proprietor discouraging any attempts to do business differently from the methods he has been following in past years. Merchandising methods are continually advancing to a higher plane, and every store must keep pace, or lose its place in the race for business.

If you cannot get all the business you want, put forth all the effort you can to get as much as possible of that which is going.

Value of an Attractive Store. That the neat, clean, bright and otherwise attractive store has an appreciable value in the promotion of trade is a fact that no dealer will deny. In the face of this generally acknowledged truth, it is surprising that many dealers do not give more attention to this particular. They believe, apparently, but do not act on their belief.

A store is judged by its appearance. If you set out to buy an article, you pick out an establishment that is bright and clean because you believe that you are likely to find goods of quality in such a store. The good appearing store attracts customers to it. Then again the more goods are sold where they are presented to advantage, and this cannot be done in a dark, untidy or unclean store. Presented in the proper way, goods will to a considerable extent sell themselves. This is where the store with attractive display facilities wins out.

Recognizing this fact, the merchant should give some study to ways and means by which the appearance of the store may be enhanced. It will mean more trade.

Preach Canadian-made furniture for Canadian Christmas presents.

Set Selling Prices According to Costs. In these days of ascending prices, the dealer must look to his costs and set his selling prices accordingly, if he would make a profit on the money invested in his business. Many a dealer declares that this is impossible, because if he advances his prices he will be unable to hold his volume of trade. He declares that he must meet competition—that he must meet the prices of his neighbors.

This is one of the greatest abuses of the hardware trade. It is unfortunate that so many dealers are so ignorant of their costs, and accordingly do not know whether or not they are making a profit. The tendency of these men is always to make their prices lower than they should be, with the result that the merchants who are aware of their costs and their profits are compelled to meet these prices if they would hold their trade.

The question of profit is one of vital importance to every retail merchant, because he cannot hope to remain in business long unless a sufficient profit is being made. The regrettable fact is that he sometimes believes he is making a profit when he is not, but at the end of the year, when the ledger has been balanced off, he finds he has been fooling himself, and in some cases very badly.

The first essential to the correct figuring of profits and the setting of selling prices at a proper figure is that the dealer know his costs and the amount it costs him to do business. At this time, when prices are tending upward, dealers should give close attention to this important question. It profits a dealer little to sell a lot of goods if he is not making a reasonable percentage of profit on every sale.

EDITORIAL BRIEFS.

If you are a business man, don't think too much about being contented. Cultivate ambition and contentment will take care of itself.

* * *

The man who does things will do some of them wrong. It is the man who never tries anything new who never makes a mistake.

* * *

Don't be afraid to spend some of your money to get good window dressing ideas. You can't think up all the good plans yourself.

* * *

Even customers who are not themselves neat, and who do not insist on neatness in a store, will sensibly or insensibly be favorably affected by it.

* * *

Don't give your show windows any days off. They ask none and need none. They are willing to work every day and all day.

* * *

Successful advertising is nothing more nor less than advertising that tells people what they want to know about your goods.

* * *

People go to the same store to buy to which they went for a mere accommodation. Don't be afraid to be accommodating, even when there is no money in it.

* * *

Black spots are bound to appear occasionally on the horizon of every business enterprise, but it is the man who meets them with a smile and determination who will find the clouds rolling away the soonest.

Promoting the Sale of Made-in-Canada Goods

Retailers should join in present campaign to promote the sale of Canadian goods—Unique window display used by Montreal dealer

DURING the past few years, the manufacturers of Canada have been putting forth steadily-increasing efforts to promote the sale of "Made-in-Canada" goods. Since the outbreak of war, realizing that the psychological moment was at hand for an appeal to the Canadian people to patronize home industry, manufacturers individually and collectively have undertaken a big campaign and in this they are receiving valuable support from the press of Canada. They also realize the valuable assistance that the retailers of Canada can give them in this work.

Why the Retailer Should Assist.

The retailer should realize that if Canadian-made goods are bought by Canadians, it will help in the employment problem of this country, and will also help to keep money in circulation in Canada. This is of indirect benefit to the merchant because the more people who are kept in continuous employment the more money they will have to spend with the retailer.

The retailer can also make the present "Made-in-Canada" campaign of direct benefit to his business by featuring Canadian goods in his store and cashing in on the present publicity that is being given to Canadian-made goods.

Montreal Dealer Makes Use of Window.

The window display is one effective medium of promoting the sale of "Made-in-Canada" goods, and was the one used by a Montreal store, in a recent effort in this direction.

The display in question not only featured Canadian goods, but drove home in a convincing manner to the passing public why they should buy Canadian goods. The unique manner in which this was done is illustrated in the accompanying sketch. A representative of this paper found that it proved very interesting to those passing the store.

In the left-hand side of the window was a miniature factory in idleness with many windows broken and in a generally dilapidated condition. Above it was a card which read:

AN IDLE FACTORY PRODUCES WANT AND PRIVATION. ARE YOU HELPING TO KEEP CANADIAN FACTORIES CLOSED BY BUYING GOODS MADE IN FOREIGN COUNTRIES?

On the right-hand side was another miniature factory, but a delightful contrast to the first. Here all was busyness, and the card above it read:

A BUSY FACTORY PRODUCES HAPPY HOMES AND PROSPEROUS PEOPLE. ARE YOU HELPING TO KEEP CANADIAN FACTORIES BUSY BY BUYING GOODS MADE IN CANADIAN FACTORIES?

Along the rear of the window was a big banner with the slogan: "Buy Made-in-Canada Goods."

Features of the Display.

The miniature factories were made out of cardboard

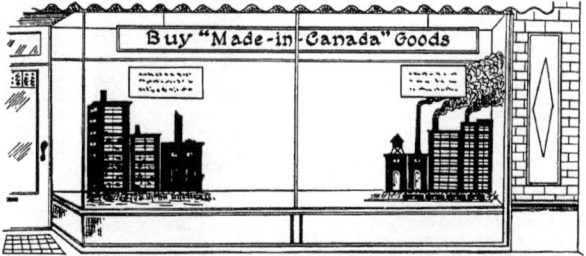

Sketch made by Canadian Furniture World's artist illustrating the central feature of a window display in a Montreal store advocating people to buy "Made-in-Canada" goods. Read about it in the accompanying article. Any kind of Canadian goods can be shown in the window.

mapped out in imitation of brick. Electric lights were placed behind the windows of the busy factory, while the idle one was in darkness. Especially at night the contrast was very conspicuous, thus assisting in driving home the point it was desired to emphasize. Canadian goods were displayed in the centre of the window. The central feature made the window a much greater attention attractor than if the display was simply of goods only.

The exports of German furniture to the United Kingdom in 1913 amounted to a value of £29,000 ($145,000), Austrian being worth £36,000 ($180,000). The combined world exports of these two countries totalled £726,000 ($3,630,000). In the opinion of British manufacturers, they can make these goods as cheaply as Austria and Germany have done.

Statuary and its Opportunities For Furniture Trade

"NO furniture store nowadays seems complete without a few of our decorations," said G. L. Irish, Toronto manufacturer and importer of statuary, to The Furniture World recently, in speaking of his and similar articles being sold through the trade. And the wonder of it was to us that more was not handled by furniture dealers, seeing that they trade in and sell everything else in the line of house furnishings. But we were a little mistaken in our surmise.

The history of the business is quite interesting. Listen to Mr. Irish as he relates his story: "I have been handling and making statuary, along with pictures and mouldings, for over 20 years," said he. "For eight years I carried the line out of Philadelphia for O. S. Bartoli, who has been retired in Italy for eleven years with a modest fortune. He was the best statuary man that ever set foot in America. I was the only one that sold his line in the United States, and we kept 40 people at work steadily in those days.

"Statuary sold at prices double and treble what they are to-day. Having made some money and getting tired of traveling, I concluded to open up a wholesale house in my home country of Canada, and for 12 years past have been located in Toronto.

"I have a number of people continually manufacturing alabastine statuary, the line of which consists of 1,500 models—copies from the leading galleries throughout the world, most of them coming from France and Italy. We imitate so closely that it needs an expert's inspection to distinguish from the genuine marble, alabaster and bronze pieces. The prices of the copies are within reach of everybody, while it is only a few who can buy the genuine article.

"There is not much statuary being imported in the genuine now, and hardly any in the imitation, as we can manufacture very cheap in this country. The men most actively employed in the line are Italians of the better class, and nearly all of them have had a world-wide experience. There is an increasing demand for the ornaments we make. The moving-picture shows have been a big factor in helping to introduce the line, as most of the leading pieces are seen and have become familiar to the people through visits to 'movie' houses showing travel pictures.

"Then, again, for the last few years the people of this country have traveled more and have seen the originals in the galleries of Europe, and statuary has been illustrated more in the magazines. In the most expensive homes you will often find from six to twelve imitation works of art such as we make in figures copying Venus de Milo, Apollo, Diana, Flying Mercury, and other subjects.

"We make a complete reproduction of the classical as well as the ornamental. The leading poets, musicians and statesmen are greatly sought after; oriental figures in colors are popular for dens and halls; electric figures in bronze are selling extensively, as also are boxes and jardinieres with zinc linings for flowers. These latter are one of the newest lines and are meeting with great success.

"Furniture stores and art galleries are our best customers, and no furniture store seems complete nowadays without a few of these decorations. They add greatly to the appearance of every store and help the sale of other goods. No home seems complete without a few pieces, new subjects of which are continually being turned out."

OLD FURNITURE

THE women are hunting for antique mahogany, old junk of that sort in our households is piled; the prices, once low are no longer toboggany, the higher they soar, as the women grow wild. Beds, for a century wobbly and rickety, dressers and chairs that are all on the blink; the owner of these is so proud and pernickety! She asks a big price, and we cough up the shink. Those creaking old beds that are wide and commodious, fitted with ropes as the old-fashioned slats! Always they seem to me wretched and odious, but when I say so, the women cry "Rats!" Bureaus so punk that they make a man serious, wapperjawed things, an offense to the eye, send the wild dames into spasms delirious: "Oh, what a sumptuous relic," they cry. How you would like to destroy all the furniture gathered from junk piles in country and towns! But if you heap it around you and burn it you're apt to retire with a dent in your crown. Rosewood, mahogany, walnut and fixtures, anything handed from ages of yore! Sadly I'm drinking my flagon of chicory, wishing the women were lucid once more.

WALT MASON.

Selling Furniture for Christmas Gifts

By WILLIAM G. COLGATE, of The Toronto Furniture Co., Ltd.

WHILE we do not in our own business specially emphasize such furniture items as might be considered suitable for Christmas gifts, believing that for retailer as well as manufacturer these are but a side issue, still we are ready to agree that from a sales standpoint the possibilities of the Christmas season as a business stimulator have been but barely realized as yet.

As a case in point, take music cabinets and sewing tables. Their practical utility, combined with their general attractiveness, appeal to almost everyone, and this in connection with their comparatively low cost should make them ready sellers amongst retailers of all classes.

To begin with, a retailer could take these or similar pieces, and, by gradually adding other articles of a like nature, such as curates, top-tilting tables, ladies' desks, serving trays, smokers' stands, and so on, could soon gather together a very respectable collection of gift furniture as would form a potent drawing card for his store. Altogether too few dealers make enough of the feature which enables them in some styles, notably period furniture, to sell individual pieces as well as complete sets. Imagine any alert jeweler forgetting to emphasize this advantage in connection with fine china or silver! Many a person might be induced to start a collection of the better class of furniture if he knew that he could add to it pieces of the same style from time to time. This point may seem rather irrelevant introduced here, but we feel that it has a bearing on the case, just the same.

In order to ensure continuity of interest in his gift department, the retailer could refer to it judiciously in his advertising, occasionally display it in his windows with appropriate window cards, and by sending out tactful, suggestive hints in the form of chatty, informative letters on the occasion of weddings, wedding anniversaries, birthdays, Christmas, etc., could make his gift furniture the centre of a good deal of interest. These are one or two ideas which have occurred to me. Doubtless the dealer himself will have thought of a great many more. But it all only serves to show what may be done in the gift department towards building up the general trade of the store when the retailer is willing to adopt measures that will bring customers to him instead of always waiting for them to take the initiative.

It marks the difference, in my opinion, between order taking and salesmanship. And that often means the difference between profit and loss.

WHAT OTHER MAKERS THINK

Furniture this year should be specially boosted, because people being in an economical state of mind, will buy necessities rather than luxuries for Xmas. In many cases family funds will be consolidated to buy a good piece of furniture. This has always been the case in off years. But unles the public first get a special invitation from the dealer, and, secondly, the dealer has the goods that are attractive, and a good selection, there will be no results.—H. W. Strudley, Imperial Rattan Co., Ltd., Stratford.

Musical Instruments and Talking Machines.

Graphophones and double disc records should fit in perfectly with the rest of the furniture dealer's line not only at the Christmas season, when they are particularly sought after, but throughout the year, and he can build up a profitable business with them, too. We feel that the furniture store is the logical place for the public to go and buy talking machines and records, and we think the furniture dealer is overlooking an excellent opportunity to increase business when he fails to put in these goods.—O. C. Dorian, Columbia Graphophone Co., Toronto.

Furniture Instead of Jewelry.

By virtue of the fact that the general money stringency has a tendency to make people consider the necessity around the home as Christmas gifts, furniture, rather than jewelry and other frivolities should be brought prominently before the purchasing public by the furniture dealer.—W. C. Willson, The Meaford Mfg. Co., Ltd., Meaford, Ont.

Display Beds in the Window.

A window display of a bedroom shown in a divided window, the arrangement of which might be in some

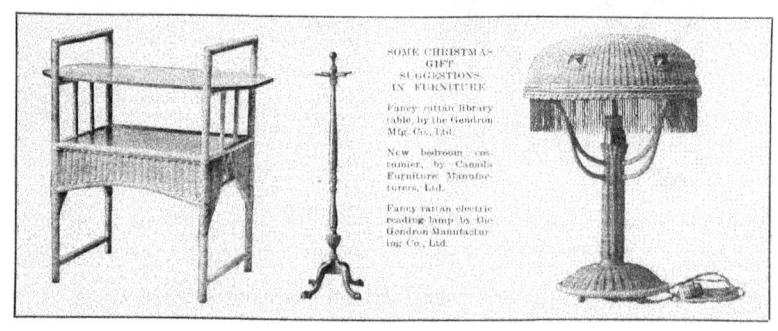

SOME CHRISTMAS GIFT SUGGESTIONS IN FURNITURE

Fancy rattan library table, by the Gendron Mfg. Co., Ltd.

New bedroom costumier, by Canada Furniture Manufacturers, Ltd.

Fancy rattan electric reading lamp by the Gendron Manufacturing Co., Ltd.

such manner as the following, should help Christmas furniture sales: In one part could be shown an outside winter scene, emphasizing coldness. In the other part could be shown a well furnished bedroom or sitting room, emphasizing comfort and illustrating articles of furniture which would make suitable gifts.

The emphasizing in advertising and displays of novelty items of furniture such as hat racks or divans as gifts for bachelor apartments, should also help in increasing furniture sales during the holiday season.—Fred A. Beckman, The Ideal Bedding Co., Ltd., Toronto.

Christmas Sales Methods

CONUNDRUM CONTEST TO PROVOKE SALES.

A large furniture store in Colorado ran a conundrum contest last year which lasted several months. Each week a coupon containing a conundrum was published in the newspapers and everyone was invited to send in solutions. The following is the announcement which was published:

"Until Christmas, we shall present each week one conundrum to be solved, fourteen in all. Some will be easy, some harder, but each has an answer.

No Buying is Necessary.

You may send in as many answers as you wish to each conundrum, but each conundrum must be accompanied by one of these coupons. This condition is positive. It will take just a few minutes each week. Worth trying, isn't it? The gifts will be delivered the day before Christmas, and the names and addresses of the lucky winners will be given in the newspapers on Christmas Day.

1st prize—To anyone solving all of the 14 conundrums correctly, we will give an elegant $200 parlor suite.

2nd prize—To anyone solving not less than 12 of the 14 conundrums correctly, we will give a handsome $125 buffet.

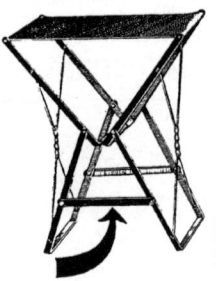

3rd prize—To anyone solving the largest number of conundrums less than twelve correctly, we will give an elegant $35 combination bookcase.

4th prize—To anyone answering the next largest number of conundrums less than twelve, we will give the choice of any $15 article in the house.

In case of a tie for any prize, the answer received first will, of course, win.

Smaller prices can be given and still net good returns.

Christmas gift suggestion: Folding chair for automobiles, made by The Ideal Bedding Co., Ltd., showing opened and closed.

EXTRA SALES FORCE ADVERTISES STORE.

A Southern merchant's extra sales force at Christmas was organized into a strong advertising department for the store. For several weeks prior to the opening of his Christmas selling season this merchant advertised for extra clerks. By December first he had engaged eight young men and women from farm families in his vicinity. It was quite a treat for these young people to get into the store for a time, and they entered upon the work with great enthusiasm.

The day the extra clerks got on the job the merchant had circulars ready which he asked them to address to their friends. He was astonished to see the liberal response these friends made to the appeal to come and buy holiday goods of the clerk who signed the circular.

POPULAR SALES PREMIUM.

A Washington, D.C., furniture concern recently put on a sales inducement feature consisting of a United States flag 4 x 6 feet, complete with pole, halyard and bracket, as a premium with a $5 purchase. Here is an idea that should prove exceedingly popular with Canadian furniture dealers who, around the holiday season, give premiums to induce sales. A Union Jack gift should take well at present.

DOLL CONTEST FOR GIRLS.

Make a store or window display of dolls, having as the central figure a large doll holding a good sized character doll dressed in infant's long clothes. The effect can be heightened by the use of doll furniture. The idea is to make a home scene.

The large doll can be seated at a table, or a living room scene can be made. A pleasing effect would be to work out the scene inside a small house. The roof should have a gable and be covered with cotton batting, sprinkled with artificial snow. The snow could be distributed through the window to represent a typical winter scene.

Interest in the display can be increased by having some prominent person select a name for the infant. The name should be deposited in an envelope in a safe place. Due publicity should be given this fact, together with an offer of a prize to the girl guessing the infant's name or a name nearest to it. One guess can be allowed with each purchase of Christmas merchandise in any amount you want to indicate.

Register the names and addresses of all the contestants, together with the date and hour they made the guess. On Christmas Eve, or whatever hour you choose, have the person who named the infant announce the name. Then have him read from the record the guesses on the name in the order they were made. The one making the first correct guess gets first prize. Continue the reading until all making a correct guess get prizes. Circularize all names received for furniture business at an early date thereafter.

SANTA CLAUS IN THE WINDOW—HOW THE FURNITURE STORE IN THE SMALL TOWN CAN MAKE A HOLIDAY DISPLAY. WINDOW TRIM MADE BY J. LETTER & SON, WATERLOO, ONT., LAST CHRISTMAS.

The Importance of the Christmas Window Display

CHRISTMAS show windows will give passersby a good or bad impression of you and your institution, so that it is most important that care and thought be given to these windows, and especially at Christmas time.

Five or ten dollars, carefully spent, some thought and some work are all that you need with the many things that are already in the store.

What to Display

Remember that practically all the Christmas gifts that will be bought are either received by or purchased

Canadian Furniture
for
Canadian Homes

Suggestion for a window card.

by women, so that it is well to bear this fact in mind in making the display.

Another thing. When people go out to buy presents they usually have no idea of what they are going to get, but look into the windows and when something appeals to them they go inside and buy. Further, the chances are that there will be other things in the store itself that will appeal to them and which they will purchase.

The great question is, of course, how to do it. The following suggestions are given in the hope that they will be of assistance to some dealers in planning their windows.

Use Price Cards.

If you use them at no other time of year, Christmas is when you should use price cards in the windows. Most any wholesale paper house can supply such cards, 2¼ by 3¼ inches, printed in three colors, with a pretty holly design around the edges, for $1.50 per 100. People want to know what a thing costs at Christmas time, more so, perhaps, than is usually the case. Not only this, but the cards mentioned will brighten up the window wonderfully.

The Christmas idea can be well conveyed by the liberal use of evergreens and holly in the back and sides of the windows, which should first be covered with white or red crepe paper tacked in place. Red bells suspended from the ceiling will add to the effect. If you want to you can get Christmas trees and put them at each end of the back of the window and hang on them various decorations.

Three Parts

Then divide your window up into three parts. Commence to dress the centre one first, by putting some good sized articles in the middle, and then fill out the remainder with smaller articles, trying always to preserve the balance one side with the other.

Treat the two other divisions similarly, with a larger article in the centre of each, and group around it goods of kindred lines. It might be well to have large show cards written, with the legends: "Useful Presents for Father, Brother, Uncle," etc. "Useful Presents for Mother, Sister, Aunt," etc. "Useful Presents for the Children," and place in each division appropriate gifts.

Just a word of caution. Do not try to get too many articles in the window. If you crowd them, all the display effect is lost, and all you will get is a "hodge-podge" without form or balance.

This matter of balance is really important in getting a good general effect. It attracts the eye, and after attracting, it pleases, so that the selling value of the window is increased.

MAKE YOUR WINDOWS SAY SOMETHING

A window trimmer had put the finishing touches on a very artistic and attractive window display of bookcases, and as was his custom, called the Boss to give

Simple background suggestion for a Christmas furniture window trim—Wallboard (colored) with holly trimmings.

it the final "Okay." After viewing the window from several angles and distances, the Boss said, "Young man, that window is pretty, it is altogether charming, but—what is it all about? You have a fine display of merchandise there and you have your window nicely spotted with color to arrest attention, but after you get the people's attention what is going to make them buy except their own desires?

"A window display can be likened to an illustration," proceeded the Boss, warming up to the subject, "which attracts attention but needs text matter to make its use profitable. Right there, my son, is the fault of this window display—of most window displays, in fact, those of other merchants as well as of ours. They don't contain enough reading matter—don't make use of the attention they have won, to put over a good selling punch. Take this window, for instance, all that it needs is a large card neatly lettered with thirty or forty well chosen words describing the advantages of sectional construction of your bookcases to make it of real selling value. Another small card inviting the people into the store to see the bookcases demonstrated would add further to its selling strength. Nine out of ten window displays could be greatly increased in selling efficiency with the addition of one or two neatly lettered cards relative to the goods on display," continued the Boss.

"Will people read the cards?" inquired the window trimmer.

The Boss answered this query with another, "Do you know how many words the average person ordinarily reads in a minute? Between two and three hundred. From this you can understand that a show card of thirty or forty words would be read at a glance. Of course people will read your show cards. They can't help reading them if they are invitingly lettered."

The window trimmer who did the listening was a good listener. He has utilized the card idea in nearly every window he has trimmed since, and every one of those windows has proved that the Boss was right. Nine out of ten windows can be improved with the addition of a well chosen and worded card relative to their merchandise.

HOLIDAY DECORATING WITH CREPE PAPER

Crepe paper is the window trimmer's best friend in Christmas displays. It helps him out of many a dilemma. When he is in doubt as to what to use for a window or store display, he is pretty safe if he makes the answer crepe paper. It takes something more than crepe paper, however, to get results from it in any kind of a display. A great many trimmers pin crepe paper on carelessly and when they do not get good results, wonder why it is.

To get the best results out of crepe paper you will have to understand the methods of handling it. You often want to use a strip of crepe paper with a ruffled edge. The way to obtain this ruffled edge is shown in Fig. 1 of accompanying illustration. Merely hold the paper between the thumb and forefinger of each hand and pull out the crepe.

To obtain a border of ruffled strips, cut strips of crepe paper of two colors; light and dark. Make the light strip five inches wide and the dark strip three inches wide. Ruffle both edges of each strip. Place the narrow strip over the wide one and fasten in the centre with a cord of twisted crepe paper made out of the light color. The method of making this cord is

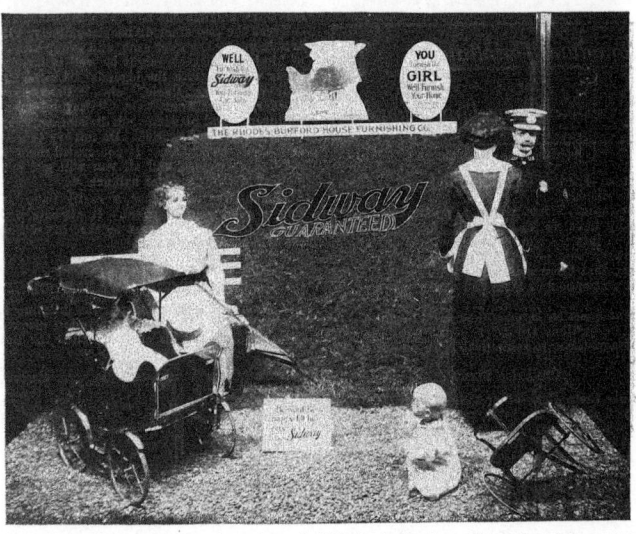

Window display of Sidway collapsible carriage made by a Louisville, Ky., furniture house which won first prize in a contest recently conducted by the Sidway Mercantile Co., Elkhart, Ind. The display is simple, yet striking and convincing.

shown in the figure below the accompanying background drawing.

A ruching border is much used. To produce this cut the crepe paper in strips about 10 inches wide. Ruffle both edges. Then fold in the centre as indicated by the dotted line, in figure three. Make three or four small

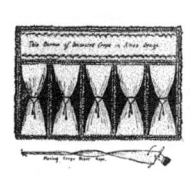

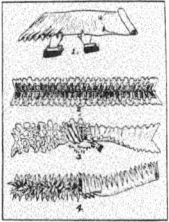

Illustrations showing how crepe paper can be used in holiday decorating.

plaits on this folded edge and pin to the border. Move along the border about four inches. Then make another bunch of plaits and pin, and continue along the whole length of the border. Spread out the edges in wide ruching as shown at the left of the figure.

Still another crepe paper effect is shown by the scissored edge in figure four. To obtain this fold a full width of crepe paper down through the centre. Then cut with scissors from the edges almost down to the centre, leaving the ends pointed. Gather in plaits and pin along the border the same as in figure three. Pin these plaits close enough together.

For the background use decorated crepe paper of holly leaf pattern along the top. Santa Claus faces or Christmas bells can be cut out and pasted along the border, in place of the wording that appears in our drawing. Below this pin strips of red crepe paper smoothly to the background. Over each strip of the red place a layer of white and gather these strips in at the centre and tie with a crepe paper cord, the making of which is illustrated below the background. To make this cord take long strips of crepe paper 10 inches wide, looping it back so as to have a double layer. Put a stick in the end of the loop. Fasten the ends to a nail and then twist the paper around until it is wound up into a rope about an inch in diameter.

Then put a border all around the window and between the strips of red. Do this by cutting white paper into three-inch strips and ruffling both edges. Fasten this to the wall by placing the crepe paper cord down through the centre of each strip and pinning it.

SELLING THE PRACTICAL GIFTS

Let us not forget the practical gifts of this season. The tendency of the public to purchase useful articles for gift purposes tends toward larger and more satisfactory sales, if catered to. While it will pay to push the specialties, and the more distinctly gift lines, let your windows show the practical, useful and staples with holiday "trimmings." Take a number of the larger pieces, the ladies' desks, the reclining chairs and rockers, the library tables and music cabinets, feature these in the windows with appropriate cards, calling specific attention to their desirability as gifts.

Everyone appreciates receiving a gift of a lasting, worth-while nature, and there is nothing more satisfying than a nice piece of furniture. While it has an individual appeal and charm, still it has a practical use for others than the recipient. There is the added value of general utility, and for this reason a larger sum will be invested in such presents than in some of the "little things."

In the store use gift cards freely on the entire stock. Even base burners have been given as gifts, and by keeping the Christmas spirit predominant throughout the store there will be many a sale for just gift purposes that would otherwise slide by.

Keep in mind that the Christmas shopper comes past your store often. Holiday buying means many a visit "down-town," and every time the man or woman, on Christmas buying bent, passes your windows they will be mentally comparing your lines and stock with others. They will be cataloging, in their mind's eye, the gift for this or that person, and if the windows are not frequently changed, you will lose out, for what might appeal to-day to one would fail to pull the other passerby. And by making use of the practical gifts, of larger value, you will be covering all channels and land the bulk of the trade.

USE PRICE TICKETS

We observe that in a very real sense the use or non-use of price tickets is the distinguishing mark between the coming and the going merchant.

Not that price tickets alone can bring back youth to a decrepit store, but when a man begins to use price tickets he naturally does the other things that make for good merchandising.

Price tickets sell goods—they sell goods—they sell goods.

An article without a price ticket will win attention only from the person who is in urgent need of that par-

Canadian furniture in New York—Window display of new Louis XII. bedroom suite in antique ivory with Wedgwood trimmings made by Toronto Furniture Co., in store of Joseph L. Herschmann, Sixth Ave.

ticular thing at that particular time. With a price ticket it will get attention from ten times as many people.

Price tickets make selling easy. Often all the clerk need do is wrap the article up and make change. With goods price-ticketed, clerks show larger daily sales, which means a smaller ratio of selling expense.

The mental attitude of the buyer is always defensive. No matter how tempting an article looks, if the price is not marked, desire is seldom strong enough to overcome the mental inertia. Price tickets make the law of suggestion work for, not against, you.

Canada imports more furniture from the United States than any other country in the world. The value of these goods for the past three (fiscal) years are: 1912, $1,092,869; 1913, $1,877,478; 1914, $1,479,319.

Collins' Course in Show Card Writing

Thirteenth of a series of articles specially prepared for this journal.

VERY attractive cards can be made with a part or the whole of the centre made transparent. The object of cards of this nature is to show at night with a light behind them. One effective way is to cut out the letters with a sharp knife and on the reverse side of the card paste brilliantly colored tissue paper. Letters like A B P R, etc., will require the centre pieces pasted on to the tissue paper after the latter has been pasted on to the back of the card. Another method is to stretch tracing or draftsman's linen or glazed signwriter's cotton on to a frame or card mat and letter on this material. This will mean that the background and not the letters will be illuminated when the sign is lighted. If electric lights are available, colored bulbs may be utilized to good advantage. Sheet celluloid may be used instead of cotton or linen. The transparent sign may be used for the sides of windows or the corners, and put next to the glass on the casing. They will then show at night as well as during the day time.

Another very attractive card of a similar character may be made by cutting the letter of a word out of cardboard, or a cut of a figure of a hat, suit, shoes, etc., then cut an oval opening or some attractive shape and paste on the back of the card a piece of black or dark brown fine threaded netting with about a one-sixteenth mesh. On to this netting, in the opening, paste the picture you have cut out. When the card is placed in position the netting is almost invisible, which gives the article or picture pasted on the appearance of being suspended in the air.

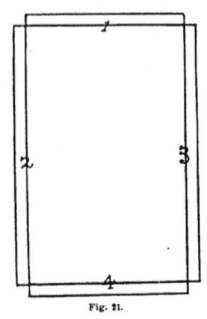

Paper Borders.

Very artistic effects may be had with cards by using wallpaper borders for the edges. These should be used only on large cards, half sheets and whole sheets. Narrow borders from one to two inches are the best widths and should be mitred at the corners. The lettering should be done in colors to harmonize with the borders.

Mounting Cards.

Cards that are mounted keep their shape, and do not curl nor fall over the same as when unmounted. One way to do this is to make wooden stretchers out of half-inch by one or one and a half inch wood. Mitre these at the corners and glue and nail together. When ready for the cards, give the top of stretcher a coat of glue. Then dampen the back of the card with a sponge or cloth and glue around the edge of card and press it on to the stretcher. Unless the card is moistened all over with water it will not lie smooth on the stretcher. After it is dry paste a border of plain green or other colored paper around the edge, allowing it to come over the face of the card, about a half or three-quarters of an inch, and lap around the edge to cover the wooden frame.

Another way to "mount" or stiffen cards is to score them about three-quarters of an inch from the edges, see 1, 2, 3, 4, Fig. 21, and turn the edges back the same as a box cover. This will necessitate cutting out a three-quarter inch square at each corner to allow the sides and ends to turn back. After turning back, paste or glue a small piece of cotton on the corners to hold them in position. Then paste a border on the edge the same as directed for the wooden stretcher. The "scoring" is done by cutting the card not quite half through

Fig. 21.

Plate 47—Fancy full block, with outline, upper case.

on the top or face side with a sharp knife. This prevents the card from breaking when you bend it back.

Pastes and Glues.

As every card writer needs paste or glue almost constantly, it is well to know how to make them. A superior paste can be made of starch. This is made the same as a laundress makes it for the clothes, only much thicker. First dissolve the starch with cold water, to remove all lumps, then pour boiling water on it, stirring all the time. A little alum water added to this or a few drops of oil of cloves will keep it for weeks from spoiling.

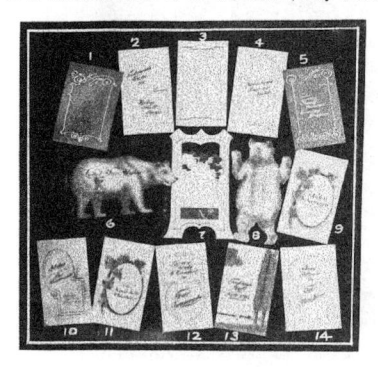

A good liquid glue can be made by dissolving a fine grade of white glue, or fish glue, in vinegar, instead of water, for at least twelve hours. Then heat it in a double boiler or glue pot until thoroughly mixed. Add a few drops of oil of cloves to keep it. This glue can be made to use cold by thinning with white wine vinegar. Use no water.

Sample Cards.

The Santa Claus card is one appropriate for the Christmas season. It is a fountain air brush design, requiring two patterns to execute it. One is a round ring and the other is a piece cut out the shape of old Santa's head and beard. Lay the pattern of the head on the card and the ring on top of it. The beard of Santa will project below the ring or circle. Air brush around the circle and the beard, then take off the pattern of the circle and allow the other pattern to remain in its place, and air brush around it inside the circle. Now finish the features by hand. The face can be flesh color and the top of the cap and tassel a bright red. The fur around the cap may be almost any fur color. You can get a quicker and even better result with a card of this type if you can get a picture or litho of old Santa and cut it out. In that case you will not need a pattern. Simply lay the picture on the card and mark around it with a pencil and air brush over the pencil marks. It will not matter if you go inside the pencil marks for the picture will cover it when it is pasted on to the card. You will have to lay a piece of paper over the beard where it projects below the circle, so you will not air brush the beard.

In the group of cards, Nos. 6 and 8 are entirely fountain air brush work, and give some idea of the wide range of work that can be accomplished with this splendid assistant of the card writer. Nos. 9, 11 and 13 and the leaves on No. 7, are also air brush designs, and further illustrate the wide range of work that can be done with it. Nos. 1 to 5 and 7, 8, 12 and 14 have plastic work on them. No. 7 is an example of an openwork design and will give some idea of how a transparent design can be made.

Plate 16—Fancy full block with outline, lower case.

PATENTED MACHINE WHICH MAKES THE FABRIC. A MASTERPIECE OF MECHANICAL ENGINEERING, FOR THE WIRE GOES IN AT ONE END AND THE COMPLETE FABRIC FOR A BED COMES OUT AT THE OTHER. THIS IS ONE OF THE MOST INTERESTING DEPARTMENTS IN THE PLANT.

Making Ideal Twisted Link Fabric

By G. L. G.

The pages of commercial history are filled with instances that relate of how certain men, makers of great discoveries, did not at first realize the importance of their "finds," until an outside, though interested, party commenced to point out their value.

We have recently pased through a like experience. First. in the development of the Ideal twisted link fabric. Second, with the super-development of the twisted link fabric into an Ideal duplex link fabric spring.

In common with all makers of bed springs, we have been striving for years to devise some type of spring that would overcome, or entirely eliminate the disadvantages of a continuous wire fabric spring. The first step in this direction was the discovery and perfecting of the Ideal double wire twisted link fabric. We found that by cutting our wire into sections 4 ins. long, and forming them into links of double thickness, joining them together in "twist" fashion, with a separate strand every two inches of the width joined by separate cross links, we secured a fabric that was by itself strong, resilient and elastic.

Then, by the process of joining up the completed fabric to the frame at both ends by a series of powerful, oil-tempered steel helical springs, we found that we had a spring that was stronger thany any continuous wire spring that we knew of. And when we proved by experiment that all danger of sagging in the fabric was eliminated, owing to the weight of the wire used in the links, and the fact that the powerful steel helical springs absorbed all the strain, we placed the spring upon the market.

We learned from experience that this spring never gave any trouble. There were never any complaints about it sagging. In fact, it was reckoned one of the strongest, most pliable and elastic bed springs on the market—for it is practically unbreakable and indestructible, and is an admirable shipping proposition, because holes cannot be punched into it anywhere.

Thus, briefly, you have the story of the development

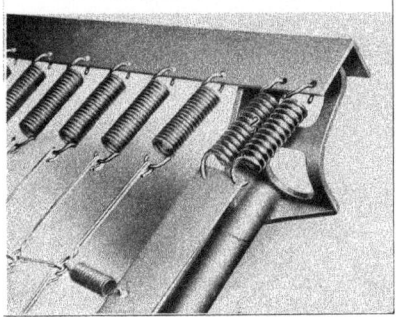

Angle and piece of Ideal twisted link fabric spring.

of the ordinary type of Ideal twisted link fabric spring.

About a year ago, we took our line of springs and commenced to experiment with a view to finding out how it would be possible to make them better without increasing the price. We spent some months and quite a little money on experiments. Finally, we evolved what we have called—and we think it is a very happy name—the Ideal duplex spring; the "spring with a backbone."

GEO. GALE & SONS' STAFF DINED

On Friday evening, Nov. 6th, the management of Geo. Gale & Sons, Ltd., Waterville, Que., gave a dinner to the staff at Riverdale Hotel, that city, covers being laid for 40. The spacious dining room was specially bedecked for the occasion, and a very generous menu was on hand, and if Russia can expedite the departure of Turkey from the map of Europe any faster than the way the staff gobbled him up, she will want to put on her skates.

W. H. Ward, vice-president and managing director, presided, and other specially invited guests were: F. R. Cromwell, M.P.; J. T. Thomas, and Peter Swanson. The toasts of the evening were: The King, Our Country, Our Guests, and Our Customers.

Mr. Ward, in his introductory remarks, said that most of the staff present had practically grown up with the firm and had been on their pay roll 20 to 25 years. He hoped the staff would have a good night and enjoy themselves thoroughly, and announced that the management would make this dinner an annual affair, which was greatly appreciated by those present. He was glad to see the firm's trade mark on the wall, with the famous guarantee, and hoped those present would look after the guarantee and see that it was kept up. He appealed to the staff to work together and pull together and everything would right itself. He then proposed the toast to the King, which was drunk with silent honors.

H. E. Sprigings, secretary-treasurer of the firm, proposed the toast of Our Country, and in an excellent speech extolled Canada as the premier colony of the British Empire, whose loyalty to the Mother Country was evidenced by the fact that we had just sent across 35,000 of our bravest sons to fight for the honor and freedom of the Empire. Continuing, he said Canada was the greatest wheat growing country in the world, and spoke of the unlimited mineral resources of Nova Scotia, Quebec and British Columbia, which made Canada practically independent and self-contained.

The toast was responded to by F. R. Cromwell, M.P., and Geo. A. Symons. Mr. Cromwell advised the audience to pay far more attention to agricultural pursuits, as they could not grow enough and the demand was greater than the supply. He instanced the fact that they had an agricultural demonstrator from Macdonald College, and that the farmers were delighted with the effect produced. He said that brains were necessary now more than ever, in order to manufacture at less cost to compete and keep up with the hard times. He then passed on to the war and in a masterly way showed what Canada was doing to help out the Mother Country.

Geo. A. Symons, who also responded, congratulated the management on giving unmistaken signs that they were going to take an interest in the men, and just as the best machinery needs oil to make the cogs work together smoothly so with human beings. The more interest a company takes in the men the better the results and the lesser the friction. He then replied to the toast after the fashion of the last speaker and gave statistics showing the vast mineral and grain wealth of the Dominion, and felt sure that Canada would emerge from the present financial depression and become a pillar of wealth, loyalty and devotion and the strong right hand of the British Empire.

Have a Nifty Trade Mark

The president, in proposing "Our Guests," said he had great pleasure in doing so and that he felt sure this gathering would produce beneficial results which would make better citizens, and help them to take a new interest in their work. He dwelt on the fact that they had a very nifty trade mark, and to keep up with the guarantee they would have to turn out very nifty goods. The new era called for greater efficiency and as the trade mark compelled them to turn out the right goods they would have to use more brain power than ever to keep up with the times. He said they had a particularly attractive town and their aim should be to make it a city. He was greatly cheered by the audience when he announced the fact that he would present a silver challenge cup to be competed for by the different departments of the factory at hockey, as all work and no play makes Jack a dull boy. His encouraging speech and reassuring remarks greatly stirred the staff present. This toast was responded to

Display of beds and parts made by Ontario Furniture Co., London, during Old Boys' Week. The company had just secured the order for furnishing the Tecumseh House addition and during the whole week The Ontario Spring Bed & Mattress Co., had men in this window putting together fifty brass beds. In their other windows the same firm had their men making fifty box springs and fifty hair mattresses. Needless to say great crowds watched the windows all week.

by Messrs. R. J. Walsh, superintendent; H. W. Fowler, and Jack Wood, who spoke in a similar vein and exhorted the men to make a special effort these bad times to turn out the best goods at the least cost, and to co-operate in every way so that the firm would come through this great financial depression with every credit.

The last toast, "Our Customers," was proposed by F. W. Bean, who is recognized in the trade as a clever, "slick" salesman. He spoke of how delighted his customers were with the new goods and of the prompt delivery that now prevailed, and spoke in a very optimistic manner of the company's future. This toast was ably responded to by Peter Swanson, who has done business with the firm since its inauguration and declared he had no kick coming and spoke of his delight at being there with the staff on that festive occasion.

J. T. Thomas, manager Bank of Commerce, replied and commented on the fact that he was a good customer of the firm, as the bank has to keep their accounts in fine shape. He was hopeful of good times coming. He said that Canada could not be held back and that we would live to see it one of the foremost nations of the world.

The musical part of the program was in good hands. Two very fine quartettes entitled "Sweet and Low" and "Far Away" were sung with great success by Messrs. Ward, Brodie, Johnston and Colbert. A duet, "Larboard Watch," was sung by Messrs. Brodie and Johnston with rare good feeling. Solo, "In Cellar Cool," was sun by L. Colbert in excellent taste; so was also "It's a Long Way to Tipperary" by Harry Bray. G. A. Symons, who supplied the comic element, brought down the house with a local rendering of Macnamara's Band, and for an encore gave "Phil the Fluter's Ball," which brought forth roars of laughter.

A final vote of thanks to W. H. Ward, for presiding, also to Frank P. Turville and A. Gowan, the auditors who were present and helped the entertainment out, was passed unanimously, and these gentlemen replied and thanked the management for the very pleasant evening they enjoyed and wished the firm every success.

FIRE IN WESTERN BED PLANT.

Fire in the Stamco Bedding Company's warehouse at Regina recently did between $5,000 and $6,000 damage, through fire, water and smoke. The cause of the fire is not known, but it started in a pile of excelsior on the second floor of the building, and before long the whole ceiling was a mass of flames. A. J. McEvoy, manager of the Stamco Company, and his little boy, were in the building at the time of the fire, but on account of the combustible nature of the material in which the fire started, the flames made great headway before the firemen arrived. It is understood that the company carries about $20,000 insurance on building and stock. The warehouse is a two-storey brick building, well built, and the fire made the greatest progress in the ceiling through which it made its way and played great havoc between the ceiling and the roof, before it could be reached. While the building was badly burned, a large percentage of the damage was done by water and smoke, ruining the stock. There was on hand at the time of the fire quite a quantity of mattresses and bedding.

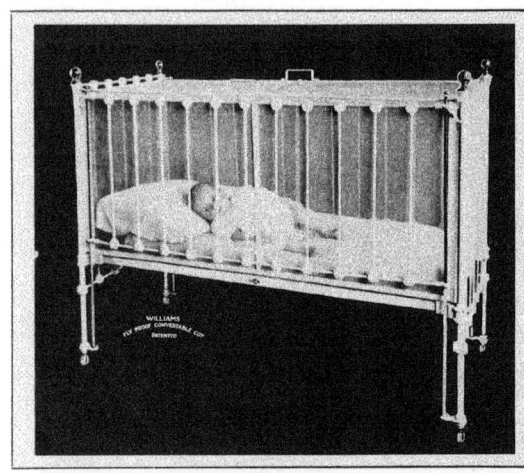

Newest thing in beds—patented fly-proof convertible cot, the invention of T. K. Williams, Winnipeg. The cot has drop sides, and the screens are removable, making it like any other baby's cot. The cot is made in a size that can be taken through any door. The inventor, by the ingenious use of simple principles, has obtained a cot which has the ordinary appearance, but can be readily and easily converted into one adapted for outdoor use. It is said to be recommended by both doctors and nurses as being perfectly sanitary and doing away with all dangers from those well recognized sources of most infantile summer complaints—the dirty, disease-spreading house fly and the blood-poisoning mosquito.

NEW WIRE SPRING MATTRESS.

To the already extensive "Ideal" line has now been added a wire spring mattress called the "Soft-Nap Inner Spring Mattress," for the making and sale of which in Canada the rights have been obtained by the Ideal Bedding Co., Ltd. The materials entering into the make-up of this mattress are best quality, highly tempered steel coil springs, specially woven in fabrics for encasing springs, best cotton felt and sterilized curled South American horse hair, and best fancy stripe and art ticking. Every section of the mattress is built by experienced workmen, and every mattress is thoroughly inspected before leaving the factory.

The mattress is made with a centre of 247 steel coil springs, each encased in a specially heavy double fabric pocket, with top and bottom made to fit snugly over the base of each spring, and without any rigid fastening, so that each works independently without coming in contact with the others, insuring freedom from noise and rendering it impossible for the springs to get out of order, or become disarranged. In the edges are gauze-covered ventilators which permit of interior circulation of air. Besides being noiseless, the "Soft-Nap" is comfortable, sanitary and is fully guaranteed.

PROMOTED TO SALES MANAGER.

The Ideal Bedding Co., Ltd., Toronto, have promoted one of the tried employes to the sales managership of the company. He is R. H. Browne, and he was manager of the Winnipeg branch. Mr. Browne made such a success in the Western field that he was brought East and

R. H. BROWNE, the Ideal Bedding Co's new sales manager.

made sales manager of the whole organization.

Those who know Mr. Browne will concur in the opinion that there is no better posted man on beds and bedding than he, for he brings to his position nearly twenty years' experience in the trade. From all accounts, Mr. Browne is becoming as popular in the East as he was, and still is, in the West—which is very gratifying to his friends and well-wishers everywhere.

MERSEREAU COMPANY BRANCHING OUT.

The Canadian Mersereau Co. have, during the past month, added three new articles to their line, and these are the first of a number of goods that will be made in addition to their regular bed lines. These articles are the "Oxford Sofa Bed," the "Harold Cot," and an "All-Iron Cot." All these goods are patented this year, and the Canadian Mersereau Co. hold the Canadian manufacturing rights.

Of the "Oxford Sofa Bed" already there is evidence that it is destined to be a good seller. It is a convertible sofa bed which a child can operate with one motion. It is a well-made, full length bed, always ready for use either as bed or sofa. It does not need adjusting, is sanitary, simple, attractive and comfortable. It has a steel frame with padded convertible mattress seat.

The "Harold Cot" is a folding cot which closes up into small space, to be put away in a corner or clothes closet out of sight, yet is always ready for use. It has a steel frame, and canvas top attached to frame with steel springs. It is made for home or camp use.

The "All-Iron Cot" is, as its name indicates, an iron framed cot with woven fabric springs. It, too, is a folding cot, made to sell a little cheaper than the "Harold." It has strength and neatness as predominating features.

WHY NOT IN CANADA TOO?

"Sell-a-Bale of mattresses" should be the slogan of the manufacturers in reply to the cry "Buy-a-Bale of Cotton." And the buying should not stop with one bale. Opportunity presents for the selling of many bales.—Furniture Manufacturer and Artisan.

BEDDING NOTES.

The Quality Mattress Co., with head office and factory at Waterloo, Ont., have opened up a branch factory and warehouse at 31-33 Front street east, Toronto.

The Alaska Western Bedding Co.'s plant at Calgary covers a total floor space of over 25,000 square feet. It has a manufacturing capacity of 45,000 mattresses and 30,000 springs annually.

A fire which broke out in the Toronto storeroom of the Gold Medal Furniture Co. a few nights ago, caused damage of $3,000 to the contents of the room. The loss is fully covered by insurance. The building was not damaged.

WARRING NATIONS BUYING AMERICAN HIDES

The Wall Street Journal in a recent issue notes a sharp advance in the price of hides. This is due, we are told, to the demand of European nations for grades of leather suited to saddlery and other articles of war equipment. It is apparent that the domestic supply of leather for upholstery and other purposes will be reduced materially by this big increase in the exportation of hides.

Shipment of the hides in their entirety—that is, without subjecting them to splitting processes—makes a very decided inroad on the stock of split leathers used by manufacturers of upholstered products, or any requiring split leathers. How much the American domestic leather supply is affected by the increased exportation of entire hides cannot be determined at a moment's estimation. It is sufficient to say that for every hide exported that are removed from the American split leather market at least two splits or sides. Obviously, the exportation of hides is developing a demand for artificial leather.

It may not be generally known that the various "splits" from an animal's hide are processed in a way that places them in the artificial class. The coating applied to the fleshy splits to give them strength and a surface for graining is very similar to the solution spread by mechanical means on the cloth backing of the best grades of artificial leather familiar to the trade and public by extensive advertising campaigns.

Three Canadian Furniture Exhibitions in January

IT is contemplated that there will be three Canadian furniture exhibitions in January, 1915, the same as last January—at Toronto, Berlin and Stratford. The decisions arrived at speak volumes for the furniture trade of the country, despite the pessimistic feeling due to the outbreak of the European war.

At Berlin a combined showing will be made of the latest productions of the Berlin and Waterloo furniture factories. This will be their fourth annual exhibition, and it speaks well for the Berlin pioneers in the exhibition field to know that the idea has given an impetus to other centres. Details of the exhibition are at present being worked out, and a full program of arrangements will appear in the next issue of Canadian Furniture World.

Commencing Monday, January 11, and continuing throughout the week, Berlin, Waterloo and outside factories are joining hands to make the coming exhibition the best yet. The main display will be held in the large factory building on Queen Street South. No effort will be spared to make the stay of visitors profitable and pleasant. J. P. Scully is secretary again this year, which means that everything will be conducted right up to the handle.

At Stratford the new factories which have been added to the furniture industry in that centre during the year will exhibit their goods for the first time, and will help complete the line of furniture for which the Classic City is famous. As at Berlin, details are in the shaping, and the program will be given later.

The Stratford furniture manufacturers intend using a large new addition to the Stratford Chair Co.'s plant for their January exhibition. Floor space of 50,000 square feet is available for display purposes, and it is the intention of all the manufacturers to attempt to make the coming exhibition, both in volume of goods shown and the number of new patterns displayed, the finest that has ever been held in Stratford or any other place in Canada.

Toronto Furniture Exhibition in January

It has been decided to hold a furniture exhibition in Toronto again, and while the exact dates are not yet set, it is likely the third and fourth weeks in January, 1915, will be the dates chosen for the second annual furniture show.

The Gregg building, at 44 York street, has been secured. It is a large, seven-storey brick building, in the down town business section, within a few minutes' walking distance of the railway station and all the hotels.

A meeting of the exhibition officers was held in the Prince George Hotel, Toronto, on November 12, to discuss details in connection with the exhibition, and also to allot space, at which the following furniture manufacturers were present:

H. B. Smith, North American Furn. Co., Owen Sound; S. M. Smyth, Strathroy Furn. Co., Strathroy; J. C. Mundell, Elora; C. M. Bell, Southampton; George Gibbard, Napanee; J. W. Abbott, Kindel Bed Co., Toronto; J. Souter, Malcolm & Souter, Hamilton; James Malcolm, Kincardine; F. E. Coombe, Kincardine; C. A. Gruetzner, Hespeler Furn. Co., Hespeler; and W. C. Willson, Geo. Graham, and J. Montgomery, of the Meaford Furn. Co.

James Malcolm was chairman of the meeting and H. B. Smith acted as secretary pro tem. When a vote was taken, everyone present was in favor of going ahead with the exhibition.

W. J. Craig, Toronto, was appointed secretary of the association, and he will look after all correspondence.

A general committee was formed consisting of the manufacturers present, with James Malcolm, of Kincardine, as chairman. The secretary, along with Mr. Abbott, of the Kindel Bed Co., and Mr. Souter, of Hamilton, were appointed a committee to look after the arrangements of the building, and to allot space.

H. B. Smith, of the North American Furn. Co., and Mr. Willson, of the Meaford Furn. Co., were appointed to make transportation arrangements.

When the manufacturers were asked what space they would require, those present offered to take the whole building, but agreed to reduce their space sufficiently to allow other manufacturers, who were not present, to come in, so that any manufacturer wanting space would do well to make application to Mr. Craig at as early a date as possible.

It is the intention of the manufacturers as a whole to exhibit mostly new patterns and medium-priced goods, and the trade will have an opportunity this coming January of seeing the finest productions of the Canadian factories under the most favorable circumstances, in a building which is perfectly heated and lighted, which has a fine elevator service, and is within a stone throw of the leading hotels.

Some of the representatives of the different firms present, who spoke very favorably of the exhibition idea, assured the meeting that the trade appreciated a first class exhibition, and that there would likely be a good attendance from all parts of the country.

CLASSIC FURNITURE FACTORY BURNED

Fire, thought to have originated in the shellac room, completely destroyed the Classic Furniture Company's factory at Stratford, on November 12. The loss is estimated at $30,000.

Supt. Mitchell had been in the factory up to 8.30, and the night watchman was on duty. Nevertheless, when discovered about 9 o'clock the fire had gained great headway in the finishing room and an east wind drove the flames back into the heart of the building.

The large stock was destroyed, this constituting the greatest loss. It is understood that the building was partly insured. The city power line passes just behind the factory from the Hydro sub-station, and for a time the city was in darkness.

The Classic Furniture, Limited, is one of Stratford's newest industrial concerns. Established but a couple of years ago, it has attained a wide reputation for the excellence of its products, which are chiefly boudoir furniture. George McLagan holds the controlling interest in the company. Julian Davies was manager. The employes were working 45 and 60 hours a week.

The management acted quickly, and before the embers were cold, had leased the premises until lately occupied by Stratford Desks, Ltd.—a building entirely equipped for furniture making—where already they are making Classic furniture. The showrooms of the Classic factory were saved, and arrangements are being made to have a complete Classic line on exhibition in January next.

Furniture Men at the Front

We publish, through the courtesy of Canada Furniture Manufacturers, Ltd., the portraits of three well known Canadian furniture men who have gone to the war's front in Europe to participate in the Empire's cause.

J. F. Nevile, of Wapella, Sask., is one of these. Having passed through the South African Campaign,

J. F. NEVILE, Wapella, Sask.

and being the proud possessor of five bars for the various engagements in which he took part, it is not likely that the husky looking soldier on the horse will be "gun shy" when he reaches the firing line. Mr. Nevile was "right on the job" when the call came for volunteers, and at present writing is in camp at Salisbury Plains, England. As before stated, Mr. Nevile is no amateur at the game, having, besides his own experience in active service, generations of Eng-

E. B. CLEGG, Peterboro.

lish fighting stock behind him, and, as he expressed it himself in a letter to a friend, is anxious to get to the front, where there is "something doing."

Mr. Nevile was one of the fortunate ones who came through the South African campaign unhurt, but has seen his comrades dropping around him, and has experienced many close calls himself, on one occasion having his horse shot from under him, so the sound of whistling bullets and bursting shells will not be much of a novelty to him. He is a member of the "Strathcona Horse," the crack cavalry regiment of the West, which is composed largely of veterans who have seen service and is noted as a regiment of hard riding, straight shooting, and seasoned men, to whom we look to give a good account of themselves when they cut loose.

A Fighting Furniture Man

Another volunteer is Lt.-Col. E. B. Clegg, the well known and popular furniture man of Peterboro, who is the commanding officer of the "57th Regiment Peterboro Rangers," and who, together with 129 other officers and men of his regiment, early responded to the call for volunteers for the overseas contingent. He, too, is in camp in England.

Lt.-Col. Clegg's regiment has the distinction of having made about the best showing of any of the regi-

M. J. NIQUET, Montreal.

ments of the Ontario cities, outside of Toronto, both in strength of numbers and in efficiency, and it speaks very highly for their commanding officer that he was appointed provisional colonel of the first battalion of the first infantry brigade, and will be in command of 1,400 men. Lt.-Col Clegg has been a resident of Peterboro practically all his life, and for a number of years has been engaged in the retail furniture business, and has hosts of friends throughout the trade whose best wishes will accompany him wherever duty calls him.

He is now Fighting

A third one of Canada's prominent furniture men to be actively engaged in the present struggle is M. Jean Niquet, of the Quebec Furniture Co., of Montreal, who left for the front to join his colors immediately on the outbreak of the war, he being a French reservist and, like the rest of his compatriots, could not get there quick enough when the call came, and although not fighting under the British flag, he is fighting alongside of it in the common cause.

M. Niquet is a native of France, and has been in Canada about twelve years, all of which he has spent in the furniture business, having been for nine years connected with the firm of "Valequette, Ltd.," of Montreal, a connection which he severed to enter into business for himself under the name of the Quebec

Library Table by The George McLagan Furniture Co., Ltd.

Furniture Co., which he has carried on with much success since its inception. During the years spent in Canada, M. Niquet has earned for himself the reputation of a progressive furniture man, not only in Montreal, but throughout the wholesale trade of Canada, by whom he is well known, and whose best wishes will accompany him throughout the campaign, hoping to see him back again safe and sound as soon as his country can spare him.

HANOVER IS ALL RIGHT

A correspondent in Hanover, Ont., writes that great injustice has been done by the circulation of reports of the alleged disloyalty of the German-Canadians of that part of Canada. The recent splendid patriotic entertainment given in Hanover was a complete refutation of such charges. Every seat in the large hall was filled. J. S. Knechtel, managing director of the Knechtel Furniture Co., occupied the chair, and he, R. J. Ball, M.P., and H. H. Miller delivered stirring patriotic addresses.

A committee which circulated a Patriotic and Relief Fund subscription list among the factory proprietors and some of the leading business men raised nearly three thousand dollars. Some of the subscriptions were as follows:

The Knechtel Furniture Co., Limited	$500 00
The Peppler Brothers, Limited	100 00
The Geutzner Light and Power Company	100 00
The Hanover Portland Cement Co., Limited	100 00
The Spiesz Furniture Co., Limited	50 00
The Knechtel Kitchen Cabinet Co., Limited	50 00
Messrs. William Knechtel and Sons	50 00
Ball Furniture Co.	100 00

One subscription was of $42.55, made by the willing contribution of one day's pay from each employe of the Peppler Bros., Limited. Hanover has sent sixteen men to the first and second contingents, and several of them are German-Canadians. The pupils of the German Baptist Sabbath School decided, by a standing vote, to forego this year their usual Christmas packages, and to allow the money thus saved, some fifty dollars, and, in addition, the proceeds of the Christmas entertainment, to go to the Belgian Relief Fund.

WAR AND FURNITURE STYLES

Apropos of the Toronto Furniture Co.'s designers now visiting European museums and art galleries seeking knowledge and information, is it not strange, says The Furniture World, of New York, "that most of our enduring styles in furniture should have been evolved during times of great public stress?

"The flight of James, or Jacobus if you prefer the Latin, marked the end of the Jacobean period and the beginning of the William and Mary style, with its pronounced Dutch characteristics. Neither of the Charles' had a peaceful reign. If they weren't participating in foreign wars, they were coping with domestic troubles. Even that famous group of eighteenth century designers, Chippendale, Hepplewhite, Sheraton, Shearer, and the Brothers Adam did much of their finest work while the country was disturbed by wars abroad and harassed by political and civil strife at home. As for Louis XVI and Marie Antoinette—but why continue? What new styles in furniture will be born as a result of the travail which at present is convulsing Europe is a question more to the point and one which no doubt is passing through the mind of more than one furniture man at this time."

MOTH-PROOF CHESTS

Perhaps the greatest peculiarity of red cedar is its odor. No matter how old the wood the odor never leaves it. This odor is most obnoxious to the moth, and for this reason it is used in the manufacture of chests to hold winter garments and clothing. This and a great deal of other useful information regarding cedar is told in a most interesting manner in a little

Bookcase, by The George McLagan Furniture Co., Ltd.

booklet just published by the Keenan Woodenware Mfg. Co., Ltd., Owen Sound, makers of "Kaybee mothproof red cedar chests." These chests, which come in various styles and sizes, are made of solid Tennessee red cedar, put together with heavy brass screws, with brass corner braces outside, end handles and lock, and lid supports—all the metal work highly polished. Some of these chests are designed to hold single fur sets or small woollen garments; others are made to hold a large family's winter furs and clothing, and there are medium sizes in between. All the chests are handmade by skilled artists.

Knobs of News

The new goods sale is a good idea at this time of year.

Mrs. Chas. Weidy has registered the Main Furniture Exchange, at Montreal.

J. F. Nevile has sold his furniture business at Wapella, Sask., to D. Hamilton.

A new plate glass front is being put in the Long furniture store at Medicine Hat, Alta.

The furniture store at Herbert, Sask., known as Paul's Place, has been sold to J. G. Peters & Son.

The London, England, Antique Furniture Co., Montreal, suffered a fire loss recently. Covered by insurance.

Albert B. Macdonald has registered as the Macdonald Stove Co., dealers in stoves and housefurnishings, at Montreal.

Herring & Simpson, furniture dealers, Montreal, recently dissolved partnership, E. W. Herring continuing the business.

Plans are being prepared for a furniture factory at Goderich, Ont., on which J. E. Bacheler proposes to spend $50,000.

Wilder's furniture store on Yonge street, Toronto, has removed to larger and more modern premises higher up the street, to No. 364.

J. E. Jacques, of the Berlin Furniture Co., is another of the Canadian furniture men traveling in Europe who was nearly caught in the war zone on the outbreak of hostilities.

H. A. Bywater has opened an upholstery store at the corner of Yonge and Scollard streets, Toronto. Mr. Bywater was, until recently, connected with the Thornton-Smith Co.

T. J. Quinsey, who recently purchased at Caledonia, Ont., the furniture business of Moore & Epps, is well-known throughout all that section, and is well liked, and no doubt will work up a large furniture and carpet business.

O. H. L. Wernicke, of the Macey Co., is chairman of the Michigan Penology Commission, and both he and Mrs. W. R. Bissell, wife of the president of the Bissell Carpet Sweeper Co., were prominent speakers at a late convention of the Michigan Charities and Correction Conference, at Grand Rapids.

R. J. Campbell, of Campbell & Campbell, furniture dealers, Brandon, Man., with his wife, has gone for a winter's stay in California. They will visit in Regina, Edmonton and Vancouver, on the way out, and will make their long stay a short distance from Oakland, Cal., where Mrs. Campbell's people reside. They will be gone until late in the spring.

The Hamel Furniture & Upholstering Company, Mildmay, Ont., have been employing the usual number of men and working full time despite the general slackness of business. Mr. Hamel was away recently on a canvassing trip and succeeded in securing a number of large orders that will keep the factory running for a twelve-hour day shift for the next six weeks.

On November 2nd A. McNiven and G. York took possession of the furniture business heretofore conducted by Hoover & Walker. The new proprietors hail from Ingersoll, and are two enterprising young business men of experience. It will be their policy to carry a complete line of furniture for the home and the office, from the best Canadian factories, all "Made in Canada" goods, and they will endeavor to make the prices sufficiently attractive to induce Guelphites to buy at home and not send money out of town for furniture.

DIRECTORY OF CARPET INDUSTRIES

Such of the carpet and furniture trades as have not as yet received a copy of the "American Buyers' Directory" (Kendrick's Directory of the Carpet and Upholstery Industries) for 1914-15, are requested to send their address to the Trades Publishing Company, 102 So. Twelfth St., Philadelphia, Pa.

THE JEFFERIES FURNITURE CO.

The business and assets of Quality Furniture Makers, Limited, Welland, Ont., which recently went into liquidation, has been sold to Edward Jefferies, managing director of the company who assumed full ownership on Monday, November 16. Mr. Jefferies will conduct the business under the name and style of The Jefferies Furniture Company, and will continue in the manufacture of medium and high grade upholstered furniture. The products of this industry have met with a very encouraging reception from the trade, and prospects are favorable for success under the new ownership and management.

CHESLEY FURNITURE CO. AGAIN OPERATE

After a temporary cessation The Chesley Furniture Co., Ltd., have resumed operations in their factory at Chesley, Ont., running the plant at full time and with a complete staff. Already they have a stock of their twin-pedestal tables ready for quick delivery to dealers wanting them immediately, or for Christmas gift selling. The officers remain unchanged. George Durst is president; Wm. Damm, vice-president; W. G. Durst, manager, and J. Houser is executive officer, and they are looking forward to big business from now on, stocks in retailers' hands throughout the country being very low.

COUNTER DISPLAY CASE FREE

The Onward Mfg. Co., Berlin, Ont., are offering to dealers handling their sliding shoes a display case free to those sending in a $25 order for shoes and slides. The case is small and compact, just large enough to hold nicely a sample of each size, yet not too big to take up too much room on the counter.

The Berlin branch factory of the Canada Furniture Manufacturers, Ltd., which has been closed since June, has been reopened and is running five days a week.

Dominion Casket Co., Limited

Telephones: Day No. 1020. Nights, Sundays and Holidays Nos. 1069-1101

Guelph, Ont.

EXPRESS ORDERS SOLICITED

No. 148

The Caskets shown by illustration on this page are goods far above the ordinary in quality and design, each case has been built from draft, making same absolutely perfect, mechanically, and of the right proportion for goods of this class.

We, at all times, endeavor to furnish our trade with goods that are strictly of the latest designs and of quality which is unquestionable. We will be pleased to answer all inquiries regarding anything needed by the Funeral Director.

No. 156

Undertakers' Department

Problems affecting the Undertaking Profession are here discussed and readers are invited to send letters expressing their views on any of the subjects dealt with—News of the profession throughout Canada.

The Doom of the Trocar

Prof. Eckels declares that the discarding of this instrument will be universal in the near future

THERE is something new in embalming—new this year; new now. There always is something new. Frequently that "something new" is "something better." Of course, all changes are not improvements. Too often the novelties pass on and are discarded almost as soon as bought. Many manufacturers are unscrupulous enough to foist upon their customers novelties which they know will not give satisfaction, but which they feel they can sell because of their novelty.

When I placed the Eckels-Genung axillary draining tubes on the market many of my would-be competitors denounced them as not practical, and freely predicted that the undertaker who bought them never would use them. As lately as a year or two ago one lecturer declared before a prominent undertakers' association that "sales" was the only object of these tubes. If this were true, they certainly would have achieved their object, because more than twenty thousand sets already have been sold, one set for almost every undertaker in the United States and Canada.

I happen to know, however, and so does practically every member of the profession, that these tubes are in daily and hourly use from Maine to California, and even beyond the seas. I feel confident, therefore, that when I say that the trocar is doomed, that my words will be given more than passing notice. The trocar is a nasty instrument. In it is summed up almost every objection which the public has conceived against embalming. At its door may be laid nine-tenths of the prejudice against the chemical disinfection and preservation of the dead human body. The undertaker does not want to use an instrument of this kind, but uses it only because he must, and then uses it with fear and trembling—behind locked doors, if possible.

It would be a bold embalmer, indeed, who would dare resort to this barbarous method in the presence of a member of the family of the deceased. I long have preached against the indiscriminate use of the trocar. I have recognized that up until this time, however, there were cases where its employment seems almost a necessity. Embalming fluids have their virtues, and a peroxide of hydrogen fluid particularly will dispose of the gases in nine out of ten cases. On that tenth case, however, and on shipping cases, where the undertaker is forced to work hurriedly, there seemed, for a long time, to be no remedy other than its use. I have realized, just as every other undertaker has, that something should be done to render it unnecessary. At last I have found it in my stomach and colon tubes.

The embalmer will find in the stomach tube just sufficient rigidity to ensure the passage of the tube down the oesophagus and into the stomach. The first move after the tube has been inserted is to attach a pump and aspirate the gas, which can be done with all of the certainty of, and none of the objections to, the trocar. The worst of the gas having been gotten rid of, the fluid can be injected through the tube, and the stomach is far more thoroughly disinfected than is possible by the older and more barbarous method.

The stomach tube is twenty inches long, entirely of metal, but its flexibility is so carefully calculated that no difficulty need be feared in securing an easy entrance. The colon tube is somewhat larger in diameter, and is forty-two inches in length.

The point is inserted in the pyloric opening, and thus its path is open all the way up to the small intestines, since it is so flexible that it will follow all of the convolutions of the ascending and descending colon. Hence all gases can be readily aspirated and the fluid injected with even more ease and certainty than if the trocar had been employed. I think I can safely claim that the trocar no longer is a necessary implement in the embalmer's kit. It had its place and had its day. In the infancy of embalming, it was as necessary as the axillary tube is at the present time. The flexible stomach and colon tubes, however, have made it as unnecessary as the fifth wheel on a wagon.

I should strongly recommend that where the stomach has been partly filled with fluid through the stomach tube, and the colon with fluid injected through the larger tube, the undertaker should gently press and massage the stomach, so as to work the fluid through the porous walls and thus assist the natural osmotic pressure of the fluid into the small intestines. This is but a moment's work, and the result will amply repay the funeral director careful and conscientious enough to resort to it. Quite aside from the fact that it produces the most excellent specimens of embalming, I always have claimed with the axillary method that one of its chief advantages is the fact that the incision is so small and in such an obscure part of the body—the armpit—that it was exceedingly difficult for a curious and prying member of the family to discover. The cruel and barbarous thrust of the trocar cannot be hidden. No method yet has been devised which will entirely cover the wound—a wound which cuts clear to the heart of every member of the family.

Why, then, inflict this wound needlessly? Why break your circulation when it can serve absolutely no good purpose, and cannot even do the work so well as can the stomach and colon tubes?

In the past I have not been so outspoken against the trocar as have some other students of embalming. This has not been because of any conviction against its use, but for the simple reason that I never care to enter a complaint when I am not in a position to suggest a remedy. A fool can find fault with things which a philosopher sometimes cannot obviate. As long as there seemed to be no way to get around the use of the trocar and nothing to take its place, I contented myself with advising care and caution in its use. Now I say that the thoughtful, earnest, conscientious, scientific, and progressive embalmer will abandon it utterly.

Get it at the Western

A Safe, Profitable Place to Buy

All Kinds of Undertakers' Supplies

Open Night and Day

Our Catalogue is with you, if not, a Post Card will bring it.

Give us a trial express order.   Phone Garry 4657.

The Western Casket Co.,
Limited

Winnipeg   Cor. Emily St., & Bannatyne Ave.   Manitoba

Impressions of National Convention

By J. B. McIntyre, St. Catharines, Ont.

In any account of my recent visit to the thirty-third annual meeting of the National Funeral Directors' Association, in the city of New Orleans, Louisiana, October 27, 28, 29, 30, 1914, I shall not attempt to describe all we saw, but I will give a brief outline of my impressions as we journeyed to and from the South.

It was a delightful morning, October 22nd, when Mrs. McIntyre and I stepped aboard the train for the West. We were joined at Hamilton by Mr. C. D. Blachford, and reached Chicago at 9 o'clock that night. We spent two days in that great metropolis, viewing her beautiful buildings and parks, and riding over her broad boulevards.

On Saturday at noon we joined the party from the American West, and our special train pulled out of Chicago prompt on schedule time. In the evening at 5.30 we were joined at Indianapolis by delegates from that city and neighboring states, and we arrived at Cincinnati at nine at night.

A wait of one hour there, and President James J. McLarney, of New York City, and the Eastern delegates joined us.

We reached the Mammoth Cave of Kentucky at 9 o'clock Sunday morning, and at this point the delegates from the south-west, who traveled by special train from St. Louis, joined the party at Glasgow Junction. Breakfast over, we transferred to the narrow gauge railway, and began to climb over the knob of the hill—up one side and down the other.

After a run of eight miles up a grade of three hundred and fifty feet, we were landed at the Mammoth Cave Hotel, a great rambling building; suits were donned by the party, and we were divided into three groups, each party selecting the route they desired to take under the direction of competent guides.

I will not attempt at this time to describe this great world of underground wonders. It is impossible to mention, less possible to describe, all the objects that interest visitors to this most gigantic cavern of the world. After four hours' journey through the Cave we returned to the Mammoth Cave Hotel, where dinner was served.

At five in the evening we again boarded our special train, which now consisted of eleven Pullman steel coaches, six standard sleepers, two compartment cars, two dining cars, and a baggage car. After an all-night run, we reached Mobile, Alabama, at 11 a.m. on Monday—a beautiful old city, with its magnificent colonial mansions, broad avenues and lovely parks. There we were entertained by P. B. Dickson and John Augwin, two of the liberal-hearted funeral directors of that city, to a steamboat ride on Mobile Bay, which was very refreshing after our long journey on the train. A substantial lunch was served on the boat, and after four hours' enjoyment in this beautiful old city we traveled through a magnificent sweep of bay-indented shore for a distance of fifty miles, where a short stay of two hours was pleasantly spent at Biloxi, Mississippi, a beautiful winter haven. We found it in the full bloom of a summer day, the magnolia trees showering down the petals of their white, sweet-scented flowers, and the live oaks festooned with long sweeping sprays of waving Spanish moss.

The beach at the riverside is lined with cottages, bungalows, villas, and hotel resorts. Running close to the water's edge is the famous shell road. We were met at the train at this beautiful city by the leading men of the Chamber of Commerce and a band of music, and they entertained us by accompanying our party for a ride by a train of trolley cars along the waterfront for several miles. On our return we were dined at the beautiful "White House" Hotel to dainty refreshments. Our short visit to the city of Biloxi was a source of delight to all.

At 9 o'clock at night we reached the quaint old city of New Orleans, which is full of interest to visitors from other sections of the country. It has a population of 350,000 people, and the city contains many modern buildings, magnificent residences, and beautiful parks and boulevards. Beyond the park are the strange and beautiful cemeteries, where all the graves are above ground, and which proved of deep interest to the modern funeral director. Seeing New Orleans

J. B. McINTYRE, St. Catharines, Ont.

is like seeing two cities—one typical of all that is modern and full of the spirit of the age; the other a city ripe with associations of old Creole days.

On our arrival at New Orleans we were met at the station by a deputation from the funeral directors' association of that city with plenty of carriages, every driver wearing a silk hat. We were driven to the beautiful Hotel Grunewald, the headquarters of the officers, and the hotel where the National Funeral Directors' Association held their four-days' session.

The opening session was held jointly with the conference of Embalmers' Examining Boards. Thursday we were entertained to a steamboat ride on the Mississippi River, leaving New Orleans at 9 a.m. and spending a delightful day at the sugar plantations and refineries, orange groves, and oyster fisheries. Luncheon was served on the boat, a fine orchestra furnishing music. The young people indulged in dancing; the members of committees held conferences; and the day passed pleasantly and enjoyably. We returned to the city at 6.30 in the evening.

Saturday was spent sightseeing around the city, and on Sunday morning those who were left of the party in the city took their departure at 8 a.m., making a stop at Louisville, Kentucky, on Monday for five hours, while we were entertained to an auto ride through the beautiful parks, and given a mid-day lunch at the Seelback Hotel by the local funeral directors.

Another stop of four hours was made at Cincinnati, and a visit was paid to ex-President Charles Miller and Aunt Beckey, who, with their sons, Hal and Warren, gave us a royal reception.

Tuesday, Nov. 2nd, we arrived in Chicago, where we spent two more enjoyable days, arriving home on Thursday, delighted with our outing, having passed through eight states and traveled three thousand four hundred miles by train.

The next annual meeting will be held in San Francisco in September or October, 1915.

Effect of War on Funeral Goods

THAT higher prices will prevail on funeral goods if the European war continues much longer, is the conclusion of The Director (New York), which thus summarizes the situation as it affects the various items entering into the manufacture of supplies:

In the embalming fluid line the most notable advance has been made in carbolic acid crystals, the cost of which, in large quantities, has leaped from 9 cents to 45 cents per pound, 55 cents being asked on small orders. Carbolic acid, or phenol, as it is chemically known, has been largely imported from Germany. It is manufactured in this country also, but the domestic product has not been equal in grade and clarity of color to the imported. Most of the large standard fluid manufacturers have either on hand or under contract a supply of this and some other chemicals sufficient to meet present demands for periods ranging from one to three months, but even they have been forced to pay greatly increased prices for some of their chemicals. Every disinfectant into which phenol enters to any appreciable extent—and there are many—must inevitably be advanced in price by the manufacturers.

Formaldehyde, which enters into the manufacture of fluids more than any other one chemical, is fortunately now a domestic product. It was formerly all imported from Germany, but of late years domestic manufacturers have entered the field and there will probably be only a slight advance in price.

Glycerin, which is incorporated in most fluids because of its quality of keeping the tissues soft and pliable, has advanced 40 per cent., from 20 cents to 28 cents per pound. Much of this was obtained from France. It is also manufactured in this country, but the withdrawal of the foreign competition will probably cause a further advance before long.

Alcohol and boric acid will be only slightly affected, but salicylic acid, which is used largely, has advanced from 24 cents to 75 cents per pound. Salicylic acid is claimed by many to have nearly as great germicidal power as phenol, and to have some advantages over the latter.

The essential oils are almost wholly of foreign manufacture, and may be utterly unobtainable when present stocks are exhausted. These include those oils used primarily to impart a pleasing color to fluids. They are not essential to the preservative or cosmetic effect, but custom has made them almost a necessary ingredient. Synthetic substitutes will probably be evolved should it become necessary.

A product of minor importance here, but which is a source of great concern in many other lines, is dye. Germany has furnished almost the entire world with its superior and cheap dyes. The custom of coloring fluids which has come into vogue of late years has almost rendered this feature an essential, although the dye, like the perfume oils, has no practical value from the preservative or cosmetic standpoint. Several propositions are now under consideration by American capitalists for the establishment of a domestic plant for the manufacture of dyes, and this will undoubtedly be done should the necessity become absolute. The cost of manufacture here, however, will be greater than abroad.

Thus it is seen that many ingredients that enter into the manufacture of embalming fluids and other disinfectants are costing the manufacturers from 10 to 400 per cent. more. The prices of these articles, if their strength and quality is to be maintained, must inevitably be increased to the jobber and undertaker. In fact, the prices to the jobber have, in many instances, already been advanced. Up to the present no advance has been made to the undertaker, and he will be wise if he stocks up while the price remains where it is.

In the manufacture of caskets the war will also have the effect of increasing costs, although not in the same great percentage as in fluids. The hardwoods will only be slightly affected. It is probable that the price of pine will rise owing to the action of Canada in prohibiting its export. Chestnut, oak, walnut and pine are all of domestic growth. African mahogany may feel the rise owing to the possible restriction of ocean transportation. Mahogany from the West Indies is not the factor it formerly was, as the supply has been diminished and the cost of getting it to tidewater has greatly increased.

The decline in the demand for cloth-covered caskets will cause less concern than would have been the case fifteen or twenty years ago, the demand now being largely for the finished cases. The cheaper black and colored cloths have been of domestic manufacture, but here again the question of dyes will make itself felt. The better grades of broadcloth are imported, and, while they can be made here, they will cost considerably more than those of foreign manufacture.

The silks and satins of quality, and much of the cheaper grades, are imported from France and Japan. With these sources of supply cut off, an unprecedented rise in price will ensue. In these goods, as in nearly every other line, domestic manufacturers can supply them, but the cost will be greater.

Even with the hardwoods and imitation finished cases there will be an increased cost due to the foreign supply of oils and gums which enter into the manufacture of paints and varnishes, to say nothing of the hardware.

Cotton gloves will soar mightily, as fully 80 per cent. of those used in this country have been imported. They can also be made here, but at an increased cost. The fleece-lined cotton gloves used in the fall and winter will be among the items on which there will be a decided advance in price. The domestic manufacturers have been unable to compete with the German product in price and quality. The winter supply is made up during the summer, but as their manufacture ceased long before the required quantity had been made up, the foreign glove will be out of the market before very long, and the higher-priced domestic product will have to be purchased.

On the imported fabrics there has been a rise of from 10 to 25 per cent., and as the cloth industry on the European Continent is at a standstill it is only a

(Continued on page 57.)

First Quality — **Dominion Manufacturers** — Prompt Service
Limited

Our Solid Oak and Mahogany Caskets are Leaders

Making a specialty of Hardwood Caskets we are able to offer you a choice, which for beauty of design and richness of finish, is unequaled.

We also manufacture a full line of Casket Hardware that is of special merit.

No. 500—Solid Oak
No. 499—Solid Mahogany

Situated as we are in the heart of Western Ontario, our well equipped factory and efficient organization place us in a position to give a very excellent service.

A Telephone order may save you time	Telephones—Factory	169
	Mr. Watson	1654
	Shipper	1020

THE GLOBE CASKET COMPANY
LONDON   ONTARIO

CANADIAN FURNITURE WORLD AND THE UNDERTAKER — December, 1914

First Quality — **Dominion Manufacturers Limited** — Prompt Service

For Quick Delivery
and Goods of Quality

A selection from our complete line of Undertakers' Supplies is sure to give you entire satisfaction.

With the express service of three great railways at our command, our facilities for quick and certain delivery are unequaled.

No. 501. Solid Oak
No. 502. Solid Mahogany

All Supplies on Shortest Notice
Competent Staff, Day and Night

The National Casket Company, Limited

93-109 Niagara Street
Toronto   Ontario

Telephones—Adelaide 454
Adelaide 455
North 5085

First Quality — **Dominion Manufacturers Limited** — **Prompt Service**

THERE'S A SAYING IN THE TRADE

"If you want something good go to Semmens & Evel"

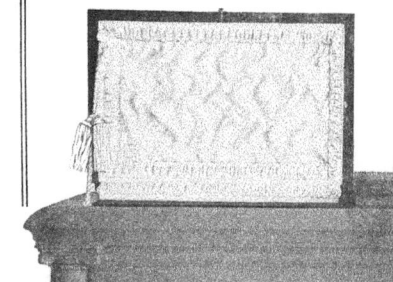

This is no idle phrase. Our workmen have had years of experience in the manufacture of the better grades of Caskets, Coffins and Funeral Furniture, and it is a matter of pride with them that the smallest detail receives the attention which has given our produce its reputation for **Superior Quality.**

No. 647

A wide range of Covered Caskets and Piano Polished Oak and Mahogany Caskets

Our Ebonet Finished Hardware Merits Your Investigation

An experienced staff at our office and factory night and day ensures the prompt execution of your order

WE NEVER MISS A TRAIN

The Semmens & Evel Casket Co., Limited

Hamilton
Telephones: 517, 3316. Nights and Sundays, 517, 3319, and 3353

Winnipeg
470 Ross Avenue
Chas. Crossland, Manager

Dominion Manufacturers Limited

First Quality — Prompt Service

High Grade Undertakers' Supplies

The D.W.T. Line stands as it has always stood, for reliable goods and efficient service. ¶ The newest and best for the undertaker.

Telephones:
ADELAIDE 454
and NORTH 5085

The
D. W. Thompson Co.
Limited
93-109 Niagara St., Toronto

Caskets, Robes and Linings

Highest quality in all Undertakers' Supplies.

Our covered Caskets are the best made.

Your order solicited

James S. Elliott & Son
Prescott   Ontario

To the *Undertakers* of Quebec

Our Plant at Three Rivers is acknowledged to be the finest in Canada. The full line of Undertakers' Supplies manufactured is a worthy product of the magnificent factory. Give us your orders and be assured of prompt and efficient service.

GIRARD & GODIN
Three Rivers, Que.

Complete Line of Burial Caskets, Hardware, Etc.

*Best Quality
Reasonable Prices*

The location of our well equipped factory enables us to provide unexcelled service for undertakers of the Maritime Provinces.

We solicit your orders by letter telegram or telephone

CHRISTIE BROS. & CO.
Amherst, N.S.

Blood Drainage

Lecture delivered at Canadian Embalmers' Convention at Toronto, by Prof. H. Moll, Chicago.

(Continued from last month).

I have tried to give you a general idea of what the blood is and the functions it performs. Now, why do we remove it from the dead human body? For just two reasons, one is to remove color, and the other is to prevent it. To remove it if it exists and to prevent it if it does not exist. Sometimes we will care for a body and everything will be in perfect condition, and when we return to it it is partially discolored because of the return of blood to the surface tissue, on account of not having been entirely removed. There is, however, a method of embalming the body without draining the blood, without drawing a drop of blood. It requires a considerable knowledge of anatomy, the location of the blood vessels, but it may be done, and probably the time will come when we will not remove the blood. It is not absolutely necessary that we should, from a scientific standpoint.

When we study histology we find that the body is composed of five different kinds of tissue. First we have the epilethium, which comprises the hair, the nails, and lining of the air and food passages. Then we have the connective tissue, the bones, ligaments, and fascia—they form a composite portion. They have little blood circulation, mostly taking up the nourishment they need from the body by absorption. The third tissue is the muscle. That is the particular part that you need to give the most attention to. That is the part of the body that becomes putrid, decomposes, as we say ordinarily. That is where the capillaries are located, between those strings called fibres.

Now, the average person thinks that you must disinfect the entire body. That is not the case; only the muscular tissue is embalmed, which, however, is in nearly every portion of the body. We find muscular tissue in the layers of the skin and in the middle wall of the artery. Therefore, it is distributed over nearly every part of the body. The next form of tissue is liquid tissue—blood, lymph, so you see that blood is a fluid tissue. It is practically of the same composition as the muscles, the red flesh of the body. If you can succeed in preserving the red flesh of the body all that is necessary is to distribute your fluid in the blood, so that when it comes to a question as to whether a body can be properly embalmed without draining of the blood, I would answer in the affirmative, but ordinarily to preserve the cosmetic effect it is necessary. Failure of preservation of the body is not due to the presence of blood, but usually to the insufficient quantity of fluid to disinfect.

How much fluid, you ask, would I use? "I would use three quarts," you say, "that ought to be enough to put the body in good shape." That would only saturate a small portion of the body. Gentlemen, I am an advocate of the liberal use of fluid in the body. I think in many instances we use our fluids too strong and don't use enough. Embalming fluid only goes as far as you force it, unless you give it the benefit of gravitation, and gravitation has a lot to do with the successful embalming of a body. But three quarts will never saturate a body thoroughly, and never did. You can distribute it in a body to keep it three or four days, and that generally serves your purpose, but that never disinfected a body, and my argument is that we should use more fluid and less strength: that is, get away from the extremely strong solutions and distribute our fluid more thoroughly and we would get better results.

Reason for Embalming

The object of our work is to protect the living, that is, to place the dead in such condition that they are no menace to the living. It is simply sanitation. When you are called into the home to disinfect the body you are called there not only for the purpose of having a satisfactory funeral, but also to protect those who are left behind, and the sooner you grasp that situation the more professional you become—that it is not only for the almighty dollar—we love it always and need it in our business—but from a professional standpoint we accomplish more, by distributing our fluid more thoroughly and embalming the body completely.

The average man figures like this: If I do the work so carefully there will be no more deaths and I will be out of business. I think the time will come when your Government will not only give you the privilege and recognize you as professional men, but will demand that all bodies be thoroughly and absolutely disinfected and made entirely harmless. A body that is unembalmed, dead of a dangerous disease, is almost as great a menace to the living in the ground as above the ground. We have evidence of where germs not entirely destroyed have caused epidemics in cities.

Now then, we will get back to the original subject of blood drainage. As you all know, the principal factor of embalment as a disinfectant is formaldehyde. We have substances in chemistry that will preserve the body equally as well as formaldehyde, but they will not hold the skin. Take carbolic acid, which is just as good a disinfectant as formaldehyde, but when you use this solely, you will have skin slip. This is one of the conditions that makes a man nervous, and I do not blame him. Therefore we are really compelled to use a certain amount of formaldehyde, and it is the disagreeable effect of formaldehyde on the coloring of the blood that causes you all your trouble.

"Well," says one man, "I leave some of the blood in the body for color." It is not desirable color he gets, I can assure you. When we study the condition of the blood after death the argument is made that there is no blood in the arteries. Soon after death the muscular tissue in the walls of the arteries is contracted, and that forces the blood into the capillaries and the veins. Now then, you have venous blood in the capillaries. If the contraction of the arteries forces that blood into the capillaries you really have no pure blood in the body, it is all more or less mixed. The blood reduces itself, it changes itself, that is due to a chemical condition. When we mix formaldehyde and blood we mix a reducing agent with blood. It has oxidizing properties, that is, it acts something similar to the sun or the outside skin of the body. The carbonic acid gas is in the impure blood. The blood keeps on changing, and is carried on mixed with impure blood. You embalm a body and the face is discolored. There is venous or impure blood in the surface skin. The embalming fluid drives that out, but there is a little dark color left in one ear, or the ear may be beautifully pink. What happens to the blood in that ear? In 24 hours it is not pink any more, but a dark color; in 48 hours it is still darker; in 72 hours it is quite a discoloration. The chemical formula for formaldehyde is CH2O. We have discovered no other chemical that is so satisfactory as formaldehyde in our embalming fluids, and still it is not just what we want in many respects, especially its bad effect on the blood.

Remove All the Blood.

There seems to be no substitute for it at the present time. Therefore, I would advise you to remove all the blood that you can, at least from the surface of the body. The little blood vessels that contain the impure blood on the surface are extremely small. If you can get the blood away from them, from the smallest blood vessels that have no valves, into the larger ones that have valves, then you succeed in removing that blood permanently. That is why it is necessary to drain the blood out of the systemic circulation, and you will be compelled to do that until we find a chemical that will take the place of formaldehyde in embalming fluids.

A lot of people are under the impression that the blood starts from the heart and all goes to the feet and comes back, or all goes to the hands and head and comes back. Most of it never reaches the hands or feet, on account of the short circuits of circulation. I advocate, continually, when you inject embalming fluid into the axillary artery you use the long tube, and that tube extends into the arch of the aorta. When the arch fills up it begins to distribute. It first goes to the arteries that nourish the heart and they are directly behind the semi-lunar valves that guard the opening. The embalming fluid goes to the heart first. What happens? That fluid is forced into the arteries, it drives the blood out of the capillaries and it embalms that tissue. The embalming is accomplished in the capillaries, and not in the arteries—the arteries are merely the channels. As soon as we realize that, we have advanced just a step in our profession.

From the capillaries of the heart the fluid forces the blood ahead of it, into the veins. You will, in this way, get some fluid mixed with your blood five minutes after you inject it. It is then carried to the lungs, then it goes on from one organ to another, so that in that process it is necessary to waste a large amount of fluid in order to get the complete circulation. Only a very small amount of the blood goes to the feet, and that portion of the extremities of your body requires very little blood in life, and they require very little embalming fluid. Connecting tissue does not have to be embalmed. It does not become putrid. Fat never becomes putrid, it can only become rancid and liquid. The ligaments, tendons, and all the material that hold the bones together simply become liquid. But it is the muscular tissue, that part of the body where you have the capillaries—and that is where you have the blood, because that requires constant nourishment, constant circulation—that is where you need your embalming fluid, and where you get rid of the embalming fluid and blood mixed from the point of distribution. The aorta we described as the main artery of the systemic circulation and all other arteries are merely branches thereof.

Question by Mr. Cobbledick: Why is it that sometimes embalming fluid will appear in the blood quicker than in other cases?

Answer by Professor Moll: This is merely an evidence that the work is going on satisfactorily, that conditions are normal and that the circulation of the fluid is not being obstructed in any way.

Blood a Friend in Life.

There are times when it is absolutely necessary to get rid of that disturbing material we call the blood. I had the pleasure of meeting Prof. Eckels the other day. Prof. Eckels is a very highly esteemed friend, and he was my preceptor, and gave me the first instruction in blood drainage. He stated that Prof. Renard, the pioneer in this kind of work, said that "blood was man's greatest friend in life and his greatest enemy in death," and that comes very near being true. The blood gives us more real trouble than any portion of the body or any component part of the body. If we could only get rid of that, it would be just as easy to embalm a body as to roll off a log.

Some men will come and tell you that they have succeeded in ridding themselves of that inconvenience or obstacle. But I am afraid that when they make the test they will fail, and I still find the necessity to drain the blood, at least in funeral work, and that is what you are interested in. I want to say to you, gentlemen, that the presence of blood in the surface tissue of the face is one of the most disquieting things. Some times it is easy to remove it, and again it is not. When we consider the disinfection of the dead human body for funeral purposes the face becomes the most important part, and my advice to you would be to spend seven-eighths of your time on the face, for, as a rule, the face gets the least of your time. That is the portion of the body that you will expose, the portion of the body that is viewed by the friends and relatives, and if it is beautiful and looks natural, compliments are showered upon you and your ability. If it is the reverse, the embalmer will be told he did not understand his work, and is censured. Of course, they do not realize the conditions when they make these remarks. So we let it pass. Criticism is one of the best things in the world. Some men hate to be criticized. The truth cuts like a sword, but if we will face the matter, criticism is one of the greatest incentives for a man to improve his conditions or his work.

I explained to you, or tried to explain to you, the composition of blood or its peculiarities. I will now continue with the matter of the drainage of the blood, strictly. Anatomically, it is figured that the amount of blood in the human body is about one-thirteenth of its weight, or approximately 10 to 15 per cent., or an average of 12½ per cent. of the body weight. In disease, when the flesh tissue or the muscular tissues of the body waste, the blood wastes in proportion. Why? It is only necessary for enough blood to nourish the muscular tissues, and if the muscular tissues waste the amount of blood will waste in proportion. So that if we have a body that weighs 150 pounds, we could figure nominally that there was 15 pounds of blood in it—nominally. The point is to get rid of that blood. The question is how much of that blood can we drain from the body? You cannot get it all.

Divisions in Blood Circulation.

The circulation of the blood is divided into five systems. There is the systemic circulation, the general circulation, which nourishes the body; the pulmonary circulation, which occurs in the lungs and purifies the blood; the capillary circulation (you cannot force embalming fluid from the arteries to the veins unless you force it through the capillaries); the portal circulation, that is located in the circulation in the abdominal cavity, and then we have the foetal circulation, or that of the unborn child.

The circulation that the embalmer uses is the systemic circulation. If he can force the embalming fluid from the arteries into the capillaries and then into the veins, he can force it through the circulatory system, providing the blood is liquid. Blood is not always liquid. Very often, and under certain conditions, it is semi-solid or thickened. All the blood that is in the systemic circulation (that is all the vessels that contain blood that has nourished the body and is then loaded with the waste matter and carried back to the lungs for purifying) can be removed. The venous blood that is carried into the right auricle of the heart, from the right auricle into the right ventricle and then to the lungs, cannot be removed. That remains. And why? Simply because you cannot exert enough pressure on the pulmonary capillaries of the lungs to force that out.

In the living body the force of the heart, which is the greatest power of the body, is lost in the capillaries. You can distinguish the heart-beat until the blood reaches the capillaries, then it is lost. You can

A New Plant and a New Line of
Undertakers' Supplies

WITH one of the largest, most modern and best equipped plants in the country we are prepared to give Canadian undertakers a standard of quality and service that cannot be equalled.

We manufacture the better grades of **Caskets, Robes, Linings, Casket Hardware**, etc., our designs being entirely new and original.

Prompt service day and night will be a pronounced feature of our business.

Write for new Calendar-Booklet at once

Canada Casket Company, Limited
Wiarton   Ontario

Toronto Office: 309-10-11 Confederation Life Building

force fluid and blood into the lungs, into the pulmonary arterial capillaries, but there is no power on earth, except, perhaps, enormous pressure that would distend the body and make it unsightly, that can force the blood from this portion of the body. The blood remains in the lungs, at least, that portion of it which is in the pulmonary circulation.

The portal circulation comprises the venous blood from the digestive tract, from the stomach, from the small and large intestines. The gastric, the splenic superior and inferior mesenteric veins, drain the blood from the digestive tract, is carried to the liver, and then into the capillaries of the liver. That blood remains in the liver, and it is in the same position that the blood is in the lungs. You cannot remove it. Therefore, you have some blood in the human body which cannot be removed.

But from the systemic circulation you can remove blood, so that in blood drainage you must always take that into consideration. Ordinarily, when you drain blood from the cadaver, how much blood should you drain? I sometimes obtain a quart, two quarts, and, in exceptional cases I have succeeded in obtaining a gallon, not all blood, but fluid and blood mixed.

This is the way the majority of embalmers figure: "Well," they say, "there is fluid mixed with the blood; the body must be embalmed." That is only evidence that you are getting the distribution of your fluid, and it would be a mistake then to discontinue to inject; that is the time that you want to continue it. In a normal condition the first organ that is embalmed is the heart. If we use the long tube in the axillary vein, passing it inward to the junction of the interjugular and subclavian veins, the fluid carries the blood out of the capillaries into the veins, and it enters into the superior vena cava, then to the tube.

It only shows that the embalment is carried out ideally and properly. Gravity is one of the greatest aids to the distribution of embalming fluid. I would lay the body perfectly level, raise the shoulders abnormally, and let the head drop so that your first fluid will go to the face. When the head and face have sufficient fluid, raise the head and shoulders high, and your fluid will drain to the lower part of the body.

The question is sometimes asked: Is there any danger of flushing the face if you allow the head to drop lower than the arch of the aorta? None whatever, if you just remember the course of the fluid through the arteries, into the capillaries, and then into the veins. The only danger of flushing the face is if you get too much fluid into the lower part of the body it becomes saturated and the vessels become engorged. For some reason Nature has not provided the internal jugular veins with a perfect valve, allowing the blood and fluid to regurgitate, and the neck in this way is liable to become discolored. A discolored neck is very undesirable because in the position that the body rests in the casket the neck is always more or less exposed. The danger of flushing is not very great if you just watch the fluid. Of course, occasionally, you have it, and you generally get it when you least expect it. Now the points where we drain blood—which are the most advantageous?

Seven Locations to Draw From

There are seven locations. You can drain blood from the basilic vein, which is alongside of the brachial artery; the axillary vein, which is in front of the axillary artery; the internal jugular in the neck; the upper femoral; and middle femoral.

You can drain blood from all those points. Some of those points have advantages over the others. The old method was to drain blood from the basilic with a long flexible tube. It was always a hit or miss sort of a job, and in the last place it was a failure because the operator would become disgusted and stop before he obtained sufficient blood.

But the axillary method was a happy medium and served the purpose of ordinary blood drainage beautifully. You probably are all familiar with the axillary method. The axillary vein is quite large, and the tube can be placed into the axillary vein to where the internal jugular and the subclavian vein meet, forming the innominate. By passing this tube into the vein we are enabled to drain the blood from the trunk vein that has no valve; and I like that because we are enabled to get the blood from the face.

You can at the same time pass the flexible tube into the axillary artery and inject fluid without stiffening the arteries. If you take up the brachial artery and inject the fluid, it is distributed in the shoulder before it reaches the general systemic circulation. When the blood is fluid there is no trouble to get it. But why is the blood not always fluid, so that it will run easily or quickly from the body? The condition of the blood is due largely to the disease, and it is affected more than any other portion of the body, and it is the first portion that is involved because it is the circulating medium. The whole body depends on that circulating medium—which carries out the work of waste or repair.

(To be continued.)

PROFESSIONAL NOTES

W. N. Knechtel, undertaker, at 1095 Yonge Street, Toronto, has added a newest model motor ambulance to his equipment.

The Central Casket Company, Ltd., Bridgeburg, Ont., has been incorporated with a capital stock of $40,000, by M. Kimball, H. R. Morwood, C. A. Hamlin and others, to manufacture undertakers' supplies.

A. B. Coffin, a retired undertaker, is dead at Maumee, Mich. He had lived in that village all his life. His sign, "A. B. Coffin, Undertaker," was known throughout the United States. Mrs. Coffin died about six years ago.

Raper, Washington, Fleury Burial Co., Ltd., of Toronto, is now the name of the concern mentioned in the November issue as having been incorporated. The directors are Jas. Robt. Fleury, F. Raper, Lottie M. Washington, Wilton Fleury and Jennie C. Derratt.

Oscar E. Klinck sued Louis Scruton at Toronto recently over the sale of an undertaking business. The trouble was over an alleged statement of Mr. Scruton that in 1913 he had had 201 funerals and in January, 1914, 17 funerals, which statement Mr. Klinck characterizes as incorrect. Scruton counterclaimed for $1,500, amount of a chattel mortgage which he claims he has not been paid.

Frank Lynett upheld the contention of the plaintiff. The defence extracted from him that 200 funerals, at an average gross profit of $30 each, would mean a total income for a year of $6,000, and as the total overhead expenses would be about $1,500, this would mean that it was expected that the purchasers in a single year would net $4,500, the exact amount of the purchase price.

In Pittsburg the ordinances give strict right of way to all funerals, and to insure proper recognition of the funeral corteges, provision is made that all carriages in the procession of funerals shall have displayed a black cross on a white background five inches square. This action by the police bureau was made at the request of the Allegheny County Funeral Directors' Association, which complained that funerals were interrupted at street crossings. Another ordinance should be adopted by all cities compelling the funeral processions to avoid the principal streets, especially in cities where there is great crowding of the thoroughfares during the business hours of the day.

EFFECT OF WAR ON FUNERAL GOODS.

(Continued from page 50.)

question of a few months when the available supply will be entirely exhausted. Domestic manufacturers, however, can furnish a satisfactory article with but few, if any, exceptions.

The hardware line is due for a rise. Hardware has been cut to pieces for several years owing to keen competition. This has been due, in part, to so many small manufacturers selling at ruinous prices in an effort to build up new business. Some casket houses have also been responsible for false prices by selling hardware at cost in order to get the casket orders.

Tin is said to have gone up 200 per cent. Much of this comes from Wales and the Malay Archipelago. The price is affected primarily by the curtailment of ocean freights, and this feature will affect every article of commerce, even though the source of supply is a neutral country.

Several other metals will be affected more or less, according to the source of supply. It is even reported that firms in this trade which contemplated another slash in hardware prices have abandoned the plan, and instead are preparing to make an advance.

Candelabra manufacturers have advanced prices to jobbers about 25 per cent., and it is logical to assume that the supply houses will follow suit.

Embalming instruments are directly affected, as they have been almost entirely imported from Europe. Instruments are made in this country and can be made in any quantity needed, but domestic manufacturers have not attempted to develop this trade, as they have been unable to compete with foreign prices. The same can be said of rubber goods.

Sizing up the whole situation, our advice to our readers is to stock up now for the next six months if finances will permit. Anyway, buy all you can afford at the present low prices.

Burglar Proof and Water Tight

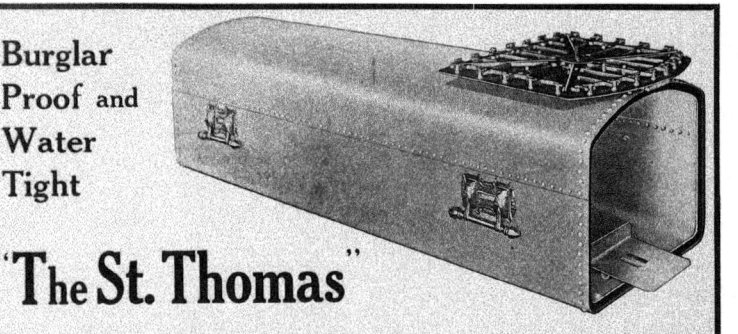

"The St. Thomas"

Original, Quick Closing End Vault

MANUFACTURED BY

The St. Thomas Metallic Vault Company, Limited

ST. THOMAS, ONTARIO

Patronize The Line of "Established Quality"

The features of the Central Line are features that make good business everywhere—honest quality, fair prices and efficient, prompt service. We specialize on

Mahogany, Oak, Plush and Cloth Covered Caskets

We can also supply anything desired in Casket Linings, Burial Robes, and a general line of Undertakers' Supplies.

Orders given our Canadian Representative, or sent to our factory at Bridgeburg by mail, telegraph or telephone will receive prompt attention.

CENTRAL CASKET COMPANY

Bridgeburg, Ont. R. S. Flint, Canadian Representative: 241 Fern Ave., Toronto

Telephone 126 Telephone Parkdale 3257

EDMONTON'S GOOD HEALTH.

In 1901 the city of Edmonton, Alberta, had a population of 2,500. It now has approximately 75,000, and covers an area of 27,000 square acres. This phenomenal growth, both in area and population, has meant heroic work on the part of its health officers to meet the problems that of necessity confronted them, such as refuse and sewage disposal, water supply, community sanitation, control of contagion, etc. It appears, however, from a recent report of the health officer of that city that he has succeeded in the face of unusual difficulties in maintaining excellent health conditions, the death rate for last year being only 10.73 per 1,000 of population.

UNDERTAKERS HEAD HEALTH PARADE.

Seventeen Indianapolis undertakers, according to a despatch in the daily press, took an important part in a recent celebration of Disease Prevention Day in that city. It is said that they headed a gigantic parade and were clad like crusaders, carrying banners with the inscription, "Disease Prevention Crusaders." By proclamation of Governor Ralston, the day was given over to attracting attention to preventable disease, and the interest displayed by the members of the profession impressed the public with the desire of the undertakers to assist in all movements for the protection of the public health.

"WHAT WE MAKE IN RED DEER"

A correspondent in the West sends us a marked copy of The Red Deer (Alta.) News, in which a writer, signing himself "Citizen," suggests the possibility of Red Deer becoming a manufacturing centre as a result of the openings due to the war. Among other suggestions "Citizen" says: "A good mechanic can build a solid oak casket complete for less than twenty-five dollars in Red Deer, and yet all the caskets used here are brought from the East at a great deal higher figure, and not as good material as could be produced at that figure. In the old land a solid British oak coffin rarely costs more than ten dollars complete, and they are all built almost without exception locally. No doubt there are many more suggestions that might be brought forward if citizens would only give the matter thought and let us all decide to, in every case possible, patronize home manufacture." We give it for what it is worth without comment.

CANADIAN FUNERAL CLAIM IN ENGLAND

At Spalding County Court His Honour Judge Sir George Sherston Baker had before him a funeral claim from British Columbia. The plaintiffs were the British Columbia Funeral Co., who sought to recover £25 from Walter William Bowman, of Spalding, for expenses incurred in connection with the burial of his son. Charles L. Harvey, for plaintiffs, stated that the claim was in respect to the burial of defendant's son, who was found drowned in April, 1912. As Mr. Merry, for defendant, was not prepared to admit certain facts, it would be necessary to obtain evidence from British Columbia, and he therefore asked for an adjournment for two months, and also for an order to put in proof by affidavit. Mr. Merry objected, stating that his client never gave an order at all, and if the case was proceeded with they wanted witnesses whom they could cross-examine. His Honour said, seeing that Mr. Merry was not satisfied, witnesses would have to be brought from British Columbia. After some discussion as to whether it was worth while going to this expense, His Honour said he should adjourn the case until the end of the moratorium.

TATTOOED WITH CEMETERY LOT.

W. R. Scott, aged about 40 years, a stranger in that community, died at the county hospital at Glendive, Mont., from paralysis. He was brought there from the vicinity of Terry, having been picked up in an unconscious condition, from which he never recovered. When taken to the local undertaking establishment it was found that Scott's chest bore an immense tattoo design in the form of a lot in a cemetery. The head and footstones of monuments were pictured at each end of a

Interior of Campbell & Campbell's undertaking parlors at Brandon, Man. This is one of the most up-to-the-minute firms in the West. There is a lady assistant, and the firm advertises in the local papers.

mound, which was covered with flowers. On the larger monument appeared the inscription, "In Memory of My Dear Dead Mother," while on the footstone was 1876." It is understood that Scott came to Montana from Toronto, Ont., and that his sister resides in that city. The body was interred in the local cemetery.

PROFESSIONAL NOTES

The B. C. Independent Undertakers, Ltd., are successors to Sill & Miller, at 652 Broadway W., Vancouver.

W. H. Richardson's furniture and undertaking parlors at Essex, Ont., were destroyed by a recent $50,000 fire, which recently occurred in that town. The firemen poured thousands of gallons of water into the building, and the stock, which included much valuable furniture, as well as costly undertakers' supplies, was a complete loss. The interior of the building is ruined, but the walls are still standing, and it is thought safe for rebuilding. Mr. Richardson carried $6,100 on the building and $16,000 on the stock.

HOSE CART USED AS HEARSE.

An old hose cart belonging to Engine Company No. 98, whose house was known as "Old Soy's," was impressed into service as a funeral car to carry the body of Charles Frederick Seyferlich, chief of the Chicago fire department since 1910, to the cemetery. Another hose cart followed in the funeral procession, bearing many floral tributes from the "boys" in the department and from city officials and friends.

"Purity Vaults"

Burglar, Vermin and Waterproof

Guaranteed against Effects of Corrosion for 50 Years

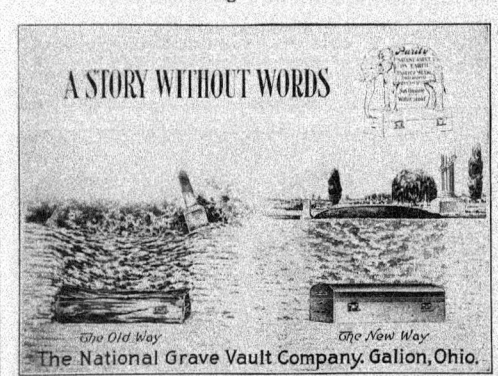

Practically indestructible. Acid tests show a ratio of 22 to 1 compared with common steel vaults.

The National Grave Vault Company, Galion, Ohio

Write for descriptive circular and how we help you sell "PURITY VAULTS"

Dominion Manufacturers, Limited
Canadian Distributors
Head Office: TORONTO

National Casket Co., Limited	Toronto
Globe Casket Co., Limited	London
Semmens & Evel Casket Co. Ltd.	Hamilton
J. S. Elliott & Son	Prescott
Girard & Godin	Three Rivers, Que.
Christie Bros. & Co.	Amherst, N.S.

A STORY WITHOUT WORDS — The Old Way / The New Way — The National Grave Vault Company, Galion, Ohio.

No Undertaker Should Overlook

the fact that he can make a full gallon of fluid of standard strength from each sixteen-ounce bottle of RE-Concentrated Dioxin. RE-Concentrated Dioxin costs no more per bottle than any standard concentrated fluid, but it is twice as strong—in other words, there are twice as many ounces of preservation in a bottle of RE-Concentrated Dioxin as there are in any bottle of merely concentrated fluid.

If economy were the only recommendation for RE-Concentrated Dioxin, however, we should not urge it upon our patrons.

As a matter of fact, it is easy to explain and equally easy to demonstrate the fact that the fluid thus produced gives a far better cosmetic effect and produces a far more life-like body than possibly could be produced by any raw formaldehyde concentrated fluid.

This is because RE-Concentrated Dioxin has a double base. When diluted to make a full gallon of fluid to the bottle, its main base is peroxide, with a secondary base of purified formaldehyde (formochloral).

Every funeral director knows that peroxide of hydrogen is the best bleacher known to chemical science. Not everyone realizes, however, that peroxide of hydrogen has blood solvent qualities far in excess of any other chemical yet discovered which is suitable for use in embalming fluid.

Peroxide of hydrogen is composed of two atoms of oxygen and two atoms of hydrogen. Since oxygen is fifteen times heavier than hydrogen, fifteen-sixteenths of the atomic weight of peroxide of hydrogen, therefore, is oxygen.

Every embalmer knows that venous blood is much darker in color, is much more sluggish and much heavier than arterial blood. What is the difference between the two?

Arterial blood is merely venous blood, which has been purified in the lungs, which has been lightened in color and rendered vastly more fluid by the oxygen which the lungs have extracted from the air we breathe.

Since fifteen-sixteenths of the atomic weight of peroxide of hydrogen is oxygen, it must be apparent, therefore, that the oxygen in the extra rich peroxide in Dioxin has a tendency to exercise the same purifying and solvent qualities upon the dark, discolored venous blood after death as the oxygen which the lungs extract from the air we breathe has upon the venous blood in life.

The result is that much more blood can be drained from a body in which RE-Concentrated Dioxin is injected than is possible from a body in which raw formaldehyde is used and in which the astringent qualities of the formaldehyde have sealed up the discolored blood corpuscles in the capillaries.

Putty color is caused by raw formaldehyde fluid sealing up the discolored corpuscles of the blood in the capillaries. It is inevitable where raw formaldehyde fluids are used unless exceeding care is used to drain blood. And even then there is great danger.

RE-Concentrated Dioxin is distinctly the most modern and the most scientific embalming fluid on the market, as well as the most economical. The progressive funeral director will not hesitate, but will order a trial shipment.

RE-Concentrated DIOXIN

H. S. ECKELS & CO. 1922 Arch St., Philadelphia, Pa.
241 Fern Ave., Toronto, Canada.

Undertakers Shipping Directory

ONTARIO

Aurora—
 Dunham, Charles.
Barrie—
 Smith, G. G. & Co.
Brockville—
 Quirmbach, Geo. R., 162 King St.
Brooklin—
 Disney, R. S.
Campbellford—
 Irwin, James.
Campden—
 Hansel, Albion.
Clinton—
 Walker, Wesley.
Coboconk—
 Greenley, A.
Copper Cliff—
 Boyd, W. C.
Dungannon—
 Sproul, William
Dutton—
 Schultz, B. L.
Elmira—
 Dreisinger, Chris.
Fenelon Falls—
 Deyman, L. & Son.

Fenwick—
 H. A. Metler.
Fergus—
 Armstrong, M. F.
 Thomson, John & Son.
Fort William—
 Cameron & Co., 711 Victoria.
 Morris, A.
Haileybury—
 Thorpe Bros.
Galt—
 Anderson, J. & Son.
 Little, T., & Son.
Hamilton—
 Green Bros., 124 King St. E.
 Robinson, J. H. & Co., 19-21 John St. N.
Hanover—
 Wunnenberg, Norman.
Hastings—
 Howard, P. N.
Hepworth—
 Downs, E. J.
Inwood—
 Lorriman, E. S.
Kemptville—
 McCaughey, Geo. A.
Kenora—
 Horn & Taylor.

Kincardine—
 Miller, E.
Kingston—
 Corbett, S. S.
Lakefield—
 Hendren, Geo. G.
Little Current—
 Sims, J. G.
Markdale—
 Oliver, M.
Newmarket—
 Millard, J. H.
North Augusta—
 Wilson, J. R.
North Bay—
 St. Pierre, E.
Oakwood—(Mariposa Station G.T.R.) Wilmot F. Webster.
Ohsweken—
 Johnson, F. L.
Oshawa—
 Disney Bros.
 Luke Bros.
Ottawa—
 Ch. R. Woodburn, 586 Bank St. Tel. Carling 600 and 1009.
 Rogers & Burney, 283 Laurier Ave. W.
Petrolia—
 Steadman Bros.
Port Arthur—
 Collin Wood, 36 Arthur St.
 Morris, A.
Prescott—
 Rankin, H. & Son.
Renfrew—
 O'Connor, Wm.
St. Mary's—
 N. L. Brandon.
St. Thomas—
 Williams, P. R. & Sons, 519 Talbot St.
Seaforth, Ont.
 W. T. Box & Co.
 Holmes, S. T.
Scotland—
 Vaughan, Jos. H. M.
Stratford—
 Greenwood & Vivian, Ltd., 88-92 Ontario St.
 White & Co., 80 Ontario St.
Sudbury—
 Henry, J. G.
Toronto—
 Cobbledick, N. B., 2068 Queen St. East and 1508 Danforth Ave. Private Ambulance.
 Raper, Washington, Fleury Burial Co., 731 Queen St. E.
 Stone, Daniel (formerly H. Stone & Son), 525 Sherbourne St.
 Vancamp, J. C., 30 Bloor St. West.
Waterloo—
 Klipper Undertaking Co.
Welland—
 Sutherland, G. W.
Woodstock—
 Meadows, T. & Sons
 Mark, Paul.
Wingham—
 Currie, R. A.
 Walker, J.

QUEBEC

Buckingham—
 Paquet, Jos.

Cowansville—
 Judson, M. B.
Montreal—
 Tees & Co., 912 St. Catherine St. West.
St. Hyacinthe—
 Cadorette, Mongeau & Leary.
St. Laurent—
 Gougeon, Jos.

NEW BRUNSWICK

Moncton—
 Tuttle Bros., 121 Lutz St.
Petitcodiac—
 Jonah, D. Allison.
Woodstock—
 Van Wart, Jacob.

NOVA SCOTIA

Ferrona—
 Fraser, D. & Co.
Halifax—
 Snow & Co., 90 Argyle St.
Sydney Mines—
 D. A. McRae, Clyde Ave.
Sydney, C.B.—
 Beaton, A. J. & Son, 374-384 George St.

MANITOBA

Brandon—
 Campbell & Campbell.
 Vincent & McPherson.
Souris—
 McCulloch, Wm.
Swan River—
 Paull, Geo.
Winnipeg—
 Bardal, A. S., 834 Sherbrooke
 Thompson, J. C., 501 Main
 Clark-Leatherdale Co., Ltd., 232 Kennedy St.

SASKATCHEWAN

Gull Lake—
 Morrow, Fred. A.
Saskatoon—
 Young, A. E.
Kamsack—
 Russell, G. E. I.
Lanigan—
 Robertson, Wm.
Moose Jaw—
 The Bellamy Co.
 Broadfoot Bros.
Rush Lake—
 Friesen, John M.
Prince Albert—
 Howard, A. C.
 Hadley, C. L.
Regina—
 Speers, George.
Semans—
 Haygarth, Jas.
Welwyn—
 LeaVens, Merritt.
Woiseley—
 Barber, B.

ALBERTA

Calgary—
 Graham & Buscomb, 611 Centre St.
Castor—
 Winter, W. G.

BRITISH COLUMBIA

Hosmer—
 Cornett, T. A.
Prince Rupert—
 Haynes, S.
Victoria—
 Hanna & Thompson, 827 Pandora Ave.

The Original Patented Concentrated Fluid

Patented Formula
Strongest and Best

Essential Oil Base, combined with Alcohol, Glycerine, Oxidized Formaldehyde and Boron-Dioxide.

Ask others for their Formula

Special Canadian Agents

National Casket Co.
Toronto, Ont.

GLOBE CASKET CO.
London, Ont.

SEMMENS & EVEL CASKET CO.
Hamilton, Ont.

GIRARD & GODIN
Three Rivers, Que.

JAS. S. ELLIOTT & SON
Prescott, Ont.

CHRISTIE BROS.
Amherst, N.S.

Larger Bottles filled up with water

Egyptian Chemical Co. Boston, U.S.A.

Canadian School of Embalming
Instruction in Practical Embalming and Funeral Directing
PREPARATION FOR EXAMINATIONS
ENTER AT ANY TIME

R. U. STONE 32 Carlton Street
Principal Toronto

INDEX TO ADVERTISEMENTS

A
Antiseptic Bedding Co. .... o.f.c.

B
Baets Bros. & Co. 22
Batavia Clamp Co. 62
Berlin Exhibition 13

C
Canada Casket Co. 56
Canadian School of Embalming ... 61
Can. H.W. Johns-Manville Co.,Ltd. 25
Central Casket Co. 58
Chesley Furniture Co. 12
Chair Craft Co. 14
Colleran Pat. Spring Mattress Co. 10
Columbia Graphophone Co. ... i.b.c.

D
Dominion Casket Co. 46
Dominion Mfrs., Limited ... 51-52-53-54

E
Eckels & Co., H. S. 60
Egyptian Chemical Co. 61
Elmira Furniture Co. 23
Elmira Interior Woodwork Co. ... 4

F
Farquharson-Gifford Co. 9

G
Gale & Son, Geo. 24
Gendron Wheel Co. 62
Gibbs-Wernicke Co. 7
Gold Medal Furn. Mfg. Co. 19

H
Hourd & Co. 15

I
Ideal Bedding Co. 26
Imperial Rattan Co. .... o.f.c.

K
Kawneer Mfg. Co. 10
Kindel Bed Co., Limited 25
Knechtel Furniture Co. 21
Knechtel Kitchen Cabinet Co. ... 20

M
Manufacturers' Exhibition Bldg. 17
Matthews Bros. 11
Menford Mfg. Co. 16
McLagan Furniture Co., Geo 3
Mundell, J. C., & Co. .... i.f.c.

N
N. A. Bent Chair Co. 6
National Grave Vault Co. 60

O
Ontario Spring Bed 4
Onward Manufacturing Co. 6

S
Shafer, D. L. & Co. 11
Sidway Mercantile Co. 62
Standard Bedding Co. 8
Stratford Brass Co. 10
Stratford Chair Co. 5
Stratford Mfg. Co. 11
St. Thomas Metallic Vault Co. ... 58

T
Textileather Co. 8
Toronto Furniture Exhibition o.b.c.

V
Victoriaville Bedding Co. 18

W
Walter & Co., B. 25
Western Casket Co. 48
Weisglass, S., Limited. 22

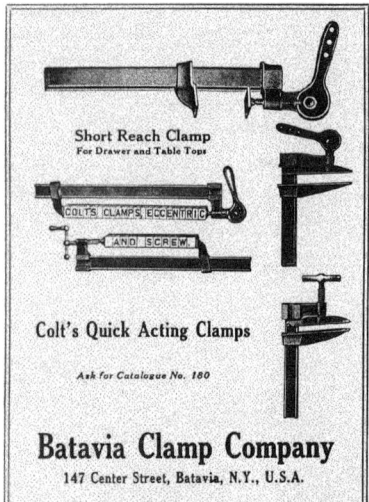

Short Reach Clamp
For Drawer and Table Tops

Colt's Quick Acting Clamps

Ask for Catalogue No. 180

Batavia Clamp Company
147 Center Street, Batavia, N.Y., U.S.A.

Invalid Chairs and Tricycles of every description.

This has been our study for thirty-five years. We build chairs that suit the requirements of any case. Write us for catalogue No. 20 and prices, if interested.

Gendron Wheel Co., Toledo, O. U.S.A.

For Sale
Wanted

TERMS FOR INSERTION
25 Cents per line, one insertion
Four lines once for $1.00, three times for $2.00.
Cash must accompany the order
No accounts booked.

MINIMUM 50 CENTS

WANTED—Commission salesman to sell on commission, in the provinces of Manitoba and Quebec, a well known line of go-carts. Must be well acquainted with the furniture and department store buyers. Answer, with references, to Box 130, Canadian Furniture World and The Undertaker, 32 Colborne St., Toronto. 14|12|2

FOR SALE—Child's white hearse and undertaker's first call light rubber-tired waggon, both in excellent condition. Less than half cost price to close an estate. A. E. Humphrey, 368 Queen St. West, Toronto. 14|12|tf

$150.00—Good undertaker's brougham—single or double. Address 1095 Yonge St., Toronto. 14|12|1

WANTED—Hearse and waggon, slightly used or in good condition. State lowest price. Box 23, Wiarton, Ont. 14|12|1

The Sidway Sellers for 1915

Will soon be shown to your buyer. You know the success you have had with the Allwin and Sidway of past seasons. The new line represents all the features which made that success plus NEW DESIGNS, IMPROVEMENTS that will appeal to the mother and help the baby and VALUES which spell substantial profits for the dealer. Don't handicap your baby carriage department by a hasty selection. Await the call from

Sidway Our Canadian Sales Organization **Allwin**
Canadian Factory, Goderich, Ontario, - F. R. HODGES, Manager
REPRESENTATIVES
In Quebec, J. J. Neander, 97 Drummond St., Montreal.
In Ontario, C. A. Coryell, 115 Wells Street, Toronto.
In Manitoba, Saskatchewan and Alberta, Miller Morse Hardware Co., Winnipeg.
West of Lake Superior, R. A. Conkey, Vancouver.

Sidway Mercantile Co., Elkhart, Ind.

COLUMBIA DEALERS THROUGHOUT CANADA ARE
REAPING A RICH HARVEST THROUGH THE SALE OF

Columbia
Patriotic Records

There is an enormous demand for records of the songs and airs beloved of our brave armies.

The Columbia Graphophone Company offers the most complete and up-to-date list of war records.

Over Twenty-Five Thousand records of *"It's A Long Way to Tipperary"* have already been sold by Columbia Dealers and it is still going strong.

Every record sold represents a substantial profit to the dealer.

Can you afford to lose the profit you could make on a Live Columbia Agency?

*Write for full particulars and free booklet "MUSIC MONEY,"
something every merchant ought to read*

Columbia Graphophone Company
Toronto, Ontario

THE FAMOUS COLUMBIA DOUBLE-DISC RECORDS ARE MADE IN CANADA

| Manufacturers are invited to make displays. | The
Second Annual | Dealers are cordially invited to attend. |

Toronto Furniture Exhibition

JANUARY 18th to FEBRUARY 1st, 1915

| About 50 manufacturers will make displays under one roof.

Eight floors, 65 x 185 ft.—about 85,000 square ft. available for displays. | **IN THE NEW**
GREGG
BUILDING
52-54 YORK ST.
TORONTO
Just around the corner from the Union Depot | Exhibition building will be thoroughly heated and well lighted.

Very convenient to the leading hotels, theatres and leading points of interest. |

A VISIT TO THE FURNITURE EXHIBITION MAY REJUVENATE YOUR BUSINESS

About 300 of the biggest buyers and livest furniture dealers in Canada attended the Furniture Exhibition in Toronto last January—and they should all be back again with many more next January.

Come and look over the new lines displayed and talk over your business problems with these men. Bring a note book for new ideas and selling stunts. Come prepared to learn and you're likely to go home with a trunk full of new plans to put ginger into your business.

A visit to the Furniture Exhibition is an investment—not an expense.

Canadian Furniture Exhibition Association

| Manufacturers who wish to exhibit should apply for space at once. | EXHIBITION COMMITTEE
J. W. ABBOTT   JAMES SOUTER
W. J. CRAIG, Sec., 215 Victoria St. Toronto | See the full list of exhibitors in the next issue of the Furniture World. |